The Law of Journalism and Mass Communication

Seventh Edition

For our families

Sara Miller McCune founded SAGE Publishing in 1965 to support the dissemination of usable knowledge and educate a global community. SAGE publishes more than 1000 journals and over 800 new books each year, spanning a wide range of subject areas. Our growing selection of library products includes archives, data, case studies and video. SAGE remains majority owned by our founder and after her lifetime will become owned by a charitable trust that secures the company's continued independence.

Los Angeles | London | New Delhi | Singapore | Washington DC | Melbourne

The Law of Journalism and Mass Communication

Seventh Edition

Susan Dente Ross

Washington State University

Amy Reynolds

Kent State University

Robert Trager

University of Colorado Boulder

FOR INFORMATION:

CQ Press

An Imprint of SAGE Publications, Inc.

2455 Teller Road

Thousand Oaks, California 91320

E-mail: order@sagepub.com

SAGE Publications Ltd.

1 Oliver's Yard

55 City Road

London EC1Y 1SP

United Kingdom

SAGE Publications India Pvt. Ltd.

B 1/I 1 Mohan Cooperative Industrial Area

Mathura Road, New Delhi 110 044

India

SAGE Publications Asia-Pacific Pte. Ltd.

18 Cross Street #10-10/11/12

China Square Central

Singapore 048423

Acquisitions Editor: Lily Norton

Content Development Editor: Jennifer Jovin-Bernstein

Editorial Assistant: Sarah Wilson

Production Editor: Tracy Buyan

Copy Editor: Melinda Masson

Typesetter: C&M Digitals (P) Ltd.

Proofreader: Barbara Coster

Indexer: Jean Casalegno

Cover Designer: Scott Van Atta

Marketing Manager: Victoria Velasquez

Cover: details of Fauve, an art quilt, © Judith Tomlinson Trager.

Printed in the United States of America

Library of Congress Cataloging-in-Publication Data

Names: Ross, Susan Dente, author. | Reynolds, Amy, author. | Trager, Robert, author.

Title: The law of journalism and mass communication / Susan Dente Ross; Amy Reynolds; Robert Trager.

Description: Seventh edition. | Thousand Oaks, California : CQ Press, an imprint of Sage Publications, Inc., [2020] | Includes bibliographical references and index.

Identifiers: LCCN 2019020903 | ISBN 9781544377582 (pbk. : alk. paper)

Subjects: LCSH: Mass media—Law and legislation—United States. | Press law—United States. | Freedom of the press—United States.

Classification: LCC KF2750 .T73 2020 | DDC 343.7309/9—dc23 LC record available at https://lccn.loc.gov/2019020903

This book is printed on acid-free paper.

19 20 21 22 23 10 9 8 7 6 5 4 3 2 1

BRIEF CONTENTS

DETAILED CONTENTS

LIST OF FEATURES

Chapter 8 • Overseeing Justice: Speech and Press Freedoms In and About the Courts

Chapter 9 • Electronic Media Regulation: From Radio to the Internet

Chapter 10 • Obscenity and Indecency: Social Norms and Legal Standards

PREFACE

This book is intended and designed primarily to serve those planning to work in journalism, public relations, advertising or marketing in new, social or traditional media. Our goal is to offer a truly readable overview of the laws of journalism and mass communication that situates the most significant aspects of that law within the social and political contexts that give them meaning. We focus sharply on the legal issues related to gathering and disseminating information in today's multimedia age that we believe are most relevant to professional communicators.

Our unique approach to "The Law of Journalism and Mass Communication" developed in response to the way we teach and the way we believe people learn. We see the law as the shifting product of specific decisions at distinct times in particular places. As such, the law is best understood when we see and feel its effects on real people in routine conflicts and through the actions of our government as well as our friends, neighbors and families.

Our hope is that "The Law of Journalism and Mass Communication" is both approachable and interesting, grounded in the traditions and rules of law but also chock-full of fresh facts and new examples that bring the law to life today. We incorporate the latest court and legislative rulings and turn attention toward the events outside of courts and beyond the judiciary to illustrate how the law works in the real world for people living their lives each day. If we have succeeded, you will find this volume both educational and interesting.

FEATURES

In this seventh edition of "The Law of Journalism and Mass Communication," readers will discover a wealth of new content—from the U.S. Supreme Court, federal and state courts, Congress, executive agencies, federal and state policymakers and advisory groups, and media organizations and allies. Readers also will discover more than 40 new photographs and dozens of new charts, graphs and tables to illustrate key trends or issues. More tightly focused breakout boxes in **International Law**, **Points of Law** and **Real World Law** highlight contemporary examples of the law in action or emphasize central concepts of law as well as intersections with international law and policy. They serve to supplement the principal discussion and to underscore important tests, breathe life into the facts and widen the lens through which we view the law.

A photograph and quotation open each chapter to illustrate and comment on a specific area of the law. A **Suppose . . .** hypothetical scenario engages readers with a question presented to the courts on the chapter's legal topic. The **Suppose** case is discussed in the chapter and resolved in one of the two case excerpts at the chapter's close. These two **Cases for Study** allow readers to engage directly with significant, often landmark, decisions to build upon the legal analysis and commentary of each chapter of "The Law of Journalism and Mass Communication." A timeline with photographs of Landmark Cases in Context accompanies each chapter to situate the law within the flow of history. Definitions in the text's margins and in a glossary at the back establish shared understanding of the specialized language of the law.

ORGANIZATION AND COVERAGE

We have refreshed the look, feel and flow of many of the chapters in this edition to provide a clearer path through sometimes fast-expanding areas of the law and to offer new examples to guide better understanding of legal complexities. Among the more notable changes in this seventh edition of "The Law of Journalism and Mass Communication," readers will find an increased emphasis in each chapter on the historical, theoretical and constitutional foundations of the legal topic as a point of departure for examination of legal evolutions, alterations and current challenges. The authors believe this grounding is especially beneficial in areas of rapid legal change. It helps readers navigate the abundance of legal decisions and details to concentrate on the core concepts and principles that endure and embody the rule of law. We hope these alterations aid comprehension and retention of the material as they facilitate classroom activities, creativity and discussion.

This edition has also moved **Emerging Law** out of breakout boxes and into the penultimate section of the chapter text, right before the **Cases for Study.** Like many of the changes we have made throughout the development of this text, this alteration comes in response to comments from our generous adopters and reviewers. The move provides a more concentrated discussion of nascent legal topics and is simple to bypass for those who wish to focus exclusively on settled law.

Beyond these shared features, each chapter benefits from unique updates that are as timely as possible, including apposite U.S. Supreme Court decisions handed down in mid-2019. More precisely, the first chapter offers revised and expanded discussions of the rule of law, stare decisis, the U.S. Constitution's role in protecting individual rights, judicial review and the personal ideologies of the justices of the U.S. Supreme Court. Chapter 2 offers a new flow and underscores the Constitution's constraint on government as a precondition for the courts' varied interpretations and applications of the core precepts of our system of law.

Building from the foundations of the preceding chapters, the chapter on speech distinctions (3) moves chronologically through the U.S. Supreme Court's evolving definitions of speech categories and their First Amendment protection. New topics here include social media as forums for hate, government (particularly police) punishment of people who show them disrespect, university speech zones and faculty use of obscenity or racial slurs in the classroom. These and other changes highlight how speech categories intended to make the law more clear and predictable are sometimes both imprecise and unstable.

New photographs, new cases and a tighter history section sharpen the chapter on libel and emotional distress (4). In particular, the discussion of actual malice has been shortened and refreshed, and the discussion of limited public figures has been revised for better clarity. The subsequent chapter (5) on defenses and privileges in libel presents a new case excerpt and new court decisions throughout to enhance coverage of anti-SLAPP litigation, fair report privilege and rhetorical hyperbole. The #MeToo movement and court trends toward earlier determinations of actual malice are among the new and emerging issues.

A crisper privacy chapter (6) provides a new summary of constitutional privacy and presents electronic privacy and U.S. Supreme Court decisions early on as a basis for new case examples and topics. The chapter offers more details and context around central rulings and examines the Fourth Amendment right to privacy as well as the recent Supreme Court decision in *Carpenter v. United States*, which is excerpted at the chapter's end. Coverage of intrusion, false light, appropriation, private facts and data privacy features new images as well as new cases.

The chapter on information gathering (7) begins with an introduction to access and its constitutional and common law roots. Exploration of the statutory right and limits to access walks through new discussion of the right to record public events, the right of access to police cameras, the privacy of specific places and records, and the protections against covert or online hacking, recording, harassment and fraud. Coverage of access to records and meetings is combined to underline the similarities and differences between them, and a more detailed discussion of the *Press-Enterprise* logic and experience test demonstrates the uncertain outcome of court decisions on access. New case examples refresh the discussion of the Freedom of Information Act.

The case history of access to courts introduces a more detailed exploration of the limits to media access to court proceedings and records (8). A clearer presentation of judicial and juror impartiality and misconduct, especially as related to social media use during trials, suggests the challenges to protecting fair trials. New case examples illustrate the broad conditions under which judges protect juror identities and issue contempt citations, and how rarely they order a change of venue. The chapter includes new treatment of the role of court media and public relations officers.

The electronic media regulation chapter (9) is reorganized to better reflect the contemporary electronic media landscape, especially in light of new technological developments. It features expanded sections on why broadcast is regulated, how the Federal Communications Commission works and what it does. It discusses in detail recent significant—and sometimes controversial—FCC decisions and related cases in the areas of net neutrality, media ownership rules, modernizing the FCC, revitalizing AM radio and updating children's television programming rules.

A more detailed explanation of early obscenity cases introduces primary concepts still relevant in obscenity law today (10). New case examples demonstrate how to apply community versus national standards and what the term "patently offensive" means when determining obscenity online and on social media. The **Emerging Law** section discusses a new federal law designed to stop human sex trafficking that may undermine Section 230 immunity for websites and internet service providers and impact other areas of media law.

Historically, the U.S. Supreme Court has decided few cases concerning intellectual property. Over the last decade, both Congress and the Supreme Court have engaged with the legal issues raised as new inventions facilitate different ways to create copyrightable works. Filled with new cases and laws, such as the Music Modernization Act, this chapter (11) simplifies this complex area of the law while highlighting important trends. Modern examples of copyright and trademark disputes include films like "Guardians of the Galaxy," television programs like "SpongeBob SquarePants" and the digital remastering of sound recordings from before 1972.

The final chapter (12) on advertising more prominently develops the place of publicity, promotion and marketing under the umbrella of commercial speech. Definitions, constitutional foundations and history of the law of commercial speech introduce the tension between the Commerce Clause and the First Amendment as context for the sometimes murky rulings of the courts. New cases and a greater emphasis on administrative agency rulemaking emphasize the complexity of legal decision making in this area. Attention is given to developments in native advertising, online and social media marketing, battles over food labeling and the legal issues relevant to promotion of businesses and professionals.

In this seventh edition of "The Law of Journalism and Mass Communication," you will discover a new breadth, diversity and dynamism of material intended to provide the tools for direct engagement with the law. As in the past, we have made every effort to ensure that this edition is lively and full of the most recent legal and policy decisions, the cutting-edge research in the field and the social, technological and economic influences upon them that transform the work and the products of professional communicators. Despite all the revisions, updates and new content, we believe this text will feel familiar to our longtime adopters. We hope you will find it in good order. As Aristotle once said, "Good law is good order."

DIGITAL RESOURCES

To supplement this text, we provide a wide range of online materials through a SAGE Edge companion website, located at **edge.sagepub.com/medialaw7e**. The site includes both student learning aids and teaching tools. The following resources have been updated and revised to enhance use of this new edition.

Password-protected **Instructor Resources** include the following:

- A **Microsoft® Word test bank** containing multiple-choice, true/false, short-answer and essay questions for each chapter. The test bank provides you with a diverse range of prewritten options as well as the opportunity for editing any question and/or inserting your own personalized questions to assess students' progress and understanding.

- Editable, chapter-specific Microsoft® **PowerPoint® slides** that offer you complete flexibility to create a multimedia presentation for your course that highlights the content and features you wish to emphasize.

- **Lecture notes** that summarize key concepts on a chapter-by-chapter basis to help you with preparation for lectures and class discussions.

- Lively and stimulating **class activities** that may be used to reinforce active, in-class learning. The activities include both individual and group opportunities.

- **Tables and figures** that may be downloaded for use in assignments, handouts and presentations.

- **Sample course syllabi** with suggested models for structuring your course that give you options to customize your course to your exact needs.

- **Links to professional resources**.

Our **Student Study Site** is completely open-access and offers a wide range of additional features:

- Mobile-friendly **eFlashcards** that reinforce understanding of key terms and concepts outlined in the chapters.

- Mobile-friendly **web quizzes** that allow for independent assessment of progress made in learning course material.

- **Links to professional resources** that guide students to materials that reinforce chapter concepts and facilitate research.

- An archive of **cases in media law** that provides the opportunity to read many of the legal decisions that construct "The Law of Journalism and Mass Communication."

ACKNOWLEDGMENTS

As with our previous editions, this book is a collaborative effort not only among its authors but also between us and the community we serve. The knowledge, insights and comments of a large and expanding group of people have helped us update and improve this book. We offer our deep respect and gratitude to all those who have shaped our understanding of the field, gently pointed out our faults of commission or omission and reinforced the strengths of this edition of "The Law of Journalism and Mass Communication." You have been more generous than we might reasonably expect.

Beyond the friends, families, students and colleagues who have encouraged and supported us in uncounted ways, we extend special thanks to all the anonymous reviewers who provided valuable feedback or, perhaps, favored our text among other books in the field. We also thank the talented editors, designers and staff at CQ Press/SAGE who helped bring this new edition to you.

Finally, and most importantly, we thank you, our readers.

The authors and SAGE also gratefully acknowledge the contributions of the following reviewers:

Caitlin Ring Carlson, *Seattle University*

Derrick Holland, *Texas Tech University*

Jonathan Kotler, *University of Southern California*

Brian Moritz, *SUNY Oswego*

David Rasmussen, *Penn State University*

J.J. Sylvia IV, *Fitchburg State University*

ABOUT THE AUTHORS

Susan Dente Ross is professor of English at Washington State University. Onetime head of the Association for Education in Journalism and Mass Communication Law Division, she is a Fulbright scholar whose work on freedom of speech and press seeks greater global equity and justice for the disempowered. She writes on law, policy and media's role in conflict transformation and reconciliation. A former owner/editor of a community newspaper, she continues to publish creative nonfiction.

Amy Reynolds is dean of the College of Communication and Information at Kent State University. Her research focuses on dissent, First Amendment history and media sociology. She has written or edited seven books. Prior to becoming a dean, she was a journalism professor at Louisiana State University and Indiana University. Before earning her PhD at the University of Texas, she worked as a reporter, producer and editor at newspapers and television stations.

Robert Trager is professor emeritus in journalism and mass communication at the University of Colorado. He taught courses in communication law, freedom of expression and media institutions. He is the founding editor of the law journal *Communication Law and Policy*. Before joining the University of Colorado faculty, he was an attorney with a major cable television company and practiced media law with a Washington, D.C., firm.

When we [Americans] talk about the rule of law, we assume that we're talking about a law that promotes freedom, that promotes justice, that promotes equality.

—U.S. Supreme Court Justice Anthony Kennedy[1]

In 2018, Brett Kavanaugh speaks before the Senate Judiciary Committee. The full Senate later confirmed him an associate justice of the U.S. Supreme Court by a vote of 52–48.

1

THE RULE OF LAW
Law in a Changing Communication Environment

SUPPOSE...

...it costs a lot to get elected, and people with money can affect election outcomes. In response, the federal government adopts laws that limit contributions to and spending by political candidates.[2] The laws try to balance the right to support candidates and the need to avoid corruption of elections.[3] Big money interests challenge the campaign finance laws in court. After decades of upholding similar laws, the U.S. Supreme Court strikes down a federal[4] ban on certain political advertisements as unconstitutional. Writing in dissent, Justice David Souter argues, "The court (and, I think, the country) loses when important precedent is overruled without good reason."[5]

The following year, a federal district court relied heavily on prior Supreme Court decisions to uphold a law that prohibited a nonprofit organization from running advertisements and airing a film about then-presidential candidate Hillary Clinton.[6] On appeal, the Supreme Court struck down the legal restrictions in *Citizens United v. Federal Election Commission*,[7] unleashing unlimited corporate and union spending on elections[8] and prompting uncertainty about the stability of the Court's decisions.[9] This chapter and the case excerpts that follow explore the relative constancy or uncertainty of the rule of law.

The ancient Greek philosopher Aristotle said people are basically self-interested; they pursue their own interests in preference to the collective good or the cause of justice. However, self-interest is ultimately shortsighted and self-destructive. A lumber company that seeks only to generate the greatest immediate profit ultimately deforests the timberlands it depends on.[10] Astute people therefore recognize that personal interests and short-term goals must sometimes give way to broader or longer-term objectives. Everyone benefits when people adopt a system of rules to promote a balance between gain and loss, between cost and benefit and between personal and universal concerns. Aristotle called this balance the "golden mean." Human interests are served and justice is best achieved when a society adopts a system of law to balance conflicting human objectives and allow people to live together successfully.[11]

rule of law
The legal standards that guide the proper and consistent creation and application of the law.

Belief in the power of law to promote this balance and restrain human injustice is the foundation of the U.S. Constitution and the **rule of law**. The U.S. Supreme Court said the notion that "our government is a government of laws, not of men" is central to our constitutional nature.[12] "Stripped of all technicalities, [the rule of law] means that government in all its actions is bound by rules fixed and announced beforehand—rules which make it possible to foresee with fair certainty how [government] will use its coercive powers in given circumstances, and to plan . . . on the basis of this knowledge."[13]

In essence, laws establish a contract that governs interactions among residents and between the people and their government. Legal rules establish the boundaries of acceptable behavior and empower government to punish violations. The rule of law limits the power of government because it prohibits government from infringing on the rights and liberties of the people. This system constrains the actions of both the people and the government to enhance liberty, freedom and justice for all.

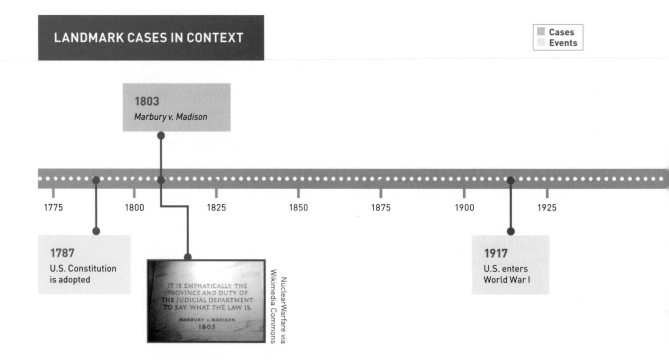

LANDMARK CASES IN CONTEXT

■ Cases
■ Events

1803
Marbury v. Madison

1775   1800   1825   1850   1875   1900   1925

1787
U.S. Constitution is adopted

IT IS EMPHATICALLY THE PROVINCE AND DUTY OF THE JUDICIAL DEPARTMENT TO SAY WHAT THE LAW IS.
MARBURY v. MADISON
1803

NuclearWarfare via Wikimedia Commons

1917
U.S. enters World War I

In 1964, as the United States expanded what many then believed was an illegal military action in Vietnam, Harvard legal scholar Lon Fuller articulated what would become a foundational understanding of the rule of law. In Fuller's view, the rule of law was a set of standards that established norms and procedures to encourage consistent, neutral decision making equally for all. Fuller's formal, conceptual definition has been criticized because it does not provide specific guidance to those drafting, interpreting or applying the law.[14] As one legal scholar noted, the rule of law is created through its application. It "cannot be [understood] in the abstract."[15]

For Fuller, the rule of law established eight "desiderata," or desired outcomes, to guide how laws should be created and employed. The rule of law requires laws to be (1) general and not discriminatory; (2) widely known and disseminated; (3) forward-looking in their application rather than retroactive; (4) clear and specific; (5) self-consistent and complementary of each other; (6) capable of being obeyed; (7) relatively stable over time; and (8) applied and enforced in ways that reflect their underlying intent.

As a mechanism for ordering human behavior, the law functions best when it makes clear, comprehensible and consistent distinctions between legal and illegal behavior. People can only obey laws that they know about and understand. Good laws must be publicly disseminated and sufficiently clear and precise to properly inform citizens of when and how the laws apply (as well as when they do not).

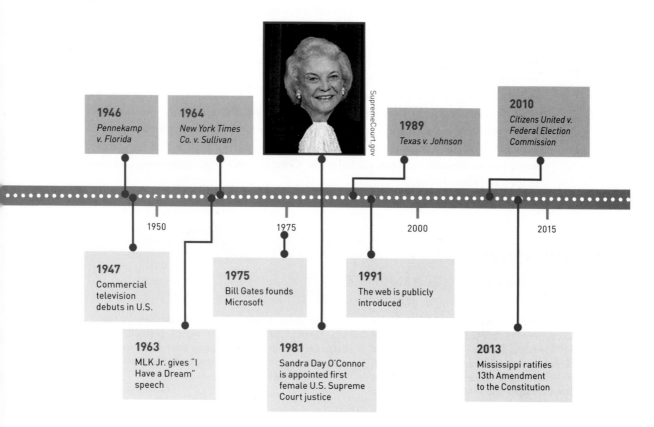

1946
Pennekamp v. Florida

1964
New York Times Co. v. Sullivan

SupremeCourt.gov

1989
Texas v. Johnson

2010
Citizens United v. Federal Election Commission

1950   1975   2000   2015

1947
Commercial television debuts in U.S.

1975
Bill Gates founds Microsoft

1991
The web is publicly introduced

1963
MLK Jr. gives "I Have a Dream" speech

1981
Sandra Day O'Connor is appointed first female U.S. Supreme Court justice

2013
Mississippi ratifies 13th Amendment to the Constitution

INTERNATIONAL LAW
FOUR FOUNDATIONS OF THE RULE OF LAW

The World Justice Project has articulated four foundations of the rule of law based on internationally accepted universal standards. Accordingly, a system of the rule of law exists when:

1. All individuals and private entities are accountable under the law.

2. The laws are fair, clear, public and stable.

3. The processes by which the laws are enacted, administered and enforced are open, robust and timely for all.

4. Those who apply the law are competent, ethical, independent, neutral and diverse.[i]

Many argue that any movement toward a universal rule of law is a form of imperialism that tramples the unique priorities of individual nations and limits the freedom of different peoples to create distinct, culturally appropriate systems of law.[ii]

vague laws
Laws that fail to define their terms or use language so general that it fails to inform citizens or judges with certainty what the laws permit or punish.

Vague laws fail to define their terms or are unclear. They are unacceptable because people may avoid participating in legal activities out of uncertainty over whether their actions are illegal. This tramples people's freedom. In 2018, the U.S. Supreme Court by a vote of 5–4 struck down a provision of the Immigration and Nationality Act[16] as unconstitutionally vague.[17] The law practically required the deportation of any immigrant convicted of an "aggravated felony" or "crime of violence." The Court reasoned that applying the provision's imprecise language "necessarily devolves into guesswork and intuition, invites arbitrary enforcement, and fails to provide fair notice,"[18] all of which violate the basic tenets of due process. These core elements of due process, Justice Neil M. Gorsuch wrote in concurrence, are foundational to the Constitution's original meaning and basic to the rule of law.[19]

INTERNATIONAL LAW
U.S. RULE OF LAW DOES NOT RANK FIRST

An international index ranks the United States 19th among 113 countries in how citizens experience the rule of law.[iii] The World Justice Project report put the United States behind the Nordic countries, Estonia, the Czech Republic and Japan but well ahead of Afghanistan, Cambodia and Venezuela.

The study found relative weaknesses in the U.S. respect for core human rights, protection of personal and property security, cost of access to civil justice, and the timeliness and impartiality of criminal justice.

Clear laws define their terms and detail their application in order to limit government officials' **discretion**. Clear laws advance the rule of law by reducing the ability of officials to apply legal rules differently to their friends and foes. "True freedom requires the rule of law and justice, and a judicial system in which the rights of some are not secured by the denial of rights to others," one observer noted.[20]

Good laws accomplish their objectives with minimum infringement on the freedoms and liberties of the people. Well-tailored laws advance specific government interests or prevent particular harms without punishing activities that pose no risk to society. A law that sought to limit noisy disturbances of residential neighborhoods at night, for example, would be poorly tailored and **overbroad** if it prohibited all discussion out of doors, anywhere at any time.

The rule of law requires the law to be internally consistent, logical and relatively stable. To ensure slow evolution rather than rapid revolution of legal rules, judges in U.S. courts interpret and apply laws based upon the **precedents** established by other court rulings. Precedent, or **stare decisis**, is the legal principle that tells courts to stand by what courts have decided previously. As the U.S. Supreme Court has written, "[T]he very concept of the rule of law underlying our own Constitution requires such continuity over time that a respect for precedent is, by definition, indispensable."[21] The principle holds that subsequent court decisions should adhere to the example and reasoning of earlier decisions in similar factual situations. Reliance on precedent is the heart of the common law (discussed later) and encourages predictable application of the law.

Although the application of prior rulings promotes the rule of law by increasing the consistency and uniformity of legal decision making,[22] it does not always happen. Sometimes precedents are unclear or seem to conflict. Then the rule of law can be ambiguous.[23] Especially where constitutional values are at issue, courts may "not allow principles of stare decisis to block correction of error," the California Supreme Court said.[24]

In 2010, for example, a "bitterly divided" U.S. Supreme Court ruled 5–4 in *Citizens United v. Federal Election Commission* (the case mentioned at the beginning and excerpted at the end of this chapter) that certain federal limits on campaign finance violated the Constitution. Observers noted that the decision made "sweeping changes in federal election law"[25] and "represented a sharp doctrinal shift."[26] Some said the Court had ignored binding precedent. Others argued that "the central principle which critics of this ruling find most offensive . . . has been affirmed by decades of Supreme Court jurisprudence."[27] Thus, the conflict centered less on *whether* to apply precedent and more on *which* precedents to apply.

Debate over the role that stare decisis plays in Supreme Court decision making arose again during the 2017–'18 term, when many said the Court had overruled four well-established precedents.[28] In *Janus v. American Federation of State, County, and Municipal Employees*,[29] for example, the Court overturned its 30-year-old holding in *Abood v. Detroit Board of Education*[30] when it held that laws forcing public employees to pay fees to their designated union violated their First Amendment right to freedom from compelled speech (see Chapter 2).

discretion
The authority to determine the proper outcome.

overbroad laws
A principle that directs courts to find laws unconstitutional if they restrict more legal activity than necessary.

precedent
The outcome of a previous case that establishes a rule of law for courts within the same jurisdiction to follow to determine cases with similar issues.

stare decisis
The doctrine that courts follow precedent; the basis of common law, it literally means to stand by the previous decision.

BODY OF THE LAW

The laws of the United States have grown in number and complexity as American society has become increasingly diverse and complicated. Many forms of communication and the laws that govern them today did not exist in the 1800s. Technology has been a driving force for change in the law of journalism and mass communication. U.S. law also has developed in response to social, political, philosophical and economic changes. Employment and advertising laws, for example, emerged and multiplied as the nation's workforce shifted and the power of corporations grew. Legislatures create new laws to reflect evolving understandings of individual rights, liberties and responsibilities. Even well-established legal concepts, such as libel—harm to another's reputation—have evolved to reflect new realities of the role of communication in society and the power of mass media to harm individuals.

The laws of journalism and mass communication generally originate from six sources.

Constitutions	**Equity Law**
Statutes	**Administrative Law**
Common Law	**Executive Orders**

Constitutions

constitutional law
The set of laws that establish the nature, functions and limits of government.

Constitutional law establishes the nature, functions and limits of government. The U.S. Constitution, the fundamental law of the United States, was framed in 1787 and ratified in 1789. Each of the states also has a constitution. These constitutions define the structure of government and delegate and limit government power to protect certain fundamental human rights. "Constitutions are checks upon the hasty action of the majority," said President William Howard Taft in 1911. "They are self-imposed restraints of a whole people upon a majority of them to secure sober action and a respect for the rights of the minority."[31]

Given the legacy of British religious oppression and the revolution against the Crown that formed this country, it should not be surprising that the U.S. Constitution protects individual liberties sometimes at the expense of much larger groups. The First Amendment, for example, generally protects an individual's right to speak very offensively, while laws in other countries are far more likely to punish hate speech, name-calling, denial of the Holocaust, criticism of government officials, anti-religious speech and much more.

The U.S. Constitution establishes the character of government, organizes the federal government, and provides a minimum level of individual rights and privileges throughout the country. It creates three separate and coequal branches of government—the executive, the legislative and the judicial—and designates the functions and responsibilities of each. The executive branch oversees government and administers, or executes, laws. The legislative branch enacts laws, and the judicial branch interprets laws and resolves legal conflicts.

political questions
Questions not subject to judicial review because they fall into areas properly handled by another branch of government.

Separation of government into branches provides checks and balances within government to support the rule of law. For example, "restrictions derived from the separation of powers doctrine prevent the judicial branch from deciding **political questions** . . . that revolve around policy choices and value determinations" because the Constitution gives the legislative and executive branches express authority to make political decisions.[32]

The **Supremacy Clause** of the Constitution establishes the Constitution as the supreme law of the land and resolves conflicts among laws by establishing that all state laws must give way to federal law, and state or federal laws that conflict with the Constitution are invalid. In a similar way, some federal laws preempt state laws, which in turn may preempt city statutes.

As the bedrock of the law, the Constitution is relatively difficult to change. There are two ways to amend the Constitution. The first and only method actually used is for both chambers of Congress to pass a proposed constitutional amendment by a two-thirds vote in each. The second method is for two-thirds of the state legislatures to vote for a Constitutional Convention, which then proposes one or more amendments. All amendments to the Constitution also must be ratified by three-fourths of the state legislatures. When Mississippi recently became the last state to ban slavery by ratifying the 13th Amendment to the Constitution, the vote was only symbolic. The needed three-fourths of states ratified the amendment in 1865.[33]

In many ways, state constitutions are distinct and independent from the U.S. Constitution they mirror. Under the principle of **federalism**, states are related to, yet independent of, the federal government and each other. Federalism encourages experimentation and variety in government. Each state has freedom to structure its unique form of government and to craft state constitutional protections that exceed the rights granted by the U.S. Constitution. For example, the U.S. Constitution says nothing about municipalities; states create and determine the authority of cities or towns. While the federal right to privacy exists only through the U.S. Supreme Court's interpretation of the protections afforded by the First Amendment to the Constitution, Washington state's constitution contains an explicit privacy clause that protects individuals from disturbances of their private affairs.[34]

Congress has approved only 33 of the thousands of proposed amendments to the U.S. Constitution, and the states have ratified only 27 of these. The first 10 amendments to the Constitution, which form the Bill of Rights, were ratified in 1791 after several states called for increased constitutional protection of individual liberties. In fewer than 500 words, the Bill of Rights expressly guarantees fundamental rights and limits government power. For example, the First Amendment (see Chapter 2) prevents government from abridging the people's right to speak and worship freely. State constitutions are amended by a direct vote of the people.

Statutes

The U.S. Constitution explicitly delegates the power to enact statutory laws to the popularly elected legislative branch of government. City, county, state and federal legislative bodies enact **statutory law**. Like constitutions, statutes are written down; both types of law are called **black-letter law**.

POINTS OF LAW
THE THREE BRANCHES OF FEDERAL GOVERNMENT

The Executive

The president, the cabinet and the administrative agencies execute laws.

The Legislative

The Senate and the House of Representatives pass laws.

The Judicial

The three levels of courts review laws and adjudicate disputes.

Supremacy Clause
Article IV, Part 2 of the U.S. Constitution establishes that federal law takes precedence over, or supersedes, state laws.

federalism
A principle according to which the states are related to yet independent of each other and are related to yet independent of the federal government.

statutory law
Written law formally enacted by city, county, state and federal legislative bodies.

black-letter law
Formally enacted, written law that is available in legal reporters or other documents.

INTERNATIONAL LAW
U.S. COURTS MAY (OR MAY NOT) APPLY INTERNATIONAL LAWS

It may seem strange, but U.S. courts do not have a certain and fixed method for dealing with international laws. Judges and academics have debated the topic for decades because the Constitution does not clearly establish how foreign laws should be applied in cases decided in the United States. Once a rather theoretical question, exploding global commerce and communications give this topic increased urgency and impact.

The Constitution delegates exclusive power over war and foreign relations to the Congress and the president.[iv] The Constitution's Supremacy Clause establishes three sources of law: the Constitution itself, "laws made in pursuance" to the Constitution and "Treaties."[v]

Because laws can be adopted only through action of the U.S. Senate or state legislatures, some argue that U.S. courts need not recognize the law of other nations.[vi]

Others claim that the Constitution's establishment of the courts[vii] implicitly conveys the responsibility to incorporate international law as enforceable common law when they generally and consistently rely upon it to guide decisions.[viii] Thus, if courts use international law, it binds. But what if some U.S. states do and others do not?

The resulting uncertainty can create inconsistency in the application of the law and undermine the rule of law.

Legislatures make laws to respond to—or predict and attempt to prevent—social problems. Statutory law may be very specific to define the legal limits of particular activities. All criminal laws are statutes, for example. Statutes also establish the rules of copyright, broadcasting, advertising and access to government meetings and information. Statutes are formally adopted through a public process and are meant to be clear and stable. They are written down in statute books and codified, which means they are compiled into topics by codes, and anyone can find and read them in public repository libraries.

Laws are not inflexible. Even the U.S. Constitution—the foundational contract between the U.S. government and the people—can be changed through amendment. Other laws—statutes, regulations and rules—may be repealed or amended by the federal, state and local bodies that adopted them, and they may be interpreted or invalidated by the courts. In its landmark 1803 ruling in *Marbury v. Madison* (excerpted at the end of this chapter), the Supreme Court established the courts' power to interpret laws. The Court held that "[i]t is emphatically the province and duty of the judicial department to say what the law is. Those who apply the rule to particular cases must of necessity expound and interpret that rule."[35]

When the language of a statute is unclear, imprecise or ambiguous, courts determine the law's meaning and application through a process called statutory **construction**. Statutes may be difficult to interpret because they fail to define key terms. For example, if the word "meeting" is not defined in an open-meetings law, it is unclear whether the law applies to virtual meetings online.[36] When a statute suggests more than one meaning, courts generally look to the law's preamble, or statement of purpose, for guidance on how the legislature intended the law to apply. Courts may use legislative committee reports, debates and public statements to guide their statutory interpretation.

Courts tend to engage in **strict construction**, which narrowly defines laws to their literal meaning and clearly stated intent. The effort to interpret laws according to the "plain meaning" of the words—the **facial meaning** of the law—limits any tendency courts might have to

construction
The process by which courts and administrative agencies determine the proper meaning and application of laws, rules and regulations.

strict construction
Courts' narrow interpretation and application of a law based on the literal meaning of its language. Especially applied in interpreting the Constitution.

facial meaning
The plain and straightforward meaning.

rewrite laws through creative or expansive interpretation. This **deference** to legislative intent reflects courts' recognition that the power to write laws lies with the publicly elected legislature. The power of courts to engage in statutory **construction** is inherently nondemocratic because judges in many states are not elected.

deference
The judicial practice of interpreting statutes and rules by relying heavily on the judgments and intentions of the administrative experts and legislative agencies that enacted the laws.

FIGURE 1.1 ■ How a Bill Becomes a Law

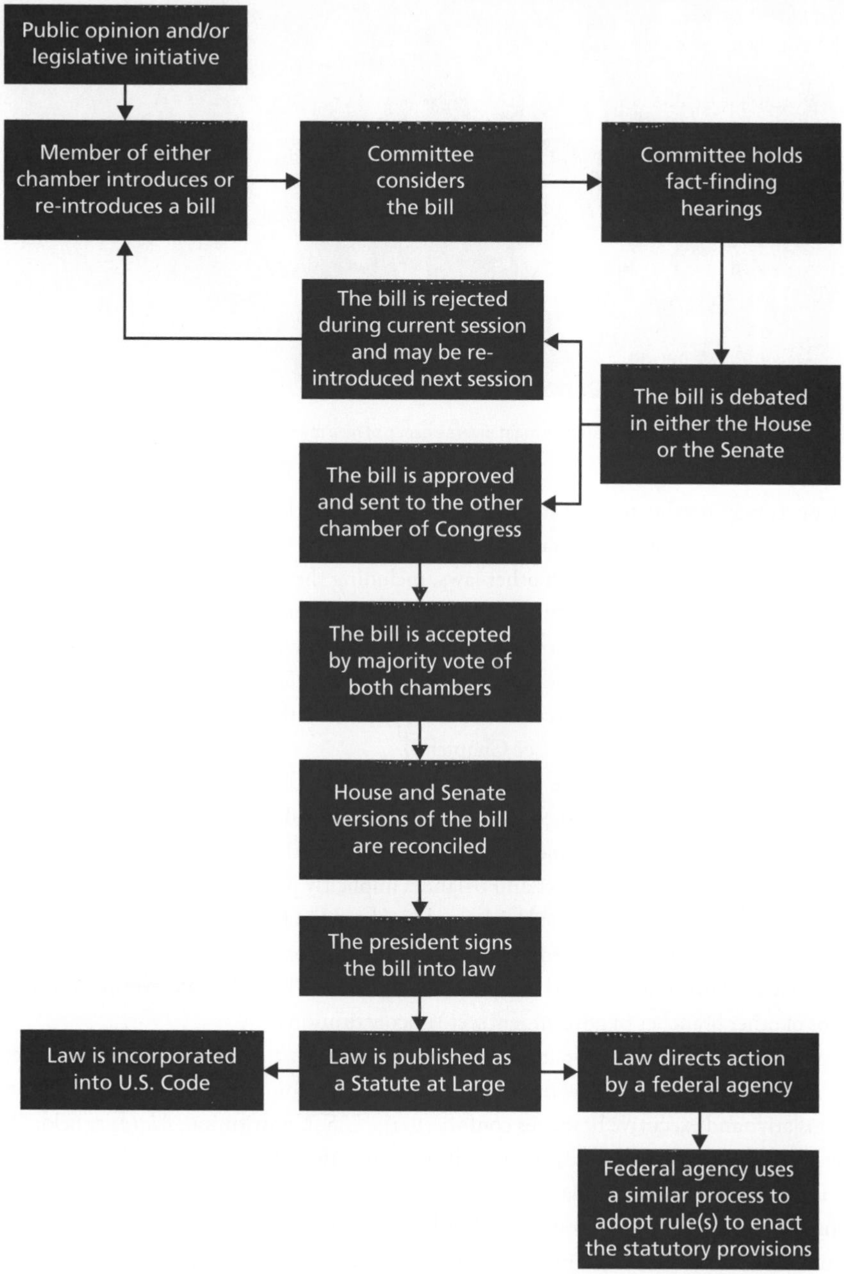

Public opinion and/or legislative initiative

Member of either chamber introduces or re-introduces a bill

Committee considers the bill

Committee holds fact-finding hearings

The bill is rejected during current session and may be re-introduced next session

The bill is debated in either the House or the Senate

The bill is approved and sent to the other chamber of Congress

The bill is accepted by majority vote of both chambers

House and Senate versions of the bill are reconciled

The president signs the bill into law

Law is incorporated into U.S. Code

Law is published as a Statute at Large

Law directs action by a federal agency

Federal agency uses a similar process to adopt rule(s) to enact the statutory provisions

Chip Somodevilla/Getty Images

In 2019, the 116th U.S. Congress seated its most diverse group of new members.

Courts may invalidate state statutes that conflict with federal laws, or city statutes that conflict with either state or federal law. However, courts try to interpret the plain meaning of a statute to avoid conflicts with other laws, including the Constitution. Courts review the constitutionality of a statute only as a last resort. When engaging in constitutional review, courts generally attempt to preserve any portions of the law that can be upheld without violating the general intent of the statute. For example, the U.S. Supreme Court struck down the Communications Decency Act[37] without undermining the balance of the comprehensive Telecommunications Act of 1996 (see Chapter 9).

In what some call "one of the greatest legal events" in U.S. history,[38] the Supreme Court in *Marbury v. Madison*[39] established the Court's power of **judicial review**—that is, the power to strike down laws the Court finds to be in conflict with the Constitution. The Court said the constitutional system of checks and balances implicitly provided the judicial branch with authority to limit the power of the legislative branch and to bar it from enacting unconstitutional laws. The Court acknowledged that the Constitution gave the legislative branch the power to make laws, but Article III empowered the judicial branch to determine whether the actions of other branches of government were unconstitutional.

judicial review
The power of the courts to determine the meaning of the Constitution and to decide whether laws violate the Constitution.

In *Marbury*, the Court gave itself the authority to limit the power of Congress to enact laws. As the final arbiters of law in the United States, the courts must ensure that actions of the legislative and executive branches conform to the U.S. Constitution, *Marbury* held. "Why courts should have this ultimate power . . . in a democratic order remains the largest and most difficult issue of constitutional law," according to one scholar.[40]

Judicial review allows all courts to examine government actions to determine their constitutionality. However, courts other than the U.S. Supreme Court rarely use this power. If a state supreme court determined that a statute was constitutional under its state constitution, the decision could be appealed to the U.S. Supreme Court, which could decide that the law did not meet the standards set by the U.S. Constitution.

Historically, the Supreme Court has used its power of judicial review sparingly and rarely struck down laws as unconstitutional. For more than half a century after *Marbury*, the Court did not use its power as chief interpreter of the Constitution. As a general rule, the Court will defer to the lawmaking authority of the executive and legislative branches of government by interpreting laws in ways that do not conflict with the Constitution. Nonetheless, it has invalidated numerous acts of Congress.

Common Law

The **common law** is judge-made law. Judges create the common law when they rely on legal custom, tradition and prior court decisions to guide their decisions in pending cases. Common law often arises in situations not covered expressly by statutes when judges base their ruling on precedent and legal **doctrines** established in similar cases. For example, under common law, judges may treat print publishers and online distributors of threatening communications differently (see Chapter 3).

The common law is not written down in one place. It consists of a vast body of legal principles created from hundreds of years of dispute resolution that reaches past the founding of this country back to England. For centuries prior to the settlement of the American colonies, English courts "discovered" the doctrines people had used throughout time to resolve disagreements. Judges then applied these "common" laws to guide court decisions. The resulting decisions, and the reasoning that supported them, was known as English common law. It became the foundation of U.S. common law.

Eventually, common law grew beyond the problem-solving principles of the common people. Today, U.S. common law rests on the presumption that prior court rulings, or precedent, should guide future courts. The essence of precedent, stare decisis, is that courts should follow each other's guidance. Once a higher court has established a principle relevant to a certain set of facts, fairness requires lower courts to try to apply the same principle to similar facts. This establishes consistency and stability in the law.

Under the rule of stare decisis, the decision of a higher court, such as the U.S. Supreme Court, establishes a precedent that binds lower court rulings. A binding precedent of the U.S. Supreme Court constrains all lower federal courts throughout the country, and the decisions of

common law
Judge-made law composed of the principles and traditions established through court rulings; precedent-based law.

doctrines
Principles or theories of law that shape judicial decision making (e.g., the doctrine of content neutrality).

REAL WORLD LAW
PRECEDENT IS A CORNERSTONE OF THE RULE OF LAW

In a 2018 dissenting opinion, Justice Elena Kagan wrote:

> The idea that today's Court should stand by yesterday's decisions is a foundation stone of the rule of law. It promotes the evenhanded, predictable and consistent development of legal doctrine. It fosters respect for and reliance on judicial decisions. And it contributes to the actual and perceived integrity of the judicial process by ensuring that decisions are founded in the law rather than in the proclivities of individuals.[ix]

each circuit court of appeals bind the district courts in that circuit. Similarly, lower state courts must follow the precedents of their own state appellate and supreme courts. However, courts from different and coequal jurisdictions do not establish binding precedent upon their peers. Courts in Rhode Island are not bound to follow precedents established in Wyoming, and federal district courts are not bound to apply precedents established by appellate courts in other federal circuits. In fact, different federal appellate courts sometimes hand down directly conflicting decisions. To avoid such conflicts, however, courts often look to each other's decisions for guidance.

Applying precedent is not clear cut. After all, the common law must be discovered through research in the thousands of court decisions collected into centuries of volumes, called court reporters. Sometimes, multiple lines of precedent seem to converge and suggest different outcomes.[41] Then a court must choose.

Even when stare decisis is clear and its power most direct, lower courts may decide not to adhere to precedent. At the risk of the judges' credibility, courts may simply ignore precedent. Courts also may depart from precedent with good reason. Courts examining a new but similar question may decide to **modify precedent**—that is, to alter the precedent to respond to changed realities. Thus, the U.S. Supreme Court might find that contemporary attitudes and practices no longer support a 20-year-old precedent permitting government to maintain the secrecy of computer compilations of public records.[42]

Courts also may **distinguish from precedent** by asserting that factual differences between the current case and the precedent case outweigh similarities. For example, the Supreme Court 40-plus years ago distinguished between newspapers and broadcasters in terms of any right of public access.[43] The Court said the public has a right to demand that broadcasters provide diverse content on issues of public importance because broadcasters use the public airwaves. The Court did not apply that reasoning when it later considered virtually the same question as applied to newspapers. Newspapers, the Court said, are independent members of the press with a protected right to control their content. The Supreme Court similarly has said "common-sense distinctions" differentiate advertising, which the courts call commercial speech, from other varieties of speech.[44]

Finally, courts very occasionally will **overturn precedent** outright and reject the fundamental premise of an earlier decision. This is a radical step and generally occurs only to remedy past errors or to reflect a fundamental rethinking of the law. In the Supreme Court's recent decision in *Janus*, the Court overruled a 30-year-old Court precedent that had required public employees to pay their "fair share" of union dues even if the employees chose not to join the union.[45] The Court said *Abood* had been poorly reasoned, produced inconsistent outcomes and violated nonmembers' right to be free from government-compelled subsidies of private speech on matters of public concern.

Equity Law

Equity law is a second form of law made by judges when they apply general principles of ethics and fairness to determine the proper remedy for a legal harm. When a court orders someone to stop using your trademark in addition to paying fines that cover the costs of actual damages caused, the order recognizes that continued use might force you out of business or associate

modify precedent
To change rather than follow or reject precedent.

distinguish from precedent
To justify an outcome in a case by asserting that differences between that case and preceding cases outweigh any similarities.

overturn precedent
To reject the fundamental premise of a precedent.

equity law
Law created by judges to decide cases based on fairness and ethics and also to determine the proper remedy.

you with products of lesser quality. Such a ruling represents the application of equity law to achieve a just result.

Equity law is intended to provide fair remedies for various harms that are not addressed in other forms of law or because fairness will not be achieved fully or at all through the rigid application of strict rules. No specific, black-letter laws dictate equity. Rather, judges use their conscience and discretion to decide what is fair and issue decrees to ensure that justice is achieved. Thus, restraining orders that require paparazzi to stay a certain distance away from celebrities are a form of equity law. An injunction in 1971 that temporarily prevented The New York Times and The Washington Post from publishing stories based on the Pentagon Papers was another form of equity relief. While the law of equity is related to common law, the rules of equity law are more flexible and are not governed by precedent.

Administrative Law

Constitutions and legislatures delegate authority to executives and to specialized executive branch agencies to make the decisions and create the rules that form **administrative law**. Administrative agencies, such as the Federal Election Commission or the Federal Trade Commission, create the rules, regulations, orders and decisions that execute, or carry out, laws enacted by Congress.

Administrative law may represent the largest proportion of contemporary law in the United States. An alphabet soup of state and federal administrative agencies—such as the Federal Communications Commission, which oversees interstate electronic communication—provides both legislative and judicial functions. These agencies adopt orders, rules and regulations with the force of law to implement the laws enacted by Congress and signed by the president.

The authority, or even the existence, of administrative agencies can change. Legislatures may adopt or amend laws to revise the responsibilities of administrative agencies. Thus, when Congress adopted the Telecommunications Act of 1996, it substantially revised the responsibilities of the FCC, originally authorized by the Communications Act of 1934.

Administrative agencies enforce the administrative rules they adopt. They conduct hearings in which they interpret their rules, grant relief, resolve disputes and levy fines or penalties. Courts generally have the power to hear appeals to the decisions of administrative agencies after agency appeal procedures are exhausted. Then courts engage in regulatory construction and judicial review. Courts generally defer to the judgment of expert administrative agencies and void agency rules and actions only when the agency clearly has exceeded its authority, violated its rules and procedures, or provided no evidence to support its ruling.

In 2015, however, the U.S. Supreme Court refused to defer to administrative interpretations of the meaning of the Affordable Care Act's precise terms.[46] The Court said the "task to determine the correct reading" of the law fell to the Court itself when, as in this case, Congress did not intend to delegate the authority to "fill in the statutory gaps" to the administrative agency.[47] Carefully parsing the meaning of the key phrases in the contested section of the law and "bearing in mind . . . that the words of a statute must be read in their context and with a view to their place in the overall statutory scheme,"[48] the Court affirmed the ruling of the Fourth Circuit Court of Appeals and found the law constitutional.[49]

administrative law
The orders, rules and regulations promulgated by executive branch administrative agencies to carry out their delegated duties.

Many saw the Court's reasoning in *King v. Burwell*, the Affordable Care Act case, as signaling a movement away from deference to administrative agency judgments. Some said the Court's shift reinforced the rule of law by counterbalancing any tendency for the new administrative agency leaders appointed by each incoming president to alter the interpretation of administrative laws.[50]

Executive Orders

executive orders
Orders from a government executive, such as the president, a governor or a mayor, that have the force of law.

Government executives, such as the president, may issue **executive orders** to create another source of law. Both President Barack Obama and President Donald Trump have used executive orders to achieve policy objectives when Congress failed to act. Their executive orders prompted frequent outcry from political opponents and protests that each was circumventing the express authority of Congress, in violation of the rule of law.

Executive Orders of Recent U.S. Presidents				
	Time Period	**Total**	**No./Yr.**	**Exec. Order No.**
William J. Clinton	Total	**364**	**46**	**12834–13197**
	Term I	200	50	12834–13033
	Term II	164	41	13034–13197
George W. Bush	Total	**291**	**36**	**13198–13488**
	Term I	173	43	13198–13370
	Term II	118	30	13371–13488
Barack Obama	Total	**276**	**35**	**13489–13764**
	Term I	147	37	13489–13635
	Term II	129	32	13636–13764
Donald J. Trump (2017–part 2018)	Total	**85**	**51**	**13765–13849**
Combined Annual AVERAGE		**39**		

Source: Washington–Trump, The American Presidency Project, presidency.proxied.lsit.ucsb.edu/data/orders.php.

The president, governors and mayors do not have unlimited power to issue executive orders. The Supreme Court long has held that executive orders must fall within the inherent powers of the executive to have the force of law.[51] The Court has said executive orders must arise from the president's explicit power under Article II, Section 2 of the Constitution, his role as commander in chief, or his responsibility to ensure that laws are properly executed. If the delegation of power to the executive is not clear, the authority to issue executive orders falls into what Justice

Robert H. Jackson once called a "zone of twilight" ambiguity.[52] However, the limits to the power to issue executive orders are largely informal and primarily a matter of self-restraint and tradition.[53]

Early in 2019, for example, the American Civil Liberties Union and 16 states filed separate lawsuits in federal court in California challenging President Trump's executive order declaring a national emergency to build a wall along the southern border.[54] The ACLU argued that the executive order unconstitutionally usurped the authority of Congress to control spending. In announcing the executive order, President Trump predicted the lawsuits and said, "We'll win in the Supreme Court."

Some executive orders are routine. For example, each president of the United States issues orders that determine what types of records will be open and which classified as secret, how long they will remain secret and who has access to them. Changes in these rules not only affect the operations of the executive agencies that create the documents; they also affect the ability of citizens to oversee and review the actions of their government (see Chapter 7).

STRUCTURE OF THE JUDICIAL SYSTEM

A basic understanding of the structure of the court system in the United States is fundamental to an appreciation of the functioning of the law. Trial courts, or federal district courts, do fact-finding, apply the law and settle disputes. Courts of appeal, including federal circuit courts and supreme courts in each system, review how lower courts applied the law. Through their judgments, courts can hand down equitable remedies, reshape laws or even throw out laws as unconstitutional.

Court Jurisdiction

An independent court system operates in each state, the District of Columbia and the federal government. The military and the U.S. territories, such as Puerto Rico, also have court systems.

Each of these court systems operates under the authority of the relevant constitution. For example, the U.S. Constitution requires the establishment of the Supreme Court of the United States and authorizes Congress to establish other courts it deems necessary to the proper functioning of the federal judiciary. **Jurisdiction** refers to a court's authority to hear a case. Every court has its own jurisdiction—that is, its own geographic or topical area of responsibility and authority.

In 2017, the U.S. Supreme Court reiterated its recognition of two types of court jurisdiction: general and specific.[55] Typically, the site or location of general jurisdiction is an individual's home or a corporation's headquarters. Given general jurisdiction, a court may hear any claim against that defendant. To be heard in a forum of specific jurisdiction, a suit must relate to the defendant's contacts with that forum. In libel, for example, the standard has been that any court in any locale where the alleged libel could be seen or heard would have jurisdiction.[56] A court may dismiss a lawsuit outside of its jurisdiction.

New technologies present new challenges to the determination of jurisdiction. Consider online libel. Given that statements published online are potentially seen anywhere, any court might claim jurisdiction (see Chapter 5). Then the plaintiff might initiate the lawsuit in any court and would likely file the suit in the court expected to render a favorable decision.

jurisdiction
The geographic or topical area of responsibility and authority of a court.

forum shopping
A practice whereby the plaintiff chooses a court in which to sue because he or she believes the court will rule in the plaintiff's favor.

In a broad ruling that could limit **forum shopping**, the practice of seeking the most favorable court to hear your case, the U.S. Supreme Court held that unless there is a substantial link between the forum of the court and the source of injury, a company may only be sued "at home."[57] Following a detailed discussion of jurisdiction, the Court unanimously held that a national newspaper's "home" is in one of only two places: where the company is incorporated or the main location of its business.[58]

As access to the internet becomes accepted as an essential public utility,[59] nations struggle individually and collectively to determine who has legal jurisdiction over international online disputes.[60] The U.S. Supreme Court test to establish specific jurisdiction often applies to such online disputes and requires courts to find that (1) the defendant intentionally acted inside the jurisdiction of the court, (2) the plaintiff's claim arose from that activity, and (3) it is reasonable for the court to exercise jurisdiction.[61]

The U.S. Constitution spells out the areas of jurisdiction of the federal courts. Within their geographic regions, federal courts exercise authority over cases that relate to interstate or international controversies or that interpret and apply federal laws, treaties or the U.S. Constitution. Thus, federal courts hear cases involving copyright laws. The federal courts also decide cases in which the federal government is a party, such as when the states bring suit against presidential directives extending protections for undocumented immigrants.[62] Cases involving controversies between states, between citizens of different states or between a state and a citizen of another state also are heard in federal courts. Thus, a libel suit brought by a resident of Pennsylvania against a newspaper in California would be heard in federal court.

Trial Courts

The state, federal and specialized court systems in the United States are organized similarly; most court systems have three tiers. At the lowest level, trial courts are the courts where nearly all cases begin. Each state contains at least one of the nation's 94 trial-level federal courts, which are called district courts. Trial courts reach decisions by finding facts and applying existing law to them. They are the only courts to use juries. They do not establish precedents. Some judges view the routine media coverage of legal actions taking place in trial courts as a threat to the fairness of trials (see Chapter 8). Some judges also fear that media coverage will cast their court in disrepute and reduce public trust in the judicial system.

de novo
Literally, "new" or "over again." On appeal, the court may review the facts de novo rather than simply reviewing the legal posture and process of the case.

Courts of Appeal

Anyone who loses a case at trial may appeal the decision. However, courts of appeal generally do not make findings of fact or receive new evidence in the case. Only in rare cases do courts of appeal review case facts **de novo**, a phrase meaning "new" or "over again." Instead,

FIGURE 1.2 ■ Comparing the Federal and State Court Systems

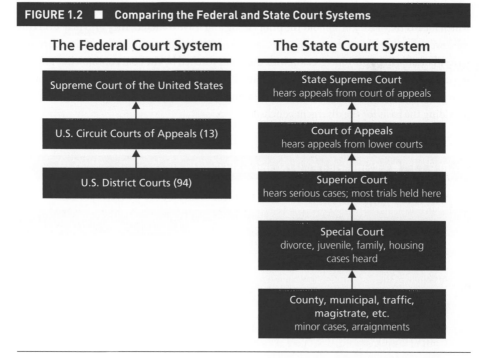

The Federal Court System

- Supreme Court of the United States
- U.S. Circuit Courts of Appeals (13)
- U.S. District Courts (94)

The State Court System

- State Supreme Court
  hears appeals from court of appeals
- Court of Appeals
  hears appeals from lower courts
- Superior Court
  hears serious cases; most trials held here
- Special Court
  divorce, juvenile, family, housing cases heard
- County, municipal, traffic, magistrate, etc.
  minor cases, arraignments

appellate courts review the legal process of the lower court. Courts of appeal examine the procedures and tests used by the lower court to determine whether **due process** was carried out—that is, whether the proper law was applied and whether the judicial process was fair and appropriate.

Decisions in appellate courts are based primarily on detailed written arguments, or briefs, and on short oral arguments from the attorneys representing each side of the case. Individuals and organizations that are not parties to the case, called **amicus curiae** ("friends of the court"), may receive court permission to submit a brief called an **amicus brief**.

Most court systems have two levels of appellate courts: the intermediate courts of appeal and the supreme court. In the federal court system, there are 13 intermediate-level appellate courts, called circuit courts. A panel of three judges hears all except the most important cases in the federal circuit courts of appeal. Only rarely do all the judges of the circuit court sit **en banc** to hear an appeal. *En banc* literally means "on the bench" but is used to mean "in full court." Twelve of the federal circuits represent geographic regions. For example, the U.S. Court of Appeals for the Ninth Circuit bears responsibility for the entire West Coast, Hawaii and Alaska, and the U.S. Court of Appeals for the D.C. Circuit covers the District of Columbia. The 13th circuit, the U.S. Court of Appeals for the Federal Circuit, handles specialized appeals. In addition, separate, specialized federal courts handle cases dealing with the armed forces, international trade or veterans' claims, among other things.

due process
Fair legal proceedings. Due process is guaranteed by the Fifth and 14th Amendments to the U.S. Constitution.

amicus brief
A submission to the court from **amicus curiae**, or "friends of the court," which are interested individuals or organizations that are parties in the case.

en banc
Literally, "on the bench" but now meaning "in full court." The judges of a circuit court of appeals will sit en banc to decide important or controversial cases.

affirm
To ratify, uphold or approve a lower court ruling.

overrule
To reverse the ruling of a lower court.

concurring opinion
A separate opinion of a minority of the court or a single judge or justice agreeing with the majority opinion but applying different reasoning or legal principles.

dissenting opinion
A separate opinion of a minority of the court or a single judge or justice disagreeing with the result reached by the majority and challenging the majority's reasoning or the legal basis of the decision.

Courts of appeal may **affirm** the decision of the lower court with a majority opinion, which means they ratify or uphold the prior ruling and leave it intact. They also may **overrule** the lower court, reversing the previous decision. Any single judge or minority of the court may write a **concurring opinion** agreeing with the result reached by the court opinion but presenting different reasoning, legal principles or issues. Judges who disagree with the opinion of the court may write a **dissenting opinion**, critiquing the majority's reasoning or judgment and providing the basis for the divergent conclusion.

TABLE 1.1 ■ Comparing Federal and State Courts
The federal government, and each state government, has its own court system.

The Federal Court System
Structure
• Article III of the Constitution invests the judicial power of the United States in the federal court system. Article III, Section 1 creates the U.S. Supreme Court and gives Congress authority to create lower federal courts. • Congress has established 13 U.S. Courts of Appeals, 94 U.S. District Courts, the U.S. Court of Claims, and the U.S. Court of International Trade. U.S. Bankruptcy Courts handle bankruptcy cases. Magistrate Judges handle some District Court matters. • Parties may appeal a decision of a U.S. District Court, the U.S. Court of Claims, and/or the U.S. Court of International Trade to a U.S. Court of Appeals. • A party may ask the U.S. Supreme Court to review a decision of the U.S. Court of Appeals, but the Supreme Court usually is under no obligation to do so.
Selection of Judges
The Constitution states that federal judges are to be nominated by the President and confirmed by the Senate. They hold office during good behavior, typically, for life. Congressional impeachment proceedings may remove federal judges for misbehavior.
Types of Cases Heard
• Cases that deal with the constitutionality of a law; • Cases involving the laws and treaties of the U.S.; • Legal issues related to ambassadors and public ministers; • Disputes between two or more states; • Admiralty law; • Bankruptcy; and • Habeas corpus issues.

The Federal Court System (Continued)

Article I Courts

Congress created several Article I, or legislative courts, that do not have full judicial power. Article I courts are:

- U.S. Court of Appeals for Veterans Claims
- U.S. Court of Appeals for the Armed Forces
- U.S. Tax Court

The State Court System

Structure

- The Constitution and laws of each state establish the state courts. Most states have a Supreme Court, an intermediate Court of Appeals, and state trial courts, sometimes referred to as Circuit or District Courts.
- States usually have courts that handle specific legal matters, e.g., probate court (wills and estates); juvenile court; family court; etc.
- Parties dissatisfied with the decision of the trial court may take their case to the intermediate Court of Appeals.
- Parties have the option to ask the highest state court to hear the case.
- Only certain cases are eligible for review by the U.S. Supreme Court.

Selection of Judges

State court judges are selected in a variety of ways, including

- election,
- appointment for a given number of years,
- appointment for life, and
- combinations of these methods, e.g., appointment followed by election.

Types of Cases Heard

- Most criminal cases, probate (involving wills and estates)
- Most contract cases, tort cases (personal injuries), family law (marriages, divorces, adoptions), etc.

State courts are the final arbiters of state laws and constitutions. Their interpretation of federal law or the U.S. Constitution may be appealed to the U.S. Supreme Court.

Article I Courts

N/A

Source: United States Courts, www.uscourts.gov/about-federal-courts/court-role-and-structure; www.uscourts .gov/aboutfederal-courts/court-role-and-structure/comparing-federal-state-courts.

Majority decisions issued by courts of appeal establish precedent for lower courts within their jurisdiction. Their rulings also may be persuasive outside their jurisdiction. If only a plurality of the judges hearing a case supports the opinion of the lower court, the decision does not establish binding precedent. Similarly, dissenting and concurring opinions do not have the force of law, but they often influence subsequent court reasoning.

FIGURE 1.3 ■ U.S. Circuit Courts of Appeal

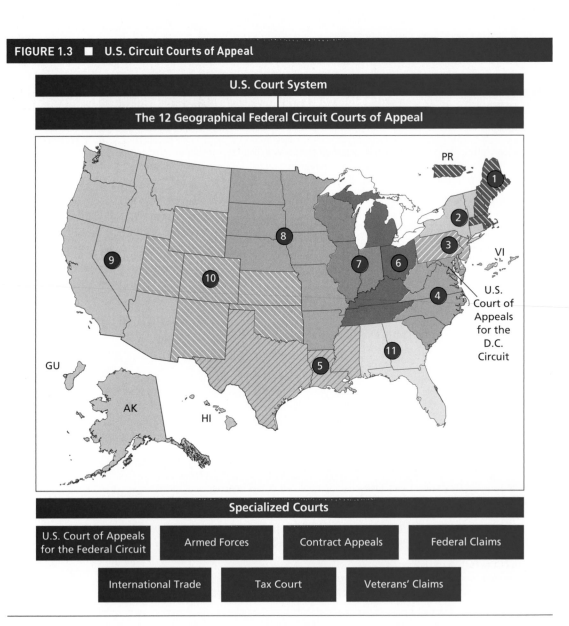

Courts of appeal also **remand**, or send back, decisions to the lower court to establish a more detailed record of facts or to reconsider the case. A decision to remand a case may not be appealed. Courts of appeal often remand cases when they believe that the lower court did not fully explore issues in the case and needs to develop a more complete record of evidence as the basis for its decision.

A circuit court of appeals decision must be signed by at least two of the three sitting judges and is final. The losing party may ask the court to reconsider the case or may request a rehearing en banc. Such requests are rarely granted. Losing parties also may appeal the verdict of any intermediate court of appeals to the highest court in the state or to the U.S. Supreme Court.

The U.S. Court of Appeals for the Ninth Circuit sits en banc in 2014 to hear the appeal in *Garcia v. Google*, which involves a demand that Google remove a video from its site.

Gina Ferazzi/Getty Images

The U.S. Supreme Court

Established in 1789, the Supreme Court of the United States functions primarily as an appellate court, although the Constitution establishes the Court's **original jurisdiction** in a few specific areas. In general, Congress has granted lower federal courts jurisdiction in these same areas, so almost no suits begin in the U.S. Supreme Court. Instead, the Court hears cases on appeal from all other federal courts, federal regulatory agencies and state supreme courts.

Cases come before the Court either on direct appeal from the lower court or through the Court's grant of a **writ of certiorari**. Certain federal laws, such as the Bipartisan Campaign Reform Act,[63] guarantee a direct right of appeal to the U.S. Supreme Court. More often, the Court grants a writ of certiorari for compelling reasons, such as when a case poses a novel or pressing legal question. The Court often grants certiorari to cases in which different U.S. circuit courts of appeal have issued conflicting opinions. The Court may consider whether an issue is ripe for consideration, meaning that the case presents a real and present controversy rather than a hypothetical concern. In addition, the Court may reject some petitions as **moot** because the controversy is no longer "live." Mootness may be an issue, for example, when a student who has challenged school policy graduates before the case is resolved. The Court sometimes accepts cases that appear to be moot if it believes the problem is likely to arise again.

The Court's Makeup. The chief justice of the United States and eight associate justices make up the Supreme Court. The president nominates and the Senate confirms the chief justice as well as the other eight members of the Court, who sit "during good behavior"[64] for life or until retirement. This gives the president considerable influence over the Court's political ideology.

remand
To send back to the lower court for further action.

original jurisdiction
The authority to consider a case at its inception, as contrasted with appellate jurisdiction.

writ of certiorari
A petition for review by the Supreme Court of the United States; *certiorari* means "to be informed of."

moot
Term used to describe a case in which the issues presented are no longer "live" or in which the matter in dispute has already been resolved; a case is not moot if it is susceptible to repetition but evades review.

TABLE 1.2 ■ The U.S. Supreme Court at a Glance, 2019

Justice	Born	Nominating President	Year Appointed
Chief Justice John G. Roberts Jr.	1955	George W. Bush	2005

Justice	Born	Nominating President	Year Appointed	Justice	Born	Nominating President	Year Appointed
Associate Justice Clarence Thomas	1948	George H. W. Bush	1991	Associate Justice Ruth Bader Ginsburg	1933	Bill Clinton	1993
Associate Justice Stephen G. Breyer	1938	Bill Clinton	1994	Associate Justice Samuel A. Alito Jr.	1950	George W. Bush	2006
Associate Justice Sonia Sotomayor	1954	Barack Obama	2009	Associate Justice Elena Kagan	1960	Barack Obama	2010
Associate Justice Neil M. Gorsuch	1967	Donald Trump	2017	Associate Justice Brett M. Kavanaugh	1965	Donald Trump	2018

Photos source: SupremeCourt.gov.

After the Senate failed to give President Obama's Supreme Court nominee a confirmation vote, President Trump took office and conservative Neil Gorsuch took the vacant seat in 2017. Combined with Justice Anthony Kennedy's retirement and the 2018 confirmation of Brett Kavanaugh, this shifted the Court toward the conservative end and made Chief Justice John Roberts the swing vote. Most observers argue this will change the direction of American jurisprudence for decades.

In 2019, Justice Sonia Sotomayor was the only true liberal among the sitting justices. She is the first Hispanic/Latina justice and one of the Court's most public facing members. Liberal justices tend to believe that government should play an active role in ensuring individual liberties. They also tend to support regulation of large businesses and corporations and to reduce emphasis on property rights. Justice Sotomayor's former experience as a prosecutor and trial judge often leads her to challenge lawyers on the facts of a case.

Supreme Court of the United States justices, fall 2018.

As the most senior justice on the court's left wing, Justice Ruth Bader Ginsburg is often in charge of assigning dissents in highly controversial cases. Once at the center of the Court's ideological spectrum, she now is the last civil rights lawyer on the Court.

Justices Elena Kagan and Stephen Breyer are seen as "center-left pragmatists."[65] Justice Kagan is the first justice in decades who did not serve previously as a judge. Her early terms on the Court displayed a willingness to inject a "critical voice that could make the case for liberals within the court and beyond"[66] and an ability to draft unanimous decisions. Justice Breyer

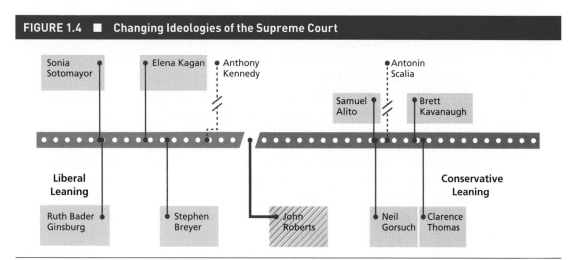

FIGURE 1.4 ■ Changing Ideologies of the Supreme Court

Source: Adapted from data collected by *The Judicial Common Space*.

INTERNATIONAL LAW
JUDICIAL SELECTION PROCESSES NEED TO SUPPORT RULE OF LAW

The World Justice Project's Rule of Law Index identified problematic trends in the judicial selection process in the United States over the last few years. Noting that judicial selection is an essential bulwark of the rule of law, particularly as related to judicial independence and accountability, the report highlighted significant differences in the U.S. process and that of most Western democratic nations.

While the United States allows almost anyone to become a judge, other countries require judges to meet certain standards for age, legal education and legal experience. In addition, most countries allow executives to appoint judges only from a list created by an independent body, which is not the case in the United States. This raises questions of judicial independence. Finally, very few countries allow public election of judges, while most states elect at least some judges. Elections make judges more accountable but also affect judicial outcomes, according to studies.

"Independence versus accountability is that tension that just runs throughout the judicial process. . . . But obviously the more independent you make the judges then in a certain sense the less accountable they can be."[xi]

tends to emphasize legal history and intent as well as substantive due process in rulings that prior to 2017 often determined the Court's majority.

Chief Justice John Roberts now is the justice closest to the center of the Court. A conservative, the chief justice tries to develop agreement across the Court by encouraging narrow rulings.

Justices Samuel Alito, Clarence Thomas, Brett Kavanaugh and Neil Gorsuch create a staunch conservative bloc in the Court.[67] Conservative justices, in general, want to reduce the role of the federal government, including the Supreme Court. They tend to favor a narrow, or close, reading of the Constitution that relies more heavily on original intent than on contemporary realities. These justices have propelled the Court's rightward shift on business, campaign finance and race.[68]

The demographics of the Supreme Court have important symbolic significance even if they do not directly influence the Court's rulings. In 2016, however, Justice Sonia Sotomayor said the Court could use more diversity. "I, for one, do think there is a disadvantage from having (five) Catholics, three Jews, everyone from an Ivy League school. . . . A different perspective can permit you to more fully understand the arguments that are before you and help you articulate your position in a way that everyone will understand."[69]

Throughout history, U.S. Supreme Court justices have been predominantly married, male, white and Protestant; only four women (3.5 percent) and two African-Americans have served on the nation's highest court. Today, the Court is more diverse than in the past. Three female justices (one Hispanic) and one African-American justice sit on the current Court, but the Court that is the final arbiter of the law in this country does not reflect the diversity of the U.S. population. Court membership overrepresents certain educational backgrounds and religious faiths. Four of the sitting justices graduated from Yale Law School and four from Harvard, which Justice Ruth Bader Ginsburg attended although she graduated from

REAL WORLD LAW
SCALIA SAID RULES, HISTORY SHOULD GUIDE COURT INTERPRETATIONS

After serving almost 30 years on the Court, Justice Antonin Scalia was one of the longest-seated justices in the Supreme Court's history when he died in 2016.[xii] His views shaped many areas of contemporary mass communication law as well as the rule of law.

Justice Scalia relied on originalism and clear rules to constrain the discretion of judges. Originalists argue that the Constitution's meaning should be determined by how the text was understood at the time it was adopted, "a historical criterion that is conceptually . . . separate from the preferences of the judge himself,"[xiii] Justice Scalia said. He argued that the Supreme Court should "curb—even reverse—the tendency of judges to imbue authoritative texts with their own policy preferences."

Clearly delineated and consistently applied rules are necessary, he said, to "provide greater certainty in the law and hence greater predictability and greater respect for the rule of law."[xiv] Concrete rules are preferable to multipart tests or balancing, he said, because "when . . . I adopt a general rule . . . I not only constrain lower courts, I constrain myself as well."[xv] The predictability of clear rules helps "enhance the legitimacy of decisions . . . [and] embolden the decision maker to resist the will of a hostile majority," one observer said.[xvi]

Columbia Law School. While 24 percent of the U.S. population is Roman Catholic, four members of the Court (45 percent), including the chief justice, profess to this faith.[70] Another third of the Court's current justices are Jewish, which is more than 20 times the percentage of Jews in the U.S. population.[71] No Supreme Court justice has self-identified as other than heterosexual and cisgender.

Granting Review. Petitioners may ask the Supreme Court for a writ of certiorari if the court of appeals or the highest state court denies them a hearing or issues a verdict against them. Writs are granted at the discretion of the Court. All seated justices consider a writ, which is granted only if at least four justices vote to hear the case. This is called the rule of four.

Neither the decision to grant nor the decision to deny a writ of certiorari indicates anything about the Court's opinion regarding the merits of the lower court's ruling. Denial of certiorari generally means that the justices do not think the issue is sufficiently important or timely to decide. In recent years, an average of 8,200 petitions have been filed with the Court, which grants fewer than 1 percent of them.[72] Approximately one-fourth of the petitions filed are accompanied by the required fee of $150. The vast majority of petitions are filed without the fee—often by prisoners who cannot pay the required filing fee.

Reaching Decisions. Once the Court agrees to hear a case, the parties file written briefs outlining the facts and legal issues in the case and summarizing their legal arguments. The justices review the briefs prior to oral argument in the case, which generally lasts one hour. The justices may sit silently during oral argument, or they may pepper the attorneys with questions.

"Our overworked Supreme Court" by Joseph Ferdinand Keppler. Published by Keppler & Schwarzmann, December 9, 1885, via SupremeCourt.gov

This 1885 lithograph shows "Our Overworked Supreme Court."

Following oral argument, the justices meet in a private, closed conference to take an initial vote on the outcome. Discussion begins with the chief justice and proceeds around the table in order of descending seniority of the associate justices. Then voting proceeds from the most junior member of the Court and ends with the chief justice. The chief justice or the most senior justice in the majority determines who will draft the majority opinion.

A majority of the justices must agree on a point of law for the Court to establish binding precedent. Draft opinions are circulated among the justices, and negotiations may attempt to shift votes. It may take months for the Court to achieve a final decision, which is then announced on decision day.

Two other options exist for the Supreme Court. It may issue a **per curiam opinion**, which is an unsigned opinion by the Court as a whole. Although a single justice may draft the opinion, that authorship is not made public. Per curiam opinions often do not include the same thorough discussion of the issues found in signed opinions. The Supreme Court also may resolve a case by issuing a **memorandum order**. A memorandum order simply announces the vote of the Court without providing an opinion. This quick and easy method to dispense with a case has become more common with the Court's growing tendency to issue fewer signed opinions.

The ideological leanings of the individual justices, and of the Court as a whole, come into play in the choice of cases granted review and the ultimate decisions of the Court.[73] The U.S. Supreme Court relies on a wide range of sources to guide its interpretation of the Constitution. **Originalists** and **textualists** seek the meaning of the Constitution primarily in its explicit text, the historical context in which the document developed and the recorded history of its deliberation and original meaning. Some justices look beyond the text to discover how best to apply the Constitution today. Their interpretation relies more expressly on deep-seated personal and societal values, ethical and legal concepts and the evolving interests of a shifting society. The Court's reasoning at times also builds on international standards, treaties or conventions, such as the Universal Declaration of Human Rights, or the decisions of courts outside the United States as well as state and other federal courts. On occasion, such as when the Court discovered a right to privacy embedded in the First Amendment, the justices refer to the views and insights of legal scholars.[74]

PROCESSES OF THE LAW

Although each court or case follows a somewhat idiosyncratic path, similar patterns of judicial process emerge. In a criminal matter, the case starts when a government agency investigates a

per curiam opinion
An unsigned opinion by the Court as a whole.

memorandum order
An order announcing the vote of the Supreme Court without providing an opinion.

originalists
Supreme Court justices who interpret the Constitution according to the perceived intent of its framers.

textualists
Judges—in particular, Supreme Court justices—who rely exclusively on a careful reading of legal texts to determine the meaning of the law.

possible crime. After gathering evidence, the government arrests someone for a crime, such as distributing false and misleading advertising through the internet. The standard of evidence needed for an arrest or to issue a search warrant is known as **probable cause**, which is more than mere suspicion.

The case then goes before a **grand jury** or a judge. Unlike trial juries (also called petit juries), grand juries do not determine guilt. Grand juries hear the state's evidence and determine whether that evidence establishes probable cause to believe that a crime has been committed. A grand jury may be convened on the county, state or federal level. If the case proceeds without a grand jury, the judge makes a probable cause determination at a preliminary hearing. If the state fails to establish probable cause, the case may not proceed. If probable cause is found, the person is indicted.

probable cause
The standard of evidence needed for an arrest or to issue a search warrant. More than mere suspicion, it is a showing through reasonably trustworthy information that a crime has been or is being committed.

grand jury
A group summoned to hear the state's evidence in criminal cases and decide whether a crime was committed and whether charges should be filed; grand juries do not determine guilt.

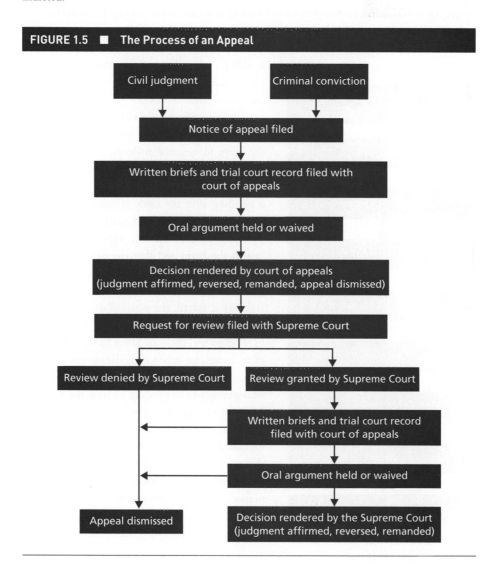

FIGURE 1.5 ■ The Process of an Appeal

Civil judgment

Criminal conviction

Notice of appeal filed

Written briefs and trial court record filed with court of appeals

Oral argument held or waived

Decision rendered by court of appeals (judgment affirmed, reversed, remanded, appeal dismissed)

Request for review filed with Supreme Court

Review denied by Supreme Court

Review granted by Supreme Court

Written briefs and trial court record filed with court of appeals

Oral argument held or waived

Appeal dismissed

Decision rendered by the Supreme Court (judgment affirmed, reversed, remanded)

Then the case moves to a court arraignment, where the defendant is formally charged and pleads guilty or not guilty. A plea bargain may be arranged in which the defendant pleads guilty to reduced charges or an agreed-upon sentence. Plea bargains account for almost 95 percent of all felony convictions in the United States.[75] If a not-guilty plea is entered, the case usually proceeds to trial. The judge may set bail.

Proof beyond a reasonable doubt is required to establish guilt in a criminal trial. A guilty verdict prompts a sentencing hearing. A criminal sentence may include jail or prison time and a fine or fines.

Civil Suits

Civil cases generally involve two private individuals or organizations asking the courts to settle a conflict. The person who files a civil complaint or sues is the **plaintiff**. The person responding to the suit is the **defendant**. The civil injury one person or organization inflicts on another is called a **tort**. Tort law provides the means for the injured party to establish fault and receive compensation.

Many communication lawsuits are civil suits in which the plaintiff must prove his or her case by the preponderance of evidence. This standard of proof is lower than in criminal cases.

Civil suits begin when the plaintiff files a pleading with the clerk of court. To receive a damage award, a plaintiff generally must show that the harm occurred, that the defendant caused the harm and that the defendant was at fault, meaning the defendant acted either negligently or with malicious intent. Under a **strict liability** standard, the plaintiff does not need to demonstrate fault on the part of the defendant in order to win the suit. Strict liability applies in cases involving inherently dangerous products or activities. Under strict liability, the individual who produced the product or took the action is liable for all resulting harms.

At a court hearing, the defendant may answer the complaint by filing a countersuit, by denying the charge, by filing a **motion to dismiss** or by filing a motion for **summary judgment** (see next page). A motion to dismiss, or **demurrer**, asks a court to reject a complaint because it is legally insufficient. For example, a defendant may admit that it distributed

plaintiff
The party who files a complaint; the one who sues.

defendant
The party accused of violating a law, or the party being sued in a civil lawsuit.

tort
A private or civil wrong for which a court can provide remedy in the form of damages.

strict liability
Liability without fault; liability for any and all harms, foreseeable or unforeseen, which result from a product or an action.

motion to dismiss
A request to a court to reject a complaint because it does not state a claim that can be remedied by law or is legally lacking in some other way.

summary judgment
The resolution of a legal dispute without a full trial when a judge determines that undisputed evidence is legally sufficient to render judgment.

demurrer
A request that a court dismiss a case on the grounds that although the claims are true, they are insufficient to warrant a judgment against the defendant.

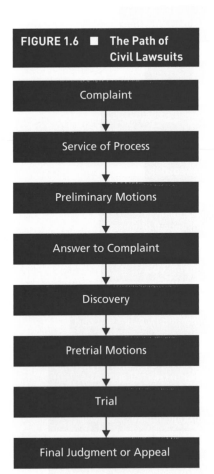

FIGURE 1.6 ■ The Path of Civil Lawsuits

Complaint

Service of Process

Preliminary Motions

Answer to Complaint

Discovery

Pretrial Motions

Trial

Final Judgment or Appeal

a story but argue that the story did not cause any legally actionable harm to the plaintiff. If the court grants the motion to dismiss, the plaintiff may appeal.

Before a case goes to trial, the disputing parties may agree to an out-of-court settlement. When this occurs, there is no public record of the outcome of the case. Out-of-court resolutions often prohibit the parties from discussing the terms of the settlement. In the 2019 settlement of the lawsuit former San Francisco 49ers quarterback Colin Kaepernick brought against the NFL, for example, a confidentiality agreement prevented the disclosure of any settlement details.[76]

Sometimes a judge will settle a civil case through a court conference. Civil suits are settled by the parties before trial almost 97 percent of the time.[77]

If the two sides do not settle, they begin to gather evidence through a process called **discovery**. In trying to build a case, one or both parties may issue a **subpoena**, which is a legal command for someone, sometimes a media professional, to appear and testify in court or turn over evidence, such as outtakes or notes. Citizens are legally obligated to comply with subpoenas, and the judge may punish noncompliance with a contempt of court citation, fines or jail.

If the parties do not reach a settlement, the case may proceed to a jury trial, which is required if either party requests it. To form a jury, the court summons individuals from a local pool, called the **venire**, that is usually based on voters' rolls. The locality where the court hears the suit is called the **venue**. The lawyers and judge select jurors through a process of questioning called **voir dire**, which literally means "to speak the truth."

While the theoretical goal is to seat an impartial jury for the trial, attorneys on both sides hope to gain advantage through the juror selection process. Attorneys may challenge potential jurors "for cause," such as when a prospective juror knows a party in the suit. They also may eliminate a limited number of potential jurors through **peremptory challenges**, in which they need not show a reason for the rejection. Expert consulting on jury selection, witness preparation, media interactions and the like help attorneys shape the jury and public messaging about the trial.

After evidence is presented at trial, the judge instructs the jury on how to apply the law to the case. Then the jury deliberates. If the jury cannot reach a verdict, the judge may order a new trial with a new jury. When a jury reaches a verdict, the judge generally enters it as the judgment of the court. However, the judge may overturn the verdict if it is contrary to the law. A successful plaintiff usually will be awarded damages.

Either party may appeal the judgment of the court. For example, if a party believes the jury was not properly instructed on the law, he or she may appeal on the basis of violation of due process. It can take years and cost hundreds of thousands of dollars to appeal a case. The person who challenges the decision of the court is called the petitioner or

Colin Kaepernick of the San Francisco 49ers takes a knee during the national anthem in Charlotte, N.C., in 2016. He settled his collusion lawsuit against the NFL in 2019.

discovery
The pretrial process of gathering evidence and facts. The word also may refer to the specific items of evidence that are uncovered.

subpoena
A command for someone to appear or testify in court or to turn over evidence, such as notes or recordings, with penalties for noncompliance.

venire
Literally, "to come" or "to appear"; the term used for the location from which a court draws its pool of potential jurors, who must then appear in court for voir dire; a change of venire means a change of the location from which potential jurors are drawn.

Jury consultant Robert Hirschorn (left) confers with George Zimmerman during Zimmerman's 2013 trial for the shooting of Trayvon Martin. Zimmerman was acquitted of second-degree murder.

appellant. The respondent to the appeal, or the **appellee**, wants the verdict to be affirmed.

Summary Judgment

When parties ask a court to dismiss a case, they file a motion for summary judgment asking the judge to decide the case on the basis of pretrial submissions when neither party disputes the underlying facts.[78] A summary judgment results in a legal determination by a court *without* a full trial and avoids the cost of trial and the risk of loss to the moving party.

venue
The locality of a lawsuit and of the court hearing the suit. Thus, a change of venue means a relocation of a trial.

voir dire
Literally, "to speak the truth"; the questioning of prospective jurors to assess their suitability.

peremptory challenge
During jury selection, a challenge in which an attorney rejects a juror without showing a reason. Attorneys have the right to eliminate a limited number of jurors through peremptory challenges.

appellant
The party making the appeal; also called the petitioner.

appellee
The party against whom an appeal is made.

A court's summary judgment may be issued based on the merits of the case as a whole or on specific issues critical to the case. In a libel case, this may occur when a plaintiff is clearly unable to meet one or more elements of the burden of proof, such as the falsity of the published material (see Chapter 4). If the judge determines evidence supports an uncontested conclusion that one party should win the case, the judge hands down a summary judgment in that party's favor.

Summary judgment may be granted at several points in litigation, but usually prior to trial. The U.S. Supreme Court has said that courts considering motions for summary judgment "must view the facts and inferences to be drawn from them in the light most favorable to the opposing party."[79] In libel cases, this means that courts must take into account the burden the plaintiff is required to meet at trial. The Court created this obstacle to summary judgment because the nonmoving party loses the opportunity to present his or her case when a judge grants summary judgment to the opposing side.[80]

In 2018, a California court of appeals affirmed summary judgment in favor of Simpson University, a religious institution that had been sued for libel and invasion of privacy when it terminated the employment of a former dean.[81] The court's judgment turned on specifics of the religious employment of the dean. Media defendants sometimes seek summary judgments to protect themselves from the high costs of frivolous lawsuits intended to harass, intimidate or affect content.[82]

For decades, courts would dismiss a case only if "no set of facts" could support the plaintiff's claim.[83] But the U.S. Supreme Court changed this standard when it decided two cases, *Bell Atlantic v. Twombly* in 2007[84] and *Ashcroft v. Iqbal* in 2009.[85] What is known as the *Twombly/Iqbal* test says a court will dismiss a case if the plaintiff cannot state a plausible claim. That requires a court to determine "exactly where plausibility falls in that gray area between possible and probable."[86] It is more difficult for plaintiffs to present plausible facts to support their claim than it is simply to show that no set of facts could prove the claim, which means that courts applying the *Twombly/Iqbal* test dismiss a case more readily. Courts continue to disagree what "plausible" means in this context.

EMERGING LAW

Early in 2019, Republican senators reintroduced a bill to reduce the number of executive agency regulations by requiring major administrative rules to be approved by both chambers of Congress.[87] If enacted, the proposed law would allow Congress to bundle rules for a single up or down vote. If either chamber failed to act, the rule would die.[88] No concurrent companion bill was introduced in the House, but an earlier version passed that chamber.[89]

For two decades, the Congressional Review Act has supported deference to executive agency rules by giving them legal force if not disapproved by Congress within 60 days.[90]

The 2019 bill and its precursor were intended to hamper overreaching by administrative agencies and to reduce proliferating rules that harm the economy, according to their sponsors.[91] Opponents argue that the law would violate the separation of powers by usurping the independent authority of executive branch agencies to implement laws duly enacted by Congress.[92] Critics say the law would also replace judicial review with congressional oversight of administrative rules.

Observers believe efforts in Congress and state legislatures to define or circumscribe the powers of the three branches of government will increase in response to growing public distrust of government and fear that the Constitution's system of checks and balances is not functioning.[93]

FINDING THE LAW

This textbook provides an introduction and overview to key areas of the law of journalism and mass communication. Many students will wish, or their professors will require them, to supplement this text with research in primary legal sources. Primary sources are the actual documents that make up the law (e.g., statutes, case decisions, administrative rules and committee reports). Legal research often begins in secondary sources that analyze, interpret and discuss the primary documents. Perhaps the most useful secondary sources for beginning researchers in communication law are "American Jurisprudence 2d," "Corpus Juris Secundum" and "Media Law Reporter." The first two are legal encyclopedias that summarize legal subjects and reference relevant cases and legal articles. "Media Law Reporter" provides both topical summaries and excerpts of key media law cases organized by subject. However, "Media Law Reporter" is not comprehensive. It contains only the cases selected by the editors to highlight prominent issues in media law. Law review articles provide invaluable scholarship and references to contemporary legal topics. However, primary source research in administrative, legislative and court documents is necessary to thoroughly research a legal topic.

This text cannot provide a detailed explanation of how to navigate these complex and diverse legal materials. However, access to primary legal materials is available online and in databases such as Westlaw and Nexis Universe.

The notes at the end of this book contain citations to many of the important cases in the law of journalism and mass communication. These legal citations provide the names of the parties in the case, the number of the volume in which the case is reported, the abbreviated name of the official legal reporter (or book) in which the case appears, the page of the reporter on which the case begins and the year in which the case was decided. For example, one citation in note 5 of this chapter looks like this: "FEC v. Wisconsin Right to Life, Inc., 551 U.S. 449, 534

SupremeCourt.gov

The main reading room in the U.S. Supreme Court Library.

(2007) (Souter, J., dissenting)." This citation shows that the first party, the Federal Election Commission, filed an appeal from a decision in favor of the second party, Wisconsin Right to Life, Inc. The decision in this case striking down a ban on issue advertising prior to elections or primaries can be found in the U.S. Reports collection, which contains U.S. Supreme Court opinions. The case appears in volume 551 (the number *before* the name of the reporter), beginning on page 449 (the number *after* the name of the reporter). The case was decided in 2007 (the number in parentheses). In addition, the page number following the comma tells you precisely what page of the decision is referenced, and the parentheses at the end indicate that the reference comes from a dissenting opinion by Justice David Souter.

READING CASE LAW

This chapter shows that the law of journalism and mass communication contains many terms and concepts that may be unfamiliar to the general reader. Key definitions in the margins and the glossary at the back of the book should help you navigate opinions for lawyers trained in legal terminology and doctrines. At first, it may be difficult to grasp the meaning and importance of a case. With practice, however, anyone can learn the language and read case law with relative ease.

The following steps will help you read the law more quickly and with better comprehension. You will understand the law far better and more easily if you give yourself sufficient time to use these three steps:

1. ***Preread the case.*** Prereading identifies the *structure* of the decision; the various *rules or doctrines* that underlie the court's reasoning; and the *outcome* of the case. These three elements highlight the most important elements of the court's reasoning. To preread, quickly skim

   a. The topic sentence of each paragraph to get the gist of the opinion and identify its most important sections

   b. The first few paragraphs of the opinion, which should establish the parties, the issues and the history of the case

   c. The last few paragraphs of the opinion to understand the **holding** (which is the legal principle taken from the decision of the court) or to get a summary of the outcome of the case

holding
The decision or ruling of a court.

2. ***Skim the entire case.*** Scan the entire case and mark the start of key sections of the case for more careful reading.

3. ***Read carefully the sections you have identified as important.*** Underline or highlight as you go. You may want to take note of the following:

    a. ***The issue.*** Knowing the issue in the case helps you know which elements of the history and facts are significant. In this text, the chapter titles generally signal the issue on which the case excerpt will focus. The case itself also often includes language that identifies the issue. Such language includes, "The question before the Court is whether . . ." and "The issue in this case is . . ."

    b. ***The facts.*** Identify which facts are central to the issue by asking yourself whether the dispute in the case is about a question of fact (e.g., what happened) or a question of law (e.g., which test, doctrine or category of speech is relevant). A libel decision that turns on the identity of the individual whose reputation was harmed would represent a question of fact, making related facts central to the holding.[94]

    c. ***The case history.*** The circumstances surrounding a decision often are pivotal to the issue before the court. Sometimes the relevant history is one of shifting legal doctrine, as when the court gradually affords commercial speech greater constitutional protection.[95] Sometimes the important context is factual, as when the court protects defamatory comments situated within a generally accurate portrayal of the violent oppression of blacks during the civil rights movement.[96]

    d. ***The common law rule***. The rule is the heart of the decision; it is the common law developed in this case. It relates to the holding but is the more general rule applied here and applicable to other cases. To identify the rule, ask whether the court has created a new test, engaged in balancing or applied an established doctrine in a new way. What are the elements of the rule, and what are its exceptions?

    e. ***The analysis.*** Here the court applies the rule to the facts. In libel law, for example, public officials must prove actual malice to win their suit. How does the court apply this element of the test?

Careful reading of the law is the first stage in conducting legal research and positions you well to write case briefs, which summarize the key elements of a court decision.

Briefing Cases

Case briefs simplify and clarify a court's opinions by selecting the five most important elements of the decision. Briefs focus on key elements and set aside content that does not directly inform the court's decision.

The five components of a case brief are often referred to as FIRAC. They are Facts, Issue, Rule of Law, Analysis and Conclusion (or holding).

1. ***The Facts.*** The facts summary should include all the information needed to understand the issue and the decision of the court. The facts statement consists of a brief but inclusive discussion of what happened in the legal dispute before it reached this court. It should include who the parties are, what happened in the trial court and the basis for appeal. What happened between the parties that gave rise to the case? Who initiated the lawsuit? What was the substance of the complaint, and what type of legal action was brought? What was the defense? What did other courts reviewing the case decide? What legal errors provide the basis for the appeal?

2. ***The Issue.*** Here, one sentence summarizes the specific question decided by the court in this case. The issue should be phrased as a single question that can be answered "yes" or "no."

3. ***The Rule of Law.*** The rule of law states, preferably in one sentence, the precedent established by this decision that will bind lower courts.

4. ***The Analysis.*** This section, also called the *rationale*, details how and why the court reached its decision. In this section, it is important to discuss the details of the court's reasoning and how it creates new law. Consider whether it establishes a new test, clarifies existing legal distinctions, defines a new category or highlights changing realities that affect the law. A thorough analysis must describe the reasoning for all the opinions in the decision and highlight the specific points on which concurring and dissenting opinions diverge from the opinion of the court.

5. ***The Conclusion.*** This is a simple declarative statement of the holding reached by the present court. What did the court decide, and did it affirm, remand or reverse? Provide the vote of the court if it is an appellate court.

Analyzing *Marbury v. Madison*

The following case brief previews the first case excerpted at the end of this chapter.

FACTS: William Marbury was one of President John Adams' 42 "midnight appointments" on the eve of his departure from the White House. The necessary paperwork and procedures to secure his and several other appointments were completed, but Secretary of State John Marshall—himself a midnight appointee—failed to deliver Marbury's commission. Upon assuming the presidency, Thomas Jefferson ordered his secretary of state—James Madison—not to deliver the commission. Under authority of the Judiciary Act of 1789, Marbury sued to ask the Supreme Court to order Madison, through a writ of mandamus, to deliver the commission. A writ of mandamus is a court order requiring an individual or organization either to perform or to stop a particular action.

ISSUE: Does the Supreme Court have the power to review acts of Congress and declare them void if they violate the Constitution?

RULE of LAW: Under Article VI, Section 2 of the U.S. Constitution, the Supreme Court is implicitly given the power to review acts of Congress and to strike them down as void if they are "repugnant" to the Constitution.

ANALYSIS: A commission signed by the president and sealed by the secretary of state is complete and legally binding. Denial of Marbury's commission violates the law, creating a governmental obligation to remedy the violation. A writ of mandamus is such a remedy. The Constitution is the "supreme law of the land" (Art. VI). As such, it is "superior" and "fundamental and paramount." It establishes "certain limits" on the power of the government it creates, including the power of Congress. The Constitution also establishes that "[it] is emphatically the province and duty of the judicial department to say what the law is." The Supreme Court, therefore, must determine the law that applies in a specific case and decide the case according to the law. If the Court finds that "ordinary" statutory law conflicts with the dictates of the Constitution, the "fundamental" constitutional law must govern. Accordingly, "a legislative act contrary to the Constitution is not law," and the Court must strike it down to give the Constitution its due weight.

Under Article III of the Constitution, Congress has the power to regulate the appellate jurisdiction, but not the original jurisdiction, of the Supreme Court. The Court's original jurisdiction is defined completely and exclusively by Article III and cannot be altered except by amendment of the Constitution. Through the Judiciary Act of 1789, Congress *added* to the original jurisdiction of the Court. Being outside the power given to Congress by the Constitution, this act is illegitimate. Because the power of mandamus was not granted to the Court by the Constitution either, the Court does not have the power to order mandamus on behalf of Marbury.

The Court held the provision of the Judiciary Act unconstitutional and declared the mandamus void.

CONCLUSION: Marshall, C.J. 6–0. Yes. Relying heavily on the inherent "logical reasoning" of the Constitution, rather than on any explicit text, the Court dismissed the case for lack of jurisdiction but found that Congress' grant of original power of mandamus to the Court violated the separation of power established in Article III of the Constitution.

CASES FOR STUDY

For study resources and a case archive, go to **edge.sagepub.com/medialaw7e**.

Thinking About It

The first case excerpt is from *Marbury v. Madison*,[101] the decision in which the Supreme Court established its own power of judicial review. A central question resolved by the Supreme Court in *Marbury v. Madison* was whether, under the Constitution, the Court had authority to void duly enacted laws that it deemed to violate the U.S. Constitution.

Critics of campaign finance regulations designed to prevent corruption in elections won several legal decisions in 2010 in the wake of the Supreme Court's ruling in *Citizens United v. Federal Election Commission*.[97] As one legal scholar noted, "The relevance of *Citizens United* has become an issue in every new campaign finance case" since the decision was handed down.[98] This aspect of the Court's decision is developed in Chapter 2 when the First Amendment implications of campaign finance laws are discussed.

Here we look instead at what *Citizens United* demonstrates about precedent and the rule of law. The debate raised in the Court's opinions has spawned vibrant public discussion about whether the doctrine of stare decisis serves "as an agent of stability" or "to destabilize the rule of law."[99] The second case excerpt below begins with Chief Justice John Roberts' concurring opinion in *Citizens United*, in which he "elaborated on when it *is* acceptable for the Court to overturn precedent."[100] Justice John Paul Stevens' rather acerbic dissent forms the second part of this contemporary Court debate on the role of precedent.

As you read these case excerpts, keep the following questions in mind:

- How do the justices differ in their interpretation of the binding nature of Supreme Court precedent?

- In the case of *Citizens United*, which justices are exercising "restraint" or "activism"? How? For what reasons?

- What are the legal foundations of the different opinions?

- What do these decisions suggest about the stability or "transformation" of the rule of law under judicial review and stare decisis?

Marbury v. Madison
SUPREME COURT OF THE UNITED STATES
5 U.S. 137 (1803)

CHIEF JUSTICE JOHN MARSHALL delivered the Court's opinion:

. . . The constitution vests the whole judicial power of the United States in one supreme court, and such inferior courts as congress shall, from time to time, ordain and establish. This power is expressly extended to all cases arising under the laws of the United States; and consequently, in some form, may be exercised over the present case; because the right claimed is given by a law of the United States.

In the distribution of this power it is declared that "the supreme court shall have original jurisdiction in all cases affecting ambassadors, other public ministers and consuls, and those in which a state shall be a party. In all other cases, the supreme court shall have appellate jurisdiction."

It has been insisted at the bar, that as the original grant of jurisdiction to the supreme and inferior courts is general, and the clause, assigning original jurisdiction to the supreme court, contains no negative or restrictive words; the power remains to the legislature, to assign original jurisdiction to that court in other cases than those specified in the article which has been recited; provided those cases belong to the judicial power of the United States.

If it had been intended to leave it to the discretion of the legislature to apportion the judicial power between the supreme and inferior courts according to the will of that body, it would certainly have been useless to have proceeded further than to have defined the judicial power, and the tribunals in which it should be vested. The subsequent part of the section is . . . entirely without meaning, if such is to be the construction. If congress remains at liberty to give this court appellate jurisdiction, where the constitution has declared their jurisdiction shall be original; and original jurisdiction where the constitution has declared it shall be appellate; the distribution of jurisdiction, made in the constitution, is form without substance. . . .

It cannot be presumed that any clause in the constitution is intended to be without effect; and therefore such a construction is inadmissible, unless the words require it. . . .

When an instrument organizing fundamentally a judicial system, divides it into one supreme, and so many inferior courts as the legislature may ordain and establish; then enumerates its powers, and proceeds so far to distribute them, as to define the jurisdiction of the supreme court by declaring the cases in which it shall take original jurisdiction, and that in others it shall take appellate jurisdiction, the plain import of the words seems to be, that in one class of cases its jurisdiction is original, and not appellate; in the other it is appellate, and not original. If any other construction would render the clause inoperative, that is an additional reason for rejecting such other construction, and for adhering to their obvious meaning.

To enable this court then to issue a mandamus, it must be shown to be an exercise of appellate jurisdiction, or to be necessary to enable them to exercise appellate jurisdiction.

It has been stated at the bar that the appellate jurisdiction may be exercised in a variety of forms, and that if it be the will of the legislature that a mandamus should be used for that purpose, that will must be obeyed. This is true; yet the jurisdiction must be appellate, not original.

It is the essential criterion of appellate jurisdiction, that it revises and corrects the proceedings in a cause already instituted, and does not create that case. Although, therefore, a mandamus may be directed to courts, yet to issue such a writ to an officer for the delivery of a paper, is in effect the same as to sustain an original action for that paper, and therefore seems not to belong to appellate, but to original jurisdiction. Neither is it necessary in such a case as this, to enable the court to exercise its appellate jurisdiction.

The authority, therefore, given to the supreme court, by the act establishing the judicial courts of the United States, to issue writs of mandamus to public officers, appears not to be warranted by the constitution; and it becomes necessary to enquire whether a jurisdiction, so conferred, can be exercised.

The question, whether an act, repugnant to the constitution, can become the law of the land, is a question deeply interesting to the United States; but, happily, not of an intricacy proportioned to its interest. It seems only necessary to recognise certain principles, supposed to have been long and well established, to decide it.

That the people have an original right to establish, for their future government, such principles as, in their opinion, shall most conduce to their own happiness, is the basis, on which the whole American fabric has been erected. The exercise of this original right is a very great exertion; nor can it, nor ought it to be frequently repeated. The principles, therefore, so established, are deemed fundamental. And as the authority, from which they proceed, is supreme, and can seldom act, they are designed to be permanent.

This original and supreme will organizes the government, and assigns to different departments their respective powers. It may either stop here; or establish certain limits not to be transcended by those departments.

The government of the United States is of the latter description. The powers of the legislature are defined, and limited; and that those limits may not be mistaken, or forgotten, the constitution is written. To what purpose are powers limited, and to what purpose is that limitation committed to writing; if these limits may, at any time, be passed by those intended to be restrained? The distinction between a government with limited and unlimited powers is abolished, if those limits do not confine the persons on whom they are imposed, and if acts prohibited and acts allowed are of equal obligation. It is a proposition too plain to be contested, that the constitution controls any legislative act repugnant to it; or, that the legislature may alter the constitution by an ordinary act.

Between these alternatives there is no middle ground. The constitution is either a superior, paramount law, unchangeable by ordinary means, or it is on a level with ordinary legislative acts, and like other acts, is alterable when the legislature shall please to alter it.

If the former part of the alternative be true, then a legislative act contrary to the constitution is not law: if the latter part be true, then written constitutions are absurd attempts, on the part of the people, to limit a power in its own nature illimitable.

Certainly all those who have framed written constitutions contemplate them as forming the fundamental and paramount law of the nation, and consequently the theory of every such government must be, that an act of the legislature repugnant to the constitution is void.

This theory is essentially attached to a written constitution, and is consequently to be considered by this court as one of the fundamental principles of our society. It is not therefore to be lost sight of in the further consideration of this subject.

If an act of the legislature, repugnant to the constitution, is void, does it, notwithstanding its invalidity, bind the courts, and oblige them to give it effect? Or, in other words, though it be not law, does it constitute a rule as operative as if it was a law? This would be to overthrow in fact what was established in theory; and would seem, at first view, an absurdity too gross to be insisted on. It shall, however, receive a more attentive consideration.

It is emphatically the province and duty of the judicial department to say what the law is. Those who apply the rule to particular cases, must of necessity expound and interpret that rule. If two laws conflict with each other, the courts must decide on the operation of each. So if a law be in opposition to the constitution; if both the law and the constitution apply to a particular case, so that the court must either decide that case conformably to the law, disregarding the constitution; or conformably to the constitution, disregarding the law; the court must determine which of these conflicting rules governs the case. This is of the very essence of judicial duty.

If then the courts are to regard the constitution; and the constitution is superior to any ordinary act of the legislature; the constitution, and not such ordinary act, must govern the case to which they both apply.

Those then who controvert the principle that the constitution is to be considered, in court, as a paramount law, are reduced to the necessity of maintaining that courts must close their eyes on the constitution, and see only the law.

This doctrine would subvert the very foundation of all written constitutions. It would declare that an act, which, according to the principles and theory of our government, is entirely void, is yet, in practice, completely obligatory. It would declare, that if the legislature shall do what is expressly forbidden, such act, notwithstanding the express prohibition, is in reality effectual. It would be giving to the legislature a practical and real omnipotence with the same breath which professes to restrict their powers within narrow limits. It is prescribing limits, and declaring that those limits may be passed at pleasure.

That it thus reduces to nothing what we have deemed the greatest improvement on political institutions—a written constitution, would of itself be sufficient, in America where written constitutions have been viewed with so much reverence, for rejecting the construction. But the peculiar expressions of the constitution of the United States furnish additional arguments in favour of its rejection.

The judicial power of the United States is extended to all cases arising under the constitution. Could it be the intention of those who gave this power, to say that, in using it, the constitution should not be looked into? That a case arising under the constitution should be decided without examining the instrument under which it arises?

This is too extravagant to be maintained. . . .

[I]t is apparent, that the framers of the constitution contemplated that instrument, as a rule for the government of courts, as well as of the legislature.

Why otherwise does it direct the judges to take an oath to support it? This oath certainly applies, in an especial manner, to their conduct in their official character. How immoral to impose it on them, if they were to be used as the instruments, and the knowing instruments, for violating what they swear to support!

The oath of office, too, imposed by the legislature, is completely demonstrative of the legislative opinion on the subject. It is in these words, "I do solemnly swear that I will administer justice without respect to persons, and do equal right to the poor and to the rich; and that I will faithfully and impartially discharge all the duties incumbent on me as according to the best of my abilities and understanding, agreeably to the constitution, and laws of the United States."

Why does a judge swear to discharge his duties agreeably to the constitution of the United States, if that constitution forms no rule for his government? If it is closed upon him, and cannot be inspected by him?

If such be the real state of things, this is worse than solemn mockery. To prescribe, or to take this oath, becomes equally a crime.

It is also not entirely unworthy of observation, that in declaring what shall be the supreme law of the land, the constitution itself is first mentioned; and not the laws of the United States generally, but those only which shall be made in pursuance of the constitution, have that rank.

Thus, the particular phraseology of the constitution of the United States confirms and strengthens the principle, supposed to be essential to all written constitutions, that a law repugnant to the constitution is void; and that courts, as well as other departments, are bound by that instrument.

The rule must be discharged.

Citizens United v. Federal Election Commission
SUPREME COURT OF THE UNITED STATES
558 U.S. 310 (2010)

JUSTICE ANTHONY KENNEDY delivered the Court's opinion.

CHIEF JUSTICE ROBERTS, with whom JUSTICE SAMUEL ALITO joined, concurring:

The Government urges us in this case to uphold a direct prohibition on political speech. It asks us to embrace a theory of the First Amendment that would allow censorship not only of television and radio broadcasts, but of pamphlets, posters, the internet, and virtually any other medium that corporations and unions might find useful in expressing their views on matters of public concern. Its theory, if accepted, would empower the Government to prohibit newspapers from running editorials or opinion pieces supporting or opposing candidates for office, so long as the newspapers were owned by corporations—as the major ones are. First Amendment rights could be confined to individuals, subverting the vibrant public discourse that is at the foundation of our democracy.

The Court properly rejects that theory, and I join its opinion in full. The First Amendment protects more than just the individual on a soapbox and the lonely pamphleteer. I write separately to address the important principles of judicial restraint and *stare decisis* implicated in this case.

Judging the constitutionality of an Act of Congress is "the gravest and most delicate duty that this Court is called upon to perform." Because the stakes are so high, our standard practice is to refrain from addressing constitutional questions except when necessary to rule on particular claims before us. This policy underlies both our willingness to construe ambiguous statutes to avoid constitutional problems and our practice "'never to formulate a rule of constitutional law broader than is required by the precise facts to which it is to be applied.'"

The majority and dissent are united in expressing allegiance to these principles. But I cannot agree with my dissenting colleagues on how these principles apply in this case.

The majority's step-by-step analysis accords with our standard practice of avoiding broad constitutional questions except when necessary to decide the case before us. The majority begins by addressing—and quite properly rejecting—Citizens United's statutory claim that [the Bipartisan Campaign Reform Act of 2002] does not actually cover its production and distribution of *Hillary: The Movie* (hereinafter *Hillary*). If there were a valid basis for deciding this statutory claim in Citizens United's favor (and thereby avoiding constitutional adjudication), it would be proper to do so. . . .

It is only because the majority rejects Citizens United's statutory claim that it proceeds to consider the group's various constitutional arguments, beginning with its narrowest claim (that *Hillary* is not the functional equivalent of express advocacy) and proceeding to its broadest claim (that *Austin v. Michigan Chamber of Commerce* (1990) should be overruled). . . .

The dissent advocates an approach to addressing Citizens United's claims that I find quite perplexing. It presumably agrees with the majority that Citizens United's narrower statutory and constitutional arguments lack merit—otherwise its conclusion that the group should lose this case would make no sense. Despite agreeing that these narrower arguments fail, however, the dissent argues that the majority should nonetheless latch on to one of them in order to avoid reaching the broader constitutional question of whether *Austin* remains good law. It even suggests that the Court's failure to adopt one of these concededly meritless arguments is a sign that the majority is not "serious about judicial restraint."

This approach is based on a false premise: that our practice of avoiding unnecessary (and unnecessarily broad) constitutional holdings somehow trumps our obligation faithfully to interpret the law. It should go without saying, however, that we cannot embrace a narrow ground of decision simply because it is narrow; it must also be right. Thus while it is true that "[i]f it is not necessary to decide more, it is necessary not to decide more," sometimes it is necessary to decide more. There is a difference between judicial restraint and judicial abdication. When constitutional questions are "indispensably necessary" to resolving the case at hand, "the court must meet and decide them." . . .

This is the first case in which we have been asked to overrule *Austin*, and thus it is also the first in which we have had reason to consider how much weight to give *stare decisis* in assessing its continued validity. The dissent erroneously declares that the Court "reaffirmed" *Austin*'s holding in subsequent cases. Not so. Not a single party in any of those cases asked us to overrule *Austin*, and as the dissent points out, the Court generally does not consider constitutional arguments that have not properly been raised. *Austin*'s validity was therefore not directly at issue in the cases the dissent cites. The Court's unwillingness to overturn *Austin* in those cases cannot be understood as a *reaffirmation* of that decision.

Fidelity to precedent—the policy of *stare decisis*—is vital to the proper exercise of the judicial function. "*Stare decisis* is the preferred course because it promotes the even-handed, predictable, and consistent development of legal principles, fosters reliance on judicial decisions, and contributes to the actual and perceived integrity of the judicial process." For these reasons, we have long recognized that departures from precedent are inappropriate in the absence of a "special justification."

At the same time, *stare decisis* is neither an "inexorable command," nor "a mechanical formula of adherence to the latest decision," especially in constitutional cases. If it were, segregation would be legal, minimum wage laws would be unconstitutional, and the Government could wiretap ordinary criminal suspects without first obtaining warrants. As the dissent properly notes, none of us has viewed *stare decisis* in such absolute terms.

Stare decisis is instead a "principle of policy." When considering whether to reexamine a prior erroneous holding, we must balance the importance of having constitutional questions *decided* against the importance of having them *decided right*. As Justice Jackson explained, this requires a "sober appraisal of the disadvantages of the innovation as well as those of the questioned case, a weighing of practical effects of one against the other."

In conducting this balancing, we must keep in mind that *stare decisis* is not an end in itself. It is instead "the means by which we ensure that the law will not merely change erratically, but will develop in a principled and intelligible fashion." Its greatest purpose is to serve a constitutional ideal—the rule of law. It follows that in the unusual circumstance when fidelity to any particular precedent does more to damage this constitutional ideal than to advance it, we must be more willing to depart from that precedent.

Thus, for example, if the precedent under consideration itself departed from the Court's jurisprudence, returning to the "'intrinsically sounder' doctrine established in prior cases" may "better serv[e] the values of *stare decisis* than would following [the] more recently decided case inconsistent with the decisions that came before it." Abrogating the errant precedent, rather than reaffirming or extending it, might better preserve the law's coherence and curtail the precedent's disruptive effects.

Likewise, if adherence to a precedent actually impedes the stable and orderly adjudication of future cases, its *stare decisis* effect is also diminished. This can happen in a number of circumstances, such as when the precedent's validity is so hotly contested that it cannot reliably function as a basis for decision in future cases, when its rationale threatens to upend our settled jurisprudence in related areas of law, and when the precedent's underlying reasoning has become so discredited that the Court cannot keep the precedent alive without jury-rigging new and different justifications to shore up the original mistake.

These considerations weigh against retaining our decision in *Austin*. First, as the majority explains, that decision was an "aberration" insofar as it departed from the robust protections we had granted political speech in our earlier cases . . . [and] does not explain why corporations may be subject to prohibitions on speech in candidate elections when individuals may not.

Second, the validity of *Austin*'s rationale—itself adopted over two "spirited dissents"—has proved to be the consistent subject of dispute among Members of this Court ever since. The simple fact that one of our decisions remains controversial is, of course, insufficient to justify overruling it. But it does undermine the precedent's ability to contribute to the stable and orderly development of the law. In such circumstances, it is entirely appropriate for the Court—which in this case is squarely asked to reconsider *Austin*'s validity for the first time—to address the matter with a greater willingness to consider new approaches capable of restoring our doctrine to sounder footing.

Third, the *Austin* decision is uniquely destabilizing because it threatens to subvert our Court's decisions even outside the particular context of corporate express advocacy. The First Amendment theory underlying *Austin*'s holding is extraordinarily broad. *Austin*'s logic would authorize government prohibition of political speech by a category of speakers in the name of equality—a point that most scholars acknowledge (and many celebrate), but that the dissent denies.

It should not be surprising, then, that Members of the Court have relied on *Austin*'s expansive logic to justify greater incursions on the First Amendment, even outside the original context of corporate advocacy on behalf of candidates running for office. The dissent in this case succumbs to the same temptation, suggesting that *Austin* justifies prohibiting corporate speech because such speech might unduly influence "the market for legislation." The dissent reads *Austin* to permit restrictions on corporate speech based on nothing more than the fact that the corporate form may help individuals coordinate and present their views more effectively. A speaker's ability to persuade, however, provides no basis for government regulation of free and open public debate on what the laws should be.

If taken seriously, *Austin*'s logic would apply most directly to newspapers and other media corporations. They have a more profound impact on public discourse than most other speakers. These corporate entities are, for the time being, not subject to [the statute's] otherwise generally applicable prohibitions on corporate political speech. But this is simply a matter of legislative grace. The fact that the law currently grants a favored position to media corporations is no reason to overlook the danger inherent in accepting a theory that would allow government restrictions on their political speech.

These readings of *Austin* do no more than carry that decision's reasoning to its logical endpoint. In doing so, they highlight the threat *Austin* poses to First Amendment rights generally, even outside its specific factual context of corporate express advocacy. Because *Austin* is so difficult to confine to its facts—and because its logic threatens to undermine our First Amendment jurisprudence and the nature of public discourse more broadly—the costs of giving it *stare decisis* effect are unusually high.

Finally and most importantly, the Government's own effort to defend *Austin*—or, more accurately, to defend something that is not quite *Austin*—underscores its weakness as a precedent of the Court. The Government concedes that *Austin* "is not the most lucid opinion," yet asks us to reaffirm its holding. But while invoking *stare decisis* to support this position, the Government never once even mentions the compelling interest that *Austin* relied upon in the first place: the need to diminish "the corrosive and distorting effects of immense aggregations of wealth that are accumulated with the help of the corporate form and that have little or no correlation to the public's support for the corporation's political ideas." *Austin*'s specific holding on the basis of two new and potentially expansive interests—the need to prevent actual or apparent quid pro quo corruption, and the need to protect corporate shareholders. Those interests

may or may not support the result in *Austin*, but they were plainly not part of the reasoning on which *Austin* relied. . . .

To its credit, the Government forthrightly concedes that *Austin* did not embrace either of the new rationales it now urges upon us. To be clear: The Court in *Austin* nowhere relied upon the only arguments the Government now raises to support that decision. . . .

To the extent that the Government's case for reaffirming *Austin* depends on radically reconceptualizing its reasoning, that argument is at odds with itself. *Stare decisis* is a doctrine of preservation, not transformation. It counsels deference to past mistakes, but provides no justification for making new ones. There is therefore no basis for the Court to give precedential sway to reasoning that it has never accepted, simply because that reasoning happens to support a conclusion reached on different grounds that have since been abandoned or discredited.

Doing so would undermine the rule-of-law values that justify *stare decisis* in the first place. It would effectively license the Court to invent and adopt new principles of constitutional law solely for the purpose of rationalizing its past errors, without a proper analysis of whether those principles have merit on their own. This approach would allow the Court's past missteps to spawn future mistakes, undercutting the very rule-of-law values that *stare decisis* is designed to protect.

None of this is to say that the Government is barred from making new arguments to support the outcome in *Austin*. On the contrary, it is free to do so. And of course the Court is free to accept them. But the Government's new arguments must stand or fall on their own; they are not entitled to receive the special deference we accord to precedent. They are, as grounds to support *Austin*, literally unprecedented. Moreover, to the extent the Government relies on new arguments—and declines to defend *Austin* on its own terms—we may reasonably infer that it lacks confidence in that decision's original justification.

Because continued adherence to *Austin* threatens to subvert the "principled and intelligible" development of our First Amendment jurisprudence,

I support the Court's determination to overrule that decision. . . .

JUSTICE JOHN PAUL STEVENS, with whom JUSTICE RUTH BADER GINSBURG, JUSTICE STEPHEN BREYER and JUSTICE SONIA SOTOMAYOR join, concurring in part and dissenting in part:

. . . The majority's approach to corporate electioneering marks a dramatic break from our past. Congress has placed special limitations on campaign spending by corporations ever since the passage of the Tillman Act in 1907. We have unanimously concluded that this "reflects a permissible assessment of the dangers posed by those entities to the electoral process," and have accepted the "legislative judgment that the special characteristics of the corporate structure require particularly careful regulation." The Court today rejects a century of history when it treats the distinction between corporate and individual campaign spending as an invidious novelty born of *Austin v. Michigan Chamber of Commerce.* Relying largely on individual dissenting opinions, the majority blazes through our precedents, overruling or disavowing a body of case law.

In his landmark concurrence in *Ashwander v. TVA* (1936), Justice Brandeis stressed the importance of adhering to rules the Court has "developed . . . for its own governance" when deciding constitutional questions. Because departures from those rules always enhance the risk of error, . . . I emphatically dissent from its principal holding.

The Court's ruling threatens to undermine the integrity of elected institutions across the Nation. The path it has taken to reach its outcome will, I fear, do damage to this institution. Before turning to the question whether to overrule *Austin* and part of *McConnell,* it is important to explain why the Court should not be deciding that question.

The first reason is that the question was not properly brought before us. . . . [T]he majority decides this case on a basis relinquished below, not included in the questions presented to us by the litigants, and argued here only in response to the Court's invitation. This procedure is unusual and inadvisable for a court. Our colleagues' suggestion that "we are asked to reconsider *Austin* and, in effect, *McConnell,*" would be more accurate if rephrased to state that "we have asked ourselves" to reconsider those cases. . . .

It is all the more distressing that our colleagues have manufactured a facial challenge, because the parties have advanced numerous ways to resolve the case that would facilitate electioneering by non-profit advocacy corporations such as Citizens United, without toppling statutes and precedents. Which is to say, the majority has transgressed yet another "cardinal" principle of the judicial process: "[I]f it is not necessary to decide more, it is necessary not to decide more." . . .

The final principle of judicial process that the majority violates is the most transparent: *stare decisis.* I am not an absolutist when it comes to *stare decisis,* in the campaign finance area or in any other. No one is. But if this principle is to do any meaningful work in supporting the rule of law, it must at least demand a significant justification, beyond the preferences of five Justices, for overturning settled doctrine. "[A] decision to overrule should rest on some special reason over and above the belief that a prior case was wrongly decided." No such justification exists in this case, and to the contrary there are powerful prudential reasons to keep faith with our precedents.

The Court's central argument for why *stare decisis* ought to be trumped is that it does not like *Austin.* The opinion "was not well reasoned," our colleagues assert, and it conflicts with First Amendment principles. This, of course, is the Court's merits argument, the many defects in which we will soon consider. I am perfectly willing to concede that if one of our precedents were dead wrong in its reasoning or irreconcilable with the rest of our doctrine, there would be a compelling basis for revisiting it. But neither is true of *Austin,* and restating a merits argument with additional vigor does not give it extra weight in the *stare decisis* calculus.

Perhaps in recognition of this point, the Court supplements its merits case with a smattering of assertions. The Court proclaims that "*Austin* is undermined by experience since its announcement." This is a curious claim to make in a case that lacks a developed record. The majority has no empirical evidence with which to substantiate the claim; we just have its *ipse dixit* that the real world has not been kind to *Austin*. Nor does the majority bother to specify in what sense *Austin* has been "undermined." Instead it treats the reader to a string of non sequiturs: "Our Nation's speech dynamic is changing"; "[s]peakers have become adept at presenting citizens with sound bites, talking points, and scripted messages"; "[c]orporations . . . do not have monolithic views." How any of these ruminations weakens the force of *stare decisis*, escapes my comprehension.

The majority also contends that the Government's hesitation to rely on *Austin*'s anti-distortion rationale "diminishe[s]" "the principle of adhering to that precedent." Why it diminishes the value of *stare decisis* is left unexplained. We have never thought fit to overrule a precedent because a litigant has taken any particular tack. Nor should we. Our decisions can often be defended on multiple grounds, and a litigant may have strategic or case-specific reasons for emphasizing only a subset of them. Members of the public, moreover, often rely on our bottom-line holdings far more than our precise legal arguments; surely this is true for the legislatures that have been regulating corporate electioneering since *Austin*. The task of evaluating the continued viability of precedents falls to this Court, not to the parties.

Although the majority opinion spends several pages making these surprising arguments, it says almost nothing about the standard considerations we have used to determine *stare decisis* value, such as the antiquity of the precedent, the workability of its legal rule, and the reliance interests at stake. It is also conspicuously silent about *McConnell*, even though the *McConnell* Court's decision to uphold [the Bipartisan Campaign Reform Act (BCRA)] relied not only on the anti-distortion logic of *Austin* but also on the statute's historical pedigree, and the need to preserve the integrity of federal campaigns.

We have recognized that "*[s]tare decisis* has special force when legislators or citizens 'have acted in reliance on a previous decision, for in this instance overruling the decision would dislodge settled rights and expectations or require an extensive legislative

response.'" *Stare decisis* protects not only personal rights involving property or contract but also the ability of the elected branches to shape their laws in an effective and coherent fashion. Today's decision takes away a power that we have long permitted these branches to exercise. State legislatures have relied on their authority to regulate corporate electioneering, confirmed in *Austin*, for more than a century. The Federal Congress has relied on this authority for a comparable stretch of time, and it specifically relied on *Austin* throughout the years it spent developing and debating BCRA. The total record it compiled was *100,000 pages* long. Pulling out the rug beneath Congress after affirming the constitutionality of [the statutory provision] six years ago shows great disrespect for a coequal branch.

By removing one of its central components, today's ruling makes a hash out of BCRA's "delicate and interconnected regulatory scheme." . . .

Beyond the reliance interests at stake, the other *stare decisis* factors also cut against the Court. Considerations of antiquity are significant for similar reasons. *McConnell* is only six years old, but *Austin* has been on the books for two decades, and many of the statutes called into question by today's opinion have been on the books for a half-century or more. The Court points to no intervening change in circumstances that warrants revisiting *Austin*. Certainly nothing relevant has changed since we decided WRTL [*Federal Election Commission v. Wisconsin Right to Life, Inc.*] two Terms ago. And the Court gives no reason to think that *Austin* and *McConnell* are unworkable.

In fact, no one has argued to us that *Austin*'s rule has proved impracticable, and not a single for-profit corporation, union, or State has asked us to overrule it. Quite to the contrary, leading groups representing the business community, organized labor and the nonprofit sector, together with more than half of the States, urge that we preserve *Austin*. As for *McConnell*, the portions of BCRA it upheld may be prolix, but all three branches of Government have worked to make §203 as user-friendly as possible. For instance, Congress established a special mechanism for expedited review of constitutional challenges; the FEC has established a standardized process, with clearly defined safe harbors, for corporations to claim that a particular electioneering communication is permissible under WRTL; and, as noted above, The Chief Justice crafted his controlling opinion in WRTL with the express goal of maximizing clarity and administrability. The case for *stare decisis* may be bolstered, we have said, when subsequent rulings "have reduced the impact" of a precedent "while reaffirming the decision's core ruling."

In the end, the Court's rejection of *Austin* and *McConnell* comes down to nothing more than its disagreement with their results. Virtually every one of its arguments was made and rejected in those cases, and the majority opinion is essentially an amalgamation of resuscitated dissents. The only relevant thing that has changed since *Austin* and *McConnell* is the composition of this Court. Today's ruling thus strikes at the vitals of *stare decisis*, "the means by which we ensure that the law will not merely change erratically, but will develop in a principled and intelligible fashion" that "permits society to presume that bedrock principles are founded in the law rather than in the proclivities of individuals."

Visit **edge.sagepub.com/medialaw7e** to help you accomplish your coursework goals in an easy-to-use learning environment.

Freedom of expression is the matrix, the indispensable condition, of nearly every other form of freedom.

—U.S. Supreme Court Justice Benjamin N. Cardozo[1]

In 2018, the U.S. Supreme Court held that a Minnesota state ban on wearing clothing like this at the polls violated the First Amendment.

2

THE FIRST AMENDMENT
Speech and Press Freedoms in Theory and Reality

SUPPOSE . . .

. . . an anonymous source gives newspapers copies of classified federal government documents that show the government has been lying publicly about U.S. casualties and the U.S. war abroad. After the newspapers begin publishing stories based on the documents, the government obtains a court order to stop further stories, on the grounds coverage will jeopardize military operations and undermine national security. The newspapers challenge the ban in court, arguing that they have a First Amendment right to publish the information and the public has a need to know the truth.

Does the government's power to classify government records as secret allow it to prevent publication of classified government information once disclosed? Does the First Amendment allow government to prevent media coverage of issues of national importance? Does it matter how the newspapers obtained the documents? Look for the answers to these questions in this chapter's discussion of *New York Times Co. v. United States* and its case excerpt at the end of the chapter.

The First Amendment to the U.S. Constitution includes only 45 words. "Congress shall make no law respecting an establishment of religion, or prohibiting the free exercise thereof; or abridging the freedom of speech, or of the press; or the right of the people peaceably to assemble, and to petition the government for a redress of grievances." Since the adoption of the Bill of Rights in 1791, thousands of articles, books and legal cases have tried to interpret the First Amendment and define the boundaries of the six freedoms it protects.[2] A literal interpretation of the First Amendment would completely ban Congress, and only Congress, from "abridging" the freedom of speech or of the press in any way. However, in 1925, the U.S. Supreme Court said the First Amendment applied to state legislatures as well as to Congress.[3] Supreme Court decisions also make clear that although the First Amendment says government "shall make no law," the First Amendment's ban is *not* absolute.[4]

WHERE THE FIRST AMENDMENT CAME FROM

Historians of the First Amendment generally agree that the First Amendment was intended to prevent the U.S. government from adopting the types of suppressive laws that flourished in England following the introduction of the printing press in 1450. Beginning in the early 1500s, the British Crown controlled all presses in England through its licensing power. King Henry VIII and the Roman Catholic Church sought to suppress challenges to their power by outlawing critical views as heresy (criticism of the church) or sedition (challenges to government). They jointly imposed a strict system of licensing of printers and prior review of all publications.

Review before printing enabled the king's officers to ban disfavored authors and ideas. Printers suspected of publishing outlawed texts faced fines, prison, torture or even

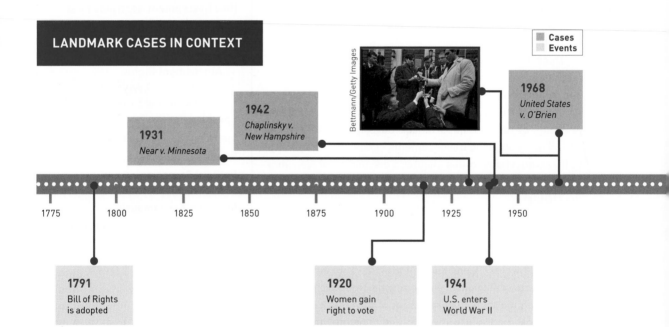

LANDMARK CASES IN CONTEXT

Cases
Events

Bettmann/Getty Images

1931
Near v. Minnesota

1942
Chaplinsky v. New Hampshire

1968
United States v. O'Brien

1775   1800   1825   1850   1875   1900   1925   1950

1791
Bill of Rights is adopted

1920
Women gain right to vote

1941
U.S. enters World War II

execution. In exchange for lucrative monopoly printing contracts, licensed printers reported and attacked unlicensed printers and destroyed their presses, but unlicensed texts continued to appear.

Foundations of First Amendment Theory

In 1643, the power of prior review shifted from the king's officers to the British Parliament. Authors and publishers protested government censorship and developed theories to justify press freedom. In 1644, English poet John Milton's unlicensed "Areopagitica" argued that an open marketplace of ideas advanced the interests of society and humankind. Milton, who was angered by church and state attempts to destroy his pamphlet advocating divorce, said the free exchange of ideas was vital to the discovery of truth. He wrote, famously,

> Though all the winds of doctrine were let loose to play upon the earth, so Truth be in the field, we do injuriously by licensing and prohibiting to misdoubt her strength. Let her and Falsehood grapple; who ever knew Truth put to the worse in a free and open encounter?[5]

By the late 1600s, English philosopher and political theorist John Locke argued that government censorship was an improper exercise of power.[6] Locke first said that all people

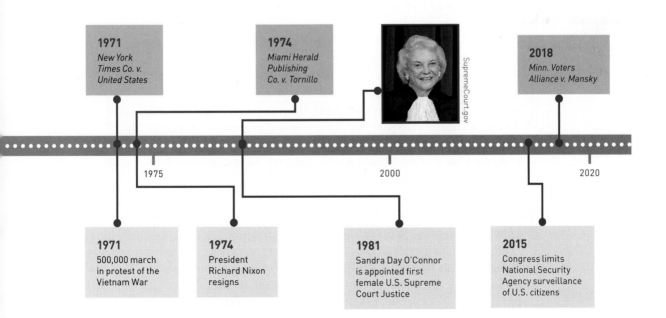

1971
New York Times Co. v. United States

1974
Miami Herald Publishing Co. v. Tornillo

SupremeCourt.gov

2018
Minn. Voters Alliance v. Mansky

1975

2000

2020

1971
500,000 march in protest of the Vietnam War

1974
President Richard Nixon resigns

1981
Sandra Day O'Connor is appointed first female U.S. Supreme Court Justice

2015
Congress limits National Security Agency surveillance of U.S. citizens

have fundamental natural rights, including life, personal liberty and self-fulfillment. Freedom of expression is central to these natural rights. Government has no innate rights or authority, and its power derives solely through grant from the people. Government actions outside the sphere of power granted by the people are illegitimate. The people do not give government the power over their natural human rights. Accordingly, government censorship is always illegitimate. Locke's vision of government was revolutionary.

In 1694, the British Parliament failed to renew the Licensing Act, and official **prior restraint** of publications ended. But for the next 100 years, the British government enacted and enforced laws that punished immoral, illegal or dangerous speech after the fact. Political thinkers of the day generally did not view punishment after the fact as censorship because it allowed people to speak and publish and held them accountable for the harms their speech was believed to cause, such as sedition, **defamation** (criticism of individuals) and blasphemy (sacrilegious speech about God).

The British licensed presses in the colonies, and government censors previewed publications until the 1720s. The crime of **seditious libel** made it illegal to publish anything harmful to the reputation of a colonial governor. Truth was not a defense because truthful criticism still harmed the governor's reputation, and the governor had a legal right to be compensated for that harm.

Nearly half a century later, French political philosopher Jean-Jacques Rousseau advanced the idea of a social contract between the people and their government in which the people limit some individual freedoms for a government that advances the collective interest.[7] Rousseau said all people are born free and equal but need the constraints of morality and law to become civilized and nonviolent. Accordingly, people form a social contract in which they remain sovereign and retain their human rights. Therefore, government censorship can never be justified.

British legal scholar Sir William Blackstone described the prevailing understanding of the free press under the common law of the day.[8] He wrote,

> The liberty of the press is indeed essential to the nature of a free state, but this consists in laying no *previous* restraints upon publications, and not in freedom from censure for criminal matter when published. Every freeman has an undoubted right to lay what sentiments he pleases before the public, to forbid this is to destroy the freedom of the press, but if he publishes what is improper, mischievous or illegal, he must take the consequences of his own temerity.[9]

Blackstone's view of freedom of the press and of British licensing, taxation and common law restraints on speech and press traveled to the American colonies.[10]

With growing independence, the colonies attempted to dismantle some British common law traditions. In the case of John Peter Zenger, this publisher of a newspaper in New York clearly had broken the sedition law by printing criticism of colonial Gov. William Cosby. Cosby jailed Zenger to stop the publications. Arguing for the defense, Andrew Hamilton said

prior restraint
Action taken by the government to prohibit publication of a specific document or text before it is distributed to the public; a policy that requires government approval before publication.

defamation
A false communication that harms another's reputation and subjects him or her to ridicule and scorn; incorporates both libel and slander.

seditious libel
Communication meant to incite people to change the government; criticism of the government.

INTERNATIONAL LAW
THE U.S. WAR ON INFORMATION?

Some see the annual Google transparency report as a barometer of internet freedom, and in 2019, it ranked the United States third in online censorship of the leading 20 industrialized nations.[i] Russia was by far the most aggressive government in removing content from the web, but the United States followed closely behind No. 2: Turkey. China ranked 14, behind Germany, France, the United Kingdom and Canada, among others.

Notions that established, Western democracies are less likely to engage in censorship are not accurate, according to a recent study of social media.[ii] Evidence suggests the contrary; there may be a greater tendency to censor in more open societies that have "more at stake." The responses of democratic nations to social media activism "have not differed significantly from the responses of authoritarian regimes," the study concluded.

The government's own records show that the United States "censored, withheld or said it couldn't find" more public records requested under the Freedom of Information Act (see Chapter 7) in 2017 than in any year in the past decade.[iii] FOIA requests for government files that year came up empty or censored 78 percent of the time, and the government spent more than $40 million defending its records denials and redactions.

no one should be jailed for publishing truthful and fair criticism of government. The jury agreed and acquitted Zenger in 1734 despite the contrary common law.

Very few trials for seditious libel followed. However, the struggle to define the acceptable limits of free speech and a free press continued in colonial legislatures that used their power to question, convict, jail and fine those who published criticism of the legislature of breach of parliamentary privilege.

This mixed history shaped First Amendment freedoms of speech and of the press. The Constitution's framers understood both the British tradition of punishment for sedition, blasphemy and libel, and the colonists' growing enthusiasm for increasingly free debate. It seems clear the authors of the First Amendment intended to provide a ban on prior restraints. Less clear is whether they intended to eliminate the common law regarding sedition, blasphemy and libel.[11]

As the 18th century ended, U.S. laws continued to punish criticism of government. Seven years after the adoption of the First Amendment, the Sedition Act imposed heavy fines and jail time on individuals who stirred up public emotions or expressed malicious views against the government. More than a dozen prosecutions and convictions under the Alien and Sedition Acts targeted outspoken publishers and political opponents of President John Adams.[12] The Alien and Sedition Acts expired without the U.S. Supreme Court reviewing their constitutionality, but more than 150 years later, Justice William J. Brennan said that "the court of history" clearly found the Sedition Act unconstitutional.[13]

WHEN "THE PRESS" CHANGES

In 1791, when the First Amendment was adopted, speaking to crowds in town squares and the printed word, the press, was *the* medium of mass communication. Printing of pamphlets, posters, books and newspapers was the primary means to distribute your message, and the masses reached were small. The largest 18th-century newspapers had circulations of no more than 200 or so readers. Word of mouth, speech, remained essential to spreading timely information.

Today, the First Amendment faces a very different reality. Observers long have decried the asserted threat new media pose to families, communities and society.[14] Established media viewed newcomers as competitors, even as new arrivals touted their ability to increase the quantity and diversity of speech and press.

New media—motion pictures, radio, television, telephone, cable, the internet, Siri—provide new types, reach, modes and uses of communication. They blur the line between press and speech, and "smart" devices challenge the "human rights" foundations of First Amendment freedoms. The bottleneck control of information by massive media conglomerates raises concerns that private owners may censor the exchange of information and ideas.[15]

For its part, the Supreme Court has struggled to decide whether and how the First Amendment protects new media.[16] For a time, the Court generally treated each medium differently on the grounds that each presented unique First Amendment capabilities. In 1949, for example, one justice argued that "the moving picture screen, the radio, the newspaper, the handbill, the sound truck and the street corner orator have differing natures, values, abuses and dangers. Each, in my view, is a law unto itself."[17] The Court accepted regulatory differences "justified by some special characteristic of the press"[18] or by specific distinctions among the media. Government could regulate broadcasters differently from newspapers because

REAL WORLD LAW
WHAT'S PUBLICATION?

When an employee clicks "like" on a Facebook post, is that speech or press?

A U.S. district court in Virginia ruled that Facebook "likes" are not expression protected by the First Amendment.[iv] Two sheriff's employees were fired after they clicked "like" on the campaign Facebook page of their boss's election opponent. They sued, saying the termination violated their free speech rights, but the district court rejected their challenge.

On appeal, the Fourth Circuit Court of Appeals disagreed.[v] It wrote:

On the most basic level, clicking on the "like" button literally published the statement that the User "likes" something, which is itself a substantive statement. . . . That a user may use a single mouse click to produce the message that he likes the page instead of typing the same message with several individual key strokes is of no constitutional significance.

Liking a political candidate's campaign page communicates the user's approval of the candidate and supports the campaign by associating the user with it. In this way, it is the internet equivalent of displaying a political sign in one's front yard, which the Supreme Court has held is substantive speech.[vi]

broadcasters act as trustees of scarce public airwaves.[19] Unique regulations on cable operators did not violate the First Amendment, the Court said, because cable threatened the survival of free over-the-air broadcasts.[20]

REAL WORLD LAW
COURTS GRAPPLE WITH MEANING/SIGNIFICANCE OF EMOJI

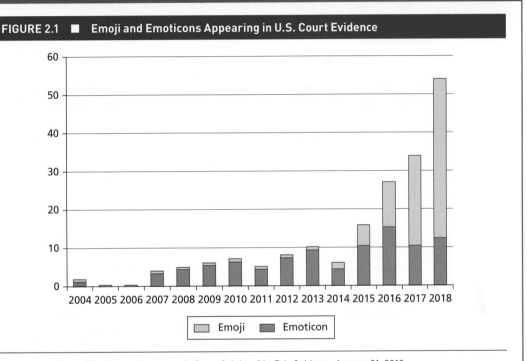

FIGURE 2.1 ■ Emoji and Emoticons Appearing in U.S. Court Evidence

Source: Adapted from "Emojis and Emoticons in Court Opinions" by Eric Goldman, January 31, 2019.

Emoji, the ubiquitous pictographs of quick messaging, are showing up more often in courts' evidence. One study found they appeared in more than 30 percent of all cases in 2018, and courts are struggling to interpret what they mean and how the First Amendment applies.[vii] Though they rarely have swayed case outcomes, the ambiguity of emoji and emoticons (their text-based cousins) may make them difficult for courts to interpret accurately and consistently.

One complexity is that "emoji usually have dialects."[viii] A crown in a text about Shakespeare's *Hamlet*, for example, may be purely representational. That same crown in a discussion of prostitution likely signifies that the "pimp is the king," according to the testimony of one sex-trafficking expert. Emoji also appear differently on different platforms, and different people may view the same emoji differently.

Appearing most frequently in cases involving sex crimes, emoji recently have been evidence in relation to threats, to a defendant's state of mind and to contract deliberations to shed light on intent. As emoji become an increasingly central part of text communications, courts will need to wrestle with how and whether they are protected speech that discloses otherwise hidden feelings and intentions.

But modern media blur or erase those distinctions. With all established news media and even online news losing audiences and the digital market gobbling up revenue,[21] the nature of U.S. media is changing even before you consider that six companies control the bulk of communications (cell, cable, films, news) across the United States.[22] Traditional media owners merge and consolidate holdings to prevent technology firms from taking over the market. But fewer owners controlling more diverse media present challenges to the Court's carefully drawn distinctions and the assumption that competition ensures an open marketplace of ideas.[23] When those below 30 often get their news from late-night comedians like Jimmy Fallon, Seth Meyers, Trevor Noah and Jimmy Kimmel, the courts are asked to reconsider what constitutes news and "the press" and how to determine its constitutional value.

FIGURE 2.2 ■ Media Ownership

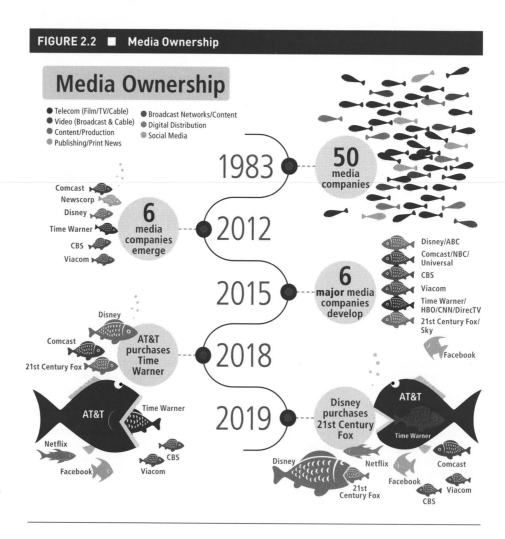

HOW THE FIRST AMENDMENT IS UNDERSTOOD

The mixed legacy of British common law and the fast-changing nature of communications create obstacles to a consistent, stable interpretation of the Constitution. Textualists assert that the First Amendment's own words are the most concrete and unwavering explanation of its meaning, but the text says nothing about whether court orders requiring WikiLeaks to disclose the source of its access to confidential government documents would "abridge" the freedom of "the press" or whether Facebook "likes" are a protected part of First Amendment "freedom of speech."[24]

Some justices look to history, seeking the **original intent** of the framers of the Constitution, to help them determine whether occupying the streets of Ferguson, Mo., or wearing bandanas and carrying AR-15 rifles at a Texas protest are protected speech.[25] Unfortunately, the authors of the First Amendment left scant records to indicate what they meant by "the freedom of speech, or of the press."

Other justices view the Constitution as a living document and argue that the ambiguity of constitutional language is its greatest strength. To them, a clear understanding of what the words of the First Amendment meant in 1791 would rarely be relevant today. Others argue that such a malleable understanding of the Constitution gives the U.S. Supreme Court too much power and poses a threat to legal predictability.

Even parts of the First Amendment that seem clear sometimes become muddy. On its face, the First Amendment limits government—"Congress shall make no law . . ." It prevents government abridging "the freedom" of expression of private individuals and organizations. It does not speak to the ability of private companies to limit speech freedoms or the ability of government to control the content of official government speech. In general, private actors cannot violate the constitutional rights of others because the Constitution requires "state action."

Generally, the Supreme Court avoids broad statements about the First Amendment and determines what the First Amendment means within the particular context of each specific case.

To reach decisions, the Supreme Court often weighs the constitutional interests on one side of a case against the competing interests on the other side. When courts make decisions by weighing the specific facts on each side of the case, their reasoning is called **ad hoc balancing**. No clear rule dictates the weight of interests in ad hoc balancing. Instead, judges determine which side has greater constitutional merit.

Courts also use categories of speech to reach some First Amendment decisions. The Supreme Court has defined several speech categories, such as political speech and commercial speech, to guide the appropriate First Amendment application. Simply put, the Court's categories give some kinds of speech a lot of protection; some, less; others, none at all. When speech falls into one of these categories, the courts do not balance the value of the speech against society's interests. Using the categorical approach, the courts' central question is whether a specific act of expression falls within a fully protected, less protected or unprotected class.

Decades ago in *Chaplinsky v. New Hampshire*,[26] the Court first noted that "certain well-defined and narrowly limited classes of speech . . . are no essential part of any exposition

original intent
The perceived intent of the framers of the Constitution that guides some First Amendment application and interpretation.

ad hoc balancing
Making decisions according to the specific facts of the case under review rather than more general principles.

WASHINGTON PRESIDING IN THE CONVENTION 1787.

George Washington presiding over debate at the Constitutional Convention in 1787.

categorical balancing
Legal reasoning that weighs different broad categories, such as political speech, against other interests, such as privacy, to create general rules that may be applied in later cases with similar facts.

of ideas, and are of such slight social value as a step to truth" that government may prevent and punish this speech without violating the First Amendment. In *Chaplinsky*, the Court did not fully develop the different "narrow" categories of speech, but subsequent rulings make clear that political speech enjoys full constitutional protection, while fighting words and obscenity are unprotected categories. The First Amendment also does not prohibit laws that punish blackmail, extortion, perjury, false advertising and disruptive speech in the public school classroom, for example.

When the category of speech is less clearly defined, the courts generally balance the nature of the speech against any competing societal values using what is called **categorical balancing**. For example, pornography is not a legal category of speech. To determine whether certain pornographic images deserve constitutional protection, courts must balance the right to freedom of sexual expression against the harms it causes in the specific circumstances of the case.[27] Judges do this on a case-by-case basis.

The U.S. Supreme Court used balancing in *Lane v. Franks* to rule that the First Amendment protects the right of public employees to testify in court on matters of public concern.[28] Weighing the interest of a government agency to control the speech of its employees against the right of the person to testify in court, the Court first clarified the boundary between government and private speech. "When public employees make statements pursuant to their official duties, the employees are not speaking as citizens for First Amendment purposes"[29] but are speaking for the government, the Court wrote. The First Amendment protection for government employee speech depends on that distinction as well as on the public value of the speech. In *Lane*, the value of public testimony about government corruption outweighed the government interest in stopping it.

The Supreme Court sidestepped an opportunity to decide the amount of First Amendment protection given to false speech when it considered whether a federal law that made it a crime to lie about being awarded U.S. military honors violated the Constitution.[30] In its decision in *United States v. Alvarez* striking down the Stolen Valor Act, only four justices held that the First Amendment absolutely protects false statements. Reasoning for this plurality, Justice Anthony Kennedy argued that speech may be excluded from First Amendment protection only in the rare and extreme circumstances of the "historic categories" that pose a grave and imminent threat. False claims about military awards do not. Congress later amended the Stolen Valor Act to make it illegal to profit from such lies.[31]

The Ninth Circuit Court of Appeals later distinguished between false action and lies to rule that the First Amendment did not prevent government from punishing the wearing of unearned military medals.[32] The First Amendment protected only false claims of military honors.

Similarly, the Sixth Circuit Court of Appeals found an Ohio law prohibiting "false statements" during a political campaign unconstitutional.[33] The court reasoned that "the First Amendment protects the 'civic duty' to engage in public debate, with a preference for counteracting lies with more accurate information, rather than by restricting lies." The First Amendment directs government not to restrict speech, and as the Supreme Court established, the "fixed star in our constitutional constellation" is that the government may not "prescribe what shall be orthodox in politics."[34]

WHY WE VALUE THE FIRST AMENDMENT

The Supreme Court has interpreted the First Amendment as an instrument to achieve specific social functions or advance certain fundamental values. Speech deserves protection because it aids the search for truth, advances self-governance, provides a check on government abuse of power and offers a safety valve for social discontent.[35] Some scholars argue that the most significant value of the First Amendment is to improve the ability of minorities to be heard[36] or to encourage the development of a tolerant society.[37] The U.S. Supreme Court applied this view of the freedoms of speech and press as instruments to advance societal objectives[38] when it upheld broadcast regulation as a constitutional means to increase the diversity of ideas reaching U.S. voters.

In recent years, theories of the Constitution as purely a limit on government power—not as a provider of personal liberties—have challenged the notion that an unregulated marketplace of ideas achieves truth or good democratic outcomes.[39] Some believe this theory aids understanding of First Amendment protections for political lies, "socially worthless untruths" and new technological forms of "cheap and abundant robotic speech" (e.g., Siri).[40] If the Constitution is solely a check on government, it has no proactive role in addressing imbalances of power between collective speakers (social media, communications conglomerates, the internet) who may overwhelm the marketplace of ideas and the sole individual. A hands-off approach to liars and animatronic speakers is justified by the notions that all "truths" are partial, the identity of speakers does not determine the value of their speech and government may not establish preferred orthodoxies.[41]

Those who value free speech in and of itself—as an end rather than a means—see free speech as a natural right. For them, the Constitution protects freedom of speech because speech is fundamental to individual natural liberty, essential to what it means to be human.[42] Such views often rely on framers' understanding of broad human liberties that rarely outweighed the public good.[43] Laws could limit basic human rights to advance collective welfare.

These two perspectives on free speech help courts determine what types of speech deserve to be protected or punished. Neither does a very good job, however. Neither provides strict guidelines or clear lines (what the law calls bright-line distinctions) to delineate protected speech. For instance, the functional approach fails to establish a clear boundary between speech that helps democratic self-governance and speech that does not. When is a march and rally in Washington, D.C., protected political expression? If speech is protected because it is the essence of being human, where are its logical boundaries? Does the Constitution protect my right to express myself by shooting guns in the middle of the city?

REAL WORLD LAW
SOME CORE VALUES OF FREE SPEECH

Experts disagree on the meaning and value(s) served by the First Amendment.[ix] Some of the frequently identified core values of free speech are as follows:

- *Human liberty.* The freedom of speech is a fundamental, inalienable natural right.[x]

- *Self-governance.* The freedom to discuss political candidates and issues is essential to "democratic self-determination."[xi]

- *Restraint on government power.* Free speech is a "check" on government overreach and an "invaluable bulwark against tyranny."[xii]

- *Attainment of truth.* Free speech is vital to the "marketplace of ideas," to the discovery of truth and to challenging orthodoxies.[xiii]

- *Safety valve.* Free speech in "the worst of times" is a mechanism for "letting off steam" that reduces violence and helps maintain social stability.[xiv]

- *Its own end.* Free speech, like clean air or beauty, is an end in and of itself.[xv]

Two apparently contradictory landmark Supreme Court rulings on a public right of access to the media demonstrate the dilemmas presented by value-based decision making. In the first of these, *Red Lion Broadcasting Co. v. Federal Communications Commission*, the Court ruled years ago that regulations requiring broadcasters to seek out and broadcast competing views on controversial public issues were constitutional.[44] Broadcasters had said FCC rules requiring them to notify and provide free broadcast time for political candidates to reply to on-air attacks violated their First Amendment right to choose what they aired. The Court disagreed and said,

> The right of free speech of a broadcaster . . . or any other individual does not embrace a right to snuff out the free speech of others. . . . [The broadcaster] has no constitutional right to . . . monopolize a radio frequency to the exclusion of his fellow citizens.[45]

Here the Court held that diverse speech over the public airwaves was of paramount value to listeners. Five years later, with three new members, the Supreme Court ruled in *Miami Herald Publishing Co. v. Tornillo* that the First Amendment protected the autonomy of the printed press and barred government from requiring newspapers to provide free reply space to political candidates attacked in the paper. The Court said that "compelling editors or publishers to publish that which 'reason tells them should not be published'" is unconstitutional.[46] Although newspapers are a platform for public debate, "press responsibility is not mandated by the Constitution, and like many other virtues it cannot be legislated."[47] The Court reasoned:

> A newspaper is more than a passive receptacle or conduit for news, comment and advertising. The choice of material to go into a newspaper, and the decisions made as

to limitations on the size and content of the paper, and treatment of public issues and public officials—whether fair or unfair—constitute the exercise of editorial control and judgment. It has yet to be demonstrated how governmental regulation of this crucial process can be exercised consistent with First Amendment guarantees of a free press.[48]

HOW GOVERNMENT RESTRAINS FIRST AMENDMENT FREEDOMS

The U.S. Supreme Court has established one bedrock principle: Freedom of speech and of the press cannot coexist with prior restraint. Prior restraints stop speech before it is spoken and halt presses before they print. They are the essence of censorship. But in today's world of Instagram and Snapchat, how should government step in to avoid the harms speech may cause?

The Court's modern understanding of prior restraint originated in 1931.[49] In *Near v. Minnesota*, the Court said that prior restraint, especially any outright ban on expression, is the least tolerable form of government intervention in the speech marketplace.[50] The case began after the publisher of a Minneapolis newspaper printed charges that city officials allowed Jewish gangsters to run gambling, bootlegging and racketeering businesses across the city. When the publisher could not show that the attacks were true and published with good intent, the court shut down the paper under a state public nuisance law that punished publication of "scandalous or defamatory material."

On review, the Supreme Court ruled that the permanent ban on future issues of the newspaper was unconstitutional. The Court said the First Amendment stands as a nearly absolute barrier to classic prior restraints. Government prohibitions before publication are unacceptable unless the government can show that the action is essential to avoid a very narrow list of harms, such as the disclosure of military movements.

In *Near*, the Supreme Court held that the First Amendment placed a heavy, but not absolute, burden on government prior restraints. While the "liberty of speech, and of the press, is not an absolute right, . . . [t]he fact that the liberty . . . may be abused by miscreant purveyors of scandal does not make any the less necessary the immunity from previous restraint in dealing with official misconduct."[51] The Court said prior restraints may be permissible but only in "exceptional cases. When a nation is at war . . . [n]o one would question but that a government might prevent actual obstruction to its recruiting service or the publication of the sailing dates of transports or the number and location

POINTS OF LAW

SUPREME COURT'S DOCTRINE IN *NEAR V. MINNESOTA*

In its 1931 decision in *Near v. Minnesota*, the U.S. Supreme Court established that government

- may not censor or prohibit a publication in advance

- except when a communication is obscene, incites violence or reveals military secrets

- *and* the government makes a specific showing that a prior restraint is justified.

In all other cases, government may punish communications only after the fact.[xvi]

Associated Press

Dr. Daniel Ellsberg (left), the U.S. Defense Department consultant who leaked the Pentagon Papers, speaks to reporters after his 1971 arraignment on charges of illegal possession of the classified documents.

injunction
A court order prohibiting a person or organization from doing some specified act.

of troops." It said that the government also could prevent the publication of obscenity, incitements to violence or overthrow of government and "words that may have all the effect of force."[52]

In 1971, the U.S. Supreme Court ruled in *New York Times Co. v. United States* (excerpted at the end of this chapter) that a court order preventing publication of news stories based on leaked Pentagon reports was an unconstitutional prior restraint.[53] The New York Times had begun a series of news stories based on a top-secret Department of Defense study of the then-ongoing U.S. involvement in Vietnam. The Nixon administration asked for a court **injunction** to stop the publication about the so-called Pentagon Papers report on the status of the war. The government said publication threatened national security and the safety of U.S. troops. The district court agreed and enjoined publication.

Many compared the WikiLeaks posting of more than 90,000 classified U.S. military documents on the war in Afghanistan to the publication of the Pentagon Papers during the Vietnam War.[54] Both leaks hinged on media providing greater transparency and credibility to information about an ongoing and controversial war involving U.S. troops.[55] However, the Pentagon Papers documents were at least three years old and were released as U.S. troops began to withdraw from Vietnam; some WikiLeaks material was only a few weeks old and appeared as the war in Afghanistan was ramping up.[56]

Acting with unusual speed in the case of the Pentagon Papers, the Supreme Court said the injunction violated the Constitution because the government had not shown that the ban was essential to prevent a real and immediate risk of harm to a compelling government interest. The Court said, "[A]ny system of prior restraints of expression comes to this Court bearing a heavy presumption against its constitutional validity."[57] The Court decision left open the possibility that prior restraints might be constitutional if the government could meet this very rigorous test.

Five years later, in *Nebraska Press Association v. Stuart*, the Court said prior restraints are generally unconstitutional because they pose too great a risk that government will censor ideas it disfavors and distort the marketplace of ideas.[58] The Court said that if "a threat of criminal or civil sanctions after publication 'chills' speech, prior restraint 'freezes' it." Prohibited prior restraints have three elements: (1) government oversight over whole categories of speech, content or publications; (2) government determination of acceptable content; and (3) government power to stop content before it reaches the public.

The First Amendment poses its greatest obstacle to direct prior restraints on the news media because every moment of a ban on reporting causes direct harm to the First Amendment rights of both the media and the public.[59] Yet news organizations report that policies imposed on government agencies, the "management" of reporters through government public relations offices and calls by government officials to punish or remove journalists all have the effect of prior restraint.[60] The government says it has the power to control the flow of information from its employees and to classify information.

Today, apparent prior restraints arise in the form of court orders that stop speech or publication. For example, the Supreme Court long ago said a state court injunction preventing the scheduled broadcast of an investigative news report was unconstitutional; indefinite delay of news was unacceptable under the First Amendment.[61] As another court noted, "News delayed is news denied."[62] The Supreme Court decision involved CBS News' intended broadcast of undercover footage of a South Dakota meatpacking plant. Although the broadcast relied on "calculated misdeeds" and might cause significant harm to the meatpacking company, the Court ruled that the "most extraordinary remedy" of an injunction was unwarranted because it was not essential.

The speed and breadth of online dissemination sometimes leads courts to impose injunctions. When a county sheriff pressured credit card companies to refuse their services to Backpage.com, the company sued.[63] Backpage argued that the sheriff's attempt to strangle website revenue because he disliked its adult advertising section violated the site's freedom of speech. The appeals court said the attempt to prevent publication of adult ads was intimidation, a threat and a prior restraint that either threatened to harm or actually harmed the plaintiff's speech. "[A] public official . . . who tries to shut down an avenue of expression of ideas and opinions through actual or threatened imposition of government power or sanction is violating the First Amendment."[64] The court ordered the sheriff to stop any attempts to silence Backpage advertising.

In a case involving an ongoing and increasingly heated dispute between two entertainment firms, a trial court ordered one party accused of cyberstalking to stop all texting and online posting to or about the other and to remove previously posted material. The communications involved one text, two emails and the reposting of several articles.[65] On review, a Florida appeals court declined to reach the First Amendment question but struck down the restraining order it called "a classic example of prior restraint . . . [that] violates the Constitution."[66]

POINTS OF LAW
WHAT IS A PRIOR RESTRAINT?

A prior restraint is good, old, garden-variety censorship. Prior restraint exists when

1. any government body or representative
2. reviews speech or press *prior* to distribution and
3. stops the dissemination of ideas *before* they reach the public.

The Supreme Court has called prior restraint "the most serious and the least tolerable infringement on First Amendment rights."[xvii]

The U.S. Supreme Court has held that a prior restraint on the media can be justified only when there is clear and convincing evidence that the speech will cause great and certain harm that cannot be addressed by less intrusive measures or when the speaker clearly engaged in criminal activity to obtain the information being banned.[67] The ban on prior restraints does not prohibit laws that silence discussion of particular topics, such as threats to national security. Judges' orders prohibiting trial participants from discussing ongoing trials also generally are acceptable. Laws that limit use of copyrighted material are mandated by the Constitution, and laws that criminalize obscenity are accepted. Police also may legally prevent the speech involved when individuals conspire to commit a crime or to incite violence.

HOW THE SUPREME COURT REVIEWS LAWS AFFECTING FIRST AMENDMENT RIGHTS

The U.S. Supreme Court does not view all government actions that appear to restrain freedom of speech in advance as prior restraints. The Court decides the constitutionality of laws by drawing a number of distinctions. It first determines whether a law involves speech at all. Minimum-wage regulations and laws that prevent monopolies fall within the power of Congress to regulate commerce.[68] The Court generally presumes that these **laws of general application** are constitutional. The Supreme Court reviews challenges to such laws under its least rigorous or minimum review, called **rational review**. Under rational review, a law is constitutional if government can show it serves a rational purpose. Laws reviewed under minimum scrutiny must be reasonable and serve a legitimate government purpose to be constitutional.

When government actions do affect the freedom of speech and press protected by the First Amendment, the Supreme Court first determines whether the law targets the ideas expressed or aims at some goal unrelated to the content of the message. The Court calls the first type of law **content based** and the second **content neutral**. Content-based laws regulate what is being said; they single out certain messages or types of speech for particular treatment. Laws that prohibit the "desecration" of the U.S. flag are content based.[69] Content-neutral laws restrict where, when and how ideas are expressed. Also called **time/place/manner laws**, content-neutral restrictions often advance public interests unrelated to speech.

Content-Based Laws

The U.S. Supreme Court generally presumes content-based laws are unconstitutional. Like prior restraints, laws that punish expression of specific ideas after the fact pose a serious threat of government censorship. To stop government infringement on disfavored ideas, the Supreme Court applies its most rigorous test to determine whether content-based laws are constitutional. The toughest standard of review, **strict scrutiny**, finds laws that apply different treatment to different types of speech unconstitutional unless they use (1) the least restrictive means (2) to advance a compelling government interest.

Laws employ the least restrictive means only if they are extremely narrowly tailored to their goals and affect the smallest possible amount of protected speech. The Supreme Court generally finds that a law is least restrictive if the government has no other reasonable method to achieve its goals that would be less harmful to free speech rights. To pass strict scrutiny, laws also must directly advance a compelling or paramount government interest. The Court has said a **compelling interest** is an interest of the highest order that relates to core constitutional concerns or the most significant functions of government. Compelling government interests include national security, the electoral process and public health and safety.

In *Simon & Schuster v. Crime Victims Board*, for example, the Supreme Court struck down a New York law that required convicted criminals to turn over the profits of publications that made even passing reference to their crimes.[70] The state said the money would compensate crime victims, increase victim compensation and decrease the "fruits" of crime. Simon & Schuster had published a true-crime autobiography of a Mafia figure and challenged the law on the grounds that it targeted specific content for punishment by the government. The Supreme Court found

---

POINTS OF LAW
STRICT SCRUTINY

The U.S. Supreme Court has said content-based laws are constitutional only if they pass strict scrutiny. To pass strict scrutiny, a law must

1. be necessary and

2. employ the least restrictive means

3. to advance a compelling government interest.

Strict scrutiny is the most rigorous test used by the courts to determine whether a law is constitutional. Few laws pass this test.

---

the law content-based law and said it advanced a compelling government interest, but it also punished writings that deserved full First Amendment protection.[71] The law was unconstitutional because it did not use the least restrictive means to achieve its goal.

Content-Neutral Laws

Laws that impose speech restrictions to advance legitimate government interests without targeting particular viewpoints or content generally are constitutional. Many laws that limit noise in school zones are content neutral and constitutional.[72] The Supreme Court applies **intermediate scrutiny** to such laws and finds them constitutional if they restrict speech as little as necessary to advance an important government interest unrelated to speech. Content-neutral laws generally regulate the non-speech elements of messages, such as the location, time of day or volume. If content-neutral laws advance a legitimate government goal and do not favor particular views, the Court generally finds them constitutional even if they reduce the method, location or quantity of speech.

The U.S. Supreme Court established its foundational First Amendment test for content-neutral laws in its review of the conviction of David Paul O'Brien for burning his draft card during an anti–Vietnam War protest. O'Brien violated a federal law that made it a crime to knowingly destroy a draft card. The government said the law aided the functioning of the draft and the U.S. military and protected the national security.[73] O'Brien argued that the law was unconstitutional on its face (see Chapter 1) and infringed his freedom of speech.

In *United States v. O'Brien*, the Supreme Court disagreed and upheld O'Brien's conviction.[74] Looking at the actual words of the law—a type of review called statutory construction (see Chapter 1)—the Supreme Court said the statute served a compelling government interest in ensuring the operation of the military draft and caused only minimal harm to O'Brien's speech. The law was content neutral because it did not target disfavored viewpoints and was

strict scrutiny
A court test for determining the constitutionality of laws aimed at speech content, under which the government must show it is using the least restrictive means available to directly advance its compelling interest.

compelling interest
A government interest of the highest order, an interest the government is required to protect.

intermediate scrutiny
A standard applied by the courts to review laws that implicate but do not directly regulate core constitutional values; also called heightened review.

Bettmann/Getty Images

David P. O'Brien (second from left), 19, was among young men on the courthouse steps in Boston in 1967 burning their draft cards in protest to the Vietnam War.

symbolic expression
Action that warrants some First Amendment protection because its primary purpose is to express ideas.

O'Brien test
A three-part test used to determine whether a content-neutral law is constitutional.

important government interest
An interest of the government that is substantial or significant (i.e., more than merely convenient or reasonable) but not compelling.

narrowly tailored because it left O'Brien free to express his opposition to the draft in other ways. Finally, the Court said the government could constitutionally place a small burden on **symbolic expression**—the combination of speech and action represented by draft-card burning.

The decision produced a new three-part test for incidental regulations of speech, known as the *O'Brien* test. Under the *O'Brien* test, courts find a law content neutral and constitutional if the law (1) is unrelated to the suppression of speech, (2) advances an important government interest, and (3) is narrowly tailored to achieve that interest while only incidentally restricting protected speech. If the Court finds a law is not directed at the content of speech and does not target ideas disfavored by government, it generally passes the first prong. Then the Court must find the law serves an **important government interest**. A government interest is important when it is weighty or significant, more than merely convenient or reasonable. Laws intended to serve government goals unrelated to content tend to meet this standard.

The third part of the *O'Brien* test, sometimes called the narrow-tailoring standard, requires a law to "fit" its purpose. A law "fits" when it advances the government interest without imposing an unnecessary burden on speech.[75] The calculation is not precise. Narrowly tailored laws must be clear and not give officials unlimited discretion.[76] They need not be the best fit, however. Historically, most laws reviewed under *O'Brien* intermediate scrutiny have been upheld.

The Court applied the *O'Brien* test to uphold a regulation requiring New York City employees to control the volume and sound mix of performers in Central Park.[77] Performers said the rule unconstitutionally allowed the city to control their expression even when it served no important government interest. The Court, however, said the city's complete control of sound was a narrowly tailored means for the city to protect nearby (wealthy) residents from disturbance. *Ward v. Rock Against Racism* established that *O'Brien* requires only a loose fit. A law is narrow tailored if the government interest would suffer without a law that serves the interest reasonably well.

In *Hill v. Colorado*, the Court held that a state law creating moving, non-protest zones around people entering abortion clinics was a valid, narrowly tailored, content-neutral restriction that directly advanced the government's important interest in protecting the public from harassment.[78] But in 2014 in *McCullen v. Coakley*, the Court held that a fixed, 35-foot buffer zone around clinics was an unconstitutional prior restraint.[79] The Supreme Court said the fixed zone imposed a serious burden on individuals seeking to "counsel" women because it was not narrowly tailored to promote "public safety, patient access to health care, and unobstructed use of public sidewalks and roadways." The difference rested on the Court's conclusion that permanent buffer zones made it "substantially more difficult" to engage in one-on-one conversations.

Courts prior to 2015 generally reviewed statutes that regulated signs to protect community safety and aesthetics under *O'Brien* and found them content neutral and constitutional.[80] In *Reed v. Town of Gilbert*, the U.S. Supreme Court changed this when it unanimously struck down a sign ordinance that established nearly two dozen categories of signs (e.g., church, temporary directional, political), each with its own restrictions.[81] In *Reed*, the Court said the law was content based on its face because it "applie[d] to particular speech because of the topic discussed or the idea or message expressed."[82] Regulations that "draw distinctions based on the message . . . [or that] defin[e] regulated speech by particular subject matter . . . [or] by its function or purpose . . . are subject to strict scrutiny."[83]

The Court held that laws that make content distinctions, regardless of the law's purpose, are always content based.[84] A law that differentiates between different types of messages cannot be viewed as content neutral even if it serves an important purpose unrelated to speech content. The purpose of the law becomes relevant only after a court decides that the law does *not* make content distinctions, the *Reed* Court said. The Supreme Court then applied strict scrutiny, its most rigorous review, and found the town of Gilbert's sign law unconstitutional.

Some said the *Reed* holding marked an "important change in First Amendment doctrine," shifted the nature of content-neutral review and "imperil[ed] hundreds, even perhaps thousands, of local, state and federal laws that make subject matter or viewpoint distinctions."[85] In the year following the decision, four U.S. circuit courts of appeal struck down laws that likely would have survived pre-*Reed* intermediate scrutiny.[86] A representative decision of the U.S. Appeals Court for the Seventh Circuit concluded that, under *Reed*, "[a]ny law distinguishing one kind of speech from another by reference to [the] meaning [of the speech] now requires a compelling justification" rather than merely the important government interest required for content-neutral restrictions to be found constitutional under *O'Brien*.[87]

POINTS OF LAW

O'BRIEN INTERMEDIATE SCRUTINY

The Supreme Court generally applies some form of intermediate scrutiny to content-neutral laws that incidentally affect the freedom of speech. A law is constitutional under *O'Brien* intermediate scrutiny if it falls within the power of government and

1. advances an important government interest

2. that is unrelated to suppression of speech and

3. is narrowly tailored to only incidentally restrict First Amendment freedoms.[xviii]

POINTS OF LAW

INTERMEDIATE SCRUTINY AFTER REED V. TOWN OF GILBERT

Following the Supreme Court's ruling in *Reed v. Town of Gilbert*, courts should follow this two-step process to determine whether to apply intermediate scrutiny to laws affecting speech.[xix] Intermediate scrutiny should be applied only if

1. the law does not distinguish between categories or types of speech and

2. the law's purpose is not related to the viewpoint or content of the speech.

SPEAKING POLITICS

Political speech lies at the "core of what the First Amendment is designed to protect."[88] The U.S. Supreme Court has said political speech involves any "communication concerning political change."[89] This encompasses ballots and voting, electioneering speeches and lobbying, campaign spending and yard signs, political advertisements, cartoons and blogs, petitions and buttons and maybe even protests. Believing that political speech is integral to democratic government, the Court generally has used strict scrutiny to review laws that seem to infringe on political speech.[90]

In 2018, the Supreme Court ruled that a Minnesota state ban on wearing political insignia or slogans inside a polling place on Election Day violated the First Amendment.[91] The Court struck down the law as poorly tailored to fit the "special purpose" of the polling place as "an island of calm." The Court accepted that government could exclude "some forms of advocacy" from the polls but said the loosely drafted Minnesota statute presented "riddles" that encouraged "haphazard interpretations."

"[I]f a State wishes to set its polling places apart as areas free of partisan discord, it must employ a more discernible approach than the one Minnesota has offered here," the Court concluded.[92] After the ruling, laws in 10 states restricted what you could wear when you went to vote.[93]

Another lawsuit began when an anti-abortion group planned a billboard campaign claiming that a candidate for the U.S. House of Representatives backed taxpayer-funded abortion because he supported the Affordable Care Act. The candidate sought a court order to block the ads as false, and the anti-abortion group challenged the constitutionality of the state law prohibiting lies in campaign ads. The Sixth Circuit Court of Appeals allowed the candidate to sue for defamation,[94] but he could not prove the defamatory statement was made with knowledge that it was false or reckless disregard for its truth, which is required for public officials to win a libel suit (see Chapter 4).

On remand from the Supreme Court,[95] the Sixth Circuit Court found the law unconstitutional because its content-based restriction on core political speech was not narrowly tailored to advance the state's compelling interest in preserving the integrity of its elections.[96] Some say the decision could affect similar laws in 15 states.[97]

Despite the Supreme Court's position that political speech deserves the highest level of constitutional protection, news organizations and government may punish employees whose political expression violates their policies. In an older ruling, the Washington State Supreme Court held that the First Amendment protection of editorial autonomy allows newspapers in Washington to prohibit reporters from engaging in political activity.[98]

SPEAKING FOR AND AS THE GOVERNMENT

Courts have attempted to distinguish the ability of government to control the speech of its employees from the freedom of individuals who work in government to engage in protected speech outside of their employment. Government employees do not lose their personal freedom of speech when they accept government work,[99] but the government has the authority to classify sensitive materials and control their distribution, especially in the name of national security. The government also may impose codes of silence and control the content of employee speech and work products to advance governmental interests.[100]

The U.S. Supreme Court has held that government control of employee speech extends only to speech directly related to government employment.[101] The Court struck down the portion of a federal law requiring nongovernmental organizations to disseminate specific messages as a condition of receiving federal funding.[102] The Court said the law unconstitutionally sought "to leverage funding to regulate speech outside the contours of the program itself."[103]

In *Garcetti v. Ceballos*, the Supreme Court clarified the distinction between speech *as* a government employee and independent speech *of* a government employee.[104] The Court said the First Amendment did not prohibit government from limiting or punishing an employee's inappropriate work-related expression. The case involved a county attorney's transfer and denial of promotion after he reported alleged inaccuracies in a sheriff's affidavit. The attorney said the actions unconstitutionally punished his protected speech; the government countered that the attorney's report was punishable employee speech. In a 5–4 ruling, the Supreme Court agreed with the government and said the government has authority "over what [expression] the employer itself has commissioned or created."[105]

Then, in 2016, the Supreme Court ruled that the First Amendment prevented a city police department from demoting an employee in order to stop the employee's "overt involvement" in a political campaign.[106] After a police officer reported seeing a detective picking up a campaign sign for a mayoral candidate opposing the chief of police, the chief demoted the detective. The Supreme Court said the purpose of obtaining the political sign was immaterial to its decision. It ruled that the police department's intention to punish protected individual, political activity was sufficient to demonstrate that it had violated the First Amendment.

In another case involving a complaint of attempted retaliatory firing by a city council, the Supreme Court denied that the action violated the Constitution and described the employee's claim as "an ordinary workplace grievance." The unanimous Court held that the right of employees to petition for redress must be balanced "against the government's interest . . . in the effective and efficient management of its internal affairs."[107] The government's need to manage its affairs "requires proper restraints on the invocation of rights by employees."[108]

In one of several recent decisions involving mandatory union payments by public employees, the Supreme Court said that the state of Illinois could not require workers hired by Medicaid clients and funded through that federal program to pay union dues if they chose not to join the union.[109] The Court reasoned that these health care workers were not full-fledged government employees. Two years later, with only eight members sitting on the Court, the justices split evenly on whether government agencies could compel their own employees to contribute to unions that used the funding to support political or ideological causes the employees disfavored.[110]

In 2017, the Supreme Court made clear that courts should use "great caution before extending government-speech precedents . . . [because] private speech could be passed off as government speech [and] silence[d] simply [by] affixing a government seal of approval."[111] The following year, the Second Circuit Court of Appeals rejected the argument that simply granting a vendor permit to an Italian-food truck, Wandering Dago, turned the vendor's speech into government speech. The appeals court held that the Constitution prevented the state from refusing to grant a permit to the vendor simply because it found the name to be an offensive, ethnic slur.[112]

Many of these rulings turn on somewhat obscure distinctions between the government's own speech and efforts to regulate private speech. In *Walker v. Texas Division, Sons of Confederate Veterans*, the Supreme Court waded directly into this "muddy" and "befuddling area of the law"[113] to establish "the outer bounds of the government-speech doctrine."[114] The case involved a Texas Department of Motor Vehicles denial of a specialty license plate bearing the image of a Confederate battle flag. The department refused to permit the plate because it was an "offensive" symbol of "hate."[115] The Court majority in *Walker* upheld the state's authority to control the content of the "quasi-government" speech on license plates because it bore a clear link to the government. Government, like private citizens, has the right to be free from association with unwanted messages.

The *Walker* majority relied on the Supreme Court's reasoning in *Pleasant Grove v. Summum*, which held that government could select the monuments it displays in its parks.[116] A religious group raised a First Amendment challenge to a city's decision not to post the group's "Seven Aphorisms" on a permanent monument.[117] In reviewing the case, the Supreme Court first said that various limitations inherent to public displays make it impractical for government to accommodate all speakers. The Court concluded "that the City's decision to accept certain privately donated monuments while rejecting respondent's is best viewed as a form of government speech . . . not subject to the Free Speech Clause."[118] The selected speakers effectively extended government speech and were subject to government control of content.

Writing in dissent in *Walker*, Justice Samuel Alito said the plates, designed and paid for by private individuals, represented private speech.[119] Along with the three other conservative justices then on the Supreme Court, he acknowledged that government had a small part in the speech but expressed doubt that vanity messages on license plates were government speech at all because they played no role in governmental functions or policies.

In 2019, *Manhattan Community Access Corp. v. Halleck* asked the U.S. Supreme Court to decide whether a municipally created and licensed company with some government-appointed directors violated the Constitution when it rejected programming for its public access channels that it deemed offensive.[120] The Second Circuit Court of Appeals had ruled that cable operator was a state actor and "the electronic version of the public square"[121] that violated the First Amendment when it refused to broadcast a film criticizing Manhattan Community Access Corp.[122]

The Supreme Court disagreed.[123] Writing for the majority in a sharply divided 5-4 decision, Justice Brett Kavanaugh concluded that the First Amendment did not apply; the cable company was not a state actor because it did not perform "a function traditionally exclusively performed by the state."[124] Providing a forum for speech is not an exclusive governmental function, and "a private entity who opens its property for speech by others is not transformed by that fact alone into a state actor," the Court concluded.[125]

The majority and dissent agreed that New York state law extensively regulates cable operators, limiting their "editorial discretion and in effect requir[ing them] to operate almost like a common carrier."[126] Still, the majority said this did not make the cable company a state actor subject to the First Amendment.[127] Justice Sotomayor disagreed sharply and said the state essentially appointed the cable company as its "agent" to provide the public forum.[128] She and three others said the Court's ruling "risks sowing confusion among the lower courts about how and when government outsourcing will render any abuses that follow beyond the reach of the Constitution."[129]

Some said the Court's decision affirmed the foundational concept that "private firms [are] not bound by the First Amendment."[130] Others said it reinforced fears about the impact of newly appointed Supreme Court justices on civil liberties.[131] One legal expert said the Court had given Facebook "carte blanche to allow hate speech or [to] delete hate speech."[132]

REQUIRING SPEECH

The U.S. Supreme Court has said, "The right to speak and the right to refrain from speaking are complementary components of the broader concept of individual freedom of mind."[133] Accordingly, government may not force citizens to express ideas with which they disagree.

More than 75 years ago, the Supreme Court issued a foundational ruling when students who were Jehovah's Witnesses challenged the then-mandatory flag salute and Pledge of Allegiance in schools as a violation of their religious beliefs. The Supreme Court agreed.[134] Despite the important role of public schools in teaching students civic values and responsibilities,[135] schools may not indoctrinate students into particular ideologies, the Court said.[136] "No official, high or petty, can prescribe what shall be orthodox in politics, nationalism, religion or other matters of opinion or force citizens to confess by word or act their faith therein."[137]

Forty years later, the Court extended that freedom to license plates. A married couple, also Jehovah's Witnesses, challenged a New Hampshire law requiring all license plates to bear the state slogan, "Live Free or Die." In violation of state law, the couple covered up the slogan because they found it "morally, ethically, religiously and politically abhorrent." The Supreme Court struck down the law, saying it required citizens to promote the state's ideological message on their own property. Individuals have a constitutional right "to refrain from speaking" and "not to be coerced by the state into advertising a slogan" that violates their beliefs.[138]

In 2018, the Supreme Court said the First Amendment prevented the state of California from forcing state-licensed "crisis pregnancy centers" to notify clients that public family-planning services were available.[139] The Court rejected the notion that noncommercial professional speech was a discrete category with its own First Amendment rules and declined to consider the case under its compelled speech or government-speech precedents. Instead, it found that the law would fail both strict and intermediate scrutiny because its numerous exemptions failed to fit the state's asserted interest in informing low-income women about state-supported services. The challenged law mandated that licensed centers inform patients of some state-sponsored services, including contraception and abortion, and required unlicensed centers to disclose their lack of licensing.

That same year, the Supreme Court's narrow ruling in *Masterpiece Cakeshop v. Colorado Civil Rights Commission* found that Colorado violated the First Amendment rights of a baker when it found him guilty of violating the state's anti-discrimination law by refusing to bake a wedding cake for a same-sex couple.[140] The case pitted the government's desire to prevent discrimination against the First Amendment's mandate that government not require individuals to express ideas to which they object. The Court found that the state's punishment of the baker was unconstitutional because it did not treat the baker's sincere religious concerns—core elements of his freedoms of speech and association—with the neutrality and care they were due. Instead, the state's hostility to the baker's beliefs violated the "fixed star" of the Constitution that government may not take sides in matters of religion.[141]

POLITICAL CAMPAIGNING AND FINANCING ELECTIONS

More than a decade ago, Congress passed the Bipartisan Campaign Reform Act, banning "soft money" contributions to national political parties and imposing limits on the amount and source of funds candidates may accept and spend. The law limited individual spending and prohibited corporate (including nonprofit and union) funding of political messages during a certain period prior to an election. In *Citizens United v. Federal Election Commission*, the Supreme Court found the law's well-established restrictions on corporate and union election spending facially unconstitutional.[142] The Court reasoned that the BCRA's requirements that political donors be disclosed adequately addressed the government's concern that unrestricted corporate election spending might lead to political corruption. Direct limits on how corporations and unions could fund campaigns violated the First Amendment. Courts have applied *Citizens United* to strike down numerous restrictions on political spending.[143]

Then in *McCutcheon v. FEC*, the Court struck down another piece of the BCRA, removing the cap on total individual political contributions.[144] The Court said the aggregate limit reduced

REAL WORLD LAW
POST–CITIZENS UNITED: OUTSIDE DONORS SHAPE POLITICAL CAMPAIGNS

Almost two decades after the Supreme Court's landmark decision in *Citizens United v. Federal Election Commission*[xx] deregulated many areas of campaign financing, dozens of scholarly articles each year examine its impact on freedom of speech, elections, corporations, democracy and more.

One report found that the total amount of money in presidential elections increased more than 1,200 percent from $225 million in 1980 to nearly $3 billion in 2012.[xxi] Initial increases were fueled by individual donors, but since 2012, "the amount

of outside spending from ideological groups" has topped all other categories. At the same time, candidates and their campaigns are spending less, meaning that outside spending plays an increasing role in elections.

One empirical study found that "removing bans on . . . outside spending increase[d] the electoral success of Republican candidates and [led] to ideologically more conservative state legislatures" but neither increased "ideological polarization" nor decreased attention to "the public good."[xxii]

an individual's ability to participate in the political process without advancing the government's interest in preventing corruption. "Congress may target only a specific type of corruption—'quid pro quo' corruption," or bribery,[145] Chief Justice John Roberts wrote for the Court.

When the state of Colorado sought to apply state campaign finance disclosure requirements to a film about the impact of political advocacy groups on state politics, the film's producer, Citizens United, sued.[146] Citizens United argued that its film was not "electioneering communication" under the law and the law violated its First Amendment freedoms. On appeal, the Tenth Circuit Court of Appeals said it could find no legitimate basis to distinguish between the advocacy group's movies on political subjects and "legitimate press functions."[147] The First Amendment, it said, required film producers to be exempt from disclosure requirements.

The Supreme Court also has ruled that government may refuse to assist employee political contributions.[148] The Court employed rational review to uphold an Idaho state ban on the use of government payroll deductions for political contributions. The majority reasoned that the Constitution imposed no affirmative obligation on government to facilitate such political activities and the ban advanced the state's interest in avoiding the appearance of partisan political activity.

Sipa via AP Images

In 2019 hearings before Congress, Rep. Alexandria Ocasio-Cortez, D-N.Y., criticized the nation's "fundamentally broken" campaign finance laws under which, she said, it's "super legal . . . to be a pretty bad guy."

SPEAKING ANONYMOUSLY

The Supreme Court has said anonymous political speech has an "honorable tradition" that "is a shield from the tyranny of the majority."[149] Finding a state ban on anonymous campaign literature unconstitutional, the Court said the state's interest in preventing fraud and political influence was sufficiently important, but the law was not narrowly tailored. A long line of cases protects anonymous political speech.[150]

In 2010, the Supreme Court suggested that citizens engaged in the political process do not have an absolute right to keep their identities secret.[151] A citizen referendum sought to repeal a Washington state law granting new rights to same-sex domestic partners. The state open records law (see Chapter 7) required release of the names of people who endorsed the referendum, but referendum supporters argued that disclosure violated their First Amendment right to anonymous political speech and increased the threat of reprisals. The Supreme Court applied strict scrutiny and ruled that public disclosure of the petitioners' names was substantially related to the important government interest in preserving the integrity of balloting and elections. On remand, the lower court ruled that the First Amendment did not protect anonymity even when disclosure might facilitate harassment.[152]

The protection sometimes afforded anonymous political speech does not extend generally to a broad right to anonymity. In an illustrative case, the Ninth Circuit Court of Appeals recently denied a request from online review site Glassdoor, Inc. to **quash** a subpoena requiring the company to disclose the identity of people criticizing a government contractor whose business was

quash
To void or nullify a legal procedure or action; a motion often made in response to subpoenas for confidential information

---

REAL WORLD LAW
RIGHT TO SPEAK ANONYMOUSLY LIKELY FAILS TO PROTECT YOUR DATA

Government requests to social media for confidential subscriber information are becoming ubiquitous. Facebook reported a 21 percent increase in worldwide requests for user data—to a total of 78,890—in the first six months of 2017.[xxiii]

In a case involving a private chat app, a federal judge approved a subpoena request filed by victims of the August 2017 car attack at a Charlottesville white-rights protest to disclose the identities of those using Discord to organize the rally.[xxiv] Violence at the rally caused one death and more than three dozen injuries. The judge said the user identification could be disclosed to the court, though not the public, because the interest in prosecuting criminal conspiracy outweighed any claimed user right to anonymous speech.[xxvi] Citing privacy provisions under the Stored Communications Act, the judge denied a subpoena to access the content of users' Discord messages.

---

under investigation.[153] The government initially sought identifying information on 125 posts but narrowed the request to eight critical reviews. Federal law generally requires online service providers to disclose customer communications and records when the government shows reasonable grounds to believe they are relevant to an ongoing criminal investigation.[154] Here, the circuit court reasoned that citizens, like journalists, do not have a First Amendment right not to testify in a grand jury investigation (see Chapter 8).[155] In contrast, a federal district court in Texas struck down a subpoena seeking subscriber data on five Twitter accounts implicated in alleged cyberharassment.[156]

ASSEMBLING AND SPEAKING IN PUBLIC AND NONPUBLIC PLACES

People across the United States assemble daily to exchange ideas on public street corners and in town parks, in elementary school cafeterias and university lecture halls. Each of these gatherings occurs in what the U.S. Supreme Court calls a **public forum**. The concept of public forums recognizes the long and central role of public oratory in the United States. The idea is that a lot of government property is essentially held in trust for use by the public; it is the public's space.

public forum
Government property held for use by the public, usually for purposes of exercising rights of speech and assembly.

An early Supreme Court decision involved a challenge to a city ordinance prohibiting the distribution of pamphlets in city streets and parks. It explained the concept as follows:

> Wherever the title of streets and parks may rest, they have immemorially been held in trust for the use of the public and, time out of mind, have been used for purposes of assembly, communicating thoughts between citizens and discussing public questions. Such use of the streets and public places has, from ancient times, been a part of the privileges, immunities, rights and liberties of citizens.[157]

The people have a First Amendment right to use public forum property to express themselves free from fear of government censorship or punishment.[158] The Court has ruled that the Constitution allows Nazis, Vietnam War protesters, civil rights activists and the homeless to march and assemble in public places.[159]

In 2011 in *Snyder v. Phelps*, the Supreme Court ruled that even "outrageous" speech on a public sidewalk about a public issue cannot be punished.[160] The father of a Marine killed in the Iraq War had sought damages from Westboro Baptist Church members for harm caused by their picketing at his son's funeral with signs reading "Thank God for dead soldiers" and "Fag troops." But the Court held that the First Amendment protects public picketing even when the messages "fall short of refined social or political commentary." The people's right to speak and assemble in public forums is not absolute; it is balanced against other considerations and must be compatible with the normal activity in that place.

The Supreme Court has established a hierarchy of three types of public forums according to the nature of the place, its primary activities and the history of public access.[161] Lands historically intended for public use—such as parks, streets and sidewalks adjacent to many public buildings—are **traditional public forums**.[162] The public has a general and presumed right to use these places for expression. Thus, in 2013, the Sixth Circuit Court of Appeals struck down Michigan's 94-year-old ban on "begging in a public place." The court said begging is a protected form of speech and the state could not ban from a traditional public forum "an entire category of activity that the First Amendment protects."

Government may set up rules, hours and policies to facilitate use of traditional public forums. Rules that close public parks after dark or require permits for gatherings are constitutional if they are fairly applied and content neutral, meaning they are tailored to their purpose and do not discriminate because of the content of the group's ideas or politics. Appeals courts have found restrictions on rallies on a town lawn[163] and disorderly gatherings in public places[164] unconstitutional because they prohibited more protected speech than necessary to serve the town objectives. Government must demonstrate a compelling interest to ban all expressive activities or assembly in a traditional public forum.

The Supreme Court has held that government may ban public picketing and protests from traditional public forums to protect core privacy, safety or health interests. The Court upheld a ban on targeted picketing outside a doctor's residence and no-protest buffer zones outside abortion clinics.[165]

The primary purpose of public schools and university classrooms, high school newspapers and fairgrounds is not to serve public assembly or speech. Yet they may provide ideal settings for public expression. When government chooses to allow public use of these spaces, it creates **designated public forums**,[166] and government may limit their public use.

The government may restrict the times and manners of public use of a designated public forum to ensure that public assemblies do not conflict with the property's primary function. Government may impose well-tailored, reasonable, content-neutral licensing and usage regulations. In general, the Supreme Court reviews regulations of designated, or limited, public forums under intermediate scrutiny, balancing the citizen right of free expression against the primary function of the facility. When the government facility is operating as a public forum, government officials do not have unfettered discretion over its use and may not make content-based discriminations among users.[167] Public access cannot be denied entirely without a compelling reason.

Two decades after the Fourth Circuit Court of Appeals described interactive, online services as "a forum for a true diversity of political discourse, unique opportunities for cultural development and myriad avenues for intellectual activity,"[168] the U.S. Supreme Court in 2017 adopted

traditional public forum
Lands designed for public use and historically used for public gathering, discussion and association (e.g., public streets, sidewalks and parks). Free speech is protected in these areas.

designated public forum
Government spaces or buildings that are available for public use (within limits).

REAL WORLD LAW
CONTROLLING SPACE TO LIMIT PROTEST?

In 2018, the National Park Service proposed new rules that would limit significantly gatherings around the White House and the National Mall, limit the number of people who could gather without a permit and prohibit demonstrations around most memorials "to preserve an atmosphere of contemplation."[xxvi] One change would reduce the area for public demonstrations adjacent to the White House by 80 percent and "would all but prohibit civic gatherings" there.[xxvii] Another would require

demonstrators to pay for permits to "cover some of the costs" of administration, which the park service previously funded.

The park service said the rules had not been updated in more than a decade and needed revision to reduce complexity and address increased public demonstrations in Washington, D.C. The number of applications for protest permits decreased 31 percent between 2010 and 2017, according to an American Civil Liberties Union study.

language that evoked public forum analysis.[169] "While in the past there may have been difficulty in identifying the most important places (in a spatial sense) for the exchange of views, today the answer is clear. It is cyberspace . . . and social media in particular," the Court said.[170] Early in 2019, the Fourth Circuit Court of Appeals picked up the language to rule that a Virginia official violated the First Amendment by banning a constituent from the official's Facebook page.[171] Describing online social media as essential platforms for speech and press freedoms, the appeals court held that the Constitution prevented government from blocking access to an official's Facebook page.

In 2018, a federal district court in New York had reached the same result in response to President Donald Trump blocking a user's access to his Twitter account because he disfavored the user's political views.[172] The court said the president's action, through an intermediary, constituted viewpoint-based government regulation of political speech in violation of the First Amendment.[173] But a federal district court in Kentucky ruled that public forum analysis did not apply to the governor's Facebook and Twitter accounts.[174]

nonpublic forum
Government-held property that is not available for public speech and assembly purposes.

Some government property simply is not available for public use. **Nonpublic forums** exist where public access, assembly and speech would conflict with the proper functioning of the government service and where there is no history of public access. Courts generally defer to the government to determine when government property is off limits. In nonpublic forums, government behaves more like a private property owner and controls the space to achieve government objectives. Military bases, prisons, post office walkways, utility poles, airport terminals and private mailboxes are all nonpublic forums.[165] Government may exclude the entire public or certain speakers or messages from nonpublic forums on the basis of a reasonable or rational, viewpoint-neutral interest.[176]

Private Property as a Public Forum

Public forums, sometimes, though rarely, exist on private property. When private property replaces or functions as a traditional public space, it may be treated as a public forum. The law in this area is unclear. However, when the open area of an enclosed shopping mall or a large private parking lot is used widely for public assembly and expression, the Supreme Court has

POINTS OF LAW

WHERE CAN I SPEAK?

The Supreme Court has designated three types of public property as held in trust for the public to provide "the liberty to discuss *publicly* and truthfully all matters of public concern without prior restraint or fear of subsequent punishment."[xxviii] The Court's public forum doctrine establishes the following:[xxix]

- *Traditional public forums* include areas historically used and created for public use or expressive activity.

- *Limited/designated public forums* exist when government permits public use under specific conditions of spaces with other primary purposes, such as school buildings.

- *Nonpublic forums* arise when government property has a primary purpose that is incompatible with public use (e.g., inside the Pentagon or a prison).

said the private property owner sometimes may be required to allow public gatherings and free expression.[177]

Funding as Forum

Sometimes government funds that subsidize expression create something like a public forum. If government funding supports broad speech and associational activities, the government generally may not discriminate on the basis of the ideas expressed.[178] Government spending may not, for example, disfavor large newspapers, general interest magazines or commercial publications.[179] Government allocation of benefits and costs must be content neutral and evenhanded. When a program provided free legal services to welfare recipients, for example, the Supreme Court held that it could not refuse services to people challenging existing welfare laws.[180]

Many government funding programs have the express purpose of discriminating among applicants according to the ideas they express. The National Endowment for the Arts, for example, funds artists based on the value and quality of submitted artistic proposals. NEA grants are designed to advance the NEA's objectives, not to create a public forum for art. Accordingly, the NEA may choose not to fund art it disfavors or finds indecent or offensive.[181] The same is true of book purchases for public school libraries. School libraries are not public forums for all printed materials; they provide curriculum- and age-appropriate materials to school students. Therefore, library choices based on the school-age appropriateness of books do not violate the Constitution.[182]

ASSOCIATING FREELY

Sometimes viewed as a "derivative" right "associated" with free speech,[183] the right to freedom of association has developed somewhat separately from freedom of speech precedents. Several U.S. Supreme Court rulings established that government generally cannot force private organizations to include individuals or to support messages with which they disagree.[184] In one famous case, organizers of the large, annual St. Patrick's Day parade in Boston refused to allow an LGBTQ alliance to participate. The alliance sued, arguing that its exclusion from the parade violated its freedom of speech. The trial court agreed. Because the parade had no expressive purpose, the court said, forced inclusion of alliance members in the event would cause no harm to the parade organizer's First Amendment rights.

A unanimous Supreme Court reversed. The Court said it was unnecessary to the alliance's message that it participate in the organizer's event. The alliance could reach the desired audience in a number of ways that would not infringe on the organizer's freedom of association and speech. The Court said, "Whatever the reason [for excluding the group], it boils down to the choice of a speaker not to propound a particular point of view, and that choice is presumed to lie beyond the government's power of control."[185] An LGBTQ alliance participated in Boston's St. Patrick's Day parade for the first time in 2015.[186]

EMERGING LAW

A pair of recent Supreme Court cases presenting challenges to the constitutionality of state electoral redistricting put freedom of association center stage. In 2018, the Supreme Court decided both *Abbott v. Perez* and *Gill v. Whitford*, which respectively challenged Texas and Wisconsin electoral redistricting as a violation of freedom of voter association and the 14th Amendment right to equal protection.[187] In both cases, challengers said the new districting, which created an "efficiency gap" in favor of Republican voters, was unconstitutional because it diluted the power of an individual Democratic voter.[188]

Reviewing statewide evidence against the equal protection challenge, the Supreme Court in *Abbott* upheld the Texas redistricting because the plaintiffs had failed to show the individual voter harm or clear discriminatory legislative intent needed to support a voter dilution challenge. In *Gill*, the Court remanded the challenge to Wisconsin's redistricting for more detailed fact finding.[189] Both majority **dicta** and a four-justice dissent encouraged a fuller presentation of the First Amendment issues.

dicta
Statements in a court opinion that are not central or essential to its reasoning or holding.

Writing for the dissent, Justice Elena Kagan said the existing statewide evidence might be sufficient for a freedom of association challenge because a statewide "gerrymander weakens [the Democratic party's] capacity to perform all its functions . . . [and] has burdened the ability of like-minded people across the State to affiliate in a political party and carry out that organization's activities and objects."[190] The Court seems poised to examine voters' right to freedom of association in this case or perhaps one of the challenges to state redistricting from Florida, North Carolina and Utah moving through the courts.[191]

In 2019, the U.S. Court of Appeals for the Third Circuit ruled that a Delaware constitutional requirement that judicial appointments maintain a political balance between the two major parties violated a judicial candidate's right to freedom of association.[192] Because open judicial seats were identified as either Democrat or Republican, a political independent was effectively blocked from pursuing a judicial appointment.[193] The court's ruling in favor of the would-be judge split from decades-old rulings in the Sixth and Seventh Circuits that found the First Amendment did not prevent governors from making politically based judicial appointments.[194]

CASES FOR STUDY

For study resources and a case archive, go to **edge.sagepub.com/medialaw7e**.

The first of this chapter's two case excerpts examines the First Amendment protection from prior restraints on the press. In *New York Times Co. v. United States*, the U.S. Supreme Court provided expedited review of a federal injunction against war reporting by The Times and The Washington Post based on leaked classified documents. The Court's careful delineation of the government's limited ability to exercise prior restraint on speech underscored the importance of the separation of powers and reaffirmed that the government has very limited authority over the press. The second excerpt, *Reed v. Town of Gilbert*, presents the Supreme Court's 2015 decision articulating what some believe is a new understanding of which laws are reviewed under strict scrutiny because they are defined as content based. Although the justices reach a unanimous decision, they do not all endorse the majority's definition of content-based laws or its automatic application of strict scrutiny to such laws.

Thinking About It

The two case excerpts explore two fundamental approaches to understanding the First Amendment. One Supreme Court decision establishes the extent and limits of the First Amendment's protection from government prior restraint on the press. The other redefines the basic distinction between laws that regulate on the basis of content and those that do not. As you read these case excerpts, keep the following questions in mind:

- What justification does the Court offer in *New York Times Co. v. United States* for the First Amendment's nearly absolute ban on prior restraints?

- In *Reed v. Town of Gilbert*, why do the justices disagree on the definition of content neutrality?

- What do the two decisions indicate about the power of the First Amendment to limit government regulations of "the press" and of the people's right to speak through signs?

- Does the Court use the same level of scrutiny in both cases? How do you know?

New York Times Co. v. United States
SUPREME COURT OF THE UNITED STATES
403 U.S. 713 (1971)

PER CURIAM OPINION:

We granted certiorari in these cases in which the United States seeks to enjoin the New York Times and the Washington Post from publishing the contents of a classified study entitled "History of U.S. Decision-Making Process on Viet Nam Policy."

"Any system of prior restraints of expression comes to this Court bearing a heavy presumption against its constitutional validity." The Government "thus carries a heavy burden of showing justification for the imposition of such a restraint." The [lower courts] held that the Government had not met that burden. We agree.

The judgment of the Court of Appeals for the District of Columbia Circuit is therefore affirmed. The order of the Court of Appeals or the Second Circuit is reversed, and the case is remanded with directions to enter a judgment affirming the judgment of the District Court for the Southern District of New York. The stays entered June 25, 1971, by the Court are vacated. The judgments shall issue forthwith.

So ordered.

**JUSTICE HUGO BLACK,
with whom JUSTICE WILLIAM
DOUGLAS joined, concurring:**

I adhere to the view that the Government's case against the Washington Post should have been dismissed, and that the injunction against the New York Times should have been vacated without oral argument when the cases were first presented to this Court. I believe that every moment's continuance of the injunctions against these newspapers amounts to a flagrant, indefensible, and continuing violation of the First Amendment. . . .

In the First Amendment, the Founding Fathers gave the free press the protection it must have to fulfill its essential role in our democracy. The press was to serve the governed, not the governors. The Government's power to censor the press was abolished so that the press would remain forever free to censure the Government. The press was protected so that it could bare the secrets of government and inform the people. Only a free and unrestrained press can effectively expose deception in government. And paramount among the responsibilities of a free press is the duty to prevent any part of the government from deceiving the people and sending them off to distant lands to die of foreign fevers and foreign shot and shell. In my view, far from deserving condemnation for their courageous reporting, the New York Times, the Washington Post, and other newspapers should be commended for serving the purpose that the Founding Fathers saw so clearly. In revealing the workings of government that led to the Vietnam War, the newspapers nobly did precisely that which the Founders hoped and trusted they would do. . . .

The word "security" is a broad, vague generality whose contours should not be invoked to abrogate the fundamental law embodied in the First Amendment. The guarding of military and diplomatic secrets at the expense of informed representative government provides no real security for our Republic. The Framers of the First Amendment, fully aware of both the need to defend a new nation and the abuses of the English and Colonial governments, sought to give this new society strength and security by providing that freedom of speech, press, religion, and assembly should not be abridged. . . .

**JUSTICE WILLIAM DOUGLAS,
with whom JUSTICE HUGO
BLACK joined, concurring:**

. . . It should be noted at the outset that the First Amendment provides that "Congress shall make no law . . . abridging the freedom of speech, or of the press." That leaves, in my view, no room for governmental restraint on the press. . . .

The dominant purpose of the First Amendment was to prohibit the widespread practice of governmental suppression of embarrassing information. It is common knowledge that the First Amendment was adopted against the widespread use of the common law of seditious libel to punish the dissemination of material that is embarrassing to the powers-that-be. The present cases will, I think, go down in history as the most dramatic illustration of that principle. . . .

Secrecy in government is fundamentally antidemocratic, perpetuating bureaucratic errors. Open debate and discussion of public issues are vital to our national health. On public questions there should be "uninhibited, robust, and wide-open" debate. . . .

**JUSTICE WILLIAM
BRENNAN, concurring:**

. . . The error that has pervaded these cases from the outset was the granting of any injunctive relief whatsoever, interim or otherwise. The entire thrust of the Government's claim throughout these cases has been that publication of the material sought to be enjoined "could," or "might," or "may" prejudice the national interest in various ways. But the First Amendment tolerates absolutely no prior judicial restraints of the press predicated upon surmise or conjecture that untoward consequences may result. Our cases, it is true, have indicated that there is a single, extremely narrow class of cases in which the First Amendment's ban on prior judicial restraint may be overridden. Our cases have thus far indicated that such cases may arise only when the Nation "is at war," during which times "[n]o one would question but that a government might prevent actual obstruction to its recruiting service or the publication of the dates of transports or the number and location of troops." Even if the present world situation were assumed to be tantamount to a time of war, or if the power of presently available armaments would justify even in peacetime the suppression of information that would set in motion a nuclear holocaust, in neither of these actions has the Government presented or even alleged that publication of items from or based upon the material at issue would cause the happening of an event of that nature. "[T]he chief purpose of [the First Amendment's] guaranty [is] to prevent previous restraints upon publication." Thus, only governmental allegation and proof that publication must inevitably, directly, and immediately cause the occurrence of an event kindred to imperiling the safety of a transport already at sea can support even the issuance of an interim restraining order. . . . Unless and until the Government has clearly made out its case, the First Amendment commands that no injunction may issue. . . .

JUSTICE POTTER STEWART, with whom JUSTICE BYRON WHITE joined, concurring:

. . . If the Constitution gives the Executive a large degree of unshared power in the conduct of foreign affairs and the maintenance of our national defense, then, under the Constitution, the Executive must have the largely unshared duty to determine and preserve the degree of internal security necessary to exercise that power successfully. It is an awesome responsibility, requiring judgment and wisdom of a high order. I should suppose that moral, political, and practical considerations would dictate that a very first principle of that wisdom would be an insistence upon avoiding secrecy for its own sake. For when everything is classified, then nothing is classified, and the system becomes one to be disregarded by the cynical or the careless, and to be manipulated by those intent on self-protection or self-promotion. I should suppose, in short, that the hallmark of a truly effective internal security system would be the maximum possible disclosure, recognizing that secrecy can best be preserved only when credibility is truly maintained. . . .

JUSTICE BYRON WHITE, with whom JUSTICE POTTER STEWART joined, concurring:

I concur in today's judgments, but only because of the concededly extraordinary protection against prior restraints enjoyed by the press under our constitutional system. I do not say that in no circumstances would the First Amendment permit an injunction against publishing information about government plans or operations. . . . But I nevertheless agree that the United States has not satisfied the very heavy burden that it must meet to warrant an injunction against publication in these cases, at least in the absence of express and appropriately limited congressional authorization for prior restraints in circumstances such as these. . . .

CHIEF JUSTICE WARREN BURGER, dissenting:

. . . As I see it, we have been forced to deal with litigation concerning rights of great magnitude without an adequate record, and surely without time for adequate treatment either in the prior proceedings or in this Court. . . .

I agree generally with Mr. Justice Harlan and Mr. Justice Blackmun, but I am not prepared to reach the merits.

JUSTICE JOHN HARLAN, with whom CHIEF JUSTICE WARREN BURGER and JUSTICE HARRY BLACKMUN join, dissenting:

. . . The power to evaluate the "pernicious influence" of premature disclosure is not, however, lodged in the Executive alone. I agree that, in performance of its duty to protect the values of the First Amendment against political pressures, the judiciary must review the initial Executive determination to the point of satisfying itself that the subject matter of the dispute does lie within the proper compass of the President's foreign relations power. . . . Moreover, the judiciary may properly insist that the determination that disclosure of the subject matter would irreparably impair the national security be made by the head of the Executive Department concerned. . . .

But, in my judgment, the judiciary may not properly go beyond these two inquiries and re-determine for itself the probable impact of disclosure on the national security. . . .

JUSTICE HARRY BLACKMUN, dissenting:

. . . The First Amendment, after all, is only one part of an entire Constitution. . . . Each provision of the

Constitution is important, and I cannot subscribe to a doctrine of unlimited absolutism for the First Amendment at the cost of downgrading other provisions. First Amendment absolutism has never commanded a majority of this Court. What is needed here is a weighing, upon properly developed standards, of the broad right of the press to print and of the very narrow right of the Government to prevent. Such standards are not yet developed.

Reed v. Town of Gilbert
SUPREME COURT OF THE UNITED STATES
135 S. Ct. 2218 (2015)

JUSTICE CLARENCE THOMAS
delivered the Court's opinion:

The town of Gilbert, Arizona (or Town), has adopted a comprehensive code governing the manner in which people may display outdoor signs (Sign Code or Code). The Sign Code identifies various categories of signs based on the type of information they convey, then subjects each category to different restrictions. One of the categories is "Temporary Directional Signs Relating to a Qualifying Event," loosely defined as signs directing the public to a meeting of a nonprofit group. The Code imposes more stringent restrictions on these signs than it does on signs conveying other messages. We hold that these provisions are content-based regulations of speech that cannot survive strict scrutiny.

The Sign Code prohibits the display of outdoor signs anywhere within the Town without a permit, but it then exempts 23 categories of signs from that requirement. These exemptions include everything from bazaar signs to flying banners. Three categories of exempt signs are particularly relevant here.

The first is "Ideological Sign[s]." This category includes any "sign communicating a message or ideas for noncommercial purposes that is not a Construction Sign, Directional Sign, Temporary Directional Sign Relating to a Qualifying Event, Political Sign, Garage Sale Sign, or a sign owned or required by a governmental agency." Of the three categories discussed here, the Code treats ideological signs most favorably, allowing them to be up to 20 square feet in area and to be placed in all "zoning districts" without time limits.

The second category is "Political Sign[s]." This includes any "temporary sign designed to influence the outcome of an election called by a public body." The Code treats these signs less favorably than ideological signs. The Code allows the placement of political signs up to 16 square feet on residential property and up to 32 square feet on nonresidential property, undeveloped municipal property, and "rights-of-way." These signs may be displayed up to 60 days before a primary election and up to 15 days following a general election.

The third category is "Temporary Directional Signs Relating to a Qualifying Event." This includes any "Temporary Sign intended to direct pedestrians, motorists, and other passersby to a 'qualifying event.'" A "qualifying event" is defined as any "assembly, gathering, activity, or meeting sponsored, arranged, or promoted by a religious, charitable, community service, educational, or other similar non-profit organization." The Code treats temporary directional signs even less favorably than political signs. Temporary directional signs may be no larger than six square feet. They may be placed on private property or on a public right-of-way, but no more than four signs may be placed on a single property at any time. And, they may be displayed no more than 12 hours before the "qualifying event" and no more than 1 hour afterward.

Petitioners Good News Community Church (Church) and its pastor, Clyde Reed, wish to advertise the time and location of their Sunday church services. The Church is a small, cash-strapped entity that owns no building, so it holds its services at elementary schools or other locations in or near the Town. In order to inform the public about its services, which are held in a variety of different locations, the Church began placing 15 to 20 temporary signs around the Town, frequently in the public right-of-way abutting the street. The signs typically displayed the Church's name, along with the time and location of the upcoming service. Church members would post the signs early in the day on Saturday and then remove them around midday on Sunday. The display of these signs requires little money and manpower, and thus has proved to be an economical and effective way for the Church to let the community know where its services are being held each week.

This practice caught the attention of the Town's Sign Code compliance manager, who twice cited the Church for violating the Code. The first citation noted that the Church exceeded the time limits for displaying its temporary directional signs. The second citation referred to the same problem, along with the Church's failure to include the date of the event on the signs. Town officials even confiscated one of the Church's signs, which Reed had to retrieve from the municipal offices.

Reed contacted the Sign Code Compliance Department in an attempt to reach an accommodation. His efforts proved unsuccessful. The Town's Code compliance manager informed the Church that there would be "no leniency under the Code" and promised to punish any future violations.

Shortly thereafter, petitioners filed a complaint . . . arguing that the Sign Code abridged their freedom of speech in violation of the First and Fourteenth Amendments. The District Court denied the petitioners' motion for a preliminary injunction. The Court of Appeals for the Ninth Circuit affirmed, holding that the Sign Code's provision regulating temporary directional signs did not regulate speech on the basis of content. . . . It then remanded for the District Court to determine in the first instance whether the Sign Code's distinctions among temporary directional signs, political signs, and ideological signs nevertheless constituted a content-based regulation of speech.

On remand, the District Court granted summary judgment in favor of the Town. The Court of Appeals again affirmed, holding that the Code's sign categories were content neutral. The court concluded that "the distinctions between Temporary Directional Signs, Ideological Signs, and Political Signs . . . are based on objective factors relevant to Gilbert's creation of the specific exemption from the permit requirement and do not otherwise consider the substance of the sign." . . . [T]he Court of Appeals concluded that the Sign Code is content neutral. As the court explained, "Gilbert did not adopt its regulation of speech because it disagreed with the message conveyed" and its "interests in regulat[ing] temporary signs are unrelated to the content of the sign." Accordingly, the court believed that the

Code was "content-neutral as that term [has been] defined by the Supreme Court." In light of that determination, it applied a lower level of scrutiny to the Sign Code and concluded that the law did not violate the First Amendment.

We granted certiorari, and now reverse.

The First Amendment, applicable to the States through the Fourteenth Amendment, prohibits the enactment of laws "abridging the freedom of speech." Under that Clause, a government, including a municipal government vested with state authority, "has no power to restrict expression because of its message, its ideas, its subject matter, or its content." Content-based laws—those that target speech based on its communicative content—are presumptively unconstitutional and may be justified only if the government proves that they are narrowly tailored to serve compelling state interests.

Government regulation of speech is content based if a law applies to particular speech because of the topic discussed or the idea or message expressed. This commonsense meaning of the phrase "content based" requires a court to consider whether a regulation of speech "on its face" draws distinctions based on the message a speaker conveys. Some facial distinctions based on a message are obvious, defining regulated speech by particular subject matter, and others are more subtle, defining regulated speech by its function or purpose. Both are distinctions drawn based on the message a speaker conveys, and, therefore, are subject to strict scrutiny.

Our precedents have also recognized a separate and additional category of laws that, though facially content neutral, will be considered content-based regulations of speech: laws that cannot be "justified without reference to the content of the regulated speech," or that were adopted by the government "because of disagreement with the message [the speech] conveys." Those laws, like those that are content based on their face, must also satisfy strict scrutiny.

The Town's Sign Code is content based on its face. It defines "Temporary Directional Signs" on the basis of whether a sign conveys the message of directing the public to church or some other "qualifying event." It defines "Political Signs" on the basis of whether a sign's message is "designed to influence the outcome of an election." And it defines "Ideological Signs" on the basis of whether a sign "communicat[es] a message or ideas" that do not fit within the Code's other categories. It then subjects each of these categories to different restrictions.

The restrictions in the Sign Code that apply to any given sign thus depend entirely on the communicative content of the sign. . . . [T]he Church's signs inviting people to attend its worship services are treated differently from signs conveying other types of ideas. On its face, the Sign Code is a content-based regulation of speech. We thus have no need to consider the government's justifications or purposes for enacting the Code to determine whether it is subject to strict scrutiny.

In reaching the contrary conclusion, the Court of Appeals offered several theories to explain why the Town's Sign Code should be deemed content neutral. None is persuasive.

The Court of Appeals first determined that the Sign Code was content neutral because the Town "did not adopt its regulation of speech [based on] disagree[ment] with the message conveyed," and its justifications for regulating temporary directional signs were "unrelated to the content of the sign." In its brief to this Court, the United States similarly contends that a sign regulation is content neutral—even if it expressly draws distinctions based on the sign's communicative content—if those distinctions can be "'justified without reference to the content of the regulated speech.'"

But this analysis skips the crucial first step in the content-neutrality analysis: determining whether the law is content neutral on its face. A law that is content based on its face is subject to strict scrutiny regardless of the government's benign motive, content-neutral justification, or lack of "animus toward the ideas contained" in the regulated speech. We have thus made clear that "[i]llicit legislative intent is not the sine qua non of a violation of the First Amendment," and a party opposing the government "need adduce no evidence of an improper censorial motive." Although "a content-based purpose may be sufficient in certain circumstances to show that a regulation is content based, it is not necessary." In other words, an innocuous justification cannot transform a facially content-based law into one that is content neutral.

That is why we have repeatedly considered whether a law is content neutral on its face before turning to the law's justification or purpose. Because strict scrutiny applies either when a law is content based on its face or when the purpose and justification for the law

are content based, a court must evaluate each question before it concludes that the law is content neutral and thus subject to a lower level of scrutiny.

The Court of Appeals and the United States misunderstand our decision in Ward [v. Rock Against Racism]. [It] had nothing to say about facially content-based restrictions because it involved a facially content-neutral ban on the use, in a city-owned music venue, of sound amplification systems not provided by the city. In that context, we looked to governmental motive, including whether the government had regulated speech "because of disagreement" with its message, and whether the regulation was "'justified without reference to the content of the speech.'" But Ward's framework "applies only if a statute is content neutral." Its rules thus operate "to protect speech," not "to restrict it."

The First Amendment requires no less. Innocent motives do not eliminate the danger of censorship presented by a facially content-based statute. . . . That is why the First Amendment expressly targets the operation of the laws—i.e., the "abridg[ement] of speech"—rather than merely the motives of those who enacted them. "The vice of content-based legislation . . . is not that it is always used for invidious, thought-control purposes, but that it lends itself to use for those purposes."

For instance, . . . one could easily imagine a Sign Code compliance manager who disliked the Church's substantive teachings deploying the Sign Code to make it more difficult for the Church to inform the public of the location of its services. Accordingly, we have repeatedly "rejected the argument that 'discriminatory . . . treatment is suspect under the First Amendment only when the legislature intends to suppress certain ideas.'"

The Court of Appeals next reasoned that the Sign Code was content neutral because it "does not mention any idea or viewpoint, let alone single one out for differential treatment." It reasoned that, for the purpose of the Code provisions, "[i]t makes no difference which candidate is supported, who sponsors the event, or what ideological perspective is asserted."

The Town seizes on this reasoning, insisting that "content based" is a term of art that "should be applied flexibly" with the goal of protecting "viewpoints and ideas from government censorship or favoritism." In the Town's view, a sign regulation that "does not censor or favor particular viewpoints or ideas" cannot be content based. The Sign Code allegedly passes this test because its treatment of temporary directional signs does not raise any concerns that the government is "endorsing or suppressing 'ideas or viewpoints,'" and the provisions for political signs and ideological signs "are neutral as to particular ideas or viewpoints" within those categories.

This analysis conflates two distinct but related limitations that the First Amendment places on government regulation of speech. Government discrimination among viewpoints—or the regulation of speech based on "the specific motivating ideology or the opinion or perspective of the speaker"—is a "more blatant" and "egregious form of content discrimination." But it is well established that "[t]he First Amendment's hostility to content-based regulation extends not only to restrictions on particular viewpoints, but also to prohibition of public discussion of an entire topic."

Thus, a speech regulation targeted at specific subject matter is content based even if it does not discriminate among viewpoints within that subject matter. For example, a law banning the use of sound trucks for political speech—and only political speech—would be a content-based regulation, even if it imposed no limits on the political viewpoints that could be expressed. The Town's Sign Code likewise singles out specific subject matter for differential treatment, even if it does not target viewpoints within that subject matter. Ideological messages are given more favorable treatment than messages concerning a political candidate, which are themselves given more favorable treatment than messages announcing an assembly of like-minded individuals. That is a paradigmatic example of content-based discrimination.

Finally, the Court of Appeals characterized the Sign Code's distinctions as turning on "the content-neutral elements of who is speaking through the sign and whether and when an event is occurring." That analysis is mistaken on both factual and legal grounds.

To start, the Sign Code's distinctions are not speaker based. The restrictions for political, ideological, and temporary event signs apply equally no matter who sponsors them. If a local business, for example, sought to put up signs advertising the Church's meetings, those signs would be subject to the same limitations as such signs placed by the Church. And if Reed had decided to display signs

in support of a particular candidate, he could have made those signs far larger—and kept them up for far longer—than signs inviting people to attend his church services. If the Code's distinctions were truly speaker based, both types of signs would receive the same treatment.

In any case, the fact that a distinction is speaker based does not, as the Court of Appeals seemed to believe, automatically render the distinction content neutral. Because "[s]peech restrictions based on the identity of the speaker are all too often simply a means to control content," we have insisted that "laws favoring some speakers over others demand strict scrutiny when the legislature's speaker preference reflects a content preference." Thus, a law limiting the content of newspapers, but only newspapers, could not evade strict scrutiny simply because it could be characterized as speaker based. Likewise, a content-based law that restricted the political speech of all corporations would not become content neutral just because it singled out corporations as a class of speakers. . . .

Nor do the Sign Code's distinctions hinge on "whether and when an event is occurring." The Code does not permit citizens to post signs on any topic whatsoever within a set period leading up to an election, for example. . . .

And, just as with speaker-based laws, the fact that a distinction is event based does not render it content neutral. . . . A regulation that targets a sign because it conveys an idea about a specific event is no less content based than a regulation that targets a sign because it conveys some other idea. Here, the Code singles out signs bearing a particular message: the time and location of a specific event. This type of ordinance may seem like a perfectly rational way to regulate signs, but a clear and firm rule governing content neutrality is an essential means of protecting the freedom of speech, even if laws that might seem "entirely reasonable" will sometimes be "struck down because of their content-based nature."

Because the Town's Sign Code imposes content-based restrictions on speech, those provisions can stand only if they survive strict scrutiny, "which requires the Government to prove that the restriction furthers a compelling interest and is narrowly tailored to achieve that interest." Thus, it is the Town's burden to demonstrate that the Code's differentiation between temporary directional signs and other types of signs, such as political signs and ideological signs, furthers a compelling governmental interest and is narrowly tailored to that end. The Town cannot do so. It has offered only two governmental interests in support of the distinctions the Sign Code draws: preserving the Town's aesthetic appeal and traffic safety. Assuming for the sake of argument that those are compelling governmental interests, the Code's distinctions fail as hopelessly underinclusive.

Starting with the preservation of aesthetics, temporary directional signs are "no greater an eyesore," than ideological or political ones. Yet the Code allows unlimited proliferation of larger ideological signs while strictly limiting the number, size, and duration of smaller directional ones. The Town cannot claim that placing strict limits on temporary directional signs is necessary to beautify the Town while at the same time allowing unlimited numbers of other types of signs that create the same problem.

The Town similarly has not shown that limiting temporary directional signs is necessary to eliminate threats to traffic safety, but that limiting other types of signs is not. The Town has offered no reason to believe that directional signs pose a greater threat to safety than do ideological or political signs. If anything, a sharply worded ideological sign seems more likely to distract a driver than a sign directing the public to a nearby church meeting.

In light of this underinclusiveness, the Town has not met its burden to prove that its Sign Code is narrowly tailored to further a compelling government interest. . . .

Our decision today will not prevent governments from enacting effective sign laws. The Town asserts that an "'absolutist'" content-neutrality rule would render "virtually all distinctions in sign laws . . . subject to strict scrutiny," but that is not the case. Not "all distinctions" are subject to strict scrutiny, only content-based ones are. Laws that are content neutral are instead subject to lesser scrutiny.

The Town has ample content-neutral options available to resolve problems with safety and aesthetics. For example, its current Code regulates many aspects of signs that have nothing to do with a sign's message: size, building materials, lighting, moving parts, and portability. And on public property, the Town may go a long way toward entirely forbidding the posting of signs, so long as it does so in an even-handed, content-neutral manner. Indeed, some lower courts have long held that similar content-based

sign laws receive strict scrutiny, but there is no evidence that towns in those jurisdictions have suffered catastrophic effects.

We acknowledge that a city might reasonably view the general regulation of signs as necessary because signs "take up space and may obstruct views, distract motorists, displace alternative uses for land, and pose other problems that legitimately call for regulation." At the same time, the presence of certain signs may be essential, both for vehicles and pedestrians, to guide traffic or to identify hazards and ensure safety. A sign ordinance narrowly tailored to the challenges of protecting the safety of pedestrians, drivers, and passengers—such as warning signs marking hazards on private property, signs directing traffic, or street numbers associated with private houses—well might survive strict scrutiny. The signs at issue in this case, including political and ideological signs and signs for events, are far removed from those purposes. As discussed above, they are facially content based and are neither justified by traditional safety concerns nor narrowly tailored.

We reverse the judgment of the Court of Appeals and remand the case for proceedings consistent with this opinion.

It is so ordered.

JUSTICE SAMUEL ALITO, with whom JUSTICE ANTHONY KENNEDY and JUSTICE SONIA SOTOMAYOR joined, concurring.

I join the opinion of the Court but add a few words of further explanation.

As the Court holds, what we have termed "content-based" laws must satisfy strict scrutiny. Content-based laws merit this protection because they present, albeit sometimes in a subtler form, the same dangers as laws that regulate speech based on viewpoint. Limiting speech based on its "topic" or "subject" favors those who do not want to disturb the status quo. Such regulations may interfere with democratic self-government and the search for truth.

As the Court shows, the regulations at issue in this case are replete with content-based distinctions, and as a result they must satisfy strict scrutiny. This does not mean, however, that municipalities are powerless to enact and enforce reasonable sign regulations. . . .*

In addition to regulating signs put up by private actors, government entities may also erect their own signs consistent with the principles that allow governmental speech. They may put up all manner of signs to promote safety, as well as directional signs and signs pointing out historic sites and scenic spots.

Properly understood, today's decision will not prevent cities from regulating signs in a way that fully protects public safety and serves legitimate esthetic objectives.

---

*Of course, content-neutral restrictions on speech are not necessarily consistent with the First Amendment. Time, place, and manner restrictions "must be narrowly tailored to serve the government's legitimate, content-neutral interests." But they need not meet the high standard imposed on viewpoint- and content-based restrictions.

JUSTICE STEPHEN BREYER, concurring.

I join JUSTICE KAGAN's separate opinion. Like JUSTICE KAGAN, I believe that categories alone cannot satisfactorily resolve the legal problem before us. The First Amendment requires greater judicial sensitivity both to the Amendment's expressive objectives and to the public's legitimate need for regulation than a simple recitation of categories, such as "content discrimination" and "strict scrutiny," would permit. In my view, the category "content discrimination" is better considered . . . as a rule of thumb, rather than as an automatic "strict scrutiny" trigger, leading to almost certain legal condemnation.

To use content discrimination to trigger strict scrutiny sometimes makes perfect sense. There are cases in which the Court has found content discrimination an unconstitutional method for suppressing a viewpoint. And there are cases where the Court has found content discrimination to reveal that rules governing a traditional public forum are, in fact, not a neutral way of fairly managing the forum in the interest of all speakers. In these types of cases, strict scrutiny is often appropriate, and content discrimination has thus served a useful purpose.

But content discrimination, while helping courts to identify unconstitutional suppression of expression, cannot and should not always trigger strict scrutiny. To say that it is not an automatic "strict scrutiny" trigger is not to argue against that concept's use. I readily concede, for example, that content discrimination, as a conceptual tool, can sometimes reveal weaknesses in the government's rationale for a rule that limits speech. . . . I also concede that, whenever government disfavors one kind of speech, it places that speech at a disadvantage, potentially interfering with the free marketplace of ideas and with an individual's ability to express thoughts and ideas that can help that individual determine the kind of society in which he wishes to live, help shape that society, and help define his place within it.

Nonetheless, in these latter instances to use the presence of content discrimination automatically to trigger strict scrutiny and thereby call into play a strong presumption against constitutionality goes too far. That is because virtually all government activities involve speech, many of which involve the regulation of speech. Regulatory programs almost always require content discrimination. And to hold that such content discrimination triggers strict scrutiny is to write a recipe for judicial management of ordinary government regulatory activity. . . .

I recognize that the Court could escape the problem by watering down the force of the presumption against constitutionality that "strict scrutiny" normally carries with it. But, in my view, doing so will weaken the First Amendment's protection in instances where "strict scrutiny" should apply in full force.

The better approach is to generally treat content discrimination as a strong reason weighing against the constitutionality of a rule where a traditional public forum, or where viewpoint discrimination, is threatened, but elsewhere treat it as a rule of thumb, finding it a helpful, but not determinative legal tool, in an appropriate case, to determine the strength of a justification. I would use content discrimination as a supplement to a more basic analysis, which, tracking most of our First Amendment cases, asks whether the regulation at issue works harm to First Amendment interests that is disproportionate in light of the relevant regulatory objectives. Answering this question requires examining the seriousness of the harm to speech, the importance of the countervailing objectives, the extent to which the law will achieve those objectives, and whether there are other, less restrictive ways of doing so. . . .

Here, regulation of signage along the roadside, for purposes of safety and beautification is at issue. There is no traditional public forum nor do I find any general effort to censor a particular viewpoint. Consequently, the specific regulation at issue does not warrant "strict scrutiny." Nonetheless, for the reasons that JUSTICE KAGAN sets forth, I believe that the Town of Gilbert's regulatory rules violate the First Amendment. I consequently concur in the Court's judgment only.

JUSTICE ELENA KAGAN, with whom JUSTICE RUTH BADER GINSBURG and JUSTICE STEPHEN BREYER joined, concurring.

Countless cities and towns across America have adopted ordinances regulating the posting of signs, while exempting certain categories of signs based on their subject matter. For example, some municipalities generally prohibit illuminated signs in residential neighborhoods, but lift that ban for signs that identify the address of a home or the name of its owner or occupant. In other municipalities, safety signs such as "Blind Pedestrian Crossing" and "Hidden Driveway" can be posted without a permit, even as other permanent signs require one. Elsewhere, historic site markers—for example, "George Washington Slept Here"—are also exempt from general regulations. And similarly, the federal Highway Beautification Act limits signs along interstate highways unless, for instance, they direct travelers to "scenic and historical attractions" or advertise free coffee.

Given the Court's analysis, many sign ordinances of that kind are now in jeopardy. Says the majority: When laws "single[] out specific subject matter," they are "facially content based"; and when they are facially content based, they are automatically subject to strict scrutiny. And although the majority holds out hope that some sign laws with subject-matter exemptions "might survive" that stringent review, the likelihood is that most will be struck down. After all, it is the "rare case[] in which a speech restriction withstands strict scrutiny." To clear that high bar, the government must show that a content-based distinction "is necessary to serve a compelling state interest and is narrowly drawn to achieve that end."

So on the majority's view, courts would have to determine that a town has a compelling interest in informing passersby where George Washington slept. . . . The consequence—unless courts water down strict scrutiny to something unrecognizable—is that our communities will find themselves in an unenviable bind: They will have to either repeal the exemptions that allow for helpful signs on streets and sidewalks, or else lift their sign restrictions altogether and resign themselves to the resulting clutter.

Although the majority insists that applying strict scrutiny to all such ordinances is "essential" to protecting First Amendment freedoms, I find it challenging to understand why that is so. This Court's decisions articulate two important and related reasons for subjecting content-based speech regulations to the most exacting standard of review. The first is "to preserve an uninhibited marketplace of ideas in which truth will ultimately prevail." The second is to ensure that the government has not regulated speech "based on hostility—or favoritism—towards the underlying message expressed." Yet the subject-matter exemptions included in many sign ordinances do not implicate those concerns. . . .

We apply strict scrutiny to facially content-based regulations of speech, in keeping with the rationales just described, when there is any "realistic possibility that official suppression of ideas is afoot." That is always the case when the regulation facially differentiates on the basis of viewpoint. It is also the case (except in non-public or limited public forums) when a law restricts "discussion of an entire topic" in public debate.

Indeed, the precise reason the majority applies strict scrutiny here is that "the Code singles out signs bearing a particular message: the time and location of a specific event." We have stated that "[i]f the marketplace of ideas is to remain free and open, governments must not be allowed to choose 'which issues are worth discussing or debating.'" And we have recognized that such subject-matter restrictions, even though viewpoint-neutral on their face, may "suggest[ ] an attempt to give one side of a debatable public question an advantage in expressing its views to the people." Subject-matter regulation, in other words, may have the intent or effect of favoring some ideas over others. When that is realistically possible—when the restriction "raises the specter that the Government may effectively drive certain ideas or viewpoints from the marketplace"—we insist that the law pass the most demanding constitutional test.

But when that is not realistically possible, we may do well to relax our guard so that "entirely reasonable" laws imperiled by strict scrutiny can survive. This point is by no means new. . . . Our cases have been far less rigid than the majority admits in applying strict scrutiny to facially content-based laws—including in cases just like this one [when] the law's enactment and enforcement revealed "not even a hint of bias or censorship. . . ." The majority could easily have taken [that] tack here.

The Town of Gilbert's defense of its sign ordinance—most notably, the law's distinctions between directional signs and others—does not pass strict scrutiny, or intermediate scrutiny, or even the laugh test. . . . The absence of any sensible basis for [the law's] distinctions dooms the Town's ordinance under even the intermediate scrutiny that the Court typically applies to "time, place, or manner" speech regulations.

Accordingly, there is no need to decide in this case whether strict scrutiny applies to every sign ordinance in every town across this country containing a subject-matter exemption.

I suspect this Court and others will regret the majority's insistence today on answering that question in the affirmative. . . . Because I see no reason why such an easy case calls for us to cast a constitutional pall on reasonable regulations quite unlike the law before us, I concur only in the judgment.

⑤SAGE edge™

Visit **edge.sagepub.com/medialaw7e** to help you accomplish your coursework goals in an easy-to-use learning environment.

The character of every act depends upon the circumstance in which it is done. . . .
The question . . . is whether the words used are used in such circumstances and are of such a nature as to create a clear and present danger that they will bring about the substantive evils that Congress has a right to prevent.

—U.S. Supreme Court Justice Oliver Wendell Holmes[1]

In 2019, leading rappers like Dr. Dre (left) and Snoop Dogg waited for the U.S. Supreme Court to decide whether lyrics protesting police violence against black men were punishable threats or protected free speech.

Jeff Kravitz/FilmMagic/Getty Images

3

SPEECH DISTINCTIONS

Different Categories Trigger Distinct Treatment

SUPPOSE . . .

. . . on his Facebook page, a man posts original rap lyrics filled with violent language about his wife and children, the police, a kindergarten class and an FBI agent. He includes statements that the lyrics are "fictitious" artistic First Amendment expression not directed toward real individuals.[2] The jury decides a reasonable reader would find the posts threatening, convicts him of the federal crime of conveying threats across state lines and sentences him to four years in jail. The appeals court affirms. But can song lyrics pose a criminal threat if you didn't intend to threaten? Does it matter that you communicated them online to your Facebook "friends"? Look for the U.S. Supreme Court's answers in the discussion and excerpt of *Elonis v. United States*[3] in this chapter.

This chapter examines how courts determine the boundaries of protected speech. It explores expression at the fringes of First Amendment protection and beyond and the special considerations given to speech in and around public schools and universities.

A cornerstone of First Amendment analysis is that it does not prohibit all laws that infringe upon speech. To determine when laws violate the First Amendment, courts may use highly fact-specific ad hoc balancing to balance the societal harms against the personal freedoms involved in the case. Alternately, courts often rely on previously established categories of speech to apply specific standards of court review to that speech. Some categories of speech—blackmail, perjury, false advertising and obscenity, for example—are unprotected categories. If the speech category is protected, courts then look to the specific context of the speech and the nature of the legal punishment to determine how best to review the case.

When the category of speech is developing or evolving, such as hate speech or threats, courts look at the language of the statute, the circumstances and the level of harm to determine whether the speech is protected. One difficulty is that the seriousness of harm caused by the speech rarely can be known in advance.

EVOLVING COURT TESTS TO PROTECT DISRUPTIVE SPEECH

The U.S. Supreme Court has developed several tests to help it and other courts decide when unpopular or disturbing speech must be protected and when it may be punished. The Court has said free expression is not protected if it causes imminent harm or plays "no essential part of any exposition of ideas, and [is] of such slight social value as a step to truth that any benefit that may be derived from [it] is clearly outweighed by the social interest in order and morality."[4] No bright lines define the boundaries of this category. The border between protected and unprotected speech is not fixed. The Court's tests afford leeway in response to changing circumstances.

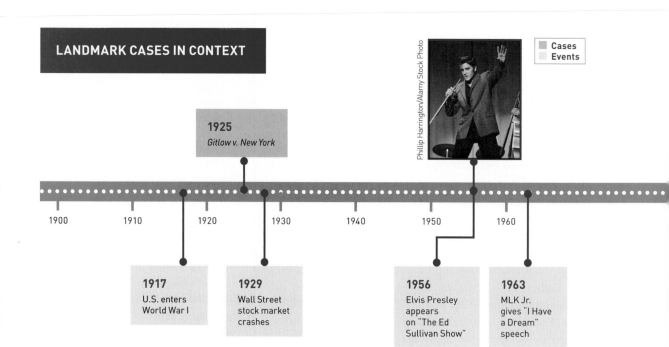

LANDMARK CASES IN CONTEXT

Philip Harrington/Alamy Stock Photo

■ Cases
■ Events

1925
Gitlow v. New York

1900   1910   1920   1930   1940   1950   1960

1917
U.S. enters
World War I

1929
Wall Street
stock market
crashes

1956
Elvis Presley
appears
on "The Ed
Sullivan Show"

1963
MLK Jr.
gives "I Have
a Dream"
speech

From a Bad Tendency to a Clear and Present Danger

A century ago, Justice Oliver Wendell Holmes wrote for a unanimous U.S. Supreme Court that government had both a right and a duty to prevent speech that presented a "**clear and present danger**" to the nation.[5] The case of *Schenck v. United States* began when Charles Schenck, a Socialist Party member, mailed anti-draft pamphlets to men in Philadelphia. The pamphlets encouraged readers to reject the government's pro-war philosophy and oppose U.S. participation in World War I. Schenck was convicted of violating the Espionage Act of 1917, which was enacted to unify the nation behind the war effort.

In affirming Schenck's conviction, the Supreme Court said the mailing had a "bad tendency" that could endanger national security. Justice Holmes said ordinarily harmless words may become criminal during times of war because of the heightened danger they pose: "It is a question of proximity and degree."[6] Common sense indicates that "the most stringent protection of free speech would not protect a man in falsely shouting fire in a theatre and causing a panic."[7] Nor would it protect an individual in a military recruitment office falsely shouting, "I have a bomb."

Under the Espionage Act, a unanimous Court affirmed other convictions for anti-war protests, speeches and pamphlets the Court said might tend to endanger the nation. In one case, the Court upheld a 10-year prison term for publishing writings that questioned the

clear and present danger
Doctrine establishing that restrictions on First Amendment rights will be upheld if they are necessary to prevent an extremely serious and imminent harm.

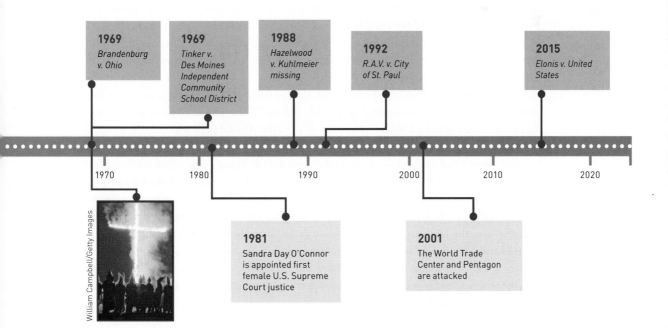

1969
Brandenburg v. Ohio

1969
Tinker v. Des Moines Independent Community School District

1988
Hazelwood v. Kuhlmeier missing

1992
R.A.V. v. City of St. Paul

2015
Elonis v. United States

1970   1980   1990   2000   2010   2020

William Campbell/Getty Images

1981
Sandra Day O'Connor is appointed first female U.S. Supreme Court justice

2001
The World Trade Center and Pentagon are attacked

REAL WORLD LAW
DEMOCRACY'S UNREASONED, UNCIVIL PROMISE

Vehement expression of opposing ideas is not the antithesis of free speech, but it does not necessarily produce informed democratic debate.[i] When raucous name-calling, hate-filled signs and near-threats in the streets replace the reasoned exchange of ideas, free speech may seem pathological.

Law professor Martin Redish suggests that concern about speech "pathology pervades the flow of American political history," and the U.S. Supreme Court rules accordingly. "Virtually all periods of strong political dissent throughout the nation's history have been met with a corresponding rise in repress[ion]."[ii]

Nonetheless, uncivil discord may be an essential cost of democracy.

"The labels 'civility' and 'incivility' . . . effectively function as exclusion instruments," according to one legal scholar. "Although they create the appearance of inclusiveness and openness to contrarian views," they work to silence dissenting voices.[iii]

constitutionality of the draft and the merits of the war.[8] The Court said the publications presented "a little breath [that] would be enough to kindle a flame" of unrest.[9] The Court also upheld the conviction of a speaker who told Socialist Party conventioneers, "You are fit for something better than slavery and cannon fodder."[10] The jury relied on the speaker's court testimony that he abhorred the war to demonstrate both his intent and the likelihood he would harm the war effort.

The Court also used this so-called bad-tendency standard to uphold a Sedition Act conviction of five friends whose pamphlets criticized U.S. interference in the Russian Revolution and encouraged strikes at U.S. munitions factories.[11] The leaflets told workers to oppose "the hypocrisy of the United States and her allies." This time writing in dissent, Justice Holmes said the "surreptitious publishing of a silly leaflet by an unknown man" did not pose a sufficiently grave and imminent danger to permit punishment.[12] The First Amendment requires government to protect diverse and loathsome opinions, he wrote, "unless they so imminently threaten immediate interference with the lawful and pressing purposes of the law that an immediate check is required to save the country."[13] This Holmes dissent in *Abrams v. United States* transformed his interpretation of the First Amendment and created the clear and present danger test.

The Court relied on the clear and present danger test for 50 years most often to affirm punishment of communists.[14] During the Red Scare of the 1920s, the Court affirmed the conviction of an immigrant for publication and distribution of Socialist Party literature urging the rise of socialism in the United States.[15] Without evidence that the pamphlets caused any harm or disruption, the Supreme Court in *Gitlow v. New York* upheld the conviction for criminal anarchy and advocacy to overthrow the government, saying that the pamphlets lit a "revolutionary spark" that might ignite a "sweeping and destructive conflagration."[16] The majority said the writings "endanger[ed] the foundations of organized government and threaten[ed] its overthrow by unlawful means."[17]

Now writing in dissent, Justice Holmes declared, "Every idea is an incitement" and most ideas "should be given their chance and have their way" in the dialogue of a free and democratic society.[18] The mere dissemination of ideas does not endanger the nation.

The majority of the Court did not embrace Holmes' view, but its *Gitlow* decision expanded free speech protection by establishing the doctrine of incorporation. The **incorporation doctrine** applies the 14th Amendment's due process clause to limit the power of state and local governments to abridge the Bill of Rights.[19] In other words, incorporation prevents the states, as well as the federal government, from abridging protected First Amendment rights.

In the years leading up to U.S. involvement in World War II, the Supreme Court used the clear and present danger test to uphold the conviction of a labor activist for participating in meetings of the Communist Labor Party.[20] In *Whitney v. California*, the Court accepted without evidence that the Communist party was violent and ruled that the First Amendment did not bar California from making it a crime to belong to a group that advocated violence. Mere party membership was sufficient to pose an imminent threat that was "relatively serious."[21] Writing in concurrence, Justice Louis Brandeis said a clear and present danger existed when previous conduct suggested a group *might contemplate* advocacy of immediate serious violence.[22]

During the anti-communist frenzy of the 1950s, the Court used the clear and present danger test to uphold a federal law that required labor union officers to swear they were not communists.[23] In dissent, Justice Hugo Black said the test did not sufficiently protect unpopular political speech or association from overzealous regulation: "Too often it is fear which inspires such passions, and nothing is more reckless or contagious. In the resulting hysteria, popular indignation tars with the same brush all those who have ever been associated with any member of the group under attack."[24]

Members of the Court increasingly questioned the ability of the clear and present danger test to protect radical speech. In several cases, the Court ruled that regulation of speech is unconstitutional if it does not address a problem more severe than abstract expressions about revolt and is not narrowly tailored to avoid infringing on protected speech.[25] While it is constitutional to regulate speech that advocates illegal action, government may not punish the mere expression of radical ideas. This doctrine was established in *Brandenburg v. Ohio*, a case involving incitement.

From Clear and Present Danger to Incitement

In 1969, the U.S. Supreme Court determined that the clear and present danger test was inadequate to protect innocent yet offensive speech.[26] In *Brandenburg v. Ohio*, the Court adopted a new test that drew a bright-line distinction between advocating violence as an abstract concept and inciting imminent violence when it ruled that the First Amendment protects the right to advocate but not to incite, or provoke, immediate violence.[27]

The case involved Clarence Brandenburg, a television repairman and Ku Klux Klan leader, who spoke to a dozen KKK members in the woods of rural Ohio. Brandenburg made vague threats to take "revengeance" against various government leaders, and his racist speech was later televised. Brandenburg was convicted under state criminal conspiracy law

incorporation doctrine
The 14th Amendment concept that most of the Bill of Rights applies equally to the states.

of attempting to violently overthrow government. He said the conviction violated his right of free speech.

The Supreme Court struck down Brandenburg's conviction, holding that the First Amendment protected people's right to advocate abhorrent ideas. Brandenburg's anti-Semitic and racist comments were highly offensive, the Court said, but "[m]ere advocacy of the use of force or violence does not remove speech from the protection of the First Amendment."[28] To protect the expression of abstract ideas about the necessity of violence from government intrusion, the Court established a test named after the case. The *Brandenburg* test permits government to punish the advocacy of violence only by showing that the advocacy was (1) intended to and (2) likely to incite imminent (3) lawless action.[29]

In a second case, *Hess v. Indiana*, Gregory Hess used profanity at an anti–Vietnam War rally after sheriff's officers moved demonstrators out of the street. On appeal, the U.S. Supreme Court overturned Hess' conviction for disorderly conduct. The First Amendment protected his speech that was not intended to, and not likely to, provoke an imminent violation of the law.[30] The Court held that unless a speaker so inflamed a crowd that people responded with immediate, illegal acts, the speech was protected.

Under *Brandenburg*, the incitement does not have to be explicit, but two recent U.S. Supreme Court decisions[31] raise the bar needed for government to show that prosecution is reasonable because a communication is sufficiently likely to be "directed to inciting or producing imminent lawless action and is likely to incite or produce such action."[32] Relying on *Bell Atlantic v. Twombly* and *Ashcroft v. Iqbal*, the Court said charges should be dismissed if judges' "common sense" and judicial experience indicated that (1) the preliminary facts (2) did not make a plausible showing (3) that the necessary elements of the crime were met.[33]

POINTS OF LAW

THE *BRANDENBURG* INCITEMENT TEST

In *Brandenburg v. Ohio*, the U.S. Supreme Court established a test to determine when it is constitutional for government to punish illegal encouragement of violence.[iv] The Court clarified the test a few years later and affirmed that government could punish speech provoking illegal activity only if facts showed that the speaker

1. intended to
2. and was likely to incite imminent
3. violent or illegal action.[v]

Under *Brandenburg*, punishable incitement exists if the facts show that intent, likelihood and imminence are probable and that the violence is so immediate that no other action would address the harm. The Court has not clearly defined these three elements.[vi] In 2007 and 2009, two Supreme Court rulings muddied the already murky *Brandenburg* test.[vii]

In a 2017 decision, the Sixth Circuit Court of Appeals applied the *Twombly/Iqbal* standard to dismiss an incitement suit brought against President Donald Trump for telling a crowd at a campaign rally to "get 'em out of here." He was referring to protesters at the event.[34] After President Trump's comment, members of the crowd pushed and shoved the protesters as they exited, and the protesters sued the president for damages for "inciting to riot."

A court may dismiss a charge of incitement using the plausibility standard if the court's common-sense interpretation of the preliminary facts establishes that intent,

In 2016, Trump supporters in Daytona Beach, Fla., "detained" a protester at a campaign rally for then-candidate Donald Trump.

likelihood and imminence are unlikely to be shown. The government's showing of these key elements must rely on facts alone, not on "legal conclusion[s]" that may be incorrect.[35] The facts must present a case that is more than speculative; it must be "plausible on its face" and provide a "reasonable" basis for the court to believe that it is "more than a sheer possibility" that the defendant is liable.[36]

The Sixth Circuit dismissed the case against the president on the grounds that the First Amendment protects speech that does not meet the *Brandenburg* standard.

When applied to claims that media provoke violence, the incitement test requires a showing that exposure to the media content would cause immediate violent or unlawful activity. That is nearly impossible to prove. Media content does not ordinarily provoke such a rapid response. When seeing, reading or hearing media material, a person must process the information before taking action. There generally is time to prevent a person from committing violent acts. The incitement test also requires proof that media content is likely to cause a reasonable person to act illegally. Rarely will a court find that a reasonable person would commit violence in response to media content.

SPEECH HARMS

Contrary to the childhood chant, words *can* hurt you. Speakers—sometimes intentionally, sometimes not—disrupt organized activities or offend, denigrate or degrade people. People call each other names; they hurl hateful insults and epithets at each other. They threaten; they harass. They fill public meetings and public streets with dissent and discontent. The words and images they use alienate, cause fear and increase conflict.

Offensive Speech

Although many different types of speech offend or cause discomfort, mental anguish or suffering, the U.S. Supreme Court has said the First Amendment protects our right to

Decades after Paul Robert Cohen became famous as the voice of free speech and anti–Vietnam War protest, he said his renown was accidental. He appealed his case to the U.S. Supreme Court because he wanted to avoid serving 30 days in jail.

express ourselves in our own words. In *Cohen v. California*,[37] Paul Robert Cohen appealed his conviction for disturbing the peace for opposing the Vietnam War by wearing a jacket bearing the phrase "Fuck the Draft" in the Los Angeles courthouse. Cohen said the First Amendment protected his pure political speech. The Supreme Court agreed. Although court officials have broad authority to maintain decorum, they cannot punish speech that does not disrupt the court's functioning simply because they find the words offensive.

The Supreme Court went further in *Cohen* and said the First Amendment protected both the content and the feelings expressed through a message. Meaningful protection for free speech goes beyond the "cognitive content" to protect the "emotive function" of a message, the Court said. It is not simply *what* you say but *how* you say it that enjoys constitutional protection. As Justice John Harlan famously wrote, "One man's vulgarity is another's lyric."[38]

In 2018, the U.S. Supreme Court ruled that a citizen's First Amendment rights might protect him from punishment for disrupting city council meetings.[39] The case began when the police arrested and removed an individual with a history of criticizing the city council from a council meeting after he repeatedly refused to stop interrupting the proceeding. The individual claimed the arrest violated his freedom of speech and retaliated for his lawsuit against the council for alleged open-meeting violations (see Chapter 7). The Supreme Court acknowledged the legitimate justification for the arrest but said probable cause did not automatically overcome a claim that the arrest was improperly motivated by retaliation for protected First Amendment activity.[40] In an 8–1 decision limited to "these facts," the Court said the case involved high-value political speech. In 2019, the Supreme Court resolved another case by concluding that "the presence of probable cause [for arrest] should generally defeat a First Amendment retaliatory arrest claim."[41]

Fighting Words

The First Amendment protects people's right to vent anger in words. Free speech serves society as a safety valve, allowing people to blow off steam before they resort to physical violence.[42] Nonetheless, the Supreme Court recognizes that to vent anger also may "set fire to reason."[43]

In a case that foreshadowed the logic of *Brandenburg*, the U.S. Supreme Court in 1942 in *Chaplinsky v. New Hampshire*[44] established that government may punish speech that provokes violent listener reaction. When residents complained that Walter Chaplinsky was distributing Jehovah's Witness pamphlets on the streets, a group of people became restless. A police officer warned Chaplinsky to stop because he was disturbing the peace, and later another officer detained him. The officer and Chaplinsky encountered the first officer, who warned Chaplinsky again, and Chaplinsky called the officer a "goddamned racketeer" and a "damned Fascist." Chaplinsky was convicted under a state law that defined disturbing the peace as publicly calling someone "any offensive, derisive or annoying word . . . or name . . . with intent to deride, offend or annoy."

In its landmark decision, the U.S. Supreme Court upheld the conviction, ruling that the First Amendment did not protect narrow categories of speech that make no contribution to the discussion of ideas or the search for truth. The Court said Chaplinsky's comments were unprotected **fighting words** that "by their very utterance inflict injury or tend to incite immediate breach of peace."[45]

fighting words
Words not protected by the First Amendment because they are directed at an individual and cause immediate harm or trigger violent response.

In 1949, the Supreme Court heard the case of a priest who was arrested for disorderly conduct when his anti-Semitic and pro-Fascist comments to a sympathetic audience riled a group outside the assembly hall to violence. Illinois courts upheld his conviction, ruling that the law punished only unprotected fighting words that "stir[] the public to anger, invite[] dispute, bring[] about a condition of unrest, . . . create[] a disturbance or . . . molest[] the inhabitants in the enjoyment of peace and quiet by arousing alarm."[46]

The U.S. Supreme Court reversed, reasoning that "a function of free speech under our system of government is to *invite* dispute."[47] The Court in *Terminiello v. Chicago* said speech "may indeed best serve its high purpose when it induces a condition of unrest, creates dissatisfaction with conditions as they are or even stirs people to anger."[48] The First Amendment protects such speech "unless shown likely to produce a clear and present danger of a serious substantive evil that rises far above public inconvenience, annoyance or unrest."[49] Subsequent Supreme Court rulings[50] have confirmed that the Constitution permits government to prohibit only those face-to-face comments that are inherently likely to trigger an immediate reaction of disorder or violence.

REAL WORLD LAW
CYBERBULLYING

Teens and preteens rely on technology to connect with peers and family, but online activity exposes them to risks of cyberbullying and cybervictimization.[viii] Cyberbullying, or repeated online aggression that is difficult to diffuse or defend against,[ix] affects fully one-third of boys and one-fourth of girls during their adolescence, a study published in 2019 reported.[x] Although cyberbullying and cybervictimization are linked with adverse health effects, psychological problems and suicide,[xi] half of all teens say their parents have no knowledge of their online activities.

In a rare case of cyberbullying that did not involve school/university students or personnel, the mother of a teen created a Myspace profile for a non-existent 16-year-old boy to flirt with and then break up with her daughter's classmate. The day the mom,

posing as the boy, told the classmate, "The world would be a better place without you in it," the girl committed suicide.

A jury convicted the woman for violating Myspace's anti-harassment rules and the Computer Fraud and Abuse Act,[xii] intended to prevent unauthorized access to, or hacking of, computer accounts. A federal district judge set aside the verdict, ruling that the law was unconstitutionally vague because it provided neither the required fair warning of what constituted illegal activity nor objective criteria by which to determine when a crime had occurred.[xiii] The judge also said the law was not intended to apply to cyberbullying.

All 50 states have laws or policies punishing cyberbullying; they differ broadly.[xiv]

Two recent cases involving leafleting at an annual Arab International Festival demonstrate the principle that listeners' reactions against speakers generally are insufficient grounds to regulate expression.[51] The cases began when police arrested members of a Christian evangelical group, Bible Believers, for distributing leaflets and preaching against Islam in ways some Muslim festivalgoers responded to with threats of violence. The police removed the Bible Believers under a recently enacted city ban on leafleting promoted by the festival sponsors. The Bible Believers challenged their arrest and removal as a violation of their freedom of speech, but the trial court found the action to be a reasonable time, place and manner restriction to maintain an orderly festival. The Sixth Circuit Court of Appeals disagreed. It struck down the law as an example of what some call a "heckler's veto," which allows unhappy listeners to abridge others' freedom of speech.

Hate Speech

hate speech
A category of speech that includes name-calling and pointed criticism that demeans others on the basis of race, color, gender, ethnicity, religion, national origin, disability, intellect or the like.

Contemporary concerns about the harms caused by intolerance, racism and bigotry have generated state and local speech codes to regulate so-called **hate speech**, but courts generally find these laws unconstitutional. *Hate speech* is not a legal term, but it is commonly understood to involve name-calling, slurs and epithets that demean others on the basis of identity. Few cases dealing squarely with hate speech have reached the U.S. Supreme Court, but lower courts consistently have found anti-bias and anti-hate-speech laws unconstitutional.

The primary Supreme Court decision dealing with a hate speech law, *R.A.V. v. City of St. Paul*, involved several white teenage boys who, late one night, made a crude wooden cross from a broken chair and set it ablaze in the yard of a black family.[52] They were convicted of

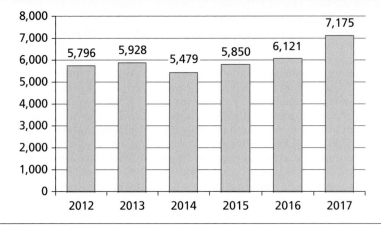

FIGURE 3.1 ■ U.S. Hate Crimes 2012–2017

Year	Hate Crimes
2012	5,796
2013	5,928
2014	5,479
2015	5,850
2016	6,121
2017	7,175

Source: Federal Bureau of Investigation, 2017 Hate Crime Statistics.

INTERNATIONAL LAW
IS ONLINE CENSORSHIP THE ANSWER?

Although major social media networks like Facebook or Twitter argue that efforts to control hate speech cost them both users and profits, others see their open, often pseudonymous platforms as a freeway for hate, fringe radical ideas and the spread of terrorism.[xv] Most social networks take steps to moderate the most vile communicators and terrorist content, but a Facebook policy manager said a joint effort of tech companies and civil society was needed to effectively curb online extremism. Speaking to the World Government Summit in 2019, she said censorship is ineffective and only fuels authors to spread their messages further.[xvi]

Following the summit, the parliament of India summoned a Twitter representative to appear before hearings on an initiative to protect "citizens' rights" on social media. The French digital minister proposed legislation to increase fines and penalties for online providers who fail to remove racist and hateful content. Google, Twitter and Facebook also jointly called on the British government to establish flexible principles to draw bright-line distinctions between legal and illegal content.[xvii] The British government began pushing online providers to remove "abusive, humiliating or intimidating content" in 2017.

violating a local statute that punished the display of symbols—such as a burning cross—that arouse "anger, alarm or resentment in others on the basis of race, color, creed, religion or gender." The Minnesota Supreme Court upheld the conviction, reasoning that the bias-motivated crime statute punished only unprotected fighting words.

A unanimous U.S. Supreme Court reversed, but the justices did not agree on why. Five justices said the law was too narrow, or **underinclusive**, because it punished only a specific subset of fighting words that the government found particularly objectionable. Thus, the law imposed unconstitutional **viewpoint-based discrimination** because it punished certain forms of racist speech (cross burnings) but not others. The remaining four justices said the law was overbroad; it punished too much speech, not too little. They said the law unconstitutionally went beyond fighting words to punish speech that did not arise in face-to-face encounters and whose only harm was to prompt "generalized reactions" of hurt or offense.

In explaining its reasoning, the *R.A.V.* Court said:

> It is not true that "fighting words" have at most a "de minimus" expressive content, or that their content is in all respects "worthless and undeserving of constitutional protection"; sometimes they are quite expressive indeed. We have not said that they constitute "no part of the expression of ideas," but only that they constitute "no essential part of any expression of ideas." . . . [T]he unprotected features of [fighting] words are, despite their verbal character, essentially a "nonspeech" element of communication.[53]

Since *R.A.V.*, most efforts to tailor a constitutional hate speech ordinance have failed. Supreme Court decisions make the precise level of protection the Constitution affords fighting words

underinclusive
A First Amendment doctrine that disfavors narrow laws that target a subset of a recognized category for discriminatory treatment.

viewpoint-based discrimination
Government censorship or punishment of expression based on the ideas or attitudes expressed. Courts will apply a strict scrutiny test to determine whether the government acted constitutionally.

Joe Kohen via Getty Images

The Department of Justice has reviewed burnings of gay pride flags to determine whether to prosecute the act as a hate crime that is not protected by the First Amendment.

unclear. They suggest that speech loses its constitutional protection when the speaker intends to provoke violence or incite immediate unrest in a targeted individual or group. The Supreme Court has shied away from using the fighting words category to judge the constitutionality of laws that attempt to regulate highly volatile speech and instead has examined the reach of the law. The Court has struck down laws that attempt to punish specific types of offensive speech on the grounds that the laws are not sufficiently narrowly tailored to prevent intrusion on protected speech.

In 2015, the Ninth Circuit Court of Appeals denied a motion to require Google to take down a film an actor said forced her to be associated with hate speech.[54] Without the actor's permission, filmmakers put her five-second performance from an action film into "Innocence of Muslims" dubbed with anti-Islamic audio in Arabic. The film sparked threats against the actor and violent protests in many countries. YouTube blocked its display in several Arab and Muslim countries, and a three-judge panel of the Ninth Circuit initially ordered its removal in the United States. Rehearing the case en banc, the full court made no reference to *R.A.V.* and struck down the injunction because the actor had not shown the irreparable harm needed to justify a presumptively unconstitutional prior restraint.

In recent years, police in Pennsylvania have relied on the state's hate crime statute against individuals showing them disrespect.[55] The law makes it a crime to intimidate someone with "malicious intention toward the[ir] race, color, religion or national origin." In a 2018 case, the police increased the charges against a 52-year-old black man they say resisted arrest for shoplifting and called them "Nazis," "skinheads" and "Gestapo." The hate crime charge transformed a first-degree misdemeanor into a third-degree felony. In another case, the state appeals court said Mike Love, a black man, had used "numerous racial epithets" when he called several undercover police officers "white boys" and "fucking crackers" and told them to "get off the corner" prior to an altercation.[56] The court affirmed Love's 23-month jail term for violating the state's ethnic intimidation law.

Intimidation and Threats

true threat
Speech directed toward an individual or historically identified group with the intent of causing fear of harm.

When speech crosses certain lines, government may restrict messages that are sufficiently detrimental to important competing interests. A decade and a half ago, the U.S. Supreme Court created a category of speech it called **true threats**. The case involved three cross burnings, one at a KKK rally and two in the yard of a black family. In *Virginia v. Black*, the Court ruled that the First Amendment allows states to punish individuals who set crosses ablaze with the intent to intimidate.[57] The Court said laws may constitutionally target a specific subset of fighting words, such as cross burnings, that is so "inextricably intertwined" with a clear and pervasive history of violence that it constitutes a threat. The Court said a burning cross is an instrument of racial terror and imminent violence whose power to intimidate overshadows free speech concerns. In *R.A.V.*, the Court had struck down a law that unconstitutionally targeted a subset of speech the city found particularly offensive.[58]

Writing for the majority in *Virginia v. Black*, Justice Sandra Day O'Connor reasoned that despite the inextricable connection between cross burnings and the KKK's "reign of terror in the South," history alone does not transform offensive speech into unprotected threats. Here the cross burning involved an intent to intimidate, which may be punished. For speech to become a punishable threat, a speaker must (1) direct the threat toward one or more individuals (2) with the intent of causing the listener(s) (3) to fear bodily harm or death.[59] In this case, cross burning was constitutionally punishable because the intimidation was intended to create pervasive fear of violence in the targeted individual or group. In dissent, Justice Clarence Thomas said the law punished only illegal acts and was unrelated to First Amendment concerns: "Those who hate cannot terrorize and intimidate to make their point."

William Campbell/Getty Images

A hooded member of the Ku Klux Klan sets a cross on fire.

In 2015, the Supreme Court remanded the First Amendment question of when internet posts constitute true threats punishable by law.[60] The case of *Elonis v. United States* involved a Pennsylvania man convicted of making Facebook threats to his estranged wife and law enforcement officers. Anthony Elonis said he did not intend any threats and was composing "therapeutic" rap lyrics to express his depression and frustration after his wife took their children and left him.[61] At trial, Elonis' wife testified that she was terrified by the posts, had filed a protective order against him and feared for her life and that of her children. The jury convicted Elonis.

On appeal, the Third Circuit Court of Appeals identified both a subjective and an objective element to threats.[62] The subjective element involves the speaker's knowing communication of an intention to cause harm. The objective standard means that a reasonable person would view the communication as a threat. The court affirmed the conviction on the grounds that the lyrics clearly met the objective standard.

But the Supreme Court disagreed. A conviction for a true threat cannot rely on the recipient's perception and the speaker's mere negligence, it said.[63] Conviction for making a threat, like any criminal conviction, requires a showing that the defendant intended to commit the crime or knew that a reasonable person would perceive the communication as a threat.[64] "Wrongdoing must be conscious to be criminal. . . . [T]his principle is as universal and persistent in mature systems of law as belief in freedom of the human will," the Court said.[65]

On remand, the Third Circuit reviewed the trial court's instructions to the jury, which said that a threat exists when a reasonable communicator would understand the receiver would perceive a threat. The court concluded that the instructions met the Supreme Court's requirement and reaffirmed Elonis' conviction.[66] Elonis was released in 2016 after serving 44 months in jail.

In 2018, the Pennsylvania Supreme Court upheld the conviction of Jamal Knox, who performed under the name Mayhem Mal, for terrorist threats toward police officers for his rap song, "Fuck the Police."[67] The song, posted widely through Facebook and YouTube, names two Pittsburgh police officers and ends with the phrase "Let's kill these cops cuz they don't do us no good."[68] The named officers said the lyrics made them "nervous," and one quit the police force. Defense attorneys argued that the rap song was pure political speech that "no reasonable person familiar with rap music would have interpreted as a true threat of violence." Knox said the song was written from his rap persona and he had no intention to threaten or harm the officers. The state's high court ruled that Knox intended to threaten and intimidate. The U.S. Supreme Court declined to review the case in 2019.[69]

In a 2018 case in Louisiana initiated by a complaint against an arresting police officer, a panel of the Fifth Circuit Court of Appeals overturned a conviction for threats under state law.[70] The court found the law unconstitutional because its definition of threats encompassed both threats of force and lawsuits filed against public employees.[71]

SYMBOLIC SPEECH

Much expression that might anger or upset people does not cross the line into incitement, fighting words or threats. Sometimes it does not even take the form of words. Nonverbal expression, in the form of burning flags, wearing armbands or marching through the public streets, is what the U.S. Supreme Court has called symbolic speech. The Court has said symbolic speech deserves First Amendment protection in some cases, but it has rejected "the view that an apparently limitless variety of conduct can be labeled speech whenever the person engaging in the conduct intends thereby to express his idea."[72] Only actions that are "closely akin to 'pure speech'" are viewed as symbolic speech.[73]

Some of the most vehement and heated debate in the 1960s involved symbolic speech. Amid the civil rights movement and protests against the Vietnam War, the Court held that the Constitution protected the rights of protest groups to express the most radical and unpopular political ideas. However, there were limits, and the line between protected political protest and illegal activity, incitement or fighting words was not always obvious.

Burning Speech

In the first of these cases (which is discussed in Chapter 2), the Supreme Court affirmed the power of government to punish David O'Brien for burning his draft card in violation of a federal law intended to facilitate the military draft. The *O'Brien* ruling established intermediate scrutiny as the standard of judicial review of content-neutral laws that incidentally infringed protected speech. In affirming O'Brien's conviction, the Court focused on why the government had enacted the law (intent) and how the law operated (effect) while acknowledging the expressive content of the public destruction of a draft card.[74]

Fast-forward 20 years, and the Court reviewed a case in which Gregory Lee Johnson had been convicted, sentenced to a year in prison and fined $2,000 for burning the American flag during a protest at the Republican National Convention in Dallas. In *Texas v. Johnson*, the Supreme Court used strict scrutiny to strike down a Texas law that made it a crime to desecrate the flag.[75] The state of Texas said its ban on flag desecration preserved an important symbol of national unity and prevented breach of the peace. Johnson argued that the law violated his right to free speech. The Supreme Court agreed. Finding flag burning to be a form of symbolic speech, the Court struck down the Texas law as unconstitutionally content based.

A sharply divided Supreme Court held that the law failed to pass strict scrutiny because it served no compelling interest. The state's interest in preserving the sanctity of the flag represented an unconstitutional attempt to punish ideas government disliked. The law's sole purpose was to prohibit expression the state found offensive. "If there is a bedrock principle underlying the First Amendment," Justice William Brennan wrote for the Court, "it is that the government may not prohibit the expression of an idea simply because society finds the idea itself offensive or disagreeable."[76] The law was unconstitutional because it neither served a compelling interest nor used the least intrusive means to advance its goals.

The Constitution also generally protects exaggeration, hyperbole and excess in speech by looking to the context to determine whether the words should be taken on their face. For example, the Court said an anti-war protester's comment to fellow marchers that "we'll take the fucking street later" did not present the clear and present danger of violence required under the incitement test because it was unlikely to prompt any immediate action.[77]

DO MEDIA INCITE HARM?

A series of Federal Trade Commission reports on violent entertainment marketed to children consistently cites research establishing "that exposure to violence in entertainment media alone does not cause a child to commit a violent act."[78] Although there is little agreement on how exposure to television, video game, music and movie violence influences youth aggression,[79] some have tied excessive exposure to these media to mass murders.[80] Lawsuits have claimed that injury resulted from imitating the violence in movies like "Natural Born Killers"

The violent images and play of video games, such as "Call of Duty," generate public and legislative concern.

and video games like "Doom," and courts have been asked to determine the level of media responsibility.[81]

Physical Harms

One lawsuit decades ago began when 13-year-old Ronny Zamora shot and killed his 83-year-old neighbor. Zamora's parents sued, claiming the television networks had failed to exercise "ordinary care to prevent their son from being impermissibly stimulated, incited and instigated to duplicate the atrocities he viewed on television."[82] A federal district court said the networks did not have a duty to stop showing violent programs and could not be held responsible for the teen's actions. To dictate a limit on violent content would violate the First Amendment rights of the networks and the public, the court held.[83]

If a court uses the incitement test when a member of the media is sued for causing physical harm, the plaintiff rarely wins. Plaintiffs generally fail to convince courts that media intentionally encouraged people to harm themselves or others. One case of media incitement involved a Hustler magazine article titled "Orgasm of Death," describing autoerotic asphyxiation. The parents of a 14-year-old boy who hanged himself with a copy of Hustler open to the story sued Hustler. The Fifth Circuit Court of Appeals said Hustler was not liable and did not incite the boy's actions.[84] The magazine not only did not urge readers to perform the act described; it repeatedly warned against it.

Courts have not found that media incited violence even when media knew criminal activity might be related to their content. For example, two decades ago Paramount Pictures continued distributing the movie "The Warriors" despite knowledge of two killings near California theaters that showed the film. When a teenager was stabbed and killed by another youth after leaving "The Warriors," the murdered boy's father sued Paramount. The Massachusetts Supreme Court held that the film's fictional portrayal of gang warfare did not constitute incitement because it did not advocate violent or unlawful acts.[85]

In a rare ruling of its kind, the Fourth Circuit Court of Appeals held a book publisher liable because it intended for criminals to buy and use the book "Hit Man: A Technical Manual for Independent Contractors" as a how-to for murder.[86] After a killer mimicked the book's detailed instructions to murder a woman, her son and the son's nurse, the court said the First Amendment did not protect Paladin Press because it encouraged, aided and abetted a crime. "[E]very court that has addressed the issue" agrees the First Amendment does not necessarily prevent finding a mass medium liable for assisting a crime, even if that aid "takes the form of the spoken or written word."[87] Paladin Press settled the case for $5 million.[88]

Negligence

negligence
Generally, the failure to exercise reasonable or ordinary care.

Plaintiffs suing the media for causing physical harm often argue that the media negligently distributed material that led to injury or death. When such suits are based on the tort of **negligence** (discussed in Chapter 4), the plaintiff must show that the media defendant had a duty of due care, the defendant breached that duty and the breach caused the plaintiff's injury. Although lawsuits have proliferated, courts rarely find the media negligent and liable for violent content.[89]

For example, one court found NBC was not negligent when a girl was raped after the network aired the film "Born Innocent." Four days after the film aired, a 9-year-old was attacked and raped on a San Francisco beach in a manner similar to central events in the film. The girl's parents sued NBC, claiming it was negligent in showing the movie when children could watch it. A state appellate court said the First Amendment barred any finding that NBC had a duty of care to the girl.[90] To do otherwise, the court said, would cause NBC to engage in self-censorship.

Foreseeability. To determine a defendant's duty of care, courts often ask whether the defendant should have foreseen that its product messages would cause harm. If a reasonable person would not foresee the harm, there was no duty.

Soldier of Fortune magazine ads promoting "GUN FOR HIRE . . . All jobs considered" preceded two murder attempts, one of which was successful. A federal district court rejected the magazine's argument that the First Amendment protected its right to publish the ads.[91] The court said free speech is not absolute, and a jury could find the ads "had a substantial probability of ultimately causing harm to some individuals."[92] The magazine had a duty of due care because it was foreseeable that the ads could lead to physical injury.

However, Soldier of Fortune could not foresee harm from an ad that read: "EX-MARINES— 67–69 'Nam Vets, Ex-DI, weapons specialist—jungle warfare, pilot, M.E., high risk assignments, U.S. or overseas."[93] In response to the ad, Robert Black paid John Wayne Hearn $10,000 to kill Black's wife. After Sandra Black's murder, her mother and son sued the magazine. The appellate court said the magazine had "no duty to refrain from publishing a facially innocuous classified advertisement when the ad's context—at most—made its message ambiguous."[94] In a third case, a federal appellate court said Soldier of Fortune was obligated to determine whether the language of an ad, on its face, created an unreasonable risk of causing violent crime.[95]

The Sixth Circuit Court of Appeals held that video game manufacturers have no duty to protect against an individual's independent decision to kill.[96] Parents of a 14-year-old video game player who shot three of his peers at their high school sued video game producers, claiming the negligent distribution of violent video games made them liable for alleged harms to the couple's son and his victims. The court held there was insufficient proof that the game producers should have foreseen that their products could prompt the shooting.[97] Even if the gameplay involved shootings, it is "simply too far a leap from shooting characters on a video screen . . . to shooting people in a classroom," the court said.[98]

Proximate Cause. If a defendant's actions led to the plaintiff's injury, the defendant caused the injury. But unless the defendant's action was the **proximate cause** of the harm, courts will not hold the defendant liable. To determine proximate cause, courts decide whether there is a direct relationship between the defendant's action and the plaintiff's injury. Courts often refuse to find proximate cause if there is a weak linkage between the defendant's action and the subsequent injury.

proximate cause
The legal determination of whether it is reasonable to conclude that the defendant's actions led to the plaintiff's injury.

In one case, a mother sued the manufacturer of "Dungeons & Dragons"[99] on the grounds that her son committed suicide when he lost touch with reality because of the game. A federal appellate court said the suicide was independent of the gameplay. Both the loss of reality and the decision to commit suicide were intervening events. Similarly, when a teenager committed suicide while listening to an Ozzy Osbourne album that includes the song "Suicide Solution," the teenager's parents sued. A California appellate court said the connection between the suicide and the song's lyrics was too tenuous to show proximate cause.[100]

The U.S. Supreme Court weighed in when it struck down a California law.[101] In *Brown v. Entertainment Merchants Association*, a video game merchants' group challenged a state law that prohibited sale of violent video games to minors and required package labeling of violent content.[102] The law targeted only violent video games that (1) appealed to deviant or morbid interests, (2) were patently offensive under contemporary community standards and (3) lacked serious artistic or other value (see discussion of related obscenity standards in Chapter 10). The state said the law was intended to advance the important government interest in preventing psychological harm to minors.

But the Supreme Court said the law unconstitutionally singled out video games from other media because of the games' interactivity and attractiveness to children.[103] In *Brown*, the Court refused to create a new category of disfavored speech for video game violence. It said violent video games deserve full First Amendment protection and California's attempt to do otherwise was both "unprecedented and mistaken."[104]

Reviewing the law under strict scrutiny, the Court found it facially unconstitutional. "It is difficult to distinguish politics from entertainment and dangerous to try. . . . Like the protected books, plays and movies that preceded them, video games communicate ideas and even social messages. . . . That suffices to confer First Amendment protection."[105]

In his concurring opinion, Justice Samuel Alito urged care when sweeping new technologies under the media umbrella. He wrote:

> In considering the application of unchanging constitutional principles to new and rapidly evolving technology, this Court should proceed with caution. . . . We should not jump to the conclusion that new technology is fundamentally the same as some older thing with which we are familiar. And we should not hastily dismiss the judgment of legislators, who may be in a better position than we are to assess the implications of new technology.[106]

In a rare decision after *Brown*, the Alabama Supreme Court allowed a civil lawsuit brought by the families of two murdered police officers to proceed against the makers of a video game. In the underlying case, the Alabama court upheld a 17-year-old's conviction and death sentence for killing the officers during his arrest for carjacking.[107] The teen used the defense that his extensive play of "Grand Theft Auto" had caused post-traumatic stress and prompted the killings.[108] The officers' families wanted to hold the game makers liable.

Harmful Images

The U.S. Supreme Court used its review of a federal statute making it a crime to profit from "depictions of animal cruelty"[109] to reaffirm its power to define categories of speech and to determine which are, and are not, fully protected by the First Amendment. In *United States v. Stevens*, the Supreme Court said Congress did not have the power to prohibit images of animal cruelty because the Constitution fully protects even violent and deeply disturbing images.[110]

In reviewing the conviction of Robert J. Stevens for compiling and selling videotapes of dogfights in violation of the Animal Crush Video Prohibition Act, the Court said it is possible "there are some categories of speech that have been historically unprotected [that] have not yet been specifically identified or discussed . . . in our case law. But if so, there is no evidence that 'depictions of animal cruelty' is among them."[111] Neither Congress nor the Supreme Court has "freewheeling authority to declare new categories of speech outside the scope of the First Amendment," the Court said. It found the law substantially overbroad and struck it down because it infringed fully protected speech.[112]

Other Harms

Any person or company involved with preparing or publishing news, entertainment and advertising may be sued for any number of legal claims. Media are not exempt when laws, such as contract laws, apply generally to any competent adult. Thus, when media make contractual agreements, they may be sued for breaching a contract.

For example, when documentary filmmakers interviewed an art critic for their film about censorship, the filmmakers signed a contract stating that the interview would not be distributed beyond a single British channel. After the film won numerous awards and was selected to open a prestigious festival, the critic sued. The filmmakers argued that the contract did not apply because they used only brief portions of the interview in the film. The court interpreted the contract to prevent reuse of the unedited interview footage, so the documentary with only interview excerpts could be exhibited wherever the producer wanted.[113]

The U.S. Supreme Court's 2018 decision in *Masterpiece Cakeshop v. Colorado Civil Rights Commission* underscores why neutral laws of general applicability apply to individuals and media firms alike.[114] The case involved a ruling of the Colorado Civil Rights Commission that a baker violated the state's anti-discrimination law by refusing to bake a wedding cake for a same-sex couple. The baker said the wedding violated his profound religious beliefs and his choice not to bake the cake was protected by the First Amendment. The Court said it was "unexceptional" that the government's power to enact anti-discrimination laws "protect[s] gay persons . . . [and] other classes of individuals in acquiring whatever products and services they choose on the same terms and conditions as are offered to other members of the public."[115] However, the Court struck down the law **as applied**. Such laws may not violate a speaker's freedom "to choose the content of his own message."[116]

as applied
A legal phrase referring to interpretation of a statute on the basis of actual effects on the parties in the present case.

In another recent decision, the Supreme Court ruled that a prior criminal conviction cannot justify government suppression of speech that does not meet either the *Brandenburg* or the *Cohen* standard. The Court ruled in *State v. Packingham* that a North Carolina law barring sex offenders from using social media websites like Facebook and Twitter was unconstitutional.[117]

Lester Packingham's conviction of taking indecent liberties with a minor made him subject to the state law.[118] After his release from prison, Packingham used Facebook to express his happiness at having a parking ticket dismissed and was arrested under the law intended to prevent sex offenders from soliciting victims online. He challenged his arrest as an unconstitutional abridgement of his First Amendment right to free speech, but the state supreme court ruled that the law was a constitutional limit on conduct, not a restriction of speech.[119] The U.S. Supreme Court reversed, holding that the law was unconstitutionally overbroad and failed to demonstrate a compelling need to prevent online speech to minors.

In another case, a federal district court relied in part on *Cohen* to rule that a state may not broadly punish speech by convicted criminals.[120] A Pennsylvania state law allowed prosecutors or crime victims to bring civil lawsuits to obtain an injunction to stop any "conduct" by a convicted criminal that perpetuates the harms of the crime and "causes a temporary or permanent state of mental anguish" to the victim.[121] The Revictimization Relief Act took effect within weeks of a small private Pennsylvania college announcing that its commencement speaker would be alumnus Mumia Abu-Jamal, who had been convicted of killing a police officer.

Jamal challenged the act, and its application to him, as unconstitutionally vague, overbroad, content based and serving no compelling government interest. The trial court agreed and said Supreme Court precedent established that when a law's action is triggered by "the impact an expression has on its listeners, [it] is the essence of content-based regulation."[122] The law's explicit, unconstitutional intent was to prevent "expression that causes mental anguish in crime victims," the court said, and imposed a permanent injunction against application of the law.

NATIONAL SECURITY AND TRANQUILITY

It is difficult to determine when speech threatens national security or what speech must be curbed to provide for the public peace and tranquility. Decisions tend to reflect the national mood and contemporary realities. During times of war or national unrest, courts often see radical speech and protest as more dangerous than they would during times of calm.[123] The U.S. Supreme Court has not created legal rules to counterbalance the urge to stifle speech during times of instability.[124] Because the country moves from peace to war and back, the relative freedom to express unpopular ideas also shifts, undermining the promised stability of the law.[125]

Threats to National Security

Government efforts to punish speech that threatens its authority or undermines the security of the nation did not end in 1801 when the Sedition Act (discussed in Chapter 2) expired.

Both federal and state legislatures have enacted laws to protect the public from speakers who would incite violence or the overthrow of government. Sometimes such laws infringe protected speech, but well-crafted laws that target speech related to illegal conspiracies, advocacy of terrorism and treason generally are constitutional.

In *Holder v. Humanitarian Law Project*, the U.S. Supreme Court upheld a federal ban on "material support" to terrorists even when the law prevented support of legal expressive activities.[126] The **USA PATRIOT Act's**[127] ban defined "material support" as *any* service, training, expert advice or assistance to a designated terrorist organization. It encompassed some types of political organizing, activism and speech as illegal support for terrorism. The Humanitarian Law Project, a nonprofit organization, said the ban prevented it from training peaceful tactics to the Kurdistan Workers' Party (PKK), which was a federally designated terrorist organization. The group said the ban was overbroad and had a **chilling effect** on speech and associations protected by the First Amendment. Government actions that discourage the exercise of a constitutional right cause a chilling effect.

In upholding the law as applied in this case, the Supreme Court deferred to the government's judgment, "given the sensitive interests in national security and foreign affairs at stake."[128] The Court said the law was neither vague nor overbroad. Although "the scope of the material-support statute may not be clear in every application, . . . the statutory terms are clear in their application to plaintiffs' proposed conduct," the Court wrote.[129] The law's ban on training of the PKK constitutionally advanced the government's compelling interest in "provid[ing] for the common defense," the Court concluded.[130]

Following the U.S. Supreme Court's ruling, the First Circuit Court of Appeals upheld Tarek Mehanna's conviction for terrorism for online postings of accurate translations of al-Qaida materials.[131] The First Circuit held that Mehanna's translations knowingly "coordinated" with and provided material support to a foreign terrorist organization.[132] Although the conviction clearly targeted Mehanna's online speech, the court said that congressional debate over the Patriot Act ensured that the law did not violate the First Amendment.

The Patriot Act was signed within weeks of the terrorist attack on the United States on September 11, 2001. Critics argue that the Patriot Act and laws increasing government surveillance to advance the war on terrorism threaten fundamental civil liberties.[133] However, as Chief Justice William H. Rehnquist once said, "It is neither desirable nor is it remotely likely that civil liberty will occupy as favored a position in wartime as it does in peacetime."[134] Some Supreme Court decisions reflect Rehnquist's view. For example, during the post–World War II Red Scare, the Court said the First Amendment did not stop some government laws requiring employees to swear loyalty oaths and reject communism.[135] The Court also ruled that the Constitution permitted excluding a foreign economist and banning his speeches at U.S. universities because he was a Marxist.[136]

When online content advances terrorism or other extreme harms, Section 230 of the Communications Decency Act may protect digital service providers from liability for third-party content. In 2016, the First Circuit Court of Appeals said the broad protections of the CDA clearly establish "the right to publish the speech of others in the information age." The court dismissed a suit brought by three minors, who were victims of sexual trafficking,

USA PATRIOT Act
The Uniting and Strengthening America by Providing Appropriate Tools Required to Intercept and Obstruct Terrorism Act of 2001. The act gave law enforcement agencies greater authority to combat terrorism.

chilling effect
The discouragement of a constitutional right, especially free speech, by any government practice that creates uncertainty about the proper exercise of that right.

against an online advertising site.[137] The court said the difficult balance between protecting young women from "circumstances that evoke outrage" and protecting the freedom of speech advanced through online platforms must be struck in favor of the speech. The Supreme Court declined to review the case.[138]

A federal district court judge similarly held that Section 230 of the CDA protected Twitter from a claim that it had materially contributed to the spread of Islamic State propaganda that led to the murder of a contractor in Jordan.[139] The court dismissed the claim that Twitter's "refusal to take any meaningful action" to deter IS pro-terrorist posts made it liable for the murder.

SPEECH IN THE SCHOOLS

There is nothing in the wording of the First Amendment to suggest that it protects the rights of minors, public school students or campus media differently from the rights of others. However, U.S. society has asserted unique interests in protecting and educating its youth. Sometimes courts have accepted the idea that the nation's interest in developing its youth outweighs the free speech rights of public school students. Courts have struggled to determine both how and where to draw the line between advancing the important concerns of parents and educators and protecting the sometimes-conflicting rights of students to freedom of speech and association.

Nearly 40 years ago, the U.S. Supreme Court said students' free speech rights prevented schools from removing books from the school library simply because someone might find them offensive.[140] Over the objections of a library review committee, a school board removed 10 books from school libraries because some board members found them "objectionable," "anti-American, anti-Christian, anti-[Semitic] and just plain filthy."[141] Several students sued, and the Supreme Court said the book removal violated the First Amendment.

Although schools must ensure that curriculum is age appropriate and of good quality, schools may not constitutionally remove library books to placate a hypersensitive few. When the readings are optional, individual student freedom of choice prevails. The Court said that "access [to controversial materials] prepares students for active and effective participation in the pluralistic, often contentious society in which they will soon be adult members."[142] Decisions to remove books may not be made "in a narrowly partisan or political manner"[143] and are more likely to be constitutional if they advance a curricular purpose.

In 2012, a U.S. district court judge required a public high school to stop using an internet filtering program that eliminated websites that expressed pro-LGBTQ concepts and values.[144] The school's filter tagged anti-gay sites under "religion," which allowed access, but tagged pro-gay sites with "sex," which triggered blocking. "These filters are a new version of book-banning or pulling books off the shelf," a spokesperson for the American Library Association said.[145]

More than 75 years ago, the U.S. Supreme Court applied its doctrine that "[t]he right to speak and the right to refrain from speaking are complementary components of the broader concept of individual freedom of mind"[146] to students. Public school students who were

Jehovah's Witnesses challenged the mandatory flag salute and Pledge of Allegiance in school as a violation of their religious beliefs. In *West Virginia State Board of Education v. Barnette*, the Court agreed.[147] Despite the important role of public schools in teaching students civic values and responsibilities,[148] schools may not indoctrinate students into particular ideologies, the Court said.[149] In *Barnette*, the Court held that "[i]f there is any fixed star in our constitutional constellation, it is that no official, high or petty, can prescribe what shall be orthodox in politics, nationalism, religion or other matters of opinion or force citizens to confess by word or act their faith therein."[150]

Public Forum Analysis

The courts have used several different approaches to determine when student press and speech are protected. In many cases, the U.S. Supreme Court has viewed public schools and universities—including school-sponsored events, publications, funding and physical spaces—as limited public forums. Under public forum doctrine, and applying the *O'Brien* test (discussed in Chapter 2), schools may impose reasonable content-neutral time, place and manner regulations on student speech activities to advance educational objectives. What this means in practice is that schools and universities may adopt regulations to advance educational goals even if the rules incidentally limit students' and teachers' freedom of speech. School officials generally may not dictate the content of student speech except to prevent speech that would directly undermine the school's educational mission. Courts have upheld public school restrictions on students' clothing, the hours school facilities may be used by outsiders, the school-related expression of teachers and the content of school-sponsored student speech and publications.

In several other approaches, the Court looked to the age, impressionability and maturity of the students; the location of the expression; the content of the speech; and the specific educational goals of the institution to determine the case outcome. Political turbulence and social unrest play a part. As one Court observer noted, sometimes "the very concept of academic freedom is under fire."[151] Such case-specific decisions do not provide clear rules of law. The variety of tests yields different outcomes among primary, secondary and postsecondary schools as well as between a high school newspaper and a university student's speech during an open public debate.

The *Tinker* Test

If *Barnette* declared students' fundamental freedom from indoctrination, *Tinker v. Des Moines Independent Community School District* established school classes as a site that is "peculiarly the marketplace of ideas" where speech may be regulated only to prevent a "substantial disruption" to school activities.[152] The U.S. Supreme Court's *Tinker* test, as it is known, arose from a 1969 decision involving symbolic anti-war protest in school.

When a brother and sister in junior and senior high school wore black armbands, a popular protest to the Vietnam War, they were suspended for violating a new policy prohibiting black armbands. The students did not disrupt classes, and they sued, claiming the suspensions violated their right to free speech.

The Tinkers (Lorena, Paul and Mary Beth, left to right) speak with the press in 1969 after learning the U.S. Supreme Court upheld the teens' right to wear anti-war armbands in school.

Bettmann/Getty Images

In what some call "the most important Supreme Court case in history protecting the constitutional rights of students,"[153] the Court in *Tinker* agreed with the students. The Court held that the symbolic expression of the armbands was "akin to pure speech" and fully protected under the First Amendment.[154] When novel or deviant issues are expressed, the First Amendment must weigh heavily in favor of the expression and against the bureaucratic urge to suppress, the Court said. The Constitution does not allow officials to suppress student expression that is unpleasant or discomfiting.[155] Under the First Amendment, it is "unmistakable" that individuals do not "shed their constitutional rights to freedom of speech or expression at the schoolhouse gate."[156] Unless student expression substantially disrupts the school's educational activities, school administrators lack authority to regulate the speech, the Court said.[157]

For nearly four decades, the rule was clear: Only when speech inside or adjacent to the school during school hours disrupts school activities may it be punished.[158] Then the Court's ruling in *Morse v. Frederick* seemed to muddy the test. In *Morse*, the Court held that the "substantial disruption" rule established in *Tinker* was not limited to speech during school hours or in the school building.[159]

The case began when high school senior Joseph Frederick displayed a banner reading "Bong Hits 4 Jesus" during a school field trip. Frederick said he did it for a laugh and to get himself on TV. The school's principal, Deborah Morse, did not find it humorous and told him to remove the banner. When he refused, she tore down the sign and suspended him for violating a school policy that banned the advocacy of illegal drug use. Frederick sued, alleging that the principal had violated his right to free speech.

The district court sided with the principal, but the Ninth Circuit Court of Appeals reversed, ruling that school officials may not "punish and censor non-disruptive" speech by students at school-sponsored events simply because they object to the message. In a 5–4 ruling, the U.S. Supreme Court sided with the principal. The Court ruled that school officials may prohibit messages that advocate illegal drug use without running afoul of the First Amendment. For the majority, Chief Justice John Roberts wrote that students' First Amendment protection does not extend to speech that directly contravenes an important school policy. The Court reasoned that the "special environment" and the educational mandate of the schools permitted officials to prohibit student speech that raises a "palpable" danger to established school anti-drug policy.[160] The sanction was constitutional because it punished advocacy of illegal drug use.

In a critical concurrence, however, Justice Samuel Alito said student speech rights may be subject to infringement in schools because schools are "places of special danger" where mandatory attendance may subject students "to threats to their physical safety they would not otherwise face."[161] As Justice John Paul Stevens suggested in dissent, the resulting "ham-handed, categorical approach [to student freedom of speech] is deaf to the constitutional imperative to permit unfettered debate, even among high-school students."[162] It permits content-based

George (Jürgen) Wittenstein / akg-images

discrimination. Since *Morse*, courts have relied on it to uphold school policies that prohibit speech related and unrelated to illegal activities.[163]

The widely watched case of Taylor Bell, a high school senior in Mississippi, began when he posted rap lyrics on Facebook and YouTube intended to reach school officials. The lyrics alleged sexual misconduct with students by two named teachers and described violence against them. Bell said his charges against the teachers were true, and he was not at school and did not use school resources to post the lyrics. The Itawamba County School Board suspended and transferred Bell to another school for threatening, harassing, intimidating and making false claims against the teachers.[164] The trial court ruled that the school had the authority to punish Bell's speech, which he could reasonably foresee would substantially disrupt the school and did so.[165]

On appeal, a panel of the Fifth Circuit Court of Appeals relied on *Tinker* and ruled that Bell's off-campus speech from home outside of school hours was protected by the First Amendment because the school failed to show that it caused a substantial disruption. But rehearing the case of *Bell v. Itawamba County School Board* en banc, the Fifth Circuit affirmed Bell's sanctions and found that the description of violent acts against two named teachers was intended to reach the school and could reasonably be foreseen to cause a substantial disruption.[166] The U.S. Supreme Court declined to review the case.

In 2019, the U.S. Supreme Court denied certiorari to review the constitutionality of a Kentucky law that made it a crime to speak to a school employee in a way that "interferes with" school functions.[167] The speech at issue involved neither students nor issues of public interest. Johnathan Masters, a graduate student and future candidate for state lieutenant governor,[168] was found guilty of violating the law when he told a school principal he would "kick [the principal's] ass" after the principal refused to allow Masters to conduct a study of the 450 students in kindergarten through twelfth grade in the Cloverdale school.[169] Masters shouted at the principal in the foyer of the school and refused to leave despite the principal's repeated requests.

The Kentucky Court of Appeals reviewed Masters' $500 fine and guilty verdict under *Chaplinsky's* fighting words doctrine.[170] "Angrily telling someone you are going to physically harm them is precisely the type of speech that would incite a reasonable person to violence.

Student protest of social injustice has a long history. During World War II, Sophie Scholl (pictured center), her brother Hans and Christoph Probst were executed by the Nazis for their "White Rose Resistance" movement urging students to rise up against the Nazi regime.

Not only that, such a threat of physical force against a principal during the school day foreseeably triggers a safety protocol which disrupts the orderly function of the classroom.[171] Finding the law to be a reasonable time/place/manner restriction, the court said it was neither overbroad nor vague. It unanimously affirmed the lower court's ruling.

The *Fraser* Approach

Decades ago, the U.S. Supreme Court was asked to determine the limits of students' right to profane or offensive speech in public schools. The case of *Bethel School District v. Fraser* involved a speech by Matthew Fraser nominating a classmate for student government.[172] Employing a number of metaphors for male sexual prowess, Fraser addressed nearly 600 high school students, including some 14-year-olds, who were required to attend the school-sponsored assembly. The assistant principal said the speech violated a school policy prohibiting obscene speech that "materially and substantially interferes with the educational process." She suspended Fraser and prohibited his selection as graduation speaker.

Fraser challenged the action as a violation of his First Amendment rights. On review, the Supreme Court upheld the school's decision. The Court said that when student speech occurs during a school-sponsored event, the student's liberty of speech may be curtailed to protect the school's educational purpose, especially when young students are in the audience. This is particularly true if the forum for the student speech suggests that the student is speaking for the school. The *Fraser* decision held that eliminating vulgarity and profanity from school events advanced the duty of schools to "inculcate . . . habits and manners of civility."[173] Rather than view student First Amendment rights as paramount, the Court said it was "perfectly appropriate" for a school to impose student sanctions to disassociate the school from speech that threatened its core purpose.

The *Hazelwood* Test

Two years later, the U.S. Supreme Court reaffirmed school authority over school-sanctioned activities and speech. In this case, students in the journalism class at Hazelwood East High School in St. Louis, Mo., published a student newspaper, Spectrum, under the supervision of a faculty adviser who reviewed the content. The principal also reviewed each issue before publication, but school policy said students enjoyed freedom of "responsible" speech.

After the principal removed two pages of the newspaper that included one story about teen pregnancy at the school and a second about the impact of divorce on students at the school, student editors sued. The principal said the targeted stories invaded the privacy of students and parents interviewed and contained material inappropriate for younger students. Other inoffensive stories were also eliminated by removal of the pages to expedite printing before the school year ended. The trial court rejected the students' challenge, but the court of appeals reversed, saying the school could edit the newspaper's content only to avoid legal liability, not to advance grammatical, journalistic or social values.

In *Hazelwood School District v. Kuhlmeier*, the Supreme Court again reversed and said school administrators, not student reporters and editors, have authority to determine the appropriate content of a school-sponsored student newspaper.[174] When a school creates and

---

POINTS OF LAW

COURT REVIEW OF NON-UNIVERSITY-STUDENT SPEECH

U.S. Supreme Court decisions generally approach non-university-student speech cases in one of three ways:

1. Is the speech disruptive? If the speech disrupts the functioning of the public school or violates the rights and interests of other students, it may be regulated under *Tinker.*[xxiii]

2. Is the speech of low value? If the speech is lewd or if it conflicts with the school's pedagogical goals or public values, it may be regulated under *Fraser.*[xxiv]

3. Is the speech sponsored by the school or perceived to reflect the school's official position and endorsement? If the speech is closely associated with the school's activities, curriculum or policies, it may be regulated under *Hazelwood.*[xxv]

---

supervises a forum for student speech, such as a student assembly or a teacher-supervised student newspaper, the school endorses that speech and is not only permitted but required to control the content to achieve educational goals, the Court said.[175] Schools must exercise their supervisory function to promote a positive educational environment in all "school-sponsored . . . expressive activities that students, parents and members of the public might reasonably perceive to bear the imprimatur of the school."[176] In a footnote, however, the Court made clear that the decision did not apply to the university student press.[177]

Choosing the Proper Test

The *Morse* decision recognizing a school's authority to punish off-campus, school-related student speech led to conflicting rulings among U.S. circuit courts because it appeared to grant school officials new latitude to sanction nondisruptive speech. In recent years, courts of appeal demonstrate increased uncertainty about when *Tinker* applies and when *Fraser, Hazelwood* or *O'Brien* should dictate the outcome. For example, the Second Circuit Court of Appeals limited the application of *Tinker* to "a student's personal expression . . . [that] happens to occur on the school premises." It applied *Hazelwood* to rule that a middle school had authority to ban a class president from a scheduled speech unless she deleted a closing religious blessing because the speech constituted school-sponsored expression.[178]

The Third Circuit Court of Appeals applied forum analysis to find unconstitutional an elementary school ban on student nondisruptive distribution of materials from nonschool organizations.[179] In another case, the Third Circuit relied on *Fraser* to find that a middle school student had a good likelihood of winning a challenge to the school's prohibition of breast-cancer-awareness bracelets reading "i ♥ boobies! (KEEP A BREAST)."[180] The school had said the bracelets were "lewd, vulgar, profane or plainly offensive." But the court said they likely were protected speech because they were nondisruptive and discussed an important social issue.

The Tenth Circuit used *Tinker* as the basis for ruling that school officials did not violate the First Amendment when they prevented high school students from distributing rubber fetus dolls in school.[181] And, again applying *Tinker*, the Fourth Circuit upheld student punishment for wearing a Confederate flag T-shirt to school because "school officials could reasonably forecast" that the shirt "would materially and substantially disrupt the work and discipline of the school."[182] In direct conflict, the Seventh Circuit Court of Appeals summarily affirmed the right of students to wear T-shirts critical of homosexuality but noted that *Tinker*'s "substantial disruption test [has not] proved a model of clarity in its application." In a pair of rulings, the Third Circuit homed in on the difficulty of locating *Tinker*'s schoolhouse gate when a court must address the "metaphysical question of where [the] speech occurred when [the student] used the internet as the medium."[183]

Increased inconsistency among court decisions in the wake of the Fifth Circuit's 2015 ruling in *Morse* "highlight[s] the murky state of student speech law" and suggests that existing tests may be too imprecise and too malleable to address concerns about student speech in the web era.[184] The U.S. Supreme Court has not reviewed any of these cases. As a consequence, the standard for deciding the free speech rights of students in public schools is less than clear. In general, rules limiting student expression in and about public schools or school policies likely are constitutional if the policies neither (1) limit expressive content that is compatible with the school's educational priorities nor (2) target specific content without a strong educational justification.

The Supreme Court has refused to grant university administrators "the same degree of deference" it grants to high school administrators to regulate student expression[185] because college students are "less impressionable than younger students"[186] and because the special characteristics of public schools require that students' rights are "not automatically coextensive with the rights of adults in other settings."[187] The Court generally protects the free speech and free press rights of university students as an essential part of their educational experience. The university and, to some degree, its faculty control the content of the curriculum. Otherwise, university policies and procedures generally must provide a neutral platform for broad discussion of issues.[188]

Campus Speech

The U.S. Supreme Court has established that universities have a greater obligation to create and maintain forums for broad public discussion than do the public schools. In *Papish v. Board of Curators of the University of Missouri*, the Supreme Court established that "the mere dissemination of ideas—no matter how offensive to good taste—on a state university campus may not be shut off in the name alone of 'conventions of decency.'"[189] The Court said the university violated the First Amendment rights of 32-year-old journalism graduate student Barbara Papish when it expelled her for distributing an underground campus newspaper that contained a political cartoon depicting policemen raping the Statue of Liberty and the Goddess of Justice, and an article under the title, "M—f— Acquitted."

The Supreme Court has distinguished universities from public schools and held that a university's "mission is well served if students have the means to engage in dynamic discussions of philosophical, religious, scientific, social and political subjects in their extracurricular campus life outside the lecture hall."[190] As a consequence, public universities not only may but must support all messages without regard to content to enhance wide-open extracurricular debate and free speech interests.[191]

In 2019, the U.S. Supreme Court declined to review an appeal from a group of students who challenged University of South Carolina student speech and assembly policies both as applied and as facially unconstitutional.[192] University policies limit student speech to limited zones on campus, require advance authorization from the university and impose a vague nondiscrimination/nonharassment policy that prohibits "unwelcome" speech and "suggestive or insulting gestures or sounds." The university had permitted the group to assemble to display and discuss symbols, including a swastika, that had provoked campus controversies elsewhere, but had interviewed the group's leader briefly in response to student complaints about the event.

The Fourth Circuit Court of Appeals affirmed the trial court ruling that the administration's minimally intrusive questioning after the fact posed no threat to the group's First Amendment rights. The group lacked standing to present a challenge to hypothetical future application of the university's nondiscrimination policies.

Almost 25 years ago, the U.S. Supreme Court held that public universities must fund student groups on the basis of content-neutral policies.[193] When a university's funding "program [is] designed to facilitate private speech," the funding creates a public forum that prohibits university control of the content of the speech.[194] Writing in concurrence, Justice David Souter said the power of school authorities "to limit expressive freedom of students . . . is confined to high schools, whose students and their schools' relation to them are different and at least arguably distinguishable from their counterparts in college education."[195] Consequently, neither university administrators nor students who contribute fees for student activities may discriminate among student groups because of the ideas they express.[196]

The Supreme Court recently reshaped this concept when it ruled in *Christian Legal Society v. Martinez* that a California law school could deny funding and other benefits to an explicitly religious student group whose members were required to sign a statement of faith.[197] The school's failure to recognize Christian Legal Society as an official student group denied the group access to university recruitment fairs, bulk emails and posting on school bulletin boards—benefits that clearly implicate First Amendment rights. Yet the Court said the law school's denial based on its requirement that recognized student groups be open to "all comers" was a reasonable, viewpoint-neutral means to advance school interests in nondiscriminatory access for students. Alternative, nonuniversity means of communication "reduce[d] the importance of [university] channels" in reaching law school students and adequately protected the group's speech interests.[198]

In what some saw as a radical expansion of *Tinker*, the Court relied on it to defer to the judgment of law school administrators "in light of the special characteristics of the school environment."[199] Writing in dissent, Justice Samuel Alito concluded that after the decision there is "no freedom for expression that offends prevailing standards of political correctness in our country's institutions of higher learning."[200]

REAL WORLD LAW
ARE CAMPUSES FREE-SPEECH-FREE ZONES?

In 2019, U.S. President Donald Trump signed an executive order barring federal grants to universities that fail to "avoid creating environments that stifle competing perspectives."[xxvi] The order "encourage[d] institutions to foster environments that promote open, intellectually engaging and diverse debate" and extended the Constitution's free speech mandate to private universities that receive federal grants. It came after the president promised the Conservative Political Action Conference that he would address what he called a campus political climate that chills discourse.[xxvii] He said the order was intended to redress the "increasingly hostile" efforts of university "professors and power structures" to prevent students from "challenging far-left ideology."

In recent years, violent student protests, walkouts, sit-ins and canceled invitations have met proposed and actual events featuring speakers including Breitbart senior editor and "right-wing provocateur" Milo Yiannopoulos.[xxviii] Universities increasingly engage in what two First Amendment scholars have called "the new censorship."[xxix] They adopt broad anti-harassment and anti-discrimination policies, create "safe spaces" free from allegedly harmful verbal confrontation or "micro-aggressions" and advocate for "trigger warnings" on sensitive or potentially disturbing speech.

The chairman of the College Republican National Committee endorsed the president's executive order as "critical" because universities "have absolutely failed to protect free speech on campus." More negative responses included statements that the order was redundant, lacked any enforcement mechanisms, was vague and subjective, and represented federal micromanagement of university affairs.[xxx]

Although student fees or university allocations generally fund student newspapers and yearbooks in whole or in part, the Supreme Court generally has viewed campus publications as forums for student expression in which universities may not control content. "Colleges and universities are supposed to be bastions of unbridled inquiry and expression," as one writer put it, "but they probably do as much to repress speech as any other institution in young people's lives."[201] The author said a recent study found that only about one-third of students and fewer than one in five faculty members strongly agreed that it is "safe to hold unpopular positions on campus."

When Kansas State University officials confiscated a student yearbook they said contained some objectionable content, the en banc Sixth Circuit Court of Appeals ruled that the confiscation violated students' First Amendment rights.[202] Declining to apply *Hazelwood* because a university "yearbook [must] be analyzed as a limited public forum—rather than [the] nonpublic forum" of a high school newspaper, the court said the university had neither the need nor the authority to control the content of speech in the student yearbook.[203]

Despite the asserted differences between schools and universities, some courts apply *Hazelwood* to review restrictions on university-subsidized and -approved publications.[204] One case began when a dean at Governors State University in Illinois required her preapproval of content before publication of the student newspaper. Student editors sued, claiming the action violated their First Amendment rights. The Seventh Circuit Court of Appeals, using *Hazelwood*, held that the student newspaper was a limited-purpose public forum beyond the control of the university's administration.

The Ninth Circuit Court of Appeals found that editors of a conservative student newspaper at Oregon State University had a legitimate First Amendment claim to nondiscriminatory access to campus to distribute their publication.[205] The case involved an independent student newspaper distributed through campus newspaper boxes. Under a new unwritten policy allegedly intended to clean up campus, university employees removed this newspaper's distribution boxes, leaving those for USA Today and others. A written OSU policy established most of the campus as a public forum. The Ninth Circuit held that university constraints on free speech in the campus public forum were subject to the most stringent scrutiny. It held that the university's "standardless policy" unconstitutionally, purposefully and arbitrarily singled out the independent newspaper.

Several court decisions establish greater latitude for colleges to punish speech by students. In *Tatro v. University of Minnesota*, the Minnesota Supreme Court upheld university sanctions on a student for "satirical commentary and violent fantasy" she posted on Facebook about a school cadaver.[206] Students in anatomy lab were required to sign a policy that allowed only "respectful and discreet" comments about cadavers. On Facebook, the student said she liked working with cadavers because it provided opportunity for "lots of aggression to be taken out" with an embalming knife that she wanted to use to "stab a certain someone in the throat."[207] In response, the student received an F in the lab, was placed on probation and was required to have a psychiatric examination. She sued, arguing that the sanctions violated her freedom of speech.[208] The university said it had authority to regulate any student speech "reasonably related to legitimate pedagogical concerns."

Rather than rely on established tests to review the case, the state supreme court held that the university's action did not violate the First Amendment because the rules were "narrowly tailored and directly related to established professional conduct standards."[209] The court said the core mission of the university program was to instill professional standards of ethics and behavior in its students.[210] Therefore, the university could "constitutionally regulate off-campus conduct that violate[s] specific professional obligations," although it could not "regulate a student's personal expression at any time, in any place, for any claimed curriculum-based reason."[211]

Although the Minnesota court in *Tatro* emphasized the narrowness of its ruling, a growing number of federal appeals courts has upheld the authority of colleges to punish or even expel college students, especially graduate students, for speech that violates the "professional standards" of their chosen field.[212] These courts recognize that greater latitude is provided to college student speech than to the free expression of less mature students[213] but split on whether to apply *Hazelwood* to these university speech cases.[214]

The Ninth Circuit Court of Appeals also crafted its own test to review sanctions on university student speech related to professional standards. In *Oyama v. University of Hawaii*, the Ninth Circuit affirmed the constitutionality of the university's effective expulsion of a student based on his unprofessional and inappropriate speech.[215] The student was denied a student teacher placement because he made disparaging remarks about students with disabilities and said he favored consensual sexual relations with children. The student sued, saying the punishment violated his First Amendment rights.

AP Photo/Robert W. Klein

In the mid-1960s, Mario Savio, leader of the Berkeley Free Speech Movement, participates in massive student protests at the University of California, Berkeley that set off the free speech movement nationwide.

The Ninth Circuit said *Hazelwood* did not apply.[216] It relied heavily on *Tatro* and found the university's punishment constitutional because it "related directly to defined and established professional standards, was narrowly tailored to serve the University's foundational mission of evaluating [student] suitability for teaching and reflected reasonable professional judgment."[217]

In 2016, the Eighth Circuit Court of Appeals relied squarely on *Hazelwood* in deciding *Keefe v. Adams*.[218] After Craig Keefe posted angry comments on Facebook that made a fellow nursing student "extremely uncomfortable and nervous," school administrators removed Keefe from the nursing program for "behavior unbecoming of the profession and transgression of professional boundaries."[219] Turning *Hazelwood* on its head, the Eighth Circuit said a "university may have an even stronger interest in the content of its curriculum and imposing academic discipline than did the high school at issue in Hazelwood."[220] The court ruled that "college administrators and educators in a professional school have discretion to require compliance with recognized standards of the profession, both on and off campus, so long as their actions are reasonably related to legitimate pedagogical concerns."[221]

The Supreme Court denied certiorari in *Keefe*,[222] allowing this and other rulings to stand that "leave[] college students with diminished free-speech protection in all forums . . . if their speech can be deemed unprofessional" even when it does not substantially disrupt school activities,[223] according to experts.

Some university administrators try to influence the content of student media by pressuring faculty or staff advisers. In a recent example, the top editors of the University of Georgia's student newspaper resigned en masse, claiming nonstudent managers hired to oversee The Red and Black had interfered with their editorial autonomy.[224] A memo on content guidelines circulating among the paper's publishing board questioned the journalistic value of "content that catches people or organizations doing bad things." Within days of the student walkout, the university reiterated its support of student control of content and reinstated the student editors.[225]

In an earlier fight over university student newspaper content, a federal district court ruled that the First Amendment did not prohibit Kansas State University from removing and reassigning the adviser of The Collegian.[226] The adviser was dismissed amid controversy over the newspaper's coverage of campus diversity issues and events.[227] Student editors and the adviser sued, claiming that the adviser's removal was unconstitutional censorship. The head of the journalism school said a content analysis of the newspaper supported the adviser's removal,[228] and university administrators said budget concerns drove the decision.[229]

Speech Codes

In what some call a concession to political correctness[230] and others consider an import-ant step toward a more safe, tolerant and inclusive society,[231] universities across the United States began adopting and strengthening campus speech codes in the 1980s.[232] The codes vary widely but generally prohibit harassment, bigotry and discrimination on campus. Courts found the speech codes that targeted offensive or disfavored speech unconstitutional because they reduced exchange of ideas based on content.[233] As one federal district court wrote, "The Supreme Court has consistently held that statutes punishing speech or conduct solely on the grounds that they are unseemly or offensive are unconstitutionally overbroad."[234] Nonetheless, campus hate speech codes continue to be adopted.[235] One study found that despite declines, nearly 60 percent of the 400 universities examined maintained policies that "seriously infringe upon the free speech rights of students."[236] The universities argue that the codes are essential to protect civil discourse and advance their educational missions.

More recently, universities have revised and adopted anti-discrimination and anti-harassment policies that may implicate free speech.[237] The rules implement federal Title VII civil rights prohibitions against workplace harassment, hostile work environments[238] and discrimination.[239] In one on-point case, the University of Wisconsin defended its Design for Diversity by asserting that Title VII required it to regulate hostile academic environments. The federal district court disagreed and held that Title VII does not supersede the First Amendment.[240]

Faculty language that provokes student protest and outrage has led some universities to examine the boundary between faculty First Amendment freedoms and university priorities to provide a setting conducive to education and equity for all.[241] In 2018, a DePaul University law professor was investigated after a group of students complained the professor used "the N word" in a class about provocation and self-defense.[242] Some students had objected earlier to the professor's use of "retard," "faggot" and "bitch" in class. A University of Chicago law pro-fessor stopped using "the N word" in 2019 after his use of it in a class discussion about fighting words prompted student backlash and calls for sanctions. The university supported his right to use the term.[243]

EMERGING LAW

A pending lawsuit brought by those injured in the 2017 "Unite the Right" rally in Charlottesville, Va., against the rally organizers asks the court to decide the extent to which the First Amendment protects those who associate to later commit violence. The federal judge denied a motion from Unite organizers to quash subpoenas for discovery in the case.[244] The court accepted the "weighty" constitutional concerns raised by the Unite movement but said their attack on the plaintiffs and the resulting injuries were not accidental but a direct result of the plaintiffs' support for minorities. The First Amendment did not protect the defendants, who included members of the KKK, several neo-Nazi groups and other white supremacists, from facing charges that they conspired to commit violence.

Amid the "rise in violent extremism perpetrated by white nationalists"[245] who often display Confederate symbols, several states passed laws to remove historical monuments to the Confederacy.[246] In 2018, a federal district court in Louisiana refused to honor an injunction request from the United Daughters of the Confederacy to stop the removal of Confederate monuments in New Orleans.[247] In 2019, a court struck down a 2017 Alabama law prohibiting the alteration or removal of Confederate monuments, saying it unconstitutionally required citizens to associate with a state message supporting the Confederacy. "Just as the state could not force any particular citizen to post a pro-Confederacy sign in his or her front lawn, so too can the state not commandeer the city's property for the state's preferred message," the court said. The state said it would appeal the ruling.[248]

In a related Mississippi case, citizens sued the state arguing that the state flag bearing the Confederate emblem was "tantamount to hateful government speech [with] discriminatory intent and disparate impact."[249] The court said the Confederate emblem was a symbol "of slavery, lynchings, pain and white supremacy," but it refused to order the state to stop using the flag because the plaintiffs had failed to show that the flag caused an injury that could be legally remedied.[250] The Fifth Circuit Court of Appeals affirmed.[251]

CASES FOR STUDY

For study resources and a case archive, go to **edge.sagepub.com/medialaw7e.**

Thinking About It

The two case excerpts that follow highlight the U.S. Supreme Court's attempts to balance the First Amendment freedom of speech with concerns for educational goals and personal safety. Both cases help identify the parameters of First Amendment protection: The first, *Tinker*, clarifies the extent to which important competing values—in this case, education of the young—may limit the freedom of speakers. The second, *Elonis*, helps define when words that express ideas, even in artistic form, may lose constitutional protection because they threaten others and engender fear.

- Consider what each decision, as well as the two taken together, demonstrates about the different categories of speech in the U.S. Supreme Court's jurisprudence.

- In these two decisions defining the extent of First Amendment freedoms, does the Supreme Court focus on the nature of the speech, the intent of the law, the impact of the regulation or something else to reach its conclusion?

- To what extent does the Supreme Court's decision in *Tinker* turn on the category of speech, the type of speaker, the location of speech or other factors involved?

- Does *Elonis* provide a workable definition of true threats and a clear test to determine when such speech is unprotected?

Tinker v. Des Moines Independent Community School District
SUPREME COURT OF THE UNITED STATES
393 U.S. 503 (1969)

JUSTICE ABE FORTAS delivered the Court's opinion:

. . . The District Court recognized that the wearing of an armband for the purpose of expressing certain views is the type of symbolic act that is within the Free Speech Clause of the First Amendment. As we shall discuss, the wearing of armbands in the circumstances of this case was entirely divorced from actually or potentially disruptive conduct by those participating in it. It was closely akin to "pure speech" which, we have repeatedly held, is entitled to comprehensive protection under the First Amendment.

First Amendment rights, applied in light of the special characteristics of the school environment, are available to teachers and students. It can hardly be argued that either students or teachers shed their constitutional rights to freedom of speech or expression at the schoolhouse gate. This has been the unmistakable holding of this Court for almost 50 years. . . .

. . . On the other hand, the Court has repeatedly emphasized the need for affirming the comprehensive authority of the States and of school officials, consistent with fundamental constitutional safeguards, to prescribe and control conduct in the schools. . . . Our problem lies in the area where students in the exercise of First Amendment rights collide with the rules of the school authorities.

The problem posed by the present case . . . does not concern aggressive, disruptive action or even group demonstrations. Our problem involves direct, primary First Amendment rights akin to "pure speech."

The school officials banned and sought to punish petitioners for a silent, passive expression of opinion, unaccompanied by any disorder or disturbance on the part of petitioners. There is here no evidence whatever of petitioners' interference, actual or nascent, with the school's work or of collision with the rights of other students to be secure and to be let alone. Accordingly, this case does not concern speech or action that intrudes upon the work of the schools or the rights of other students. . . .

. . . Outside the classrooms, a few students made hostile remarks to the children wearing armbands, but there were no threats or acts of violence on school premises.

The District Court concluded that the action of the school authorities was reasonable because it was based upon their fear of a disturbance from the wearing of the armbands. But, in our system, undifferentiated fear or apprehension of disturbance is not enough to overcome the right to freedom of expression. Any departure from absolute regimentation may cause trouble. Any variation from the majority's opinion may inspire fear. Any word spoken, in class, in the lunchroom, or on the campus, that deviates from the views of another person may start an argument or cause a disturbance. But our Constitution says we must take this risk; and our history says that it is this sort of hazardous freedom—this kind of openness—that is the basis of our national strength and of the independence and vigor of Americans who grow up and live in this relatively permissive, often disputatious, society.

In order for the State in the person of school officials to justify prohibition of a particular expression of opinion, it must be able to show that its action was caused by something more than a mere desire to avoid the discomfort and unpleasantness that always accompany an unpopular viewpoint. Certainly where there is no finding and no showing that engaging in the forbidden conduct would "materially and substantially interfere with the requirements of appropriate discipline in the operation of the school," the prohibition cannot be sustained.

. . . [T]he record fails to yield evidence that the school authorities had reason to anticipate that the wearing of the armbands would substantially interfere with the work of the school or impinge upon the rights of other students. . . .

On the contrary, the action of the school authorities appears to have been based upon an urgent wish to avoid the controversy which might result from the expression, even by the silent symbol of armbands, of opposition to this Nation's part in the conflagration in Vietnam. It is revealing, in this respect, that the meeting at which the school principals decided to issue the contested regulation was called in response to a student's statement to the journalism teacher in one of the schools that he wanted to write an article on Vietnam and have it published in the school paper. (The student was dissuaded.)

It is also relevant that the school authorities did not purport to prohibit the wearing of all symbols of political or controversial significance. The record shows that students in some of the schools wore buttons relating to national political campaigns, and some even wore the Iron Cross, traditionally a symbol of Nazism. . . . Instead, a particular symbol—black armbands worn to exhibit opposition to this Nation's involvement in Vietnam—was singled out for prohibition. Clearly, the prohibition of expression of one particular opinion, at least without evidence that it is necessary to avoid material and substantial interference with schoolwork or discipline, is not constitutionally permissible.

In our system, state-operated schools may not be enclaves of totalitarianism. School officials do not possess absolute authority over their students. Students in school as well as out of school are "persons" under our Constitution. They are possessed of fundamental rights, which the State must respect, just as they themselves must respect their obligations to the State. In our system, students may not be regarded as closed-circuit recipients of only that which the State chooses to communicate. They may not be confined to the expression of those sentiments that are officially approved. In the absence of a specific showing of constitutionally valid reasons to regulate their speech, students are entitled to freedom of expression of their views. . . .

. . . A student's rights, therefore, do not embrace merely the classroom hours. When he is in the cafeteria, or on the playing field, or on the campus during the authorized hours, he may express his opinions, even on controversial subjects like the conflict in Vietnam, if he does so without "materially and substantially interfer[ing] with the requirements of appropriate discipline in the operation of the school" and without colliding with the rights of others. But conduct by the student, in class or out of it, which for any reason—whether it stems from time, place, or type of behavior—materially disrupts class work or involves substantial disorder or invasion of the rights of others is, of course, not immunized by the constitutional guarantee of freedom of speech.

Under our Constitution, free speech is not a right that is given only to be so circumscribed that it exists in principle but not in fact. Freedom of expression would not truly exist if the right could be exercised only in an area that a benevolent government has provided as a safe haven for crackpots. . . . [W]e do not confine the permissible exercise of First Amendment rights to a telephone booth or the four corners of a pamphlet, or to supervised and ordained discussion in a school classroom.

If a regulation were adopted by school officials forbidding discussion of the Vietnam conflict, or the expression by any student of opposition to it anywhere on school property except as part of a prescribed classroom exercise, it would be obvious that the regulation would violate the constitutional rights of students, at least if it could not be justified by a showing that the students' activities would materially and substantially disrupt the work and discipline of the school. In the circumstances of the present case, the prohibition of the silent, passive "witness of the armbands," as one of the children called it, is no less offensive to the Constitution's guarantees. . . .

JUSTICE POTTER STEWART, concurring:
Although I agree with much of what is said in the Court's opinion, and with its judgment in this case, I cannot share the Court's uncritical assumption that, school discipline aside, the First Amendment rights of children are coextensive with those of adults. . . . I continue to hold the view [that] . . . [a] State may permissibly determine that, at least in some precisely delineated areas, a child—like someone in a captive audience—is not possessed of that full capacity for individual choice which is the presupposition of First Amendment guarantees.

JUSTICE BYRON WHITE, concurring:

While I join the Court's opinion, I deem it appropriate to note, first, that the Court continues to recognize a distinction between communicating by words and communicating by acts or conduct which sufficiently impinges on some valid state interest. . . .

JUSTICE HUGO BLACK, dissenting:

The Court's holding in this case ushers in what I deem to be an entirely new era in which the power to control pupils by the elected "officials of state supported public schools . . ." in the United States is in ultimate effect transferred to the Supreme Court. The Court brought this particular case here on a petition for certiorari urging that the First and Fourteenth Amendments protect the right of school pupils to express their political views all the way "from kindergarten through high school." Here, the constitutional right to "political expression" asserted was a right to wear black armbands during school hours and at classes in order to demonstrate to the other students that the petitioners were mourning because of the death of United States soldiers in Vietnam and to protest that war which they were against. . . .

. . . [T]he crucial . . . questions are whether students and teachers may use the schools at their whim as a platform for the exercise of free speech—"symbolic" or "pure"—and whether the courts will allocate to themselves the function of deciding how the pupils' school day will be spent. While I have always believed that, under the First and Fourteenth Amendments, neither the State nor the Federal Government has any authority to regulate or censor the content of speech, I have never believed that any person has a right to give speeches or engage in demonstrations where he pleases and when he pleases. . . .

I think the record overwhelmingly shows that the armbands did exactly what the elected school officials and principals foresaw they would, that is, took the students' minds off their class work and diverted them to thoughts about the highly emotional subject of the Vietnam War. And I repeat that, if the time has come when pupils of state-supported schools, kindergartens, grammar schools, or high schools, can defy and flout orders of school officials to keep their minds

on their own schoolwork, it is the beginning of a new revolutionary era of permissiveness in this country fostered by the judiciary. . . .

It may be that the Nation has outworn the old-fashioned slogan that "children are to be seen, not heard," but one may, I hope, be permitted to harbor the thought that taxpayers send children to school on the premise that at their age they need to learn, not teach. . . . Iowa's public schools . . . are operated to give students an opportunity to learn, not to talk politics by actual speech, or by "symbolic" speech. And, as I have pointed out before, the record amply shows that public protest in the school classes against the Vietnam War "distracted from that singleness of purpose which the State [here Iowa] desired to exist in its public educational institutions." . . .

This case, therefore, wholly without constitutional reasons, in my judgment, subjects all the public schools in the country to the whims and caprices of their loudest-mouthed, but maybe not their brightest, students. I, for one, am not fully persuaded that school pupils are wise enough. . . . I wish, therefore, wholly to disclaim any purpose on my part to hold that the Federal Constitution compels the teachers, parents, and elected school officials to surrender control of the American public school system to public school students. I dissent.

JUSTICE JOHN HARLAN, dissenting:

I certainly agree that state public school authorities in the discharge of their responsibilities are not wholly exempt from the requirements of the Fourteenth Amendment respecting the freedoms of expression and association. At the same time I am reluctant to believe that there is any disagreement between the majority and myself on the proposition that school officials should be accorded the widest authority in maintaining discipline and good order in their institutions. To translate that proposition into a workable constitutional rule, I would, in cases like this, cast upon those complaining the burden of showing that a particular school measure was motivated by other than legitimate school concerns—for example, a desire to prohibit the expression of an unpopular point of view, while permitting expression of the dominant opinion.

Finding nothing in this record which impugns the good faith of respondents in promulgating the armband regulation, I would affirm the judgment below.

Elonis v. United States

SUPREME COURT OF THE UNITED STATES
135 S. Ct. 2001 (2015)

CHIEF JUSTICE JOHN ROBERTS delivered the opinion of the Court.

Federal law makes it a crime to transmit in interstate commerce "any communication containing any threat . . . to injure the person of another." 18 U. S. C. § 875(c). Petitioner was convicted of violating this provision under instructions that required the jury to find that he communicated what a reasonable person would regard as a threat. The question is whether the statute also requires that the defendant be aware of the threatening nature of the communication, and—if not—whether the First Amendment requires such a showing.

Anthony Douglas Elonis was an active user of the social networking web site Facebook. . . . In May 2010, Elonis' wife of nearly seven years left him, [and] . . . Elonis began "listening to more violent music" and posting self-styled "rap" lyrics . . . [that] included graphically violent language and imagery. This material was often interspersed with disclaimers that the lyrics were "fictitious," with no intentional "resemblance to real persons." Elonis posted an explanation to another Facebook user that "I'm doing this for me. My writing is therapeutic."

Elonis' co-workers and friends viewed the posts in a different light. Around Halloween of 2010, Elonis posted a photograph of himself and a co-worker at a "Halloween Haunt" event at the amusement park where they worked. In the photograph, Elonis was holding a toy knife against his co-worker's neck, and in the caption Elonis wrote, "I wish." . . . [The] chief of park security was a Facebook "friend" of Elonis, saw the photograph, and fired him.

In response, Elonis posted a new entry on his Facebook page:

"Moles! Didn't I tell y'all I had several? Y'all sayin' I had access to keys for all the f***in' gates. That I have sinister plans for all my friends and must have taken home a couple. Y'all think it's too dark and foggy to secure your facility from a man as mad as me? You see, even without a paycheck, I'm still the main attraction. Whoever thought the Halloween Haunt could be so f***in' scary?" . . .

Elonis' posts frequently included crude, degrading, and violent material about his soon-to-be ex-wife. Shortly after he was fired, Elonis posted an adaptation of a satirical sketch that he and his wife had watched together. In the actual sketch, called "It's Illegal to Say . . . ," a comedian explains that it is illegal for a person to say he wishes to kill the President, but not illegal to explain that it is illegal for him to say that. When Elonis posted the script of the sketch, however, he substituted his wife for the President. The posting was part of the basis for Count Two of the indictment, threatening his wife:

> "Hi, I'm Tone Elonis.
>
> Did you know that it's illegal for me to say I want to kill my wife? . . .
>
> It's one of the only sentences that I'm not allowed to say. . . .
>
> Now it was okay for me to say it right then because I was just telling you that it's illegal for me to say I want to kill my wife. . . .
>
> Um, but what's interesting is that it's very illegal to say I really, really think someone out there should kill my wife. . . .
>
> But not illegal to say with a mortar launcher.
>
> Because that's its own sentence. . . .
>
> I also found out that it's incredibly illegal, extremely illegal to go on Facebook and say

something like the best place to fire a mortar launcher at her house would be from the cornfield behind it because of easy access to a getaway road and you'd have a clear line of sight through the sun room. . . .

Yet even more illegal to show an illustrated diagram [of the house]. . . ."

The details about the home were accurate. At the bottom of the post, Elonis included a link to the video of the original skit, and wrote, "Art is about pushing limits. I'm willing to go to jail for my Constitutional rights. Are you?"

After viewing some of Elonis' posts, his wife felt "extremely afraid for [her] life." A state court granted her a three-year protection-from-abuse order against Elonis (essentially, a restraining order). Elonis referred to the order in another post on his "Tone Dougie" page, also included in Count Two of the indictment:

"Fold up your [protection-from-abuse order] and put it in your pocket

Is it thick enough to stop a bullet?

Try to enforce an Order

that was improperly granted in the first place

Me thinks the Judge needs an education

on true threat jurisprudence

And prison time'll add zeros to my settlement . . .

And if worse comes to worse

I've got enough explosives to take care of the State Police and the Sheriff's Department."

At the bottom of this post was a link to the Wikipedia article on "Freedom of speech." . . . That same month, . . . Elonis posted [this] entry . . . :

"That's it, I've had about enough

I'm checking out and making a name for myself

Enough elementary schools in a ten mile radius to initiate the most heinous school shooting ever imagined

And hell hath no fury like a crazy man in a Kindergarten class

The only question is . . . which one?"

. . . A grand jury indicted Elonis for making threats to injure . . . in violation of 18 U. S. C. §875(c). In the District Court, Elonis moved to dismiss the indictment for failing to allege that he had intended to threaten anyone. The District Court denied the motion, holding that Third Circuit precedent required only that Elonis "intentionally made the communication, not that he intended to make a threat." At trial, Elonis testified that his posts emulated the rap lyrics of the well-known performer Eminem . . . In Elonis' view, he had posted "nothing . . . that hasn't been said already." The Government presented as witnesses Elonis' wife and co-workers, all of whom said they felt afraid and viewed Elonis' posts as serious threats.

Elonis requested a jury instruction that "the government must prove that he intended to communicate a true threat." The District Court denied that request. The jury instructions instead informed the jury that

"A statement is a true threat when a defendant intentionally makes a statement in a context or under such circumstances wherein a reasonable person would foresee that the statement would be interpreted by those to whom the maker communicates the statement as a serious expression of an intention to inflict bodily injury or take the life of an individual."

The Government's closing argument emphasized that it was irrelevant whether Elonis intended the postings to be threats—"it doesn't matter what he thinks." A jury convicted Elonis . . . [and] sentenced [him] to three years, eight months' imprisonment and three years' supervised release.

Elonis renewed his challenge to the jury instructions in the Court of Appeals, contending that the jury should have been required to find that he intended his posts to be threats. The Court of Appeals disagreed, holding that the intent required by Section 875(c) is only the intent to communicate words that the defendant understands, and that a reasonable person would view as a threat.

We granted certiorari.

. . . This statute requires that a communication be transmitted and that the communication contain a threat. It does not specify that the defendant must have any mental state with respect to these elements. In particular, it does not indicate whether the defendant must intend that his communication contain a threat.

Elonis argues that the word "threat" itself in Section 875(c) imposes such a requirement. According to Elonis, every definition of "threat" or "threaten" conveys the notion of an intent to inflict harm. . . . For its part, the Government argues that Section 875(c) should be read in light of its neighboring provisions . . . [that] expressly include a mental state requirement of an "intent to extort." According to the Government, the[se] express "intent to extort" requirements . . . should preclude courts from implying an unexpressed "intent to threaten" requirement in Section 875(c).

. . . The most we can conclude from the language of Section 875(c) and its neighboring provisions is that Congress meant to proscribe a broad class of threats in Section 875(c), but did not identify what mental state, if any, a defendant must have to be convicted. . . .

The fact that the statute does not specify any required mental state, however, does not mean that none exists. We have repeatedly held that "mere omission from a criminal enactment of any mention of criminal intent" should not be read "as dispensing with it." This rule of construction reflects the basic principle that "wrongdoing must be conscious to be criminal." . . . The "central thought" is that a defendant must be "blameworthy in mind" before he can be found guilty. . . . Although there are exceptions, the "general rule" is that a guilty mind is "a necessary element in the indictment and proof of every crime." We therefore generally "interpret[] criminal statutes to include broadly applicable scienter requirements, even where the statute by its terms does not contain them."

This is not to say that a defendant must know that his conduct is illegal before he may be found guilty. The familiar maxim "ignorance of the law is no excuse" typically holds true. Instead, our cases have explained that a defendant generally must "know the facts that make his conduct fit the definition of the offense," even if he does not know that those facts give rise to a crime. . . .

[I]n *United States v. X-Citement Video* (1994), we considered a statute criminalizing the distribution of visual depictions of minors engaged in sexually explicit conduct. We rejected a reading of the statute which would have required only that a defendant knowingly send the prohibited materials, regardless of whether he knew the age of the performers. We held instead that a defendant must also know that those depicted were minors, because that was "the crucial element separating legal innocence from wrongful conduct."

When interpreting federal criminal statutes that are silent on the required mental state, we read into the statute "only that *mens rea* which is necessary to separate wrongful conduct from 'otherwise innocent conduct.'" . . .

Section 875(c), as noted, requires proof that a communication was transmitted and that it contained a threat. . . . The parties agree that a defendant under Section 875(c) must know that he is transmitting a communication. But communicating *something* is not what makes the conduct "wrongful." Here "the crucial element separating legal innocence from wrongful conduct" is the threatening nature of the communication. The mental state requirement must therefore apply to the fact that the communication contains a threat.

Elonis' conviction, however, was premised solely on how his posts would be understood by a reasonable person. Such a "reasonable person" standard is a familiar feature of civil liability in tort law, but is inconsistent with "the conventional requirement for criminal conduct—*awareness* of some wrongdoing." Having liability turn on whether a "reasonable person" regards the communication as a threat—regardless of what the defendant thinks—"reduces culpability on the all-important element of the crime to negligence," and we "have long been reluctant to infer that a negligence standard was intended in criminal statutes." Under these principles, "what [Elonis] thinks" does matter.

The Government is at pains to characterize its position as something other than a negligence standard, emphasizing that its approach would require proof that a defendant "comprehended [the] contents and context" of the communication. . . . Elonis can be convicted, the Government contends, if he himself knew the contents and context of his posts, and a reasonable person would have recognized that the posts would be read as genuine threats. That is a negligence standard.

In light of the foregoing, Elonis' conviction cannot stand. The jury was instructed that the Government need prove only that a reasonable person would regard Elonis' communications as threats, and that was error. Federal criminal liability generally does not turn solely on the results of an act without considering the defendant's mental state. That understanding "took deep and early root in American soil" and Congress left it intact here: Under Section 875(c), "wrongdoing must be conscious to be criminal." . . .

Our holding makes clear that negligence is not sufficient to support a conviction under Section 875(c), contrary to the view of nine Courts of Appeals. . . . The judgment of the United States Court of Appeals for the Third Circuit is reversed, and the case is remanded for further proceedings consistent with this opinion.

It is so ordered.

JUSTICE ALITO, concurring in part and dissenting in part.

. . . The Court's disposition of this case is certain to cause confusion and serious problems. . . . The Court holds that the jury instructions in this case were defective because they required only negligence in conveying a threat. But the Court refuses to explain what type of intent was necessary. Did the jury need to find that Elonis had the *purpose* of conveying a true threat? Was it enough if he *knew* that his words conveyed such a threat? Would *recklessness* suffice? The Court declines to say. Attorneys and judges are left to guess. . . .

This Court has not defined the meaning of the term "threat" in §875(c), but in construing the same term in a related statute, the Court distinguished a "true 'threat'" from facetious or hyperbolic remarks. In my view, the term "threat" in §875(c) can fairly be defined as a statement that is reasonably interpreted as "an expression of an intention to inflict evil, injury,

or damage on another." Conviction under §875(c) demands proof that the defendant's transmission was in fact a threat, *i.e.*, that it is reasonable to interpret the transmission as an expression of an intent to harm another. In addition, it must be shown that the defendant was at least reckless as to whether the transmission met that requirement. . . . I would hold that a defendant may be convicted under §875(c) if he or she consciously disregards the risk that the communication transmitted will be interpreted as a true threat. . . .

There remains the question whether interpreting §875(c) to require no more than recklessness with respect to the element at issue here would violate the First Amendment. . . .

Elonis argues that the First Amendment protects a threat if the person making the statement does not actually intend to cause harm. . . .

Elonis also claims his threats were constitutionally protected works of art. Words like his, he contends, are shielded by the First Amendment because they are similar to words uttered by rappers and singers in public performances and recordings. . . . But context matters. "Taken in context," lyrics in songs that are performed for an audience or sold in recorded form are unlikely to be interpreted as a real threat to a real person. Statements on social media that are pointedly directed at their victims, by contrast, are much more likely to be taken seriously. . . .

Threats of violence and intimidation are among the most favored weapons of domestic abusers, and the rise of social media has only made those tactics more commonplace. A fig leaf of artistic expression cannot convert such hurtful, valueless threats into protected speech. . . .

We have sometimes cautioned that it is necessary to "exten[d] a measure of strategic protection" to otherwise unprotected false statements of fact in order to ensure enough "'breathing space'" for protected speech. A similar argument might be made with respect to threats. But we have also held that the law provides adequate breathing space when it requires proof that false statements were made with reckless disregard of their falsity. Requiring proof of recklessness is similarly sufficient here.

Finally, because the jury instructions in this case did not require proof of recklessness, I would vacate the judgment below and remand for the Court of Appeals to decide in the first instance whether Elonis' conviction could be upheld under a recklessness standard.

JUSTICE THOMAS, dissenting.

We granted certiorari to resolve a conflict in the lower courts over the appropriate mental state for threat prosecutions under 18 U. S. C. §875(c). . . . Rather than resolve the conflict, the Court casts aside the approach used in nine Circuits and leaves nothing in its place. Lower courts are thus left to guess at the appropriate mental state for §875(c). All they know after today's decision is that a requirement of general intent will not do. But they can safely infer that a majority of this Court would not adopt an intent-to-threaten requirement, as the opinion carefully leaves open the possibility that recklessness may be enough.

This failure to decide throws everyone from appellate judges to everyday Facebook users into a state of uncertainty. . . . Because the Court of Appeals properly applied the general-intent standard, and because the communications transmitted by Elonis were "true threats" unprotected by the First Amendment, I would affirm the judgment below. . . .

Because §875(c) criminalizes speech, the First Amendment requires that the term "threat" be limited to a narrow class of historically unprotected communications called "true threats." To qualify as a true threat, a communication must be a serious expression of an intention to commit unlawful physical violence, not merely "political hyperbole"; "vehement, caustic, and sometimes unpleasantly sharp attacks"; or "vituperative, abusive, and inexact" statements. It also cannot be determined solely by the reaction of the recipient, but must instead be "determined by the interpretation of a *reasonable* recipient familiar with the context of the communication," lest historically protected speech be suppressed at the will of an eggshell observer. There is thus no dispute that, at a minimum, §875(c) requires an objective showing: The communication must be one that "a reasonable observer would construe as a true threat to another." And there is no dispute that the posts at issue here meet that objective standard. . . .

Our default rule in favor of general intent applies with full force to criminal statutes addressing speech. Well over 100 years ago, this Court considered a conviction under a federal obscenity statute that punished

anyone "'who shall knowingly deposit, or cause to be deposited, for mailing or delivery,'" any "'obscene, lewd, or lascivious book, pamphlet, picture, paper, writing, print, or other publication of an indecent character.'" In that case, as here, the defendant argued that, even if "he may have had . . . actual knowledge or notice of [the paper's] contents" when he put it in the mail, he could not "be convicted of the offence . . . unless he knew or believed that such paper could be properly or justly characterized as obscene, lewd, and lascivious." The Court rejected that theory . . .

Applying ordinary rules of statutory construction, I would read §875(c) to require proof of general intent. To "know the facts that make his conduct illegal" under §875(c), a defendant must know that he transmitted a communication in interstate or foreign commerce that contained a threat. . . . A defendant like Elonis, however, who admits that he "knew that what [he] was saying was violent" but supposedly "just wanted to express [him]self," acted with the general intent required under §875(c), even if he did not know that a jury would conclude that his communication constituted a "threat" as a matter of law. . . .

Requiring general intent in this context is not the same as requiring mere negligence. . . . [T]he defendant must *know*—not merely be reckless or negligent with respect to the fact—that he is committing the acts that constitute the . . . offense.

But general intent requires *no* mental state (not even a negligent one) concerning the "fact" that certain words meet the *legal* definition of a threat. . . .

Elonis also insists that we read an intent-to-threaten element into §875(c) in light of the First Amendment. But our practice of construing statutes "to avoid constitutional questions . . . is not a license for the judiciary to rewrite language enacted by the legislature." . . .

Elonis does not contend that threats are constitutionally protected speech, nor could he: "From 1791 to the present, . . . our society . . . has permitted restrictions upon the content of speech in a few limited areas," true threats being one of them. Instead, Elonis claims that only *intentional* threats fall within this particular historical exception. . . .

Elonis also insists that our precedents require a mental state of intent when it comes to threat prosecutions under §875(c). . . .

We generally have not required a heightened mental state under the First Amendment for historically unprotected categories of speech. For instance, the Court has indicated that a legislature may constitutionally prohibit "'fighting words,' those personally abusive epithets which, when addressed to the ordinary citizen, are, as a matter of common knowledge, inherently likely to provoke violent reaction," without proof of an intent to provoke a violent reaction. Because the definition of "fighting words" turns on how the "ordinary citizen" would react to the language, this Court has observed that a defendant may be guilty of a breach of the peace if he "makes statements likely to provoke violence and disturbance of good order, even though no such eventuality be intended," and that the punishment of such statements "as a criminal act would raise no question under [the Constitution]." . . . I see no reason why we should give threats pride of place among unprotected speech.

⑤SAGE edge™

Visit **edge.sagepub.com/medialaw7e** to help you accomplish your coursework goals in an easy-to-use learning environment.

[D]ebate on public issues should be uninhibited, robust and wide-open, and . . . it may well include vehement, caustic, and sometimes unpleasantly sharp attacks on government and public officials.

—U.S. Supreme Court Justice William Brennan[1]

Montgomery, Ala., police commissioner L.B. Sullivan (second from right) sued The New York Times for libel in the 1960s. The U.S. Supreme Court decision in *New York Times Co. v. Sullivan* is one of the most important legal cases in the history of U.S. constitutional law.

4

LIBEL AND EMOTIONAL DISTRESS
The Plaintiff's Case

. . . that a civil rights group buys space in a major national newspaper. Its full-page editorial calls attention to the plight of people engaged in nonviolent demonstrations. Some recent events are described. The overall thrust of the text is accurate, but it also contains some minor factual errors. The editorial is critical of how some public officials—police officers, in particular—handled one demonstration. Several public officials, including the police commissioner, believe the editorial damaged their reputations and sue for defamation. Given the factual errors in the text, should the plaintiffs win their lawsuit? Should it make any difference that they are public officials? Look for the answers to these questions when the case of *New York Times Co. v. Sullivan* is discussed later in this chapter and in an excerpt at the end of this chapter.

Libel law is meant to protect an individual's reputation. It allows a person who believes his or her reputation has been injured to file a claim against the party responsible, asking for monetary damages to compensate for harm and to restore his or her reputation.

The idea that a person's reputation is valuable and worth protecting is a centuries-old concept. Throughout the course of Western civilization, people have closely associated reputation with one's ability to participate in social and economic life.[2] "The right of a man to the protection of his own reputation from unjustified invasion and wrongful hurt reflects no more than our basic concept of the essential dignity and worth of every human being—a concept at the root of any decent system of ordered liberty," wrote former U.S. Supreme Court Chief Justice William Rehnquist.[3]

According to the U.S. Supreme Court, the common law of slander and libel is designed to achieve society's "pervasive and strong interest in preventing and redressing attacks upon reputation."[4] The challenge becomes "balanc[ing] the State's interest in compensating private individuals for injury to their reputation against the First Amendment interest in protecting this type of expression."[5]

One important consideration in libel claims is truth. Centuries ago, truthful statements that damaged reputation could be libelous. That is no longer the case.

The word "defamation" generally refers to false communication about another person that damages that person's reputation or brings him or her into disrepute. Both slander and libel are forms of defamation.

Historically, people associated "slander" with spoken words that damage reputation and "libel" with written defamation. The laws governing each are similar but distinct. The distinction between libel and slander is largely a historical artifact. Slander lawsuits rarely emerge today because most spoken word claims arise in the context of mass media.

The general purpose of libel laws is to allow people who are defamed to restore their reputations. Libel laws also serve as a deterrent. When a successful plaintiff—the party initiating the lawsuit—is awarded damages, three objectives are served: The plaintiff is compensated for his or her reputational and other losses, the defendant is punished, and the defendant and others are discouraged from committing the same kind of libelous conduct in the future. Thus, a societal benefit may result, particularly if as much attention is given to setting the record straight as was given to the reputation-damaging remarks.

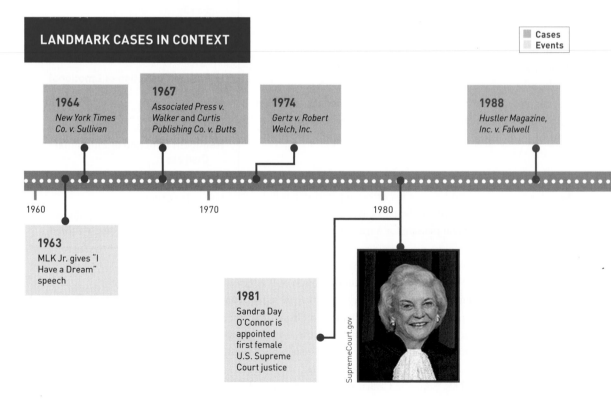

LANDMARK CASES IN CONTEXT

Cases
Events

1964
New York Times Co. v. Sullivan

1967
Associated Press v. Walker and Curtis Publishing Co. v. Butts

1974
Gertz v. Robert Welch, Inc.

1988
Hustler Magazine, Inc. v. Falwell

1960

1970

1980

1963
MLK Jr. gives "I Have a Dream" speech

1981
Sandra Day O'Connor is appointed first female U.S. Supreme Court justice

SupremeCourt.gov

A BRIEF HISTORY

Western civilization's earliest recorded prosecution for reputation-damaging remarks is arguably the trial and execution of Socrates in 399 B.C. In response to charges of slandering Greek gods and corrupting Athens youth, the philosopher was brought before a public court. He admitted his "slanderous" teachings and, by a vote of 277 to 224, was found guilty. Socrates accepted his execution to dramatize the primacy of the life of the mind and the need for freedom of thought.[6]

The word "libel" means "little book" in Latin. The legal term comes from the ancient Roman practice of publishing booklets that one Roman used to defame another. Although ancient Greek as well as Roman law contributed to the development of libel law in Western societies, the English common law is where American libel law finds its most significant roots.

In 15th-century England, one of two courts heard defamation complaints: the court of common law or the infamous court of the Star Chamber. The court of the Star Chamber evolved from the meetings of the king's royal council. Established in 1487, it was named after the star painted on the ceiling of the room in which it met. In the early 1600s, the court of the Star Chamber declared libel a criminal offense because it tended to cause breach of the peace. If the libel was "against a magistrate, or other public person, it [was] a greater offence."[7]

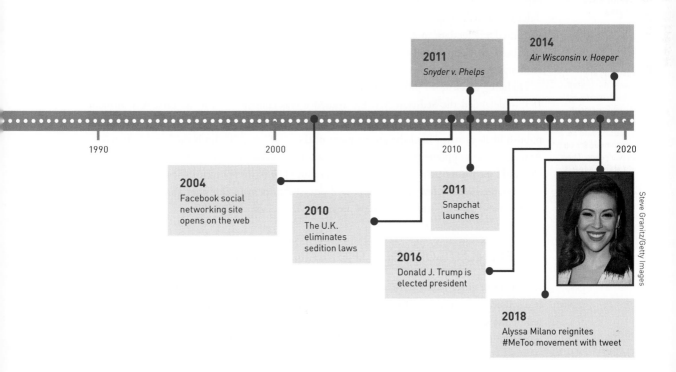

2014
Air Wisconsin v. Hoeper

2011
Snyder v. Phelps

1990   2000   2010   2020

2004
Facebook social networking site opens on the web

2010
The U.K. eliminates sedition laws

2011
Snapchat launches

2016
Donald J. Trump is elected president

2018
Alyssa Milano reignites #MeToo movement with tweet

Steve Granitz/Getty Images

The court of the Star Chamber generally viewed written defamation as more serious than spoken. Penalties for defamation included the possibility that the defamer "may be punished by fine and imprisonment, and if the case be exorbitant, by pillory and loss of his ears."[8] The Star Chamber was disbanded in 1641, and common law courts resumed their jurisdiction over defamation cases.[9]

Eighteenth-century English judge Sir William Blackstone and his "Commentaries on the Law of England" played a major role in the development of law in the United States. Libel law is no exception. Punishment for defamation was not inconsistent with the concept of freedom of the press. A free press, Blackstone wrote, "consists in laying no previous restraints upon publications, and not in freedom from censure for criminal matter when published."[10] Anyone can express his sentiments to the public, he added, "but if he publishes what is improper, mischievous, or illegal, he must take the consequences of his own temerity."[11]

damages
Monetary compensation that may be recovered in court by any person who has suffered loss or injury. Damages may be compensatory for actual loss or punitive as punishment for outrageous conduct.

Those consequences were to take the form of monetary **damages** sought by a plaintiff in compensation for a tarnished reputation. As a chief justice of the U.S. Supreme Court later described its evolution, "Defamation law developed not only as a means of allowing an individual to vindicate his good name, but also for the purpose of obtaining redress for harm caused by such statements."[12]

That legal principle was brought to the American colonies and into the states after independence. But England also provided America with legal theories that were less desirable in a republic committed to individual freedoms. Among them was the concept of seditious libel. At various times throughout American history, authorities have been especially sensitive to criticism of the government. In response, laws have been passed to criminalize such expression. For example, the **Sedition Act of 1798** made it a crime to write "any false, scandalous and malicious" statements against either the president or Congress.[13] While the act permitted a defendant to escape penalty by proving the truth of the writing, and juries were permitted to decide critical questions of law and fact, the law was intended to silence critics of entrenched political powers.

Sedition Act of 1798
Federal legislation under which anyone "opposing or resisting any law of the United States, or any act of the President of the United States," could be imprisoned for up to two years. The act also made it illegal to "write, print, utter, or publish" anything that criticized the president or Congress.

Echoing Blackstone, John Marshall—chief justice of the United States between 1801 and 1835—defended the Sedition Act. He argued it was consistent with the First Amendment because it did not impose a prior restraint.[14] "It is known to all," he wrote, that those who publish libels or who "libel the government of the state" may "be both sued and indicted."[15] Among the act's opponents was James Madison, the principal author of the First Amendment: "It would seem a mockery to say that no laws should be passed preventing publications from being made, but that laws might be passed punishing them in case they should be made."[16] Madison and his supporters ultimately prevailed. The act expired in 1801.

THE ELEMENTS OF LIBEL: THE PLAINTIFF'S CASE

Libel is a tort governed by state law, with some protection under the First Amendment, which is discussed later in this chapter. Just as defamation was recognized first as a harm committed by the spoken word and later as one that could also be committed through writing, the opportunities for libelous speech have increased exponentially with the development of communication technologies. Because of the ease and speed of communicating in today's global digital age, possibilities for libel are on the rise.

Libel law serves to check the power of the media by opening its newsgathering and decision-making processes to public scrutiny and accountability. Although the best cure for bad speech may be more speech,[17] contemporary American society is often unwilling to rely only on corrective speech as a remedy for false and damaging statements to reputations. Libel law is one of the checks and balances in that process. The right of individuals to be secure in their reputations is weighed against the rights of others to be heard on issues of importance.

Unlike in the era of common law libel, when the defendant was required to prove that a defamatory statement was true, the **burden of proof** is now on the plaintiff. To win, the plaintiff must prove that all of the required elements apply to the allegedly libelous material. Each of these elements requires definition and explanation.

Statement of Fact

In order to be libelous, a statement must make an assertion of fact. During the 2016 presidential election, many politicians and their partisan supporters argued about facts and sometimes presented opinions as facts. The hashtag #alternativefacts went viral in 2016 after President Donald Trump's senior adviser used the phrase in response to allegations that the White House was providing false information to the public.

The dictionary defines a fact as "a piece of information presented as having objective reality"[18] and opinion as "a view, judgment or appraisal formed in the mind about a particular matter; a belief stronger than impression and less strong than positive knowledge."[19] Understanding the difference between fact and opinion is important because an expression of opinion cannot be libelous.

burden of proof The requirement for a party to a case to demonstrate one or more claims by the presentation of evidence. In libel law, the plaintiff has the burden of proof.

REAL WORLD LAW
WHAT IS FAKE NEWS?

The phrase "fake news" is now a common part of American political discourse, and while it is not a new concept, it is often so broadly applied that its meaning can get lost. Fake news is misinformation, or intentionally false information intended to mislead. President Donald Trump falsely claims he invented the term.[i] According to Merriam-Webster, the term was generally used in the 19th century by local newspapers to identify misinformation. In the 16th century, people used the term "false news."[ii] The Nazis used the German equivalent "Lügenpresse" in the 1930s to advance their propaganda campaigns.[iii]

Political actors and movements around the globe have breathed new life into the phrase in an attempt to undermine public confidence in mainstream news media and advance their own political agendas. Others correctly use the term to identify misleading false information and propaganda as well as link the concept to fake social media accounts designed to spread misinformation. Facebook and Twitter now report regularly on how they are trying to stop the spread of fake news from fake accounts and profiles on their platforms.[iv]

What is the best antidote to fake news? "A free and independent press . . . is the best means to ensure an informed citizenry, and to hold institutions and individuals to account," according to one First Amendment expert.[v]

How can you tell the difference between fact and opinion? If you write that in January 2019 the U.S. unemployment rate was 4 percent, you are offering an assertion of fact that can be proven true or false. If you write that you think the U.S. unemployment rate is too high, that is opinion. Opinion is not libelous because an opinion cannot be false—and falsity is another requirement of the plaintiff's libel case. (The opinion defense is explained in detail in Chapter 5.) For now, it is enough to understand that whether material can be considered an expression of opinion requires a rigorous analysis.

Publication

In order for a statement to be libelous, the plaintiff must show that the statement was made public. To satisfy this standard, only one person in addition to the source and subject of the allegedly defamatory statement must have seen or heard the information in question. When information is presented through the mass media, including social media, publication is presumed. Under the law of libel, material is considered published any time it is printed in a periodical, broadcast over the airwaves or posted on the internet.

Republication. Repeating libelous information is as potentially harmful to someone's reputation as publishing it in the first place. Thus, the person who republishes can be held just as responsible as the originator. Republishing libelous information is seen as a new publication in the eyes of the law. This is true even when careful attribution occurs. The law's rationale is to prevent individuals or the media from freely committing defamation simply by attributing the libelous material to another source.

In a 2010 New Jersey defamation lawsuit, the chief executive officer of a company filed a defamation claim against eBossWatch.com, which published an annual "America's Worst Bosses" list on which he was named. The original defamation claim was dismissed, but when the same website years later published a story about the lawsuit, the CEO again sued for defamation.[20] The trial court held the story to be a second publication, but an appellate court disagreed and noted that minor modifications to the story did not transform the article into a new publication. On appeal in 2018, the New Jersey Supreme Court held that the article's change was material and substantive and that it did constitute a republication, although it also affirmed the case's dismissal on different grounds.[21]

Republication on the internet illustrates how new technologies and platforms can open the door to refinements in the law. For example, in New York, a judge held that new comments made to older messages in order to return them to prominent positions on a website to keep a conversation alive—"bump messages"—do not count as republication in the context of libel.[22] However, a 2016 decision in Utah held that a defendant did meet the requirement of republication when she updated text on a website on which she had posted numerous defamatory statements about a residential youth treatment facility.[23]

In another case, a New York trial court held that adding a "share button" to online archived articles is not republication, even though the buttons facilitate content sharing. The court based its decision on the idea that the target audience, newspaper readers, did not change with the addition of the button. Moreover, readers always had the option to share even without the button; they could print, email or distribute articles in other ways. The court said the use of a share button was "akin to a delayed circulation of the original rather than republication."[24]

Is retweeting a form of republication? Many legal experts say that retweets are protected as long as new defamatory remarks are not added, although this is still an open legal question and no cases have yet determined this. Courts now generally apply the same logic to hyperlinking. The New York Court of Appeals, the state's highest court, has held that continuous access to an article posted via hyperlinks is not a republication. This typically changes, however, if new content is added. For example, a New York district court held that a software company could proceed with a defamation claim after a computer support website added potentially defamatory statements to a post that contained an old hyperlink.[25]

In an age of rapidly changing communication technologies, the republication rule would seem at odds with the wish to promote the free flow of ideas—a tenet of the First Amendment. Section 230 of the **Communications Decency Act**, the fair report privilege, the neutral reportage defense and the wire service defense, all discussed in Chapter 5, confront this issue.

Vendors and Distributors. Publisher liability in libel is determined by whether publishers are or should be aware of the material they disseminate, possibly including a presumption that they have read and edited the content. To prove publication, a libel plaintiff must show not just that libelous material was published; the plaintiff must also identify a specific person, group or business responsible for the publication. Among those who are granted a republication exception are vendors and distributors. For example, booksellers like Amazon.com, libraries and newsstands are not publishers of the works they stock. They cannot be sued for libel based on the works they make available because they do not control the content of those products.

Before passage of the Communications Decency Act more than 20 years ago, internet service providers were regarded as both publishers[26] and distributors of information that others published.[27] This issue was resolved when Section 230 of the CDA was tested by a libel claim against AOL (then America Online, Inc.).[28]

Kenneth Zeran claimed AOL injured his reputation by not quickly removing false information about him. His claim arose after an anonymous AOL user posted an advertisement for T-shirts with images and a slogan glorifying the 1995 Oklahoma City bombing. The ad included Zeran's telephone number. Zeran said he had no knowledge of the ad. "By its plain language, Section 230 creates a federal immunity to any cause of action that would make service providers liable for information originating with a third-party user of that service," the First Circuit Court of Appeals noted.[29] The court said Section 230 prevents courts from considering an ISP a publisher[30] because Congress recognized that to do so would create an "obvious chilling effect" on speech.[31]

Nearly a decade after the *Zeran* decision, the First Circuit Court of Appeals ruled that the definition of "provider of an interactive computer service" includes service providers who do not directly connect their users to the internet.[32] Unlike AOL in the *Zeran* case, the defendant

Communications Decency Act
The part of the 1996 Tele-communications Act that largely attempted to regulate internet content. The Communications Decency Act was successfully challenged in *Reno v. American Civil Liberties Union* (1997).

here only managed a series of websites. The court reasoned that narrowing protection only to services that provide internet access undermined congressional intent and held that Section 230 immunity should be broadly construed.[33] (Section 230 as a defense is discussed in detail in Chapter 5.)

Unknown Publisher/Anonymous Speech.   Sometimes material is published, but the speaker is unknown. A hallmark of the internet and interaction through some mobile applications and social media is anonymous communication. The ability to speak anonymously can allow ideas and viewpoints that otherwise might remain unexpressed to enter the marketplace of ideas by reducing the fear of reprisal. "Under our constitution, anonymous pamphleteering is not a pernicious, fraudulent practice, but an honorable tradition of advocacy and of dissent," U.S. Supreme Court Justice Antonin Scalia once wrote. "Anonymity is a shield from the tyranny of the majority."[34] As Chapter 2 notes, the Supreme Court has recognized a First Amendment right to anonymous speech. But what happens when the wish to protect anonymous speech collides with the imperative of holding people accountable for libelous expression?

Generally speaking, state courts have taken three approaches to "unmasking" anonymous posters on the internet in libel cases. In *Dendrite v. John Doe #3*, a court in New Jersey held that the plaintiff must present the court with prima facie ("on its face") evidence sufficient to prove the plaintiff has a case that can withstand a motion to dismiss. A motion to dismiss is a formal request to the court to dismiss a case. It is often filed immediately by a defendant after a plaintiff files suit, although it may be filed at any time during legal proceedings by either party.

REAL WORLD LAW
THE PRESIDENT AND DEFAMATION

In 2018, a New York appeals court held that the defamation lawsuit against President Donald Trump brought by Summer Zervos, a former contestant on "The Apprentice," could proceed. President Trump's lawyers argued that the president cannot be sued for unofficial acts while in office. The New York court disagreed and applied the U.S. Supreme Court decision in *Clinton v. Jones* as precedent.[vi] That case involved a sexual harassment lawsuit brought against then-President Bill Clinton while in office. The Supreme Court held in *Clinton* that a sitting president does not have temporary immunity from civil litigation while in office.[vii] On further appeal in 2019, the decision to let the case proceed was upheld. A five-justice panel wrote, "We reject defendant President Trump's argument that the Supremacy Clause of the United States Constitution prevents a New York State court—and every other state court in the country—from exercising its authority under its state constitution."[viii]

Zervos has accused President Trump of sexual misconduct. When President-elect Trump publicly denied her claims, he also suggested she made up her story for publicity. The court held that his statements were clearly susceptible to defamatory meaning and cited precedent for defamation claims maintained against people who call purported victims of sexual assault liars.[ix] The outcome of the case is still pending.

In a separate case, adult film actress Stephanie Clifford lost her defamation lawsuit against Trump on grounds that an allegedly defamatory tweet about her was rhetorical hyperbole (see Chapter 5).[x]

President Donald Trump (left) faces defamation allegations from former "The Apprentice" contestant Summer Zervos (right).

Grounds for dismissing a lawsuit are determined by each jurisdiction's laws. If the plaintiff's case can withstand a motion to dismiss, then the court should balance the First Amendment rights of the anonymous speaker against the strength of the prima facie case and the need to disclose the anonymous speaker.[35]

Two recent cases in California illustrate how the *Dendrite* holding may be applied. In one case, Yelp, Inc. petitioned an appeals court to overturn a court order that required the company to produce documents that Yelp argued would reveal the identity of an anonymous reviewer.[36] The court agreed that Yelp had standing to assert a First Amendment right on behalf of its anonymous reviewer, but it also said the plaintiff succeeded in making a **prima facie** showing that the Yelp review in question was actionable. The prima facie showing established that the plaintiff was entitled to discovery of the reviewer's identity because the review could constitute defamation.[37]

Another case involved the Glassdoor job recruiting and review website. A software and email archiving company filed a defamation lawsuit against several unnamed individuals based on critical reviews posted on Glassdoor's website.[38] ZL Technologies, Inc. subpoenaed Glassdoor records to identify and provide contact information for the anonymous posters and Glassdoor resisted. The trial court denied ZL's motion to compel Glassdoor to provide the information, noting that the defendants had a First Amendment right to remain anonymous.[39] An appeals court disagreed. In addition to applying *Dendrite* and holding that ZL Technologies had made a prima facie showing of an actionable claim, the appeals court added a new requirement. The court said that reasonable efforts must be made to notify the anonymous defendants before they are unmasked in order to give them an opportunity to respond.[40]

prima facie
Latin for "at first look," or "on its face"; evidence before a trial that is sufficient to prove the case unless substantial contradictory evidence is presented.

Virginia takes a different approach. To unmask anonymous users, plaintiffs must show they have a legitimate, good faith basis to claim an actionable offense within the court's jurisdiction, and the identity of the anonymous speaker is central to advancing their case.[41] Most other state courts have rejected this standard because it does not offer the speaker sufficient First Amendment protection.

A third approach is the most protective of anonymous speech. The Delaware Supreme Court has held that a defamation plaintiff must "satisfy a 'summary judgment' standard before obtaining the identity of an anonymous defender." Under a summary judgment standard, a judge must view certain points in the light most favorable to the defendant and make a judgment from that perspective. The Delaware Supreme Court wrote, "Indeed, there is reason to believe that many defamation plaintiffs bring suit merely to unmask the identities of anonymous critics. . . . The goals of this new breed of libel action are largely symbolic, the primary goal being to silence John Doe and others like him."[42]

Identification

A libel plaintiff is required to show that he or she was the specific person whose reputation was harmed or, possibly, that he or she was a member of a small group that was defamed. Early common law asked whether the statement was "of and concerning" the plaintiff—a standard still employed. This test asks whether the statement reasonably refers to the plaintiff. People can be identified by name, by title, through photographic images or within a context in which their identity can be inferred. Someone other than the plaintiff and the defendant must recognize that the content is about the plaintiff. In addition, the intention of the publisher is not critical to this determination; a publisher may not have intended to implicate the plaintiff, but identification might have occurred nonetheless.

Group Identification. In some circumstances, libel law allows any member of a group to sue when the entire group has been libeled. The key is whether in libeling the group, the information is also "of and concerning" the specific individual bringing the lawsuit. In general, the smaller the group, the more likely it is that its individual members have been identified. According to one authority, "It is not possible to set definite limits as to the size of the group or class, but the cases in which recovery [of damages] has been allowed usually have involved numbers of 25 or fewer."[43]

A court will evaluate each situation on its specific facts. Some rulings in this category indicate that if a group has fewer than 25 members, any one of them could file a successful libel claim, depending on the libelous material in question. As a group grows in size, the inclusiveness of the language that allegedly libeled its members becomes a factor.[44]

In 2014, after Rolling Stone magazine published and then retracted an article titled "A Rape on Campus," several defamation lawsuits emerged. The article detailed a gang rape at a University of Virginia fraternity house that was later determined to be fabricated. The most recently settled defamation lawsuits focused on group libel and identification.

Three former members of the Phi Kappa Psi fraternity sued the magazine, its owner and the article's author for defamation, claiming that the article identified them individually as participants in the alleged rape and collectively as members of the fraternity where the alleged rape occurred. While they were not named in the article, they argued that anyone at the University of Virginia familiar with the fraternity would have been able to identify them. For example, the article detailed the setting of the rape in a room on top of a staircase and claimed one alleged rapist was an avid swimmer.[45]

A district court dismissed the lawsuit, but the Second Circuit Court of Appeals held that two of the three men and the fraternity could continue their lawsuit. The court said one of the men lived in the only room on the second floor of the fraternity house that met the description of the room where the alleged rape occurred. A second plaintiff was an avid swimmer who had a prominent role in the fraternity's initiation process, and that process was implicated in the article. The circuit court agreed with the lower court that the third man's claim of identification based on the description that he frequently rode his bike to campus was not sufficient to identify him. Because the article suggested that all members of the fraternity knew about the alleged rape, even if they did not participate, the group libel claim made by the members of the fraternity was allowed to proceed on small group defamation theory.[46] The case was settled out of court.[47]

Rolling Stone magazine recently settled the final defamation lawsuit tied to its 2014 article about a gang rape at the University of Virginia that proved to be false.

Defamation

Another element in the plaintiff's case involves the allegedly libelous content itself. In order for the plaintiff to win, the material at issue must be defamatory. The challenge is defining and establishing a standard of defamation. The standard begins with the premise that when reputation is damaged, defamation occurs.

Some words by themselves may qualify as defamatory. Some kinds of statements convey such defamatory meaning that they are considered to be defamatory as a matter of law; on its face and without further proof, the content is defamatory. This is **libel per se**. Libel per se typically involves accusations of criminal activity, unethical activity or practice, unprofessional behavior and/or immoral actions (sometimes called moral turpitude, which is conduct contrary to community standards).

libel per se
A statement whose injurious nature is apparent and requires no further proof.

For example, in 2018, the New York Supreme Court held that HIV infection fell under the "loathsome disease" category of libel per se. A model posed for photos on an unrelated topic, and two years later, her image was sold to Getty Images, which then licensed one of the photos to the New York City Division of Human Rights. The DHR used the image in print and digital ads about HIV/AIDS that read, "I AM POSITIVE (+)" and "I HAVE RIGHTS" along with additional information. The appeals court noted that while it did not consider HIV loathsome, it acknowledged that people who suffer from an HIV diagnosis are often ostracized and targets of discrimination. The court granted summary judgment for defamation per se.[48]

Distinguishing defamatory from nondefamatory statements is more art than science. Within various contexts, the following definitions of "defamatory" have been offered:

- Words or images that are false and injurious to another

- Words or images that expose another person to hatred, contempt or ridicule

- Words or images that tend to harm the reputation of another so as to lower him or her in the estimation of the community or deter third persons from associating or dealing with him or her[49]

- Words or images that subject a person to the loss of goodwill or confidence from others[50]

- Words or images that subject a person to scorn or ridicule

- Words or images that tend to expose a person to hatred, contempt or aversion, or tend to induce an evil opinion of him or her in the minds of a substantial number of people in the community

- Words or images that tend to prejudice someone in the eyes of a substantial and respectable minority of the community[51]

Whatever the standard, courts traditionally have said that the matter must be viewed from the perspective of "right-thinking" people.[52] Some examples of recent cases that explored the meaning of defamation include a New York appellate court's decision that a false allegation of homosexuality is no longer defamatory per se. The court cited New York's Marriage Equality Act as evidence of changing attitudes toward homosexuality.[53] Rhode Island's Supreme Court held that deliberately and falsely stating that a political event is "off the record" is not defamatory. A plaintiff argued that a newspaper portrayed him falsely as "someone to be

REAL WORLD LAW
LESSONS LEARNED FROM THE ROLLING STONE DEFAMATION LAWSUIT

In 2016, a jury awarded a University of Virginia administrator $3 million in damages for a discredited Rolling Stone article, "A Rape on Campus." The jury ordered both the magazine and the reporter to pay damages. The article relied on a single source when it reported the story of a gang rape at a fraternity party. The rape never happened.[xi]

In 2015, a report by the Columbia University Graduate School of Journalism called the article a "failure of journalism." This resulted in Rolling Stone retracting the story and removing it from its website.[xii]

Libel defense attorneys suggested that several lessons came from the Rolling Stone case:[xiii]

- Reporters should be aware that what they say in post-publication interviews and on their

social media feeds can bring the possibility of individual liability in defamation cases, as it did in this case. Media defense attorneys discourage reporters from talking on the record about their work.

- After concerns about the original article came to light, Rolling Stone published two editor notes to clarify/apologize. These notes generated additional publicity and brought the article to the attention of a new audience. This was considered republication.

- The Rolling Stone verdict is unusual because of the focus on the individual reporter. She was found to be an independent publisher for a post-publication remark in interviews with the media.

disliked because he is a political insider who attacks the First Amendment."[54] Similarly, in Massachusetts, an appellate court held that when a newspaper wrote that it could not reach a person for comment, such a statement isn't defamatory even if it is false. In Florida, a state court said that reporting that a plaintiff refused to cooperate or comment in a televised news story is not defamatory.[55]

In contrast with libel per se is **libel per quod**. It arises when the matter by itself does not appear to be defamatory, but knowledge of additional information would damage the plaintiff's reputation. An example of libel per quod would be a news article in which the plaintiff was reported to have visited 123 Main Street. By itself, the report is not defamatory. But if most readers are aware this is a place to buy and sell heroin, then the report would have accused the plaintiff of involvement in illegal activity.

Gilbert Carrasquillo/Getty Images

Central to different defamation lawsuits against comedian Bill Cosby in several states are his public statements that several of his alleged victims of sexual assault lied when they accused him.

libel per quod
Libel that is actionable only when the plaintiff introduces additional facts to show defamation.

Article headlines can occasionally be the source of successful libel claims. As with captions and teasers, their abbreviated nature and shortened message may still be interpreted in a defamatory way. Whether the headline is "of and concerning" the plaintiff becomes material—as do the other elements of the plaintiff's case. For example, in the manhunt that ensued after the 2013 Boston Marathon bombing, a picture of two young men who attended the Boston Marathon appeared on the front page of the New York Post under the headline "BAG MEN." Although a small text box on the front page noted that no evidence linked them to the bombing, the article that accompanied the image said that police investigators had been circulating photos of two men whom witnesses saw chatting near the finish line.[56]

The First Circuit Court of Appeals held that a reasonable reader could interpret the article to suggest the two men were suspects. "When taken in context of the widespread reporting on the bombing, the 'BAG MEN' headline could be construed to imply that the plaintiffs' bags had been used to carry the bombs."[57] The New York Post settled the case out of court.

Article illustrations and photographs can also result in libel if they are juxtaposed in a way that creates a defamatory impression. A New York court held that an archived crime scene photo used as a visual with an article about gang violence was capable of defamatory meaning. The photo of a 10-year-old African-American boy looking over yellow police tape at a crime scene was placed underneath the headline "Call to Get Tougher on Gang Activities." The appeals court said that the juxtaposition of the photo and the text could create a defamatory impression and that connecting a person to a serious crime like gang activity constitutes libel per se.[58]

Among the challenges for a court is deciding what the words or images at issue in a libel case mean and whether they can be considered defamatory. Whether they are actionable cannot simply be determined according to whether they harmed the plaintiff's reputation. The allegedly libelous matter may conceivably harm reputation without rising to the level of defamation. Thus, another element of defamation that plaintiffs must show is that the material "is reasonably capable of sustaining defamatory meaning."[59] A judge decides whether the words constituting the statement at issue are capable of conveying defamatory meaning. If so, the case may move to trial to determine whether, in fact, the words did convey a defamatory meaning.

Business Reputation. While businesses and corporations do not have reputations in the same sense that individuals do, they can suffer reputational harm that can impair their ability to conduct business. In addition, individuals within businesses and corporations may have a legitimate libel claim when criticism of the business falsely implies wrongdoing on their part.

Trade Libel. Trade libel pertains to criticism of products rather than criticism of people or businesses. When it applies to food products, it is sometimes colloquially called "veggie libel." These are state laws that became popular in the 1990s. In one of the most famous cases, a group of Texas cattlemen sued Oprah Winfrey for remarks she made about mad cow disease. During that time, international media had reported on the disease after several people in the United Kingdom died from eating infected beef. An episode of "The Oprah Winfrey Show" titled "Dangerous Food" explored the topic of diseased beef. Although neither Texas nor any of the plaintiffs was mentioned, the Texas Beef Group and several other Texas-based cattle companies filed suit. They claimed the show's producers "intentionally edited . . . much of the factual and scientific information that would have calmed the hysteria it knew one guest's false exaggerations would create."[60] The plaintiffs added that this "malicious" treatment "caused markets to immediately" crash and they suffered damages as a result.[61] When Winfrey commented during the show that the information about tainted beef had "just stopped me cold from eating another burger,"[62] the flames were fanned. The plaintiffs sought $100 million in damages. Winfrey won at trial and on appeal. The Texas cattlemen were unable to meet the burden of proof.[63]

A series of reports by ABC News that called a processed meat product "pink slime" were the focus of a recent trade libel suit brought by Beef Products, Inc. (BPI). The company sought $1.2 billion in damages under South Dakota's "veggie libel" law. BPI says it was defamatory to call its "lean finely textured beef," made from raw chunks of meat and fat beef trimmings, "pink slime," a term that originated from a U.S. Department of Agriculture (USDA) microbiologist.[64]

BPI's product was used by many fast-food chains and sold by large grocery store chains. ABC News reports said the product was made with "low grade" meat, including scraps and waste, and was supposedly made partially from connective animal tissue. BPI maintained that the product was made from muscle, or meat. The public pressured fast-food chains to eliminate the textured beef product, and BPI's revenues plummeted, resulting in the closure of three of its processing plants and the loss of 700 jobs.[65]

Jordan Strauss/Invision/AP

Oprah Winfrey

ABC argued that the use of the term "pink slime" was protected expression of opinion and sought to have the complaint dismissed. A South Dakota court held that "the use of the term 'pink slime' with a food product can be reasonably interpreted as implying that the food product is not meat and is not fit to eat, which are objective facts which can be proven." The court allowed the lawsuit to move forward[66] against ABC, news anchor Diane Sawyer and one ABC news correspondent. In 2017, BPI settled out of court. ABC News did not retract or apologize for its report, noting that the company reached "an amicable resolution" with BPI.[67]

Falsity

For a statement to be libelous, it must be false. The plaintiff is responsible for demonstrating that the statement at issue is false rather than the defendant proving the statement is true.

Historically, this was reversed: The burden of proof to show a statement is true was placed on the defendant. Libel law in the United States now clearly places the burden of proof regarding falsity on the plaintiff. The U.S. Supreme Court has emphatically reinforced this aspect of libel law. Justice Sandra Day O'Connor emphasized the importance of protecting and encouraging the free flow of information and ideas:

> We believe that the Constitution requires us to tip [the scales] in favor of protecting free speech. . . . The burden of proving truth upon media defendants who publish speech of public concern deters such speech because of the fear that liability will unjustifiably result. . . . Because such a "chilling" effect would be antithetical to the First Amendment's protection of true speech on matters of public concern . . . a plaintiff must bear the burden of showing that the speech at issue is false before recovering damages for defamation from a media defendant. To do otherwise could only result in a deterrence of the speech which the Constitution makes free.[68]

The burden of proof of falsity occasionally serves as a deterrent to potential plaintiffs. The requirement to delve deeply into the allegedly libelous statement and refute its veracity is sometimes so distasteful that would-be plaintiffs choose not to file libel claims in the first place.

Substantial Truth. Libel law provides some latitude with regard to falsity. Minor error or discrepancy does not necessarily make a statement false. As long as the statement is substantially true, it cannot meet the standard for falsity and therefore cannot be libelous. The U.S. Supreme Court said that substantial truth "would absolve a defendant even if she cannot justify every word of the alleged defamatory matter; it is sufficient if the substance of the charge is proved true, irrespective of the slight inaccuracy in the details. . . . Minor inaccuracies do not amount to falsity so long as the substance, the gist, the sting of the libelous charge can be justified."[69]

For example, in 2018, a woman sued CNN and one of its reporters for defamation after the network reported that she participated in a Trump rally, was improperly given a press credential and later hung up on a reporter asking her questions. The woman said she was a freelance artist. A Maryland court dismissed the case because the plaintiff did not present plausible evidence that CNN's coverage was substantially false. She had participated in a Trump rally, and she did have a press credential. And, while the suggestion that she hung up on a reporter was in dispute, the court said that even if it were true, it was not damaging.[70]

Libel by Implication. While individual statements may be factually accurate, taken together they sometimes may paint a different picture. Through implication or innuendo, one can create libelous messages. In a case dismissed by a Washington state appeals court, for example, a crane operator sued a newspaper for what he said was implied in headlines. After an accident, Seattle Post-Intelligencer headlines read, "Operator in crane wreck has history of drug abuse" and "Man completed mandated rehab program after his last arrest in 2000." The crane operator's tests for drugs after the accident were negative. He filed several claims including libel, though he admitted that there were no false statements in the newspaper. Still, he claimed "defamation by implication" due to the juxtaposing of true statements in a way that created a false impression.[71] This case followed an Iowa Supreme Court ruling that public plaintiffs there can sue for "defamation by implication." The court said that if a true fact is not properly and thoroughly explained, it can become defamatory if, when read in a particular way, it carries false implications.[72]

Libel by implication can also happen through the juxtaposition of images. In 2016, the Third Circuit Court of Appeals concluded that the juxtaposition of a photo did create a defamatory impression in a case that involved a Philadelphia firefighter who appeared in a picture next to a story about a sex scandal within the city's fire department. The court decided that a reasonable person could conclude that the inclusion of the firefighter's picture and name juxtaposed to the story would incorrectly implicate him in the sex scandal.[73]

The Ninth Circuit Court of Appeals unanimously decided in favor of an unidentified performer in the pornography industry after a stock photo of her appeared within a story about a female performer testing positive for HIV, which temporarily shut down the porn industry in California. The unidentified performer was one of the most popular soft porn actresses on the internet. While the story text noted that the unidentified performer who tested positive was new to the industry, the court held that the photo juxtaposition resulted in a reasonable implication that the statements in the story referred to the model/actress used in the stock photo, even though she was not named.[74]

Fault

To support a libel claim, a plaintiff must show that the defendant was at fault in making public the allegedly false and defamatory statement of fact. Prior to *New York Times Co. v. Sullivan,* fault was not an element of common law libel. That landmark case eliminated the concept of libel as a no-fault tort, and subsequent U.S. Supreme Court cases explained what level of fault is used in libel suits. As a general rule, public officials and public figures must prove actual malice as a standard of fault, and private individuals must prove negligence.

New York Times Co. v. Sullivan. One of the most important legal cases in the history of American constitutional law is a libel case, *New York Times Co. v. Sullivan.*[75] The U.S.

Supreme Court's ruling in that case has had monumental impact, not just on journalism but on democracy and society as a whole.

The circumstances of *New York Times Co. v. Sullivan* arose within the context of the civil rights movement of the 1960s. African-American groups seeking racial equality under the law frequently engaged in nonviolent marches in Southern states. These events were minimized or ignored by the local Southern press but were covered elsewhere, including frequently in The New York Times. Many Southern leaders resented the Times and national news outlets that covered the marches.

Against that backdrop, a coalition of civil rights leaders purchased space in The New York Times for a full-page statement. Carrying the headline "Heed Their Rising Voices," the "advertorial" made charges against officials in Southern states who they claimed used violent and illegal methods to suppress the marches. Although the gist of the statement was factually accurate, there were some errors of fact. Asserting he had been defamed, L.B. Sullivan, the police commissioner of Montgomery, Ala., filed a libel claim against the Times and some of the civil rights leaders who had purchased the newspaper space.

Although Sullivan was not identified by name in the statement, he maintained that it was "of and concerning" him. The ad criticized public officials who used illegal tactics and violence to counter peaceful demonstrations. Sullivan maintained that the statements implicated him. He and his attorneys were able to file a libel claim in Alabama because several copies of the paper had been circulated in Montgomery County. A trial court quickly ruled in Sullivan's favor, awarding him $500,000 in damages. The Alabama Supreme Court upheld both the verdict and the award.

The New York Times appealed the case to the U.S. Supreme Court, arguing that because Sullivan was a public official, a higher standard should be applied. The case came at a critical time both in the history of the civil rights movement and for The New York Times, which could have suffered crippling financial damage if the judgment against it was affirmed. In a landmark ruling that rewrote U.S. libel law, the Court ruled 9–0 in favor of the Times, reversing the judgment of the Alabama Supreme Court.

The Court's decision in *Sullivan* was based on the premise that to readily punish a media organization for publishing criticism of government officials was contrary to "the central meaning of the First Amendment," an argument that for the first time applied the protections of the First Amendment to libel law. The Court's decision rested on the principle that media defendants did not have sufficient protection from libel suits. Awarding victories to libel plaintiffs too easily, the Court reasoned, threatened to choke off the free flow of information that is essential to the maintenance of a democratic society. Fear of making even minor errors would result in a chilling effect on the media, unduly restricting press freedom. Moreover, this freedom was especially important when it came to criticism of the government and government officials. This kind of political speech is a core First Amendment value.[76] To allow libel plaintiffs who are government officials to be successful without a showing of fault would be tantamount to reinstituting seditious libel—prohibiting criticism of the government.

REAL WORLD LAW
CONTEMPORARY THREATS TO *TIMES V. SULLIVAN*

Writing alone in a concurring opinion in 2019, U.S. Supreme Court Justice Clarence Thomas called for the Court to reconsider *New York Times Co. v. Sullivan*. Justice Thomas, an originalist (see Chapter 1), argued that the landmark ruling has no basis in the Constitution as understood by the framers. "*New York Times* and the court's decisions extending it were policy-driven decisions masquerading as constitutional law," Thomas wrote.[xiv]

Justice Thomas' opinion appeared in his concurrence to the Court's decision not to hear an appeal in Kathrine McKee's defamation lawsuit against comedian Bill Cosby. Lower courts determined that McKee is a public figure for defamation purposes. She claims Cosby raped her. He called her a liar.[xv]

"Although the Court [in *Times v. Sullivan*] held that its newly minted actual-malice rule was required by the First and Fourteenth Amendments," Justice Thomas wrote, "it made no attempt to base that rule on the original understanding of those provisions. . . . There are sound reasons to question whether either the First or Fourteenth Amendment, as originally understood, encompasses an actual-malice standard for public figures or otherwise displaces vast swaths of state defamation law."[xvi]

For Sullivan to win his case, Justice William Brennan wrote, the police commissioner would have to prove that The New York Times published the editorial-advertisement knowing it contained false information or with reckless disregard for its truth. This new standard of fault, Brennan wrote, is "**actual malice**." Media defendants must have some room for error—"breathing space."[77] After this ruling, plaintiffs who are public officials must prove that defamatory content is published with actual malice—a new level of fault.

actual malice
In libel law, a statement made knowing it is false or with reckless disregard for its truth.

Justice Brennan explained: "We consider this case against the background of a profound national commitment to the principle that debate on public issues should be uninhibited, robust, and wide-open."[78] This debate should be open not just to members of the press but also to members of the public.[79] If libel plaintiffs were not required to show actual malice before they could win libel suits, such debate would be unduly limited because of self-censorship by both the public and the press, he wrote.[80] The Supreme Court's opinion emphasized that when people enter government service, they assume roles in which their job performance is rightly scrutinized and often criticized. Thus, the open debate the Court sought to protect "may well include vehement, caustic, and sometimes unpleasantly sharp attacks on government and public officials."[81]

Furthermore, because public officials have easy access to the news media, they have an avenue by which to correct any reputational harm they may have suffered. Thus, they must meet a more difficult standard than the one applied to cases involving private plaintiffs.

The opinion emphasized that the First Amendment permitted—even encouraged—an aggressive press. This was especially true with regard to the media's role as a "watchdog" in democratic society, keeping an eye on those in government. Allowing libel suits to proceed too easily would damage democracy. Referring to the consequences of large damage awards

THE NEW YORK TIMES, TUESDAY, MARCH 29, 1960

> **"** *The growing movement of peaceful mass demonstrations by Negroes is something new in the South, something understandable.... Let Congress heed their rising voices, for they will be heard.* **"**
>
> —*New York Times editorial*
> *Saturday, March 19, 1960*

Heed Their
Rising Voices

AS the whole world knows by now, thousands of Southern Negro students are engaged in widespread non-violent demonstrations in positive affirmation of the right to live in human dignity as guaranteed by the U. S. Constitution and the Bill of Rights. In their efforts to uphold these guarantees, they are being met by an unprecedented wave of terror by those who would deny and negate that document which the whole world looks upon as setting the pattern for modern freedom...

In Orangeburg, South Carolina, when 400 students peacefully sought to buy doughnuts and coffee at lunch counters in the business district, they were forcibly ejected, tear-gassed, soaked to the skin in freezing weather with fire hoses, arrested en masse and herded into an open barbed-wire stockade to stand for hours in the bitter cold.

In Montgomery, Alabama, after students sang "My Country, 'Tis of Thee" on the State Capitol steps, their leaders were expelled from school, and truckloads of police armed with shotguns and tear-gas ringed the Alabama State College Campus. When the entire student body protested to state authorities by refusing to re-register, their dining hall was padlocked in an attempt to starve them into submission.

In Tallahassee, Atlanta, Nashville, Savannah, Greensboro, Memphis, Richmond, Charlotte, and a host of other cities in the South, young American teenagers, in face of the entire weight of official state apparatus and police power, have boldly stepped forth as pro-

tagonists of democracy. Their courage and amazing restraint have inspired millions and given a new dignity to the cause of freedom.

Small wonder that the Southern violators of the Constitution fear this new, non-violent brand of freedom fighter... even as they fear the upswelling right-to-vote movement. Small wonder that they are determined to destroy the one man who, more than any other, symbolizes the new spirit now sweeping the South—the Rev. Dr. Martin Luther King, Jr., world-famous leader of the Montgomery Bus Protest. For it is his doctrine of non-violence which has inspired and guided the students in their widening wave of sit-ins; and it is this same Dr. King who founded and is president of the Southern Christian Leadership Conference—the organization which is spearheading the surging right-to-vote movement. Under Dr. King's direction the Leadership Conference conducts Student Workshops and Seminars in the philosophy and techniques of non-violent resistance.

Again and again the Southern violators have answered Dr. King's peaceful protests with intimidation and violence. They have bombed his home almost killing his wife and child. They have assaulted his person. They have arrested him seven times—for "speeding," "loitering" and similar "offenses." And now they have charged him with "perjury"—a *felony* under which they could imprison him for *ten years.* Obviously, their real purpose is to remove him physically as the leader to whom the students and millions

of others—look for guidance and support, and thereby to intimidate *all* leaders who may rise in the South. Their strategy is to behead this affirmative movement, and thus to demoralize Negro Americans and weaken their will to struggle. The defense of Martin Luther King, spiritual leader of the student sit-in movement, clearly, therefore, is an integral part of the total struggle for freedom in the South.

Decent-minded Americans cannot help but applaud the creative daring of the students and the quiet heroism of Dr. King. But this is one of those moments in the stormy history of Freedom when men and women of good will must do more than applaud the rising-to-glory of others. The America whose good name hangs in the balance before a watchful world, the America whose heritage of Liberty these Southern Upholders of the Constitution are defending, is *our* America as well as theirs...

We must heed their rising voices—yes—but we must add our own.

We must extend ourselves above and beyond moral support and render the material help so urgently needed by those who are taking the risks, facing jail, and *even death* in a glorious re-affirmation of our Constitution and its Bill of Rights.

We urge you to join hands with our fellow Americans in the South by supporting, with your dollars, this combined appeal for all three needs—the defense of Martin Luther King—the support of the embattled students—and the struggle for the right-to-vote.

Your Help Is Urgently Needed . . . NOW!!

Stella Adler	Dr. Alan Knight Chalmers	Anthony Franciosa	John Killens	L. Joseph Overton	Maureen Stapleton
Raymond Pace Alexander	Richard Coe	Lorraine Hansberry	Eartha Kitt	Clarence Pickett	Frank Silvera
Harry Van Arsdale	Nat King Cole	Rev. Donald Harrington	Rabbi Edward Klein	Shad Polier	Hope Stevens
Harry Belafonte	Cheryl Crawford	Nat Hentoff	Hope Lange	Sidney Poitier	George Tabor
Julie Belafonte	Dorothy Dandridge	James Hicks	John Lewis	A. Philip Randolph	Rev. Gardner C.
Dr. Algernon Black	Ossie Davis	Mary Hinkson	Viveca Lindfors	John Raitt	Taylor
Marc Blitzstein	Sammy Davis, Jr.	Van Heflin	Carl Murphy	Elmer Rice	Norman Thomas
William Branch	Ruby Dee	Langston Hughes	Don Murray	Jackie Robinson	Kenneth Tynan
Marlon Brando	Dr. Philip Elliott	Morris Iushewitz	John Murray	Mrs. Eleanor Roosevelt	Charles White
Mrs. Ralph Bunche	Dr. Harry Emerson	Mahalia Jackson	A. J. Muste	Bayard Rustin	Shelley Winters
Diahann Carroll	Fosdick	Mordecai Johnson	Frederick O'Neal	Robert Ryan	Max Youngstein

We in the south who are struggling daily for dignity and freedom warmly endorse this appeal

Rev. Ralph D. Abernathy *(Montgomery, Ala.)*	Rev. Matthew D. McCollom *(Orangeburg, S.C.)*	Rev. Walter L. Hamilton *(Norfolk, Va.)*	Rev. A. L. Davis *(New Orleans, La.)*
Rev. Fred L. Shuttlesworth *(Birmingham, Ala.)*	Rev. William Holmes Borders *(Atlanta, Ga.)*	I. S. Levy *(Columbia, S.C.)*	Mrs. Katie E. Whickham *(New Orleans, La.)*
Rev. Kelley Miller Smith *(Nashville, Tenn.)*	Rev. Douglas Moore *(Durham, N.C.)*	Rev. Martin Luther King, Sr. *(Atlanta, Ga.)*	Rev. W. H. Hall *(Hattiesburg, Miss.)*
Rev. W. A. Dennis *(Chattanooga, Tenn.)*	Rev. Wyatt Tee Walker *(Petersburg, Va.)*	Rev. Henry C. Bunton *(Memphis, Tenn.)*	Rev. J. E. Lowery *(Mobile, Ala.)*
Rev. C. K. Steele *(Tallahassee, Fla.)*		Rev. S.S. Seay, Sr. *(Montgomery, Ala.)*	Rev. T. J. Jemison *(Baton Rouge, La.)*
		Rev. Samuel W. Williams *(Atlanta, Ga.)*	

COMMITTEE TO DEFEND MARTIN LUTHER KING AND THE STRUGGLE FOR FREEDOM IN THE SOUTH

312 West 125th Street, New York 27, N.Y. UNiversity 6-1700

Chairmen: A. Philip Randolph, Dr. Gardner C. Taylor; *Chairmen of Cultural Division:* Harry Belafonte, Sidney Poitier; *Treasurer:* Nat King Cole; *Executive Director:* Bayard Rustin; *Chairmen of Church Division:* Father George B. Ford, Rev. Harry Emerson Fosdick, Rev. Thomas Kilgore, Jr., Rabbi Edward E. Klein; *Chairman of Labor Division:* Morris Iushewitz

Please mail this coupon TODAY!

```
Committee To Defend Martin Luther King
                     and
The Struggle For Freedom in The South
     312 West 125th Street, New York 27, N.Y.
                UNiversity 6-1700

I am enclosing my contribution of $
for the work of the Committee.

Name _____
Address _____
City          Zone         State

☐ I want to help    ☐ Please send further information

        Please make checks payable to:
     Committee to Defend Martin Luther King
```

Originally published in The New York Times, Mar. 29, 1960

The New York Times "advertorial" that prompted L.B. Sullivan's libel lawsuit against the newspaper.

against newspapers, Brennan wrote, "Whether or not a newspaper can survive a succession of such judgments, the pall of fear and timidity imposed upon those who would give voice to public criticism is an atmosphere in which the First Amendment freedoms cannot survive."[82]

Enjoying added protection from lawsuits in public official libel cases, the news media were more aggressive in the wake of the *Sullivan* case. In the years immediately following the ruling, aggressive coverage of events such as the civil rights movement, the Vietnam War and the Watergate scandal followed.[83]

New York Times Co. v. Sullivan "constitutionalized" libel law. The decision gave new meaning to the phrase "freedom of the press." Restricting the flow of information, as the Supreme Court observed was possible under prior libel standards, is antithetical to the First Amendment.

Actual Malice

"Actual malice" is defined as knowledge of falsity or reckless disregard for the truth. Although the examination of this concept began within the discussion of *New York Times Co. v. Sullivan*, additional scrutiny is required given the developments that followed the landmark ruling.

Knowledge of Falsity. Knowledge of falsity is nothing more than lying—publishing information knowing it is false. Knowledge of falsity is uncommon in the news media, where truth and accuracy are universal standards. Intentionally distorted representation may rise to the level of knowledge of falsity. During the 1964 presidential campaign, for example, some people questioned Republican Party nominee Sen. Barry Goldwater's fitness for office. Fact magazine's publisher asked hundreds of psychiatrists to analyze Goldwater's mental condition in a questionnaire. He received a variety of responses but published only those that reflected poorly on the senator. When Goldwater sued for libel, the Second Circuit Court of Appeals concluded that the publisher's conduct qualified as knowledge of falsity.[84]

Does knowingly changing the quoted statements of an interview subject also qualify as knowledge of falsity? Reporter Janet Malcolm did just that in articles published in The New Yorker. The articles were based on more than 40 hours of taped interviews with psychoanalyst Jeffrey Masson. The U.S. Supreme Court noted that in those hours of recorded interviews, no statements identical to the challenged passages appeared. In its decision, the Court ruled that while readers presume that words within quotation marks are verbatim reproductions of what the interviewee said, it would be unrealistic for the law to require the press to meet such a standard. Justice Anthony Kennedy wrote, "A deliberate alteration of the words uttered by a plaintiff does not equate with knowledge of falsity . . . unless the alteration results in a material change in the meaning conveyed by the statement."[85] Absent an alteration that changes the meaning, the words remain substantially true. Courts today often refer to the outcome in the *Masson* case as the material change of meaning doctrine.

In 2014, the U.S. Supreme Court further clarified the material change of meaning doctrine in a case involving a former pilot who sued an airline for defamation after the airline reported his "suspicious" behavior to the Transportation Security Administration.[86] The Aviation and Transportation Security Act has an immunity provision for reporting suspicious behavior to the TSA. In a 6–3 vote, the Supreme Court said the ATSA provided immunity to the airline unless the disclosure to the TSA was made with actual malice. The court applied the *New York Times Co. v. Sullivan* actual malice standard and wrote that immunity applied unless the statements to the TSA were materially false.[87] Writing for the majority, Justice Sonia Sotomayor said that to accept the plaintiff's demand for precise wording in reporting suspicious behavior to the TSA "would vitiate the purpose of ATSA immunity," and that "baggage handlers, flight attendants, gate agents and other airline employees who report suspicious behavior to the TSA should not face financial ruin if, in the heat of a potential threat, they fail to choose their words with exacting care."[88]

Reckless Disregard for the Truth. Reckless disregard for the truth may be thought of as very sloppy journalism. The sloppiness must be both careless and irresponsible. In its *New York Times Co. v. Sullivan* ruling, the U.S. Supreme Court made it clear that the failure by the newspaper in that case to check the advertisement against its own records did not rise to the level of reckless disregard. A few years later, the Court considered two cases simultaneously that added to the understanding of reckless disregard. In the first, a weekly magazine, The Saturday Evening Post, published an article in 1963 about an attempt to fix a 1962 college football game. The magazine's source claimed he had been "patched" into a telephone conversation between the athletic director at the University of Georgia, Wally Butts, and the head football coach at the University of Alabama, Paul "Bear" Bryant. Moreover, the source claimed that in the call he heard the two men arranging the fix. The source, George Burnett, said he took careful notes of the conversation.

The Saturday Evening Post based its article on Burnett's recollection but never asked to see his notes. No effort was made by the magazine to corroborate the information with other sources, nor were other potential sources of information consulted, such as football experts, game films or witnesses. Burnett's credibility also went unchecked. It turned out he had a criminal record. The magazine's editors failed to do their jobs adequately. As Justice John Harlan wrote for the Court, "In short, the evidence is ample to support a finding of highly unreasonable conduct constituting an extreme departure from the standards of investigation and reporting ordinarily adhered to by responsible publishers."[89] The Court indicated that the omissions of responsibility by The Saturday Evening Post clearly qualified as conduct that rises to the level of reckless disregard for the truth.

In the second case, a retired major general, Edwin Walker, sued The Associated Press for its reports on his role in incidents surrounding efforts to keep the peace at the University of Mississippi when it was enrolling its first African-American student in 1962. The AP reported that Walker had taken command of a violent crowd of protesters and had personally led a charge against federal marshals sent there to enforce a court decree and to assist in preserving order. The report also described Walker as encouraging rioters to use violence and giving them technical advice on combating the effects of tear gas.[90] These false statements were distributed to several other media outlets.

In distinguishing the two cases, the Supreme Court cited one significant factor: "The evidence showed that the Butts story was in no sense 'hot news,' and the editors of the magazine recognized the need for a thorough investigation of the serious charges. . . . In contrast to the Butts article, the dispatch which concerns us in *Walker* was news which required immediate dissemination. . . . Considering the necessity for rapid dissemination, nothing in this series of events gives the slightest hint of a severe departure from accepted publishing standards."[91]

Thus, the urgency of a story has a significant bearing on whether the methods used by the news media defendant exhibit reckless disregard for the truth. The Court is willing to allow the news media some "wiggle room" when there is deadline pressure. In addition, the reliability of a story's source and the believability of the information are factors in the judgment.

The following year, the U.S. Supreme Court further developed its reckless disregard standard. The Court admitted that "reckless disregard" cannot be summarized in a single definition. "There must be sufficient evidence to permit the conclusion that the defendant in fact entertained serious doubts as to the truth of his publication," according to the Court. "Publishing with such doubts shows reckless disregard for the truth or falsity and demonstrates actual malice."[92]

In determining the publisher's state of mind, the Supreme Court infused an element of subjectivity. The Court said the purpose of the actual malice standard was to emphasize free expression. If it erred in its definition of reckless disregard, the Court said it would do so on the side that enhanced rather than chilled expression.

Four decades ago, the Supreme Court ruled that a defendant's state of mind is relevant and can be considered as evidence.[93] Ten years later, the Court held that reckless disregard does not necessarily need to focus on any single lapse by the defendant. It could rest on an evaluation of the record as a whole—the more mistakes that are made, the more readily a court may conclude that a defendant acted with reckless disregard. The case involved an Ohio newspaper that acted with actual malice when it failed to interview the one witness who could have verified its story about alleged corruption in a local election for a judgeship. The newspaper did not listen to a tape it had been told would exonerate the plaintiff, a tape that the plaintiff delivered to the newspaper at the newspaper's request. An editorial the newspaper published prior to the libelous report indicated the editor had already decided to publish the allegations at issue regardless of evidence to the contrary. Discrepancies in the testimony of the defendant's own witnesses supported the idea that the defendant had failed to conduct a complete investigation with the deliberate intent of avoiding the truth.[94]

Conceptually, reckless disregard for the truth, rather than knowledge of falsity, is more commonly present in actual malice libel claims. The reliability of sources and the believability of information are still key considerations when courts consider actual malice claims today. For example, in 2018, the Second Circuit Court of Appeals held that relying on anonymous sources alone does not automatically support a claim of actual malice.[95] Recently, a

Texas appeals court noted that not investigating source credibility or working to corroborate a source's story, as well as omitting material from a press release issued after a story was published, does constitute actual malice.[96] A Washington, D.C., court concluded that if a defendant has obvious reasons to doubt the accuracy of a source's statements, then this could constitute actual malice.[97]

Public Officials. New York Times Co. v. Sullivan also established that not only is the content of the allegedly libelous material important, so is the nature of the plaintiff. The ruling said the standard of fault for public official plaintiffs is actual malice. Private figures, on the other hand, are usually required to show some lesser, easier-to-prove level of fault, typically negligence.

"It is clear that the 'public official' designation applies at the very least to those among the hierarchy of government employees who have or appear to have to the public substantial responsibility for or control over the conduct of governmental affairs," wrote Justice Brennan.[98] The U.S. Supreme Court defined public officials as people whom the public is justified in wanting to know about because they serve the public. Information about them may relate to the officials' qualifications, conduct and character. Not all individuals paid by the government for their work will meet the criteria.

Conversely, one can meet the public official standard without being a government employee. For example, the U.S. Supreme Court held that a libel plaintiff in New Hampshire hired by three elected county commissioners to supervise a county-owned public recreation facility is a public official. "Where a position in government has such apparent importance that the public has an independent interest in the qualifications and performance of the person who

INTERNATIONAL LAW
U.S. JURISDICTION AND LIBEL TOURISM

The nonprofit Electronic Frontier Foundation published a series titled the "Stupid Patent of the Month." EFF says the purpose is to draw attention to questionable patents that could stifle innovation. When EFF featured a patent held by global equity firm GEMSA, the company sued EFF for defamation in Australia, where GEMSA is located. The Australian court issued an injunction and ordered EFF to remove its post.

EFF argued that the Australian injunction violated its free speech rights and sought relief from the removal order in federal court. EFF argued that the statements in its article were true, were hyperbole and constituted protected opinion under the First Amendment.[xvii] The federal district court in Northern California concluded it had jurisdiction

because the Australian court's injunction required EFF to take significant steps in California; the Australian injunction caused harm that would be suffered in California; and EFF's claims arose out of GEMSA's California-related activities.[xviii]

The judge lifted the order because EFF would not have been found liable for defamation under U.S. and California laws, and EFF's speech is protected by the First Amendment and under the U.S. libel tourism law.[xix] Libel tourism is the practice of filing a libel claim in a country where it is easier for a plaintiff to win. Congress enacted the SPEECH Act to stop libel tourism. According to the law, foreign orders are not enforceable in the U.S. unless they are consistent with U.S. and state constitutions and laws.[xx]

holds it, beyond the general public interest in the qualifications, conduct and performance of all government employees, both elements we identified in New York Times are present, and the New York Times malice standards apply," the Court wrote.[99]

A person usually remains a public official even after leaving a position that includes substantial responsibility for or control over the conduct of governmental affairs, as long as the allegedly libelous material pertains to the person's conduct while in that post. The U.S. Supreme Court has said that it is possible, though rare, for the passage of time to erode the public's interest in the official's conduct in office. In these unusual circumstances, the actual malice standard would no longer apply.[100]

Public Figures. In two cases decided after *New York Times Co. v. Sullivan*, the U.S. Supreme Court determined that public figures also must prove actual malice. The Court determined this in *Curtis Publishing Co. v. Butts* and *Associated Press v. Walker*, the two cases described previously and considered simultaneously by the Court. Chief Justice Earl Warren wrote, "To me, differentiation between 'public figures' and 'public officials' and the adoption of separate standards of proof for each has no basis in law, logic, or First Amendment policy. Increasingly in this country, the distinctions between governmental and private sectors are blurred."[101] This is perhaps even more true in 2020 than in the 1960s. One reason a higher level of fault is required of public officials is that they typically have access to the media to correct damage to their reputation. **Public figures**, Warren claimed, are no different:

> "Public figures," like "public officials," often play an influential role in ordering society. And surely as a class these "public figures" have as ready access as "public officials" to the mass media of communication, both to influence policy and to counter criticism of their views and activities. Our citizenry has a legitimate and substantial interest in the conduct of such persons, and freedom of the press to engage in uninhibited debate about their involvement in public issues and events is as crucial as it is in the case of "public officials." The fact that they are not amenable to the restraints of the political process only underscores the legitimate and substantial nature of the interest, since it means that public opinion may be the only instrument by which society can attempt to influence their conduct.[102]

While the Court determined in the *Butts* and *Walker* decisions in 1967 that public figures should meet the same standard of fault as public officials, the Court identified more specific categories of public figures in subsequent cases.

All-Purpose Public Figures. The U.S. Supreme Court has defined categories of public figures required to prove actual malice as the standard of fault if they sue for libel. In *Gertz v. Robert Welch, Inc.*, the Court said that some people "occupy positions of such persuasive power and influence that they are deemed public figures for all purposes."[103] An **all-purpose public figure** is anyone whom a court labels to be "public" under all circumstances. That is, no matter the context, the individual's name is widely recognizable to at least some

public figure
In libel law, a plaintiff who is in the public spotlight, usually voluntarily, and must prove the defendant acted with actual malice in order to win damages.

all-purpose public figure
In libel law, a person who occupies a position of such persuasive power and influence as to be deemed a public figure for all purposes. All-purpose public figure libel plaintiffs are required to prove actual malice.

segments of the public. Because the Supreme Court has said that a public figure is someone with widespread fame or notoriety, the individual's prominence is important in determining public figure status. Some courts add an additional requirement: The person must also have written or spoken about a broad range of issues. These are people who have acquired some degree of fame outside the public official sphere—"celebrities," for example. This could include not only those in the entertainment field but also some athletes, activists, religious leaders and business leaders.

Limited-Purpose Public Figures. More common than all-purpose public figures are those people who have attained public figure status only within a narrow set of circumstances. These people, in the words of the Court, "have thrust themselves to the forefront of particular public controversies in order to influence the resolution of the issues involved."[104] Like an all-purpose public figure, a **limited-purpose public figure** invites attention and comment. An individual may be a limited-purpose public figure within a particular community or a particular field. In the *Gertz* ruling, Justice Lewis Powell echoed Justice Brennan's *New York Times Co. v. Sullivan* rationale, noting that an individual who seeks government office must accept "certain necessary consequences of that involvement in public affairs. He runs the risk of closer public scrutiny than might otherwise be the case."[105] He then added the key declaration: "Those classed as public figures stand in a similar position."[106]

Unlike an all-purpose public figure, a limited-purpose public figure's prominence may apply only to a narrowly drawn context. Merely being an executive within a prominent and influential company, for example, does not by itself make one an all-purpose public figure. Professionals are typically not all-purpose public figures, but under certain circumstances, they can be limited-purpose public figures. For example, voluntary use of controversial or unorthodox techniques may be enough to confer limited-purpose public figure status. Publicly defending such methods or adopting other controversial stands also tends to bring about limited-purpose public figure status. A doctor who had written extensively on health issues as a newspaper columnist, who had authored several journal articles on the subject and who had appeared on at least one nationally broadcast television program discussing health and nutrition issues was held to be a limited-purpose public figure for a limited range of issues—those pertaining to health and nutrition.[107]

An individual may assume limited-purpose public figure status within small publics but may revert to being a private figure in larger spheres. For example, a university professor may be a public figure on campus and in the adjacent academic community but a private person beyond those boundaries. The professor's public figure status is limited.

Although the groundwork had already been established,[108] another series of rulings by the U.S. Supreme Court more precisely articulated who qualifies as a public figure. In one case, a man had been in the news 16 years prior to a false characterization in a book, but he had not voluntarily thrust himself into the public eye. The Supreme Court ruled he was not a public figure.[109] In another case, when a wealthy and well-known socialite sued for libel over a report about her behavior that led to divorce, the Court said she was private because her involvement in the divorce was not voluntary.[110] In a third case,

limited-purpose public figure
In libel law, a plaintiff who has attained public figure status within a narrow set of circumstances by thrusting him- or herself to the forefront of particular public controversies in order to influence the resolution of the issues involved; this kind of public figure is more common than the all-purpose public figure.

the Court held that a scientist who had received federal grants and who had published papers in scientific journals was a private figure. The defendant claimed the scientist had become a public figure through the notoriety of his libel suit. The Court ruled that libel defendants cannot, in effect, create a public figure through the defamation claim itself or media coverage of it.[111]

POINTS OF LAW

PLAINTIFFS AND STANDARD OF FAULT[XXI]

Category of Plaintiff	Standard of Fault	How to Identify
Public Officials	Actual Malice	Government employees who have substantial responsibility for or control over the conduct of governmental affairs
		People who do not work for the government but are implicated when the public has an independent interest in their qualifications and performance (e.g., government contractors)
		Not ALL government employees—based on the public importance of position
All-Purpose Public Figures	Actual Malice	A person a court labels to be public under all circumstances
		People who occupy positions of pervasive power and influence
		Sometimes an additional requirement that the person has commented publicly about a broad range of issues
		Common examples: celebrities, professional athletes, activists, business and religious leaders
Limited-Purpose Public Figures	Actual Malice	People who have attained public status only within a narrow set of circumstances
		People who have received attention and comment by engaging or participating in a matter of public concern
		Most common category
Private Figures	Negligence, but Sometimes Actual Malice	All those who do not qualify as public
		Standard of fault depends on state law, typically negligence
		Strict liability OK in some cases involving private individuals and private speech

This and similar cases illustrate **bootstrapping**. Bootstrapping occurs when media defendants "attach" themselves to the protection of the actual malice standard by citing media coverage of the plaintiff as evidence that the plaintiff is a public figure. Courts have noted that the public controversy at issue must have existed prior to the publication upon which the defamation claim is based in order for the plaintiff to be categorized as a public figure.[112] Courts attempt to carefully decide which came first: the controversy or the allegedly libelous story about the controversy.

Just as media are not permitted to bootstrap themselves onto their own material to strengthen their defense, a plaintiff may not avoid the actual malice standard by claiming that the attention was unwanted. The proper question for a court is not whether the plaintiff volunteered for the publicity but whether the plaintiff volunteered for an activity from which publicity would foreseeably arise.

Even if an individual is not active in a particular field of endeavor, presence within that field may satisfy a court's limited-purpose public figure requirements. One court explains, if a person has "chosen to engage in a profession which draws him regularly into regional and national view and leads to fame and notoriety in the community . . . he invites general public discussion. . . . If society chooses to direct massive public attention to a particular sphere of activity, those who enter that sphere inviting such attention overcome the *Times* standard."[113]

Drawing public attention to matters of public concern almost always results in a court making some kind of public figure determination because of the significance of the Supreme Court's *Gertz* precedent. For example, after more than 20 other women had come forward with public accusations of sexual assault against comedian Bill Cosby, Kathrine McKee told the New York Daily News that Cosby raped her in 1974.[114] The Daily News subsequently published an article describing McKee's account of the alleged rape. Cosby's attorney emailed the Daily News a letter refuting McKee's claims.

McKee alleged that the attorney also leaked the letter to other media. Within hours, she claimed, various news organizations reported on the letter. McKee said this harmed her reputation and that her dispute with Cosby was a matter of private concern. A federal district court disagreed and dismissed McKee's defamation lawsuit, holding that she was a limited-purpose public figure who could not show actual malice.[115] The First Circuit Court of Appeals upheld the trial court ruling. "[T]he web of sexual assault allegations implicating Cosby, an internationally renowned comedian commonly referred to as 'America's Dad,' constitutes a public controversy. . . . By purposefully disclosing to the public her own rape accusation against Cosby via an interview with a reporter, McKee 'thrust' herself to the 'forefront' of this controversy, seeking to 'influence its outcome.'"[116]

Involuntary Public Figures. In *Gertz*, the U.S. Supreme Court also suggested that there may be a third category: **involuntary public figures.** These are people who do not necessarily thrust themselves into public controversies voluntarily but who are drawn into specific issues.[117] An individual could be drawn into a matter of public controversy through unforeseen or unintended circumstances, becoming a public figure through no

bootstrapping
In libel law, the forbidden practice of a defendant claiming that the plaintiff is a public figure solely on the basis of the statement that is the reason for the lawsuit.

involuntary public figure
In libel law, a person who is involuntarily drawn into a given issue. This category of plaintiff is rare.

purposeful action. The Court added, however, that the occurrence of such public figures is "exceedingly rare."[118] Cases surface only occasionally where plaintiffs are declared involuntary public figures.[119]

Losing Public Figure Status. It is theoretically possible for one-time public figures to revert to private status with the passage of time. However, the courts have been inconsistent in their application of this concept. One consideration is whether the person's role in a particular matter remains in the public consciousness or is of public concern. To return to private status, a plaintiff would likely need to demonstrate not only that he or she is no longer a subject of public concern but also that his or her libel claim is not connected to events or controversies of which the public remains aware.

Private Figures. A libel plaintiff who does not qualify as a public official or public figure is considered a **private figure**. Private figures usually do not have to prove actual malice as the level of fault. Typically, they need to show only that the libel defendant acted with negligence.

private figure
In libel law, a plaintiff who cannot be categorized as either a public figure or a public official. Generally, in order to recover damages, a private figure is required to prove negligence on the part of the defendant.

While the definition of negligence varies from state to state, it is easier to prove than actual malice. Negligence is the failure to exercise reasonable or ordinary care. No single definition clearly establishes what constitutes negligence in news reporting. Media operate according to a variety of professional standards, especially as new forms of media continue to emerge. What is "acceptable" for social media may not be for television news reporting. Unlike professions in medicine or law, no single authoritative code of conduct guides reporters, public relations practitioners or even the late-night comedians who increasingly discuss news events. Examples of negligence may include, but are not limited to, relying on a single or anonymous source; making careless misstatements about the contents of documents; failing to follow established internal practices and policies; and making errors when taking notes or quoting sources.

The Nature of the Statement. Whether a plaintiff is considered an all-purpose or limited-purpose public figure in a libel suit can depend on the nature of the material being published—specifically whether it relates to a matter of public concern. In a case that reached the U.S. Supreme Court, a credit reporting agency issued a credit report that erroneously reported the bankruptcy filing of a Vermont construction contractor. The credit report had been sent to five subscribers who, by agreement, could not repeat the information. The contractor sued for libel. The U.S. Supreme Court upheld a lower court ruling that the contractor was a private figure because the statement about its supposed bankruptcy was not a matter of public concern.[120] The Court wrote that the status of the speaker, the purpose of the speech, the nature of the statement and the size of the audience are relevant in determining matters of public concern.[121]

Additionally, in its 5–4 decision in *Dun & Bradstreet, Inc. v. Greenmoss Builders, Inc.*, the Supreme Court explored the question of whether strict liability could apply in private defamation claims involving non-media defendants. As noted in Chapter 1, under a strict liability standard, the plaintiff does not need to demonstrate fault on the part of the defendant in order to win the suit. The Court held that if a defendant's statement did not involve a matter of public concern, then presumed punitive damages could be awarded without a showing of actual malice.[122]

Generally speaking, a majority of lower court decisions involving libel in the private person–private information context have concluded that states can impose liability without fault in line with the Court's *Dun & Bradstreet* decision. In a federal district court in Oregon in 2011, the application of strict liability to a libel case raised questions about bloggers and their status as media defendants.[123] Kevin Padrick, a senior executive with Obsidian Finance Group, sued blogger Crystal Cox for criticisms she posted about him and Obsidian on her personal, issue-specific website www.obsidianfinancesucks.com, as well as on some third-party websites. Cox suggested, among other things, that Padrick and Obsidian committed fraud, were corrupt and paid off the media and politicians, as well as that Padrick had hired a hit man to kill her.[124]

The court rejected Cox's claim that she was a media defendant. The court determined Cox to be a private figure because she provided no evidence of education in journalism, no connections with established news organizations and no adherence to basic journalistic standards. The court also held that her post about Obsidian Finance did not involve matters of public concern.[125] A jury awarded damages of $1 million to Obsidian Finance and $1.5 million to Padrick.

Cox filed a motion for a new trial, arguing that the jury instructions misstated the law and that the verdict was excessive. That motion was denied. Subsequently, both Cox and Obsidian appealed to the Ninth Circuit Court of Appeals. In 2014, the circuit court agreed with First Amendment scholar Eugene Volokh, who argued that Cox was entitled to the same protection afforded media defendants in the *Gertz* case. He said the court must apply at least a negligence standard of fault and that the speech at issue was a matter of public concern.[126]

The Ninth Circuit decision held that bloggers are entitled to the protection provided by *Gertz* when a blog post involves a matter of public concern. Rejecting the notion that First Amendment protection applies only to trained and credentialed journalists, the panel quoted the U.S. Supreme Court's ruling in *Citizens United v. Federal Election Commission*: "We have consistently rejected the proposition that the institutional press has any constitutional privilege beyond that of other speakers. . . . As the Supreme Court has accurately warned, a First Amendment distinction between the institutional press and other speakers is unworkable. . . . In defamation cases, the public-figure status of a plaintiff and the public importance of the statement at issue—not the identity of the speaker—provide the First Amendment touchstones."[127]

EMOTIONAL DISTRESS

Sometimes people who bring a libel lawsuit will also claim a harm that does not simply involve reputation. A news story could cause **emotional distress** even though it is not defamatory.

emotional distress
Serious mental anguish.

Or a libelous story injuring a plaintiff's reputation might also upset him or her emotionally. There are two categories of emotional distress suits: **intentional infliction of emotional distress** and **negligent infliction of emotional distress**.

Just as a libel defendant may act with actual malice—that is, intentionally or recklessly publishing false material—so may an intentional or **reckless** act or statement cause emotional distress. Acting recklessly is not caring what the result of an action will be. Also, being negligent—an act or statement made by mistake or without anticipating the possible harm the act or statement could cause—may inflict emotional distress, just as a negligently published article may defame someone. Emotional distress cases sometimes are called "emotional injury" or "mental distress" suits.

The law defines "emotional distress" as being frightened or extremely anxious. A plaintiff must show the emotional injury is very serious or severe, that she or he experienced considerable mental pain or anguish.[128] Merely being upset, angry, embarrassed or resentful is not enough to win a lawsuit based on infliction of emotional distress.[129] However, emotions such as severe disappointment or an intense feeling of shame or humiliation may cause the extreme mental pain that the emotional distress tort requires.[130]

INTENTIONAL INFLICTION OF EMOTIONAL DISTRESS

Intentional or reckless conduct that is extreme and outrageous and causes severe emotional harm can be grounds for a successful lawsuit.[131] The key to intentional infliction of emotional distress (IIED) is that the defendant's actions must have been outrageous—that is, actions a civilized society considers intolerable and beyond all bounds of decency.[132]

Usually, insults do not amount to outrageous conduct, nor do words that annoy, or even statements that are mild threats. Courts understand that people are not always polite. The high standard plaintiffs must meet—the defendant's conduct must be beyond all possible bounds of decency—is meant to prevent lawsuits being filed over mere insults, annoying comments and other remarks that are aggravating but not outrageous.[133] In addition to outrageousness, an IIED plaintiff must prove severe emotional distress caused by the defendant's action or expression. This requires more than mild annoyance or embarrassment.

Outrageousness

Media defendants win most IIED cases primarily because courts do not find the media acted in an outrageous manner. For example, there was nothing extreme or outrageous when a photographer on assignment for Harper's Magazine took a picture of a soldier's body lying in an open casket at the soldier's funeral. The soldier, who died while serving in Iraq, was the first member of the Oklahoma National Guard to be killed in action in more than 50 years. Harper's published the photograph along with others showing Americans and Iraqis mourning those killed in the war. The Tenth Circuit Court of Appeals rejected a lawsuit for intentional infliction of emotional distress brought by the soldier's family, ruling that the photograph was not "so extreme and outrageous as to go beyond all possible bounds of decency."[134]

---

intentional infliction of emotional distress Extreme and outrageous intentional or reckless conduct causing plaintiffs severe emotional harm; public official and public figure plaintiffs must show actual malice on the defendant's part.

negligent infliction of emotional distress Careless breach of a duty that causes the plaintiff severe emotional harm.

reckless Word used to describe actions taken with no consideration of the legal harms that might result.

Broadcasting the identity of undercover narcotics police officers has not been found outrageous. The Tenth Circuit court said publishing "upsetting but true news reports" is not "so extreme and outrageous as to permit recovery" in an IIED lawsuit.[135]

Not even incorrectly suggesting that a scientist sent anthrax-laced letters was deemed outrageous. In a series of newspaper columns, New York Times columnist Nicholas Kristof wrote that the FBI should focus on a Mr. Z in the investigation into the mailing of letters containing anthrax that caused five deaths. The columnist later identified Mr. Z as Dr. Steven J. Hatfill, a research scientist employed by the U.S. Department of Defense. Hatfill sued the Times for IIED and other torts. The Fourth Circuit Court of Appeals found Hatfill could not show that publishing the columns constituted extreme and outrageous conduct.[136] The U.S. government exonerated Hatfill in 2008 and awarded him $4.6 million to settle a lawsuit he brought against the government.[137]

In West Virginia, a court dismissed a defamation and IIED case against HBO and comedian John Oliver for statements made on an episode of "Last Week Tonight with John Oliver." Oliver made several critical comments about the coal industry and said that a federal Mine Safety and Health Administration investigation contradicted coal company owner Robert Murray's view that an earthquake had caused a mine collapse. The court dismissed the IIED claim on several grounds, including that the plaintiffs did not prove the statements were highly offensive and outrageous.[138]

Plaintiffs have proved outrageousness in several IIED cases brought against the media. Eran Best sued for intentional infliction of emotional distress based on an episode of the A&E network reality program "Female Forces." The program follows female police officers through their workday. In one episode, a male Naperville, Ill., police officer stopped Best and called for a female officer, who arrived with a "Female Forces" camera crew. The camera crew recorded as officers gave Best a field sobriety test and arrested her for driving on a suspended driver's license. They handcuffed Best, searched her car and took her to the police station.

In the police car, the male officer told Best her arrest would not be on "Female Forces" if she did not sign a consent form. At the police station, a "Female Forces" producer urged Best to sign. Best repeatedly refused and did not sign a consent form. Despite that, footage including the sobriety test and her being handcuffed appeared on "Female Forces." Best's face is visible and her voice heard. The program also included a scene in which the two officers kidded about Best's "expensive taste" while searching her car. One officer said Best "likes Coach purses, bags, and shoes." The other commented on Best's driving a Jaguar. The court held that Best could show outrageousness based on the program's airing footage that included the mocking comments, knowing Best objected, and ignoring the assurances given her that the footage would not be televised.[139]

Courts have ruled that some newsgathering techniques by themselves are outrageous. For instance, a television news reporter and cameraman approached a house next door to one where, earlier in the day, a woman had murdered her two small children and then committed suicide. The reporter talked with a 5-year-old child, her 7-year-old sister and their 11-year-old babysitter, who were home without an adult present. The reporter asked the children what had happened next door. After the children said they knew nothing about it, the reporter said,

"Well, the mom has killed the two little kids and herself." With the camera continuing to film, the reporter asked about the family next door.

Although the station did not show the videotape, the children's parents sued for intentional infliction of emotional distress. Ruling in favor of the plaintiff, a California appellate court noted that the reporter approached the children suddenly and with no warning; a cameraman pointed bright lights at the children; the reporter pushed the door open; the reporter blurted out "information with emotionally devastating potential"; and the children were not allowed to object to being interviewed on videotape and were too young to understand they could refuse.[140] The court said these actions could be seen as extreme and outrageous, especially because they involved children under 12 years old.

Entertainment programs as well as news reports may be the basis of intentional infliction of emotional distress cases. A court may find that remarks are extreme and outrageous if the person who made the statements knew or should have known that the plaintiff was particularly susceptible to emotional distress. For instance, after Melinda Duckett's 2-year-old son disappeared, CNN's Nancy Grace recorded a telephone conversation with Duckett. The recording was for Grace's show the following day. Just before the program aired, Duckett committed suicide. CNN ran the recording as scheduled and several times after that. Duckett's estate, her parents and her sister sued CNN and Grace for intentional infliction of emotional distress. The federal district court said if the defendants knew Duckett already suffered emotional and psychological stress because her son had disappeared, as the plaintiffs alleged, "'the potential for severe emotional distress is enormously increased.'"[141]

In addition to proving that the defendant's actions or statements were outrageous, a plaintiff suing for IIED must prove the defendant acted intentionally or recklessly.[142]

Actual Malice

The U.S. Supreme Court requires public people to prove actual malice in addition to the tort's other elements. As discussed earlier in this chapter, in *New York Times Co. v. Sullivan*, the Supreme Court defined "actual malice" as publishing with knowledge of falsity or a reckless disregard for the truth.[143] When the Rev. Jerry Falwell sued Larry Flynt and Hustler magazine for intentional infliction of emotional distress, the Court extended its actual malice ruling to IIED cases in *Hustler Magazine, Inc. v. Falwell*.[144] Flynt published what he claimed was a parody of a Campari advertising campaign. At the time, Campari, a liquor manufacturer, published ads in which celebrities discussed their "first time," an obvious double entendre about tasting Campari and having sex.

In Flynt's satire, Falwell, the leader of a national organization named the Moral Majority, described his "first time" as being with his mother in an outhouse. The magazine portrayed Falwell, who was known for speaking out against immorality, as a hypocrite for engaging in immoral activities. Hustler included a disclaimer saying "ad parody—not to be taken seriously," and the magazine's table of contents cited the page as "Fiction—Ad and Personality Parody."

Falwell sued Flynt for libel, appropriation and intentional infliction of emotional distress. A federal district court jury rejected the libel claim because the satire was so outlandish no one would believe it was a statement of fact. At trial on that issue, a jury said Flynt intentionally inflicted emotional distress, and it awarded Falwell $100,000 in compensatory damages and $100,000 in punitive damages.[145] A federal appellate court affirmed, saying the satire was outrageous and intentionally published.[146]

But the Supreme Court reversed that decision, holding that as a public figure Falwell had to present proof of actual malice.[147] The Court found that, as satire, the First Amendment protected the magazine's Campari ad. Biting, even hurtful, humor is the stock-in-trade of satirical works, the Court found, and it was simply not possible to create a constitutionally valid distinction between political cartoons and satires and the arguably tasteless Campari ad spoof. If juries were permitted to award damages for such satires, the Court warned, jurors could decide what was outrageous based on their political leanings, which would violate the First Amendment.

Not all parodies and satires were protected, the *Falwell* Court said. A public figure or public official who could prove that a satire included a false statement of fact published with actual malice could win a lawsuit

The satire that prompted Jerry Falwell to sue Larry Flynt and Hustler magazine.

for IIED. Because the jury in this case had found there were no factual statements in the piece—it was just a parody—Falwell could not successfully sue for IIED.

The Court also suggested Falwell might have used the IIED tort as a replacement for his rejected libel claim. The Court reasoned that if public figures had to prove actual malice to win libel cases, they should carry that burden for IIED as well.

In 2011, the U.S. Supreme Court again ruled that an IIED claim infringed the First Amendment. The Court said in *Snyder v. Phelps* that speech about matters of public concern, even "particularly hurtful" expression, is protected against an IIED lawsuit.[148] In *Snyder v. Phelps*, protesters from Westboro Baptist Church in Kansas picketed the funeral of a Marine killed in action in Iraq. Westboro's 75 congregants, most of whom were church founder Fred Phelps' family members, believed "God hates and punishes the United States for its tolerance of homosexuality, particularly in America's military," according to the Court.[149] The group expressed its views by picketing, frequently near military funerals.

Westboro Baptist Church members in front of the U.S. Supreme Court building as the Court hands down its *Snyder v. Phelps* decision.

Chip Somodevilla/Getty Images

Phelps and six of his family members picketed 1,000 feet from the Marine's hometown Catholic church for 30 minutes before the funeral. They displayed signs saying, for example, "God Hates the USA/ Thank God for 9/11," "Thank God for Dead Soldiers," "Pope in Hell" and "Priests Rape Boys." Another sign said "God Hates Fags," although the Marine was not gay. Only the tops of the signs were visible to those in the funeral procession as it passed close to the protesters. Later that evening, while watching a televised news report about the demonstration, the Marine's father, Albert Snyder, saw what the signs said.

Snyder sued for IIED and other torts. He said several of the signs, such as those saying "You're Going to Hell" and "God Hates You," were directed at him. The jury granted a multimillion-dollar award for the IIED and other claims. Westboro appealed. The Fourth Circuit Court of Appeals reversed, holding that the First Amendment protected Westboro's statements because they dealt with matters of public concern, could not be proven false and were hyperbole.[150]

The U.S. Supreme Court agreed with the appellate court. Westboro's signs related to matters of public concern, and as *New York Times Co. v. Sullivan* emphasized, the First Amendment stands for "a profound national commitment to the principle that debate on public issues should be uninhibited, robust, and wide-open," the Court ruled.[151] Citing *Hustler Magazine, Inc. v. Falwell*, the Court said the First Amendment may be a defense against an IIED claim.

In response to the *Snyder* decision, Congress adopted a law forbidding protests two hours before or after a military funeral and demonstrations closer than 300 feet from such funerals with a possible award of $50,000 in statutory damages.[152]

The Court did not decide whether expression directed to a private individual or during disorderly demonstrations would be protected against an IIED claim even if the content addressed matters of public concern. The *Snyder* Court said it did not consider whether the Marine's father was a public or private figure. Had he been found a public figure, he would have had to prove actual malice, as the Court said in *Falwell*. But in *Snyder*, the Court said the Westboro picketers were aiming their expression at the general public, not at Albert Snyder or his family. Because the expression was about matters of public concern and was directed toward a broad audience, the speech was protected regardless of what elements Snyder had to prove to win an IIED lawsuit.

NEGLIGENT INFLICTION OF EMOTIONAL DISTRESS

If one person carelessly causes another emotional harm, the injured person may sue using a tort called negligent infliction of emotional distress (NIED). The law asks whether the defendant should have anticipated that her or his careless action would injure the plaintiff. More formally, a plaintiff suing for NIED must prove (1) the defendant had a duty to use due care, (2) the defendant negligently breached that duty, (3) the breach caused the plaintiff's injury and (4) the breach was the proximate cause of the plaintiff's severe emotional distress.[153]

A "duty of due care" means the defendant should have foreseen that negligence could cause harm to the person or people to whom he or she owed a duty. Breaching the duty means the defendant did not act as a reasonable person would. Causing the plaintiff's emotional distress means the defendant's actions were the direct reason the plaintiff was emotionally harmed. This may be called "cause-in-fact." Proximate cause is the law's way of asking if it is reasonable to conclude the defendant caused the plaintiff's injury. NIED suits against the media often turn on the proximate cause question. Courts usually find that actions taken by a media organization are only tangentially related to the plaintiff's injury. If the connection between what the organization did and how the plaintiff was injured is too indirect to find the mass medium responsible, the plaintiff cannot prove proximate cause.

Courts in some states also require plaintiffs to show a degree of physical harm.[154] The harm may be that the defendant physically injured (or even just touched) the plaintiff, caused emotional harm or caused emotional harm resulting in physical symptoms.[155] The plaintiff's challenge is convincing courts that an emotional distress claim is real. Courts see the NIED tort as caught between two important concerns. First, the law wants to compensate people whose emotional injuries are caused by others' negligence. But second, judges want to avoid suits for trivial or fraudulent emotional harm claims.[156] These competing interests have "caused inconsistency and incoherence in the law," one court said.[157]

POINTS OF LAW
IIED AND NIED

Plaintiff's Case (IIED)
Defendant's intentional or reckless conduct

- was extreme and outrageous—beyond the bounds of decency tolerated in civilized society;
- involved actual malice, if plaintiff is a public official or public figure; and
- caused plaintiff's severe emotional distress.

Plaintiff's Case (NIED)

- Defendant had a duty to use care.
- Defendant negligently breached that duty.
- The breach caused the plaintiff's injury.
- The breach was the proximate cause of the plaintiff's severe emotional distress.

NIED suits against the media usually fail, although plaintiffs have successfully sued for NIED when the media have put them in harm's way. For example, after a woman had been physically attacked, but before the assailant was apprehended by police, a newspaper published the woman's name and address. After the newspaper published the article, the assailant terrorized his victim several more times. A Missouri appellate court upheld the victim's NIED suit.[158]

EMERGING LAW

A significant challenge to defamation law today is how to deal with defamatory content online that is easily shared. Courts have seen a surge of defamation cases in which plaintiffs seek not only damages but also a court order (called injunctive relief) to stop future publication of defamatory content on the internet or via social media.[159] Most of these cases do not involve the media but rather involve attacks by and about private people. The outcomes of these rulings sometimes conflict.

In 2014, the Supreme Court of Texas held that while injunctions against future publication of defamatory content are a form of prior restraint (see Chapter 2), post-trial orders to remove defamatory speech from websites are a permissible remedy.[160] A year later, in Washington, a state appellate court held that a permanent injunction against posting defamatory material is not a prior restraint.[161] In 2016, a California appeals court required Yelp to remove a defamatory post, a decision consistent with the Texas Supreme Court ruling.[162]

The precedent more commonly used in these cases now comes from the Seventh Circuit Court of Appeals' 2015 ruling against a broad injunction in a complicated case filed in 2008. The case involved a Catholic nun who claimed to have seen a series of apparitions of the Virgin Mary more than 50 years earlier. The circuit court struck down the injunction and held that "[a]n injunction against defamatory statements, if permissible at all, must not through careless drafting forbid statements not yet determined to be defamatory, for by doing so it could restrict lawful expression."[163] Affirming that an injunction would harm not only the speaker but also listeners, the court nonetheless opened the door for trial judges to determine whether an injunction is appropriate. In a concurrence, one judge wrote, "[T]he question whether an injunction is permissible *at all* in this context is a sensitive and difficult matter of First Amendment law."[164]

In 2018, the First Circuit Court of Appeals considered whether a court could impose a permanent injunction when prior defamatory claims are likely to be repeated.[165] The case involved two women who published a series of false accusations against Dr. Hayat Sindi, a Saudi scientist and entrepreneur and a visiting scholar at Harvard at the time. The allegations included a claim that Dr. Sindi hired a colleague to ghostwrite her dissertation, repeatedly lied about her age to win awards meant for younger scientists and inflated her résumé. Dr. Sindi won her libel and IIED lawsuits, and the lower court ordered a permanent injunction against the defendants to stop them from repeating their libelous claims.[166]

On appeal, the First Circuit vacated the permanent injunction, writing that it "cannot survive the strict scrutiny that the Constitution demands for prior restraints on speech."[167] The *Sindi* decision has already served as a precedent to reject other requests for a broad injunction on defamatory speech on the basis that they constitute prior restraints.[168]

Legal experts suggest that the approach most courts will take is consistent with the approach from the Seventh and First Circuits.[169] The bar for an injunction is very high because of concerns about prior restraint. The experts emphasize the importance of context in these cases. "By its very nature, defamation is an inherently contextual tort," the First Circuit wrote in *Sindi*. "Words that were false and spoken with actual malice on one occasion might be true on a different occasion or might be spoken without actual malice. What is more, language that may subject a person to scorn, hatred, ridicule or contempt in one setting may have a materially different effect in some other setting. The cardinal vice of the injunction entered by the district court is its failure to make any allowance for contextual variation."[170]

CASES FOR STUDY

For study resources and a case archive, go to **edge.sagepub.com/medialaw7e**.

Thinking About It

The two case excerpts that follow are considered landmark cases about both libel and intentional infliction of emotional distress. As you read these case excerpts, keep the following questions in mind:

- How do the two decisions help define the meaning of actual malice as it applies to public officials and public figures?

- What are the important concepts that each of these decisions adds to laws about libel and intentional infliction of emotional distress?

- According to the U.S. Supreme Court in *New York Times Co. v. Sullivan* and in *Hustler Magazine, Inc. v. Falwell*, how does libel law implicate the First Amendment?

- What approach does the Supreme Court take in trying to balance First Amendment rights against the right not to be emotionally harmed and to protect your reputation?

New York Times Co. v. Sullivan
SUPREME COURT OF THE UNITED STATES
376 U.S. 254 (1964)

JUSTICE WILLIAM BRENNAN delivered the Court's opinion:

We are required in this case to determine for the first time the extent to which the constitutional protections for speech and press limit a State's power to award damages in a libel action brought by a public official against critics of his official conduct.

Respondent L.B. Sullivan is one of the three elected Commissioners of the City of Montgomery, Alabama. He testified that he was "Commissioner of Public Affairs and the duties are supervision of the Police Department, Fire Department, Department of Cemetery and Department of Scales." He brought this civil libel action against the four individual petitioners, who are Negroes and Alabama clergymen, and against petitioner the New York Times Company, a New York corporation which publishes the New York Times, a daily newspaper. A jury in the Circuit Court of Montgomery County awarded him damages of $500,000, the full amount claimed, against all the petitioners, and the Supreme Court of Alabama affirmed. . . .

Of the 10 paragraphs of text in the advertisement, the third and a portion of the sixth were the basis of respondent's claim of libel. . . .

It is uncontroverted that some of the statements contained in the two paragraphs were not accurate descriptions of events which occurred in Montgomery. Although Negro students staged a demonstration on the State Capitol steps, they sang the National Anthem and not "My Country, 'Tis of Thee." Although nine students were expelled by the State Board of Education, this was not for leading the demonstration at the Capitol, but for demanding service at a lunch counter in the Montgomery County Courthouse on another day. Not the entire student body, but most of it, had protested the expulsion, not by refusing to register, but by boycotting classes on a single day; virtually all the students did register for the ensuing semester. . . .

Because of the importance of the constitutional issues involved, we granted the separate petitions for certiorari of the individual petitioners and of the Times. We reverse the judgment. We hold that the rule of law applied by the Alabama courts is constitutionally deficient for failure to provide the safeguards for freedom of speech and of the press that are required by the First and Fourteenth Amendments in a libel action brought by a public official against critics of his official conduct. We further hold that under the proper safeguards the evidence presented in this case is constitutionally insufficient to support the judgment for respondent. . . .

The publication here was not a "commercial" advertisement . . . [that] communicated information, expressed opinion, recited grievances, protested claimed abuses, and sought financial support on behalf of a movement whose existence and objectives are matters of the highest public interest and concern. That the Times was paid for publishing the advertisement is as immaterial in this connection as is the fact that newspapers and books are sold. . . . Any other conclusion would discourage newspapers from carrying "editorial advertisements" of this type, and so

might shut off an important outlet for the promulgation of information and ideas by persons who do not themselves have access to publishing facilities—who wish to exercise their freedom of speech even though they are not members of the press. . . . To avoid placing such a handicap upon the freedoms of expression, we hold that, if the allegedly libelous statements would otherwise be constitutionally protected from the present judgment, they do not forfeit that protection because they were published in the form of a paid advertisement. . . .

The general proposition that freedom of expression upon public questions is secured by the First Amendment has long been settled by our decisions. The constitutional safeguard, we have said, "was fashioned to assure unfettered interchange of ideas for the bringing about of political and social changes desired by the people. . . ."

. . . The First Amendment, said Judge Learned Hand, "presupposes that right conclusions are more likely to be gathered out of a multitude of tongues, than through any kind of authoritative selection. To many this is, and always will be, folly; but we have staked upon it our all." . . .

Thus we consider this case against the background of a profound national commitment to the principle that debate on public issues should be uninhibited, robust, and wide-open, and that it may well include vehement, caustic, and sometimes unpleasantly sharp attacks on government and public officials. The present advertisement, as an expression of grievance and protest on one of the major public issues of our time, would seem clearly to qualify for the constitutional protection. The question is whether it forfeits that protection by the falsity of some of its factual statements and by its alleged defamation of respondent. . . .

That erroneous statement is inevitable in free debate, and . . . it must be protected if the freedoms of expression are to have the "breathing space" that they "need . . . to survive. . . ."

Injury to official reputation affords no more warrant for repressing speech that would otherwise be free than does factual error. . . .

If neither factual error nor defamatory content suffices to remove the constitutional shield from criticism of official conduct, the combination of the two elements is no less inadequate. . . .

. . . A rule compelling the critic of official conduct to guarantee the truth of all his factual assertions—and to do so on pain of libel judgments virtually unlimited in amount—leads to a comparable "self-censorship." Allowance of the defense of truth, with the burden of proving it on the defendant, does not mean that only false speech will be deterred. . . . The constitutional guarantees require, we think, a federal rule that prohibits a public official from recovering damages for a defamatory falsehood relating to his official conduct unless he proves that the statement was made with "actual malice"—that is, with knowledge that it was false or with reckless disregard of whether it was false or not. . . .

. . . As Madison said, "the censorial power is in the people over the Government, and not in the Government over the people." It would give public servants an unjustified preference over the public they serve, if critics of official conduct did not have a fair equivalent of the immunity granted to the officials themselves. . . .

We hold today that the Constitution delimits a State's power to award damages for libel in actions brought by public officials against critics of their official conduct. Since this is such an action, the rule requiring proof of actual malice is applicable. . . .

Applying these standards, we consider that the proof presented to show actual malice lacks the convincing clarity which the constitutional standard demands, and hence that it would not constitutionally sustain the judgment for respondent under the proper rule of law. . . .

Finally, there is evidence that the Times published the advertisement without checking its accuracy against the news stories in the Times' own files. The mere presence of the stories in the files does not, of course, establish that the Times "knew" the advertisement was false, since the state of mind required for actual malice would have to be brought home to the persons in the Times' organization having responsibility for the publication of the advertisement. . . .

The judgment of the Supreme Court of Alabama is reversed and the case is remanded to that court for further proceedings not inconsistent with this opinion.

Reversed and remanded.

Hustler Magazine, Inc. v. Falwell
SUPREME COURT OF THE UNITED STATES
485 U.S. 46 (1988)

CHIEF JUSTICE WILLIAM REHNQUIST delivered the Court's opinion:

Petitioner Hustler Magazine, Inc., is a magazine of nationwide circulation. Respondent Jerry Falwell, a nationally known minister who has been active as a commentator on politics and public affairs, sued petitioner and its publisher, petitioner Larry Flynt, to recover damages for invasion of privacy, libel, and intentional infliction of emotional distress. . . .

The inside front cover of the November 1983 issue of Hustler Magazine featured a "parody" of an advertisement for Campari Liqueur that contained the name and picture of respondent and was entitled "Jerry Falwell talks about his first time." This parody was modeled after actual Campari ads that included interviews with various celebrities about their "first times." Although it was apparent by the end of each interview that this meant the first time they sampled Campari, the ads clearly played on the sexual double entendre of the general subject of "first times." Copying the form and layout of these Campari ads,

Hustler's editors chose respondent as the featured celebrity and drafted an alleged "interview" with him in which he states that his "first time" was during a drunken incestuous rendezvous with his mother in an outhouse. The Hustler parody portrays respondent and his mother as drunk and immoral, and suggests that respondent is a hypocrite who preaches only when he is drunk. In small print at the bottom of the page, the ad contains the disclaimer, "ad parody—not to be taken seriously." The magazine's table of contents also lists the ad as "Fiction; Ad and Personality Parody."

[Falwell sued. He failed on the libel and privacy claims.] The jury ruled for respondent on the intentional infliction of emotional distress claim, however, and stated that he should be awarded $100,000 in compensatory damages, as well as $50,000 each in punitive damages. . . .

On appeal, the United States Court of Appeals for the Fourth Circuit affirmed the judgment against petitioners. . . .

At the heart of the First Amendment is the recognition of the fundamental importance of the free flow of ideas and opinions on matters of public interest and concern. . . . We have therefore been particularly vigilant to ensure that individual expressions of ideas remain free from governmentally imposed sanctions. . . .

The sort of robust political debate encouraged by the First Amendment is bound to produce speech that is critical of those who hold public office or those public figures who are "intimately involved in the resolution of important public questions or, by reason of their fame, shape events in areas of concern to society at large." . . . Such criticism, inevitably, will not always be reasoned or moderate; public figures as well as public officials will be subject to "vehement, caustic, and sometimes unpleasantly sharp attacks." . . .

Of course, this does not mean that any speech about a public figure is immune from sanction in the form of damages. Since *New York Times Co. v. Sullivan*, we have consistently ruled that a public figure may hold a speaker liable for the damage to reputation caused by publication of a defamatory falsehood, but only if the statement was made "with knowledge that it was false or with reckless disregard of whether it was false or not." False statements of fact are particularly valueless; they interfere with the truth-seeking function of the marketplace of ideas, and they cause damage to an individual's reputation that cannot easily be repaired by counterspeech, however persuasive or effective. But even though falsehoods have little value in and of themselves, they are "nevertheless inevitable in free debate," and a rule that would impose strict liability on a publisher for false factual assertions would have an undoubted "chilling" effect on speech relating to public figures that does have constitutional value. "Freedoms of expression require 'breathing space.'" This breathing space is provided by a constitutional rule that allows public figures to recover for libel or defamation only when they can prove both that the statement was false and that the statement was made with the requisite level of culpability. . . .

Generally speaking, the law does not regard the intent to inflict emotional distress as one which should receive much solicitude, and it is quite understandable that most if not all jurisdictions have chosen to make it civilly culpable where the conduct in question is sufficiently "outrageous." But in the world of debate about public affairs, many things done with motives that are less than admirable are protected by the First Amendment. . . .

[Although] a bad motive may be deemed controlling for purposes of tort liability in other areas of the law, we think the First Amendment prohibits such a result in the area of public debate about public figures.

Were we to hold otherwise, there can be little doubt that political cartoonists and satirists would be subjected to damages awards without any showing that their work falsely defamed its subject. . . .

. . . Several famous examples of this type of intentionally injurious speech were drawn by Thomas Nast, probably the greatest American cartoonist to date, who was associated for many years during the post–Civil War era with Harper's Weekly. In the pages of that publication Nast conducted a graphic vendetta against William M. "Boss" Tweed and his corrupt associates in New York City's "Tweed Ring." It has been described by one historian of the subject as "a sustained attack which in its passion and effectiveness stands alone in the history of American graphic art." . . .

Despite their sometimes caustic nature, from the early cartoon portraying George Washington as an ass down to the present day, graphic depictions and satirical cartoons have played a prominent role in public and political debate. . . .

Respondent contends, however, that the caricature in question here was so "outrageous" as to distinguish it from more traditional political cartoons. There is no doubt that the caricature of respondent and his mother published in Hustler is at best a distant cousin of the political cartoons described above, and a rather poor relation at that. If it were possible by laying down a principled standard to separate the one from the other, public discourse would probably suffer little or no harm. But we doubt that there is any such standard, and we are quite sure that the pejorative description "outrageous" does not supply one. "Outrageousness" in the area of political and social discourse has an inherent subjectiveness about it which would allow a jury to impose liability on the basis of the jurors' tastes or views, or perhaps on the basis of their dislike of a particular expression. An "outrageousness" standard thus runs afoul of our longstanding refusal to allow damages to be awarded because the speech in question may have an adverse emotional impact on the audience. . . .

We conclude that public figures and public officials may not recover for the tort of intentional infliction of emotional distress by reason of publications such as the one here at issue without showing in addition that the publication contains a false statement of fact which was made with "actual malice," *i.e.,* with knowledge that the statement was false or with reckless disregard as to whether or not it was true. This is not merely a "blind application" of the *New York Times* standard, it reflects our considered judgment that such a standard is necessary to give adequate "breathing space" to the freedoms protected by the First Amendment.

Here it is clear that respondent Falwell is a "public figure" for purposes of First Amendment law. The jury found against respondent on his libel claim when it decided that the Hustler ad parody could not "reasonably be understood as describing actual facts about [respondent] or actual events in which [he] participated." The Court of Appeals interpreted the jury's finding to be that the ad parody "was not reasonably believable," and in accordance with our custom we accept this finding. Respondent is thus relegated to his claim for damages awarded by the jury for the intentional infliction of emotional distress by "outrageous" conduct. But, for reasons heretofore stated, this claim cannot, consistently with the First Amendment, form a basis for the award of damages when the conduct in question is the publication of a caricature such as the ad parody involved here. The judgment of the Court of Appeals is accordingly

Reversed.

⑤SAGE edge™

Visit **edge.sagepub.com/medialaw7e** to help you accomplish your coursework goals in an easy-to-use learning environment.

Under the First Amendment there is no such thing as a false idea. . . . But there is no constitutional value in false statements of fact.

—U.S. Supreme Court Justice Lewis Powell[1]

In 2018, a federal judge dismissed a defamation lawsuit against BuzzFeed News, citing protection under the fair report privilege. The lawsuit came after BuzzFeed published the infamous "Trump Dossier," alleging links between Russia and then-President-elect Donald Trump.

5

LIBEL
Defenses and Privileges

SUPPOSE...

... that a newspaper columnist writes about a school board hearing that is investigating possible neglect or wrongdoing on the part of school employees. The column contains accusations that some people lied at the hearing. One of the accused, believing that the statement was false and damaged his reputation, sues the columnist and his newspaper for libel. The defendants claim the column is an expression of opinion and the First Amendment protects their opinion. These were the circumstances in *Milkovich v. Lorain Journal Co.*, discussed in this chapter and excerpted at the end.

Plaintiffs in a libel lawsuit must prove all the elements explained in Chapter 4 to have a chance for their claim to prevail. When plaintiffs fail to prove even one element of a libel claim, they lose. Even if plaintiffs are able to prove each element of a libel claim, that may not be sufficient to win. Parties sued for libel can use many defenses, any of which has the potential to be successful, depending on the circumstances of the case. There is one important difference between the plaintiff's case and the defendant's challenges: Although the plaintiff must prove every element of his or her case, a successful defendant needs only one suitable defense.

TRUTH

Defending a libel suit may consist of merely taking the elements of the plaintiff's case, explained in Chapter 4, and proving their opposite. A libel defendant may be able to demonstrate that there is no liability for publishing the statement at issue if it is not defamatory, it was not published or the plaintiff was not identified. Truth or substantial truth is the appropriate counterargument to the plaintiff's claim that the material at issue is false.

Truth is sometimes viewed as the most basic and ironclad of all libel defenses. As noted in Chapter 4, the plaintiff is responsible for demonstrating that the statement at issue is false rather than the defendant proving the statement is true. A minor error or discrepancy does not necessarily make a statement false. As long as the statement is substantially true, it cannot meet the standard for falsity and therefore cannot be libelous.

As part of a defense strategy, a libel defendant may attempt to demonstrate to a court that it conducted itself in a responsible way in gathering and reporting the news. The defendant is then more likely to garner support for its argument that it should not be found at fault, or legally responsible for committing libel. The media defendant, for example, may need to disprove the plaintiff's claim that its employees acted with reckless disregard for the truth or that they were negligent.

In attempting to prove that a libel defendant acted with reckless disregard, a plaintiff is likely to attempt to build a case bit by bit, demonstrating a series of irresponsible or careless acts in the newsgathering and publishing process. Courts have said that no single element is sufficient to prove clearly and convincingly that a defendant acted with reckless disregard, but each can be used as evidence to build a case.

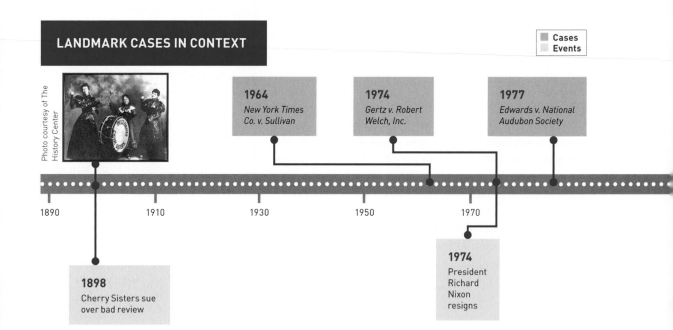

LANDMARK CASES IN CONTEXT

■ Cases
■ Events

Photo courtesy of The History Center

1964
New York Times Co. v. Sullivan

1974
Gertz v. Robert Welch, Inc.

1977
Edwards v. National Audubon Society

1890　　1910　　1930　　1950　　1970

1898
Cherry Sisters sue over bad review

1974
President Richard Nixon resigns

News media libel defendants want to strengthen their position by showing as many of the following as possible:

- They thoroughly investigated the story.

- They conducted interviews with people who had knowledge of facts related to the story, including the subject of the story.

- They did not solely rely on previously published material.

- They did not solely rely on biased stories.

- Their reporting was careful, systematic and painstaking.

- They sought multiple viewpoints, which were included in the story when possible.

- They showed a willingness to retract or correct a story when facts warranted such action.

- If applicable, there was a demonstrable deadline.

In addition to defending a libel case on the elements, those accused of libel have several defenses at their disposal that may not directly correspond with any specific element of the plaintiff's case.

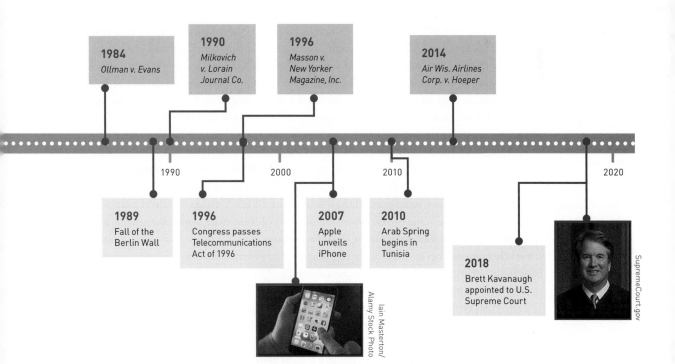

1984
Ollman v. Evans

1990
Milkovich v. Lorain Journal Co.

1996
Masson v. New Yorker Magazine, Inc.

2014
Air Wis. Airlines Corp. v. Hoeper

1990   2000   2010   2020

1989
Fall of the Berlin Wall

1996
Congress passes Telecommunications Act of 1996

2007
Apple unveils iPhone

2010
Arab Spring begins in Tunisia

2018
Brett Kavanaugh appointed to U.S. Supreme Court

Iain Masterton/ Alamy Stock Photo

SupremeCourt.gov

Attorney Gloria Allred (right) represented several women suing comedian Bill Cosby for defamation after he called them liars for alleging sexual misconduct or assault. Central to their claims is the notion of truth.

ANTI-SLAPP PROTECTION

Chilling speech is the goal of some defamation lawsuits. In those cases, libel law is used not as a shield against threatened harms or as a means of correcting them, but as a weapon to prevent speech from occurring in the first place. Called **SLAPPs** (strategic lawsuits against public participation),[2] they are meant to silence critics. For example, a news media outlet publishes a story critical of a large corporation. That corporation sues the media outlet for libel, even though the corporation knows it cannot win on the elements. The lawsuit is really meant to discourage or silence any further criticism by forcing the media outlet into court where it must pay high attorney's fees and spend time defending itself. This would be a SLAPP.

SLAPP (strategic lawsuit against public participation)
A lawsuit whose purpose is to harass critics into silence, often to suppress those critics' First Amendment rights.

Plaintiffs rarely win these cases. Noting that SLAPPs are often used to suppress First Amendment rights, some states have enacted anti-SLAPP legislation.[3] Generally, **anti-SLAPP laws** allow defendants to make a motion to strike a lawsuit because it involves a matter of public concern. Plaintiffs have the burden to show that they will prevail in the lawsuit; otherwise, the suit is dismissed. If a defendant prevails, some anti-SLAPP laws allow him or her to collect attorney's fees from the plaintiff.

anti-SLAPP laws
State laws meant to provide a remedy for a SLAPP. Plaintiffs have the burden to show that they will prevail in the lawsuit; otherwise, the suit is dismissed.

Courts have generally upheld the constitutionality of anti-SLAPP laws. More recently, however, the Washington and Minnesota Supreme Courts struck down their states' anti-SLAPP laws by holding that the laws violated a plaintiff's right to a jury trial.[4] Both state supreme courts struck down the laws on their face, meaning that none of the other provisions within the anti-SLAPP laws survived. Neither state legislature has proposed a new version of an anti-SLAPP law in light of these court decisions. In 2019, political groups in Texas encouraged the state legislature to limit the reach of that state's anti-SLAPP statute, called the Texas Citizens Participation Act.[5]

Currently, 29 states, the District of Columbia and one U.S. territory (Guam) either have enacted an anti-SLAPP statute or have state courts that recognize anti-SLAPP protections as a matter of case law. State courts consider new anti-SLAPP statutes as they emerge.

In the past few years, some plaintiffs have brought anti-SLAPP claims in federal court, and the outcome is mixed.[6] The primary question in many of these cases is whether anti-SLAPP laws conflict with the **Federal Rules of Civil Procedure**. These are the general rules that govern all civil proceedings in the U.S. district courts. The Federal Rules of Civil Procedure date back to the 1930s. Some federal courts have determined that these rules prevent the application of state-law protections like those provided by anti-SLAPP laws.[7]

Federal Rules of Civil Procedure
General rules that govern all civil proceedings in the U.S. district courts.

The First, Fifth and Ninth U.S. Circuit Courts have applied anti-SLAPP laws in part or in whole.[8] President Donald Trump in 2018 filed an anti-SLAPP motion against Stephanie Clifford, an adult film star who goes by the stage name Stormy Daniels. Clifford lost her defamation lawsuit against President Trump in a federal court in California. The court ordered her to pay the president nearly $300,000 in legal fees because of his anti-SLAPP motion. The Ninth Circuit Court of Appeals upheld the application of California's anti-SLAPP law and the financial judgment against Clifford. The state's anti-SLAPP law requires that the plaintiff pay the defendant's legal costs when a defendant succeeds on an anti-SLAPP motion in California. Clifford has appealed.[9]

The D.C. Tenth and Eleventh U.S. Circuit Courts have each rejected the application of anti-SLAPP laws in federal court. For example, the Eleventh Circuit Court has held that part of Georgia's anti-SLAPP law conflicted with the Federal Rules of Civil Procedure and therefore could not apply in federal court.[10]

The D.C. Circuit Court ruled similarly that a federal court could not apply a state or locality's anti-SLAPP provisions because applying both the Federal Rules and the anti-SLAPP statute was too burdensome on courts.[11] Even though the circuit court did not apply the D.C. anti-SLAPP statute, it still found that the defamation claim brought by the son of current Palestinian leader Mahmoud Abbas should be dismissed because his case was not based on factual representations.[12]

In another D.C. Circuit case, a different panel of judges held that the *Abbas* ruling got it wrong, noting instead that the burden is the same, whether applying the Federal Rules or the D.C. anti-SLAPP statute.[13] Additionally, the court held that the denial of an anti-SLAPP

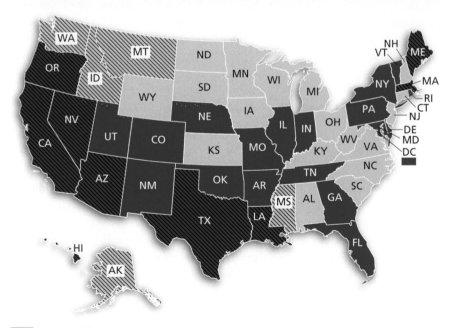

MAP 5.1 ■ Anti-SLAPP Protection by State

■ States with anti-SLAPP protection

▢ States without anti-SLAPP protection

▨ States in a federal circuit that apply anti-SLAPP laws in federal court

Stephanie Clifford, known by her stage name Stormy Daniels, and her then-attorney, Michael Avenatti.

motion is immediately appealable. The case originated when noted climate scientist Michael E. Mann filed a libel suit against the National Review and Competitive Enterprise Institute. Dr. Mann claimed that their articles criticizing his conclusions about global warming and accusing him of deception and academic and scientific misconduct defamed him.[14]

The D.C. Circuit Court applied the D.C. anti-SLAPP statute and concluded that Dr. Mann "hurdled the Anti-SLAPP statute's threshold, showing likelihood of success on the merits" because he presented legally sufficient evidence to support the fact that the articles were defamatory and published with actual malice.[15] Subsequent anti-SLAPP decisions in the D.C. district court have followed both the *Abbas* and *Mann* precedents, even though they conflict. Recent decisions show that the D.C. Circuit Court has more often relied on *Abbas* and has refused to apply the D.C. anti-SLAPP law.[16]

Given these different applications of anti-SLAPP statutes in various federal courts, legal experts thought this issue was ripe for hearing by the U.S. Supreme Court.[17] However, in 2018, the Supreme Court declined to hear a Tenth Circuit Court case out of New Mexico that rejected the application of that state's anti-SLAPP law in federal court.[18] For now, the application of state anti-SLAPP laws in federal courts varies based on the different circuit court jurisdictions.

FAIR REPORT PRIVILEGE

fair report privilege
A privilege for accurate and fair reports on the content of official records and proceedings. Sometimes called "conditional privilege."

absolute privilege
A complete exemption from liability for defamation because the statement was made within the performance of official government duties.

An open society demands that members of the public have access to information relating to government proceedings. Citizens in a participatory democracy are entitled to such information.[19] The **fair report privilege** is based on the idea that keeping citizens informed about matters of public interest is sometimes more important than avoiding incidental damage to individual reputations. Under the fair report privilege, accurate and fair reporting of official government records or proceedings provides protection from defamation and related claims. If a contributor to an official proceeding makes a statement that is false and defamatory—or if an official government record does the same—reports that rely exclusively on the statement will not be liable for defamation as long as they are accurate and fair.

The justification for the fair report privilege stems from another privilege. This privilege—called **absolute privilege**—typically occurs within the context of carrying out the business of government and grants immunity from liability. For those working in various government arenas, for example legislatures and courts, it is vitally important that they communicate information without the fear of being sued for libel.

POINTS OF LAW
FAIR REPORT PRIVILEGE

1. The information must come from an "official" record or proceeding.

2. The news report must fairly and accurately reflect information from the public record or the official proceeding.

3. The source of the statement should be clearly noted in the news report.

Not all states recognize the fair report privilege. Recent cases have trended toward a broader definition of records and proceedings and have upheld the fair report privilege in a variety of contexts because of its critical role in reporting on public affairs.

The fair report privilege is a qualified or conditional extension of absolute privilege. The condition or qualification to absolute privilege, as noted above, is that official records must be accurately and fairly reported. The fair report privilege covers officials and proceedings in the executive, judicial and legislative branches of state, local and federal governments and, often, private individuals communicating with the government. Media accounts of judicial proceedings, including testimony, depositions, attorney arguments, trials, verdicts, opinions and orders—those aspects that are typically open or available to the public—are usually covered. Also, documents that relate to the judicial branch are typically included under the fair report privilege.

For example, a Pennsylvania state court applied the fair report privilege to an article about a convicted drug dealer, even though there was a minor discrepancy between the news account and the court record. The newspaper said the plaintiff owned the car in which he was arrested, but the court report stated that the plaintiff was actually a passenger. The court said the fact difference was minor and immaterial.[20] A New York court came to a similar conclusion when it held that minor inaccuracies, including when those errors are about the precise legal significance of court orders and filings, are protected by the state's fair report privilege.[21]

Law enforcement agencies are also covered by the fair report privilege, including reports of police activity. For example, a former Belleville, Ill., police chief sued the local newspaper for libel after the newspaper reported that he was the subject of a rape investigation. A three-judge panel of the state appellate court unanimously dismissed the case, ruling that the newspaper was protected by the fair report privilege because its article was a fair and accurate report based on a local prosecutor's comments.[22]

Not every statement by a police officer is privileged. Privilege is generally determined on a case-by-case fact basis with different outcomes in different states. One state supreme court, for example, refused to apply the fair report privilege to statements made by a police officer to a reporter during an interview.[23] The court ruled that the officer's participation in the interview and his remarks were not considered to be part of his official duties—a key determinant in deciding whether the privilege applies.

In South Carolina, a court held that the fair report privilege applied to an email the sheriff's department sent to a newspaper and was not limited to official records and press releases. In Michigan, a U.S. district court applied the privilege to unofficial statements made to the press by police officers.[24] The Sixth Circuit Court of Appeals, applying Tennessee law, upheld a summary judgment in favor of a local TV news station that videotaped a story based on a ride-along with the U.S. Marshals Service during which the marshals erroneously arrested an individual with the same name as the fugitive. A day after the ride-along, the station aired its report of the arrest. Although the arrest itself was in error, the court held that the television report was a fair and accurate account of an official government action. Because the station didn't know the marshals had arrested the wrong person, the court found no evidence of actual malice to overcome the privilege.[25]

Recently, a West Virginia court held that a showing of actual malice cannot defeat the fair report privilege. That case involved comedian John Oliver's HBO show "Last Week Tonight With John Oliver."[26]

A Massachusetts court did not recognize the fair report privilege in the "BAG MEN" case (noted in Chapter 4). In the manhunt that ensued after the 2013 Boston Marathon bombing, the New York Post published a picture of two young men who attended the Boston Marathon on the front page under the headline "BAG MEN."[27] The New York Post argued that the fair report privilege applied because the photograph it used came from an FBI email. The court said the article had not fairly and accurately reported the information, so the fair report privilege did not apply. The case was ultimately settled out of court.[28]

Various media outlets, including the celebrity gossip website TMZ, accurately reported information from a press conference held by the attorney general of New York. In that press conference and in a subsequent press release, the attorney general discussed the arrest of a woman for her alleged involvement in a drug and prostitution ring. TMZ's headline for its story read, "Super Bowl Prostitution Bust Was Asian Invasion."

The problem: The attorney general indicted and arrested the wrong person, and the woman identified by TMZ and others sued for defamation and other claims. A federal district court in New Jersey dismissed the claims under fair report privilege. The court held that the media defendants accurately reported the information from the attorney general's press conference and press release, even though the attorney general presented inaccurate information.[29] In 2017, the Third Circuit Court of Appeals upheld the application of the fair report privilege, noting that privilege does not hinge on the accuracy of the underlying official statement or document.[30]

Over the past several years, fair report privilege decisions tend to uphold the privilege in a broad variety of contexts. In Rhode Island, for example, a federal district court applied the privilege to reporting on a nongovernment official who participated in a press panel at a state prison. The panel highlighted a drug treatment program for inmates. The court determined that articles about the panel were fair and accurate and that the panel was an official proceeding because two government agencies sponsored it, it included government officials as participants and it promoted the government's drug treatment program. The court held that the privilege applied to all speakers on the panel, even if they were not "responsible authoritative decisionmaker[s]."[31]

The court noted that the privilege is rooted in access to accurate information and not the reliability of speakers.[32]

More recently, the fair report privilege has been extended to include hyperlinks to other news articles that cite an official proceeding.[33] For example, casino magnate Sheldon Adelson sued a political group for defamation based on its online petition that encouraged then-presidential candidate Mitt Romney to reject financial contributions from Adelson because his money was "tainted" and "dirty."[34] In 2017, the Second Circuit Court of Appeals upheld the Nevada Supreme Court's ruling that a hyperlink to an Associated Press story, which described a sworn declaration made in a lawsuit by an ex-employee against Adelson's company, was sufficient to invoke the fair report privilege. The circuit court upheld the dismissal of Adelson's defamation claim.[35]

In a recent case against BuzzFeed, Russian businessmen sued for defamation for the publication of an article about the existence of a dossier containing unverified allegations against then-President-elect Donald Trump. The dossier alleged contact between Trump campaign staff and Russian operatives. A New York court applied the fair report privilege, noting: "BuzzFeed alleges that the Dossier was part of briefings to President Obama, Vice President Biden and President-Elect Trump on January 6, 2017 and that the Dossier was given to the FBI Director[.] . . . These allegations suggest that the article reported on an issue of national public interest and are therefore sufficient to defeat plaintiffs' motion to dismiss."[36]

Legal experts say that the fair report privilege is critical to reporting on public affairs and its broader application by the courts is a significant development. They note that New York and California have the largest bodies of case law about the fair report privilege and that other states are increasingly looking at those decisions as precedents.[37] Even so, different outcomes—including the failure to recognize the fair report privilege—occur in different states and court systems.[38] As noted earlier, not all states recognize the fair report privilege.[39]

OPINION

Justice Louis Brandeis wrote early in the 20th century, "[F]reedom to think as you will and speak as you think are means indispensable to the discovery and spread of political truth."[40] Historically, the common law provided a fair comment and criticism privilege to afford legal immunity for the honest expression of opinion on matters of legitimate public interest based on a true or privileged statement of fact.[41] Today, holding and expressing opinions is a right guaranteed by the First Amendment. "Under the First Amendment there is no such thing as a false idea. However pernicious an opinion may seem, we depend for its correction not on the conscience of judges and juries but on the competition of other ideas," wrote U.S. Supreme Court Justice Lewis Powell in *Gertz* (also discussed in Chapter 4).[42]

Although the *Gertz* decision constitutionalized the opinion defense, it did not provide specific guidance on how to apply it. Even today, after subsequent cases have offered guidance, the foundational difficulty comes in attempting to distinguish statements of fact from statements of opinion. Stating an opinion involves far more than attaching "In my opinion," "I believe" or similar qualifiers to a statement. More than 35 years ago, the D.C. Circuit Court of Appeals

Fair comment and criticism is a common law privilege that protects critics from lawsuits brought by individuals in the public eye. Historically, the fair comment and criticism privilege was incorporated into the common law to afford legal immunity for the honest expression of opinion on matters of legitimate public interest based on a true or privileged statement of fact.[i] Comment was generally privileged when it addressed a matter of public concern, was based on true or privileged facts, represented the actual opinion of the speaker and was not made solely for the purpose of causing harm.[ii] The privilege of fair comment applied only to an expression of opinion and not to a false statement of fact, whether it was expressly stated or implied from an expression of opinion.[iii] As the U.S. Supreme Court has stated, "The privilege of 'fair comment' was the device employed to strike the appropriate balance between the need for vigorous public discourse and the need to redress injury to citizens wrought by invidious or irresponsible speech."[iv] Practically speaking, this common law defense is rarely used today because the stronger constitutional opinion defense that first emerged in *Gertz*[v] and was subsequently clarified in *Milkovich*[vi] (discussed later in the chapter) offers more protection. Some legal scholars have argued that the fair comment and criticism common law privilege could have newfound relevance if states utilized it to prevent SLAPPs.[vii]

began to develop the attributes of opinion. That court articulated a four-part test to determine whether a statement was one of fact or an expression of opinion.[43] Not all of the test's elements needed to be satisfied; rather, the answers to its questions were to be evaluated in total.

Named for the case from which it stems, *Ollman v. Evans*,[44] the *Ollman* test appeared to provide a sound and relatively straightforward instrument, in four parts, to assess opinion:

1. Is the statement verifiable—can the statement be proved either true or false? Opinion is indirectly linked to the falsity/truth element of libel. That is, if a statement cannot be proved true or false, then it may satisfy the legal definition of an expression of opinion.

2. What is the common usage or meaning of the words?

3. What is the journalistic context in which the statement occurs? This element is especially important for the media. It provides added weight for an opinion defense when the material in question appears in a part of a publication (or, e.g., a broadcast or website) traditionally reserved for opinions—for example, the op-ed pages, personal columns, social media or blogs. The statement must be considered within the material taken as a whole. The language of an entire opinion column, for example, may signal that a specific statement, standing alone, which would appear to be factual, is actually an expression of opinion.

4. What is the broader social context into which the statement fits? For example, was the statement at issue made within a context or in a place where the expression of opinions is common or expected? Or was it made within a context in which statements are presumed to be statements of fact?

Soon after the *Ollman* test was established, courts granted opinion a wide berth of protection. Newsweek magazine, for example, was vindicated in publishing a reference to a false accusation that a former South Dakota governor had sexually assaulted a teenage girl. The words appeared to some people to constitute a statement of fact, but the court found them to be "imprecise, unverifiable" and "presented in a forum where spirited writing is expected and involves criticism of the motives and intentions of a public official."[45] Other plaintiffs who sued because they were called unscrupulous charlatans, neo-Nazis, sleazebags, and ignorant and spineless politicians lost their cases because courts determined these charges to be expressions of opinion rather than statements of fact.[46]

Photo courtesy of The History Center

In 1898, a well-known stage act, the Cherry Sisters, lost their libel lawsuit because the fair comment and criticism privilege protected a bad review that appeared in an Iowa newspaper.

Six years after the D.C. Circuit Court created the *Ollman* test, the U.S. Supreme Court reframed what had appeared to be a nearly absolute opinion defense. The case involved a high school wrestling team that brawled with a competing team during a match. Several people were injured. After a hearing, the coach of one team was censured, and his team was placed on probation. A lawsuit was filed in an attempt to prevent the team probation.

At a hearing, the coach, Michael Milkovich, denied that he had incited the brawl. In the next day's newspaper, a local sports columnist wrote that Milkovich, along with a school superintendent, misrepresented the truth in an effort to keep the team off probation. "Anyone who attended the meet . . . knows in his heart that [they] lied at the hearing after each having given his solemn oath to tell the truth," the column read. "But they got away with it." The columnist added that the episode provided a lesson for the student body: "If you get in a jam, lie your way out."[47]

The coach sued for libel. After 15 years and several appeals, the Ohio Court of Appeals held that the column was constitutionally protected opinion, but the U.S. Supreme Court reversed.[48] The Court rejected the broad application of the concept that there is "no such thing as a false idea." "[T]his passage has become the opening salvo in all arguments for protection from defamation actions on the ground of opinion, even though [the original] case did not remotely concern the question," Chief Justice William Rehnquist wrote for the Court.[49] The passage from *Gertz* was not intended to create a wholesale defamation exemption for anything that might be labeled opinion. "Not only would such an interpretation be contrary to the tenor and context of the passage, but it would also ignore the fact that expressions of 'opinion' may often imply an assertion of objective fact," according to the Court.[50]

Chief Justice Rehnquist wrote that facts can disguise themselves as opinions. Merely embedding statements of fact in a column does not transform those statements into expressions of opinion. They remain statements of fact and, if false, may be the basis of a libel suit. Whether the material is verifiable—whether it can be proved true or false—is paramount. The Supreme Court said the key question in this case was whether a reasonable reader could conclude that the statements in the column implied that Milkovich had lied in the judicial proceeding. The Court believed that such an implication had been made and ruled for Milkovich. Even though the material was in a column and thus satisfied the "journalistic context" part of the *Ollman* test, the Court said it was not opinion.[51]

Since the *Milkovich* decision (excerpted at the end of the chapter), courts have provided First Amendment protection to two broad categories of opinion: (1) statements that are not provably false and (2) statements that "cannot reasonably [be] interpreted as stating actual facts."[52]

For example, in 2018, the Supreme Court of Texas dismissed a defamation lawsuit against The Dallas Morning News on grounds that it was opinion based on true facts.[53] The lawsuit originated after the paper ran a column suggesting that the parents of a teenager who committed suicide had acted deceptively when they omitted that information from his obituary. The court noted that the column did include an implication of defamatory content and the writer did not follow journalistic ethical standards, yet the implication in the column was true and therefore protected as opinion.[54] This case, *Dallas Morning News v. Tatum* (excerpted at the end of this chapter), illustrates how courts apply *Milkovich* and analyze defamatory meaning and statements of fact and opinion.

Letters to the Editor and Online Comments

The approach that courts take to applying protection to online comments is based primarily on earlier cases that focused on letters to the editor of a newspaper. Letters to the editor are typically viewed as expressions of opinion rather than statements of fact. For that reason, historically, newspapers and magazines have won most cases based on the publication of such letters. Courts have sought to provide protection for the publication of letters, often viewing them as part of an open forum for the general public. In many cases in which letters to the editor were not protected as opinion, courts have held that those letters combined opinion and facts.[55]

Today, based on the same rationale, courts generally offer the same protection for opinions published as opinion blogs or as comments on review or comment-based websites, as well as comments that appear below news articles on newspaper or related websites. The location of a letter or comment within a publication is likely to have a significant bearing in determining whether it qualifies as opinion. This stems directly from the "journalistic context" element of the *Ollman* test. By appearing within a section of a publication that is clearly set aside for the expression of opinions—including opinions from readers—a letter (versus an article) or an online comment (that appears below an article) or even a review is much more likely to be viewed by a court as an expression of opinion. The same is true in the context of publication of comments on specific websites.

For example, a court in New York held that two women who called an ex-boyfriend a liar and a cheater were expressing opinion because their words appeared in the context of a website whose sole purpose is to air complaints about dishonest romantic partners.[56] In another case, a New York trial court dismissed a libel case on the grounds that criticism published on an online review website amounted to pure opinion and did not include provable defamatory facts. In that case, a medical doctor sued over comments that claimed she was "a terrible doctor" and was "mentally unstable and has poor skills." The court held that the comments were opinion in the context of the internet and said that anonymous comments on the web "can be understood as a platform for 'unsupported and often baseless assertions of opinion' rather than fact."[57]

An appellate court in California affirmed the dismissal of a libel case against the Gizmodo tech blog. In that case, the plaintiff challenged an article that criticized him for overhyping his startups and new tech products. Gizmodo's use of the word "scam" was central to the plaintiff's argument, but the court looked at the article as a whole and said it was opinion that had "the tone and style of a sarcastic product or movie review." The court also noted that Gizmodo allowed readers to draw their own conclusions about the plaintiff's products through links to product source materials.[58]

Rhetorical Hyperbole, Parody and Satire

If the material on which a libel claim is based is so outrageous that no reasonable person could believe it, then a plaintiff cannot show damage to his or her reputation. The most infamous example of this is from *Hustler Magazine, Inc. v. Falwell*,[59] discussed in Chapter 4.

The U.S. Supreme Court first recognized rhetorical hyperbole as protected speech—and therefore a libel defense—when a developer sued the publisher of a newspaper after the newspaper printed articles reporting that some people characterized the developer's negotiating tactics as blackmail.[60] The developer argued that the word "blackmail" implied that the developer had committed the crime of blackmail. The Supreme Court rejected the developer's argument, holding that the word "blackmail" was defamatory when reported because "even the most careless reader must have perceived that the word was no more than rhetorical hyperbole, a vigorous epithet used by those who considered [the developer's] negotiating position extremely unreasonable."[61]

Hyperbole, or rhetorical hyperbole, is a figure of speech that uses extreme exaggeration to make a point or show emphasis. Hyperbole is rampant on the internet and social media. For example, would you stay at a hotel labeled the No. 1 Dirtiest Hotel of the year by online reviewers? When the Grand Resort Hotel and Convention Center in Pigeon Forge, Tenn., nabbed this top spot on a list, major television news outlets and websites reported the distinction. The list on TripAdvisor.com included a link to the hotel with a photograph of a ripped bedspread and a user quote that read, "There was dirt at least ½ inch thick in the bathtub which was filled with lots of dark hair."[62]

NBC's "Saturday Night Live" is famous for its political parody and satire. In 2017, actress Melissa McCarthy made a surprise appearance as then-White House Press Secretary Sean Spicer.

The Grand Resort took issue with a system of online reviews that resulted in this ranking. It argued that such a distinction "maliciously" caused customers to lose confidence in the resort and the TripAdvisor rating caused "great injury and irreparable damage to . . . destroy [its] business and reputation by false and misleading means."[63] The hotel sued TripAdvisor for libel and said the numerical ranking system the site used to determine each year's top 10 dirtiest hotels was based solely on customer reviews.

A federal district court in Tennessee dismissed the hotel's libel suit, holding that the online ranking was clearly rhetorical hyperbole, even though it offered a numerical ranking system. The appeals court agreed: "TripAdvisor's placement of Grand Resort on the '2011 Dirtiest Hotels' list is not capable of being defamatory." The court added that the list is protected opinion because "the list employs loose, hyperbolic language and its general tenor undermines any assertion . . . that the list communicates anything more than the opinions of TripAdvisor's users."[64]

If the president-elect of the United States calls you a "major loser" or a "real dummy" on Twitter, is that defamatory content? In 2017, a New York judge dismissed a defamation suit filed against then-President-elect Donald Trump by a veteran political strategist and TV pundit, writing that Trump's Twitter insults are generally viewed as hyperbolic opinion. "His tweets about his critics . . . are rife with vague and simplistic insults such as 'loser' or 'total loser' or 'totally biased loser,' 'dummy' or 'dope' or 'dumb,' 'zero/no credibility,' 'crazy' or 'wacko' and 'disaster,' all deflecting serious consideration," the judge wrote.[65]

Trump launched a Twitter tirade toward Cheryl Jacobus after she made critical comments about him and his campaign on CNN. Trump's insults included a claim that Jacobus had "begged" his campaign for a job and was only critical of him because his campaign didn't hire her. Jacobus said that was false. The judge determined that while "the intemperate tweets are clearly intended to belittle and demean the plaintiff," she failed to show that they had damaged her reputation even if the claim about her wanting a job was false.[66]

Similar to rhetorical hyperbole, satire or parody meant to be humorous or offer social commentary is often not libelous. For example, an artist was sued for libel because one of his paintings portrayed the plaintiffs holding knives and attacking a young woman. The artist knew the plaintiffs, also artists, but had become embroiled in a spat with them over their views on art. The painting was meant to satirize the views of those depicted. An appellate court considered the context and identified it as symbolic expression with no accusation of criminal conduct.[67]

Compare that to a situation in which a newspaper published a fictional article describing a Texas juvenile court judge who ordered the detention of a first grader for making a threat in a book report. The fictional student was described as appearing before the judge in handcuffs and ankle shackles.[68] The problem arose because the judge named in this otherwise made-up story was real. The satirical article came out after a real court case in which that same judge had ordered the detention of a 13-year-old student who wrote a Halloween horror story depicting the shooting death of a teacher and two students.

The newspaper did not dispute that its article on the first grader was completely made up. It was meant to be a commentary on the judge and his heavy-handed justice. But the judge and a district attorney sued for libel, claiming that the article could be understood by a reasonable reader as making false statements of fact about them and that they were made with actual malice. The newspaper defended itself by claiming the article was satire and parody and therefore protected by the First Amendment. Ultimately, the Texas Supreme Court ruled for the newspaper.[69] The court cited clues in the article that would alert a reasonable reader that the article was not a statement of fact but instead a criticism or opinion. Though the article did have a superficial degree of plausibility, the court said, that is the hallmark of satire.

SECTION 230 IMMUNITY

Section 230 of the federal Communications Decency Act (CDA) of 1996[70] is critical to the functioning of the internet.[71] As mentioned in Chapter 4, Section 230 offers immunity to websites in libel claims, although the protection is not absolute. Section 230 generally provides legal protection to website operators and internet service providers when issues arise from content created by others. For 20 years, courts have rejected attempts to limit the application of Section 230 to only "traditional" ISPs like Verizon or AT&T. Instead, they have extended protection to the many diverse entities commonly called "interactive computer service providers."[72] Under this broader definition, blog sites and other interactive services that rely on user-generated content, information provided from third-party RSS feeds or reader comments also may receive immunity from libel claims under Section 230. This broader definition includes social media platforms like YouTube, Facebook and Twitter as well as review websites like Yelp.

The key to determining whether Section 230 protects against a libel claim is to identify the source of the content and the extent to which the ISP interacted directly with the content. For example, courts have ruled that when bloggers allow third parties to add readers' comments or other materials to their blogs, then Section 230 protects them. What is less clear is whether those who edit comments or selectively publish reader comments also would fall under Section 230 immunity.[73]

In 2011, a California state court considered whether Facebook qualified for immunity under Section 230 for its "Sponsored Story" advertising system. Five plaintiffs sued Facebook for placing their usernames and profile pictures in Sponsored Stories on friends' Facebook pages. For example, plaintiff Angel Fraley "liked" Rosetta Stone's Facebook profile in order to receive a free software demonstration. Subsequently, Fraley's friends' Facebook pages showed a Sponsored Story advertisement with the Rosetta Stone logo and her "like" for Rosetta Stone.[74]

Facebook argued that it is protected under Section 230 because it is an "interactive computer service" with content provided by third parties. But, the court disagreed in the context of the Sponsored Story feature, saying that because Facebook creates and develops the commercial content without user consent, Facebook is not immune. "Although Facebook meets

In California, Courtney Love won the first Twitter libel case to ever go before a jury because the plaintiff could not prove actual malice.

the definition of an interactive computer service under the CDA . . . it also meets the statutory definition of an information content provider. . . . Furthermore, [the fact that members] are information content providers does not preclude [Facebook] from also being an information content provider by helping develop at least in part the information posted in the form of Sponsored Stories."[75] In this case, the court is making a clear distinction between content creation and distribution.

A ruling by the Sixth Circuit Court of Appeals further extends Section 230 protection if the operator of a website creates or adds content to a post that is potentially libelous. In a case that involved TheDirty.com, a U.S. district court in Kentucky held that the website was not immune from liability for potentially defamatory comments third-party posters made on the website. TheDirty.com is a popular website that allows users to "anonymously upload comments, photographs, and video, which [the website owner] then selects and publishes along with his own distinct, editorial comments. In short, the website is a user-generated tabloid primarily targeting non-public figures."[76]

The Sixth Circuit panel reversed the lower court decision, holding that the website owner's additional comments did not materially contribute to the defamatory content of the third-party statements. According to this ruling, Section 230 immunity remained even if an ISP encouraged defamatory posts, selected the defamatory posts for publication and/or "adopted or ratified" the defamatory posts through its own comments.[77] This is called the "material contribution test," which means that a website operator does not forgo Section 230 immunity unless the operator "materially contributes" to the defamatory content produced by the users.[78]

Although Section 230 is a robust defense for ISPs and information content providers, it is far from ironclad. In 2016, the Ninth Circuit Court of Appeals refused to grant immunity under Section 230 to Internet Brands, Inc. in a case that involved the Model Mayhem networking website it operated for people in the modeling industry. The plaintiff in the case, identified as Jane Doe, posted her information to the site and was then contacted by two men posing as talent scouts who lured her to a fake audition where they drugged her, raped her and recorded the rape for sale and distribution as pornography. Doe sued Internet Brands under a California law that requires a warning of harm when a person has a "special relationship to either the person whose conduct needs to be controlled or . . . to the foreseeable victim of that conduct."[79] Doe asserted that Internet Brands knew its website was being used by sexual predators and failed to warn users. "The duty to warn allegedly imposed by California law would not require Internet Brands to remove any user content or otherwise affect how it publishes or monitors such content," according to the Ninth Circuit. "Any alleged obligation to warn could have been satisfied without changes to the content posted by the website's users and without

POINTS OF LAW

DOES SECTION 230 IMMUNITY APPLY?

Section 230[ix] immunity applies to internet service providers and websites if

- the ISP/website is a content distributor, not a content creator; or
- the ISP/website did not interact directly with the content.

Section 230 immunity also applies when

- ISPs/websites correct, edit, add or remove content—so long as they do not substantially alter the meaning of the content;
- ISPs/websites solicit or encourage users to submit content;
- ISPs/websites pay a third party to create or submit content—so long as they do not substantially alter the meaning of the content; or
- ISPs/websites provide forms or drop-downs to facilitate content submission by users—so long as the forms and drop-downs are neutral.

conducting a detailed investigation. Internet Brands could have given a warning to Model Mayhem users, perhaps by posting a notice on the website or by informing users by email what it knew."[80] This ruling applies only under state law in California.

OTHER DEFENSES

Neutral Reportage

As explained in Chapter 4, someone who repeats libelous information is potentially as responsible as the originator of that same information. Republication is not a valid libel defense. But that longtime rule of libel law was loosened somewhat by the doctrine of neutral reportage.

Neutral reportage recognizes the importance of the First Amendment principle of the free flow of information. The doctrine suggests that accusations made by one individual about another should be available to the public. In some circumstances, the news value lies not in whether the accusation is true but simply in the fact that the accusation was made or who made it. According to neutral reportage, the news media should not be restrained from merely reporting an accusation as long as the reporting is done in a fair, objective and balanced (i.e., neutral) manner. Even if the publisher of the reported accusations has serious doubts about their veracity, the neutral reportage doctrine could provide a successful defense.

The neutral reportage defense was established in 1977 and applied only to cases involving public figures.[81] Since then, the scope of that application has sometimes expanded beyond public figures, although courts have not uniformly embraced neutral reportage. Its recognition

neutral reportage In libel law, a defense accepted in some jurisdictions that provides First Amendment protection for reporting of an accusation made by a responsible and prominent organization, even when it turns out the accusation was false and libelous.

The First Amendment is a defense in a libel case in some jurisdictions if the following apply:

- The story is newsworthy and related to a public controversy.

- The accusation is made by a responsible person or group.

- The charge is about a public official, public figure or public organization.

- The story is accurate, containing denials or other views.

- The reporting is neutral.

has been spotty. The U.S. Supreme Court has not heard a neutral reportage case, so individual state and federal districts determine how to handle neutral reportage.[82] While neutral reportage remains an option in the libel defendant's arsenal, the inconsistent manner in which courts have accepted it makes its application in a specific case questionable. Much depends on how a court in a given jurisdiction may have ruled on neutral reportage previously. The neutral reportage defense has received renewed attention recently because of the #MeToo movement and the trend of people making allegations, typically on social media, of sexual misconduct by public figures. Legal experts note that both the fair report privilege and neutral reportage may protect media reporting on #MeToo allegations that have emerged on social media, but only in limited situations and depending on jurisdiction.[83]

Wire Service Defense

The wire service defense is related to the neutral reportage doctrine. It provides a defense for republication on the condition that the reporting meets certain standards. The wire service defense reflects and acknowledges the extent to which news media are dependent on news services, such as The Associated Press, particularly for nonlocal news. To expect verification of every report is unreasonable. This defense holds that the accurate republication of a story provided by a reputable news agency does not constitute fault as a matter of law. The wire defense is available to libel defendants if four factors are met: (1) The defendant received material containing the defamatory statements from a reputable newsgathering agency, (2) the defendant did not know the story was false, (3) nothing on the face of the story reasonably could have alerted the defendant that it may have been incorrect and (4) the original wire service story was republished without substantial change.

The wire service defense has succeeded even when a newspaper published a story that relied on past wire service articles[84] and when a network affiliate broadcast news reports of its parent network.[85] Like the neutral reportage privilege, the wire service defense has been accepted only in a limited number of jurisdictions.

single-publication rule
A rule that limits libel victims to only one cause of action even with republications of the libel in the same outlet; common in the mass media and on websites.

Single-Publication Rule

Another issue related to republication is the availability of an article subsequent to its initial publication. Does the republication of a work weeks, months or years after its original publication constitute a publication, therefore subjecting it to additional, separate libel claims? According to the **single-publication rule**, no. The rule holds that the entire edition of a newspaper or magazine is a single publication. Subsequent sales or reissues are not new publications. Courts across the United States also apply the single-publication rule to internet publications and to emerging online publishing platforms as well as with digital archiving.[86]

Thus, a new libel suit with merit is not possible in any of these circumstances. However, if the republication involves content changes that create a new libel, the single-publication rule is unlikely to apply.

The Libel-Proof Plaintiff

When an individual's reputation is already so bad that additional false accusations could not harm it further, the individual may be unable to win a defamation suit. Under these circumstances, a libel defendant may be able to invoke the concept of the **libel-proof plaintiff**. The U.S. Supreme Court has held that states are free to adopt the doctrine as they see fit.[87]

Since the concept was first articulated as a libel defense,[88] two different ways to implement it have emerged.

One application of the libel-proof concept occurs when any reputational harm to the plaintiff caused by a false accusation only incrementally adds to the already damaged reputation. Suppose, for example, that an individual is identified in an article as a thief, child molester and tax evader. If all of those charges are true, does it make any difference if the article also falsely identifies the individual as a kidnapper? Not likely—in such a case, the publisher could probably win, arguing that the single false statement causes negligible (or incremental) harm beyond what already exists and therefore is not grounds for a libel suit. The plaintiff is libel-proof.

Several media organizations argued in 2019 that former Maricopa County Sheriff Joe Arpaio is libel-proof. Arpaio garnered national attention for his aggressive stance on immigration. A federal district court found him guilty of contempt after he disobeyed a court order to stop making immigration-related arrests. President Donald Trump pardoned Arpaio in 2017 before he was sentenced for the misdemeanor. Various national media outlets, including CNN, Rolling Stone and HuffPost, called Arpaio a "convicted felon" and an "ex-felon," which they argued was substantially true. HuffPost also noted that Arpaio should be considered libel-proof specific to the issue of his contempt of court conviction. The case is still pending.[89]

Like other common law libel privileges, the acceptance of this part of the doctrine has not been universal. In an early ruling, the D.C. Circuit Court of Appeals rejected the libel-proof plaintiff doctrine. A journalist described the founder of an organization as a racist, fascist, anti-Semitic neo-Nazi. The defense argued that previous publications had already so irreparably tarnished the plaintiff's reputation that the libel-proof doctrine should apply. In an opinion written by then-Judge Antonin Scalia, the court rejected the claim, ruling that "we cannot envision how a court would go about determining that someone's reputation had already been 'irreparably' damaged—i.e., that no new reader could be reached by the freshest libel."[90] In writing that no matter how bad one's reputation is, it can always be worsened, Scalia offered an analogy: "It is shameful that Benedict Arnold was a traitor; but he was not a

POINTS OF LAW
THE WIRE SERVICE DEFENSE

The wire service defense may be applied in some jurisdictions as long as the following are present:

1. The defendant received material containing the defamatory statements from a reputable newsgathering agency.

2. The defendant did not know the story was false.

3. Nothing on the face of the story reasonably alerted the defendant that it may have been incorrect.

4. The original wire service story was republished without substantial change.

libel-proof plaintiff A plaintiff whose reputation is deemed to be so damaged that additional false statements of and concerning him or her cannot cause further harm.

INTERNATIONAL LAW
INTERNATIONAL JURISDICTION IN LIBEL ACTIONS

Because U.S. libel law is more protective of defendants than are laws in other countries, U.S. citizens have historically been more susceptible to libel verdicts against them in foreign courts. International plaintiffs have been known to engage in "libel tourism," shopping for a country other than the United States in which to file a libel claim.

A decade ago, the U.S. Congress passed a bill to stop libel tourism by preventing federal courts from enforcing a foreign libel judgment against an American journalist, author or publisher if it is inconsistent with the First Amendment. The law also allows individuals who have a foreign judgment levied against them to demonstrate that it is not enforceable in the United States.[x]

What about libel actions that cross the U.S. borders? In 2017, the Texas Supreme Court held that a Mexican recording artist living in Texas could sue TV Azteca because the Mexican multimedia company intentionally targeted the Texas market and it was not unreasonable or burdensome for TV Azteca to have to comply with the laws of the jurisdiction in which it does business and in which the Mexican recording artist lived.[xi]

shoplifter to boot, and one should not have been able to make that charge while knowing its falsity with impunity."[91]

Courts may also recognize a second way to apply the libel-proof doctrine—libel plaintiffs with tarnished reputations with regard to a particular issue are libel-proof only with respect to that issue. Libel claims pursued in this context present the question of whether previous publicity and the issue before the court are within the same framework.

For example, a plaintiff challenged a newspaper report that he had tested positive for drug use. In this 40-year-old decision, the court found that although the report was incorrect, the plaintiff was libel-proof regarding this specific issue because he had previously admitted using drugs.[92] Had the new report falsely damaged his reputation regarding a topic unrelated to drug use, the libel-proof plaintiff doctrine could not have been invoked. The plaintiff still had a positive reputation to protect in other areas.

ADDITIONAL DEFENSE CONSIDERATIONS

Summary Judgment

A libel defendant can ask a court to dismiss a lawsuit by filing a motion for summary judgment. As noted in Chapter 1, a summary judgment is just what the name implies: A judge promptly decides certain elements of a case and grants the motion to dismiss the case. It can occur at any of several points in litigation but usually occurs prior to trial.

A judge may issue a summary judgment on grounds that there is no genuine dispute about any material fact. With libel, this generally means a plaintiff is clearly unable to meet at least one element in his or her burden of proof. On numerous occasions, the U.S. Supreme Court said that when considering motions for summary judgment, courts "must view the facts and inferences to be drawn from them in the light most favorable to the opposing party."[93] Particularly in libel cases, this means that courts must take into account the burden the plaintiff must meet at trial. The rationale behind this view is that if the summary judgment is granted, the plaintiff's opportunity to prove a case ends, but if a defendant's motion for summary judgment is denied, the defendant still has an opportunity to prove his or her case at trial.[94]

Summary judgments can be important tools for protecting free expression, particularly in an environment in which plaintiffs have harassed the media by filing frivolous lawsuits (e.g., see the description of SLAPPs earlier in this chapter). One federal judge wrote that summary procedures are essential in First Amendment cases. Free debate is at stake if the harassment succeeds. One purpose of the *New York Times Co. v. Sullivan* actual malice principle, the judge wrote, is to prevent people from being discouraged in the full and free exercise of their First Amendment rights.[95]

Motion to Dismiss for Actual Malice

Until 1979, summary judgment was a preferred method of dealing with libel cases involving actual malice. When the defense submitted a motion for summary judgment—based on the contention that the plaintiff could not prove actual malice—the judge would either grant or deny it. If granted, the case was over. In 1979, the U.S. Supreme Court cast doubt on the appropriateness of summary judgment in libel cases because any examination of actual malice "calls a defendant's state of mind into question."[96] Although some lower courts took the admonition to heart—using it as a basis for denying summary judgment—motions for summary judgment are still granted more often than not. In 1986, the Court ruled that in determining whether to grant motions for summary judgment, trial judges should decide whether public plaintiffs who file lawsuits claiming they have been libeled can meet the actual malice standard by "clear and convincing evidence." If not, summary judgment should be granted.[97]

This issue was revisited by the U.S. Supreme Court more than a decade ago. In 2007, the Supreme Court significantly changed the standard for the motion to dismiss in *Bell Atlantic Corp. v. Twombly*.[98] Two years later, it affirmed its decision in *Ashcroft v. Iqbal*.[99] Under *Twombly* and *Iqbal*, judges should use "judicial common sense" to determine the plausibility of a claim and the sufficiency of the evidence. The Supreme Court justified the change by noting the increasing legal costs to defendants. One study suggested that more motions to dismiss have succeeded in courts since *Twombly* and *Iqbal* in many different areas of the law.[100]

In 2012, two federal appeals courts applied *Twombly* and *Iqbal* to actual malice proceedings. The First Circuit Court of Appeals dismissed a case involving a political candidate's complaint that a political attack ad defamed him. The court said that the use of "actual malice buzzwords" was not sufficient to make a claim and that the candidate must "lay out enough facts from which [actual] malice might reasonably be inferred."[101] The Fourth Circuit Court of Appeals granted a motion to dismiss a case involving NASCAR driver Jeremy Mayfield, who sued NASCAR for reporting that he tested positive for recreational or performance-enhancing drugs. Mayfield said NASCAR knew the test result was a false positive because he was taking prescription medication at the time. The court said Mayfield's evidence was insufficient.[102]

NASCAR driver
Jeremy Mayfield

In 2016, the Eleventh Circuit Court of Appeals joined six other circuits in holding that the standard from *Twombly* and *Iqbal* applies to the actual malice element in defamation cases.[103] Legal experts now consider *Twombly* and *Iqbal* another form of defense for defamation claims, but note that motions to dismiss remain uncommon.[104]

Jurisdiction

A court may dismiss a lawsuit on the grounds that the court lacks jurisdiction. Traditionally in libel, the standard has been that wherever the material in question could be seen or heard, a court in any of those locales would have jurisdiction.[105] Thus, a plaintiff could go "forum shopping" in an attempt to find a jurisdiction most favorable to his or her case.

Given that statements published on the internet can potentially be seen anywhere, any court could claim jurisdiction. A plaintiff could initiate the lawsuit in any court, including those that might be most favorable. But early in the 21st century, significant restrictions were placed on this practice. The Fourth Circuit Court of Appeals applied a three-pronged test for determining the exercise of jurisdiction: (1) whether the defendant purposefully conducted activities in the state, (2) whether the plaintiff's claim arises out of the defendant's activities there and (3) whether the exercise of jurisdiction would be constitutionally reasonable.[106]

To understand the test, it is helpful to examine the circumstances surrounding the case in which it was first applied. Two Connecticut newspapers were investigating conditions of confinement at a Virginia prison. The story was relevant in Connecticut because some of the overflow prison population in Connecticut was being transferred to a Virginia facility. Articles that included content critical of the Virginia prison and its management appeared in the newspaper in both its print and online editions. The Virginia prison warden sued in federal court in Virginia, claiming that the online content was seen in Virginia and had defamed him there. The appeals court ruled that because the newspapers did not direct their website content to a Virginia audience, courts there had no jurisdiction. The court carefully reviewed the articles and determined they were aimed at a local (Connecticut) audience.[107] Placing content online, the court ruled, is not sufficient by itself to subject a person to the jurisdiction in another state just because the information could be accessed there.[108] Otherwise, a person who places information on the internet could be sued anywhere the information could be accessed. The bottom line, according to this ruling, is that jurisdiction rests where the publication's intended audience is located.

Statutes of Limitations

Statutes of limitations apply for virtually all crimes and civil actions. Charges of most criminal activity and civil actions can be filed only during a limited time after the alleged violation of the law. Courts do not like old claims. While not a defense per se, delay in filing a libel lawsuit can work to the benefit of a defendant, sometimes requiring dismissal where the lawsuit is barred by the statute of limitations.

In libel, the length of statutes of limitations is one, two or three years, depending on the state. The clock begins ticking on the date the material was made available to the public. With some printed publications, this can be prior to the date of publication on the cover. Many monthly magazines, for example, are mailed to subscribers and appear on newsstands or online well before the official publication date.

Statutes of limitations arguments have arisen in the context of adding new defendants to libel lawsuits as well as to the filing of anti-SLAPP motions.[109] The single-publication rule also applies to statutes of limitations. The reissue of a printed publication or a post online does not restart the statute of limitations calendar as a truly new publication would. A modification to a website—when the modification is unrelated to the allegedly defamatory statement—does not amount to a new publication. For purposes of libel claims and statutes of limitations, the date of publication remains the date on which the material was originally posted.

Retractions

While not a libel defense per se, retractions and corrections published to correct content can play a role in helping libel defendants by mitigating the damage to the plaintiff

MAP 5.2 ■ Length of Statutes of Limitations in Libel Actions

One year
Two years
Three years

*The statute of limitations in libel actions in Washington, D.C., is one year.

Sarah Palin,
former vice
presidential
candidate

**retraction
statutes**
In libel law, state
laws that limit
the damages
a plaintiff may
receive if the
defendant
has issued a
retraction of
the material at
issue. Retraction
statutes are
meant to
discourage the
punishment of any
good-faith effort
of admitting a
mistake.

that resulted from the libelous publication. The degree to which a retraction is offered promptly, is displayed prominently and is plainly stated will likely help the defendant's cause. The rationale is that a retraction can help reduce the damage to the plaintiff's reputation; the defendant therefore should be required to pay less in damages.

While issuing a retraction is certainly the responsible action to undertake, doing so may work against the defendant if the offended party files a lawsuit. Depending on their wording, retractions may be viewed as an admission of guilt. Consequently, libel defense attorneys may advise against issuing them in the first place. In part as a response to this paradox, a majority of states have adopted **retraction statutes**. Increasingly, these laws prevent plaintiffs from recovering some damages after publication of a retraction.[110] Retraction statutes vary in their strength and coverage.[111] The protection they offer differs in many ways, from prohibitions on punitive damages to restricting damages to out-of-pocket losses.[112] Most of these statutes look favorably on media defendants who issue retractions. Rather than penalizing media organizations that indirectly acknowledge some degree of negligence, these statutes offer a kind of compensation by reducing their obligation to pay damages.

Some retraction statutes have been found unconstitutional. The Arizona Supreme Court, for example, ruled that the retraction statute in that state violated the state constitution.[113] The law limited plaintiffs to recovering only special damages when retractions were published.[114] But the Arizona Constitution holds that "[t]he right of action to recover damages for injuries shall never be abrogated, and the amount recovered shall not be subject to any statutory limitation."[115] Because the law conflicted with the Arizona Constitution, it did not survive judicial scrutiny. Although a retraction or correction of a news report in Arizona may no longer immunize a libel defendant from all punitive damage claims, it may serve to reduce those damages.

EMERGING LAW

As noted in Chapter 4, a significant challenge is how to deal with defamatory content online that is easily shared. Courts have seen a surge of defamation cases in which plaintiffs seek not only damages but also a court-ordered prohibition (called injunctive relief) to stop future publication of defamatory content on the internet or via social media. In many of these cases, internet-based defendants have argued that Section 230 immunity protects them.

In 2018, the California Supreme Court upheld the application of Section 230 immunity in *Hassell v. Bird*, a case involving an order that implicated the review website Yelp. The case involved Dawn Hassell, an attorney, who sued Ava Bird, a former client who posted a negative review of Hassell on Yelp. When Bird failed to show up in court twice, the court awarded Hassell more than a half-million dollars in damages and ordered Bird to remove the negative reviews.[116] When Hassell approached Yelp to remove the reviews, Yelp attempted to intervene in the case, arguing that it was protected under Section 230. The case is procedurally complicated because Yelp was never a party in the original lawsuit. The court rejected Yelp's First Amendment argument that it was a content curator. Instead, the court said it was unprotected as a passive technology conduit required to comply with an injunction against speech already deemed to be defamatory, and therefore unprotected.[117]

Without discussing the First Amendment implications in its 4–3 decision, the California Supreme Court reversed, noting that if Hassell had initially named Yelp in the case, Yelp could have promptly received Section 230 immunity. "We must decide whether plaintiffs' litigation strategy allows them to accomplish indirectly what Congress has clearly forbidden them to achieve directly. We believe the answer is no."[118] Because of the close 4–3 decision, legal experts caution reading long-term implications into the ruling.[119] Experts say the practice of excluding internet-based content distributors from libel lawsuits to try to avoid questions of Section 230 immunity could continue.

Media law defendants pushing for actual malice determinations earlier in the legal process is another emerging trend. For example, in 2017, a federal district court dismissed former vice-presidential candidate Sarah Palin's defamation lawsuit against The New York Times. The claim stemmed from an editorial by the Times editorial board that alleged a link between Palin's political action committee circulation of an electoral map with crosshairs and recent mass shootings. The newspaper quickly apologized to Palin and issued a correction to clarify that no link had been established.[120]

In dismissing the case, the district court acknowledged that the editorial contained false statements of fact, but did not meet the requirements of actual malice.[121] This was partly because the editorial had no individual author (the byline was "the editorial board"). The district judge called an evidentiary hearing to determine who authored the editorial and his or her motivation for making the erroneous link between the shootings and Palin's PAC. During oral arguments on appeal, the panel of judges hearing the case at the Second Circuit Court of Appeals called this evidentiary hearing "highly unusual."[122]

The New York Times argued to the Second Circuit panel that *Twombly* and *Iqbal* allowed the district judge to determine if the pleadings added up to a plausible claim. The Second Circuit panel noted that while the evidentiary hearing was an attempt to get inside the head of the editorial writer to determine whether the mistake was innocent and without actual malice, the judge's questioning failed to provide opportunities for cross-examination by the two sides.[123]

Attorneys for both parties suggest that the case demonstrates that media defendants are pushing harder for actual malice determinations earlier in the process, largely to save legal costs.[124] The Second Circuit panel implied it would return the case to the district court for rehearing, but has yet to issue a decision.

CASES FOR STUDY

For study resources and a case archive, go to **edge.sagepub.com/medialaw7e**.

Thinking About It

One of the case excerpts that follow is from the U.S. Supreme Court. The other is from the Supreme Court of Texas. At the center of each is the libel defense of opinion. As you read these case excerpts, keep the following questions in mind:

- How does the *Milkovich* decision help define the meaning of opinion? Did it expand or narrow the definition of opinion?

- *Dallas Morning News v. Tatum* offers an example of how a state court determines defamatory meaning and statements of fact. What was most important to its conclusion that the column was opinion?

- How did the *Dallas Morning News* case apply the *Milkovich* precedent?

Milkovich v. Lorain Journal Co.
SUPREME COURT OF THE UNITED STATES
497 U.S. 1 (1990)

CHIEF JUSTICE WILLIAM REHNQUIST
delivered the Court's opinion:

Respondent J. Theodore Diadiun authored an article in an Ohio newspaper implying that petitioner Michael Milkovich, a local high school wrestling coach, lied under oath in a judicial proceeding about an incident involving petitioner and his team which occurred at a wrestling match. Petitioner sued Diadiun and the newspaper for libel, and the Ohio Court of Appeals affirmed a lower court entry of summary judgment against petitioner. This judgment was based in part on the grounds that the article constituted an "opinion" protected from the reach of state defamation law by the First Amendment to the United States Constitution. We hold that the First Amendment does not prohibit the application of Ohio's libel laws to the alleged defamations contained in the article.

This case is before us for the third time in an odyssey of litigation spanning nearly 15 years. Petitioner Milkovich, now retired, was the wrestling coach at Maple Heights High School in Maple Heights, Ohio. In 1974, his team was involved in an altercation at a home wrestling match with a team from Mentor High

School. Several people were injured. In response to the incident, the Ohio High School Athletic Association (OHSAA) held a hearing at which Milkovich and H. Don Scott, the Superintendent of Maple Heights Public Schools, testified. Following the hearing, OHSAA placed the Maple Heights team on probation for a year and declared the team ineligible for the 1975 state tournament. OHSAA also censured Milkovich for his actions during the altercation. Thereafter, several parents and wrestlers sued OHSAA in the Court of Common Pleas of Franklin County, Ohio, seeking a restraining order against OHSAA's ruling on the grounds that they had been denied due process in the OHSAA proceeding. Both Milkovich and Scott testified in that proceeding. The court overturned OHSAA's probation and ineligibility orders on due process grounds.

The day after the court rendered its decision, respondent Diadiun's column appeared in the News-Herald, a newspaper which circulates in Lake County, Ohio, and is owned by respondent Lorain Journal Co. The column bore the heading "Maple beat the law with the 'big lie,'" beneath which appeared Diadiun's photograph and the words "TD Says." The carryover page headline announced ". . . Diadiun says Maple told a lie." The column contained the following passages:

. . . [A] lesson was learned (or relearned) yesterday by the student body of Maple Heights High School, and by anyone who attended the Maple-Mentor wrestling meet of last Feb. 8.

A lesson which, sadly, in view of the events of the past year, is well they learned early.

It is simply this: If you get in a jam, lie your way out.

If you're successful enough, and powerful enough, and can sound sincere enough, you stand an excellent chance of making the lie stand up, regardless of what really happened.

The teachers responsible were mainly head Maple wrestling coach, Mike Milkovich, and former superintendent of schools H. Donald Scott.

. . .

Anyone who attended the meet, whether he be from Maple Heights, Mentor, or impartial observer, knows in his heart that Milkovich and Scott lied at the hearing after each having given his solemn oath to tell the truth.

But they got away with it.

Is that the kind of lesson we want our young people learning from their high school administrators and coaches?

I think not.[125]

Petitioner commenced a defamation action against respondents in the Court of Common Pleas of Lake County, Ohio, alleging that the headline of Diadiun's article and the nine passages quoted above "accused plaintiff of committing the crime of perjury, an indictable offense in the State of Ohio, and damaged plaintiff directly in his life-time occupation of

coach and teacher, and constituted libel *per se*." The action proceeded to trial, and the court granted a directed verdict to respondents on the ground that the evidence failed to establish the article was published with "actual malice" as required by *New York Times Co. v. Sullivan*. The Ohio Court of Appeals for the Eleventh Appellate District reversed and remanded, holding that there was sufficient evidence of actual malice to go to the jury. The Ohio Supreme Court dismissed the ensuing appeal for want of a substantial constitutional question, and this Court denied certiorari.

On remand, relying in part on our decision in *Gertz v. Robert Welch, Inc.* (1974), the trial court granted summary judgment to respondents on the grounds that the article was an opinion protected from a libel action by "constitutional law," and alternatively, as a public figure, petitioner had failed to make out a *prima facie* case of actual malice. The Ohio Court of Appeals affirmed both determinations. On appeal, the Supreme Court of Ohio reversed and remanded. The court first decided that petitioner was neither a public figure nor a public official under the relevant decisions of this Court. The court then found that "the statements in issue are factual assertions as a matter of law, and are not constitutionally protected as the opinions of the writer. . . . The plain import of the author's assertions is that Milkovich, *inter alia*, committed the crime of perjury in a court of law." This Court again denied certiorari.

Meanwhile, Superintendent Scott had been pursuing a separate defamation action through the Ohio courts. Two years after its Milkovich decision, in considering Scott's appeal, the Ohio Supreme Court reversed its position on Diadiun's article, concluding that the column was "constitutionally protected opinion." Consequently, the court upheld a lower court's grant of summary judgment against Scott.

The *Scott* court decided that the proper analysis for determining whether utterances are fact or opinion was set forth in the decision of the United States Court of Appeals for the District of Columbia Circuit in *Ollman v. Evans* (1984). Under that analysis, four factors are considered to ascertain whether, under the "totality of circumstances," a statement is fact or opinion. These factors are: (1) "the specific language used"; (2) "whether the statement is verifiable"; (3) "the general context of the statement"; and (4) "the broader context in which the statement appeared." The court found that application of the first two factors to the column militated in favor of deeming the challenged passages actionable assertions of fact. That potential outcome was trumped, however, by the court's consideration of the third and fourth factors. With respect to the third factor, the general context, the court explained that "the large caption 'TD Says' . . . would indicate to even the most gullible reader that the article was, in fact, opinion." As for the fourth factor, the "broader context," the court reasoned that because the article appeared on a sports page—"a traditional haven for cajoling, invective, and hyperbole"—the article would probably be construed as opinion.

Subsequently, considering itself bound by the Ohio Supreme Court's decision in *Scott*, the Ohio Court of Appeals in the instant proceedings affirmed a trial court's grant of summary judgment in favor of respondents, concluding that "it has been decided, as a matter of law, that the article in question was constitutionally protected opinion." The Supreme Court of Ohio dismissed petitioner's ensuing appeal for want of a substantial constitutional question. We granted certiorari, to consider the important questions raised by the Ohio courts' recognition of a constitutionally required "opinion" exception to the application of its defamation laws. We now reverse. . . .

Respondents would have us recognize, in addition to the established safeguards discussed above, still another First-Amendment-based protection for defamatory statements which are categorized as "opinion" as opposed to "fact." For this proposition they rely principally on the following dictum from our opinion in *Gertz:*

"Under the First Amendment there is
no such thing as a false idea. However
pernicious an opinion may seem, we depend
for its correction not on the conscience of
judges and juries but on the competition of
other ideas. But there is no constitutional
value in false statements of fact."

Judge Friendly appropriately observed that this passage "has become the opening salvo in all arguments for protection from defamation actions on the ground of opinion, even though the case did not remotely concern the question." Read in context, though, the fair meaning of the passage is to equate the word "opinion" in the second sentence with the word "idea" in the first sentence. Under this view, the language was merely a reiteration of Justice Holmes' classic "marketplace of ideas" concept. . . . ("[T]he ultimate good desired is better reached by free trade in ideas . . . the best test of truth is the power of the thought to get itself accepted in the competition of the market").

Thus, we do not think this passage from *Gertz* was intended to create a wholesale defamation exemption for anything that might be labeled "opinion." . . . (The "marketplace of ideas" origin of this passage "points strongly to the view that the 'opinions' held to be constitutionally protected were the sort of thing that could be corrected by discussion"). Not only would such an interpretation be contrary to the tenor and context of the passage, but it would also ignore the fact that expressions of "opinion" may often imply an assertion of objective fact.

If a speaker says, "In my opinion John Jones is a liar," he implies a knowledge of facts which lead to the conclusion that Jones told an untruth. Even if the speaker states the facts upon which he bases his opinion, if those facts are either incorrect or incomplete, or if his assessment of them is erroneous, the statement may still imply a false assertion of fact. Simply couching such statements in terms of opinion does not dispel these implications; and the statement, "In my opinion Jones is a liar," can cause as much damage to reputation as the statement, "Jones is a liar." As Judge Friendly aptly stated: "[It] would be destructive of the law of libel if a writer could escape liability for accusations of [defamatory conduct] simply by using, explicitly or implicitly, the words 'I think.'" It is worthy of note that, at common law, even the privilege of fair comment did not extend to "a false statement of fact, whether it was expressly stated or implied from an expression of opinion."

. . . [R]espondents do not really contend that a statement such as, "In my opinion John Jones is a liar," should be protected by a separate privilege for "opinion" under the First Amendment. But they do contend that in every defamation case the First Amendment mandates an inquiry into whether a statement is "opinion" or "fact," and that only the latter statements may be actionable. They propose that a number of factors developed by the lower courts (in what we hold was a mistaken reliance on the *Gertz* dictum) be considered in deciding which is which. But we think the "'breathing space'" which "'freedoms of expression require in order to survive'" is adequately secured by existing constitutional doctrine without the creation of an artificial dichotomy between "opinion" and fact.

Foremost, we think [precedent] stands for the proposition that a statement on matters of public concern must be provable as false before there can be liability under state defamation law, at least in situations, like the present, where a media defendant is involved. Thus, unlike the statement, "In my opinion Mayor Jones is a liar," the statement, "In my opinion Mayor Jones shows his abysmal ignorance by accepting the teachings of Marx and Lenin," would not be actionable. [Precedent] ensures that a statement of opinion relating to matters of public concern which does not contain a provably false factual connotation will receive full constitutional protection. . . .

We are not persuaded that, in addition to these protections, an additional separate constitutional privilege for "opinion" is required to ensure the freedom of expression guaranteed by the First Amendment. The dispositive question in the present case then becomes whether a reasonable factfinder could conclude that the statements in the Diadiun column imply an assertion that petitioner Milkovich perjured himself in a judicial proceeding. We think this question must be answered in the affirmative. As the Ohio Supreme Court itself observed, "The clear impact in some nine sentences and a caption is that [Milkovich] 'lied at the hearing after . . . having given his solemn oath to tell the truth.'" This is not the sort of loose, figurative, or hyperbolic language which would negate the impression that the writer was seriously maintaining that

petitioner committed the crime of perjury. Nor does the general tenor of the article negate this impression.

We also think the connotation that petitioner committed perjury is sufficiently factual to be susceptible of being proved true or false. A determination whether petitioner lied in this instance can be made on a core of objective evidence by comparing, *inter alia*, petitioner's testimony before the OHSAA board with his subsequent testimony before the trial court. As the *Scott* court noted regarding the plaintiff in that case, "Whether or not H. Don Scott did indeed perjure himself is certainly verifiable by a perjury action with evidence adduced from the transcripts and witnesses present at the hearing. Unlike a subjective assertion, the averred defamatory language is an articulation of an objectively verifiable event." So too with petitioner Milkovich.

[Previous] decisions . . . establishing First Amendment protection for defendants in defamation actions surely demonstrate the Court's recognition of the Amendment's vital guarantee of free and uninhibited discussion of public issues. But there is also another side to the equation; we have regularly acknowledged the "important social values which underlie the law of defamation," and recognized that "[s]ociety has a pervasive and strong interest in preventing and redressing attacks upon reputation." . . .

We believe our decision in the present case holds the balance true. The judgment of the Ohio Court of Appeals is reversed, and the case is remanded for further proceedings not inconsistent with this opinion.

Reversed.

Dallas Morning News v. Tatum
SUPREME COURT OF TEXAS
554 S.W.3d 614 (2018)

JUSTICE JEFFREY V. BROWN delivered the court's opinion:

> *Words—so innocent and powerless as they are, as standing in a dictionary, how potent for good and evil they become in the hands of one who knows how to combine them.*
>
> —Nathaniel Hawthorne

In this libel-by-implication case, we must determine whether the defamatory meanings the Tatums allege are capable of arising from the words that Steve Blow combined in a column that The Dallas Morning News published.[126] We conclude that the column is reasonably capable of meaning that the Tatums acted deceptively and that the accusation of deception is reasonably capable of defaming the Tatums. However, as we further conclude that the accusation is an opinion, we reverse the court of appeals' judgment and reinstate the trial court's summary judgment for petitioners Steve Blow and The Dallas Morning News. . . .

Paul Tatum was the son of John and Mary Ann Tatum. At seventeen years old, Paul was a smart, popular, and athletic high-school student. By every indication, he was a talented young man with a bright future. One mid-May evening, Paul, driving alone, crashed his parents' vehicle on his way home from a fast-food run. The vehicle's airbag deployed, and the crash was so severe that investigators later discovered Paul's eyelashes and facial tissue at the scene. The crash's cause has never been conclusively established and no evidence suggests that Paul was intoxicated or otherwise under the influence of any substance when the crash occurred.

Paul found his way home on foot. He began drinking and he called a friend. The phone call indicated to the friend that Paul was behaving erratically. The friend, concerned, traveled to Paul's house to see him in person. The friend found Paul at the Tatums' house in a confused state and holding one of the Tatum family's firearms. The friend left the room . . . to report Paul's irrational behavior to [his] parent, who was waiting in a car outside the Tatums' house. Soon after, the friend heard a gunshot. Paul had killed himself.

In the wake of Paul's death, the Tatums discovered medical literature positing a link between traumatic brain injury and suicide. The Tatums concluded that the car accident caused irrational and suicidal ideations in Paul, which in turn led to his death. . . . Paul's mother, a mental-health professional, had never noticed any suicidal tendencies in Paul. By her account, and by all others, Paul was a normal, healthy, and mentally stable young man. For the Tatums, these observations underscored the plausibility of their theory that Paul's car crash generated a brain injury that led to his suicide.

. . . [T]he Tatums sought to memorialize Paul by writing an obituary, which they published by purchasing space in The Dallas Morning News. The obituary stated that Paul died "as a result of injuries sustained in an automobile accident." The Tatums chose this wording to reflect their conviction that Paul's suicide resulted from suicidal ideation arising from a brain injury rather than from any undiagnosed mental illness. The Dallas Morning News published the obituary on May 21, 2010. More than 1,000 people attended Paul's funeral.

Steve Blow is a columnist for The Dallas Morning News. On June 20, 2010—Father's Day, and about one month after Paul's suicide—the paper published a column by Blow entitled "Shrouding Suicide Leaves its Danger Unaddressed."

The column characterized suicide as the "one form of death still considered worthy of deception." While it did not refer to the Tatums by name, it quoted from Paul's obituary and referred to it as "a paid obituary in this newspaper." Although those who knew Paul already knew the truth, the column revealed what the obituary left out: Paul's death "turned out to have been a suicide." After providing another example of an undisclosed suicide, the column went on to lament that "we, as a society, allow suicide to remain cloaked in such secrecy, if not outright deception." The reason we should be more open, according to the column, is that "the secrecy surrounding suicide leaves us greatly underestimating the danger there" and that "averting our eyes from the reality of suicide only puts more lives at risk." The reason we are not open about suicide, the column speculated, is that "we don't talk about the illness that often underlies it—mental illness." . . . Blow wrote that we should not feel embarrassed by suicide and that "the last thing I want to do is put guilt on the family of suicide victims." The column concluded with an exhortation: "Awareness, frank discussion, timely intervention, treatment—those are the things that save lives. Honesty is the first step."

Blow drafted the column without attempting to contact the Tatums and the paper published it without letting the Tatums know that it was going to print. Those who knew the Tatums immediately recognized that the obituary the column referenced was Paul's. . . .

The Tatums filed suit. They alleged libel and libel per se against Blow and the paper. In particular, the Tatums alleged the column defamed them by its "gist." . . . The News filed a motion for traditional and no-evidence summary judgment. The News asserted several traditional grounds. Among them were that the column was not reasonably capable of a defamatory meaning and that the column was an opinion. Without specifying why, the trial court granted the News's motion.

The Tatums appealed. The court of appeals . . . reversed and remanded the Tatums' claims that were based on libel and libel per se. . . .

It held the column was not an opinion because "the column's gist that the Tatums were deceptive when they wrote Paul's obituary is sufficiently verifiable to be actionable in defamation." The News's defenses based on fair comment, official proceedings, truth, substantial truth, actual malice, and negligence fared no better. Thus, the court of appeals rejected every possible ground on which the trial court might have based its grant of summary judgment.

The News petitioned this Court for review. It argues that the court of appeals was wrong on four fronts: the column is not reasonably capable of defamatory meaning; it is non-actionable opinion; it is substantially true; and the court of appeals did not properly analyze actual malice.

II

Defamation is a tort, the threshold requirement for which is the publication of a false statement of fact to a third party. The fact must be defamatory concerning the plaintiff, and the publisher must make the statement with the requisite degree of fault. And in some cases, the plaintiff must also prove damages. . . .

Texas recognizes the common-law rule that defamation is either per se or per quod. . . .

In a defamation case, the threshold question is whether the words used "are reasonably capable of a defamatory meaning." In answering this question, the "inquiry is objective, not subjective." But if the court determines the language is ambiguous, the jury should determine the statement's meaning. If a statement is not verifiable as false, it is not defamatory. Similarly, even when a statement *is* verifiable as false, it does not give rise to liability if the "entire context in which it was made" discloses that it is merely an opinion masquerading as a fact.

Both the U.S. Constitution and the Texas Constitution "robustly protect freedom of speech," and the Texas Constitution expressly acknowledges a cause of action for defamation. . . .

III

"Meaning is the life of language." Thus, the first question in a libel action is whether the words used are "reasonably capable of a defamatory meaning." In answering it, the "inquiry is objective, not subjective." We note that the question involves two independent steps. The first is to determine whether the meaning the plaintiff alleges is reasonably capable of arising from the text of which the plaintiff complains. . . . The second step is to answer whether the meaning—if

it is reasonably capable of arising from the text—is reasonably capable of defaming the plaintiff.

In the typical defamation case, the determination of what a publication means involves little beyond browsing the publication's relevant portions in search of the defamatory content of which the plaintiff complains. That is, defamatory meanings are ordinarily transmitted the same way that other meanings are—explicitly. But this is not the typical defamation case. Rather, the Tatums allege that the column defames them by its "gist."

. . . [F]or clarity, we introduce the following terms. To begin, "textual defamation" refers to the common-law concept of defamation per se, that is, defamation that arises from the statement's text without reference to any extrinsic evidence. On the other hand, "extrinsic defamation" refers to the common-law concept of defamation per quod, which is to say, defamation that *does* require reference to extrinsic circumstances. . . . This case concerns, in part, the distinction between textual defamation and extrinsic defamation.

Extrinsic defamation occurs when a statement whose textual meaning is innocent becomes defamatory when considered in light of "other facts and circumstances sufficiently expressed before" or otherwise known to the reader. The requirements for proving an extrinsic-defamation case—including the torts professor's perennial favorites of innuendo, inducement, and colloquium—are somewhat technical. Only two are of interest here. First, it must be remembered that an extrinsically defamatory statement *requires* extrinsic evidence to be defamatory at all.

Textual defamation occurs when a statement's defamatory meaning arises from the words of the statement itself, without reference to any extrinsic evidence. The ordinary textual defamation involves a statement that is explicitly defamatory. Explicit textual-defamation cases share two common attributes. First, none necessarily involve any extrinsic evidence. Thus, none necessarily involve extrinsic defamation. Second, the defamatory statement's literal text and its communicative content align—what the statement *says* and what the statement *communicates* are the same. In other words, the defamation is both *textual* and *explicit*. . . . When a publication's text implicitly communicates a defamatory statement, we refer to the plaintiff's theory as "defamation by implication."

In a defamation-by-implication case, the defamatory meaning arises from the statement's text, but it does so implicitly. Defamation by implication is not the same thing as textual defamation. Rather, it is a subset of textual defamation. . . .

. . . [A] defendant may be liable for a "publication that gets the details right but fails to put them in the proper context and thereby gets the story's 'gist' wrong.". . . Thus, [our prior cases] recognize that a plaintiff can rely on an entire publication to prove that a defendant has implicitly communicated a defamatory statement.

However, and of special importance in this case, there is no reason that implicit meanings must arise only from an entire publication or not at all. . . .

[W]e acknowledge that in a textual-defamation case, a plaintiff may allege that meaning arises in one of three ways. First, meaning may arise explicitly. . . . Second, meaning may arise implicitly as a result of the article's entire gist. . . . Third, as in this case, the plaintiff may allege that the defamatory meaning arises implicitly from a distinct portion of the article rather than from the article's as-a-whole gist. As other courts have recognized, the distinction between "as-a-whole" gist and "partial" implication is important.

. . . Accordingly, we use the following terms. "Gist" refers to a publication or broadcast's main theme, central idea, thesis, or essence. . . . [We] use "gist" in its colloquial sense. In this usage, publications and broadcasts typically have a single gist.

"Implication," on the other hand, refers to the inferential, illative, suggestive, or deductive meanings that may emerge from a publication or broadcast's discrete parts. . . . "Defamation by implication," as a subtype of textual defamation, covers both "gist" and "implication."

The difference between gist and implication is especially important in two contexts. The first relates to the substantial-truth doctrine. "A broadcast with specific statements that err in the details but that correctly convey the gist of a story is substantially true." . . . We have never held, nor do we today, that a true implication—as opposed to a true gist—can save a defendant from liability for publishing an otherwise factually defamatory statement. Second, the difference between gist and implication matters when considering the requirements that the U.S. Constitution imposes on defamation law.

By nature, defamations by implication require construction. . . . Thus, to determine whether a defamation by implication has occurred, the question is the same as it is for defamatory content generally: is the publication "reasonably capable" of communicating the defamatory statement? But to whose "reason" does "reasonably capable" refer?

Sometimes we have said that "reasonably capable" requires us to construe a publication "based upon how a person of ordinary intelligence *would* perceive it." . . . The "would" standard recognizes that gist, in particular, is the type of implication that no reasonable reader would fail to notice. But the "would" standard falls short when applied to implications. Not all readers will pick up on all reasonable implications in all publications. In fact, it seems apparent that *no* reader *would* internalize every implication from a single article—or even a single sentence.

. . . Instead, when the plaintiff claims defamation by implication, the judicial task is to determine whether the meaning the plaintiff alleges arises from an objectively reasonable reading. . . . Even reasonable readers do not internalize every single implication that a publication conveys. . . . So in an implication case, the judicial role is not to map out every single implication that a publication is capable of supporting. Rather, the judge's task is to determine whether the implication the plaintiff alleges is among the implications that the objectively reasonable reader would draw. . . .

Meanings sometimes terminate in ambiguities. And because defamation involves meaning, ambiguity is often an issue in defamation cases. . . .

Questions of meaning and ambiguity recur in three different types. First, if a court determines that a statement is capable of defamatory meaning and *only* defamatory meaning—that it is unambiguous—then the jury plays no role in determining the statement's meaning. Second, courts sometimes determine that a statement is capable of at least one defamatory and at least one non-defamatory meaning. . . . Third, a court may determine that the statement . . . is not capable of any defamatory meanings. . . .

Our point in reciting these black-letter applications of our defamation law is to emphasize that the analytical framework for considering ambiguities does not evaporate simply because the plaintiff alleges an implicit meaning. . . .

The potential chilling effect is especially strong in defamation-by-implication cases. Unlike explicit statements, publishers cannot be expected to foresee every implication that may reasonably arise from a certain publication. To avoid this chilling effect, the *First Amendment* "imposes a special responsibility on judges whenever it is claimed that a particular communication is [defamatory]." For appellate judges, one of these responsibilities is to comply with the "requirement of independent appellate review reiterated" in *New York Times v. Sullivan* as a matter of "federal constitutional law." Although *Sullivan* emphasized the "actual malice" requirement that applies when the plaintiff, defendant, or subject matter are sufficiently "public," we recognize that its reasoning extends to the *First Amendment* concerns that defamation by implication raises.

The Constitution requires protection beyond that which the "objectively reasonable reader" standard provides. . . .

One way of cabining the dangers that defamation by implication poses would be to subsume the constitutional question within the question of meaning. However, we see no reason for thinking that either the U.S. Constitution or the Texas Constitution has anything to do with what a word in its everyday usage *means*. . . . We cannot solve the constitutional challenges that the tort of defamation by implication presents simply by heightening our standard of meaning. Doing so would be to swim against the current of our traditional jurisprudence that favors "plain meaning." Consequently, we reject a heightened standard of "meaning" as a workable limit on the chilling effect that defamation by implication poses.

A second category of protection disallows defamation by implication, whether altogether or in certain contexts. Some states have taken this approach. . . . Our cases allow public figures—and by extension, private figures, to bring cases alleging defamation by implication. These precedents prevent us from relying on wholesale rejection of defamation by implication to protect the freedoms that the *First Amendment* enshrines.

Still other courts have taken a third path by suggesting that defamatory implications might presumptively constitute opinion in some contexts. We reject the view that implications are opinions, either necessarily or presumptively. Publishers cannot avoid liability for defamatory statements simply by couching their implications within a subjective opinion. Thus, after the U.S. Supreme Court's landmark decision in *Milkovich v. Lorain Journal Co.*, the opinion inquiry seeks to ascertain whether a statement is "verifiable," not whether it manifests a personal view. But no court can decide whether a statement is verifiable until the court decides what the statement *is*—that is, until it conducts an inquiry into the publication's meaning. Of course, implications may frequently turn out to be non-verifiable opinions, but we disagree that implications are presumptively opinion simply by virtue of being implicit. So we see little hope that asking a court to decide from the outset whether a statement is an opinion will limit the number of defamation-by-implication claims that reach a jury.

A fourth and final limit is to rely on or adjust the culpability standards that *Sullivan* lays out. . . . [W]e decline to recognize "culpability" as a limit on our meaning inquiry.

In place of these tests, we believe the D.C. Circuit was correct when it stated the following limit on the inquiry into meaning:

> [I]f a communication, viewed in its entire context, merely conveys materially true facts from which a defamatory inference can reasonably be drawn, the libel is not established. But if the communication, by the particular manner or language in which the true facts are conveyed, supplies additional, affirmative evidence suggesting that the defendant *intends* or *endorses* the defamatory inference, the communication will be deemed capable of bearing that meaning.

Thus, a plaintiff who seeks to recover based on a defamatory implication—whether a gist or a discrete implication—must point to "additional, affirmative evidence" within the publication itself that suggests the defendant "intends or endorses the defamatory inference." . . .

First, the evidence of intent must arise from the publication itself. In considering whether the publication demonstrates such an intent, the court must, as always, "evaluate the publication as a whole rather than focus on individual statements." . . .

Second, in consonance with our precedent and in accord with the judiciary's traditional role when considering plain meaning, the intent or endorsement inquiry "is objective, not subjective." . . . [T]he question is whether the publication indicates by its plain language that the publisher intended to convey the meaning that the plaintiff alleges.

Third, the rule may vary in application depending on the type of defamation that the plaintiff alleges. It does not apply in cases of explicit defamation because when the defendant speaks explicitly, the court indulges the presumption that the defendant intended the communicatory content that he conveyed. . . .

Finally, in a discrete-implication case, it becomes especially relevant for the court to apply the requirement that the publication's text demonstrates the publisher's intent to convey the meaning the plaintiff alleges. In applying the requirement, courts must bear its origin in mind. The especially rigorous review that the requirement implements is merely a reflection of the "underlying principle" that obligates "judges to decide when allowing a case to go to a jury would, in the totality of the circumstances, endanger *first amendment* freedoms."

At the time of summary judgment, the Tatums' live petition alleged that the column defamed them by implicitly communicating the following "gist":

> [The Tatums] created a red herring in the obituary by discussing a car crash in order to conceal the fact that Paul's untreated mental illness—ignored by Plaintiffs—resulted in a suicide that Plaintiffs cannot come to terms with. Defendants led their readers to believe it is people like Plaintiffs—and their alleged inability to accept that their loved ones suffer from mental illness—who perpetuate and exacerbate the problems of mental illness, depression, and suicide.

From this paragraph we discern that the Tatums construe the column to mean that:

- The Tatums acted deceptively in publishing the obituary;

- Paul had a mental illness, which the Tatums ignored and which led to Paul's suicide; and

- The Tatums' deception perpetuates and exacerbates the problem of suicide in others.

None of these meanings appear in the column's explicit text. Nor do they depend on any extrinsic evidence. Thus, while the Tatums allege a textual defamation, their claim rests on defamation by implication rather than on explicit meaning.

The column's gist has nothing to do with the Tatums. Rather, the column's gist is that our society ought to be more forthcoming about suicide and that by failing to do so, our society is making the problem of suicide worse, not better. So none of the meanings the Tatums allege arise from the column's gist.

As to the first meaning the Tatums allege, we agree that the column's text supports the discrete implication that the Tatums acted deceptively. The standard is whether an objectively reasonable reader would draw the implication that the Tatums allege. Here, the gist of Blow's column is that bereaved families often do society a disservice by failing to explicitly mention when suicide is the cause of death. Blow holds up the Tatums as an example of the very phenomenon that his column seeks to discourage. Blow would have no reason to mention the Tatums' obituary except to support his point that suicide often goes undiscussed. . . . Here, an objectively reasonable reading must end with the conclusion that Blow points to the Tatums as one illustration of his thesis that suicide is often "shrouded in secrecy." . . . [W]e conclude that the publication's text objectively demonstrates an intent to convey that the Tatums were deceptive.

But we do not agree that the second and third meanings the Tatums allege are implications that an objectively reasonable reader would draw.

The second alleged meaning rests on the premise that the column means that Paul had a mental illness. We do not agree that the column conveys that meaning. Though the column does say that "mental illness" "often" underlies suicide, the column does so immediately after citing the statistic that suicide is "the third-leading cause of death among young people." The author's use of the word "often" means the column does not logically entail that all suicides are the result of mental illness. And we think the space between the discussion of the Tatums and the discussion of mental illness negates the inferential construction that the Tatums allege—especially since the reference to mental illness follows a citation to a population-level statistic rather than the example paragraphs. . . [W]e conclude that the second meaning the Tatums allege does not arise from an objectively reasonable reading of the column.

Nor does their third. The column declares that "the last thing I want to do is put guilt on the family of suicide victims." An objectively reasonable reader must conclude that the column is about our society as a whole, not about the Tatums in particular. Blow wrote the column to affect future conduct, not to direct blame at any particular family (including the Tatums) for past conduct.

Because the column is "reasonably capable" of communicating the meaning that the Tatums were deceptive, the next question is whether that meaning is "reasonably capable" of defaming the Tatums. We conclude that it is.

. . . We agree with the Tatums and with the court of appeals that the column's accusation of deception is "reasonably capable" of injuring the Tatums' standing in the community. . . . Thus, the accusation is reasonably capable of being defamatory. "Deception" and "honesty" are antonyms. Blow's statement accusing the Tatums of the first is capable of impeaching their character for the second.

We conclude that of the defamatory meanings the Tatums allege, the only one capable of arising from Blow's column is the implicit statement that the Tatums acted deceptively. However, "statements that are not verifiable as false" are not defamatory. And even when a statement is verifiable, it cannot give rise to liability if "the entire context in which it was made" discloses that it was not intended to assert a fact. A statement that fails either test—verifiability or context—is called an opinion.

The News, of course, denies that it has accused the Tatums of deception. But even if the column explicitly levied that accusation, the News argues that the deception in this case is inherently unverifiable. The Tatums' mental states in the hours following Paul's death simply cannot be factually verified. Unlike in *Milkovich*, which involved perjury, no "core of objective evidence" exists from which a jury could draw any conclusions about the Tatums' mental states. The News also argues that the column's context clearly discloses that it contains opinions, and that even if the accusation is capable of verification, it is protected because it is among the opinions that the column contains.

The Tatums contend that the charge of deception is verifiable. The accusation turns on whether the Tatums drafted the obituary with a deceptive mental state. Though the News argues this makes the accusation unverifiable, the law determines mental states all the time. Defamation, the very body of law at issue, has developed a robust process for determining whether a defendant's mental state constitutes actual malice. It cannot be the case, the Tatums argue, that defamation law can ascertain a defendant's mental state but not a plaintiff's. As for context, the Tatums argue that "a reasonable reader . . . would conclude that Blow is making objectively verifiable assertions regarding the Tatums and their deliberate misrepresentations of fact in the Obituary." Thus, in the Tatums' view, the statement is both verifiable and contextually stated as a fact.

. . . "[S]tatements that are not verifiable as false cannot form the basis of a defamation claim." However, *Milkovich* requires courts to focus not only "on a statement's verifiability," but also on "the entire context in which it was made." And even when a statement *is* verifiable as false, it does not give rise to liability if the "entire context in which it was made" discloses that it is merely an opinion masquerading as fact. ("[*Milkovich* protects] statements that cannot 'reasonably [be] interpreted as stating actual facts.' . . ." (second alteration in original) (citations omitted)). Thus, statements that cannot be verified, as well as statements that cannot be understood to convey a verifiable fact, are opinions. Whether a statement is an opinion is a question of law. Finally, the type of writing at issue, though not dispositive, must never cease to inform the reviewing court's analysis.

The column's context manifestly discloses that any implied accusation of deception against the Tatums is opinion. Thus, we need not decide whether the accusation is wholly verifiable.

The column does not implicitly accuse the Tatums of being deceptive people in the abstract or by nature. Instead, it accuses them of a single, understandable act of deception, undertaken with motives that should not incite guilt or embarrassment. And it does so using language that conveys a personal viewpoint rather than an objective recitation of fact. The first sentence begins "So I guess," the column uses various versions of "I think" and "I understand," and near the column's close Blow states "the last thing I want to do is put guilt on the family of suicide victims." This first-person, informal style indicates that the format is subjective rather than objective. Nor does the column imply any undisclosed facts. The Tatums list several "exculpatory" facts that they say Blow should have included in the column. But Blow did not imply that he had personal knowledge that any of the facts the Tatums assert were false. Instead, he compared a quotation from the obituary against an account of Paul's suicide. These two accounts diverged, which Blow noted. Any speculation as to *why* the accounts diverged—if it appears in the column at all—was reasonably based on these disclosed facts. Thus, the column's words indicate that the statement is an opinion. The column's title does the same. The column as a whole, though it includes facts, argues in support of the opinion that the title conveys—society ought to be more frank about suicide. It is an opinion piece through and through.

The court of appeals ignored the column's context, opting instead to focus on decontextualized words which it—not Blow—emphasized. . . . [U]nder our precedent recognizing *Milkovich*'s joint tests, the accusation is not actionable.

Blow's column is an opinion because it does not, in context, defame the Tatums by accusing them of perpetrating a morally blameworthy deception. But to the extent that the column states that the Tatums acted deceptively, it is true. Implicit defamatory meanings—like explicit defamatory statements—are not actionable if they are either true or substantially true. . . .

The statement at issue, which arises implicitly, is that the Tatums acted deceptively when they published the obituary. . . . In our view, the statement that the Tatums were deceptive is both literally and substantially true.

The statement is literally true because the Tatums' obituary is deceptive. It leads readers to believe something that is not true. It states that Paul died from injuries arising from a car accident when in fact Paul committed suicide. . . . The Tatums respond that they earnestly believed that the obituary was true. But the Tatums' beliefs, however sincere, do not make the obituary's message any less deceptive. Indeed, the Tatums argue that Blow should have included all kinds of background facts about the Tatums' beliefs concerning traumatic brain injuries, cause of death, and other matters. But the Tatums themselves did not include any of this information in Paul's obituary. The Tatums cannot argue both that the obituary was true

without this background information and that the column is false for failing to include it.

The Tatums also respond that deception implies intentionality. We agree. But the Tatums plainly and intentionally omitted from the obituary the crucial fact that Paul committed suicide. Their motive with regard to the omission is immaterial to whether the obituary is deceptive. . . .

The column does not accuse the Tatums of being deceptive people in general, but instead of buckling to the current societal pressure to avoid disclosing suicide when it occurs. And to the extent that readers thought less of the Tatums after reading the column, it would be because they concluded on their own that the Tatums acted deceptively, not because they decided to believe the column's implied assertion to that effect. . . .

The Tatums respond that a literally truthful column would have included many caveats beyond the fact that the Tatums did not intend to deceive. These facts all relate to whether the Tatums' view of Paul's death was reasonable or scientifically justified. . . .

Blow's column was callous, certainly, but it was not false.

The publication of Blow's column may have run afoul of certain journalistic, ethical, and other standards. But the standards governing the law of defamation are not among them. Accordingly, we reverse the judgment of the court of appeals and reinstate the trial court's summary judgment in favor of petitioners Steve Blow and The Dallas Morning News, Inc.

JUSTICE JEFFREY S. BOYD, joined by JUSTICE DEBRA LEHRMANN and JUSTICE JAMES BLACKLOCK, concurring:

I imagine it's no surprise by now that many courts and commentators have complained that defamation law is a "quagmire," lacks "clarity and certainty," is "overly confusing" and "convoluted," leaves courts "hopelessly and irretrievably confused," and "has spawned a morass of case law in which consistency and harmony have long ago disappeared." I'm afraid [part] of the Court's opinion in this case—in which the Court addresses whether Steve Blow's column was reasonably capable of a defamatory meaning—tends to prove their point. . . . I fear its effort to advance the law by introducing new terminology and addressing concepts unnecessary to this decision only makes things worse.

The Court begins its twenty-five-page analysis by introducing the new labels "textual defamation" and "extrinsic defamation" for what courts have always called "defamation per se" and "defamation per quod." . . . Textual defamation by implication involves the publication's gist, which may arise implicitly because of the article's as-a-whole gist . . . but only if it is reasonably capable of a defamatory meaning, which does not mean it is or is not ambiguous, but does mean it is capable of at least one defamatory meaning. . . . Or defamation by implication may arise from a partial or discrete implication, which really means the gist of a part of the article (but the Court doesn't call that a gist), to which implication the substantial-truth doctrine does not apply. . . . But regardless of whether the defamation by implication arises from the as-a-whole gist or a discrete implication, the decision whether it is reasonably capable of a defamatory meaning must not exert too great a chilling effect on *First Amendment* activities—a particular concern in implication cases. So the plaintiff has an especially rigorous burden in such cases . . . [and] the court must conduct an especially vigorous review to confirm the defendant's intent to convey the meaning the plaintiff alleges.

Got it?

. . . I'm not yet ready to scrap our convoluted principles. I can accept the idea that defamation law must be fairly complicated due to its "frequent collision . . . with the overriding constitutional principles of free speech and free press." Despite its "technical complexity," defamation law has "shown remarkable stamina in the teeth of centuries of acid criticism," which "may reflect one useful strategy for a legal system forced against its ultimate better judgment to deal with dignitary harms." But we should always do our best to reduce the confusion, or, at least, avoid adding to it.

The question in this case is pretty simple: For summary-judgment purposes, was Blow's column reasonably capable of a defamatory meaning? We need not—and the Court does not—announce any new substantive legal principles to decide that issue. . . .

I agree that the Tatums provided some evidence that Blow's column was reasonably capable of conveying the defamatory meaning that the Tatums published a deceptive obituary. I also agree, however, that if the column expressed that assertion, it expressed it as Blow's opinion, not as a fact. Because the column only expressed a potentially defamatory opinion, the Tatums cannot recover for defamation, and we need not also consider whether Blow's opinion was correct or substantially true. . . .

Modern cellphones are not just another technological convenience. With all they contain and all they may reveal, they hold for many Americans "the privacies of life."

—**U.S. Supreme Court Chief Justice John Roberts**[1]

In a recent U.S. Supreme Court ruling about cellphone privacy, Chief Justice John Roberts remarked, "The proverbial visitor from Mars might conclude [cellphones] were an important feature of human anatomy."[2]

6 PROTECTING PRIVACY
Conflicts Among the Press, the Government and the Right to Privacy

SUPPOSE...

. . . your smartphone or cellphone connects to your carrier's wireless network through a cell tower multiple times a minute, even when you're not using it. All of this cell-site location information (CSLI) is kept by your wireless carrier for years. After police arrested several men for multiple suspected robberies, they used CSLI to connect the group's ringleader to the crime scenes. The police obtained 127 days of location data through a subpoena, or court order, as required under the Stored Communications Act, and used the CSLI to track his every move. The ringleader was convicted and sentenced to more than 100 years in prison. Could the government access those data without probable cause—sufficient reason to think a crime was committed based on facts—to obtain a search warrant?

The Fourth Amendment protects against "unreasonable searches and seizures." Does the Fourth Amendment protect CSLI from warrantless searches? Because people consent to share CSLI with their wireless carriers when they sign up for service, do they forfeit any "reasonable expectation of privacy"? More broadly, how has technology changed society's understanding of a "reasonable expectation of privacy"? Look for the answers to these questions when you read the discussion of *Carpenter v. United States* in this chapter and an excerpt of the case decision at the end of the chapter.[3]

Although libel has been recognized for more than 400 years, the notion that courts or legislatures should protect privacy rights is only about 130 years old.[4] In 1890, two Boston lawyers—Samuel Warren and his partner, then-future U.S. Supreme Court Justice

Louis Brandeis—wrote "The Right to Privacy" for the prestigious Harvard Law Review.[5] Warren and Brandeis knew that no statutes shielded people's private lives, but the lawyers contended that the common law should recognize privacy rights.[6] They argued that human dignity required protecting individual privacy.[7]

In the 20th century, the U.S. Supreme Court formally recognized a constitutional right to privacy. During the seven decades after the Warren and Brandeis article, a few state courts accepted a common law right of privacy, and several other states adopted privacy laws.[8] In recent decades, federal agencies have also started to play a greater role in protecting privacy. Today, the Federal Trade Commission has the power to police companies' data security practices, and it enforces various laws that address data security and personal privacy.

CONSTITUTIONAL RIGHT TO PRIVACY

Americans have always valued privacy rights. This is reflected in the U.S. Constitution, even though the word "privacy" is not explicitly stated. For example, the framers adopted the Fourth Amendment, protecting "the right of the people to be secure in their persons, houses, papers, and effects, against unreasonable searches and seizures."[9] Founding Father and second President John Adams recalled in his papers that it was the British writs of assistance, or generic court orders, during colonial times that allowed British officers to conduct random searches of shops, warehouses and private homes. President Adams suggested that

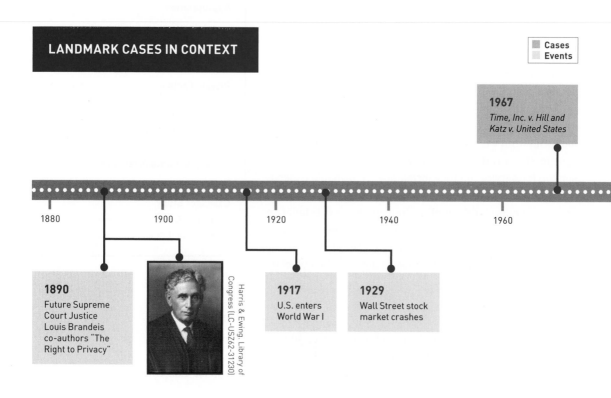

LANDMARK CASES IN CONTEXT

☐ Cases
☐ Events

1967
Time, Inc. v. Hill and Katz v. United States

1880   1900   1920   1940   1960

1890
Future Supreme Court Justice Louis Brandeis co-authors "The Right to Privacy"

Harris & Ewing, Library of Congress (LC-USZ62-31230)

1917
U.S. enters World War I

1929
Wall Street stock market crashes

public outrage over this practice "helped spark the Revolution itself" and is the reason for the Fourth Amendment.[10]

The Third and Fifth Amendments also protect different aspects of privacy.[11] Fifty years ago, in *Griswold v. Connecticut*, the U.S. Supreme Court said the word "liberty" in the 14th Amendment also includes personal privacy—"[N]or shall any State deprive any person of life, liberty, or property, without due process of law."[12] In *Griswold*, the Supreme Court struck down a state's ban on the use of birth control, noting that it violated the privacy rights of married people. The Court said in *Griswold* that a right to privacy was implicit in the various amendments previously mentioned, as well as the Ninth Amendment and even the First Amendment's "freedom to associate and privacy in one's associations."[13]

Most Americans associate the U.S. Supreme Court's *Roe v. Wade* decision with abortion rights.[14] In coming to its judgment in *Roe*, the Court also affirmed the qualified constitutional protection for personal privacy established in *Griswold*. Justice Harry Blackmun wrote for the Court:

> This right to privacy, whether it be founded in the Fourteenth Amendment's concept of personal liberty and restrictions upon state action, as we feel it is, or, as the District Court determined, in the Ninth Amendment's reservation of rights to the people, is broad enough to encompass a woman's decision whether or not to terminate her pregnancy.[15]

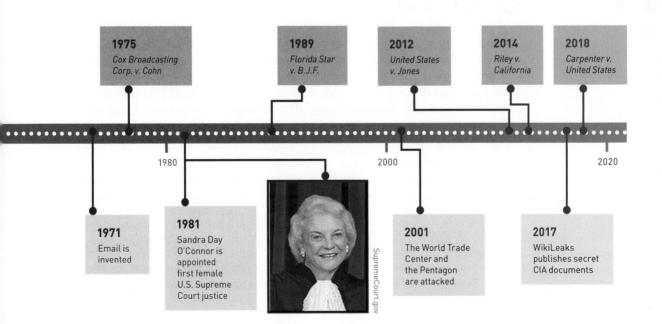

1975 Cox Broadcasting Corp. v. Cohn

1989 Florida Star v. B.J.F.

2012 United States v. Jones

2014 Riley v. California

2018 Carpenter v. United States

1980

2000

2020

1971 Email is invented

1981 Sandra Day O'Connor is appointed first female U.S. Supreme Court justice

SupremeCourt.gov

2001 The World Trade Center and the Pentagon are attacked

2017 WikiLeaks publishes secret CIA documents

In *Roe*, the Court emphasized that the right of personal privacy is qualified and must be weighed against important state interests in regulation.[16]

The earliest U.S. Supreme Court case that explored Fourth Amendment privacy-related protections focused on property and not people. Fourth Amendment cases often hinge on what constitutes a search under the law. Judges issue **search warrants** authorizing law enforcement officers to search locations and seize items. A valid search warrant must be based on probable cause—sufficient information and facts to think a crime was committed based on reliable information and facts.

In 1928, the Court held that an electronic eavesdropping device did not amount to a search under the Fourth Amendment because placing the device did not involve physical entry into the defendant's home.[17] Justice Brandeis dissented, writing that "every unjustifiable intrusion by the Government upon the privacy of the individual, whatever the means employed," was an unconstitutional search under the Fourth Amendment.[18]

In the 1960s, the Court's approach shifted. In *Silverman v. United States*, the U.S. Supreme Court held that it was a search when federal officers eavesdropped on defendants by using a microphone placed through the wall of a home. This search, the Court held, violated the Fourth Amendment.[19] In *Katz v. United States*, the defendant was convicted of illegal betting over a telephone line in a public phone booth. The government recorded his phone conversations without a warrant, which led to his conviction. The Supreme Court threw out that evidence, calling it a Fourth Amendment violation. In his concurrence, Justice John Marshall Harlan II wrote, "[A] person has a constitutionally protected reasonable expectation of privacy," and "electronic as well as physical intrusion into a place that is in this sense private may constitute a violation of the Fourth Amendment."[20]

Courts have recognized Justice Harlan's concurrence in *Katz* as the Harlan "reasonable expectation of privacy test." The test requires that an individual have an actual expectation of privacy and that society is prepared to recognize this as reasonable.[21] In a recent case, Chief Justice John Roberts wrote, "Justice Harlan's concurrence profoundly changed our Fourth Amendment jurisprudence."[22]

Thirty years ago, the Court said a search of a public employee's desk and filing cabinet did not violate his or her Fourth Amendment rights.[23] Courts have said the First Amendment does not bar private employers from examining email messages on an employee's computer because the company's interest in preventing illegal activity or unprofessional comments outweighs an employee's privacy interest.[24]

In *City of Ontario v. Quon*, the U.S. Supreme Court held that government employers may see public employees' text messages sent and received on government-issued equipment if the searches have a legitimate work-related purpose and public employees have been told not to expect privacy.[25] The case involved a police officer who used a department-issued pager to communicate with fellow officers. When the city audited officers' pagers, it found one officer had exchanged sexually explicit text messages with both his wife and his mistress. The officer claimed the city violated his reasonable expectation of privacy. The Court

search warrant
A legal order by a judge to authorize law enforcement to search locations and seize items. Only issued with probable cause.

said even if the officer did have a reasonable expectation of privacy, the city's search of his pager did not violate it. Although the Court said its ruling was narrowly applied to the case facts, subsequent cases have applied the ruling to government-issued computers and other communication technologies.[26]

Today, many challenges to privacy involve communication via new technologies. Recent U.S. Supreme Court cases have tackled questions about how courts should apply decades-old precedents to technology that did not exist at the time of those decisions. For example, the Court held that the government must have a search warrant to use a thermal imaging device on a home because use of this technology constituted a search.[27] In *United States v. Jones*, the Supreme Court unanimously held that physically mounting a GPS transmitter on a car amounts to a search and violates the Fourth Amendment.[28]

In *Riley v. California*, a unanimous Supreme Court said law enforcement may not search a person's cellphone without a warrant. The decision involved convictions of two suspects for criminal activity based on evidence found on their cellphones—one a smartphone, the other a flip phone. The government argued that searching a cellphone found on a person at the time of arrest fell under the "incident to arrest" exception, which allows for a search of a person without a warrant at the time of an arrest. Writing for the Court, Chief Justice Roberts said the "incident to arrest" exception does not apply to a cellphone:

> Modern cellphones, as a category, implicate privacy concerns far beyond those implicated by the search of a cigarette pack, a wallet, or a purse. Cellphones differ in both a quantitative and a qualitative sense from other objects that might be kept on an arrestee's person.[29]

In *Carpenter v. United States* (excerpted at the end of this chapter), the Supreme Court in 2018 extended Fourth Amendment protection to cell-site location information (CSLI), produced when your cellphone connects to your carrier's wireless network through a cell tower.[30] As required under the Stored Communications Act, the police obtained a subpoena, or court order, to get months of Timothy Carpenter's CSLI. Police then used CSLI to connect Carpenter to various robbery crime scenes. He was convicted, largely because of the CSLI.[31]

Writing for the majority in a 5–4 decision, Chief Justice Roberts said using a subpoena to obtain CSLI is not enough—instead, this constitutes a search under the Fourth

---

POINTS OF LAW

CONSTITUTIONAL RIGHT TO PRIVACY

- The U.S. Constitution protects from governmental invasion of privacy.

- Protection comes from the Third, Fourth, Fifth, Ninth and 14th Amendments.

- The U.S. Supreme Court has said personal privacy rights are qualified and not absolute (see *Griswold*[i]).

- Justice John Harlan's "reasonable expectation of privacy" test from *Katz*[ii] establishes a Fourth Amendment right to privacy when

  1. a person has an actual expectation of privacy that
  2. society recognizes as reasonable.

Amendment and requires a search warrant. "The seismic shifts in digital technology that made possible the tracking of not only Carpenter's location but also everyone else's, not for a short period but for years and years [is] unlike the nosy neighbor who keeps an eye on comings and goings," he wrote. Wireless carriers "are ever alert, and their memory is nearly infallible."[32]

In *Carpenter*, the Court noted that the case did not fit neatly with existing precedents, specifically two cases decided in the 1970s: *United States v. Miller* and *Smith v. Maryland*.[33] The Court held in both cases that an individual has no expectation of privacy in bank and phone company records kept by third parties (e.g., the bank or phone company).[34] Called the **third-party doctrine**, the concept holds that people who voluntarily give information to third parties, such as banks, phone companies or internet service providers, forfeit any reasonable expectation of privacy.

The Supreme Court rejected the application of the third-party doctrine to CSLI in *Carpenter*:

third-party doctrine
A legal concept that holds that people who voluntarily give information to third parties, such as banks or phone companies, forfeit any reasonable expectation of privacy in that information.

We decline to extend *Smith* and *Miller*[.] . . . Given the unique nature of cell phone location records, the fact that the information is held by a third party does not by itself overcome the user's claim to *Fourth Amendment* protection. . . . Although [CSLI] records are generated for commercial purposes, that distinction does not negate Carpenter's anticipation of privacy in his physical location. . . . [T]he time-stamped data provides an intimate window into a person's life, revealing not only his particular movements, but through them his "familial, political, professional, religious, and sexual associations." These location records "hold for many Americans the privacies of life." . . . [C]ell phone tracking is remarkably easy, cheap, and efficient compared to traditional investigative tools. With just the click of a button, the Government can access each carrier's deep repository of historical location information at practically no expense.[35]

The Court noted that the decision in *Carpenter* does not overturn *Miller* and *Smith* or the section of the Stored Communications Act that allowed law enforcement to obtain most records with a subpoena. The decision should be applied narrowly to CSLI rather than all third-party records. In four separate dissents, the four dissenting justices disagreed on why the majority was in error. Justices Anthony Kennedy and Samuel Alito argued primarily that the third-party doctrine should apply.[36] Justice Clarence Thomas said the framers of the U.S. Constitution did not intend privacy to be incorporated into the Fourth Amendment in the way the Court has done so over the years, particularly in its application of the *Katz* "reasonable expectation of privacy."[37] Justice Neil Gorsuch said property law precedents provide a better avenue for determining privacy concerns with new technologies.[38]

PRIVACY TORTS

The dictionary defines privacy as "freedom from unauthorized intrusion" and the "state of being let alone and able to keep certain especially personal matters to oneself."[39] This common definition of privacy reflects the evolution of privacy law, whether constitutional or based on state statutes. Sixty years ago, William Prosser, a torts expert and law school dean, suggested that states should divide privacy law into four categories: intrusion, false light, appropriation and private facts.[40] Intrusion is defined as physically or technologically disturbing another's reasonable expectation of privacy. False light is the privacy tort that involves making a person seem to be someone he or she is not in the public eye. Appropriation is generally using a person's name, picture or voice without permission for commercial purposes. Private facts is publicizing highly offensive, true private information that is not newsworthy or lawfully obtained from a public record. Courts and state legislatures adopted and continue to use Prosser's categories, but not all states allow plaintiffs to sue for each of the four privacy torts. Additionally, the appropriation tort currently includes two different torts: commercialization and right to publicity.

In 2019, 42 states recognized the intrusion tort, while two have rejected it; 34 states recognized the false light tort, and 10 have rejected it; 46 states recognized private facts, and four have rejected that doctrine; and 46 states recognized appropriation torts, while four states have not ruled on the issue. The District of Columbia and the U.S. Virgin Islands both recognize all four privacy torts, while Puerto Rico only recognizes appropriation.[41]

Only living individuals may sue for three of the privacy torts: intrusion, private facts and false light.[42] Like a person's reputation in a libel case, privacy is considered a personal right. The dead do not have personal rights. Also, businesses, associations, unions and other groups generally do not have personal rights and most often cannot sue for a privacy tort.[43] Only individuals may sue for appropriation in many states. But a few states allow businesses, nonprofit organizations and associations to bring appropriation lawsuits. Additionally, in many states, the right of publicity is extended to heirs.

INTRUSION

While many of the U.S. Supreme Court cases discussed earlier focus on the limits to government intrusion, the news media have utilized some of the same techniques to report on issues of public concern. What limits exist for investigative newsgathering techniques that can include, for example, hidden microphones and cameras?

intrusion upon seclusion
Physically or technologically disturbing another's reasonable expectation of privacy.

reasonable person
The law's version of an average person.

Invasive newsgathering techniques may amount to **intrusion upon seclusion**.[44] (Information-gathering techniques that may be classified as intrusion are discussed further in Chapter 7.) Journalists may be sued for intrusion if they intentionally interfere with another person's solitude or meddle in the person's private concerns in a way that would be highly offensive to a **reasonable person** (the law's version of an average person). The intrusion may be physical, such as entering someone's house without permission, or technological, such as using a geolocation device. The intrusion tort is intended to ensure people retain their dignity by preventing unwanted encroachment into an individual's personal physical space and private affairs. Only New York and Virginia have refused to recognize the intrusion tort.[45]

The more technology develops, the more ways intrusion can occur. For example, 41 states have enacted laws addressing a variety of concerns, including privacy protection, with unmanned aircraft systems or drones.[46] But even older technology, such as a camera's telephoto lens, can intrude.

In one case, a woman's sister-in-law, husband and children visited her home after she disappeared. They swam in the home's pool, surrounded by a seven-foot-high fence, while a CBS television network cameraman stood on a neighbor's porch and videotaped them using a telephoto lens. A federal district court permitted the family to sue CBS for intrusion, saying:

> We find that the plaintiffs' allegations that they were swimming in the backyard pool of a private home surrounded by a seven-foot privacy fence are sufficient to allege both that they believed they were in a secluded place and that the activity was private.[47]

Recent Federal Aviation Administration rules have made it easier for businesses to fly lightweight drones.

Intrusion suits have been brought based on news reporters finding information in public records. Courts have held that there is no reasonable expectation of privacy in public records.[48]

Intrusion on Private Property

Journalists might obtain information by intentionally entering private property without permission. Anyone who does so has committed intrusion, an act similar to trespass (discussed in Chapter 7). Trespass is both a crime and a tort. A trespasser may be sued for intrusion. Intrusion occurs only if a person has a reasonable expectation of privacy. For example, people have a reasonable expectation that others will not enter into their private property, such as a house or apartment, without consent. That may not be the case, however, for private land to which the public has access. In a lawsuit involving Google's Street View feature, which provides searchable panoramic street views, a couple sued Google for intrusion. Street

View showed the couple's house and swimming pool. The couple claimed the pictures could be obtained only by driving up the private street on which their home is located, a street marked as "Private Road, No Trespassing." However, no reasonable person would be highly offended by Google's entry onto the road, the Third Circuit Court of Appeals said, because guests and delivery trucks entered the road and saw what Street View's pictures showed.[49]

Ordinarily, there is not a reasonable expectation of privacy on public streets and sidewalks and in public parks where people can be seen or overheard. However, there may be circumstances when people do have a reasonable expectation of privacy in public places. For example, the U.S. Supreme Court upheld a Colorado law that created an eight-foot bubble around individuals entering a health care facility.[50] The statute made it illegal to approach within eight feet of a person going into an abortion clinic—the law's primary focus—to hand out a leaflet, display a sign or interact without the person's consent. The law applied within a 100-foot radius around a health care facility's entrance. In *Hill v. Colorado*, the Court said the law was neither content nor viewpoint based. Therefore, the Court did not apply a strict scrutiny standard. The state needed to show only a substantial interest. The Court said Colorado's interests in public health and in protecting the rights of individuals to avoid unwanted communication met the intermediate scrutiny test. Colorado's law implies that people entering health clinics have a reasonable expectation of privacy.

Courts may not permit journalists to exceed acceptable means of obtaining information. Following Princess Diana's death, California passed an anti-paparazzi law.[51] The California law said that offensively trespassing to photograph or record a person's personal or family activities is an invasion of privacy. Another California statute made it a misdemeanor to attempt to photograph or videotape the children of celebrities in a harassing manner.[52]

Journalists should not assume people involved in a news event occurring on public property do not have a reasonable expectation of privacy. For example, an automobile accident victim reasonably expected discussions with emergency personnel to be private even if medical treatment took place on the side of a public road, a court held.[53]

It is not always easy to determine whether property is private or public. Taxpayers own government land, but they may not always be permitted on the property. A federal district court ruled that police could arrest reporters entering a naval base without permission to cover protests.[54]

Defenses

Consent is the only defense for an intrusion suit based on trespass in nearly all cases. Newsworthiness is not a defense because publishing is not an element of the tort. The intrusion happens in the newsgathering process. However, the Ninth Circuit Court of Appeals said a story's newsworthiness may reduce the intrusion's offensiveness.[55] This is important because a plaintiff must prove the intrusion was highly offensive.

POINTS OF LAW
INTRUSION BY TRESPASS

Plaintiff's Case

- A reasonable expectation of privacy
- Intentional intrusion on privacy
- that would be highly offensive to a reasonable person

Defense

- Consent

Consent. A person cannot claim a reasonable expectation of privacy if he or she gave consent for someone to be on his or her private property. For example, a restaurant owner allowed a television news crew to videotape a health inspector evaluating the restaurant. After the station ran an unflattering story, the restaurant sued for intrusion. Because a trial jury found that the restaurant owner had given the television crew consent to enter the premises, an appeals court rejected the restaurant's claim.[56] Consent can also be implied. For example, if a journalist enters private property and the property owner responds to the reporter's questions, there is implied consent to remain and continue the interview.[57]

False Pretenses. Using false pretenses to enter private property is a long-standing reporting technique. Courts are not in agreement, but generally have said reporters can deceptively gain entry without invading privacy. In one case, a producer for the ABC television network program "Primetime Live" sent seven people, posing as patients and equipped with hidden cameras, to eye clinics owned by Dr. J.H. Desnick. "Primetime Live" used portions of the hidden video recordings in a story it aired suggesting that Desnick's clinics performed unnecessary cataract surgery. Desnick sued ABC for intrusion and other torts. The clinics were open to anyone who wanted an eye examination, the Seventh Circuit Court of Appeals said. The people posing as patients were allowed into the clinics, just like anyone else. The people posing as patients meant to deceive, but that did not invalidate consent to enter, the court held.[58]

The Seventh Circuit noted that people sometimes use deception to enter private or semi-private premises. For example, a restaurant owner might refuse entry to a food critic known to write harsh reviews. But restaurant critics usually do not identify themselves to the owner when they enter. The court said this deception does not negate the restaurant owner's consent. The court said this analysis might not apply to someone using false pretenses to enter for no substantive reason, for example someone who pretends to be a utilities meter reader to enter a private home. In contrast, the hypothetical restaurant critic—and the people posing as eye clinic patients—had valid reasons to be on private property, the court said.

In a different case, a photographer dressed in hospital apparel recorded a video of emergency room personnel treating a man who had a bad reaction to a drug. He asked the patient to sign a release form. The photographer said the video would be used to train hospital personnel. The patient signed the release. After the video ran on a cable program, "Trauma: Life in the ER," the patient sued for intrusion and other claims. A court agreed that the patient had a reasonable expectation of privacy in a hospital emergency room. The court said the photographer's deception invalidated the patient's consent.[59]

Entering a home or office using false pretenses may provide grounds for an intrusion suit. At least one court said that combining false pretenses with surreptitious image and audio recording after entering a home was intrusive. To investigate a person practicing medicine without a license, a Life magazine reporter and a photographer claimed to be patients and were admitted to the man's home. The reporter had a microphone in her purse, and the photographer used a small, concealed camera to take pictures. A federal appellate court ignored the false pretenses question and focused on the surreptitious reporting. The court said people have a reasonable expectation of privacy in their homes. Even though a person might expect a visitor to repeat what is seen and heard in the house, it is not expected that "what is heard and seen will be transmitted by photograph or recording . . . to the public at large."[60] The court added, "The First Amendment is not a license to trespass, to steal, or to intrude by electronic means into the precincts of another's home or office."[61]

Most states have laws making it illegal to pretend to be a law enforcement officer. In some states, it is unlawful to pretend to be any public official.

FALSE LIGHT

False light is a first cousin to libel. A misleading story or a YouTube video that represents a person as someone he or she is not may be grounds for a false light suit.[62] False light often involves the misattribution of a person's actions or beliefs. Typically, a false light tort does not require a plaintiff to show injury to reputation, although California sees false light and libel as such close relatives that a false light plaintiff must prove reputational injury.[63] Some state courts say the false light tort is too similar to defamation and refuse to recognize it. They also say false light is so vague it encroaches on First Amendment rights. A number of courts allow a plaintiff to sue for both defamation and false light based on the same facts.

false light
A privacy tort that involves making a person seem in the public eye to be someone he or she is not. Not recognized in all states.

Plaintiff's Case

Most states recognizing false light require a plaintiff to prove (1) the material was published, (2) the plaintiff was identified, (3) the published material was false or created a false impression, (4) the statements or pictures put the plaintiff in a false light that would be highly offensive to a reasonable person and (5) the defendant acted with actual malice—he or she knew the material was false or recklessly disregarded its falsity.[64] Only individuals can bring a false light suit.[65]

Publication. The false light tort requires material to have been widely distributed to the public generally or to a large segment of the community.[66] Generally, communication to a few people does not amount to publication for the false light tort, although courts in a few states allow publication to be proved by dissemination to just one person or a few people.[67] For these courts, that smaller group must have a special relationship with the plaintiff so the plaintiff would be highly offended if the group saw or heard the publication.[68]

Identification. The plaintiff must prove the material in question was about her or him. The courts of some states, such as California, define identification for false light just as they do for libel. It is sufficient if one or more people say the communication identified the plaintiff.[69] Most courts hold that because the publication requirement means many people must be exposed to the story, a large segment of the public must reasonably believe the false material refers to the plaintiff.

Falsity. Published material supporting a false light suit must be false or imply false information. If the publication is true, it cannot be grounds for a false light suit even if the material emotionally upsets the plaintiff. Minor errors ordinarily do not make a story sufficiently incorrect to meet the falsity standard.

Some courts hold that true facts can lead to false implications if the defendant intended that result. For example, The New York Times published a story implying that a businessman named Robert Howard might be using an alias and really was another person, Howard Finkelstein, a convicted felon. The story included only true statements: Records showed that Finkelstein used the name Robert Howard; Howard denied he was Finkelstein, yet rumors circulated saying he might be. A jury found that the reporter did not libel Howard because the story did not absolutely say he was Finkelstein. A federal appellate court said the story's implication that the businessman might be the felon could sustain a false light suit.[70] However, there must be a clear connection between the statements leading to a false light suit and the implied falsehood the plaintiff claims.

fact finder
In a trial, a judge or the jury determining which facts presented in evidence are accurate.

Highly Offensive. At a false light trial, the **fact finder**—the jury, if there is one, or the judge—must determine whether the published material would be highly offensive to a reasonable person. There are no definite standards. Defining "highly offensive" is a very subjective task. Some legal scholars try to clarify the term "highly offensive" by using three categories: embellishment, distortion and fictionalization.[71] These are not legal categories, but they can help to recognize a circumstance that could potentially give rise to a false light claim.

A story is embellished when false material is added to otherwise true facts. For example, a series of newspaper columns told a true story of a mother giving up a baby for adoption, the baby being adopted, a court giving the natural father custody four years later and the father hiring a psychologist to help the child adjust to a new home. One column falsely said the psychologist "has readily admitted that she sees her job as doing whatever the natural parents instruct her to do." A jury could find it highly offensive to a reasonable person to suggest a psychologist would ignore her professional commitments, a court ruled.[72]

Distortion occurs when facts are omitted or the context in which material is published makes an otherwise accurate story appear false. For example, a young woman consented to having a photographer take her picture for his portfolio. A magazine later used the picture to illustrate a story headlined "In Cold Blood—An Exposé of the Baltimore Teen Murders." The accompanying article said the high murder rate among the city's African-American teenagers was due to drug abuse and poor economic conditions. Used in other circumstances, the photo might not have led to a lawsuit. This context, however, implied that the young woman was poor, abused drugs or perhaps even was connected to a murder.[73]

Fictionalization is taking real facts and making them fiction. This can result in a false light claim when a person's name or other identifying characteristics, for example, are part of a largely fictional piece. In one case, a supermarket tabloid newspaper published a picture of 97-year-old Arkansas resident Nellie Mitchell to illustrate a story with the headline, "Pregnancy Forced Granny to Quit Work at Age 101." The story was a fictional account of an Australian woman who left her paper route at the age of 101 because she became pregnant during an extramarital affair with a rich client. Mitchell, in fact, delivered newspapers in her hometown for nearly 50 years. Mitchell won her false light suit and, after the newspaper's appeals, was awarded $1 million in damages.[74]

Fault. Decades ago, the U.S. Supreme Court decided two false light cases: *Time, Inc. v. Hill* and *Cantrell v. Forest City Publishing Co.* Both cases involved private individual plaintiffs, not public officials or public figures, and the Court held that they had to prove actual malice to win.

The Hill family sued Time, Inc., publisher of Life magazine, for a story and photographs about a play's account of the family's experience of being held hostage for 19 hours by escaped convicts. The convicts did not harm the Hills, and the family later said they were treated with respect. The play portrayed a fictional Hilliard family held hostage, beaten and verbally abused by escaped convicts. The Hills claimed that the text and accompanying photographs suggested the convicts treated the real Hill family as ruthlessly as the fictional hostages and this put the family in a false light. The Hills sued and won.[75]

The U.S. Supreme Court reversed, saying the jury should have been told that the Hills could win only if they proved actual malice.[76] The First Amendment protects the press from being sued for negligent misstatements when reporting stories of public interest, the Court reasoned.

Seven years after *Hill*, the U.S. Supreme Court again said a private plaintiff had to prove actual malice. In *Cantrell v. Forest City Publishing Co.*, the Supreme Court upheld a jury verdict in the Cantrell family's favor because the trial judge correctly told the jury to apply the actual malice standard. The case involved a feature in the Cleveland Plain Dealer newspaper about the impact of a bridge collapse on a small community in West Virginia. The article and accompanying photographs featured the Cantrell family and highlighted their abject poverty. The Court said there was sufficient evidence to show that portions of the article were false and were published with knowing falsity or reckless disregard for the truth.[77]

Lower courts are supposed to follow U.S. Supreme Court rulings. Courts in at least 11 states follow the Supreme Court precedents in *Hill* and *Cantrell*, requiring all false light plaintiffs to show actual malice.[78] For example, a court in Tennessee dismissed a case in 2018 because a former "American Idol" contestant could not prove actual malice in his false light claim against E! Entertainment television. The former contestant sued for libel and false light after the network aired an "E! True Hollywood Story" that said that "American Idol" producers disqualified the former contestant because he did not disclose a prior arrest. The docudrama on Paula Abdul also dismissed the former contestant's claim that he had an affair with her, which she denied. His false light claim alleged that these discrepancies presented him in a false light, but the court said the former contestant presented no evidence to support a showing of actual malice.[79]

Some state courts are divided on requiring private persons to prove actual malice in false light cases. Courts in at least five states and the District of Columbia have applied *Gertz v. Robert Welch, Inc.* (discussed in Chapter 4) to false light cases. They have suggested that the U.S. Supreme Court

POINTS OF LAW
FALSE LIGHT

Plaintiff's Case

- Publication of
- false facts
- about the identified individual
- that would be highly offensive to a reasonable person
- with actual malice, for both private and public plaintiffs (although a few state courts only require negligence for private plaintiffs)[iii]

Defense

- Libel defenses

An appeals court held that "The Hurt Locker" was transformative. An army sergeant said Jeremy Renner's character was based on him.

would apply *Gertz* today if it heard another false light appeal.[80] These state courts would require only that a private individual prove negligence in a false light suit, not actual malice.

Defenses

Because not all state courts recognize the false light tort, parts of it remain in flux. However, many courts say that if a false light plaintiff proves all elements of his or her case, a media defendant may use the libel defenses discussed in Chapter 5 to defeat the claim.[81] For example, media defendants can utilize the fair report privilege.[82] People with absolute privilege if sued for libel—those involved in judicial proceedings or government meetings, certain public officials and others—also have absolute privilege in false light suits. Truth is also defense in a false light suit. Only a few courts have decided whether opinion is a defense for a false light claim, and they disagree.[83]

More recently, some appellate courts have also applied anti-SLAPP statutes to false light claims. As noted in Chapter 5, anti-SLAPP laws generally allow a defendant to make a motion to strike a lawsuit because it involves a matter of public concern. The plaintiff has the burden to show that they will prevail in the lawsuit, otherwise the suit is dismissed. If a defendant prevails, some anti-SLAPP laws allow them to collect attorney's fees from the plaintiff.

In 2016, the Ninth Circuit Court of Appeals said California's anti-SLAPP statute applied to a lawsuit filed against the producers and distributers of the film "The Hurt Locker." Army sergeant Jeffrey Sarver alleged that the main character in the film was based on him, and he sued for defamation, false light, intentional infliction of emotional distress and other torts.

With respect to defamation and false light, Sarver alleged that the film's depiction of his work with improvised explosive devices during the Iraq War was false. The Ninth Circuit applied the anti-SLAPP statute to the lawsuit noting that the Iraq War was an issue of public concern.[84] "'The Hurt Locker' film and the narrative of its central character Will James spoke directly to issues of a public nature," the court wrote. Additionally, the film is "speech that was fully protected by the First Amendment, which safeguards the storytellers and artists who take the raw materials of life and transform them into art, such as movies."[85]

APPROPRIATION

Appropriation includes two different torts: **commercialization** and the **right of publicity**. Most people do not want their names or pictures to be in advertisements because they want to remain private. Generally using a person's name, picture or voice without permission for commercial or trade purposes is appropriation, an area of privacy tort law that is currently a "hot mess," according to one privacy law expert.[86] Why? Because the Supreme Court has decided only one appropriation case (*Zacchini v. Scripps-Howard Broadcasting Co.*, discussed later in this section), and that case predates many of the modern technologies and media platforms to which the Supreme Court has since given First Amendment protection.

State courts take a range of approaches to resolve appropriation cases, often based on whether the alleged appropriation arises in a commercial context (see Chapter 12) or another First Amendment context. The courts often apply strict scrutiny, rather than a balancing of interests, when reviewing cases involving the media (see Chapter 3). However, many courts apply a balancing approach to resolve some right of publicity claims.[87] Before addressing these issues, the next section will define the commercialization and right of publicity torts as well as what plaintiffs are required to prove.

Commercialization and Right of Publicity

The appropriation tort that protects people who want privacy is called "commercialization" or "misappropriation." Commercialization, the word this chapter uses, prohibits using another person's name or likeness for commercial purposes without permission. No state has refused to allow appropriation suits, though courts in some states have not yet ruled on the issue.[88]

Some people, however, want their names and pictures to be publicized, and they want to control when, how and where their names and pictures will be used for advertising and other commercial purposes. They also want to be paid for giving their permission. Courts often refer to this part of the appropriation tort as the "right of publicity."[89]

New York state adopted the country's first appropriation law in 1903.[90] Two years later, Georgia became the first state to recognize appropriation as a common law privacy tort. A federal appeals court judge, Jerome Frank, first used the phrase "right of publicity" nearly 70 years ago.[91] The court ruled that professional baseball players had a right to earn money when their names were used on baseball cards. Courts generally find that everyone has both a right to protect his or her privacy and a right to decide when his or her name or picture may or may not be used commercially by others.[92] The commercial value of a celebrity's name or picture, though, will be much greater than that of a relatively unknown individual. Courts also have said a right of publicity could be transferred, as a car can be sold, but the right of privacy cannot.

Although both commercialization and the right of publicity prevent the use of someone's name, picture, likeness, voice or identity for advertising or other commercial purposes without permission, they differ in two important ways. First, commercialization protects an individual's dignity connected with personal privacy, while the right of publicity protects the monetary value of using well-known individuals' names and pictures. Second, courts generally consider commercialization a personal right, one that does not survive a person's death. However, the right of publicity may be considered a property right. In many states, the right of publicity survives death. Just as a person may determine who gets his or her car after he or she dies—through a will or by state law—a person may choose who will control his or her right of publicity after death.[93] In many states, the right of publicity survives death.[94] The right may last for a specific number of years (from 20 to 100 years, depending on the state), as long as the right is used, or, in at least one state, forever.[95]

Recently, a handful of state legislatures have explored efforts to extend or alter the right of publicity after death, or **post-mortem**. Maryland, Massachusetts and New Hampshire failed

post-mortem
After death. Post-mortem right of publicity generally refers to a famous person's ability to control the commercial use of his or her name, picture, likeness, voice and identity after death.

to extend the application of their statutes to 70 years beyond death, but Indiana lawmakers passed an amendment to the state's existing statute and applied post-mortem publicity rights retroactively.[96] That law excludes people who became famous as a result of a criminal charge or conviction. Federal courts have recently resolved issues of jurisdiction in post-mortem right of publicity cases. For example, a few years ago, the Ninth Circuit Court of Appeals ruled that Marilyn Monroe's publicity rights died with her more than 50 years ago. Monroe's legal residence was New York, and New York does not recognize a right of publicity after death. Her estate argued that because she died in California, that state's post-mortem right of publicity statute should apply.[97] Similar cases have applied the law of the state of primary residence of the celebrity at the time of death.[98]

Legal disputes over post-mortem publicity rights have intensified in recent years. The estates of musicians Prince, Whitney Houston and Michael Jackson have been tied up in court for years over various post-mortem right of publicity issues.[99] Many of the cases center on the taxable value of the post-mortem publicity right to the estate. For example, Michael Jackson's estate valued his post-mortem image or likeness at $2,105, but the IRS determined the value to be more than $434 million.[100] Comedian Robin Williams bequeathed his post-mortem publicity rights to a charitable organization and restricted the use of these rights for 25 years. Legal experts say this was a creative way for a celebrity to exercise post-mortem control over the digital use of a celebrity's likeness in a movie or advertisement. It would also prevent the use of Williams' image as a hologram or some other not-yet-developed digital format.[101]

Recently, an Arizona appeals court held that the right of publicity is a property right that can be transferred to a descendant.[102] After the death of Prince in 2016, the Minnesota legislature tried to push through a right of publicity bill that extended post-mortem rights because of concerns about a lack of protection for Prince's estate. The bill was pulled weeks later after the bill's sponsor decided it was more prudent to leave the matter for state courts to decide.[103]

Plaintiff's Case

To win a commercialization or right of publicity case, a plaintiff must prove his or her name or likeness was used for commercial purposes without permission. The plaintiff must also show the commercial use was of and concerning him or her and was widely distributed.

In recent years, rapper 50 Cent has filed multiple lawsuits in multiple jurisdictions to protect his right of publicity.

Name or Likeness. Appropriation occurs most obviously when a person's name, picture or likeness—clearly identifying the person—is used commercially without permission. Having the same name that is used in an advertisement is usually not enough to show identification. Something in the ad must show the ad was of and concerning that plaintiff.[104] A name can sometimes be the primary basis of a claim. For example, Hasbro and Fox News anchor Harris Faulkner recently settled a case in New Jersey after Faulkner accused the toy maker of violating her right of publicity. A New Jersey court refused to dismiss Faulkner's claim, based largely on the use of her name. Hasbro had named a toy hamster from its "Littlest Pet

Shop" line Harris Faulkner. Legal experts predicted that arguments claiming the hamster looked like Faulkner would probably fail but suggested that Faulkner had a strong claim on a name-based right of publicity.[105]

It is not sufficient that the commercial use only hints at the plaintiff's identity or may remind some people of the plaintiff.[106] Rather, there must be reasonable grounds for identifying the plaintiff. For example, in a recent case involving the rapper 50 Cent, a court held that his likeness was invoked for commercial purposes when a website posted reproduced and screened photos of the rapper in its masthead. The court said that even though the images were of poor visual quality, visitors to the website could still see that the pictures were of 50 Cent.[107]

A court in Illinois dismissed a right of publicity case brought by a Guinness World Records record holder against Wendy's. The fast-food chain ran a kid's meal promotion that included Guinness-themed toys, one of which was a footbag. An accompanying card listed Guinness facts about the footbag, including this: "How many times in a row can you kick this footbag without it hitting the ground? Back in 1997, Ted Martin made his world record of 63,326 kicks in a little less than nine hours!"[108] The court said that the use of Martin's name on the instruction card did not amount to an endorsement and did not violate Martin's right of publicity. Rather, the instruction card was part of a product, not an advertisement, and it never suggested that Martin endorsed anything. The Seventh Circuit Court of Appeals upheld the dismissal, noting that the Illinois right of publicity law does not apply to the use of a person's name when it truthfully identifies a person as an author or performer.[109]

Generally, courts have held that names and associated information widely available to the public are not protected by right of publicity. For example, the Eighth Circuit Court of Appeals ruled that an online fantasy baseball league operator could use Major League Baseball players' names and statistics without MLB's permission.[110] The court said the information was widely available in the public domain, making it factual rather than personal to the players.

What about the use of a private person's name without consent in generic online advertising? Although their names were not used, two plaintiffs in Illinois sued several internet companies that offer online reports about people using information compiled from public records and other sources. The companies, including Intelius, pay internet search engines to advertise their people-search reports. When a user on one of these websites types a person's name into the search engine, the first and last name of the person being searched will appear in the defendants' advertisements through an automated process. The defendant companies designed the ads to look like they contained valuable information about the searched-for person, including items like criminal record, divorce record, background checks and bankruptcy. The district court dismissed the right of publicity claim because the advertisements failed to identify the specific plaintiffs in the case, as opposed to identifying anyone who shared their same names.[111]

Fox News anchor Harris Faulkner; Hasbro's Harris Faulkner hamster.

sound-alike
Someone whose voice sounds like another person's voice. Sound-alikes require permission or a disclaimer for commercial use.

Voice. Individuals' voices are protected against commercial use without consent. Further, advertisers may not use **sound-alikes** without permission or a disclaimer. For example, singer and actress Bette Midler refused to allow Ford Motor Co. to use her hit recording "Do You Want to Dance?" in a commercial. Ford's advertising agency then hired a member of Midler's backup singing group to imitate Midler's rendition of the song. After the radio commercial aired, a number of people told Midler they thought she had performed in the ad, which failed to say Midler was not the singer. Midler sued Ford and its advertising agency. A federal appellate court said they appropriated part of Midler's identity.[112]

POINTS OF LAW
APPROPRIATION

Plaintiff's Case

- Using a person's name, picture, likeness, voice or identity
- for advertising or other commercial uses
- without permission

Defenses

- News
- First Amendment
- Incidental use
- Mass media advertising
- Consent

Identity. People have characteristics beyond their face or voice that the appropriation tort protects. Game show host Vanna White sued Samsung Electronics for appropriation after the company ran a series of magazine ads showing its products in futuristic settings. A robot standing by a "Wheel of Fortune"-style letter board wore an evening gown, jewelry and a long blond wig. A federal appellate court said the ad appropriated White's identity, even though it did not use her name, image or voice.[113]

Actors George Wendt and John Ratzenberger, Norm and Cliff from the television show "Cheers," brought a similar lawsuit several years later. A company received permission from the studio that owned the "Cheers" copyright to install two animatronic figures resembling Norm and Cliff in airport bars. They did not have consent from the two actors. The animatronic figures resembled Wendt's and Ratzenberger's characters in their size, clothing and sitting positions at the bar, but had different faces. Wendt and Ratzenberger sued. A federal appellate court said the figures sufficiently resembled the actors and that Wendt and Ratzenberger could claim appropriation.[114] The parties settled the case out of court.[115]

Actors impersonating celebrities in noncommercial or non-advertising situations, such as in a satire or parody, are not appropriating the celebrities' likenesses or voices. The First Amendment protects such expression.[116] But the Vanna White case shows that protection does not extend to impersonations in advertisements or other commercial situations. The appellate court specifically rejected Samsung's contention that the robot ad was meant as a satire.

avatar
An icon or image that represents a person in a video game or other computer-generated content.

Two recent court decisions established that computer-generated images and **avatars** in video games can constitute a portrait under New York's right of publicity statute.[117] An avatar is an icon or image that represents a person in a video game or other computer-generated content. New York's highest court dismissed two cases in 2018 involving the video game "Grand Theft Auto V." Actress Lindsay Lohan and reality television star Karen Gravano from the show "Mob Wives" both filed lawsuits against the video game maker for images that they said depicted them. Gravano said the game's character "Andrea Bottino" appropriated her image, and Lohan argued that two scenes in the game that featured a blonde woman flashing a peace sign and taking a selfie represented her.[118] In both cases, the court said the computer-generated images could constitute a portrait under the law. However, in Gravano's case, the court said the avatar was not recognizable as Gravano. In Lohan's case, the court said the character was a generic artistic depiction of "a twenty-something woman without any particular identifying physical characteristics."[119] Both cases were dismissed.

Defenses

Even if a plaintiff can prove that his or her name or likeness was used for commercial purposes without permission, there are several defenses for appropriation.

Newsworthiness. Newsworthiness is the most common defense. Media publish newsworthy material despite having a commercial purpose.[120] Courts have defined the word "newsworthy" broadly, and the newsworthiness defense sometimes shows up in unlikely cases. For example, rapper 50 Cent argued that his creation of an explicit sex video directed at rival rapper Rick Ross was newsworthy. A New York state court disagreed, specifically noting that the posting of explicit sex tapes is not newsworthy.[121]

Judges do not carefully analyze content to determine whether it is newsworthy. The U.S. Supreme Court has heard only one appropriation case and rejected a television station's claim of a newsworthiness defense to a right of publicity suit when a local newscast showed an entertainment act in its entirety without consent or compensation.[122] The television station recorded and subsequently broadcast all 15 seconds of human cannonball Hugo Zacchini's act, including the most critical part—his flight from the cannon to the net. The Supreme Court said that people who saw the entire act on television were less likely to attend the performance in person and focused on the economic value of his act.

> There is no doubt that entertainment, as well as news, enjoys First Amendment protection. It is also true that entertainment itself can be important news. . . . But, it is important to note that neither the public nor [the television station] will be deprived of the benefit of [Zacchini's] performance as long as his commercial stake in his act is appropriately recognized.[123]

The television station's First Amendment rights were not more important than protecting Zacchini's financial interest in his performance, the Court said.[124]

The U.S. Supreme Court said human cannonball Hugo Zacchini could win an appropriation lawsuit against a television station that aired his performance in its entirety.

Bettmann/Getty Images

REAL WORLD LAW
DOES POTENTIAL ILLEGALITY IMPACT NEWSWORTHINESS?

The Indiana Supreme Court recently considered whether fantasy sports operators need the consent of college athletes when using their names, pictures and statistics in the context of online gambling.[iv]

Indiana's right of publicity statute has an exemption for newsworthy material and for reporting on events of public interest. Former college football players sued several fantasy sports companies, arguing that they used the players' names, pictures and game statistics without consent. Before deciding *Daniels v. FanDuel, Inc.*, the Seventh Circuit Court of Appeals asked the Indiana Supreme Court to decide whether the potential illegality of gambling operations impacts Indiana's newsworthiness exemption for right of publicity. The Indiana Supreme Court answered that the newsworthiness exemption would include an online fantasy sports operator's use of players' names, pictures and statistics, so the Seventh Circuit then terminated the lawsuit.[v]

One legal expert noted, however, that the Seventh Circuit "left open the possibility that . . . the players might still have a claim if there was likely confusion as to sponsorship by the athletes of the fantasy sports sites."[vi]

First Amendment. First Amendment defenses in right of publicity cases are common today, particularly in the context of artistic works such as movies and video games. Over the years, courts have also considered whether commercial products—such as posters, dolls, T-shirts and games—have First Amendment protection.[125]

Courts most often have decided posters do not have First Amendment protection. Courts have said the First Amendment protects selling posters with pictures of newsworthy individuals or events, such as a poster with a picture of former San Francisco 49ers quarterback Joe Montana celebrating the team's 1990 Super Bowl victory.[126] Courts drew a distinction between merchandise exploiting celebrities' names or likenesses and posters conveying newsworthy information of public interest. Courts found appropriation when posters of singer Elvis Presley, model Christie Brinkley and professional wrestlers were distributed without permission.[127]

The question of First Amendment protection versus right of publicity arises most frequently when a well-known person is used in an artistic work. For example, recently, a federal judge in New York ruled that hip-hop star Pitbull did not violate actress Lindsay Lohan's right of publicity by including the line "I'm toptoein', to keep flowin', I got it locked up, like Lindsay Lohan" in his hit song "Give Me Everything." Rather, the song is a work of art protected by the First Amendment.[128]

artistic relevance test
A test to determine whether the commercial use of a celebrity's name, picture, likeness, voice or identity is relevant to a disputed work's artistic purpose.

One approach used to resolve this kind of conflict is the **artistic relevance test.** This test asks whether using a celebrity's name or picture is relevant to a work's artistic purpose. If it is, the First Amendment, which applies to artistic as well as journalistic works, may allow using the celebrity's name without permission. However, consent is needed if the name or celebrity's likeness is used primarily to give the work commercial appeal. For example, in Italian movie director Federico Fellini's film "Ginger and Fred," two cabaret dancers used the nicknames Ginger and Fred because they imitated Ginger Rogers and Fred Astaire. Rogers sued, claiming the movie title infringed on her right to use her name for commercial purposes. The Second Circuit Court of Appeals applied the artistic relevance test and said Rogers could not win unless the movie title had no artistic relevance to the film itself or misled consumers about the film's content.[129] The movie's title and contents were artistically related, the court held.

Sometimes, song titles do not relate to a song's lyrics. For example, the rap duo OutKast recorded a song titled "Rosa Parks." Parks, a major figure during the civil rights movement, refused to give her seat to a white person and move to the back of the bus, as city law in racially segregated Montgomery, Ala., then required. Her defiant act touched off boycotts, sit-ins and demonstrations throughout the South.[130] Applying the *Rogers* test, a federal appellate court concluded that a jury could find that the title "Rosa Parks" had no artistic relevance to the lyrics, despite the chorus repeatedly using the phrase "move to the back of the bus." The use of Rosa Parks' name in the title of a profane and sexually explicit song was misleading, the court held, because the song was not about her.

Instead of the *Rogers* artistic relevance test, more courts today apply the **transformative use test** to decide whether a challenged work has First Amendment protection against a right of publicity suit.[131] The California Supreme Court proposed the transformative use test to distinguish protected artistic expression about celebrities from expression that encroaches on the right of publicity in a case involving the Three Stooges. The First Amendment protects a work that adds enough new elements to the original to transform it. Changing the original by giving it a new meaning or a different message justifies First Amendment protection. Transformative works may be satires, news reports, fictional works, social criticism or video games.

In the California Supreme Court case, an artist created a charcoal sketch of the Three Stooges, transferred the sketch to T-shirts and lithographs and sold thousands. A company owning the Three Stooges' publicity rights sued.[132] The California court acknowledged the conflict between the artist's First Amendment right to express himself and the right of celebrities to protect their property and financial interests in their images. The court concluded, "When artistic expression takes the form of a literal depiction or imitation of a celebrity for commercial gain, directly trespassing on the right of publicity without adding significant expression beyond that trespass," the celebrity's rights outweigh First Amendment protections.[133] The court found that the Three Stooges drawing was a "literal, conventional" depiction of the three men, with no discernible transformative elements. Because the drawing did not transform the Three Stooges' pictures, it had no First Amendment protection.

Courts have heard several cases that test the application of the transformative use test to athletes and video games. The earliest and most prominent cases settled for $60 million after a lengthy appeals process in the Ninth Circuit Court of Appeals. They involved three college athletes who filed **class action lawsuits** against the video game company Electronic Arts, the National Collegiate Athletic Association and the Collegiate Licensing Company (now known as IMG College Licensing).[134] Class action lawsuits are filed by individuals acting on behalf of a larger group with a common legal interest. A decade ago, Ed O'Bannon, the star of UCLA's 1995 championship basketball team, and Sam Keller, former quarterback from Arizona State University and the University of Nebraska, argued in a U.S. district court in California that EA's NCAA-themed video games violated their right of publicity because their likenesses were

transformative use test
A test to determine whether the First Amendment protects a work that uses a person's name, picture, likeness, voice or identity for artistic purposes. Changing the original to give it new meaning or a different message justifies First Amendment protection.

class action lawsuit
A lawsuit in which a group of people with similar injuries caused by the same product or action sue a defendant as a group.

used without compensation.[135] The players noted that the video games depicted every distinctive characteristic of them except their names. At the same time, former Rutgers quarterback Ryan Hart made the same claim in a U.S. district court in New Jersey.[136]

In both cases, EA argued that its First Amendment rights trumped the players' right of publicity. Although the facts in both cases are nearly identical and both courts applied the transformative use test, the two courts came to different decisions. In California, the court applied the transformative use test and held that EA's use of Keller was not transformative and did not deserve First Amendment protection. In New Jersey, the court ruled in favor of EA and criticized the California decision, which it suggested "[il]logically . . . consider[ed] the setting in which the character sits . . . yet ignore[d] the remainder of the game."[137] The Third Circuit Court of Appeals eventually reversed the New Jersey district court's summary judgment decision.[138] Both cases settled out of court with agreements to pay millions of dollars to the student athletes named in the class action suits.[139]

On the heels of the settlements, 10 former college football and basketball players filed a similar right of publicity lawsuit in federal court against major broadcast companies, athletic conferences and licensers. Former Vanderbilt University football player Javon Marshall was the lead plaintiff in the lawsuit, which sought damages for the misappropriation of the names, images and likenesses of college athletes in broadcasts and advertisements without their consent.[140] In 2016, the Sixth Circuit Court of Appeals affirmed a Tennessee district court ruling, which dismissed the case and noted that a common law right of publicity does not exist in that state.[141]

Recently, the NCAA appealed the Ninth Circuit's decision in the O'Bannon case to the U.S. Supreme Court, arguing the case was wrongly decided, but the Supreme Court declined to hear it. The NCAA's interest in the ruling stemmed from additional claims that the organization's rules violate antitrust laws by not allowing student athletes compensation for the use of their names and likenesses.[142]

Soon after the college athlete lawsuits, a group of former NFL players sued EA for the alleged use of their likenesses and identities in the "Madden NFL" video games. The video game gave users the ability to play as a historic football team, which the former NFL players said went beyond the NFL's licensing agreement with EA and violated their right of publicity. On appeal to the Ninth Circuit, the court rejected EA's transformative use and artistic relevance arguments and returned the case to the district court.[143] In 2018, the district court denied EA's motion to dismiss the case, but did decide that the case could not continue because the former NFL players did not constitute a class under the Federal Rules of Civil Procedure.[144] These general rules govern all civil proceedings in the U.S. district courts, and they require a sizable number of people to share a common legal issue to constitute a group for a class action claim.

Nonetheless, courts still generally apply the transformative use test to affirm First Amendment rights in lawsuits that involve movies, television and video games. In 2018, a court in California applied the transformative use test to protect a television miniseries, "Feud: Bette and Joan," inspired by the real-life, old Hollywood rivalry between actors Bette Davis and Joan Crawford.[145] Actor Olivia de Havilland sued the series creators and producers for depicting her as a character. The court rejected de Havilland's argument that by creating a character based on a real person the expressive work implied her endorsement of the work. The state appeals court concluded that the work was transformative and protected by the First Amendment, "which safeguards the storytellers and artists who take the raw materials of life—including the stories of real individuals, ordinary or extraordinary—and transform them into art."[146]

A few years ago, the Weinstein Co. prevailed in a lawsuit brought by legendary soul singer Sam Moore who said the film "Soul Men" violated his right of publicity because it told his life story. A federal appeals court applied the transformative use test and said the film added "significant expressive elements," so it was protected on First Amendment grounds.[147]

The transformative use test also provides protection for artists. Nearly two decades ago, the California Supreme Court used the test to rule that a comic book artist transformed images of two musicians, Johnny and Edgar Winter.[148] The California Supreme Court said, "An artist depicting a celebrity must contribute something more than a 'merely trivial' variation" of the celebrity's image. The artist "must create something recognizably 'his own'" for a court to find "significant transformative elements" in the artist's work.[149]

Another way to balance the First Amendment and the right of publicity is the **predominant use test**. The question is whether a person's name or image is used more for commercial purposes or substantive expression. The Missouri Supreme Court applied this test in ruling that a comic book creator named a character "Antonio 'Tony Twist' Twistelli" more to sell the comics than for free speech purposes. In the comic, Twistelli was portrayed as an organized crime leader. A real Tony Twist, a former professional hockey player, sued for misuse of his name. A jury awarded $15 million in damages, and the state's high court affirmed the ruling.[150]

Courts have long held that the First Amendment protects using celebrities' names in biographies and fiction, including movies and television programs. Although this was part of appropriation law long before the California Supreme Court used the transformative use test, the reasons are similar. Books, news stories, movies and television programs add transformative elements by putting the names in a context. For example, a movie called "Panther," combining fact and fiction, portrayed several members of the Black Panther Party, a political group active in the 1960s and 1970s that promoted black power and social activism. Bobby Seale, a prominent member of the Black Panthers, sued. A federal district court rejected Seale's appropriation claim, saying the First Amendment protected using his name in the film.[151]

Some celebrities, such as the now-deceased wealthy recluse Howard Hughes, have tried to limit who may write their biographies.[152] But no person, or deceased person's relative, has the right to prevent anyone from writing about another's life.[153]

Ads for the Media. Another First Amendment–based appropriation defense holds that mass media may run advertisements for themselves without consent when using the names and likenesses of public figures if those figures were part of their original content. Courts recognized this defense when a magazine, Holiday, ran ads for itself in two other publications. One ad urged people to subscribe, and the other ad suggested advertising agencies place their clients' ads in Holiday. Both ads included pictures of actress Shirley Booth that Holiday had

predominant use test
In a right of publicity lawsuit, a test to determine whether the defendant used the plaintiff's name or picture more for commercial purposes or protected expression.

published in one of its issues. Booth sued under New York's appropriation law. The state's highest court said that in order to stay in business and to use its First Amendment rights, the magazine had to attract subscribers and advertisers. Illustrating the magazine's contents and quality by showing what it publishes did not violate Booth's rights, the court concluded.[154]

Holiday magazine won the suit in part because it did not suggest Booth endorsed the magazine. However, a men's magazine's advertisement for itself used a picture of the actress and singer Cher that had accompanied a published interview with her. A cartoon balloon over Cher's head included the words, "So join Cher and FORUM's hundreds of thousands of other adventurous readers today." Cher sued, saying the magazine had implied her endorsement of the magazine without permission. A federal appellate court agreed with her.[155]

More recently, former Chicago Bulls star Michael Jordan sued a grocery store chain based on a magazine ad in which Jewel Food Stores congratulated him for being inducted into the Basketball Hall of Fame. The Seventh Circuit Court of Appeals found that because the grocery store's logo was prominently featured along with its marketing slogan and then linked in the ad text to Jordan, it constituted image advertising. The case was remanded to the lower court, but the Seventh Circuit said a First Amendment defense would not apply in the case.[156]

Consent. The best appropriation defense is consent. That is why professional photographers use releases—contracts prepared by lawyers and signed by all parties involved—when taking pictures for advertisements or other commercial use. Oral consent can be a defense, but proving it can be difficult if the plaintiff claims she or he did not give permission. Also, the law does not allow certain people to give consent, such as minors and those who are not mentally or emotionally capable of agreeing. And consent is limited to the agreement's terms. Consent to use a picture in an ad throughout 2020, for example, does not allow its use in 2022. Similarly, if a person gives consent to use a picture in a smartphone ad, the picture cannot be used to advertise shoes. If a person gives sweeping consent—to use a picture at any time in the future in any advertisement—a court likely will hold that the agreement is more limited than indicated.

Consent most often is explicit; a person agrees to allow his or her name to be used. But consent may also be implied. For example, a man sued the owner of a smartphone app that would send the user's contacts a text message invitation to join the app. The invitation included the user's name so people invited to join could see who sent the message. The man argued that including his name in the text message invitation exceeded the scope of his consent. The app did not allow him to view the text message invitation before the app sent it. A court in Illinois held that because the man decided to use the app to send the text messages, a reasonable user would understand his name was necessary for the invitation process to work.[157]

Incidental Use. The use of a person's name or likeness may be incidental to a work's primary purpose. Incidental use typically arises in appropriation claims and not right of publicity. A court could rule that a person's name or likeness was used so briefly that the purpose was not to make a profit or gain commercial benefit. For example, a name applied to a fictional terrorist in a comic book appeared in 1 of 116 panels spanning 24 pages. A person who said the comic book applied his name to the terrorist sued under New York's appropriation law.

A federal district court said the name's use was incidental to the comic book's primary purpose and could not sustain a privacy suit.[158] Similarly, if a photograph of a large crowd of people is used in an advertisement, it is unlikely one person in the group could claim successfully that her picture is being used for commercial purposes.

In a recent case, an Ohio couple sued Amazon.com and others for false light and appropriation for the use of their engagement photo on the cover of a self-published novel. The novel was a satirical, erotic account of a married woman's fascination with New England Patriots player Rob Gronkowski, titled "A Gronking to Remember." The court observed that the novel was alleged to be "less than tasteful" and "offensive."[159] The book was the butt of jokes on late-night talk shows before the 2014 Super Bowl and received some national media attention. The author of the self-published novel argued that his use of the photo on the cover was incidental. The district court disagreed.

> This argument confuses and misstates the issue in this case—it would be relevant if the plaintiff in the case were Rob Gronkowski, a public figure. The incidental use doctrine applies, however, only to persons with celebrity or other notorious status— which plaintiffs did not have.[160]

Rather, the couple argued that the novel's author appropriated their engagement photo "for his own commercial benefit." On appeal, the Sixth Circuit Court of Appeals held that the couple was not able to demonstrate the commercial value of their image to the corporate defenders in the case and granted Amazon and the other publishers summary judgment.[161]

PRIVATE FACTS

A court first recognized the private facts tort in 1927.[162] Journalists and others can be sued for the **private facts** tort if they publish truthful private information that is not of legitimate public concern and is highly offensive to a reasonable person.[163] The private facts tort is intended to protect a person's dignity and peace of mind by discouraging the publication of intimate facts. If intimate private facts are publicized, a jury may award monetary damages to compensate for the resulting emotional injury.[164] Courts recognize a First Amendment defense to a private facts lawsuit.[165]

private facts
Publicizing highly offensive, true private information that is not newsworthy or lawfully obtained from a public record.

Publicity

A private facts plaintiff must prove that the defendant publicized intimate information. Publicity in the private facts tort is not the same as publication in a libel suit. In libel, publication to a third party, someone other than the plaintiff and defendant, is sufficient. For the private facts tort, most courts require widespread publicity.[166] Revealing intimate information in the media will meet the definition of publicity.[167] Some courts hold that revealing private facts to small groups of people who have a special relationship with the plaintiff is sufficient. This could include the plaintiff's fellow workers, church members, colleagues in a social organization or neighbors.[168]

Intimate Facts

Intimate facts are those that a person would not want the community to know. Private facts suits, for example, could relate to a person's financial condition,[169] medical information[170] or domestic difficulties.[171] Often, private facts suits concern sexual activities.[172] The question before a court hearing a private facts case is: Would it outrage the community's notions of decency if the intimate information were published?[173]

Not all facts about a person are private. Information in a public record, such as a court filing or an arrest record, is public information. Facts are not private if a person made them public. Information told to a few close relatives or friends remains private, and a person may define his or her own circle of intimacy, according to courts.[174] But if a person reveals intimate facts publicly, the private facts tort does not limit the media from publishing the information.

For example, a friendship between two high school girls deteriorated into a bitter feud. The first girl accused the second of being pregnant, and that girl teased the first about her Jewish heritage, seeking psychological counseling and having plastic surgery. The second girl's family self-published a book about the feud. The book included school, police and legal documents connected with the situation. The first girl sued for private facts, among other torts. She claimed the book included "1) excerpts and summaries from her Myspace.com webpage; 2) three statements related to her Jewish ancestry; 3) her enrolment (sic) at [a university]; 4) two statements regarding Plaintiff's decision to seek professional psychological care or counseling; 5) Plaintiff's transfer from one high school to another under a superintendent's agreement; and 6) two statements regarding plastic surgery on Plaintiff's nose."[175] The court held that categories 1, 2, 3 and 5 were not private. The plaintiff wrote on her Myspace page that she sought psychological help and agreed that she could not conceal what she posted there. As to plastic surgery, the court said it "questions whether this matter is truly private: cosmetic surgery on one's face is by its nature exposed to the public eye."[176]

Can a victim of revenge porn win a private facts lawsuit? Websites featuring nonconsensual pornography, commonly known as revenge porn, allow people to post sexually explicit videos or nude pictures of others without their consent. The owner of the pioneering revenge porn site IsAnybodyUp.com said at the site's peak he was earning $10,000 a month in advertising revenue based on 30 million reported page views. That site is no longer active, but the owner of a different site modeled after it says he makes $3,000 a month, with some of that money coming from fees he charges people to remove pictures or videos from the site.[177]

Legal experts say a private facts lawsuit is hard to win in revenge porn cases because often the victim initially shared the explicit image with someone, usually a friend or sexual partner. Many courts have found that the act of voluntarily sharing the image makes it no longer private.[178] Many organizations, like the Cyber Civil Rights Initiative, are fighting revenge porn

INTERNATIONAL LAW
GLOBAL DATA PROTECTION REGULATION IN THE EU

Recently, the European Union implemented a new framework for consumer data protection. The Global Data Protection Regulation (GDPR) significantly changed how companies handle consumer privacy and gave EU citizens the right to control their own data. Data privacy experts have hailed the GDPR as one of the most powerful data privacy laws in the world. The GDPR requires companies to explain how they store and use consumers' personal data, allows people to request that companies delete their personal data and allows people to object to their personal data being used for direct marketing purposes (such as personally tailored ads on the internet).[vii]

The GDPR expands the concept of the "right to be forgotten." An EU Court of Justice (in essence, a "supreme court" for the European Union) decision about a decade ago required Google to unlink articles from its searches that people claimed are irrelevant or no longer accurate.[viii] Since 2014, this "right to be forgotten" has resulted in more than three million URL delisting requests to Google, which has approved about 55 percent of those.[ix]

by appealing to state legislatures. In 2019, 43 states, the District of Columbia and one territory had laws that criminalized revenge porn.[179]

Legitimate Public Concern

A plaintiff cannot win a private facts lawsuit if the information is newsworthy or of legitimate public concern. The media help determine what is newsworthy through their reporting behaviors. Courts give the media considerable leeway to determine what is newsworthy. Stories about crimes, suicides, divorces, catastrophes, diseases and other topics may include intimate information people do not want published. If newsworthy, these private facts cannot be the basis of a successful private facts suit.[180]

Many courts have said the First Amendment will not protect the publication of highly intimate facts unless they are of public concern. In defining newsworthiness, the court distinguished between information the public is entitled to know and facts publicized for a morbid or sensational reason. For example, a Sports Illustrated story included information about Mike Virgil, who bodysurfed at the Wedge, a public beach near Newport Beach, Calif., considered one of the world's most dangerous places for bodysurfing. To illustrate the surfers' daredevil attitudes, the story reported that Virgil put out a cigarette on his tongue, dove headfirst down a flight of stairs to impress women, ate spiders and jumped off billboards. Virgil spoke with the Sports Illustrated reporter but withdrew his consent to the story before publication and then sued the magazine for publishing private facts.[181]

The federal appeals court sent the case back to the trial court to decide whether public concern about surfing at the Wedge justified revealing intimate details of Virgil's life.[182] The trial court held that the personal information in the article, for example eating spiders, was embarrassing but not sensational. The facts helped describe people who bodysurfed at the Wedge, the court said in ruling for Sports Illustrated.[183]

Hulk Hogan

Several courts have taken a slightly different approach to defining newsworthiness about people involuntarily put in the public eye. These courts determine whether there is a logical connection between the news event and the private facts. Well-known people are inherently more newsworthy than others. Even celebrities, though, have a right to keep private those facts that would be highly embarrassing if publicized.

For example, in part based on a private facts claim, actress Pamela Anderson Lee and rock musician Bret Michaels successfully prevented distribution of their sex tape.[184] More recently, former professional wrestler Hulk Hogan, whose real name is Terry Bollea, sued Gawker Media for reporting on and showing excerpts of a sex tape that showed him having sex with the wife of a friend, Todd Clem, who is a radio shock jock named Bubba the Love Sponge. Clem made the recording and gave Gawker the tape; the media outlet did not pay for it. Bollea sued Clem and his wife for invasion of privacy and settled out of court after Clem acknowledged that Bollea did not know his sexual encounter was being recorded. Bollea also sued Gawker for invasion of privacy, seeking $100 million in damages.[185]

Initially, the case focused on whether issuing an injunction to prevent the publication of the tape was appropriate under the First Amendment. In ruling on the injunction, the judge wrote that Hogan's public discussions—with TMZ, on the Howard Stern show and in his autobiography—about his many affairs showed that the subject was not truly private and that reporting on the sex tape was a matter of public concern.[186]

When Bollea's privacy lawsuit went before a jury, he argued that his celebrity status as Hulk Hogan should not deprive him of privacy protections, that he did not know the sexual encounter was being recorded, that Gawker did not seek his permission to publish the video and that Gawker was not a journalist but rather was acting solely for its own commercial gain. The jury found in favor of Bollea, determining that the publication of the sex tape was offensive and not a matter of legitimate public concern. It recommended awarding $140 million in both actual and punitive damages, an award later upheld by a judge. Privacy law experts say it is more common for juries, rather than judges, to determine newsworthiness, which has recently resulted in larger jury verdicts in privacy cases.[187]

Nick Denton, Gawker's CEO, appealed the Bollea verdict and later declared personal bankruptcy, as did Gawker Media. In late 2016, Gawker and Bollea settled the invasion of privacy lawsuit for $31 million, ending the appeals process. Ultimately, the new owner of Gawker.com shut down the site and took down all of the other articles involved in the litigation.[188] Many legal experts suggest that Gawker and Denton might have prevailed on appeal based on First Amendment grounds but that the legal fight would be too costly after the revelation that billionaire Peter Thiel, the founder of PayPal, was financing Bollea's lawsuit.[189]

Recently, sports broadcaster Erin Andrews won $55 million in damages from a stalker and from a hotel owner and management group after she was the victim of unlawful videotaping. Andrews' serial stalker secretly recorded her in adjacent hotel rooms and leaked nude videos of Andrews, which went viral. The stalker went to prison, and a jury awarded Andrews damages for invasion of privacy and other torts.[190]

In 2017, New York Giants defensive end Jason Pierre-Paul settled an invasion of privacy suit with ESPN after reporter Adam Schefter tweeted photos of Pierre-Paul's hospital records from a 2015 hand injury. ESPN argued that its report-

Frank Sinatra's mug shot from an arrest in 1938 for having an affair with a married woman.

ing was newsworthy, and while a federal judge dismissed Pierre-Paul's claim that the tweet violated Florida's medical privacy statute, she allowed the privacy claim to move forward.[191]

Newsworthiness can be a defense to a private facts suit. In the past, media defendants had the burden of showing that the facts were of legitimate public interest, and some courts continue to put the newsworthiness burden on the defendant. Other courts require the plaintiff in a private facts suit to prove that the intimate facts were not newsworthy. In one example, a newspaper reported that a student body president was transgender.[192] Toni Diaz, born Antonio Diaz, underwent sex reassignment surgery before entering a community college. Elected student body president, she charged school administrators with mishandling student funds. A local newspaper columnist wrote of Diaz, "Now I realize, that in these times, such a matter is no big deal, but I suspect his female classmates in P.E. 97 may wish to make other showering arrangements." Diaz, who had told only close relatives and friends of her operation, sued the paper and columnist.

A court ruled that Diaz, as plaintiff, had to prove the private facts were not newsworthy because putting the burden on the media could lead to self-censorship. The court ruled that Diaz could show it was not newsworthy to publish remarks about her gender and that her gender had no connection with her ability to be student body president.

When a news media outlet publishes a mug shot (the police photo of an arrested person's face), it is considered newsworthy and not a violation of privacy. Mug shots are usually considered public records, not private facts. In the past few years, dozens of for-profit mug shot websites have emerged, posting publicly available mug shots for widespread viewing. Some of the websites charge people money to have their mug shots removed.[193] Several states have passed laws prohibiting companies that publish mug shots from charging fees to remove or correct information.

Several plaintiffs have also filed various privacy-related lawsuits against these websites. A federal court in Pennsylvania dismissed one lawsuit but left open the question of whether mug shot websites constitute a form of a news report.[194] In 2017, a district court in Illinois decided in a right of publicity claim that Mugshots.com and its second website, Unpublisharrest.com, which removed listings from Mugshots.com for a fee, were commercial enterprises not entitled to First Amendment protection.[195]

Some private facts plaintiffs have argued that the passage of time may mean that information is no longer of legitimate concern to the public. Either the plaintiff was newsworthy many years before the media published the intimate information, or the private facts relate to events that happened long ago. Courts have rejected this contention, saying that newsworthiness does not disappear over time.[196]

First Amendment Defense

public record
A government record, particularly one that is publicly available.

One way to balance privacy interests against First Amendment interests is to focus on the source of the information. Should the press lose a private facts suit if the intimate information came from a **public record**? The U.S. Supreme Court has said the First Amendment protects publishing truthful information of public significance lawfully obtained from public records, unless punishing the media would serve a compelling state interest. Court decisions have not held that the First Amendment always will protect publishing truthful information taken from public records,[197] but the Supreme Court has not yet found a compelling state interest that overrides the press's First Amendment rights.

In *Florida Star v. B.J.F.*, for example, the Supreme Court held that the First Amendment protected a newspaper that published the name of a rape victim, reasoning that violent crime is a publicly significant topic.[198] A woman identified as B.J.F. reported to a Florida sheriff's department that she had been robbed and sexually assaulted. The sheriff's department prepared an incident report that identified B.J.F. by her full name and placed the report in its pressroom, which was open to the public. An inexperienced reporter for The Florida Star saw the report, and the paper published a brief story on the case, including B.J.F.'s full name. This was contrary to the paper's policy of not naming rape victims. B.J.F. sued the sheriff's department and The Florida Star under a state law making it illegal for media to publish the name of a sexual assault victim. The sheriff's department settled before trial, and B.J.F. won her case against the newspaper, a result that was upheld by a Florida appellate court.[199]

The newspaper appealed the case to the U.S. Supreme Court, which reversed, holding that the First Amendment protects a newspaper that publishes truthful information lawfully obtained from public records, provided no compelling state interest requires otherwise.[200] Although protecting the identity of a sexual assault victim could serve a compelling state interest, the Court said, three factors worked against that conclusion. First, the government itself supplied the information. Second, the state law forbidding names from being published had no exceptions, even if the community already knew the victim's name. Third, the state law applied only to the media, allowing others to disseminate a victim's name. Under these circumstances, the Court said, the right to a free press outweighed the state's interest in preventing publication of B.J.F.'s name.

Information in government records available to the public cannot be considered private. Facts presented in public meetings also are not secret. Unless a judge seals a record, making it unavailable, court records are public. A private facts suit cannot be based on intimate information contained in publicly accessible records.

Some government records are not publicly accessible and may not be considered public records in a private facts lawsuit. Similarly, not all publicly accessible places are "public." Publishing a picture and a conversation obtained by entering a private hospital room may not be protected even if the hospital generally is open to the public.[201]

Lawfully Obtained. In three other decisions, the U.S. Supreme Court ruled that where the press had legally obtained truthful information from public records, it was not liable for publishing private facts. Nearly 50 years ago in *Cox Broadcasting Corp. v. Cohn*, excerpted at the end of this chapter, the Court said for the first time that truthful information lawfully obtained from a public record could not be the basis of a private facts lawsuit.[202] The case involved the rape and murder of a 17-year-old girl in Georgia. At a court proceeding some months after the crime, a reporter covering the incident learned the name of the victim from indictments filed against six defendants and reported it. The victim's father sued the television station for broadcasting the name. He won at trial and again on the television station's appeal to the Georgia Supreme Court. But the U.S. Supreme Court reversed, noting that the First Amendment protects the press against a private facts tort if the information is obtained from generally available public records.

In a separate case originating in Oklahoma, news media violated a juvenile court judge's order by publishing the name and picture of an 11-year-old boy charged with second-degree murder for shooting a railroad employee. Reporters were in the courtroom when the juvenile appeared, and the court put his name on the public record. Photographers took pictures as the minor left the courthouse. The Supreme Court said the press had lawfully obtained information available to the public and held that the First Amendment prohibits punishing the press for revealing information taken from public records.[203]

In another case, newspaper reporters who were monitoring a police scanner in West Virginia responded to a crime scene and learned from witnesses and investigators the name of a 14-year-old boy charged with killing a classmate. State prosecutors obtained an indictment against the press for publishing the boy's name in violation of a state law. The Supreme Court, however, ruled in favor of the newspaper, reasoning that the First Amendment protects news reports where journalists have lawfully obtained truthful information from publicly available sources. The Court said protecting the minor's privacy was not a compelling reason to restrict the freedom of the press.[204]

The Supreme Court has also held that the First Amendment sometimes protects publication of private information even where it was not lawfully obtained—so long as the media were not involved in illegally acquiring the information. In *Bartnicki v. Vopper* (discussed further in Chapter 7), the Court said the media were not liable for publishing an intercepted cellphone conversation between two labor negotiators. Punishing the media for publishing information they obtained without acting illegally would not further a compelling government interest, the Court said.[205]

PRIVACY AND DATA PROTECTION

data broker
An entity that collects and stores personal information about consumers, then sells that information to other organizations.

Today, people's concerns about privacy persist alongside an additional threat from marketers, **data brokers** and other businesses that amass personally identifiable data. Data brokers collect, store and sell billions of pieces of personal data that cover nearly every U.S. consumer. In addition, courts have allowed websites and advertisers to put cookies—technology that tracks what websites people visit—on computers.[206] Many smartphone applications send users' sensitive information to advertisers and third-party data collectors.[207]

A few years ago, the Federal Trade Commission issued a substantive report about consumer privacy protection and called on companies to adopt its recommended best practices. The FTC is the chief federal agency that protects consumer privacy and enforces federal privacy laws. The FTC report suggested that at all stages of product development, companies build in consumer privacy protections, including consumer data security, limited data collection and retention, and procedures to promote data accuracy. The report also recommended giving consumers the option to control how they share their information and the ability to choose a "Do Not Track" mechanism, and the FTC encouraged companies to strive toward transparency in how they collect and use consumer information.[208] Current federal and state privacy laws do not sufficiently protect American consumers, according to the FTC. The burden of understanding websites' privacy policies is with online users who must affirmatively try to ensure their own privacy.[209]

The FTC issued a report on data brokers to educate the public about how these companies use, maintain and disseminate the personal data they collect. The report noted that none of the nine major data brokers obtained their data directly from consumers. Instead, the data originated from both public and private sources, online and offline. Information collected included Social Security numbers, interest in health issues, voter records, viewed news reports, social media posts, information from travel websites and transaction data from retailers.[210]

Data brokers analyze and repackage the information they collect for sale for marketing or risk mitigation purposes and/or for people searches. The FTC said consumers could benefit from the data these brokers collect and analyze but found little transparency in the industry. Additionally, the report said these brokers unnecessarily store consumer data indefinitely, which can increase security risks for consumers (e.g., increased risk of identity theft).[211]

Recently, the U.S. Supreme Court ruled in favor of a people search engine in *Spokeo, Inc. v. Robins.*[212] Spokeo's

online search engine contains personal information about people for its users, who include employers seeking to evaluate prospective employees. Thomas Robins filed a class action suit against Spokeo after he determined that the search engine contained incorrect information that misrepresented his marital and employment status and inflated both his income and his level of education. Robins argued that the inaccuracies violated the Fair Credit Reporting Act.

In a 6–2 decision, the Supreme Court held that Robins did not have standing to sue for damages because he could not show that he suffered "concrete" harm as a result of Spokeo's alleged FCRA violation.[213] Legal experts noted that the ruling could extend to numerous other statutes used in class action lawsuits when those lawsuits are based on alleged technical violations of the law that do not cause harm. They added that the decision did not give much guidance for other cases involving the increased risk to individuals when personal data are misused or incorrect.[214]

EMERGING LAW

One statute that could be subjected to the outcome in *Spokeo* is the Video Privacy Protection Act, which courts have revived in the context of online streaming video websites and mobile applications. Congress enacted the VPPA after U.S. Supreme Court nominee Robert Bork's video rental records were disclosed to the media during his confirmation hearing in 1987. The law prevents video service providers from knowingly disclosing a consumer's personally identifiable information to a third party (with a few exceptions).[215]

While at the time of its enactment the VPPA was meant to apply only to physical video rentals, a few years ago, a federal court in California applied the law to streaming websites and mobile applications because they were sharing personally identifiable information with third-party advertisers and data brokers.[216] The First, Third, Ninth and Eleventh Circuit Courts of Appeals have come to different determinations about whether the VPPA applies to streaming websites and mobile apps, highlighting the difficulty in applying the decades-old law in a digital context.[217]

Americans tend to think that global laws do not directly impact them. With the enforcement of the Global Data Protection Regulation by the European Union (EU) starting in 2018, legal experts predict the United States will need to enact a federal data privacy law similar in scope since most U.S. corporations compete globally and must comply with the GDPR to do business in the EU. In 2018, California enacted a sweeping privacy law that goes into effect in 2020, containing many of the same provisions as the GDPR. That law gives consumers the right to know what information companies collect about them, why they are collecting data and with whom they are sharing data. It also makes it difficult to share or sell data about children younger than 16, and it makes it easier for consumers to sue companies after a data breach.[218]

CASES FOR STUDY

For study resources and a case archive, go to **edge.sagepub.com/medialaw7e.**

Thinking About It

The two case excerpts that follow are landmark privacy cases. As you read these case excerpts, keep the following questions in mind:

- Why does the majority in *Carpenter v. United States* think that cell-site location information should not be covered by the third-party doctrine? Might the U.S. Supreme Court also exclude other categories of data or personal information from the third-party doctrine concept? Why do you think these categories would or should be excluded, based on the Court's rationale in *Carpenter*?

- How do the two decisions in *Cox Broadcasting Corp. v. Cohn* and *Carpenter* differ in how they try to balance the right of privacy against other important rights?

- How does the Court suggest technology has changed our societal understanding of a "reasonable expectation of privacy"?

Cox Broadcasting Corp. v. Cohn
SUPREME COURT OF THE UNITED STATES
420 U.S. 469 (1975)

JUSTICE BYRON WHITE delivered the Court's opinion:

The issue before us in this case is whether, consistently with the First and Fourteenth Amendments, a State may extend a cause of action for damages for invasion of privacy caused by the publication of the name of a deceased rape victim which was publicly revealed in connection with the prosecution of the crime.

In August 1971, appellee's 17-year-old daughter was the victim of a rape and did not survive the incident. Six youths were soon indicted for murder and rape. Although there was substantial press coverage of the crime and of subsequent developments, the identity of the victim was not disclosed pending trial, perhaps because of Ga. Code Ann. § 26-9901 (1972), which makes it a misdemeanor to publish or broadcast the name or identity of a rape victim. In April 1972, some eight months later, the six defendants appeared in court. Five pleaded guilty to rape or attempted rape, the charge of murder having been dropped. The guilty pleas were accepted by the court, and the trial of the defendant pleading not guilty was set for a later date.

In the course of the proceedings that day, appellant Wassell, a reporter covering the incident for his employer, learned the name of the victim from an examination of the indictments which were made available for his inspection in the courtroom. That the name of the victim appears in the indictments and that the indictments were public records available for inspection are not disputed. Later that day, Wassell broadcast over the facilities of station WSB-TV, a television station owned by appellant Cox Broadcasting Corp., a news report concerning the court proceedings. The report named the victim of the crime and was repeated the following day.

In May 1972, appellee brought an action for money damages against appellants, relying on § 26-9901 and claiming that his right to privacy had been invaded by the television broadcasts giving the name of his deceased daughter. Appellants admitted the broadcasts but claimed that they were privileged under both state law and the First and Fourteenth Amendments.

The trial court, rejecting appellants' constitutional claims and holding that the Georgia statute gave a civil remedy to those injured by its violation, granted summary judgment to appellee as to liability, with the determination of damages to await trial by jury.

On appeal, the Georgia Supreme Court, in its initial opinion, held that the trial court had erred in construing § 26-9901 to extend a civil cause of action for invasion of privacy and thus found it unnecessary to consider the constitutionality of the statute. . . . Upon motion for rehearing the Georgia court countered the argument that the victim's name was a matter of public interest and could be published with impunity by relying on § 26-9901 as an authoritative declaration of state policy that the name of a rape victim was not a matter of public concern. This time the court felt compelled to determine the constitutionality of the statute and sustained it as a "legitimate limitation on the right of freedom of expression contained in the First Amendment." The court could discern "no public interest or general concern about the identity of the victim of such a crime as will make the right to disclose the identity of the victim rise to the level of First Amendment protection."

. . . [W]e conclude that we have jurisdiction to review the judgment of the Georgia Supreme Court rejecting the challenge under the First and Fourteenth Amendments to the state law authorizing damage suits against the press for publishing the name of a rape victim whose identity is revealed in the course of a public prosecution. . . .

Georgia stoutly defends both § 26-9901 and the State's common-law privacy action challenged here. Its claims are not without force, for powerful arguments can be made, and have been made, that however it may be ultimately defined, there *is* a zone of privacy surrounding every individual, a zone within which the State may protect him from intrusion by the press, with all its attendant publicity. Indeed, the central thesis of the root article by Warren and Brandeis, The Right to Privacy, was that the press was overstepping its prerogatives by publishing essentially private information and that there should be a remedy for the alleged abuses.

More compellingly, the century has experienced a strong tide running in favor of the so-called right of privacy. In 1967, we noted that "[it] has been said that a 'right of privacy' has been recognized at common law

in 30 States plus the District of Columbia and by statute in four States." We there cited the 1964 edition of Prosser's Law of Torts. The 1971 edition of that same source states that "[in] one form or another, the right of privacy is by this time recognized and accepted in all but a very few jurisdictions." Nor is it irrelevant here that the right of privacy is no recent arrival in the jurisprudence of Georgia, which has embraced the right in some form since 1905 when the Georgia Supreme Court decided the leading case of *Pavesich v. New England Life Ins. Co.*

These are impressive credentials for a right of privacy, but we should recognize that we do not have at issue here an action for the invasion of privacy involving the appropriation of one's name or photograph, a physical or other tangible intrusion into a private area, or a publication of otherwise private information that is also false although perhaps not defamatory. The version of the privacy tort now before us—termed in Georgia "the tort of public disclosure"—is that in which the plaintiff claims the right to be free from unwanted publicity about his private affairs, which, although wholly true, would be offensive to a person of ordinary sensibilities. Because the gravamen of the claimed injury is the publication of information, whether true or not, the dissemination of which is embarrassing or otherwise painful to an individual, it is here that claims of privacy most directly confront the constitutional freedoms of speech and press. The face-off is apparent, and the appellants urge upon us the broad holding that the press may not be made criminally or civilly liable for publishing information that is neither false nor misleading but absolutely accurate, however damaging it may be to reputation or individual sensibilities. In this sphere of collision between claims of privacy and those of the free press, the interests on both sides are plainly rooted in the traditions and significant concerns of our society. Rather than address the broader question whether truthful publications may ever be subjected to civil or criminal liability consistently with the First and Fourteenth Amendments, or to put it another way, whether the State may ever define and protect an area of privacy free from unwanted publicity in the press, it is appropriate to focus on the narrower interface between press and privacy that this case presents, namely, whether the State may impose sanctions on the accurate publication of the name of a rape victim obtained from public records—more specifically, from judicial records which are maintained in connection with a public prosecution and which themselves are open to public inspection. We are convinced that the State may not do so.

In the first place, in a society in which each individual has but limited time and resources with which to observe at first hand the operations of his government, he relies necessarily upon the press to bring to him in convenient form the facts of those operations. Great responsibility is accordingly placed upon the news media to report fully and accurately the proceedings of government, and official records and documents open to the public are the basic data of governmental operations. Without the information provided by the press, most of us and many of our representatives would be unable to vote intelligently or to register opinions on the administration of government generally. With respect to judicial proceedings in particular, the function of the press serves to guarantee the fairness of trials and to bring to bear the beneficial effects of public scrutiny upon the administration of justice.

Appellee has claimed in this litigation that the efforts of the press have infringed his right to privacy by broadcasting to the world the fact that his daughter was a rape victim. The commission of crime, prosecutions resulting from it, and judicial proceedings arising from the prosecutions, however, are without question events of legitimate concern to the public and consequently fall within the responsibility of the press to report the operations of government.

The special protected nature of accurate reports of judicial proceedings has repeatedly been recognized. This Court, in an opinion written by MR. JUSTICE DOUGLAS, has said:

"A trial is a public event. What transpires in the court room is public property. If a transcript of the court proceedings had been published, we suppose none would claim that the judge could punish the publisher for contempt. And we can see no difference though the conduct of the attorneys, of the jury, or even of the judge himself, may have reflected on the court. *Those who see and hear what transpired can report it with impunity.* There is no special perquisite of the judiciary which enables it, as distinguished from other institutions of democratic government, to suppress, edit, or censor events which transpire in proceedings before it."

The developing law surrounding the tort of invasion of privacy recognizes a privilege in the press to report the events of judicial proceedings. The Warren and Brandeis article noted that the proposed new right would be limited in the same manner as actions for libel and slander where such a publication was a privileged communication: "the right to privacy is not invaded by any publication made in a court of justice . . . and (at least in many jurisdictions) reports of any such proceedings would in some measure be accorded a like privilege."

The Restatement of Torts, § 867, embraced an action for privacy. . . . According to this draft, ascertaining and publishing the contents of public records are simply not within the reach of these kinds of privacy actions.

Thus even the prevailing law of invasion of privacy generally recognizes that the interests in privacy fade when the information involved already appears on the public record. The conclusion is compelling when viewed in terms of the First and Fourteenth Amendments and in light of the public interest in a vigorous press. The Georgia cause of action for invasion of privacy through public disclosure of the name of a rape victim imposes sanctions on pure expression—the content of a publication—and not conduct or a combination of speech and nonspeech elements that might otherwise be open to regulation or prohibition. The publication of truthful information available on the public record contains none of the indicia of those limited categories of expression, such as "fighting" words, which "are no essential part of any exposition of ideas, and are of such slight social value as a step to truth that any benefit that may be derived from them is clearly outweighed by the social interest in order and morality."

By placing the information in the public domain on official court records, the State must be presumed to have concluded that the public interest was thereby being served. Public records by their very nature are of interest to those concerned with the administration of government, and a public benefit is performed by the reporting of the true contents of the records by the media. The freedom of the press to publish that information appears to us to be of critical importance to our type of government in which the citizenry is the final judge of the proper conduct of public business. In preserving that form of government, the First and Fourteenth Amendments command nothing less than that the States may not impose sanctions on the publication of truthful information contained in official court records open to public inspection.

We are reluctant to embark on a course that would make public records generally available to the media but forbid their publication if offensive to the sensibilities of the supposed reasonable man. Such a rule would make it very difficult for the media to inform citizens about the public business and yet stay within the law. The rule would invite timidity and self-censorship and very likely lead to the suppression of many items that would otherwise be published and that should be made available to the public. At the very least, the First and Fourteenth Amendments will not allow exposing the press to liability for truthfully publishing information released to the public in official court records. If there are privacy interests to be protected in judicial proceedings, the States must respond by means which avoid public documentation or other exposure of private information. Their political institutions must weigh the interests in privacy with the interests of the public to know and of the press to publish. Once true information is disclosed in public court documents open to public inspection, the press cannot be sanctioned for publishing it. In this instance, as in others, reliance must rest upon the judgment of those who decide what to publish or broadcast.

Appellant Wassell based his televised report upon notes taken during the court proceedings and obtained the name of the victim from the indictments handed to him at his request during a recess in the hearing. Appellee has not contended that the name was obtained in an improper fashion or that it was not on an official court document open to public inspection. Under these circumstances, the protection of freedom of the press provided by the First and Fourteenth Amendments bars the State of Georgia from making appellants' broadcast the basis of civil liability.

Reversed.

CHIEF JUSTICE WARREN BURGER concurs in the judgment.

JUSTICE LEWIS POWELL, Jr., concurring, with whom JUSTICE WILLIAM DOUGLAS joins. . . .

JUSTICE WILLIAM DOUGLAS, concurring in the judgment.

I agree that the state judgment is "final," and I also agree in the reversal of the Georgia court. On the merits, the case for me is on all fours with *New Jersey State Lottery Comm'n v. United States.* For the reasons I stated in my dissent from our disposition of that case, there is no power on the part of government to suppress or penalize the publication of "news of the day."

JUSTICE WILLIAM REHNQUIST, dissenting.

Because I am of the opinion that the decision which is the subject of this appeal is not a "final" judgment or decree, as that term is used in 28 U. S. C. § 1257, I would dismiss this appeal for want of jurisdiction. . . .

Carpenter v. United States
SUPREME COURT OF THE UNITED STATES
138 S. Ct. 2206 (2018)

CHIEF JUSTICE JOHN ROBERTS delivered the Court's opinion:

This case presents the question whether the Government conducts a search under the *Fourth Amendment* when it accesses historical cell phone records that provide a comprehensive chronicle of the user's past movements.

There are 396 million cell phone service accounts in the United States—for a Nation of 326 million people.

Cell phones perform their wide and growing variety of functions by connecting to a set of radio antennas called "cell sites." Although cell sites are usually mounted on a tower, they can also be found on light posts, flagpoles, church steeples, or the sides of buildings. . . .

Cell phones continuously scan their environment looking for the best signal, which generally comes from the closest cell site. Most modern devices, such as smartphones, tap into the wireless network several times a minute whenever their signal is on, even if the owner is not using one of the phone's features. Each time the phone connects to a cell site, it generates a time-stamped record known as cell-site location information (CSLI). The precision of this information depends on the size of the geographic area covered by the cell site. The greater the concentration of cell sites, the smaller the coverage area. As data usage from cell phones has increased, wireless carriers have installed more cell sites to handle the traffic. That has led to increasingly compact coverage areas, especially in urban areas.

Wireless carriers collect and store CSLI for their own business purposes, including finding weak spots in their network. . . . In addition, wireless carriers often sell aggregated location records to data brokers, without individual identifying information of the sort at issue here. While carriers have long retained CSLI for the start and end of incoming calls, in recent years phone companies have also collected location information from the transmission of text messages and routine data connections. Accordingly, modern cell phones generate increasingly vast amounts of increasingly precise CSLI.

In 2011, police officers arrested four men suspected of robbing a series of Radio Shack and (ironically enough) T-Mobile stores. . . . The suspect identified 15 accomplices who had participated in the heists and gave the FBI some of their cell phone numbers; the FBI then reviewed his call records to identify additional numbers that he had called around the time of the robberies.

Based on that information, the prosecutors applied for court orders under the Stored Communications Act to obtain cell phone records for petitioner Timothy Carpenter and several other suspects. That statute, as amended in 1994, permits the Government to compel the disclosure of certain telecommunications records. . . . Federal Magistrate Judges issued two orders directing Carpenter's wireless carriers—MetroPCS and Sprint—to disclose [CSLI] . . . during the four-month period when the string of robberies occurred. . . . Altogether the Government obtained 12,898 location points cataloging Carpenter's movements—an average of 101 data points per day.

Carpenter was charged with six counts of robbery and an additional six counts of carrying a firearm during a federal crime of violence. Prior to trial, Carpenter . . . argued that the Government's seizure of the records violated the Fourth Amendment because they had been obtained without a warrant supported by probable cause. The District Court denied the motion.

At trial . . . FBI agent Christopher Hess . . . produced maps that placed Carpenter's phone near four of the charged robberies. In the Government's view, the location records clinched the case. . . . Carpenter was convicted on all but one of the firearm counts and sentenced to more than 100 years in prison.

The Court of Appeals for the Sixth Circuit affirmed. The court held that Carpenter lacked a reasonable expectation of privacy in the location information collected by the FBI because he had shared that information with his wireless carriers. Given that cell phone users voluntarily convey cell-site data to their carriers as "a means of establishing communication," the court concluded that the resulting business records are not entitled to Fourth Amendment protection. . . .

The Fourth Amendment protects "[t]he right of the people to be secure in their persons, houses, papers, and effects, against unreasonable searches and seizures." The "basic purpose of this Amendment" . . . "is to safeguard the privacy and security of individuals against arbitrary invasions by governmental officials."

. . . For much of our history, Fourth Amendment search doctrine was "tied to common-law trespass" and focused on whether the Government "obtains information by physically intruding on a constitutionally protected area." More recently, the Court has recognized that "property rights are not the sole measure of Fourth Amendment violations." In [Katz], we established that "the Fourth Amendment protects people, not places," and expanded our conception of the Amendment to protect certain expectations of privacy as well. . . .

[The Fourth] Amendment seeks to secure "the privacies of life" against "arbitrary power." . . . [A] central aim of the Framers was "to place obstacles in the way of a too permeating police surveillance."

We have kept this attention to Founding-era understandings in mind when applying the Fourth Amendment to innovations in surveillance tools. . . .

[I]n Riley, the Court recognized the "immense storage capacity" of modern cell phones in holding that police officers must generally obtain a warrant before searching the contents of a phone. . . .

The case before us involves the Government's acquisition of wireless carrier cell-site records revealing the location of Carpenter's cell phone whenever it made or received calls. This sort of digital data—personal location information maintained by a third party—does not fit neatly under existing precedents. Instead, requests for cell-site records lie at the intersection of two lines of cases, both of which inform our understanding of the privacy interests at stake.

The first set of cases addresses a person's expectation of privacy in his physical location and movements. [W]e [have] considered the Government's use of a "beeper" to aid in tracking a vehicle through traffic. . . . The Court concluded [in *Knotts*] that the "augment[ed]" visual surveillance did not constitute a search because "[a] person traveling in an automobile on public thoroughfares has no reasonable expectation of privacy in his movements from one place to another." . . .

This Court in *Knotts*, however, was careful to distinguish between the rudimentary tracking facilitated by the beeper and more sweeping modes of surveillance. . . . Significantly, the Court reserved the question whether "different constitutional principles may be applicable" if "twenty-four hour surveillance of any citizen of this country [were] possible."

Three decades later, the Court considered more sophisticated surveillance of the sort envisioned in *Knotts* and found that different principles did indeed apply. In *United States* v. *Jones* . . . the Court decided the case based on the Government's physical trespass of the vehicle. At the same time, five Justices agreed that related privacy concerns would be raised by, for example, "surreptitiously activating a stolen vehicle detection system" in Jones's car to track Jones himself, or conducting GPS tracking of his cell phone. Since GPS monitoring of a vehicle tracks "every movement" a person makes in that vehicle, the concurring Justices concluded that "longer term GPS monitoring in investigations of most offenses impinges on expectations of privacy"—regardless whether those movements were disclosed to the public at large.

In a second set of decisions, the Court has drawn a line between what a person keeps to himself and what he shares with others. We have previously held that "a person has no legitimate expectation of privacy in information he voluntarily turns over to third parties." . . . As a result, the Government is typically free to obtain such information from the recipient without triggering Fourth Amendment protections.

This third-party doctrine largely traces its roots to *Miller*. While investigating Miller for tax evasion, the Government subpoenaed his banks, seeking several months of canceled checks, deposit slips, and monthly statements. The Court rejected a Fourth Amendment challenge to the records collection. For one, Miller could "assert neither ownership nor possession" of the documents; they were "business records of the banks." For another, the nature of those records confirmed Miller's limited expectation of privacy, because the checks were "not confidential communications but negotiable instruments to be used in commercial transactions," and the bank statements contained information "exposed to [bank] employees in the ordinary course of business." . . .

Three years later, *Smith* applied the same principles in the context of information conveyed to a telephone company. . . .

The question we confront today is how to apply the Fourth Amendment to a new phenomenon: the ability to chronicle a person's past movements through the record of his cell phone signals. Such tracking partakes of many of the qualities of the GPS monitoring we considered in *Jones*. Much like GPS tracking of a vehicle, cell phone location information is detailed, encyclopedic, and effortlessly compiled.

At the same time, the fact that the individual continuously reveals his location to his wireless carrier implicates the third-party principle of *Smith* and *Miller*. But while the third-party doctrine applies to telephone numbers and bank records, it is not clear whether its logic extends to the qualitatively different category of cell-site records. After all, when *Smith* was decided in 1979, few could have imagined a society in which a phone goes wherever its owner goes, conveying to the wireless carrier not just dialed digits, but a detailed and comprehensive record of the person's movements.

We decline to extend *Smith* and *Miller* to cover these novel circumstances. Given the unique nature of cell phone location records, the fact that the information is held by a third party does not by itself overcome the user's claim to *Fourth Amendment* protection. Whether the Government employs its own surveillance technology as in *Jones* or leverages the technology of a wireless carrier, we hold that an individual maintains a legitimate expectation of privacy in the record of his physical movements as captured through CSLI. The location information obtained from Carpenter's wireless carriers was the product of a search. . . .

A person does not surrender all *Fourth Amendment* protection by venturing into the public sphere. . . . Prior to the digital age, law enforcement might have pursued a suspect for a brief stretch, but doing so "for any extended period of time was difficult and costly and therefore rarely undertaken." For that reason, "society's expectation has been that law enforcement agents and others would not—and indeed, in the main, simply could not—secretly monitor and catalogue every single movement of an individual's car for a very long period."

Allowing government access to cell-site records contravenes that expectation. . . . [L]ike GPS monitoring, cell phone tracking is remarkably easy, cheap, and efficient compared to traditional investigative tools. With just the click of a button, the Government can access each carrier's deep repository of historical location information at practically no expense.

In fact, historical cell-site records present even greater privacy concerns than the GPS monitoring of a vehicle we considered in *Jones*. . . . A cell phone faithfully follows its owner beyond public thoroughfares and into private residences, doctor's offices, political headquarters, and other potentially revealing locales. . . . Accordingly, when the Government tracks the location of a cell phone it achieves near perfect surveillance, as if it had attached an ankle monitor to the phone's user.

Moreover, the retrospective quality of the data here gives police access to a category of information otherwise unknowable. . . . Critically, because location information is continually logged for all of the 400 million devices in the United States—not just those belonging to persons who might happen to come under investigation—this newfound tracking capacity runs against everyone. . . .

Whoever the suspect turns out to be, he has effectively been tailed every moment of every day for five years, and the police may—in the Government's view—call upon the results of that surveillance without regard to the constraints of the Fourth Amendment. Only the few without cell phones could escape this tireless and absolute surveillance.

The Government and Justice Kennedy contend, however, that the collection of CSLI should be permitted because the data is less precise than GPS information. . . .

While the records in this case reflect the state of technology at the start of the decade, the accuracy of CSLI is rapidly approaching GPS-level precision. As the number of cell sites has proliferated, the geographic area covered by each cell sector has shrunk, particularly in urban areas. In addition, with new technology measuring the time and angle of signals hitting their towers, wireless carriers already have the capability to pinpoint a phone's location within 50 meters.

Accordingly, when the Government accessed CSLI from the wireless carriers, it invaded Carpenter's reasonable expectation of privacy in the whole of his physical movements.

The Government's primary contention to the contrary is that the third-party doctrine governs this case. . . .

The Government's position fails to contend with the seismic shifts in digital technology that made possible the tracking of not only Carpenter's location but also everyone else's, not for a short period but for years and years. Sprint Corporation and its competitors are not your typical witnesses. Unlike the nosy neighbor who keeps an eye on comings and goings, they are ever alert, and their memory is nearly infallible. There is a world of difference between the limited types of personal information addressed in *Smith* and *Miller* and the exhaustive chronicle of location information casually collected by wireless carriers today. The Government thus is not asking for a straightforward application of the third-party doctrine, but instead a significant extension of it to a distinct category of information. . . .

The Court has in fact already shown special solicitude for location information in the third-party context. In *Knotts*, the Court relied on *Smith* to hold that an individual has no reasonable expectation of privacy in public movements that he "voluntarily conveyed to anyone who wanted to look." But when confronted with more pervasive tracking, five Justices agreed [in *Jones*] that longer term GPS monitoring of even a vehicle traveling on public streets constitutes a search. Justice Gorsuch wonders why "someone's location when using a phone" is sensitive, and Justice Kennedy assumes that a person's discrete movements "are not particularly private." Yet this case is not about "using a phone" or a person's movement at a particular time. It is about a detailed chronicle of a person's physical presence compiled every day, every moment, over several years. Such a chronicle implicates privacy concerns far beyond those considered in *Smith* and *Miller*.

. . . Cell phone location information is not truly "shared" as one normally understands the term. In the first place, cell phones and the services they provide are "such a pervasive and insistent part of daily life" that carrying one is indispensable to participation in modern society. Second, a cell phone logs a cell-site record by dint of its operation, without any affirmative act on the part of the user beyond powering up. Virtually any activity on the phone generates CSLI, including incoming calls, texts, or e-mails and countless other data connections that a phone automatically makes when checking for news, weather, or social media updates. Apart from disconnecting the phone from the network, there is no way to avoid leaving behind a trail of location data. As a result, in no meaningful sense does the user voluntarily "assume[ ] the risk" of turning over a comprehensive dossier of his physical movements.

We therefore decline to extend *Smith* and *Miller* to the collection of CSLI. Given the unique nature of cell phone location information, the fact that the Government obtained the information from a third party does not overcome Carpenter's claim to Fourth Amendment protection. The Government's acquisition of the cell-site records was a search within the meaning of the Fourth Amendment.

Our decision today is a narrow one. . . . We do not disturb the application of *Smith* and *Miller* or call into question conventional surveillance techniques and tools, such as security cameras. Nor do we address other business records that might incidentally reveal location information. Further, our opinion does not consider other collection techniques involving foreign affairs or national security. As Justice Frankfurter noted when considering new innovations in airplanes and radios, the Court must tread carefully in such cases, to ensure that we do not "embarrass the future."

Having found that the acquisition of Carpenter's CSLI was a search, we also conclude that the Government must generally obtain a warrant supported by probable cause before acquiring such records. . . .

At some point, the dissent should recognize that CSLI is an entirely different species of business record—something that implicates basic Fourth Amendment concerns about arbitrary government power much more directly than corporate tax or payroll ledgers. When confronting new concerns wrought by digital technology, this Court has been careful not to uncritically extend existing precedents. . . .

This is certainly not to say that all orders compelling the production of documents will require a showing of probable cause. The Government will be able to use subpoenas to acquire records in the overwhelming majority of investigations. We hold only that a warrant is required in the rare case where the suspect has a legitimate privacy interest in records held by a third party.

Further, even though the Government will generally need a warrant to access CSLI, case-specific exceptions may support a warrantless search of an individual's cell-site records under certain circumstances. . . .

As a result, if law enforcement is confronted with an urgent situation, such fact-specific threats will likely justify the warrantless collection of CSLI. Lower courts, for instance, have approved warrantless searches related to bomb threats, active shootings, and child abductions. Our decision today does not call into doubt warrantless access to CSLI in such circumstances. While police must get a warrant when collecting CSLI to assist in the mine-run criminal investigation, the rule we set forth does not limit their ability to respond to an ongoing emergency. . . .

We decline to grant the state unrestricted access to a wireless carrier's database of physical location information. In light of the deeply revealing nature of CSLI, its depth, breadth, and comprehensive reach, and the inescapable and automatic nature of its collection, the fact that such information is gathered by a third party does not make it any less deserving of Fourth Amendment protection. The Government's acquisition of the cell-site records here was a search under that Amendment.

The judgment of the Court of Appeals is reversed, and the case is remanded for further proceedings consistent with this opinion.

It is so ordered.

JUSTICE ANTHONY KENNEDY, with whom JUSTICE CLARENCE THOMAS and JUSTICE SAMUEL ALITO join, dissenting.[219]

This case involves new technology, but the Court's stark departure from relevant *Fourth Amendment* precedents and principles is, in my submission, unnecessary and incorrect, requiring this respectful dissent.

The new rule the Court seems to formulate puts needed, reasonable, accepted, lawful, and congressionally authorized criminal investigations at serious risk in serious cases, often when law enforcement seeks to prevent the threat of violent crimes. . . .

The Court has twice held that individuals have no Fourth Amendment interests in business records which are possessed, owned, and controlled by a third party. This is true even when the records contain personal and sensitive information. So when the Government uses a subpoena to obtain, for example, bank records, telephone records, and credit card statements from the businesses that create and keep these records, the Government does not engage in a search of the business's customers within the meaning of the Fourth Amendment.

. . . Cell-site records, however, are no different from the many other kinds of business records the Government has a lawful right to obtain by compulsory process. Customers like petitioner do not own, possess, control, or use the records, and for that reason have no reasonable expectation that they cannot be disclosed pursuant to lawful compulsory process. . . .

In concluding that the Government engaged in a search, the Court unhinges Fourth Amendment doctrine from the property-based concepts that have long grounded the analytic framework that pertains in these cases. In doing so it draws an unprincipled and unworkable line between cell-site records on the one hand and financial and telephonic records on the other. According to today's majority opinion, the Government can acquire a record of every credit card purchase and phone call a person makes over months or years without upsetting a legitimate expectation of privacy. But, in the Court's view, the Government crosses a constitutional line when it obtains a court's approval to issue a subpoena for more than six days of cell-site records in order to determine whether a person was within several hundred city blocks of a crime scene. That distinction is illogical and will frustrate principled application of the Fourth Amendment in many routine yet vital law enforcement operations.

It is true that the Cyber Age has vast potential both to expand and restrict individual freedoms in dimensions not contemplated in earlier times. . . .

Here the only question necessary to decide is whether the Government searched anything of Carpenter's when it used compulsory process to obtain cell-site records from Carpenter's cell phone service providers. This Court's decisions in *Miller* and *Smith* dictate that the answer is no, as every Court of Appeals to have considered the question has recognized. . . .

Based on *Miller* and *Smith* . . . it is well established that subpoenas may be used to obtain a wide variety of records held by businesses, even when the records contain private information. Credit cards are a prime example. State and federal law enforcement, for instance, often subpoena credit card statements to develop probable cause to prosecute crimes ranging from drug trafficking and distribution to healthcare fraud to tax evasion. . . . Subpoenas also may be used to obtain vehicle registration records, hotel records, employment records, and records of utility usage, to name just a few other examples.

. . . In my respectful view the majority opinion misreads this Court's precedents, old and recent, and transforms *Miller* and *Smith* into an unprincipled and unworkable doctrine. . . .

The Court appears . . . to read *Miller* and *Smith* to establish a balancing test. For each "qualitatively different category" of information, the Court suggests, the privacy interests at stake must be weighed against the fact that the information has been disclosed to a third party. When the privacy interests are weighty enough to "overcome" the third-party disclosure, the Fourth Amendment's protections apply.

That is an untenable reading of *Miller* and *Smith*. . . .

[T]he Court maintains, cell-site records are "unique" because they are "comprehensive" in their reach; allow for retrospective collection; are "easy, cheap, and efficient compared to traditional investigative tools"; and are not exposed to cell phone service providers in a meaningfully voluntary manner. But many other kinds of business records can be so described. Financial records are of vast scope. Banks and credit card companies keep a comprehensive account of almost every transaction an individual makes on a daily basis. "With just the click of a button, the Government can access each [company's] deep repository of historical [financial] information at practically no expense." And the decision whether to transact with banks and credit card companies is no more or less voluntary than the decision whether to use a cell phone. Today, just as when *Miller* was decided, "'it is impossible to participate in the economic life of contemporary society without maintaining a bank account.'" But this Court, nevertheless, has held that individuals do not have a reasonable expectation of privacy in financial records. . . .

Technological changes involving cell phones have complex effects on crime and law enforcement. Cell phones make crimes easier to coordinate and conceal, while also providing the Government with new investigative tools that may have the potential to upset traditional privacy expectations. How those competing effects balance against each other, and how property norms and expectations of privacy form around new technology, often will be difficult to determine during periods of rapid technological change. . . . Congress weighed the privacy interests at stake and imposed a judicial check to prevent executive overreach. The Court should be wary of upsetting that legislative balance and erecting constitutional barriers that foreclose further legislative instructions. . . . The Court's decision runs roughshod over the mechanism Congress put in place to govern the acquisition of cell-site records and closes off further legislative debate on these issues.

The Court says its decision is a "narrow one." But its reinterpretation of *Miller* and *Smith* will have dramatic consequences for law enforcement, courts, and society as a whole. . . .

The Court's decision also will have ramifications that extend beyond cell-site records to other kinds of information held by third parties, yet the Court fails "to provide clear guidance to law enforcement" and courts on key issues raised by its reinterpretation of *Miller* and *Smith*. . . .

This case should be resolved by interpreting accepted property principles as the baseline for reasonable expectations of privacy. Here the Government did not search anything over which Carpenter could assert ownership or control. Instead, it issued a court-authorized subpoena to a third party to disclose information it alone owned and controlled. That should suffice to resolve this case. . . .

These reasons all lead to this respectful dissent.

---

⑤SAGE edge™

Visit **edge.sagepub.com/medialaw7e** to help you accomplish your coursework goals in an easy-to-use learning environment.

[W]ithout freedom to acquire information, the right to publish would be impermissibly compromised. Accordingly, a right to gather news, of some dimensions, must exist.

—U.S. Supreme Court Justice Lewis Powell[1]

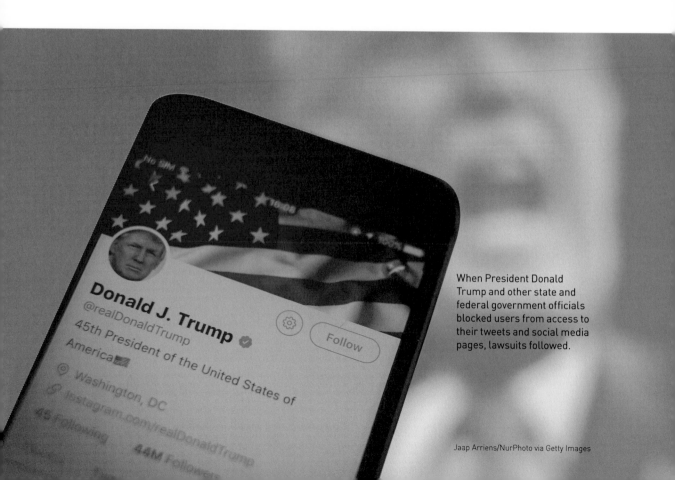

When President Donald Trump and other state and federal government officials blocked users from access to their tweets and social media pages, lawsuits followed.

Jaap Arriens/NurPhoto via Getty Images

7

GATHERING INFORMATION
Opportunities and Obstacles

SUPPOSE...

. . . that a team of law enforcement officers executes a search warrant on what they believe is the home of a suspect. A newspaper reporter and photographer accompany the officers, who forcibly enter the home in the early morning, awakening two residents, who are the suspect's parents. The couple assures the officers their son is not there. The photographer takes several pictures, though none are published. After a search of the home, the officers and journalists leave. Was the journalists' presence illegal? If so, who is liable for the illegal act—the journalists or the law enforcement agency? Look for the answers to these questions when the case of *Wilson v. Layne* is discussed later in this chapter and excerpted at the end of the chapter.[2]

BRIEF OVERVIEW OF ACCESS

While the Constitution authorized Congress to keep some records secret and courts had a history of openness (see Chapter 8), no history or law ensured the openness of information from the executive branch. The first Congress in 1789 adopted only a "housekeeping" statute that empowered federal departments to establish their own rules and policies for keeping and sharing documents.[3] Few questions about access to government information presented themselves until World War II ended and the Cold War spread global distrust.[4] Congress enacted its first substantive records law, the Administrative Procedure Act of 1946, to give federal officials discretion to make records public except "for good cause" or "in the public interest."[5] The law generally enabled federal government agencies to keep all unpublished records secret.

In the mid-1960s in a case involving a ban on travel to Cuba, the U.S. Supreme Court held that weighty national security considerations required that "the right to speak and publish does not carry with it the unrestrained right to gather information."[6] As Congress itself struggled to obtain government information, it began to enact laws to improve interagency, interbranch and public access to government records. Congress enacted the Freedom of Information Act (called FOIA, pronounced foy-yuh) in 1966.[7] The law created a presumption of access to all official executive agency records unless the material met the requirements of nine narrow exemptions. In the 1970s, two federal laws established access to meetings of federal advisory committees[8] and policymaking bodies,[9] and the Privacy Act protected seven types of personal information held by government agencies from this openness.[10]

Although the U.S. Supreme Court has never defined the precise parameters of a First Amendment right of access to government information, the Court in 1972 said that freedom of the press would be "eviscerated" without some protection for gathering information.[11] A few years later, the Supreme Court explained that

> the public's interest in knowing about its government is protected by the guarantee of a free press, but the protection is indirect. The Constitution itself is neither a Freedom of Information Act nor an official secrets act.[12]

Many countries, though not the United States, have official secrets laws to protect state secrets and information related to national security. The U.S. Supreme Court's rulings on public access relate to specific laws and to particular government information, institutions and events.

LANDMARK CASES IN CONTEXT

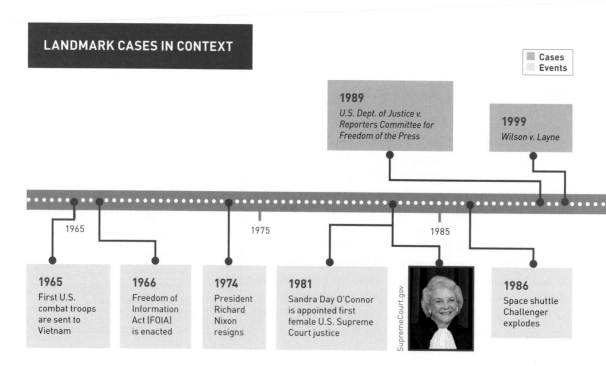

Cases
Events

1989
U.S. Dept. of Justice v. Reporters Committee for Freedom of the Press

1999
Wilson v. Layne

1965

1975

1985

1965
First U.S. combat troops are sent to Vietnam

1966
Freedom of Information Act (FOIA) is enacted

1974
President Richard Nixon resigns

1981
Sandra Day O'Connor is appointed first female U.S. Supreme Court justice

SupremeCourt.gov

1986
Space shuttle Challenger explodes

While some states adopted "sunshine laws," as access laws are called, much earlier than FOIA, many enacted open-records and open-meetings laws echoing the foundational federal statutes during the '60s and '70s.[13] In the four decades since, both federal and state legislatures have amended laws to respond to the changing nature of recordkeeping in the electronic age[14] and passed exemptions[15] that create significant differences of access among states and between them and the federal government.[16]

Since the terrorist attacks of Sept. 11, 2001, courts have struggled to reconcile the need for national security with the uncertain First Amendment guarantee of government openness.[17] A recent study found that, in most states, "open records laws are riddled with loopholes while the government agencies meant to enforce them are often toothless and underfunded."[18] One state records act included 260 exemptions. In 2015, the USA Freedom Act that restored post-9/11 anti-terrorism provisions also increased public access to the government's national security apparatus.[19] For example, Section 402 of the act required the federal government to declassify and release "significant" opinions of the secret proceedings of the Foreign Intelligence Surveillance Court that reviews the legality of national security operations.

FIRST AMENDMENT RIGHT OF ACCESS

While legal scholars and media advocates argue that the First Amendment should be understood to protect the right to gather information and report the news,[20] the U.S. Supreme Court has said merely that newsgathering plays an important role in advancing First Amendment interests.[21] Courts consistently rule that no explicit newsgathering right exists under the First

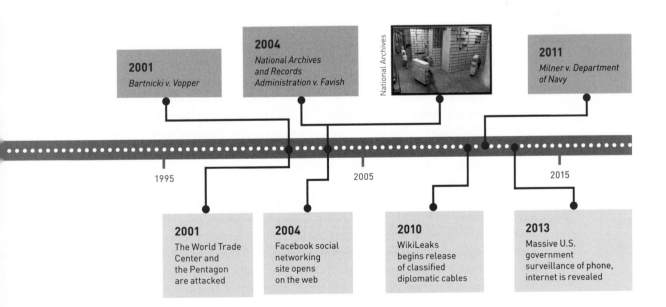

2001
Bartnicki v. Vopper

2004
National Archives and Records Administration v. Favish

National Archives

2011
Milner v. Department of Navy

1995

2005

2015

2001
The World Trade Center and the Pentagon are attacked

2004
Facebook social networking site opens on the web

2010
WikiLeaks begins release of classified diplomatic cables

2013
Massive U.S. government surveillance of phone, internet is revealed

Amendment, and the Supreme Court has not clearly defined the First Amendment right of access to government information and institutions. However, several circuit courts of appeal have found a First Amendment right of public access to administrative proceedings.[22] In one case, the Second Circuit Court of Appeals ruled that the public's right of access applies to New York City Transit Authority hearings on violation of its rules.[23] Applying a test established to generally support a public right of access to judicial proceedings (see discussion of the *Press-Enterprise* test in Chapter 8),[24] the court said the transit authority had failed to show that either the logic of ensuring the proper functioning of the hearings or their history of openness supported a ban on public attendance at its adjudication hearings.

Some rulings differentiate between the public access provided to a government proceeding and the information related to it. In 2017, for example, a federal district court said the public had the right to view the entirety of executions in Arizona but that right did not extend to information about the specific drugs, personnel and procedures used.[25] In a similar case in Alabama, however, the Eleventh Circuit Court of Appeals held that the public enjoyed a common law right of access to the death-penalty protocol.[26] Long-standing bans on the reporting of military troop locations and movements also withstand scrutiny as do policies on "pool reporting" and embedding reporters with the military.[27]

Access to Public and Quasi-Public Places

A complex array of statutes and court precedents establish protections for access to public and quasi-public spaces. Public sidewalks, public parks and much public property constitute First Amendment public forums established for use by the public, with some limitations (see Chapter 2). Government may restrict access to these to ensure the proper functioning of public services and to protect public safety. Accordingly, police and other public safety officials may order individuals, including the press, to stay away from a crime scene or other event on public land or in public forums, but they may not apply policies in an arbitrary or discriminatory fashion. Police may arrest anyone who disobeys a lawful order and interferes with police functions.

Public officials do not have unlimited power over individuals at a location. In one case, the city of New York agreed to pay an $18 million settlement for the arrest and detention—from a couple of hours to more than a day—of nearly 1,800 protesters, journalists and onlookers at the 2004 Republican National Convention.[28] In another case, the Seventh Circuit Court of Appeals found unconstitutional a Chicago ordinance that made it a crime for an individual to knowingly disregard police orders to disperse near a site of disorderly conduct. The case involved an individual's arrest for refusal to stay on the sidewalk near where an officer arrested protesters causing "serious inconvenience, annoyance or alarm."[29] The court said the law was too broad, vague and subjective to pass constitutional review.

Recent court decisions turn on fact determinations of the nature of the location involved. Some government lands and buildings, such as military bases, prisons and polling sites, are not broadly open to the public. A representative case involved two separate arrests of individuals for photographing Customs and Border Protection operations at the U.S./Mexico border.[30] The plaintiffs argued that CBP policies ban photography from "large swaths" of public streets and sidewalks adjacent to border entry points. In 2018, the Ninth Circuit Court of Appeals remanded the case to determine, among other things, whether CBP regulations violate First Amendment rights in traditional public forums.[31]

The U.S. Court of Appeals for the Sixth Circuit struck down an Ohio law that required all nonvoters to stay well away from the polls.[32] Applying strict scrutiny to what the court viewed as a content-based restriction on nonvoter speech, the court found the law violated the press's First Amendment rights. The state had a compelling interest in ensuring orderly elections, but the law was not narrowly drawn to achieve that end, the court said.

Some of the estimated 900 bison culled from Yellowstone in 2015 awaiting slaughter in the Stephens Creek Capture Facility in Montana.

When the Third Circuit Court of Appeals reviewed Pennsylvania's law requiring people to remain 10 feet away from the polls unless voting, it saw the law as a limit on information gathering that could interfere with the primary purpose of the polling place.[33] In reviewing both the logic and experience of public access to the polls, the Third Circuit said (1) openness might reduce voter fraud but also discourage some people from voting and (2) the secrecy of the ballot had increased through time. The court concluded that both elements supported the limit on public access to the polls.

Some seemingly public property sometimes may be closed to the public. In one case, the Wisconsin Supreme Court upheld a photojournalist's conviction for disorderly conduct for circumventing a roadblock, then jumping a fence to take pictures of an airplane crash at a publicly owned airport. Officers had limited access to authorized personnel, but the journalist refused to leave or stop taking pictures. The court rejected the argument that the First Amendment requires news media access to emergency sites. Access was restricted, not denied, the court said, and journalists who followed the airport's media guidelines were taken to the crash site.[34]

The Ninth Circuit Court of Appeals said both logic and experience should be used "to evaluate attempts to access a wide range of civil and administrative government activities" when it held that Bureau of Land Management rules did not violate the rights of reporters seeking access to BLM holding facilities for wild horses.[35] Despite finding that public access enhanced the horse roundups and that the roundups had been open traditionally,[36] the Ninth Circuit said the limits appropriately advanced the BLM's overriding interest in safety and did not unduly infringe First Amendment rights.

A recent federal district court ruling similarly allowed the U.S. National Park Service to ban observers from the annual cull of buffalo from Yellowstone.[37] The court reasoned that the culls historically had been closed to the public and closures were narrowly tailored to protect the safety of workers and the public. "Viewing the culling of bison is not protected First Amendment speech or activity." Even if it applied the First Amendment, the court said, it would find the park was a nonpublic forum and the ban was content-neutral.

Right to Record

It generally is legal to record whatever can be viewed or heard on or from public property, but the recording of certain events may be restricted. For example, some years ago, reporters challenged the Maryland Legislature's ban on recording legislative sessions, and the state appeals court said that although newsgathering enjoys some First Amendment protection, banning recorders does not infringe on that right.[38] It called the ban "a mere inconvenience."[39] Similar reasoning guides the U.S. Supreme Court, the federal court system and the few state judiciaries that continue to limit or prohibit cameras in courtrooms, as explained in Chapter 8.[40]

In recent years, conflicts with police over the right to record police actions have increased. Police have detained or arrested those recording anything from large public protests to traffic stops and confiscated or destroyed their footage. Most U.S. circuit courts of appeal have concluded that the First Amendment protects individuals from punishment for recording police activity in public.[41]

When the First Circuit Court of Appeals reviewed the arrest of a woman who sat in her car and used her cellphone to film an officer's nearby traffic stop of her friend, the court said the First Amendment protected her right to peacefully and nondisruptively record public police activity.[42] Three years earlier, the First Circuit ruled that the First Amendment requires police to justify an arrest for recording by showing that filming hindered performance of their duties.[43] Applying similar reasoning, the Fifth Circuit Court of Appeals upheld charges against a man who refused repeated orders to stop recording police when recording interfered with performance of their duties.[44] The man was a member of a community group in Austin, Texas, dedicated to holding police officers accountable for misconduct. At two separate events the same evening, several officers told the man he was "interfering" with their official actions because he did not stay an arm's length away from them. He said he remained farther away than the required arm's length. However, the court ruled that the officers were immune from liability for violating his First Amendment rights because he repeatedly disobeyed the officers' orders to step back.

The Seventh Circuit Court of Appeals found that the First Amendment also protected audio recording of police officers, even when state law required the consent of all parties.[45] The Seventh Circuit ruled that a law prohibiting public recording of police activities in a traditional public forum violated the First Amendment because the burden on speech outweighed any substantial state interest in prohibiting recording of what other witnesses might readily overhear.

In 2017, the Third Circuit Court of Appeals joined this "growing consensus" upholding the right to record when it found that the First Amendment protected the right of bystanders to film arrests by Philadelphia police officers.[46] The court said such filming advanced important public interests in (1) improving observation of police activities and (2) enhancing public discourse about them.[47] The Third Circuit also held that the "unsettled" state of First Amendment rights at the time of the arrests entitled the officers to qualified immunity from liability.[48] In dissent, one judge wrote:

> [I]n light of the social, cultural and legal context in which this case arose, I am
> convinced that . . . no reasonable officer could have denied at the time of the incidents

underlying these cases that efforts to prevent people from recording their activities infringed rights guaranteed by the First Amendment. For these reasons, I dissent from the majority's conclusion that the police officers are immune from suit.[49]

In 2017, the Supreme Court of Hawaii affirmed the broad First Amendment and state constitutional rights of the publisher of Maui Time to be protected from arrest for disorderly conduct and disobeying a police officer for filming traffic stops.[50] A Texas court of appeals also struck down a state law prohibiting "improper photography" without the person's consent and "with intent to . . . arouse or gratify the sexual desire of any person."[51] The court said the state law against "upskirting," or surreptitious photography of people's privates, unconstitutionally restricted an individual's thoughts and the right to take photographs.

STATUTORY RIGHT OF ACCESS

In 1822, James Madison articulated the need for openness in a democratic society. "Knowledge will forever govern ignorance," he said, "and a people who mean to be their own governors must arm themselves with the power which knowledge gives."[52] It was not until the mid-20th century, however, that the size and complexity of government prompted citizens to seek laws to require public access to government decision making and records. Then state and federal laws developed to obligate governments to open their business to the public.[53]

Today, two sets of laws—at both the federal and state levels—establish boundaries for public access to government meetings and records. (Access to judicial proceedings and records is addressed separately in Chapter 8.) Other statutes determine the particular conditions under which recordings (audio or video) are permitted. The following provides an introduction to the general principles and concepts advanced by these laws. However, federal and state laws differ in significant ways, and professional communicators should become familiar with the laws in their locale.

Access to Federal and State Records

Congress passed the **Freedom of Information Act** more than 50 years ago with the intention of allowing anyone access to records held by federal executive branch agencies.[54] The law established, according to the U.S. Supreme Court, that "disclosure, not secrecy, is the dominant objective."[55] Accordingly, exemptions and exclusions that allow government to withhold information must be interpreted narrowly to afford the greatest possible access. The law has been modified through the Open Government Act of 2007 to clarify its exemptions,[56] to specify its application to electronic records[57] and to limit fees and response times.[58] The federal FOIA Improvement Act of 2016 mandates a "presumption of openness" that permits agencies to withhold records only if it is "reasonably foreseeable" that disclosure would harm one of the interests protected by FOIA's exemptions.[59] In a 2018 FOIA case, a federal district court admonished the General Services Administration for releasing emails but not their supporting attachments. The court said "GSA's blinkered literalism,

Freedom of Information Act The federal law that requires records held by federal government agencies to be made available to the public unless covered by one of nine exemptions.

The Lenexa Federal Records Center in Kansas is a major holding facility for federal government documents.

distinguishing emails from email attachments, is at odds with the agency's 'duty to construe a FOIA request liberally.'"[60]

The language of FOIA provides access to "agency records," which raises two questions: (1) What is an agency? and (2) What is a record? Under the law, "agency" is defined as "any executive department, military department, government corporation, government-controlled corporation, or other establishment in the executive branch of the government, including the Executive Office of the President or any independent regulatory agency."[61] This includes all federal executive offices, such as the Office of Management and Budget and the Office of Policy Development.

The law excludes the White House itself, including the president's closest advisers and their staffs. It also excludes Congress, the federal courts and the myriad of quasi-executive organizations that receive federal funding but are not under the direct control of the federal government—for example, the Corporation for Public Broadcasting.[62] Covered government entities include cabinet-level departments such as Defense, Homeland Security and Justice; regulatory agencies such as the Federal Communications Commission and the Securities and Exchange Commission; and NASA and the U.S. Postal Service.

legislative history Congressional reports and records of deliberations about proposed legislation.

Neither the text of FOIA nor its **legislative history** defines "record,"[63] but courts have interpreted the act to apply to all tangible or fixed items that (a) document government actions and (b) may be reproduced. Thus, computer files, paper reports, films, videotapes, photographs and audio recordings are records under the law. A record already exists; it is not something government might compile from the information it holds.

While the definitions of agency and record are relatively clear, the criteria necessary to link an agency and a record in order for something to qualify as an "agency record" remain in dispute. The "statutory silence"[64] on the precise definition of covered agency records leaves courts to construe this key legal phrase.[65] The U.S. Supreme Court has said that "[t]he use of the word 'agency' as a modifier demonstrates that Congress contemplated some relationship between an 'agency' and the 'record' requested."[66] In Senate hearings, the term "agency record" was assumed to include "all papers which an agency preserves in the performance of its functions."[67]

The key is that the record pertains to the agency's functions. In a decision shortly after the law's passage, a federal court of appeals ruled that a congressional transcript held by the CIA was not a covered agency record.[68] The agency's mere possession of a document did not transform it into an agency record.[69] Nonetheless, FOIA requests disclose a vast array of information. They have led government to release data related to NASA mishaps,[70] design deficiencies in the Hubble Space Telescope, dangers to local communities from nuclear weapons plants, hazardous lead levels in wines, misuse of government resources and emails exchanged between regulators and the industries they regulate.[71]

POINTS OF LAW

RECORDS UNDER FOIA

In light of the Freedom of Information Act's unclear definition of agency record, courts have developed the following criteria:

- A record is anything in a fixed form (video, audio, digital, paper).

- An agency record must be part of the legitimate conduct of the agency's official duties.

- An agency record likely is any document created and possessed by the agency.

- A record possessed but not created by an agency may not be an agency record.

- An agency is not required to create a record that does not exist or to obtain a record not under agency control.

Requesting a record from a federal government agency is relatively easy. (Obtaining the record may be another matter.) FOIA requests may be made by telephone, email or mail. Agencies enjoy some discretion on whether to release records, so it may help to begin with a friendly telephone call to identify the record holder and perhaps obtain the records without further effort.[72] A written request helps record the date of the request, the precise records requested and the agency's responses, all of which are essential if you later sue the agency to obtain the records.

Requests should be as detailed as possible because the agency has the option to charge for records searches and/or duplicating fees at cost, or the agency may waive the fees. FOIA provides for fee waivers for news media and fee reductions for nonprofit organizations. Others find that requests for fee waivers may trigger lengthy delays. Many federal agency websites offer instructions on how to file FOIA requests. The Reporters Committee for Freedom of the Press also provides a useful online guide,[73] with an online FOIA letter generator[74] and step-by-step help with letter preparation.

Agencies have 20 working days to respond to FOIA requests. "Respond" does not mean comply, but the D.C. Circuit Court of Appeals held that the agency "must at least indicate within the relevant time period the scope of the documents it will produce and the exemptions it will claim with respect to any withheld documents."[75] Appeals may be filed for unreasonable delays, and records denials may be challenged in federal court.

In 2018, after the U.S. Department of Education failed to comply fully with requests to provide records relevant to any gun lobby role in the department's decision to allow schools to use federal education funds to arm teachers, the Southern Poverty Law Center filed a FOIA suit. The lawsuit sought "all records discussing or revealing communications or [DOE] meetings with the National Rifle Association, the National Shooting Sports Foundation [and] Gun Owners of America" as well as communications with NRA President Oliver North and CEO Wayne LaPierre. After a very partial response and more than a month later, the SPLC sued when DOE said it was "unable to provide an estimated completion date."[76]

When FBI agents reportedly posed as reporters to bait a bombing suspect into clicking email links filled with malware, the Reporters Committee for Freedom of the Press filed FOIA requests for records on agency media impersonation policies. The FBI said its search found no relevant records. In 2017, the D.C. Circuit Court of Appeals relied on the FBI's description of its cursory search to find insufficient basis to conclude that the FBI actually searched for the records. The FBI's failure to search the FBI Director's Office was unacceptable because the "record reveals [that] office directly and conspicuously weigh[ed] in" on the issue of media impersonation.[77]

The law's presumption of access places the burden of proof on the agency to show why any delay or nondisclosure is valid. The agency must cite the specific exemption that justifies nondisclosure and must limit nondisclosure to only those narrow portions of the requested records that qualify. For example, a federal judge ruled that the National Nuclear Security Administration unreasonably delayed response to numerous requests for records on nuclear waste sites in New Mexico. The vague justification that the records were complex and sensitive did not meet the agency's FOIA obligations.[78]

Courts have allowed federal agencies essentially to say, "We don't have to tell you if we have the documents." This nonreply response is called a "Glomar" response, taken from the CIA's refusal to disclose whether it had information related to rumored involvement of Howard Hughes' Glomar Explorer in U.S. attempts to recover a lost Soviet submarine. More recently, though, the D.C. Circuit Court of Appeals refused to allow the CIA to use the Glomar response when the American Civil Liberties Union requested documents about drones used for targeted killings. The court said national security would not be harmed by the CIA's revealing whether it had such documents given that public officials had revealed the CIA's involvement in the drone program.[79]

Electronic Freedom of Information Act A 1996 amendment to the Freedom of Information Act that applies the act to electronically stored information.

Some 24 years ago, Congress passed an amendment to FOIA known as the **Electronic Freedom of Information Act** to extend FOIA to computer records.[80] The law established that computer searches to retrieve records do not constitute creation of a new record, a justification some agencies had used to deny access to electronic records. EFOIA requires agencies to deliver documents in "any form or format requested" that is "readily reproducible by the agency." A federal appeals court said this required the DOD to provide files in zipped format because the agency used such files as part of its "business as usual."[81]

EFOIA requires federal agencies to create a FOIA section on their websites and to provide "electronic reading rooms" filled with online copies of records, policy statements, administrative opinions and indexes of frequently sought documents. The law encourages agencies to provide expedited access to records when the requester can demonstrate a compelling safety or public interest need for rapid access. Following EFOIA, many states adopted specific provisions to ensure and improve electronic access to state records.[82] Some states also followed the federal government's use of Glomar responses.

Every state and the District of Columbia has an access-to-information/open records statute. Some follow the model of FOIA; others look very different. Some require more or less disclosure than FOIA. In Texas, for example, a state agency has only 10 days to comply with a request.[83] The tradition of state open records is deeper than the federal version. As early

REAL WORLD LAW
SAMPLE FOIA REQUEST LETTER[i]

Agency Head [or Freedom of Information Act Officer]
  Name of Agency
  Address of Agency
  City, State, Zip Code
  Re: Freedom of Information Act Request
  Dear _____:
  This is a request under the Freedom of Information Act.

  I request that a copy of the following documents [or documents containing the following information] be provided to me: [identify the documents or information as specifically as possible].

  In order to help to determine my status to assess fees, you should know that I am [insert a suitable description of the requester and the purpose of the request].

  [Sample requester descriptions:
  a representative of the news media affiliated with the _____ newspaper (magazine, television station, etc.), and this request is made as part of newsgathering and not for a commercial use.

  affiliated with an educational, nonprofit or noncommercial scientific institution, and this request is made for a scholarly, public service or scientific purpose and not for a commercial use.

  an individual seeking information for personal use and not for a commercial use.

  affiliated with a private corporation and am seeking information for use in the company's business.]

  [Optional] I am willing to pay fees for this request up to a maximum of $_____. If you estimate that the fees will exceed this limit, please inform me first.

  [Optional] I request a waiver of all fees for this request. Disclosure of the requested information to me is in the public interest because it is likely to contribute significantly to public understanding of the operations or activities of the government and is not primarily in my commercial interest. [Include a specific explanation.]

  Thank you for your consideration of this request.
  Sincerely,
  Name
  Address
  City, State, Zip Code
  Telephone number [Optional]

as 1849, Wisconsin provided for inspection of public records. The explicit purpose of state open-records laws tends to be government accountability. Illinois links the right of access to enabling "people to fulfill their duties of discussing public issues fully and freely" and making "informed political judgments."[84]

Because there is so much state-to-state variation in open-records laws, characterizing them broadly is virtually impossible. Even those that appear similar may, in reality, differ in their details. Generally speaking, however, some observations are helpful:

- Like federal agencies, state agencies are not required to create or acquire records in response to a request.

- Few states require agencies to produce record indexes.

- Some states require that requesters be state residents.

- Many states have exemptions similar to those of FOIA.

- Most state open-records laws cover electronic and computer-stored records, but some states do not require that these records be transformed into a user-friendly format.

- Some state open-records laws cover the legislature, executive branch and courts.

- Some state laws do not specify response time limits. Delays can be lengthy.

- Some states do not specify penalties for agencies violating the law.

State open-records laws apply not only to state government agencies and departments but also to cities, school districts and other state authorities. Like FOIA, most apply to digital records. The law in Tennessee covers "all documents, papers, letters, maps, books, photographs, microfilms, electronic data processing files and output, sound recordings, or other materials regardless of physical form made or received pursuant to law or ordinance or in connection with the transaction of official business by a governmental agency."[85]

metadata
A set of data that describes and gives information about other data.

A question raised in one case was whether hidden **metadata** that record the creation date, authorship and edit history of a digital file were a public record.[86] The case began when a Phoenix police officer sought the metadata because he suspected information had been altered in the city records he received in response to a records request. The city argued that metadata were not part of the record and therefore not subject to the state open-records law. The Arizona Supreme Court disagreed, ruling that metadata are "part of the underlying document; [meta information] does not stand on its own."[87]

In a decision establishing that the public records act applied to public information stored on a personal computer, the Washington Supreme Court ruled that metadata are subject to disclosure because they may contain information that relates to the conduct of government.[88] In 2016, the Washington Supreme Court found that a prosecutor's call logs and work-related voice and text messages related to his official duties and stored on his private cellphone also were subject to disclosure.[89] "An individual has no constitutional privacy interest in a *public* record," the court said, but the employee had a legitimate privacy interest in his personal information.[90] To accommodate the personal privacy interest, the court said "an employee's good-faith search for public records on his personal device can satisfy an agency's obligation" for disclosure under the public records law.[91]

A growing number of states have ruled that government employees cannot avoid disclosure under state open-records laws by using personal devices to conduct the public's business.[92] In 2017, the California Supreme Court relied on the Washington Supreme Court decision to hold that when a government "employee uses a personal account to communicate about the conduct of public business the writings may be subject to disclosure under the California Public Records Act."[93]

Timely response and effective enforcement of open-records laws are important. Thirty-four states and the District of Columbia provide civil and/or criminal sanctions for failure to comply with records requests.[94] In 2019, media and open government groups in Nevada fought against state and local government officials over proposed fee reductions and increased responsiveness and penalties for noncompliance under the state open-records law.[95] In Alabama, a proposed major overhaul of the state open-records law would ensure faster, less expensive and more enforceable citizen access to records.[96]

Access to Federal and State Meetings

The foundational law establishing public access to federal government meetings is the **Government in the Sunshine Act**—also known as the "Federal Open Meetings Law." It was passed almost 45 years ago.[97] Because the processes of meetings as well as their results are of legitimate public interest, the act requires the 50 or so federal executive branch agencies, commissions and boards to conduct their business in public. To fall under the law, the boards or agencies must exercise independent authority and have members appointed by the president. The law requires them to give advance public notice of their meetings, to make most decisions in public and to record decisions.

Approximately 1,000 advisory boards provide expert guidance to the federal government. They play a major role in the development of government policy but are not covered by the Government in the Sunshine Act because they have no independent authority. The Federal Advisory Committee Act opens their meetings and records to the public unless the committee is "composed wholly of full-time officers or employees of the federal government."[98]

All states and the District of Columbia have laws or constitutional provisions ensuring some degree of public access to government meetings.[99] The laws vary widely, as do the penalties for violating them. In general, open-meetings laws trigger public access whenever a quorum of a decision-making body deliberates public business. The laws permit attendance but do not require public participation. Boards may meet the need for public access either through space in their meeting room or through electronic access. Applying this logic, some observers believe open-meetings laws should apply to online chats.

Most state laws require agencies to provide public notice in advance of meetings and to record minutes of their business. A few states also require boards to keep minutes of their executive (closed, nonvoting) sessions, which become available to the public if closure is improper or once the need for closure has passed. Most state laws define a meeting as either a physical gathering or a videoconference that allows members to interact in real time.[100]

In a detailed 2019 decision carefully parsing both the meaning of "meeting" under the Alabama open-meetings law and exceptions to the requirement that deliberations be conducted in open public sessions, the state supreme court ruled that a state health care board's closed "training session" violated the law.[101] The court invalidated board actions discussed during the closed session. It said the board had attempted to shield substantive deliberations about a projected $220 million budget shortfall from public scrutiny by calling its meeting a training session, which is exempted under state law.

Most state open-meetings laws are applied to allow audio and video recordings of meetings. In Utah and Oklahoma, for example, statutes permit the recording of meetings.[102] Court rulings in New York and New Jersey similarly recognize a right to record, but some states have no express guarantee for the right to record.[103] Recording generally may not disrupt proceedings.

Government in the Sunshine Act Sometimes referred to as the Federal Open Meetings Law, it mandates that meetings of federal government agencies be open to the public unless exempted under specific provisions of the law.

POINTS OF LAW

STATE OPEN-MEETINGS LAWS: THE NEW YORK EXAMPLE

The following is excerpted from the New York Open Meetings Law's section on opening meetings and executive sessions:

(a) Every meeting of a public body shall be open to the general public, except that an executive session of such body may be called and business transacted thereat in accordance with section one hundred five of this article. (b) Public bodies shall make or cause to be made all reasonable efforts to ensure that meetings are held in facilities that permit barrier-free physical access to the physically handicapped, as defined in subdivision five of section fifty of the public buildings law. (c) A public body that uses videoconferencing to conduct its meetings shall provide an opportunity to attend, listen and observe at any site at which a member participates. (d) Public bodies shall make or cause to be made all reasonable efforts to ensure that meetings are held in an appropriate facility which can adequately accommodate members of the public who wish to attend such meetings.[ii]

Several states outline provisions for the enforcement of open-meetings laws. In Michigan, for example, any citizen may challenge in court a decision made by a public body to deny access. If the court determines that the closure violated the law, the court can invalidate that decision and any actions taken during the closure. In addition, a public official who intentionally breaks the law is subject to a fine up to $1,000. A second deliberate violation can result in a fine up to $2,000, a jail term of up to one year or both.[104]

In a ruling related to open meetings, the Ninth Circuit Court of Appeals recently struck down a California city ordinance that permitted the city council to evict members of the public from its meetings for "disorderly, insolent or disruptive behavior."[105] The court said the law was unconstitutionally overbroad because it permitted the counsel to expel citizens who were merely "impertinent, insolent or essentially offensive" but caused no disruption.

Face-to-Face and Participant Recording

The durable record of events and conversations created by audio and video recording is a staple of much professional communication. Recording audio or video with plainly visible equipment generally does not violate any state or federal law. Both federal law and the Federal Communications Commission have authority over telephone calls that cross state lines. Although federal law allows recording with one-party consent, an FCC rule requires notification and consent of all parties or the use of a repeating beeping tone to inform all parties the call is being recorded.[106] The FCC says the federal law helps law enforcement officers listen to calls as part of their duties, while the commission rule discourages the public from recording calls without permission.[107]

Hidden recordings and recordings of telephone calls are regulated by U.S. Congress and most states through statutes meant to prohibit eavesdropping, wiretapping and telephone interception to protect privacy interests (see Chapter 6). The federal anti-wiretapping statute prevents third-party recording when no participant has consented.[108] Some states require notice and consent of all parties, but 38 states allow recording with one-party consent when the person doing the recording has consented.[109] Another 13 states specifically outlaw the use of hidden cameras in private places.[110] Twelve states are all-party states that require all participants in a conversation to give consent.[111] Some all-party laws apply only to confidential conversations. Some state courts apply that state's laws even to interstate phone calls.[112]

Vermont is the only state without a law specifically addressing audio or video recording of conversations, but the state's highest court has held that hidden recordings of communications in a home violate personal privacy.[113] However, the court ruled in another case that recording a conversation in a parking lot "subject to the eyes and ears of passersby" is legal.[114]

In general, the law in the location of the recording device applies. Because this is not universally true, however, it is wise to follow the strictest of the laws that might apply. In one recent case, the California Supreme Court held that a Georgia company that routinely recorded business calls with clients in California must comply with California's stricter statute.[115] Georgia allows recording with one-party consent. California requires all parties to agree, and the court said application of the stricter law protected "the degree of privacy afforded to California residents" without unduly harming any Georgia interests.

The FCC requires broadcasters to notify callers if the station intends to broadcast a call live or record the call for later broadcast. Consent is not necessary, only notification. There is an exception for programs that customarily air calls live or broadcast recorded calls, such as radio call-in shows. These callers have a reasonable expectation that their conversations will be aired or recorded.[116]

In *Bartnicki v. Vopper*, the U.S. Supreme Court ruled that the First Amendment allows media to use an illegal recording so long as they were not involved in its production. The case involved a third-party surreptitious recording of a phone conversation between two teachers' union negotiators about a difficult collective bargaining agreement. One negotiator said, "[W]e're gonna have to go to their, their homes . . . [t]o blow off their front porches; we'll have to do some work on some of those guys."[117] Local radio stations played the tape, and newspapers printed its contents. The negotiator sued, arguing that the media intentionally "disclosed" a private exchange they should have known was obtained in violation of the federal wiretap law.[118] The media claimed the First Amendment allowed the use of the taped discussion of matters of significant concern because journalists were not involved in the wiretapping.

The Supreme Court agreed with the media. The First Amendment protects a journalist who shares or reports on illegally intercepted private conversations when the conversation is newsworthy and the journalist was not involved in the interception. The Court said the media were protected because they (1) played no part in the illegal interception, (2) had lawful access to the information on the tapes and (3) correctly judged the conversation to be of public concern.[119]

The Court held that the ban on disclosure of illegally intercepted communications failed to serve the government's alleged compelling interest of dissuading people from intercepting private communications. The Court said the government's important interest in minimizing harm to private callers by discouraging distribution of illegally intercepted calls was outweighed by the need to inform people of matters of public interest. "[A] stranger's illegal conduct does not suffice to remove the First Amendment shield from speech about a matter of public concern,"[120] the Court concluded.

Under federal and many state laws, a recording made to commit a crime or a tort is illegal regardless of who consents. For example, rap artists Andre Young, Snoop Dogg, Ice Cube and Eminem were scheduled to perform in Detroit as part of a nationwide tour. In each of

MAP 7.1 ■ Recording Laws by State

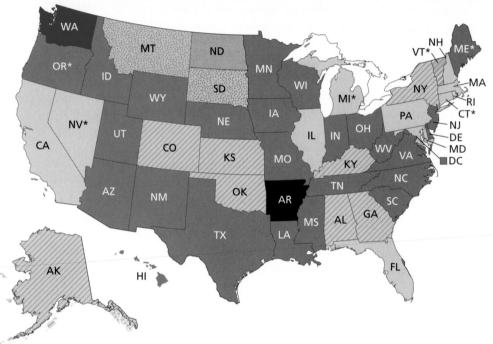

* Rules on consent vary; for more information, please visit rcfp.org/recording.

☐ Consent of all parties required. Criminal penalties. Statute allows for civil suits. Specific hidden camera law. Additional penalties for disclosing or publishing information.

☐ Criminal penalties. Statute allows for civil suits. Specific hidden camera law. Additional penalties for disclosing or publishing information.

☐ Consent of all parties required. Criminal penalties. Statute allows for civic suits. Specific hidden camera law.

☐ Criminal penalties. Statute allows for civil suits. Additional penalties for disclosing or publishing information.

☐ Criminal penalties. Specific hidden camera law. Additional penalties for disclosing or publishing information.

☐ Consent of all parties required. Criminal penalties. Specific hidden camera law.

☐ Criminal penalties. Additional penalties for disclosing or publishing information.

☐ Criminal penalties. Specific hidden camera law.

☐ Specific hidden camera law.

■ No additional penalties for disclosing or publishing information.

Source: Reporters Committee for Freedom of the Press, *Reporter's Recording Guide*, Aug. 1, 2012, www.rcfp.org/reporters-recording-guide.

POINTS OF LAW

MEDIA DISTRIBUTION OF ILLEGALLY INTERCEPTED CALLS

Under the U.S. Supreme Court's ruling in *Bartnicki v. Vopper*,[iii] the First Amendment protects media from liability for distributing illegally intercepted communications when

- the media had no involvement in the interception,
- the media gained access to the intercepted calls legally, and
- the content of the intercepted calls relates to matters of public concern.

10 cities before Detroit, a short video introduced Andre Young and Snoop Dogg. But Detroit police told tour producers the video violated obscenity laws and could not be shown. Tour representatives secretly recorded the meeting and included parts of the recording in a music video sold internationally.

In response to the music video, city officials sued under the federal wiretap law that makes it illegal to record a private conversation without the consent of at least one party.[121] Tour representatives said they gave themselves permission, but the court said one-party consent is not sufficient if recording is for an illegal purpose or to commit a tort.[122] Here the tour representatives made the video intending to use it to commit the tort of appropriation—taking the material without consent for commercial purposes (see Chapter 6).

In a California case, two reporters with a hidden camera and cellphone recorder claimed they wanted help obtaining a home mortgage from the Association of Community Organizations for Reform Now.[123] They said they wanted to speak confidentially with the ACORN employee. They then said "they intended to fill the house with underage girls working as prostitutes . . . [and] needed help filling out tax forms so the income from this illegal operation would appear legitimate." The reporters later posted the tape online showing the ACORN employee "conspiring to promote an underage prostitution business," according to the federal district court.

The key question before the court was whether the taping violated California law because the ACORN employee had a reasonable expectation that the conversation would be confidential. The court reasoned that a reasonable expectation of confidentiality attached to a discussion about personal client matters inside the employee's office. Therefore, the employee's agreement to discuss the matter did not amount to consent to recording. The case settled out of court with a payment of $100,000 to the ACORN employee.[124]

Some state laws on recording are complicated. In Delaware, for example, both civil and criminal statutes apply.[125] State privacy law requires all parties to consent to recording, but a federal district court applied the law years ago to find that individuals have a right to record their own conversations.[126] Delaware criminal law makes it a felony to "intercept" a call without consent from all parties unless you are a participant or have received prior permission to record. In Illinois, the state supreme court recently found the state's law was unconstitutionally overbroad because it made it a crime to record any conversation without everyone's permission.[127] Subsequent amendments to the law distinguished recording of private and public communications and applied criminal penalties only to recording "in a surreptitious manner."

STATUTORY LIMITS TO ACCESS

Statutes at the federal and state levels both guarantee and prohibit access to property, government records and meetings. Physical access to private property is circumscribed by common law, the Constitution and state statutes and rulings. Distinct rules apply to specific types of records and to the means of obtaining or recording information. Professional communicators should be familiar with this complex of laws but need to recognize that many are in nearly constant flux. Thus, when concerned about legal limits, it may be wise to seek expert legal advice.

Intrusion and Trespass Laws

Permission to enter private property may be given or denied only by the owner or the resident, who may not be the owner. Entering private property without permission is trespass.[128] The law against trespass is generally applicable; no one may trespass. Law enforcement officials with a search warrant or exercising emergency control over property are authorized to enter without permission, but that authority does not extend to others.

ride-along
The practice of private citizens, especially professional communicators, accompanying law enforcement or emergency personnel as they carry out their duties.

The media **ride-along**—in which media representatives accompany officers to various scenes—long has provided material for news and entertainment as well as police public relations campaigns. However, when police operations occur on private property, the residents' Fourth Amendment protection against unreasonable searches and unreasonable intrusion or trespass on their privacy comes into play. Although some courts have held that the silence of the property owner implies consent, especially if the events are newsworthy, other courts disagree.[129] Rulings that balance residents' right to be free from intrusion against the media's First Amendment rights to gather information generally curtail media access to private property.

In one recent case, however, the Sixth Circuit Court of Appeals affirmed that Tennessee state law protected a broadcasting station from liability for claims arising from a ride-along.[130] At the invitation of federal marshals, a reporter from the Nashville station videoed the arrest of fugitives rounded up as part of a weeklong national sweep. The subsequent broadcast featured a woman who was misidentified and mistakenly arrested in her home. She sued for defamation and false light. The appeals court dismissed the case and held that the broadcaster's accurate report on the botched arrest was protected from liability under the state's fair report privilege (see Chapter 5 on fair report privilege).

In contrast, a television crew that accompanied Los Angeles Fire Department paramedics and broadcast their unsuccessful efforts to resuscitate a heart attack victim on the local news was guilty of trespass. In ruling for the victim's family, a California appeals court said, "Personal security in a society saturated daily with publicity about its members requires protection not only from governmental intrusion but some basic bulwark of defense against private commercial enterprises which derive profits from gathering and disseminating information."[131] The court said

> [t]he First Amendment has never been construed to accord newsmen immunity from torts or crimes committed during the course of newsgathering. The First Amendment is not a license to trespass, to steal or to intrude by electronic means into the precincts of another's home or office.[132]

The U.S. Supreme Court reinforced that doctrine in *Hanlon v. Berger*.[133] When U.S. Fish and Wildlife Service agents searched a Montana ranch, agents carried CNN cameras and microphones without the residents' knowledge. Officials suspected the family had shot or poisoned eagles, violating federal wildlife laws.[134] The family sued for intrusion, and the Supreme Court said a jury should decide the case. CNN was not protected by the agents' privilege because the recording was not intended to aid law enforcement, the Court said. The case settled out of court.[135]

In *Wilson v. Layne*, excerpted at the end of this chapter, the Supreme Court dealt another blow to ride-alongs.[136] Law enforcement officers with a search warrant allowed a Washington Post photographer to accompany their early morning raid of a private home to arrest a fugitive. The photographer took pictures as officers wrestled a man to the floor and a woman emerged from the bedroom. The pair were the parents of the fugitive, who was not at home. None of the photos were published. The couple sued on the grounds that the presence of journalists violated their Fourth Amendment protection. The U.S. Supreme Court agreed.

A warrant entitles officers to enter the home but does not authorize those officers to invite civilians along, the Court said.[137] The presence of reporters was unrelated to the warrant's purpose and the limited intrusion it allowed.[138] Any benefits ride-alongs provided to suspects or law enforcement activities were too far removed from the warrant's objective to override the residents' Fourth Amendment rights.[139] The decision established that it generally violates the Fourth Amendment for civilians to accompany officials into a home during the execution of

---

POINTS OF LAW

WILSON V. LAYNE:[v] THE STATE OF RIDE-ALONGS

- A search warrant entitles officers, but not reporters, to enter a home.
- The presence of reporters is unrelated to the authorized intrusion.
- The presence of reporters serves no legitimate law enforcement purposes.
- Inviting reporters for the execution of a search warrant violates the Fourth Amendment.

a warrant unless they are there to help execute the warrant.[140] Third parties, including media representatives, have greater leeway to accompany police on public property, but they are not immune from liability even in those circumstances.[141]

In 2018, following remand from the Tenth Circuit Court of Appeals, a federal district court reversed itself and struck down recent revisions to Wyoming trespass laws that made it a crime to enter private or public "open land" without permission to gather "resource data" on land and water use.[142] The laws targeted environmental and animal groups seeking to "unlawfully collect resource data," such as water samples, to test E. coli contamination from cattle waste runoff. The Tenth Circuit drew a parallel to right-to-record-in-public cases and reasoned that "collection of resource data constitutes the protected creation of speech."[143]

Certain properties also may be protected by laws specifically limiting recording. The federal Animal Enterprise Terrorism Act of 2014 prohibits damage to "real or personal property" of an animal facility, defines activities intended to "harm or interfere with" animal facilities as terrorism and imposes penalties of prison and substantial fines. The law states that it should not be "construed to prohibit any expressive activity."[144] In a 2017 decision, the Seventh Circuit Court of Appeals upheld the law against a First Amendment challenge because it "does not criminalize speech or expressive activity."[145]

State "ag-gag" laws, however, prohibit recording, photographing or entering agricultural facilities to document animal abuse or other illegal activity without the owners' informed permission. Idaho's law, one of three original ag-gag laws challenged as unconstitutional, was struck down for violating both the First Amendment and the equal protection clause by penalizing lawful employees who wanted to expose "matters of utmost public concern."[146] The case involved a video of commercial dairy workers in Hansen, Idaho, dragging a cow by the neck across the floor behind a tractor and repeatedly beating, kicking and jumping on cows.[147]

The Idaho dairy farmers' association promptly sponsored a second state law in 2016.[148] The new Idaho law, similar to those in seven other states,[149] "criminalize[d] activities that facilitate undercover investigations" of livestock operations.[150] The new statute made it a crime (1) to gain access to a livestock operation without disclosing "media or political affiliations" and/or (2) to videotape "animal abuse or life-threatening safety violations."[151] These so-called disclosure laws require individuals to reveal their identities before they gather sufficient evidence to demonstrate the pattern of abuse needed for successful prosecution. A federal district court struck down this Idaho law as unconstitutionally content and viewpoint based, and the Ninth Circuit Court of Appeals affirmed the core ruling.[152] The district court also ordered the state to pay the plaintiffs' legal expenses[153] and concluded:

> Given the public's interest in the safety of the food supply, worker safety and the humane treatment of animals, it would contravene strong First Amendment values to say the state has a compelling interest in affording these heavily regulated facilities extra protection from public scrutiny.[154]

In one high-profile arrest, internationally renowned photojournalist George Steinmetz was charged with trespassing after photographing a cattle feedlot in Kansas while paragliding.[155] He was on assignment for National Geographic magazine. "It was quite a surprise to me," Steinmetz said. "I've been detained in Iran and Yemen, and questioned about spying, but never arrested. And then I get thrown in jail in America."[156]

Federal Aviation Administration rules governing the use of drones prohibit drone flights over "any persons" not directly involved in their operation.[157] Drones may not fly above national parks, military bases, stadiums, sporting events or sites of emergencies. There is also a no-fly zone within five miles of airports (except with prior authorization) and in Washington, D.C. Subject to these restrictions, noncommercial drone photographers and news operations generally may photograph from drones. Commercial operators—including photographers and public relations and advertising professionals—must apply for FAA exemptions to photograph and to fly in controlled airspace.

The FAA recently sought a $1.9 million fine from SkyPan, a company providing aerial photography for real estate purposes.[158] The FAA said the company had flown scores of unapproved flights over highly congested airspace above New York and Chicago. The dispute settled with a $200,000 fine.[159] In 2019, the FAA issued stricter guidelines for oversight of improper drone usage, but a FOIA request showed the FAA had not issued a single enforcement action against drone pilots in 2018.[160]

Many state and municipal laws impose additional limits on drone photography.[161] A 2017 national legislative roundup identified 27 states with regulations addressing the use of drones.[162] These laws vary dramatically in their breadth and focus. California was among the first to ban drone recording.[163] In the most stringent of these laws, Texas generally bans drone recording for any use except education, research, limited development and commercial purposes and for police, military and state reasons.[164]

In 2019, a national organization advocated that states revise trespass and intrusion statutes to incorporate drones.[165] Wisconsin was the first state to make it a criminal misdemeanor to use a drone to record another *person* in a place where the person has a reasonable expectation of privacy.[166] New Jersey was considering adding drones to both its trespass and privacy laws in 2019.[167] "The popular use of drones has warranted the need to clarify that flying a drone over private property without permission is still trespassing and an invasion of privacy of anyone on that property," one New Jersey senator said.

George Steinmetz

George Steinmetz's paragliding photograph of Brookover Ranch Feed Yard and adjacent crop circles in Garden City, Kan.

Exemptions to Open Records

Federal agencies are not compelled to hand over every record requested under the Freedom of Information Act. Although the law presumes public access to records, nine FOIA exemptions *permit*—they do not require—agencies to refuse to disclose specific types of information. The law requires agencies to interpret the exemptions narrowly and to limit withholding only to those sections of records covered by an exemption. Record keepers are required to strike out, or redact, the covered portions of records rather than withhold the record in its entirety. Agencies judge what must be withheld and often exercise their discretion in favor of nondisclosure.

When an agency denies all or part of a FOIA request, the law requires the agency to explain why the record falls under one or more specific exemptions. Presidential elections and major events often trigger shifts in policies directing how agencies respond to FOIA requests. Shortly after the Sept. 11, 2001, terrorist attacks, for example, a memo from the U.S. attorney general encouraged federal agencies to withhold records whenever a "sound legal basis" might justify secrecy under one or more exemptions.[168] Another post–Sept. 11 development was the passage of the Homeland Security Act, which provides broad exemptions from FOIA disclosure for information related to critical infrastructure, including bridges, dams and computer systems.[169] Although President Barack Obama declared "profound national commitment to ensuring an open government,"[170] his promise of openness did not significantly enhance public access.[171] Instead, the federal government set records for nondisclosure and censorship of public records.[172]

Each of FOIA's nine exemptions and agency interpretations of them that have generated court challenges are discussed in the following section. In 2019, the U.S. Supreme Court decision in *Kisor v. Wilkie* said courts should exercise increased, independent review of executive agencies' interpretations of their own rules.[173] Observers argued that the ruling might also signal the end of deference to executive agency interpretations of applicable federal laws.[174]

Exemption 1: National Security. Records fall under the exemption of national security if they are classified as confidential, secret or top secret. Members of the executive branch use each classification to reflect the rising sensitivity of the information and the potential for harm if released.[175] Records requests denied on the basis of this exemption have been the most difficult to overturn.

FOIA empowers judges to determine whether information was properly classified as a potential threat to national security. Typically, judges rule in favor of classification. The U.S. Supreme Court, for example, referred to the exemption as the "keystone of a congressional scheme that balances deference to the executive's interest in maintaining secrecy with continued judicial and congressional oversight."[176] Even when information is widely known, such as the CIA's use of waterboarding and other "enhanced interrogation techniques [of military detainees], an agency may refuse a FOIA request on the basis of national security," the Second Circuit Court of Appeals ruled.[177]

In 2013, after disclosure of the U.S. government's vast surveillance activities within the United States, Twitter sought to publish information it said would clarify incomplete government reporting of its national security surveillance. Because recipients of government surveillance orders and National Security Letters are barred from publicizing these orders, Twitter wanted to publish a standing statement identifying the types of national security orders it had *not* received. Twitter planned to remove the statement if it received any such orders.

After the Department of Justice prevented Twitter's publication, citing national security concerns, Twitter sued, arguing that the action was an unconstitutional prior restraint. In 2019, in a recent action in the pending lawsuit, the U.S. attorney general claimed "state secrets" privilege to stop Twitter's disclosure and said the court could "in no event" authorize Twitter to disclose classified information.[178] The federal district court reiterated the courts' authority to independently review government secrecy classifications and said no "state secrets" privilege exists.[179]

The Second Circuit Court of Appeals in 2018 declared its independent review of national security claims but relied entirely on Department of Defense classifications to uphold refusal to disclose already leaked DOD photographs of military detainees in Afghanistan and Iraq.[180] In California, a federal district court held that the access provisions of the USA Freedom Act did not require the government to disclose any content from six Foreign Intelligence Surveillance Court (national security) rulings while a FOIA request was pending.[181] Similarly, courts have rejected efforts of the American Civil Liberties Union to use FOIA to obtain information about government warrantless surveillance of civilians, but lawsuits continue.[182]

Exemption 2: Internal Agency Rules and Procedures. The exemption related to internal agency rules is a "housekeeping" exemption. It covers records related exclusively to the practices of the agency itself: vacation policies, lunch break rules, parking space assignments and so on. Its purpose is not so much to prevent any harm from disclosure but to eliminate the time and expense of retrieving these mundane records. The exemption also covers any internal policy that might be used inappropriately. For example, break or shift change procedures used by federal prison guards could conceivably be used to breach facility security.

This exemption cannot be used to conceal all agency practices. If an agency policy or procedure is of public concern and its disclosure would not undermine agency regulations, a court could rule that related records do not qualify for Exemption 2 and order their release. In a case seeking records related to Air Force Academy honor and ethics hearings, the U.S. Supreme Court said, "[T]he general thrust of the exemption is simply to relieve agencies of the burden of assembling and maintaining for public inspection matters in which the public could not reasonably be expected to have an interest."[183]

In another decision, the Supreme Court ruled that Exemption 2 applies only to human resource and "employee relations" records, not to other records an agency might possess.[184] Therefore, the Court said, the U.S. Navy could not use Exemption 2 to reject a FOIA request for information about explosives at a naval base in Puget Sound, Wash. The location of the munitions is unrelated to employee records.

Exemption 3: Disclosures Forbidden by Other Statutes. This exemption stipulates that FOIA cannot override other laws that forbid the disclosure of certain information. When litigation surfaces related to this exemption, courts usually require the government to show that

(1) the information being sought falls within the scope of the statute being cited and (2) the statute grants no discretionary authority to the government agency holding the information (i.e., the nondisclosure is mandatory). If those standards are met, the decision to withhold records generally is upheld.

In 2018, for example, a federal district court upheld a decision of the Bureau of Alcohol, Tobacco, Firearms and Explosives to withhold records related to the bureau's firearms tracing database.[185] The court said the withholding was acceptable under a recurring congressional appropriation even though the appropriation did not explicitly reference Exemption 3. The OPEN FOIA Act of 2009 requires all statutes passed after 2009 with specific exemptions from disclosure to cite the amended language of FOIA Exemption 3.

Exemption 4: Trade Secrets. The private business information provided to government agencies—such as profit-and-loss statements, market-share information and secret formulas—is generally exempt from disclosure under FOIA. Agencies collect and keep the information to assist government objectives, such as enforcement of copyright law, unrelated to the recipient agency's specific duties. Trade secret information is commercially useful and confidential. Its release is likely to cause competitive harm to a business.

The Eighth Circuit Court of Appeals in 2018 granted a newspaper's appeal for release of the names, addresses and annual food-stamp sales of retail groceries participating in the U.S. Department of Agriculture's Supplemental Nutrition Assistance Program, commonly known as SNAP. The court said agencies withholding records as trade secrets needed to show that disclosure was almost certain to cause "substantial competitive harm."[186] The USDA did not appeal the order to release the records. In 2019, the U.S. Supreme Court ruled that the appeal of a grocery-industry group could proceed.[187] Four decades earlier, the Supreme Court said FOIA is a disclosure statute that does not include a mechanism for private individuals to sue to protect confidentiality.[188]

In that earlier Exemption 4 case, Chrysler Corp. had turned over documents related to its affirmative-action program and workforce composition to a government agency. Chrysler challenged agency release of those records in response to a FOIA request. In *Chrysler v. Brown,* the U.S. Supreme Court remanded the case to determine whether statutory protection for trade secrets applied.[189] Courts generally have required agencies seeking to withhold material under Exemption 4 to show that the information is, in fact, a trade secret.

Exemption 5: Agency Memoranda. Sometimes referred to as the "working papers" or "discovery" exemption, Exemption 5 protects from disclosure agency memoranda, studies or drafts that are prepared and used inside agencies to create final reports or policies. One court ruled that this exemption protects both the decision-making process and the need to avoid public confusion through disclosure of preliminary decisions.[190] In 2016, Congress limited the exemption for records of "deliberative process" to 25 years.[191]

In a recent Exemption 5 case, a federal district court held that the exemption allowed withholding of some, but not all, records related to the Department of Justice Terrorist Surveillance Program.[192] Because the DOJ had failed to fully identify the processes that needed shielding, the court said it would conduct closed, *in camera* review of the records.

When an association seeking documents related to tribal water allocation faced an Exemption 5 denial from the Department of the Interior and the Bureau of Indian Affairs, the U.S. Supreme Court ruled in favor of full disclosure. The Court said the documents did not qualify as "inter-agency or intra-agency memoranda or letters," and Exemption 5 was not intended to protect government secrets.[193]

This exemption does protect presidential communications and information exchanged between an agency and its attorney(s). Exemption 5 recognizes that the traditional attorney–client privilege is not waived merely because the client is a federal agency. Anything that is considered discovery material—the evidence gathered in a civil trial and made available to both sides as part of the trial process—is covered by this exemption.

Exemption 6: Personal Privacy. Privacy is at the heart of Exemptions 6 and 7. Exemption 6 allows withholding of "personnel and medical . . . and similar files, the disclosure of which would constitute a clearly unwarranted invasion of personal privacy." The phrase "similar files" has been the source of much dispute. It has generally been interpreted broadly to include lists, files, records and letters.

Courts attempt to balance privacy concerns against the purpose of FOIA. Sometimes courts consider the purpose of the request and any public interest in disclosure. "Exemption Six overwhelmingly favors the disclosure of information relating to a violation of the public trust by a government official," one federal appeals court ruled.[194] However, the U.S. Supreme Court favored privacy when it recognized that FOIA's purpose is allowing the activity of government—not private citizens—to be open to public scrutiny.[195]

Exemption 7: Law Enforcement Records. Records compiled within the context of law enforcement investigations may be exempt from FOIA disclosure. There are limits, however, to the exemption. For the government to deny disclosure, release of a record must reasonably be expected to

a.   interfere with enforcement proceedings,

b.   deprive a person of the right to a fair trial,

c.   constitute an unwarranted invasion of privacy,

d.   disclose the identity of a confidential source,

e.   disclose law enforcement techniques and procedures or

f.   endanger the life or physical safety of any individual.

At one time, items such as rap sheets, arrest records, convictions records and department manuals were not exempt. In *U.S. Department of Justice v. Reporters Committee for Freedom of the Press*,[196] excerpted at the end of this chapter, a journalist filed a FOIA request with the FBI for its criminal records on four members of a family suspected of criminal activity. The FBI disclosed only the records of the three deceased family members. Challenged on the grounds that the records might disclose the survivor's involvement in political corruption,

TOP SECRET

confinement box. The other inquiry involved claims that the SERE training caused two individuals to engage in criminal behavior, namely, felony shoplifting and downloading child pornography onto a military computer. According to this official, these claims were found to be baseless. Moreover, he has indicated that during the three and a half years he spent as ███████ of the SERE program, he trained 10,000 students. Of those students, only two dropped out of the training following the use of these techniques. Although on rare occasions some students temporarily postponed the remainder of their training and received psychological counseling, those students were able to finish the program without any indication of subsequent mental health effects.

You have informed us that you have consulted with ███████████ who has ten years of experience with SERE training ██ He stated that, during those ten years, insofar as he is aware, none of the individuals who completed the program suffered any adverse mental health effects. He informed you that there was one person who did not complete the training. That person experienced an adverse mental health reaction that lasted only two hours. After those two hours, the individual's symptoms spontaneously dissipated without requiring treatment or counseling and no other symptoms were ever reported by this individual. According to the information you have provided to us, this assessment of the use of these procedures includes the use of the waterboard.

Additionally, you received a memorandum from the ████████████████████████ ████████████████████████████ which you supplied to us. ██████ has experience with the use of all of these procedures in a course of conduct, with the exception of the insect in the confinement box and the waterboard. This memorandum confirms that the use of these procedures has not resulted in any reported instances of prolonged mental harm, and very few instances of immediate and temporary adverse psychological responses to the training. ██████████ reported that a small minority of students have had temporary adverse psychological reactions during training. Of the 26,829 students trained from 1992 through 2001 in the Air Force SERE training, 4.3 percent of those students had contact with psychology services. Of those 4.3 percent, only 3.2 percent were pulled from the program for psychological reasons. Thus, out of the students trained overall, only 0.14 percent were pulled from the program for psychological reasons. Furthermore, although ███████████ indicated that surveys of students having completed this training are not done, he expressed confidence that the training did not cause any long-term psychological impact. He based his conclusion on the debriefing of students that is done after the training. More importantly, he based this assessment on the fact that although training is required to be extremely stressful in order to be effective, very few complaints have been made regarding the training. During his tenure, in which 10,000 students were trained, no congressional complaints have been made. While there was one Inspector General complaint, it was not due to psychological concerns. Moreover, he was aware of only one letter inquiring about the long-term impact of these techniques from an individual trained

TOP SECRET

5

An example of a redacted document that was released under FOIA. This is one page from a memo to the CIA's general counsel written by the assistant attorney general in 2002.

Memo excerpt from "Interrogation of al Qaeda operative" by Jay S. Bybee, Assistant Attorney General, OLC to John Rizzo, Acting General Counsel of the Central Intelligence Agency. August 1, 2002. Available online at http://www.fas.org/irp/agency/doj/olc/zubaydah.pdf.

the U.S. Supreme Court said, "Disclosure of records regarding private citizens, identifiable by name, is not what the framers of FOIA had in mind."[197] It upheld the denial of access.

In 2004, the U.S. Supreme Court affirmed the authority of several federal agencies and organizations to withhold death scene photographs of the former legal counsel to President Bill Clinton.[198] Multiple independent government and private investigations concluded that the adviser committed suicide. In affirming denial of access to the photos, the Supreme Court held that the right of personal privacy under FOIA extends to surviving family members. Those seeking information that implicates personal privacy interests must demonstrate a significant public interest in the information sought. In cases of alleged government malfeasance, the Court said, "the requester must establish more than a bare suspicion . . . [and] must produce evidence that would warrant a belief by a reasonable person that the alleged government impropriety might have occurred."[199]

FOIA does not facilitate fishing expeditions into government-held information about private individuals. Its objective is to provide access to "official information that sheds light on an agency's performance of its statutory duties, . . . [which] is not fostered by disclosure of information about private citizens that . . . reveals little or nothing about an agency's own conduct."[200]

In 2011, the U.S. Supreme Court narrowed and clarified this privacy exemption. AT&T argued that, as a corporation, it qualified for Exemption 7 withholding of records to protect "personal privacy." In a unanimous decision, the Supreme Court held that Exemption 7 applies to individuals, not corporations, because the ordinary meaning of the word "personal" refers to human beings.[201] Federal agencies, then, cannot use this exemption to reject FOIA requests for information about corporations and other businesses.

Exemption 8: Financial Records. This exemption allows for nondisclosure of sensitive financial reports or audits held by government. To support nondisclosure, the government agency must show that the release of records would undermine public confidence in banks and other financial institutions. This sweeping exemption left many questions unanswered during the savings and loan collapse of the 1980s. In 2010, Congress repealed portions of the Dodd-Frank Act that had exempted the Securities and Exchange Commission from FOIA and allowed Exemption 8 to apply to the SEC.[202]

Exemption 9: Geological Data. Exemption 9 rarely comes into play within a news media context although it is broad. It is designed to prevent oil and gas exploration companies from obtaining information from federal agencies that can provide them a competitive advantage. Much like the trade secrets exemption, this exemption protects potentially profitable confidential geological information from being obtained through FOIA.

Exemptions to Open Meetings

Ten exemptions allow boards to close meetings or hold closed, nonvoting executive sessions on specific topics. Exemptions 1 through 9 are similar to those of the federal Freedom of

Information Act detailed above.[203] Exemption 10 applies to agency litigation or arbitration. A frequent reason for closure is that the board will discuss matters related to personnel, and closure protects the privacy of those involved.

Privacy

Federal and state laws aimed at protecting personal privacy intentionally create barriers to gathering personally identifiable information. The federal Privacy Act of 1974 limits federal agency collection of private information, allows the subject of the records to review and amend their content, and requires government agencies to use individual, personal information only for the reason(s) it was collected.[204]

Agencies may not release the information to anyone other than the subject of the record without the written consent of the person involved. Exceptions to the privacy provisions are for law enforcement or congressional investigations, census or labor statistics and archival of historically significant material. If FOIA mandates disclosure of information protected under the Privacy Act, FOIA prevails. Individuals may sue for "actual damages" caused by violations of the law. In a case involving interagency sharing of a pilot's HIV status, the U.S. Supreme Court recently ruled that damage awards are limited to financial costs and do not compensate for mental anguish or suffering.[205]

Student Records

Family Educational Rights and Privacy Act
A federal law that protects the privacy of student education records. Also known as the Buckley Amendment.

The **Family Educational Rights and Privacy Act** of 1974, sometimes called the Buckley Amendment,[206] forbids any school that receives federal funding from releasing students' academic records unless the subjects, as adults, or their parents provide consent. Adult students and the parents of minor children are permitted to review and amend the records. The law shields records that contain personally identifiable information, which the Department of Education defines to include a family member's name, the student's Social Security or student ID number and personal characteristics or other information that would make it easy to determine the student's identity.[207]

Government-supported schools also are forbidden from releasing grades or information related to a student's health. In 2012, amendments to the law protected student IDs and email addresses from disclosure and clarified that "directory" information such as a student's name, address, telephone number, date and place of birth, major field of study, dates of attendance and degrees and awards received may be released.

Violating the law puts an institution's government funding at risk. University officials often cite FERPA as an obstacle to release of campus police records or student disciplinary records. Although nondisclosure may protect individual privacy, the law does not mandate it. Many argue that state open-records laws require release of campus crime and justice system information the public has a right to know.

Such campus information is more difficult to obtain in the wake of a Sixth Circuit Court of Appeals ruling that student disciplinary records are shielded by FERPA.[208] The weekly Chronicle of Higher Education and the Miami University of Ohio student newspaper sought the records of the university's internal discipline committees to examine crime trends on campus. The Sixth Circuit said the law's language made clear that disciplinary proceedings were part of student records and could not be released without consent. In 2014, the Eighth Circuit Court of Appeals declined to determine whether release of student records to the Board of Immigration Appeals considering deportation of an immigrant student violated FERPA.[209]

Campus Crime

The federal Campus Security Policy and Campus Crime Statistics Act of 1990, or the **Clery Act** as it is now known, requires universities that receive federal funds to compile and publish statistics on campus crime each year.[210] Campus security must maintain a log of all crimes for public review and provide timely warnings of threats to safety. Campus police logs and annual statistics have uncovered significant problems on campuses, such as excesses in fraternity hazing and gay bashing at the University of Georgia uncovered when student journalists obtained records of university disciplinary hearings.[211] The Georgia Supreme Court held that disciplinary records were not student records under FERPA because they were not concerned with student academic performance, financial aid or academic probation.[212]

> **Clery Act**
> The federal law that requires most universities to maintain up-to-date police logs and report campus crimes annually.

The Department of Education reviews campus compliance with the act and levies fines for noncompliance. In 2019, for example, DOE continued to investigate Michigan State University for routine and "serious violations" of reporting on crimes involving athletics, Greek life and residence halls.[213] In 2018, the University of Montana received a fine of almost $1 million for failure to report crimes. Pennsylvania State University received the largest fine on record, $2.4 million, in 2016 for failure to properly report long-standing sexual abuses by assistant football coach Jerry Sandusky.[214]

Medical Records

The **Health Insurance Portability and Accountability Act** prevents health professionals and institutions from revealing individuals' personal medical records.[215] After Congress passed HIPAA in 1996, the Department of Health and Human Services crafted the first federal medical privacy regulations, called the Standards for Privacy of Individually Identifiable Health Information. These rules were designed to give patients more control over their health information and to limit the use and release of health records to third parties. Generally, the privacy standards established a federal requirement that most health care providers obtain a patient's written consent before disclosing the patient's personal health information. The rules restrict the use of such records for marketing and research purposes.

> **Health Insurance Portability and Accountability Act**
> A federal law protecting against health professionals and institutions revealing individuals' private medical records.

Drivers' Information

The federal **Drivers' Privacy Protection Act** of 1994 prohibits states from "knowing disclosure" of information obtained from driver's license and vehicle registration records without permission except under specific circumstances.[216] At one time, many states sold this information for millions of dollars annually. Congress stopped this practice in part to prevent stalkers from obtaining information about potential targets. However, the law prevents anyone from using these records to find information valuable to the public. The U.S. Supreme Court

> **Driver's Privacy Protection Act**
> Federal legislation that prohibits states from disclosing personal information that drivers submit in order to obtain a driver's license.

upheld the law against a constitutional challenge, finding that Congress' power over interstate commerce allowed it to adopt the statute.[217]

In 2015, the Seventh Circuit Court of Appeals refused to dismiss a district court ruling that the Sun-Times newspaper of Chicago was punishable for disclosing "private information" from the driver's licenses of several police officers.[218] The Sun-Times received photographs and physical descriptions of the officers after the state attorney general required their release under the state's freedom of information law. In its published criticism of the officers' participation in a homicide lineup, the Sun-Times included each officer's birth date, height, weight, hair and eye color, details it said were essential to demonstrate the problematic composition of the police lineup. The newspaper argued that it had published accurate, legally obtained information that was not defined as private under the law.

The Seventh Circuit held that the DPPA's ban on disclosure of private information applied and the newspaper enjoyed no First Amendment protection from penalty. The court reasoned that the ban was both content-neutral and rationally related to the government's legitimate interest in protecting the information from unauthorized disclosure. The Supreme Court declined to review the decision.

Covert Recording or Intercepting "Wire" Communications

Covert recording, which is unknown to some of the parties, always involves some deception; recording devices are hidden, and informed parties can shape their comments with knowledge of the recording. The ubiquity of cellphone cameras and recording today increases the opportunity for covert recording and prompted laws meant to protect against video voyeurism.

Described in various ways, the crime of video voyeurism includes knowingly photographing in/to private locations and covert photos of people's intimate anatomy, such as photos up a woman's skirt.[219] The federal Video Voyeurism Prevention Act[220] prohibits unauthorized photography of an individual's anatomy when there is a legitimate expectation of privacy. A total of 24 states also have laws that specifically address this issue. The remaining 26 states have general "anti-voyeurism" or "peeping" laws.[221] The Connecticut statute came under review in 2016 in a case that asked whether surreptitious filming of a partner during consensual sex violated the law.[222] The state appellate court upheld the trial court's ruling that voyeurism did not occur because the alleged violation occurred "in plain view" of the defendant and involved no surreptitious invasion.

After a Texas appellate court struck down as overbroad that state's sweeping "improper photography" law in 2014,[223] the state revised the law. The state's more targeted "invasive photography" law now makes it illegal to take or distribute, without the person's consent, images (1) of the person's intimate areas, (2) when a person is in a changing room or bathroom or (3) with the intention of invading the person's privacy.[224]

Some media organizations enforce policies about the use of hidden recordings or recordings without consent. In addition, various state and federal laws come into play. While the use of hidden cameras by media does not itself constitute an illegal intrusion, 13 states specifically prohibit the unauthorized use or installation of cameras in private places.[225] Recording may be acceptable in one state but not another.[226] Covert recording also may violate federal laws.

REAL WORLD LAW
CHILLING HOSPITAL PR: PATIENT APPROVAL REQUIRED

In 2016, New York–Presbyterian Hospital agreed to pay $2.2 million in fines to federal regulators for recording patients without patient consent. The decision involved ABC's reality show "NY Med" airing the dying moments of an 83-year-old man who had been struck by a car.[vi]

The U.S. Department of Health and Human Services used the fine to clarify that medical facilities violate the rights of patients if they allow media into treatment areas without patient approval. Many said the ruling would end popular television and cable shows recorded in hospitals.

"I think this will have a chilling effect on hospitals going forward," said the chairman of the ethics committee of the American College of Emergency Physicians. "Any hospital legal counsel worth his salt or any P.R. director would be committing malpractice in order to allow it to occur. It's now embodied in a federal directive."[vii]

Federal laws also protect the privacy of "wire communications," which include technologies that may not be wired but transfer voice from one point to another.[227] Landline telephones, cellphones and computer-based voice services such as Skype, Google Hangouts and FaceTime[228] all fall under this regulatory umbrella. The federal **Wiretapping and Electronic Surveillance Act**[229] prohibits the interception (and recording) of a "wire" voice communication. The law allows the government to bring criminal charges, and private individuals may sue for civil damages. It does not protect messages that are stored after transmission. The data packets stored following internet calls are subject to the Stored Communications Act,[230] which offers "considerably less protection" than the Wiretap Act.[231] Investigative agencies may access live or stored calls with warrants and subpoenas.

The federal Electronic Communications Privacy Act also prohibits the unauthorized interception of an electronic communication while it is in transit or storage.[232] Both the ECPA and the Computer Fraud and Abuse Act prohibit computer and phone hacking, which violate a user's expectation of privacy.[233] All 50 states also make it illegal to hack into someone's computer or phone to obtain previously recorded conversations or messages or to gain access to another person's phone records by misrepresenting your identity.[234]

Alleged violation of the ECPA has been among the claims in suits against internet service providers who reveal the identity of anonymous communicators. Courts generally have favored ISPs that disclose identities according to the standards outlined in the act. In one case, the plaintiff posted a message on AOL (then America Online) that harassed the soon-to-be ex-wife of the plaintiff's lover. When AOL investigated, it terminated the poster's contract for violating AOL's "Rules of the Road." Under subpoena and in compliance with an exception provided by the ECPA, AOL provided the identity of the poster to the subject of the post. A federal court ruled that such disclosure did not violate the poster's privacy.[235]

Wiretapping and Electronic Surveillance Act A federal law that makes it illegal to intercept, record, disseminate or use a private communication without a participant's permission.

In recent years, Pennsylvania courts have heard a number of wiretapping cases.[236] One 2018 decision established that the state law is modeled on the federal law to "emphasize[] the protection of privacy."[237] However, both laws expressly exempt interceptions by police and prisons that follow established procedures. In addition, the Foreign Intelligence Surveillance Act allows government investigators to use wiretaps, surveillance and tracking of personal communications without a court order.[238] Journalists are subject to FISA, as are professional communications firms, and the extent to which the government uses FISA to surveil journalists and obtain their sources is unknown, according to the Reporters Committee for Freedom of the Press.[239]

OTHER LIMITS TO GATHERING INFORMATION

Individuals who value their privacy or wish to avoid contact or publicity may seek protection under criminal harassment and stalking laws designed to protect crime victims.[240] The Kansas Protection From Stalking Act, for example, prohibits stalking and harassment.[241] It defines stalking as "intentional harassment . . . that places the other person in reasonable fear" and harassment as two or more "knowing and intentional [acts] . . . that seriously alarm, annoy, torment or terrorize . . . that serve no legitimate purpose."[242] While prosecutors and judges tend to strike down the application of these laws to journalists who persist in asking questions, anti-harassment statutes in nine states leave the door open for prosecution for repeated, aggressive contacts to gather information.[243]

Harassment and Stalking

Notable examples of aggressive newsgathering that cross the line involve "paparazzi" photographers pursuing celebrities. Decades ago, a court ordered a photographer to stay a fixed distance away from former first lady Jacqueline Kennedy Onassis, her children and their homes and schools.[244] Both Onassis and the Secret Service sued the photographer for continually interfering with the agents performing their protective duties. The court flatly rejected the photographer's claim that the First Amendment was a complete defense to his behavior.[245]

In a recent California case, a state court upheld a law increasing penalties for reckless driving "with the intent to capture an image [or] sound recording . . . of another person for a commercial purpose."[246] A commercial photographer challenged the provision as unconstitutionally intended to infringe on the First Amendment activities of celebrity photographers.[247] The court disagreed and said the law broadly applied to anyone engaged in the specified activities that interfere with safe driving.

tortious newsgathering The use of reporting techniques that are wrongful and unlawful and for which the victim may obtain damages in court.

The concept of **tortious newsgathering** developed in response to the "ambush-and-surveillance" journalism practiced by some journalists and television programs. The tort broadly encompasses the range of problematic behaviors explored in this chapter. One case symbolizes the evolution of the law—and the media—in this area. When insurance company executives denied interviews from the television program "Inside Edition," show producers staked out the home of two executives, followed them and their 3-year-old, and made recordings using hidden cameras, powerful microphones and extreme telephoto lenses. The crew then followed the family to Florida and anchored a boat 50 yards offshore of the family house.

A judge in Philadelphia granted the family an injunction.[248] The "*legal* newsgathering activities" of the "Inside Edition" crew would not be "irreparably harmed by an injunction narrowly tailored to preclude them from continuing their harassing conduct" because, the judge said, the injunction targeted only illegal newsgathering tactics.

Fraud and Misrepresentation

Years ago, ABC News magazine reporters used false names and fake work histories to go undercover in Food Lion grocery stores to investigate alleged unsanitary practices.[249] They wore hidden cameras and microphones.[250] Their jobs gave them access to nonpublic areas of the stores, where they filmed meat-handling practices. Food Lion denied the accusations and sued for fraud, trespass, unfair trade practices and breach of a duty of loyalty to "attack[] the methods used by defendants to gather the information ultimately aired on 'PrimeTime Live.'"[251] Because Food Lion chose not to sue for defamation (which requires falsity), the trial court said the truth of the story was not at issue.[252] The jury found for Food Lion, awarding the grocery chain more than $5.5 million in punitive damages. The judge reduced the award to $315,000.

ABC appealed the verdict, and the Court of Appeals for the Fourth Circuit reversed on all but the trespass and breach of loyalty claims.[253] It remains a cautionary tale. Not only did the lower court call some newsgathering techniques illegal, but a dissenting judge on the federal appeals court panel would have sustained the fraud claim and the punitive damages against ABC.[254] Although ABC ultimately paid only $2 in damages, some factors should be kept in mind:

- First, the attorney fees were costly.[255]

- Second, those costs and the verdict should raise serious questions about newsgathering techniques that involve deception.

- Third, the jury showed real animosity toward the news media, particularly toward big, powerful and seemingly well-to-do news organizations.[256]

- ABC's successful appeal relied on specific state laws. A different result might arise in a different state.

In Minnesota, a court ruled against a Minneapolis television station whose employee hid her media job to work as a volunteer in a facility for the mentally disabled. She wore a hidden camera and used the video in broadcasts critical of the facility. The facility sued for fraud and trespass, and the Minnesota appeals court ruled that the station misrepresented itself and trespassed on private property.[257] The parties reached a confidential settlement.

Misrepresentation also can occur when journalists disclose who they are but disguise the nature of the story they are developing. When truckers declined to participate in an NBC

A group of bronze paparazzi dogs roves the globe to suggest that the pack behaviors of photojournalists are unreasonable, according to the artists, Gillie and Marc.

"Dateline" story about the trucking industry, NBC promised one truck driver and his boss that their report would be positive and would not include comments from anyone from Parents Against Tired Truckers. The "Dateline" segment was not positive. It included statements like "American highways are a trucker's killing field."[258] It also contained interviews with PATT members. The trucking company sued NBC for fraud and misrepresentation. The First Circuit Court of Appeals favored NBC on nearly every point and ruled that the network's vague promise to produce a "positive portrayal" was insufficient basis for a claim.[259] But the court said damages could be awarded based on NBC's specific and unequivocal promise not to include anyone from PATT. The parties settled for an undisclosed amount.[260]

Problems With Sources and Confidentiality

Using material from social media may be perilous because many of the circulated claims are both anonymous and without supporting evidence. The Washington Post, among other prominent media, has been caught publishing material based on tweets only to find the purported tweeter did not exist. One media critic discovered that his intentionally planted misinformation with no named source took 10 minutes to go viral. Two 2019 studies found that fewer than 1 percent of Twitter or Facebook users spread or read the vast majority of misinformation parading as news.[261] Older, extremely right-wing Twitter users are most likely to circulate fakery, with one in five routinely doing so, one study found.

Many professional communications firms prohibit or caution practitioner use of social media content. The Associated Press, for example, says, "Fake accounts are rampant in the social media world. . . . [N]ever lift quotes, photos or video from social networking sites and attribute them to the name on the profile or feed where you found the material."[262] In 2019, internet companies including Pinterest also took steps to stop the spread of medical misinformation in the wake of measles outbreaks believed fueled by anti-vaccine falsehoods.[263] Facebook said its new policies would reject ads and deny recommendations to pages that spread hoaxes and anti-vaccine propaganda.

When professional communicators seek sensitive information or whistleblower tips, a promise of anonymity may be the only way to gain access to key information. In exchange for information, communicators may agree to limit how the information is used or provide confidentiality for the source.[264] The promise of confidentiality is a "form of currency" used to free up tips and insights.[265] One estimate indicates that at least one-third of newspaper accounts and the vast majority of newsmagazine stories conceal source attribution.[266] Reporters and their news organizations typically keep promises of confidentiality, even when courts ask them to break them (see Chapter 8). Keeping such promises is both ethical and practical. Individuals and organizations that break promises develop a reputation for being untrustworthy. Sources vanish.

promissory estoppel
A legal doctrine requiring liability when a clear promise is made and relied on and injury results from the broken promise.

When an organization breaks a promise and reveals the identity of a source promised anonymity, the source may sue and win.[267] Promises, even unwritten promises, can be legally binding under the principle of **promissory estoppel**. Promissory estoppel requires courts to enforce a promise if the individual who received the promise relied on it and its breach created a harm that should be remedied by law. Promissory estoppel is a generally applicable law that applies with equal force to news organizations as to anyone else.

The U.S. Supreme Court ruled years ago that the First Amendment does not protect journalists from the consequences of broken promises.[268] The case of *Cohen v. Cowles Media Co.* involved a political campaign worker's offer of prejudicial information about a political opponent to four reporters just days before the election. On the condition that his identity be kept secret, the campaign worker disclosed that the opposing candidate had been arrested for unlawful assembly and petty theft more than 10 years earlier. Two newspapers ran the stories and clearly identified the source because they said the public deserved to know who was engaged in political "dirty tricks."

When the campaign worker was fired, he sued, claiming the newspapers broke a contractual agreement. At trial, the jury agreed and awarded $200,000 in compensatory damages and $500,000 in punitive damages. On review, the Minnesota Supreme Court struck down the award on the grounds that the application of promissory estoppel to newspapers would abridge First Amendment interests. On appeal, the U.S. Supreme Court reversed. The Court said the First Amendment imposed no bar to the application of promissory estoppel to the press. "Generally applicable laws do not offend the First Amendment simply because their enforcement against the press has incidental effects on its ability to gather and report the news," Justice Byron White wrote in *Cohen*.[269]

EMERGING LAW

Government officials may use arrest or even physical assault to deter media coverage. Some believe such interference with media has increased in recent years. In 2016, for example, six journalists faced felony charges for inciting a riot during Inauguration Day protests in Washington, D.C.[270] A reporter was arrested at the West Virginia State Capitol for repeatedly asking Health and Human Services Secretary Tom Price about Affordable Care Act coverage of domestic violence.[271] A Montana congressman was convicted of assaulting a reporter for The Guardian at a campaign event just before the special election.[272]

In 2019, the U.S. Supreme Court in *Nieves v. Bartlett* determined when individuals can bring a First Amendment challenge to an arrest on the grounds that the arrest illegally restrained their protected speech.[273] The case involved the arrest of Russell Bartlett for "aggressive" behavior at a large outdoor festival. Finding that the police had probable cause to arrest Bartlett, the Supreme Court reversed the Ninth Circuit Court of Appeals ruling and barred Bartlett from pursuing a retaliatory arrest claim.[274]

Bartlett argued that the police arrested him for disorderly conduct in retaliation for his earlier comments to the officer confronting a minor suspected of underage drinking. Bartlett also had refused to respond to the officer's questions. Bartlett said the officer's comment during the arrest—"Bet you wish you would have talked to me now"—established that the arrest would not have occurred "but-for" the officer's animus.[275]

Writing for a plurality of the Court, Chief Justice John Roberts argued that causation is difficult to determine in claims of retaliatory arrest because protected speech is often "a wholly legitimate consideration" in determining whether to make an arrest.[276] A majority of the Court then concluded that "the presence of probable cause should generally defeat a First Amendment retaliatory arrest claim."[277]

This photo by a journalist named in the U.S. government database of individuals subject to additional screening at the U.S./Mexico border shows a Border Patrol sign and concertina wire keeping migrants back from the U.S. border in Nogales, Ariz.

Alone in dissent in the fractured *Nieves* ruling, Justice Sonia Sotomayor said the vague decision would not adequately protect freedom of speech. She argued that the Court's logic would permit retaliatory arrests to go unpunished "unless the plaintiff can muster evidence that he was arrested when otherwise similarly situated individuals not engaged in the same sort of speech had not been."[278] Absent such comparative evidence, *Nieves* will leave plaintiffs "out of luck, even if they could offer other, unassailable proof of an officer's unconstitutional statements and motivations" for the arrest, she said.[279]

Immediately following the ruling, media advocates expressed concern that *Nieves* would have a severe chilling effect on citizens and journalists attempting to record or protest police actions.[280] They said it would shield police officers from liability for arresting individuals out of anger prompted by protected First Amendment activities.

In 2018 and 2019, in response to the "climate of extreme hostility toward the press," Congress introduced the Journalist Protection Act to make attacks on reporters a federal crime.[281] In 2018, the United States was listed, for the first time, as one of the five deadliest countries in the world for journalists and as one of only three where journalists were killed in cold blood outside a war zone.[282] The deadliest attack was at the Capital Gazette in Maryland, where a man walked into the newspaper office and shot five employees.[283]

In 2019, news media disclosed that Customs and Border Protection had compiled a list of journalists and activists to be stopped and questioned at the U.S./Mexico border.[284] Ten journalists who were covering the migrant caravan were labeled "instigators" who should be subject to extended questioning "to collect evidence . . . for future legal actions." Some journalists reported that they were told to give officers access to their cellphones. A spokesperson for the American Civil Liberties Union called the targeted questioning "an egregious violation of the First Amendment" that could have a significant chilling effect on coverage of important matters of public concern.[285]

In Georgia, legislators introduced a bill in 2019 to establish a state board to oversee journalists' work, consider complaints and issue "formal advisory opinions."[286] The board also might establish voluntary accreditation for journalists, according to the bill's sponsor. A member of the Georgia First Amendment Foundation said the bill was intended to limit scrutiny of the legislature.

Another issue working its way through state courts involves the public's right of access to police camera footage. In 2019, for example, the New Jersey Supreme Court was asked to review whether the public has a common law or statutory right of access to police camera videos.[287] The lower court ruled that dashcam recordings are public records but did not determine whether the recording at issue should be released under the state's open-records law.

In Pennsylvania, a 2017 state supreme court decision held that police vehicle recordings were not automatically exempt from disclosure under the "investigative information" exclusion to the state's open-records requirements.[288] The court reiterated that recent amendments to the law expanded public access to increase government transparency, and exemptions must be determined on a case-by-case basis. The court limited the investigative exemption to materials related directly to the "systematic inquiry or examination into a potential crime."

In 2018, a federal district court ruled that President Donald Trump cannot block critics from his Twitter account without violating the First Amendment.[289] The court said the Twitter account was the equivalent of a public forum in which the president communicated with the public and to which the public should have access. While an appeal in that case is pending,[290] state courts are grappling with how recordkeeping and disclosure requirements of their open-records laws apply to officials' various email and social media accounts.

In 2019, several cases pitted the Trump administration against congressional efforts to gather information about the president's finances, activities and initiatives. Two federal judges refused to accept President Trump's arguments that congressional subpoenas to his accounting firm and banks "served no legislative purpose." Citing the broad investigative authority of Congress and the need for courts to defer to congressional judgment, the courts upheld the subpoenas.[291] "The power of Congress to conduct investigations is inherent in the legislative process," one judge declared.[292] In a separate action, the president used executive privilege to block a congressional subpoena for records related to a new citizenship question on the 2020 census.[293] The U.S. Supreme Court remanded the case in 2019.[294]

A Vermont case involved a request for communications within the attorney general's office "received or sent on a private email account . . . or private text messaging account."[295] Reversing lower court rulings, the state supreme court held that state law required agencies to conduct a reasonable search of all "records produced or acquired in the course of agency business . . . regardless of whether they are located in private accounts of state employees or officials or on the state system."[296] In a similar case in Washington, a state appeals court held that "a public official's posts on a personal Facebook page can constitute an agency's public records subject to disclosure . . . if the posts relate to the conduct of government and are prepared within a public official's scope of employment or official capacity." However, city council members' personal posts on personal social media accounts do not constitute public records.[297]

CASES FOR STUDY

For study resources and a case archive, go to **edge.sagepub.com/medialaw7e**.

Thinking About It

The two case excerpts that follow cover different subsets in the broad area of information gathering. The first case relates to the Freedom of Information Act. The second addresses the concept of the ride-along. As you read these case excerpts, keep the following questions in mind:

- Just how much information does the Freedom of Information Act provide? Are the limits that have been established fair?

- In the *Reporters Committee* case, what factor does the U.S. Supreme Court identify as critical in deciding whether to disclose a private document?

- The *Reporters Committee* case was decided in 1989. Has the nature of privacy changed in such a way that might change the ruling today?

- Note that in the *Wilson* ride-along case, a media organization is not a party to the case. Nevertheless, it is a ruling that affects the media significantly. How and why?

U.S. Department of Justice v. Reporters Committee for Freedom of the Press
SUPREME COURT OF THE UNITED STATES
489 U.S. 749 (1989)

JUSTICE JOHN PAUL STEVENS
delivered the Court's opinion:

The Federal Bureau of Investigation (FBI) has accumulated and maintains criminal identification records, sometimes referred to as "rap sheets," on over 24 million persons. The question presented by this case is whether the disclosure of the contents of such a file to a third party "could reasonably be expected to constitute an unwarranted invasion of personal privacy" within the meaning of the Freedom of Information Act (FOIA).

In 1924 Congress appropriated funds to enable the Department of Justice (Department) to establish a program to collect and preserve fingerprints and other criminal identification records. That statute authorized the Department to exchange such information with "officials of States, cities and other institutions." . . . Congress created the FBI's identification division, and gave it responsibility for "acquiring, collecting, classifying, and preserving criminal identification and other crime records and the exchanging of said criminal identification records with the duly authorized officials of governmental agencies, of States, cities, and penal institutions." Rap sheets compiled pursuant to such authority contain certain descriptive information, such as date of birth and physical characteristics, as well as a history of arrests, charges, convictions, and incarcerations of the subject. Normally a rap sheet is preserved until its subject attains age 80. Because of the volume of rap sheets, they are sometimes incorrect or incomplete and sometimes contain information about other persons with similar names.

The local, state, and federal law enforcement agencies throughout the Nation that exchange rap-sheet

data with the FBI do so on a voluntary basis. The principal use of the information is to assist in the detection and prosecution of offenders; it is also used by courts and corrections officials in connection with sentencing and parole decisions. As a matter of executive policy, the Department has generally treated rap sheets as confidential and, with certain exceptions, has restricted their use to governmental purposes. Consistent with the Department's basic policy of treating these records as confidential, Congress in 1957 amended the basic statute to provide that the FBI's exchange of rap-sheet information with any other agency is subject to cancellation "if dissemination is made outside the receiving departments or related agencies."

As a matter of Department policy, the FBI has made two exceptions to its general practice of prohibiting unofficial access to rap sheets. First, it allows the subject of a rap sheet to obtain a copy, and second, it occasionally allows rap sheets to be used in the preparation of press releases and publicity designed to assist in the apprehension of wanted persons or fugitives. . . .

Although much rap-sheet information is a matter of public record, the availability and dissemination of the actual rap sheet to the public is limited. Arrests, indictments, convictions, and sentences are public events that are usually documented in court records. In addition, if a person's entire criminal history transpired in a single jurisdiction, all of the contents of his or her rap sheet may be available upon request in that jurisdiction. That possibility, however, is present in only three States. All of the other 47 States place substantial restrictions on the availability of criminal-history summaries even though individual events in those summaries are matters of public record. Moreover, even in Florida, Wisconsin, and Oklahoma, the publicly available summaries may not include information about out-of-state arrests or convictions.

The statute known as FOIA is actually a part of the Administrative Procedure Act. Section 3 of the APA as enacted in 1946 gave agencies broad discretion concerning the publication of governmental records. In 1966 Congress amended that section to implement "'a general philosophy of full agency disclosure.'" The amendment required agencies to publish their rules of procedure in the Federal Register, and to make available for public inspection and copying their opinions, statements of policy, interpretations, and staff manuals and instructions that are not published in the Federal Register. . . . In addition, [it] requires every agency "upon any request for records which . . . reasonably describes such records" to make such records "promptly available to any person." If an agency improperly withholds any documents, the district court has jurisdiction to order their production. Unlike the review of other agency action that must be upheld if supported by substantial evidence and not arbitrary or capricious, FOIA expressly places the burden "on the agency to sustain its action" and directs the district courts to "determine the matter de novo."

Congress exempted nine categories of documents from FOIA's broad disclosure requirements. Three of those exemptions are arguably relevant to this case. Exemption 3 applies to documents that are specifically exempted from disclosure by another statute. Exemption 6 protects "personnel and medical files and similar files the disclosure of which would constitute a clearly unwarranted invasion of personal privacy." Exemption 7(C) excludes records or information compiled for law enforcement purposes, "but only to the extent that the production of such [materials] . . . could reasonably be expected to constitute an unwarranted invasion of personal privacy."

Exemption 7(C)'s privacy language is broader than the comparable language in Exemption 6 in two respects. First, whereas Exemption 6 requires that the invasion of privacy be "clearly unwarranted," the adverb "clearly" is omitted from Exemption 7(C). This omission is the product of a 1974 amendment adopted in response to concerns expressed by the President. Second, whereas Exemption 6 refers to disclosures that "would constitute" an invasion of privacy,

Exemption 7(C) encompasses any disclosure that "could reasonably be expected to constitute" such an invasion. This difference is also the product of a specific amendment. Thus, the standard for evaluating a threatened invasion of privacy interests resulting from the disclosure of records compiled for law enforcement purposes is somewhat broader than the standard applicable to personnel, medical, and similar files.

This case arises out of requests made by a CBS news correspondent and the Reporters Committee for Freedom of the Press (respondents) for information concerning the criminal records of four members of the Medico family. The Pennsylvania Crime Commission had identified the family's company, Medico Industries, as a legitimate business dominated by organized crime figures. Moreover, the company allegedly had obtained a number of defense contracts as a result of an improper arrangement with a corrupt Congressman.

FOIA requests sought disclosure of any arrests, indictments, acquittals, convictions, and sentences of any of the four Medicos. Although the FBI originally denied the requests, it provided the requested data concerning three of the Medicos after their deaths. In their complaint in the district court, respondents sought the rap sheet for the fourth, Charles Medico (Medico), insofar as it contained "matters of public record." . . .

Exemption 7(C) requires us to balance the privacy interest in maintaining, as the government puts it, the "practical obscurity" of the rap sheets against the public interest in their release.

The preliminary question is whether Medico's interest in the nondisclosure of any rap sheet the FBI might have on him is the sort of "personal privacy" interest that Congress intended Exemption 7(C) to protect. As we have pointed out before, "[t]he cases sometimes characterized as protecting 'privacy' have in fact involved at least two different kinds of interests. One is the individual interest in avoiding disclosure of personal matters, and another is the interest in independence in making certain kinds of important decisions." Here, the former interest, "in avoiding disclosure of personal matters," is implicated. Because events summarized in a rap sheet have been previously disclosed to the public, respondents contend that Medico's privacy interest in avoiding disclosure of a federal compilation of these events approaches zero. We reject respondents' cramped notion of personal privacy.

To begin with, both the common law and the literal understandings of privacy encompass the individual's control of information concerning his or her person. In an organized society, there are few facts that are not at one time or another divulged to another. Thus the extent of the protection accorded a privacy right at common law rested in part on the degree of dissemination of the allegedly private fact and the extent to which the passage of time rendered it private. According to Webster's initial definition, information may be classified as "private" if it is "intended for or restricted to the use of a particular person or group or class of persons: not freely available to the public." Recognition of this attribute of a privacy interest supports the distinction, in terms of personal privacy, between scattered disclosure of the bits of information contained in a rap sheet and revelation of the rap sheet as a whole. The very fact that federal funds have been spent to prepare, index, and maintain these criminal-history files demonstrates that the individual items of information in the summaries would not otherwise be "freely available" either to the officials who have access to the underlying files or to the general public. Indeed, if the summaries were "freely available," there would be no reason to invoke FOIA to obtain access to the information they contain. Granted, in many contexts the fact that information is not freely available is no reason to exempt that information from a statute generally requiring its dissemination. But the issue here is whether the compilation of otherwise hard-to-obtain information alters the privacy interest implicated by disclosure of that information. Plainly there is a vast difference between the public records that might be found after a diligent search of courthouse files, county archives, and local police stations throughout the country and a computerized summary located in a single clearinghouse of information.

This conclusion is supported by the web of federal statutory and regulatory provisions that limits the disclosure of rap-sheet information. That is, Congress has authorized rap-sheet dissemination to banks, local licensing officials, the securities industry, the nuclear-power industry, and other law enforcement agencies. Further, the FBI has permitted such disclosure to the subject of the rap sheet and, more generally, to assist in the apprehension of wanted persons or fugitives. Finally, the FBI's exchange of rap-sheet information "is subject to cancellation if dissemination is made outside the receiving departments or related agencies." This careful and limited pattern of authorized rap-sheet disclosure fits the dictionary definition

of privacy as involving a restriction of information "to the use of a particular person or group or class of persons." Moreover, although perhaps not specific enough to constitute a statutory exemption under FOIA Exemption 3, these statutes and regulations, taken as a whole, evidence a congressional intent to protect the privacy of rap-sheet subjects, and a concomitant recognition of the power of compilations to affect personal privacy that outstrips the combined power of the bits of information contained within.

Other portions of FOIA itself bolster the conclusion that disclosure of records regarding private citizens, identifiable by name, is not what the framers of FOIA had in mind. Specifically, FOIA provides that "[t]o the extent required to prevent a clearly unwarranted invasion of personal privacy, an agency may delete identifying details when it makes available or publishes an opinion, statement of policy, interpretation, or staff manual or instruction." Additionally, FOIA assures that "[a]ny reasonably segregable portion of a record shall be provided to any person requesting such record after deletion of the portions which are exempt under Section (b)." These provisions, for deletion of identifying references and disclosure of segregable portions of records with exempt information deleted, reflect a congressional understanding that disclosure of records containing personal details about private citizens can infringe significant privacy interests.

Also supporting our conclusion that a strong privacy interest inheres in the nondisclosure of compiled computerized information is the Privacy Act of 1974. The Privacy Act was passed largely out of concern over "the impact of computer data banks on individual privacy." The Privacy Act provides generally that "[n]o agency shall disclose any record which is contained in a system of records . . . except pursuant to a written request by, or with the prior written consent of, the individual to whom the record pertains." Although the Privacy Act contains a variety of exceptions to this rule, including an exemption for information required to be disclosed under FOIA, Congress' basic policy concern regarding the implications of computerized data banks for personal privacy is certainly relevant in our consideration of the privacy interest affected by dissemination of rap sheets from the FBI computer.

Given this level of federal concern over centralized data bases, the fact that most States deny the general public access to their criminal-history summaries should not be surprising. As we have pointed out, in

47 States nonconviction data from criminal-history summaries are not available at all, and even conviction data are "generally unavailable to the public." State policies, of course, do not determine the meaning of a federal statute, but they provide evidence that the law enforcement profession generally assumes—as has the Department of Justice—that individual subjects have a significant privacy interest in their criminal histories. It is reasonable to presume that Congress legislated with an understanding of this professional point of view.

In addition to the common-law and dictionary understandings, the basic difference between scattered bits of criminal history and a federal compilation, federal statutory provisions, and state policies, our cases have also recognized the privacy interest inherent in the nondisclosure of certain information even where the information may have been at one time public. . . .

In sum, the fact that "an event is not wholly 'private' does not mean that an individual has no interest in limiting disclosure or dissemination of the information." The privacy interest in a rap sheet is substantial. The substantial character of that interest is affected by the fact that in today's society the computer can accumulate and store information that would otherwise have surely been forgotten long before a person attains age 80, when the FBI's rap sheets are discarded.

Exemption 7(C), by its terms, permits an agency to withhold a document only when revelation "could reasonably be expected to constitute an unwarranted invasion of personal privacy." We must next address what factors might warrant an invasion of the interest described in Part IV.

Our previous decisions establish that whether an invasion of privacy is warranted cannot turn on the purposes for which the request for information is made. Except for cases in which the objection to disclosure is based on a claim of privilege and the person requesting disclosure is the party protected by the privilege, the identity of the requesting party has no bearing on the merits of his or her FOIA request. Thus, although the subject of a presentence report can waive a privilege that might defeat a third party's access to that report, and although the FBI's policy of granting the subject of a rap sheet access to his own criminal history is consistent with its policy of denying access to all other members of the general public, the rights of the two press respondents in this case are no different from those that might be asserted by any other third party, such as a neighbor or prospective employer. As we have repeatedly stated, Congress "clearly intended" FOIA "to give any member of the public as much right to disclosure as one with a special interest [in a particular document]." . . . "The Act's sole concern is with what must be made public or not made public."

Thus whether disclosure of a private document under Exemption 7(C) is warranted must turn on the nature of the requested document and its relationship to "the basic purpose of the Freedom of Information Act 'to open agency action to the light of public scrutiny'" . . . rather than on the particular purpose for which the document is being requested. In our leading case on FOIA, we declared that the Act was designed to create a broad right of access to "official information." . . .

This basic policy of "'full agency disclosure unless information is exempted under clearly delineated statutory language'" indeed focuses on the citizens' right to be informed about "what their government is up to." Official information that sheds light on an agency's performance of its statutory duties falls squarely within that statutory purpose. That purpose, however, is not fostered by disclosure of information about private citizens that is accumulated in various governmental files but that reveals little or nothing about an agency's own conduct. In this case—and presumably in the typical case in which one private citizen is seeking information about another—the requester does not intend to discover anything about the conduct of the agency that has possession of the requested records. Indeed, response to this request would not shed any light on the conduct of any Government agency or official. . . .

Respondents argue that there is a twofold public interest in learning about Medico's past arrests or convictions: He allegedly had improper dealings with a corrupt Congressman, and he is an officer of a corporation with defense contracts. But if Medico has, in fact, been arrested or convicted of certain crimes, that information would neither aggravate nor mitigate his allegedly improper relationship with the Congressman; more specifically, it would tell us nothing directly about the character of the Congressman's behavior. Nor would it tell us anything about the conduct of the Department of Defense (DOD) in awarding one or more contracts to the Medico Company. Arguably a FOIA request to the DOD for records relating to those contracts, or for documents describing the agency's procedures, if any, for determining whether officers of a prospective contractor have criminal records, would constitute an appropriate request for "official information." Conceivably Medico's rap sheet would provide details to include in a news story, but, in itself, this is not the kind of public interest for which Congress enacted FOIA. In other words, although there is undoubtedly some public interest in anyone's criminal history, especially if the history is in some way related to the subject's dealing with a public official or agency, FOIA's central purpose is to ensure that the Government's activities be opened to the sharp eye of public scrutiny, not that information about private citizens that happens to be in the warehouse of the Government be so disclosed. Thus, it should come as no surprise that in none of our cases construing FOIA have we found it appropriate to order a Government agency to honor a FOIA request for information about a particular private citizen.

What we have said should make clear that the public interest in the release of any rap sheet on Medico that may exist is not the type of interest protected by FOIA. Medico may or may not be one of the 24 million persons for whom the FBI has a rap sheet. If respondents are entitled to have the FBI tell them what it knows about Medico's criminal history, any other member of the public is entitled to the same disclosure—whether for writing a news story, for deciding whether to employ Medico, to rent a house to him, to extend credit to him, or simply to confirm or deny a suspicion. There is, unquestionably, some public interest in providing interested citizens with answers to their questions about Medico. But that interest falls outside the ambit of the public interest that FOIA was enacted to serve.

Finally, we note that Congress has provided that the standard fees for production of documents under FOIA shall be waived or reduced "if disclosure of the information is in the public interest because it is likely to contribute significantly to public understanding of the operations or activities of the government and is not primarily in the commercial interest of the requester." Although such a provision obviously implies that there will be requests that do not meet such a "public interest" standard, we think it relevant to today's inquiry regarding the public interest in release of rap sheets on private citizens that Congress once again expressed the core purpose of FOIA as "contribut[ing] significantly to public understanding of the operations or activities of the government."

Both the general requirement that a court "shall determine the matter de novo" and the specific reference to an "unwarranted" invasion of privacy in Exemption 7(C) indicate that a court must balance the public interest in disclosure against the interest Congress intended the Exemption to protect. Although both sides agree that such a balance must be undertaken, how such a balance should be done is in dispute. The Court of Appeals majority expressed concern about assigning federal judges the task of striking a proper case-by-case, or ad hoc, balance between individual privacy interests and the public interest in the disclosure of criminal-history information without providing those judges standards to assist in performing that task. Our cases provide support for the proposition that categorical decisions may be appropriate and individual circumstances disregarded when a case fits into a genus in which the balance characteristically tips in one direction. . . .

. . . [W]e hold as a categorical matter that a third party's request for law enforcement records or information about a private citizen can reasonably be expected to invade that citizen's privacy, and that when the request seeks no "official information" about a Government agency, but merely records that the Government happens to be storing, the invasion of privacy is "unwarranted." The judgment of the Court of Appeals is reversed.

It is so ordered.

Wilson v. Layne
SUPREME COURT OF THE UNITED STATES
526 U.S. 603 (1999)

CHIEF JUSTICE WILLIAM REHNQUIST delivered the Court's opinion:
While executing an arrest warrant in a private home, police officers invited representatives of the media to accompany them. We hold that such a "media ride-along" does violate the Fourth Amendment, but that because the state of the law was not clearly established at the time the search in this case took place, the officers are entitled to the defense of qualified immunity.

In early 1992, the Attorney General of the United States approved "Operation Gunsmoke," a special national fugitive apprehension program in which United States Marshals worked with state and local police to apprehend dangerous criminals. The "Operation Gunsmoke" policy statement explained that the operation was to concentrate on "armed individuals wanted on federal and/or state and local warrants for serious drug and other violent felonies." This effective program ultimately resulted in over 3,000 arrests in 40 metropolitan areas.

One of the dangerous fugitives identified as a target of "Operation Gunsmoke" was Dominic Wilson, the son of petitioners Charles and Geraldine Wilson. Dominic Wilson had violated his probation on previous felony charges of robbery, theft, and assault with intent to rob, and the police computer listed "caution indicators" that he was likely to be armed, to resist arrest, and to "assault police." The computer also listed his address as 909 North Stone Street Avenue in Rockville, Maryland. Unknown to the police, this was actually the home of petitioners, Dominic Wilson's parents. Thus, in April 1992, the Circuit Court for Montgomery County issued three arrest warrants for Dominic Wilson, one for each of his probation violations. The warrants were each addressed to "any duly authorized peace officer," and commanded such officers to arrest him and bring him "immediately" before the Circuit Court to answer an indictment as to his probation violation. The warrants made no mention of media presence or assistance.

In the early morning hours of April 16, 1992, a Gunsmoke team of Deputy United States Marshals and Montgomery County Police officers assembled to execute the Dominic Wilson warrants. The team was accompanied by a reporter and a photographer from the Washington Post, who had been invited by the Marshals to accompany them on their mission as part of a Marshal's Service ride-along policy.

At around 6:45 a.m., the officers, with media representatives in tow, entered the dwelling at 909 North Stone Street Avenue in the Lincoln Park neighborhood of Rockville. Petitioners Charles and Geraldine Wilson were still in bed when they heard the officers enter the home. Petitioner Charles Wilson, dressed only in a pair of briefs, ran into the living room to investigate. Discovering at least five men in street clothes with guns in his living room, he angrily demanded that they state their business, and repeatedly cursed the officers. Believing him to be an angry Dominic Wilson, the officers quickly subdued him on the floor. Geraldine Wilson next entered the living room to investigate, wearing only a nightgown. She observed her husband being restrained by the armed officers.

When their protective sweep was completed, the officers learned that Dominic Wilson was not in the house, and they departed. During the time that the officers were in the home, the Washington Post photographer took numerous pictures. The print reporter was also apparently in the living room observing the confrontation between the police and Charles Wilson. At no time, however, were the reporters involved in the execution of the arrest warrant. The Washington Post never published its photographs of the incident.

Petitioners sued the law enforcement officials in their personal capacities for money damages. . . . They contended that the officers' actions in bringing members of the media to observe and record the attempted execution of the arrest warrant violated their Fourth Amendment rights. . . .

. . . [G]overnment officials performing discretionary functions generally are granted a qualified immunity and are "shielded from liability for civil damages insofar as their conduct does not violate clearly established statutory or constitutional rights of which a reasonable person would have known."

. . . A court evaluating a claim of qualified immunity "must first determine whether the plaintiff has alleged the deprivation of an actual constitutional right at all, and if so, proceed to determine whether that right was clearly established at the time of the alleged violation." This order of procedure is designed to "spare a defendant not only unwarranted liability, but unwarranted demands customarily imposed upon those defending a long drawn-out lawsuit." Deciding the constitutional question before addressing the qualified immunity question also promotes clarity in the legal standards for official conduct, to the benefit of both the officers and the general public. We now turn to the Fourth Amendment question.

In 1604, an English court made the now-famous observation that "the house of every one is to him as his castle and fortress, as well for his defence against injury and violence, as for his repose." In his Commentaries on the Laws of England, William Blackstone noted that

the law of England has so particular and
tender a regard to the immunity of a man's
house, that it stiles it his castle, and will

never suffer it to be violated with impunity: agreeing herein with the sentiments of ancient Rome. . . . For this reason no doors can in general be broken open to execute any civil process; though, in criminal causes, the public safety supersedes the private.

The Fourth Amendment embodies this centuries-old principle of respect for the privacy of the home: "The right of the people to be secure in their persons, houses, papers, and effects, against unreasonable searches and seizures, shall not be violated, and no Warrants shall issue, but upon probable cause, supported by Oath or affirmation, and particularly describing the place to be searched, and the persons or things to be seized."

Our decisions have applied these basic principles of the Fourth Amendment to situations, like those in this case, in which police enter a home under the authority of an arrest warrant in order to take into custody the suspect named in the warrant. In *Payton v. New York* (1980), we noted that although clear in its protection of the home, the common-law tradition at the time of the drafting of the Fourth Amendment was ambivalent on the question of whether police could enter a home without a warrant. We were ultimately persuaded that the "overriding respect for the sanctity of the home that has been embedded in our traditions since the origins of the Republic" meant that absent a warrant or exigent circumstances, police could not enter a home to make an arrest. We decided that "an arrest warrant founded on probable cause implicitly carries with it the limited authority to enter a dwelling in which the suspect lives when there is reason to believe the suspect is within."

Here, of course, the officers had such a warrant, and they were undoubtedly entitled to enter the Wilson home in order to execute the arrest warrant for Dominic Wilson. But it does not necessarily follow that they were entitled to bring a newspaper reporter and a photographer with them. . . .

Certainly the presence of reporters inside the home was not related to the objectives of the authorized intrusion. Respondents concede that the reporters did not engage in the execution of the warrant, and did not assist the police in their task. The reporters therefore were not present for any reason related to the justification for police entry into the home—the apprehension of Dominic Wilson.

This is not a case in which the presence of the third parties directly aided in the execution of the warrant. Where the police enter a home under the authority of a warrant to search for stolen property, the presence of third parties for the purpose of identifying the stolen property has long been approved by this Court and our common-law tradition.

Respondents argue that the presence of the Washington Post reporters in the Wilsons' home nonetheless served a number of legitimate law enforcement purposes. They first assert that officers should be able to exercise reasonable discretion about when it would "further their law enforcement mission to permit members of the news media to accompany them in executing a warrant." But this claim ignores the importance of the right of residential privacy at the core of the Fourth Amendment. It may well be that media ride-alongs further the law enforcement objectives of the police in a general sense, but that is not the same as furthering the purposes of the search. Were such generalized "law enforcement objectives" themselves sufficient to trump the Fourth Amendment, the protections guaranteed by that Amendment's text would be significantly watered down.

Respondents next argue that the presence of third parties could serve the law enforcement purpose of publicizing the government's efforts to combat crime, and facilitate accurate reporting on law enforcement activities. There is certainly language in our opinions interpreting the First Amendment which points to the importance of "the press" in informing the general public about the administration of criminal justice. . . . But the Fourth Amendment also protects a very important right, and in the present case it is in terms of that right that the media ride-alongs must be judged.

Surely the possibility of good public relations for the police is simply not enough, standing alone, to justify the ride-along intrusion into a private home. And even the need for accurate reporting on police issues in general bears no direct relation to the constitutional justification for the police intrusion into a home in order to execute a felony arrest warrant.

Finally, respondents argue that the presence of third parties could serve in some situations to minimize police abuses and protect suspects, and also to protect the safety of the officers. While it might be reasonable for police officers to themselves videotape home entries as part of a "quality control" effort to ensure that the rights of homeowners are being respected, or even to preserve evidence, such a situation is significantly different from the media presence in this case. The Washington Post reporters in the Wilsons' home were working on a story for their own purposes. They were not present for the purpose of protecting the officers, much less the Wilsons. A private photographer was acting for private purposes, as evidenced in part by the fact that the newspaper and not the police retained the photographs. Thus, although the presence of third parties during the execution of a warrant may in some circumstances be constitutionally permissible, the presence of these third parties was not.

The reasons advanced by respondents, taken in their entirety, fall short of justifying the presence of media inside a home. We hold that it is a violation of the Fourth Amendment for police to bring members of the media or other third parties into a home during the execution of a warrant when the presence of the third parties in the home was not in aid of the execution of the warrant.

Since the police action in this case violated the petitioners' Fourth Amendment right, we now must decide whether this right was clearly established at the time of the search. As noted above, government officials performing discretionary functions generally are granted a qualified immunity and are "shielded from liability for civil damages insofar as their conduct does not violate clearly established statutory or constitutional rights of which a reasonable person would have known." What this means in practice is that "whether an official protected by qualified immunity may be held personally liable for an allegedly unlawful official action generally turns on the 'objective legal reasonableness' of the action, assessed in light of the legal rules that were 'clearly established' at the time it was taken." . . .

We hold that it was not unreasonable for a police officer in April 1992 to have believed that bringing media observers along during the execution of an arrest warrant (even in a home) was lawful. First, the constitutional question presented by this case is by no means open and shut. The Fourth Amendment protects the rights of homeowners from entry without a warrant, but there was a warrant here. The question is whether the invitation to the media exceeded the scope of the search authorized by the warrant. Accurate media coverage of police activities serves an important public purpose, and it is not obvious from the general principles of the Fourth Amendment that the conduct of the officers in this case violated the Amendment.

Second, although media ride-alongs of one sort or another had apparently become a common police practice, in 1992 there were no judicial opinions holding that this practice became unlawful when it entered a home. . . .

Finally, important to our conclusion was the reliance by the United States marshals in this case on a Marshal's Service ride-along policy which explicitly contemplated that media who engaged in ride-alongs might enter private homes with their cameras as part of fugitive apprehension arrests. The Montgomery County Sheriff's Department also at this time had a ride-along program that did not expressly prohibit media entry into private homes. Such a policy, of course, could not make reasonable a belief that was contrary to a decided body of case law. But here the state of the law as to third parties accompanying police on home entries was at best undeveloped, and it was not unreasonable for law enforcement officers to look and rely on their formal ride-along policies.

Given such an undeveloped state of the law, the officers in this case cannot have been "expected to predict the future course of constitutional law." Between the time of the events of this case and today's decision, a split among the Federal Circuits in fact developed on the question whether media ride-alongs that enter homes subject the police to money damages. If judges thus disagree on a constitutional question, it is unfair to subject police to money damages for picking the losing side of the controversy.

For the foregoing reasons, the judgment of the Court of Appeals is affirmed.

It is so ordered.

Due process requires that the accused receive a trial by an impartial jury free from outside influences. . . . Given . . . the difficulty of effacing prejudicial publicity from the minds of the jurors, the trial courts must take . . . remedial measures that will prevent [] prejudice at its inception.

—U.S. Supreme Court Justice Tom Clark[1]

A trial judge in Arapahoe County, Colo., sealed all court records of prosecutorial misconduct in the capital murder conviction of Sir Mario Owens. District Attorney Carol Chambers led the prosecution.[2]

8

OVERSEEING JUSTICE
Speech and Press Freedoms
In and About the Courts

. . . a man convicted of three murders and sentenced to death has confirmed evidence of misconduct by the prosecution during his trials. The court sealed much of the record of his trials because one murder was gang related and the others were of a witness and the witness's fiancée. Seeking to appeal the verdicts and the death sentence, the defendant asked the court to disqualify the prosecution and order a new trial. In response, the trial judge issued an extensive ruling detailing evidence of significant prosecutorial misconduct, including the withholding of exculpatory evidence from the defense. But the judge denied the disqualification motion, finding that none of the misconduct affected the trial outcome.

In a short ruling citing only "countervailing interests," the judge also sealed all of the records related to the disqualification hearing. Both the defendant and a newspaper sued for access. Does the defendant have a First Amendment right to see the prosecution's response to his motion to disqualify? Should the transcript of the disqualification hearing and the related records be open to the defendant, the media and the public? Look for answers to these and other questions when the case of *People v. Owens* is discussed later and the decision is found at the end of this chapter.[3]

The Sixth Amendment to the U.S. Constitution gives criminal defendants the right to a speedy public trial by an impartial jury of their peers in the locale of the crime. In the 50 years since U.S. Supreme Court Justice Tom Clark suggested that courts must remedy the inherent conflict between fair trials and robust news coverage of trials and crime, we have moved to instant memes and real-time media clips of unfolding trials that circulate the globe.[4] Trial observers describe crime scenes and evidence. Reporters interview neighbors, family, police and victims throughout investigations. Media disseminate gory photographs, and public relations experts carefully craft an image of the victim.[5]

Media inform; they persuade; sometimes they convince.[6] The stories they tell affect suspects' lives and even the charges filed. Media affect attitudes toward policing and the criminal justice system, although demographic traits exert similar or stronger influences.[7] Exemplary media coverage of "unequal justice,"[8] prosecutors' discretion, the prevalence of plea bargains,[9] overcrowded and violent prisons[10] and more does not correct public misunderstanding of the criminal justice system.

Studies show that people who rely on media coverage to understand crime—most people—misunderstand the nature and frequency of crime and the identity of criminals.[11] Potential jurors read and see coverage of crime that presents the accused in overwhelmingly negative ways, focuses on community fear and outrage, and contains information that will not be admissible at trial.[12] Black males and Latinos are overrepresented in media reports on crime, especially violent crime.[13] Yet judges almost uniformly reject defense requests to delay or relocate a trial away from coverage, which "means that 'trial by media' is often going to affect . . . jurors."[14]

ACCESS TO COURTS AND COURT RECORDS

Together the Fifth, Sixth and Seventh Amendments to the U.S. Constitution guarantee the right to a fair and open public trial.[15] Four decades ago, the U.S. Supreme Court said

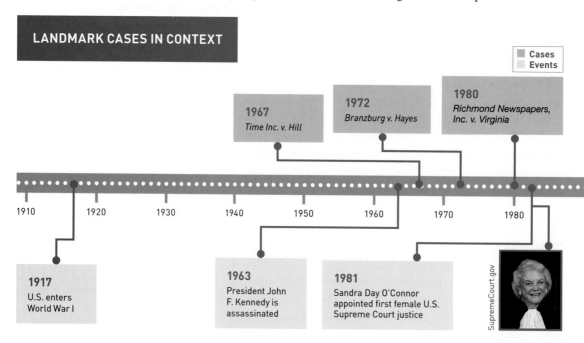

LANDMARK CASES IN CONTEXT

Cases
Events

1967
Time Inc. v. Hill

1972
Branzburg v. Hayes

1980
Richmond Newspapers, Inc. v. Virginia

1910 1920 1930 1940 1950 1960 1970 1980

1917
U.S. enters World War I

1963
President John F. Kennedy is assassinated

1981
Sandra Day O'Connor appointed first female U.S. Supreme Court justice

SupremeCourt.gov

the public's long-standing common law right to view public trials must be balanced against protection of a fair trial.[16] The Court's landmark ruling in *Gannett v. DePasquale* arose after Judge Daniel DePasquale granted pretrial motions to suppress evidence and confessions and to exclude the public and the press from the trial for the murder of an off-duty police officer. No one at the pretrial hearing, including a Gannett reporter, objected to the court's rulings.

After Gannett later objected to the court closure, the judge upheld the motions and said the defendant's right to a fair trial outweighed the right of the press to cover the hearing. On review, the Supreme Court considered whether a criminal defendant may waive his right to a public trial regardless of whether the public, including the media, wants to attend. Because publicity could prejudice the defendant's right to a fair trial, judges should use means that "are not strictly and inescapably necessary" to protect a fair trial, the Court concluded.[17] Justice Potter Stewart wrote:

> There can be no blinking the fact that there is a strong societal interest in public trials. Openness in court proceedings may improve the quality of testimony, induce unknown witnesses to come forward with relevant testimony, cause all trial participants to perform their duties more conscientiously, and generally give the public an opportunity to observe the judicial system. But there is a strong societal interest in other constitutional guarantees extended to the accused as well.[18]

While concurring with the Court's opinion to uphold closure, Justice Harry Blackmun argued that closing a courtroom "may implicate interests beyond those of the accused, . . . [including] important social interests relating to the integrity of the trial process."[19] He said judges must weigh those competing interests fully even if no one objects to closure. Judges should presume

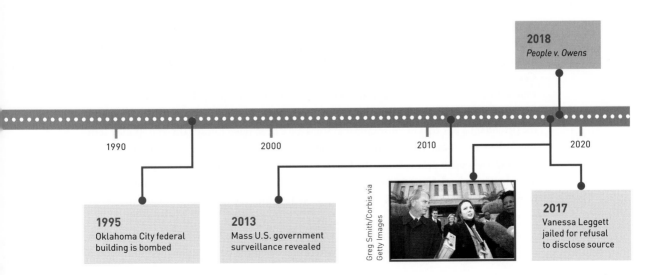

2018
People v. Owens

1990   2000   2010   2020

1995
Oklahoma City federal building is bombed

2013
Mass U.S. government surveillance revealed

Greg Smith/Corbis via Getty Images

2017
Vanessa Leggett jailed for refusal to disclose source

that court processes should be open and require the party seeking closure to show convincingly (1) the probability that publicity would infringe on the right to a fair trial, (2) the inadequacy of alternatives to closure and (3) the effectiveness of closure.

Presuming the Openness of Trials

In a series of cases beginning with *Gannett*, the U.S. Supreme Court largely adopted Justice Blackmun's concurring opinion that "[p]ublic confidence cannot long be maintained where important judicial decisions are made behind closed doors and then announced in conclusive terms to the public, with the record supporting the court's decision sealed from public view."[20] These Supreme Court decisions establish a qualified First Amendment right of public access to judicial proceedings when (a) the proceeding traditionally has been open to the public and (b) openness advances the proceeding's goals. This **experience and logic test**, as it is called, holds that closure of such proceedings should be a last resort used only when (a) essential (b) to avoid a substantial probability of harm (c) to some overriding interest where (d) no effective alternative exists.

experience and logic test
A doctrine that evaluates both the history of openness and the role it plays in ensuring the credibility of a judicial process to determine whether it is presumptively open.

In *Richmond Newspapers, Inc. v. Virginia*,[21] the Supreme Court held that the Sixth Amendment right to a public trial does not belong to the defendant alone. The Court said criminal trials are presumptively open and the First Amendment prohibits their closure without a full exploration of alternatives.[22] Chief Justice Warren Burger wrote that "absent an overriding interest articulated in findings, the trial of a criminal case must be open to the public."[23] Open criminal trials serve the public interest and advance the core First Amendment goal of protecting "freedom of communications on matters relating to the functioning of government."[24] Access to the criminal process enables citizens to evaluate government performance, to maintain faith in the judicial system and to seek catharsis for the trauma of crimes.[25]

The Supreme Court of South Dakota applied this reasoning to recognize a qualified First Amendment right of access to civil trials in that state.[26] The state high court found that the presumption of openness outweighed the agreement of all trial parties and the judge to close the trial about a popular tourist attraction. In addition, the desire to reduce prejudicial publicity does not justify gag orders in civil cases decided by a judge, the court said.

On the heels of *Richmond Newspapers, Inc.*, the U.S. Supreme Court ruled that states may not require closure of specific portions of criminal trials.[27] In *Globe Newspaper Co. v. Superior Court for Norfolk County*, the Supreme Court struck down a Virginia law that closed courtrooms during all testimony of any minor who was a sexual assault victim. The Court said the automatic closure of a sexual assault trial involving testimony by a juvenile defendant denied the defendant a fair trial because criminal trials have been open historically and "public scrutiny enhances the quality and safeguards the integrity" of trials.[28] To justify closure of such presumptively open proceedings, the Court said, the First Amendment requires the state to provide a "weighty" showing that (1) closure is necessary (2) to protect "a compelling government interest and (3) is narrowly tailored to serve that interest."[29] The decision must be made on a case-by-case basis.

A pair of cases involving the Press-Enterprise newspaper in California settled the application of the experience and logic test to determine when the constitutional presumption of

---

POINTS OF LAW

OPEN COURTS

According to the U.S. Supreme Court's rulings in two Press-Enterprise newspaper cases, court proceedings are presumptively open if experience and logic dictate openness. Accordingly, court processes are presumed to be open if

1. the proceeding traditionally has been open, and

2. openness advances the goals and functioning of the proceeding itself.[i]

---

openness applies. In those two cases, the U.S. Supreme Court applied the qualified right of access to transcripts of trial proceedings.[30] Under the *Press-Enterprise* decisions, court procedures and their associated records are presumptively open when (1) they "have historically been open to the press and general public" and (2) "public access plays a significant positive role in the functioning of the particular process in question."[31] The Supreme Court also ruled that the presumptive public right of access applied to both jury selection and preliminary hearings, which determine whether there is sufficient evidence to proceed to trial.[32] Eleven federal courts of appeals have extended the qualified right of access to other judicial records.[33]

The U.S. Supreme Court has held that the right of access to trials and trial records may be overcome by compelling "overriding interests." The Court has said "safeguarding the physical and psychological well-being of a minor" and protecting the right to a fair trial are overriding interests that may warrant narrowly tailored limits on public access.[34]

The Court said access to the hearings themselves, not simply to transcripts released later, is vital to ensure public confidence. Some particularly sensitive questions to potential jurors during jury selection, or voir dire, might raise privacy concerns sufficient to warrant closure. However, such closures must be narrowly tailored to protect only those matters that raise serious concerns. Some courts justify closed voir dire and juror anonymity, saying that access to jury selection and juror identity erodes the candor of potential jurors and harms an integral judicial process. In 2010, the Supreme Court's decision in *Presley v. Georgia* reiterated that "the public has a right to be present whether or not any party has asserted the right."[35] The Court reaffirmed that the Sixth Amendment right to a public trial applies to voir dire.[36] "Courts are obligated to take every reasonable measure to accommodate public attendance at criminal trials."[37]

Recent court rulings provide a glimpse into the procedures and standards by which the state of Colorado determined the openness of court proceedings related to the triple murders and capital sentence of Sir Mario Owens, excerpted at the end of the chapter.[38] Concurrent proceedings against Owens and two other defendants span more than a decade and presented the probability that information disclosed in one might prejudice the others.[39] For example, before the trials began and in response to defense requests to restrict pretrial publicity, the trial court found that the "nature" of the pending cases and of existing publicity demanded the court take steps to protect a fair trial process.[40]

The courts prohibited all trial participants, court personnel and others associated with trial attorneys from disclosing to the public any information or opinion that might prejudice the trial, including (1) prior criminal record, (2) defendants' statements, (3) defendants' results or refusal to participate in examinations, (4) identity or credibility of witnesses, (5) possibility of plea deals, (6) opinions of guilt or (7) predictions of outcomes. The order expressly forbid the release of any information not a part of the public court record, including any sealed records, *in camera* discussions or hearings held without the public present. The limits applied for 90 days prior to trial. The court also cautioned the attorneys to seal discovery information and to consider carefully what documents should or should not be made public. It allowed extrajudicial comment only on public records and trial proceedings to the extent they did not violate the above limits.

After the defendants were convicted and sentenced to death, they sought access to the prosecutor's files to support their claim that the prosecution had withheld evidence that mediated their crimes and might have reduced their sentences.[41] The trial court confirmed evidence of extensive prosecutorial misconduct but sealed all records relating to the motion for dismissal or disclosure because it ruled that the misconduct affected neither the verdict nor the death sentence.[42] The court sealed all transcripts, exhibits and actions in the challenge to the government's decision to execute the defendants.

In 2018, the Colorado Supreme Court affirmed a separate court order refusing to release witness identification and other information related to the defendants' challenge to their death-penalty sentences.[43] Some of the witnesses were in a witness protection program.[44] Without employing the two-part experience and logic test established in *Press-Enterprise*, the state supreme court held in *People v. Owens* that neither the state constitution nor the First Amendment guaranteed the defendants or news organization access to sealed records in the capital murder case.[45]

Despite saying that it would review the legal issue de novo, the Colorado Supreme Court summarily dismissed "constitutional arguments for mandatory disclosure of records sealed in this matter" in its two-page decision.[46] The court limited its analysis of federal court decisions to two decisions of the Tenth Circuit Court of Appeals and without mention of relevant U.S. Supreme Court rulings. Its limited analysis of its own state precedent on a right of access to court records also cited two cases. Without discussing the first,[47] the court dismissed its second cited precedent in three sentences, emphasizing that the earlier decision found "no absolute right to examine" records.[48] However, that earlier court decision held that a ban on disclosure "would raise serious questions of constitutional law involving freedom of the press and the separation of governmental power."[49] Despite the lack of an absolute right of access, the court decision in that earlier case ordered release of the records to avoid "such [constitutional] difficulty."[50]

In its 2018 decision in *People v. Owens*, the Colorado Supreme Court said that "while presumptive access to judicial proceedings is a right recognized under both the state and federal constitutions, neither the U.S. Supreme Court nor the Colorado Supreme Court has ever held that records filed with a court are treated the same way."[51] In 2019, the U.S. Supreme Court denied certiorari to review the decision.[52]

In 2019 in a high-profile defamation case arising from BuzzFeed reporting on Russian hacking into Democratic National Committee computers during the 2016 U.S. presidential campaign, a federal district court in Florida unsealed documents kept confidential pending the trial conclusion.[53] The judge dismissed as speculative arguments that disclosure would endanger some foreign individuals who provided evidence and taint the jury in any potential retrial.[54]

Broadcasting and Recording Court Proceedings

Although the First Amendment provides a right of access to courts, openness is not absolute. Judges may limit attendance, including the number of media present, and they may exclude recording devices to ensure decorum in their courts.

In 1981 in *Chandler v. Florida*, the U.S. Supreme Court said the right of access to public trials does not include presumptive access for cameras.[55] The Court noted that electronic coverage affects the trial process and participants in unpredictable ways. Although the Court no longer presumed cameras would be inherently prejudicial, it said individual states should determine whether to permit cameras in courtrooms; it said print coverage sufficiently protects the public interest in open trials. The U.S. Supreme Court does not permit still or video cameras during its oral arguments.

In 2016, the U.S. Judicial Conference ended a four-year national trial project[56] allowing cameras in civil proceedings in 14 federal district courts.[57] Despite majority support for cameras from participants, the national policy body continued the ban on recording in federal trial courts.[58] Federal Rule of Criminal Procedure 53 generally prohibits cameras in federal criminal trial courts, and federal policy bans televised civil proceedings. The 13 federal circuit courts of appeal each decide whether to allow televised or other news media coverage.

INTERNATIONAL LAW
INDIA'S SUPREME COURT ALLOWS (SECURITY) CAMERAS IN COURTS

A much-publicized 2017 initiative of the Supreme Court of India to install closed-circuit TV cameras in 24 courts across the country was intended to increase security, not public access to trials.[ii] The original order said the cameras would be installed to monitor the courts, the judges' chambers and "such important locations of the court complexes."[iii] However, it exempted the recordings from disclosure under India's Right to Information Act without permission of the court involved.

The order followed a petition from a man seeking to record the trial of his "matrimonial dispute to ensure a fair trial" and years of government pressure to record the courts to increase transparency. In 2017, India's Department of Justice said cameras would keep an eye on trial participants' conduct and provide electronic records of proceedings. The high court had resisted audio-video recordings and said "wider consultation" was needed to ensure that cameras did not imperil fair trials.

TABLE 8.1 ■ Cameras in Federal Courts	
U.S. Supreme Court	No cameras
U.S. Circuit Courts	Civil trials at judges' discretion; barred from criminal proceedings by Federal Rule of Criminal Procedure 53
U.S. District Courts	Cameras in some proceedings in Second and Ninth Circuit trial courts

Judges in federal appellate courts generally permit cameras in the courtroom at least some of the time. Court rules determine the specific conditions that apply when cameras are allowed. Video coverage of some district court proceedings is allowed in the Second and Ninth Circuits.[59]

In a narrow ruling, the U.S. Supreme Court prevented the broadcast of a federal district court trial on a California ballot measure banning same-sex marriage. The defense opposed the coverage. The Court said the trial court's decision to permit live streaming of the proceeding failed to "follow the appropriate procedures set forth in federal law,"[60] and public viewing might cause harassment of trial participants. The trial court struck down the voter-approved same-sex marriage ban.[61]

Cameras are allowed in some courtrooms some of the time in all 50 states.[62] Many states limit the number and location of cameras. Roughly 20 states are extremely permissive about cameras in the courtroom. In Florida, a judicially created presumption permits camera coverage of virtually all cases.[63] Massachusetts rules generally permit journalists to record or provide real-time transmission of court proceedings unless there is evidence of a "substantial likelihood of harm" to parties or a fair trial.[64] South Dakota rules allow broadcast coverage of trials with the consent of the judge and all parties, except for recording of jurors or proceedings when the jury is excluded.[65] The Illinois code of judicial conduct limits broadcasting of court proceedings to "the extent authorized by order of the Supreme Court"[66] and prohibits broadcasting or recording of any compelled witness testimony.[67]

States from Alabama to Utah limit camera coverage of trials based on the type of case or the ages of the witnesses. In nine states, judges may limit the number and location of cameras, prohibit recording of jurors or vulnerable witnesses or require pooled cameras. In another six states, including Delaware and Illinois, courts are virtually closed to cameras. To ensure they do not violate court rules, those wishing to record court proceedings must be familiar with the details of the laws in the states where they report.

Using Newer Technologies in the Courts

Studies of the effects on courts of accelerating news cycles, 24-hour news coverage, blogs, webcasts and other "new media" mechanisms suggest these media sensationalize rather than educate or inform the public.[68] A recent study said that the ubiquity of social media threatens the impartiality of the jury,[69] and courts concerned about their uncertain impact are not racing to embrace new media.[70] In one recent case, the Tennessee Supreme Court sent a first-degree murder conviction back for review by the trial court because the judge had failed to question a juror who had exchanged Facebook messages with one of the state's witnesses during jury deliberation.[71] Jury deliberations are sealed.

REAL WORLD LAW
MANAGING NEW MEDIA IN COURTS

A Media Law Resource Center model policy for electronic media in the court system makes the following recommendations:

1. People in courtrooms may use electronic devices to silently take notes and/or transmit texts without prior authorization from the presiding judge.

2. A judge may prohibit or restrict use of electronic devices if they pose any threat to safety or security or compromise the integrity of the proceeding.

3. Use of electronic devices by reporters, bloggers and other court observers to post online commentary during the proceedings is presumptively permitted so long as it meets the above conditions.[iv]

Led by California and Massachusetts, courts are integrating social media into their administrative offices, their courtrooms and their public outreach, but policies vary widely.[72] Courts use closed-circuit coverage of sensitive witnesses, and some stream or have blogs that offer instant public access. Some state and federal courts allow reporters to webcast and use social media posts to provide play-by-play coverage of unfolding trials.[73] One judge—overseeing a $1 million recording industry lawsuit against a Boston University student for copyright infringement through Kazaa—echoed the *Press-Enterprise* standard and said nothing in "life or logic" prevents live streaming of court proceedings, especially in a case involving digital technology.[74] However, the First Circuit Court of Appeals refused to allow webcasting of the appeal.[75] The Ninth Circuit Court of Appeals began live streaming en banc proceedings several years ago.[76]

The Michigan Supreme Court became the first to ban all electronic communication by jurors during trials, and a number of courts declared mistrials because of juror use of new media during trial.[77] Similar bans were spreading across the country,[78] and courts struggle to determine whether to use new media evidence in trials.

Accessing Court Records

The public right to access court records is grounded in common law and the U.S. and state constitutions. Decisions to close, or seal, court records generally are subject to the same constitutional limits as court closure. They are strongly disfavored and must pass the stringent *Press-Enterprise* experience and logic test.

In a case related to the event that ended the Nixon presidency, the U.S. Supreme Court limited the common law right of access to court records. The 1974 criminal trial of some aides to then-President Richard Nixon for the Watergate Hotel break-in and conspiracy relied on the former president's White House tape recordings as evidence. Federal law provides

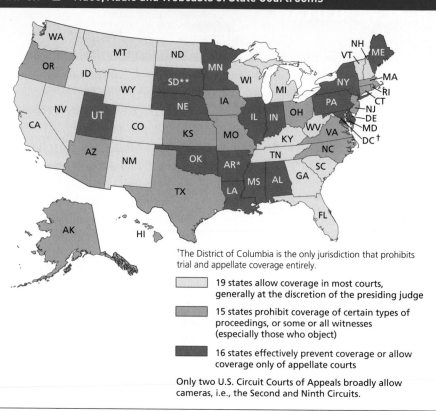

MAP 8.1 ■ Video, Audio and Webcasts of State Courtrooms

†The District of Columbia is the only jurisdiction that prohibits trial and appellate coverage entirely.

19 states allow coverage in most courts, generally at the discretion of the presiding judge

15 states prohibit coverage of certain types of proceedings, or some or all witnesses (especially those who object)

16 states effectively prevent coverage or allow coverage only of appellate courts

Only two U.S. Circuit Courts of Appeals broadly allow cameras, i.e., the Second and Ninth Circuits.

Source: Cameras in the Court: A State-by-State Guide, Nov. 15–26, 2012, rtdna.org/article/cameras_in_the_court_a_state_by_state_guide_updated#.Uielybx1Ets.

delayed public access to presidential records, including the Nixon tapes, but the district court denied media access to the tapes during the trial. It said broadcast of the tapes might prejudice defense appeals.

The court of appeals reversed. In *Nixon v. Warner Communications,* the Supreme Court held that courts are not required to provide access to all records in their custody, particularly when the records are available through alternative means.[79] The Court said the press had no First Amendment right to inspect or copy the tapes because the media have no rights of access superior to those of the general public.[80]

In 2019, the Eleventh Circuit Court of Appeals held that a common law right of access required the courts to release Alabama Department of Corrections records detailing the state's execution protocol.[81] The court said the state's legal injection procedure submitted—though not formally filed—with the court during litigation was a judicial record subject to disclosure "because it was submitted to the district court to resolve disputed substantive motions, . . . was discussed and analyzed by all parties in evidentiary hearings and arguments, and was unambiguously integral to the court's resolution" of the issue.[82] In addition, the state failed to show sufficient interests in secrecy to overcome the public's presumptive right of access. Court records that do not unduly harm due process or privacy rights should be open.

Both federal and state courts tend to require government to provide a specific showing of a compelling need to maintain the secrecy of presumptively open court records. In 2017, for example, the Ninth Circuit Court of Appeals upheld the secrecy of testimony related to a defendant's cooperation in providing information about organized drug smuggling into the United States.[83] The appeals court found that the risk of harm to the defendant's family outweighed the qualified First Amendment right of access to the criminal court records.

State court rules and policies generally determine the openness of court records. To limit harms to trial fairness and invasion of privacy, rules generally seal court records of information disclosed mandatorily or under discovery unless the material is presented in open court. States generally impose penalties on judicial employees who violate these rules. Three decades ago, the U.S. Supreme Court ruled in *Florida Star v. B.J.F.* that states may not punish media for publishing truthful information obtained legally from court files unless the penalty is "narrowly tailored to a state interest of the highest order."[84] (See Chapter 6 for a discussion of this case.)

After the "Undisclosed" blog, which reports on wrongful convictions, was denied the right to copy court recordings of a murder trial, the Georgia Supreme Court in 2017 held that the state law that provides public access to court records also provides a right to copy the record.[85] The state supreme court said the public's protected right to inspect is "not complete unless it includes the right to copy." However, the court refused to release the court clerk's recording of the trial. Because the recording had not been filed with the trial court, it was not a court record. In a footnote, however, the court said a trial recording *might* be disclosable if the official transcript failed to provide a full record of what occurred in open court.

Unclear judicial standards lead to wide disparities in the sealing of court records.[86] Although the U.S. Supreme Court has said access restrictions must be narrowly tailored to meet a compelling interest, few courts require detailed evidence to justify records closures. In Hawaii, the state supreme court struck down a trial court's sealing of "the entire legal file" in the prosecution of a Honolulu police officer charged with drug-related crimes.[87] The trial court said complete secrecy was needed to protect the ongoing investigation, but the Hawaii Supreme Court said a narrower secrecy ruling would be adequate and the state must provide a specific showing of a compelling need for nondisclosure.

A New York trial court unsealed records of a state legislator's extramarital affairs while he was awaiting sentencing for fraud, extortion and money laundering.[88] The court said disclosure threatened neither the defendant's privacy right nor his right to a fair trial in any potential retrial. Public access to the evidence submitted under seal advanced the public interest because the evidence itself is often "as important as the trial" in ensuring public confidence in judicial procedures, the court said. The court order required the redaction of the identity of two Jane Does to preserve their legitimate privacy interest.

In 2018, a Pennsylvania appeals court ordered the unsealing of all trial court records connected to the sexual assault proceedings against former Pennsylvania State University assistant football coach Jerry Sandusky.[89] The trial court refused to unseal the records that related to grand jury testimony, but the appeals court held that there was "no question" that the records were covered by both a common law and First Amendment right of access.

Former Penn State assistant football coach Jerry Sandusky leaves the Pennsylvania courthouse where he was sentenced for child sexual abuse in 2012.

Some courts exclude sealed cases from their dockets and electronic case management systems, effectively preventing challenges to closure or even knowledge that the cases exist. Where state open-records laws do apply, these rules also vary. In Indiana, the open-records law covers all court records not closed by a specific exemption.[90] An Ohio Supreme Court ruling said neither the constitution nor the state's open-records law prevented a judge from sealing an entire court record weeks after the defendant was acquitted of criminal charges.[91] The court said that "limit[ing] the life of a particular record" did not harm the public's right to know. Washington's broad Public Records Act excludes the courts.[92]

Electronically Accessing Court Records

Numerous national court and judicial organizations have worked to facilitate online public access to court records while protecting important interests in privacy.[93] Both the National Center for State Courts and the Justice Management Institute advocated that court records be posted online and be presumptively open.

The Public Access to Court Electronic Records site (www.pacer.gov) provides online access to federal court records, but electronic access to state court records is "remarkably disparate."[94] State rules vary broadly on which records are online and for what purposes and to whom they are open. For example, about half of Florida circuit and county courts have their court records online.[95] Minnesota maintains a searchable online database of all public information on its courts that includes some court records.[96] Most states provide some access to civil and family law case records online.[97] Recent decisions in Maine, Oklahoma and Virginia increased public access to online court records.[98] Some states' online access systems are free and comprehensive; many others charge fees.

Electronic access to public records has increased fears about how easily searchable data compilations alter the nature and extent of access to courts. Many states limit access to records containing sensitive information, such as the financial records or addresses of individuals, especially when it is aggregated online.[99] Information gatherers wanting detailed information on state laws on access to court records on- and offline may find it through the National Center for State Courts.[100]

In a foundational decision in 1989, long before online access to court records was common, the Supreme Court ruled in *U.S. Department of Justice v. Reporters Committee for Freedom of the Press* that federal law did not allow journalists access to an FBI electronic compilation of rap (arrest) sheets.[101] The reporter wanted to compile the background of a suspected mobster, but the Court said access to the aggregated information posed an impermissible threat to individual privacy.

A Virginia Supreme Court ruling in 2017 held that the state Freedom of Information Act similarly required a newspaper to seek access to court records from each court jurisdiction rather than from the state's court-records database.[102] The question before the court was about the source of disclosure, "not whether [the] records should be made public," because the records were unquestionably covered by the state open-records act. However, the court concluded that access could be obtained only from the designated records custodians, which the law established to be the clerk of each court jurisdiction.

State court rules may also affect electronic access. For example, the Minnesota court records committee suggests that large fees be charged for court databases in order to make money.[103] A Washington state court rule requires people who request criminal conviction data to agree to use the information responsibly.[104] The uneven and fast-shifting pattern of electronic access to court records requires those seeking records to know their state rules and procedures.

ADVANCING FAIRNESS IN TRIALS

Potential jurors do not live in a vacuum. Like everyone, they swim daily in a sea of crime coverage. The U.S. Supreme Court recognized the potential harms media publicity might cause to fair trials in the early days of television. More than 50 years ago in *Estes v. Texas*, the Supreme Court ruled that televised coverage of the criminal trial of a Texas financier charged with a multimillion-dollar con was inherently prejudicial.[105]

A huge, highly publicized national investigation preceded the case, with the financier appearing on the cover of Time magazine in 1962. A Texas newspaper editor won the 1963 Pulitzer Prize for bringing the fraud "to national attention with resultant investigation, prosecution and conviction of [Billie Sol] Estes."[106] Despite defense requests to ban cumbersome television cameras in those early days of TV from the court, cameras and reporters swarmed the trial where Estes was convicted of conspiracy and fraud.

On appeal, the U.S. Supreme Court found that intensive broadcast coverage prior to the trial *automatically* altered juror perceptions of the case and created prejudice and a form of harassment of the defendant. While the media play an important role in "informing the citizenry of public events and occurrences, including court proceedings," the Court said media had no independent or greater right of access to trials than anyone else.[107] Moreover, facts demonstrated that television crews caused sufficient disruption to the trial to undermine due process, the search for truth and a just outcome.

Banning cameras did not harm press coverage because "[t]he right of the communications media to comment on court proceedings does not bring with it the right to inject themselves into the fabric of the trial process to alter the purpose of that process," wrote Justice Marshall Harlan in a concurring opinion.[108] The *Estes* decision did not impose a blanket ban on television coverage, especially if and when it became so commonplace that it seemed vital to the public's right to know.[109] Instead, the Court said judges must take steps to reduce the significant potential harms of publicity on trials.

The Court later rejected the assumption that all broadcast coverage of trials is inevitably prejudicial,[110] but it continued to emphasize that judges must ensure that media publicity does not undermine trial fairness. The year after *Estes*, the Supreme Court overturned a murder

REAL WORLD LAW
DOES PUBLICITY BIAS JURORS?

Studies do not support the claim that pretrial publicity regularly alters the outcome of a trial.[v] Pretrial publicity affects verdicts only when

- jurors are exposed to heavy pretrial publicity,

- evidence in court does not point convincingly to a clear verdict,

- information provided by the media seems more convincing or reliable than the evidence in court,

- the media consistently lean toward one verdict and

- all the remedies available to the court fail at the same time.

conviction when a judge allowed extensive pretrial and trial publicity to turn the proceedings into a "Roman holiday."[111] The case of *Sheppard v. Maxwell* reviewed the conviction of prominent Cleveland physician Sam Sheppard for the beating death of his wife. Dr. Sheppard said a stranger had broken into their home, knocked him unconscious and committed the crime.

The media frenzy began the day of the crime and pervaded every aspect of what was called "the trial of the century."[112] Months before the trial, a televised five-hour inquest examined the defendant without counsel before hundreds of spectators, and media published juror names and addresses weeks prior to the trial. Media practically overtook the small courtroom during the trial, broadcast live coverage and printed verbatim transcripts. The jury was not sequestered, and the judge said he could not restrict dissemination of prejudicial information by the media. The jury deliberated five days before handing down a conviction. The court sentenced Sheppard to life imprisonment.

The U.S. Supreme Court overturned his conviction, concluding that intense and prejudicial press coverage prevented a fair trial.[113] The Court said judges must protect fair trials by controlling the trial process and participants, including the media. The Court acknowledged the important role of free press in a democracy and in the administration of justice. However, the Court said the press has no right to inflame the minds of jurors, jeopardize trial fairness or make a mockery of judicial process. After 10 years in jail, Sheppard was retried and found not guilty.

While limited press coverage may coexist with a fair trial, the Court said "massive and pervasive" coverage that reaches the jurors and permeates the trial may be *presumed* to be prejudicial when "the totality of circumstances" presents the likelihood of prejudice.[114] The *Sheppard* Court said trial judges must supervise their courtrooms carefully and use the many narrowly tailored measures they have available to guarantee a fair trial.[115] It encouraged courts to insulate witnesses, limit comments outside of the courtroom by trial participants and government employees, and impose rules on media behavior inside the court.[116] The Court recommended the following measures:

1. **Continuance,** or delay, of the trial until publicity has subsided

2. Change of the venue, or location, of the trial to avoid areas permeated by media coverage

3. **Sequestration,** or isolation, of the jury from the public

4. Extensive voir dire, or questioning, of potential jurors to identify prejudice

5. **Gag orders** on participants to limit discussion of the case outside the courtroom

6. Protection of potential witnesses from outside influences

7. Instructions, or **admonitions,** to the jury to avoid prejudicial influences and to set aside any preconceptions they may have

8. Retrial if the jury or the judicial process has been contaminated by media coverage

9. Limitations on press attendance, through measures such as pool reporting, to reduce the impact of their presence on jurors and witnesses

Following *Sheppard*

The *Sheppard* ruling was applauded for its protection of defendants' rights and criticized for prompting judges to limit the openness of judicial proceedings. Judges apply the measures suggested by the Supreme Court in *Sheppard* to prevent or correct prejudice in the jury by establishing where and how the jury is chosen, as well as where and when the trial takes place, and by limiting the amount of speech freedom jury members and other trial participants have during the trial.

In one case, media were barred from a pretrial hearing in Miami involving four men accused of the murder of Washington Redskins star Sean Taylor.[117] The judge agreed with defense attorneys that media coverage of the hearing on the admissibility of alleged confessions might prejudice prospective jurors. Attorneys for the Miami Herald and Post-Newsweek unsuccessfully argued that Miami's juror pool was large enough to find unbiased jurors even if the admissions were publicized.

Selecting Jurors

When a court wants to select a jury for a trial, the clerk of court selects names at random from a list, such as adult licensed drivers or registered voters, in the county where the trial will be held. The location of the pool of jurors is called the venire. Each potential juror receives a **summons** to appear in court.

The judge and/or attorneys for both sides question members of the jury pool in what is called voir dire. Public relations specialists may help identify favorable jurors. The voir dire process allows either side to pose a **for-cause challenge** to a potential juror if the individual's responses suggest a prejudice relevant to the case. Juror prejudice may not be assumed simply because of a juror's race or gender.[118] An impartial juror does not need to be completely uninformed about the case. Impartial jurors instead must persuade the court that they have

continuance
Postponement of a trial to a later time.

sequestration
The isolation of jurors to avoid prejudice from publicity in a sensational trial.

gag orders
A nonlegal term used to describe court restraining orders that prohibit publication or discussion of specific materials.

admonitions
Judges' instructions to jurors warning them to avoid potentially prejudicial communications.

summons
A notice asking an individual to appear at a court. Potential jurors receive such a summons.

for-cause challenge
In the context of jury selection, the ability of attorneys to remove a potential juror for a reason the law finds sufficient, as opposed to a peremptory challenge.

no fixed opinion of the guilt or innocence of the defendant.[119] They will give the facts full and unbiased consideration and reach a verdict based solely on the evidence presented in court. A limited number of peremptory challenges enable attorneys to remove potential jurors without any explanation. The selected jurors then are **impaneled** and sworn in.

In a Kentucky case that received extensive media coverage and social media debate, the state supreme court remanded a man's conviction for killing a young girl while driving impaired. The appeal involved a seated juror who lied during voir dire about being a Facebook "friend" with the victim's mother.[120] Reviewing only the issue of whether the dishonest voir dire response created "reversible error" in due process, the high court said "'friendships' on Facebook and other similar social networking websites do not *necessarily* carry the same weight as true friendships or relationships in the community" and do not automatically create impermissible bias.[121]

Rehearing the case, the lower court found the juror's lie inadvertent and allowed the conviction to stand. On review of the entire trial record, the Kentucky Supreme Court reversed on the grounds that for-cause release of 50 potential jurors had exhausted the entire jury pool. One seated juror knew the defendant had a history of substance abuse and reckless behavior.[122] The state supreme court admonished lower courts that "trial judges are possessed of great authority to enlarge jury panels or change venues. They don't have to imperil their cases with such miserly voir dire practices."[123]

Instructing the Jury

Judges routinely issue admonitions, or instructions and warnings, to jurors to tell them to avoid potential prejudice. Typical admonitions tell jurors not to view news coverage and not to discuss the case among themselves or with others prior to jury deliberations. The judge in a recent murder and child-abuse case refused to find prejudice despite a juror's almost daily tweets about the case throughout the trial.[124] During the second week of the trial, one tweet read: "In my book, everybody's guilty until proven innocent."[125] Although the judge acknowledged the juror's use of Twitter violated his instructions, he refused to grant a retrial. The appellate court found the lower court's review of the juror's alleged misconduct reasonable and affirmed the trial court's conclusion.[126]

Judges also give instructions to the jury prior to deliberation. These instructions generally outline the applicable law and remind jurors of their duty to reach a verdict based only on the evidence presented in court.

Sequestering the Jury

Sometimes, though rarely, a judge will sequester, or isolate, a jury during a trial and prohibit jurors from having unsupervised contact with anyone outside of court. Sequestration may protect trial fairness, but it may alter juror attitudes and the outcome of the trial.

Relocating the Trial

Although the Sixth Amendment protects a criminal defendant's right to a trial in the location where the crime occurred, either the prosecution or the defense may request a change of venue, or location. If media coverage creates a substantial likelihood of harming a fair trial, judges may order an expensive change of venue, but they rarely do.

For example, when selection of unbiased jurors in the Boston Marathon bombing trial of Dzhokhar Tsarnaev proved difficult, the judge three times denied defense requests to move the trial out of Boston.[127] Although almost 70 percent of nearly 1,400 prospective jurors identified a personal connection to the case and belief in the defendant's guilt, the First Circuit Court of Appeals affirmed the judge's decision that the defense failed to demonstrate that irreparable harm would occur if the trial were not moved.[128]

Delaying the Trial

In 2016, the U.S. Supreme Court ruled that the Sixth Amendment right to a speedy trial does not require speedy sentencing.[129] The case involved a man who waited in jail for more than 14 months for sentencing. He appealed his sentence of seven years in prison, arguing that the sentencing delay was unconstitutional. The Supreme Court disagreed. Its short, unanimous ruling said the "heart" of the Sixth Amendment is the desire to protect the "presumption of innocence and therefore loses force upon conviction."[130]

Criminal defendants may waive their Sixth Amendment right to a speedy trial. Defendants and their attorneys may seek a delay, or continuance, to try to reduce the prejudicial impact of publicity. The prosecution may oppose a continuance because postponements often reduce the availability and recall of witnesses.[131]

In 2015, a Delaware trial court found that court-requested delays of nearly three years between an arrest for drunk driving and the trial unfairly prejudiced a defendant.[132] "When a trial is delayed, a defendant is presumed to be prejudiced to some degree. . . . [Although] 'time's erosion of exculpatory evidence and testimony can rarely be shown,' it is nonetheless the 'most serious' type of prejudice."[133]

Making Jurors Anonymous

A tradition of openly identifying members of juries reaches back to colonial days.[134] Anonymous juries once were extremely rare and considered "a drastic measure"[135] but became commonplace late in the 20th century.[136] Today, the question of a constitutional or common law right of access to juror information remains unsettled. Two federal appellate courts have held that the public has a First Amendment right to timely access to juror names in a criminal proceeding,[137] but only the Tenth Circuit Court of Appeals has failed to approve the use of anonymous juries.[138]

Some courts refuse to release the names and identities of jurors in high-profile cases or in cases where jurors may legitimately be concerned for their personal safety.[139] In 2018, for example, the federal judge overseeing the highly publicized fraud trial of Paul Manafort, former campaign chair for President Donald Trump, refused to release the identities of jurors. Juror "peace and safety" as well as "the integrity of the process" of jury deliberation required protection of jurors' personal information, the judge said, but jurors were free to initiate contact with media if they wished.[140] The jury found Manafort guilty on eight of 18 counts charged.

In contrast, the Pennsylvania court hearing sexual assault charges against Bill Cosby said the public had a constitutional right of access to juror names.[141] However, the court withheld the information for three weeks after Cosby was found guilty "to provide a cooling off period and to permit the jurors to return to their private lives."

Some courts justify juror anonymity on grounds that release of personal information violates jurors' privacy interests. Although criminal defense attorneys argue that juror anonymity increases juror anxiety and perception that the defendant is guilty, few courts accept that anonymous juries are inherently prejudicial. In Texas, the criminal code requires anonymous juries unless there is a showing that openness serves the public good.[142]

Limiting Speech Outside of Court

Judges tend to believe that when government and court officials—police and attorneys, for example—publicly discuss ongoing trials, their speech influences jurors' perceptions of witnesses' guilt or innocence. In *Sheppard*, the Supreme Court encouraged judges to use **restraining orders**, or gag orders, to prevent trial participants from discussing potentially prejudicial information outside the courtroom.

restraining order
A court order forbidding an individual or group of individuals from doing a specified act until a hearing can be conducted.

Some 25 years ago, the U.S. Supreme Court ruled in *Mu'Min v. Virginia* that restraining attorneys' speech outside the courtroom during a trial did not violate the First Amendment.[143] The Court reasoned that insiders to a vital government process have special access to sensitive information and unique power to derail justice. Consequently, courts may control their trial-related speech when it poses a "substantial likelihood" of jeopardizing a fair trial.[144]

Gag orders on trial participants generally are upheld if (1) narrowly drawn and (2) supported by evidence that unfettered speech poses a substantial likelihood of jeopardizing a fair trial and (3) by careful consideration of alternatives. Narrowly drawn restraining orders end as soon as the threat to the trial process passes.[145] A different test applies to gag orders on the media.

In high-profile cases, judges concerned about prejudicial pretrial publicity may issue sweeping gag orders on all trial participants. Thus, the judge in the murder trial of the Aurora, Colo., theater shooter banned all parties from disseminating any information about the case.[146] Despite prominent opposition to the ban,[147] the judge let it stand throughout the trial.[148]

In 2016, the Michigan Supreme Court lifted a judge's sweeping gag order in the criminal corruption trial of two government officials.[149] The order prevented "all potential trial participants from making any extra judicial statements regarding this case to members of the media."[150] Although the appeals court upheld the order and said it "placed no direct restraint of any kind on the free press,"[151] the state supreme court vacated the order as an impermissible prior restraint.

In 2015, the U.S. Court of Appeals for the Fourth Circuit vacated[152] a West Virginia judge's "extensive" ban on comments to the media about a criminal trial related to the 2010 Upper Big Branch Mine disaster that killed 29 miners.[153] The trial judge said the ban "restricting the parties and potential trial participants' statements to the press at the outset helps preserve the defendant's right to a fair and just tribunal."[154] But the Fourth Circuit required the showing set out in the *Press-Enterprise* decision that "specific findings . . . demonstrat[e] that, first, there is a substantial probability that the defendant's right to a fair trial will be prejudiced by publicity

REAL WORLD LAW
JUDICIAL IMPARTIALITY AND "FRIENDS" OF THE COURT

In recent years, courts have disagreed on whether Facebook "friendships" pose a risk of prejudice to a fair trial. One appeals court in Florida required a judge in a criminal case to recuse himself because he was a Facebook "friend" of the prosecutor.[vi] The court said:

> Judges do not have the unfettered social freedom of teenagers. . . . Maintenance of

the appearance of impartiality requires the avoidance of entanglements and relationships that compromise that appearance.[vii]

In contrast, a federal district court in Pennsylvania refused to put any weight on Facebook relationships because "'Friendships' on Facebook may be as fleeting as the flick of a delete button."[viii]

that closure would prevent and, second, reasonable alternatives to closure cannot adequately protect the defendant's fair trial rights."[155]

Judging Impartially

Sometimes the fairness of the judge is cast into doubt. In *Sheppard*, the U.S. Supreme Court said the fact that both the judge and the prosecutor were running for election during the trial posed the potential for prejudice.[156] The Supreme Court also has ruled that the Constitution requires judges to disqualify or recuse themselves from hearing a case when a risk of prejudice exists because "a person with a personal stake [in the case outcome] . . . had a significant and disproportionate influence" in the judge's election or appointment to the bench.[157] But the Supreme Court struck down a Minnesota state law that banned judges from campaigning on issues that might come before their court.[158] The Court said the law violated the First Amendment by directly limiting speech vital to elections.[159]

BALANCING INTERESTS

Decades ago, the U.S. Supreme Court said for centuries it has been a "fundamental maxim that the public has a right to every man's evidence."[160] While law enforcement is responsible for identifying relevant evidence, judges must determine which evidence may be admitted into court. Judges may use their power to require individuals to testify or to produce relevant evidence. It is unequivocally "the obligation of all citizens to give relevant testimony with respect to criminal conduct," the Court said.[161]

Requiring Evidence

Many argue that the First Amendment's recognition of the value of newsgathering should protect journalists from forced disclosure of information in court. This rationale holds that

REAL WORLD LAW
YOUR DATA ARE NOT SAFE FROM GOVERNMENT (SP)EYES

A long legal battle between the U.S. Department of Justice and Apple over access to the iPhone used by one of the shooters in a terrorist attack ended when the DOJ paid hackers to break into Apple's encrypted system. A DOJ official said the break-in was appropriate "on both national security and on law enforcement grounds because of the potential use [of encryption] by terrorists and other national security concerns" to thwart government law enforcement.[ix]

In another case, the FBI subpoenaed and gagged Open Whisper Systems to obtain access to information in iPhones protected by the software developer's encryption system, Signal, which is used by many people in the media.[x] Major media and tech industry players joined a lawsuit by Microsoft that said bans on discussion of governmental snooping into customers' information violated the First Amendment.[xi] Microsoft said the government had subpoenaed its customer data 5,600 times in 18 months, with almost half of the requests accompanied by gag orders. Most of the gags never expire.

reporter's privilege
The concept that reporters may keep information such as source identity confidential. The rationale is that the reporter–source relationship is similar to doctor–patient and lawyer–client relationships.

a requirement to testify infringes the First Amendment guarantee of freedom of the press, which provides a **reporter's privilege** not to divulge confidential information. The U.S. Supreme Court has recognized only a limited constitutional protection for reporter confidentiality. Courts tend to reason that justice often depends on evidence that sometimes is held by journalists.

Courts provide search warrants and subpoenas to collect evidence and ensure that it is presented in court. A search warrant permits law enforcement officers to search a specified place for particular items or people. The Fourth Amendment to the U.S. Constitution requires that searches be conducted reasonably. To receive a search warrant, investigators must show probable cause that the items or people are vital to the investigation and are likely to be found in the specified location. Search warrants demand immediate compliance. There is no legal way to delay, resist or prevent a legally warranted search. Some national security mechanisms allow searches and seizures without a warrant or with a secret warrant.[162]

A search warrant implies greater urgency than a subpoena. Subpoenas do not require on-the-spot compliance. They order the person to appear at a future judicial proceeding. In the interim, the recipient can file a motion to quash, or vacate, the subpoena. Concern that evidence might be destroyed by the lapse between service of a subpoena and the date of the required court appearance is one justification for search warrants.

Forty years ago, the U.S. Supreme Court ruled directly on the amount of protection the First Amendment provides from searches of newsrooms.[163] Investigators with a search warrant sought unpublished photographs of a campus demonstration taken by the Stanford University student newspaper staff. The Stanford Daily sued the police, claiming the search violated the newspaper's First and Fourth Amendment rights. The Fourth Amendment protects against unreasonable searches and seizures.

Because no one at the newspaper was suspected of a crime, the trial judge ruled that the search warrant was unreasonable unless government could show that a subpoena was impractical. The appellate court agreed. The court's decision reasoned that police search of newsrooms would disrupt timely publication, dry up confidential sources, deter reporters from keeping records and chill the dissemination of news.

In *Zurcher v. Stanford Daily*, the U.S. Supreme Court rejected this reasoning and ruled that newsrooms are entitled to no special treatment beyond that afforded any citizen.[164] The Court said that nothing in the Fourth Amendment restricted searches of newsrooms. Implicitly, the ruling suggested that nothing in the First Amendment did either.

Penalizing Failure to Disclose

As professional collectors of news and information, journalists may be more likely than most to have information of importance to a court.[165] If reporters refuse to testify and disclose information sought under subpoena, judges may use their power of contempt to punish them.[166] A finding of criminal contempt results in a fixed jail term and/or fine. Under civil contempt, journalists are jailed until they comply with the order to disclose or until the matter is resolved. Contempt citations must be obeyed.

When former New York Times reporter Judith Miller refused to comply with a subpoena to testify before a grand jury about her knowledge of a White House leak that outed an undercover CIA agent, she was cited with contempt and spent 85 days in jail.[167] The prosecutor argued that "journalists are not entitled to promise complete confidentiality—no one in America is."[168] The U.S. Supreme Court rejected her appeal.[169] Miller was released from jail and testified after her source relieved her of her confidentiality agreement.[170]

In 2019, former Army intelligence analyst Chelsea Manning was jailed for contempt for refusal to testify in an ongoing grand jury investigation of WikiLeaks.[171] The Fourth Circuit Court of Appeals upheld Manning's contempt charge and denied bail for failure to comply with a subpoena to testify about her role in disclosing more than half a million classified and sensitive military and diplomatic documents to the public via WikiLeaks.[172] Manning testified at length in 2013 during her court martial for violating the Espionage Act, and her attorneys argued that she had "no further knowledge of any relevant people or events." The court said she would remain in jail until she testified or the grand jury concluded.

In 2017, the Ninth Circuit Court of Appeals required Glassdoor to respond to a federal grand jury subpoena and provide the names of anonymous users who criticized their employer, a federal contractor under investigation.[173] Glassdoor argued that the subpoena violated users' First Amendment rights and should be reviewed under strict scrutiny, but the Ninth Circuit applied the *Branzburg* standard that subpoenas issued as part of a "good faith" grand jury investigation do not warrant privilege.[174] While the subpoenas did implicate the users' right to speak anonymously, the Ninth Circuit said that right does not cloak individuals from their duty to testify before an ongoing grand jury investigation.

Also in 2017, a federal district court upheld a subpoena for Twitter subscriber data on one of three anonymous users implicated in cyberharassment of an FBI agent.[175] Applying *Branzburg*, the court said the government's compelling interest in investigating the harassment

POINTS OF LAW

CONTEMPT OF COURT

Judges have broad, discretionary power to cite individuals with contempt of court for failure to obey a court order or any misconduct that interferes with the court. This power is limited by some state laws and the First Amendment.[xii]

- **Civil contempt** citations may compel an individual to do something, such as name a source or turn over notes. Civil contempt sometimes is called "indirect contempt" because the instigating event generally occurs outside the direct supervision of the judge.

- **Criminal contempt** is conduct in or near the court that obstructs court proceedings. Because it generally interferes directly with court proceedings, it sometimes is called "direct contempt."

Under the First Amendment, judges may issue contempt citations against negative news coverage only if the comments intimidate jurors or undermine the fairness of the trial. Individuals given lengthy jail terms for contempt have a right to a jury trial.[xiii]

outweighed the harm to the right to speak anonymously for the one subscriber who tweeted directly with the alleged harasser. The court said this user demonstrated the "substantial relationship" to the crime needed to uphold a subpoena.

Protecting Juveniles

Courts generally limit access to legal proceedings involving juveniles to advance the government's substantial interest in reducing trauma that might impede rehabilitation and healing of juvenile victims, defendants and witnesses. The U.S. Supreme Court has said that historically confidential juvenile processes reduce the stigmatization of minors.[176] Fifty years ago, the Supreme Court said juvenile court procedures must ensure that minors receive the full "reach of constitutional guarantees applicable to adults."[177] The Court also held that juvenile defendants have the right to counsel and notice.[178]

Federal law permits, but does not require, closure of juvenile proceedings and records on a case-by-case basis. Most federal courts do not consider juvenile proceedings to be presumptively open, and about a third of the states presume that juvenile proceedings are closed while another third provide a broad right of public access to juvenile courts.[179] Georgia and Los Angeles County, for example, have open juvenile courts, and in 2014, Kentucky initiated a pilot project to explore whether juvenile courts should be presumptively open.[180] Washington state presumes that juvenile proceedings will be open.

All states allow certain juveniles to be treated as adults within the justice system, but Maryland, New Jersey and Wisconsin may prohibit the media from revealing the identity of a juvenile. Communicators who legally obtain sealed information about juveniles may publish the information without fear of punishment. A recent Massachusetts Supreme Court decision confirmed that state courts cannot ban media from releasing the legally obtained name of a minor.[181] Most states bar cameras from juvenile courts.[182]

In Massachusetts (where the law makes juvenile murder trials presumptively open, while other juvenile proceedings are presumptively closed), a trial judge denied a 14-year-old murder suspect's motion to seal the highly prejudicial video recording and transcript of his police interview.[183] The court said the records were presumptively open once entered into evidence. Police had interviewed the teen alone. He received life in prison for the rape and murder of a math teacher.[184]

Jailed for more than five months for refusal to disclose her sources to a grand jury, aspiring crime writer Vanessa Leggett later received the PEN First Amendment Award for her protection of freedom of the press.

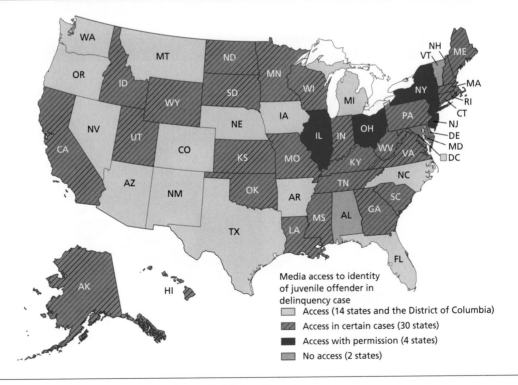

MAP 8.2 ■ State-by-State Media Access to Juvenile Offender Identities

Media access to identity of juvenile offender in delinquency case
- Access (14 states and the District of Columbia)
- Access in certain cases (30 states)
- Access with permission (4 states)
- No access (2 states)

Source: NCJJ/OJJPD Juvenile Offenders and Victims: 2006 National Report.

To determine the applicable right of access to juvenile proceedings, individuals should consult state laws and reports on juvenile justice from the Reporters Committee for Freedom of the Press and the National Center for Juvenile Justice.[185] Connecticut, Illinois, Massachusetts and Vermont in 2017 considered raising the juvenile court age to 21.[186]

Protecting Sexual Assault Victims

In cases of sexual assault, all the states and the District of Columbia have a rape shield law to protect the alleged victim from questions that might prejudice jurors against the victim.[187] Except for Mississippi, every state has a statute excluding evidence of the complaining witness's past sexual activity.[188] Some states also shield the victim's identity and other personal information.[189]

The Sixth Circuit Court of Appeals recently rejected a challenge to Michigan's rape shield law.[190] The court ruled that the Sixth Amendment permitted limits on the extent and nature of the defendant's cross-examination of his minor nephew, the molestation victim who experienced a nervous breakdown.

Protecting State Secrets and National Security

Sixty-seven years ago, the U.S. Supreme Court granted the executive branch power to keep secret—with little judicial review—information that it said would present a "reasonable

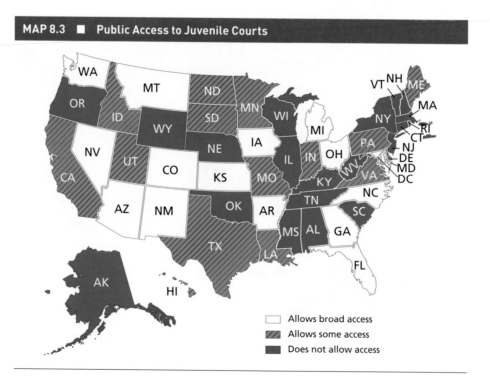

MAP 8.3 ■ Public Access to Juvenile Courts

Legend:
- Allows broad access
- Allows some access
- Does not allow access

danger" to national security.[191] One study found that administrations since the Sept. 11, 2001, terrorist attack have "aggressively used the 'state secrets' privilege, insisting that entire cases could be exempt from judicial review."[192] Another study said administrations use the power to declare "state secrets" to thwart open judicial proceedings and even prevent cases from going to trial.[193]

Forty years ago, the Foreign Intelligence Surveillance Act established broad government power to conduct covert physical and electronic surveillance of foreign nationals and countries suspected of espionage.[194] Cases involving the act are heard in special FISA courts where proceedings and records are secret. National security concerns justify the secrecy of virtually all FISA court actions. The courts are presumptively closed, and the court docket is "super-sealed" to hide evidence of even the existence of the case.[195] In 2015, the U.S. Supreme Court declined to review a sweeping ban on public release of information from the secret Foreign Intelligence Surveillance Court trials of alleged terrorists.[196]

A case outside the FISA courts involved the federal government's extraordinary rendition program that covertly transferred individuals out of the United States for detention and interrogation on foreign soil. In its review of the government's asserted national security privilege, the Ninth Circuit Court of Appeals held that the privilege may (1) completely bar lawsuits in which "the very subject matter of the action" is highly threatening to national security or (2) require the exclusion of all privileged evidence.[197] To exclude evidence rather than dismiss a trial requires courts to determine that only "some of the matters [government] seeks to protect from disclosure in th[e] litigation are valid state secrets."[198] The Ninth Circuit dismissed the case, holding that evidence about government abduction and torture was privileged and there was no way to litigate the case "without creating an unjustifiable risk of divulging state secrets."[199]

In 2017, the D.C. Circuit Court of Appeals reversed a trial court ruling that had unsealed videotape of government treatment of a Guantanamo Bay detainee on hunger strike.[200] The government had submitted the classified tape in the detainee's civil challenge to forced feeding. The three circuit court judges disagreed on whether any qualified First Amendment right of access applied to the videotape, but they agreed unanimously that the government's interest in secrecy outweighed any such right.

In another case, the Ninth Circuit Court of Appeals upheld the Obama administration's use of national security secrets to shield details of the Bush administration's extraordinary rendition program during a criminal prosecution of a Boeing subsidiary for removing alleged terrorists from the United States.[201]

Closing Courts

In *Press-Enterprise I* and *II*, the U.S. Supreme Court said, "The presumption of openness may be overcome only by an overriding interest based on findings that closure is essential to preserve higher values and is narrowly tailored to serve that interest."[202] *Press-Enterprise II* established that general privacy concerns alone do not justify closing a courtroom or voir dire. Anyone seeking to close a presumptively open hearing must show that (1) the openness has a "substantial probability" of significantly threatening the fair trial process and (2) closure is a last resort "essential" to preserving fair trial rights.[203] Before closing a courtroom, judges must determine that facts demonstrate *all* of the following:

- Openness poses a substantial threat to a fair proceeding.

- No alternative exists that would effectively eliminate the threat to fairness.

- Closure will effectively eliminate the threat.

- Closure will be narrowly tailored to protect maximum public access to the judicial process.

Before closing any or all of a trial, judges must permit interested parties and the public to raise objections.

Despite this high standard, courts continue to close their doors and seal their records. Courts generally accept the commonsense notion that media coverage has an effect on the fairness of a trial.[204] Judges sometimes close trials of their own accord, called *sua sponte*, without hearings or findings of prejudice.[205] Studies, however, show that the effects of media coverage appear to be highly specific and inconsistent.[206]

When the trial judge banned media from voir dire in the fraud trial of home décor guru Martha Stewart, the Second Circuit Court of Appeals ruled the judge's actions unconstitutional. "The mere fact of intense media coverage of a celebrity defendant, without further compelling justification, is simply not enough to justify closure."[207]

Courts sometimes close trials and records in business cases that involve trade secrets and proprietary information. When the parties settled the "landmark monopolization case of the 21st Century"[208] between computer industry giant Intel and its chief competitor, Advanced Micro Devices, media argued that the court's seal improperly shielded Intel business practices from public scrutiny.[209] The case settled, ending the media request to unseal "hundreds of millions of pages of documentation" held in the court's records.[210] In a related case heard in the European Union, the U.S. Supreme Court ordered disclosure to AMD of some 600,000 pages of Intel records.[211]

POINTS OF LAW

THE *PRESS-ENTERPRISE* TEST FOR COURT CLOSURE

In *Press-Enterprise (II) v. Superior Court of California*,[xiv] the U.S. Supreme Court established that an individual seeking to close open court records or proceedings, including pretrial hearings, must provide

1. specific, on-the-record findings that there is a "substantial probability" that openness will jeopardize the defendant's right to a fair trial and

2. convincing evidence that closure is "essential" to preserve the trial's fairness.

In another business case, a federal judge closed the courtroom and sealed documents to protect the secrets of Facebook and ConnectU. The case settled with Facebook allegedly paying $65 million.[212] Another federal judge sealed the courtroom and records in a lawsuit brought by the Motion Picture Association of America to prevent RealDVD from selling decryption software.[213]

The right of public access does not extend to all criminal trial proceedings. Grand jury hearings and their documents generally are sealed. The U.S. Supreme Court has not ruled directly on whether hearings to consider the suppression of evidence or plea bargains must be open. At least one federal appeals court has ruled that judges may hold conferences in closed chambers or conduct whispered bench conferences in the courtroom during the trial.

Courts also protect the secrecy of jury deliberations. In 2016, however, the Supreme Court held that a conviction should be reviewed when it is discovered that a juror reached the verdict based on racial animus toward the defendant.[214]

ADVANCING THE FLOW OF NEWS

In the years following *Sheppard v. Maxwell*, state media, bar associations and members of the judiciary developed agreements to guide reporting on the courts. The so-called bench/bar/press guidelines aimed to limit prejudicial media coverage by restricting both the content and the tone of trial coverage. They balanced the media and public interest in information against the courts' concerns about privacy and fairness. State rules vary, but some agreements create boards able to punish media violations.

Fifty years ago, a neighbor almost immediately confessed to the murder of six family members in Nebraska. National news media converged on the murder trial, and the judge issued an order barring publication of specific evidence and ordering the media to follow Nebraska's bench/bar/press guidelines. The voluntary guidelines encouraged media not to disclose information about confessions, guilt or innocence, lab tests, witness credibility or statements that reasonably would be expected to influence the outcome of the trial.

POINTS OF LAW

CLOSING MEDIA MOUTHS: THE *NEBRASKA PRESS ASSOCIATION* STANDARD

Nebraska Press Association v. Stuart established that a judge must justify gags imposed on the media with convincing evidence that

1. disclosure of the information would present a substantial threat to a fair trial,
2. there is no effective alternative to a gag on the press,
3. the gag will effectively eliminate the danger to the fair trial and
4. the gag is narrowly tailored to restrict only the information that must be kept secret.[xv]

New York Times
General Counsel
James C. Goodale
arrives at court
June 17, 1971, to
oppose the court's
restraining order
on continued
publication of the
Pentagon Papers
(the Supreme
Court ruling
discussed in
Chapter 2).

The state press association appealed. The Nebraska Supreme Court upheld the order, and in *Nebraska Press Association v. Stuart* the U.S. Supreme Court reversed.[215] The Supreme Court said decisions about news content are the domain of editors, not judges. That remains the law. The Court has never said courts may bind media to bench/bar/press guidelines.

Some courts continue to enforce the voluntary bench/bar/press guidelines on media. One state court in Washington excluded the press from a pretrial hearing after it ruled that its prior pretrial coverage violated the guidelines.[216] Another trial judge made press adherence to the guidelines a condition for media to attend a pretrial hearing open to the public. The Washington Supreme Court upheld this procedure.[217]

Guiding Media Coverage of Courts

The U.S. Supreme Court's landmark decision in *Nebraska Press Association* called press gags an extraordinary remedy that is presumptively unconstitutional.[218] The Supreme Court classified gag orders on the media as the most serious and least tolerable prior restraint on First Amendment rights. Court orders that bar the media from publicizing legally obtained information about ongoing trials must meet the highest standard of review. For example, states may not punish witnesses to secret grand juries who discuss their own testimony after the conclusion of the grand jury investigation.[219] Court bans on press photographs of jurors outside the courtroom generally must pass strict scrutiny because they constitute a form of prior restraint on a free press.

But the U.S. Supreme Court declined to review a press appeal challenging two Florida court orders directing that "no party shall further disclose the contents of the transcript of testimony before the grand jury" that had been leaked to the press.[220] In his opinion, Justice Anthony Kennedy denied certiorari "despite indications that a prior restraint may have been imposed."[221] The Supreme Court also upheld a restraining order that prevented two newspapers from publicizing the confidential membership and donor list of a religious group obtained from the discovery process in a libel lawsuit.[222] The Court unanimously found the restraining order constitutional because it did not prevent the newspapers from publishing the same information if they obtained it outside of trial discovery.

After *Nebraska Press Association*, courts must consider three things before imposing a media gag: (1) the quantity and content of media coverage, (2) the potential effectiveness of alternatives to a gag and (3) the likelihood that a gag would remedy the harmful publicity. Judges must determine that the gag is a last resort that narrowly targets information that poses a clear threat to the fair trial and limits as little press freedom as possible. Constitutionally valid media gag orders are rare.

POINTS OF LAW

WHAT IS FAIR COVERAGE OF CRIMINAL TRIALS?

Media standards of professional and ethical performance as well as bench/bar/press guidelines establish fair reporting standards on criminal proceedings. Most guidelines say that only an overwhelming justification should lead media to report

1. the existence or content of a confession;

2. statements or opinions of guilt or innocence;

3. the results of lab tests;

4. statements or opinions on the credibility of witnesses, the evidence or the investigative process or personnel; or

5. other information reasonably likely to affect the trial verdict.

Courts continue to place gags on the media. An Alabama trial judge briefly banned two newspapers from publishing information in the public record about the age and condition of gas pipes across Alabama.[223] The judge entered the gag in response to Alabama Gas Corp.'s claim that publication of the information raised a risk to national security of sabotage and terrorism.

The National Center for State Courts, a nonprofit clearinghouse and information resource for courts, produces several guides on court management of high-profile cases, sharing information, managing a court's image and shaping media coverage.[224] Directed primarily toward court public information and media relations officers, the center's web resources encourage court personnel to "serve as liaisons between the courts and the media," ensure fair and accurate reporting and prevent any infringement on court proceedings, especially in highly publicized and notorious trials.[225]

In 2016, Florida launched a new plan to improve communication by and from the courts to enhance public confidence in its judiciary.[226] Goals established by court public information officers included improving public outreach, enhancing court websites, strengthening relations with the media and increasing public educational programming.

Protecting Confidential Information

Although individuals who receive subpoenas are expected to comply, recipients may move to quash the subpoena. When journalists are subpoenaed to testify about confidential information, they may use either a state reporter's privilege or state shield laws in efforts to quash the subpoena.

Recently, screenwriter and producer of NPR's podcast "Serial" Mark Boal settled his six-month lawsuit against the government to stop a subpoena for 25 hours of unedited tapes of his interviews with accused U.S. Army deserter Bowe Bergdahl.[227] Bergdahl was a prisoner of the Taliban in Afghanistan and Pakistan for five years. The military court trying Bergdahl had

Mark Boal's interviews with U.S. Army Sgt. Bowe Bergdahl became the basis of the second season of the investigative podcast "Serial."

threatened Boal with a contempt citation. Military courts do not recognize reporter's privilege, but Boal argued that federal court precedents should apply. The settlement details were not released, but the government agreed to drop the subpoena and to allow Boal to protect all confidential material from his interviews with Bergdahl.

Providing a Limited Privilege

The concept of reporter's privilege, sometimes called "journalist's privilege," is an extension of other forms of privilege. Courts long have granted certain privileges not to testify to parties in a special relationship—lawyer–client, doctor–patient, husband–wife or clergy–parishioner, for example. Journalists argue that the reporter–source relationship is precisely one of these privileged relationships[228] that the First Amendment protects. Compelling a journalist to violate a promise of confidentiality, they say, impinges on freedom of the press and harms the flow of information. One distinction between lawyer–client and reporter–source relationships is that lawyer–client privilege "belongs" to the client, and reporter's privilege belongs to both the source and the reporter. A client may release an attorney from the agreement while a journalist may argue for privilege even after release from the promise.[229]

Reporter's privilege as we know it originated in the landmark U.S. Supreme Court case *Branzburg v. Hayes*.[230] *Branzburg* consolidated four cases. Two involved Paul Branzburg's sources on illegal drug use reported in The (Louisville) Courier-Journal. Two were related to sources within the Black Panthers contacted in separate reporting by TV reporter Paul Pappas and New York Times reporter Earl Caldwell. All three refused to testify before grand juries and were cited with contempt.

All three reporters claimed the First Amendment provided a privilege that protected them from revealing confidential information. They argued that their ability to report news would be irreparably harmed. Sources would dry up. Mere appearance before a closed grand jury could chill their access to sources who would never know what the reporter revealed. Forced grand jury appearance alone would reduce the information available to the public in violation of the First Amendment.

By a 5–4 majority, the U.S. Supreme Court disagreed.[231] The Court balanced the benefits of a reporter's privilege not to testify before a grand jury against the public interest in justice and favored the latter. Obtaining evidence is critical to justice, the Court said. The fact that the necessary evidence is held by a reporter is immaterial. Writing in concurrence, Justice Lewis Powell emphasized "the limited nature" of the Court's holding.[232] Reporter's privilege to withhold information should be determined case by case. Refusal to provide information may be permissible if the information fails to serve "a legitimate need of law enforcement."[233]

Writing in dissent, only Justice William Douglas argued that journalists have an absolute privilege to withhold information, including sources' names.[234] Three justices criticized

INTERNATIONAL LAW
CANADA SAYS STOP TRAMPLING ON REPORTERS' RIGHTS

Without providing a broad statement on reporter's privilege, the Supreme Court of Canada urged judges to use caution when forcing journalists to reveal sources.[xvi] In a ruling in a libel lawsuit brought against a Globe and Mail reporter, the court said:

> If relevant information is available by other means and, therefore, could

be obtained without requiring a journalist to break the undertaking of confidentiality, then those avenues ought to be exhausted. The necessity requirement . . . acts as a further buffer against fishing expeditions and any unnecessary interference with the work of the media.[xvii]

the "Court's crabbed view of the First Amendment"[235] and said reporters have a limited First Amendment privilege to refuse to reveal sources.[236] The First Amendment guarantee is "not for the benefit of the press so much as for the benefit of all of us."[237] Writing for the three, Justice Potter Stewart said a First Amendment privilege to withhold information should exist unless officials could meet "a heavy burden of justification" to overcome the privilege.[238] He said that burden could be met only when (1) there is probable cause to believe the reporter has information clearly relevant to a specific violation of law, (2) the information being sought cannot be obtained by other means that are less intrusive of First Amendment values and (3) there is a compelling and overriding interest in the information.[239]

Many courts adopted this approach, which is called the "reporter's privilege test." Among federal appellate courts, only the Sixth Circuit Court of Appeals has not recognized some journalists' privilege to protect confidential sources.[240]

The *Branzburg* decision is narrow, speaking only to a journalist being called before a grand jury. The various *Branzburg* opinions did not make clear how to determine privilege beyond grand juries, but an "unofficial majority" of the Court said a qualified reporter's privilege may be contemplated outside grand jury circumstances. Court application of privilege is highly fact specific. A decade ago, the Pennsylvania Supreme Court broke ground when it rejected the assumption that shield laws do *not* protect against grand jury subpoenas. After a newspaper reporter used a confidential source to report on a grand jury proceeding, the state high court ruled that the Pennsylvania shield law grants an absolute privilege to journalists and protects their sources in all cases.[241]

In 2016, a federal district court in Massachusetts ordered radio and television commentator Glenn Beck to provide the identities of at least two of the confidential sources he relied on to link the plaintiff, Abdulrahman Alharbi, to the 2013 Boston Marathon bombing.[242] Alharbi sued Beck for libel for repeatedly reporting that Alharbi helped finance the bombing. Beck claimed qualified privilege from disclosure and sought summary judgment on the libel charge, asserting that the stories were accurate reports of information from confidential

MAP 8.4 ■   Reporter's Privilege Protections by State

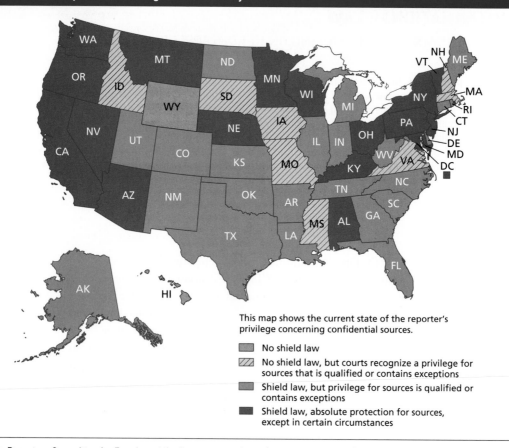

This map shows the current state of the reporter's privilege concerning confidential sources.

- No shield law
- No shield law, but courts recognize a privilege for sources that is qualified or contains exceptions
- Shield law, but privilege for sources is qualified or contains exceptions
- Shield law, absolute protection for sources, except in certain circumstances

Source: Reporters Committee for Freedom of the Press, www.rcfp.org/reporters-privilege/

government sources. The court said disclosure of two of Beck's six sources was necessary due to Beck's vague and often contradictory testimony about their identities and the information they provided. Accurate reports of what they said were essential to Alharbi's case.

In a highly visible case, the Justice Department investigated, questioned and subpoenaed Pulitzer Prize–winning New York Times reporter James Risen for more than six years to discover the source of classified information used in his book, "State of War: The Secret History of the CIA and the Bush Administration."[243] The government dropped charges against Risen only after convicting former CIA agent Jeffrey Sterling for the leak.

In *United States v. Sterling*, the Fourth Circuit Court of Appeals said no First Amendment or common law privilege exists for journalists.[244] The Fourth Circuit said Risen did not have protection against testifying because he could provide a "direct, firsthand account of the [alleged] criminal conduct . . . [that] cannot be obtained by alternative means, as [Risen] is without dispute the only witness who can offer this critical testimony."[245]

Recently, a New York appeals court held that reporter's privilege protected a New York Times reporter from forced disclosure of information from her jailhouse interview of a man charged with a decades-old high-profile murder. The court said Frances Robles' notes of interviews with the "Baby Hope" murder suspect were neither "critical [n]or necessary" to the prosecution.[246] An Arizona appellate court also recognized a qualified First Amendment privilege for newsgathering materials and held that the trial court should have quashed a subpoena for the interview notes of a Phoenix reporter.[247]

Relying on Delaware's Reporters' Privilege Act, a state trial court used a balancing test to let stand a subpoena against the New Journal for the unedited video of one reporter's entire interview with murder suspect Christopher Rivers.[248] The court said the newspaper failed to show how release of the information in the interview would chill its reporting. Moreover, the information was material to the prosecution, unavailable elsewhere and intended for public display.

Some lower courts have balanced *Branzburg*'s three factors (possession, alternatives and relevance) against the asserted damage to newsgathering and the First Amendment. If one factor clearly favors the journalist, the journalist may have reporter's privilege protection. For example, one federal district court ruled that reporter's privilege shielded a journalist from being questioned because there were alternative ways to obtain the information.[249] Another federal district court upheld reporter's privilege on the grounds that the information sought was not materially relevant to the charges involved in the case.[250]

When faced with subpoenas to identify those who posted anonymously on their websites, news organizations discover that reporter's privilege may not protect them. In Idaho, for example, a county Republican Committee official sought the source of allegedly defamatory comments about her that appeared on a blog administered by a reporter of The Spokesman-Review. The newspaper claimed reporter's privilege protection under the First Amendment and the state constitution. The court denied protection, reasoning that the privilege did not apply to the journalist who was "not acting as a reporter" but serving as "a facilitator of commentary."[251]

POINTS OF LAW
THE REPORTER'S PRIVILEGE TEST

A reporter's privilege to withhold information likely does not exist if the government can demonstrate all of the following:

1. Possession: Probable cause to believe that the reporter has information clearly connected to a specific violation of law

2. No Alternatives: That the information sought cannot be obtained by alternative means less destructive of First Amendment values

3. Relevance: That there is a compelling and overriding interest in the information[xviii]

Reporter's privilege may not protect freelance journalists or filmmakers. The U.S. Court of Appeals for the Second Circuit ruled that a documentary filmmaker could not use reporter's privilege because attorneys representing the film's subjects helped with the movie's production. That meant the filmmaker was not a journalist because he did not function with journalistic independence, the court said.[252] However, a federal district court refused to rule that documentary filmmaker Ken Burns had become an advocate and thereby lost his reporter's privilege protection when he produced "The Central Park Five," a film about five men convicted of raping a jogger in New York's Central Park.[253] The court quashed a subpoena for outtakes from the Burns film. The court rejected the argument that the filmmaker was not independent, and therefore unprotected by privilege, simply because he held an opinion about the men's guilt or innocence.[254]

Applying Shield Laws

shield laws
State laws that protect journalists from being found in contempt of court for refusing to reveal sources.

Almost 50 years ago, the U.S. Supreme Court's opinion in *Branzburg* essentially invited legislatures to determine whether "a statutory newsman's privilege is necessary and desirable."[255] Although 17 states had enacted **shield laws** prior to *Branzburg*, most others passed laws to protect journalists in some situations from contempt citations for refusing to reveal a source.[256] Wyoming is the only holdout, but Hawaii's shield law expired in 2013.[257] The struggle to enact effective shield laws to protect confidential sources and information has been difficult and has produced what one scholar called "a haphazard system of limited protection."[258]

There is no federal shield law to protect journalists involved in federal proceedings. Journalists involved in federal proceedings may rely on the uncertain common law privilege. Efforts to pass a federal shield law have highlighted the problems inherent in broadly establishing those who would be protected and narrowly defining the conditions in which the shield would not apply.[259] Legislators flounder when attempting to protect legitimate sources of news without shielding illegal leakers of secret government information, for example. They struggle to allow government to engage in secret surveillance and data gathering in the name of national security while prohibiting covert government fishing expeditions into the private communications of newsgatherers.

These problems are global, according to a recent study by UNESCO, which found that most laws are outdated both in how they define "journalist" and in their failure to protect against government surveillance and data delivery laws targeting phone companies and internet service providers.[260] Montana recently became the first state in the nation to specifically protect reporters' privileged electronic communications from government intrusion.[261] The revised law no longer permits state or local governments to request reporters' confidential information from third parties such as email providers and social networking sites. Recent attempts to strengthen shield laws in Colorado and Maryland failed.[262]

State laws vary widely. Shield statutes all grant some degree of reporter's privilege and reduce the discretion of the court about whether privilege exists and for whom. No laws protect everyone providing news to the public from every subpoena. The wording of shield laws often limits who and what they protect and in what situations, and courts tend to require compliance with a subpoena when withholding information may be seen as a threat to the Sixth Amendment right to a fair trial. Court rulings also are highly fact specific and do not lend themselves to broad, predictive conclusions even under a single state's well-adjudicated law.

For example, a federal court did not apply California's strong shield law to a reporter's 2018 challenge to a subpoena to testify about her reporting on inmate deaths in San Diego County jails.[263] The court quashed the subpoena based on the reporter's qualified First Amendment privilege because the state had not exhausted other sources for the information. In another San Diego case, prosecutors in a drunk driving case claimed that a reporter who witnessed a car wreck, called 911 and encouraged the driver to push the car to the side of the road thereby lost his reporter's privilege.[264] The reporter argued that he did not "abandon his craft" by engaging with those on the scene and removal of his privilege would create "a perverse disincentive" for reporters to help at emergencies. While some states have eyewitness exceptions to their shield laws, California does not. The judge quashed the subpoena.

In a high-profile case in Florida in 2017, BuzzFeed argued that both Florida and New York shield laws and the First Amendment protected it from forced disclosure of the source of the Christopher Steele "Trump dossier" it used in reporting on Russian hacking into Democratic National Committee computers during the 2016 presidential campaign.[265] The plaintiffs demanded disclosure of the source on the grounds that the Florida shield law did not apply to online news publications. In refusing to force disclosure of BuzzFeed's source, the federal district court wrote:

> There is nothing in the statute that limits the privilege to traditional print media. Because BuzzFeed writes stories and publishes news articles on its website, it qualifies as a "news agency," "news journal" or "news magazine." Accordingly, BuzzFeed is covered under the Florida Shield Law.[266]

The court said forced disclosure was unwarranted because the plaintiffs had failed to meet "their burden of making a clear and specific showing that the identity of the source cannot be obtained through alternative sources."[267]

In a dozen legal battles in Minnesota, a county attorney demanded that reality crime television show "The First 48" turn over all of its footage of several criminal defendants. The show's producers refused the request and argued that the footage was protected by the state's shield law. But the county said the footage was critical to both sides of the case and the shield should not apply because the show "is an entertainment device; it's not a device seeking truth or justice. It gets in the way of us doing our job."[268] One district court judge agreed, requiring disclosure of the footage relevant to the double-murder case of Antonio Fransion Jenkins Jr.[269]

REAL WORLD LAW
THE QUESTIONABLE TRUTH OF "TRUE CRIME"

Crime is big entertainment business. True crime, as the subject of podcasts like "Undisclosed" and "Serial" or documentaries like "Making a Murderer" and "Paradise Lost," has exploded in popularity, producing both greater public awareness of police or judicial misconduct and unfairness and increased desensitization to the grisly details and victims of crime.[xix]

True crime "reenactments" or dramas rarely present the entire case. Prosecutors, in particular, criticize the true crime genre for producing profound misunderstandings in the minds of the general public and potential jurors about trials and the imperfect search for truth. True crime stories often exaggerate the availability of solid facts and definitive tests to create a seeming certainty about what actually happened.[xx] Media critics note that true crime stories tend to wrap everything up neatly, but fewer than 60 percent of real murders are actually solved.

Both "Serial" and "Making a Murderer" have been criticized for failing to provide a full view of the case and omitting incriminating evidence presented at trial.[xxi] In response, a producer of "Making a Murderer" said the series "hold[s] a mirror up" to the investigative and prosecutorial processes and highlights legislative reforms and advances in DNA testing that allow reinvestigation of potentially wrongful convictions.[xxii]

In a divided opinion, New York state's highest court held that the state shield law did not allow a reporter to appeal a trial court's refusal to quash a subpoena while the criminal case was proceeding.[270] The majority criticized the state legislature for failure to act on its "repeated recommendations" to permit such appeals. The dissent said the ruling ran contrary to "our settled law and against our state's strong historical protections of journalists and the news gathering process."

A journalist successfully quashed a subpoena to testify in the perjury trial of one of the organizers of the 2017 Unite the Right rally in Charlottesville, Va.[271] The challenge relied on the qualified reporter's privilege established by both state and federal court precedents there that covers both sources and unpublished information, regardless of confidentiality.

Some shield laws recognize the difficulty of defining "journalist" by applying protection to several categories of people. The Minnesota shield law protects anyone "directly engaged in the gathering, procuring, compiling, editing or publishing of information . . . to the public."[272] Some states shield those who report or write "motion picture news." Freelance writers, book authors, internet writers and many others are left out of many shield laws. Some states also exclude magazine writers.

In Arizona, an ex-mobster demanded the notes of an author writing a book about political corruption in the state. An Arizona appellate court let the subpoena stand because its shield law did not protect authors who do not report news or regularly disseminate information.[273]

In 2017, a Pennsylvania court found that the state's shield law made no distinction based on the form of publication. Two people brought suit against a blogger to obtain the identity of individuals who made allegedly libelous comments to his posts.[274] The court said the state

Foundational definitions in state shield laws determine the breadth and application of the law. For example, West Virginia's law includes the following:

"Reporter" means a person who regularly gathers, prepares, collects, photographs, records, writes, edits, reports or publishes news or information that concerns matters of public interest for dissemination to the public for a substantial portion of the person's livelihood, or a supervisor or employer of that person in that capacity: Provided that a student reporter at an accredited educational institution who meets all of the requirements of this definition, except that his or her reporting may not provide a portion of his or her livelihood, meets the definition of reporter for purposes of this section.[xxiii]

On its face, this law applies only to individuals who disseminate news for a living (including freelancers whose major income comes from news) and those working in and with campus media.

shield law protected the blog operator because he was an author who gathered, compiled and published news through a general-circulation publication comparable to a newspaper. The shield law protected sources to whom the blogger had promised confidentiality but did not automatically protect commenters who were not confidential sources.[275]

Several state courts have excluded bloggers from shield protection. A New Jersey court found that the state's shield law did not protect an online bulletin-board poster who did not employ customary journalistic practices such as checking facts, including different views or promising sources confidentiality.[276] The New Jersey Supreme Court said the law shields only those connected with or employed by "news media."[277] Electronic bulletin boards are "little more than forums for discussion" and do not meet this definition, the court said. The state supreme court said the law applied to individuals who communicate to the public on- or offline and have a relationship to their publication similar to that of reporters with traditional media.[278]

One judge initially said the Illinois shield law did not protect bloggers on a website containing technology news and commentary. The decision was reversed when the website disclosed that it also included reviews and undertook fact checking. When a blog contributes to information flow by reporting recent events, it can be considered a news medium, according to the court.[279] Courts in Indiana and Kentucky have ruled that their states' shield laws do not apply to anonymous posters.[280] Shield laws in Colorado, Florida, Montana, Oregon and North Carolina protect the identities of anonymous posters by broadly defining what they protect.[281]

A federal district court in Oregon said the state's shield law did not protect a self-identified investigative blogger who was a defendant in a libel suit.[282] The blog was not a "medium of communication," the court said, because it was not "affiliated with any newspaper, magazine, periodical, book, pamphlet, news service, wire service, news or feature syndicate, broadcast station or network, or cable, television system." The court also said the blogger was not a journalist because she presented no evidence of journalistic training, affiliation or practices.[283] In a related decision, the same judge defended his narrow reading of the Oregon shield law. He said he did not mean "that a person who 'blogs' could never be considered 'media.'"[284] Rather, the absence of *any* journalistic practice prevented her categorization as a journalist.

A Texas court said the state's shield law did not apply to someone who blogged about oil and gas drilling's impact on the environment. The blogger was an activist, not a journalist, because she had no journalism background, was not objective and did not adhere to journalistic ethics, the court said.[285]

In Washington, an appellate court applied the state's shield law to protect the identity of hackers who posted Kazakh government emails online that a newspaper used to write articles critical of the government.[286] The court said the hackers were protected sources despite the fact that they did not provide the information directly to the newspaper.

Courts are most likely to protect source confidentiality in civil cases in which journalists are not parties to the litigation. In such cases, courts tend to assume the existence of alternative sources for the information that do not implicate the First Amendment. Applying the state's shield law, an Illinois appellate court vacated a contempt order against a journalist whose testimony was sought in a multiple murder case.[287]

Like other privileges, reporter's privilege can be waived. Particularly when a journalist is on the verge of going to jail, confidential sources may grant permission to the reporter to disclose their identities. Courts tend to diminish the weight of privilege once a source releases a reporter from the promise of secrecy.

Clarifying What Shield Laws Cover

The information protected by shield laws also varies by state. Tennessee's shield law applies to any information or source of information used for publication or broadcast. Most statutes do not protect journalists called to testify about events they witnessed, especially crimes. Also, the shield often crumbles when journalists are defendants—for example, in a libel case. Access to the reporter's knowledge, notes and sources may be vital to the plaintiff's effort to prove the journalist acted with negligence or actual malice.

In a complex defamation and right-to-record suit involving NBC Universal's "Dateline" show, the Tenth Circuit Court of Appeals said Colorado's shield law protects confidential sources but does not prevent legitimate discovery of nonconfidential information even from journalists.[288] Courts in at least three states have ruled that their state shield laws did not prevent subpoenas for newsgathering records or confidential sources.[289]

Finding Other Protections

Other defenses may protect journalists from revealing information. Any subpoena in a federal criminal case must comply with Rule 17(c) of the Federal Rules of Criminal Procedure. The rule says a subpoena may be issued only for materials "admissible as evidence." The U.S. Supreme Court said that to justify a subpoena, the materials must be relevant, otherwise unavailable and necessary for the trial. The subpoena may not be a "fishing expedition."[290] Rule 26 of the Federal Rules of Civil Procedure prohibits a judge from granting a subpoena for materials in a civil trial if the materials can be obtained elsewhere or if the burden to get the materials outweighs any benefit.

The Privacy Protection Act

After the *Stanford Daily* newsroom search case, Congress passed the Privacy Protection Act of 1980 that significantly limits both state and federal agencies' use of search warrants against public communicators. The law prohibits government agents from searching or seizing a journalist's "work product" or "documentary materials" in the journalist's possession as part of a criminal investigation. Work product includes notes and drafts of news stories. Documentary materials include videotapes, audiotapes and computer files.[291] The law also protects outtakes not included in the final product.

Limited exceptions under the Privacy Protection Act apply if the news organization has refused an order to disclose and all other remedies have been exhausted. Agents may seize certain information related to national security, child pornography or evidence that a journalist committed a crime. Investigators also may seize documentary materials to prevent their destruction or the death or other serious injury of individuals. Journalists may sue government employees for violating the law and seek damages, attorney's fees and court costs.

In at least one case, the U.S. Department of Justice accused a reporter of a crime in an effort to circumvent the Privacy Protection Act. To justify a targeted search of a Fox News reporter's emails, the DOJ claimed the reporter conspired with a State Department analyst to obtain classified documents.[292] Subsequent rules prevented the FBI and others from using an accusation of conspiracy to obtain a search warrant for a reporter's materials.[293]

Yet searches continue. In 2016, police in New Brunswick, N.J., armed with a warrant seized materials from a newspaper after it reported on alleged corruption in a city water department.[294] The online story included images of a stolen water meter the paper said a water department employee claimed was "proof that a crime has been committed." The police chief said the interest of "a criminal investigation kind of outweighs" any investigation by the newspaper.

Facing National Security Claims

As discussed elsewhere, national security claims often trump other legal protections. However, the U.S. Court of Appeals for the Ninth Circuit recently ruled that the Department of Homeland Security's border agents do not have unlimited power to search people's electronic devices.[295] The case involved finding child pornography on a laptop, but the court signaled that the DHS must have "reasonable suspicion" before searching individuals' electronic devices. However, the Ninth Circuit said "a quick look" or "unintrusive search of a laptop," such as asking that the computer be turned on, is acceptable.

A Washington Times reporter settled her lawsuit against the DHS for seizure of news-gathering materials—including information about a whistleblower. The materials were taken from her home under a warrant seeking evidence in a case unrelated to the reporter.[296] Under a secret settlement, the DHS agreed to improve its protection of newsgathering materials in future searches.

The Department of Justice informed the Associated Press only after the fact that it had obtained two months of records from 20 AP phone lines, including general switchboard numbers and an office-wide shared fax line.[297] The DOJ never justified the seizure or explained how it obtained the records. DOJ regulations require notice and notification and that subpoenas of journalists' records be narrowly tailored and used as a last resort.

Challenging Closures

The public has a right to challenge court closures, sealed public records and seizures of personal materials. Anyone may challenge a judge's order closing records or criminal proceedings. Such requests should be made in writing and/or in open court. When challenging court closures, individuals should stand and request recognition by the judge and then state an objection to the closure. Anyone also may ask the court to delay proceedings to seek the advice of an attorney in order to object to the closure.

EMERGING LAW

Today, only 50 members of the public can view U.S. Supreme Court sessions in person.[298] Everyone else receives news of the Court's oral arguments secondhand. Some Supreme Court observers predicted that recent appointees to the Court might modify its ban on cameras in the high court, and a 2018 poll found that two-thirds of Americans believe the U.S. Supreme Court should televise oral arguments.[299] Failing that, almost three-quarters want the Court to release same-day audio recording.

Both seem unlikely; none of the current justices supports the idea. During their Senate confirmation hearings, Justices Elena Kagan and Sonia Sotomayor expressed support, and Justice Neil Gorsuch said he had an "open mind" about broadcasts of Supreme Court sessions, but all have since backed away.[300] In 2018, Supreme Court nominee Brett Kavanaugh broke precedent during his confirmation hearings by declining to take a stance on cameras in the Supreme Court. Congress has failed many times to pass laws that would presume broadcast access to the U.S. Supreme Court unless a majority of the justices voted for closure to protect specific, enumerated interests.[301] Justice Anthony Kennedy said a congressional mandate would violate established "etiquette" if not the letter of the law.

The near ubiquity of cellphones and their associated social media platforms inside courtrooms presents difficult questions about First and Sixth Amendment rights and new opportunities for covert juror misconduct.[302] Social media give individual jurors private access to potentially prejudicial information at the touch of a screen. A judge may sanction a juror whose actions are likely to substantially prejudice ongoing litigation, but the judge must be aware of the problem to take effective action against it.[303] And remedies, such as declaring a mistrial, are costly and may jeopardize the defendant's right to a fair and timely trial.[304]

Several recent cases highlight the growing problem. During a Florida drug trial, nine jurors searched the internet for information about the case, the lawyers, the defendant and even evidence specifically excluded from court. One juror explained the violation of court instructions by saying, "Well, I was curious."[305] In another case, one juror tweeted about the jury's deliberations during a death penalty case, prompting reversal of the death sentence.[306]

In the very high-profile trial that found Dzhokhar Tsarnaev guilty of the 2013 Boston Marathon bombings, Tsarnaev challenged his conviction and sentence partly on the basis "that the jurors should be presumed to have been prejudiced because of social media activity."[307] The judge dismissed the social media threat as both "overblown" and presumptive because the defense presented no evidence of actual juror misconduct or prejudice. Nonetheless, the potential threat of social media interactions by jurors is a growing problem.[308] One study concluded that "there is no perfect solution to the growing risk of juror misconduct associated with social media."[309]

Almost half a century ago, the U.S. Supreme Court declared that "one man's vulgarity is another's lyric."[310] The ruling involved the intentional, and the Court said effective, use of the phrase "Fuck the Draft," then a popular statement of opposition to both the military draft and the Vietnam War. In *Cohen v. California*, the Supreme Court established that the First Amendment protected not simply the content of a message but also the shockingly offensive impact of some ways of expressing oneself.

Some fear the Supreme Court's recent decision not to hear the appeal of Jamal Knox, a Pittsburgh rapper sentenced to two to six years in prison for his lyrics, signals a willingness to step back from this broad endorsement of the freedom to express oneself in highly offensive ways.[311] Dozens of recent criminal trials of amateur rappers, generally young men of color, have used rap lyrics as evidence of "either autobiographical confessions of illegal behavior or evidence of a defendant's knowledge, motive or identity with respect to the alleged crime."[312] Prosecutors' use of rappers' artistic self-expression as evidence of bad character or criminal motive reflects "a long tradition of antagonism between the legal establishment and hip-hop culture," according to scholars studying the trend.[313] They argue that it misconstrues the role of hyperbole in hip-hop and threatens the freedom of artistic expression.

Because of the potential for lyrics to be inflammatory or to incite racial animus among jurors, some courts are excluding hip-hop lyrics. In one recent case, the New Jersey Supreme Court overturned the attempted murder conviction of Vonte Skinner, a rapper, because the prosecution's heavy reliance on Skinner's "violent, profane and disturbing rap lyrics" was "highly prejudicial" and provided little or no evidence of "any motive or intent."[314] Another court held that rap lyrics may be presented as evidence "only if they demonstrate 'a strong nexus' to the crime."[315]

CASES FOR STUDY

For study resources and a case archive, go to **edge.sagepub.com/medialaw7e**.

Thinking About It

The two case excerpts that follow address different aspects of access to trials. The first is the U.S. Supreme Court ruling about the right of the public, independent from the parties at trial, to attend criminal trials. The second, *People v. Owens*, is a recent decision of the Colorado Supreme Court examining whether either the state constitution or the First Amendment provides a right of access to criminal court records. As you read these case excerpts, keep the following questions in mind:

- What foundations does the U.S. Supreme Court draw upon in *Richmond Newspapers, Inc. v. Virginia* to conclude that the public has a right of access to criminal trials?

- What does the Court's decision in *Richmond Newspapers* suggest about any broader public right of access to judicial proceedings?

- How does the reasoning of the Colorado Supreme Court in *People v. Owens* compare to that of the U.S. Supreme Court in *Richmond Newspapers*?

- How do these two decisions balance a defendant's right to a fair trial against the public's right to know?

Richmond Newspapers, Inc. v. Virginia
SUPREME COURT OF THE UNITED STATES
448 U.S. 555 (1980)

**CHIEF JUSTICE WARREN BURGER
delivered the Court's opinion:**

The narrow question presented in this case is whether the right of the public and press to attend criminal trials is guaranteed under the United States Constitution. . . .

Stevenson was indicted for the murder of a hotel manager who had been found stabbed to death on December 2, 1975. Tried promptly in July, 1976, Stevenson was convicted of second-degree murder in the Circuit Court of Hanover County, Va. The Virginia Supreme Court reversed the conviction in October, 1977, holding that a bloodstained shirt purportedly belonging to Stevenson had been improperly admitted into evidence. Stevenson was retried in the same court. This second trial ended in a mistrial on May 30, 1978, when a juror asked to be excused after trial had begun and no alternate was available. A third trial, which began in the same court on June 6, 1978, also

ended in a mistrial . . . because a prospective juror had read about Stevenson's previous trials in a newspaper and had told other prospective jurors about the case before the retrial began.

Stevenson was tried in the same court for a fourth time beginning on September 11, 1978. Present in the courtroom when the case was called were . . . reporters for appellant Richmond Newspapers, Inc. Before the trial began, counsel for the defendant moved that it be closed to the public:

"[T]here was this woman that was with the family of the deceased when we were here before. She had sat in the Courtroom. I would like to ask that everybody be excluded from the Courtroom because I don't want any information being shuffled back and forth when we have a recess as to what—who testified to what."

The trial judge, who had presided over two of the three previous trials, asked if the prosecution had any objection to clearing the courtroom. The prosecutor stated he had no objection and . . . the trial judge . . . ordered "that the Courtroom be kept clear of all parties except the witnesses when they testify." The record does not show that any objections to the closure order were made by anyone present at the time. . . .

Later that same day, however, appellants sought a hearing on a motion to vacate the closure order. The trial judge granted the request and scheduled a hearing to follow the close of the day's proceedings. When the hearing began, the court ruled that the hearing was to be treated as part of the trial; accordingly, he again ordered the reporters to leave the courtroom, and they complied.

At the closed hearing, counsel for appellants observed that no evidentiary findings had been made by the court prior to the entry of its closure order, and pointed out that the court had failed to consider any other, less drastic measures within its power to ensure a fair trial. Counsel for appellants argued that constitutional considerations mandated that before ordering closure, the court should first decide that the rights of the defendant could be protected in no other way.

Counsel for defendant Stevenson pointed out that this was the fourth time he was standing trial. He also referred to "difficulty with information between the jurors," and stated that he "didn't want information to leak out," be published by the media, perhaps inaccurately, and then be seen by the jurors. Defense counsel argued that these things, plus the fact that "this is a small community," made this a proper case for closure.

The trial judge noted that counsel for the defendant had made similar statements at the morning hearing. The court also stated: "One of the other points that we take into consideration in this particular Courtroom is layout of the Courtroom. I think that having people in the Courtroom is distracting to the jury. Now, we have to have certain people in here and maybe that's not a very good reason. When we get into our new Court Building, people can sit in the audience so the jury can't see them. The rule of the Court may be different under those circumstances. . . ."

The prosecutor again declined comment, and the court summed up by saying: "I'm inclined to agree with [defense counsel] that, if I feel that the rights of the defendant are infringed in any way, [when] he makes the motion to do something and it doesn't completely override all rights of everyone else, then I'm inclined to go along with the defendant's motion." The court denied the motion to vacate and ordered the trial to continue the following morning "with the press and public excluded."

What transpired when the closed trial resumed the next day was disclosed in the following manner by an order of the court entered September 12, 1978:

"[In] the absence of the jury, the defendant, by counsel, made a Motion that a mistrial be declared, which motion was taken under advisement."

"At the conclusion of the Commonwealth's evidence, the attorney for the defendant moved the Court to strike the Commonwealth's evidence on grounds stated to the record, which Motion was sustained by the Court."

"And the jury having been excused, the Court doth find the accused NOT GUILTY of Murder, as charged in the Indictment, and he was allowed to depart." . . .

The Virginia Supreme Court . . . finding no reversible error, denied the petition for appeal. . . .

The criminal trial which appellants sought to attend has long since ended, and there is thus some suggestion that the case is moot. This Court has frequently recognized, however, that its jurisdiction is not necessarily defeated by the practical termination of a contest which is short-lived by nature. If the underlying dispute is "capable of repetition, yet evading review," it is not moot. . . .

In prior cases the Court has treated questions involving conflicts between publicity and a defendant's right to a fair trial. . . . But here for the first time the Court is asked to decide whether a criminal trial itself may be closed to the public upon the unopposed request of a defendant, without any demonstration that closure is required to protect the defendant's superior right to a fair trial, or that some other overriding consideration requires closure.

The origins of the proceeding which has become the modern criminal trial in Anglo-American justice can be traced back beyond reliable historical records. . . . What is significant for present purposes is that, throughout its evolution, the trial has been open to all who cared to observe. . . . From these early times, although great changes in courts and procedure took place, one thing remained constant: the public character of the trial at which guilt or innocence was decided. . . .

We have found nothing to suggest that the presumptive openness of the trial, which English courts were later to call "one of the essential qualities of a court of justice," was not also an attribute of the judicial systems of colonial America. . . . In some instances, the openness of trials was explicitly recognized as part of the fundamental law of the Colony. . . . Other contemporary writings confirm the recognition that part of the very nature of a criminal trial was its openness to those who wished to attend. . . .

As we have shown, . . . the historical evidence demonstrates conclusively that, at the time when our organic laws were adopted, criminal trials both here and in England had long been presumptively open. This is no quirk of history; rather, it has long been recognized as an indispensable attribute of an Anglo-American trial. . . . Jeremy Bentham not only recognized the therapeutic value of open justice but regarded it as the keystone:

"Without publicity, all other checks are insufficient: in comparison of publicity, all other checks are of small account. Recordation, appeal, whatever other institutions might present themselves in the character of checks, would be found to operate rather as cloaks than checks; as cloaks in reality, as checks only in appearance." . . .

. . . The early history of open trials in part reflects the widespread acknowledgment . . . that public trials had significant community therapeutic value. . . . [P]eople sensed from experience and observation that, especially in the administration of criminal justice, the means used to achieve justice must have the support derived from public acceptance of both the process and its results.

When a shocking crime occurs, a community reaction of outrage and public protest often follows. Thereafter the open processes of justice serve an important prophylactic purpose, providing an outlet for community concern, hostility, and emotion. Without an awareness that society's responses to criminal conduct are underway, natural human reactions of outrage and protest are frustrated and may manifest themselves in some form of vengeful "self-help," as indeed they did regularly in the activities of vigilante "committees" on our frontiers. . . .

Civilized societies withdraw both from the victim and the vigilante the enforcement of criminal laws, but they cannot erase from people's consciousness the fundamental, natural yearning to see justice done—or even the urge for retribution. The crucial prophylactic aspects of the administration of justice cannot function in the dark; no community catharsis can occur if justice is "done in a corner [or] in any covert manner." It is not enough to say that results alone will satiate the natural community desire for "satisfaction." A result considered untoward may undermine public confidence, and where the trial has been concealed from public view, an unexpected outcome can cause a reaction that the system at best has failed and at worst has been corrupted. To work effectively, it is important that society's criminal process "satisfy the appearance of justice," and the appearance of justice can best be provided by allowing people to observe it. . . .

People in an open society do not demand infallibility from their institutions, but it is difficult for them to accept what they are prohibited from observing. When a criminal trial is conducted in the open, there is at least an opportunity both for understanding the system in general and its workings in a particular case: "The educative effect of public attendance is a material advantage. Not only is respect for the law increased and intelligent acquaintance acquired with the methods of government, but a strong confidence in judicial remedies is secured which could never be inspired by a system of secrecy.". . .

. . . Instead of acquiring information about trials by firsthand observation or by word of mouth from those who attended, people now acquire it chiefly through the print and electronic media. In a sense, this validates the media claim of functioning as surrogates for the public. While media representatives enjoy the same right of access as the public, they often are provided special seating and priority of entry so that they may report what people in attendance have seen and heard. This "[contributes] to public understanding of the rule of law and to comprehension of the functioning of the entire criminal justice system. . . ."

From this unbroken, uncontradicted history, supported by reasons as valid today as in centuries past, we are bound to conclude that a presumption of openness inheres in the very nature of a criminal trial under our system of justice. . . .

Despite the history of criminal trials being presumptively open since long before the Constitution, the State presses its contention that neither the Constitution nor the Bill of Rights contains any provision which, by its terms, guarantees to the public the right to attend criminal trials. Standing alone, this is correct, but there remains the question whether, absent an explicit provision, the Constitution affords protection against exclusion of the public from criminal trials. . . .

The Bill of Rights was enacted against the backdrop of the long history of trials being presumptively open. Public access to trials was then regarded as an important aspect of the process itself; . . . In guaranteeing freedoms such as those of speech and press, the First Amendment can be read as protecting the right of everyone to attend trials so as to give meaning to those explicit guarantees. "The First Amendment goes beyond protection of the press and the self-expression of individuals to prohibit government from limiting the stock of information from which members of the public may draw." Free speech carries with it some freedom to listen. . . . What this means in the context of trials is that the First Amendment guarantees of speech and press, standing alone, prohibit government from summarily closing courtroom doors which had long been open to the public at the time that Amendment was adopted. . . .

. . . It is not crucial whether we describe this right to attend criminal trials to hear, see, and communicate observations concerning them as a "right of access," or a "right to gather information," for we have recognized that "without some protection for seeking out the news, freedom of the press could be eviscerated." The explicit, guaranteed rights to speak and to publish concerning what takes place at a trial would lose much meaning if access to observe the trial could, as it was here, be foreclosed arbitrarily.

The right of access to places traditionally open to the public, as criminal trials have long been, may be seen as assured by the amalgam of the First Amendment guarantees of speech and press; and their affinity to the right of assembly is not without relevance. . . . [A] trial courtroom also is a public place where the people generally—and representatives of the media—have a right to be present, and where their presence historically has been thought to enhance the integrity and quality of what takes place.

The State argues that the Constitution nowhere spells out a guarantee for the right of the public to attend trials, and that, accordingly, no such right is protected. . . . But arguments such as the State makes have not precluded recognition of important rights not enumerated. . . . We hold that the right to attend criminal trials is implicit in the guarantees of the First Amendment; without the freedom to attend such trials, which people have exercised for centuries, important aspects of freedom of speech and "of the press could be eviscerated."

Having concluded there was a guaranteed right of the public under the First and Fourteenth Amendments to attend the trial of Stevenson's case, we return to the closure order challenged by appellants. . . . Despite the fact that this was the fourth trial of the accused, the trial judge made no findings to support closure; no inquiry was made as to whether alternative solutions would have met the need to ensure fairness; there was no recognition of any right under the Constitution for the public or press to attend the trial.

There exist in the context of the trial itself various tested alternatives to satisfy the constitutional demands of fairness. . . . There was no suggestion that any problems with witnesses could not have been dealt with by their exclusion from the courtroom or their sequestration during the trial. Nor is there anything to indicate that sequestration of the jurors would not have guarded against their being subjected to any improper information. All of the alternatives admittedly present difficulties for trial courts, but none of the factors relied on here was beyond the realm of the manageable. Absent an overriding interest articulated in findings, the trial of a criminal case must be open to the public. Accordingly, the judgment under review is

Reversed. . . .

JUSTICE JOHN PAUL STEVENS concurring:

This is a watershed case. Until today, the Court has accorded virtually absolute protection to the dissemination of information or ideas, but never before has it squarely held that the acquisition of newsworthy matter is entitled to any constitutional protection whatsoever. . . .

Today, however, for the first time, the Court unequivocally holds that an arbitrary interference with access to important information is an abridgment of the freedoms of speech and of the press protected by the First Amendment. . . .

. . . I agree that the First Amendment protects the public and the press from abridgment of their rights of access to information about the operation of their government, including the Judicial Branch; given the total absence of any record justification for the closure order entered in this case, that order violated the First Amendment.

JUSTICE WILLIAM BRENNAN, with whom JUSTICE THURGOOD MARSHALL joined, concurring:

. . . I agree with those of my Brethren who hold that, without more, agreement of the trial judge and the parties cannot constitutionally close a trial to the public.

While freedom of expression is made inviolate by the First Amendment, and, with only rare and stringent exceptions, may not be suppressed, the First Amendment has not been viewed by the Court in all settings as providing an equally categorical assurance of the correlative freedom of access to information. Yet the Court has not ruled out a public access component to the First Amendment in every circumstance. Read with care and in context, our decisions must therefore be understood as holding only that any privilege of access to governmental information is subject to a degree of restraint dictated by the nature of the information and countervailing interests in security or confidentiality. These cases neither comprehensively nor absolutely deny that public access to information may at times be implied by the First Amendment and the principles which animate it.

The Court's approach in right-of-access cases simply reflects the special nature of a claim of First Amendment right to gather information. . . . [T]he First Amendment . . . has a structural role to play in securing and fostering our republican system of self-government. Implicit in this structural role is not only "the principle that debate on public issues should be uninhibited, robust, and wide-open," but also the antecedent assumption that valuable public debate—as well as other civic behavior—must

be informed. The structural model links the First Amendment to that process of communication necessary for a democracy to survive, and thus entails solicitude not only for communication itself, but also for the indispensable conditions of meaningful communication. . . .

First, the case for a right of access has special force when drawn from an enduring and vital tradition of public entree to particular proceedings or information. Such a tradition commands respect, in part, because the Constitution carries the gloss of history. More importantly, a tradition of accessibility implies the favorable judgment of experience. Second, the value of access must be measured in specifics. Analysis is not advanced by rhetorical statements that all information bears upon public issues; what is crucial in individual cases is whether access to a particular government process is important in terms of that very process.

To resolve the case before us, therefore, we must consult historical and current practice with respect to open trials, and weigh the importance of public access to the trial process itself. . . . [S]ignificantly for our present purpose, [the Court has] recognized that open trials are bulwarks of our free and democratic government: public access to court proceedings is one of the numerous "checks and balances" of our system, because "contemporaneous review in the forum of public opinion is an effective restraint on possible abuse of judicial power." Indeed, the Court focused with particularity upon the public trial guarantee "as a safeguard against any attempt to employ our courts as instruments of persecution," or "for the suppression of political and religious heresies." Thus, . . . open trials are indispensable to First Amendment political and religious freedoms. . . .

Publicity serves to advance several of the particular purposes of the trial (and, indeed, the judicial) process. . . . But, as a feature of our governing system of justice, the trial process serves other, broadly political, interests, and public access advances these objectives as well. To that extent, trial access possesses specific structural significance. . . . Secrecy is profoundly inimical to this demonstrative purpose of the trial process. . . .

But the trial is more than a demonstrably just method of adjudicating disputes and protecting rights. . . . It follows that the conduct of the trial is preeminently a matter of public interest. . . .

. . . [R]esolution of First Amendment public access claims in individual cases must be strongly influenced by the weight of historical practice and by an assessment of the specific structural value of public access in the circumstances. With regard to the case at hand, our ingrained tradition of public trials and the importance of public access to the broader purposes of the trial process, tip the balance strongly toward the rule that trials be open. What countervailing interests might be sufficiently compelling to reverse this presumption of openness need not concern us now, for the statute at stake here authorizes trial closures at the unfettered discretion of the judge and parties. Accordingly, [the law] violates the First and Fourteenth Amendments, and the decision of the Virginia Supreme Court to the contrary should be reversed.

JUSTICE POTTER STEWART concurring:

. . . [The presumption of open criminal proceedings] does not mean that the First Amendment right of members of the public and representatives of the press to attend civil and criminal trials is absolute. Just as a legislature may impose reasonable time, place, and manner restrictions upon the exercise of First Amendment freedoms, so may a trial judge impose reasonable limitations upon the unrestricted occupation of a courtroom by representatives of the press and members of the public. Much more than a city street, a trial courtroom must be a quiet and orderly place. Moreover, every courtroom has a finite physical capacity, and there may be occasions when not all who wish to attend a trial may do so. And while there exist many alternative ways to satisfy the constitutional demands of a fair trial, those demands may also sometimes justify limitations upon the unrestricted presence of spectators in the courtroom.

Since, in the present case, the trial judge appears to have given no recognition to the right of representatives of the press and members of the public to be present at the Virginia murder trial over which he was presiding, the judgment under review must be reversed.

JUSTICE HARRY BLACKMUN concurring:

. . . I remain convinced that the right to a public trial is to be found where the Constitution explicitly placed it—in the Sixth Amendment.

The Court, however, has eschewed the Sixth Amendment route. The plurality turns to other possible constitutional sources and invokes a veritable potpourri of them—the Speech Clause of the First Amendment, the Press Clause, the Assembly Clause, the Ninth Amendment, and a cluster of penumbral guarantees recognized in past decisions. This course is troublesome, but it is the route that has been selected and, at least for now, we must live with it. . . .

. . . [W]ith the Sixth Amendment set to one side in this case, I am driven to conclude, as a secondary position, that the First Amendment must provide some measure of protection for public access to the trial. . . . It is clear and obvious to me, on the approach the Court has chosen to take, that, by closing this criminal trial, the trial judge abridged these First Amendment interests of the public.

I also would reverse, and I join the judgment of the Court.

JUSTICE WILLIAM REHNQUIST dissenting:

. . . I do not believe that either the First or Sixth Amendment, as made applicable to the States by the Fourteenth, requires that a State's reasons for denying public access to a trial, where both the prosecuting attorney and the defendant have consented to an order of closure approved by the judge, are subject to any additional constitutional review at our hands. . . .

The issue here is not whether the "right" to freedom of the press conferred by the First Amendment to the Constitution overrides the defendant's "right" to a fair trial conferred by other Amendments to the Constitution; it is, instead, whether any provision in the Constitution may fairly be read to prohibit what the trial judge in the Virginia state-court system did in this case. Being unable to find any such prohibition in the First, Sixth, Ninth, or any other Amendment to the United States Constitution, or in the Constitution itself, I dissent.

People v. Owens
SUPREME COURT OF COLORADO
420 P.3D 257 (COLO. 2018)

JUSTICE MELISSA HART delivered the court's en banc opinion:

We accepted jurisdiction in this original proceeding to consider The Colorado Independent's contention that the Arapahoe County District Court erred in refusing to grant public access to certain records maintained under seal in a capital murder case.

The Colorado Independent contends that the federal and state constitutions grant a presumptive right of access to documents filed in criminal cases. While presumptive access to judicial proceedings is a right recognized under both the state and federal constitutions, neither the United States Supreme Court nor this court has ever held that records filed with a court are treated the same way. We decline to conclude here that such unfettered access to criminal justice records is guaranteed by either the First Amendment or Article II, section 10 of the Colorado Constitution.

Defendant Sir Mario Owens was convicted of first-degree murder and sentenced to death in 2008. In 2017, the trial court denied Mr. Owens's motion for post-conviction relief . . . as well as his related motion to disqualify the District Attorney's Office for the 18th Judicial District and to appoint a special prosecutor. The basis for the motion to disqualify was an allegation that the District Attorney had failed to disclose evidence that would have been favorable to Mr. Owens's defense. Over Mr. Owens's objection, the trial court issued a protective order, which remains in place today, sealing portions of the post-conviction motions practice.

In 2017, The Colorado Independent ("petitioner") filed a motion with the district court, asking the court to unseal the records, arguing that public access to the records was required by the First Amendment, Article II, section 10 of the Colorado Constitution, common law, and the Colorado Criminal Justice Records Act. The district court denied that motion, and petitioner filed for relief . . . , limiting its request for relief to the argument that presumptive access to judicial records is a constitutional guarantee.

Relief [to stay all lower court proceedings] is an extraordinary remedy limited in purpose and availability. Our exercise of original jurisdiction is discretionary. We have previously exercised our original jurisdiction to address public access to court documents. Here, we do so once again.

Because the availability of First Amendment protection presents a legal question, we review such challenges de novo. De novo review is also appropriate for alleged violations of Article II, section 10 of the Colorado Constitution.

Here, we reject petitioner's constitutional arguments for mandatory disclosure of the records sealed in this matter. We find no support in United States Supreme Court jurisprudence for petitioner's contention that the First Amendment provides the public with a constitutional right of access to any and all court records in cases involving matters of public concern. Petitioner cites none. The Tenth Circuit has more than once declined to recognize a First Amendment right of access to court records.

Moreover, we have never recognized any such constitutional right—whether under the First Amendment or Article II, section 10 of the Colorado Constitution. Petitioner's near-exclusive reliance on this court's opinion in [*Times-Call Publishing Co. v. Wingfield*] is misplaced. In *Wingfield*, we analyzed a statutory prohibition against the inspection of court records in pending cases by non-parties. We concluded that while no "absolute right to examine" court records exists, inspection may be permitted "at the discretion of the court." Contrary to petitioner's assertion, this court did not hold in *Wingfield* that limiting access to court records violates the First Amendment. We decline to do so now in the absence of any indication from the nation's high court that access to all criminal justice records is a constitutionally guaranteed right belonging to the public at large.

We also see no compelling reason to interpret our state constitution as guaranteeing such a sweeping—and previously unrecognized—right of unfettered access to criminal justice records. On the contrary, such a ruling would do violence to the comprehensive open-records laws and administrative procedures currently in place—including, but not limited to, the Colorado Criminal Justice Records Act—that are predicated upon the absence of a constitutionally guaranteed right of access to criminal justice records.

We affirm the denial of The Colorado Independent's motion to unseal the subject records.

⑤SAGE edge™

Visit **edge.sagepub.com/medialaw7e** to help you accomplish your coursework goals in an easy-to-use learning environment.

[T]he media and entertainment landscape has been completely transformed by the digital revolution. . . . There's something . . . that differentiates broadcasters. . . . You're not just there for your communities, you're there for free. . . . I believe a strong broadcasting industry serves the interest of the American people.

—FCC Chair Ajit Pai[1]

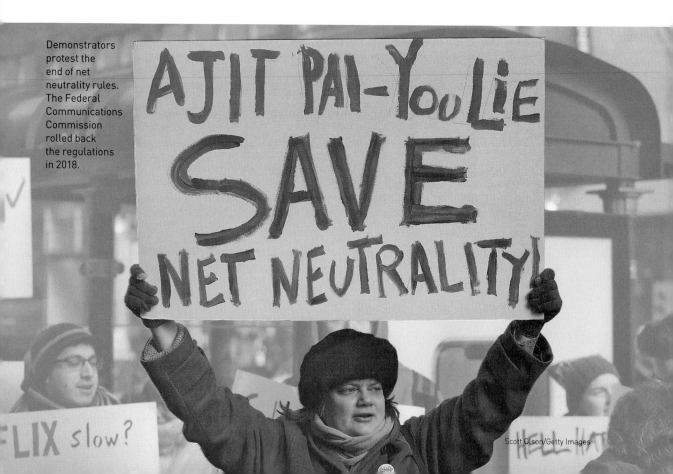

Demonstrators protest the end of net neutrality rules. The Federal Communications Commission rolled back the regulations in 2018.

ELECTRONIC MEDIA REGULATION

From Radio to the Internet

SUPPOSE . . .

. . . that a radio station airs a program that personally attacks the author of a book critical of a presidential candidate. The book author demands free airtime to respond to the personal attack, but the radio station refuses. The author challenges the radio station's decision with the Federal Communications Commission, the agency that regulates radio. The FCC agrees with the book author, citing the requirements of the fairness doctrine—a rule that requires contrasting viewpoints on controversial issues of public importance and allows free airtime to respond to personal attacks. The radio station challenges the fairness doctrine on First Amendment grounds. What differentiates broadcast stations from other forms of media? Would the First Amendment disallow the fairness doctrine if it applied to a different form of media, for example, a printed newspaper? Look for answers to these questions in the discussion of *Red Lion Broadcasting Co., Inc. v. Federal Communications Commission* and in the case excerpt at the end of the chapter.

BRIEF OVERVIEW OF ELECTRONIC MEDIA

Digital technologies have transformed the distribution channels, platforms and devices through which most people consume media, news and entertainment. Today, consumers do not think about making meaningful distinctions between electronic and print media because content is so readily available in a variety of formats. Yet, the distinction between electronic and print media is still important within mass communication law.

As explained in Chapter 1, precedent is the legal principle that tells courts to stand by what they have decided previously.

Because precedents are established over time, sometimes they do not quickly or easily guide new or emerging technological challenges. Throughout this book, you have read numerous examples of how courts, state legislatures, Congress and administrative agencies have adapted or changed existing laws, administrative rules and precedents to address new challenges created by emerging technologies. What is different within the context of electronic media is that the technologies themselves are interwoven into the legal and regulatory framework established over the past century. That framework does not always adapt quickly, yet technological innovation and change happen at a rapid pace.

electronic media
All forms of media that utilize electronics or digital encoding to distribute news and entertainment.

Electronic media include all forms of media that utilize electronics or digital encoding to distribute news and entertainment. However, they do not include media that have historically been distributed through printed means, even though most print media today are created electronically and live on the internet. For example, The New York Times is considered part of the print media, even though many of its users access its content through a mobile app or on a website.

The term "electronic media" itself may seem outdated in 2020, but it acknowledges the history and evolution of media technologies and has a distinct meaning in the area of mass communication law. Within the broad category of electronic media, not all are treated the same under the law. For example, broadcast radio and television stations must comply with more regulations designed to protect the public interest than some other forms of both electronic and print media. Radio and television station licensees often tell courts there is no valid reason to regulate broadcasting because the First Amendment should apply equally to all mass

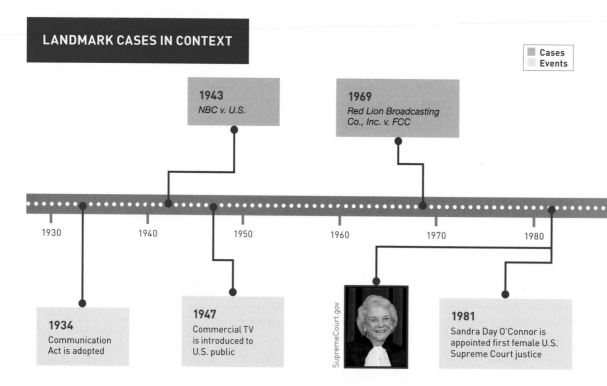

LANDMARK CASES IN CONTEXT

Cases
Events

1943
NBC v. U.S.

1969
Red Lion Broadcasting Co., Inc. v. FCC

1930   1940   1950   1960   1970   1980

1934
Communication Act is adopted

1947
Commercial TV is introduced to U.S. public

SupremeCourt.gov

1981
Sandra Day O'Connor is appointed first female U.S. Supreme Court justice

media. The U.S. Supreme Court has rejected this argument, and its decisions have allowed for the different treatment of mass media under the First Amendment. The Supreme Court has held that movies, for example, do not have the same First Amendment rights as print media.[2] Each mass medium has its own peculiarities, although each has basic free speech protection, the Court has said (as discussed in Chapter 3).

This chapter explains the distinct legal issues and regulations that govern electronic media, which include radio, television, satellite, cable, wire and broadband.

HISTORY OF BROADCAST REGULATION

The general concept of broadcasting, or the transmission of programs using the **electromagnetic spectrum**, emerged in the late 19th century after European physicists began to understand how to use the spectrum to transmit signals.[3] The spectrum is made up of different types of energy that radiate from where they are produced—called electromagnetic radiation. Together, they form the electromagnetic spectrum, which consists of electromagnetic waves we cannot see, for example, microwaves and radio waves. In 1897, Nikola Tesla, after whom Elon Musk named his global electric car company Tesla, filed U.S. patents that explained how electrical energy could be transmitted without wires, and later realized that his patents could be used for wireless communication.[4]

At the turn of the 20th century, Italian inventor Guglielmo Marconi transmitted radio signals using radio frequencies, which are part of the electromagnetic spectrum. Often, messages

electromagnetic spectrum
The range of wavelengths or frequencies over which electromagnetic radiation extends. It is used to send both analog and digital signals.

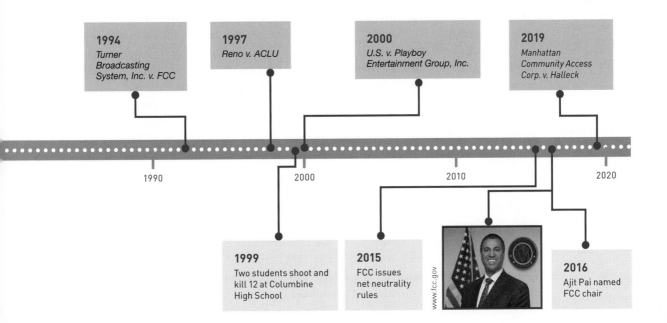

1994
Turner Broadcasting System, Inc. v. FCC

1997
Reno v. ACLU

2000
U.S. v. Playboy Entertainment Group, Inc.

2019
Manhattan Community Access Corp. v. Halleck

1990   2000   2010   2020

1999
Two students shoot and kill 12 at Columbine High School

2015
FCC issues net neutrality rules

www.fcc.gov

2016
Ajit Pai named FCC chair

interfered with each other during this early period of experimentation. In 1902, an American physicist applied his knowledge of telegraphs to advance radio tuning to try to overcome the problem of interference. A few years later, in what is hailed as the birth of public radio in the United States, the first public broadcast was transmitted in New York City in 1910. The broadcast featured the voices of the Metropolitan Opera. Members of the public and the press used earphones to listen at locations across the city.[5]

Congress passed the first federal regulation of broadcast in 1910. The Wireless Ship Act required oceangoing vessels to carry radio equipment and operators, but Congress had not considered the law's impact on the spectrum, especially given that the mandate had global implications.[6] Other nations pressured Congress to establish standards that everyone could adopt, allowing messages to reach their destinations without interference. Then tragedy struck. In 1912, the Titanic hit an iceberg, plunging thousands to their deaths. The Titanic sent a distress signal, but it did not reach authorities because of interference and because the radio operator on the nearest ship was off-duty and did not hear the message.[7]

The Titanic disaster prompted Congress to pass the Radio Act of 1912, which required oceangoing ships to have 24-hour radio operators.[8] It also gave the U.S. secretary of commerce power to grant radio station licenses, assigning each licensee a specific frequency. A **radio frequency** is any one of the electromagnetic wave frequencies that lie within a specified range that is used for communication. The intent was to prevent message interference.[9]

However, the law did not give the secretary power to refuse a license or substantially regulate radio. Anyone applying for a license would get one, as long as no two applications were for the same frequency. The commerce secretary also had no authority to limit the power used to broadcast, which allowed the most powerful stations to drown out others. Amateur radio operators began ignoring the law, changing the frequencies they used and even relocating to other cities without the secretary's approval.[10]

Because radio was playing an increasingly important role in American commerce, Congress adopted the Radio Act of 1927 to solve these growing issues.[11] The law established the **Federal Radio Commission**, a federal agency charged with issuing or denying radio licenses and assigning frequencies to prevent stations from interfering with each other. The law gave the FRC the power to regulate stations as necessary to allow radio's development.

The 1927 law included several provisions that remain in effect today. First, the act said the FRC could not censor radio content. Second, it said the public, not station licensees, owned the electromagnetic spectrum. That is, the spectrum is considered a public resource. Because of this, the law required the FRC to make decisions based on the "public interest, convenience and necessity."[12] A federal court interpreted the 1927 act to say the federal government, not the states, had exclusive control over radio broadcasting.[13]

Shortly after passing the 1927 act, Congress realized that radio needed continued oversight. In addition to the FRC, a number of different federal agencies had authority over various aspects of the radio industry. To resolve these problems, Congress rescinded the 1927 act and adopted the Communications Act of 1934.[14] The 1934 act established the **Federal Communications Commission** as a federal agency, directly responsible to Congress and charged with regulating interstate and international communications. Today, the FCC oversees radio, television, wire, satellite, cable and broadband.

radio frequency
Any one of the electromagnetic wave frequencies that lie in the range extending from around 3 kHz to 300 GHz, which includes those frequencies used for communications or radio signals.

Federal Radio Commission
A federal agency established by the Radio Act of 1927 to oversee radio broadcasting. The Federal Communications Commission succeeded the FRC in 1934.

Federal Communications Commission
A U.S. government agency, directly responsible to Congress and charged with regulating interstate and international communications by radio, television, wire, satellite, cable and broadband.

REASONS TO REGULATE BROADCASTING

Congress established the FCC and began to regulate **broadcasting** because it used the spectrum—a limited, public resource. Unlike print media or even the internet today—anyone with enough money can print a newspaper or publish a website—only a select few companies in a geographical area may use the spectrum.

Broadcasting is formally defined by the Communications Act of 1934 as use of the electromagnetic spectrum to send signals to many listeners and viewers simultaneously.[15]

The Titanic.

It is not a broadcast when the CBS television network sends a signal to the CBS station in Des Moines, Iowa. That is a private transmission from the network to the station.[16] It is a broadcast when the Des Moines station sends the signal through its transmitter to thousands of television sets and to the local cable system. CBS, then, does not broadcast; rather, the stations owned by or affiliated with CBS broadcast. The FCC's broadcast regulations apply to radio and television stations.

Spectrum Scarcity

More than 75 years ago, the U.S. Supreme Court first established **spectrum scarcity** as the principal reason the government can regulate broadcasters.[17] After the Communications Act of 1934 created the FCC, radio station owners expected the commission to prevent interference by carefully choosing licensees and controlling the power that stations used to broadcast. The commission took more control over the radio industry than expected. Among other decisions, the FCC adopted rules regulating the relationship between the emerging radio networks and local stations. The commission was concerned that networks exerted too much control over stations, requiring the stations to carry all network programs, for example.[18]

The networks sued the FCC, claiming that it overstepped its statutory responsibilities.[19] The U.S. Supreme Court supported the FCC. "[T]he radio spectrum simply is not large enough to accommodate everybody," the Supreme Court said.[20] The few companies using the spectrum have a special privilege, making it reasonable to regulate them, the Court decided.[21]

In the 1920s, the FRC also said radio stations should broadcast various views about public issues.[22] The FCC subsequently adopted regulations in 1949 stating how that policy, called the **fairness doctrine**, should be put into effect. The FCC's 1949 rule said that television and radio stations must (1) air programs discussing public issues and (2) include a variety of views about controversial issues of public importance.[23] Different views did not have to be presented in one program, but the station's overall programming had to reflect important opinions about controversial topics. The commission justified the fairness doctrine by pointing to licensees' responsibilities to the public.[24]

broadcasting Defined by the Communications Act of 1934 as use of the electromagnetic spectrum to send signals to many listeners and viewers simultaneously.

spectrum scarcity The limitation to the number of segments of the broadcast spectrum that may be used for radio or television in a specific geographical area without causing interference.

fairness doctrine The Federal Communications Commission rule requiring broadcast stations to air programs discussing public issues and include a variety of views about controversial issues of public importance.

President Franklin D. Roosevelt signed the Communications Act of 1934.

The U.S. Supreme Court upheld the fairness doctrine and reinforced the spectrum scarcity rationale in *Red Lion Broadcasting Co., Inc. v. FCC* (excerpted at the end of this chapter).[25] The audience's right to hear both sides of an issue was more important than the licensee's First Amendment freedom, according to the Court.[26] The Supreme Court reiterated that the limitations of the spectrum prevent everyone who wants to broadcast from doing so and that the spectrum is a public resource. As noted in Chapter 2, the Court ruled five years later that print media do not have the same right-of-reply requirement as broadcasters.[27]

The FCC changed its rules in 1987, finding that the fairness doctrine violated broadcasters' First Amendment rights.[28] The commission said that broadcasters censored themselves under the fairness doctrine, choosing not to present discussions about important public issues rather than be forced to air a variety of opinions about those issues. Two years later, the District of Columbia Circuit Court of Appeals agreed with the broadcasters, and the fairness doctrine ended.[29]

Two features of the fairness doctrine formally remained on the books for another decade. First, the commission's personal attack rule, the *Red Lion* decision's focus, required broadcast stations to provide free reply time to any person or group whose integrity, honesty or character was attacked on the air. The rule did not apply to public officials. Second, the political editorial rule required broadcasters to give free time for a legally qualified candidate to respond to an editorial opposing the candidate or promoting any of the candidate's rivals.

In 2000, the D.C. Circuit Court said the FCC had not justified the rules and ordered their elimination.[30] Public stations still may not endorse or oppose a political candidate, although they may air editorials about public issues.[31] In 2011, the FCC formally eliminated the fairness doctrine, noting that the rule had not been enforced since the late 1980s.[32] Spectrum scarcity remains the reason courts most often give for allowing broadcast regulation. Not everyone who wants a license to operate a television or radio station may have one because the spectrum has only enough room to accommodate a limited number of stations.[33]

In continuing to use this reasoning, courts seem to ignore the development of direct broadcast satellite service, satellite radio, radio and television low-power stations (broadcasting signals available within a few miles of the transmitter), the internet and other emerging technologies. Although the U.S. Supreme Court has recognized these newer technologies, the Court said it would not alter its spectrum scarcity rationale "without some signal from Congress or the FCC that technological developments have advanced so far that some revision of the system of broadcast regulation may be required."[34]

In addition to spectrum scarcity, courts use two other rationales to justify regulating broadcast radio and television. First, the broadcast media are pervasive. Without regulation, children in particular could be exposed to inappropriate content.[35] A second reason is the perception that broadcast media have a greater influence on audiences—a "special impact"—than do print media.[36] Again, this rationale is especially concerned with children.

Although broadcasting remains the most regulated mass medium, the courts have permitted the FCC to roll back many regulations during the past three decades. However, the Supreme Court has yet to clearly state that spectrum scarcity is no longer a valid rationale for regulating broadcast radio and television.

Today, 93 percent of Americans listen to radio. Additionally, more than one-third of Americans currently use their mobile phones to stream music. Pandora is one of the most popular music streaming services in the United States.

The Public Interest Standard

In both the 1927 Radio Act and the 1934 Communications Act, Congress said the public interest comes before a station's interests. Both laws say federal regulation is to be guided by the "public interest, convenience and necessity."[37] Neither law defined the term "public interest." Through its first 50 years overseeing broadcasters, the FCC justified adopting regulations by citing public interest. Then, in the 1980s, the commission said the public interest required deregulating the broadcast industry. The FCC's focus shifted more to the market to help regulate broadcasting in the public interest.[38]

Even in a market-driven model, public interest considerations persist. For example, Congress authorized the creation of the First Responder Network Authority, commonly called FirstNet, nearly a decade ago. FirstNet is an independent **broadband** network dedicated exclusively to the public safety community. Broadband is a high-capacity transmission technique that uses a wide range of frequencies on the spectrum, which enables a large number of messages to be communicated simultaneously. Broadband allows for faster connection to networks, for example, the internet.

broadband
A high-capacity transmission technique using a wide range of spectrum frequencies to enable a large number of messages to be communicated simultaneously.

Congress allocated spectrum and provided $7 billion to construct the secure FirstNet system in all U.S. cities and rural communities. The 9/11 Commission recommended FirstNet in response to reports from police, firefighters and emergency medical personnel of communication failures because they could not access broadband networks during the Sept. 11 terrorist attacks. Public safety officials' access to broadband was also a problem after Hurricane Katrina in New Orleans.[39]

FirstNet's Nationwide Public Safety Broadband Network is not yet complete, but emergency communications during the Boston Marathon bombing in 2013 showed the network's progress.[40] Immediately after the bombings, the Boston Police Department was able to access broadband to issue warnings and alerts to the public via social media, and the FBI was able to receive information through video streams and tools like Google Person Finder.[41] In a major step forward in 2018, the network launched its core, the brain and nervous system of the network that separates the public safety broadband network from commercial broadband traffic.[42]

FEDERAL COMMUNICATIONS COMMISSION

The FCC "is the United States' primary authority for communications law, regulation and technological innovation."[43] The FCC adopts and enforces regulations affecting large segments of the electronic media, and it licenses spectrum users. The U.S. president selects the FCC's five commissioners, who are appointed to five-year terms. The president also designates one of the commissioners to be FCC chair—the commission's CEO. The U.S. Senate must approve commissioner nominations, including the chair. No more than three sitting commissioners may be from the same political party. Commissioners may not have financial interests in any company or industry the FCC oversees and must be U.S. citizens. The FCC operates under the Administrative Procedure Act, a law telling federal agencies how they may propose and adopt regulations and giving federal courts power to rule on challenges to those decisions. Congress gives the FCC its funding, increasing or decreasing the budget each year as Congress chooses.

How Does the FCC Work?

notice of proposed rulemaking
A notice issued by the Federal Communications Commission announcing that it is considering changing certain of its regulations or adopting new rules.

At the most basic level, the commissioners adopt rules and regulations. The process starts when commissioners identify a problem or receive a petition from the public that warrants attention. Problems can include an industry behavior that adversely affects consumers, difficulty in enforcing an existing rule or the need to update a rule because of changes in technology. Congress can also mandate the FCC to take action and initiate the rulemaking process.[44] FCC staff members prepare a **notice of proposed rulemaking** explaining what the commissioners plan to do and why. Members of the public, interested companies and industry organizations may submit comments to the commission. The FCC also provides an opportunity to submit replies that respond to the original comment submissions. FCC staff members consider all the submissions and draft a report and order. The commissioners discuss the draft, suggest changes and vote on a final version in a public meeting. Companies, organizations and individuals who object to the commission's final decision may ask the commissioners to reconsider. The FCC rarely reconsiders its decisions. The final regulations then become part of the FCC's rules. The commission's rules have the effect of law. Companies, industries and individuals must comply with the FCC's rules or face sanctions.

A company, an industry association or an individual affected by a commission decision may challenge the FCC policy in a federal appellate court. Usually the appeal is to the U.S. Court of Appeals for the District of Columbia Circuit, although other circuits also may hear an appeal of a commission decision. A federal court ruling overrides an FCC decision.

President Donald Trump nominated sitting FCC Commissioner Ajit Pai to become the Federal Communications Commission chair in 2017. Pai joined the FCC as a commissioner in 2012. Among Pai's priorities for the FCC are making broadband service available to all Americans; pushing for "Next Generation 911," which ensures people can always reach emergency services; leading the modernization of media regulation initiatives; and speeding up the agency's decision-making process, which can take years.[i]

In addition to Pai (a Republican), the other commissioners are

- Michael O'Rielly (Republican), first appointed in 2013 by President Barack Obama and currently serving his second term (which began in 2015);[ii]

- Brendan Carr (Republican), appointed by President Trump to his first term in 2017, who prior to becoming a commissioner served as FCC general counsel;[iii]

- Jessica Rosenworcel (Democrat), first appointed in 2012 by President Obama and currently serving her second term (which began in 2017);[iv] and

- Geoffrey Starks (Democrat), appointed by President Trump to his first term in 2019, who prior to becoming a commissioner served as assistant bureau chief in the FCC's Enforcement Bureau.[v]

What Does the FCC Do?

In addition to adopting rules and regulations, another important responsibility of the FCC is to grant a license to broadcast. The FCC acts on behalf of the public in allowing a licensee to use the spectrum for the license period. The FCC's broadcast regulations apply to radio and television stations. It is unlawful to operate any broadcast station in the United States without an FCC license, which is granted for an eight-year period and may be renewed for subsequent eight-year periods. Renewal is ensured unless the licensee has not operated in the public interest, has repeatedly violated FCC rules or has shown a pattern of abusing the law. There is no limit on the number of renewals a station owner may receive; a corporate owner may retain a station license as long as the corporation exists. An FCC license is not transferable: A licensee wanting to sell a broadcast station may sell the building, equipment, transmitter and trucks—but not the license. The FCC acts on behalf of the public in allowing a licensee to use the spectrum for the license period.

Federal Communications Commission Chair Ajit Pai.

If two or more competing applicants want a license for the frequency that is not already used for broadcasting, the FCC holds an auction.[45] The bidder offering to pay the government the most money is awarded the station license.

To obtain a license, an individual must be an American citizen.[46] A foreign corporation may not hold a license, nor may a corporation with more than 20 percent foreign ownership. A foreign government may not be a licensee, nor may a corporation controlled by another corporation with more than 25 percent foreign ownership.[47] These foreign ownership restrictions, first adopted in the 1927 law and continued in the 1934 act, were justified by national security concerns. Congress did not want U.S. media used for foreign propaganda.

The Telecommunications Act of 1996 required the FCC to review its ownership rules every two years. About 15 years ago, Congress amended the requirement. Today, the FCC conducts a review of its ownership rules every four years, called the Quadrennial Regulatory Review.[48]

FCC Ownership Rules

cross-ownership rule
A Federal Communications Commission rule that governs when one entity can own two or more companies with related interests.

For decades, the FCC has limited the number of stations a single licensee can own, both in one metropolitan area and nationally. The broadcast and newspaper industries long have maintained that the FCC's ownership rules are overly burdensome in the fast-evolving and highly competitive modern media marketplace. Public interest groups have argued that the ownership rules are necessary to preserve the public interest in viewpoint diversity.

The FCC's rationale for limiting ownership is rooted in public interest considerations. For example, when the FCC passed its first **cross-ownership rule** that prohibited the ownership of a newspaper and a broadcast station that served the same local community, it emphasized the need for a diversity of voices to be heard via different media outlets in each market.[49] However, FCC Chair Ajit Pai said recently that the cross-ownership rule "might have made sense when it was adopted in 1975, but it ha[s] become an anachronism in the internet age."[50]

REAL WORLD LAW
MODERNIZATION OF THE FCC

As technology rapidly advances, how has the Federal Communications Commission adapted? The FCC website states that "[i]n its work facing economic opportunities and challenges associated with rapidly evolving advances in global communications, the agency capitalizes on its competencies in

- Promoting competition, innovation and investment in broadband services and facilities
- Supporting the nation's economy by ensuring an appropriate competitive

framework for the unfolding of the communications revolution

- Encouraging the highest and best use of spectrum domestically and internationally
- Revising media regulations so that new technologies flourish alongside diversity and localism
- Providing leadership in strengthening the defense of the nation's communications infrastructure"[vi]

Recently, through a series of reconsideration orders, reviews and amendments, the FCC has eliminated or modified many of its ownership rules that were either slightly adapted or upheld during the 2014 Quadrennial Regulatory Review process.[51] The ownership rules impacted by the FCC's recent actions include the national television ownership rule, the local newspaper/broadcast cross-ownership rule, the local radio/television cross-ownership rule, the local television ownership rule, the local radio ownership rule and rules that govern joint sales agreements. JSAs allow one station to sell some or all advertising time on another station in the same market.

The FCC attributed its recent actions to the "explosive growth of the number and variety of sources of local news and information in the modern marketplace"[52] and its Modernization of Media Regulation Initiative, launched in 2017.[53] The objective of the modernization initiative is "to eliminate or modify regulations that are outdated, unnecessary or unduly burdensome," the FCC announced. "By initiating this review [of rules], the Commission takes another step to advance the public interest by reducing unnecessary regulations and undue regulatory burdens that can stand in the way of competition and innovation in media markets."[54]

The national television ownership rule does not limit the number of television stations a single entity may own. Rather, the entity, usually a corporation that owns multiple television stations in different U.S. media markets, cannot reach more than 39 percent of all U.S. television households. As a result of the 2017 Order on Reconsideration, the FCC maintained the 39 percent national ownership cap, but it changed the way it calculates stations' collective audience reach.

If a station group owns UHF channels, which use a specific part of the spectrum that has historically been considered inferior to VHF, those UHF channels are counted as having a 50 percent smaller reach than VHF channels when the FCC determines compliance with the 39 percent ownership cap. This practice, which the FCC has utilized in the past, is called the UHF discount.[55]

In 2016, the FCC eliminated the UHF discount. It said that while analog UHF stations did historically have a disadvantage compared to VHF stations, the advent of cable, satellite and digital broadcasting had resulted in UHF frequencies becoming stronger and better than VHF frequencies.[56]

Despite the technology-related enhancement of UHF frequencies, under the current rule adopted in 2017, the FCC reinstated the UHF discount. Several public interest groups challenged the reinstatement of the UHF discount in court. They argued that the rule was obsolete and harmed the FCC's ability to promote diversity, competition and localism over public airwaves because media companies could use the UHF discount to collect a greater number of stations and still meet the 39 percent cap.[57]

The D.C. Circuit Court of Appeals dismissed the appeal because it said the public interest groups did not have standing—they could not demonstrate that they would be directly harmed by the FCC's decision.[58] During oral arguments in the case, the D.C. Circuit Court panel raised substantive questions about the reinstatement of the UHF discount and its impact on localism, but did not answer those questions in the dismissal.[59]

TABLE 9.1 ■ Current FCC Media Ownership Rules		
FCC Rule	**Definition**	**Rule Status**
National Television Ownership Rule	Limits a single entity to reaching no more than 39 percent of all U.S. TV households.	**Reinstated** the 50 percent UHF channel discount in calculations of audience reach (called the UHF discount). No longer subject to quadrennial review.
Newspaper/ Broadcast Cross-Ownership Rule	Prohibits ownership of both a broadcast station (AM, FM, TV) and a daily newspaper in the same relevant market.	**Eliminated** as "outdated considering the explosive growth of the number and variety of sources of local news and information in the modern marketplace."
Radio/ Television Cross-Ownership Rule	Prohibits joint ownership of more than two television stations and one radio station in the same market (with some exceptions).	**Eliminated** because local radio and TV ownership rules continue to restrict how many radio and TV stations a single entity may own.
Local Television Ownership Rule	Limits ownership to two TV stations in the same market, but one must not be ranked among the top four stations in the market (Top Four Prohibition) *and* at least eight independently owned TV stations must remain in the market following the combination of two TV stations in the market (Eight Voices Test).	**Modified Top Four Prohibition** by allowing for "case-by-case review . . . to account for [special] circumstances." **Eliminated Eight Voices Test** as "unsupported by the record or any reasoned basis."
Local Radio Ownership Rule	Limits (by tiers) total number of radio stations jointly owned in a local market, depending on the number of stations in the market.	**No change** except that FCC adopted a "narrow presumption" in favor of a waiver of the rule in certain circumstances in the Washington, D.C., and New York City markets.
Television JSA Attribution	Television JSAs that involve the sale of more than 15 percent of the weekly advertising time of a station are counted toward the brokering station's ownership totals.	**Eliminated** because JSAs provide "an important source of financing and tangible public interest benefits, particularly in small and medium-sized markets."

Sources: 2014 Quadrennial Regulatory Review–Review of the Commission's Broadcast Ownership Rules and Other Rules Adopted Pursuant to Section 202 of the Telecommunications Act of 1996, Order on Reconsideration, 32 FCC Rcd. 9802 (2017). See also FCC, FCC Fact Sheet: Review of the Commission's Broadcast Ownership Rules, Joint Sales Agreements, and Shared Services Agreements, and Comment Sought on an Incubator Program, May 5, 2019, www.fcc.gov/consumers/guides/fccs-review-broadcast-ownership-rules.

The recent proposed Sinclair Broadcast Group merger with Tribune Media is an example that highlighted the potential impact of the reinstatement of the UHF discount on efforts of big companies to expand their national reach. Sinclair, the country's largest broadcaster, operating 192 television stations in 89 markets, sought regulatory approval for its proposed acquisition of Tribune Media soon after the FCC reinstated the UHF discount.[60] Critics of the proposed merger noted that if the merger succeeded, Sinclair would own many more stations with significantly greater national audience reach.[61] The reinstatement of the UHF discount aided Sinclair in growing its national footprint while still meeting the 39 percent cap, which critics argued would harm localism and diversity of voices.

The timing of the UHF discount announcement and Sinclair's proposed merger with Tribune triggered the FCC Inspector General, an internal auditor, to investigate whether the FCC coordinated with Sinclair or was politically pressured to make the UHF discount decision.[62] The investigation concluded that the decision was not a result of pressure from Sinclair or the Trump administration, but rather reflected long-standing conservative policy beliefs that were becoming FCC policy under Pai and the conservative majority on the commission.[63]

The politically charged environment that surrounded the proposed merger process was partially due to Sinclair's history of injecting the political perspectives of its owners into local news operations. For example, when Senator John Kerry ran against President George W. Bush in the 2004 presidential election, Sinclair created a corporate publication center that produced news reports and commentary that it required all of its stations to air. All of the mandatory commentary pieces criticized Kerry and liberal media bias.[64]

More recently, Sinclair reportedly forced dozens of its local news anchors to read the same speech to their millions of collective viewers. The speech warned about fake news and suggested that some "media use their platforms to push their own personal bias." The "forced read" mirrored commentary by President Donald Trump about fake news and media bias.[65]

In the end, the merger failed because the FCC issued an order that accused Sinclair of misrepresenting its efforts to divest certain stations to stay underneath the 39 percent cap.[66]

The FCC 2017 Order on Reconsideration also eliminated the local newspaper/broadcast cross-ownership rule and the local radio/television cross-ownership rule. The newspaper/broadcast cross-ownership rule prohibited common ownership of a full-power broadcast station and a daily newspaper in the same market.[67] The radio/television cross-ownership rule prohibited ownership of more than two television stations and one radio station in the same market, unless the market met certain size criteria that would allow for additional, proportional ownership. The FCC said the rules were eliminated because they were "outdated" and local radio and television ownership rules would continue to restrict how many radio and television stations a single entity may own.[68]

Under the local television ownership rule, a company may own up to two television stations in the same market if at least one of the stations is not ranked among the top four stations in the market. This is called the Top Four Prohibition. The 2017 order kept the Top Four rule in place but allowed for case-by-case review of exceptions under special circumstances.[69] Previously, at least eight independently owned television stations also had to remain in the market following the combined ownership of stations. The 2017 order eliminated this requirement, commonly called the Eight Voices Test, as "unsupported by the record or any reasoned basis."[70]

The 2017 order did not substantively change the local radio ownership rule. Under the current radio ownership rule, the total number of radio stations commonly owned in a local radio market is tiered, depending on the total number of stations in the market. For example, in markets with 45 or more radio stations, a company may own up to 8 commercial radio stations, as many as 5 of which can be in the same AM/FM service area. The 2017 order adopted a new, narrow presumption in favor of a waiver of the local radio ownership rule in certain circumstances in the New York City and Washington, D.C., markets.[71]

In 2014, the FCC voted 3–2 along party lines to adopt a rule to cut down on joint sales agreements between television stations. A joint sales agreement, or JSA, is an agreement between stations to jointly sell advertising. The FCC saw these agreements as unfair to small companies, especially new entrants, and as a way to circumvent the FCC's limit on owning more than one full-power television station in the same market.[72]

The FCC's 2014 rule barred companies from using one advertising sales staff for two or more stations in the same local market. This effectively meant that any television station that handled more than 15 percent of ad sales for another station would be considered an owner of both stations under FCC rules. The FCC gave stations two years to seek a waiver to the rules or to unwind cooperative ad sales agreements. The FCC encouraged waivers to JSAs that would enhance diversity in media ownership.

In 2016, the Third Circuit Court of Appeals struck down the 2014 rule, noting that the FCC expanded the reach of the ownership rules without first justifying the change in policy through quadrennial review. The 2010 and 2014 quadrennial reviews of the media ownership rules had not happened when the FCC issued the new joint sales rule in 2014.[73]

The 2017 order eliminated the JSA rule, arguing against the FCC's position from just a few years earlier. Instead, the 2017 order suggested that by eliminating the JSA rule the FCC is "preserving an important source of financing and tangible public interest benefits, particularly in small- and medium-sized markets."[74]

The 2017 order also eliminated the main studio rule, which required television stations to maintain at least one local studio in licensed markets.[75] The elimination of this 80-year-old rule allows station owners to create centralized newsrooms with centralized distribution models. The FCC called the studio rule outdated in the digital age and burdensome on broadcasters to maintain so many physical addresses. Critics argued that the elimination of the rule would lessen stations' presence in and commitment to their local communities.[76]

Additionally, the 2017 order created an incubator program to promote ownership diversity in the broadcast industry. Commissioner Geoffrey Starks, appointed in 2019, said recently that ownership diversity would be one of his primary areas of focus while at the FCC.[77]

The FCC's 2018 Quadrennial Regulatory Review is currently underway,[78] with a focus on continued scrutiny of the local radio ownership rule and the local television ownership rule and reconsideration of the dual network rule, which forbids a company from owning more than one of the top four broadcast television networks—ABC, CBS, Fox and NBC.[79]

REAL WORLD LAW
MEDIA CONSOLIDATION AND DIVERSITY

Currently, Nexstar Media Group is seeking approval to buy Tribune Media for $4.1 billion. As part of the merger process, Nexstar must sell some stations to remain below the Federal Communications Commission's 39 percent audience cap. Prior to the proposed merger with Tribune Media, Nexstar sold three stations to Marshall Broadcasting Group, a minority-owned broadcast company. The FCC has encouraged station sales to minority owners because underrepresented groups own less than 10 percent of broadcast stations nationwide.[vii]

In 2019, MBG sued Nexstar in New York, claiming breach of contract and fraudulent misrepresentation. The lawsuit alleges that Nexstar sold the three stations to MBG only to gain FCC approval to buy other stations, then engaged in FCC-prohibited practices in an attempt to drive down the value of the three stations it sold to MBG so it could buy them back at a lower price.[viii] In its lawsuit, MBG alleges that Nexstar is intentionally selling stations to minority-owned station groups as a strategy to reduce FCC scrutiny.[ix]

Nexstar denied the allegations. In 2019, Nexstar sold two additional stations to a newly formed minority-owned broadcast company as part of its proposed merger with Tribune Media. If the Nexstar–Tribune Media merger is approved, Nexstar will become the nation's largest television station owner.[x]

Public Broadcasting

More than 50 years ago, Congress created the Corporation for Public Broadcasting, a private, nonprofit corporation whose purpose is to ensure universal, public access to free news, information and entertainment programming.[80] The CPB is the "steward of the federal government's investment in public broadcasting and the largest . . . source of funding for public radio, television and related online and mobile services."[81] The Public Broadcasting Act says public stations must strictly adhere to "objectivity and balance in all programs or series of programs of a controversial nature."[82] Despite this "objectivity" language, the U.S. Supreme Court has allowed public stations to air editorials favoring or opposing public and political issues.[83] Public stations have "important journalistic freedoms which the First Amendment jealously protects," the Supreme Court said.[84] The CPB supports NPR and PBS, which provide programming to public broadcast stations.

The FCC oversees public broadcasting stations, which must comply with most of the same rules commercial broadcasters follow. Public stations do not carry advertising.[85] However, corporations and individuals make financial contributions to noncommercial stations and may receive on-air acknowledgments of those contributions.[86] A federal district court decision in California upheld this advertising ban. The FCC fined a public television station in San Francisco for what the commission said amounted to paid ads. The license holder of the station, Minority Television Project, appealed the fine and also challenged the law that prohibits all advertising—both political and commercial—on public television. The Ninth Circuit Court of Appeals affirmed the lower court decision that upheld the ban on all ads on noncommercial stations.[87]

A few years ago, hackers broke into the Emergency Alert Systems in Montana and Michigan and sent out an emergency alert of a zombie attack. Hoaxes like this are forbidden by Federal Communications Commission rules.

BROADCAST PROGRAMMING RULES

The FCC is not allowed to censor broadcast content.[88] But the FCC may set general programming rules, such as prohibiting hoaxes,[89] requiring children's programming and regulating politicians' radio and television appearances.

Since the FCC adopted its current ban on broadcast hoaxes nearly 30 years ago, it has not punished a single station for broadcasting a hoax. The FCC's definition of a hoax is knowingly broadcasting false reports of crimes or catastrophes that "directly cause" foreseeable, "immediate, substantial and actual public harm."[90]

Political Broadcasting Regulations

In both the Radio Act of 1927 and the Communications Act of 1934, Congress ensured that broadcasters could not favor one political candidate for an elective office over another. Section 315 of the 1934 act guarantees equal opportunity rather than equal time to **legally qualified candidates**.[91] Section 315 does not apply to ballot issues, such as referendums, state constitutional amendments, initiatives and recalls of elected officials.

legally qualified candidate
Someone who has publicly announced a bid for office, has her or his name on the ballot or is a serious write-in candidate. The candidate also must be legally qualified to hold the office.

"Equal opportunity" means all candidates are given the opportunity to reach approximately the same audience as an opponent. Being allowed to purchase a minute of time at midnight is not equal opportunity if the candidate's opponent purchased a minute at 9 p.m. Nor is being given one minute an equal opportunity if the candidate's opponent has used 30 minutes. Equal opportunity also means getting free time if a candidate's opponent appeared on a station or cable system without paying (with some exceptions). During the general election, every legally qualified candidate may use the equal opportunity rule if another candidate for the office uses a broadcast station or cable system.

"Use" is defined as the candidate or the candidate's picture being seen or the candidate's voice being heard on a broadcast station or cable system. The broadcasting of a candidate's name without the candidate's picture or voice is not a use.

This applies to more than candidates' commercials. If candidates appear on a television station's lifestyles program to give a cooking demonstration, candidates have used the station. This is true even if the candidates do not mention that they are a candidate, discuss their platform or refer to politics in any way. Potential voters might have a more favorable impression of candidates when proving themselves a master chef instead of discussing their political platform in a commercial. Their legally qualified opponents, then, may request equal opportunity, or an equal amount of airtime for an equivalent price.

Sixty years ago, Congress adopted four exceptions to the use rule. First, regularly scheduled news programs are exempt. This exemption was meant for local news programs. But when the commission defined this category as including "programs reporting about some area of current events, in a manner similar to more traditional newscasts,"[92] it also included such programs as "Entertainment Tonight"[93] and "Celebrity Justice."[94]

Second, regularly scheduled news interview programs are exempt. These must have been regularly scheduled for some time before the election. For example, scheduling four interview shows, one each week for a month before an election, does not qualify a program as "regularly scheduled." Although this exemption initially was for programs such as "Meet the Press" and "Face the Nation," the FCC has included "Jerry Springer"[95] and "The Howard Stern Show."[96]

Third, live coverage of bona fide news events is exempt. If a candidate's campaign speech is covered live, the candidate's on-air appearance will not be considered a use. Nor is it a use if candidates participate in a televised debate, no matter who sponsors the debate. Because debates are exempt, the debate organizers may include and exclude any candidates they want.[97]

Fourth, candidates' appearances in documentaries do not trigger Section 315 if the appearance is incidental to the program's topic. For example, if a mayoral candidate is an expert on the state's fishing industry and appears in a documentary about that topic, it will not be considered a use. Of course, if the documentary is about the candidate's childhood in a housing project, the candidate's appearance would not be incidental to the program's topic and would be use.

Candidates who want equal opportunity must request time from the station or cable system within seven days of their opponent's appearance. The station or cable system is under no obligation to notify opponents of a political candidate's use of the station.

To reduce negative political advertising, a federal law requires candidates to promise stations they will refer to their opponents in a commercial only under specific conditions. To refer to an opponent, a candidate's (1) radio commercial must include the candidate's voice approving the commercial's contents or (2) television commercial must show the candidate or the candidate's picture with a printed statement approving the commercial.[98] FCC regulations require any commercial on a broadcast station to identify who paid for the ad.[99] This rule applies to political advertisements as well. A candidate's ad, then, must say on radio or show in print for a televised ad something like "This advertisement paid for by the Pat Smith for Congress Committee."

POINTS OF LAW
SECTION 315 OF THE COMMUNICATIONS ACT OF 1934

Section 315 of the Communications Act of 1934

- guarantees "equal opportunity" to "legally qualified candidates" for elective office
- to reach approximately the same audience
- when another legally qualified candidate "uses" a broadcast station or cable system
- to advertise or when they appear on any of the station's programming.

Exceptions to "use" include

- regularly scheduled news programs,
- regularly scheduled interview programs,
- live coverage of bona fide news and debates, and
- when the legally qualified candidate's appearance is incidental to the program's topic.

Legally qualified candidates must request equal opportunity from the station or cable system within seven days of their opponent's appearance. The station or cable system is under no obligation to notify opponents of a political candidate's use of the station.

This ad from the 2016 U.S. presidential election prominently displays the sponsorship identification required by the Federal Communications Commission.

Broadcast stations and cable systems cannot edit or censor political appearances. Because stations are not permitted to edit or censor, they also are not responsible for what candidates say. For example, if candidates libel their opponent, the opponent may sue the candidate but not the station.[100] If the first legally qualified candidate running for an office does not appear on a station, Section 315 would not be triggered for other candidates. Although this is legal under Section 315, the FCC has suggested that stations should allow candidates airtime because it is in the public interest.

Congress recognized this Section 315 loophole and closed it—at least for itself. Section 312(a)(7) of the Communications Act requires radio and television stations to provide federal candidates with reasonable access.[101] This means even the first candidate for a federal office asking to buy commercial time must be sold the advertising spot.[102] The federal elective offices are senator, representative and president. Section 312(a)(7) exempts noncommercial and cable stations from complying with the section's requirements.

Section 312(a)(7)'s requirement that commercial stations provide candidates for federal office with "reasonable access" is not clear.[103] Broadcasters must consider each federal candidate's request "on an individualized basis, and broadcasters are required to tailor their responses to accommodate, as much as reasonably possible, a candidate's stated purposes in seeking air time." However, broadcasters also may "give weight to such factors as the amount of time previously sold to the candidate, the disruptive impact on regular programming and the likelihood of requests for time by rival candidates."[104] Broadcasters may not use these criteria as an excuse to deny federal candidates the time requested. Rather, "broadcasters must cite a realistic danger of substantial program disruption" or the likelihood of too many requests.[105] Aside from being assured they can get on the air, federal candidates are treated under Section 315 just as are candidates for state and local offices.

The FCC has determined that an opposing candidate's supporters may ask for equal opportunity under the same standards that Section 315 requires when the candidate's supporters use airtime. This means the candidates cannot ask for equal opportunity if their opponents' supporters use a station, but each candidate's supporters can ask for time. This is called the **Zapple rule**, named after a congressional staff attorney who first asked the FCC about these circumstances.

Zapple rule
A political broadcasting rule that allows a candidate's supporters equal opportunity to use broadcast stations if the candidate's opponents' supporters use the stations.

Children's Programming Requirements

Thirty years ago, Congress passed the Children's Television Act.[106] The law set general requirements for children's programming on broadcast television stations. The statute required broadcast television stations to provide programming intended for children up to 17 years old

INTERNATIONAL LAW
EXPAND FOREIGN OWNERSHIP?

FCC Commissioner Michael O'Rielly has suggested that the FCC consider reducing barriers to foreign investment in the U.S. communications marketplace.[xi] He noted that the FCC has the authority to permit a higher foreign ownership limit (above the current 25 percent cap) or to waive the limit altogether. O'Rielly argued that greater foreign investment in U.S. communications companies would provide new sources of funding for growth and job creation, add new diverse voices to the marketplace and help remove other international trade barriers.[xii]

The FCC has chosen to consider broadcast licensee requests to exceed the cap on foreign investment on a case-by-case basis.

that met their "educational and informational needs."[107] The law also limited commercial time before, during and after children's programs on broadcast and cable television. For children 12 years old and younger, advertising during children's programming was limited to 12 minutes per hour during the week and 10 1/2 minutes per hour on the weekends.

The FCC also has ruled that characters in children's programs cannot appear in commercials before, during or after children's programs.[108] Cartoon characters in children's programs or children's program hosts also may not sell products in commercials during or adjacent to shows in which the character or host appears.[109]

The FCC allowed individual stations to decide how much children's programming to carry[110] until 1996, when it adopted standards for complying with the Children's Television Act.[111] The commission ruled that broadcast television stations must carry three hours per week, averaged over a six-month period, of programming specifically intended to meet children's intellectual/cognitive and social/emotional needs. The programs must be at least 30 minutes long, regularly scheduled weekly and broadcast between 7 a.m. and 10 p.m. local time. The commission identified this as "core programming."

A station not meeting the core programming standard may substitute shorter programs, public service announcements for children and programs not scheduled weekly. The FCC may choose not to renew a station's license if it does not meet the requirements. When the core programming standard was enacted, the FCC said its children's programming rules were "reasonable, viewpoint-neutral" requirements for licensees who must operate in the public interest.[112]

Recently, Commissioner O'Rielly suggested that the 30-year-old children's television regulations are "ineffective and burdensome" to broadcasters and are no longer needed given the proliferation of children's programming across various media channels and platforms.[113] In 2018, the FCC adopted a notice of proposed rulemaking to change the children's television rules as part of the FCC's media modernization initiative. The NPRM sought comment on every aspect of the children's television rules.[114] The NPRM did not propose the elimination of the rules, but it did tentatively conclude that reporting requirements for licensees be

The long-running, popular children's show "Sesame Street" has aired on PBS since 1969. Recently, the show moved its first-run episodes to HBO, but the show still appears on PBS.

simplified, that the core programming requirement that programs are at least 30 minutes in length be maintained and that regularly scheduled, weekly core programming requirements should be eliminated. The NPRM recognized the importance of children's programming, but it also acknowledged that broadcasters need greater flexibility and the current rules are outdated.[115]

In 2019, the FCC approved changes to the core programming requirements. Broadcasters are now allowed to begin airing children's programming at 6 a.m. (instead of 7 a.m.); stations may count some children's programming not regularly scheduled (for example, educational specials) toward the annual core programming requirement; and stations can count some short-form programming toward the core programming requirement.[116]

The FCC eliminated the requirement that a station air an additional three hours of children's programming for each 24/7 multicast stream. The FCC also revised the reporting requirements for children's programming, retained rules that require program guides and eliminated the rule that required on-air notification of core programs on non-commercial stations.[117]

MULTICHANNEL VIDEO PROGRAMMING DISTRIBUTOR REGULATION

multichannel video programming distributor
An entity, including cable or direct broadcast satellite services, that provides multiple channels of video programming for purchase.

In addition to regulating broadcast media, the FCC regulates satellite and cable. As new forms of video distribution have emerged, the FCC began referring to these channels collectively as **multichannel video programming distributors**. The FCC defines both cable and direct broadcast satellite services as MVPDs. An MVPD is an entity that makes available for purchase multiple channels of video programming. According to the FCC, the major MVPDs today offer hundreds of linear television channels and thousands of nonlinear video-on-demand and pay-per-view programs. In addition to delivering video programming to television sets, MVPDs deliver video programming to computer screens, tablets and mobile devices. The FCC notes that MVPDs also offer internet and phone services as core elements of their business models.[118]

History of Cable and Satellite Regulation

The MVPD regulation of today has evolved from early cable regulation. Cable systems send signals through a wire—coaxial cable or fiber-optic lines—and do not use the spectrum. Cable television emerged because some people could not get a broadcast television signal, particularly in rural areas. In the 1940s, a power company employee built a large antenna in the Appalachian Mountains of Pennsylvania that received signals from Philadelphia television stations. A wire ran from the antenna to a building and from there to homes, giving birth to cable television.[119] For decades, it was called "community antenna television" or CATV.

Initially, the FCC decided it had no jurisdiction over CATV.[120] But broadcast television station owners feared CATV could take away their viewers and advertisers and urged the FCC to reconsider. In 1962, noting that some CATV operators used the spectrum to transmit signals from stations to cable system antennas, the FCC decided it had jurisdiction over at least part of the CATV business.[121] When the commission adopted several CATV rules, cable operators challenged the commission's authority to control CATV, but the U.S. Supreme Court upheld the FCC's jurisdiction.[122] The Court said that because the FCC was responsible for protecting the public's interest in broadcasting, it had the right to oversee CATV as ancillary to its responsibility toward broadcasting.

FCC rule changes in the mid-1970s allowed cable systems to move beyond delivery of local television signals to carry the signals of stations outside the local community. For example, HBO launched a pay cable service in 1975. With distant station signals and HBO, cable television could offer programming not available on local television stations.

About 40 years ago, communities wanted to regulate cable, arguing that system wires ran over public streets and sidewalks, and telephone companies wanted to offer cable services throughout the country. Cable operators did not want regulation. Trying to strike a compromise, Congress adopted the Cable Communications Policy Act of 1984.[123] The law gave local and state governments and the federal government shared authority over cable.

A few years later, critics said the 1984 law gave the cable industry monopoly power in communities and allowed cable companies to raise rates without limit, provide poor customer service and prevent competition. Congress responded by re-regulating cable in the Cable Television Consumer Protection and Competition Act of 1992.[124] The 1992 law regulated rates cable systems charged subscribers. It also required cable systems to carry local broadcast television stations and to deliver other programming, such as ESPN and MTV, to direct broadcast satellite companies and other cable competitors. The law also barred local governments from allowing one cable system to monopolize service if others wanted to compete.

When Congress adopted the Telecommunications Act of 1996, it loosened many of the cable regulations imposed in 1992.[125] Designed primarily to foster competition in the telephone industry, the 1996 law also deregulated cable subscriber rates, again allowing cable companies to raise most prices without government permission.

The 1984, 1992 and 1996 laws did not define cable's First Amendment status. The U.S. Supreme Court first decided the cable industry had protection similar to the print media,[126] then suggested it was not certain what First Amendment analysis should be applied to cable television[127] and finally applied strict scrutiny to cable content regulations.[128]

Just as the emergence of cable required the FCC to consider its role in regulation, so did the emergence of direct broadcast satellite services to consumers. DBS uses a small dish attached to a roof or the side of a house to receive signals from a high-powered satellite. More than 34 million American households receive their television programming by subscribing to a DBS service.[129]

Years ago, the FCC encouraged DBS service to develop as a cable competitor by declining to classify satellite service as broadcasting. The commission's decision relieved DBS of the regulatory burdens that broadcasters, and to a lesser extent cable, faced. The commission instead categorized DBS as a point-to-multipoint nonbroadcast service, a ruling upheld in court.[130] Dissatisfied with the FCC's decision not to impose regulations on DBS, Congress passed the Cable Television Consumer Protection and Competition Act of 1992. The law required DBS providers to abide by the political broadcasting rules in Sections 315 and 312(a)(7), discussed earlier in this chapter.

DBS emerged as a challenger to cable's dominance when Congress allowed satellite services to offer subscribers their local television stations as well as satellite programming.[131] As DBS grew, the FCC imposed additional regulations. For example, the FCC required satellite operators to set aside 4 percent of their channel capacity for educational or informational programming.[132] The commission said carrying noncommercial or public broadcast stations would not satisfy this requirement. The FCC also required DBS systems to comply with the same advertising limits during children's programming the commission applied to broadcast television stations.[133]

Must-Carry and Retransmission Consent

must-carry rule Regulations enacted under the federal cable law that require multichannel video programming distributors to transmit local broadcast television stations. Also called the cable carriage requirement.

retransmission consent Part of the federal cable law allowing broadcast stations to negotiate a fee for retransmission of their programs.

The Cable Television Consumer Protection and Competition Act of 1992 contained two provisions that required the carriage of broadcast stations on cable, DBS and all MVPD systems—the **must-carry rule** and **retransmission consent**. The 1992 law prohibits these providers from retransmitting a broadcast station without the broadcaster's explicit permission. The law instead gives the broadcaster the ability to negotiate with the MVPD for carriage. When the 1992 law passed, broadcast programming was the most popular content available on cable and DBS systems. One of the key concepts behind retransmission consent was the idea that broadcasters like ABC or CBS were producing popular content carried on large cable systems such as Comcast and Time Warner, but very few consumers received their broadcast programs over

REAL WORLD LAW
FCC OVERTURNS SPORTS BLACKOUT RULES

Recently, the Federal Communications Commission ended its 40-year enforcement of sports blackout rules, meaning it would allow multichannel video programming distributors to transmit sports programming even if a sports event was blacked out on a local broadcast station. According to the FCC, "This action removes Commission protection of the private blackout policies of sports leagues, which require local broadcast stations to black out a game if a team does not sell a certain percentage of tickets by a certain time prior to the game."[xiii]

The FCC said the decision offers transparency to sports fans and allows sports leagues to choose to continue the blackout policies through private agreements with programming distributors. In the absence of FCC rules, MVPDs must still obtain the necessary rights to distribute a sporting event from an alternative source.[xiv]

the air using an antenna. This meant that the broadcasters did not receive advertising revenue for their programming. The 1992 law allowed broadcasters to negotiate with cable systems to permit retransmission of their content generally for a fee and did not give the FCC authority to force broadcasters to consent to carriage.[134]

Because not all broadcast channels were popular enough to be sought after by an MVPD, the law also granted broadcasters the option to require MVPDs to carry their programming rather than negotiating for retransmission. Must-carry, also called the cable carriage requirement, means that if a broadcast station chooses must-carry status, it may not be dropped from an MVPD's channel lineup. By asserting its must-carry rights, the broadcaster cannot demand payment for its content from the MVPD.

Every three years, commercial broadcast stations choose between must-carry and retransmission consent. Noncommercial stations may not choose retransmission consent; they are carried under the must-carry provision.

In the 1990s, the cable industry fought the must-carry rule in court. Cable companies argued that a system can carry only a limited number of networks. Finding room to carry a local station's signal could force a cable system to eliminate other programming it already carried—Food Network, for example. Cable companies also said the must-carry rules were content-specific regulations, forcing cable to choose a local station over some other programming. Congress would have to show it had a compelling interest to justify imposing a content-specific rule, cable companies argued, and no such compelling interest existed.

Nearly 25 years ago, the U.S. Supreme Court upheld the must-carry rules in *Turner Broadcasting System, Inc. v. FCC* (excerpted at the end of this chapter). The Supreme Court applied the First Amendment test it uses for print media to cable: If the regulation affects speech because of its content, apply strict scrutiny; if the regulation is content neutral, apply an intermediate standard.[135] (Strict scrutiny and intermediate scrutiny are discussed in Chapter 2.)

In the second *Turner Broadcasting System, Inc. v. FCC* decision, in 1997, the U.S. Supreme Court refused to accept the cable industry's argument that the must-carry rules were content specific.[136] The must-carry rules are content neutral because they do not dictate specific programming, the Court said. To determine the rules' constitutionality, the Court applied the test it established in *United States v. O'Brien* (Chapter 2).[137] The *O'Brien* test applies to regulations incidentally affecting speech when that is not the regulation's primary purpose. The rules protect broadcast stations, which is an important objective, the Court said. In enacting them, Congress did not intend to directly affect cable systems' speech. Rather, Congress needed to adopt the rules to achieve its purpose of ensuring consumers' access to local broadcast stations.[138]

When the cable industry again challenged the must-carry rules in 2009, the U.S. Court of Appeals for the Second Circuit rejected the argument that must-carry rules violate cable operators' First Amendment rights.[139] The U.S. Supreme Court refused to hear the case.

In 2015, the FCC implemented the requirements of the Satellite Television Extension and Localism Act Reauthorization Act of 2014, which aimed to modernize the must-carry and retransmission consent rules but maintain the basic framework of the 1992 Cable Act.[140]

satellite market modification rule
Part of the Satellite Television Extension and Localism Act Reauthorization Act of 2014 that allows a television station, satellite operator or county government to request the addition or deletion of communities from a broadcast station's local television market.

Specifically, the law added a new **satellite market modification rule**, which allows a television station, satellite operator or county government to request the addition or deletion of communities from a broadcast station's local television market to better reflect current market realities. For example, in many communities, existing satellite delivery of a local broadcast television station doesn't exist because it is not technically or economically feasible.[141]

When the FCC receives a market modification request, it considers five factors that would allow a petitioner to demonstrate it provides local service to the community, including the consideration of access to television stations located in the same state. Additionally, the FCC initiated a review of the current process for evaluating whether broadcasters and MVPDs are negotiating for retransmission consent in good faith. The goal of the review of the retransmission consent rule is to ensure that negotiations are conducted fairly and "in a way that benefits consumers of video programming services."[142]

Recently, several networks have challenged MVPD decisions about placement of their networks within subscription packages, which determine viewer access. In 2016, the D.C. Circuit Court of Appeals decided that when a network brings forward a complaint about carriage requirements, it must show that its request for carriage would provide a net benefit to the MVPD. The case involved a claim by the Tennis Channel that Comcast discriminated against it in favor of affiliated networks.[143]

Earlier, the Game Show Network alleged that Cablevision discriminated against it when the cable company repositioned the network to a premium sports tier, which meant viewers

REAL WORLD LAW
ONLINE VIDEO DISTRIBUTORS

Online video distributors are entities that provide video programming using the internet. Currently, the Federal Communications Commission groups video content distribution into broadcast television stations, multichannel video programming distributors and online video distributors. Consumers need a broadband connection to receive video content from OVDs. The FCC recently asked for comment on whether to expand its MVPD definition to include OVDs,[xv] but has not yet taken any action.

Under the FCC's current definition, an OVD is different from an MVPD.[xvi] OVDs are diverse and include a variety of types of distributors, such as movie companies that release their films online instead of distributing them for viewing in a movie theater. Examples of OVDs are Sling TV, Apple TV and Sony's PlayStation Vue.

The FCC noted that OVDs may "be involved in providing video storage and delivery services, content creation or aggregation (i.e., networks, studios, and sports leagues), or device manufacturing. Several technology companies, notably Amazon, Apple, Google, and Microsoft, also serve as OVDs. Each company takes a slightly different approach to integrating its online video services with storage services, apps, and devices to attract and retain customers."[xvii]

OVDs attempting to enter the marketplace face several challenges, including access to sufficient internet capacity to allow for a high-quality viewing experience. Recently, the FCC began an inquiry to determine whether it should address issues that independent video programmers face in gaining carriage in the current marketplace.[xviii]

would have to pay more to access the network's programming. The Game Show Network said WE tv and Wedding Central, comparable networks, remained on a less expensive, expanded basic tier.[144] Cablevision said it moved the network because of low viewership. An administrative law judge decided in favor of the Game Show Network, citing evidence of discrimination, and ordered Cablevision to put the channel back on the expanded basic tier and pay a fine.[145] FCC commissioners reviewed the decision and reversed. They said that the Game Show Network failed to produce evidence of discrimination.[146]

The Federal Communications Commission has regulatory power over emerging internet-based video services like Sling TV because these services use a high-speed internet connection to deliver video content to consumers.

In two decisions, one in 2017 and one in 2018, the FCC's Media Bureau denied two complaints filed by The Word Network, which provides original, African-American ministry programming. The FCC Media Bureau develops, recommends and administers the FCC's policy and licensing programs related to the media industry. In both complaints, The Word Network alleged that Comcast violated FCC carriage requirements by replacing The Word Network with Impact Network, which features the same kind of programming. The network also complained that when Comcast demanded exclusive digital distribution rights to The Word Network, it was asserting a financial interest in the network. The Media Bureau concluded that The Word Network did not demonstrate that Comcast had discriminated against it when it replaced The Word Network with Impact. The Media Bureau also decided that Comcast's demand for an exclusive license for digital distribution did not amount to a demand for a financial interest in the network.[147]

Public Access Channels

By the time Congress adopted the Cable Communications Policy Act of 1984, most cable franchises already included provisions for public, educational or governmental access channels. The 1984 statute made that reality the law. Congress saw **PEG access channels** as a way to allow the public, various educational institutions and local governments to have access to cable systems in ways Congress does not require for newspapers, magazines, radio and television stations and other mass media. The 1984 law sets aside channels for public, educational or governmental use.[148] Although the law does not require cable system operators to agree to carry PEG channels, they usually do.

Public access channels generally allow local citizens, on a first-come basis, to put on programming they choose. Many municipalities have a government official or nonprofit organization oversee public channel programming.[149] Local school boards and colleges use educational channels. Government channels often carry city council and county board meetings. The 1984 cable act prohibits cable system operators from exercising any editorial control over PEG or leased access programming.[150]

PEG access channels
Channels that cable systems set aside for public, educational and governmental use.

The Cable Television Consumer Protection and Competition Act of 1992 also required DBS operators to offer leased access channels for noncommercial educational purposes,[151] but a federal appellate court rejected the PEG and leased access requirements as infringing on DBS providers' First Amendment rights.[152]

As noted in Chapter 2, in 2019 the U.S. Supreme Court considered whether a municipally licensed public access television channel's denial of access to programming it deemed offensive violated the First Amendment rights of the employees who submitted the content. The Second Circuit Court of Appeals determined that the cable public access television channel was "the electronic version of the public square," so its denial of access violated the First Amendment.[153]

The Supreme Court disagreed. In a 5–4 decision, Justice Brett Kavanaugh concluded that the First Amendment did not apply; the cable operator was not a state actor because it did not perform "a function traditionally exclusively performed by the state."[154] Both the majority and the dissent acknowledged that New York law extensively regulates cable operators, limiting their "editorial discretion and in effect requir[ing them] to operate almost like a common carrier."[155] Still, the majority said this did not make the cable company a state actor subject to the First Amendment.

INTERNET REGULATION

The U.S. Supreme Court held in *Reno v. American Civil Liberties Union* that the internet has complete First Amendment protection.[156] *Reno v. ACLU* decided a challenge to the Communications Decency Act, a provision of the Telecommunications Act of 1996.[157] The CDA prohibited transmitting indecent, patently offensive or obscene material to minors over the internet.

To determine the CDA's constitutionality, the Court had to decide what First Amendment protections applied to the internet. The U.S. Supreme Court has said each mass medium has its own peculiarities, so there may need to be adjustments to a medium's First Amendment rights. Broadcasting, as discussed throughout this chapter, uses public spectrum, which justifies its limited First Amendment protection. In *Reno*, the Supreme Court said that the internet did not use the spectrum and was not as invasive as broadcasting. Families not wanting their children to have internet access do not need to subscribe to an internet service. Unlike broadcasting, the internet does not have any special characteristics that require decreasing its First Amendment rights, the *Reno* Court held. Historically, the internet has not been "subject to the type of government supervision and regulation that has attended the broadcast industry."[158]

Justice John Paul Stevens, writing for the Court majority, characterized the internet as "a unique medium" that is "a vast platform from which to address and hear from a worldwide audience of millions of readers, viewers, researchers and buyers. Any person or organization with a computer connected to the internet can 'publish' information."[159]

Having held that internet content has full First Amendment protection, the Court overturned the CDA's restrictions on transmitting indecent and patently offensive material using the internet. The Court upheld the ban on obscene content sent over the internet. The

First Amendment does not protect obscene material on the internet or in any medium (see Chapter 10).[160]

For the past 15 years, the FCC has considered and reconsidered its role in internet regulation. While Congress has not given the commission explicit authority over the internet, the FCC has said it had ancillary jurisdiction under the Communications Act of 1934.[161] As noted earlier in the chapter, years before Congress adopted the first cable television law in 1984, the U.S. Supreme Court held that the 1934 act's language gave the FCC jurisdiction over cable as "ancillary" to its statutory right to regulate broadcasting.[162]

Although initially the FCC took a "hands off the internet" approach, more recently it claimed ancillary jurisdiction over broadband. The FCC's claim of jurisdiction over broadband has been both upheld and rejected by courts.

About 15 years ago, the U.S. Supreme Court held that cable television systems do not have to give their customers a choice of internet service providers.[163] The case before the Supreme Court turned on determining the legal category for cable internet services. The Telecommunications Act of 1996 said telecommunications services are utilities that can be more strictly regulated than broadcast. This could include requiring them to sell access to their networks.[164] However, the FCC determined in 2002 that cable internet access is not a telecommunications service but an information service.[165] Information services, according to the FCC, provide enhanced services, like web hosting, and are more than a basic utility that provides nothing more than transmission, like a telephone wire.

One way to gain high-speed internet access is through a cable modem offered by a cable television system. An ISP provides the internet connection. Many cable systems wanted their customers to use only an ISP they owned or with which they had an agreement. But other ISPs might want to use a cable system to provide high-speed internet access through cable modems. Must cable systems allow these other ISPs to offer access?

The U.S. Supreme Court said the 1996 law was ambiguous and the FCC had a right to interpret how the law applied to ISPs. The Court's ruling affirmed the authority of the FCC to categorize cable modem service as an information service, permitting cable system operators to choose which ISPs may offer high-speed internet access through cable modems. The ruling also prevented local cable television franchising authorities from regulating high-speed internet access through cable modems.

The way the FCC categorizes internet services has an impact on how it will regulate the internet. Five years ago, as part of its 2015 Open Internet Order, the FCC changed the classification of internet services from an information service to a basic telecommunications service. This classification change allowed the FCC to regulate broadband providers as common carriers, meaning they were treated like landline telephone providers and other utilities.[166] As such, they must make their services available to everyone on the same terms.

In 2018, under new leadership, the FCC reversed the 2015 classification. The Restoring Internet Freedom Order reinstated the information service classification of broadband internet.[167] As a result of the classification change back to an information service, the FCC restored its earlier determination that broadband is not a commercial service subject to strict regulation. It also restored the authority of the Federal Trade Commission to provide oversight of ISPs' privacy practices.[168]

Net Neutrality

The 2018 FCC order also rolled back **net neutrality** rules. At its core, net neutrality simply means that ISPs cannot charge content providers to speed up the delivery of their content. Supporters of net neutrality say that the concept is important for the internet to maintain its democratic status. They argue that ISPs should not favor some content providers over others simply because they can charge them more money to deliver their content, even if that content takes up a lot of broadband space (for example, video). Notable corporate supporters of net neutrality principles include Google, Microsoft, Netflix and Twitter.[169]

Opponents of net neutrality say that if ISPs cannot charge more money for different kinds of transmissions such as those required by online video distributors, then it stifles innovation and runs against the ISPs' financial interests. Opponents to net neutrality principles include Verizon, AT&T and Comcast. The net neutrality issue also tends to fall along political party lines with Democrats supporting net neutrality principles and Republicans opposing them.[170]

The FCC issued its first net neutrality order more than a decade ago.[171] In the first court challenge to that order, the D.C. Circuit Court of Appeals held that the FCC did not have jurisdiction to regulate ISP broadband services.[172] After that court decision, the FCC tried again, issuing new net neutrality rules in its 2010 Open Internet Report and Order.[173] Verizon challenged the 2010 order. In 2014, the D.C. Circuit Court struck down the FCC's new net neutrality rules.[174] The court said the FCC's Open Internet Orders failed to justify its shift away from the commission's previous decision to categorize ISPs as information services. The court's decision left open the door for the FCC to pursue new net neutrality rules if it adequately justified its reclassification of ISPs as a telecommunications service.[175]

The FCC's 2015 Open Internet Order reclassified high-speed internet service as a telecommunications service under Title II of the Telecommunications Act of 1996 and effectively began treating broadband service providers like a public utility.[176] The 2015 FCC order banned throttling, blocking and paid prioritization of content. This meant providers were not permitted to "impair or degrade" or block lawful internet traffic on the basis of content. The ban on paid prioritization cuts to the heart of net neutrality and prohibited broadband providers from creating paid "fast lanes" to favor some kinds of traffic over others.[177]

The FCC's 3–2 vote on the 2015 order divided along party lines. The three Democrats on the commission voted in favor of the order,[178] while the two Republicans on the commission voted against the order.[179] Nearly 50 organizations sued to block the rules that took effect in 2015; the D.C. Circuit Court consolidated all of the lawsuits[180] and in 2016 denied the petitions for review of the 2015 order.[181] When President Trump nominated Pai to lead the FCC in 2017, many speculated that net neutrality would end. In

Viewers of comedian John Oliver's weekly HBO show have twice crashed the Federal Communications Commission's system by submitting thousands of comments on net neutrality.

mid-2017, Pai announced that the FCC would begin the process of loosening net neutrality enforcement regulations.[182]

In 2018, the FCC adopted the Restoring Internet Freedom Order that eliminated the net neutrality rules against blocking, throttling and paid prioritization as well as the general conduct rule, which applied on a case-by-case basis to practices that harmed consumers.[183] The 3–2 vote in 2018 remained along party lines, with Republicans now in the majority. The 2018 order took effect in June of that year, amid 22 state attorneys general, several companies and several public interest groups filing lawsuits in various courts to challenge the new order.[184]

Currently, 34 states and the District of Columbia have introduced a total of 120 bills and resolutions regarding net neutrality. Five states—California, New Jersey, Oregon, Vermont and Washington—have enacted legislation or adopted resolutions. In Vermont, legislation required an ISP to certify it was in compliance with net neutrality standards, as articulated in the 2015 order, to receive a government contract to provide internet service. The state also requires the attorney general to review an ISP's network management practices to ensure they are in compliance with the 2015 rules.[185]

California and New Jersey both passed resolutions urging Congress to restore net neutrality.[186]

In 2019, supporters of net neutrality in both the House and Senate introduced the Save the Internet Act. The legislation would overturn the 2018 rules and restore net neutrality protections from the 2015 order.[187] The bill passed in the House in 2019, but the Senate majority leader said it would be "dead on arrival" in the Senate and the White House said it would veto the bill if it were passed.[188]

EMERGING LAW

Seven years ago, the FCC sought to revitalize AM radio services. AM radio broadcasting is a radio technology that is more prone to interference and has inferior sound quality to FM radio broadcasting. Since the launch of the AM Radio Revitalization Initiative, the FCC has made several rule changes. The new rules give AM stations more flexibility, for example, the ability to purchase an FM translator in a secondary market to extend an AM station's reach.[189] An FM translator is a receiver that rebroadcasts the AM signal to a surrounding area.

AM radio is often an important source of news and information during disasters. For example, when Hurricanes Harvey and Irma recently impacted nine major media markets along the Gulf Coast, radio listening surged. When Hurricanes Irma and Maria devastated Puerto Rico, the broadcast radio audience increased 11 percent, with local stations adding nearly 100,000 listeners.[190]

AM revitalization remains a priority for the FCC, which recently proposed additional new rules to solve interference problems as more AM stations have purchased FM translators.[191] Digital radio, or using digital technology to transmit a clearer and more efficient radio signal over the spectrum, is well positioned for substantial growth over the next decade. Recently, the FCC approved the use of digital radio technology for AM and FM radio. In the next few years,

AM and FM stations will begin to broadcast a digital signal alongside their current analog signals on the same frequency.[192]

In 2017, the FCC gave the go-ahead for the voluntary adoption of ATSC 3.0, a new broadcast transmission standard commonly called Next Generation TV. The FCC's Advanced Television Systems Committee developed the new standard, which gives broadcasters the ability to support interactivity, a superior 4K picture, targeted advertising and content, transmission to mobile devices and the integration of broadcast programming with other internet protocol services.[193]

The move to ATSC 3.0 updates technologies that are more than 20 years old. FCC Chair Pai said the new standard, supported by broadcasters, would also allow for ultrahigh definition and immersive audio, better access to content for the disabled and the development of a substantially more advanced emergency alert system.[194]

Along with the Next Generation TV authorization, the FCC implemented a series of rules to facilitate a transition from ATSC 1.0 to ATSC 3.0. For example, broadcasters who choose to implement Next Generation TV are required to air a local simulcast of the primary ATSC 3.0 video programming stream in the current ATSC 1.0 format. One of the challenges with the implementation is that ATSC 3.0 cannot use the older ATSC 1.0 interface. So, to meet the simulcast requirement, Next Generation TV stations must partner with another "host" station in their local market. This local simulcasting requirement only applies to the primary video programming stream aired by Next Generation TV broadcasters on their ATSC 3.0 channels.[195]

The FCC's Next Generation TV rules went into effect in 2018. Phoenix, Ariz., served as the first "model market" for Next Generation TV, with 10 participating television stations.[196] In 2019, 40 markets announced they would begin to roll out Next Generation TV.[197]

For more than 25 years, the FCC has conducted different kinds of auctions that allow companies to buy spectrum allocation to meet changing needs of both industry and consumers. Recently, the FCC auctioned off a substantial amount of advanced wireless service (AWS-3) spectrum, freed up by transferring U.S. Defense Department and other government agencies to different bands. AWS-3 is the "high-frequency band" of the spectrum that carries lots of data but loses quality performance when it travels through building walls. A spectrum auction works like other auctions—spectrum goes to the highest bidder.[198]

In 2017, the FCC concluded its incentive auction, which under the Spectrum Act of 2012 allowed the FCC to provide broadcasters with the ability to voluntarily relinquish their spectrum usage rights (in a reverse auction), then auction those rights to companies that need flexible-use wireless licenses in a forward auction. The FCC has used this process to "repack" the spectrum, reorganizing and reassigning broadcast television stations to channels in the TV band while allocating the blocks of cleared spectrum in the flexible wireless use band to wireless providers.[199]

In 2019, the verified cost of the repacking process was $1.8 billion, nearly $100 million more than Congress authorized in the Spectrum Act. Congress passed the RAY BAUM's Act in 2018 to cover the shortfall and provide additional funding for 2019. The spectrum repacking process will continue in the coming years. The Spectrum Pipeline Act of 2015 requires the FCC to hold more auctions to make additional spectrum available for mobile services by 2024.[200]

CASES FOR STUDY

For study resources and a case archive, go to **edge.sagepub.com/medialaw7e**.

Thinking About It

The two case excerpts that follow deal with broadcasting and cable television. As you read these case excerpts, keep the following questions in mind:

- What reasons does the U.S. Supreme Court give for the way it applies the First Amendment to broadcasting and cable?

- Do these two decisions logically lead to the Supreme Court ruling in *Reno v. ACLU* that the internet should have full First Amendment protection? Why or why not?

- In what ways are these two cases still relevant today, as technology has fundamentally changed the electronic media landscape?

Red Lion Broadcasting Co., Inc. v. Federal Communications Commission
SUPREME COURT OF THE UNITED STATES
395 U.S. 367 (1969)

**JUSTICE BYRON WHITE
delivered the Court's opinion:**

The Federal Communications Commission has for many years imposed on radio and television broadcasters the requirement that discussion of public issues be presented on broadcast stations, and that each side of those issues must be given fair coverage. This is known as the fairness doctrine, which originated very early in the history of broadcasting and has maintained its present outlines for some time. It is an obligation whose content has been defined in a long series of FCC rulings in particular cases, and which is distinct from the statutory requirement of Section 315 of the Communications Act that equal time be allotted all qualified candidates for public office. Two aspects of the fairness doctrine, relating to personal attacks in the context of controversial public issues and to political editorializing, were codified more precisely in the form of FCC regulations in 1967. The two cases before us now, which were decided separately below, challenge the constitutional and statutory bases of the doctrine and component rules. *Red Lion* involves the application of the fairness doctrine to a particular broadcast, and *RTNDA* [*Radio and Television News Directors Association*] arises as an action to review the FCC's 1967 promulgation of the personal attack and political editorializing regulations, which were laid down after the *Red Lion* litigation had begun.

The Red Lion Broadcasting Company is licensed to operate a Pennsylvania radio station, WGCB. On November 27, 1964, WGCB carried a 15-minute broadcast by the Reverend Billy James Hargis as part of a "Christian Crusade" series. A book by Fred J. Cook entitled "Goldwater—Extremist on the Right" was discussed by Hargis, who said that Cook had been fired by a newspaper for making false charges against city officials; that Cook had then worked for a Communist-affiliated publication; that he had defended Alger Hiss and attacked J. Edgar Hoover and the Central Intelligence Agency; and that he had now written a "book to smear and destroy Barry Goldwater." When Cook heard of the broadcast he concluded that he had been personally attacked and demanded free reply time, which the station refused. After an exchange of letters among Cook, Red Lion, and the FCC, the FCC declared that the Hargis broadcast constituted a personal attack on Cook; that Red Lion had failed to meet its obligation under the fairness doctrine . . . to send a tape, transcript, or summary of the broadcast to Cook and offer him reply time; and that the station must provide reply time whether or not Cook would pay for it. On review in the Court of Appeals for the District of Columbia Circuit, the FCC's position was upheld as constitutional and otherwise proper. . . .

Believing that the specific application of the fairness doctrine in *Red Lion*, and the promulgation of the regulations in *RTNDA*, are both authorized by Congress and enhance rather than abridge the freedoms of speech and press protected by the First Amendment, we hold them valid and constitutional, reversing the judgment below in *RTNDA* and affirming the judgment below in *Red Lion*.

The history of the emergence of the fairness doctrine and of the related legislation shows that the Commission's action in the *Red Lion* case did not exceed its authority, and that in adopting the new regulations the Commission was implementing congressional policy rather than embarking on a frolic of its own.

Before 1927, the allocation of frequencies was left entirely to the private sector, and the result was chaos. It quickly became apparent that broadcast frequencies constituted a scarce resource whose use could be regulated and rationalized only by the Government. Without government control, the medium would be of little use because of the cacophony of competing voices, none of which could be clearly and predictably heard. Consequently, the Federal Radio Commission was established to allocate frequencies among competing applicants in a manner responsive to the public "convenience, interest, or necessity."

Very shortly thereafter the Commission expressed its view that the "public interest requires ample play for the free and fair competition of opposing views, and the commission believes that the principle applies . . . to all discussions of issues of importance to the public." This doctrine was applied through denial of license renewals or construction permits, both by the FRC, and its successor FCC. After an extended period during which the licensee was obliged not only to cover and to cover fairly the views of others, but also to refrain from expressing his own personal views, the latter limitation on the licensee was abandoned and the doctrine developed into its present form.

There is a twofold duty laid down by the FCC's decisions and described by the 1949 Report on Editorializing by Broadcast Licensees. The broadcaster must give adequate coverage to public issues, and coverage must be fair in that it accurately reflects the opposing views. This must be done at the broadcaster's own expense if sponsorship is unavailable. Moreover, the duty must be met by programming obtained at the licensee's own initiative if available from no other source. . . .

When a personal attack has been made on a figure involved in a public issue, . . . [it is required] that the individual attacked himself be offered an opportunity to respond. Likewise, where one candidate is endorsed in a political editorial, the other candidates must themselves be offered reply time to use personally or through a spokesman. These obligations differ from the general fairness requirement that issues be presented, and presented with coverage of competing views, in that the broadcaster does not have the option of presenting the attacked party's side himself or choosing a third party to represent that side. But insofar as there is an obligation of the broadcaster to see that both sides are presented, and insofar as that is an affirmative obligation, the personal attack doctrine and regulations do not differ from the preceding fairness doctrine. The simple fact that the attacked men or unendorsed candidates may respond themselves or through agents is not a critical distinction, and indeed, it is not unreasonable for the FCC to conclude that the objective of adequate presentation of all sides may best be served by allowing those most closely affected to make the response, rather than leaving the response in the hands of the station which has attacked their candidacies, endorsed their opponents, or carried a personal attack upon them. . . .

The broadcasters challenge the fairness doctrine and its specific manifestations in the personal attack and political editorial rules on conventional First Amendment grounds, alleging that the rules abridge their freedom of speech and press. Their contention is that the First Amendment protects their desire to use their allotted frequencies continuously to broadcast whatever they choose, and to exclude whomever they choose from ever using that frequency. No man may be prevented from saying or publishing what he thinks, or from refusing in his speech or other utterances to give equal weight to the views of his opponents. This right, they say, applies equally to broadcasters.

Although broadcasting is clearly a medium affected by a First Amendment interest, differences in the characteristics of new media justify differences in the standards applied to them. For example, the ability of new technology to produce sounds more raucous than those of the human voice justifies restrictions on the sound level, and on the hours and places of use, of sound trucks so long as the restrictions are reasonable and applied without discrimination.

Just as the Government may limit the use of sound-amplifying equipment potentially so noisy that it drowns out civilized private speech, so may the Government limit the use of broadcast equipment. The right of free speech of a broadcaster, the user of a sound truck, or any other individual does not embrace a right to snuff out the free speech of others. . . .

It was . . . the chaos which ensued from permitting anyone to use any frequency at whatever power level he wished, which made necessary the enactment of the Radio Act of 1927 and the Communications Act of 1934. It was this reality which at the very least necessitated first the division of the radio spectrum into portions reserved respectively for public broadcasting and for other important radio uses such as amateur operation, aircraft, police, defense, and navigation; and then the subdivision of each portion, and assignment of specific frequencies to individual users or groups of users. Beyond this, however, because the frequencies reserved for public broadcasting were limited in number, it was essential for the Government to tell some applicants that they could not broadcast at all because there was room for only a few.

Where there are substantially more individuals who want to broadcast than there are frequencies to allocate, it is idle to posit an unabridgeable First Amendment right to broadcast comparable to the right of every individual to speak, write, or publish. If 100 persons want broadcast licenses but there are only 10 frequencies to allocate, all of them may have the same "right" to a license; but if there is to be any effective communication by radio, only a few can be licensed and the rest must be barred from the airwaves. It would be strange if the First Amendment, aimed at protecting and furthering communications, prevented the Government from making radio communication possible by requiring licenses to broadcast and by limiting the number of licenses so as not to overcrowd the spectrum.

This has been the consistent view of the Court. Congress unquestionably has the power to grant and deny licenses and to eliminate existing stations. No one has a First Amendment right to a license or to monopolize a radio frequency; to deny a station license because "the public interest" requires it "is not a denial of free speech."

By the same token, as far as the First Amendment is concerned those who are licensed stand no better than those to whom licenses are refused. A license permits broadcasting, but the licensee has no constitutional right to be the one who holds the license or to monopolize a radio frequency to the exclusion of his fellow citizens. There is nothing in the First Amendment which prevents the Government from requiring a licensee to share his frequency with others and to conduct himself as a proxy or fiduciary with obligations to present those views and voices which are representative of his community and which would otherwise, by necessity, be barred from the airwaves.

This is not to say that the First Amendment is irrelevant to public broadcasting. On the contrary, it has a major role to play as the Congress itself recognized in forbidding FCC interference with "the right of free speech by means of radio communication." Because of the scarcity of radio frequencies, the Government is permitted to put restraints on licensees in favor of others whose views should be expressed on this unique medium. But the people as a whole retain their interest in free speech by radio and their collective right to have the medium function consistently with the ends and purposes of the First Amendment. It is the right of the viewers and listeners, not the right of the broadcasters, which is paramount. It is the purpose of the First Amendment to preserve an uninhibited marketplace of ideas in which truth will ultimately prevail, rather than to countenance monopolization of that market, whether it be by the Government itself or a private licensee. "Speech concerning public affairs is more than self-expression; it is the essence of self-government." It is the right of the public to receive suitable access to social, political, esthetic, moral, and other ideas and experiences which is crucial here. That right may not constitutionally be abridged either by Congress or by the FCC.

Rather than confer frequency monopolies on a relatively small number of licensees, in a Nation of 200,000,000, the Government could surely have decreed that each frequency should be shared among all or some of those who wish to use it, each being assigned a portion of the broadcast day or the broadcast week. The ruling and regulations at issue here do not go quite so far. They assert that under specified circumstances, a licensee must offer to make available a reasonable amount of broadcast time to those who have a view different from that which has already been expressed on his station. The expression of a political endorsement, or of a personal attack while dealing with a controversial public issue, simply triggers this time sharing. As we have said, the *First Amendment* confers no right on licensees to prevent others from broadcasting on "their" frequencies and no right to an unconditional monopoly of a scarce resource which the Government has denied others the right to use.

In terms of constitutional principle, and as enforced sharing of a scarce resource, the personal attack and political editorial rules are indistinguishable from the equal-time provision of Section 315, a specific enactment of Congress requiring stations to set aside reply time under specified circumstances and to which the fairness doctrine and these constituent regulations are important complements. That provision, which has been part of the law since 1927, has been held valid by this Court as an obligation of the licensee relieving him of any power in any way to prevent or censor the broadcast, and thus insulating him from liability for defamation. The constitutionality of the statute under the First Amendment was unquestioned.

Nor can we say that it is inconsistent with the First Amendment goal of producing an informed public capable of conducting its own affairs to require a broadcaster to permit answers to personal attacks occurring in the course of discussing controversial issues, or to require that the political opponents of those endorsed by the station be given a chance to communicate with the public. Otherwise, station owners and a few networks would have unfettered power to make time available only to the highest bidders, to communicate only their own views on public issues, people and candidates, and to permit on the air only those with whom they agreed. There is no sanctuary in the First Amendment for unlimited private censorship operating in a medium not open to all. "Freedom of the press from governmental interference under the First Amendment does not sanction repression of that freedom by private interests."

It is strenuously argued, however, that if political editorials or personal attacks will trigger an obligation in broadcasters to afford the opportunity for expression to speakers who need not pay for time and whose views are unpalatable to the licensees, then broadcasters will be irresistibly forced to self-censorship and their coverage of controversial public issues will be eliminated or at least rendered wholly ineffective. Such a result would indeed be a serious matter, for should licensees actually eliminate their coverage of controversial issues, the purposes of the doctrine would be stifled.

At this point, however, as the Federal Communications Commission has indicated, that possibility is at best speculative. The communications industry, and in particular the networks, have taken pains to present controversial issues in the past, and even now they do not assert that they intend to abandon their efforts in this regard. It would be better if the FCC's encouragement were never necessary to induce the broadcasters to meet their responsibility. And if experience with the administration of these doctrines indicates that they have the net effect of reducing rather than enhancing the volume and quality of coverage, there will be time enough to reconsider the constitutional implications. The fairness doctrine in the past has had no such overall effect.

That this will occur now seems unlikely, however, since if present licensees should suddenly prove timorous, the Commission is not powerless to insist that they give adequate and fair attention to public issues. It does not violate the First Amendment to treat licensees given the privilege of using scarce radio frequencies as proxies for the entire community, obligated to give suitable time and attention to matters of great public concern. To condition the granting or renewal of licenses on a willingness to present representative community views on controversial issues is consistent with the ends and purposes of those constitutional provisions forbidding the abridgment of freedom of speech and freedom of the press. Congress need not stand idly by and permit those with licenses to ignore the problems which beset the people or to exclude from the airways anything but their own views of fundamental questions. The statute, long administrative practice, and cases are to this effect.

Licenses to broadcast do not confer ownership of designated frequencies, but only the temporary privilege of using them. . . . The statute mandates the issuance of licenses if the "public convenience, interest, or necessity will be served thereby." . . . [In 1943] the Court considered the validity of the Commission's chain broadcasting regulations, which among other things forbade stations from devoting too much time to network programs in order that there be suitable opportunity for local programs serving local needs. The Court upheld the regulations, unequivocally recognizing that the Commission was more than a traffic policeman concerned with the technical aspects of broadcasting and that it neither exceeded its powers under the statute nor transgressed the First Amendment in interesting itself in general program format and the kinds of programs broadcast by licensees. . . .

It is argued that even if at one time the lack of available frequencies for all who wished to use them justified the Government's choice of those who would best serve the public interest by acting as proxy for those who would present differing views, or by giving the latter access directly to broadcast facilities, this condition no longer prevails so that continuing control is not justified. To this there are several answers.

Scarcity is not entirely a thing of the past. Advances in technology . . . have led to more efficient utilization of the frequency spectrum, but uses for that spectrum have also grown apace. Portions of the spectrum must be reserved for vital uses unconnected with human communication, such as radio-navigational aids used by aircraft and vessels. Conflicts have even emerged between such vital functions as defense preparedness and experimentation in methods of averting midair collisions through radio warning devices. . . .

The rapidity with which technological advances succeed one another to create more efficient use of spectrum space on the one hand, and to create new uses for that space by ever growing numbers of people on the other, makes it unwise to speculate on the future allocation of that space. It is enough to say that the resource is one of considerable and growing importance whose scarcity impelled its regulation by an agency authorized by Congress. . . .

Even where there are gaps in spectrum utilization, the fact remains that existing broadcasters have often attained their present position because of their initial government selection in competition with others before new technological advances opened new opportunities for further uses. Long experience in broadcasting, confirmed habits of listeners and viewers, network affiliation, and other advantages in program procurement give existing broadcasters a substantial advantage over new entrants, even where new entry is technologically possible. These advantages are the fruit of a preferred position conferred by the Government. Some present possibility for new entry by competing stations is not enough, in itself, to render unconstitutional the Government's effort to assure that a broadcaster's programming ranges widely enough to serve the public interest.

In view of the scarcity of broadcast frequencies, the Government's role in allocating those frequencies, and the legitimate claims of those unable without governmental assistance to gain access to those frequencies for expression of their views, we hold the regulations and ruling at issue here are both authorized by statute and constitutional. . . .

Turner Broadcasting System, Inc. v. Federal Communications Commission

SUPREME COURT OF THE UNITED STATES
512 U.S. 622 (1994)

JUSTICE ANTHONY KENNEDY
delivered the opinion of the Court:

. . . [T]he Cable Television Consumer Protection and Competition Act of 1992 requires cable television systems to devote a portion of their channels to the transmission of local broadcast television stations. This case presents the question whether these provisions abridge the freedom of speech or of the press, in violation of the First Amendment. . . .

The role of cable television in the Nation's communications system has undergone dramatic change over the past 45 years. Given the pace of technological advancement and the increasing convergence between cable and other electronic media, the cable industry today stands at the center of an ongoing telecommunications revolution with still undefined potential to affect the way we communicate and develop our intellectual resources.

The earliest cable systems were built in the late 1940's to bring clear broadcast television signals to remote or mountainous communities. The purpose was not to replace broadcast television but to enhance it. Modern cable systems do much more than enhance the reception of nearby broadcast television stations. With the capacity to carry dozens of channels and import distant programming signals via satellite or microwave relay, today's cable systems are in direct competition with over-the-air broadcasters as an independent source of television programming.

Broadcast and cable television are distinguished by the different technologies through which they reach viewers. Broadcast stations radiate electromagnetic signals from a central transmitting antenna. These signals can be captured, in turn, by any television set within the antenna's range. Cable systems, by contrast, rely upon a physical, point-to-point connection between a transmission facility and the television sets of individual subscribers. Cable systems make this connection much like telephone companies, using cable or optical fibers strung above ground or buried in ducts to reach the homes or businesses of subscribers. The construction of this physical infrastructure entails the use of public rights-of-way and easements and often results in the disruption of traffic on streets and other public property. As a result, the cable medium may depend for its very existence upon express permission from local governing authorities.

Cable technology affords two principal benefits over broadcast. First, it eliminates the signal interference sometimes encountered in over-the-air broadcasting and thus gives viewers undistorted reception of broadcast stations. Second, it is capable of transmitting many more channels than are available through broadcasting, giving subscribers access to far greater programming variety. . . .

The cable television industry includes both cable operators (those who own the physical cable network and transmit the cable signal to the viewer) and cable programmers (those who produce television programs and sell or license them to cable operators). In some cases, cable operators have acquired ownership of cable programmers, and vice versa. Although cable operators may create some of their own programming, most of their programming is drawn from outside sources. These outside sources include not only local or distant broadcast stations, but also the many national and regional cable programming networks that have emerged in recent years, such as CNN, MTV, ESPN, TNT, C-Span, The Family Channel, Nickelodeon, Arts and Entertainment, Black Entertainment Television, CourtTV, The Discovery Channel, American Movie Classics, Comedy Central, The Learning Channel, and The Weather Channel. Once the cable operator has selected the programming sources, the cable system functions, in essence, as a conduit for the speech of others, transmitting it on a continuous and unedited basis to subscribers.

In contrast to commercial broadcast stations, which transmit signals at no charge to viewers and generate revenues by selling time to advertisers, cable systems charge subscribers a monthly fee for the right to receive cable programming and rely to a lesser extent on advertising. In most instances, cable subscribers choose the stations they will receive by selecting among various plans, or "tiers," of cable service. In a typical offering, the basic tier consists of local broadcast stations plus a number of cable programming networks selected by the cable operator. For an additional cost, subscribers can obtain channels devoted to particular subjects or interests, such as recent-release feature movies, sports, children's programming, sexually explicit programming, and the like. Many cable systems also offer pay-per-view service, which allows an individual subscriber to order and pay a one-time fee to see a single movie or program at a set time of the day.

On October 5, 1992, Congress overrode a Presidential veto to enact the Cable Television Consumer Protection and Competition Act of 1992. Among other things, the Act subjects the cable industry to rate regulation by the Federal Communications Commission (FCC) and by municipal franchising authorities; prohibits municipalities from awarding exclusive franchises to cable operators; imposes various restrictions on cable programmers that are affiliated with cable operators; and directs the FCC to develop and promulgate regulations imposing minimum technical standards for cable operators. At issue in this case is the constitutionality of the so-called must-carry provisions, which require cable operators to carry the signals of a specified number of local broadcast television stations. . . .

Congress enacted the 1992 Cable Act after conducting three years of hearings on the structure and operation of the cable television industry. . . . Congress found that the physical characteristics of cable transmission, compounded by the increasing concentration of economic power in the cable industry, are endangering the ability of over-the-air broadcast television stations to compete for a viewing audience and thus for necessary operating revenues. Congress determined that regulation of the market for video programming was necessary to correct this competitive imbalance.

In particular, Congress found that over 60 percent of the households with television sets subscribe to cable, and for these households cable has replaced over-the-air broadcast television as the primary provider of video programming. This is so, Congress found, because "most subscribers to cable television systems do not or cannot maintain antennas to receive broadcast television services, do not have input selector switches to convert from a cable to antenna reception system, or cannot otherwise receive broadcast television services." In addition, Congress concluded that due to "local franchising requirements and the extraordinary expense of constructing more than one cable television system to serve a particular geographic area," the overwhelming majority of cable operators exercise a monopoly over cable service. "The result," Congress determined, "is undue market power for the cable operator as compared to that of consumers and video programmers."

According to Congress, this market position gives cable operators the power and the incentive to harm broadcast competitors. The power derives from the cable operator's ability, as owner of the transmission facility, to "terminate the retransmission of the broadcast signal, refuse to carry new signals, or reposition a broadcast signal to a disadvantageous channel position." The incentive derives from the economic reality that "cable television systems and broadcast television stations increasingly compete for television advertising revenues." By refusing carriage of broadcasters' signals, cable operators, as a practical matter, can reduce the number of households that have access to the broadcasters' programming, and thereby capture advertising dollars that would otherwise go to broadcast stations. . . .

In light of these technological and economic conditions, Congress concluded that unless cable operators are required to carry local broadcast stations, "[t]here is a substantial likelihood that . . . additional local broadcast signals will be deleted, repositioned, or not carried"; the "marked shift in market share" from broadcast to cable will continue to erode the advertising revenue base which sustains free local broadcast television; and that, as a consequence, "the economic viability of free local broadcast television and its ability to originate quality local programming will be seriously jeopardized." . . .

There can be no disagreement on an initial premise: Cable programmers and cable operators engage in and transmit speech, and they are entitled to the protection of the speech and press provisions of the First Amendment. Through "original programming or by exercising editorial discretion over which stations or programs to include in [their] repertoire," cable programmers and operators "seek to communicate messages on a wide variety of topics and in a wide variety of formats." By requiring cable systems to set aside a portion of their channels for local broadcasters, the must-carry rules regulate cable speech in two respects: The rules reduce the number of channels over which cable operators exercise unfettered control, and they render it more difficult for cable programmers to compete for carriage on the limited channels remaining. Nevertheless, because not every interference with speech triggers the same degree of scrutiny under the First Amendment, we must decide at the outset the level of scrutiny applicable to the must-carry provisions.

We address first the Government's contention that regulation of cable television should be analyzed under the same First Amendment standard that applies to regulation of broadcast television. It is true that our cases have permitted more intrusive regulation of broadcast speakers than of speakers in other media. . . . But the rationale for applying a less rigorous standard of First Amendment scrutiny to broadcast regulation, whatever its validity in the cases elaborating it, does not apply in the context of cable regulation.

The justification for our distinct approach to broadcast regulation rests upon the unique physical limitations of the broadcast medium. As a general matter, there are more would-be broadcasters than frequencies available in the electromagnetic spectrum. And if two broadcasters were to attempt to transmit over the same frequency in the same locale, they would interfere with one another's signals, so that neither could be heard at all. The scarcity of broadcast frequencies thus required the establishment of some regulatory mechanism to divide the electromagnetic spectrum and assign specific frequencies to particular broadcasters. In addition, the inherent physical limitation on the number of speakers who may use the broadcast medium has been thought to require some adjustment in traditional First Amendment analysis to permit the Government to place limited content restraints, and impose certain affirmative obligations, on broadcast licensees. As we said in *Red Lion*, "where there are substantially more individuals who want to broadcast than there are frequencies to allocate, it is idle to posit an unabridgeable First Amendment right to broadcast comparable to the right of every individual to speak, write, or publish." . . .

. . . The broadcast cases are inapposite in the present context because cable television does not suffer from the inherent limitations that characterize the broadcast medium. Indeed, given the rapid advances in fiber optics and digital compression technology, soon there may be no practical limitation on the number of speakers who may use the cable medium. Nor is there any danger of physical interference between two cable speakers attempting to share the same channel. . . .

This is not to say that the unique physical characteristics of cable transmission should be ignored when determining the constitutionality of regulations affecting cable speech. They should not. But whatever relevance these physical characteristics may have in the evaluation of particular cable regulations, they do not require the alteration of settled principles of our First Amendment jurisprudence. . . .

. . . Our precedents thus apply the most exacting scrutiny to regulations that suppress, disadvantage, or impose differential burdens upon speech because of its content. Laws that compel speakers to utter or distribute speech bearing a particular message are subject to the same rigorous scrutiny. In contrast, regulations that are unrelated to the content of speech are subject to an intermediate level of scrutiny, because in most cases they pose a less substantial risk of excising certain ideas or viewpoints from the public dialogue. . . .

As a general rule, laws that by their terms distinguish favored speech from disfavored speech on the basis of the ideas or views expressed are content-based. By contrast, laws that confer benefits or impose burdens on speech without reference to the ideas or views expressed are in most instances content-neutral.

Insofar as they pertain to the carriage of full-power broadcasters, the must-carry rules, on their face, impose burdens and confer benefits without reference to the content of speech. Although the provisions interfere with cable operators' editorial discretion by compelling them to offer carriage to a certain minimum number of broadcast stations, the extent of the interference does not depend upon the content of the cable operators' programming. The rules impose obligations upon all operators, save those with fewer than 300 subscribers, regardless of the programs or stations they now offer or have offered in the past. Nothing in the Act imposes a restriction, penalty, or burden by reason of the views, programs, or stations the cable operator has selected or will select. The number of channels a cable operator must set aside depends only on the operator's channel capacity; hence, an operator cannot avoid or mitigate its obligations under the Act by altering the programming it offers to subscribers.

The must-carry provisions also burden cable programmers by reducing the number of channels for which they can compete. But, again, this burden is unrelated to content, for it extends to all cable programmers irrespective of the programming they choose to offer viewers. And finally, the privileges conferred by the must-carry provisions are also unrelated to content. The rules benefit all full power broadcasters who request carriage—be they commercial or noncommercial, independent or network-affiliated, English or Spanish language, religious or secular. The aggregate effect of the rules is thus to make every full power commercial and noncommercial broadcaster eligible for must-carry, provided only that the broadcaster operates within the same television market as a cable system. . . .

That the must-carry provisions, on their face, do not burden or benefit speech of a particular content does not end the inquiry. Our cases have recognized that even a regulation neutral on its face may be content-based if its manifest purpose is to regulate speech because of the message it conveys.

Appellants contend, in this regard, that the must-carry regulations are content-based because Congress' purpose in enacting them was to promote speech of a favored content. We do not agree. Our review of the Act and its various findings persuades us that Congress' overriding objective in enacting must-carry was not to favor programming of a particular subject matter, viewpoint, or format, but rather to preserve access to free television programming for the 40 percent of Americans without cable. . . .

In short, Congress' acknowledgment that broadcast television stations make a valuable contribution to the Nation's communications system does not render the must-carry scheme content-based. The scope and operation of the challenged provisions make clear, in our view, that Congress designed the must-carry provisions not to promote speech of a particular content, but to prevent cable operators from exploiting their economic power to the detriment of broadcasters, and thereby to ensure that all Americans, especially those unable to subscribe to cable, have access to free television programming—whatever its content. . . .

JUSTICE SANDRA DAY O'CONNOR, with whom JUSTICE ANTONIN SCALIA and JUSTICE RUTH BADER GINSBURG joined, and with whom JUSTICE CLARENCE THOMAS joined in part, concurring in part and dissenting in part:

There are only so many channels that any cable system can carry. If there are fewer channels than programmers who want to use the system, some programmers will have to be dropped. In the must-carry provisions of the Cable Television Consumer Protection and Competition Act of 1992, Congress made a choice: By reserving a little over one-third of the channels on a cable system for broadcasters, it ensured that in most cases it will be a cable programmer who is dropped and a broadcaster who is retained. The question presented in this case is whether this choice comports with the commands of the First Amendment.

The 1992 Cable Act implicates the First Amendment rights of two classes of speakers. First, it tells cable operators which programmers they must carry, and keeps cable operators from carrying others that they might prefer. Though cable operators do not actually originate most of the programming they show, the Court correctly holds that they are, for First Amendment purposes, speakers. Selecting which speech to retransmit is, as we know from the example of publishing houses, movie theaters, bookstores, and Reader's Digest, no less communication than is creating the speech in the first place.

Second, the Act deprives a certain class of video programmers—those who operate cable channels rather than broadcast stations—of access to over one-third of an entire medium. Cable programmers may compete only for those channels that are not set aside by the must-carry provisions. A cable programmer that might otherwise have been carried may well be denied access in favor of a broadcaster that is less appealing to the viewers but is favored by the must-carry rules. It is as if the Government ordered all movie theaters to reserve at least one-third of their screening for films made by American production companies, or required all bookstores to devote one-third of their shelf space to nonprofit publishers. As the Court explains, cable programmers and operators stand in the same position under the First Amendment as do the more traditional media. . . .

I agree with the Court that some speaker-based restrictions—those genuinely justified without reference to content—need not be subject to strict scrutiny. But looking at the statute at issue, I cannot avoid the conclusion that its preference for broadcasters over cable programmers is justified with reference to content. . . .

Preferences for diversity of viewpoints, for localism, for educational programming, and for news and public affairs all make reference to content. They may not reflect hostility to particular points of view, or a desire to suppress certain subjects because they are controversial or offensive. They may be quite benignly motivated. But benign motivation, we have consistently held, is not enough to avoid the need for strict scrutiny of content-based justifications. The First Amendment does more than just bar government from intentionally suppressing speech

of which it disapproves. It also generally prohibits the government from excepting certain kinds of speech from regulation because it thinks the speech is especially valuable.

This is why the Court is mistaken in concluding that the interest in diversity—in "access to a multiplicity" of "diverse and antagonistic sources"—is content neutral. Indeed, the interest is not "related to the *suppression* of free expression," but that is not enough for content neutrality. The interest in giving a tax break to religious, sports, or professional magazines, is not related to the suppression of speech; the interest in giving labor picketers an exemption from a general picketing ban, is not related to the suppression of speech. But they are both related to the *content* of speech—to its communicative impact. The interest in ensuring access to a multiplicity of diverse and antagonistic sources of information, no matter how praiseworthy, is directly tied to the content of what the speakers will likely say. . . .

Having said all this, it is important to acknowledge one basic fact: The question is not whether there will be control over who gets to speak over cable—the question is who will have this control. Under the FCC's view, the answer is Congress, acting within relatively broad limits. Under my view, the answer is the cable operator. Most of the time, the cable operator's decision will be largely dictated by the preferences of the viewers; but because many cable operators are indeed monopolists, the viewers' preferences will not always prevail. Our recognition that cable operators are speakers is bottomed in large part on the very fact that the cable operator has editorial discretion. . . .

But the First Amendment as we understand it today rests on the premise that it is government power, rather than private power, that is the main threat to free expression; and as a consequence, the Amendment imposes substantial limitations on the Government even when it is trying to serve concededly praiseworthy goals. Perhaps Congress can to some extent restrict, even in a content-based manner, the speech of cable operators and cable programmers. But it must do so in compliance with the constitutional requirements, requirements that were not complied with here. Accordingly, I would reverse the judgment below.

⑤SAGE edge™

Visit **edge.sagepub.com/medialaw7e** to help you accomplish your coursework goals in an easy-to-use learning environment.

I shall not today attempt further to define the kinds of material I understand to be [obscene]; and perhaps I could never succeed in intelligibly doing so. But I know it when I see it.

—U.S. Supreme Court Justice Potter Stewart[1]

Ninety million people witnessed Janet Jackson's Super Bowl halftime show "wardrobe malfunction." For a fraction of a second her breast was exposed, leading to more than 500,000 viewer complaints to the Federal Communications Commission.

AP Photo/David Phillip

10

OBSCENITY AND INDECENCY
Social Norms and Legal Standards

SUPPOSE...

... that a singer-actress and a television personality say four-letter expletives on live television broadcasts and a TV cop program briefly shows female nudity. These are words most people have heard and images most teenagers and adults have seen, but federal law has banned broadcasting such words and pictures for decades. Should the Federal Communications Commission find the broadcasts indecent? Should the FCC punish stations for airing expletives and brief nudity? Look for the answers to these questions when *Federal Communications Commission v. Fox Television Stations, Inc.* is discussed later in this chapter and excerpted at the end of the chapter.

Sexual expression is ubiquitous in contemporary societies—as it has been for centuries. It can be found in art, theater, beer commercials, text messages and memes; on websites and social media; in television programs and in movies. Legal experts observe that changing technology and social conventions now allow "virtually limitless" access to sexually explicit content.[2]

Some believe sexually explicit material does not deserve First Amendment protection. Others argue sexual expression is just that—expression.[3] The law as it applies to sexual expression comes from the U.S. Supreme Court's First Amendment decisions as well as administrative law. Increasingly, issues surrounding sexual expression may also intersect with privacy (see Chapter 6) and other tort laws. For example, revenge porn is the act of publicly sharing sexually explicit images or videos, usually of a sexual partner, without consent. In 2019, 46 states, the District of Columbia and Guam had laws that criminalized revenge porn.[4]

First Amendment decisions about sexual expression primarily focus on obscenity, a category of speech not protected by the First Amendment. The dictionary defines obscenity simply as "relating to sex in an indecent or offensive way," or "very offensive in usually a shocking

pornography
A vague—not legally precise—term for sexually oriented material.

indecency
A narrow legal term referring to sexual expression and expletives inappropriate for children on broadcast radio and television.

obscenity
The dictionary defines it as relating to sex in an indecent, very offensive or shocking way. The legal definition of obscenity comes from *Miller v. California*—material is determined to be obscene if it passes the *Miller* test.

way."[5] The legal definition of obscenity comes from *Miller v. California*, a U.S. Supreme Court case decided in 1973 and discussed in detail later in this chapter.

Administrative laws that apply to sexual expression come from the FCC (see Chapter 9) and focus on indecency. Broadly, indecency refers to content some people find offensive. It is not synonymous with obscenity. For regulatory purposes, the FCC defines indecency and determines the rules for how indecency regulation is applied to different media—most notably, broadcasting.[6]

Generally speaking, there is not agreement on what word to use in describing all offensive sexual expression. What's the difference between obscenity, pornography and indecency? The word **pornography** is vague—not legally precise—because it encompasses both protected and unprotected sexual material. The term **indecency** has only a narrow legal meaning, referring to sexual expression and expletives inappropriate for children on broadcast radio and television. Until the mid-20th century, American courts used a broad definition of **obscenity**, allowing government officials to ban a wide range of materials.

OBSCENITY

Two centuries ago, American society considered religious blasphemy and heresy to be more troublesome than sexual expression. With few exceptions, governments—state and federal—did not adopt laws or bring criminal charges related to sexual material.

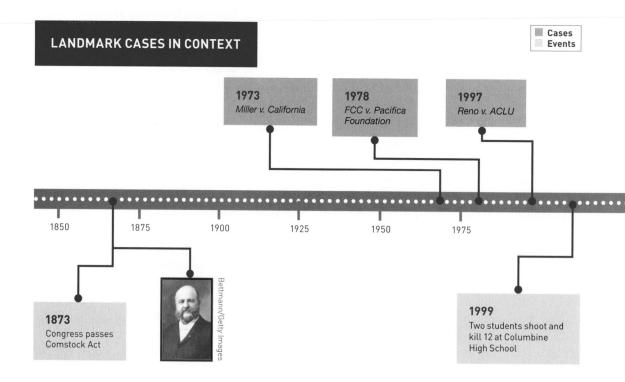

LANDMARK CASES IN CONTEXT

■ Cases
■ Events

1973
Miller v. California

1978
FCC v. Pacifica Foundation

1997
Reno v. ACLU

1850   1875   1900   1925   1950   1975

1873
Congress passes Comstock Act

Bettmann/Getty Images

1999
Two students shoot and kill 12 at Columbine High School

Comstock and *Hicklin*

After the Civil War, Anthony Comstock, a store clerk, became the champion of young men's decency and launched an anti-obscenity movement.[7] He believed that "anything remotely touching upon sex was . . . obscene."[8] In 1872, Comstock convinced the Young Men's Christian Association to support his campaign against sexual content in art, newspapers, books, magazines and other media. Comstock became secretary of the New York Society for the Suppression of Vice, funded in part by prominent and wealthy businessmen.[9]

Although federal laws already banned importing and mailing obscene material, Comstock vigorously lobbied Congress to further tighten mailing restrictions. His campaign culminated in the Comstock Act, a federal law adopted in 1873 prohibiting the mailing of "obscene, lewd, or lascivious" material.[10] Initially used only to stop mailings concerning contraception and abortion, the law was amended in 1876 to ensure that it banned the mailing of pornographic materials.[11]

After the law's adoption, Congress appointed Comstock as a special postal inspector to help enforce the statute. He held the post for 42 years. As a U.S. Postal Service special agent, Comstock prosecuted many people for selling and mailing material that he said was lewd. Comstock would order items through the mail and then, with the illicit item as evidence, take the seller to court.[12]

In the late 1860s, when the post–Civil War United States began hearing cases involving sexually explicit material, it became clear that judges would not protect obscene publications under

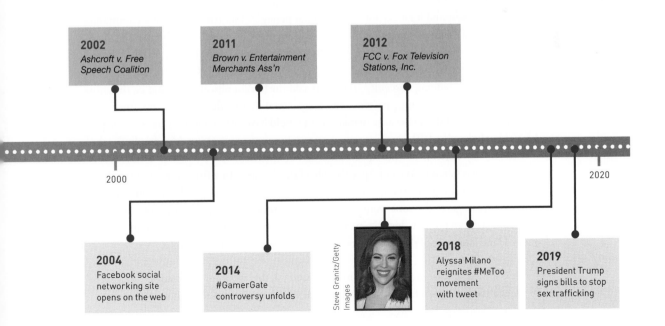

2002
Ashcroft v. Free Speech Coalition

2011
Brown v. Entertainment Merchants Ass'n

2012
FCC v. Fox Television Stations, Inc.

2000

2020

2004
Facebook social networking site opens on the web

2014
#GamerGate controversy unfolds

Steve Granitz/Getty Images

2018
Alyssa Milano reignites #MeToo movement with tweet

2019
President Trump signs bills to stop sex trafficking

Bettmann/Getty Images

In addition to successfully lobbying Congress to pass what became the Comstock Act, Anthony Comstock effectively pushed all states to pass obscenity laws.

Hicklin **rule**
Taken from a mid-19th-century English case and used in the United States until the mid-20th century, a rule that defines material as obscene if it tends to corrupt children.

the First Amendment. The question was how to define obscenity. Beginning in the late 19th century and continuing for more than 60 years, federal courts applied the *Hicklin* **rule** to decide obscenity cases. The rule came from an 1868 British case, *Regina v. Hicklin*, stating that "the test of obscenity is this, whether the tendency of the matter charged as obscenity is to deprave and corrupt those whose minds are open to such immoral influences and into whose hands a publication of this sort may fall."[13]

In essence, the *Hicklin* rule meant adults could be exposed only to material acceptable for the most susceptible minds—the young. U.S. courts commonly held that if even a portion of a publication met the *Hicklin* rule, the entire publication was obscene.

Although the *Hicklin* rule remained the primary test used to determine obscenity into the 1930s, it was not always applied. In a 1913 case that involved an American literary work whose publisher was prosecuted under the Comstock Act, federal Judge Learned Hand noted that the *Hicklin* standard "does not seem to me to answer to the understanding and morality of the present time" and that its application would "reduce our treatment of sex to the standard of a child's library."[14]

Judge Hand argued that courts should approach obscenity "like other kinds of conduct" and consider applying community standards that are "subject to the social sense of what is right." He added, "To put thought in leash to the average conscience of the time is perhaps tolerable, but to fetter it by the necessities of the lowest and least capable seems a fatal policy."[15] His articulation of a community standard would eventually reappear in later U.S. Supreme Court decisions about obscenity.

Deciding whether U.S. customs officials could prevent James Joyce's novel "Ulysses" from being imported, a federal district court in 1933 rejected the *Hicklin* rule and proposed a new standard for judging obscenity. The court said the test for obscenity should be the entire work's impact on an "average person." The judge noted that while the book contained four-letter profanities, it did so because that language would have been habitually used by the people the book described. The explicit sexual material in the book was not "dirt for dirt's sake." The court said "Ulysses" was literary art and was not obscene.[16]

The Second Circuit Court of Appeals upheld the decision. In writing for the court, Judge Augustus Hand (Judge Learned Hand's cousin) considered the entire work. He said that while numerous passages in the book would be obscene by any definition, taking the book as a whole it did not "tend to promote lust . . . even though it justly may offend many."[17] In his opinion, Judge Hand laid some of the groundwork for future obscenity tests. He wrote,

It is settled, at least so far as this court is concerned, that works of physiology, medicine, science and sex instruction are not within the statute, though to some extent and among some persons they may tend to promote lustful thoughts. We think the same immunity should apply to literature as to science, where the presentation, when viewed objectively, is sincere, and the erotic matter is not introduced to promote lust and does not furnish the dominant note of the publication. The question in each case is whether a publication taken as a whole has a libidinous effect. The book before us has such portentous length, is written with such evident truthfulness in its depiction of certain types of humanity, and is so little erotic in its result, that it does not fall within the forbidden class.[18]

The "Ulysses" decision suggested that courts should determine what is obscene by reviewing the material in its entirety instead of assessing isolated passages or pictures. The decision also suggested the test should ascertain a work's effect on an average person instead of on children. Despite the ruling, many federal and state courts continued to apply the *Hicklin* rule into the 1950s, reflecting the political and social climate of the times as well as the difficulty in drawing a line between obscenity and other forms of sexual expression.[19]

Current Obscenity Definition

The assumption throughout the 19th and early to mid-20th century was that the First Amendment did not protect obscene publications and materials.[20] The U.S. Supreme Court confirmed this in 1957 in *Roth v. United States*. At the same time, it definitively rejected *Hicklin* and narrowed the obscenity definition to give sexual expression more freedom. Even though the court upheld Samuel Roth's conviction for violating the Comstock Act by mailing sexually explicit literature, the decision represented the Court's first full attempt to distinguish between unprotected obscenity and protected sexual expression.[21] The Court said material was obscene if, first, an "average person, applying contemporary community standards," found the work taken as a whole appealed to **prurient interest**, meaning that it "excites lustful thoughts." Second, obscene material must be "utterly without redeeming social importance."[22]

prurient interest
Lustful thoughts or sexual desires.

The test remained difficult for government prosecutors to meet, however, and there were relatively few obscenity convictions after *Roth*. The Court refined the *Roth* test several times over the next two decades, but those refinements caused confusion and continued to raise questions about how to determine the social importance or social value of sexual expression.[23]

For example, in 1964, the U.S. Supreme Court overturned the conviction of a movie theater manager who showed an internationally acclaimed French film that the state of Ohio deemed obscene. The film told the story of an adulterous affair between a middle-aged woman and a young man. The six justices who voted to reverse the obscenity conviction offered five different rationales. In his concurrence in *Jacobellis v. Ohio*, Justice Potter Stewart famously expressed the challenge in creating a clear test for determining obscenity. "I shall not today attempt further to define the kinds of material I understand to be [obscene]; and perhaps I could never succeed in intelligibly doing so," he wrote. "But I know it when I see it, and the motion picture involved in this case is not that."[24]

Several other U.S. Supreme Court decisions in the 1960s further muddied the water.[25] Finally, in 1973, the Court reconsidered obscenity law again in *Miller v. California* and established the definition of obscenity that remains to this day.[26] Defendant Marvin Miller mass mailed advertising brochures for four adult books and a film to people who had not requested them. The brochures included pictures, drawings and text "very explicitly depicting men and women in groups of two or more engaging in a variety of sexual activities, with genitals often prominently displayed."[27] The manager of a Newport Beach, Calif., restaurant opened the mail one morning with his mother standing at his side. Five brochures slipped out of an unmarked envelope for all to see. The manager called the police. A jury convicted Miller of violating a California statute that forbid the intentional distribution of obscene materials. Miller appealed to the U.S. Supreme Court.

In *Miller*, the justices established a complex, three-part definition of obscenity. Under the *Miller* test, to find material obscene a court must consider whether (1) "the average person, applying contemporary community standards," would find that the work, taken as a whole, appeals to prurient interests; (2) the work depicts or describes, in a patently offensive way, sexual conduct specifically defined by the applicable state law; and (3) the work, taken as a whole, lacks serious literary, artistic, political or scientific value.[28]

A work must meet every part of the test to be obscene. That is, the government must show a work, considered in its entirety, (1) arouses sexual lust, (2) is hard-core pornography and (3) has no serious social value. If the government cannot prove any part of this test, the work is not obscene, and the First Amendment protects it.

The *Miller* Test

The first part of the *Miller* test requires showing that an average person would find that the work, taken in its entirety, appeals to prurient interests, or "lustful thoughts." The Court said "prurient" refers to "morbid or lascivious longings."[29] Material arousing morbid or shameful sexual thoughts meets this part of the *Miller* test.

INTERNATIONAL LAW
U.K. PORNOGRAPHY BAN

In 2019, the British government began to enforce a provision in the Digital Economy Act of 2017 that blocks access to pornography by users under the age of 18.[i] Under the new law, internet users in the country who visit a pornography website must first provide their age, then provide proof. To verify age, users can submit credit card information or government IDs online, or they can verify their age in person at a participating store, in exchange for a pass.

The government said the ban is the "world's first" and that it will "help make Britain the safest place in the world for children."[ii] Critics argue that the law creates user data privacy concerns and that it will be difficult to enforce. The government appointed the British Board of Film Classification, a nongovernmental organization that has some experience with online regulation of pornography in video, films and music, as the regulatory agency to enforce the ban. The ban does not apply to social media or to users outside the United Kingdom.[iii]

The *Miller* case confirmed what the U.S. Supreme Court held in earlier cases: To determine whether material appeals to prurient interests, the content must be considered as a whole, not as discrete pictures or words. An assessment of whether the material appeals to prurient interests must be based on conclusions drawn by an average person in the community, not a child or a particularly sensitive person.[30] The Court has not explained how a juror can know the standards of an average person. Some courts allow survey results to help jurors understand community attitudes, but not all courts permit social science data as evidence.

Legislatures and courts decide what geographic area comprises the community for setting obscenity standards. The Supreme Court has said the community may be the city or county where jurors live. In the *Miller* decision, the Court allowed California to use statewide standards. Other states, such as Illinois, also have permitted statewide obscenity standards.[31] Even a "deviant sexual group, rather than the public at large," may be a community for determining appropriate standards, the Court has said.[32]

The internet has made the determination of a geographically bound community more challenging. Even so, courts have not established precedent for use of a national standard to determine a community standard.[33] For example, in a recent case before the Fifth Circuit Court of Appeals, a man found guilty of sharing obscene content with a minor challenged his conviction on grounds that the court improperly applied the community standard.[34] A jury found him guilty of sharing, in an internet chat room, webcam videos of himself masturbating. The recipient of the videos was an undercover police officer posing as a 14-year-old girl.

The man argued that the community standard in his case should have been defined as a national community of people who participate in internet chat rooms. The court rejected his argument, noting that no court has yet set a binding precedent for use of a national standard.[35]

About a decade ago in a case that is an outlier, the Ninth Circuit Court of Appeals suggested that jury instructions could include national community standard considerations.[36] In that case, jurors were instructed to consider contemporary community standards outside of their physical district. The appeals court said that in that instance the jury should have been allowed to apply a national community standard, but the court did not invalidate the jurors' approach of applying their own sense of what contemporary community standards should be.[37]

Several U.S. Supreme Court justices have acknowledged the challenges of applying community standards in the internet age. Where a person sends, receives or accesses content could be wide-ranging and have very different community standards. Recently retired U.S. Supreme Court Justice Anthony Kennedy, joined by Justices Ruth Bader Ginsburg and David Souter, recognized that the "national variation in community standards constitutes a particular burden on internet speech."[38] Similarly, Justice Stephen Breyer said applying "the community standards of every locality in the United States would provide the most puritan of communities with a heckler's internet veto affecting the rest of the Nation."[39] Former Justice Sandra Day O'Connor also favored a national community for judging internet communications.[40] Nonetheless, the U.S. Supreme Court has not adopted a national community standard in cases of internet obscenity, so local and statewide community standards still prevail.

POINTS OF LAW

THE *MILLER* TEST

To find material obscene under the *Miller* test, a court must review the work as a whole, and consider whether

1. "the average person, applying contemporary community standards," would find that the work appeals to prurient interests;

2. the work depicts or describes, in a patently offensive way, sexual conduct specifically defined by the applicable state law; and

3. the work lacks serious literary, artistic, political or scientific value (often called the SLAPS test).[iv]

patently offensive
Term describing material with hard-core sexual conduct.

serious social value
Material cannot be found obscene if it has serious literary, artistic, political or scientific value determined using national, not local/community, standards.

The second part of the *Miller* test requires the government to show the material is **patently offensive** according to state law. In *Miller*, the U.S. Supreme Court provided examples of patent offensiveness: (1) "representations or descriptions of ultimate sexual acts, normal or perverted, actual or simulated" or (2) "representations or descriptions of masturbation, excretory functions and lewd exhibition of the genitals."[41] As in the first part of the *Miller* test, patent offensiveness is to be determined by contemporary community standards, the Court said.

Patently offensive material at least has to include hard-core sexual conduct. The Supreme Court made this clear when it rejected a jury's finding that the 1971 movie "Carnal Knowledge" was obscene.[42] The award-nominated and critically acclaimed movie featured some partial nudity but had no sex scenes. An Albany, Ga., jury convicted a theater operator for showing the film. The Supreme Court said the jury had the right to use local community standards in deciding whether the film appealed to prurient interests. However, the jury could not find that the movie was patently offensive unless at a minimum it met the Supreme Court's understanding of that term, as illustrated by the Court's examples.

The Court has said the *Miller* examples of patently offensive material were not an exhaustive list. Sexually explicit material not included in the Court's list of sexual acts could be patently offensive.[43] "It would be a serious misreading of *Miller* to conclude that juries have unbridled discretion in determining what is 'patently offensive,'" the Court said.[44]

Recently, courts have found Snapchat videos that show genitalia and masturbation are patently offensive,[45] as are photographs of genitalia sent through text message.[46] In both of these cases, the intended recipients of the sexually explicit material were minors.

The third part of the *Miller* obscenity test says material cannot be found obscene if it has serious literary, artistic, political or social value. There is a wide gap between any social value and serious social value. Material falling in the space between "any social value" and "serious social value" could be found obscene if it also meets the first two parts of the *Miller* test.

In *Pope v. Illinois*, decided after *Miller*, the U.S. Supreme Court said serious social value should be decided using national standards, not local criteria.[47] The *Pope* decision also said a determination of **serious social value** should be based on what a reasonable person would decide. Because this suggests an objective, rather than a subjective, analysis of a work's social value, juries may consider testimony of expert witnesses who express their opinions about a work's social value.

At the request of a county sheriff in Florida, a federal district court found a 2 Live Crew album, "As Nasty as They Wanna Be," to be obscene. On review, the Eleventh Circuit Court of Appeals observed that 2 Live Crew presented several expert witnesses at trial who testified the album had serious social value. The sheriff played the album at trial but offered no expert witnesses to support his contention that the recording was obscene. The appellate court said simply listening to a recording was not enough to determine whether the recording possessed serious social value. Expert witnesses' testimony was required.[48]

Sexually Explicit Material and Children

More than six decades ago, the U.S. Supreme Court held that government officials may not limit adults to seeing only material acceptable for children. In 1957, the Court struck down a Michigan law making it illegal to distribute sexual material "tending to incite minors to violent or depraved or immoral acts."[49] The Court said the law violated the First Amendment because its effect "is to reduce the adult population of Michigan to reading only what is fit for children."[50]

In 1992, a Florida county sheriff asked a court to find 2 Live Crew's "As Nasty as They Wanna Be" album obscene but did not provide any evidence.

Jeff Kravitz/FilmMagic, Inc./Getty Images

However, the opposite is not true—material not obscene for adults may be obscene if the same material is given to minors. Restricting minors' access to sexual material is sometimes called **variable obscenity**. In *Ginsberg v. New York*, the Court said minors do not have a First Amendment right to sexually explicit material acceptable for adults. Under its power to protect the well-being of minors, the Court said, a state may "adjust the definition of obscenity to social realities."[51]

Under federal law, making, selling, distributing or possessing child pornography is illegal. Federal law defines **child pornography** as "any visual depiction . . . involving the use of a minor engaging in sexually explicit conduct . . . or such visual depiction [that] has been created . . . to appear that an identifiable minor is engaging in sexually explicit conduct."[52] The question is not whether children are appearing in videos, films or photographs that would be obscene under the *Miller* test. Rather, the question is whether minors are being sexually exploited. In addition to the federal law, all states and the District of Columbia have child pornography laws.

Courts, Congress and child welfare organizations have recognized the harm child pornography causes. Harm comes not only from the initial sexual act or depiction but also from the availability of the images. Today, pornographic content can be widely shared through social media. For example, some of the most popular pornography sites on the internet are "tube sites," which allow users to upload their own videos that can then be easily shared.[53]

Nearly four decades ago, in *New York v. Ferber*, the U.S. Supreme Court upheld New York's child pornography law, one of the nation's strictest.[54] Paul Ferber sold pornographic films of young boys to an undercover officer. Hearing Ferber's appeal of his conviction, the Supreme Court said child pornography laws are essential to protecting minors. Using children

variable obscenity
The concept that sexually oriented material not obscene for adults may be obscene if distributed to minors.

child pornography
Any image showing children in sexual or sexually explicit situations.

Paul Archuleta/Getty Images

Recently, actress Mischa Barton won a restraining order to prevent her ex-boyfriend, who secretly recorded them having sex, from selling the video.

in sexual material harms minors' "physiological, emotional and mental health," the Court said.[55] First, the children endure psychological harm, knowing there is a permanent record of their participation in sexual activity. Second, making, selling and obtaining pornography showing children in sexual situations helps to perpetuate the sexual exploitation of children and encourages pedophilia.

Federal law is applied to visual depictions and defines child pornography as any image showing minors in "sexually explicit conduct."[56] The conduct may be actual or simulated "sexual intercourse," "masturbation" or lewd "exhibition of the genitals or pubic area."[57]

Courts strictly interpret child pornography laws. "Unlike the Court's obscenity standards, child pornography laws involve no fuzzy facts like 'community standards' or 'artistic value,' and prosecutors can make a case with little more than proof that the defendant possessed or made a visual depiction of sexual conduct by a minor," wrote a First Amendment scholar.[58] For example, a film showed preteen and teenaged girls younger than 17 years old wearing bikinis, leotards or underwear (but not nude) and gyrating to music. The "photographer would zoom in on the children's . . . genital area and display a close-up view for an extended period of time," a federal appellate court said.[59] The film was child pornography. The federal child pornography law does not require nudity, the court said, holding that this broad interpretation of federal law does not make the law unconstitutionally overbroad.[60]

More than 20 years ago, Congress adopted the Child Pornography Prevention Act, criminalizing the possession of digital images of children in sexual poses or activities, even if the images were of young-looking adults and not of real children. The U.S. Supreme Court found the law unconstitutional, noting that two provisions in the law that dealt with virtual images of children were too broad.[61]

Congress tried again and 15 years ago passed the Prosecutorial Remedies and Other Tools to End the Exploitation of Children Today (PROTECT) Act in response to the Supreme Court's decision. The PROTECT Act made it a crime to offer or solicit sexually explicit images of children. The narrow focus of the new law was on pandering. If someone offers material as child pornography, he or she could be convicted regardless of whether the material uses or depicts real children. Under review, the Supreme Court held that the PROTECT Act was constitutional and did not violate the First Amendment because it was narrowly tailored. The Court noted that "the emergence of new technology and the repeated retransmission of picture files over the internet . . . could make it nearly impossible to prove that a particular image was produced using real children [even though] there is no substantial evidence that any of the child pornography images being trafficked today were made other than by the abuse of real children."[62]

Courts continue to hear cases about child pornography and technology. For example, six years ago, a defendant in the Eighth Circuit Court of Appeals challenged the federal definition of child pornography that includes "visual depictions . . . modified to appear" like a minor engaged in sexual conduct.[63] The defendant argued that the definition was overly broad because morphed images are not real, so sexual abuse cannot occur. The Eighth Circuit disagreed, noting that the government did not have a less restrictive means "to protect this child from the exploitation and psychological harm resulting from the distribution of the morphed image than to prevent [the defendant] from disseminating it."[64]

U.S. law allows child pornography victims to seek restitution not only from the person who created the sexually explicit images but also from those who possess them.[65] The victim may recover for physical and psychological medical services, temporary housing, childcare, lost income, attorney's fees and other expenses. The person who created the images will be liable for these damages.[66] Ten U.S. courts of appeals have ruled that the victim must show that a person who possessed or transmitted the illegal images caused specific harms.[67] The Fifth Circuit Court of Appeals is the only federal appellate court to disagree.[68] It ruled that if the victim showed that he or she was harmed by the fact that the image was shared, then anyone found guilty of possessing that image might be liable for damages.

In 2014, the U.S. Supreme Court took a closer look at the specific statutory language in the mandatory restitution provision of the federal law[69] and concluded in *Paroline v. United States* that Congress intended to limit restitution to only those losses proximately caused by the defendant.[70] A proximate cause is a cause that most directly produces the effect. The possession of child pornography containing a plaintiff's image, unlike the creation of that image, may not qualify as a proximate cause that entitles the victim to compensation. Or, if it does, it might not justify awarding the full amount of damages the plaintiff claims.

The Supreme Court said a victim should receive restitution only in an amount that represents the extent of loss the defendant caused the victim.[71] The court was split 5–4, with two dissenting opinions. In one, Chief Justice John G. Roberts, joined by Justices Antonin Scalia and Clarence Thomas, argued that the Court's *Paroline* ruling simply asks lower courts to pick "arbitrary" amounts for restitution. That is not "good enough for the criminal law," they said, and would ultimately result in no restitution for victims who are repeatedly victimized in cases when many offenders (sometimes thousands) possess images of the child pornography victim.[72]

In her dissent, Justice Sonia Sotomayor argued that the Court's opinion could not be reconciled with the law Congress passed, which she said requires full restitution for a victim's losses. "Given the very nature of the child pornography market—in which a large class of offenders contribute jointly to their victims' harm by trading their images—[the Court's approach leaves] victims with little hope of recovery," she wrote.[73]

One legal scholar has suggested that restitution for victims of child pornography is not as straightforward as restitution for victims of other criminal acts. She suggested, as did the dissenting justices, that Congress should revisit the law. The appellate courts that have heard these cases have also urged Congress to clarify the language in the law to provide for its consistent application.[74]

REAL WORLD LAW
SEXTING AND TEENS

A recent study in the Journal of the American Medical Association shows that more than one in four teens reports receiving a "sext."[v] Sexting is sending someone sexually explicit photographs or messages via a mobile phone. Sometimes prosecutors classify sexting involving those under 18 years old as child pornography.[vi] If the act of sexting is child pornography, those who receive and retain sexually explicit images can be charged with possessing child pornography, a felony under state and federal laws.

Currently, 25 states have laws that specifically target sexting.[vii] Some state legislatures—including those in Arizona, Connecticut, Louisiana and Illinois—have adopted laws imposing lighter sentences on teenage sexters. Other states, for example Texas and Florida, take a rehabilitative approach to teen sexting and require education and community service as part of their accountability efforts.[viii]

Other Considerations

Although courts have upheld laws against making, distributing, selling and exhibiting obscene material, the U.S. Supreme Court said the First Amendment protects possession of obscene material, except child pornography, in the privacy of one's home.

More than 50 years ago, overturning a conviction for possessing obscene films, the U.S. Supreme Court in *Stanley v. Georgia* said that merely categorizing films as obscene did not justify "a drastic invasion of personal liberties guaranteed by the First Amendment."[75] Police had found the obscene films during a search of a suspected bookmaker's home. The Court said there are reasons to have obscenity statutes, but the reasons do not allow authorities to "reach into the privacy of one's own home."[76] Government may not tell people what books they may read or films they may watch, the Court said.

The First Amendment protects filmmakers (see Chapter 2).[77] Nonetheless, the U.S. Supreme Court once allowed government censorship boards to license films for exhibition. That is, in some states and communities, a theater had to obtain board approval before it could show a film.[78] When they were active, some censorship boards assumed a given film was obscene and required the movie producer to prove it was not. This violated the movie producer's rights, the Supreme Court said.[79]

The last movie censorship board, the Maryland State Board of Censors, stopped functioning nearly four decades ago. But the procedural safeguards the Supreme Court required of those boards set the standard for all obscenity prosecutions. For example, government officials must prove in court that a work is obscene. Officials cannot merely claim material is obscene and then ban it. Additionally, any prior restraint on allegedly obscene material must be for as short a time as possible until a court decides whether the work meets the obscenity definition.

Authorities also have tried to control obscenity using laws that target organized crime. Fifty years ago, Congress adopted the Racketeer Influenced and Corrupt Organizations Act.[80] Thirty-two states also have RICO acts. The RICO laws forbid using money earned from illegal activities—racketeering—to finance legal or illegal businesses or nonprofit enterprises engaged in interstate commerce.[81]

RICO laws implicate the First Amendment because the laws allow the government to seize all assets acquired through racketeering activity. In one case, the owner of a dozen adult theaters and bookstores was convicted of violating obscenity laws. Under the state's RICO law, authorities seized the contents of the defendant's theaters and bookstores. The defendant claimed the seizure violated his First Amendment rights. In part, he said the seizure amounted to a prior restraint because not all the seized books and his theaters' films were obscene. The Supreme Court disagreed. The seizure was for past criminal acts—selling obscene material, the Supreme Court said.[82] If the defendant wanted to open a new adult bookstore that sold sexually explicit but not obscene material, he could do so in the future. Therefore, there was no prior restraint.

INDECENCY

The U.S. Supreme Court has made clear that the First Amendment does not protect obscenity. Does the First Amendment protect indecency? Indecent speech is protected in print media, in movies, in recordings and on the internet. The Communications Act of 1934 makes it illegal to broadcast indecent material.[83] As with obscenity, the problem is defining "indecency."

According to the U.S. Supreme Court, "The normal definition of 'indecent' merely refers to nonconformance with accepted standards of morality."[84] "Indecency" is not a synonym for "obscenity," the Court said.[85] Rather, indecency is content some people find offensive. Material that is patently offensive but does not have prurient appeal is not obscene, but it may be indecent.[86] Material may also be indecent even if it has serious social value. The FCC once defined indecency as "language or material that, in context, depicts or describes in terms patently offensive as measured by contemporary community standards for the broadcast medium, sexual or excretory activities or organs."[87]

In both the Radio Act of 1927 and the Communications Act of 1934, Congress prohibited broadcasting "any obscene, indecent, or profane language."[88] Congress later eliminated this provision but inserted the ban on indecent broadcasts into the federal criminal code.[89] In 1960, Congress gave the FCC power to impose civil fines on broadcasters who violated the commission's indecency regulations.[90]

The FCC and the courts, with Congress' acquiescence, said the reason for limiting indecent programs on broadcast radio or television is to protect children.[91] For example, in fining

George Carlin.

a radio station for discussing oral sex during an afternoon program, the commission emphasized "the presence of children in the broadcast audience."[92] The First Amendment protects indecent material in other media because these media can separate children from adults in their audiences. Minors can be prevented from having access to indecent books, magazines and movies, for example. But broadcast radio and television are too pervasive; they are available everywhere, and children continually are exposed to them. Those concerned about indecency, then, had to balance potential harms to children against broadcasters' First Amendment rights.

Federal Communications Commission Regulation

The FCC did not act against indecency until 1975. The commission responded to a father's complaint that he and his young son heard a New York City radio station playing comedian George Carlin's "Filthy Words" monologue at 2 p.m. Carlin's 12-minute live performance contained the seven "words you couldn't say on television."[93] He then said them repeatedly.[94] The FCC fined the station's operator, Pacifica Foundation, for indecency because it broadcast "language that describes, in terms patently offensive as measured by contemporary community standards for the broadcast medium, sexual or excretory activities and organs, at times of the day when there is a reasonable risk that children may be in the audience."[95]

FCC v. Pacifica Foundation (excerpted at the end of the chapter) reached the U.S. Supreme Court, which said broadcasters have First Amendment protection, but the protection is limited because of spectrum scarcity (see Chapter 9). This allows courts to restrict indecency in broadcasting but not in other media, the Court said.

In determining whether the Carlin recording was indecent, the Court said the context of the challenged material is "all-important" and that an "occasional expletive" need not lead to sanctioning a broadcaster.[96] The Court focused on the "repetitive, deliberate use" of words that refer to "excretory or sexual activities or organs" in a "patently offensive" manner.[97] This suggested that indecency applied only to a Carlin-like monologue—defining indecency as "filthy words." The Court emphasized radio and television's "uniquely pervasive presence in the lives of all Americans" and focused on children. The nature of broadcasting made it "uniquely accessible to children, even those too young to read." That concern and the specific facts of the case—Carlin's repeatedly saying the seven words—justified the FCC's fining the radio station, the Court said.[98]

For a decade after *Pacifica*, the FCC defined indecency as the intentional repetition of dirty words. The commission said, "[D]eliberate and repetitive use in a patently offensive manner is a requisite to a finding of indecency."[99] When the words were only expletives—a single swear word or exclamation—the use was not indecent.

In 1987, the FCC expressed concern that the "filthy words" indecency definition did not sufficiently protect children. The commission adopted a new, broader standard to define indecency.[100] The commission said it would consider a broadcast's context and tone as well as its language.[101] Because the *Pacifica* Court did not define "patently offensive" as measured by "community standards for the broadcast medium," broadcasters had little guidance beyond knowing the seven words Carlin used in his monologue.[102]

U2 lead singer Bono.

About 20 years ago, the FCC tried to clarify its indecency standard by adopting broadcast industry indecency guidelines. The commission again said material is indecent if it met the generic *Pacifica* test, adding that it would consider several factors in determining whether broadcast material was patently offensive: (1) how explicitly or graphically the material described sexual activities, (2) whether the material dwelt on sexual activities and (3) whether the material was meant to shock or sexually excite the audience. The FCC said it would consider the full context in which the material appeared.[103]

Just two years after the FCC adopted the new indecency guidelines, it took action against several live broadcasts that would bring more refinement to the FCC's indecency standard. At the 2003 Golden Globes Awards, U2 lead singer Bono said, "This is really, really, fucking brilliant," in accepting an award. Viewer complaints poured in to the FCC. The FCC enforcement bureau concluded that the singer's comment was not indecent because it did not describe a sexual activity and the utterance was "fleeting and isolated."[104] The full commission reviewed and then reversed that decision.

In doing so, the FCC asserted for the first time that a "fleeting expletive"—a single, non-literal use of a curse word—could be indecent.[105] The FCC said the "'F-Word' is one of the most vulgar, graphic and explicit descriptions of sexual activity in the English language," and therefore "inherently has a sexual connotation." The decision overruled previous decisions that did not find a fleeting expletive indecent.

Shortly after making its decision about Bono's use of a fleeting expletive at the Golden Globes, the FCC determined that two Billboard Music Awards programs were patently offensive because two celebrities uttered fleeting expletives that were shocking and gratuitous. Singer and actress Cher's unscripted exclamation in 2002—"People have been telling me I'm on the way out every year, right? So fuck 'em"—and television personality Nicole Richie's remark at the 2003 awards—"Have you ever tried to get cow shit out of a Prada purse? It's not so fucking simple"—were both found to be indecent and profane.[106]

On appeal, the Second Circuit Court of Appeals rejected the FCC's decision, saying the commission "failed to adequately explain why it had changed its nearly-30-year policy on fleeting expletives." The court noted that the FCC ruling "bore 'no rational connection to the Commission's actual policy,' because the FCC had not instituted a blanket ban on expletives."[107]

The U.S. Supreme Court overturned the Second Circuit's decision. The Supreme Court said the FCC did not act arbitrarily or capriciously and supplied sufficient reasons for its new policy. The FCC admitted it overturned a long-standing regulation that a single, fleeting expletive was not indecent. But the commission said the "F-Word" has a sexual meaning no matter how it is used, a meaning that insults and offends. That was enough justification for the Court, in a 5–4 decision, to uphold the FCC's new rule.[108]

The Supreme Court sent the case back to the Second Circuit, which on rehearing accepted a new argument from broadcasters—that the fleeting-expletives rule violated their First Amendment rights. This was a question the Supreme Court had not addressed.[109] The appellate court held that the commission's fleeting-expletives policy violated the First Amendment because it was vague, not allowing broadcasters to know what content would be found indecent and thus causing a chilling effect. The court said the chilling effect went beyond the fleeting-expletives regulation, forcing broadcasters not to take risks but rather to self-censor content that might or might not be found indecent under the FCC's definition.[110]

The FCC appealed the Second Circuit's decision to the U.S. Supreme Court. In 2012, the Supreme Court told the FCC it could not fine broadcasters for carrying the Bono, Cher and Richie utterances because the FCC adopted the fleeting-expletives rule after those programs were aired.[111] The Court also said broadcasters could not be held liable for violating a rule they did not know would change. The Supreme Court did not determine whether indecency regulations infringe broadcasters' First Amendment rights. The Court also did not define indecency, nor did it give the FCC guidance for defining indecency. Aside from telling the FCC it could not apply new rules retroactively, the Court did no more than say the FCC may modify its indecency regulations, considering the public interest and legal requirements, and courts may review the current or modified indecency rules when appropriate cases arise.[112]

Fifteen years ago, while the question about whether Bono, Cher and Richie's fleeting expletives were indecent was bouncing back and forth in the courts, Justin Timberlake ever-so-briefly (for 9/16 of one second) and accidentally exposed Janet Jackson's breast during the 2004 Super Bowl halftime show. A frenzy ensued. Congress increased the maximum fine the FCC could impose for broadcasting indecent material "by a factor of 10."[113] Reacting to public and congressional outrage, the FCC said Jackson's partial nudity violated its indecency standard and imposed $550,000 in fines against Viacom-owned television stations that aired the Super Bowl.[114] Viacom, Inc. owns CBS, the network that carried the Super Bowl in 2004.

The Third Circuit Court of Appeals overturned the commission's decision, saying that for three decades the FCC punished broadcasters for indecent programming only when the material was "so pervasive as to amount to 'shock treatment' for the audience. . . . [T]he Commission consistently explained that isolated or fleeting material did not fall within the scope of actionable indecency."[115]

The U.S. Supreme Court told the Third Circuit to reconsider its decision in light of its 2009 ruling concerning Bono, Cher and Richie's fleeting expletives.[116] In 2011, the Third

Circuit issued a new ruling that said the 2009 *Fox* decision supported its conclusion in the Super Bowl case that the FCC could not impose fines for airing a fleeting image of Jackson's breast.[117] However, both the FCC and the U.S. Supreme Court acknowledged that the commission changed the definition of indecency in its fleeting-expletives ruling, which applied to both words and images. Additionally, as with the Bono, Cher and Richie broadcasts, the Jackson incident occurred before the FCC announced its new fleeting-expletives rule, so the CBS network and stations could not have anticipated the change. On this basis, the Third Circuit affirmed its previous ruling that the FCC could not impose fines for airing a fleeting image of Jackson's breast. The Supreme Court refused to hear an appeal of the Third Circuit's 2011 decision.

The Supreme Court's 2012 *Fox Television* decision (excerpted at the end of this chapter) and the Court's refusal to review the Third Circuit's Super Bowl ruling left broadcasters with little guidance. The Court gave the FCC a suggestion, though, when it said in *Fox Television*, "[T]his opinion leaves the Commission free to modify its current indecency policy in light of its determination of the public interest and applicable legal requirements."[118] In 2013, the FCC began reconsidering its indecency regulations again. The commission sought public comment on whether the FCC should change its broadcast indecency policies but failed to take any action and has not revisited its indecency policies since the public comment period more than seven years ago.[119]

The FCC has issued few indecency rulings or fines since the Supreme Court's 2012 *Fox Television* decision. One notable fine occurred in 2015, after the FCC concluded that a local Roanoke, Va., station was liable for accidentally airing three seconds of a sexually explicit, pornographic video clip.[120] The station broadcast a news story about a porn star who volunteered with a local rescue organization. It intended to use an acceptable still image from a porn website, but instead the image came with boxes that auto-loaded pornographic films. As a result, the station accidentally aired an image of a naked man with "a hand moving up and down the length of the shaft of the erect penis."[121] The FCC fined the station the maximum $325,000.[122]

In all of the U.S. Supreme Court decisions about broadcasting and indecency, the Court balanced a broadcaster's free speech rights against concerns for children. In 1993, the FCC adopted a **safe harbor policy** to comply with a congressional mandate. The safe harbor policy holds that the FCC will not punish a broadcast station that airs indecent, but not obscene, material between 10 p.m. and 6 a.m. local time.[123] With court approval, the FCC agreed not to take action against indecent broadcasts aired at a time when few children should be in the audience.[124]

As noted in Chapter 9, the FCC regulates multichannel video programming distributors differently from broadcasting. Before the FCC created the current MVPD definition and framework, its indecency decisions focused on cable.

HBO's development in 1975 spurred cable's popularity. Certain movies that HBO showed offended some state legislators and local officials, and by the early 1980s they adopted laws forbidding cable indecency. Courts uniformly rejected these restrictions. For example, a Miami, Fla., ordinance prohibited cable systems from distributing "obscene or indecent" material.[125] A federal appellate court said the *Pacifica* restrictions on broadcasting indecent material did not

safe harbor policy
A Federal Communications Commission policy designating 10 p.m. to 6 a.m. as a time when broadcast radio and television stations may air indecent material without violating federal law or FCC regulations.

REAL WORLD LAW
TECHNOLOGY AND PARENTAL CONTROL

When Congress passed the Telecommunications Act of 1996, it required all television manufacturers to include an electronic chip that would allow parents to block reception of certain programs they did not want their children to view. The V-chip, as it was commonly known, was heralded as a big step toward reducing a minor's exposure to sex, violence and vulgar language.[ix]

Various studies showed that the V-chip did not work well with the Federal Communications Commission ratings system that also emerged at the time. That voluntary ratings system still exists to help parents know what audience is appropriate for a program, from TV-MA (for mature audiences) to TV-Y (for the youngest audience).[x]

Today, V-chip technology is considered a relic, and concerns about the content children consume have focused on social media channels like YouTube. After complaints that children might accidentally stumble across YouTube user-created graphic parody videos tied to popular children's programs like "Peppa Pig," YouTube introduced filters and age restrictions.[xi] About five years ago, YouTube also created a special app for children's content called YouTube Kids.

In 2019, after reports of sexual predatory behavior arose, YouTube disabled its comments function from tens of millions of videos that featured minors.[xii] Investigations showed that YouTube's filter algorithm directed people to videos of young children playing once someone started searching related terms, which sent people down "a wormhole into a soft-core pedophile ring."[xiii]

apply to cable television. Parents could prevent their children from watching cable television by not subscribing.

The court also said the Miami law was overbroad because it did not allow any period when a cable system could transmit indecent material. Courts struck down several similar laws that the Utah Legislature and many Utah cities adopted to ban indecent material on cable television.[126] Congress adopted the first federal law regulating cable in 1984 but did not use the statute to limit indecent content on cable television. Rather, the law said only that cable systems could not transmit obscene material.[127] The 1984 Cable Communications Policy Act's one concession to those concerned about indecency was to require cable system operators to provide a method for subscribers to block individual cable channels.[128]

The FCC has not attempted to extend its broadcast indecency regulations to cable television.[129] However, more than 25 years ago, Congress decided that indecent cable content required its attention. A 1992 federal law included three provisions limiting indecent content on two specific types of cable channels. First, Congress allowed cable operators to ban indecent programming on the cable channels provided for community, local school and government agency use, the PEG access channels. Second, the law said cable systems could ban any programming a cable operator believed "describes or depicts sexual or excretory activities or organs in a patently offensive manner" from the cable channels individuals and companies could rent to display their own content, the leased-access channels (see Chapter 9).

In *Denver Area Educational Telecommunications Consortium, Inc. v. Federal Communications Commission*,[130] the U.S. Supreme Court upheld the leased-access provision. However, the Court said cable systems could not prohibit indecent programming on PEG access channels.[131]

The Court's *Denver Area* decision was fractious. Even when a group of justices agreed on a result, they could not agree on a reason for the outcome. Subsequently, Congress continued its efforts to limit indecency on PEG access channels. In the Telecommunications Act of 1996, Congress said cable operators could not exercise editorial control over PEG content, but they "may refuse to transmit any public access program or portion of a public access program which contains obscenity, indecency, or nudity."[132] This provision has yet to be challenged in court.

Mark Boster/Los Angeles Times via Getty Images

Recently, some viewers complained to the Federal Communications Commission about the use of the word "goddamn" in promos for "RuPaul's Drag Race."

The U.S. Supreme Court overturned other sections of the 1996 act dealing with sexually explicit cable programming. Congress required cable operators to scramble the signal of any indecent programming on adult-oriented channels.[133] In part, Congress said, this was to prevent adult programming signals from bleeding into channels that children could see even in homes that did not subscribe to adult channels. Alternatively, Congress said, cable programmers could offer adult programming only during hours when children are unlikely to be watching. The FCC said the period would be 10 p.m. to 6 a.m.[134]

A unanimous Supreme Court said those provisions of the 1996 act were content-based regulations requiring a strict scrutiny analysis.[135] Protecting children from exposure to sexually explicit programming was a compelling state interest, but Congress had not adopted the least restrictive approach. Instead, the Court said, cable subscribers could ask cable companies to block channels and request the mechanism to block channels themselves. The availability of these alternatives made the 1996 act's scrambling and late-night provisions unconstitutional, the Court ruled.

OBSCENITY, INDECENCY AND THE INTERNET

The internet has made it easy to access sexually explicit content. For example, Pornhub, the most popular pornography video-sharing website, reported 33.5 billion visits to the site in 2018, up 5 billion from 2017. Users conducted 30.3 billion searches and uploaded 4.79 million new videos in 2018. Worldwide, 80 percent of the site's users accessed content from smartphones and tablets.[136] According to one legal scholar, society remains mostly concerned with protecting nonconsenting adults and children from sexually explicit content. He notes, "[T]he government can constitutionally prohibit the sale or exhibition to children of material that is obscene for minors, but only if it can do so without significantly interfering with the rights of adults." He adds that the government can prohibit the production, distribution and possession of child pornography. "Beyond that, though, there are effectively no limits on what consenting adults can see" in the internet age.[137]

Local and state governments across the United States have initiated public awareness campaigns, like this one in California, to end sex trafficking.

Congress first attempted to regulate internet indecency with the Communications Decency Act, Title V of the Telecommunications Act of 1996.[138] The CDA made it illegal to knowingly transmit "obscene or indecent messages to any recipient under 18 years of age" or to make available "patently offensive messages" to anyone under 18 years old.

The U.S. Supreme Court rejected the indecency provision of the CDA, finding it unconstitutionally overbroad in *Reno v. American Civil Liberties Union*.[139] The Supreme Court first said that, unlike broadcasting, the internet had full First Amendment protection. The internet is not limited by spectrum scarcity, as is broadcasting. Also, the internet is not as intrusive as broadcasting. Families not wanting children to access the internet at home need not subscribe to an internet service provider, the Court said. For these reasons, the Court refused to find the internet bound by the *Pacifica* case and rejected the CDA's complete ban on indecent internet content.

Because the CDA directly restricted speech, the Court used a strict scrutiny analysis. The Court acknowledged that Congress had a compelling interest in protecting children from sexually explicit content. But the Court decided the law was too sweeping. The CDA denied adults access to protected speech as a way to prevent minors from being exposed to potentially harmful content. The Court noted that (at that time) there was no technology allowing adults to see internet material while preventing children from doing so. The Court also said the CDA was overbroad because Congress had not carefully defined the words "indecent" and "offensive."[140] The Court's decision did not apply to the CDA's restriction on sending obscene material over the internet. This limitation remains part of the federal law.

Congress enacted the Child Online Protection Act in 1998, intending to correct the CDA's constitutional problems.[141] Courts consistently have found the COPA unconstitutional. The COPA differed from the CDA in two important ways. First, the COPA banned internet distribution to children of material "harmful to minors," defined in part as being designed to pander to prurient interest, determined by applying contemporary community standards. Second, the COPA's restriction on transmitting harmful content applied only to people intending to profit from using the internet. The law also defined minors as 16 and younger, not 17 and younger.

The COPA definition of harmful to minors resembled the *Miller* obscenity definition. This meant the COPA affected a narrower range of materials than did the CDA. But the definition focused on all materials inappropriate for minors, so the COPA reduced adult access to only materials appropriate for children—just as the CDA had.

Courts consistently found the COPA unconstitutional. Challenges to the COPA stayed in the courts for a decade. First, a federal district court preliminarily stopped the government from enforcing the law.[142] The Third Circuit Court of Appeals affirmed the decision, concluding that the community standards language was overbroad.[143] The U.S. Supreme Court disagreed with the Third Circuit and vacated the decision.[144] Reviewing the case again, the Third Circuit issued an injunction blocking the COPA's enforcement. The court said there were technological methods of limiting children's access to websites containing inappropriate material and that a sweeping ban on "material harmful to children" was not the least restrictive way to achieve Congress' purpose.[145]

On review, the U.S. Supreme Court left the preliminary injunction in place, saying that blocking and filtering software could effectively limit children's access to harmful material. However, the Supreme Court sent the case back to the trial court to update information about internet technology. Courts must have current information to decide if the COPA limits more speech than necessary to protect children, the Court said.

The Court saw the COPA as a content-based speech regulation (see Chapter 2) and required the government to show there were no alternatives less restrictive of First Amendment rights. For example, filters could prevent children from seeing harmful material while allowing adults access to internet content, the Supreme Court said. Also, filters would not chill speech. Websites could include content unacceptable for children but constitutionally protected for adults, and it would be difficult for the government to show that the COPA would be more effective and less restrictive than filters, the Supreme Court concluded.[146]

A federal district court in 2007 found that the COPA was not narrowly tailored and not the least restrictive or most effective way to achieve Congress' compelling interest in protecting children.[147] The government once again appealed the decision.

Hearing the case one more time, the Third Circuit affirmed the district court's decision.[148] Applying strict scrutiny, the appellate court agreed that the government had a compelling interest in protecting children from exposure to harmful material on the internet. But the court said the COPA was not narrowly tailored to achieve that goal. The court also held that several words and phrases in the law, such as "minor," were vague and not clearly defined.[149]

The U.S. Supreme Court refused to hear the government's appeal of the Third Circuit's decision.[150] More than a decade after the COPA's adoption, courts definitively ruled it unconstitutional.

Even before Congress adopted the COPA, it took another, indirect route to keep sexual material off the internet. The Child Pornography Prevention Act, adopted in 1996, made it illegal to send or possess digital images of child pornography.[151] The law made it illegal to send or possess an image that "is, or appears to be, of a minor engaging in sexually explicit conduct," or if the image is advertised or distributed in a way "that conveys the impression" that a minor is "engaging in sexually explicit conduct."[152]

The U.S. Supreme Court said the CPPA abridged First Amendment rights and found it unconstitutional.[153] In *Ashcroft v. Free Speech Coalition*, the Court said the language making it illegal to send or possess images that were not obscene was overbroad. The law would prevent adults from seeing constitutionally protected content in order to block children's exposure. Because the CPPA was a content-based regulation, the Supreme Court applied strict scrutiny. It said Congress had a compelling interest in protecting children from being involved in the sex trade. However, the Court said, since computer-generated pictures of minors are outlawed, the CPPA would prohibit child pornography that does not harm an actual child. That also would be true when adults who appear to be children are pictured.

As noted earlier in the chapter, Congress adopted the PROTECT Act of 2003 in response to the Court's decision.[154] The PROTECT Act makes it illegal to provide someone with or request from someone an image that "is indistinguishable from that of a minor" in a sexual situation. This wording differs from the "appears to be" and "conveys the impression" language in the CPPA. In 2008, the Supreme Court found the PROTECT Act constitutional. The Court said the act focused not on the material but on the speech—offering or requesting child pornography—that could put the material into distribution. The First Amendment does not protect offers to engage in illegal transactions, the Court said, because offering to give or receive unlawful material has no social value.[155]

In addition to the PROTECT Act, the U.S. Supreme Court found constitutional one other congressional attempt to deal with online content. Congress enacted the Children's Internet Protection Act in 2000. This law focused on schools and libraries that receive federal money. The CIPA would stop federal funding from going to schools and libraries that did not install "technology protection measures" on their computers with internet access. Those schools and libraries wanting to continue receiving federal funds would have to install filtering software that blocked obscenity, child pornography or material "harmful to minors."[156]

The Supreme Court held in *United States v. American Library Association* that Congress had the right to set conditions for receipt of federal money.[157] The Court said public libraries already choose to purchase or not purchase certain books and other materials. For example, most libraries exclude pornographic material from their print collections, the Court said. Limiting what internet sites were available on the computers that libraries provided to the public was an equivalent decision. The Court also said requiring adults to ask a librarian to unblock a computer did not infringe on adults' First Amendment rights.

EMERGING LAW

Recently, Congress, state governments and the courts have turned their attention to websites that feature "adult sections" through which advertisers solicit sexual services. Backpage.com and Craigslist are the two websites that have received the most attention. For example, in 2017, a Senate investigative committee concluded that Backpage was knowingly assisting human traffickers. Backpage called the subcommittee's findings "unconstitutional government censorship."[158] Soon after, however, the website said it would close its adult section while it fought several lawsuits in federal courts.[159]

In Washington and Massachusetts, Backpage successfully argued that the First Amendment protected it from enforcement of state laws that created criminal liability for anyone who knowingly advertises "sexual abuse of a minor."[160] Backpage argued that the law would chill permissible ads and that Section 230 of the CDA (see Chapter 5) protected it from liability. Federal courts have agreed.

In 2018, President Trump signed a bill into law that ended the

protection that Section 230 provided for Backpage and others who allowed third-party users to sell sex-related services on their sites. The Allow States and Victims to Fight Online Sex Trafficking Act of 2017, known as FOSTA, allows victims to sue websites that knowingly supported sex trafficking on their sites. The law amended Section 230 by removing protection for online companies for content they host on their websites or services as it relates to the sexual exploitation of children and/or sex trafficking.[161] "Removing the unwarranted shield from legal responsibility will save countless children from horrific tragedy, both physical and emotional," one of the bill's co-sponsors said.[162]

Upon passage of the bill, Craigslist suspended its "personals" section, writing,

> US Congress just passed [a bill] seeking to subject websites to criminal and civil liability when third parties (users) misuse online personals unlawfully. Any tool or service can be misused. We can't take such risk without jeopardizing all our other services, so we are regretfully taking craigslist personals offline.[163]

Several organizations, including anti-trafficking advocates, civil liberties groups and technology scholars, challenged the law on the grounds that it violates the First Amendment because it is overly broad. The D.C. Circuit Court of Appeals dismissed their suit for lack of standing.[164] An appeal was pending in mid-2019.[165]

While law enforcement officials praised the shutdown of adult-oriented advertising, such as what appeared on Backpage, they also said the platform had been a key tool for identifying and charging sexual predators. Sex workers said they used the sites for screening, providing them some additional protections from violence.[166] Legal experts have raised concerns about broader harms FOSTA might cause to Section 230 immunity for websites and internet service providers and also suggested the law was overbroad and violated the First Amendment.[167]

Surrounded by victims and their families, President Donald Trump signs the Allow States and Victims to Fight Online Sex Trafficking Act of 2017.

Chris Kleponis/picture-alliance/dpa/AP Images

CASES FOR STUDY

For study resources and a case archive, go to **edge.sagepub.com/medialaw7e**.

Thinking About It

The two case excerpts that follow offer the U.S. Supreme Court's definition of indecency and demonstrate how the FCC has applied the concept of indecency in specific contexts over time. As you read these case excerpts, keep the following questions in mind:

- Is the rationale of protecting children and the intrusiveness of broadcasting in the home, put forth by the Court in *FCC v. Pacifica Foundation*, still relevant today? Could new technologies and different ways to deliver content such as George Carlin's monologue change the outcome in this case if it were heard by the Supreme Court today?

- Considering the different views from the justices in *Pacifica Foundation*, what are the various ways that each sees indecency as distinct from obscenity with respect to the First Amendment?

- In *FCC v. Fox Television Stations, Inc.*, does the Supreme Court clearly justify why the law forbids indecency?

- If you were in charge of a broadcast channel, would you have enough specific guidance from the *Fox* decision to help you determine how to avoid getting fined for airing indecent content? Why or why not?

Federal Communications Commission v. Pacifica Foundation

SUPREME COURT OF THE UNITED STATES
438 U.S. 726 (1978)

JUSTICE JOHN PAUL STEVENS
delivered the Court's opinion:

This case requires that we decide whether the Federal Communications Commission has any power to regulate a radio broadcast that is indecent but not obscene.

A satiric humorist named George Carlin recorded a 12-minute monologue entitled "Filthy Words" before a live audience in a California theater. He began by referring to his thoughts about "the words you couldn't say on the public, ah, airwaves, um, the ones you definitely wouldn't say, ever." He proceeded to list those words and repeat them over and over again in a variety of colloquialisms. The transcript of the recording . . . indicates frequent laughter from the audience.

At about 2 o'clock in the afternoon on Tuesday, October 30, 1973, a New York radio station, owned by respondent Pacifica Foundation, broadcast the "Filthy Words" monologue. A few weeks later a man, who stated that he had heard the broadcast while driving with his young son, wrote a letter complaining to the Commission. . . .

The complaint was forwarded to the station for comment. In its response, Pacifica explained that the monologue had been played during a program about contemporary society's attitude toward language and that, immediately before its broadcast, listeners had been advised that it included "sensitive language which might be regarded as offensive to some." Pacifica characterized George Carlin as "a significant social satirist" who . . . "examines the language of ordinary people. . . . Carlin is not mouthing obscenities, he is merely using words to satirize as harmless and essentially silly our attitudes towards those words." . . .

On February 21, 1975, the Commission issued a declaratory order granting the complaint and holding that Pacifica "could have been the subject of administrative sanctions." The Commission did not impose formal sanctions. . . .

In its memorandum opinion the Commission stated that it intended to "clarify the standards which will be utilized in considering" the growing number of complaints about indecent speech on the airwaves.

Advancing several reasons for treating broadcast speech differently from other forms of expression, the Commission found a power to regulate indecent broadcasting in two statutes, [one] which forbids the use of "any obscene, indecent, or profane language by means of radio communications," and [another] which requires the Commission to "encourage the larger and more effective use of radio in the public interest."

The Commission characterized the language used in the Carlin monologue as "patently offensive," though not necessarily obscene, and expressed the opinion that it should be regulated by principles analogous to those found in the law of nuisance. . . .

Applying these considerations to the language used in the monologue as broadcast by respondent, the Commission concluded that certain words depicted sexual and excretory activities in a patently offensive manner, noted that they "were broadcast at a time when children were undoubtedly in the audience (i.e., in the early afternoon)," and that the prerecorded language, with these offensive words "repeated over and over," was "deliberately broadcast." In summary, the Commission stated: "We therefore hold that the language as broadcast was indecent and prohibited."

After the order issued, the Commission was asked to clarify its opinion by ruling that the broadcast of indecent words as part of a live newscast would not be prohibited. The Commission issued another opinion in which it pointed out that it "never intended to place an absolute prohibition on the broadcast of this type of language, but rather sought to channel it to times of day when children most likely would not be exposed to it." The Commission noted that its "declaratory order was issued in a specific factual context," and declined to comment on various hypothetical situations presented by the petition. It relied on its "long standing policy of refusing to issue interpretive rulings or advisory opinions when the critical facts are not explicitly stated or there is a possibility that subsequent events will alter them."

The United States Court of Appeals for the District of Columbia Circuit reversed, with each of the three judges on the panel writing separately. . . .

Having granted the Commission's petition for certiorari, we must decide: (1) whether the scope of judicial review encompasses more than the Commission's determination that the monologue was indecent "as broadcast"; (2) whether the Commission's order was a form of censorship . . . ; (3) whether the broadcast was indecent . . . ; and (4) whether the order violates the First Amendment of the United States Constitution.

. . . [A] statutory question presented by this case is whether the afternoon broadcast of the "Filthy Words" monologue was indecent. . . . Even that question is narrowly confined by the arguments of the parties.

The Commission identified several words that referred to excretory or sexual activities or organs, stated that the repetitive, deliberate use of those words in an afternoon broadcast when children are in the audience was patently offensive, and held that the broadcast was indecent. Pacifica takes issue with the Commission's definition of indecency, but does not dispute the Commission's preliminary determination that each of the components of its definition was present. Specifically, Pacifica does not quarrel with the conclusion that this afternoon broadcast was patently offensive. Pacifica's claim that the broadcast was not indecent within the meaning of the statute rests entirely on the absence of prurient appeal.

The plain language of the statute does not support Pacifica's argument. The words "obscene, indecent, or profane" are written in the disjunctive, implying that each has a separate meaning. Prurient appeal is an element of the obscene, but the normal definition of "indecent" merely refers to nonconformance with accepted standards of morality.

Pacifica argues, however, that this Court has construed the term "indecent" in related statutes to mean "obscene," as that term was defined in *Miller v. California*. . . . In holding that the statute's coverage is limited to obscenity, the Court followed the lead of Mr. Justice Harlan [who] . . . thought that the phrase "obscene, lewd, lascivious, indecent, filthy or vile," taken as a whole, was clearly limited to the obscene, a reading well grounded in prior judicial constructions. . . .

. . . [T]he Commission has long interpreted [the statute] as encompassing more than the obscene. The former statute deals primarily with printed matter enclosed in sealed envelopes mailed from one individual to another; the latter deals with the content of public broadcasts. It is unrealistic to assume that Congress intended to impose precisely the same limitations on the dissemination of patently offensive matter by such different means.

Because neither our prior decisions nor the language or history of [the statute] supports the conclusion that prurient appeal is an essential component of indecent language, we reject Pacifica's construction of the statute. When that construction is put to one side, there is no basis for disagreeing with the Commission's conclusion that indecent language was used in this broadcast.

Pacifica makes two constitutional attacks on the Commission's order. First, it argues that the Commission's construction of the statutory language broadly encompasses so much constitutionally protected speech that reversal is required even if Pacifica's broadcast of the "Filthy Words" monologue is not itself protected by the First Amendment. Second, Pacifica argues that inasmuch as the recording is not obscene, the Constitution forbids any abridgment of the right to broadcast it on the radio.

The first argument fails because our review is limited to the question whether the Commission has the authority to proscribe this particular broadcast. . . .

It is true that the Commission's order may lead some broadcasters to censor themselves. At most, however, the Commission's definition of indecency will deter only the broadcasting of patently offensive references to excretory and sexual organs and activities. While some of these references may be protected, they surely lie at the periphery of First Amendment concern. . . . Invalidating any rule on the basis of its hypothetical application to situations not before the Court is "strong medicine" to be applied "sparingly and only as a last resort." We decline to administer that medicine to preserve the vigor of patently offensive sexual and excretory speech.

When the issue is narrowed to the facts of this case, the question is whether the First Amendment denies government any power to restrict the public broadcast of indecent language in any circumstances. . . .

The words of the Carlin monologue are unquestionably "speech" within the meaning of the First Amendment. It is equally clear that the Commission's objections to the broadcast were based in part on its content. The order must therefore fall if, as Pacifica argues, the First Amendment prohibits all governmental regulation that depends on the content of speech. Our past cases demonstrate, however, that no such absolute rule is mandated by the Constitution.

. . . The government may forbid speech calculated to provoke a fight. It may pay heed to the "'common-sense differences' between commercial speech and other varieties." It may treat libels against private citizens more severely than libels against public officials. Obscenity may be wholly prohibited. . . .

The question in this case is whether a broadcast of patently offensive words dealing with sex and excretion may be regulated because of its content. Obscene materials have been denied the protection of the First Amendment because their content is so offensive to contemporary moral standards.

But the fact that society may find speech offensive is not a sufficient reason for suppressing it. Indeed, if it is the speaker's opinion that gives offense, that consequence is a reason for according it constitutional protection. For it is a central tenet of the First Amendment that the government must remain neutral in the marketplace of ideas. If there were any reason to believe that the Commission's characterization of the Carlin monologue as offensive could be traced to its political content—or even to the fact that it satirized contemporary attitudes about four-letter words—First Amendment protection might be required. But that is simply not this case. These words offend for the same reasons that obscenity offends. . . .

Although these words ordinarily lack literary, political, or scientific value, they are not entirely outside the protection of the First Amendment. Some uses of even the most offensive words are unquestionably protected. Indeed, we may assume, *arguendo*, that this monologue would be protected in other contexts. Nonetheless, the constitutional protection accorded to a communication containing such patently offensive sexual and excretory language need not be the same in every context. . . . Words that are commonplace in one setting are shocking in another. To paraphrase Mr. Justice Harlan, one occasion's lyric is another's vulgarity.

In this case it is undisputed that the content of Pacifica's broadcast was "vulgar," "offensive," and "shocking." Because content of that character is not entitled to absolute constitutional protection under all circumstances, we must consider its context in order to determine whether the Commission's action was constitutionally permissible.

We have long recognized that each medium of expression presents special First Amendment problems. And of all forms of communication, it is broadcasting that has received the most limited First Amendment protection. . . . [A]lthough the First Amendment protects newspaper publishers from being required to print the replies of those whom they criticize, it affords no such protection to broadcasters;

on the contrary, they must give free time to the victims of their criticism.

The reasons for these distinctions are complex, but two have relevance to the present case. First, the broadcast media have established a uniquely pervasive presence in the lives of all Americans. Patently offensive, indecent material presented over the airwaves confronts the citizen, not only in public, but also in the privacy of the home, where the individual's right to be left alone plainly outweighs the First Amendment rights of an intruder.

Because the broadcast audience is constantly tuning in and out, prior warnings cannot completely protect the listener or viewer from unexpected program content. To say that one may avoid further offense by turning off the radio when he hears indecent language is like saying that the remedy for an assault is to run away after the first blow. One may hang up on an indecent phone call, but that option does not give the caller a constitutional immunity or avoid a harm that has already taken place.

Second, broadcasting is uniquely accessible to children, even those too young to read. Although Cohen's written message might have been incomprehensible to a first grader, Pacifica's broadcast could have enlarged a child's vocabulary in an instant. Other forms of offensive expression may be withheld from the young without restricting the expression at its source. Bookstores and motion picture theaters, for example, may be prohibited from making indecent material available to children. . . . The ease with which children may obtain access to broadcast material . . . amply justif[ies] special treatment of indecent broadcasting.

It is appropriate, in conclusion, to emphasize the narrowness of our holding. This case does not involve a two-way radio conversation between a cab driver and a dispatcher, or a telecast of an Elizabethan comedy. We have not decided that an occasional expletive in either setting would justify any sanction or, indeed, that this broadcast would justify a criminal prosecution. The Commission's decision rested entirely on a nuisance rationale under which context is all-important. The concept requires consideration of a host of variables. The time of day was emphasized by the Commission. The content of the program in which the language is used will also affect the composition of the audience, and differences between radio, television, and perhaps closed-circuit transmissions, may also be relevant. . . . We . . . hold that when the Commission finds that a pig has entered the parlor, the exercise of its regulatory power does not depend on proof that the pig is obscene.

The judgment of the Court of Appeals is reversed.

It is so ordered.

JUSTICE LEWIS POWELL, with whom JUSTICE HARRY BLACKMUN joined, concurring in part and concurring in the judgment.

. . . The Court today reviews only the Commission's holding that Carlin's monologue was indecent "as broadcast" at two o'clock in the afternoon, and not the broad sweep of the Commission's opinion. . . .

I also agree with much that is said in Part IV of MR. JUSTICE STEVENS' opinion, and with its conclusion that the Commission's holding in this case does not violate the First Amendment. Because I do not subscribe to all that is said in Part IV, however, I state my views separately.

It is conceded that the monologue at issue here is not obscene in the constitutional sense. . . . Some of the words used have been held protected by the First Amendment in other cases and contexts. I do not think Carlin, consistently with the First Amendment, could be punished for delivering the same monologue to a live audience composed of adults who, knowing what to expect, chose to attend his performance. And I would assume that an adult could not constitutionally be prohibited from purchasing a recording or transcript of the monologue and playing or reading it in the privacy of his own home.

But it also is true that the language employed is, to most people, vulgar and offensive. . . . The Commission did not err in characterizing the narrow category of language used here as "patently offensive" to most people regardless of age.

The issue, however, is whether the Commission may impose civil sanctions on a licensee radio station for broadcasting the monologue at two o'clock in the afternoon. The Commission's primary concern was to prevent the broadcast from reaching the ears of unsupervised children who were likely to be in the audience at that hour. . . .

In most instances, the dissemination of this kind of speech to children may be limited without also limiting willing adults' access to it. Sellers of printed and recorded matter and exhibitors of motion pictures and live performances may be required to shut their doors to children, but such a requirement has no effect on adults' access.

The difficulty is that such a physical separation of the audience cannot be accomplished in the broadcast media. During most of the broadcast hours, both adults and unsupervised children are likely to be in the broadcast audience, and the broadcaster cannot reach willing adults without also reaching children. This, as the Court emphasizes, is one of the distinctions between the broadcast and other media to which we often have adverted as justifying a different treatment of the broadcast media for First Amendment purposes.

In my view, the Commission was entitled to give substantial weight to this difference in reaching its decision in this case.

A second difference, not without relevance, is that broadcasting—unlike most other forms of communication—comes directly into the home, the one place where people ordinarily have the right not to be assaulted by uninvited and offensive sights and sounds. Although the First Amendment may require unwilling adults to absorb the first blow of offensive but protected speech when they are in public before they turn away, a different order of values obtains in the home. . . .

. . . In short, I agree that on the facts of this case, the Commission's order did not violate respondent's First Amendment rights.

. . . In my view, the result in this case does not turn on whether Carlin's monologue, viewed as a whole, or the words that constitute it, have more or less "value" than a candidate's campaign speech. This is a judgment for each person to make, not one for the judges to impose upon him.

The result turns instead on the unique characteristics of the broadcast media, combined with society's right to protect its children from speech generally agreed to be inappropriate for their years, and with the interest of unwilling adults in not being assaulted by such offensive speech in their homes. Moreover, I doubt whether today's decision will prevent any adult who wishes to receive Carlin's message in Carlin's own words from doing so, and from making for himself a value judgment as to the merit of the message and words. These are the grounds upon which I join the judgment of the Court as to Part IV.

JUSTICE WILLIAM BRENNAN and JUSTICE POTTER STEWART, with whom JUSTICE THURGOOD MARSHALL joined, dissenting.
I agree with MR. JUSTICE STEWART that . . . the word "indecent" must be construed to prohibit only obscene speech. I would, therefore, normally refrain from expressing my views on any constitutional issues implicated in this case. However, I find the Court's misapplication of fundamental First Amendment principles so patent, and its attempt to impose *its* notions of propriety on the whole of the American people so misguided, that I am unable to remain silent.

For the second time in two years, the Court refuses to embrace the notion, completely antithetical to basic First Amendment values, that the degree of protection the First Amendment affords protected speech varies with the social value ascribed to that speech by five Members of this Court. Moreover, as do all parties, all Members of the Court agree that the Carlin monologue aired by Station WBAI does not fall within one of the categories of speech, such as "fighting words," or obscenity, that is totally without First Amendment protection. This conclusion, of course, is compelled by our cases expressly holding that communications containing some of the words found condemnable here are fully protected by the First Amendment in other contexts. Yet despite the Court's refusal to create a sliding scale of First Amendment protection calibrated to this Court's perception of the worth of a communication's content, and despite our unanimous agreement that the Carlin monologue is protected speech, a majority of the Court nevertheless finds that, on the facts of this case, the FCC is not constitutionally barred from imposing sanctions on Pacifica for its airing of the Carlin monologue. This majority apparently believes that the FCC's disapproval of Pacifica's afternoon broadcast of Carlin's "Dirty Words" recording is a permissible time, place, and manner regulation. Both the opinion of my Brother STEVENS and the opinion of my Brother POWELL rely principally on two factors in reaching this conclusion: (1) the capacity of a radio broadcast to intrude into the unwilling listener's home, and (2) the presence of children in the listening audience. Dispassionate analysis, removed from individual notions as to what is proper and what is not, starkly reveals that these justifications, whether individually or together, simply do not support even the professedly moderate degree of governmental homogenization of radio communications—if, indeed, such homogenization can ever be moderate given the pre-eminent status of the right of free speech in our constitutional scheme—that the Court today permits.

Without question, the privacy interests of an individual in his home are substantial and deserving of significant protection. In finding these interests sufficient to justify the content regulation of protected speech, however, the Court commits two errors. First, it misconceives the nature of the privacy interests involved where an individual voluntarily chooses to admit radio communications into his home. Second, it ignores the constitutionally protected interests of both those who wish to transmit and those who desire to receive broadcasts that many—including the FCC and this Court—might find offensive.

. . . Even if an individual who voluntarily opens his home to radio communications retains privacy interests of sufficient moment to justify a ban on protected speech if those interests are "invaded in an essentially intolerable manner," the very fact that those interests are threatened only by a radio broadcast precludes any intolerable invasion of privacy; for unlike other intrusive modes of communication, such as sound trucks, "[the] radio can be turned off"—and with a minimum of effort.

. . . The Court's balance, of necessity, fails to accord proper weight to the interests of listeners who wish to hear broadcasts the FCC deems offensive. It permits majoritarian tastes completely to preclude a protected message from entering the homes of a receptive, unoffended minority. No decision of this Court supports such a result. . . .

. . . Because the Carlin monologue is obviously not an erotic appeal to the prurient interests of children, the Court, for the first time, allows the government to prevent minors from gaining access to materials that are not obscene, and are therefore protected, as to them. . . .

The opinion of my Brother POWELL acknowledges that there lurks in today's decision a potential for "'[reducing] the adult population . . . to [hearing] only what is fit for children,'" but expresses faith that the FCC will vigilantly prevent this potential from ever becoming a reality. I am far less certain than my Brother POWELL that such faith in the Commission is warranted; and even if I shared it, I could not so easily shirk the responsibility assumed by each Member of this Court jealously to guard against encroachments on First Amendment freedoms.

In concluding that the presence of children in the listening audience provides an adequate basis for the FCC to impose sanctions for Pacifica's broadcast of the Carlin monologue, the opinions of my Brother POWELL, and my Brother STEVENS, both stress the time-honored right of a parent to raise his child as he sees fit—a right this Court has consistently been vigilant to protect. Yet this principle supports a result directly contrary to that reached by the Court. [Prior decisions] hold that parents, *not* the government, have the right to make certain decisions regarding the upbringing of their children. As surprising as it may be to individual Members of this Court, some parents may actually find Mr. Carlin's unabashed attitude towards the seven "dirty words" healthy, and deem it desirable to expose their children to the manner in which Mr. Carlin defuses the taboo surrounding the words. Such parents may constitute a minority of the American public, but the absence of great numbers willing to exercise the right to raise their children in this fashion does not alter the right's nature or its existence. Only the Court's regrettable decision does that.

As demonstrated above, neither of the factors relied on by both the opinion of my Brother POWELL and the opinion of my Brother STEVENS—the intrusive nature of radio and the presence of children in the listening audience—can, when taken on its own terms, support the FCC's disapproval of the Carlin monologue. . . . Taken to their logical extreme, these rationales would support the cleansing of public radio of any "four-letter words" whatsoever, regardless of their context. The rationales could justify the banning from radio of a myriad of literary works, novels, poems, and plays by the likes of Shakespeare, Joyce, Hemingway, Ben Jonson, Henry Fielding, Robert Burns, and Chaucer; they could support the suppression of a good deal of political speech, such as the Nixon tapes; and they could even provide the basis for imposing sanctions for the broadcast of certain portions of the Bible.

In order to dispel the specter of the possibility of so unpalatable a degree of censorship, and to defuse Pacifica's overbreadth challenge, the FCC insists that it desires only the authority to reprimand a broadcaster on facts analogous to those present in this case . . . For my own part, even accepting that this case is limited to its facts, I would place the responsibility and the right to weed worthless and offensive communications from the public airways where it belongs and where, until today, it resided: in a public free to choose those communications worthy of its attention from a marketplace unsullied by the censor's hand.

The absence of any hesitancy in the opinions of my Brothers POWELL and STEVENS to approve the FCC's censorship of the Carlin monologue on the basis of two demonstrably inadequate grounds is a function of their perception that the decision will result in little, if any, curtailment of communicative exchanges protected by the First Amendment. . . .

. . . [E]ven if an alternative phrasing may communicate a speaker's abstract ideas as effectively as those words he is forbidden to use, it is doubtful that the sterilized message will convey the emotion that is an essential part of so many communications.

. . . The airways are capable not only of carrying a message, but also of transforming it. A satirist's monologue may be most potent when delivered to a live audience; yet the choice whether this will in fact be the manner in which the message is delivered and received is one the First Amendment prohibits the government from making.

It is quite evident that I find the Court's attempt to unstitch the warp and woof of First Amendment law in an effort to reshape its fabric to cover the patently wrong result the Court reaches in this case dangerous as well as lamentable. Yet there runs throughout the opinions of my Brothers POWELL and STEVENS another vein I find equally disturbing: a depressing inability to appreciate that in our land of cultural pluralism, there are many who think, act, and talk differently from the Members of this Court, and who do not share their fragile sensibilities. It is only an acute ethnocentric myopia that enables the Court to approve the censorship of communications solely because of the words they contain.

. . . The words that the Court and the Commission find so unpalatable may be the stuff of everyday conversations in some, if not many, of the innumerable subcultures that compose this Nation. Academic research indicates that this is indeed the case. As one researcher concluded, "[words] generally considered obscene like 'bullshit' and 'fuck' are considered neither obscene nor derogatory in the [black] vernacular except in particular contextual situations and when used with certain intonations."

. . . In this context, the Court's decision may be seen for what, in the broader perspective, it really is: another of the dominant culture's inevitable efforts to force those groups who do not share its mores to conform to its way of thinking, acting, and speaking.

Pacifica, in response to an FCC inquiry about its broadcast of Carlin's satire on "'the words you couldn't say on the public . . . airways,'" explained that "Carlin is not mouthing obscenities, he is merely using words

to satirize as harmless and essentially silly our attitudes towards those words." In confirming Carlin's prescience as a social commentator by the result it reaches today, the Court evidences an attitude toward the "seven dirty words" that many others besides Mr. Carlin and Pacifica might describe as "silly." Whether today's decision will similarly prove "harmless" remains to be seen. One can only hope that it will.

JUSTICE POTTER STEWART, with whom JUSTICE WILLIAM BRENNAN, JUSTICE BYRON WHITE and JUSTICE THURGOOD MARSHALL join, dissenting.

. . . The statute pursuant to which the Commission acted makes it a federal offense to utter "any obscene, indecent, or profane language by means of radio communication." The Commission held, and the Court today agrees, that "indecent" is a broader concept than "obscene" as the latter term was defined in *Miller v. California*, because language can be "indecent" although it has social, political, or artistic value and lacks prurient appeal. But this construction of [the statute], while perhaps plausible, is by no means compelled. To the contrary, I think that "indecent" should properly be read as meaning no more than "obscene." Since the Carlin monologue concededly was not "obscene," I believe that the Commission lacked statutory authority to ban it. Under this construction of the statute, it is unnecessary to address the difficult and important issue of the Commission's constitutional power to prohibit speech that would be constitutionally protected outside the context of electronic broadcasting.

This Court has recently decided the meaning of the term "indecent" in a closely related statutory context [and held] that "indecent" . . . has the same meaning as "obscene" as that term was defined in the *Miller* case. . . .

I would hold, therefore, that Congress intended, by using the word "indecent" in § 1464, to prohibit nothing more than obscene speech. Under that reading of the statute, the Commission's order in this case was not authorized, and on that basis I would affirm the judgment of the Court of Appeals.

Federal Communications Commission v. Fox Television Stations, Inc.
SUPREME COURT OF THE UNITED STATES
567 U.S. 239 (2012)

JUSTICE ANTHONY KENNEDY
delivered the Court's opinion:

In FCC v. Fox Television Stations, Inc. (2009) (*Fox I*), the Court held that the Federal Communication[s] Commission's decision to modify its indecency enforcement regime to regulate so-called fleeting expletives was neither arbitrary nor capricious. The Court then declined to address the constitutionality of the policy, however, because the United States Court of Appeals for the Second Circuit had yet to do so. On remand, the Court of Appeals [in 2010] found the policy was vague and, as a result, unconstitutional. The case now returns to this Court for decision upon the constitutional question.

[The U.S. Criminal Code] provides that "[w]hoever utters any obscene, indecent, or profane language by means of radio communication shall be fined . . . or imprisoned not more than two years, or both." The Federal Communications Commission (Commission) has been instructed by Congress to enforce [that provision] between the hours of 6 a.m. and 10 p.m. And the Commission has applied its regulations to radio and television broadcasters alike. . . .

This Court first reviewed the Commission's indecency policy in FCC v. Pacifica Foundation (1978). In *Pacifica*, the Commission determined that George Carlin's "Filthy Words" monologue was indecent. It contained "language that describes, in terms patently offensive as measured by contemporary community standards for the broadcast medium, sexual or excretory activities and organs, at times of the day when there is a reasonable risk that children may be in the audience." This Court upheld the Commission's ruling. . . .

In 1987, the Commission determined it was applying the *Pacifica* standard in too narrow a way. It stated that in later cases its definition of indecent language would "appropriately includ[e] a broader range of material than the seven specific words at issue in [the Carlin monologue]." Thus, the Commission indicated it would use the "generic definition of indecency" articulated

in its 1975 *Pacifica* order and assess the full context of allegedly indecent broadcasts rather than limiting its regulation to a "comprehensive index . . . of indecent words or pictorial depictions."

Even under this context based approach, the Commission continued to note the important difference between isolated and repeated broadcasts of indecent material. In the context of expletives, the Commission determined "deliberate and repetitive use in a patently offensive manner is a requisite to a finding of indecency." For speech "involving the description or depiction of sexual or excretory functions . . . [t]he mere fact that specific words or phrases are not repeated does not mandate a finding that material that is otherwise patently offensive . . . is not indecent."

In 2001, the Commission issued a policy statement intended "to provide guidance to the broadcast industry regarding [its] caselaw interpreting [the indecency law] and [its] enforcement policies with respect to broadcast indecency." In that document the Commission restated that for material to be indecent it must depict sexual or excretory organs or activities and be patently offensive as measured by contemporary community standards for the broadcast medium. Describing the framework of what it considered patently offensive, the Commission explained that three factors had proved significant:

> "(1) [T]he explicitness or graphic nature of
> the description or depiction of sexual or
> excretory organs or activities; (2) whether
> the material dwells on or repeats at length
> descriptions of sexual or excretory organs or
> activities; (3) whether the material appears
> to pander or is used to titillate, or whether
> the material appears to have been presented
> for its shock value."

As regards the second of these factors, the Commission explained that "[r]epetition of and persistent focus on sexual or excretory material have been cited consistently as factors that exacerbate the potential offensiveness of broadcasts. In contrast, where sexual or excretory references have been made once or have been passing or fleeting in nature, this characteristic has tended to weigh against a finding of indecency." The Commission then gave examples of material that was not found indecent because it was fleeting and isolated, and contrasted it with fleeting references that were found patently offensive in light of other factors.

It was against this regulatory background that the three incidents of alleged indecency at issue here took place. First, in the 2002 Billboard Music Awards, broadcast by respondent Fox Television Stations, Inc., the singer Cher exclaimed during an unscripted acceptance speech: "I've also had my critics for the last 40 years saying that I was on my way out every year. Right. So f*** 'em." Second, Fox broadcast the Billboard Music Awards again in 2003. There, a person named Nicole Richie made the following unscripted remark while presenting an award: "Have you ever tried to get cow s*** out of a Prada purse? It's not so f***ing simple." The third incident involved an episode of NYPD Blue, a regular television show broadcast by respondent ABC Television Network. The episode broadcast on February 25, 2003, showed the nude buttocks of an adult female character for approximately seven seconds and for a moment the side of her breast. During the scene, in which the character was preparing to take a shower, a child portraying her boyfriend's son entered the bathroom. A moment of awkwardness followed. The Commission received indecency complaints about all three broadcasts.

After these incidents, but before the Commission issued Notices of Apparent Liability to Fox and ABC, the Commission issued a decision sanctioning NBC for a comment made by the singer Bono during the 2003 Golden Globe Awards. Upon winning the award for Best Original Song, Bono exclaimed: "'This is really, really, f***ing brilliant. Really, really great.'" Reversing a decision by its enforcement bureau, the Commission found the use of the F-word actionably indecent. The Commission held that the word was "one of the most vulgar, graphic and explicit descriptions of sexual activity in the English language," and thus found "any use of that word or a variation, in any context, inherently has a sexual

connotation." Turning to the isolated nature of the expletive, the Commission reversed prior rulings that had found fleeting expletives not indecent. The Commission held "the mere fact that specific words or phrases are not sustained or repeated does not mandate a finding that material that is otherwise patently offensive to the broadcast medium is not indecent."

Even though the incidents at issue in these cases took place before the *Golden Globes* Order, the Commission applied its new policy regarding fleeting expletives and fleeting nudity. It found the broadcasts by respondents Fox and ABC to be in violation of this standard.

As to Fox, [in 2006] the Commission found the two Billboard Awards broadcasts indecent. Numerous parties petitioned for a review of the order in the United States Court of Appeals for the Second Circuit. The Court of Appeals granted the Commission's request for a voluntary remand so that it could respond to the parties' objections. In its remand order, the Commission applied its tripartite definition of patently offensive material from its 2001 Order and found that both broadcasts fell well within its scope. As pertains to the constitutional issue in these cases, the Commission noted that under the policy clarified in the *Golden Globes* Order, "categorically requiring repeated use of expletives in order to find material indecent is inconsistent with our general approach to indecency enforcement." Though the Commission deemed Fox should have known Nicole Richie's comments were actionably indecent even prior to the *Golden Globes* Order, it declined to propose a forfeiture in light of the limited nature of the Second Circuit's remand. The Commission acknowledged that "it was not apparent that Fox could be penalized for Cher's comment at the time it was broadcast." And so, as in the Golden Globes case it imposed no penalty for that broadcast.

Fox and various intervenors returned to the United States Court of Appeals for the Second Circuit, raising administrative, statutory, and constitutional challenges to the Commission's indecency regulations. In a 2-to-1 decision, with Judge Leval dissenting, the Court of Appeals found the *Remand* Order arbitrary and capricious because "the FCC has made a 180-degree turn regarding its treatment of 'fleeting expletives' without providing a reasoned explanation justifying the about-face." While noting its skepticism as to whether the Commission's fleeting expletive regime "would pass constitutional muster," the Court of Appeals found it unnecessary to address the issue.

The case came here on certiorari. Citing the Administrative Procedure Act, this Court noted that the Judiciary may set aside agency action that is arbitrary or capricious. In the context of a change in policy (such as the Commission's determination that fleeting expletives could be indecent), the decision held an agency, in the ordinary course, should acknowledge that it is in fact changing its position and "show that there are good reasons for the new policy." There is no need, however, for an agency to provide detailed justifications for every change or to show that the reasons for the new policy are better than the reasons for the old one.

Judged under this standard, the Court in *Fox I* found the Commission's new indecency enforcement policy neither arbitrary nor capricious. The Court noted the Commission had acknowledged breaking new ground in ruling that fleeting and nonliteral expletives could be indecent under the controlling standards; the Court concluded the agency's reasons for expanding the scope of its enforcement activity were rational. Not only was it "certainly reasonable to determine that it made no sense to distinguish between literal and nonliteral uses of offensive words," but the Court agreed that the Commission's decision to "look at the patent offensiveness of even isolated uses of sexual and excretory words fits with the context-based approach [approved] . . . in *Pacifica*." Given that "[e]ven isolated utterances can . . . constitute harmful 'first blow[s]' to children," the Court held that the Commission could "decide it needed to step away from its old regime where non-repetitive use of an expletive was *per se* nonactionable." Having found the agency's action to be neither arbitrary nor capricious, the Court remanded for the Court of Appeals to address respondents' First Amendment challenges.

On remand from *Fox I*, the Court of Appeals held the Commission's indecency policy unconstitutionally vague and invalidated it in its entirety. The Court of Appeals found the policy, as expressed in the 2001 Guidance and subsequent Commission decisions, failed to give broadcasters sufficient notice of what would be considered indecent. Surveying a number of Commission adjudications, the court found the

Commission was inconsistent as to which words it deemed patently offensive. It also determined that the Commission's presumptive prohibition on the F-word and the S-word was plagued by vagueness because the Commission had on occasion found the fleeting use of those words not indecent provided they occurred during a bona fide news interview or were "demonstrably essential to the nature of an artistic or educational work." The Commission's application of these exceptions, according to the Court of Appeals, left broadcasters guessing whether an expletive would be deemed artistically integral to a program or whether a particular broadcast would be considered a bona fide news interview. The Court of Appeals found the vagueness inherent in the policy had forced broadcasters to "choose between not airing . . . controversial programs [or] risking massive fines or possibly even loss of their licenses." And the court found that there was "ample evidence in the record" that this harsh choice had led to a chill of protected speech.

The procedural history regarding ABC is more brief. On February 19, 2008, the Commission issued a forfeiture order finding the display of the woman's nude buttocks in NYPD Blue was actionably indecent. The Commission determined that, regardless of medical definitions, displays of buttocks fell within the category of displays of sexual or excretory organs because the depiction was "widely associated with sexual arousal and closely associated by most people with excretory activities." The scene was deemed patently offensive as measured by contemporary community standards, and the Commission determined that "[t]he female actor's nudity is presented in a manner that clearly panders to and titillates the audience." Unlike in the Fox case, the Commission imposed a forfeiture of $27,500 on each of the 45 ABC-affiliated stations that aired the indecent episode. In a summary order the United States Court of Appeals for the Second Circuit vacated the forfeiture order, determining that it was bound by its *Fox* decision striking down the entirety of the Commission's indecency policy.

. . . These are the cases before us.

A fundamental principle in our legal system is that laws which regulate persons or entities must give fair notice of conduct that is forbidden or required. This requirement of clarity in regulation is essential to the protections provided by the Due Process Clause of the

Fifth Amendment. It requires the invalidation of laws that are impermissibly vague. A conviction or punishment fails to comply with due process if the statute or regulation under which it is obtained "fails to provide a person of ordinary intelligence fair notice of what is prohibited, or is so standardless that it authorizes or encourages seriously discriminatory enforcement." As this Court has explained, a regulation is not vague because it may at times be difficult to prove an incriminating fact but rather because it is unclear as to what fact must be proved.

Even when speech is not at issue, the void for vagueness doctrine addresses at least two connected but discrete due process concerns: first, that regulated parties should know what is required of them so they may act accordingly; second, precision and guidance are necessary so that those enforcing the law do not act in an arbitrary or discriminatory way. When speech is involved, rigorous adherence to those requirements is necessary to ensure that ambiguity does not chill protected speech.

These concerns are implicated here because, at the outset, the broadcasters claim they did not have, and do not have, sufficient notice of what is proscribed. And leaving aside any concerns about facial invalidity, they contend that the lengthy procedural history set forth above shows that the broadcasters did not have fair notice of what was forbidden. Under the 2001 Guidelines in force when the broadcasts occurred, a key consideration was "'whether the material dwell[ed] on or repeat[ed] at length'" the offending description or depiction. In the 2004 *Golden Globes* Order, issued after the broadcasts, the Commission changed course and held that fleeting expletives could be a statutory violation. In the challenged orders now under review the Commission applied the new principle promulgated in the *Golden Globes* Order and determined fleeting expletives and a brief moment of indecency were actionably indecent. This regulatory history, however, makes it apparent that the Commission policy in place at the time of the broadcasts gave no notice to Fox or ABC that a fleeting expletive or a brief shot of nudity could be actionably indecent; yet Fox and ABC were found to be in violation. The Commission's lack of notice to Fox and ABC that its interpretation had changed so the fleeting moments of indecency contained in their broadcasts were a violation of

[the indecency law] as interpreted and enforced by the agency "fail[ed] to provide a person of ordinary intelligence fair notice of what is prohibited." This would be true with respect to a regulatory change this abrupt on any subject, but it is surely the case when applied to the regulations in question, regulations that touch upon "sensitive areas of basic First Amendment freedoms."

The Government raises two arguments in response, but neither is persuasive. As for the two fleeting expletives, the Government concedes that "Fox did not have reasonable notice at the time of the broadcasts that the Commission would consider non-repeated expletives indecent." The Government argues, nonetheless, that Fox "cannot establish unconstitutional vagueness on that basis . . . because the Commission did not impose a sanction where Fox lacked such notice." As the Court observed when the case was here three Terms ago, it is true that the Commission declined to impose any forfeiture on Fox, and in its order the Commission claimed that it would not consider the indecent broadcasts either when considering whether to renew stations' licenses or "in any other context." This "policy of forbearance," as the Government calls it, does not suffice to make the issue moot. Though the Commission claims it will not consider the prior indecent broadcasts "in any context," it has the statutory power to take into account "any history of prior offenses" when setting the level of a forfeiture penalty. Just as in the First Amendment context, the due process protection against vague regulations "does not leave [regulated parties] . . . at the mercy of *noblesse oblige.*" Given that the Commission found it was "not inequitable to hold Fox responsible for [the 2003 broadcast]," and that it has the statutory authority to use its finding to increase any future penalties, the Government's assurance it will elect not to do so is insufficient to remedy the constitutional violation.

In addition, when combined with the legal consequence described above, reputational injury provides further reason for granting relief to Fox. As respondent CBS points out, findings of wrongdoing can result in harm to a broadcaster's "reputation with viewers and advertisers." This observation is hardly surprising given that the challenged orders, which are contained in the permanent Commission record, describe in strongly disapproving terms the indecent material broadcast by Fox, and Fox's efforts to protect children from being exposed to it. Commission sanctions on broadcasters for indecent material are widely publicized. The challenged orders could have an adverse impact on Fox's reputation that audiences and advertisers alike are entitled to take into account.

With respect to ABC, the Government with good reason does not argue no sanction was imposed. The fine against ABC and its network affiliates for the seven seconds of nudity was nearly $1.24 million. The Government argues instead that ABC had notice that the scene in NYPD Blue would be considered indecent in light of a 1960 decision where the Commission declared that the "televising of nudes might well raise a serious question of programming contrary to [the indecency law]." This argument does not prevail. An isolated and ambiguous statement from a 1960 Commission decision does not suffice for the fair notice required when the Government intends to impose over a $1 million fine for allegedly impermissible speech. . . .

The Commission failed to give Fox or ABC fair notice prior to the broadcasts in question that fleeting expletives and momentary nudity could be found actionably indecent.

Therefore, the Commission's standards as applied to these broadcasts were vague, and the Commission's orders must be set aside.

It is necessary to make three observations about the scope of this decision. First, because the Court resolves these cases on fair notice grounds under the Due Process Clause, it need not address the First Amendment implications of the Commission's indecency policy. It is argued that this Court's ruling in *Pacifica* (and the less rigorous standard of scrutiny it provided for the regulation of broadcasters) should be

overruled because the rationale of that case has been overtaken by technological change and the wide availability of multiple other choices for listeners and viewers. The Government for its part maintains that when it licenses a conventional broadcast spectrum, the public may assume that the Government has its own interest in setting certain standards. These arguments need not be addressed here. In light of the Court's holding that the Commission's policy failed to provide fair notice it is unnecessary to reconsider *Pacifica* at this time.

This leads to a second observation. Here, the Court rules that Fox and ABC lacked notice at the time of their broadcasts that the material they were broadcasting could be found actionably indecent under then-existing policies. Given this disposition, it is unnecessary for the Court to address the constitutionality of the current indecency policy as expressed in the *Golden Globes* Order and subsequent adjudications. The Court adheres to its normal practice of declining to decide cases not before it.

Third, this opinion leaves the Commission free to modify its current indecency policy in light of its determination of the public interest and applicable legal requirements. And it leaves the courts free to review the current policy or any modified policy in light of its content and application.

* * *

The judgments of the United States Court of Appeals for the Second Circuit are vacated, and the cases are remanded for further proceedings consistent with the principles set forth in this opinion.

It is so ordered.

Justice Sotomayor took no part in the consideration or decision of these cases.

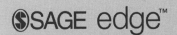

Visit **edge.sagepub.com/medialaw7e** to help you accomplish your coursework goals in an easy-to-use learning environment.

We're going to aggressively protect our intellectual property. Our single greatest asset is the innovation and the ingenuity and creativity of the American people.

—Barack Obama, former president of the United States[1]

In an intellectual property case against Disney, Marvel Studios and others, a judge recently ruled that the use of a specific motion-picture technology in blockbuster films like "Guardians of the Galaxy" violated the patent rights of the technology's inventors but did not violate copyright.

Photo 13/Alamy Stock Photo

11 INTELLECTUAL PROPERTY
Protecting and Using Intangible Creations

SUPPOSE...

... that a startup tech company has developed an individualized antenna system that allows customers to watch over-the-air television broadcasts via the internet on any device. Broadcast television networks claim this new system violates copyright law, specifically their public performance rights under the 1976 Copyright Act. If the individualized antenna system persists, broadcasters could lose millions of dollars in licensing fees they receive from cable companies, who have to pay for the right to carry the broadcasters' copyrighted programming. Does this new system violate the public performance rights of broadcasters? Or does this innovative technology simply provide customers a more individualized, less expensive and more convenient way to watch broadcast programs? Look for the answer to these questions in the case of *American Broadcasting Companies, Inc. v. Aereo, Inc.* discussed later in this chapter and excerpted at the end of the chapter.

P atent, trademark and copyright statutes all are categorized as **intellectual property law**. Generally, intellectual property laws—particularly patent and copyright statutes—are intended to encourage creativity. Ensuring that people will benefit financially from their creations encourages them to continue being creative.

A **copyright** is an exclusive legal right protecting intellectual creations from unauthorized use. U.S. copyright law protects the rights of creators of "original works of authorship" to use their creations.[2] The work's creator—the copyright holder—determines who can use the work, for what purpose and for how long. The U.S. Constitution grants creators control over their works for a "limited time."[3] Today, copyright for many works lasts for the creator's life plus 70 years. Copyright law balances the creator's right to restrict the use of his or her work and society's belief that some uses should be allowed without the creator's permission.[4]

intellectual property law
The legal category including copyright, trademark and patent law.

copyright
An exclusive legal right used to protect intellectual creations from unauthorized use.

Achieving the balance has been difficult since the United States adopted its first copyright law in 1790.

Trademarks help businesses protect their brands and identity. A **trademark** is a word, name, symbol or design used to identify a company's goods and distinguish them from similar products other companies make.[5]

Intellectual property law is increasingly complex because of technological advances, but as with other areas of the law, core principles still apply. Historically, the U.S. Supreme Court has decided few cases concerning intellectual property. However, over the last decade, as new inventions that facilitate new ways to create copyrightable works have brought forward new legal questions, both Congress and the U.S. Supreme Court have engaged these issues.

trademark
A word, name, symbol or design used to identify a company's goods and distinguish them from similar products other companies make.

COPYRIGHT

The concept of protecting creators' works emerged in the 15th century, when the invention of the printing press enabled cheaper copying. In England, the monarchy held that printers would control publication and the Crown would control printers. Authors might be paid for a manuscript, but then they dropped out of the picture.[6] Copyright's initial purpose was to prevent sedition—criticizing the king or queen. The Crown gave a group of printers, called the

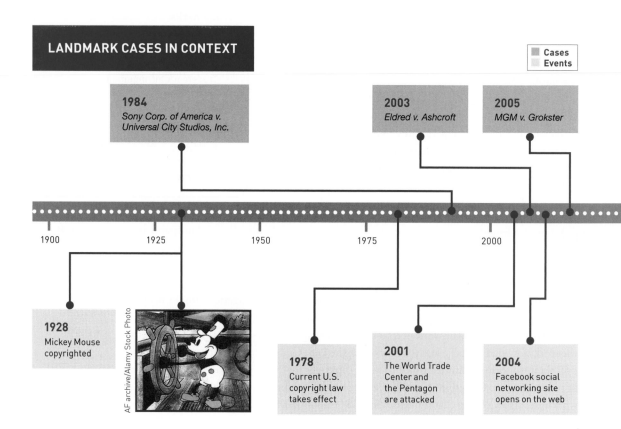

LANDMARK CASES IN CONTEXT

■ Cases
■ Events

1984
Sony Corp. of America v. Universal City Studios, Inc.

2003
Eldred v. Ashcroft

2005
MGM v. Grokster

1900   1925   1950   1975   2000

1928
Mickey Mouse copyrighted

AF archive/Alamy Stock Photo

1978
Current U.S. copyright law takes effect

2001
The World Trade Center and the Pentagon are attacked

2004
Facebook social networking site opens on the web

Stationers' Company, control over printing. Licensed printers received the right to publish a work in perpetuity.

The license requirement ended in 1694, but the Stationers' Company did not disappear. Rather, it shifted its focus from printers to authors. The first copyright law in England, the **Statute of Anne** of 1710, protected authors' works and granted authors copyright protection if they registered their works with the government.[7] Under the Statute of Anne, authors controlled their creations but often sold their rights to printers to make money. When the copyright period ended, the work entered the **public domain**, and anyone could use it without permission. The public domain concept still exists today.

The U.S. Constitution followed England's lead, allowing Congress to adopt copyright and patent laws to encourage authors to create new works.[8] Before the Constitution was ratified, 12 of the 13 states passed copyright laws. The first Congress in 1790 adopted a law giving books, maps and charts a 14-year copyright.[9] The U.S. Supreme Court later ruled that the federal law superseded state statutes and common law copyright claims.[10]

During the 19th century, Congress amended the copyright law to protect musical compositions, photographs and paintings.[11] The 1870 act established the Library of Congress, giving it the power to register copyrights and requiring creators to deposit with the library two copies of a copyrighted published work.

Statute of Anne
The first copyright law, adopted in England in 1710, protected authors' works if the authors registered them with the government.

public domain
Refers to creative materials that are not protected by intellectual property laws. The public can use public domain work without permission.

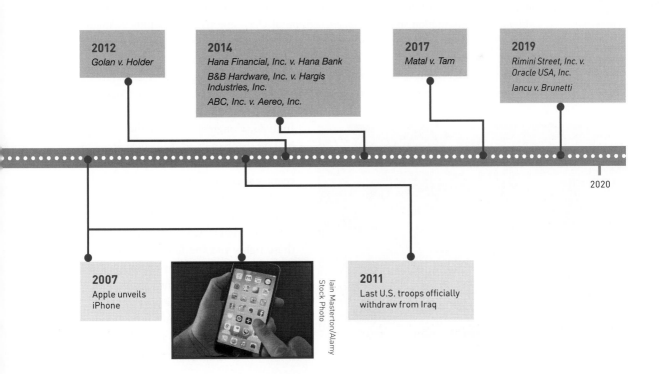

2012
Golan v. Holder

2014
Hana Financial, Inc. v. Hana Bank
B&B Hardware, Inc. v. Hargis Industries, Inc.
ABC, Inc. v. Aereo, Inc.

2017
Matal v. Tam

2019
Rimini Street, Inc. v. Oracle USA, Inc.
Iancu v. Brunetti

2020

2007
Apple unveils iPhone

Iain Masterton/Alamy Stock Photo

2011
Last U.S. troops officially withdraw from Iraq

INTERNATIONAL LAW
SAMSUNG ELECTRONICS CO. V. APPLE

Worldwide patents do not exist. A patent, or right granted to an inventor, must be filed in each country where protection is sought. Large technology companies like Apple and Samsung have annually registered as many as 5,000 patents worldwide.[i]

It is perhaps no surprise that Samsung, a South Korean company, and Apple, a U.S. company, have sued each other over various intellectual property claims, including patent violations, for nearly a decade. The lawsuits span the globe and include court decisions in Australia, Germany and the Netherlands. One tech commentator said these cases are less about money than about control of the mobile device market.[ii]

In its first design patent decision in more than a century, the U.S. Supreme Court recently tried to clarify how Apple could recover damages from Samsung for infringement under the U.S. Patent Act.[iii] Design patents focus on how an article, or product, looks. In 2012, a jury held that Samsung infringed Apple's design patents. Samsung faced nearly $1 billion in penalties based on total profits from all of its phones that infringed.[iv]

In a narrow ruling in 2016, a unanimous U.S. Supreme Court held that Samsung needed only to pay damages on the infringing components rather than on the entire phone. In 2018, on rehearing the case after the Supreme Court decision, a jury awarded Apple $539 million in damages.[v] Samsung did not appeal the verdict, and Apple and Samsung settled their remaining claims out of court. The amount of the final settlement was not disclosed.[vi]

Berne Convention The primary international copyright treaty adopted by many countries in 1886 and by the United States in 1988.

In 1886, several countries signed the **Berne Convention** for the Protection of Literary and Artistic Works in a step toward protecting works globally. The United States did not join, although the convention spurred a major revision of U.S. copyright law in 1909.[12] Among other changes, the law extended copyright protection to 28 years, with a renewal period of another 28 years.

As the 20th century progressed, entertainment, news, technology and other industries pressured Congress to update copyright law. In response, Congress adopted the Copyright Act of 1976, which took effect Jan. 1, 1978. In 1988, Congress amended the 1976 act in ways that permitted the United States to join the Berne Convention—more than a century after the treaty's initial adoption.[13]

The 1976 Copyright Act specifies what may be protected by copyright, what rights that protection includes, any restrictions on those rights and the formalities necessary to exercise the rights. The act remains the backbone of U.S. copyright law today.

In 1998, Congress adopted the Digital Millennium Copyright Act in an attempt to integrate the internet and other digital media more squarely into copyright law.[14]

Sean Pavone/Alamy

The copyright law passed in 1870 established the Library of Congress.

The DMCA bans software and hardware that facilitate circumventing copyright protection technology, with certain exceptions.[15] For example, the act forbids software that would disable anti-copying features in software that enables the copying of digital video.[16] The DMCA also prohibits removing or changing copyright information, such as the copyright owner's name.[17]

What Does a Copyright Protect?

U.S. copyright law protects a wide variety of works. Congress provided two broad criteria, offered some examples and left it to the courts to provide more clarity. The 1976 law says that copyright protection applies to "original works of authorship" that are "fixed in any tangible medium of expression."[18] Congress used the word "authorship" to include artists, composers, journalists, sculptors and many other creators.

A work must be substantially original to be protected.[19] Copyright law does not define "original." As one court said, "originality" simply means "a work independently created by its author, one not copied from pre-existing works, and a work that comes from the exercise of the creative powers of the author's mind."[20] Explained recently by another court, "The *sine qua non* of copyright is originality. . . . [It] means only that the work was independently created by the author (as opposed to copied from other works), and that it possesses at least some minimal degree of creativity."[21]

POINTS OF LAW
THE 1976 COPYRIGHT ACT

Copyright protection applies to "original works of authorship" that are "fixed in any tangible medium of expression."[vii]
The following works are protected by copyright:

- Literary works

- Musical works, including any accompanying words

- Dramatic works, including any accompanying music

- Pantomimes and choreographic works

- Pictorial, graphic and sculptural works

- Motion pictures and other audiovisual works

- Sound recordings

- Architectural works

The U.S. Copyright Office suggests viewing these categories broadly. For example, computer software is considered a literary work protected by copyright law.[viii] In a 2017 decision, the U.S. Supreme Court said clothing design elements could receive copyright protection as pictorial, graphic and sculptural works.[ix]

Design 299B
Registration No. VA 1-319-226

Design 299A
Registration No. VA 1-319-228

Two cheerleading uniforms were at the center of a recent U.S. Supreme Court decision to allow copyright of clothing design elements when perceived as a work of art.

In addition to being original, a work must be "fixed in a tangible medium." This means a work must be capable of being seen, "reproduced, or otherwise communicated, either directly or with the aid of a machine or device"—for example, words or images on paper, software in the cloud, a quilt made of cloth, a statue made of marble or music fixed in a digital file.[22]

The 1976 Copyright Act lists eight categories of eligible works: (1) literary works; (2) musical works, including any accompanying words; (3) dramatic works, including any accompanying music; (4) pantomimes and choreographic works; (5) pictorial, graphic and sculptural works; (6) motion pictures and other audiovisual works; (7) sound recordings and (8) architectural works.[23] These categories are more illustrative than definitive. For example, software may be copyrighted (typically it is considered a literary work because it is written code), even though it is not listed separately among the eight categories. Designs, patterns and shapes also may have copyright protection.

In a 6–2 decision, the U.S. Supreme Court recently held that design features in clothing could be eligible for copyright protection if those features are perceived as a work of art separate from the "useful article."[24] According to the U.S. Copyright Office, a useful article is an object that has a utilitarian function "that is not merely to portray the appearance of the article or to convey information."[25] Clothing and furniture are examples of useful articles.

At issue in the case was whether stripes, zigzags and chevrons on a cheerleading uniform could receive copyright protection. Before the case reached the Supreme Court, various circuit courts of appeal had reached different conclusions on the broader issue of clothing design, resulting in nine different variability tests to determine whether copyright protection was appropriate.[26]

The U.S. Supreme Court said it accepted the case to resolve the widespread disagreement. Writing for the majority, Justice Clarence Thomas said, "[A] feature incorporated into the design of a useful article is eligible for copyright protection only if the feature (1) can be perceived as a two- or three-dimensional work of art separate from the useful article and (2) would qualify as protectable pictorial, graphic, or sculptural work—either on its own or fixed in some other tangible medium of expression—if it were imagined separately from the useful article into which it is incorporated."[27] Legal experts said the Supreme Court's decision is significant for the fashion industry, which has asserted for years that clothing not only is a useful article in that it protects the body, but also is a form of creative expression.[28]

For many years, sound recordings—the actual recordings, as opposed to the music and lyrics—were not protected by copyright. This changed in 1971, when an update to the federal copyright law gave protection for songs recorded in 1972 or later. Songs recorded prior to 1972 have some limited protection under state laws. Recently, the Ninth Circuit Court of Appeals considered whether digitally remastered, pre-1972 sound recordings were original enough to justify copyright protection.[29] Reversing a district court decision, the Ninth Circuit ruled that despite a sound engineer's remastering that could include aesthetic changes, these changes were not substantial enough to be considered original. "A digitally remastered sound recording made as a copy of the original analog sound recording will rarely exhibit the necessary originality to qualify for independent copyright protection," the court said.[30]

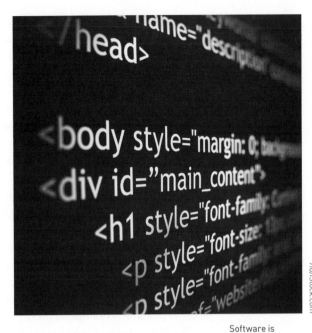

Software is copyrightable as a literary work because it is written code.

The 1976 statute protects all works eligible for copyright, both published and unpublished.[31] Before the 1976 statute was adopted, unpublished works were protected by state common law, not the federal statute. Common law protection for unpublished works and protection lasted forever.[32] The new law changed this, giving unpublished creations the same protection as published works.

A work that is not original or is not fixed in a tangible medium cannot be copyrighted. For example, a telephone directory's contents of names, addresses and phone numbers lacked originality, the U.S. Supreme Court ruled. There was insufficient creativity in an alphabetical list.[33]

A collection of previously created works can be protected if there is substantial originality in the choice or arrangement of the works.[34] The copyright law refers to this as a "compilation."[35] An example of a compilation is a book of poetry that includes poems written by several different poets arranged around a common theme, such as love. Newspapers and magazines are also considered compilations. The statute permits a copyright of the creation of the compilation, but each work included in the collection retains its own copyright protection. Ideas, history and facts cannot be copyrighted.[36] To qualify for copyright protection, there must be originality or novelty in the compiling or organizing of facts.[37]

As technology advances, new questions arise in this area—for example, is an individual point of interest within a GPS database copyrightable? A federal district court said "yes" because of the originality in selecting, categorizing and arranging the database.[38] In another case, a federal district court held that the HTML code and cascading style sheets (commonly called CSS) underlying an online advertiser's website were sufficiently original and creative to allow them to be copyrighted.[39]

A news story reporting an automobile accident can receive copyright protection. But the underlying facts—the accident itself—cannot be copyrighted. A reporter's description of the accident is original and is fixed in a tangible medium when typed into a computer or smartphone. However, the reporter may not successfully claim he or she was first on the scene and therefore no other journalist may write about the accident. Nor may a scholar write a book about a historical incident—even one that has not been described previously—and prevent anyone else from writing about the incident.

The law does not give copyright protection to words and phrases, including advertising slogans and titles of books, movies and television programs, because they lack sufficient originality to qualify for copyright protection. However, a trademark, discussed later in this chapter, can protect these creations. Also, works created by the U.S. government are not eligible for copyright protection.[40]

A work's creator owns the work's copyright—with some exceptions.[41] For example, if two or more people create a work, the copyright is jointly owned, and all creators share the copyright protection.

work made for hire
Work created when working for another person or company. The copyright in a work made for hire belongs to the employer, not the creator.

When a person creates a work as part of her or his employment, the law gives the copyright to the employer.[42] The copyright law calls such a creation a **work made for hire**.[43] A work may also be for hire if the creator and employer agree to that in writing and if the work is specially ordered or commissioned for use in, for example, a compilation, a motion picture, a textbook or any of several other categories the law specifies.[44]

The U.S. Supreme Court has listed a number of factors for courts to consider in determining whether a person acted as an employee.[45] These include (1) the organization's right to control how the work is accomplished, (2) who owns the equipment used to create the work, (3) where the work took place, (4) who determined the days and hours worked, (5) whether there was a long-term relationship between the two parties, (6) who hired any assistants that may have been used and several other factors. The more the company or organization controls the factors, the more the balance tips toward a work made for hire. Freelancers, today often hired as independent contractors, will own the copyrights to their works, absent a work made for hire or other agreement. It is common, however, for the employer or hiring entity to require a written agreement that establishes the employer's copyright ownership. Freelancers and independent contractors should carefully read agreements they sign to understand who owns the copyright to their work.[46]

The copyright law allows copyright ownership to be changed by contract. However, contracts transferring copyrights in freelancer material to a newspaper or magazine do not automatically transfer control to media organizations' online publications. The copyright law calls newspapers and magazines "collective works."[47]

More than 15 years ago, in *New York Times Co., Inc. v. Tasini*, the U.S. Supreme Court said online publications are reproduced and distributed individual articles. The Court said when the Times placed articles published in its paper onto the internet, it took articles out of context because the website presented individual articles rather than articles in the context of the original newspaper page. The freelance writers retained their copyrights in the individual articles, the Court said. If a contract between a freelancer and a newspaper did not specifically include online publications, the agreement covered only the initial publication.[48]

Exclusive Rights and Limitations

The law specifies six exclusive rights copyright holders have in their works. This includes (1) the right to reproduce the work, (2) the right to make derivative works, (3) the right to distribute the work publicly, (4) the right to perform a work publicly, (5) the right to display a work publicly and (6) the right to transmit a sound recording through digital audio means.[49] No one may copy a work without the copyright holder's permission. There are exceptions to this copyright protection. For example, the U.S. Supreme Court allowed home recording of broadcast programming for personal use.[50] Congress amended the Copyright Act to permit making a single copy of an analog or digital recording for personal use.[51]

A **derivative work** is a work that is obtained from or created in relation to an original work. Without the copyright holder's permission, no one may use a copyrighted work to create a related work. For example, HBO reportedly paid "Game of Thrones" novelist George R.R. Martin millions of dollars for the rights to use his stories as a basis for its "Game of Thrones" series. The HBO series is a derivative work from the novels, for which Martin received compensation.[52]

derivative work
A work that is obtained from or created in relation to an original work.

Recently, a federal court held that an e-book is not a derivative work because it does not recast, transform or adapt a preexisting work and it is not an original work of authorship.[53] In 2018, the Ninth Circuit Court of Appeals held that the digital remastering of pre-1972 sound recordings did not create derivative works.[54] That determination was tied to the court's reasoning, mentioned earlier, that the digital copy is not original:

> If an allegedly derivative sound recording does not add or remove any sounds from the underlying sound recording, does not change the sequence of the sounds, and does not remix or otherwise alter the sounds in sequence or character, the recording is likely to be nothing more than a copy . . . and is presumptively devoid of the original sound recording authorship required for copyright protection. . . . This presumption may, of course, be overcome, by showing that the work contains independent creative content, recognizable contributions of sound recording authorship or variations in defining aspects that give a derivative sound recording a new and different essential character and identity.[55]

In another case that involved the use of modern technology, a federal judge recently ruled that the creative output from a computer program is not a derivative work unless the software does the "lion's share" of the creative work.[56] The case involved a complicated mix of copyright and patent infringement claims that centered on the MOVA Contour system, software that captures the motion of the human face to create computer-generated imagery, or CGI. The software's inventor sued several major motion picture studios for alleged unauthorized use of the CGI program, cases that are still tied up in court and have broader intellectual property implications for patent owners. However, the judge rejected the software creator's argument that the software's CGI output—for example, characters in blockbuster films like "Deadpool" and "Guardians of the Galaxy"—was a derivative work of the software itself. The judge said that actors and directors substantially contributed to the facial motions shown in the films.[57]

After this monkey selfie emerged and a copyright claim followed, a federal judge said animals do not have copyright privileges under the current law.

Transmit Clause
Part of the 1976 Copyright Act that says broadcast networks, local broadcasters and cable television systems perform a work when they transmit content to viewers.

In addition to controlling derivative works, the copyright owner also determines when a work will be publicly distributed. This includes public distribution of a work on social media. For example, a federal district court said merely posting photos on Twitter does not allow others to use them without permission.[58] Daniel Morel photographed scenes after the Haiti earthquake in 2010. He posted these photos to his Twitter account. Without Morel's permission, an employee of Agence France-Presse, an international news agency, sent eight of Morel's photos to the AFP photo desk. Morel sued AFP and several other media organizations for copyright infringement.

AFP argued that when Morel posted his photos on Twitter, he accepted Twitter's terms of service, and those terms automatically granted permission to use the photos. A federal district court disagreed, holding that Twitter's terms of service do not state or mean that content posted to a Twitter account essentially falls into the public domain.[59] AFP infringed Morel's copyrights, the court ruled.[60]

The right to publicly perform a work applies to "literary, musical, dramatic and choreographic works, pantomimes, and motion pictures and other audiovisual works."[61] This restricts anyone from transmitting a movie to the public, for example, without the copyright holder's permission.

One important consideration in this area of copyright law as a result of new technology is how to apply the Transmit Clause. When Congress passed the 1976 Copyright Act, it added the **Transmit Clause** to clarify how broadcasters and cable television systems "perform" within this area of copyright law. Congress said that, under the Transmit Clause, a broadcast network is performing when it transmits content; a local broadcaster is performing when it transmits the network broadcast; and a cable television system performs when it retransmits a broadcast to its subscribers.[62]

In cable television's infancy, the U.S. Supreme Court held that cable did not infringe anyone's copyright when it retransmitted broadcast station signals to subscribers.[63] The Court said retransmitting broadcast signals was not a performance under the 1909 copyright law and did not require copyright holder permission. Congress agreed to override the Court's decisions in the 1976 law and adopted a compromise that cable system owners had reached with the producers and broadcasters.[64] That 1976 law allows cable operators to retransmit radio and television broadcast signals without obtaining permission in exchange for a compulsory fee based on a percentage of a cable system's annual revenues. The U.S. Copyright Office collects and distributes the fees to the copyright holders of the programs and other material cable broadcasts and retransmits. Multichannel video program distributors have a similar compulsory license to retransmit broadcast signals.[65] For example, direct broadcast satellite services pay royalties according to their number of subscribers.

The application of the Transmit Clause to new technology is at the heart of the U.S. Supreme Court's 2014 decision in *American Broadcasting Companies, Inc. v. Aereo, Inc.* (excerpted at the end of this chapter).[66] At issue was whether Aereo's innovative system of utilizing thousands of dime-sized antennas to offer its subscribers broadcast television content over the internet violated the Transmit Clause and constituted a public performance of copyrighted works. The Court held that it did, comparing Aereo's service to a cable system.[67] Immediately following the decision, Aereo suspended its video streaming service[68] and asked the Federal Communications Commission to grant it a license to retransmit broadcast material as a MVPD (see Chapter 9), which required Aereo to apply for compulsory licensing (like a cable system) under the Copyright Act.[69] The Copyright Office concluded that internet-based retransmission services are not eligible for a blanket license, like MVPDs, effectively putting them out of business.[70]

FilmOn X, a service nearly identical to Aereo, made arguments similar to Aereo's in various courts at about the same time. After the Supreme Court's *Aereo* decision, FilmOn X's appeal to the Ninth Circuit Court of Appeals ended with a full-court rehearing that resulted in the same ultimate outcome—"a service that captures copyrighted works broadcast over the air, and then retransmits them to paying subscribers over the internet without the consent of the copyright holders, is not a 'cable system' eligible for a compulsory license under the Copyright Act."[71]

In addition to public performance rights, copyright holders have the right to publicly display a work. This applies to "literary, musical, dramatic and choreographic works [and] pantomimes," as does the right to perform a work publicly. The right to display adds protection for "pictorial, graphic, or sculptural works, including the individual images of a motion picture

POINTS OF LAW

EXCLUSIVE RIGHTS IN COPYRIGHTED WORKS

The copyright holder with exclusive rights may do the following:[x]

1. Reproduce the copyrighted work

2. Prepare derivative works based upon the copyrighted work

3. Distribute copies of the copyrighted work to the public by sale or other transfer of ownership, or by rental, lease or lending (except CDs and computer software)

4. Perform the copyrighted work publicly in the case of literary, musical, dramatic and choreographic works; pantomimes; and motion pictures and other audiovisual works

5. Display the copyrighted work publicly in the case of literary, musical, dramatic and choreographic works; pantomimes; and pictorial, graphic or sculptural works, including the individual images of a motion picture or other audiovisual work

6. Perform the copyrighted work publicly by means of a digital audio transmission in the case of sound recordings

or other audiovisual work."[72] Under this provision, no one may display a painting, sculpture, photograph or similar work without the copyright owner's permission.

A common practice on websites today is called inline linking, or the practice of using a linked object, for example an image, that appears on one site but is hosted on another site's server. Sometimes this happens through the use of embedding tools, made available on social media platforms. Does this practice violate a copyright holder's display right? About a decade ago, the Ninth Circuit Court of Appeals created what has come to be called the server test. The server test maintains that a copyright holder's display right for an image is not infringed when it is embedded or linked from a third-party server.[73]

In 2018, a federal district court chose not to apply the server test and held that Breitbart News Network violated a copyright holder's display right when it embedded a tweet featuring a photograph of New England Patriots quarterback Tom Brady on its website.[74] The candid photo of Brady and other well-known athletes was first posted to the photographer's Snapchat. The photo went viral after the image was connected to speculation that Brady might have been recruiting a free agent basketball player for Boston. The photo ended up on Reddit and then Twitter, shared without permission. Eventually, several news websites used Twitter's embed tool to display the tweets and the image in their articles about Brady and the free agent player.[75]

The court said that embedding a tweet that contains a potentially infringing copy of a photo can constitute infringement, unless it is fair use (discussed later in the chapter). In rejecting the server test, the district court noted, "The plain language of the Copyright Act . . . and subsequent Supreme Court jurisprudence [i.e., *Aereo*] provide no basis for a rule that allows the physical location or possession of an image to determine who may or may not have 'displayed'" it.[76]

The defendants argued that the server test is well-settled law and that providing HTML instructions, which is effectively what the inline linking or embedding process does, is not the same as displaying the image.[77] The Second Circuit Court of Appeals denied an appeal.[78]

The final exclusive right maintained by a copyright holder is the right to transmit a sound recording through digital audio means.[79] This provision requires obtaining permission from a recording company to play one of its recordings via the internet, satellite radio or other digital media, including interactive services. Permission is not required to play a recording over a broadcasting station or in a live performance, but permission is required to play the composition embedded within the recording (unless its copyright protection has expired).

Some protections are not absolute under U.S. copyright law. For example, libraries open to the public have a limited right to make photocopies for certain purposes.[80] Though not part of the law, Congress provided guidelines for teachers in not-for-profit educational institutions. A teacher may, no more than twice per term, copy one chapter from a book for the teacher's own use or copy an excerpt of no more than 1,000 words or 10 percent of a book to distribute to a class. The guidelines do not allow students to copy materials.[81]

Copyright owners do not have the right to control individual copies of their works after distribution—with a few exceptions. A person who buys a copy of a novel may give away that book, sell it, rent it or throw it away.[82] The author has no right to stop the purchaser from taking any of those actions. This is called the **first-sale doctrine**.[83] The copyright law says that once creators have distributed copies of a work, they no longer can regulate what happens to those copies. However, when copyright holders agree to transfer the physical object containing the copyrighted work—the printed book containing a novel, for example—they do not transfer any rights in the copyrighted content. For example, the law still restricts copying the novel or making derivative works. The first-sale doctrine distinguishes between the physical object and the intellectual creation itself. The doctrine does not change the copyright holder's control of the creation; it changes only control of the object containing the creation. The U.S. Supreme Court has said the first-sale doctrine also allowed the purchase of foreign-manufactured books and the sale of them in the United States.[84]

The first-sale doctrine, like some other parts of the copyright law, was meant for a pre-digital world. When a digital copy is sent from one computer to another, the receiving computer makes an additional copy of the document, something the law does not allow.

Concerns about people making cheap copies of computer software, music or movies prompted Congress to limit the first-sale doctrine by restricting the ability to share digital copies without the copyright holder's permission.[85] Several years ago, the U.S. Court of Appeals for the Second Circuit ruled that a company called ReDigi infringed Capitol Records' copyrights in its sound recordings. ReDigi allowed people to "sell their legally acquired digital music files and buy used digital music from others at a fraction of the price currently available on iTunes." Essentially, ReDigi acted as a used digital music store. The Second Circuit held that when a digital music file moves from one person's computer to another computer, the file is reproduced. Because reproduction is one of the rights guaranteed to a copyright owner, ReDigi infringed Capitol's rights under the copyright law, the court said.[86]

Duration, Licensing and Scope

A copyright is a property right. Just like a car, a copyright can be given away, sold or leased.

Rights protected by copyright can be thought of as a bundle that includes a number of rights. For example, an author writes a novel and has the right, among others, to prevent unauthorized copying. If the author sells the right to reproduce the novel as a hardback book, the author still holds all the other copying rights. The author may sell the paperback copying rights to another publisher. The author may sell to a film studio one of the rights to a derivative work—the right to make a movie from the novel. That still leaves the author with many other rights. Or the author may choose to sell all of his or her rights to one person or company. Each time the author sells a right, he or she receives a lump sum payment or, often, a percentage of revenue from sales.

Whoever buys a right from the author then owns that right unless a contract between the author and the buyer says otherwise. If the buyer wants to sell the right to a third person, the author cannot refuse to allow the sale unless the author has a contractual right to do so. A copyright does not disappear when the copyright holder dies. The copyright holder may transfer the right to someone else through a will.

Not only may copyright holders completely transfer their rights; they may license or lease rights. A license is a contract giving limited permission for use. The 1976 copyright law

first-sale doctrine
Once a copyright owner sells a copy of a work, the new owner may possess, transfer or otherwise dispose of that copy without the copyright owner's permission.

recognizes that creators often do not have equal bargaining rights with the large corporations purchasing creators' copyrights. To strike a more equal balance, the law gives creators a termination right.[87] This allows creators, or their heirs, to require that the transferred rights be returned 35 to 40 years after the original transfer. This does not apply to works made for hire.

Licensing music in the age of streaming has challenged existing laws and norms. Popular recording artists like Adele have barred their work from streaming services like Spotify because song royalties from streaming are low.[88] For example, in 2016, artists earned 17 cents for every 100 plays on free, ad-supported music-streaming services. In 2018, Congress passed the Music Modernization Act to update music licensing and royalty rules and address royalty problems.[89] The new law, the first major update of copyright law since the DMCA in 1998, ensures that songwriters and artists receive royalties for songs recorded before 1972 and creates a new, independent entity, called the Mechanical Licensing Collective, to help streaming services, like Apple Music and Spotify, pay copyright holders.[90]

The MMA requires the creation of a new blanket license for streaming music that will be created and managed by the new MLC. This new blanket license will cover activities related to making permanent and limited downloads and interactive streams of "musical works embodied in sound recordings."[91] The MLC will

> (i) collect, distribute and audit the royalties generated from these licenses to and for the respective musical work owners; (ii) create and maintain a public database that identifies musical works with their owners along with ownership share information; (iii) provide information to help with and engage in matching musical works with their respective sound recordings; and (iv) hold unclaimed royalties for at least 3 years before distributing them on a market-share basis to copyright owners.[92]

In addition, the MMA improves royalty compensation to songwriters and provides royalties for record producers and sound engineers. Music creators, artists, the recording industry and the tech industry all supported the MMA as an important first step to fix many of the challenges that evolved as the digital music revolution took shape over the past decade.[93]

The U.S. Constitution gives Congress the right to adopt copyright and patent laws "for limited times."[94] The 1976 copyright law gave copyright protection for the creator's lifetime plus 50 years after the creator's death with no renewal. The Sonny Bono Copyright Term Extension Act of 1998 extended all copyright periods by 20 years. Sonny Bono, formerly an entertainer and singer-actress Cher's first husband, was a member of the U.S. House of Representatives when he died. Congress named the copyright extension act in Bono's honor because Bono believed copyrights should last forever.[95]

Mickey Mouse's copyright protection would have expired in 2003 if Congress had not passed the Bono Act.[96] The copyright originally was granted in 1928 when Mickey's first cartoon, "Steamboat Willie," was shown. After the Bono Act took effect, the copyright period for works created on or after Jan. 1, 1978, became the author's lifetime plus 70 years.[97] The Bono Act protects Mickey's copyright until 2023.

Works made for hire are protected for 95 years from publication or 120 years from creation, whichever is shorter.[98] Copyright protection's duration depends on several factors. First, the current law did not affect works created in the United States that were in the public domain on Jan. 1, 1978. When the current copyright statute took effect, the public domain included many works because their copyrights had expired—such as Herman Melville's "Moby-Dick." Also, some works copyrighted under the 1909 law lost protection because their creators failed to renew copyrights.

The U.S. Supreme Court upheld the Bono Act against claims that it violates the constitutional copyright clause and the First Amendment.[99] In *Eldred v. Ashcroft*, the Supreme Court said extending the copyright period is constitutional. Congress has the right to determine what "limited" means as long as the copyright period is not forever, the

Mickey Mouse as Steamboat Willie in the first Mickey cartoon.

Court said. Congress could justify extending the copyright period because people live longer now. Also, technological changes make copyrighted works last longer.

The creator's life plus 70 years is a limited time within the meaning of the Constitution's copyright clause, the Court said.[100] The phrase "limited time" does not mean a fixed time. The copyright period may be flexible. However, the Court did not define "limited time," nor did it offer a test for determining what period might go beyond "limited."

The Court also rejected First Amendment arguments against the Bono Act. The Constitution's adopters found no tension between the First Amendment and the copyright clause, according to the Court. The current law balances free speech and copyright protection concerns. And the fair use defense, discussed later in this chapter, allows the public to use portions of copyrighted works under certain circumstances, the Court said.

When the United States joined the Berne Convention, many works created in other countries had fallen into the public domain in the United States but not in their creators' countries.[101] That allowed orchestras on limited budgets and school programs, for example, to perform compositions by 20th-century composers such as Dmitri Shostakovich and Igor Stravinsky without paying a royalty fee. Films Alfred Hitchcock directed in England and Pablo Picasso's paintings also were freely available. In 1994, Congress gave copyright protection to these foreign works.[102] Works affected generally were those produced between 1923 and 1989 that remained under copyright in the country where they were created.[103]

Groups directly affected by losing free access to these works sued, arguing Congress' action was unconstitutional. In *Golan v. Holder*, the U.S. Supreme Court disagreed.[104] The Court said the Constitution's language allows Congress to give copyright protection to works that once were in the public domain. Congress' action did no more than put the United States in the same position as other countries that are parties to the Berne Convention.

The Court also said Congress might reasonably assert that the comportment of U.S. copyright law with the laws of other Berne members would help create a well-functioning international system and thus inspire new works. The Court rejected the plaintiffs' argument that their First Amendment rights were abridged because they no longer could perform the newly

AF archive/Alamy Stock Photo

protected works. The Court said any work Congress brought under copyright protection remained available, just for a fee. The Court also emphasized Congress' freedom to broadly interpret the Constitution's copyright clause.[105]

Copyright Infringement

infringement
The unauthorized manufacture, sale or distribution of an item protected by copyright, patent or trademark law.

Using any part of a copyrighted work is **infringement** unless there is an applicable defense. The copyright statute allows a court to award **statutory damages** even if the infringer does not make a profit from the creator's work.[106]

In addition to statutory damages, the successful party in a copyright infringement lawsuit may recover some of its legal costs. In 2019, the U.S. Supreme Court held unanimously that Section 505 of the Copyright Act allows the prevailing party in copyright litigation to recover only the costs of the legal action that are specifically listed in the six categories in Section 505.[107]

statutory damages
Damages specified in certain laws. Under these laws, copyright being an example, a judge may award statutory damages even if a plaintiff is unable to prove actual damages.

In *Rimini Street v. Oracle USA*, Oracle had argued that it was entitled to the "full costs" of its legal action, which the lower courts awarded as $29 million in attorney's fees, $3.4 million in taxable costs and $13 million in additional nontaxable costs, such as covering expert witness costs or jury consultation costs. Justice Brett Kavanaugh wrote for the Court that the $13 million in nontaxable costs was not allowed under Section 505.[108]

Copyright automatically begins for an original work the moment it is created and fixed in a tangible medium. However, if an entity infringes upon the copyright, the copyright holder cannot sue under the law unless the copyright has been registered. To sue for copyright infringement, the plaintiff first must show proof of a valid, registered copyright prior to bringing a lawsuit. After several circuit court decisions left unclear the point in the copyright application process at which an infringement claim may begin, the U.S. Supreme Court weighed in. In 2019, the Supreme Court unanimously held that a copyright claimant may only commence a copyright infringement lawsuit after the copyright is registered by the U.S. Copyright Office. Copyright owners may recover for infringements that occurred before and after the copyright's registration, but they may not bring an infringement claim until the Register of Copyrights has approved a properly filed application and registered the copyright.[109]

Nearly 70 years ago, a landmark decision in the Second Circuit Court of Appeals defined the basic structure of most copyright infringement claims.[110] Called the *Arnstein* test, it first requires a determination of whether a plaintiff's work was actually copied. Without proof of copying, there is no infringement. To prove that something was copied, juries and judges consider whether a defendant had access to the work and whether the works are substantially similar. Today, expert witness testimony is allowed as part of the process to help better understand differences in various contexts. For example, the context of a copyright infringement claim about music sampling could be different than a claim about software. It is common for courts to recognize the need for expert testimony in cases that are highly technical.[111]

Over the years, courts have created several different tests to help refine the definition of substantial similarity.[112] Regardless of the test applied, the keys to determining infringement are access and substantial similarity. Legal experts note that the *Arnstein* decision deliberately empowered juries to play a central role in determining the answer to both questions. The question of access to a copyrighted work always comes before consideration of substantial similarity.

In a well-publicized infringement case a few years ago, a Los Angeles jury awarded the estate of Motown legend Marvin Gaye $7.3 million for copyright infringement. At issue was substantial similarity between the 2013 smash hit "Blurred Lines," written and performed by Robin Thicke, Pharrell Williams and Clifford Harris (better known as rapper T.I.), and Gaye's 1977 classic "Got to Give It Up."[113]

Thicke, Williams and Harris ended months of arguing with Gaye's family by filing a lawsuit asking the federal court to declare that their song did not infringe "Got to Give It Up." The three argued that what they were trying to capture with "Blurred Lines" was a specific "feel," paying tribute to an era and a genre. Gaye's estate filed a counterclaim, arguing that the two songs contained eight similarities that infringed, including a signature phrase in the main vocal melodies, hooks with similar notes and backup vocals and similarity of the core themes of the songs, among other similarities.[114] The case wound up before a jury.

> ### POINTS OF LAW
> ### INFRINGING COPYRIGHT
>
> A copyright plaintiff must prove
>
> 1. the work used is protected by a valid copyright—meaning it is an original work fixed in a tangible medium;
>
> 2. the plaintiff owns the copyright;
>
> 3. the valid copyright is registered with the Copyright Office; *and*
>
> 4. there is evidence that the defendant directly copied the copyrighted work *or* the infringer had access to the copyrighted work, and the two works are substantially similar.

Because Gaye's estate owned only the composition (the sheet music), not the sound recording, the court allowed the jury only to hear a stripped-down version of Gaye's recording of "Got to Give It Up." The jury sided with Gaye's estate, deciding that Thicke and Williams had infringed but Harris had not, nor had the distributors of the song (Universal Music Group, Interscope Records and Williams' Star Trak Entertainment).[115]

Experts argue that copyright law today has become so complex that jury decisions create ad hoc and arbitrary results. The U.S. Supreme Court has never weighed in on copyright infringement analyses, which is why courts differ in their approach to determining infringement.

A plaintiff does not have to prove that a copyright infringement was deliberate. Accidental infringement violates the law. A court may reduce statutory damages imposed on a person who unintentionally infringed on another person's copyright and waive statutory damages completely if the innocent infringer works for a nonprofit library or public broadcaster.[116]

In addition to direct copyright infringement, other forms of infringement can occur. Showing that the defendant knowingly aided or contributed to copyright infringement is sufficient for **contributory infringement**. Although contributory infringement is not specifically banned in the copyright law, the statute implies that contributory infringement violates the law, and courts long have held it actionable.[117]

contributory infringement
The participation in, or contribution to, the infringing acts of another person.

Contributory infringement may be difficult to prove. Several television program producers sued Sony for making VCRs that allowed viewers to tape copyrighted programs without permission. The producers claimed the VCRs enabled unauthorized copying. In *Sony Corp. of America v. Universal City Studios, Inc.*, the U.S. Supreme Court said Sony might have known that viewers used VCRs to record television programs, but it could be fair use (discussed later in this chapter) to record programs to watch later—time shifting.[118] Sony was not liable because the VCRs could be used for noninfringing purposes, the Court ruled.[119]

YouTube has created a copyright center (www.youtube .com/yt/ copyright/) to teach users about copyright infringement and avoid video removals.

A quarter-century later, Cablevision Systems faced a similar challenge to its digital video recorder system. A group of movie studios and broadcast and cable networks argued that Cablevision's DVRs directly infringed on program copyrights by making unauthorized copies on computers and publicly performing the programs when customers later watched them. The U.S. Court of Appeals for the Second Circuit ruled that the cable customer, rather than Cablevision, copied the program. Cablevision's computers acted as a modern VCR. Because only one customer at a time viewed the program, the program was not publicly performed, "public" being a group larger than just one customer.[120]

Embedding a video image on a website is not contributory infringement, the Seventh Circuit Court of Appeals ruled.[121] Recently, a gay pornography site sued MyVidster, a "social bookmarking" service. MyVidster subscribers can "bookmark" videos uploaded with or without permission to a server. The MyVidster site finds the embed code and stores it with an image from the video. MyVidster patrons can select the video, transmitted for viewing from the server, without going through any computer controlled by MyVidster. The pornography site claimed MyVidster contributed to copyright infringement by linking to websites containing illegal copies of the videos. The court disagreed. Just as newspapers used to list theaters where a movie was playing, MyVidster was not helping customers either copy or perform the videos, the court said.

Another form of infringement is **vicarious infringement**, based on a common law principle that holds companies responsible for the acts of employees if the acts are within the nature and scope of the employment. To establish liability, direct infringement must occur. In cases of vicarious infringement, the company has a financial interest in the infringement and the ability to control it even if the company does not have direct knowledge of the infringement.

vicarious infringement
Under common law principles, companies are responsible for the acts of employees if the acts are within the nature and scope of their employment and the company has a financial interest in the infringement and the ability to control it.

Early digital music file-sharing services are examples of vicarious infringement. Napster, one of the first music file-sharing services, allowed users to reach into each other's computers to retrieve files containing copyrighted music. Before the Ninth Circuit Court of Appeals ruled that Napster's operation violated copyright law, millions of people used this peer-to-peer network to make unauthorized copies of sound recordings.[122] Napster's sole purpose was to aid copyright infringement by allowing users to share copyrighted music, according to the court.

About 15 years ago, the recording and movie industries filed a copyright infringement lawsuit against two peer-to-peer networks, Grokster and Morpheus, claiming they contributed to copyright infringement by allowing network users to illegally download copyrighted songs and movies. In the *Metro-Goldwyn-Mayer Studios, Inc. v. Grokster, Ltd.* decision, the U.S. Supreme Court held that Grokster infringed on MGM's copyright because it knew people used its software to download music files. The Supreme Court said it did not matter that the software could be used for legal purposes because Grokster induced, or encouraged, users to infringe on copyrights.[123] Courts call this **infringement by inducement**. Infringement by inducement is when a person or entity who does not directly infringe induces others to do so and can be held liable for that infringement.[124]

Websites allowing users to illegally download movies violate the *Grokster* decision's inducement rule, the Ninth Circuit Court of Appeals held in 2013.[125] Seven major movie studios showed that the defendant's peer-to-peer file-sharing sites directly helped site users locate specific movies and television programs to upload copyrighted works and burn copyrighted material onto DVDs to play on television sets. The court said this and other evidence showed the defendant induced site users to infringe the movie studio's copyrights.

In 2018, a federal court in California issued an injunction against the makers of TickBox, a television streaming device that allowed users to download apps that facilitated free access to copyrighted content.[126] The court said TickBox was inducing infringement. TickBox subsequently agreed to a $25 million judgment to settle a copyright infringement case brought against it by the major studios.[127]

Fair Use Defense

A person sued for copyright infringement might claim that the plaintiff did not file within the law's three-year statute of limitations (or five years for criminal charges).[128] Or a defendant may argue that the copyright holder knowingly has abandoned the copyright, placing the work in the public domain.[129] The most common defense, however, is **fair use**.

Courts recognized the fair use defense long before Congress wrote it into the 1976 copyright law.[130] Courts understood that the copyright statutes—from 1790 to the present—give copyright holders the right to forbid any use of their works without permission. But what if an English teacher copies a few paragraphs from a novel for a class discussion? Or a movie reviewer shows 15 seconds of a film on television to illustrate a point about the movie? Or a comedian sings a portion of a song's lyrics in a parody? Courts have decided that these and similar uses could be fair to the copyright holder and to society. The 1976 Copyright Act included fair use as a defense.[131]

Fair use is difficult to define. One judge has said that to be fair "the use must be of a character that serves the copyright objective of stimulating productive thought and public instruction without excessively diminishing the incentives for creativity."[132] The 1976 law set out four criteria courts use in balancing the plaintiff's rights to forbid any use of a work without permission and the defendant's right to use a portion of the work under certain circumstances: (1) the purpose and character of the use, (2) the nature of the copyrighted work, (3) the amount and substantiality of the portion used and (4) the effect on the plaintiff's potential market.

1. The Purpose and Character of the Use. In determining the purpose and character of the defendant's use of the copyrighted material, courts consider several factors, including whether the use is for commercial or nonprofit purposes. The law gives examples of uses that would tilt the balance toward a fair use: criticism, comment, news reporting, teaching (including multiple copies for classroom use), scholarship, parody, searchable databases and research.[133]

infringement by inducement
Sometimes just called inducement. When a person or entity who does not directly infringe can be held liable for inducing others to infringe.

fair use
A test courts use to determine whether using another's copyrighted material without permission is legal or an infringement. Also used in trademark infringement cases.

transformative use
When the reuse of an original copyrighted work has transformed the work's appearance or nature to such a degree that the use is not infringing.

News reporting may be considered a fair use, but this is not clear. For example, more than 30 years ago, The Nation magazine used 300 to 400 words from President Gerald R. Ford's memoirs without the book publisher's permission. The publisher had sold Time magazine the exclusive right to run excerpts. The U.S. Supreme Court acknowledged that Ford's thoughts were news, but that alone was not sufficient to qualify The Nation's copying as fair use.[134] The Supreme Court said it was not.

In a case involving a cover version of a popular song, the U.S. Supreme Court considered whether a parody changes the work it mocks or merely repeats without permission the copyrighted material.[135] In its decision, the Supreme Court made **transformative use** a key part of fair use's first element (the concept of transformative use is also discussed in Chapter 6, related to the right of publicity). The more the parody transforms the work it mimics, the more likely it is that the nature of the use is fair.

The Court said fair use is more likely if the new work "adds something new, with a further purpose or different character, altering the [copyrighted work] with new expression, meaning, or message."[136] A 2 Live Crew parody of Roy Orbison's song "Oh, Pretty Woman" might be fair use because it did transform the original, the Supreme Court said.[137] The Court emphasized the importance of 2 Live Crew's transformation of the original but said the district court must reconsider whether the other fair use elements established fair use. The parties settled the case.[138]

Eight years ago, the Seventh Circuit Court of Appeals ruled that a parody by the animated television program "South Park" of a viral video, "What What (In the Butt)," was fair use because the program's intent was "to comment on and critique the social phenomenon that is the 'viral video.'"[139] In 2015, the Second Circuit held that an unauthorized derivative work of the film "Point Break" was also fair use and could itself be copyrighted because the parody added sufficient originality.[140]

Arguments for transformative use go beyond parodies, and they do not always succeed. For example, in a bench trial in federal court in New York, the judge found that a celebrity gossip website infringed on the copyrights of the owners of celebrity photos it used. The website argued that its unauthorized use of the paparazzi images in website banners and as thumbnail images along with "clickbait" headlines was transformative, but the court disagreed.[141]

A federal judge held that the legal databases Lexis and Westlaw did not

AF archive/Alamy Stock Photo

A federal court of appeals found a "South Park" parody to be fair use.

POINTS OF LAW

TRANSFORMATIVE USE[xi]

Transformative use is one of the primary defenses used today when arguing fair use. Transformative use is generally fair use if the answer to two questions is "yes":

1. Has the material you have taken from the original work been transformed by adding new expression or meaning?

2. Was value added to the original by creating new information, new aesthetics or new insights and understandings?

Courts must also apply the other fair use factors (discussed in this section) to transformative use, but frequently it is the transformative use determination that carries the most weight.

violate copyright law when they copied legal briefs in their entirety to create an interactive legal research tool. Although the use of the legal briefs was commercial (or for profit), the judge said the transformative nature of the database carried greater weight.[142]

Recently, a federal district court in New York held that a service that monitors and records television and radio broadcasts to turn them into a searchable database for its users amounts to fair use because the database is transformative.[143] On appeal, however, the Second Circuit Court of Appeals reversed.[144] The court said that while the service was developed and offered for transformative purposes, the service's watch function, which allowed viewers to watch the recorded video clips, was not fair use.[145]

Five years ago, the Second Circuit Court of Appeals held that Google's mass digitization of millions of books, in connection with providing brief excerpts of books used in Google's search function, was a transformative fair use.[146] Several book publishers and the Authors Guild, which represents authors whose works were made into digital books without their permission, sued Google, claiming copyright infringement. A federal district judge ruled that scanning the books amounted to fair use for purposes of preserving the works, making the books available to those with sight impairment and enabling the works to be searched.[147] The Second Circuit agreed and noted that Google's "snippet" view of the books added value and context to the basic transformative search function.[148]

2. The Nature of the Copyrighted Work. This factor examines whether the copyrighted work is largely creative, such as a feature film, or more informational or functional, like a compilation of court decisions.[149] Courts often find more copyright protection for creative works. Copying portions of factually based materials may tilt the balance toward a fair use.

The question of whether unpublished materials should have special protection against a fair use defense arose when a court allowed J.D. Salinger, the author of "The Catcher in the

Rye," to stop distribution of an unauthorized biography including excerpts from his letters.[150] A federal appellate court held that unpublished materials are entitled to more protection than published works. Congress later amended the Copyright Act to clarify that while unpublished materials are afforded more protection than published materials, fair use is still an appropriate defense if a person can meet all four factors.[151]

3. The Amount and Substantiality of the Portion Used. Courts ask two questions with regard to the amount and substantiality factor. First, how much of the copyrighted work was used without permission? Courts may count how many lines of code from a computer program, words from a story or seconds from a movie were used. A court may also consider what percentage of the original was used. Second, what particular portion of the copyrighted work was used, and how important was it to the copyrighted work? If the most important portion of a work is used without permission, the balance tips toward infringement.

Copying the entirety of a copyrighted work does not necessarily mean the use was not fair. A group of students sued the company that owns Turnitin, a plagiarism detection service, because Turnitin archived their work in the company's computers. The students claimed the archiving effectively copied their work, thus infringing their copyrights. The Fourth Circuit Court of Appeals disagreed.[152] Although the company copied each student paper in its entirety, the court found Turnitin's archiving to be fair use. In general, the court said, "as the amount of the copyrighted material that is used increases, the likelihood that the use will constitute a 'fair use' decreases."[153] However, the court balanced the amount used against other fair use factors, particularly the purpose of the use. Turnitin uses each student paper for a limited purpose, that is, to enable students and teachers to expose plagiarism. In the database-related transformative use cases noted earlier, courts reinforced the idea that fair use can apply even if works are copied in their entirety.[154]

Similarly, a federal appellate court said reprinting full pictures of Grateful Dead posters and concert tickets did not preclude finding fair use when the images were scattered throughout a book in collages of images, text and graphic art. The court said the use was transformative because images were shown in reduced size and only a few unauthorized copyrighted works were published among 2,000 images.[155]

Professors, film and media studies students and documentary filmmakers generally may use short clips from movies for criticism, for commentary or even to make new, noncommercial videos, the Librarian of Congress ruled.[156]

4. The Effect on the Plaintiff's Potential Market. Many courts consider the extent to which the unauthorized copying diminished the copyright holder's likely profits from his or her creation. Historically, this was the most important of the four fair use factors. Today, it is typically the second most important factor behind transformative use. When a Kinko's store responded to professors' requests to make course packets by copying chapters from numerous books without permission, several publishers sued for copyright infringement. A court rejected Kinko's fair use defense, finding the fourth factor the "single most important" part of the fair use test in that particular case.[157] If students purchased the professor's course packet, they were not purchasing the textbook from which the chapters came.

The U.S. Supreme Court has said copying a substantial portion of a copyrighted work without permission may prove a "greater likelihood of market harm under the fourth" element of the fair use test.[158] That is, typically, the more of a work that someone copies, the less likely it is someone else will purchase the original. This would cause market harm to the copyright holder. With the increase in the application of transformative use in the first part of the fair use test (purpose and character of the use), some courts have acknowledged that under the fourth part of the test the transformative use of the work actually expands the market for the original work.[159] That is, copying the entire work for a searchable database, as Google has done, can make the full work more widely available in the marketplace, and that enhances the value of the copyrighted work.

DMCA Safe Harbor Protections

As noted earlier in this chapter, the Digital Millennium Copyright Act was an attempt to bring the internet and other digital media under copyright law.[160] One of the concerns the DMCA addresses is whether internet service providers can lose copyright suits based on content their users post.

The DMCA shields ISPs and video-sharing sites from copyright infringement claims if they remove material that a copyright holder tells them is posted without permission.[161] This is called a "takedown notice." This protection is available if a website names an agent to receive takedown requests, lets site users know of the site's copyright infringement policy and complies with takedown requests it receives. ISPs must comply with takedown requests that clearly identify the work claimed to infringe copyright and provide the URL of the infringing work.[162] A customer cannot sue the ISP for removing material even if the customer later shows the material did not violate a copyright holder's rights. ISPs that knowingly transmit material that violates copyright are not protected.

The DMCA offers other protection to video-sharing websites such as YouTube and Vimeo. It protects video-sharing websites from monetary damages when a user, rather than the site, posts copyrighted material without permission. The copyright holder cannot successfully sue the site operator if the operator (1) did not know the content infringed someone's copyright, (2) did not earn money directly from the posted material and (3) promptly complied with a takedown notice. These takedown protections, also known as **safe harbor**, limit video-sharing sites' liability.

Seven years ago, the DMCA's safe harbor saved Veoh Networks, an internet-based video-sharing service, from losing a copyright infringement suit. Universal Music Group, one of the world's largest recording companies, sued Veoh over user-uploaded videos that included UMG-copyrighted songs. Veoh had implemented a copyright infringement policy and taken down videos when notified of violations but was not able to prevent all infringements. Despite failure to notify Veoh of all infringing videos, UMG said Veoh should have known some of its videos infringed copyright. The Ninth Circuit Court of Appeals said the DMCA requires specific notification to Veoh of videos that need to be removed.[163] Absent such notification, Veoh had neither the right nor the ability to prevent users from posting videos that infringed copyright, the court said.

safe harbor
The takedown notification provision of the Digital Millennium Copyright Act that protects internet service providers and video-sharing websites from claims of infringement when they do not know about or profit from the infringement and promptly comply with a takedown notice.

The DMCA's safe harbor provision also kept Google-owned YouTube from losing a $1 billion suit filed by Viacom in 2013. A district judge in 2013 held that YouTube's removal of 100,000 videos that Viacom said infringed its copyrights did not show that YouTube knew it carried Viacom's copyrighted material.[164] Without that knowledge, the safe harbor protected YouTube.

In 2016, the Second Circuit Court of Appeals ruled that the DMCA safe harbor did not protect a handful of infringing videos that Vimeo employees viewed and did not flag for possible infringement.[165] This is sometimes called **red-flag knowledge**. The phrase refers to an ISP or website being "subjectively aware of facts that would have made the specific infringement 'objectively' obvious to a reasonable person."[166] If the website has red-flag knowledge of infringing material and does not remove it, then a court could find it responsible for infringement. Vimeo argued that the videos reviewed by the employees did not contain "objectively obvious" infringement and should be protected by the safe harbor provision, but the court disagreed.[167]

Another aspect of the Second Circuit's decision in the Vimeo case involved pre-1972 sound recordings. As noted earlier in the chapter, state copyright laws have applied to pre-1972 sound recordings because of a gap in the federal law. In its decision, the Second Circuit Court of Appeals said the DMCA safe harbor applies to state copyrights, reversing a lower court ruling that said DMCA safe harbor did not apply. As a result of the Second Circuit decision, Vimeo invoked the DMCA safe harbor to dismiss the infringement claims when the case was remanded to the lower court. The lower court then dismissed all the state copyright claims under the DMCA safe harbor except those that demonstrated Vimeo had red-flag knowledge of infringement.[168]

The DMCA safe harbor does not offer protection if an ISP or sharing service does not implement its policies for enforcement. For example, in 2018, the Fourth Circuit Court of Appeals rejected Cox Communications' safe harbor defense in a case that involved its subscribers' use of BitTorrent, a peer-to-peer file sharing system used mostly for the sharing of copyrighted material without permission. While the ISP had a policy for terminating repeat infringers, evidence showed it did not act to actually terminate users who received multiple notices of infringing behavior.[169]

In the context of a news website, the Tenth Circuit Court of Appeals held in 2016 that Examiner.com was protected under the DMCA safe harbor provision after individuals contributing to the website posted photographs without permission. The court's decision was based on the fact that the site's contributors are considered users under the DMCA and that the infringing photos were posted at their discretion. The website did not have red-flag knowledge.[170]

red-flag knowledge
When an internet service provider or website is aware of facts that would make infringement obvious to a reasonable person.

TRADEMARKS

As mentioned at the start of the chapter, a trademark is a word, name, symbol or design used to identify a company's goods and distinguish them from similar products other companies make.[171] A service mark accomplishes the same purpose for services a firm provides. A trade name identifies a particular company rather than the company's product or service. Federal law also protects trade dress, which describes a product's total look, including size, shape, color, texture and graphics. The word "trademark" may be used generally to include all four of these categories. However, the law does not protect trade names or trade dress as completely as it protects trademarks and service marks.

Photo 12/Alamy Stock Photo

When a company filed to register "The Krusty Krab" as a trademark for a future restaurant chain, Viacom, the owner of "SpongeBob SquarePants" trademarks, sued for trademark infringement and won.

Trademarks may be brand names or logos designed to identify a company's product. The Nike "swoosh" is a well-known logo. But the list of what can be trademarked is lengthy: letters (CBS), numbers (VO5), domain names (Amazon.com), slogans ("Just do it"), shapes (Coke bottle), colors (Corning fiberglass pink insulation),[172] sounds (quacking noise made by guides and participants in duck boat tours)[173] and smells ("fresh cut grass" for tennis balls).[174]

Trademarks are valuable. For example, consider the importance of McDonald's, Google, Nike, Amazon, Kleenex, Starbucks and Coke as trademarks. Companies use trademarks to advertise their products and services. Customers use trademarks to ensure they are getting the goods or services from a particular company. The federal Lanham Act protects trademarks that are eligible for registration with the U.S. Patent and Trademark Office.[175] The law ensures that if a company complies with certain requirements, no other company may use the trademarked word, symbol, slogan or other such item that will confuse consumers about who supplies a particular product or service. The Lanham Act also prevents using a mark to falsely suggest a product's source even if the mark is not registered.[176]

Distinctiveness Requirement

Distinctive words, designs or other indicators of a product or service's origin are eligible for trademark registration.[177] A trademark will be protected only if it is distinctive. A trademark is distinctive if it distinguishes one company's goods from another's.

There is a spectrum of distinctiveness in trademark law. The less unique—that is, the more broadly descriptive—a mark is, the less likely it is to be eligible for trademark registration. The most distinctive category is "fanciful marks." These are invented marks, including made-up words. Lexus, Xerox and Exxon are examples of fanciful marks. A court found that Peterbilt and Kenworth are fanciful marks applied to trucks.[178] The trucks' manufacturer sued a website operator who used the words "Peterbilt" and "Kenworth" in the site's address without permission. Because fanciful marks are the strongest and most distinctive trademarks possible, the greatest trademark protection should be applied to fanciful marks, the court said. When a strong mark is infringed, it is more likely consumers will be confused, the court concluded.

"Arbitrary marks," the next most distinctive category, are words that have ordinary meanings unrelated to the product or service. For example, an apple is a fruit, but Apple is a trademark for computers and other products manufactured by Apple, Inc. A dictionary will define the word "apple" as a fruit, but not as a computer. Numbers and letters arranged in a distinctive order may be arbitrary marks, such as bebe for clothes[179] or V8 for vegetable juice.[180]

"Suggestive marks" suggest a product's qualities or a manufacturer's business but do not describe either. A suggestive mark requires consumers to use their imaginations to discern the company's exact business.[181] One court said Coppertone, Orange Crush and Playboy are good examples of suggestive marks "because they conjure images of the associated products without directly describing those products."[182] A court held that the word "CarMax" is a suggestive mark for a used car dealership.[183] The word suggests that CarMax is involved in the automobile business but does not say the company sells used cars.

A "descriptive mark" leaves little to a consumer's imagination. The mark describes the product or service and may or may not suggest what company provided it. Generally, commonly used descriptive terms cannot be trademarked. For example, many soft drink companies may use the word "refreshing" to describe their products. However, a descriptive mark may be a trademark if it has acquired a distinctive connection to the product for which it is used. Courts call this a **secondary meaning** beyond the word's common meaning. Distinctive, arbitrary and suggestive marks do not require a secondary meaning.

To obtain a secondary meaning, the public must associate a word with a product's source or producer, not the product. Courts do not agree on a test for finding a secondary meaning, but the Ninth Circuit Court of Appeals' approach is illustrative. It considers "(1) whether actual purchasers of the product bearing the claimed trademark associate the trademark with the producer; (2) the degree and manner of advertising under the claimed trademark; (3) the length and manner of use of the claimed trademark; and (4) whether use of the claimed trademark has been exclusive."[184]

In 2018, the Fifth Circuit Court of Appeals held that Viacom held the common law trademark to "The Krusty Krab," the name of the restaurant central to the Viacom-owned animated show "SpongeBob SquarePants."[185] Viacom had sued a corporation that sought to register the trademark "The Krusty Krab" for its planned chain of restaurants. The court said that "The Krusty Krab" was distinctive and had acquired secondary meaning. The public associates "The Krusty Krab" with "SpongeBob SquarePants" because it is a significant element in the show that has aired for 18 years, it is depicted in advertisements that promote franchise sales and it is used on social media platforms by the "SpongeBob" franchise, as well as in mobile apps and games, the court said. The court rejected the argument from the restaurant owner that the public would find the cartoon distinct from the restaurant.[186]

secondary meaning
Meaning beyond a word's common meaning. To obtain secondary meaning, the public must associate a word with a product's source or producer, not the product.

POINTS OF LAW

TYPES OF MARKS

A trademark is only protected if it is distinctive. The more distinct or unique a mark, the more likely it will be eligible for trademark registration.

- **Fanciful marks**—invented marks, including made-up words (for example, "Lexus") most likely to receive trademark protection

- **Arbitrary marks**—words that have ordinary meanings unrelated to the product or service (for example, "Apple")

- **Suggestive marks**—marks that suggest a product's source or manufacturer's business but do not describe what the product is (for example, "Playboy")

- **Descriptive marks**—marks that describe the product or service and leave little to a consumer's imagination and that must attach a distinctive meaning to the product or service (called secondary meaning) to be trademarked

Certain groups of descriptive words, such as geographic terms, rarely acquire the secondary meaning needed to be a registered trademark if they only describe where the goods or services are made or offered.

For example, a court refused to find that the word "Boston" had a secondary meaning in the phrase "Boston Beer."[187] Although the beer is manufactured in Boston, "Boston" means the Massachusetts city and is not connected in the public's mind with that brand of beer, the court said. The court did not allow "Boston Beer" to become a trademark. A geographic term also cannot be a registered trademark if it is deceptive. For example, a ham processor located in Nebraska cannot use the term "Danish ham" as a trademark for its product.

Similarly, people's names must acquire a secondary meaning to be protected. In one case, Fabrikant & Sons, a jewelry company, trademarked the word "Fabrikant." Several years later, Fabrikant Fine Diamonds began business as a buyer and seller of jewelry. Both companies are located in New York City, and both are owned by individuals named Fabrikant. A court ruled that Fabrikant Fine Diamonds had to either stop using the name Fabrikant or use a first name in front of the word to distinguish it from Fabrikant & Sons.[188] Otherwise the public would be confused, the court said. Courts often consider three factors to rule in competing name cases. As one court put it, the factors are "(a) the interest of the plaintiff in protecting the good will which has attached to his personal name trademark, (b) the interest of the defendant in using his own name in his business activities and (c) the interest of the public in being free from confusion and deception."[189]

Finally, generic words will not be given trademark protection. A graham cracker manufacturer cannot use the word "cracker" as a trademark, for example. A manufacturer is not allowed to take a word commonly used to describe a product category and use it exclusively for the company's own purpose. For instance, Harley-Davidson could not use the word "hog" as a mark for its motorcycles,[190] nor could a concert promoter obtain a trademark for the term "summer jam" to advertise its summer concerts.[191]

Some marks that once were protected became generic when the public used the mark to mean a category of goods rather than a particular manufacturer's product. "Thermos," "cellophane," "brassiere," "aspirin," "shredded wheat" and "monopoly" (the board game) all once were protected copyrights that became generic words.[192] Courts ask what a word's primary significance is to the public. If the public thinks of a word as describing a class of goods—a vacuum bottle is a thermos—the word is generic and cannot be a protected mark. If the word primarily means a particular manufacturer—Xerox makes Xerox copying machines—the word will remain a trademark.[193]

Companies often take several steps to prevent a trademark from becoming generic. Among other actions, a company may select a distinctive mark, advertise the goods using both the trademark and the product's generic word (Kleenex facial tissue), use advertisements to educate the public that the product's trademark is not a generic word and use the trademark on several different products.[194]

Registering a Trademark

A history of using a distinctive mark to identify a product can give the mark protection even if it is not registered. The first person or company to use the mark owns it. State courts recognize common law rights in marks within the geographic area where the mark is used. It is not necessary to register a mark to give it common law protection. An owner of a mark protected by common law may use the symbols ™ (trademark) or ﹩ᴹ (service mark), but these are not recognized by statute.

A mark must be registered with the U.S. Patent and Trademark Office to have statutory protection under the Lanham Act.[195] Registering a mark requires submitting an application form, a drawing of the mark and a filing fee to the PTO. Trademark law's complexity means a trademark attorney needs to be involved in registering a mark. Trademark registration excludes marks with a flag or other insignia of any country or U.S. state or city, marks with a name or other identification of a living person without the individual's consent or marks that are only descriptive without secondary meaning.[196] Nor will the PTO register a mark identical to or similar to an existing mark.[197]

disparaging marks
Trademarks considered immoral, disparaging or deceptive under the Lanham Act. Recently, the U.S. Supreme Court has ruled that the First Amendment protects immoral and disparaging marks.

Section 2(a) of the Lanham Act prevents the PTO from registering a mark that is considered immoral, disparaging or deceptive.[198] These kinds of trademarks are often referred to as **disparaging marks**.

In 2017, the U.S. Supreme Court considered whether the Lanham Act's ban on disparaging trademarks violates the First Amendment.[199] Simon Tam and his Asian-American band the Slants applied for a trademark to protect the band name. The band says it used the name to reappropriate the slur sometimes applied to Asians. The PTO refused to register the trademark because it was disparaging. Sitting en banc, the D.C. Circuit Court of Appeals reversed and held that the PTO's ban on disparaging marks was an unconstitutional viewpoint-based restriction on speech.[200] "Courts have been slow to appreciate the expressive power of trademarks," the D.C. Circuit Court wrote. "The government cannot refuse to register disparaging marks because it disapproves of the expressive messages conveyed by the marks."[201]

The government argued that trademarks, like license plates, are a form of government speech. Government's power to operate the trademark program includes the power to reject the disparaging mark. In *Matal v. Tam*, excerpted at the end of the chapter, the U.S. Supreme Court held that the disparagement clause violates the First Amendment. "Contrary to the Government's contention, trademarks are private, not government speech," Justice Samuel Alito wrote for the Court. "Because the "Free Speech Clause . . . does not regulate government speech," the government is not required to maintain viewpoint neutrality on its own speech. This Court exercises great caution in extending its government-speech precedents, for if private speech could be passed off as government speech by simply affixing a government seal of approval, government could silence or muffle the expression of disfavored viewpoints."[202]

While the Court's decision in *Matal v. Tam* addressed disparaging trademarks, Section 2(a) of the Lanham Act also prevents the PTO from registering a mark that is considered immoral.

In 2019, the U.S. Supreme Court considered whether the registration of "immoral" or "scandalous" marks violates the First Amendment. The case involved the PTO's rejection of the trademark FUCT under Section 2(a). Los Angeles, Calif., artist Erik Brunetti founded the FUCT clothing brand in 1991. Brunetti sought trademark protection in 2011. The PTO rejected the trademark because it viewed the mark as a scandalous, four-letter word.[203]

After the Supreme Court's ruling in *Matal*, the D.C. Circuit Court of Appeals ruled in Brunetti's favor, finding that Section 2(a)'s ban on immoral trademarks violated the First Amendment because it was a content-based restriction that should be subject to strict scrutiny.[204] In oral arguments before the Supreme Court, the government argued that registering a trademark is a government benefit that does not prevent Brunetti from selling his clothes with the FUCT brand. By not registering his trademark, the government is placing a valid condition on participation in a federal program, the government argued.[205]

The Supreme Court disagreed. Justice Elena Kagan, writing for the majority, said that the Lanham Act's ban was viewpoint-based and overly broad and violated the First Amendment. She highlighted the PTO's inconsistent application of the ban—for example, the PTO's rejection of a mark that promoted the use of medical marijuana, but approval of a mark used to discourage drug use; or, the approval of a mark with the words "War on Terrorism Memorial," but the rejection of a mark that reflected support for the terrorist group al-Qaeda. "These decisions are understandable. The rejected marks express opinions that are, at the least, offensive to many Americans," Kagan wrote. "But as the Court made clear in *Tam*, a law disfavoring 'ideas that offend' discriminates based on viewpoint, in violation of the First Amendment."[206]

All of the justices agreed that the Lanham Act's provision violated the First Amendment. Three justices concurred in part and dissented in part, writing separate opinions. Chief Justice John Roberts and Justices Stephen Breyer and Sonia Sotomayor all said the Court should have accepted the government's argument that a narrow construction of the definition of "scandalous" would not violate the First Amendment—it would only regulate marks that are obscene,

In addition to raising First Amendment concerns, the Oregon-based band the Slants said it needed its name trademarked to land a record label deal.

vulgar or profane.[207] "Freedom of speech is a cornerstone of our society and the First Amendment protects Brunetti's right to use words like the one at issue here," wrote Justice Sotomayor. "The Government need not, however, be forced to confer on Brunetti's trademark . . . when 'scandalous' can reasonably be read to bar the registration of only those marks that are obscene, vulgar or profane."[208]

Federal registration provides more protection for a mark than does common law. Registration establishes the date of the mark's first use, protects nationwide use and lets competitors know that a company owns the mark.[209] A company may use the statutory symbol for registered marks. The symbol ® or the phrase "Registered U.S. Patent and Trademark Office" is acceptable. If a registered mark is infringed, its owner may sue in federal court. After five years of use, the mark gains nearly complete protection.[210] During the sixth year after registration, a mark owner must file an affidavit confirming the mark has been in continued use.[211] Marks registered after Nov. 16, 1989, have a 10-year term. Registrations may be renewed indefinitely.[212]

Domain Names and Keywords

Congress adapted trademark law to the internet, but website addresses, or domain names, have been a particular problem for trademark law. Domain names may be trademarked and protected against infringement, although the domain name suffixes, such as .com or .org, are not considered part of a trademarked domain name.

Cybersquatters claim domain names that include trademarks or famous people's names. Before Congress passed the Anticybersquatting Consumer Protection Act, trademark owners often sued cybersquatters, frequently successfully, to try to stop the practice.[213] The ACPA provides civil and criminal remedies for registering a domain name with the intention of selling it to the trademark owner. The law applies to a domain name identical or confusingly similar to a trademark or that disparages or injures a well-known trademark. A defendant must have acted in bad faith to be liable under the statute.

In one ACPA case, a company named Spider Webs registered hundreds of domain names, including ErnestandJulioGallo.com. The Gallo winery sued. A federal appellate court held the ACPA constitutional and said the unauthorized domain name could injure Gallo's trademark.[214] Spider Webs admitted it registered the domain name hoping the ACPA would be found unconstitutional. That showed bad faith, the appellate court said, and it upheld a $25,000 damage award and a court order preventing Spider Webs from registering any domain name that used "Gallo" or "Ernest and Julio."

If two companies have identical or similar trademarks for two different products, the companies' domain names might be the same—chip.com for a computer chip company or for a potato chip company. In such a case, one court said trademark law takes precedence over domain registration. The court gave a disputed domain name—moviebuff—to the company that first used the mark.[215] However, if two domain names are similar and both describe the companies' products, courts may allow the firms to continue using the names. For example, the manufacturer of Beanie Babies sued a company using bargainbeanies.com as a domain name. The bargain beanies company sold used beanbag animals. A federal appellate court said preventing a firm from using a domain name describing its business would be like "forbidding a used car dealer who specializes in selling Chevrolets to mention" the car's name in the dealer's advertising.[216] The court allowed both companies to use their domain names.

More recently, lawsuits have arisen around trademarks and keywords used for internet searches. A federal court in California held that use of a competitor's trademark as an advertising keyword in a search is not likely to cause consumer confusion and is not a trademark infringement.[217] For example, in 2018, a court held that the Alzheimer's Foundation of America's purchase of the Alzheimer's Disease and Related Disorders Association trademarks as search engine keywords, as well as purchasing the two-word phrase "Alzheimer's Foundation" as search engine keywords, did not violate the Lanham Act.[218]

Trademark Infringement

Anyone may use a protected trademark in a way that is not confusing. The Lanham Act says trademark infringement occurs when a mark "is likely to cause confusion, or to cause a mistake, or to deceive as to the affiliation, connection, or association of such person with another person, or as to the origin, sponsorship, or approval of his or her goods, services, or commercial activities by another person."[219] Including the words "Starbucks," "Prada" and "Chipotle" in this paragraph is not a trademark infringement. Using marks for informational purposes is a fair use.

The First Amendment protects using a competitor's trademark in comparative advertising, courts have ruled.[220] However, a competitor may not alter a mark in a comparative ad. In one case, a competitor to John Deere's lawn tractor business aired a comparative ad that distorted and animated Deere's trademarked deer logo, showing the deer jumping through a hoop that breaks apart, for instance. The ad diminished Deere's logo in consumers' minds, a court ruled.[221]

Facebook claimed likelihood of confusion and won a trademark infringement lawsuit against a social networking site named Teachbook. Teachbook marketed to teachers, stating that many schools forbid teachers from using Facebook because students might learn teachers' personal information. A federal district court found a likelihood of confusion between the two marks because the "Teachbook mark is highly similar to the registered Facebook mark in appearance, sound, meaning, and commercial impression."[222]

Similar—even identical—marks may not cause confusion if the goods for which the marks are used are not the same. Wendy's automobile parts may coexist with Wendy's restaurants if a court says consumers would not think the restaurant company also owns the auto parts store.

Companies may redesign or refresh logos and retain the original trademark. Trademark **tacking** allows a trademark owner to slightly alter a trademark without abandoning ownership of the original mark. In order to "tack" a trademark, the owner must show that "the two trademarks

tacking
Allows a trademark owner to slightly alter a trademark without abandoning ownership of the original mark.

famouslogos.us

The evolution of the Pepsi logo would likely qualify as tacking.

create the same, continuing commercial impression, and the later mark should not materially differ from or alter the character of the mark attempted to be tacked."[223] Courts review tacking claims with a higher likelihood of confusion standard. That is, rather than establishing the likelihood of confusion in the marketplace, when a trademark owner is arguing for tacking, that owner must show that consumers believe both trademarks represent the same company or product and that there is no marketplace confusion. A business owner can show tacking by demonstrating that the new trademark is basically the same as the original in the eyes of consumers.

For example, "Pepsi-Cola" was trademarked in 1903. Since then, the company's logo has evolved from the soda's name appearing in cursive font to a circle-shaped logo with "Pepsi" in the center. Since the 1940s, the logos have incorporated red, white and blue as part of the circle.[224] Pepsi would likely be able to "tack" its logos since changes always incorporate previous, recognizable logo elements. The logo the company uses today combines the colors it started using in the 1940s with a font that contains a modern look but incorporates elements of the original logo.[225]

In 2015, the U.S. Supreme Court ruled unanimously that a jury should decide questions of tacking because it involves a question of fact—whether the two marks create the same commercial impression to consumers.[226] As one trademark expert observed, "This makes sense: A jury is comprised of 12 ordinary people, and questions about trademarks usually revolve around whether ordinary consumers would be confused."[227]

Courts use a variety of criteria to determine whether consumers likely will be confused by similar marks used by different products or services. These include the marks' similarities, the similarities of products or services for which the marks are used, how consumers purchase the goods (impulse buying or careful consideration), how well known the first-used mark is, actual confusion that can be proved and how long both marks have been used without confusion.[228]

dilution
Using a famous trademark in a way that disparages or diminishes the mark's effectiveness in the market. Can happen from blurring or tarnishment.

tarnishment
A poorly made or unsavory product using a mark similar to a famous trademark that could cause consumers to think less of the well-known product.

Using a famous trademark in a way that disparages or diminishes the mark's effectiveness is known as **dilution**. Dilution may happen in two ways.[229] First, a product name similar to a well-known trademark could make the famous mark less distinctive. What the law calls blurring whittles away a trademark's selling power. Second, a poorly made or unsavory product using a name similar to a famous trademark could cause consumers to think less of the well-known mark. This is **tarnishment**.[230]

Congress revised federal anti-dilution law in response to a U.S. Supreme Court decision involving an "adult novelties" store in Elizabethtown, Ky., called Victor's Secret. After the Victoria's Secret franchise asked the store's owners not to use the name Victor's Secret, the owners called it Victor's Little Secret. Victoria's Secret sued for trademark dilution. The Supreme Court said Victoria's Secret had to show actual dilution of its trademark, which might be difficult for the large corporation to do.[231] The Court said there is "a complete absence of evidence of any lessening of the capacity of the Victoria's Secret mark to identify . . . goods . . . sold in Victoria's Secret stores or advertised in its catalogs."[232]

Congress rejected that approach. It revised anti-dilution law to require companies with famous trademarks to show only a likelihood of dilution, not actual dilution of trademark effectiveness. But the core of the anti-dilution law remains the same: A company does not have to prove it is likely consumers will be confused between a famous trademark and a similar product or service name. Rather, the company has to show only that another firm's similar mark has diminished the well-known mark's distinctiveness or injured its reputation.

Nearly half the states have anti-dilution statutes. These laws protect dilution of all marks used in the state, not just the famous marks the federal anti-dilution law protects.

Defenses

The Lanham Act lists nine defenses to a trademark infringement action.[233] Most turn on disputed facts. For example, a defendant might argue that the registered trademark was obtained fraudulently, that the trademark has been abandoned and no longer is in use or that the mark misrepresents a product's origin. A defendant also might claim to have used and registered the mark first.

The Lanham Act also provides a fair use defense.[234] This allows one company's trademark to describe another company's product. Courts will accept the fair use defense if the defendant used the mark to describe its goods and not as a trademark. Also, the use cannot cause customer confusion. For example, a federal court in Utah recently held that NoMoreRack.com's use of the word "overstock" in its advertisements was a fair use and did not infringe on Overstock.com's trademark. The court said that use of such a general term, even though the websites directly compete with each other, did not create a likelihood of confusion.[235]

In another recent case, the Ninth Circuit Court of Appeals held that use of the phrase "web celeb" as part of an entertainment website and as a television award show category was fair use even though "webceleb" is a trademark attached to a website that provides a marketplace for independent musicians and fans to buy music. The court held that the phrase "web celeb" was merely a common descriptive phrase for internet celebrities.[236]

Referring to the defendant's own product or service by using the plaintiff's mark without permission also may be a fair use. This may be done in comparative advertising, or in other contexts. In one case, two newspapers used the trademarked name of a band, New Kids on the Block, to promote the newspapers' telephone polls about the band. The papers used the band's name to describe the papers' own product: the telephone poll. A court found this a fair use because the band could not be identified without using its trademarked name and the papers did not suggest that the band endorsed the poll.[237]

The anti-dilution law also provides a fair use exception. Using a famous trademark for comparative advertising, parody or all forms of news reporting and commentary is not an infringement.[238]

EMERGING LAW

API stands for "application programming interface." Basically, APIs are computer operating system tools that enable developers to create software applications that communicate with each other. One well-known API is Oracle's Java. Google's Android, a popular mobile phone platform, is software written in Java but containing its own APIs.[239]

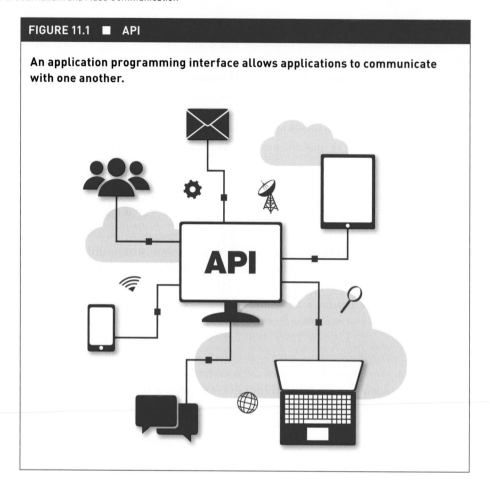

FIGURE 11.1 ■ API

An application programming interface allows applications to communicate with one another.

In 2010, Oracle sued Google for copyright infringement, arguing that the Android API copied the Java code along with the "structure, sequence and organization" of 37 Java API packages. A jury heard portions of the case and decided that Google did infringe, but at the same time a district court judge ruled that APIs like Java are a method of operation and are not copyrightable.[240]

These conflicting results generated several appeals. In 2014, a federal court of appeals reversed the district court judge's decision and said the Java API, including its structure, sequence and organization, did qualify for copyright protection because it included creative expression separate from its function. The appeals court reinstated the jury's verdict. Google had argued that its use of the API constituted a fair use, and that claim resulted in a hung jury. So, the appeals court remanded that specific question to the district court.[241]

Google appealed to the U.S. Supreme Court, but after inviting the solicitor general to file a brief in the case,[242] the Court denied the petition. In 2016, a jury found Google's use of Oracle's API was fair use. The jury instructions in that case defined transformative use and noted that "when purely functional elements are embedded in copyrighted work and it is necessary to copy associated creative elements to utilize functional elements, [this] favors fair use."[243]

On appeal, the Federal Circuit Court held that Google's use of Oracle's API did not constitute fair use. It reversed both the jury verdict and a district court's decision to uphold the verdict.[244] The Federal Circuit Court concluded, "There is nothing fair about taking a copyrighted work verbatim and using it for the same purpose and function as the original in a competing platform."[245] In 2018, the Federal Circuit denied Google's motion for reconsideration, and in mid-2019, Google asked the U.S. Supreme Court to review the case.[246]

CASES FOR STUDY

For study resources and a case archive, go to **edge.sagepub.com/medialaw7e**.

Thinking About It

Historically, the U.S. Supreme Court has decided few cases concerning intellectual property, but as technology advances rapidly, the Supreme Court has heard multiple cases in the past few terms. Both of these case excerpts are recent decisions. As you read them, keep the following questions in mind:

- How does the Supreme Court's ruling about disparaging trademarks in *Matal v. Tam* address the issue of viewpoint discrimination?

- Do you agree with the Supreme Court's reasoning in *American Broadcasting Companies, Inc. v. Aereo, Inc.*? Does it make sense to consider Aereo's service a public performance? Why or why not?

- Do you think the *Aereo* decision could stimulate or stifle the development of new technology?

Matal v. Tam
SUPREME COURT OF THE UNITED STATES
137 S. CT. 1744 (2017)

JUSTICE SAMUEL ALITO (joined by CHIEF JUSTICE JOHN ROBERTS, JUSTICE CLARENCE THOMAS and JUSTICE STEPHEN BREYER) delivered the Court's opinion:
This case concerns a dance-rock band's application for federal trademark registration of the band's name, "The Slants." "Slants" is a derogatory term

for persons of Asian descent, and members of the band are Asian-Americans. But the band members believe that by taking that slur as the name of their group, they will help to "reclaim" the term and drain its denigrating force.

The Patent and Trademark Office (PTO) denied the application based on a provision of federal law prohibiting the registration of trademarks that may "disparage . . . or bring . . . into contemp[t] or disrepute" any "persons, living or dead." We now hold that this provision violates the Free Speech Clause of the First Amendment. It offends a bedrock First Amendment principle: Speech may not be banned on the ground that it expresses ideas that offend.

"The principle underlying trademark protection is that distinctive marks—words, names, symbols, and the like—can help distinguish a particular artisan's goods from those of others."

"[F]ederal law does not create trademarks." Trademarks and their precursors have ancient origins, and trademarks were protected at common law and in equity at the time of the founding of our country. . . . The foundation of current federal trademark law is the Lanham Act, enacted in 1946. By that time, trademark had expanded far beyond phrases that do no more than identify a good or service. Then, as now, trademarks often consisted of catchy phrases that convey a message.

Under the Lanham Act, trademarks that are "used in commerce" may be placed on the "principal register," that is, they may be federally registered. . . . "[N]ational protection of trademarks is desirable," we have explained, "because trademarks foster competition and the maintenance of quality by securing to the producer the benefits of good reputation." . . .

The Lanham Act contains provisions that bar certain trademarks from the principal register. . . .

At issue in this case is one such provision, which we will call "the disparagement clause." This provision prohibits the registration of a trademark "which may disparage . . . persons, living or dead, institutions, beliefs, or national symbols, or bring them into contempt, or disrepute." This clause appeared in the original Lanham Act and has remained the same to this day.

When deciding whether a trademark is disparaging, an examiner at the PTO generally applies a "two-part test." The examiner first considers "the likely meaning of the matter in question, taking into account not only dictionary definitions, but also the relationship of the matter to the other elements in the mark, the nature of the goods or services, and the manner in which the mark is used in the marketplace in connection with the goods or services." "If that meaning is found to refer to identifiable persons, institutions, beliefs or national symbols," the examiner moves to the second step, asking "whether that meaning may be disparaging

to a substantial composite of the referenced group." If the examiner finds that a "substantial composite, although not necessarily a majority, of the referenced group would find the proposed mark . . . to be disparaging in the context of contemporary attitudes," a prima facie case of disparagement is made out, and the burden shifts to the applicant to prove that the trademark is not disparaging. What is more, the PTO has specified that "[t]he fact that an applicant may be a member of that group or has good intentions underlying its use of a term does not obviate the fact that a substantial composite of the referenced group would find the term objectionable."

Simon Tam is the lead singer of "The Slants." He chose this moniker in order to "reclaim" and "take ownership" of stereotypes about people of Asian ethnicity. The group "draws inspiration for its lyrics from childhood slurs and mocking nursery rhymes" and has given its albums names such as "The Yellow Album" and "Slanted Eyes, Slanted Hearts."

Tam sought federal registration of "THE SLANTS," on the principal register, but an examining attorney at the PTO rejected the request, applying the PTO's two-part framework and finding that "there is . . . a substantial composite of persons who find the term in the applied-for mark offensive." The examining attorney relied in part on the fact that "numerous dictionaries define 'slants' or 'slant-eyes' as a derogatory or offensive term." The examining attorney also relied on a finding that "the band's name has been found offensive numerous times"—citing a performance that was canceled because of the band's moniker and the fact that "several bloggers and commenters to articles on the band have indicated that they find the term and the applied-for mark offensive."

Tam contested the denial of registration before the examining attorney and before the PTO's Trademark Trial and Appeal Board (TTAB) but to no avail. Eventually, he took the case to federal court, where the en banc Federal Circuit ultimately found the disparagement clause facially unconstitutional under the First Amendment's Free Speech Clause. The majority found that the clause engages in viewpoint-based discrimination, that the clause regulates the expressive component of trademarks and consequently cannot be treated as commercial speech, and that the clause is subject to and cannot satisfy strict scrutiny. The majority also rejected the Government's argument that registered trademarks constitute government speech, as well as the Government's contention that federal registration is a form of government subsidy. And the majority opined that even if the disparagement clause were analyzed under this Court's commercial speech cases, the clause would fail the "intermediate scrutiny" that those cases prescribe. . . .

The Government filed a petition for certiorari, which we granted in order to decide whether the disparagement clause "is facially invalid under the Free Speech Clause of the First Amendment." . . .

Because the disparagement clause applies to marks that disparage the members of a racial or ethnic group, we must decide whether the clause violates the Free Speech Clause of the First Amendment. And at the outset, we must consider three arguments that would either eliminate any First Amendment protection or result in highly permissive rational-basis review. Specifically, the Government contends (1) that trademarks are government speech, not private speech, (2) that trademarks are a form of government subsidy, and (3) that the constitutionality of the disparagement clause should be tested under a new "government-program" doctrine. We address each of these arguments below.

The First Amendment prohibits Congress and other government entities and actors from "abridging the freedom of speech"; the First Amendment does not say that Congress and other government entities must abridge their own ability to speak freely. . . .

As we have said, "it is not easy to imagine how government could function" if it were subject to the restrictions that the First Amendment imposes on private speech. "'[T]he First Amendment forbids the government to regulate speech in ways that favor some viewpoints or ideas at the expense of others,'" but imposing a requirement of viewpoint-neutrality on government speech would be paralyzing. When a government entity embarks on a course of action, it necessarily takes a particular viewpoint and rejects others. . . .

But while the government-speech doctrine is important—indeed, essential—it is a doctrine that is susceptible to dangerous misuse. If private speech could be passed off as government speech by simply affixing a government seal of approval, government could silence or muffle the expression of disfavored viewpoints. For this reason, we must exercise great caution before extending our government-speech precedents.

At issue here is the content of trademarks that are registered by the PTO, an arm of the Federal Government. The Federal Government does not dream up these marks, and it does not edit marks submitted for registration. Except as required by the statute involved here, an examiner may not reject a mark based on the viewpoint that it appears to express. Thus, unless that section is thought to apply, an examiner does not inquire whether any viewpoint conveyed by a mark is consistent with Government policy or whether any such viewpoint is consistent with that expressed by other marks already on the principal register. Instead, if the mark meets the Lanham Act's viewpoint-neutral requirements, registration is mandatory. And if an examiner finds that a mark is eligible for placement on the principal register, that decision is not reviewed by any higher official unless the registration is challenged. Moreover, once a mark is registered, the PTO is not authorized to remove it from the register unless a party moves for cancellation, the registration expires, or the Federal Trade Commission initiates proceedings based on certain grounds.

In light of all this, it is far-fetched to suggest that the content of a registered mark is government speech. If the federal registration of a trademark makes the mark government speech, the Federal Government is babbling prodigiously and incoherently. It is saying many unseemly things. It is expressing contradictory views. It is unashamedly endorsing a vast array of commercial products and services. And it is providing Delphic advice to the consuming public.

For example, if trademarks represent government speech, what does the Government have in mind when it advises Americans to "make.believe" (Sony), "Think different" (Apple), "Just do it" (Nike), or "Have it your way" (Burger King)? Was the Government warning about a coming disaster when it registered the mark "EndTime Ministries"?

The PTO has made it clear that registration does not constitute approval of a mark. And it is unlikely that more than a tiny fraction of the public has any idea what federal registration of a trademark means. None of our government speech cases even remotely supports the idea that registered trademarks are government speech. . . .

Trademarks have not traditionally been used to convey a Government message. With the exception of the enforcement of 15 U.S.C. § 1052(a), the viewpoint expressed by a mark has not played a role in the decision whether to place it on the principal register. And there is no evidence that the public associates the contents of trademarks with the Federal Government.

This brings us to the case on which the Government relies most heavily, *Walker*, which likely marks the outer bounds of the government-speech doctrine. Holding that the messages on Texas specialty license plates are government speech, the *Walker* Court cited three factors. . . . First, license plates have long been used by the States to convey state messages. Second, license plates "are often closely identified in the public mind" with the State, since they are manufactured and owned by the State, generally designed by the State, and serve as a form of "government ID." Third, Texas "maintain[ed] direct control over the messages conveyed on its specialty plates." . . . [N]one of these factors are present in this case. . . .

Perhaps the most worrisome implication of the Government's argument concerns the system of copyright registration. If federal registration makes a trademark government speech and thus eliminates all First Amendment protection, would the registration of the copyright for a book produce a similar transformation?

The Government attempts to distinguish copyright on the ground that it is "'the engine of free expression,'" but as this case illustrates, trademarks often have an expressive content. Companies spend huge amounts to create and publicize trademarks that convey a message. It is true that the necessary brevity of trademarks limits what they can say. But powerful messages can sometimes be conveyed in just a few words.

Trademarks are private, not government, speech. We next address the Government's argument that this case is governed by cases in which this Court has upheld the constitutionality of government programs that subsidized speech expressing a particular viewpoint. These cases implicate a notoriously tricky question of constitutional law. "[W]e have held that the Government 'may not deny a benefit to a person on a basis that infringes his constitutionally protected . . . freedom of speech even if he has no entitlement to that benefit.'" But at the same time,

government is not required to subsidize activities that it does not wish to promote. Determining which of these principles applies in a particular case "is not always self-evident," but no difficult question is presented here.

Unlike the present case, the decisions on which the Government relies all involved cash subsidies or their equivalent. . . . In other cases, we have regarded tax benefits as comparable to cash subsidies.

The federal registration of a trademark is nothing like the programs at issue in these cases. The PTO does not pay money to parties seeking registration of a mark. Quite the contrary is true: An applicant for registration must pay the PTO a filing fee of $225–$600. And to maintain federal registration, the holder of a mark must pay a fee of $300–$500 every 10 years. The Federal Circuit concluded that these fees have fully supported the registration system for the past 27 years. . . .

Finally, the Government urges us to sustain the disparagement clause under a new doctrine that would apply to "government-program" cases. For the most part, this argument simply merges our government-speech cases and the . . . subsidy cases in an attempt to construct a broader doctrine that can be applied to the registration of trademarks. The only new element in this construct consists of two cases involving a public employer's collection of union dues from its employees. But those cases occupy a special area of First Amendment case law, and they are far removed from the registration of trademarks. . . .

Potentially more analogous are cases in which a unit of government creates a limited public forum for private speech. When government creates such a forum, in either a literal or "metaphysical" sense, some content- and speaker-based restrictions may be allowed. However, even in such cases, what we have termed "viewpoint discrimination" is forbidden.

Our cases use the term "viewpoint" discrimination in a broad sense, and in that sense, the disparagement clause discriminates on the bases of "viewpoint." To be sure, the clause evenhandedly prohibits disparagement of all groups. It applies equally to marks that damn Democrats and Republicans, capitalists and socialists, and those arrayed on both sides of every possible issue. It denies registration to any mark that is offensive to a substantial percentage of the members of any group. But in the sense relevant here, that is viewpoint discrimination: Giving offense is a viewpoint.

We have said time and again that "the public expression of ideas may not be prohibited merely because the ideas are themselves offensive to some of their hearers." For this reason, the disparagement clause cannot be saved by analyzing it as a type of government program in which some content- and speaker-based restrictions are permitted.

Having concluded that the disparagement clause cannot be sustained under our government-speech or subsidy cases or under the Government's proposed "government-program" doctrine, we must confront a dispute between the parties on the question whether trademarks are commercial speech. . . . The Government and *amici* supporting its position argue that all trademarks are commercial speech. They note that the central purposes of trademarks are commercial and that federal law regulates trademarks to promote fair and orderly interstate commerce. Tam and his *amici*, on the other hand, contend that many, if not all, trademarks have an expressive component. In other words, these trademarks do not simply identify the source of a product or service but go on to say something more, either about the product or service or some broader issue. The trademark in this case illustrates this point. The name "The Slants" not only identifies the band but expresses a view about social issues.

We need not resolve this debate between the parties because the disparagement clause cannot withstand even *Central Hudson* review. Under *Central Hudson*, a restriction of speech must serve "a substantial interest," and it must be "narrowly drawn." The disparagement clause fails this requirement.

It is claimed that the disparagement clause serves two interests. The first is phrased in a variety of ways in the briefs. Echoing language in one of the opinions below, the Government asserts an interest in preventing "'underrepresented groups'" from being "'bombarded with demeaning messages in commercial advertising.'" An *amicus* supporting the Government refers to "encouraging racial tolerance and protecting the privacy and welfare of individuals." But no matter how the point is phrased, its unmistakable thrust is this: The Government has an interest in preventing speech expressing ideas that offend. And,

as we have explained, that idea strikes at the heart of the First Amendment. Speech that demeans on the basis of race, ethnicity, gender, religion, age, disability, or any other similar ground is hateful; but the proudest boast of our free speech jurisprudence is that we protect the freedom to express "the thought that we hate."

The second interest asserted is protecting the orderly flow of commerce. Commerce, we are told, is disrupted by trademarks that "involv[e] disparagement of race, gender, ethnicity, national origin, religion, sexual orientation, and similar demographic classification." Such trademarks are analogized to discriminatory conduct, which has been recognized to have an adverse effect on commerce.

A simple answer to this argument is that the disparagement clause is not "narrowly drawn" to drive out trademarks that support invidious discrimination. The clause reaches any trademark that disparages *any person, group, or institution*. It applies to trademarks like the following: "Down with racists," "Down with sexists," "Down with homophobes." It is not an anti-discrimination clause; it is a happy-talk clause. In this way, it goes much further than is necessary to serve the interest asserted.

The clause is far too broad in other ways as well. The clause protects every person living or dead as well as every institution. Is it conceivable that commerce would be disrupted by a trademark saying: "James Buchanan was a disastrous president" or "Slavery is an evil institution"?

There is also a deeper problem with the argument that commercial speech may be cleansed of any expression likely to cause offense. The commercial market is well stocked with merchandise that disparages prominent figures and groups, and the line between commercial and non-commercial speech is not always clear, as this case illustrates. If affixing the commercial label permits the suppression of any speech that may lead to political or social "volatility," free speech would be endangered.

* * *

For these reasons, we hold that the disparagement clause violates the Free Speech Clause of the First Amendment. The judgment of the Federal Circuit is affirmed.

It is so ordered.

JUSTICE ANTHONY KENNEDY and JUSTICE CLARENCE THOMAS, with whom JUSTICE RUTH BADER GINSBURG, JUSTICE SONIA SOTOMAYOR and JUSTICE ELENA KAGAN join, concurring in part and concurring in the judgment.

The Patent and Trademark Office (PTO) has denied the substantial benefits of federal trademark registration to the mark THE SLANTS. The PTO did so under the mandate of the disparagement clause. . . .

As the Court is correct to hold, § 1052(a) constitutes viewpoint discrimination—a form of speech suppression so potent that it must be subject to rigorous constitutional scrutiny. The Government's action and the statute on which it is based cannot survive this scrutiny.

The Court is correct in its judgment, and I join Parts I, II, and III-A of its opinion. This separate writing explains in greater detail why the First Amendment's protections against viewpoint discrimination apply to the trademark here. . . .

Those few categories of speech that the government can regulate or punish—for instance, fraud, defamation, or incitement—are well established within our constitutional tradition. Aside from these and a few other narrow exceptions, it is a fundamental principle of the First Amendment that the government may not punish or suppress speech based on disapproval of the ideas or perspectives the speech conveys.

The First Amendment guards against laws "targeted at specific subject matter," a form of speech suppression known as content based discrimination. This category includes a subtype of laws that go further, aimed at the suppression of "particular views . . . on a subject." A law found to discriminate based on viewpoint is an "egregious form of content discrimination," which is "presumptively unconstitutional."

At its most basic, the test for viewpoint discrimination is whether—within the relevant subject category—the government has singled out a subset of messages for disfavor based on the views expressed. In the instant case, the disparagement clause the Government now seeks to implement and enforce identifies the relevant subject as "persons, living or dead, institutions, beliefs, or national symbols." Within that category, an applicant may register a positive or benign mark but not a derogatory one. The law thus reflects the Government's disapproval of a subset of messages it finds offensive. This is the essence of viewpoint discrimination.

The Government disputes this conclusion. It argues, to begin with, that the law is viewpoint neutral because it applies in equal measure to any trademark that demeans or offends. This misses the point. A subject that is first defined by content and then regulated or censored by mandating only one sort of comment is not viewpoint neutral. To prohibit all sides from criticizing their opponents makes a law more viewpoint based, not less so. The logic of the Government's rule is that a law would be viewpoint neutral even if it provided that public officials could be praised but not condemned. The First Amendment's viewpoint neutrality principle protects more than the right to identify with a particular side. It protects the right to create and present arguments for particular positions in particular ways, as the speaker chooses. By mandating positivity, the law here might silence dissent and distort the marketplace of ideas.

The Government next suggests that the statute is viewpoint neutral because the disparagement clause applies to trademarks regardless of the applicant's personal views or reasons for using the mark. Instead, registration is denied based on the expected reaction of the applicant's audience. In this way, the argument goes, it cannot be said that Government is acting with hostility toward a particular point of view. For example, the Government does not dispute that respondent seeks to use his mark in a positive way. Indeed, respondent endeavors to use The Slants to supplant a racial epithet, using new insights, musical talents, and wry humor to make it a badge of pride. Respondent's application was denied not because the Government thought his object was to demean or offend but because the Government thought his trademark would have that effect on at least some Asian-Americans.

The Government may not insulate a law from charges of viewpoint discrimination by tying censorship to the reaction of the speaker's audience. The Court has suggested that viewpoint discrimination occurs when the government intends to suppress a speaker's beliefs, but viewpoint discrimination need not take that form in every instance. The danger of viewpoint discrimination is that the government is attempting to remove certain ideas or perspectives from a broader debate. That danger is all the greater if the ideas or perspectives are ones a particular audience might think offensive, at least at first hearing. An initial reaction may prompt further reflection, leading to a more reasoned, more tolerant position.

Indeed, a speech burden based on audience reactions is simply government hostility and intervention in a different guise. The speech is targeted, after all, based on the government's disapproval of the speaker's choice of message. And it is the government itself that is attempting in this case to decide whether the relevant audience would find the speech offensive. For reasons like these, the Court's cases have long prohibited the government from justifying a First Amendment burden by pointing to the offensiveness of the speech to be suppressed.

The Government's argument in defense of the statute assumes that respondent's mark is a negative comment. In addressing that argument on its own terms, this opinion is not intended to imply that the Government's interpretation is accurate. From respondent's submissions, it is evident he would disagree that his mark means what the Government says it does. The trademark will have the effect, respondent urges, of reclaiming an offensive term for the positive purpose of celebrating all that Asian-Americans can and do contribute to our diverse Nation. While thoughtful persons can agree or disagree with this approach, the dissonance between the trademark's potential to teach and the Government's insistence on its own, opposite, and negative interpretation confirms the constitutional vice of the statute.

. . . To the extent trademarks qualify as commercial speech, they are an example of why that term or category does not serve as a blanket exemption from the First Amendment's requirement of viewpoint neutrality. Justice Holmes' reference to the "free trade in ideas" and the "power of . . . thought to get itself accepted in the competition of the market," was a metaphor. In the realm of trademarks, the metaphorical marketplace of ideas becomes a tangible, powerful reality. Here that real marketplace exists as a matter of state law and our common-law tradition, quite without regard to the Federal Government. These marks make up part of the expression of everyday life, as with the names of entertainment groups, broadcast networks, designer

clothing, newspapers, automobiles, candy bars, toys, and so on. Nonprofit organizations—ranging from medical-research charities and other humanitarian causes to political advocacy groups—also have trademarks, which they use to compete in a real economic sense for funding and other resources as they seek to persuade others to join their cause. To permit viewpoint discrimination in this context is to permit Government censorship.

. . . It is telling that the Court's precedents have recognized just one narrow situation in which viewpoint discrimination is permissible: where the government itself is speaking or recruiting others to communicate a message on its behalf. The exception is necessary to allow the government to stake out positions and pursue policies. But it is also narrow, to prevent the government from claiming that every government program is exempt from the First Amendment. These cases have identified a number of factors that, if present, suggest the government is speaking on its own behalf; but none are present here.

There may be situations where private speakers are selected for a government program to assist the government in advancing a particular message. That is not this case either. The central purpose of trademark registration is to facilitate source identification. To serve that broad purpose, the Government has provided the benefits of federal registration to millions of marks identifying every type of product and cause. Registered trademarks do so by means of a wide diversity of words, symbols, and messages. Whether a mark is disparaging bears no plausible relation to that goal. While defining the purpose and scope of a federal program for these purposes can be complex, our cases are clear that viewpoint discrimination is not permitted where, as here, the Government "expends funds to encourage a diversity of views from private speakers."

* * *

A law that can be directed against speech found offensive to some portion of the public can be turned against minority and dissenting views to the detriment of all. The First Amendment does not entrust that power to the government's benevolence. Instead, our reliance must be on the substantial safeguards of free and open discussion in a democratic society.

For these reasons, I join the Court's opinion in part and concur in the judgment.

American Broadcasting Companies, Inc. v. Aereo, Inc.
SUPREME COURT OF THE UNITED STATES
134 S. CT. 2498 (2014)

JUSTICE STEPHEN BREYER delivered the Court's opinion:

The Copyright Act of 1976 gives a copyright owner the "exclusive righ[t]" to "perform the copyrighted work publicly." . . .

We must decide whether respondent Aereo, Inc., infringes this exclusive right by selling its subscribers a technologically complex service that allows them to watch television programs over the Internet at about the same time as the programs are broadcast over the air. We conclude that it does.

For a monthly fee, Aereo offers subscribers broadcast television programming over the Internet, virtually as the programming is being broadcast. Much of this programming is made up of copyrighted works. Aereo neither owns the copyright in those works nor holds a license from the copyright owners to perform those works publicly.

Aereo's system is made up of servers, transcoders, and thousands of dime-sized antennas housed in a central warehouse. It works roughly as follows: First, when a subscriber wants to watch a show that is currently being broadcast, he visits Aereo's website and selects, from a list of the local programming, the show he wishes to see.

Second, one of Aereo's servers selects an antenna, which it dedicates to the use of that subscriber (and that subscriber alone) for the duration of the selected show. A server then tunes the antenna to the over-the-air broadcast carrying the show. The antenna begins to receive the broadcast, and an Aereo transcoder translates the signals received into data that can be transmitted over the Internet.

Third, rather than directly send the data to the subscriber, a server saves the data in a subscriber-specific folder on Aereo's hard drive. In other words, Aereo's system creates a subscriber-specific copy—that is, a "personal" copy—of the subscriber's program of choice.

Fourth, once several seconds of programming have been saved, Aereo's server begins to stream the saved copy of the show to the subscriber over the Internet. . . . The subscriber can watch the streamed program on the screen of his personal computer, tablet, smart phone, Internet-connected television, or other Internet-connected device. The streaming continues, a mere few seconds behind the over-the-air broadcast, until the subscriber has received the entire show. . . .

Aereo emphasizes that the data that its system streams to each subscriber are the data from his own personal copy, made from the broadcast signals received by the particular antenna allotted to him. . . .

Petitioners are television producers, marketers, distributors, and broadcasters who own the copyrights in many of the programs that Aereo's system streams to its subscribers. They brought suit against Aereo for copyright infringement in Federal District Court. They sought a preliminary injunction, arguing that Aereo was infringing their right to "perform" their works "publicly," as the Transmit Clause defines those terms.

The District Court denied the preliminary injunction. Relying on prior Circuit precedent, a divided panel of the Second Circuit affirmed. In the Second Circuit's view, Aereo does not perform publicly within the meaning of the Transmit Clause because it does not transmit "to the public." Rather, each time Aereo streams a program to a subscriber, it sends a *private* transmission that is available only to that subscriber. The Second Circuit denied rehearing en banc, over the dissent of two judges. We granted certiorari.

This case requires us to answer two questions: First, in operating in the manner described above, does Aereo "perform" at all? And second, if so, does Aereo do so "publicly"? We address these distinct questions in turn.

Does Aereo "perform"? . . . Phrased another way, does Aereo "transmit . . . a performance" when a subscriber watches a show using Aereo's system, or is it only the subscriber who transmits? In Aereo's view, it does not perform. . . . Like a home antenna and DVR, Aereo's equipment simply responds to its subscribers' directives. So it is only the subscribers who "perform" when they use Aereo's equipment to stream television programs to themselves.

Considered alone, the language of the Act does not clearly indicate when an entity "perform[s]" (or "transmit[s]") and when it merely supplies equipment that allows others to do so. But when read in light of its purpose, the Act is unmistakable: An entity that engages in activities like Aereo's performs.

History makes plain that one of Congress' primary purposes in amending the Copyright Act in 1976 was to overturn this Court's determination that community antenna television (CATV) systems (the precursors of modern cable systems) fell outside the Act's scope. In *Fortnightly Corp. v. United Artists Television, Inc.* (1968), the Court considered a CATV system that carried local television broadcasting, much of which was copyrighted, to its subscribers in two cities. . . .

Asked to decide whether the CATV provider infringed copyright holders' exclusive right to perform their works publicly, the Court held that the provider did not "perform" at all. . . . The Court reasoned that CATV providers were unlike broadcasters:

> "Broadcasters select the programs to be viewed; CATV systems simply carry, without editing, whatever programs they receive. Broadcasters procure programs and propagate them to the public; CATV systems receive programs that have been released to the public and carry them by private channels to additional viewers."

Instead, CATV providers were more like viewers. . . . Viewers do not become performers by using "amplifying equipment," and a CATV provider should not be treated differently for providing viewers the same equipment.

In *Teleprompter Corp. v. Columbia Broadcasting System, Inc.* (1974), the Court considered the copyright liability of a CATV provider that carried broadcast television programming into subscribers' homes from hundreds of miles away. Although the Court recognized that a viewer might not be able to afford amplifying equipment that would provide access to those distant signals, it nonetheless found that the CATV provider was more like a viewer than a broadcaster. . . .

The Court also recognized that the CATV system exercised some measure of choice over what to transmit. But that fact did not transform the CATV system into a broadcaster. A broadcaster exercises significant creativity in choosing what to air, the Court reasoned. . . .

In 1976 Congress amended the Copyright Act in large part to reject the Court's holdings in *Fortnightly* and *Teleprompter.* . . . Congress enacted new language that erased the Court's line between broadcaster and viewer, in respect to "perform[ing]" a work. The amended statute clarifies that to "perform" an audiovisual work means "to show its images in any sequence or to make the sounds accompanying it audible." . . . Under this new language, *both* the broadcaster *and* the viewer of a television program "perform," because they both show the program's images and make audible the program's sounds. . . .

Congress also enacted the Transmit Clause, which specifies that an entity performs publicly when it "transmit[s] . . . a performance . . . to the public." Cable system activities, like those of the CATV systems in *Fortnightly* and *Teleprompter*, lie at the heart of the activities that Congress intended this language to cover. . . . The Clause thus makes clear that an entity that acts like a CATV system itself performs, even if when doing so, it simply enhances viewers' ability to receive broadcast television signals.

Congress further created a new section of the Act to regulate cable companies' public performances of copyrighted works. Section 111 creates a complex, highly detailed compulsory licensing scheme that sets out the conditions, including the payment of compulsory fees, under which cable systems may retransmit broadcasts. . . . Congress made these three changes to achieve a similar end: to bring the activities of cable systems within the scope of the Copyright Act.

This history makes clear that Aereo is not simply an equipment provider. . . . Aereo's activities are substantially similar to those of the CATV companies that Congress amended the Act to reach. . . .

We recognize, and Aereo and the dissent emphasize, one particular difference between Aereo's system and the cable systems at issue in *Fortnightly* and *Teleprompter*. The systems in those cases transmitted constantly; they sent continuous programming to each subscriber's television set. In contrast, Aereo's system remains inert until a subscriber indicates that she wants to watch a program. . . .

This is a critical difference, says the dissent. . . . In our view, however, the dissent's . . . argument, in whatever form, makes too much out of too little. . . .

Next, we must consider whether Aereo performs petitioners' works "publicly," within the meaning of the Transmit Clause. Under the Clause, an entity performs a work publicly when it "transmit[s] . . . a performance . . . of the work . . . to the public." Aereo denies that it satisfies this definition. . . .

As we have said, an Aereo subscriber receives broadcast television signals with an antenna dedicated to him alone. . . . The fact that each transmission is to only one subscriber, in Aereo's view, means that it does not transmit a performance "to the public."

. . . The text of the Clause effectuates Congress' intent. Aereo's argument to the contrary relies on the premise that "to transmit . . . a performance" means to make a single transmission. But the Clause suggests that an entity may transmit a performance through multiple, discrete transmissions. That is because one can "transmit" or "communicate" something through a *set* of actions. . . .

The fact that a singular noun ("a performance") follows the words "to transmit" does not suggest the contrary. . . .

The Transmit Clause must permit this interpretation, for it provides that one may transmit a performance to the public "whether the members of the public capable of receiving the performance . . . receive it . . . at the same time or at different times." . . .

Finally, we note that Aereo's subscribers may receive the same programs at different times and locations. This fact does not help Aereo, however, for the Transmit Clause expressly provides that an entity may perform publicly "whether the members of the public capable of receiving the performance . . . receive it in the same place or in separate places and at the same time or at different times." In other words, "the public" need not be situated together, spatially or temporally. For these reasons, we conclude that Aereo transmits a performance of petitioners' copyrighted works to the public, within the meaning of the Transmit Clause.

. . . In sum, having considered the details of Aereo's practices, we find them highly similar to those of the CATV systems in *Fortnightly* and *Teleprompter.* And those are activities that the 1976 amendments

sought to bring within the scope of the Copyright Act. Insofar as there are differences, those differences concern not the nature of the service that Aereo provides so much as the technological manner in which it provides the service. We conclude that those differences are not adequate to place Aereo's activities outside the scope of the Act.

For these reasons, we conclude that Aereo "perform[s]" petitioners' copyrighted works "publicly," as those terms are defined by the Transmit Clause. We therefore reverse the contrary judgment of the Court of Appeals, and we remand the case for further proceedings consistent with this opinion.

It is so ordered.

JUSTICE ANTONIN SCALIA, with whom JUSTICE CLARENCE THOMAS and JUSTICE SAMUEL ALITO join, dissenting.

This case is the latest skirmish in the long-running copyright battle over the delivery of television programming. . . .

There are two types of liability for copyright infringement: direct and secondary. As its name suggests, the former applies when an actor personally engages in infringing conduct. Secondary liability, by contrast, is a means of holding defendants responsible for infringement by third parties, even when the defendants "have not themselves engaged in the infringing activity." It applies when a defendant "intentionally induc[es] or encourag[es]" infringing acts by others or profits from such acts "while declining to exercise a right to stop or limit [them]."

Most suits against equipment manufacturers and service providers involve secondary-liability claims. . . .

This suit, or rather the portion of it before us here, is fundamentally different. The Networks claim that Aereo *directly* infringes their public-performance right. Accordingly, the Networks must prove that Aereo "perform[s]" copyrighted works when its subscribers log in, select a channel, and push the "watch" button. That process undoubtedly results in a performance; the question is *who* does the performing. If Aereo's subscribers perform but Aereo does not, the claim necessarily fails.

. . . A comparison between copy shops and video-on-demand services illustrates the point. A copy shop rents out photocopiers on a per-use basis.

One customer might copy his 10-year-old's drawings—a perfectly lawful thing to do—while another might duplicate a famous artist's copyrighted photographs—a use clearly prohibited. Either way, *the customer* chooses the content and activates the copying function; the photocopier does nothing except in response to the customer's commands. Because the shop plays no role in selecting the content, it cannot be held directly liable when a customer makes an infringing copy.

Video-on-demand services, like photocopiers, respond automatically to user input, but they differ in one crucial respect: *They choose the content*. When a user signs in to Netflix, for example, "thousands of . . . movies [and] TV episodes" carefully curated by Netflix are "available to watch instantly." That selection and arrangement by the service provider constitutes a volitional act directed to specific copyrighted works and thus serves as a basis for direct liability.

The distinction between direct and secondary liability would collapse if there were not a clear rule for determining whether *the defendant* committed the infringing act. . . .

So which is Aereo: the copy shop or the video-on-demand service? In truth, it is neither. Rather, it is akin to a copy shop that provides its patrons with a library card. Aereo offers access to an automated system consisting of routers, servers, transcoders, and dime-sized antennae. Like a photocopier or VCR, that system lies dormant until a subscriber activates it. . . .

Unlike video-on-demand services, Aereo does not provide a prearranged assortment of movies and television shows. Rather, it assigns each subscriber an antenna that—like a library card—can be used to obtain whatever broadcasts are freely available. Some of those broadcasts are copyrighted; others are in the public domain. The key point is that subscribers call all the shots: Aereo's automated system does not relay any program, copyrighted or not, until a subscriber selects the program and tells Aereo to relay it. Aereo's operation of that system is a volitional act and a but-for cause of the resulting performances, but, as in the case of the copy shop, that degree of involvement is not enough for direct liability.

In sum, Aereo does not "perform" for the sole and simple reason that it does not make the choice of content. And because Aereo does not perform, it cannot be held directly liable for infringing the Networks' public-performance right. That conclusion does not necessarily mean that Aereo's service complies with the Copyright Act. Quite the contrary. The Networks' complaint alleges that Aereo is directly *and* secondarily liable for infringing their public-performance rights *and also* their reproduction rights. Their request for a preliminary injunction—the only issue before this Court—is based exclusively on the direct-liability portion of the public-performance claim. . . .

The Court's conclusion that Aereo performs boils down to the following syllogism: (1) Congress amended the Act to overrule our decisions holding that cable systems do not perform when they retransmit over-the-air broadcasts; (2) Aereo looks a lot like a cable system; therefore (3) Aereo performs. . . .

I share the Court's evident feeling that what Aereo is doing (or enabling to be done) to the Networks' copyrighted programming ought not to be allowed. But perhaps we need not distort the Copyright Act to forbid it.

. . . [T]he proper course is not to bend and twist the Act's terms in an effort to produce a just outcome, but to apply the law as it stands and leave to Congress the task of deciding whether the Copyright Act needs an upgrade. . . .

I respectfully dissent.

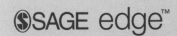

Our question is whether speech which does "no more than propose a commercial transaction" is so removed from an "exposition of ideas" and from "truth, science, morality and arts in general, in its diffusion of liberal sentiments on the administration of government," that it lacks all protection. Our answer is that it is not.

—U.S. Supreme Court Justice Harry Blackmun[1]

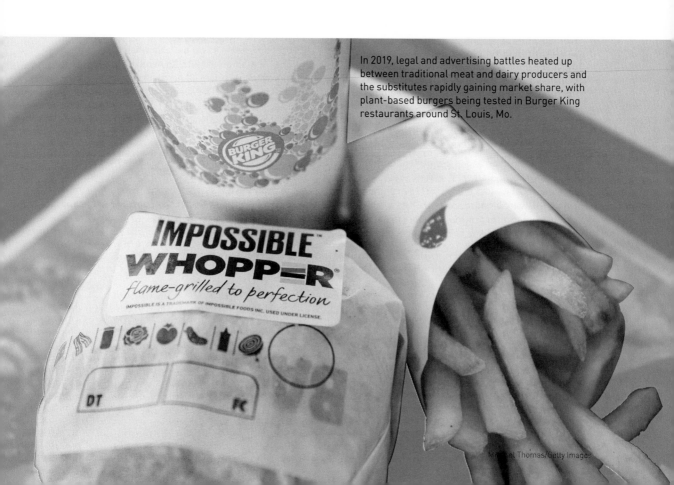

In 2019, legal and advertising battles heated up between traditional meat and dairy producers and the substitutes rapidly gaining market share, with plant-based burgers being tested in Burger King restaurants around St. Louis, Mo.

12

ADVERTISING
When Speech and Commerce Converge

SUPPOSE . . .

. . . a state law prohibits drug marketers and data-mining companies from buying doctors' prescription records from pharmacies to help protect the privacy of doctors and prevent aggressive drug marketing to them. The law allows anyone other than drug company marketers or data compilers to access the prescription records. Legislative history shows that the law is intended to encourage sales of generic over costlier brand-name drugs.[2]

Does the law regulate commerce, business activities or commercial speech? If it regulates speech, is it a constitutional use of government authority, or does it unconstitutionally target speech because of government disfavor with its content? Look for answers to these questions when the case of *Sorrell v. IMS Health, Inc.*[3] is discussed later in this chapter and excerpted at the chapter's end.

DEFINING COMMERCIAL SPEECH

Speech categories (as discussed in Chapter 3) are intended to help courts determine the proper application of First Amendment protections in specific cases. Speech categories work best to create clarity and stability in the law when they, themselves, are clear and unambiguously defined. That is not the case with commercial speech, which has evolved across decades through a series of fact-specific and sometimes confusing U.S. Supreme Court decisions.

In the 1940s and '50s, the U.S. Supreme Court reluctantly began crafting a speech category to help define the boundaries between the constitutionally approved regulation of commerce and the constitutionally protected freedom of speech. The

Commerce Clause—Article 1, Section 8 of the U.S. Constitution—enumerates to Congress the power "to regulate commerce with foreign nations, and among the several states."[4] Commerce generally is defined as the provision of goods or services in exchange for compensation, usually payment.

Commercial transactions routinely and necessarily involve speech between the parties that often begins with solicitation, promotion and advertising; encompasses negotiations, agreements and contracts; and concludes with exchange and compensation. The U.S. Supreme Court initially avoided deciding when such speech is so intricately interconnected with commerce that it is regulable and when it is not. The distinction between commercial and noncommercial speech often is complex and difficult, especially since the Supreme Court's decision in *Citizens United v. Federal Election Commission* (see Chapter 1) found that some spending is the equivalent of speech.[5]

In its ruling first suggesting the category of commercial speech 75 years ago, the U.S. Supreme Court did not use that term and only mentioned "speech" once.[6] The case involved distribution of a handbill encouraging people on the streets of New York to pay to tour a decommissioned U.S. Navy submarine docked at a city pier. City law prohibited commercial handbill distribution except when "solely devoted to information or a public protest," so the promoter printed a protest to that law on the flip side of the ad.[7] Lower courts ruled that the

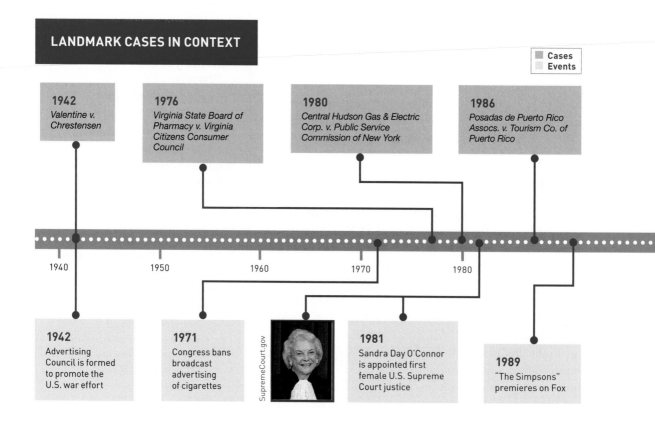

LANDMARK CASES IN CONTEXT

■ Cases
■ Events

1942
Valentine v. Chrestensen

1976
Virginia State Board of Pharmacy v. Virginia Citizens Consumer Council

1980
Central Hudson Gas & Electric Corp. v. Public Service Commission of New York

1986
Posadas de Puerto Rico Assocs. v. Tourism Co. of Puerto Rico

1940   1950   1960   1970   1980

1942
Advertising Council is formed to promote the U.S. war effort

1971
Congress bans broadcast advertising of cigarettes

SupremeCourt.gov

1981
Sandra Day O'Connor is appointed first female U.S. Supreme Court justice

1989
"The Simpsons" premieres on Fox

inclusion of this "political speech" immunized him from prosecution, but the U.S. Supreme Court reversed.

In its six-paragraph opinion in *Valentine v. Chrestensen*, the Supreme Court described the handbill as "commercial advertising" and "soliciting," as prohibited by the law, and emphasized the public's right to be free of interference on public thoroughfares.[8] By "attempting to use the streets of New York by distributing commercial advertising, the prohibition of the code provision was lawfully invoked against [the respondent's] *conduct*," the Court said.[9] Moreover, because "affixing of the protest against official conduct to the advertising circular was with the intent, and for the purpose, of evading" the law, the Court said the city could legally prevent its distribution.[10]

Many interpreted *Chrestensen* to mean that a message whose primary purpose was to promote commerce did not receive First Amendment protection. Then, in *Breard v. Alexandria*, the Supreme Court upheld a law banning unsolicited door-to-door sales of magazines.[11] The Court acknowledged the First Amendment value of magazines but reasoned that the "primary purpose" of the activity was commercial and, therefore, regulable.[12]

New York Times Co. v. Sullivan, which involved a paid ad promoting the civil rights movement in the midst of violent, national upheaval (see Chapter 2), presented the question of whether the payment for the ad or the nature of the message established its primary purpose.[13]

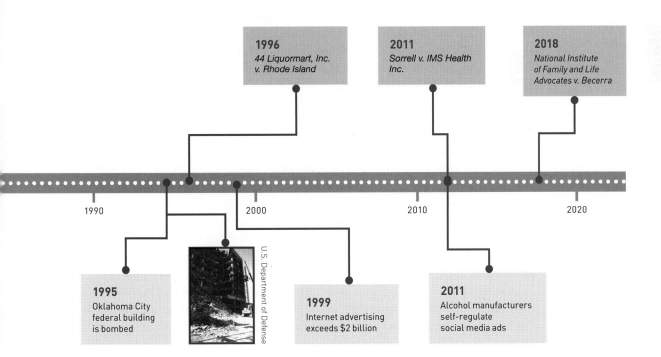

1996
44 Liquormart, Inc. v. Rhode Island

2011
Sorrell v. IMS Health Inc.

2018
National Institute of Family and Life Advocates v. Becerra

1990 2000 2010 2020

1995
Oklahoma City federal building is bombed

U.S. Department of Defense

1999
Internet advertising exceeds $2 billion

2011
Alcohol manufacturers self-regulate social media ads

In its landmark ruling in *Sullivan*, the U.S. Supreme Court distinguished the civil rights ad from *Chrestensen*'s overt "commercial advertising." The Court described the *Sullivan* ad as communicating information and opinions and seeking support "on behalf of a movement whose existence and objectives are matters of the highest public interest and concern."[14] The fact "that the Times was paid for publishing the advertisement is as immaterial in this connection as is the fact that newspapers and books are sold," the Court concluded.[15] While recognizing the often multiple and complicated nature of paid messages, the Court in *Sullivan* affirmed the notion that government could regulate commercial messages more readily than noncommercial messages.

In a subsequent case, the Supreme Court said the holding in *Chrestensen* was limited and established only that government could regulate "the *manner* in which commercial advertising could be distributed."[16] In *Bigelow v. Virginia*, as in *Sullivan*, the Court looked beyond commercial motivation to the political nature and public interest in advertising about legal abortions in New York state to determine that neither payment for nor the format of such commercial speech deprived it of First Amendment protection.[17] The *Bigelow* decision used the commercial purpose of the ad as a factor to be balanced against the public interest in the speech and "clearly establish[ed] that speech is not stripped of First Amendment protection merely because it appears in [the] form" of paid commercial advertisements.[18] The Court said *Chrestensen* had never been intended to permit any and all government regulation of commercial advertising.[19]

The Supreme Court overturned *Chrestensen* and provided commercial speech explicit First Amendment protection in *Virginia State Board of Pharmacy v. Virginia Citizens Consumer Council*.[20] Reviewing a Virginia state ban on pharmacists' advertising of prescription drug prices, the Court said the ban violated the public's right to receive factual information and the need for a free flow of commercial information to aid intelligent consumer decisions.[21] The Court clarified that commercial speech does not fall "wholly outside the protection" of the First Amendment.[22] Commercial speech has value within the economic marketplace and as a venue for debate.[23] The Court explained,

> If there is a kind of commercial speech that lacks all First Amendment protection,
> therefore, it must be distinguished by its content. Yet the speech whose content
> deprives it of protection cannot simply be speech on a commercial subject. . . . [The]
> question is whether speech [that] does no more than propose a commercial
> transaction is so removed from any exposition of ideas and from truth, science,
> morality, and arts in general, in its diffusion of liberal sentiments on the
> administration of government that it lacks all protection.[24]

In a test that looked something like intermediate scrutiny, the U.S. Supreme Court found the government's asserted interest in fostering high professional standards among pharmacists insufficient to support a ban on price advertising and found the law overbroad in achieving its stated goal. The Court added that its ruling allowed the government to continue to regulate false, deceptive or misleading speech that was "*purely* commercial."[25]

Applying this reasoning, the Court then struck down laws prohibiting "for sale" signs on lawns, ads for contraceptives and lawyer advertising.[26] In the last of these, however, the Supreme Court said that "there are commonsense differences between commercial speech and other varieties" of speech that make commercial speech more resilient in the face of government regulation.[27] In another case involving attorney solicitation of clients, the Court said that it "afforded commercial speech a limited measure of protection, commensurate with its subordinate position in the scale of First Amendment values."[28]

Some 40 years after its initial foray into commercial speech, the U.S. Supreme Court had failed to define the category clearly. In *Central Hudson Gas & Electric Corp. v. Public Service Commission*, the decision widely touted as the cornerstone of modern commercial speech law, the Court said commercial speech was "expression related *solely* to the economic interests of the speaker and its audience" and/or "speech proposing a commercial transaction."[29] The Supreme Court described commercial speech as generally an advertisement for the sale of goods and services.[30] That ambiguous definition remains to this day.

> **POINTS OF LAW**
> ### THE 1976 U.S. SUPREME COURT DEFINITION OF COMMERCIAL SPEECH
>
> More than half a century ago, the U.S. Supreme Court decision in *Virginia State Board of Pharmacy v. Virginia Citizens Consumer Council* said the purely commercial speech that warranted reduced First Amendment protection
>
> 1. did nothing more than propose a commercial transaction and
>
> 2. was unrelated to the exploration of ideas, truth, science and the arts.[i]

Today, ads come in a wide variety of forms and media, with many intended to be difficult to recognize or avoid.[31] **Native advertising**, which represented the greatest share of the roughly $44 billion online advertising market in 2019,[32] disguises commercial advertising content by mirroring the tone, style and design of the nonadvertising copy in which it is embedded. Sponsored content, a subcategory of native advertising, is paid for by a third party but written to echo the editorial content of the site or publication in which it appears.[33] The Wall Street Journal, BuzzFeed, HuffPost and others have employees dedicated to generating this paid content.[34] All of this content may be categorized as commercial speech, as are the tweets and posts of celebrities who receive compensation for saying they love Gucci shoes or for posing in front of a Casper Sleep mattress.[35]

native advertising Ads designed to resemble the editorial content of the medium where they appear.

Ads are difficult to identify today for another reason. As advertising and promotion have grown in their economic impact, they also have taken on social issues like "toxic masculinity," teen suicide and gun control.[36] Some publicists argue that the resulting public controversy strategically fuels both the viewing and the impact of ads, even if it requires public relations teams to step in to smooth ruffled feathers.[37] This mingling of commerce with public issues also moves the speech away from being "*purely* commercial," which the U.S. Supreme Court has said may be regulated.

Lower courts struggle to define what is, and is not, commercial speech. In one case, the Fifth Circuit Court of Appeals ruled that one company's claim that the chief employee of another firm was a "deadbeat dad" was commercial speech because the individual "made [the posted comment] with the economic interest of harming" the other's business.[38] The court held that the First Amendment permitted legal action against the commenter.[39]

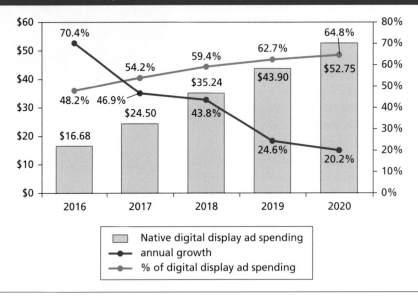

FIGURE 12.1 ■ U.S. Native Digital Display Ad Spending, 2016–2020 (in billions of dollars)

Source: eMarketer, March 2019.

In another recent case, former Chicago Bulls star Michael Jordan sued a grocery store for printing his photograph and a message congratulating him for being inducted into the Basketball Hall of Fame in a magazine ad bearing the store's logo and marketing slogan.[40] Without determining the store's liability, the Seventh Circuit Court of Appeals found that the paid content was commercial speech even though it did not "propose a commercial transaction."[41] On remand, the trial court found for the store.[42]

When Army Sgt. Jeffrey Sarver sued the producers of the Oscar-winning film "The Hurt Locker" for appropriating his image as a lead character, he categorized the film as commercial speech that deserved reduced First Amendment protection. The Ninth Circuit Court of Appeals disagreed. It said the film was not commercial speech because it did not propose a commercial transaction.[43]

When the Enigma Software Group sued Bleeping Computer for false advertising through its online forum discussing software firms and products, Bleeping moved for dismissal, claiming that user comments were not commercial speech.[44] The federal district court, however, said a "hybrid" combination of commercial and noncommercial speech could be regulated under commercial speech standards if the (1) advertisement (2) referenced a specific product or service (3) to advance the speaker's economic interests.[45] Because the user comments "lambasted" Enigma and recommended "a trustworthy alternative," the court said the false advertising claim could proceed to trial.[46]

TESTING COMMERCIAL SPEECH PROTECTION

In the 1970s, the U.S. Supreme Court established that when truthful commercial speech is of core public interest, the First Amendment protection for the speech outweighs the government's interest in regulating advertising.[47] But the Court did not make clear exactly what level of First Amendment protection such nondeceptive advertising enjoys.

In *Central Hudson*, the Court designed a new test. The *Central Hudson* test established that regulation of (1) nondeceptive advertising for legal products and services is constitutional *only* if (2) government demonstrates a "substantial" state interest in the regulation, (3) the regulation "directly advance[s]" that interest and (4) the regulation is "no more extensive than necessary to serve that interest."[48] Applying the new test, which bears a striking resemblance to the *O'Brien* test for content-neutral regulations of speech (see Chapter 2),[49] the Court found a New York state ban on energy-use advertising unconstitutional.

In *Posadas de Puerto Rico Associates v. Tourism Co. of Puerto Rico*, the U.S. Supreme Court walked through the steps it set out in *Central Hudson*. It first reaffirmed that "commercial speech receives a limited form of First Amendment protection so long as it concerns a lawful activity and is not misleading or fraudulent."[50] The advertising at issue in *Posadas* was for casino gambling, a lawful activity for the targeted residents of Puerto Rico, and the ad was neither misleading nor fraudulent. Such commercial speech "may be restricted only if the government's interest in doing so is substantial, the restrictions directly advance the government's asserted interest, and the restrictions are no more extensive than necessary to serve that interest," the Court said.[51]

The government interest in regulating casino advertising was to reduce demand from Puerto Rico residents for casino gambling, and the Supreme Court said this "interest in the health, safety and welfare of its citizens constitutes a 'substantial' governmental interest" as required under *Central Hudson*.[52] The remainder of the test examines

> the "fit" between the legislature's *ends* and the *means* chosen to accomplish those ends. Step three asks . . . whether the challenged restrictions on commercial speech "directly advance" the government's asserted interest. . . . [T]he restrictions on advertising of casino gambling "directly advance" the legislature's interest in reducing demand for games of chance. . . . [T]he legislature felt that for Puerto Ricans the risks associated with casino gambling were significantly greater than those associated with the more traditional kinds of gambling in Puerto Rico. In our view, the legislature's separate classification of casino gambling, for purposes of the advertising ban, satisfies the third step of the *Central Hudson* analysis.[53]

The Court said the regulation certainly passed the final step of the test as "no more extensive than necessary" because the law was aimed only at residents, not tourists, and because the Puerto Rico Legislature surely could have prohibited casino gambling by the residents of Puerto Rico altogether. "In our view, the greater power to completely ban casino gambling necessarily includes the lesser power to ban advertising of casino gambling."[54]

The U.S. Supreme Court has tinkered with, clarified or altered the "fit," or "no more extensive than necessary," requirement of the *Central Hudson* test almost since its adoption. In *Board of Trustees of the State University of New York v. Fox*, the Court attempted to clarify that element of the test.[55] In *Fox*, the Court said advertising regulation did not need to employ the "least restrictive means" available.[56] Instead, regulation must demonstrate a "reasonable fit" to the state interest. Citing *Posadas*, the Court explained, "What our decisions require is a 'fit' between the legislature's ends and the means chosen to accomplish those ends—a fit that is not necessarily perfect, but reasonable."[57] This revision displayed deference to legislative judgments and made it easier for advertising regulations to be found constitutional.

In subsequent commercial speech rulings, the U.S. Supreme Court tried to help lower courts grapple with the determination. It said a law does not "fit" its objective when alternatives are available "which could advance the government's asserted interest in a manner less intrusive to . . . First Amendment rights."[58] Alternately, "the scope of the restriction on speech must be reasonably, though it need not be perfectly, targeted to address the harm intended to be regulated."[59] Or the required match between the law and its goals must be one of "narrow tailoring" where courts "carefully calculate the costs and benefits associated with the burden on speech."[60] It's a matter of "proportionality," some justices said.[61] And in the case of *Sorrell v. IMS Health, Inc.* (discussed again later and excerpted at the end of the chapter), the Court sidestepped the definition of fit to explain its objective: the proper "fit" ensures "not only that the State's interests are proportional to the resulting burdens placed on speech but also that the law does not seek to suppress a disfavored message."[62]

Lower courts and scholars criticized the Supreme Court's shifting definition of *Central Hudson*'s required "fit" because it made consistent decisions difficult and altered the level of First Amendment protection given to truthful commercial speech about legal products.

The U.S. Supreme Court further increased confusion about the protection of commercial speech in cases where it considered the nature of the advertised product. In *44 Liquormart, Inc. v. Rhode Island*, a case about the state's ban on price advertising for alcohol, the Supreme Court emphasized that government could not ban advertising even for dangerous or disfavored "vice" products, such as alcohol, "to keep people in the dark for what the government perceives to be their own good."[63] The Court said advertising bans were the most egregious regulatory approach and courts should use "special care" in review of their use to achieve government goals unrelated to the speech involved.[64] Justice Clarence Thomas went further; he said all regulations that prohibit truthful advertising for legal products are per se unconstitutional.[65]

Then, in *Sorrell v. IMS Health, Inc.*, the Supreme Court said strict scrutiny applies to government attempts to prohibit dissemination of truthful, nonmisleading information about a lawful product even when the speech is commercial.[66] The Vermont law at issue placed a ban on the sale, disclosure and use of the prescribing patterns of physicians. The law specifically sought to prevent drug marketers from using information gathered by pharmacists about which drugs specific doctors prescribed to tailor their marketing and promotional efforts.[67] Both the marketers for pharmaceutical companies and the data-mining firms that collected and sold the prescribing information challenged the law as a First Amendment violation.

The Supreme Court identified the law as both a content- and a speaker-based restriction on speech as well as an attempt to prohibit certain uses of truthful information. After acknowledging *Central Hudson*'s intermediate-level scrutiny as the standard test for review of restrictions on commercial speech, the Court said that "commercial speech, including advertising, has an informational function and is not valueless in the marketplace of ideas."[68] The Court then said that "strict" or "heightened" scrutiny was the appropriate standard to review "a specific, content-based burden on protected expression."[69] Strict scrutiny was justified, the Court said, because the government was trying to suppress the flow of information "out of disagreement with the message it conveys."[70]

Examining the law as a content-based regulation, the Court found the law unconstitutional without relying on its commercial speech precedents.[71] In passing, at the end of its lengthy decision, the Court dismissed its commercial speech decisions as relevant only to laws with a "neutral justification" intended to prevent "commercial harms" or false, deceptive or misleading advertising.[72] In broad disagreement, the dissent said the law was an economic regulation that should be upheld if it used a reasonable means to achieve the government's objective.[73]

Scholars have called *Sorrell* "incoherent," arguing that it introduced "a new rationale so jarring"[74] that it "pinched the already-narrow space between the First Amendment protection accorded commercial and non-commercial speech."[75] Some said the decision eviscerated well-developed precedent that speech intended solely to generate profits and sales should not receive the full constitutional protection afforded to political, artistic or scientific speech.[76] Only a year after it was handed down, observers said the *Sorrell* decision led courts to heighten the scrutiny applied to laws that regulated truthful, nondeceptive advertising, twisting the outcomes in cases on both advertising and product labeling.[77]

Circuit courts seemed uncertain when to apply *Sorrell* and when to rely on *Central Hudson*. For example, the Ninth Circuit Court of Appeals recently remanded a case with guidance to review a California restriction on alcohol advertising under *Sorrell*'s heightened scrutiny.[78] A year earlier, the Ninth Circuit said the *Central Hudson* test should apply to consideration of whether an ordinance restricting in-window alcohol advertising by stores along a pedestrian mall "fit" the city's stated goals.[79]

Ruling after *Sorrell*, an en banc D.C. Circuit Court of Appeals also applied the *Central Hudson* test, ignoring its "directly advances" element, to affirm the constitutionality of U.S. Department of Agriculture meat-labeling requirements.[80] The court said the merchants' minimal First Amendment interest in refusing to disclose factual information was easily overcome by the consumer benefits of the information.[81]

POINTS OF LAW

THE *CENTRAL HUDSON* TEST AFTER *SORRELL*

In *Sorrell v. IMS Health, Inc.*,[iii] the U.S. Supreme Court instructed courts ruling on the constitutionality of a commercial speech regulation to ask:

1. Is the commercial speech false or related to an illegal activity?
   a. If yes, the speech may be banned or strictly regulated.
   b. If no, proceed with the test.
2. Is the regulation of commercial speech based on its content?
   a. If yes, the court must apply heightened, or strict, scrutiny and presume that the regulation is unconstitutional.
   b. If no, proceed with the test.
3. Is the regulation of commercial speech content neutral?
   a. If yes, the court must apply the *Central Hudson*[iv] test and strike down the regulation unless the answer to all of the following is yes.
      i. Does the rule relate to a significant government interest?
      ii. Does the rule directly advance that government interest?
      iii. Is the regulation unrelated to the suppression of speech?
      iv. Does the regulation "fit" the government interest without unduly infringing on speech?

This new standard makes it very difficult for regulations of truthful commercial speech to survive First Amendment review unless the speech promotes an illegal activity.

COMPELLING COMMERCIAL SPEECH

For more than 30 years, the U.S. Supreme Court has held that government efforts to compel speech and government efforts to silence speech are equally suspect. The freedom of speech "necessarily compris[es] the decision of both what to say and what not to say," the Supreme Court said.[82] Government-mandated disclosures—such as loyalty oaths, safety recall notifications or cigarette warning labels—threaten First Amendment freedoms in two ways. First, they alter the speaker's coherent message. "For instance, by compelling newspaper editors or parade organizers to include certain material," they "unduly intrude" on the editors' or organizers' ability to communicate their chosen message.[83] Second, they force a speaker to declare something as fact that the speaker disputes.[84] Mandated speech also prevents silence by those who prefer not to speak at all. The U.S. Supreme Court has said that speech mandates are content-based regulations subject to strict scrutiny review.[85]

However, for the past three-plus decades, the Supreme Court has applied a relaxed standard of review to government mandates for "purely factual and uncontroversial" commercial

REAL WORLD LAW

UNCERTAIN TRUTHS, LABELS AND LAWSUITS

Monsanto's multimillion-dollar 2019 advertising campaign defended its popular weed killer, Roundup, against lawsuits that the product causes cancer.[v] Roundup product labels also stated that the active ingredient, "glysophate, targets an enzyme found in plants but not in people or pets."[vi]

California was the first state to list glysophate as an agent that may cause cancer, requiring product warning labels.[vii] A federal judge in 2018 blocked the required labeling because Monsanto likely would win its First Amendment argument that the label was controversial and could mislead consumers.[viii]

In 2019, a California jury ordered Monsanto to pay $2 billion to a couple who said using Roundup according to label instructions caused their cancer.[ix] Soon after, Monsanto sought to relocate Roundup trials outside the reach of California's "liberal" consumer-protection laws.[x]

disclosures.[86] In *Zauderer v. Office of Disciplinary Counsel of Supreme Court of Ohio*, the Court established that

> [b]ecause the extension of First Amendment protection to commercial speech is justified principally by the value to consumers of the information such speech provides . . . [and the advertiser's] protected interest in *not* providing any particular factual information in his advertising is minimal, [the government has some freedom] to prescribe what shall be orthodox in commercial advertising.[87]

When government requires only truthful, uncontroversial commercial information intended to assist informed consumer choice, courts should defer to the government's judgment, the Supreme Court held. Required factual disclosures infringe "much more narrowly" on the First Amendment interests of commercial speakers than other forms of compelled speech, the Court said, so government may require warnings or disclaimers that are "reasonably related to the state's interest in preventing deception of consumers."[88]

Lower courts struggled to distinguish *Zauderer*'s purely factual disclosures needing only rational review from government mandates that imposed intrusive or ideological messages that triggered strict scrutiny review.[89] The courts did not agree on how to apply *Zauderer*'s lesser review for an "uncontroversial" disclosure that (1) was factually accurate or (2) reflected a commonly accepted understanding.[90] Some limited *Zauderer* review to disclosures intended to prevent deception.[91] Others applied *Zauderer* to disclosures that informed consumers of basic information, such as product origin.[92]

In 2018, in *National Institute of Family and Life Advocates v. Becerra*, the Supreme Court suggested that *Zauderer*'s departure from strict scrutiny review of government-compelled commercial disclosures should apply narrowly and only to disclosures that were unrelated to a subject of disagreement.[93] In *NIFLA*, the Supreme Court struck down a California law requiring commercial, pregnancy-crisis centers to provide factual information about public abortion services without deciding what standard of review applied.[94] The Court explained that compelled disclosures must "remedy a harm that is *potentially real* not purely hypothetical" and be "no broader than reasonably necessary" to survive constitutional review.[95] California could not require pro-life centers to inform women of low-cost abortions, the Court said, because the state had failed to draft a narrow law that served a substantial state interest.

In 2018, the Supreme Court's one-sentence opinion in *CTIA—The Wireless Association v. City of Berkeley* instructed the Ninth Circuit Court of Appeals to reconsider a Berkeley city commercial speech mandate and to use *NIFLA* rather than *Zauderer* to guide the outcome. The Berkeley ordinance required cellphone retailers to tell customers that carrying a cellphone in certain ways could expose them to radiation beyond Federal Communications Commission recommended limits.[96]

The Ninth Circuit had relied on the *Zauderer* test even though the required disclosure was not justified by the need to prevent consumer deception.[97] The circuit court reasoned that both the FCC and the city had found a substantial interest "in this compelled disclosure [that] is reasonably related to protection of the health and safety of consumers."[98] The court said the purpose of the forced disclosure did not need to be prevention of consumer deception. "Any governmental interest will suffice so long as it is substantial, . . . given that the purpose of the compelled disclosure is to provide accurate factual information to the consumer."[99] The U.S. Supreme Court disagreed and remanded the case. On reconsideration in 2019, the Ninth Circuit again said the disclosure requirement did not violate CTIA's First Amendment rights.[100]

Prior to the Supreme Court's *NIFLA* and *CTIA* opinions, the Ninth Circuit Court of Appeals had relied on *Zauderer* to find that the First Amendment challenge to a San Francisco ordinance requiring health warnings on sugar-sweetened beverage products and their fixed advertising (billboards) was likely to succeed because the ordinance "was unjustified or unduly burdensome."[101] The Ninth Circuit found that a health warning on soda pop and other sweetened beverages but not on other sugar-laden food products was neither an "uncontroversial" nor a "purely factual" disclosure, as *Zauderer* requires.[102] When rehearing the case late in 2018, the Ninth Circuit suggested that it might remand it for reconsideration in light of *NIFLA*.[103]

PROMOTING DISFAVORED PRODUCTS

vice products
Products related to activities generally considered unhealthy or immoral or whose use is restricted by age or other condition. The category includes alcohol, tobacco, firearms, sexually explicit materials and drugs.

Controversial commercial speech—such as advertising for **vice products** or advertising to susceptible audiences—is a prime arena for testing the limits of constitutional protection for commercial speech. The U.S. Supreme Court must often determine the limits of permissible regulation of advertising for alcohol, tobacco, drugs, gambling, guns and, more recently, marijuana.

Tobacco

The Lorillard brothers began advertising their tobacco products in a New York daily newspaper in 1789. Nearly two centuries later, the D.C. Circuit Court of Appeals ruled that the federal Public Health Cigarette Smoking Act's ban on broadcast TV and radio ads for cigarettes did not violate the free speech rights of tobacco companies because other outlets existed for their advertising.[104] The appeals court said the government had the power to regulate tobacco advertising to protect minors and others from the lure of tobacco. Tobacco producers responded by increasing advertising via print media, billboards and other means.

More recently, Lorillard Tobacco Co. challenged a Massachusetts law that limited point-of-sale tobacco ads and banned outdoor tobacco ads within 1,000 feet of schools or playgrounds. The U.S. Supreme Court reviewed the law under *Central Hudson* and held that the limits on ads at the point of purchase advanced a legitimate state interest in preventing minors from accessing tobacco products that were illegal for them to consume. In *Lorillard Tobacco Co. v. Reilly*, the Court said the restrictions addressed a state interest "unrelated to the communication of ideas."[105] However, the ban on outdoor advertising was unconstitutional because it did not reasonably fit the state's interest.

In 2013, a quarter century after federal law prohibited cigarette ads on TV, R.J. Reynolds Tobacco Co. launched a campaign for its e-cigarette, Vuse.

In 2017, one federal district court upheld the authority of the Food and Drug Administration (discussed later in this chapter) to regulate all tobacco products, including cigars, e-cigarettes and vaping materials.[106] The Trump administration, however, blocked enforcement of new FDA rules that prohibited the sale of cigars, e-cigarettes and vaping materials to anyone under 18 and required the products to provide ingredient labels, addictiveness warnings and proof of claims that they were "light" or "mild."[107] At least one First Amendment challenge to the FDA rules was pending in mid-2019.[108]

Gambling

The case of *Posadas* discussed earlier involved casino advertising in Puerto Rico, where gambling is legal.[109] But a few years later, the U.S. Supreme Court reviewed the constitutionality of a federal law that banned a radio station in North Carolina, where gambling was illegal, from advertising lotteries even when most of the station's listeners lived in Virginia, where lotteries were legal. The station was only three miles from Virginia.

The U.S. Supreme Court upheld the ban, finding that the state power to ban gambling provided a legitimate government interest in discouraging gambling promotion.[110] The Court said that

> Congress surely knew that stations in one state could often be heard in another
> but expressly prevented each and every North Carolina station, including Edge,
> from carrying lottery ads . . . [because] each North Carolina station would have an
> audience in that state, even if its signal reached elsewhere.[111]

In addition to finding that the state's greater power to ban gambling encompassed the lesser power to ban its promotion, the Court said that the radio station's audience-based argument "has no logical stopping point once state boundaries are ignored." The Court declined "to start down that road."[112]

Alcohol

More than 20 years ago, when Coors Brewing Co. wanted to advertise and label its beer with the percentage of alcohol content, a federal law stood in the way. Coors challenged the law on First Amendment grounds, and the federal government said the law was a reasonable means to prevent "strength wars" that might increase beer potency and harm society. In *Rubin v. Coors Brewing Co.*, the U.S. Supreme Court held for Coors.[113] The Court said that while combating "strength wars" might be a substantial interest, a ban on alcohol content advertising or labeling did not "fit" that goal as well as would alternatives "less intrusive to the First Amendment's protections for commercial speech."[114]

In the case of *44 Liquormart, Inc. v. Rhode Island* mentioned earlier, Rhode Island fined a liquor store owner who tried to evade a state ban on ads that made "reference to the price" of liquor by placing the exclamation "Wow" instead of prices next to bargain products in newspaper ads. The owner raised a First Amendment challenge to the law, and the state argued that the ban advanced the government's substantial interest in promoting temperance by preventing bargain-priced alcohol promotions designed to increase consumption.

The U.S. Supreme Court favored the liquor store.[115] The Court first surveyed "the role commercial speech has long played" in American culture,[116] noted the Court's own long-standing hostility to commercial speech regulation of this type and "decline[d] to give force to [the] highly deferential approach" the Court utilized in *Posadas*.[117] It concluded that the state's

---

REAL WORLD LAW
DOES ADVERTISING INCREASE PRODUCT DEMAND?

A key justification for government regulation of advertising is that it alters consumer choices and increases product demand. Policy and empirical studies find mixed results. One study suggested that advertising increases demand for cigarettes. Another found that alcohol advertising instead shifts consumption among brands.[xi] The Food and Drug Administration found a correlation between advertising and increased product demand, but other federal agencies were "not convinced."[xii]

Nonetheless, U.S. Supreme Court's rulings have reasoned that

- companies "believe that promotion would increase sales";[xiii]

- legislatures have a "reasonable" belief that advertising "would serve to increase the demand for the product advertised";[xiv] and

- "[p]roduct advertising stimulates demand for products, while suppressed advertising may have the opposite effect."[xv]

"paternalistic assumption that the public will use truthful, non-misleading commercial information unwisely cannot justify a decision to suppress it."[118] The Supreme Court ruled the law unconstitutional because it did "not agree with the assertion that the price advertising ban [would] significantly advance the state's interest in promoting temperance."[119]

Almost 25 years later, the Fourth Circuit Court of Appeals held that Virginia's ban on alcohol ads in college newspapers violated the First Amendment because it was not narrowly tailored to the state's interest in reducing alcohol abuse on college campuses.[120] The same court earlier held that the ban was facially constitutional.[121] The later decision found the regulation was unconstitutional as applied because most readers of the Virginia Tech newspaper were 21 or older. Both the newspaper and its readers "have a protected interest" in "truthful, non-misleading" alcohol advertising, the court ruled.

Prescription Drugs

The U.S. Supreme Court applied strict scrutiny in its recent review of a Vermont law that prohibited only certain marketers from buying doctors' prescription records from pharmacies.[122] The state law limited access to specific brand-name drug sales data to protect doctors' privacy and prevent drug marketing designed to quash demand for cheaper generic drugs.[123] In *Sorrell v. IMS Health, Inc.* (discussed earlier and excerpted at the end of this chapter), the Supreme Court found that "the state has burdened a form of protected expression that it found too persuasive. At the same time, the state has left unburdened those speakers whose messages are in accord with its own views. This the state cannot do."[124]

Guns

A California law established that "[n]o handgun or imitation handgun, or placard advertising the sale or other transfer thereof, shall be displayed in any part of [commercial] premises where it can readily be seen from the outside."[125] When two gun stores were forced to remove in-store signs, the owners sued. Applying *Central Hudson,* a federal trial court in California said the advertising at issue was lawful and nonmisleading and the state's interest in reducing handgun suicide was substantial.[126] However, the court found "paternalistic" and "highly speculative" the government's theory

> that an impulsive person will see a handgun sign outside a store, will impulsively buy the gun (although the Government does not identify a specific purpose for the purchase), and then, at some unspecified future time likely years later, the person's impulsive temperament will lead him to impulsively misuse the handgun that he bought in response to seeing the sign.[127]

The law was unconstitutional, the court concluded, because it did not substantially advance the state's legitimate interest and was intended to suppress truthful speech that the government found too persuasive. In an earlier ruling, the court said the First Amendment challenge to the law would likely succeed because the state's goals of dampening demand and reducing violence were tenuous and only indirectly advanced by limiting the merchants' speech.[128]

ADVERTISING ON GOVERNMENT PROPERTY

A number of recent cases address the rights of individuals, especially proponents of controversial positions, to advertise in space offered by the government. Case outcomes vary with those favoring advertisers often determined by the nature of speech involved and those favoring government focused on the nature of the forum. For example, a divided Ninth Circuit Court of Appeals upheld the authority of Seattle Metro Transit to prohibit ads on its buses that criticized Israeli policies toward Palestinians.[129] In rejecting ads that read "ISRAELI WAR CRIMES . . . YOUR TAX DOLLARS AT WORK," the court said the county applied viewpoint-neutral, content-based review of speech in a limited public forum. The SMT ruling responded to "real and substantial" fears that the ads' display "presented a reasonably foreseeable threat of disruption" to transit passengers.[130]

The First Circuit Court of Appeals also affirmed a Massachusetts ban on ads that "demean or disparage" individuals or groups from its transit vehicles.[131] One banned ad read "IN ANY WAR BETWEEN THE CIVILIZED MAN AND THE SAVAGE, SUPPORT THE CIVILIZED MAN. ★ SUPPORT ISRAEL ★ DEFEAT JIHAD." The court said the ad space was a nonpublic forum and the ban a constitutional application of "reasonable, viewpoint-neutral limits."

In contrast, a federal district court ruled that the Philadelphia public transit authority's refusal to display ads that read "Islamic Jew-Hatred: It's in the Quran. Two Thirds of All US Aid Goes to Islamic Countries" violated the First Amendment.[132] The court reasoned that the ad was "exactly the sort of political expression that lies at the heart of the First Amendment . . . regardless of its alleged falsity."[133] The court then enjoined the city's ban on the ads.[134]

PROMOTING AND PUBLICIZING BUSINESSES AND PROFESSIONALS

The U.S. Supreme Court has distinguished the First Amendment right of a business to communicate political messages from its commercial speech. For example, when a bank wanted to pay to support a voter referendum, including public advertising for it, the Supreme Court affirmed the bank's constitutional right.[135] Relying on the public's right to free-flowing information and the nearly impossible differentiation of media companies from others, the Court provided businesses' noncommercial speech with greater protection than afforded under the commercial speech doctrine.[136] The Supreme Court's decision in *Citizens United v. Federal Election Commission* (see Chapters 1 and 2) also increased the First Amendment protection for corporate funding of political speech.[137]

Some years ago, in the midst of a large public controversy about Nike's offshore factories, Nike issued press releases and letters to newspapers and university athletic directors in an attempt to place itself in a positive light. In *Nike, Inc. v. Kasky*, the U.S. Supreme Court was asked to determine whether Nike's published communications responding to accusations of illegal, unsafe and abusive conditions in its overseas plants could be punished as false advertising.[138]

The trial court dismissed the case, but the California Supreme Court ruled that the speech contained statements of fact that might be punishable under the state's false advertising and unfair competition laws. The court said Nike's published statements to potential customers were commercial speech intended to maintain or increase sales.[139] Nike appealed to the U.S. Supreme Court and argued that, even if false, its speech was political and protected by the First Amendment. The Supreme Court dismissed the case without addressing the core question. Nike reportedly settled and paid $1.5 million to the Fair Labor Association.

Workers in a Nike factory near Ho Chi Minh City, Vietnam.

Corporate, business and professional ads designed to enhance sales and revenue generally are commercial speech. When state bar associations of lawyers and judges prohibited advertising by lawyers, the U.S. Supreme Court struck down the ban.[140] The Court said the absolute prohibition on truthful advertising was unconstitutional, although "[r]easonable" restrictions—such as those pertaining to false advertising—might survive First Amendment scrutiny."[141] The Court did not indicate how it would review professional association limits on advertising by professionals in other fields, such as public relations or marketing.

When a dentist with a specialty in endodontics was denied permission to list both "dentist" and "endodontist" on his signs, he raised a First Amendment challenge to the Ohio law that prohibited dentists from advertising both general and specialized practices. The trial court dismissed the claim, but the Sixth Circuit Court of Appeals reversed. It instructed the trial court to apply the *Central Hudson* test, which it said must place the burden on the government to justify the law's restraint of speech.[142]

In recent decades, corporate and professional self-promotion and branding have grown in economic and social importance, and business and professional advertising and publicity campaigns have stepped increasingly into public debates on social issues like teen suicide and gun control.[143] If such advertising goes awry, it may or may not land companies in court, but some publicists argue that the public attention and even legal controversy effectively increase both the viewing and the impact of their commercial messages.[144] For example, Gillette's recent "The Best Men Can Be" ad campaign targeting "toxic masculinity" generated a lot of buzz, although it did not lead to obviously increased sales.[145] That slogan is also an example of **puffery**.

Puffed-up claims that a company, its products or its benefits for consumers are the best or the greatest generally are legal if they do not imply factual claims. When they suggest facts or involve competitors, they can generate lawsuits that are expensive. In one recent case, a Papa John's ad campaign with the slogan "Better Ingredients. Better Pizza." claimed the company used "clear filtered water," while its competition used "whatever comes out of the tap."[146] Pizza Hut sued.

puffery
Exaggerated but generally legal subjective advertising claims that no reasonable person would take literally.

At trial, the jury said the slogan was puffery consumers would not take literally, but the claims about competitors were misleading. The Fifth Circuit Court of Appeals agreed. It described puffery as the perfectly legal "exaggerated advertising, blustering and boasting by a manufacturer upon which no consumer could reasonably rely."[147] However, the court said that when the slogan was combined with Papa John's claims about the quality of its dough and sauce, the slogan changed from legal puffery into fact statements about the comparative superiority of its ingredients over those of competitors that could be legally actionable.[148]

RESTRICTING FALSE OR MISLEADING COMMERCIAL SPEECH

deceptive advertising Material claims made in the promotion, advertising or marketing of products or services that are likely to deceive consumers.

Since the 1970s, the U.S. Supreme Court has provided increasing First Amendment protection for commercial speech. Neither the definition of the category nor the precise test applied to government constraints on commercial speech is clear and stable, but the Court has steadfastly held that the Constitution does not protect false or **deceptive advertising**.[149] In *Virginia State Board of Pharmacy*, the Supreme Court established that government could regulate commercial lies and deceptions because

> the advertiser's access to the truth about his product and its price substantially eliminates any danger that governmental regulation of false or misleading price or product advertising will chill accurate and nondeceptive commercial expression. There is, therefore, little need to sanction some falsehood in order to protect speech that matters.[150]

The Court developed this thought further in *Lorillard Tobacco Co.* when it wrote,

> [I]n the context of commercial speech, it is less necessary to tolerate inaccurate statements for fear of silencing the speaker, and also . . . it is more appropriate to

INTERNATIONAL LAW
MISLEADING ADVERTISING IN EUROPE

According to the European Commission, anyone advertising, marketing, promoting or selling goods and services is required to provide consumers with enough accurate information to make an informed purchase.[xvi] The European Union identifies "bait advertising, phony 'free' offers, manipulation of children, false claims of cures, hidden [native] advertisements in media, . . . [and] false offers of prizes" as among the most prominent misleading or aggressive practices that are prohibited.[xvii]

Recent EU regulations bar "unfair commercial practices" in advertising and marketing that are likely to materially distort the purchase decisions of a reasonable consumer.[xviii] The EC found that earlier policies failed to prevent deceptive online practices such as misleading internet offers, false product and price comparisons, fake internet domain name sales, use of competitors' trademarks and other internet-based fraud.[xix]

require that a commercial message appear in such a form, or include such additional information, warnings and disclaimers, as are necessary to prevent its being deceptive.[151]

For four decades, U.S. Supreme Court opinions have flatly stated that commercial speech loses its First Amendment protection if it is misleading, fraudulent, false, deceptive or coercive. In reviewing a city ordinance that prohibited the distribution of "commercial handbills," but not newspapers, on public property, the Court discussed the expanse of permitted government regulation.

> Obviously, much commercial speech is not provably false, or even wholly false, but only deceptive or misleading. We foresee no obstacle to a state's dealing effectively with this problem. The First Amendment, as we construe it today, does not prohibit the state from insuring that the stream of commercial information flow[s] cleanly as well as freely.[152]

In *Zauderer*, the Court said government could justify regulation if an ad had a "tendency to mislead" consumers.[153] Then *Cincinnati v. Discovery Network* seemed to suggest that regulation of a "literally true but misleading disclosure [that] creates the *possibility* of consumer deception" might also be permitted.[154]

The Supreme Court rarely attempted to define when advertising became impermissibly deceptive or misleading. Circuit courts of appeal have wrestled to decide when advertising "is inherently likely to deceive or where the record indicates that a particular form or method . . . of advertising has in fact been deceptive."[155] Determining the truth or falsity of an ad involves a relatively straightforward, fact-based inquiry. For example, in 2018, the makers of Canada Dry Ginger Ale faced a number of lawsuits because of the label and advertising claim that the carbonated soft drink is "Made from Real Ginger." Independent tests showed no "detectable" amount of ginger in the beverage.[156]

Identifying deceptive advertising that misleads potential customers requires the difficult determination of probable audience response. The courts do not provide consistent guidance.

REGULATING COMMERCIAL SPEECH CONCERNS

More than half a century before the U.S. Supreme Court established that the First Amendment protected truthful, nonmisleading commercial speech about legal products and services, Congress began enacting laws to protect consumers from unscrupulous business practices.[157] Because commercial speech often crosses state lines and falls under the U.S. Constitution's Commerce Clause, the federal government generally preempts state regulation of advertising and other commercial speech.[158] Congress has enacted scores of laws to ensure that companies provide consumers with essential and accurate information. Consumers and competing firms initiate lawsuits when they believe they have been harmed or treated unfairly contrary to the provisions of these laws.

Eighty years ago, Congress passed the **Lanham Act** that prohibits any false or misleading description or promotion of goods, services or commercial activities.[159] At the outset, the law was seldom used to curtail advertising practices, but it became the foundation for lawsuits, especially over ads using price or product comparisons.

The U.S. Supreme Court has determined that the Lanham Act does not require a party to be either a direct corporate competitor or a consumer of the product to sue under the law.[160] In a case that involved printer toner cartridges, the Supreme Court said a plaintiff has standing to sue when the defendant allegedly caused an injury to the plaintiff's commercial interest that lies in the law's "zone of interest."[161] The Court did not define "zone of interest" but suggested it is roughly equivalent to legislative intent. The intent of the Lanham Act is broadly to prevent commercial deception.

In another case, the Supreme Court interpreted the federal Food, Drug and Cosmetic Act[162] to complement the goals and mechanisms of the Lanham Act and allowed POM Wonderful to sue Coca-Cola over the labeling of its Minute Maid pomegranate blueberry juice.[163] The FDCA allowed the product, which contained only 0.3 percent pomegranate and 0.2 percent blueberry juice, to be labeled "a flavored blend of five juices."[164] But the Court said the law did not prevent POM Wonderful from pursuing a claim that the label violated the Lanham Act ban on deceptive and misleading advertising.

The Supreme Court said Coca-Cola was incorrect in arguing "that because food and beverage labeling is involved, it has no Lanham Act liability here for practices that allegedly mislead and trick customers, all to the injury of the competitor."[165] The Court went further. It said the Lanham Act did not require the false advertising to directly cause the injury at the heart of the suit. Rather, the injury must be "proximately caused" by the false advertising.[166] Consumer response to a defendant's false advertising that harms a company's sales or reputation is sufficient to establish the "injury in fact" necessary to bring suit.

Some recent cases illustrate what constitutes deceptive advertising. In one, several employees changed firms and sent emails to their former clients falsely claiming that their new employer would be working with their previous firm. The original company sued for false advertising. On appeal, the Sixth Circuit Court of Appeals allowed the false advertising claim to proceed.[167] The court said false advertising claims may be raised when speech is "disseminated either widely enough to the relevant purchasing public to constitute advertising or promotion within that industry or to a substantial portion of the plaintiff's or defendant's existing customer or client base."[168]

When the National Association for the Advancement of Colored People sued anti-abortion advocates for false advertising to stop an online article titled "NAACP: National Association for the Abortion of Colored People," the Fourth Circuit Court of Appeals held that the speech did not violate the Lanham Act because it was not published "in connection with" the promotion or sale of goods or services.[169] It therefore was not advertising. In another case, a federal trial court in California allowed a suit to

Coca-Cola

proceed against Uber to examine whether the "safest rides," "safe pickups" and other statements it made in ads and on its receipts were puffery or advertising claims that would be punishable if false or deceptive.[170]

The Federal Trade Commission

Multiple federal executive-branch agencies oversee specific industries or parts of the U.S. economy and administer federal laws regulating their commercial speech. Congress established the **Federal Trade Commission** in 1914 and expanded its powers in 1938 under the Lanham Act. A primary function of the FTC is to prohibit "unfair or deceptive acts or practices in or affecting commerce."[172] The FTC protects consumers by ensuring that advertisers have evidence to support their claims.[173]

A 2019 report found that the FTC "continued to be one of Washington's most aggressive regulators" but that because "all five of the FTC's current commissioners" joined in 2018, future activity was uncertain.[174] In 2017 and 2018, almost 70 percent of FTC enforcement actions focused on "financial services, web services and emerging technologies, data security and consumer privacy, telecommunications and health care."[175] Deceptive online advertising practices and misleading business opportunities ranked high among FTC enforcement priorities, the report concluded.

Thirty-five years ago, the FTC defined deceptive, false or misleading advertising as advertising that (1) makes a "material" claim or omission that (2) affects consumers' conduct or decisions and that (3) is likely to mislead a reasonable consumer.[175] Under the Lanham Act, the FTC distinguishes puffery from deception. As one former FTC commissioner said,

> The FTC does not pursue subjective claims. . . . But if there is an objective component to the claim—such as "more consumers prefer our hairspray to any other" or "our hairspray lasts longer than the most popular brands"—then you need to be sure that the claim is not deceptive and that you have adequate **substantiation** *before* you make the claim. These requirements apply both to explicit or express claims and to implied claims.[176]

While complaints, congressional inquiries or publicity often alert the FTC to potentially problematic advertisements, the commission also initiates inquiries into products, services or advertising practices. Some issues arise directly from advertisers seeking advice to avoid problems. FTC inquiries and fact-findings, like grand jury investigations, generally are closed to protect the privacy of those investigated. FTC powers range from rulemaking to investigation to enforcement, and

Federal Trade Commission
A federal agency created in 1914. Its purpose is to promote free and fair competition in interstate commerce; this includes preventing false and misleading advertising.

substantiation
Support of a claim with objective data or evidence.

POINTS OF LAW

FALSE AND MISLEADING?

A Federal Trade Commission policy statement establishes the three-part federal definition of false and misleading advertising:

- First, the ad must involve a "material" representation, omission or practice.

- Second, the material representation must be likely to affect the consumer's conduct or decision with regard to a product or service.

- Third, the representation must be likely to mislead a reasonable consumer acting reasonably in the circumstances.[xx]

their enforcements run from quite informal letters to serious, official legal actions. The FTC acts both preventatively and correctively.

The least formal FTC preventive action is a nonbinding opinion letter sent to an advertiser seeking advice about advertising and promotions. The next step up is an official FTC advisory opinion that is part of the public record. Advisory opinions inform individuals beyond those directly involved about various trade-related issues, and they often require advertisers to adhere to the opinion or face potential legal liability.

FTC industry guides suggest policies about particular products or services. FTC trade regulation rules target an entire trade to mandate a particular practice. A recent FTC industry guide on advertising testimonials and endorsements established that endorsers, especially celebrity endorsers, may be personally liable for false claims.[177] New media users, specifically bloggers and social media and viral campaigners, are subject to FTC enforcement action, as are "nontraditional" advertising endorsers, such as "on-air DJs."[178]

The FTC generally seeks voluntary compliance with its actions and asks advertisers to provide evidence of their own corrective steps before initiating investigations or corrective measures. If an advertiser fails to comply voluntarily, the FTC may initiate corrections and sanctions through a consent decree or agreement. Consent decrees often contain a cease and desist order requiring an advertiser to stop particular practices. For example, the FTC ordered American Nationwide Mortgage Co. to cease and desist its direct mail ad campaign that stated, "30-Year Fixed. 1.95%." In a virtually illegible footnote on the ad's reverse side, the text stated, "4.981% Annual Percentage Rate."[179] Under the FTC order, the mortgage company agreed to discontinue the advertisement.

A consent decree is for settlement purposes only. It does not constitute an admission of guilt by the advertiser. The FTC issued its first consent decree for deceptive online advertising 25 years ago after a service placed advertisements on the internet advising consumers to take illegal steps to repair their credit records.[180] The FTC required the advertiser to provide consumer compensation, to cease misrepresentations and to cooperate in FTC investigations of the sellers of the credit program materials.

In 2017, Uber signed an FTC consent order and agreed to establish strict privacy practices to settle FTC charges that it had deceived customers about Uber drivers' access to customers' private information.[181] In 2018, after Uber failed to inform the FTC of a major breach of customer data, Uber signed an expanded agreement that included possible penalties for failure to maintain customer privacy and inform the FTC of security breaches.[182]

Later in 2018, the FTC found that Uber had failed to comply with the agreements and ordered Uber to implement a privacy program.[183] The order mandated specific corrective provisions, including Uber recordkeeping and reporting, FTC monitoring and independent external assessment of Uber compliance for up to 20 years. The FTC also filed a formal complaint against Uber for false or misleading claims about the security of customer information.[184] In an earlier FTC action, Uber paid $20 million to settle claims that its online advertising for drivers falsely inflated their hourly earnings.[185]

The FTC recently sued Volkswagen for false and deceptive "clean diesel" vehicle advertising and promotions.[186] The action followed public disclosure that the car manufacturer falsified its vehicle emission-test results for years.[187]

FTC actions like these produce negative publicity for the companies involved and may result in court- or FTC-imposed fines, which the FTC often publicizes. For example, when the FTC concluded that Rite Aid pharmacies failed to provide their advertised protection for the privacy of individuals' prescription drug information, the resulting consent order mandated specific corrective measures by Rite Aid and fined the company $1 million.[188]

If advertisers refuse to sign a consent order, the FTC may issue a litigated order. The FTC files litigated orders in an administrative court. If the court affirms the order, the advertiser may appeal to a federal court. Failure to follow a litigated order upheld by the courts may result in fines of up to $10,000 per day. In one litigated action, the promoters of two dietary supplements advertised for weight loss and disease prevention agreed to pay the FTC $4.5 million for their false or unsubstantiated product claims and deceptively formatted infomercials.[189]

The FTC uses substantiation requirements to demand that advertisers prove their claims with "competent and reliable evidence."[190] The FTC's demand to "prove it" was central to its case against Tropicana's Healthy Heart orange juice. Through both television and print, Tropicana advertised that drinking its product increased "good" cholesterol and lowered blood pressure. The FTC said the clinical study Tropicana used to substantiate its claims was inadequate.[191] The FTC said the ads were false or misleading and ordered Tropicana to stop making the claims.

If an advertiser fails to substantiate its advertised claims, the FTC may impose fines, initiate court action and/or order **corrective advertising** that requires the advertiser to correct the misleading claims through new ads or other means.

Decades ago, the FTC used corrective advertising against a then-famous Listerine mouthwash ad campaign. The FTC found that Listerine misled the public for more than half a century with ad claims that the mouthwash killed germs and helped prevent colds and sore throats. A federal appeals court ruled that the FTC-ordered corrective advertising did not violate the First Amendment because "Listerine's advertisements play[ed] a substantial role in creating or reinforcing in the public's mind a false belief about the product . . . [that would] linger on after the false advertising ceases."[192] Nearly a year of required corrective advertising was not "an unreasonably long time in which to correct a hundred years of cold claims," the court ruled.[193] The company spent $10 million on those ads.

The FTC issued a litigated corrective advertising order for unsubstantiated superiority claims in advertisements and packaging claims for Doan's analgesic products.[194] The commission said substantial evidence supported its finding that the ads' deceptive claims were material, affected consumer beliefs and created lingering effects that required remedy.[195] The order required Doan's to spend its average annual advertising budget on corrective ads for a minimum of one year.

The FTC also may seek court injunctions or restraining orders to stop advertising that is false or misleading and may cause immediate harm. These orders generally stop the advertising until a full hearing takes place. The FTC, however, sought permanent injunctions to stop companies from making unsubstantiated claims that required consumers to pay thousands of dollars in up-front fees to receive promised reductions in credit card debt.[196]

corrective advertising The Federal Trade Commission power to require an advertiser to advertise or otherwise distribute information to correct false or misleading advertisement claims.

More than 40 years ago, government attempts to protect susceptible people, especially children, from tobacco promotions targeted Camel's use of the cartoon character Joe Camel.[197] The FTC asked an administrative law judge to issue a cease and desist order to stop R.J. Reynolds Tobacco Co. from using Joe Camel in any way that "would have a substantial appeal to children . . . below the age of 18."[198] Critics said Joe Camel prompted smoking by minors, for whom smoking was illegal. In fact, Camel cigarettes' share of the youth market rose from 4 percent to 13 percent after the introduction of Joe Camel.[199] The tobacco industry settled, agreeing to end all use of cartoon characters and all billboard and transit ads promoting tobacco products in all 50 states.

Vintage Camel cigarette advertising featuring Joe Camel.

Viviane Moos/Getty Images

Online Advertising

The internet provides fertile ground for fraud and unwanted ads, and the cost-effectiveness of online advertising is attractive to companies. Internet ads can reach an enormous audience of consumers targeted because their online behavior indicates interest in relevant activities or products. Clicking on online ads also provides advertisers with marketable user data and a back door to illegal snooping.

The FTC recently reported that it had initiated more than 130 spyware and spam cases.[200] In one example, the FTC settled its action against the Canadian dating site Ashley Madison after AM created fake profiles of members to lure others—including 19 million Americans—to pay to initiate or end memberships. The FTC settled, with AM paying $1.6 million and agreeing to correct its "lax" data security.[201]

In 2015, the FTC settled a complaint that app developers violated the Children's Online Privacy Protection Act[202] by enabling advertisers to use "persistent identifiers," or trackers, to target ads toward children.[203] The FTC's rules under COPPA classify persistent identifiers as personal information and prohibit their collection from children under 13 without parental notice and consent.[204]

For several years, the FTC has asked internet platforms and their advertisers voluntarily to give consumers "effective and meaningful privacy protection" via an easy, internet-wide "Do Not Track" option.[205] The FTC has said that because mechanisms targeting advertising to consumers are invisible, consumers should have an easy way to opt out.[206] The FTC promised Congress a simple, global solution for consumers, but its proposed rules allowed Facebook, Google and other "internet publishers with a direct relationship with consumers" to collect a wide array of data.[207]

In 2019, Facebook faced a settlement of up to $5 billion for improperly sharing the data of more than 80 million of its users in what top members of the Senate Judiciary Committee called another in the company's "history of broken and under-enforced consent decrees."[208] A few years earlier, Facebook settled FTC charges and agreed to stop sharing users' personal information with advertisers without permission.[209]

In 2019, the FTC completed its first review of the opt-out, labeling and identification requirements it imposed on commercial senders of unsolicited email, or spam advertising.[210] The review found that the rules that implemented the 2004 federal Controlling the Assault of Non-Solicited Pornography and Marketing Act[211] were effective and did not need to be modified.[212] The CAN-SPAM law prohibits "the transmission . . . of a commercial electronic mail message . . . that contains, or is accompanied by, header information that is materially false or materially misleading."[213] The law also empowers internet service providers and the government to sue spammers and requires unsolicited messages to include opt-out instructions.

Penalties for violations include up to five years' imprisonment and fines of up to $6 million.[214] In addition, the FTC requires employees who send out personal messages about company products to disclose their conflict of interest and make clear that they are not speaking on behalf of the employer.[215]

Most states have their own anti-spam laws.[216] In Virginia, where laws target unsolicited commercial bulk emails,[217] Jeremy Jaynes, a man once considered one of the world's most prolific spammers,[218] was charged with violating the law after he sent more than 55,000 unsolicited emails to subscribers of AOL (then America Online). The Virginia Supreme Court overturned Jaynes' conviction, finding the law's prohibition on false labeling of routing information overbroad and facially unconstitutional because it infringed the First Amendment right to engage in anonymous speech and targeted not only unsolicited commercial bulk emails but "the anonymous transmission of all unsolicited bulk e-mails including those containing political, religious or other speech protected by the First Amendment to the United States Constitution."[219]

For almost two decades, Congress and the Federal Trade Commission have worked to implement a simple, global way to eliminate unwanted commercial email and social media spam.

The U.S. Court of Appeals for the Eighth Circuit addressed a similar problem related to fax advertisements. The Telephone Consumer Protection Act requires all unsolicited faxed ads to include instructions on how to opt out.[220] The appeals court said the opt-out provision applied even when the recipient consented to the faxes because the rule was intended to prevent recipients' limited consent from becoming global or permanent.[221] On remand, the sender faced a multimillion-dollar class action suit for failure to include opt-out language in faxes for which the recipient had given prior explicit consent.

Required Disclosures

The FTC generally requires advertising on any platform to include disclosures to ensure that tweets and posts and endorsements as well as traditional ads do not mislead consumers about the nature or the source of the content they are viewing. More than 30 years ago in *Zauderer v. Office of Disciplinary Counsel of Supreme Court of Ohio* (discussed earlier in this chapter), the U.S. Supreme Court affirmed that government may force disclosures that are reasonably related to a substantial government interest.[222]

FTC rules require companies to disclose any payment for endorsements of their products, and publishers must identify any content they produce or display in exchange for compensation. FTC guidelines require that disclosures for ads on websites, social media and mobile devices be sufficiently clear and conspicuous that a reasonable consumer will see them and understand that they apply to the appropriate content, even if the disclosure cannot be immediately adjacent to the ad. Space limitations, for example on Twitter, do not justify failure to provide appropriate disclosures.[223]

When the FTC recently told Ellen DeGeneres and Nicki Minaj, among almost two dozen celebrities, that they needed to be transparent about all "material connections" to the products they promote through their social media, publicists scrambled to reshape Instagram and Facebook posts to comply with disclosure requirements.[224] A year later, an FTC report found that only one fourth of celebrities were following its regulations that require clear notification of compensation for content on social media.[225]

In 2015, the FTC announced that its disclosure requirements applied to native advertising in which ads resemble the editorial content of the medium in which they appear. The FTC said native ads are deceptive when their overall impression so closely mimics nonpaid content as to be likely to confuse consumers.[226]

In its first enforcement against native ads, the FTC in 2016 issued a complaint against clothing retailer Lord & Taylor.[227] Lord & Taylor's marketing of a new women's clothing line included blog posts, digital photos, video uploads, native ads in online fashion magazines and a team of online "fashion influencers recruited for their fashion style and extensive base of followers on social media platforms."[228] The FTC said the "influencers" received undisclosed payment and free clothing to send preapproved Lord & Taylor posts and hashtags that reached an estimated 11.4 million Instagram users. Lord & Taylor also preapproved at least one online article and an Instagram photo without disclosing that the content was paid.

In settling the case, the FTC prohibited Lord & Taylor from making any representations that suggest that paid content is independent or objective. The FTC required Lord & Taylor to ensure that all endorsers disclosed their paid relationship with the retailer.[229] The settlement punished only Lord & Taylor (the advertiser), not the influencers or the publishers, although FTC policy allows liability for all of these parties.[230]

In another case involving paid "influencers," an FTC order required Machinima, a multi-channel YouTube network about video games and gaming culture, to ensure its ad campaigns carried proper disclosure. Microsoft and its advertising agency paid influencers to promote Microsoft's Xbox One through a Machinima video campaign. The FTC said that many influencers "gave the impression that their videos were independently produced and that their comments reflected the influencer's personal views."[231] The FTC's settlement punished the publisher, Machinima, not Microsoft, the ad agency or the influencers.[232]

A study conducted in 2016 found that 40 percent of publishers were not complying with FTC rules requiring labeling of native ads.[233] In 2017, the FTC sent out more than 90 warning letters in one week to remind broadcasters, advertisers, marketers and "influencers" of their obligation to disclose all sponsored promotions and endorsements they distribute through social media. The letters are the first to target the influencers themselves and emphasize the shared responsibility for disclosure.[234] In 2018, an FTC study found that "a significant percentage" of consumers could not identify some native advertising as advertising even with prominent labeling.[235]

A handful of FTC investigations suggest that the FTC also applies disclosure requirements to word-of-mouth campaigns by bloggers and noncelebrities.[236] In word-of-mouth marketing, a company encourages (and generally compensates) users of its products to "talk them up" on social media to their friends on the theory that recommendations from friends and real product users are more persuasive than other sources.[237]

The Federal Communications Commission

The Federal Communications Commission is among the numerous other federal agencies that impose requirements on advertisers to prevent consumer deception. The FCC's oversight of broadcast television includes regulation of certain types of advertising, marketing and promotional content to serve the public interest (see Chapter 9).

FCC rules prohibit paid, for-profit business and campaign advertising on public television stations.[238] The U.S. Supreme Court denied certiorari to review the Ninth Circuit Court of Appeals' summary judgment upholding the FCC ban against a public television station's First Amendment challenge. The Ninth Circuit found that substantial evidence supported the FCC's conclusion that commercial and political advertising posed a legitimate threat to the noncommercial, educational "essence" of public television.[239] The court accepted the decades-old rationale that the scarcity of broadcast airwaves supports government's increased regulation of television.

The FCC also regulates offensive broadcast advertising, but no federal agency or law controls offensive nonbroadcast ads or advertising of disfavored activities, such as violence or pornography. FCC guidelines suggest that offensiveness can arise from the nature of the product, the time at which the ad appears or the manner in which it is presented.[240] In recent years, the FCC has reported no enforcement actions against offensive broadcast ads.

Two decades ago, FCC rules banned broadcasters in Louisiana from airing ads for private casino gambling because the ads reached states where such gambling was illegal. In a case brought by an association of broadcasters, a unanimous U.S. Supreme Court held that although the state had a substantial interest in reducing the social costs of gambling, the rules failed the *Central Hudson* test because they did not advance that interest.[241] The rules were underinclusive because they prohibited only advertising for private casinos (not for casinos operated by Native American tribes and not advertising of other forms of gambling). The rules simply directed gamblers to favored outlets, the Court said. Moreover, the rules were not as narrowly tailored as they could be.[242]

The Federal Election Commission

In a recent decision, the U.S. Court of Appeals for the D.C. Circuit affirmed Federal Election Commission rules requiring disclosure of corporate and union funding, but not other types of funding, for broadcast "electioneering communications." The court said Congress had "spoke[n] plainly" about its intentions, and the FEC rules were not "capricious" or "arbitrary" or unsupported by a substantial government interest.[243]

In its opinion, the court focused significant attention on the tension between unfettered free speech and forced disclosures, whose "deleterious effects . . . have been ably catalogued."[244] The opinion opens by declaring that

> [d]isclosure chills speech. Speech without disclosure risks corruption [or deception]. And the Supreme Court's track record of expanding who may speak while simultaneously blessing robust disclosure rules has set these two values on an ineluctable collision course.[245]

The D.C. Circuit Court suggested that the U.S. Supreme Court has failed to provide clear guidance to lower courts on when the First Amendment does and does not permit government-compelled disclosures.

One of the proposed cigarette-package images abandoned by the Food and Drug Administration.

The Food and Drug Administration and Others

When the Food and Drug Administration initiated rules "designed to stop sales and marketing of cigarettes and smokeless tobacco to children," a federal district court in North Carolina said the FDA had authority to impose only some of the rules.[246] The court said the FDA could regulate access and labeling of tobacco products as part of its authority over sales and use, but FDA authority "cannot be so broadly construed as to encompass conditions on advertising and promotion."[247]

A decade later, as regulators struggled to balance consumer protection and tobacco company speech rights, Congress enacted the Family Smoking Prevention and Tobacco Control Act.[248] Under the new law, the FDA adopted graphic labeling requirements for cigarettes.[249] The U.S. Courts of Appeals for the D.C. and Sixth Circuits disagreed on the constitutionality of the FDA rules requiring tobacco companies to "emblazon cigarette packaging with images of people dying from smoking-related disease, mouth and gum damage linked to smoking and other graphic portrayals of the harms of smoking."[250]

Applying *Central Hudson*, the Sixth Circuit upheld most of the new labeling requirements because they regulated only commercial speech about risky tobacco products. The D.C. Circuit applied strict scrutiny to this compelled speech and found the labeling requirement largely unconstitutional.[251] Both courts said the rules required speech that was neither purely factual nor uncontroversial.[252] The Supreme Court declined review of both cases.[253]

As mentioned earlier, the FDA in 2016 applied its tobacco label rules to all "e-cigarettes, vaping devices and other electronic nicotine delivery systems," including hookahs.[254] In 2017 and 2018, two federal district court decisions upheld the FDA's inclusion of vaping devices under "tobacco products" subject to its disclosure and other advertising requirements.[255] One applied *Zauderer* and found that the FDA had made the necessary showing to support its required factual and uncontroversial disclosures that reasonably advanced the government's significant interest in informing the public about health and safety risks.[256] Other consolidated First Amendment challenges to the FDA's health safety warning labels were pending in mid-2019 in the federal district court in Washington, D.C.[257]

REAL WORLD LAW
IT IS THE AGE OF INFLUENCERS AND E-SMOKING

Philip Morris tobacco company halted a global "media influencer" marketing campaign for its electronic nicotine-delivery product in 2019 after the Reuters news agency reported that one of the people promoting the product was 21.[xxi] Philip Morris said it halted all influencer campaigns to avoid similar incidents in the future."[xxii]

Alina Tapilina, a 21-year-old Russian model and social media personality with more than 80,000 Instagram followers, was paid to post a picture of herself holding Philip Morris's iQOS device on Instagram. Other photos show Tapilina posed suggestively, drinking wine, swimming and wearing "little clothing in luxurious settings."[xxiii]

Company marketing standards prohibit tobacco-related promotions by individuals "who are or appear to be under the age of 25."[xxiv] Earlier, the U.S. Food and Drug Administration permitted U.S. sales of the iQOS device after Philip Morris agreed to warn young people away from the product.[xxv] Company marketing submitted for FDA review featured models "appearing at least a decade older and wearing modest, professional clothes."[xxvi] The company also publicized that "all tobacco and e-cigarette companies . . . do their part to guard against youth nicotine use." [xxvii]

The Reuters investigation suggested that Philip Morris had conducted a coordinated marketing and lobbying effort to combat anti-smoking and e-cigarettes initiatives.[xxviii]

The government interest in promoting certain messages in favor of healthy eating, for example, generally does not outweigh a company's First Amendment right to refuse to carry government speech.[258] The free speech rights of food producers have blocked government efforts to impose advertising and labeling requirements on "foodstuffs" marketed to children.[259]

In 2019, the U.S. Department of Health and Human Services announced a new rule under the Lanham Act requiring TV prescription drug ads to contain specific price information.[260] Enforcement of the rule will occur primarily through lawsuits from competitors who believe the price disclosures are false or misleading.[261] The Association of National Advertisers opposed the rule on the grounds that price disclosures, without information on rebates and discounts, would not inform consumers but "lead to a large part of the public being misinformed."[262] The ANA also argued that the rule would not meet *Zauderer*'s requirement that compelled disclosures be "factual and uncontroversial."[263]

EMERGING LAW

Some scholars suggest that changes in the U.S. Supreme Court's application of content neutrality in recent rulings, including *Sorrell* and *NIFLA*, undermine the constitutional protection of advertising regulation.[264] They see a Court shift away from relaxed, deferential review of commercial speech regulations[265] toward the application of a strict content-neutrality rule to the commercial and compelled speech categories, which, "almost by definition, [are] content- and speaker-focused."[266]

Many scholars believe the Supreme Court has moved toward much more rigorous oversight of the restrictions on commercial speech that long have been viewed as "reasonable social and economic regulations."[267] Stricter review of commercial speech regulations would require stronger government justification to support regulation and likely mean that fewer government regulations would survive court First Amendment scrutiny. One scholar concluded that "some aspects of the compelled speech doctrine . . . seem hard to wrestle into a fully coherent pattern."[268]

In 2019, the FDA was considering new rules to prevent consumer deception when plant-based products use "milk" or "cheese" in their labeling. One FDA commissioner joked that almond milk should not be called milk because "an almond doesn't lactate."[269] Between 2012 and 2017, sales of nondairy milks—like almond, coconut and soy—grew more than 60 percent while dairy milk sales fell.[270] Dairy farmers led the movement to call such products nut juice.[271]

Arguing that labeling alternately sourced protein products "meat" was misleading, the U.S. Cattlemen's Association asked the U.S. Department of Agriculture to prohibit the "meat" label on "plant-based" substitutes.[272] By 2019, half a dozen states had joined the movement to impose labeling requirements on laboratory-produced, meat-substitute products, several of which had not yet hit market shelves.[273] At least two states passed resolutions asking Congress to adopt federal legislation to give the USDA authority over meat labeling and to distinguish animal products from cell-cultured meat products.[274] Parties said a settlement was close in a First Amendment challenge to the first "real meat" law passed in Missouri in 2018.[275]

In 2016, the National Bioengineered Food Disclosure Standard preempted state authority to regulate labeling of genetically engineered food or seed.[276] The law was a compromise between those who wanted explicit labels on all products containing genetically modified organisms and those who argued that such labels increased consumers' misperceptions of GMOs. The law requires identification of all genetically engineered foods and ingredients through a package "QR code" that can be scanned by a smartphone, not through specific language printed on the label. Genetically engineered or genetically modified and laboratory-produced food products generally need specific labels to that effect only if they differ in their nutritional value or allergens from the conventional foods they replace.[277]

In 2018, the USDA had yet to establish standards for implementing the law. The department was struggling to develop non-GMO-labeling standards to advance consumers' interest in knowing what they are eating while protecting the producers' constitutional right to remain silent about certain aspects of their products.[278] However, several courts were hearing challenges to "natural" and "non-GMO" food product labels, including one asserting that the label on Kind products was deceptive and misleading because independent tests identified GMO ingredients.[279]

In 2018, the Alcohol and Tobacco Tax and Trade Bureau proposed extensive rule changes to modernize, clarify and reorganize regulations on the labeling and advertising of alcoholic beverages.[280] The new rules would treat all alcoholic beverages similarly and modify existing limits on strength claims on beer that were struck down by the U.S. Supreme Court more than 20 years ago in *Rubin v. Coors Brewing Co.*[281]

Although TTB said its new language codified "longstanding interpretations" to ensure adequate protection of commercial speech, its proposed prohibition on disparaging, false, misleading, obscene or indecent statements on labels or in advertisements drew strong criticism from advertisers.[282] One alcohol-industry spokesman said the rule would not pass the "heightened scrutiny" required by the U.S. Supreme Court to uphold restrictions that "discriminate against specific speakers or content."[283] Comments on the proposed rule change were scheduled to close in mid-2019.[284]

CASES FOR STUDY

For study resources and a case archive, go to **edge.sagepub.com/medialaw7e**.

Thinking About It

The two case excerpts that follow address the regulation of commercial speech and whether specific regulations are consistent with the First Amendment. The first is the U.S. Supreme Court case that established the test for answering that question. In the second case, the U.S. Supreme Court declines to apply that test and shifts toward the scrutiny it employs in "pure" speech cases. As you read these case excerpts, keep the following questions in mind:

- What are the circumstances surrounding each case?

- Specifically, what type of speech is involved, and in what ways is it intermingled with commerce?

- What is the nature of the regulations being challenged?

- What is the state interest in each case? Are those interests legitimate?

- How does the Court's review in *Sorrell* differ from the test established by *Central Hudson*? What implications does this difference have for First Amendment protection of commercial speech?

Central Hudson Gas & Electric Corp. v. Public Service Commission of New York
SUPREME COURT OF THE UNITED STATES
447 U.S. 557 (1980)

JUSTICE LEWIS POWELL
delivered the Court's opinion:

This case presents the question whether a regulation of the Public Service Commission of the State of New York violates the First and Fourteenth Amendments because it completely bans promotional advertising by an electrical utility.

In December, 1973, the Commission, appellee here, ordered electric utilities in New York State to cease all advertising that "promot[es] the use of electricity." The order was based on the Commission's finding that "the interconnected utility system in New York State does not have sufficient fuel stocks or sources of supply to continue furnishing all customer demands for the 1973–1974 winter."

Three years later, when the fuel shortage had eased, the Commission requested comments from the public on its proposal to continue the ban on promotional advertising. Central Hudson Gas & Electric Corp., the appellant in this case, opposed the ban on First Amendment grounds. After reviewing the public comments, the Commission extended the prohibition in a Policy Statement issued on February 25, 1977.

The Policy Statement divided advertising expenses "into two broad categories: promotional—advertising intended to stimulate the purchase of utility services . . . and institutional and informational, a broad category inclusive of all advertising not clearly intended to promote sales." The Commission declared all promotional advertising contrary to the national policy of conserving energy. It acknowledged that the ban is not a perfect vehicle for conserving energy.

For example, the Commission's order prohibits promotional advertising to develop consumption during periods when demand for electricity is low. By limiting growth in "off-peak" consumption, the ban limits the "beneficial side effects" of such growth in terms of more efficient use of existing powerplants. And since oil dealers are not under the Commission's jurisdiction and thus remain free to advertise, it was recognized that the ban can achieve only "piecemeal conservationism." Still, the Commission adopted the restriction because it was deemed likely to "result in some dampening of unnecessary growth" in energy consumption.

The Commission's order explicitly permitted "informational" advertising designed to encourage "shifts of consumption" from peak demand times to periods of low electricity demand. Informational advertising would not seek to increase aggregate consumption, but would invite a leveling of demand throughout any given 24-hour period. The agency offered to review "specific proposals by the companies for specifically described [advertising] programs that meet these criteria."

When it rejected requests for rehearing on the Policy Statement, the Commission supplemented its rationale for the advertising ban. The agency observed that additional electricity probably would be more expensive to produce than existing output. Because electricity rates in New York were not then based on marginal cost, the Commission feared that additional power would be priced below the actual cost of generation. The additional electricity would be subsidized by all consumers through generally higher rates. The state agency also thought that promotional advertising would give "misleading signals" to the public by appearing to encourage energy consumption at a time when conservation is needed. . . .

The Commission's order restricts only commercial speech, that is, expression related solely to the economic interests of the speaker and its audience. The First Amendment, as applied to the States through the Fourteenth Amendment, protects commercial speech from unwarranted governmental regulation. Commercial expression not only serves the economic interest of the speaker, but also assists consumers and furthers the societal interest in the fullest possible dissemination of information. In applying the First Amendment to this area, we have rejected the "highly paternalistic" view that government has complete power to suppress or regulate commercial speech. . . .

Nevertheless, our decisions have recognized "the 'commonsense' distinction between speech proposing a commercial transaction, which occurs in an area traditionally subject to government regulation, and other varieties of speech." . . . The Constitution therefore accords a lesser protection to commercial speech than to other constitutionally guaranteed expression. The protection available for particular commercial expression turns on the nature both of the expression and of the governmental interests served by its regulation.

The First Amendment's concern for commercial speech is based on the informational function of advertising. Consequently, there can be no constitutional objection to the suppression of commercial messages that do not accurately inform the public about lawful activity. The government may ban forms of communication more likely to deceive the public than to inform it, or commercial speech related to illegal activity.

If the communication is neither misleading nor related to unlawful activity, the government's power is more circumscribed. The State must assert a substantial interest to be achieved by restrictions on commercial speech. Moreover, the regulatory technique must be in proportion to that interest. The limitation on expression must be designed carefully to achieve the State's goal. Compliance with this requirement may be measured by two criteria. First, the restriction must directly advance the state interest involved; the regulation may not be sustained if it provides only ineffective or remote support for the government's purpose. Second, if the governmental interest could be served as well by a more limited restriction on commercial speech, the excessive restrictions cannot survive. . . .

The second criterion recognizes that the First Amendment mandates that speech restrictions be "narrowly drawn." The regulatory technique may extend only as far as the interest it serves. The State cannot regulate speech that poses no danger to the asserted state interest, nor can it completely suppress information when narrower restrictions on expression would serve its interest as well. . . .

In this case, the Commission's prohibition acts directly against the promotional activities of Central Hudson, and, to the extent the limitations are unnecessary to serve the State's interest, they are invalid. . . .

In commercial speech cases, then, a four-part analysis has developed. At the outset, we must determine whether the expression is protected by the First Amendment. For commercial speech to come within that provision, it at least must concern lawful activity and not be misleading. Next, we ask whether the asserted governmental interest is substantial. If both inquiries yield positive answers, we must determine whether the regulation directly advances the governmental interest asserted, and whether it is not more extensive than is necessary to serve that interest.

We now apply this four-step analysis for commercial speech to the Commission's arguments in support of its ban on promotional advertising.

The Commission does not claim that the expression at issue either is inaccurate or relates to unlawful activity. Yet the New York Court of Appeals questioned whether Central Hudson's advertising is protected commercial speech. Because appellant holds a monopoly over the sale of electricity in its service area, the state court suggested that the Commission's order restricts no commercial speech of any worth. The court stated that advertising in a "noncompetitive market" could not improve the decisionmaking of consumers. The court saw no constitutional problem with barring commercial speech that it viewed as conveying little useful information.

This reasoning falls short of establishing that appellant's advertising is not commercial speech protected by the First Amendment. Monopoly over the supply of a product provides no protection from competition with substitutes for that product. . . .

Even in monopoly markets, the suppression of advertising reduces the information available for consumer decisions and thereby defeats the purpose of the First Amendment. The New York court's argument appears to assume that the providers of a monopoly service or product are willing to pay for wholly ineffective advertising. Most businesses—even regulated monopolies—are unlikely to underwrite promotional advertising that is of no interest or use to consumers. Indeed, a monopoly enterprise legitimately may wish to inform the public that it has developed new services or terms of doing business. A consumer may need information to aid his decision whether or not to use the monopoly service at all, or how much of the service he should purchase. In the absence of factors that would distort the decision to advertise, we may assume that the willingness of a business to promote its products reflects a belief that consumers are interested in the advertising. Since no such extraordinary conditions have been identified in this case, appellant's monopoly position does not alter the First Amendment's protection for its commercial speech.

The Commission offers two state interests as justifications for the ban on promotional advertising. The first concerns energy conservation. Any increase in demand for electricity—during peak or off-peak periods—means greater consumption of energy. The Commission argues, and the New York court agreed, that the State's interest in conserving energy is sufficient to support suppression of advertising designed to increase consumption of electricity. In view of our country's dependence on energy resources beyond our control, no one can doubt the importance of energy conservation. Plainly, therefore, the state interest asserted is substantial.

The Commission also argues that promotional advertising will aggravate inequities caused by the failure to base the utilities' rates on marginal cost. The utilities argued to the Commission that if they could promote the use of electricity in periods of low demand, they would improve their utilization of generating capacity. The Commission responded that promotion of off-peak consumption also would increase consumption during peak periods. If peak demand were to rise, the absence of marginal cost rates would mean that the rates charged for the additional power would not reflect the true costs of expanding production. Instead, the extra costs would be borne by all consumers through higher overall rates. Without promotional advertising, the Commission stated, this inequitable turn of events would be less likely to occur. The choice among rate structures involves difficult and important questions of economic supply and distributional fairness. The State's concern that rates be fair and efficient represents a clear and substantial governmental interest.

Next, we focus on the relationship between the State's interests and the advertising ban. Under this criterion, the Commission's laudable concern over the equity and efficiency of appellant's rates does not provide a constitutionally adequate reason for restricting protected speech. The link between the advertising prohibition and appellant's rate structure is, at most, tenuous. The impact of promotional advertising on the equity of appellant's rates is highly speculative. Advertising to increase off-peak usage would have to increase peak usage, while other factors that directly affect the fairness and efficiency of appellant's rates remained constant. Such conditional and remote eventualities simply cannot justify silencing appellant's promotional advertising.

In contrast, the State's interest in energy conservation is directly advanced by the Commission order at issue here. There is an immediate connection between advertising and demand for electricity. Central Hudson would not contest the advertising ban unless it believed that promotion would increase its sales. Thus, we find a direct link between the state interest in conservation and the Commission's order.

We come finally to the critical inquiry in this case: whether the Commission's complete suppression of speech ordinarily protected by the First Amendment is no more extensive than necessary to further the State's interest in energy conservation. The Commission's order reaches all promotional advertising, regardless of the impact of the touted service on overall energy use. But the energy conservation rationale, as important as it is, cannot justify suppressing information about electric devices or services that would cause no net increase in total energy use. In addition, no showing has been made that a more limited restriction on the content of promotional advertising would not serve adequately the State's interests.

Appellant insists that, but for the ban, it would advertise products and services that use energy efficiently. These include the "heat pump," which both parties acknowledge to be a major improvement in electric heating, and the use of electric heat as a "backup" to solar and other heat sources. Although the Commission has questioned the efficiency of electric heating before this Court, neither the Commission's Policy Statement nor its order denying rehearing made findings on this issue. In the absence of authoritative findings to the contrary, we must credit as within the realm of possibility the claim that electric heat can be an efficient alternative in some circumstances.

The Commission's order prevents appellant from promoting electric services that would reduce energy use by diverting demand from less efficient sources, or that would consume roughly the same amount of energy as do alternative sources. In neither situation would the utility's advertising endanger conservation or mislead the public. To the extent that the Commission's order suppresses speech that in no way impairs the State's interest in energy conservation, the Commission's order violates the First and Fourteenth Amendments, and must be invalidated.

The Commission also has not demonstrated that its interest in conservation cannot be protected adequately by more limited regulation of appellant's commercial expression. To further its policy of conservation, the Commission could attempt to restrict the format and content of Central Hudson's advertising. It might, for example, require that the advertisements include information about the relative efficiency and expense of the offered service, both under current conditions and for the foreseeable future. In the absence of a showing that more limited speech regulation would be ineffective, we cannot approve the complete suppression of Central Hudson's advertising.

Our decision today in no way disparages the national interest in energy conservation. We accept without reservation the argument that conservation, as well as the development of alternative energy sources, is an imperative national goal. Administrative bodies empowered to regulate electric utilities have the authority—and indeed the duty—to take appropriate action to further this goal. When, however, such action involves the suppression of speech, the First and Fourteenth Amendments require that the restriction be no more extensive than is necessary to serve the state interest. In this case, the record before us fails to show that the total ban on promotional advertising meets this requirement.

Accordingly, the judgment of the New York Court of Appeals is

Reversed. . . .

JUSTICE WILLIAM REHNQUIST, dissenting:

The Court today invalidates an order issued by the New York Public Service Commission designed to promote a policy that has been declared to be of critical national concern. The order was issued by the Commission in 1973 in response to the Mideastern oil embargo crisis. It prohibits electric corporations "from promoting the use of electricity through the use of advertising, subsidy payments . . . or employee incentives." Although

the immediate crisis created by the oil embargo has subsided, the ban on promotional advertising remains in effect. The regulation was re-examined by the New York Public Service Commission in 1977. Its constitutionality was subsequently upheld by the New York Court of Appeals, which concluded that the paramount national interest in energy conservation justified its retention.

The Court's asserted justification for invalidating the New York law is the public interest discerned by the Court to underlie the First Amendment in the free flow of commercial information. Prior to this Court's recent decision in *Virginia Pharmacy Board v. Virginia Citizens Consumer Council*, however, commercial speech was afforded no protection under the First Amendment whatsoever. Given what seems to me full recognition of the holding of *Virginia Pharmacy Board* that commercial speech is entitled to some degree of First Amendment protection, I think the Court is nonetheless incorrect in invalidating the carefully considered state ban on promotional advertising in light of pressing national and state energy needs. . . .

This Court has previously recognized that, although commercial speech may be entitled to First Amendment protection, that protection is not as extensive as that accorded to the advocacy of ideas. . . . "We have not discarded the 'common-sense' distinction between speech proposing a commercial transaction, which occurs in an area traditionally subject to government regulation, and other varieties of speech. To require a parity of constitutional protection for commercial and noncommercial speech alike could invite dilution, simply by a leveling process, of the force of the Amendment's guarantee with respect to the latter kind of speech. Rather than subject the First Amendment to such a devitalization, we instead have afforded commercial speech a limited measure of protection, commensurate with its subordinate position in the scale of First Amendment values, while allowing modes of regulation that might be impermissible in the realm of noncommercial expression."

The Court's decision today fails to give due deference to this subordinate position of commercial speech. The Court in so doing returns to the bygone era . . . in which it was common practice for this Court to strike down economic regulations adopted by a State based on the Court's own notions of the most appropriate means for the State to implement its considered policies.

I had thought by now it had become well established that a State has broad discretion in imposing economic regulations. . . . The State of New York has determined here that economic realities require the grant of monopoly status to public utilities in order to distribute efficiently the services they provide, and in granting utilities such status it has made them subject to an extensive regulatory scheme. When the State adopted this scheme and when its Public Service Commission issued its initial ban on promotional advertising in 1973, commercial speech had not been held to fall within the scope of the First Amendment at all. . . .

The Court today holds not only that commercial speech is entitled to First Amendment protection, but also that when it is protected a State may not regulate it unless its reason for doing so amounts to a "substantial" governmental interest, its regulation "directly advances" that interest, and its manner of regulation is "not more extensive than necessary" to serve the interest. The test adopted by the Court thus elevates the protection accorded commercial speech that falls within the scope of the First Amendment to a level that is virtually indistinguishable from that of noncommercial speech. . . .

An ostensible justification for striking down New York's ban on promotional advertising is that this Court has previously "rejected the 'highly paternalistic' view that government has complete power to suppress or regulate commercial speech. '[P]eople will perceive their own best interests if only they are well enough informed and . . . the best means to that end is to open the channels of communication, rather than to close them. . . .'" Whatever the merits of this view, I think the Court has carried its logic too far here. . . .

While it is true that an important objective of the First Amendment is to foster the free flow of information, identification of speech that falls within its protection is not aided by the metaphorical reference to a "marketplace of ideas." There is no reason for believing that the marketplace of ideas is free from market imperfections any more than there is to believe that the invisible hand will always lead to optimum economic decisions in the commercial market. . . . Indeed, many types of speech have been held to fall outside the scope of the First Amendment, thereby subject to governmental regulation, despite this Court's references to a marketplace of ideas. . . .

I remain of the view that the Court unlocked a Pandora's Box when it "elevated" commercial speech to the level of traditional political speech by according it First Amendment protection in *Virginia Pharmacy Board v. Virginia Citizens Consumer Council*. The line between "commercial speech," and the kind of speech that those who drafted the First Amendment had in mind, may not be a technically or intellectually easy one to draw, but it surely produced far fewer problems than has the development of judicial doctrine in this area since *Virginia Pharmacy Board*. . . .

The notion that more speech is the remedy to expose falsehood and fallacies is wholly out of place in the commercial bazaar, where if applied logically the remedy of one who was defrauded would be merely a statement, available upon request, reciting the Latin maxim "*caveat emptor.*" But since "fraudulent speech" in this area is to be remediable under *Virginia Pharmacy Board*, the remedy of one defrauded is a lawsuit or an agency proceeding based on common-law notions of fraud that are separated by a world of difference from the realm of politics and government. What time, legal decisions, and common sense have so widely severed, I declined to join in *Virginia Pharmacy Board*, and regret now to see the Court reaping the seeds that it there sowed. For in a democracy, the economic is subordinate to the political, a lesson that our ancestors learned long ago, and that our descendants will undoubtedly have to relearn many years hence.

The Court concedes that the state interest in energy conservation is plainly substantial, as is the State's concern that its rates be fair and efficient. It also concedes that there is a direct link between the Commission's ban on promotional advertising and the State's interest in conservation. The Court nonetheless strikes down the ban on promotional advertising because the Commission has failed to demonstrate, under the final part of the Court's four-part test, that its regulation is no more extensive than necessary to serve the State's interest. In reaching this conclusion, the Court conjures up potential advertisements that a utility might make that conceivably would result in net energy savings. The Court does not indicate that the New York Public Service Commission has in fact construed its ban on "promotional" advertising to preclude the dissemination of information that clearly would result in a net energy savings, nor does it even suggest that the Commission has been confronted with and rejected such an advertising proposal. The final part of the Court's test thus leaves room for so many hypothetical "better" ways that any ingenious lawyer will surely seize on one of them to secure the invalidation of what the state agency actually did. . . .

Ordinarily it is the role of the State Public Service Commission to make factual determinations concerning whether a device or service will result in a net energy savings and, if so, whether and to what extent state law permits dissemination of information about the device or service. Otherwise, as here, this Court will have no factual basis for its assertions. And the State will never have an opportunity to consider the issue and thus to construe its law in a manner consistent with the Federal Constitution. . . .

It is, in my view, inappropriate for the Court to invalidate the State's ban on commercial advertising here, based on its speculation that in some cases the advertising may result in a net savings in electrical energy use, and in the cases in which it is clear a net energy savings would result from utility advertising, the Public Service Commission would apply its ban so as to proscribe such advertising. Even assuming that the Court's speculation is correct, I do not think it follows that facial invalidation of the ban is the appropriate course. . . .

For the foregoing reasons, I would affirm the judgment of the New York Court of Appeals.

Sorrell v. IMS Health, Inc.
SUPREME COURT OF THE UNITED STATES
131 S. CT. 2653 (2011)

JUSTICE ANTHONY KENNEDY delivered the Court's opinion:

. . . Pharmaceutical manufacturers promote their drugs to doctors through a process called "detailing." This often involves a scheduled visit to a doctor's office to persuade the doctor to prescribe a particular pharmaceutical. Detailers bring drug samples as well as medical studies that explain the "details" and potential advantages of various prescription drugs. Interested physicians listen, ask questions, and receive followup data. Salespersons can be more effective when they know the background and purchasing preferences of their clientele, and pharmaceutical salespersons are no exception. Knowledge of a physician's prescription practices—called "prescriber-identifying information"—enables a detailer better to ascertain which doctors are likely to be interested in a particular drug and how best to present a particular sales message. Detailing is an expensive undertaking, so pharmaceutical companies most often use it to promote high-profit brand-name drugs protected by patent. Once a brand-name drug's patent expires, less expensive bioequivalent generic alternatives are manufactured and sold.

Pharmacies, as a matter of business routine and federal law, receive prescriber-identifying information when processing prescriptions. Many pharmacies sell this information to "data miners," firms that analyze prescriber-identifying information and produce reports on prescriber behavior. Data miners lease these reports to pharmaceutical manufacturers subject to nondisclosure agreements. Detailers, who represent the manufacturers, then use the reports to refine their marketing tactics and increase sales.

In 2007, Vermont enacted the Prescription Confidentiality Law. The measure is also referred to as Act 80. It has several components. The central provision of the present case is § 4631(d).

> A health insurer, a self-insured employer, an electronic transmission intermediary, a pharmacy, or other similar entity shall not sell, license, or exchange for value regulated records containing prescriber-identifiable information, nor permit the use of regulated records containing prescriber-identifiable information for marketing or promoting a prescription drug, unless the prescriber consents. . . . Pharmaceutical manufacturers and pharmaceutical marketers shall not use prescriber-identifiable information for marketing or promoting a prescription drug unless the prescriber consents. . . .

The quoted provision has three component parts. The provision begins by prohibiting pharmacies, health insurers, and similar entities from selling prescriber-identifying information, absent the prescriber's consent. The parties here dispute whether this clause applies to all sales or only to sales for marketing. The provision then goes on to prohibit pharmacies, health insurers, and similar entities from allowing prescriber-identifying information to be used for marketing, unless the prescriber consents. This prohibition in effect bars pharmacies from disclosing the information for marketing purposes. Finally, the provision's second sentence bars pharmaceutical manufacturers and pharmaceutical marketers from using prescriber-identifying information for marketing, again absent the prescriber's consent. The Vermont attorney general may pursue civil remedies against violators.

Separate statutory provisions elaborate the scope of the prohibitions. . . . "Marketing" is defined to include "advertising, promotion, or any activity" that is "used to influence sales or the market share of a prescription drug." § 4631(d) further provides that Vermont's Department of Health must allow "a prescriber to give consent for his or her identifying information to be used for the purposes" identified. . . . Finally, the Act's prohibitions on sale, disclosure, and use are subject to a list of exceptions. For example, prescriber-identifying information may be disseminated or used for "health care research"; to enforce "compliance" with health insurance formularies, or preferred drug lists; for "care management educational communications provided to" patients on such matters as "treatment options"; for law enforcement operations; and for purposes "otherwise provided by law."

Act 80 also authorized funds for an "evidence-based prescription drug education program" designed to provide doctors and others with "information and education on the therapeutic and cost-effective utilization of prescription drugs." An express aim of the program is to advise prescribers "about commonly used brand-name drugs for which the patent has expired" or will soon expire. Similar efforts to promote the use of generic pharmaceuticals are sometimes referred to as "counter-detailing." The counter-detailer's recommended substitute may be an older, less expensive drug and not a bioequivalent of the brand-name drug the physician might otherwise prescribe. Like the pharmaceutical manufacturers whose efforts they hope to resist, counterdetailers in some states use prescriber-identifying information to increase their effectiveness. States themselves may supply the prescriber-identifying information used in these programs. . . .

Act 80 was accompanied by legislative findings. Vermont found, for example, that the "goals of marketing programs are often in conflict with the goals of the state" and that the "marketplace for ideas on medicine safety and effectiveness is frequently one-sided in that brand-name companies invest in expensive pharmaceutical marketing campaigns to doctors." Detailing, in the legislature's view, caused doctors to make decisions based on "incomplete and biased information." Because they "are unable to take the time to research the quickly changing pharmaceutical market," Vermont doctors "rely on information provided by pharmaceutical representatives." The legislature further found that detailing increases the cost of health care and health insurance; encourages hasty and excessive reliance on brand-name drugs, before the profession has observed their effectiveness as compared with older and less expensive generic alternatives; and fosters disruptive and repeated marketing visits tantamount to harassment. . . . Use of prescriber-identifying data also helps detailers shape their messages by "tailoring" their "presentations to individual prescriber styles, preferences, and attitudes."

The present case involves two consolidated suits. One was brought by three Vermont data miners, the other by an association of pharmaceutical manufacturers that produce brand-name drugs. . . . Contending that § 4631(d) violates their First Amendment rights as incorporated by the Fourteenth Amendment, the respondents sought declaratory and injunctive relief. . . .

After a bench trial, the United States District Court for the District of Vermont denied relief. The District Court found that "[p]harmaceutical manufacturers are essentially the only paying customers of the data vendor industry" and that, because detailing unpatented generic drugs is not "cost-effective," pharmaceutical sales representatives "detail only branded drugs." . . . The United States Court of Appeals for the Second Circuit reversed and remanded. It held that § 4631(d) violates the First Amendment by burdening the speech of pharmaceutical marketers and data miners without an adequate justification. . . . The decision of the Second Circuit is in conflict with decisions of the United States Court of Appeals for the First Circuit concerning similar legislation enacted by Maine and New Hampshire. Recognizing a division of authority regarding the constitutionality of state statutes, this Court granted certiorari.

The beginning point is the text of § 4631(d). In the proceedings below, Vermont stated that the first sentence . . . prohibits pharmacies and other regulated entities from selling or disseminating prescriber-identifying information for marketing. The information, in other words, could be sold or given away for purposes other than marketing. . . . At oral argument in this Court, however, the state for the first time advanced an alternative reading . . . namely, that pharmacies, health insurers, and similar entities may not sell prescriber-identifying information for any purpose, subject to the statutory exceptions set out [in the law]. It might be argued that the state's new-found interpretation comes too late in the day. . . . For the state to change its position is particularly troubling in a First Amendment case, where plaintiffs have a special interest in obtaining a prompt adjudication of their rights, despite potential ambiguities of state law.

In any event, § 4631(d) cannot be sustained even under the interpretation the state now adopts. As a consequence this Court can assume that the opening clause . . . prohibits pharmacies, health insurers, and similar entities from selling prescriber-identifying information, subject to the statutory exceptions set out . . . Under that reading, pharmacies may sell the information to private or academic researchers, but not, for example, to pharmaceutical marketers. There is no dispute as to the remainder of § 4631. It prohibits pharmacies, health insurers, and similar entities from disclosing or otherwise allowing prescriber-identifying information to be used for marketing. And it bars pharmaceutical manufacturers and detailers from using the information for marketing. The questions now are whether § 4631(d) must be tested by heightened judicial scrutiny and, if so, whether the state can justify the law.

On its face, Vermont's law enacts content- and speaker-based restrictions on the sale, disclosure, and use of prescriber-identifying information. The provision first forbids sale subject to exceptions based in large part on the content of a purchaser's speech. For example, those who wish to engage in certain "educational communications" may purchase the information. The measure then bars any disclosure when recipient speakers will use the information for marketing. Finally, the provision's second sentence prohibits pharmaceutical manufacturers from using the information for marketing. The statute thus disfavors marketing, that is, speech with a particular content. More than that, the statute disfavors specific speakers, namely pharmaceutical manufacturers. As a result of these content- and speaker-based rules, detailers cannot obtain prescriber-identifying information, even though the information may be purchased or acquired by other speakers with diverse purposes

and viewpoints. Detailers are likewise barred from using the information for marketing, even though the information may be used by a wide range of other speakers. For example, it appears that Vermont could supply academic organizations with prescriber-identifying information to use in countering the messages of brand-name pharmaceutical manufacturers and in promoting the prescription of generic drugs. But § 4631(d) leaves detailers no means of purchasing, acquiring, or using prescriber-identifying information. The law on its face burdens disfavored speech by disfavored speakers.

Any doubt that § 4631(d) imposes an aimed, content-based burden on detailers is dispelled by the record and by formal legislative findings. As the District Court noted, "[p]harmaceutical manufacturers are essentially the only paying customers of the data vendor industry"; and the almost invariable rule is that detailing by pharmaceutical manufacturers is in support of brand-name drugs. Vermont's law thus has the effect of preventing detailers—and only detailers—from communicating with physicians in an effective and informative manner. Formal legislative findings accompanying § 4631(d) confirm that the law's express purpose and practical effect are to diminish the effectiveness of marketing by manufacturers of brand-name drugs. . . . The legislature designed § 4631(d) to target those speakers and their messages for disfavored treatment. "In its practical operation," Vermont's law "goes even beyond mere content discrimination, to actual viewpoint discrimination." Given the legislature's expressed statement of purpose, it is apparent that § 4631(d) imposes burdens that are based on the content of speech and that are aimed at a particular viewpoint.

Act 80 is designed to impose a specific, content-based burden on protected expression. It follows that heightened judicial scrutiny is warranted. The Court has recognized that the "distinction between laws burdening and laws banning speech is but a matter of degree" and that the "Government's content-based burdens must satisfy the same rigorous scrutiny as its content-based bans."

The First Amendment requires heightened scrutiny whenever the government creates "a regulation of speech because of disagreement with the message it conveys." . . . Even if the hypothetical measure on its face appeared neutral as to content and speaker, its purpose to suppress speech and its unjustified burdens on expression would render it unconstitutional. Commercial speech is no exception. A "consumer's concern for the free flow of commercial speech often may be far keener than his concern for urgent political dialogue." That reality has great relevance in the fields of medicine and public health, where information can save lives.

The State argues that heightened judicial scrutiny is unwarranted because its law is a mere commercial regulation. It is true that restrictions on protected expression are distinct from restrictions on economic activity or, more generally, on nonexpressive conduct. It is also true that the First Amendment does not prevent restrictions directed at commerce or conduct from imposing incidental burdens on speech. . . . But § 4631(d) imposes more than an incidental burden on protected expression. Both on its face and in its practical operation, Vermont's law imposes a burden based on the content of speech and the identity of the speaker. While the burdened speech results from an economic motive, so too does a great deal of vital expression. Vermont's law does not simply have an effect on speech, but is directed at certain content and is aimed at particular speakers. . . .

Vermont further argues that § 4631(d) regulates not speech but simply access to information. Prescriber-identifying information was generated in compliance with a legal mandate, the state argues, and so could be considered a kind of governmental information. . . . An individual's right to speak is implicated when information he or she possesses is subjected to "restraints on the way in which the information might be used" or disseminated. . . . It is true that the respondents here . . . do not themselves possess information whose disclosure has been curtailed. That information, however, is in the hands of pharmacies and other private entities. There is no question that the "threat of prosecution . . . hangs over their heads." . . . [R]estrictions on the disclosure of government-held information can facilitate or burden the expression of potential recipients and so transgress the First Amendment. Vermont's law imposes a content- and speaker-based burden on respondents' own speech. That consideration . . . requires heightened judicial scrutiny.

The state also contends that heightened judicial scrutiny is unwarranted in this case because sales, transfer, and use of prescriber-identifying information are conduct, not speech. Consistent with that submission, the United States Court of Appeals for the First Circuit has characterized prescriber-identifying information as a mere "commodity" with no greater entitlement to First Amendment protection than "beef jerky." In contrast the courts below concluded that a prohibition on the sale of prescriber-identifying information is a content-based rule akin to a ban on the sale of cookbooks, laboratory results, or train schedules.

This Court has held that the creation and dissemination of information are speech within the meaning of the First Amendment. Facts, after all, are the beginning point for much of the speech that is most essential to advance human knowledge and to conduct human affairs. There is thus a strong argument that prescriber-identifying information is speech for First Amendment purposes.

The state asks for an exception to the rule that information is speech, but there is no need to consider that request in this case. The state has imposed content- and speaker-based restrictions on the availability and use of prescriber-identifying information. So long as they do not engage in marketing, many speakers can obtain and use the information. But detailers cannot. Vermont's statute could be compared with a law prohibiting trade magazines from purchasing or using ink. Like that hypothetical law, § 4631(d) imposes a speaker- and content-based burden on protected expression, and that circumstance is sufficient to justify application of heightened scrutiny. As a consequence, this case can be resolved even assuming, as the state argues, that prescriber-identifying information is a mere commodity.

In the ordinary case it is all but dispositive to conclude that a law is content-based and, in practice, viewpoint-discriminatory. The state argues that a different analysis applies here because, assuming § 4631(d) burdens speech at all, it at most burdens only commercial speech. As in previous cases, however, the outcome is the same whether a special commercial speech inquiry or a stricter form of judicial scrutiny is applied. For the same reason there is no need to determine whether all speech hampered by § 4631(d) is commercial, as our cases have used that term.

Under a commercial speech inquiry, it is the state's burden to justify its content-based law as consistent with the First Amendment. To sustain the targeted, content-based burden § 4631(d) imposes on protected expression, the state must show at least that the statute directly advances a substantial governmental interest and that the measure is drawn to achieve that interest. There must be a "fit between the legislature's ends and the means chosen to accomplish those ends." As in other contexts, these standards ensure not only that the state's interests are proportional to the resulting burdens placed on speech but also that the law does not seek to suppress a disfavored message.

The state's asserted justifications for § 4631(d) come under two general headings. First, the state contends that its law is necessary to protect medical privacy, including physician confidentiality, avoidance of harassment, and the integrity of the doctor-patient relationship. Second, the state argues that § 4631(d) is integral to the achievement of policy objectives— namely, improved public health and reduced health-care costs. Neither justification withstands scrutiny.

Vermont argues that its physicians have a "reasonable expectation" that their prescriber-identifying information "will not be used for purposes other than . . . filling and processing" prescriptions. It may be assumed that, for many reasons, physicians have an interest in keeping their prescription decisions confidential. But § 4631(d) is not drawn to serve that interest. Under Vermont's law, pharmacies may share prescriber-identifying information with anyone for any reason save one: They must not allow the information to be used for marketing. Exceptions further allow pharmacies to sell prescriber-identifying information for certain purposes, including "health care research." § 4631(e). And the measure permits insurers, researchers, journalists, the state itself, and others to use the information. . . .

Perhaps the state could have addressed physician confidentiality through "a more coherent policy." . . . But the state did not enact a statute with that purpose or design. Instead, Vermont made prescriber-identifying information available to an almost limitless audience. The explicit structure of the statute allows the information to be studied and used by all but a narrow class of disfavored speakers. Given the information's widespread availability and many permissible uses, the state's asserted interest in physician confidentiality does not justify the burden that § 4631(d) places on protected expression.

The State points out that it allows doctors to forgo the advantages of § 4631(d) by consenting to the sale, disclosure, and use of their prescriber-identifying information. See § 4631(c)(1). . . . Vermont has given its doctors a contrived choice: Either consent, which will allow your prescriber-identifying information to be disseminated and used without constraint; or, withhold consent, which will allow your information to be used by those speakers whose message the state supports. Section 4631(d) may offer a limited degree of privacy, but only on terms favorable to the speech the state prefers. . . . [T]he state has conditioned privacy on acceptance of a content-based rule that is not drawn to serve the state's asserted interest. To obtain the limited privacy allowed by § 4631(d), Vermont physicians are forced to acquiesce in the state's goal of burdening disfavored speech by disfavored speakers.

. . . Rules that burden protected expression may not be sustained when the options provided by the state are too narrow to advance legitimate interests or too broad to protect speech. As already explained, § 4631(d) permits extensive use of prescriber-identifying information and so does not advance the state's asserted interest in physician confidentiality. The limited range of available privacy options instead reflects the state's impermissible purpose to burden disfavored speech.

The state also contends that § 4631(d) protects doctors from "harassing sales behaviors." "Some doctors in Vermont are experiencing an undesired increase in the aggressiveness of pharmaceutical sales representatives," the Vermont Legislature found, "and a few have reported that they felt coerced and harassed." It is doubtful that concern for "a few" physicians who may have "felt coerced and harassed" by pharmaceutical marketers can sustain a broad content-based rule like § 4631(d). Many are those who must endure speech they do not like, but that is a necessary cost of freedom. In any event the State offers no explanation why remedies other than content-based rules would be inadequate. Physicians can, and often do, simply decline to meet with detailers, including detailers who use prescriber-identifying information. Doctors who wish to forgo detailing altogether are free to give "No Solicitation" or "No Detailing" instructions to their office managers or to receptionists at their places of work. . . .

Vermont argues that detailers' use of prescriber-identifying information undermines the doctor-patient relationship by allowing detailers to influence treatment decisions. According to the state, "unwanted pressure occurs" when doctors learn that their prescription decisions are being "monitored" by detailers. Some physicians accuse detailers of "spying" or of engaging in "underhanded" conduct in order to "subvert" prescription decisions. And Vermont claims that detailing makes people "anxious" about whether doctors have their patients' best interests at heart. But the state does not explain why detailers' use of prescriber-identifying information is more likely to prompt these objections than many other uses permitted by § 4631(d). In any event, this asserted interest is contrary to basic First Amendment principles. Speech remains protected even when it may "stir people to action," "move them to tears," or "inflict great pain." The more benign and, many would say, beneficial speech of pharmaceutical marketing is also entitled to the protection of the First Amendment. If pharmaceutical marketing affects treatment decisions, it does so because doctors find it persuasive. Absent circumstances far from those presented here, the fear that speech might persuade provides no lawful basis for quieting it.

The state contends that § 4631(d) advances important public policy goals by lowering the costs of medical services and promoting public health. If prescriber-identifying information were available for use by detailers, the state contends, then detailing would be effective in promoting brand-name drugs that are more expensive and less safe than generic alternatives. This logic is set out at length in the legislative findings accompanying § 4631(d). Yet at oral argument here, the state declined to acknowledge that § 4631(d)'s objective purpose and practical effect were to inhibit detailing and alter doctors' prescription decisions. The state's reluctance to embrace its own legislature's rationale reflects the vulnerability of its position.

While Vermont's stated policy goals may be proper, § 4631(d) does not advance them in a permissible way. As the Court of Appeals noted, the "state's own explanation of how" § 4631(d) "advances its interests cannot be said to be direct." The state seeks to achieve its policy objectives through the indirect means of restraining certain speech by certain speakers—that is, by diminishing detailers' ability to influence prescription decisions. Those who seek to censor or burden free expression often assert that disfavored speech has adverse effects. But the "fear that people would make bad decisions if given truthful information" cannot justify content-based burdens on speech. These precepts apply with full force when the audience, in this case prescribing physicians, consists of "sophisticated and experienced" consumers.

As Vermont's legislative findings acknowledge, the premise of § 4631(d) is that the force of speech can justify the government's attempts to stifle it. Indeed the state defends the law by insisting that "pharmaceutical marketing has a strong influence on doctors' prescribing practices." This reasoning is incompatible with the First Amendment. In an attempt to reverse a disfavored trend in public opinion, a state could not ban campaigning with slogans, picketing with signs, or marching during the daytime. Likewise the state may not seek to remove a popular but disfavored product from the marketplace by prohibiting truthful, nonmisleading advertisements that contain impressive endorsements or catchy jingles. That the state finds expression too persuasive does not permit it to quiet the speech or to burden its messengers.

The defect in Vermont's law is made clear by the fact that many listeners find detailing instructive. Indeed the record demonstrates that some Vermont doctors view targeted detailing based on prescriber-identifying information as "very helpful" because it allows detailers to shape their messages to each doctor's practice. Even the United States, which appeared here in support of Vermont, took care to dispute the state's "unwarranted view that the dangers of [n]ew drugs outweigh their benefits to patients." There are divergent views regarding detailing and the prescription of brand-name drugs. Under the Constitution, resolution of that debate must result from free and uninhibited speech. . . . The choice "between the dangers of suppressing information, and the dangers of its misuse if it is freely available," is one that "the First Amendment makes for us."

Vermont may be displeased that detailers who use prescriber-identifying information are effective in promoting brand-name drugs. The state can express that view through its own speech. But a state's failure to persuade does not allow it to hamstring the opposition. The state may not burden the speech of others in order to tilt public debate in a preferred direction. "The commercial marketplace, like other spheres of our social and cultural life, provides a forum where ideas and information flourish. Some of the ideas and information are vital, some of slight worth. But the general rule is that the speaker and the audience, not the government, assess the value of the information presented."

It is true that content-based restrictions on protected expression are sometimes permissible, and that principle applies to commercial speech. Indeed the government's legitimate interest in protecting consumers from "commercial harms" explains "why commercial speech can be subject to greater governmental regulation than noncommercial speech." Here, however, Vermont has not shown that its law has a neutral justification. The state nowhere contends that detailing is false or misleading within the meaning of this Court's First Amendment precedents. Nor does the state argue that the provision challenged here will prevent false or misleading speech. The state's interest in burdening the speech of detailers instead turns on nothing more than a difference of opinion.

* * *

The capacity of technology to find and publish personal information, including records required by the government, presents serious and unresolved issues with respect to personal privacy and the dignity it seeks to secure. In considering how to protect those interests, however, the state cannot engage in content-based discrimination to advance its own side of a debate.

If Vermont's statute provided that prescriber-identifying information could not be sold or disclosed except in narrow circumstances then the state might have a stronger position. Here, however, the state gives possessors of the information broad discretion and wide latitude in disclosing the information, while at the same time restricting the information's use by some speakers and for some purposes, even while the state itself can use the information to counter the speech it seeks to suppress. Privacy is a concept too integral to the person and a right too essential to freedom to allow its manipulation to support just those ideas the government prefers.

When it enacted § 4631(d), the Vermont Legislature found that the "marketplace for ideas on medicine safety and effectiveness is frequently one-sided in that brand name companies invest in expensive pharmaceutical marketing campaigns to doctors." "The goals of marketing programs," the legislature said, "are often in conflict with the goals of the state." The text of § 4631(d), associated legislative findings, and the record developed in the District Court establish that Vermont enacted its law for this end. The state has burdened a form of protected expression that it found too persuasive. At the same time, the state has left unburdened those speakers whose messages are in accord with its own views. This the state cannot do.

The judgment of the Court of Appeals is affirmed.
It is so ordered.

JUSTICE STEPHEN BREYER, with whom JUSTICE RUTH BADER GINSBURG and JUSTICE ELENA KAGAN join, dissenting.

The Vermont statute before us adversely affects expression in one, and only one, way. It deprives pharmaceutical and data-mining companies of data, collected pursuant to the government's regulatory mandate, that could help pharmaceutical companies create better sales messages. In my view, this effect on expression is inextricably related to a lawful governmental effort to regulate a commercial enterprise. The First Amendment does not require courts to apply a special "heightened" standard of review when reviewing such an effort. And, in any event, the statute meets the First Amendment standard this Court has previously applied when the government seeks to regulate commercial speech. For any or all of these reasons, the Court should uphold the statute as constitutional.

GLOSSARY

absolute privilege: A complete exemption from liability for defamation because the statement was made within the performance of official government duties.

actual malice: In libel law, a statement made knowing it is false or with reckless disregard for its truth.

ad hoc balancing: Making decisions according to the specific facts of the case under review rather than more general principles.

administrative law: The orders, rules and regulations promulgated by executive branch administrative agencies to carry out their delegated duties.

admonitions: Judges' instructions to jurors warning them to avoid potentially prejudicial communications.

affirm: To ratify, uphold or approve a lower court ruling.

all-purpose public figure: In libel law, a person who occupies a position of such persuasive power and influence as to be deemed a public figure for all purposes. All-purpose public figure libel plaintiffs are required to prove actual malice.

amicus brief: A submission to the court from **amicus curiae**, or "friends of the court," which are interested individuals or organizations that are parties in the case.

anti-SLAPP laws: State laws meant to provide a remedy for a SLAPP. Plaintiffs have the burden to show that they will prevail in the lawsuit; otherwise, the suit is dismissed.

appellant: The party making the appeal; also called the petitioner.

appellee: The party against whom an appeal is made.

appropriation: Using a person's name, picture, likeness, voice or identity for commercial or trade purposes without permission.

artistic relevance test: A test to determine whether the commercial use of a celebrity's name, picture, likeness, voice or identity is relevant to a disputed work's artistic purpose.

as applied: A legal phrase referring to interpretation of a statute on the basis of actual effects on the parties in the present case.

avatar: An icon or image that represents a person in a video game or other computer-generated content.

Berne Convention: The primary international copyright treaty adopted by many countries in 1886 and by the United States in 1988.

black-letter law: Formally enacted, written law that is available in legal reporters or other documents.

bootstrapping: In libel law, the forbidden practice of a defendant claiming that the plaintiff is a public figure solely on the basis of the statement that is the reason for the lawsuit.

broadband: A high-capacity transmission technique using a wide range of spectrum frequencies to enable a large number of messages to be communicated simultaneously.

broadcasting: Defined by the Communications Act of 1934 as use of the electromagnetic spectrum to send signals to many listeners and viewers simultaneously.

burden of proof: The requirement for a party to a case to demonstrate one or more claims by the presentation of evidence. In libel law, the plaintiff has the burden of proof.

categorical balancing: Legal reasoning that weighs different broad categories, such as political speech, against other interests, such as privacy, to create general rules that may be applied in later cases with similar facts.

child pornography: Any image showing children in sexual or sexually explicit situations.

chilling effect: The discouragement of a constitutional right, especially free speech, by any government practice that creates uncertainty about the proper exercise of that right.

class action lawsuit: A lawsuit in which a group of people with similar injuries caused by the same product or action sue a defendant as a group.

clear and present danger: Doctrine establishing that restrictions on First Amendment rights will be upheld if they are necessary to prevent an extremely serious and imminent harm.

Clery Act: The federal law that requires most universities to maintain up-to-date police logs and report campus crimes annually.

commercialization: The appropriation tort used to protect people who want privacy; prohibits using another person's name or likeness for commercial purposes without permission.

common law: Judge-made law composed of the principles and traditions established through court rulings; precedent-based law.

Communications Decency Act: The part of the 1996 Telecommunications Act that largely attempted to regulate internet content. The Communications Decency Act was successfully challenged in *Reno v. American Civil Liberties Union* (1997).

compelling interest: A government interest of the highest order, an interest the government is required to protect.

concurring opinion: A separate opinion of a minority of the court or a single judge or justice agreeing with the majority opinion but applying different reasoning or legal principles.

constitutional law: The set of laws that establish the nature, functions and limits of government.

construction: The process by which courts and administrative agencies determine the proper meaning and application of laws, rules and regulations.

content based: A term used to describe government actions prompted by the ideas, subject matter or position of the message.

content neutral: A term used to describe government actions that incidentally and unintentionally affect speech as they advance other important government interests unrelated to the content of speech.

continuance: Postponement of a trial to a later time.

contributory infringement: The participation in, or contribution to, the infringing acts of another person.

copyright: An exclusive legal right used to protect intellectual creations from unauthorized use.

corrective advertising: The Federal Trade Commission power to require an advertiser to advertise or otherwise distribute information to correct false or misleading advertisement claims.

cross-ownership rule: A Federal Communications Commission rule that governs when one entity can own two or more companies with related interests.

damages: Monetary compensation that may be recovered in court by any person who has suffered loss or injury. Damages may be compensatory for actual loss or punitive as punishment for outrageous conduct.

data broker: An entity that collects and stores personal information about consumers, then sells that information to other organizations.

de novo: Literally, "new" or "over again." On appeal, the court may review the facts de novo rather than simply reviewing the legal posture and process of the case.

deceptive advertising: Material claims made in the promotion, advertising or marketing of products or services that are likely to deceive consumers.

defamation: A false communication that harms another's reputation and subjects him or her to ridicule and scorn; incorporates both libel and slander.

defendant: The party accused of violating a law, or the party being sued in a civil lawsuit.

deference: The judicial practice of interpreting statutes and rules by relying heavily on the judgments and intentions of the administrative experts and legislative agencies that enacted the laws.

demurrer: A request that a court dismiss a case on the grounds that although the claims are true, they are insufficient to warrant a judgment against the defendant.

derivative work: A work that is obtained from or created in relation to an original work.

designated public forum: Government spaces or buildings that are available for public use (within limits).

dicta: Statements in a court opinion that are not central or essential to its reasoning or holding.

dilution: Using a famous trademark in a way that disparages or diminishes the mark's effectiveness in the market. Can happen from blurring or tarnishment.

discovery: The pretrial process of gathering evidence and facts. The word also may refer to the specific items of evidence that are uncovered.

discretion: The authority to determine the proper outcome.

disparaging marks: Trademarks considered immoral, disparaging or deceptive under the Lanham Act. Recently, the U.S. Supreme Court has ruled that the First Amendment protects immoral and disparaging marks.

dissenting opinion: A separate opinion of a minority of the court or a single judge or justice disagreeing with the result reached by the majority and challenging the majority's reasoning or the legal basis of the decision.

distinguish from precedent: To justify an outcome in a case by asserting that differences between that case and preceding cases outweigh any similarities.

doctrines: Principles or theories of law that shape judicial decision making (e.g., the doctrine of content neutrality).

Driver's Privacy Protection Act: Federal legislation that prohibits states from disclosing personal information that drivers submit in order to obtain a driver's license.

due process: Fair legal proceedings. Due process is guaranteed by the Fifth and 14th Amendments to the U.S. Constitution.

electromagnetic spectrum: The range of wavelengths or frequencies over which electromagnetic radiation extends. It is used to send both analog and digital signals.

Electronic Freedom of Information Act: A 1996 amendment to the Freedom of Information Act that applies the act to electronically stored information.

electronic media: All forms of media that utilize electronics or digital encoding to distribute news and entertainment.

emotional distress: Serious mental anguish.

en banc: Literally, "on the bench" but now meaning "in full court." The judges of a circuit court of appeals will sit en banc to decide important or controversial cases.

equity law: Law created by judges to decide cases based on fairness and ethics and also to determine the proper remedy.

executive orders: Orders from a government executive, such as the president, a governor or a mayor, that have the force of law.

experience and logic test: A doctrine that evaluates both the history of openness and the role it plays in ensuring the credibility of a judicial process to determine whether it is presumptively open.

facial meaning: The plain and straightforward meaning.

fact finder: In a trial, a judge or the jury determining which facts presented in evidence are accurate.

fair report privilege: A privilege for accurate and fair reports on the content of official records and proceedings. Sometimes called "conditional privilege."

fair use: A test courts use to determine whether using another's copyrighted material without permission is legal or an infringement. Also used in trademark infringement cases.

fairness doctrine: The Federal Communications Commission rule requiring broadcast stations to air programs discussing public issues and include a variety of views about controversial issues of public importance.

false light: A privacy tort that involves making a person seem in the public eye to be someone he or she is not. Not recognized in all states.

Family Educational Rights and Privacy Act: A federal law that protects the privacy of student education records. Also known as the Buckley Amendment.

Federal Communications Commission: A U.S. government agency, directly responsible to Congress and charged with regulating interstate and international communications by radio, television, wire, satellite, cable and broadband.

Federal Radio Commission: A federal agency established by the Radio Act of 1927 to oversee radio broadcasting. The Federal Communications Commission succeeded the FRC in 1934.

Federal Rules of Civil Procedure: General rules that govern all civil proceedings in the U.S. district courts.

Federal Trade Commission: A federal agency created in 1914. Its purpose is to promote free and fair competition in interstate commerce; this includes preventing false and misleading advertising.

federalism: A principle according to which the states are related to yet independent of each other and are related to yet independent of the federal government.

fighting words: Words not protected by the First Amendment because they are directed at an individual and cause immediate harm or trigger violent response.

first-sale doctrine: Once a copyright owner sells a copy of a work, the new owner may possess, transfer or otherwise dispose of that copy without the copyright owner's permission.

for-cause challenge: In the context of jury selection, the ability of attorneys to remove a potential juror for a reason the law finds sufficient, as opposed to a peremptory challenge.

forum shopping: A practice whereby the plaintiff chooses a court in which to sue because he or she believes the court will rule in the plaintiff's favor.

Freedom of Information Act: The federal law that requires records held by federal government agencies to be made available to the public unless covered by one of nine exemptions.

gag orders: A nonlegal term used to describe court restraining orders that prohibit publication or discussion of specific materials.

Government in the Sunshine Act: Sometimes referred to as the Federal Open Meetings Law, it mandates that meetings of federal government agencies be open to the public unless exempted under specific provisions of the law.

grand jury: A group summoned to hear the state's evidence in criminal cases and decide whether a crime was committed and whether charges should be filed; grand juries do not determine guilt.

hate speech: A category of speech that includes name-calling and pointed criticism that demeans others on the basis of race, color, gender, ethnicity, religion, national origin, disability, intellect or the like.

Health Insurance Portability and Accountability Act: A federal law protecting against health professionals and institutions revealing individuals' private medical records.

Hicklin **rule:** Taken from a mid-19th-century English case and used in the United States until the mid-20th century, a rule that defines material as obscene if it tends to corrupt children.

holding: The decision or ruling of a court.

impanel: To select and seat a jury.

important government interest: An interest of the government that is substantial or significant (i.e., more than merely convenient or reasonable) but not compelling.

incorporation doctrine: The 14th Amendment concept that most of the Bill of Rights applies equally to the states.

indecency: A narrow legal term referring to sexual expression and expletives inappropriate for children on broadcast radio and television.

infringement: The unauthorized manufacture, sale or distribution of an item protected by copyright, patent or trademark law.

infringement by inducement: Sometimes just called inducement. When a person or entity who does not directly infringe can be held liable for inducing others to infringe.

injunction: A court order prohibiting a person or organization from doing some specified act.

intellectual property law: The legal category including copyright, trademark and patent law.

intentional infliction of emotional distress: Extreme and outrageous intentional or reckless conduct causing plaintiffs severe emotional harm; public official and public figure plaintiffs must show actual malice on the defendant's part.

intermediate scrutiny: A standard applied by the courts to review laws that implicate but do not directly regulate core constitutional values; also called heightened review.

intrusion upon seclusion: Physically or technologically disturbing another's reasonable expectation of privacy.

involuntary public figure: In libel law, a person who is involuntarily drawn into a given issue. This category of plaintiff is rare.

judicial review: The power of the courts to determine the meaning of the Constitution and to decide whether laws violate the Constitution.

jurisdiction: The geographic or topical area of responsibility and authority of a court.

Lanham Act: A federal law that regulates the trademark registration process but also contains a section permitting business competitors to sue one another for false advertising.

laws of general application: Laws such as tax and equal employment laws that fall within the express power of government. Laws of general application are generally reviewed under minimum scrutiny.

legally qualified candidate: Someone who has publicly announced a bid for office, has her or his name on the ballot or is a serious write-in candidate. The candidate also must be legally qualified to hold the office.

legislative history: Congressional reports and records of deliberations about proposed legislation.

libel per quod: Libel that is actionable only when the plaintiff introduces additional facts to show defamation.

libel per se: A statement whose injurious nature is apparent and requires no further proof.

libel-proof plaintiff: A plaintiff whose reputation is deemed to be so damaged that additional false statements of and concerning him or her cannot cause further harm.

limited-purpose public figure: In libel law, a plaintiff who has attained public figure status within a narrow set of circumstances by thrusting him- or herself to the forefront of particular public controversies in order to influence the resolution of the issues involved; this kind of public figure is more common than the all-purpose public figure.

memorandum order: An order announcing the vote of the Supreme Court without providing an opinion.

metadata: A set of data that describes and gives information about other data.

modify precedent: To change rather than follow or reject precedent.

moot: Term used to describe a case in which the issues presented are no longer "live" or in which the matter in dispute has already been resolved; a case is not moot if it is susceptible to repetition but evades review.

motion to dismiss: A request to a court to reject a complaint because it does not state a claim that can be remedied by law or is legally lacking in some other way.

multichannel video programming distributor: An entity, including cable or direct broadcast satellite services, that provides multiple channels of video programming for purchase.

must-carry rule: Regulations enacted under the federal cable law that require multichannel video programming distributors to transmit local broadcast television stations. Also called the cable carriage requirement.

native advertising: Ads designed to resemble the editorial content of the medium where they appear.

negligence: Generally, the failure to exercise reasonable or ordinary care.

negligent infliction of emotional distress: Careless breach of a duty that causes the plaintiff severe emotional harm.

net neutrality: The principle that holds that internet service providers cannot charge content providers to speed up the delivery of their goods—all internet traffic is treated equally.

neutral reportage: In libel law, a defense accepted in some jurisdictions that provides First Amendment protection for reporting of an accusation made by a responsible and prominent organization, even when it turns out the accusation was false and libelous.

nonpublic forum: Government-held property that is not available for public speech and assembly purposes.

notice of proposed rulemaking: A notice issued by the Federal Communications Commission announcing that it is considering changing certain of its regulations or adopting new rules.

O'Brien test: A three-part test used to determine whether a content-neutral law is constitutional.

obscenity: The dictionary defines it as relating to sex in an indecent, very offensive or shocking way. The legal definition of obscenity comes from *Miller v. California*—material is determined to be obscene if it passes the *Miller* test.

original intent: The perceived intent of the framers of the Constitution that guides some First Amendment application and interpretation.

original jurisdiction: The authority to consider a case at its inception, as contrasted with appellate jurisdiction.

originalists: Supreme Court justices who interpret the Constitution according to the perceived intent of its framers.

overbroad laws: A principle that directs courts to find laws unconstitutional if they restrict more legal activity than necessary.

overrule: To reverse the ruling of a lower court.

overturn precedent: To reject the fundamental premise of a precedent.

patently offensive: Term describing material with hard-core sexual conduct.

PEG access channels: Channels that cable systems set aside for public, educational and governmental use.

per curiam opinion: An unsigned opinion by the Court as a whole.

peremptory challenge: During jury selection, a challenge in which an attorney rejects a juror without showing a reason. Attorneys have the right to eliminate a limited number of jurors through peremptory challenges.

plaintiff: The party who files a complaint; the one who sues.

political questions: Questions not subject to judicial review because they fall into areas properly handled by another branch of government.

pornography: A vague—not legally precise—term for sexually oriented material.

post-mortem: After death. Post-mortem right of publicity generally refers to a famous person's ability to control the commercial use of his or her name, picture, likeness, voice and identity after death.

precedent: The outcome of a previous case that establishes a rule of law for courts within the same jurisdiction to follow to determine cases with similar issues.

predominant use test: In a right of publicity lawsuit, a test to determine whether the defendant used the plaintiff's name or picture more for commercial purposes or protected expression.

prima facie: Latin for "at first look," or "on its face"; evidence before a trial that is sufficient to prove the case unless substantial contradictory evidence is presented.

prior restraint: Action taken by the government to prohibit publication of a specific document or text before it is distributed to the public; a policy that requires government approval before publication.

private facts: Publicizing highly offensive, true private information that is not newsworthy or lawfully obtained from a public record.

private figure: In libel law, a plaintiff who cannot be categorized as either a public figure or a public official. Generally, in order to recover damages, a private figure is required to prove negligence on the part of the defendant.

probable cause: The standard of evidence needed for an arrest or to issue a search warrant. More than mere suspicion, it is a showing through reasonably trustworthy information that a crime has been or is being committed.

promissory estoppel: A legal doctrine requiring liability when a clear promise is made and relied on and injury results from the broken promise.

proximate cause: The legal determination of whether it is reasonable to conclude that the defendant's actions led to the plaintiff's injury.

prurient interest: Lustful thoughts or sexual desires.

public domain: Refers to creative materials that are not protected by intellectual property laws. The public can use public domain work without permission.

public figure: In libel law, a plaintiff who is in the public spotlight, usually voluntarily, and must prove the defendant acted with actual malice in order to win damages.

public forum: Government property held for use by the public, usually for purposes of exercising rights of speech and assembly.

public record: A government record, particularly one that is publicly available.

puffery: Exaggerated but generally legal subjective advertising claims that no reasonable person would take literally.

quash: To void or nullify a legal procedure or action; a motion often made in response to subpoenas for confidential information

radio frequency: Any one of the electromagnetic wave frequencies that lie in the range extending from around 3 kHz to 300 GHz, which includes those frequencies used for communications or radio signals.

rational review: A standard of judicial review that assumes the constitutionality of reasonable legislative or administrative enactments and applies minimum scrutiny to their review.

reasonable person: The law's version of an average person.

reckless: Word used to describe actions taken with no consideration of the legal harms that might result.

red-flag knowledge: When an internet service provider or website is aware of facts that would make infringement obvious to a reasonable person.

remand: To send back to the lower court for further action.

reporter's privilege: The concept that reporters may keep information such as source identity confidential. The rationale is that the reporter–source relationship is similar to doctor–patient and lawyer–client relationships.

restraining order: A court order forbidding an individual or group of individuals from doing a specified act until a hearing can be conducted.

retraction statutes: In libel law, state laws that limit the damages a plaintiff may receive if the defendant has issued a retraction of the material at issue. Retraction statutes are meant to discourage the punishment of any good-faith effort of admitting a mistake.

retransmission consent: Part of the federal cable law allowing broadcast stations to negotiate a fee for retransmission of their programs.

ride-along: The practice of private citizens, especially professional communicators, accompanying law enforcement or emergency personnel as they carry out their duties.

right of publicity: The appropriation tort protecting a celebrity's right to have his or her name, picture, likeness, voice and identity used for commercial or trade purposes only with permission.

rule of law: The legal standards that guide the proper and consistent creation and application of the law.

safe harbor: The takedown notification provision of the Digital Millennium Copyright Act that protects internet service providers and video-sharing websites from claims of infringement when they do not know about or profit from the infringement and promptly comply with a takedown notice.

safe harbor policy: A Federal Communications Commission policy designating 10 p.m. to 6 a.m. as a time when broadcast radio and television stations may air indecent material without violating federal law or FCC regulations.

satellite market modification rule: Part of the Satellite Television Extension and Localism Act Reauthorization Act of 2014 that allows a television station, satellite operator or county government to request the addition or deletion of communities from a broadcast station's local television market.

secondary meaning: Meaning beyond a word's common meaning. To obtain secondary meaning, the public must associate a word with a product's source or producer, not the product.

Sedition Act of 1798: Federal legislation under which anyone "opposing or resisting any law of the United States, or any act of the President of the United States," could be imprisoned for up to two years. The act also made it illegal to "write, print, utter, or publish" anything that criticized the president or Congress.

seditious libel: Communication meant to incite people to change the government; criticism of the government.

sequestration: The isolation of jurors to avoid prejudice from publicity in a sensational trial.

serious social value: Material cannot be found obscene if it has serious literary, artistic, political or scientific value determined using national, not local/community, standards.

shield laws: State laws that protect journalists from being found in contempt of court for refusing to reveal sources.

single-publication rule: A rule that limits libel victims to only one cause of action even with republications of the libel in the same outlet; common in the mass media and on websites.

SLAPP (strategic lawsuit against public participation): A lawsuit whose purpose is to harass critics into silence, often to suppress those critics' First Amendment rights.

sound-alike: Someone whose voice sounds like another person's voice. Sound-alikes require permission or a disclaimer for commercial use.

spectrum scarcity: The limitation to the number of segments of the broadcast spectrum that may be used for radio or television in a specific geographical area without causing interference.

stare decisis: The doctrine that courts follow precedent; the basis of common law, it literally means to stand by the previous decision.

Statute of Anne: The first copyright law, adopted in England in 1710, protected authors' works if the authors registered them with the government.

statutory damages: Damages specified in certain laws. Under these laws, copyright being an example, a judge may award statutory damages even if a plaintiff is unable to prove actual damages.

statutory law: Written law formally enacted by city, county, state and federal legislative bodies.

strict construction: Courts' narrow interpretation and application of a law based on the literal meaning of its language. Especially applied in interpreting the Constitution.

strict liability: Liability without fault; liability for any and all harms, foreseeable or unforeseen, which result from a product or an action.

strict scrutiny: A court test for determining the constitutionality of laws aimed at speech content, under which the government must show it is using the least restrictive means available to directly advance its compelling interest.

subpoena: A command for someone to appear or testify in court or to turn over evidence, such as notes or recordings, with penalties for noncompliance.

substantiation: Support of a claim with objective data or evidence.

summary judgment: The resolution of a legal dispute without a full trial when a judge determines that undisputed evidence is legally sufficient to render judgment.

summons: A notice asking an individual to appear at a court. Potential jurors receive such a summons.

Supremacy Clause: Article IV, Part 2 of the U.S. Constitution establishes that federal law takes precedence over, or supersedes, state laws.

symbolic expression: Action that warrants some First Amendment protection because its primary purpose is to express ideas.

tacking: Allows a trademark owner to slightly alter a trademark without abandoning ownership of the original mark.

tarnishment: A poorly made or unsavory product using a mark similar to a famous trademark that could cause consumers to think less of the well-known product.

textualists: Judges—in particular, Supreme Court justices—who rely exclusively on a careful reading of legal texts to determine the meaning of the law.

third-party doctrine: A legal concept that holds that people who voluntarily give information to third parties, such as banks or phone companies, forfeit any reasonable expectation of privacy in that information.

time/place/manner laws: A First Amendment concept that laws regulating the conditions of speech are more acceptable than those regulating content; also, the laws that regulate these conditions.

tort: A private or civil wrong for which a court can provide remedy in the form of damages.

tortious newsgathering: The use of reporting techniques that are wrongful and unlawful and for which the victim may obtain damages in court.

trademark: A word, name, symbol or design used to identify a company's goods and distinguish them from similar products other companies make.

traditional public forum: Lands designed for public use and historically used for public gathering, discussion and association (e.g., public streets, sidewalks and parks). Free speech is protected in these areas.

transformative use: When the reuse of an original copyrighted work has transformed the work's appearance or nature to such a degree that the use is not infringing.

transformative use test: A test to determine whether the First Amendment protects a work that uses a person's name, picture, likeness, voice or identity for artistic purposes. Changing the original to give it new meaning or a different message justifies First Amendment protection.

Transmit Clause: Part of the 1976 Copyright Act that says broadcast networks, local broadcasters and cable television systems perform a work when they transmit content to viewers.

true threat: Speech directed toward an individual or historically identified group with the intent of causing fear of harm.

underinclusive: A First Amendment doctrine that disfavors narrow laws that target a subset of a recognized category for discriminatory treatment.

USA PATRIOT Act: The Uniting and Strengthening America by Providing Appropriate Tools Required to Intercept and Obstruct Terrorism Act of 2001. The act gave law enforcement agencies greater authority to combat terrorism.

vague laws: Laws that fail to define their terms or use language so general that it fails to inform citizens or judges with certainty what the laws permit or punish.

variable obscenity: The concept that sexually oriented material not obscene for adults may be obscene if distributed to minors.

venire: Literally, "to come" or "to appear"; the term used for the location from which a court draws its pool of potential jurors, who must then appear in court for voir dire; a change of venire means a change of the location from which potential jurors are drawn.

venue: The locality of a lawsuit and of the court hearing the suit. Thus, a change of venue means a relocation of a trial.

vicarious infringement: Under common law principles, companies are responsible for the acts of employees if the acts are within the nature and scope of their employment and the company has a financial interest in the infringement and the ability to control it.

vice products: Products related to activities generally considered unhealthy or immoral or whose use is restricted by age or other condition. The category includes alcohol, tobacco, firearms, sexually explicit materials and drugs.

viewpoint-based discrimination: Government censorship or punishment of expression based on the ideas or attitudes expressed. Courts will apply a strict scrutiny test to determine whether the government acted constitutionally.

voir dire: Literally, "to speak the truth"; the questioning of prospective jurors to assess their suitability.

Wiretapping and Electronic Surveillance Act: A federal law that makes it illegal to intercept, record, disseminate or use a private communication without a participant's permission.

work made for hire: Work created when working for another person or company. The copyright in a work made for hire belongs to the employer, not the creator.

writ of certiorari: A petition for review by the Supreme Court of the United States; *certiorari* means "to be informed of."

Zapple rule: A political broadcasting rule that allows a candidate's supporters equal opportunity to use broadcast stations if the candidate's opponents' supporters use the stations.

NOTES

CHAPTER 1 BOXED FEATURES

i. *What Is the Rule of Law?*, World Justice Project, worldjusticeproject.org/about-us/overview/what-rule-law, accessed Feb. 5, 2019.

ii. Rosa Ehrenreich Brooks, *The New Imperialism: Violence, Norms, and the "Rule of Law,"* 101 Mich. L. Rev. 2275 (2003); *but see* David Pimental, *Rule of Law Reform Without Cultural Imperialism?*, 2 Hague J. on Rule L. 1 (2010).

iii. *Rule of Law Index 2017–18*, World Justice Project, data.worldjusticeproject.org.

iv. U.S. Const. art. 1, § 8, cl. 11; *id.* art. II, § 2.

v. *Id.* art. VI, cl. 2.

vi. Anthony Bellia Jr. & B.R. Clark, *Why Federal Courts Apply the Law of Nations Even Though It Is Not the Supreme Law of the Land*, 106 Geo. L. J. 1915, 1960 (2017–18), www.law.georgetown.edu/georgetown-law-journal/wp-content/uploads/sites/26/2018/10/Why-Federal-Courts-Apply-the-Law-of-Nations.pdf.

vii. U.S. Const. art. III.

viii. David Moore, *The Supremacy Clause and International Law*, Jurist, July 1, 2012, www.jurist.org/commentary/2012/07/david-moore-international-law/; *but see* John Harrison, *The Constitution and the Law of Nations*, 106 Geo. L. J. 1659 (2018).

ix. Janus v. AFSCME, 138 S. Ct. 2448, 2497 (2018) (Kagan, J., dissenting) (internal citations omitted).

x. Calder v. Jones, 465 U.S. 783, 789 (1983).

xi. *Rule of Law Talk: Professor Jack Knight on Judicial Selection*, World Justice Project, Sept. 5, 2018, worldjusticeproject.org/about-us/connect/podcast/rule-law-talk-episode-1-judicial-selection.

xii. John G. Roberts, Jr., *Statement by Chief Justice John G. Roberts, Jr.*, Feb. 13, 2016, www.supremecourt.gov/publicinfo/press/pressreleases/pr_02-13-16. (William O. Douglas, the longest-serving justice, served 36 and a half years.) *See also* Supreme Court of the United States, *Frequently Asked Questions*, Mar. 14, 2016, www.supremecourt.gov/about/faq_justices.aspx.

xiii. Antonin Scalia, *Originalism: The Lesser Evil*, 57 U. Cin. L. Rev. 849, 862–64 (1989).

xiv. Antonin Scalia & Bryan A. Garner, Reading Law: The Interpretation of Legal Texts, xxviii–xxix (2012).

xv. Antonin Scalia, *The Rule of Law as a Law of Rules*, 56 U. Chi. L. Rev. 1175 (1989).

xvi. Alex Kozinski, *My Pizza With Nino*, 12 Cardoza L. Rev. 1583, 1588–89 (1991).

CHAPTER 1

1. *Interview with ABA President William Neukom*, ABA Dialogue on the Rule of Law, n.d., at 5, www.americanbar.org/content/dam/aba/administrative/public_education/resources/FinalDialogueROLPDF.pdf.

2. Planned Parenthood of Southeastern Pa. v. Casey, 505 U.S. 833, 854 (1992).

3. Alberto Luperon, *Election Law Expert: If Electoral College Abandons Trump, May Go Against Rule of Law*, Law Newz, Nov. 25, 2016, lawnewz.com/high-profile/election-law-expert-if-electoral-college-abandons-trump-may-go-against-rule-of-law; Garrett Epps, *The Electoral College Wasn't Meant to Overturn Elections*, Atlantic, Nov. 27, 2016, www.theatlantic.com/politics/archive/2016/11/the-electoral-college-shouldnt-save-us-from-trump/508817.

4. 2 U.S.C. § 441b (McCain–Feingold Act).

5. FEC v. Wisconsin Right to Life, Inc., 551 U.S. 449, 534 (2007) (Souter, J., dissenting).

6. Citizens United v. FEC, 530 F. Supp. 2d 274 (D.D.C. 2008).

7. 558 U.S. 310 (2010).

8. Libby Watson, *Six Years Later, the Impact of* Citizens United *Still Looms Large*, Sunlight Found., Jan. 21, 2016, sunlightfoundation.com/2016/01/21/6-years-later-the-impact-of-citizens-united-still-looms-large/.

9. Brandon J. Murrill, *The Supreme Court's Overruling of Constitutional Precedent*, Cong. Res. Serv., Sept. 24, 2018, fas.org/sgp/crs/misc/R45319.pdf.

10. *See* Dr. Seuss, The Lorax (1971). (Dr. Seuss is Theodor Seuss Geisel's pseudonym.)

11. Kenneth Grady, *The Election, the Rule of Law, and the Role of Lawyers*, Seytlines, Nov. 17, 2016, www .seytlines.com/2016/11/the-election-the-rule-of-law-and-the-role-of-lawyers.

12. Marbury v. Madison, 5 U.S. 137, 163 (1803).

13. Freidrich A. Hayek, The Road to Serfdom 54 (1944).

14. *See, e.g.,* John Gardner, *The Supposed Formality of the Rule of Law, in* Law as a Leap of Faith 205 (2012).

15. Moeen H. Chema, *The Politics of the Rule of Law*, 24 Mich. St. J. Int'l L. 449, 492 (2015).

16. 18 U.S.C. § 16(b).

17. Sessions v. Dimaya, 138 S. Ct. 1204 (2018).

18. *Id.* at 1222–3.

19. *Id.* at 1225.

20. Chief Rabbi Lord Sacks, *Passover Tells Us: Teach Your Children Well*, HuffPost Blog, Apr. 17, 2011, www.huffingtonpost.com/chief-rabbi-lord-sacks/ passover-message-for-huff_b_849623.html.

21. Planned Parenthood of Southeastern Pa. v. Casey, 505 U.S. 833, 854 (1992).

22. Brandon J. Murrill, *The Supreme Court's Overruling of Constitutional Precedent*, Cong. Res. Serv., Sept. 24, 2018, fas.org/sgp/crs/misc/R45319.pdf.

23. Kenneth Grady, *The Election, the Rule of Law, and the Role of Lawyers*, Seytlines, Nov. 17, 2016, www .seytlines.com/2016/11/the-election-the-rule-of-law-and-the-role-of-lawyers.

24. Johnson v. Department of Justice, 341 P.3d 1075, 1082 (Cal. 2015).

25. Lisa McElroy, *Citizens United v. FEC in Plain English*, SCOTUS Blog, Jan. 22, 2010, www.scotusblog.com/ 2010/01/citizens-united-v-fec-in-plain-english/.

26. Adam Liptak, *Justices, 5–4, Reject Corporate Spending Limit*, N.Y. Times, Jan. 21, 2010, www .nytimes.com/2010/01/22/us/politics/22scotus .html.

27. Glenn Greenwald, *What the Supreme Court Got Right*, Salon, Jan. 22, 2010, www.salon.com/2010/01/22/ citizens_united/.

28. Brandon J. Murrill, *The Supreme Court's Overruling of Constitutional Precedent*, Cong. Res. Serv., Sept. 24, 2018, fas.org/sgp/crs/misc/R45319.pdf.

29. 138 S. Ct. 2448 (2018).

30. 431 U.S. 209 (1977).

31. H.R.J. Res. 4, 62nd Cong., 1st Sess., 47 Cong. Rec. 4 (1911).

32. Aktepe v. United States, 105 F.3d 1400, 1402 (11th Cir. 1997) (*citing* Japan Whaling Ass'n v. American Cetacean Soc., 478 U.S. 221, 230 (1986)).

33. Stephanie Condon, *After 148 Years, Mississippi Finally Ratifies 13th Amendment*, CBS News, Feb. 18, 2013, www.cbsnews.com/8301-250_162-57569880/ after-148-years-mississippi-finally-ratifies-13th-amendment-which-banned-slavery/.

34. Wash. St. Const. art. 1, § 7.

35. 5 U.S. 137, 177 (1803).

36. Susan Dente Ross, *Access and New Media Technology: Teleconferencing, Telecommuting, and Public Access, in* Access Denied: Freedom of Information in the Information Age 65 (Charles Davis & Sig Splichal, eds., 2000).

37. Reno v. American Civil Liberties Union, 521 U.S. 844 (1997).

38. Paul W. Kahn, The Reign of Law: *Marbury v. Madison* and the Construction of America 4 (1997).

39. 5 U.S. 137 (1803).

40. Kahn, Reign of Law.

41. *See, e.g.,* Miller v. Alabama, 567 U.S. 460, 469 (2012) ("The cases before us implicate two strands of precedent reflecting our concern with proportionate punishment").

42. Dept. of Justice v. Rep. Committee for Freedom of the Press, 489 U.S. 749 (1989).

43. *See, e.g.,* Red Lion Broadcasting Co. v. FCC, 395 U.S. 367 (1969); Miami Herald Pub. Co. v. Tornillo, 418 U.S. 241 (1974).

44. *See* Bolger v. Youngs Drug Products Corp., 463 U.S. 60 (1983); Central Hudson Gas & Electric Corp. v. Public Service Commission of New York, 447 U.S. 557, 562–63 (1980); Ohralik v. Ohio State Bar Assn., 436 U.S. 447, 455–56 (1978); Virginia Pharmacy Bd. v. Virginia Citizens Consumer Council, Inc., 425 U.S. 748, 771–72, n. 24 (1976).

45. Janus v. Am. Fed. of State, County, and Mun. Employees, 138 S. Ct. 2448 (2018) (*rev'g* Abood v. Detroit Bd. of Ed., 431 U.S. 209 (1997)).

46. King v. Burwell, 135 S. Ct. 2480, 2488 (2015) (*rejecting* Chevron v. Natural Resource Defense Council, 467 U.S. 837, 842–43 (1984), two-stage process of (1) finding ambiguity and (2) deferring to reasonable administrative interpretations).

47. *Id.* at 2489.

48. *Id.* at 2492.

49. *Id.* at 2496.

50. Richard J. Pierce Jr., *The Future of Deference*, 84 Geo. Wash. L. Rev. 1293 (2016).

51. *See, e.g,* Panama Refining Co. v. Ryan, 293 U.S. 388, 431–34 (1935) (tying ambiguous presidential authority to explicit findings of fact and substantive due process).

52. Youngstown v. Sawyer, 343 U.S. 579, 637 (1952) (Jackson, J., concurring).

53. Kenneth Mayer, With the Stroke of a Pen: Executive Orders and Presidential Power (2001).

54. Charlie Savage & Robert Pear, *16 States Sue to Stop Trump's Use of Emergency Powers to Build Border Wall*, N.Y. Times, Feb. 18, 2019, nytimes.com/2019/02/18/us/politics/national-emergency-lawsuits-trump.html; Dartunorro Clark, *ACLU Sues Trump Over His National Emergency for Border Wall*, NBC News, Feb. 19, 2019, www.nbcnews.com/politics/politics-news/aclu-sues-trump-over-his-national-emergency-border-wall-n973306.

55. Bristol-Myers Squibb Co. v. Superior Court, 137 S. Ct. 1773 (2017).

56. *See, e.g.,* Keeton v. Hustler Magazine, Inc., 465 U.S. 770 (1984) (overturning lower court ruling dismissing libel suit filed by resident of New York against Ohio corporation in New Hampshire court). *See also* New York Times Co. v. Sullivan, 376 U.S. 254 (1964) (in which trial and first appeal were heard in Alabama courts).

57. Rich Samp, *With* Bauman v. Daimler Chrysler, *High Court May Have Put Brakes on Forum Shopping*, Forbes, Feb. 4, 2014, www.forbes.com/sites/wlf/2014/02/04/with-bauman-v-daimlerchrysler-high-court-may-have-put-brakes-on-forum-shopping.

58. Daimler AG v. Bauman, 571 U.S. 117 (2014).

59. Dashiell Bennett, *Obama: The Internet Is a Utility*, Atlantic, Nov. 10, 2014, www.theatlantic.com/technology/archive/2014/11/obama-internet-utility-fcc-regulation-net-neutrality/382561.

60. Matthew Chivvis, *Reexamining the Yahoo! Litigations: Toward an Effects Test for Determining International Cyberspace Jurisdiction*, 41 U.S.F.L. Rev. 699 (2007).

61. Calder v. Jones, 465 U.S. 783, 789 (1983).

62. Silva Mathema, *Assessing the Economic Impacts of Granting Deferred Action Through DACA and DAPA*, Ctr. for Am. Progress, June 15, 2016, uslegalsolutions.com/wp-content/uploads/2016/06/Assessing-the-Economic-Impacts-of-Granting-Deferred-Action-Through-DACA-and-DAPA-_-Center-for-American-Progress1.pdf.

63. 28 U.S.C. § 1292(a)(1).

64. U.S. Const. art. III, § 1.

65. *Briefing Paper*, SCOTUS Blog, June 28, 2010, www.scotusblog.com/wp-content/uploads/2010/06/Kagan-issues_ideology-June-29.pdf; *see also* Mark Tushnet, In the Balance: Law and Politics on the Roberts Court (2013).

66. Joan Biskupic, *Analysis: Justice Kagan—Giving Liberals a Rhetorical Lift*, Thompson Reuters, Apr. 5, 2012, www.reuters.com/article/us-usa-court-kagan/analysis-justice-kagan-giving-liberals-a-rhetorical-lift-idUSBRE83410E20120405?feedType=RSS&feedName=healthNews.

67. Mark Tushnet, *Opinions: Five Myths About the Roberts Court*, Wash. Post, Oct. 11, 2013, www.washingtonpost.com/opinions/five-myths-about-the-roberts-court/2013/10/11/69924370-30f4-11e3-8627-c5d7de0a046b_story.html.

68. Alicia Parlapiano & Karen Yourish, *Where Neil Gorsuch Would Fit on the Supreme Court*, N.Y. Times, Feb. 1, 2017, www.nytimes.com/interactive/2017/01/31/us/politics/trump-supreme-court-nominee.html?_r=0.

69. Katie Reilly, *Justice Sotomayor Calls for More Supreme Court Diversity*, Time, Apr. 9, 2016, time.com/4287655/sonia-sotomayor-supreme-court-diversity/.

70. David Masci & Gregory A. Smith, *Seven Facts About U.S. Catholics*, Pew Res. Ctr., Oct. 10, 2018, www.pewresearch.org/fact-tank/2018/10/10/7-facts-about-american-catholics/.

71. *Jews in America: By the Numbers*, PBS: Wash. Week, Feb. 21, 2017, www.pbs.org/weta/washingtonweek/blog-post/jews-america-numbers.

72. Richard Wolf, *About 2,000 Petitions Await Supreme Court's Return*, USA Today, Sept. 23, 2013, www.usatoday.com/story/news/nation/2013/09/23/supreme-court-petitions-prisoners-clerks/2843401/.

73. *See, e.g.,* Gregory A. Caldeira & John R. Wright, *The Discuss List: Agenda Building in the Supreme Court*, 24 Law & Society Rev. 807 (1990).

74. Samuel D. Warren & Louis D. Brandeis, *The Right to Privacy*, 4 Harv. L. Rev. 193 (1890).

75. Gabe Del Valle, *Most Criminal Cases End in Plea Bargains, Not Trials*, Outline, Aug. 7, 2017, theoutline.com/post/2066/most-criminal-cases-end-in-plea-bargains-not-trials?zd=1&zi=nxl77iqo.

76. Matt Vautour, *Colin Kaepernick, Eric Reid and NFL Reach Confidential Settlement in Collusion Case*, Mass. Live, Feb. 15, 2019, masslive.com/patriots/2019/02/colin-kaepernick-nfl-reach-confidential-settlement-in-collusion-case.html.

77. *Government Survey Shows 97 Percent of Civil Cases Settled*, Phoenix Bus. J., May 27, 2004, www.bizjournals.com/phoenix/stories/2004/05/31/newscolumn5.html?page=all.

78. Fed. R. Civ. P. 56(a).

79. Mourning v. Family Publishing Service, 411 U.S. 356, 382 (1973). *See also* Adickes v. Kress & Co., 398 U.S. 144, 157 (1970); United States v. Diebold, Inc., 369 U.S. 654, 655 (1962).

80. *See* Anderson v. Liberty Lobby, Inc., 477 U.S. 242 (1986).

81. Sumner v. Simpson University, 27 Cal. App. 5th 577 (2018).

82. Washington Post Co. v. Keogh, 365 F.2d 965, 968 (D.C. Cir. 1966).

83. Conley v. Gibson, 355 U.S. 41 (1957).

84. 550 U.S. 544 (2007).

85. 556 U.S. 662 (2009).

86. Joseph A. Seiner, *After* Iqbal, 45 Wake Forest L. Rev. 179, 180–81 (2010).

87. *GOP Senators' Bipartisan Bill Aims to Rein in Regulations From Unelected Federal Bureaucrats*, Ripon Advance News Serv., Jan. 15, 2019, riponadvance.com/stories/gop-senators-bipartisan-bill-aims-to-rein-in-regulations-from-unelected-federal-bureaucrats/.

88. *League Opposes H.R. 26, REINS Act of 2017*, lwv.org/content/league-opposes-hr-26-reins-act-2017.

89. Lisa Lambert & Richard Cowan, *Republicans Act to Curb U.S. Regulation*, Reuters, Jan. 5, 2017, www.reuters.com/article/us-usa-congress-regulations/republicans-act-to-curb-u-s-regulation-democrats-poised-for-fight-idUSKBN14Q07B.

90. 5 U.S.C. § 801(a)(1)(A).

91. H.R. 26, 115th Cong. (2017) (Regulations from the Executive in Need of Scrutiny Act).

92. *REINS Act Fact Sheet*, Public Citizen, n.d., citizen.org/sites/default/files/public_citizen_reins_act_fact_sheet.pdf.

93. Richard H. Pildes, *The Supreme Court's Contribution to the Confrontation Over Emergency Powers*, LawFare Blog, Feb. 19, 2019, lawfareblog.com/supreme-courts-contribution-confrontation-over-emergency-powers; Matt Latimer, *Trump's National Emergency Is Great News for Future President Alexandria Ocasio-Cortez*, Politico, Feb. 14, 2019, www.politico.com/magazine/story/2019/02/14/trump-national-emergency-border-precedent-225055.

94. *See* New York Times Co. v. Sullivan, 376 U.S. 254 (1964).

95. *See, e.g.,* 44 Liquormart v. Rhode Island, 517 U.S. 484 (1996).

96. *See* New York Times Co., 376 U.S. 254.

97. *See, e.g.,* Dan Eggen & T. W. Farnam, *More Setbacks for Campaign Finance Rules*, Wash. Post, July 15, 2010, at A17; Green Party of Connecticut v. Garfield, 616 F.3d 189 (2d Cir. 2010); Long Beach Area Chamber of Commerce v. City of Long Beach, 603 F.3d 684 (9th Cir.), *cert. denied*, 562 U.S. 896 (2010); SpeechNow.org v. FEC, 599 F.3d 686 (D.C. Cir.), *cert. denied*, 562 U.S. 1003 (2010); Citizens United v. FEC, 558 U.S. 310 (2010).

98. *Connecticut Campaign Finance Decisions From Second Circuit:* Green Party v. Garfield, Const. L. Prof Blog, July 13, 2010, lawprofessors.typepad.com/conlaw/2010/07/connecticut-campaign-finance-decisions-from-second-circuit-green-party-v-garfield.html.

99. Michael Cummins, *Citizens United and the Roberts Court*, Campaign for Liberty, June 30, 2010, www.campaignforliberty.com/article.php?view=978.

100. Damon W. Root, *Citizens United, Stare Decisis, and the Chicago Gun Case*, Reason, Jan. 22, 2010, reason.com/blog/2010/01/22/citizens-united-stare-decisis.

101. 5 U.S. 137 (1803).

CHAPTER 2 BOXED FEATURES

i. Sara Fischer, *U.S. Ranks Third Among G20 Nations in Google Censorship Requests*, Axios, Mar. 5, 2019, www.axios.com/google-government-censorship-requests-1dac73c4-0f94-455d-9245-ea2d36cbd10d.html.

ii. Archie L. Dick et al., *Are Established Democracies Less Vulnerable to Internet Censorship Than Authoritarian Regimes? The Social Media Test*, FAIFE Spotlight, www.ifla.org/files/assets/faife/publications/spotlights/2%20FAIFE_Dick_Oyieke_Bothma.pdf.

iii. Ted Bridis, *U.S. Sets New Record for Censoring, Withholding Gov't Files*, U.S. News & World Report, Mar. 12, 2018, www.usnews.com/news/business/articles/2018-03-12/us-sets-new-record-for-censoring-withholding-govt-files.

iv. Bland v. Roberts, 730 F.3d 368, 386 (4th Cir. 2013).

v. *Id.*

vi. *See, e.g.,* City of Ladue v. Gilleo, 512 U.S. 43 (1994).

vii. Eric Goldman, *Surveying the Law of Emojis*, Santa Clara Univ. Legal Studies Research Paper 8–17, May 1, 2017, papers.ssrn.com/sol3/papers.cfm?abstract_id=2961060.

viii. Eric Goldman, *Emoji Law 2018 Year-in-Review*, Tech. and Mkg. L. Blog, Jan. 31, 2019, blog.ericgoldman.org/archives/2019/01/emoji-law-2018-year-in-review.htm. *See also* Eric Goldman, *Emojis and the Law*, 93 Wash. L. Rev. 1227 (2018).

ix. Thomas I. Emerson, *Toward a General Theory of the First Amendment*, 72 Yale L.J. 877 (1963).

x. *See* John Locke, Two Treatises of Government 4 (Peter Laslett ed., Cambridge Univ. Press 1988) (1698).

xi. For detailed discussion, *see* Alexander Meiklejohn, Free Speech and Its Relation to Self-Government (1948); Robert Post, *Managing Deliberation: The Quandary of Democratic Dialogue*, 103 Ethics 654, 672 (1993).

xii. James Madison, *Report on the Virginia Resolutions* (Jan. 1800), reprinted in 5 The Founders' Constitution (Philip B. Kurland & Ralph Lerner eds., 1987); Vincent Blasi, *The Checking Value in First Amendment Theory*, 1977 Am. B. Found. Res. J. 521, 523 (1977).

xiii. Zechariah Chafee Jr., *Freedom of Speech in War Time*, 32 Harv. L. Rev. 932 (1919); Zechariah Chafee Jr., Freedom of Speech 37 (1920).

xiv. Vincent Blasi, *The Pathological Perspective and the First Amendment*, 85 Colum. L. Rev. 449, 464 (1985); C. Edwin Baker, *Scope of the First Amendment Freedom of Speech*, 25 UCLA L. Rev. 964 (1978).

xv. Ronald Dworkin, A Moral Reading of the American Constitution (1996).

xvi. Near v. Minnesota, 283 U.S. 697 (1931).

xvii. Nebraska Press Ass'n v. Stuart, 427 U.S. 539, 559 (1976).

xviii. United States v. O'Brien, 391 U.S. 367 (1968).

xix. 135 S. Ct. 2218 (2015).

xx. 558 U.S. 310 (2010).

xxi. Zachary Albert, *Trends in Campaign Financing, 1980–2016*, Campaign Finance Task Force, Oct. 12, 2017, bipartisanpolicy.org/wp-content/uploads/2018/01/Trends-in-Campaign-Financing-1980-2016.-Zachary-Albert.pdf.

xxii. Nour Abdul-Razzak et al., *After Citizens United: How Outside Spending Shapes American Democracy*, SSRN, Apr. 17, 2018, papers.ssrn.com/sol3/papers.cfm?abstract_id=2823778.

xxiii. Hillary Grigonis, *Government Requests for Facebook Data Continues* (sic) *to Grow*, Digital Trends, Dec. 12, 2017, www.digitaltrends.com/social-media/facebook-transparency-report-2017-first-half.

xxiv. Ben Lovejoy, *Secure Chat App Could Prove Key to Unmasking Charlottesville White Supremacists*, 9To5Mac, Aug. 8, 2018, 9to5mac.com/2018/08/08/discord-app-charlottesville.

xxv. Sines v. Kessler, 2018 WL 3730434 (N.D. Cal. Aug. 6, 2018).

xxvi. Special Regulations, Areas of the National Park System, National Capital Region, Special Events and Demonstrations, 83 Fed. Reg. 40,460 (proposed Aug. 15, 2018) (to be codified at 36 C.F.R. 7). *See* Olivia Paschal, *The Backlash to New Rules on Protests in D.C.*, Atlantic, Oct. 13, 2018, www.theatlantic.com/politics/archive/2018/10/new-rules-could-curb-protests-dc/572944.

xxvii. Kriston Capps, *White House to Protesters: "Get Off My Lawn?,"* CityLab, Oct. 16, 2018, www.citylab.com/design/2018/10/white-house-to-protesters-get-off-my-lawn/573040.

xxviii. Thornhill v. Alabama, 310 U.S. 88, 101–02 (1940) (emphasis added).

xxix. *See, e.g.,* Madsen v. Women's Health Ctr., 512 U.S. 753 (1994); United States v. Kokinda, 497 U.S. 720 (1990); Frisby v. Schultz, 487 U.S. 474 (1988); United States v. Grace, 461 U.S. 171 (1983); Cox v. Louisiana, 379 U.S. 536 (1965); Schneider v. New Jersey, 308 U.S. 147 (1939).

CHAPTER 2

1. Planned Parenthood of Southeastern Pa. v. Casey, 505 U.S. 833, 854 (1992).

2. Palko v. Connecticut, 302 U.S. 319 (1937).

3. Gitlow v. New York, 268 U.S. 652 (1925).

4. *See, e.g.,* Schenck v. United States, 249 U.S. 47 (1919); Brandenburg v. Ohio, 395 U.S. 444 (1969); Miller v. California, 413 U.S. 15 (1973); Nat'l Endowment for the Arts v. Finley, 524 U.S. 569 (1998). Note that even Justice Hugo Black, viewed as nearly a First Amendment absolutist, acknowledged that the authors of the First Amendment accepted some restraints on speech.

5. John Milton, *Areopagitica* (1st ed. n.p. 1644), in Great Books of the Western World 409 (1952).

6. John Locke, The Second Treatise of Civil Government (1690).

7. Jean-Jacques Rousseau, The Social Contract (1762).

8. 4 William Blackstone, Commentaries 151–52 (London: 1769).

9. *Id.* (emphasis added).

10. Frederick S. Siebert, Freedom of the Press in England 1476–1776, at 10 (1952); Leonard Levy, Legacy of Suppression (1960).

11. *See, e.g.,* Leonard Levy, Legacy of Suppression (1960); Leonard Levy, Emergence of a Free Press (1985). *But see* Zechariah Chafee, Free Speech in the United States 2 (1941) (arguing First Amendment was designed to eliminate law of sedition forever).

12. *See* James Morton Smith, Freedom's Fetters (1956).

13. *See* New York Times Co. v. Sullivan, 376 U.S. 254 (1964).

14. Ithiel de Sola Pool, Technologies of Freedom (1983).

15. *See, e.g.,* Philip M. Napoli, *What If More Speech Is No Longer the Solution?: First Amendment Theory Meets Fake News and the Filter Bubble*, 70 Fed. Com. L.J. 55 (2018).

16. *See* Lovell v. Griffin, 303 U.S. 444, 452 (1938); Burstyn v. Wilson, 343 U.S. 495 (1952).

17. Kovacs v. Cooper, 336 U.S. 77, 97 (1949) (Jackson, J., concurring).

18. Minneapolis Star & Tribune Co. v. Minnesota Comm'r of Revenue, 460 U.S. 575, 585 (1983).

19. *See, e.g.,* Red Lion Broadcasting Co. v. FCC, 395 U.S. 367 (1969).

20. *See, e.g.,* Turner Broadcasting Sys., Inc. v. FCC, 512 U.S. 622 (1994); Turner Broadcasting Sys., Inc. v. FCC, 520 U.S. 180 (1997).

21. Michael Barthel, *5 Facts About the State of the News Media in 2017*, FactTank, Aug. 21, 2018, www.pew research.org/fact-tank/2018/08/21/5-facts-about-the-state-of-the-news-media-in-2017.

22. Nicholas Rapp & Aric Jenkins, *These 6 Companies Control Much of U.S. Media*, Fortune, July 24, 2018, fortune.com/longform/media-company-ownership-consolidation.

23. Project for Excellence in Journalism of the Columbia University Graduate School of Journalism, *Overview: The State of the News Media 2005, An Annual Report on American Journalism*, www.journalism.org.

24. *See* Haleigh Jones, *Public Officials' Facebook "Likes": The Case for Leaving Regulation of Official "Likes" to the Torches and Pitchforks of Constituents*, 18 SMU Sci. & Tech. L. Rev. 263 (2015); Jonathan Peters, *WikiLeaks, the First Amendment, and the Press*, Harv. L. & Pol'y Rev., Apr. 18, 2011, hlpronline.com; Bland v. Roberts, 857 F. Supp. 2d 599 (E.D. Va. 2012).

25. *See, e.g.,* Angela Rulffes, *The First Amendment in Times of Crisis: An Analysis of Free Press Issues in Ferguson, Missouri*, 68 Syracuse L. Rev. 607 (2018); Katlyn E. DeBoer, *Clash of the First and Second Amendments: Proposed Regulation of Armed Protests*, 45 Hastings Const. L.Q. 333 (2017–18).

26. 315 U.S. 568, 571–72 (1942).

27. *See, e.g.,* United States v. Williams, 553 U.S. 285 (2008).

28. 573 U.S. 228 (2014).

29. 537 U.S. 228, 234 (2014) (*quoting* Garcetti v. Ceballos, 547 U.S. 410, 421 (2006)).

30. United States v. Alvarez, 567 U.S. 709 (2012).

31. 18 U.S.C. § 704(b).

32. United States v. Swisher, 771 F.3d 514 (9th Cir. 2014).

33. Susan B. Anthony List v. Driehaus, 814 F.3d 466, 472 (6th Cir. 2016).

34. West Virginia State Bd. of Educ. v. Barnette, 319 U.S. 624, 642 (1943).

35. *See, e.g.,* Vincent Blasi, *The Checking Value in First Amendment Theory*, 1977 Am. Bar Found. Res. J. 521 (1977).

36. *See, e.g.,* Catharine MacKinnon, Feminism Unmodified: Discourses on Life and Law (1987); Words That Wound: Critical Race Theory, Assaultive Speech, and the First Amendment (Mari J. Matsuda et al. eds., 1993).

37. *See, e.g.,* Lee C. Bollinger, The Tolerant Society: Freedom of Speech and Extremist Speech in America (1986).

38. *See, e.g.,* John Stuart Mill, On Liberty (1859); Alexander Meiklejohn, Free Speech and Its Relation to Self-Government (1948); Thomas I. Emerson, The System of Free Expression (1970); Cass Sunstein, Democracy and the Problem of Free Speech (1993).

39. *See,* Eugene Cerruti, *Dancing in the Courthouse: The First Amendment Right of Access Opens a New Round*, 29 U. Rich. L. Rev. 237 (1994–95); Steven G. Gey, *The First Amendment and the Dissemination of Socially Worthless Untruths*, 36 Fla. St. U. L. Rev. 1 (2008); Steven G. Gey, *Procedural Annihilation of Structural Rights*, 61 Hastings L.J. 1 (2009); Helen Norton, *Lies and the Constitution*, 2012 Sup. Ct. Rev.

161 (2012); Philip M. Napoli, *What If More Speech Is No Longer the Solution: First Amendment Theory Meets Fake News and the Filter Bubble*, 70 Fed. Comm. L.J. 55 (2018); Clay Calvert et al., *Fake News and the First Amendment: Reconciling a Disconnect Between Theory and Doctrine*, 86 U. Cinn. L. Rev. 99 (2018).

40. Steven G. Gey, *The First Amendment and the Dissemination of Socially Worthless Untruths*, 36 Fla. St. U. L. Rev. 1 (2008); Toni M. Massaro et al., *SIRI-OUSLY 2.0: What Artificial Intelligence Reveals About the First Amendment*, 101 Minn. L. Rev. 2481 (2017). *But see* Bruce E. H. Johnson et al., *Panel 1: Robotic Speech and the First Amendment*, 41 Seattle U. L. Rev. 1075 (2018), digitalcommons. law.seattleu.edu/sulr/vol41/iss4/4/ (arguing that whether viewed negatively or positively, the First Amendment protection is for listeners, not for speakers).

41. West Virginia State Bd. of Educ. v. Barnette, 319 U.S. 624, 642 (1943).

42. *See, e.g.,* C. Edwin Baker, *Scope of the First Amendment Freedom of Speech*, 25 UCLA L. Rev. 964 (1978).

43. Jud Campbell, *Natural Rights and the First Amendment*, 127 Yale L.J. 246 (2017–18).

44. 395 U.S. 367 (1969).

45. *Id.* at 387, 389.

46. 418 U.S. 241, 256 (1974).

47. *Id.*

48. *Id.* at 258.

49. 283 U.S. 697 (1931).

50. *Id.*

51. *Id.* at 708, 720.

52. *Id.* at 716.

53. 403 U.S. 713 (1971).

54. Janie Lorber, *Early Word: WikiLeaked*, N.Y. Times, July 30, 2010, thecaucus.blogs.nytimes.com.

55. Adam Kirsch, *Why Wikileaks Still Needs "The New York Times,"* New Republic, July 25, 2010, new republic.com/article/76562/why-wikileaks-still-needs-the-new-york-times.

56. WikiLeaks, wikileaks.org.

57. 403 U.S. at 714.

58. Nebraska Press Ass'n v. Stuart, 427 U.S. 539, 559 (1976).

59. New York Times Co. v. Jascalevich, 439 U.S. 1317 (1978); Nebraska Press Ass'n v. Stuart, 427 U.S. 539 (1976).

60. *See* National Writers Union, *Who Will Rid Me of This Troublesome Reporter?*, Trentonian, Feb. 20, 2019, www.trentonian.com/news/local/national-writers-union-who-will-rid-me-of-this-troublesome/article_5e810062-3534-11e9-ac48-03a151496542 .html; Kathryn Foxhall, *When Censorship Becomes a Cultural Norm*, Editor & Publisher, May 16, 2014, www.editorandpublisher.com/feature/when-censorship-becomes-a-cultural-norm2014-05-15t11-11-19.

61. CBS v. Davis, 510 U.S. 1315 (1994) (Blackmun, J., Circuit Justice).

62. Miami Herald Publ'g Co. v. McIntosh, 340 So. 2d 904, 910 (Fla. 1977).

63. Backpage.com, LLC v. Dart, 807 F.3d 229 (7th Cir. 2015).

64. *Id.* at 230.

65. David v. Textor, 189 So.3d 871, 873-874 (4th Dist. Fla. 2016).

66. *Id.* at 876.

67. CBS v. Davis, 510 U.S. 1315, 1320 (1994).

68. U.S. Const. art. I, § 8 (giving Congress authority "to regulate Commerce with foreign nations, and among the several states, and with the Indian Tribes").

69. Texas v. Johnson, 491 U.S. 397 (1989).

70. 502 U.S. 105 (1991).

71. *Id.*

72. Grayned v. City of Rockford, 408 U.S. 104 (1972).

73. United States v. O'Brien, 391 U.S. 367 (1968).

74. *Id.*

75. Ward v. Rock Against Racism, 491 U.S. 781 (1989). *See also* Matthew D. Bunker & Emily Erickson, *The Jurisprudence of Precision: Contrast Space and Narrow Tailoring in First Amendment Doctrine*, 6 Comm. L. & Pol'y 259 (2001).

76. Forsyth County v. The Nationalist Movement, 505 U.S. 123 (1992).

77. Ward v. Rock Against Racism, 491 U.S. 781 (1989).

78. 530 U.S. 703 (2000).

79. 573 U.S. 464 (2014).

80. Brown v. Town of Cary, 706 F.3d 294 (4th Cir. 2013).

81. 135 S. Ct. 2218 (2015).

82. *Id.* at 2227.

83. *Id.*

84. *Id.*

85. Genevieve Lakier, Reed v. Town of Gilbert, *Arizona, and the Rise of the Anticlassificatory First Amendment*, 1 Sup. Ct. Rev. 2016, www.journals .uchicago.edu/doi/full/10.1086/691625. *See also* Adam Liptak, *Court's Free-Speech Expansion Has Far-Reaching Consequences*, N.Y. Times, Aug. 17, 2015, www.nytimes.com/2015/08/18/us/politics/ courts-free-speech-expansion-has-far-reaching- consequences.html.

86. *See* Free Speech Coalition, Inc. v. Attorney Gen. United States, 825 F.3d 149 (3rd Cir. 2016); Sarver v. Chartier, 813 F.3d 891, 905–06 (9th Cir. 2016); Central Radio Co. v. City of Norfolk, 811 F.3d 625, 631 (4th Cir. 2016); Norton v. City of Springfield, Ill., 806 F.3d 411 (7th Cir. 2015).

87. Norton v. City of Springfield, Ill., 806 F.3d 411 (7th Cir. 2015).

88. Virginia v. Black, 538 U.S. 343, 365 (2003).

89. Meyer v. Grant, 486 U.S. 414 (1988).

90. *See, e.g.,* Buckley v. Valeo, 424 U.S. 1 (1976).

91. Minnesota Voters Alliance v. Mansky, 138 S. Ct. 1876, 1885–92 (2018).

92. *Id.* at 1891. *See also* Michael R. Dimino, Minnesota Voters Alliance v. Mansky *Strikes Down a Vague Ban on Speech in Polling Places, But Future Bans May Be Upheld*, 19 Fed. Society Rev. 2018 (9 Widener L. Commonwealth Res. Paper No. 18–16), poseidon01 .ssrn.com.

93. Torey Van Oot, *There Are Laws About What You Can Wear to Vote*, InStyle, Oct. 30, 2018, www .instyle.com/news/what-to-wear-voting-laws- electioneering.

94. Susan B. Anthony List v. Driehaus, 779 F.3d 628 (6th Cir. 2015).

95. Susan B. Anthony List v. Driehaus, 525 Fed. App'x 415 (6th Cir. 2013); *rev'd*, 573 U.S. 616 (2014).

96. Susan B. Anthony List v. Driehaus, 814 F.3d 466 (6th Cir. 2016).

97. Associated Press, *U.S. Supreme Court to Consider Ohio Ban on Campaign Lies*, Times-Picayune, Apr. 16, 2014, www.nola.com/politics/index.ssf/2014/04/ us_supreme_court_to_consider_o.html.

98. Nelson v. McClatchy, 936 P.2d 1123 (Wash. 1997).

99. *See, e.g.,* Perry v. Sindermann, 408 U.S. 593 (1972). For discussion of parallel treatment of public school students, see Chapter 3 and Tinker v. Des Moines Independent Community School Dist., 393 U.S. 503 (1969).

100. *See, e.g.,* Pickering v. Bd. of Educ., 391 U.S. 563 (1968); Snepp v. United States, 444 U.S. 507 (1980); Toni M. Massaro, *Significant Silences: Freedom of Speech in the Public Sector Workplace*, 61 S. Cal. L. Rev. 1 (1987). *But see* Daniel N. Hoffman, Governmental Secrecy and the Founding Fathers: A Study in Constitutional Controls (1981); Kermit L. Hall, *The Virulence of the National Appetite for Bogus Revelation*, 56 Md. L. Rev. 1 (1997).

101. Agency for Int'l Dev. v. Alliance for Open Society Int'l, Inc., 570 U.S. 205 (2013).

102. *Id.*

103. *Id.*

104. 547 U.S. 410 (2006).

105. *Id.* at 422.

106. Heffernan v. City of Paterson, 136 S. Ct. 1412 (2016).

107. *Id.*

108. *Id.*

109. Harris v. Quinn, 573 U.S. 616 (2014).

110. Friedrichs v. California Teachers Ass'n, 135 S. Ct. 2993 (2016).

111. Matal v. Tam, 137 S. Ct. 1744, 1758 (2017).

112. Wandering Dago v. Destito, 879 F.3d 20 (2d Cir. 2018). *See* Matal v. Tam, 137 S. Ct. 1744 (2017).

113. Eric Sundin, Note: *To Alito, or Not to Alito: An Analysis of Government Speech in a Post-Walker World*, 8 Houston L. Rev. 31, 42 (2017).

114. Matal v. Tam, 137 S. Ct. 1744, 1760 (2017) (characterizing Walker v. Texas Div., Sons of Confed. Veterans, 135 S. Ct. 2239 (2015)).

115. *Walker*, 135 S. Ct. at 2245.

116. Pleasant Grove City v. Summum, 555 U.S. 460 (2009).

117. *Id.*

118. *Id.* at 481.

119. Walker, 135 S. Ct. at 2255 (Alito, J., dissenting).

120. Manhattan Cmty. Access Corp. v. Halleck, 2019 U.S. LEXIS 4178 (2019).

121. 882 F.3d 300, 304 (2d Cir. 2018).

122. *Id.*

123. *Halleck*, 2019 U.S. LEXIS 4178.

124. *Id.* at *5.

125. *Id.*

126. *Id.* at *18.

127. *Id.* at *19.

128. *Id.* at *40, *39.

129. *Id.* at *46.

130. Charles Fain Lehman, *SCOTUS: Private Firms Not Bound by First Amendment*, WASHINGTON FREE BEACON, June 17, 2019, freebeacon.com/issues/scotus-private-firms-not-bound-by-first-amendment/.

131. Elliot Mincbert, *Kavanaugh and Gorsuch Cast Deciding Votes to Allow Public Access Cable TV Censorship*, CONFIRMED JUDGES, CONFIRMED FEARS, June 17, 2019, www.pfaw.org/blog-posts/confirmed-judges-confirmed-fears-kavanaugh-and-gorsuch-cast-deciding-votes-to-allow-public-access-cable-tv-censorship/.

132. Tony Mauro, *SCOTUS Ruling Could Let Tech Platforms Avoid First Amendment Constraints*, NAT'L L. J., June 17, 2019, www.law.com/nationallawjournal/2019/06/17/scotus-ruling-could-let-tech-platforms-avoid-first-amendment-constraints/.

133. Wooley v. Maynard, 430 U.S. 705, 714 (1977).

134. West Virginia State Bd. of Educ. v. Barnette, 319 U.S. 624 (1943).

135. Ambach v. Norwick, 441 U.S. 68 (1979).

136. *See, e.g.,* Epperson v. Arkansas, 393 U.S. 97 (1968); Edwards v. Aguillard, 482 U.S. 578 (1987); Pickering v. Bd. of Educ., 391 U.S. 563 (1968).

137. West Virginia State Bd. of Educ. v. Barnette, 319 U.S. 624, 642 (1943).

138. Wooley v. Maynard, 430 U.S. 705, 714 (1977).

139. Nat'l Instit. of Family & Life Advocates v. Becerra, 138 S. Ct. 2361 (2018).

140. 138 S. Ct. 1719 (2018).

141. *See* Scott W. Gaylord, *Is a Cake Worth a Thousand Words? Masterpiece Cakeshop and the Impact of Antidiscrimination Laws on the Marketplace of Ideas*, 85 TENN. L. REV. 361 (2018); John G. Culhane, *The Right to Say, But Not to Do: Balancing First Amendment Freedom of Expression With the Anti-Discrimination Imperative*, 24 WIDENER L. REV. 235 (2018).

142. 558 U.S. 310 (2010).

143. *See, e.g.,* Am. Tradition Partnership v. Bullock, 132 S. Ct. 2490 (2012) (per curiam); Texans for Free Enter. v. Tex. Ethics Comm'n, 732 F.3d 535 (5th Cir. 2013); Wis. Right to Life v. Barland, 751 F.3d 804 (7th Cir. 2014); *c.f.* Bluman v. FEC, 132 S. Ct. 1087 (2012) (summary judgment upholding ban on foreign political contributions); Republican Party v. King, 741 F.3d 1089 (10th Cir. 2013).

144. McCutcheon v. FEC, 572 U.S. 185 (2014).

145. *Id.* at 224.

146. Citizens United v. Gessler, 773 F.3d 200 (10th Cir. 2014).

147. *Id.*

148. Ysursa v. Pocatello Educ. Ass'n, 555 U.S. 353 (2009).

149. McIntyre v. Ohio Election Comm'n, 514 U.S. 334, 357 (1995).

150. *See* Talley v. California, 362 U.S. 60 (1960); Buckley v. Am. Const. L. F., 525 U.S. 182 (1999); Watchtower v. Stratton, 536 U.S. 150 (2002).

151. Doe v. Reed, 561 U.S. 186 (2010).

152. Doe v. Reed, 823 F. Supp. 2d 1195 (W.D. Wash. 2011).

153. *In re* Grand Jury Subpoena, 875 F.3d 1179 (9th Cir. 2017).

154. 18 U.S.C. § 2703. *But see* 47 U.S.C. § 551(c) (potentially establishing a higher standard for forced disclosure of identifying information on cable subscribers).

155. Branzburg v. Hayes, 408 U.S. 665 (1972).

156. *In re* Grand Jury Subpoena Issued to Twitter, Inc., 2017 WL 9485553 (N.D. Tex. Nov. 7, 2017); *see also* Music Grp. Macao Commercial Offshore, Ltd. v. Does, 82 F. Supp. 3d 979, 983 (N.D. Cal. 2015) (denying motion to compel Twitter to disclose anonymous website posters).

157. Hague v. Comm. for Industrial Org., 307 U.S. 496, 515 (1939).

158. *See, e.g.,* Susan Dente Ross, *An Apologia to Radical Dissent and a Supreme Court Test to Protect It*, 7 COMM. L. & POL'Y 401 (2002); Ronald J. Krotoszynski Jr., *Essay: Celebrating Selma: The Importance of Context in Public Forum Analysis*, 104 YALE L.J. 1411 (1995).

159. *See, e.g.,* Skokie v. Nat'l Socialist Party of America, 439 U.S. 916 (1978); Hess v. Indiana, 414 U.S. 105

(1973); Brown v. Louisiana, 383 U.S. 131 (1966); Edwards v. South Carolina, 371 U.S. 229 (1963); NAACP v. Claiborne Hardware Co., 458 U.S. 886 (1982); Gregory v. City of Chicago, 394 U.S. 111 (1969); Grayned v. Rockford, 408 U.S. 104 (1972).

160. 562 U.S. 443 (2011).

161. Grayned v. Rockford, 408 U.S. 104, 116 (1972); Perry Educ. Ass'n v. Perry Local Educators' Ass'n, 460 U.S. 37 (1983).

162. *See, e.g.,* Hague v. Comm. for Industrial Org., 307 U.S. 496 (1939).

163. Coe v. Town of Blooming Grove, 429 F. App'x 55 (2d Cir. 2011).

164. Bell v. Keating, 697 F.3d 445 (7th Cir. 2012).

165. *See, e.g.,* Frisby v. Schultz, 487 U.S. 474 (1988); Madsen v. Women's Health Center, Inc., 512 U.S. 753 (1994). *But see* Scheidler v. Nat'l Org. for Women, 537 U.S. 393 (2003) (removing civil injunction on anti-abortion protesters and rejecting claim that their protests constituted illegal extortion and racketeering).

166. *See, e.g.,* Greer v. Spock, 424 U.S. 828 (1976).

167. *See, e.g.,* Smith v. Exec. Dir. of the Indiana War Memorials Comm'n, 742 F.3d 282 (7th Cir. 2014); Miller v. City of Cincinnati, 622 F.3d 524 (6th Cir. 2010), *cert. denied*, 536 U.S. 974 (2011).

168. Zeran v. America Online, 129 F.3d 327, 330 (4th Cir. 1997).

169. Packingham v. North Carolina, 137 S. Ct. 1730 (2017).

170. *Id.* at 1732.

171. Davison v. Randall, 912 F.3d 666 (4th Cir. 2019).

172. Knight First Amend. Institute v. Trump, 302 F. Supp. 3d 541 (S.D. N.Y. 2018).

173. *See* Eric Goldman, *Of Course the First Amendment Protects Google and Facebook (and It's Not a Close Question)*, Knight First Amendment Institute's Emerging Threats Series, Feb. 2018; Dawn C. Nunziato, *From Town Square to Twittersphere: The Public Forum Doctrine Goes Digital*, 25 B.U. J. Sci. & Tech. L. (2019) (Forthcoming;GWULegalStudiesResearchPaperNo. 2018-40); Micah Telegen, *You Can't Say That!: Public Forum Doctrine and Viewpoint Discrimination in the Social Media Era*, 52 U. Mich. J. L. Reform 235 (2018), repository.law.umich.edu/mjlr/vol52/iss1/7.

174. Morgan v. Bevin, 2018 U.S. Dist. LEXIS 204657.

175. *See, e.g.,* United States v. Albertini, 472 U.S. 675 (1985); Los Angeles City Council v. Taxpayers for Vincent, 466 U.S. 789 (1984); United States v. Kokinda, 497 U.S. 720 (1990).

176. *See, e.g.,* Adderley v. Florida, 385 U.S. 39 (1966).

177. *See, e.g.,* Amalgamated Food Employees Union v. Logan Valley Plaza, Inc., 391 U.S. 308 (1968); Hudgens v. Nat'l Labor Relations Bd., 424 U.S. 507 (1976); PruneYard Shopping Center v. Robins, 447 U.S. 74 (1980). *But see* Lloyd Corp., Ltd. v. Tanner, 407 U.S. 551 (1972).

178. *See, e.g.,* Bd. of Regents of the Univ. of Wis. v. Southworth, 529 U.S. 217 (2000); Rosenberger v. Rector & Visitors of the Univ. of Virginia, 515 U.S. 819 (1995).

179. *See, e.g.,* Grosjean v. Am. Press Co., 297 U.S. 233 (1936); Minneapolis Star & Tribune Co. v. Minnesota Comm'r of Revenue, 460 U.S. 575 (1983); Arkansas Writers' Project v. Ragland, 481 U.S. 221 (1987). *But see* Leathers v. Medlock, 499 U.S. 439 (1991).

180. Legal Services Corp. v. Velasquez, 532 U.S. 533 (2001).

181. NEA v. Finley, 524 U.S. 569 (1998).

182. Island Trees Union Free School Dist. Bd. of Ed. v. Pico, 457 U.S. 853 (1982).

183. Brandon T. Metroka, *The Roberts Court Constitution of Freedom of Speech: Preferences, Principles, and the Study of Supreme Court Decision-Making*, Surface 268 No. 1 (2017) (Ph.D. dissertation, Syracuse University) surface.syr.edu/cgi/viewcontent.cgi? referer=https://scholar.google.com/scholar? hl=en&as_sdt=0%2C48&as_ylo=2015&q=SCOTUS+ %22freedom+of+association%22+underdeveloped &btnG=&httpsredir=1&article=1695&context=etd.

184. *See, e.g.,* Boy Scouts of America v. Dale, 530 U.S. 640 (2000).

185. Hurley v. Irish-American Gay, Lesbian and Bisexual Group of Boston, 515 U.S. 557, 575 (1995).

186. Brian MacQuarrie & Laura Krantz, *Strife Forgotten Amid Inclusive St. Patrick's Day Parade*, Boston Globe, Mar. 18, 2015, www.bostonglobe .com/metro/2015/03/15/preparations-under-way-for-this-afternoon-patrick-day-parade/ XBloZY1z2vTe9SZnev8qyN/story.html.

187. Abbott v. Perez, 138 S. Ct. 1916 (2018); Gill v. Whitford, 138 S. Ct. 2305 (2018).

188. Abigail Aguilera, *Drawing the Line:* Whitford v. Gill and *the Search for Manageable Partisan Gerrymandering Standards*, 86 U. Cinn. L. Rev. 775 (2018).

189. Gill v. Whitford, 138 S. Ct. at 1934 (Kagan, J., dissenting).

190. *Id.* at 1939.

191. Republican Party v. Cox, 885 F. 3d 1219 (10th Cir. 2018); Hand v. Scott, 285 F. Supp. 3d 1289 (N.D. Fla. 2018); N.C. Common Cause v. Rucho, 284 F. Supp. 3d 780 (M.D.N.C. 2018).

192. Adams v. Governor of Delaware, 914 F.3d 827 (3d Cir. 2019); Delaware Const. art. IV, § 3. *See* Steven D. Schwinn, *Third Circuit Says Political Balancing on Bench Violates Free Association*, Const. LawProf Blog, Feb. 6, 2019, lawprofessors.typepad.com/conlaw/2019/02/third-circuit-says-political-balancing-on-bench-violates-free-association.html.

193. Randy J. Holland, The Delaware State Constitution 149 (2011).

194. Newman v. Voinovich, 986 F.2d 159 (6th Cir. 1993); Kurowski v. Krajewski, 848 F.2d 767, 771 (7th Cir. 1988) (finding that selection and termination of judges may apply political criteria), *cert. denied*, 488 U.S. 926 (1988)).

CHAPTER 3 BOXED FEATURES

i. David Estlund, *Democracy and the Real Speech Situation*, in Deliberative Democracy and Its Discontents 76 (Samantha Besson & Jose Luis Marti eds., 2006).

ii. Martin Redish, The Logic of Persecution: Free Expression and the McCarthy Era 54, 62 (2006).

iii. Barack Orbach, *On Hubris, Civility, and Incivility*, 54 Ariz. Law Rev. 443 (2012).

iv. Brandenburg v. Ohio, 395 U.S. 444 (1969).

v. Hess v. Indiana, 414 U.S. 105 (1973) (per curiam).

vi. Richard A. Wilson, Brandenburg *in an Era of Populism: Risk Analysis in the First Amendment* (last revised Apr. 7, 2019), forthcoming in U. Penn. J.L. & Pub. Aff., dx.doi.org/10.2139/ssrn.3330195.

vii. Bell Atl. Corp. v. Twombly, 550 U.S. 544 (2007); Ashcroft v. Iqbal, 556 U.S. 662 (2009).

viii. C.H. Stein et al., *Understanding Young Adults' Reports of Contact With Their Parents in a Digital World: Psychological and Familial Relationship*, 25 J. Child and Fam. Stud. 1802 (2016).

ix. P.K. Smith et al., *Cyberbullying: Its Nature and Impact in Secondary School Pupils*, 49 J. Child Psych. & Psychiatry 376 (2008).

x. Anna Constanza Baldry et al., *Cyberbullying and Cybervictimization Versus Parental Supervision, Monitoring and Control of Adolescents' Online Activities*, 96 Children & Youth Services Rev. 302 (2019), www.sciencedirect.com/science/article/pii/S0190740918307035.

xi. S. Horner et al., *The Impact and Response to Electronic Bullying and Traditional Bullying Among Adolescents*, 49 Computers in Hum. Behav. 288 (2015).

xii. 18 U.S.C. § 1030.

xiii. United States v. Drew, 259 F.R.D. 449, 451 n.2 (C.D. Calif. 2009).

xiv. *Laws, Policies & Regulations*, Stop Bullying, Jan. 7, 2018, www.stopbullying.gov/laws/index.html#1.

xv. Naganna Chetty, *Hate Speech Review in the Context of Online Social Networks*, 40 Aggression & Violent Behav. 108 (2018).

xvi. David Goldman, *Big Tech Made the Social Media Mess. It Has to Fix It*, CNN Business, Oct. 29, 2018, www.cnn.com/2018/10/29/tech/social-media-hate-speech/index.html.

xvii. *Facebook Calls Upon Joint Effort to Curb Hate Speech*, Digital Watch, Feb. 13, 2019, dig.watch/issues/content-policy.

xviii. 538 U.S. 343 (2003).

xix. United States v. Elonis, 841 F.3d 589 (3d Cir. 2016), *cert. denied*, 138 S. Ct. 67 (2017).

xx. *See* United States v. Wheeler, 776 F.3d 736 (10th Cir. 2015).

xxi. *See* United States v. Magleby, 241 F.3d 1306 (10th Cir. 2001).

xxii. Knox v. Pennsylvania, 203 L. Ed. 2d 746 (2019).

xxiii. Tinker v. Des Moines Indep. Cmty. Sch. Dist., 393 U.S. 503, 509 (1969).

xxiv. Bethel Sch. Dist. v. Fraser, 478 U.S. 675 (1986); Hazelwood Sch. Dist. v. Kuhlmeier, 484 U.S. 260 (1988).

xxv. *Hazelwood*, 484 U.S. 260; Lemon v. Kurtzman, 403 U.S. 602 (1971); Bd. of Regents of Univ. of Wis. System v. Southworth, 529 U.S. 217 (2000).

xxvi. *Exec. Order on Improving Free Inquiry, Transparency, and Accountability at Colleges and Universities*, White House, Mar. 21, 2019, www.whitehouse .gov/presidential-actions/executive-order-improving-free-inquiry-transparency-accountability-colleges-universities; Beth McMurtrie, *Trump's Free-Speech Order Could Have Been Harsher, But Higher-Ed Leaders Still Don't Approve*, Chronicle of Higher Ed., Mar. 21, 2019, www.chronicle.com/article/Trump-s-Free-Speech-Order/245956?cid=at&utm_ source=at&utm_medium=en&cid=at.

xxvii. Matthew S. Schwartz, *Trump and Universities in Fight Over Free Speech, Federal Research Funding*, NPR, Mar. 22, 2019, www.npr.org/2019/03/22/ 705739383/trump-and-universities-in-fight-over-free-speech-federal-research-funding.

xxviii. Kasia Kovacs, *Inflammatory and Turned Away*, Inside Higher Ed, Oct. 21, 2016, www.insidehighered.com/ news/2016/10/21/several-universities-cancel-appearances-conservative-writer-milo-yiannopoulos; Adam Tamurin, *Breitbart's Milo Yiannopoulos Inspires Tennessee "Free Speech" Bill*, Tennessean, Feb. 9, 2017, www.tennessean.com/story/news/politics/ 2017/02/09/breitbarts-milo-yiannopolous-inspires-tennessee-free-speech-bill/97690656; Peter Beinart, *Everyone Has a Right to Free Speech, Even Milo*, Atlantic, Feb. 3, 2017, www.theatlantic.com/politics/ archive/2017/02/everyone-has-a-right-to-free-speech-even-milo/515565.

xxix. Erwin Chemerinsky & Howard Gillman, Free Speech on Campus (2017).

xxx. Matthew S. Schwartz, *Trump and Universities in Fight Over Free Speech, Federal Research Funding*, NPR, Mar. 22, 2019, www.npr.org/2019/03/22/705739383/ trump-and-universities-in-fight-over-free-speech-federal-research-funding.

CHAPTER 3

1. Schenck v. United States, 249 U.S. 47, 52 (1919).

2. *Id.*

3. Elonis v. United States, 135 S. Ct. 2001 (2015), *conviction aff'd on remand*, 841 F.3d 589 (3d Cir. 2016).

4. Chaplinsky v. New Hampshire, 315 U.S. 568, 572 (1942).

5. *Schenck*, 249 U.S. 47, 52 (1919).

6. *Id.*

7. *Id.*

8. Frohwerk v. United States, 249 U.S. 204 (1919).

9. *Id.* at 208–09.

10. Debs v. United States, 249 U.S. 211 (1919).

11. Abrams v. United States, 250 U.S. 616 (1919).

12. *Id.* at 628 (Holmes, J., dissenting).

13. *Id.* at 630.

14. Dennis v. United States, 341 U.S. 494 (1951); Scales v. United States, 367 U.S. 203 (1961). *See also* Whitney v. California, 274 U.S. 357 (1927).

15. Gitlow v. New York, 268 U.S. 652 (1925).

16. *Id.* at 669.

17. *Id.* at 667.

18. *Id.* at 673 (Holmes, J., dissenting).

19. *Id.* at 666.

20. Whitney v. California, 274 U.S. 357 (1927).

21. *Id.* at 377–78 (Brandeis, J., concurring).

22. *Id.* at 379 (emphasis added).

23. Am. Commc'n Ass'n v. Douds, 339 U.S. 382 (1950).

24. *Id.* at 448–49 (Black, J., dissenting).

25. Dennis v. United States, 341 U.S. 494 (1951); Kunz v. New York, 340 U.S. 290, 300 (1951); Yates v. United States, 354 U.S. 298 (1957).

26. *See* Liezl Irene Pangilinan, Note: *"When a Nation Is at War": A Context-Dependent Theory of Free Speech for the Regulation of Weapon Recipes*, 22 Cardozo Arts & Ent. L.J. 683 (2004).

27. 395 U.S. 444 (1969).

28. *Id.* at 447.

29. *Id.* at 448.

30. 414 U.S. 105 (1973) (per curiam).

31. Bell Atl. Corp. v. Twombly, 550 U.S. 544 (2007); Ashcroft v. Iqbal, 556 U.S. 662 (2009).

32. Brandenburg v. Ohio, 395 U.S. 444, 447 (1969).

33. *Bell Atl. Corp.*, 550 U.S. 544; *Ashcroft*, 556 U.S. 662.

34. Nwanguma v. Trump, 903 F.3d 604 (6th Cir. 2018), *rehearing en banc denied*, 2018 U.S. App. LEXIS 33603 (6th Cir., Nov. 29, 2018).

35. *Bell Atl. Corp.*, 550 U.S. at 555.

36. *Ashcroft*, 556 U.S. at 678.

37. Cohen v. California, 403 U.S. 15 (1971).

38. *Id.* at 25.

39. Lozman v. City of Riviera Beach, Fla., 138 S. Ct. 1945 (2018).

40. *Id.* (citing Mt. Healthy City Bd. of Educ. v. Doyle, 429 U.S. 274 (1977)).

41. Nieves v. Bartlett, 2019 U.S. LEXIS 3557 at *22 (2019).

42. Martin H. Redish, *Advocacy of Unlawful Conduct and the First Amendment: In Defense of Clear and Present Danger*, 70 CAL. L. REV. 1159, 1162 (1982).

43. Gitlow v. New York, 268 U.S. 652, 673 (1925).

44. Chaplinsky v. New Hampshire, 315 U.S. 568 (1942).

45. *Id.* at 571–72.

46. Terminiello v. Chicago, 337 U.S. 1, 3 (1949).

47. *Id.* at 4 (emphasis added).

48. *Id.*

49. *Id.*

50. *See, e.g.,* Gooding v. Wilson, 405 U.S. 518 (1972).

51. Saieg v. City of Dearborn, 641 F.3d 727 (6th Cir. 2011); Bible Believers v. Wayne County, 805 F.3d 228, 264 (6th Cir. 2015), *cert. denied*, 136 S. Ct. 2013 (2016).

52. R.A.V. v. City of St. Paul, 505 U.S. 377 (1992).

53. *Id.* at 384–85, 386.

54. Garcia v. Google, 786 F.3d 727, 728–29 (9th Cir. 2015) (en banc).

55. Joshua Vaughn, *A Black Man Called the Cops Nazis—and Was Charged With a Hate Crime*, THE APPEAL, June 28, 2018, theappeal.org/a-black-man-called-the-cops-nazis-and-was-charged-with-a-hate-crime/?fbclid=IwAR1m0G5NwQhNC8BiTjCEqyu3UkoT2e6nqqlXzTxPDpzzOlYrv6Zc5VXGMiE.

56. Commonwealth v. Love, No. 3529 EDA 2014, 2015 Pa. Super. Unpub. LEXIS 4348 (Nov. 23, 2015).

57. Virginia v. Black, 538 U.S. 343 (2003).

58. *Id.* at 394.

59. *See* Watts v. United States, 394 U.S. 705 (1969).

60. Elonis v. United States, 135 S. Ct. 2001 (2015).

61. Two representative posts read: "There's one way to love you/but a thousand ways to kill you./I'm not going to rest/until your body is a mess,/soaked in blood and dying from all the little cuts." And: "That's it, I've had about enough/I'm checking out and making a name for myself/Enough elementary schools in a ten mile radius to initiate the most heinous school shooting ever imagined/And hell hath no fury like a crazy man in a Kindergarten class/The only question is . . . which one?"

62. United States v. Elonis, 730 F.3d 321 (3d Cir. 2013).

63. *Elonis*, 135 S. Ct. 2001.

64. *Id.* at 2012.

65. *Id.* at 2009.

66. United States v. Elonis, 841 F.3d 589.

67. Commonwealth v. Knox, 190 A.3d 1146 (Pa. 2018).

68. Veronica Stracqualursi, *Killer Mike, Chance the Rapper, Meek Mill to Supreme Court: Pittsburgh Rapper's Lyrics Are Not "a True Threat of Violence,"* CNNPOLITICS, Mar. 7, 2019, www.cnn.com/2019/03/07/politics/supreme-court-first-amendment-rappers/index.html.

69. Pennsylvania v. Knox, 190 A.3d 1146 (Pa. 2018), *petition for cert. filed*, No. 18-949 (U.S. Jan. 18, 2019), *cert. denied*, Knox v. Pennsylvania, 203 L. Ed. 2d 746 (2019).

70. Seals v. McBee, 898 F. 3d 587 (5th Cir. 2018), *reh'g en banc denied*, 907 F.3d 685 (5th Cir. 2018).

71. La. Rev'd Stat. § 14:122.

72. United States v. O'Brien, 391 U.S. 367, 376 (1968).

73. Tinker v. Des Moines Indep. Cmty. Sch. Dist., 393 U.S. 503, 505 (1969).

74. *O'Brien*, 391 U.S. 367.

75. Texas v. Johnson, 491 U.S. 397 (1989). The Supreme Court has said symbolic speech exists and warrants First Amendment protection when (1) speech and action combine, (2) there is an intent to convey a message and (3) witnesses are likely to understand that message.

76. *Id.* at 414.

77. Hess v. Indiana, 414 U.S. 105 (1973).

78. *See Marketing Violent Entertainment to Children: A Sixth Follow-up Review of Industry Practices in the Motion Picture, Music Recording & Electronic Game Industries*, FED. TRADE COMM'N, Dec. 2009, www.ftc.gov/sites/default/files/documents/reports/marketing-violent-entertainment-children-sixth-follow-review-industry-practices-motion-picture-music/p994511violententertainment.pdf.

79. *Sunday Dialogue: Mayhem on Our Screens,* N.Y. TIMES, Jan. 27, 2013, at SR2; Tracy Reilly, *The "Spiritual Temperature" of Contemporary Popular Music: An Alternative to the Legal Regulation of Death-Metal and Gangsta-Rap Lyrics*, 11 VAND. J. ENT. & TECH. L. 335 (2009).

80. *See, e.g.,* Ty Burr, *An Uncertain Line Between Fantasy's Lure, Nightmare*, BOSTON GLOBE, July 21, 2012, at A1; Nolan Finley, *Missing the Real Lessons From Arizona*, DETROIT NEWS, Jan. 20, 2011, at B1; Marc Fisher et al., *Lanza's Isolated Life Stymies Investigators*, WASH. POST, Dec. 23, 2012, at A1.

81. *See generally* John Charles Kunich, *Shock Torts Reloaded*, 6 Appalachian J.L. 1 (2006); John Charles Kunich, *Natural Born Copycat Killers and the Law of Shock Torts*, 78 Wash. U.L.Q. 1157 (2000).

82. Zamora v. Columbia Broadcasting System, 480 F. Supp. 199, 200 (S.D. Fla. 1979).

83. *Id.* at 201, 205.

84. Herceg v. Hustler Magazine, 814 F.2d 1017 (5th Cir. 1987), *cert. denied*, 485 U.S. 959 (1988).

85. Yakubowicz v. Paramount Pictures Corp., 536 N.E.2d 1067 (Mass. 1989).

86. Rice v. Paladin Enterprises, Inc., 128 F.3d 233 (4th Cir. 1997), *cert. denied*, 523 U.S. 1074 (1998).

87. *Id.* at 244.

88. Martin Garbus, *State of the Union for the Law of the New Millennium, the Internet, and the First Amendment*, 1999 Ann. Surv. Am. L. 169, 173–74.

89. Timothy D. Reeves, *Tort Liability for Manufacturers of Violent Video Games*, Ala. L. Rev. 519 (2009); Jonathan M. Proman, *Liability of Media Companies for the Violent Content of Their Products Marketed to Children*, 78 St. John's L. Rev. 426 (2004).

90. Olivia N. v. Nat'l Broad. Co., 126 Cal. App. 3d 488 (1981).

91. Norwood v. Soldier of Fortune Magazine, Inc., 651 F. Supp. 1397 (W.D. Ark. 1987).

92. *Id.* at 1403.

93. Eimann v. Soldier of Fortune Magazine, Inc., 880 F.2d 830, 834 (5th Cir. 1989), *cert. denied*, 493 U.S. 1024 (1990).

94. *Id.*

95. Braun v. Soldier of Fortune Magazine, Inc., 968 F.2d 1110 (11th Cir. 1992), *cert. denied*, 506 U.S. 1071 (1993).

96. James v. Meow Media, Inc., 300 F.3d 683 (6th Cir. 2002), *cert. denied*, 537 U.S. 1159 (2003).

97. *Id.*

98. *Id.* at 693.

99. Watters v. TSR, Inc., 904 F.2d 378 (6th Cir. 1990).

100. *See* April M. Perry, Comment: *Guilt by Saturation: Media Liability for Third-Party Violence and the Availability Heuristic*, 97 NW. U.L. Rev. 1045, 1055–56 (2003).

101. Brown v. Ent. Merchants Ass'n, 564 U.S. 786 (2011).

102. *Id.*

103. *Id.*

104. *Id.* at 794.

105. *Id.* at 790.

106. *Id.* at 806.

107. Dana Beyerle, *"Grand Theft Auto" Killer's Sentence Upheld*, Gadsden Times, Feb. 17, 2012, www.gadsdentimes.com/news/20120217/grand-theft-auto-killers-sentence-upheld.

108. *Alabama Top Court Denies Industry Motion to Dismiss GTA Killer Suit*, Game Politics, Mar. 29, 2006, gamepolitics.livejournal.com/244744.html.

109. Animal Crush Video Prohibition Act, 18 U.S.C. § 48.

110. 559 U.S. 460 (2010).

111. *Id.* at 472.

112. *Id.*

113. Wildmon v. Berwick Universal Pictures, 803 F. Supp. 1167 (D. Miss. 1992), *aff'd without opinion*, 979 F.2d 21 (5th Cir. 1992).

114. Scott W. Gaylord, *Is a Cake Worth a Thousand Words? Masterpiece Cakeshop and the Impact of Antidiscrimination Laws on the Marketplace of Ideas*, 85 Tenn. L. Rev. 361 (2018); John G. Culhane, *The Right to Say, But Not to Do: Balancing First Amendment Freedom of Expression With the Anti-Discrimination Imperative*, 24 Widener L. Rev. 235 (2018).

115. Masterpiece Cakeshop v. Colorado Civil Rights Comm'n, 138 S. Ct. 1719, 1728 (2018).

116. *Id.* (citing Hurley v. Irish-American Gay, Lesbian and Bisexual Group of Boston, 515 U.S. 557, 573 (1995)).

117. Packingham v. North Carolina, 137 S. Ct. 1730 (2017).

118. State v. Packingham, 748 S.E. 2d 146 (N.C. 2013); 777 S.E.2d 738 (N.C. 2015).

119. *Packingham*, 777 S.E.2d 738 (2015).

120. Jamal v. Kane, 105 F. Supp. 3d 448 (M.D. Pa. 2015).

121. Revictimization Relief Act, 18 Pa. Cons. Stat. § 11.101 *et seq.* (2014).

122. *Id.*, citing Simon & Schuster, Inc. v. Members of N.Y. State Crime Victims Bd., 502 U.S. 105, 118 (1991).

123. Geoffrey R. Stone, *Free Speech and National Security*, 84 Ind. L.J. 939 (2009).

124. Vincent Blasi, *The Pathological Perspective and the First Amendment*, 85 Colum. L. Rev. 449, 450 (1985).

125. Margaret A. Blanchard, Revolutionary Sparks 489 (1992); Margaret A. Blanchard, *"Why Can't We Ever Learn?" Cycles of Stability, Stress and Freedom of Expression in United States History*, 7 Comm. L. & Pol'y 347 (2002); Martin E. Halstuk, *Policy of Secrecy—Pattern of Deception: What Federalist Leaders Thought About a Public Right to Know, 1794–98*, 7 Comm. L. & Pol'y 51 (2002); Susan D. Ross, *An Apologia to Radical Dissent and a Supreme Court Test to Protect It*, 7 Comm. L. & Pol'y 401 (2002).

126. Holder v. Humanitarian Law Project, 561 U.S. 1 (2010).

127. The Uniting and Strengthening America by Providing Appropriate Tools Required to Intercept and Obstruct Terrorism Act of 2001, Pub. L. No. 107–56, 115 Stat. 272; USA PATRIOT Improvement and Reauthorization Act of 2005, 18 U.S.C. § 2709, Pub. L. No. 109–177, 120 Stat. 192 (2006).

128. *Humanitarian Law Project*, 561 U.S. at 6.

129. *Id.* at 3.

130. *Id.*

131. United States v. Mehanna, 735 F.3d 32 (1st Cir. 2013).

132. USA PATRIOT Act, 18 U.S.C. § 2339A.

133. *See, e.g.,* Marguerite Rigoglioso, *Civil Liberties and the Law in the Era of Surveillance*, 49 Stan. L. (Nov. 13, 2014), law.stanford.edu/stanford-lawyer/articles/civil-liberties-and-law-in-the-era-of-surveillance; *Top Ten Abuses of Power Since 9/11*, Am. Civil Liberties Union, www.aclu.org/other/top-ten-abuses-power-911.

134. William H. Rehnquist, All the Laws But One 224 (1998).

135. *See, e.g.,* Garner v. Bd. of Public Works of Los Angeles, 341 U.S. 716 (1951); Cole v. Richardson, 405 U.S. 676 (1972). *But see* Cramp v. Bd. of Public Instruction of Orange County, 368 U.S. 278 (1961); Communist Party of Indiana v. Whitcomb, 414 U.S. 441 (1974).

136. Kleindienst v. Mandel, 408 U.S. 753, 773 (1972) (Douglas, J., dissenting).

137. Doe v. Backpage.com, 817 F.3d 12 (1st Cir. 2016), *cert. denied*, 137 S. Ct. 622 (2017).

138. *Id.*

139. 104 F. Supp. 3d 149 (D. Mass. 2015), *aff'd*, 817 F.3d 12 (1st Cir. 2016), *cert. denied*, 137 S. Ct. 622 (2017) (mem.).

140. Bd. of Educ., Island Trees Union Free Sch. Dist. v. Pico 457 U.S. 853 (1982).

141. *Id.* at 857.

142. *Id.* at 868.

143. *Id.* at 870.

144. Parents, Families and Friends of Lesbians and Gays v. Camdenton R-111 Sch. Dist., 853 F. Supp. 2d 888 (W.D. Mo. 2012).

145. Michael Winerip, *School District Told to Replace Web Filter Blocking Pro-Gay Sites*, N.Y. Times, Mar. 26, 2012, www.nytimes.com/2012/03/26/education/missouri-school-district-questioned-over-anti-gay-web-filter.html.

146. Wooley v. Maynard, 430 U.S. 705, 714 (1977) (Burger, C.J.).

147. West Virginia State Bd. of Educ. v. Barnette, 319 U.S. 624 (1943).

148. Ambach v. Norwick, 441 U.S. 68 (1979).

149. *See, e.g.,* Epperson v. Arkansas, 393 U.S. 97 (1968); Edwards v. Aguillard, 482 U.S. 578 (1987); Pickering v. Bd. of Educ., 391 U.S. 563 (1968).

150. *Barnette*, 319 U.S. at 642.

151. Mark C. Rahdert, Point of View: *The Roberts Court and Academic Freedom*, Chronicle Higher Educ., July 27, 2007, eric.ed.gov/?q=retraction&pg=2&id=EJ773860.

152. Tinker v. Des Moines Indep. Cmty. Sch. Dist., 393 U.S. 503 (1969).

153. Erwin Chemerinsky, *Students Do Leave Their First Amendment Rights at the Schoolhouse Gates: What's Left of* Tinker?, 48 Drake L. Rev. 527 (2000).

154. Tinker v. Des Moines Indep. Cmty. Sch. Dist., 393 U.S. 503, 508 (1969).

155. *Id.*

156. *Id.* at 506.

157. *Id.* at 509.

158. Grayned v. Rockford, 408 U.S. 104 (1972).

159. Morse v. Frederick, 551 U.S. 393 (2007).

160. *Id.* at 410.

161. *Id.* at 445 (Stevens, J., dissenting).

162. *Id.*

163. Caroline B. Newcombe, Morse v. Frederick *One Year Later: New Limits on Student Speech and the "Columbine Effect,"* 42 Suffolk U. L. Rev. 427 (2009).

164. Bell v. Itawamba Cty. Sch. Bd., 774 F.3d (5th Cir. 2014).

165. Bell v. Itawamba Cty. Sch. Bd., 859 F.Supp. 2d 834 (N.D. Miss. 2012).

166. *Bell*, 774 F. 3d 280 (5th Cir. 2014), *reh'g en banc* 799 F.3d 379 (5th Cir. 2015).

167. Masters v. Commonwealth, 551 S.W.3d 458 (Ky. Ct. App. 2017), *cert. denied*, 2019 WL 135352 (Feb. 19, 2019).

168. Joseph Gerth, *Lt. Gov. Candidate Faces Charges Over Outbursts*, Courier Journal, Feb. 15, 2015, www.courier-journal.com/story/news/politics/elections/kentucky/2015/02/13/democrat-johnathan-masters-faces-charges/23354647.

169. Frank LoMonte, *Supreme Court Asked to Hear Case About Criminalizing "Disruptive" Speech to School Employees*, SPLC *Signs Onto Brief Siding With Students*, Student Press L. Ctr., Feb. 19, 2019, splc.org/2019/02/supreme-court-asked-to-hear-first-amendment-challenge-to-law-criminalizing-disruptive-speech-to-school-employees.

170. Chaplinsky v. New Hampshire, *315 U.S. 568, 573 (1942).*

171. *Id.* at 461.

172. Bethel Sch. Dist. v. Fraser, 478 U.S. 675 (1986).

173. *Id.*

174. Hazelwood Sch. Dist. v. Kuhlmeier, 484 U.S. 260 (1988).

175. *Id.* at 271.

176. *Id.* at 270.

177. *Id.* at 273 n.7.

178. A.M. v. Taconic Hills Cent. Sch. Dist., 510 F. App'x 3 (2d Cir. 2013), *cert. denied*, 571 U.S. 828 (2013).

179. K.A. *ex. rel.* Ayers v. Pocono Mt. Sch. Dist., 710 F. 3d 99 (3d Cir. 2013).

180. B.H. *ex rel.* Hawk v. Easton Area Sch. Dist., 725 F.3d 293 (3d Cir. 2013), *cert. denied*, 572 U.S. 1002 (2014).

181. Taylor v. Roswell Ind. Sch. Dist., 713 F.3d 25 (10th Cir. 2013).

182. Hardwick v. Heyward, 711 F.3d 426 (4th Cir.), *cert. denied*, 571 U.S. 829 (2013).

183. Snyder v. Blue Mountain Sch. Dist., 650 F.3d 915 (3d Cir. 2011) (en banc), *cert. denied*, 565 U.S. 1156 (2012); Layshock v. Hermitage Sch. Dist., 593 F.3d 249 (3d Cir. 2010), *cert. denied*, 565 U.S. 1156 (2012).

184. Margaret Malloy, Note: Bell v. Itawamba County School Board: *Testing the First Amendment Protection of Off-Campus Student Speech*, 2016 Wis. L. Rev. 1251 (2016). *See, e.g.,* Kowalski v. Berkeley County Schools, 652 F.3d 565 (4th Cir. 2011), *cert. denied*, 565 U.S. 1173 (2012); D.J.M. v. Hannibal Pub. Sch. Dist. #60, 647 F.3d 754 (8th Cir. 2011); Snyder v. Blue Mountain Sch. Dist., 650 F.3d 915 (3d Cir. 2011) (en banc), *cert. denied*, 565 U.S. 1156 (2012); Layshock v. Hermitage Sch. Dist., 593 F.3d 249 (3d Cir. 2010), *cert. denied*, 565 U.S. 1156 (2012); Doninger v. Niehoff, 527 F.3d 41 (2d Cir. 2008).

185. Bd. of Regents of Univ. of Wis. System v. Southworth, 529 U.S. 217, 234 n.7 (2000).

186. Widmar v. Vincent, 454 U.S. 263, 274 (1981).

187. Bethel Sch. Dist. v. Fraser, 478 U.S. 675, 683 (1986). *See also* Edwards v. Aguillard, 482 U.S. 578, 583 (1987).

188. *See, e.g.,* Bd. of Regents, 529 U.S. 217 (2000); Rosenberger v. Rector and Visitors of the Univ. of Va., 515 U.S. 819 (1995).

189. Papish v. Bd. of Curators of the Univ. of Missouri, 410 U.S. 667, 670 (1973).

190. *Id.; see also* Bd. of Regents, 529 U.S. at 233.

191. *Bd. of Regents*, 529 U.S. at 242–43 (Souter, J., dissenting). Note that the Court said this public forum also enhanced the university's curricular goals, but public forum analysis typically protects precisely those types of speech that would not be embraced by the government agency providing the forum.

192. Abbott v. Pastides, 900 F.3d 160 (4th Cir. 2018), *cert. denied*, 2019 U.S. LEXIS 1614 (U.S., Mar. 4, 2019).

193. Rosenberger v. Rector and Visitors of the Univ. of Va., 515 U.S. 819 (1995).

194. *Id.* at 833.

195. *Bd. of Regents*, 529 U.S. at 239 (Souter, J., concurring).

196. *See, e.g., Bd. of Regents*, 529 U.S. 217; *Rosenberger*, 515 U.S. 819.

197. Christian Legal Society v. Martinez, 561 U.S. 661 (2010).

198. *Id.* at 686.

199. Tinker v. Des Moines Indep. Cmty. Sch. Dist., 393 U.S. 503, 506 (1969).

200. *Christian Legal Society*, 561 U.S. at 706 (Alito, J., dissenting).

201. Greg Lukianoff, *Feigning Free Speech on Campus*, N.Y. TIMES, Oct. 25, 2012, www.nytimes.com/2012/10/25/opinion/feigning-free-speech-on-campus.html.

202. Kincaid v. Gibson, 236 F.3d 342 (6th Cir. 2001) (en banc).

203. *Id.* at 346.

204. Hosty v. Carter, 412 F.3d 731 (7th Cir. 2005), *cert. denied*, 546 U.S. 1169 (2006).

205. OSU Student Alliance v. Ray, 699 F.3d 1053 (9th Cir. 2012), *cert denied*, 571 U.S. 819 (2013).

206. Tatro v. Univ. of Minn., 816 N.W.2d 509 (Minn. 2012).

207. *Id.* at 517.

208. *Id.* at 513.

209. *Id.* at 521.

210. *Id.* at 511–12.

211. *Id.* at 521.

212. *See* Oyama v. Univ. of Hawaii, 813 F.3d 850 (9th Cir. 2015), *cert. denied*, 136 S. Ct. 2520 (2016); Keefe v. Adams, 840 F.3d 523 (8th Cir. 2016), *cert. denied*, 137 S. Ct. 1448 (2017).

213. Hazelwood Sch. Dist. v. Kuhlmeier, 484 U.S. 260 (1988).

214. *Compare, e.g.,* Keefe, 840 F.3d at 532 (relying on Hazelwood to affirm the authority of the university to expel a student for unprofessional off-campus Facebook posts about classmates that were reasonably related to and materially disrupted the graduate nursing program), *with* Oyama, 813 F.3d at 863 (not relying on Hazelwood and creating a new test to affirm the authority of the university to deny student teacher placement for a student's inappropriate remarks). *See also* Ward v. Polite, 667 F.3d 727, 733–34 (6th Cir. 2012) (applying Hazelwood to establish authority of the university to impose regulations on speech that are "reasonably related to legitimate pedagogical concerns. . . . Nothing in *Hazelwood* suggests a stop-go distinction between student speech at the high school and university levels, and we decline to create one"); Keeton v. Anderson-Wiley, 664 F.3d 865, 875–76 (11th Cir. 2011) (relying on Hazelwood to reject graduate student claim to affirm university authority to

control of graduate student speech within a "school-sponsored expressive activity" because graduate program standards constitute a nonpublic forum for government speech); Flint v. Dennison, 488 F.3d 816, 829 n.9 (9th Cir. 2007) (applying Hazelwood to college student campaign spending); Hosty v. Carter, 412 F.3d 731, 735 (7th Cir. 2005) (en banc) ("We hold . . . that *Hazelwood*'s framework applies to subsidized student newspapers at colleges as well as elementary and secondary schools"); Axson-Flynn v. Johnson, 356 F.3d 1277, 1285, 1289–93 (10th Cir. 2004) (concluding that a graduate student's speech "constitutes 'school-sponsored speech' and is thus governed by *Hazelwood*"); Student Gov't Ass'n v. Bd. of Trs. of Univ. of Mass., 868 F.2d 473, 480 n.6 (1st Cir. 1989) ("*Hazelwood* . . . is not applicable to college newspapers").

215. *Oyama*, 813 F.3d at 862.

216. *Id.* at 863.

217. *Id.* at 855, 860.

218. *Keefe*, 840 F.3d at 532 (8th Cir. 2016), *cert denied*, 137 S. Ct. 1448 (2017).

219. *Id.* at 526, 528.

220. *Id.* at 531.

221. *Id.*

222. *Id. See also* Conner Mitchell, *Supreme Court Declines to Hear Free Speech Case*, STUDENT PRESS L. CTR., Apr. 4, 2017, splc.org/2017/04/keefe-certiorari-denied/.

223. Roxann Elliott, *Court of Appeals Rules in Favor of Community College That Removed Nursing Student Over Facebook Posts*, STUDENT PRESS L. CTR., Nov. 3, 2016, www.splc.org/blog/splc/2016/11/keefe-eighth-circuit; Frank LoMonte, *Appeals Court Won't Apply Hazelwood to Teacher Trainee's Case, Instead Creates New "Professional Standards" Exception*, STUDENT PRESS L. CTR., Dec. 29, 2015, www.splc.org/blog/splc/2015/12/oyama-hawaii-ninth-circuit-college-hazelwood-ruling.

224. Richard Pérez-Peña, *Student Paper Editors Quit at University of Georgia*, N.Y. TIMES, Aug. 16, 2012, www.nytimes.com/2012/08/17/us/georgia-student-newspaper-editors-quit-over-interference.html.

225. Alexis Steven, *Editors Rejoin UGA Student Newspaper*, ATLANTA J. CONST., Aug. 20, 2012, www.ajc.com.

226. Michele Nagar, *Fired for Diversity's Sake*, ACCURACY IN ACADEMIA, July 22, 2004, www.academia.org/fired-for-diversitys-sake/.

227. *SPJ Members Issue Resolution Condemning Kansas Adviser's Firing*, STUDENT PRESS L. CTR., Oct. 6, 2004, www.splc.org/2004/10/spj-members-issue-resolution-condemning-kan-advisers-firing/?id=877; *SPLC Condemns Censorship at Kansas State*, STUDENT PRESS L. CTR., Aug. 1, 2004, splc.org/2004/08/splc-condemns-censorship-at-kansas-state/.

228. Marnette Federis, *Court to Review Kansas State Adviser Dismissal Case*, STUDENT PRESS L. CTR., Sept. 29, 2006, splc.org/2006/09/court-to-review-kansas-state-adviser-dismissal-case.

229. *See* Lane v. Simon, 2005 U.S. Dist. LEXIS 11330 (D. Kan. 2005), *vacated and remanded*, 2007 U.S. App. LEXIS 17814 (10th Cir., July 26, 2007).

230. *See, e.g.,* DINESH D'SOUZA, ILLIBERAL EDUCATION: THE POLITICS OF RACE AND SEX ON CAMPUS (1992).

231. *See, e.g.,* THE PRICE WE PAY: THE CASE AGAINST RACIST SPEECH, HATE PROPAGANDA, AND PORNOGRAPHY (Laura Lederer & Richard Delgado eds., 1994).

232. *See, e.g.,* Andrew Altman, *Liberalism and Campus Hate Speech*, in CAMPUS WARS: MULTICULTURALISM AND THE POLITICS OF DIFFERENCE (John Arthur & Amy Shapiro eds., 1993).

233. *See, e.g.,* Doe v. Univ. of Mich., 721 F. Supp. 852 (E.D. Mich. 1989); UWM Post v. Bd. of Regents of Univ. of Wis., 774 F. Supp. 1163 (E.D. Wis. 1991); Dambrot v. Central Mich. Univ., 839 F. Supp. 477 (E.D. Mich. 1993).

234. *Doe*, 721 F. Supp. 852, 864 (E.D. Mich. 1989).

235. ARATI R. KORWAR, WAR OF WORDS: SPEECH CODES AT PUBLIC COLLEGES AND UNIVERSITIES (1994); Jon B. Gould, *The Precedent That Wasn't: College Hate Speech Codes and the Two Faces of Legal Compliance*, 35 LAW & SOC'Y REV. 345 (2001).

236. Greg Lukianoff, *Spotlight on Speech Codes 2013: The State of Free Speech on Our Nation's Campuses*, THE FOUND. FOR INDIV. RIGHTS IN EDUC., www.thefire.org.

237. *See, e.g.,* Jeremy Bauer-Wolf, *A University's New Rules on Rape*, INSIDE HIGHER ED, Oct. 18, 2017, www.insidehighered.com/news/2017/10/18/university-minnesota-revises-sexual-harassment-policies; *Exec. Pol. 15 Prohibiting Discrimination, Sexual Harassment and Sexual Misconduct*, WASH. STATE UNIV., Dec. 18, 2014, policies.wsu.edu/prf/index/manuals/executive-policy-manual-contents/ep15-discrimination-sexual-harassment-sexual-misconduct.

238. Civil Rights Act of 1964, 42 U.S.C. § 2000e-2(a)(1). *See* Vance v. Ball State Univ., 570 U.S. 421 (2013).

239. *See* Johnson v. Univ. of Cincinnati, 215 F. 3d 561 (6th Cir. 2000) (finding noncompliance with affirmative-action requirements a matter of public interest but that effective hiring procedures outweighed plaintiff's free speech interests).

240. UWM Post v. Bd. of Regents of Univ. of Wis., 774 F. Supp. 1163 (1991).

241. Sarah Brown, *When Professors Stir Outrage, What's a University to Do?*, CHRONICLE OF HIGHER ED., June 26, 2018, www.chronicle.com/article/When-Professors-Stir-Outrage/243764.

242. Claire Bushey, *DePaul Investigating Law Professor's Racial Slur*, CHICAGO BUS., Feb. 28, 2018, www.chicagobusiness.com/article/20180228/NEWS04/180229894/depaul-investigating-law-professors-racial-slur.

243. Matthew Pinna, *University of Chicago Defends the Academic Freedom of Constitutional Law Professor Who Used the N-word in Class*, COLLEGE FIX, Mar. 7, 2019, www.thecollegefix.com/university-of-chicago-defends-constitutional-law-professor.

244. Sines v. Kessler, 324 F.Supp.3d 765 (W.D. Va. 2018).

245. *White Nationalist*, SOUTHERN POVERTY L. CTR., 2018, www.splcenter.org/fighting-hate/extremist-files/ideology/white-nationalist.

246. Jessica Suerth, *Here Are the Confederate Memorials That Will Be Removed After Charlottesville*, CNN.com, Aug. 15, 2017.

247. Michael Kunzelman, *Judge Refused to Block Removal of Confederate Monuments*, ASSOCIATED PRESS, Jan. 26, 2017.

248. Alabama ex rel. Marshall v. City of Birmingham, No. 01-CV-2017-903426.00 (Jefferson Cty. Cir. Ct. Aug. 16, 2017); *Alabama Appeals Confederate Monument Ruling*, ASSOCIATED PRESS, Jan. 25, 2019.

249. Moore v. Bryant, 205 F. Supp. 3d 834 (S.D. Miss. 2016), *aff'd*, 853 F.3d 245 (5th Cir.), *cert. denied*, 138 S. Ct. 468 (2017).

250. *Id.* at 848.

251. *Moore*, 853 F.3d 245.

CHAPTER 4 BOXED FEATURES

i. *Words We're Watching: The Real Story on "Fake News,"* MERRIAM-WEBSTER, Mar. 1, 2019, www.merriam-webster.com/words-at-play/the-real-story-of-fake-news.

ii. *Id.*

iii. Jane E. Kirtley, *Getting to the Truth: Fake News, Libel Laws, and "Enemies of the American People,"* Am. Bar Ass'n, Mar. 1, 2019, www.american bar.org/groups/crsj/publications/human_rights_ magazine_home/the-ongoing-challenge-to-define-free-speech/getting-to-the-truth/.

iv. *See, e.g., New Research Shows Facebook Making Strides Against False News*, Facebook Newsroom, Feb. 7, 2019, newsroom.fb.com/news/2018/10/ inside-feed-michigan-lemonde/.

v. Kirtley, *supra*, note iii.

vi. Zervos v. Trump, 74 N.Y.S.3d 442 (Sup. Ct. 2018).

vii. *See* Clinton v. Jones, 520 U.S. 681 (1997).

viii. Kevin McCoy, *NY Appeals Court Rules President Donald Trump Must Face Summer Zervos' Defamation Lawsuit*, USA Today, Mar. 14, 2019, www.usatoday .com/story/news/2019/03/14/president-donald-trump-must-face-summer-zervos-defamation-case-ny-court-rules/3162078002/.

ix. *Zervos*, 74 N.Y.S.3d 442.

x. Clifford v. Trump, 339 F.Supp.3d 915 (C.D. Cal. 2018).

xi. Hawes Spencer and Ben Sisario, *In Rolling Stone Defamation Case, Magazine and Reporter Ordered to Pay $3 Million*, N.Y. Times, Nov. 7, 2016, www .nytimes.com/2016/11/08/business/media/in-rolling-stone-defamation-case-magazine-and-reporter-ordered-to-pay-3-million.html.

xii. Sheila Coronel, Steve Coll & Derek Kravitz, *Rolling Stone and UVA: The Columbia University Graduate School of Journalism Report: An Anatomy of a Journalistic Failure*, Rolling Stone, Apr. 5, 2015, www.rollingstone.com/culture/features/a-rape-on-campus-what-went-wrong-20150405.

xiii. *Defamation and Related Claims*, Comm. L. in the Digital Age 2016 (Nov. 10, 2016).

xiv. McKee v. Cosby, 874 F.3d 54 (1st Cir. 2017), *cert. denied*, 139 S. Ct. 675 (Thomas, J., concurring).

xv. *Id.*

xvi. *Id.*

xvii. Electronic Frontier Found. v. Global Equity Mgmt. (SA) Pty Ltd., 290 F. Supp. 3d 923 (N.D. Cal. 2017).

xviii. Kevin T. Baine, *Defamation Law Case Summaries (September 2017–August 2018)*, 6 Comm. L. in the Digital Age 430 (2018).

xix. *See* Elec. Frontier Found., 290 F. Supp. 3d 923.

xx. 28 U.S.C. §§ 4101–4105 (2012).

xxi. Involuntary public figures are not included in the table because these cases are rare. The standard of fault for these plaintiffs is actual malice.

CHAPTER 4

1. New York Times Co. v. Sullivan, 376 U.S. 254, 270–72 (1964).

2. *See, e.g.,* Diane Leenheer Zimmerman, *Defamation in Fiction: Real People in Fiction: Cautionary Words About Troublesome Old Torts Poured Into New Jugs*, 51 Brooklyn L. Rev. 355 (1985).

3. Milkovich v. Lorain Journal Co., 497 U.S. 1, 22 (1990) (Rehnquist, C.J.).

4. Rosenblatt v. Baer, 383 U.S. 75, 86 (1966).

5. Dun & Bradstreet, Inc. v. Greenmoss Builders, Inc., 472 U.S. 749, 757 (1985).

6. *See* Gavin Clark, Famous Libel and Slander Cases of History (1950).

7. Van Vechten Veeder, *The History and Theory of the Law of Defamation*, 3 Colum. L. Rev. 546, 565 (1903) (quoting De Libellis Famosis, 5 Co. Rep. 125 (1606)).

8. *Id.*

9. J.H. Baker, An Introduction to English Legal History 506 (3d ed. 1990).

10. 4 William Blackstone, Commentaries 152 (1979).

11. *Id.*

12. Milkovich v. Lorain Journal Co., 497 U.S. 1, 12 (1990) (Rehnquist, C.J.).

13. Sedition Act of 1798, ch. 74, 1 Stat. 596 (1798).

14. John Marshall, *Report of the Minority on the Virginia Resolutions*, 6 J. House of Delegates (Va.) 93–95 (Jan. 22, 1799), *reprinted in* 5 The Founders' Constitution 136–38 (Philip B. Kurland & Ralph Lerner eds., 1987).

15. *Id.* at 138.

16. James Madison, *The Virginia Report of 1799–1800, Touching the Alien and Sedition Laws, reprinted in* The Founders' Constitution 141–42 (1986).

17. *See, e.g.,* Whitney v. California, 274 U.S. 357, 374–77 (1927) (Brandeis, J., concurring) ("The best answer for bad speech is more speech").

18. *Fact*, Merriam-Webster, Jan. 24, 2017, www.merri-am-webster.com/dictionary/fact.

19. *Opinion*, Merriam-Webster, Feb. 2, 2017, www.merri-am-webster.com/dictionary/opinion.

20. Petro-Lubricant Testing Labs, Inc. v. Adelman, 184 A.3d 457 (N.J. 2018).

21. *Id.*

22. *New Developments 2012*, MLRC Bulletin, Dec. 2012, at 65; *see, e.g.,* Martin v. Daily News, 951 N.Y.S.2d 87 (N.Y. Sup. 2012).

23. Diamond Ranch Academy, Inc. v. Filer, 44 Med. L. Rep. 1486 (D. Utah Feb. 17, 2016).

24. *New Developments 2012*, MLRC Bulletin, Dec. 2012, at 65; *see, e.g.,* Martin v. Daily News, 951 N.Y.S.2d 87 (N.Y. Sup. 2012).

25. Enigma Software Group USA, LLC v. Bleeping Computer, LLC, 194 F. Supp. 3d 263 (S.D.N.Y. 2016).

26. Stratton Oakmont v. Prodigy Servs. Co., 1995 N.Y. Misc. LEXIS 229 (N.Y. Sup. Ct., May 24, 1995) (holding that because Prodigy claimed to monitor its content, the ISP is placed in the role of publisher).

27. Cubby, Inc. v. CompuServe, Inc., 776 F. Supp. 135 (S.D.N.Y. 1991) (holding that the ISP is not responsible for content posted).

28. Zeran v. America Online, Inc., 129 F.3d 327, 330 (4th Cir. 1997).

29. *Id.* at 330.

30. *Id.*

31. *Id.* at 331.

32. Universal Communication Systems, Inc. v. Lycos, Inc., 478 F.3d 413 (1st Cir. 2007).

33. *Id.* at 418–19.

34. McIntyre v. Ohio Elections Comm'n, 514 U.S. 334, 357 (1995).

35. Dendrite Int'l, Inc. v. Doe No. 3, 342 N.J. Super. 134 (July 11, 2001).

36. Yelp, Inc. v. Superior Court, 224 Ca. Rptr. 3d 887 (Cal. Ct. App. 2017), *review denied* (Feb. 14, 2018).

37. *Id.*

38. ZL Techs., Inc. v. Does 1–7, 220 Cal. Rptr. 3d 569 (Ct. App. 2017).

39. *Id.*

40. Kevin T. Baine, *Defamation Law Case Summaries (September 2017–August 2018)*, 6 Comm. L. in the Digital Age 445 (2018).

41. Ashley I. Kissinger, Katharine Larsen & Matthew E. Kelley, *Protections for Anonymous Online Speech*, 2 Comm. L. in the Digital Age 532 (2012). (Good faith is only applied in the state of Virginia.)

42. Doe v. Cahill, 884 A.2d 451, 457 (Del. 2005).

43. Restatement (Second) of Torts § 564A cmt. b (1976).

44. Neiman-Marcus v. Lait, 13 F.R.D. 311, 316 (S.D.N.Y. 1952).

45. Elias v. Rolling Stone, LLC, 872 F.3d 97 (2d Cir. 2017).

46. *Id.*

47. Eriq Gardner, *Rolling Stone Settles Last Remaining Lawsuit Over UVA Rape Story*, Hollywood Rep., Dec. 21, 2017, www.hollywoodreporter.com/thr-esq/rolling-stone-settles-last-remaining-lawsuit-uva-rape-story-1069880.

48. Nolan v. State of New York, 158 A.D.3d 186 (N.Y. App. Div. 2018)

49. *See* Restatement (Second) of Torts § 559 (1997).

50. *See* W. Page Keeton et al., Prosser and Keeton on the Law of Torts § 111, at 773–78 (5th ed. 1984).

51. *See* Restatement (Second) of Torts § 559 cmt. e.

52. *See, e.g.,* Kimmerle v. New York Evening Journal, Inc., 262 N.Y. 99 (1933).

53. Yonaty v. Mincolla, N.Y.S. 2d 774 (N.Y. App. 2012).

54. Burke v. Gregg, 55 A.3d 212 (R.I. 2012).

55. *New Developments 2012*, MLRC Bulletin, Dec. 2012, at 51.

56. Kevin T. Baine et al., *Defamation Law Case Summaries for PLI*, 2 Comm. L. in the Digital Age 15 (2014); Barhoum v. NYP Holdings, Inc., 2014 Mass. Super. LEXIS 52 (Mass. Super. Ct. Mar. 10, 2014).

57. *Id.*

58. Knutt v. Metro Int'l, 938 N.Y.S.2d 134 (N.Y. App. Div. 2012).

59. Cochran v. NYP Holdings, Inc., 58 F. Supp. 2d 1113, 1121 (C.D. Cal. 1998).

60. Texas Beef Group v. Oprah Winfrey, 11 F. Supp. 2d 858, 862 (N.D. Tex. 1998). The program had been tape recorded on Apr. 11, 1996.

61. *Id.*

62. *Id.*

63. *Id.* The ruling was also based on the failure of the plaintiffs to prove that cattle are perishable food, a requirement under the Texas False Disparagement of Perishable Food Products Act. The plaintiffs sued for the alleged violation of this provision of the act.

64. *Trade Libel Basics: The Pink Slime Case*, Kelly/Warner Law, July 16, 2013, kellywarnerlaw.com/trade-libel-basics/.

65. Amanda Radke, *Update on BPI Lawsuit Against ABC*, Beef Daily, Oct. 12, 2016, www.beefmagazine.com/blog/update-bpi-lawsuit-against-abc.

66. Beef Prods., Inc. v. ABC, No. CIV12292, 2014 WL 1245307 (S.D. Cir. Mar. 27, 2014).

67. Daniel Victor, *ABC Settles With Meat Producer in "Pink Slime" Defamation Case*, N.Y. Times, June 28, 2017, www.nytimes.com/2017/06/28/business/media/pink-slime-abc-lawsuit-settlement.html?_r=0.

68. Philadelphia Newspapers, Inc. v. Hepps, 475 U.S. 767, 776–77 (1986).

69. Masson v. New Yorker Magazine, Inc., 501 U.S. 496, 516–17 (1991).

70. Kevin T. Baine et al., *Defamation Law Case Summaries (September 2017–August 2018)*, 6 Comm. L. in the Digital Age 406 (2018); Watkins v. CNN, Inc., 46 Med. L. Rep. (BNA) 1753 (D. Md. 2018).

71. Yeakey v. Hearst Communications, Inc., 234 P.3d 332 (Wash. App. 2010).

72. Stevens v. Iowa Newspapers, Inc., 728 N.W.2d 823 (Iowa 2007).

73. Cheney v. Daily News, LP, 654 Fed. Appx. 578 (3d Cir. July 19, 2016).

74. Manzari v. Assoc. Newspapers, Ltd., 830 F.3d 881 (9th Cir. 2016).

75. 376 U.S. 254 (1964).

76. *See, e.g.*, Harry Kalven Jr., *The New York Times Case: A Note on "The Central Meaning of the First Amendment,"* 1964 Sup. Ct. Rev. 191.

77. New York Times Co. v. Sullivan, 376 U.S. 254, 272 (1964).

78. *Id.* at 270.

79. *Id.* at 266.

80. *Id.* at 279.

81. *Id.* at 270.

82. *Id.* at 278.

83. *See, e.g.*, Lawrence Friedman, Am. Law in the 20th Century 341 (2002).

84. Goldwater v. Ginzburg, 414 F.2d 324 (2d Cir. 1969), *cert. denied*, 396 U.S. 1049 (1970).

85. Masson v. New Yorker Magazine, Inc., 501 U.S. 496, 517 (1991).

86. Air Wis. Airlines Corp. v. Hoeper, 571 U.S. 237 (2014).

87. *Id.* at 253–54.

88. *Id.* at 864.

89. Curtis Publ'g Co. v. Butts, 388 U.S. 130, 158 (1967).

90. Associated Press v. Walker, 388 U.S. 130, 140 (1967).

91. *Id.* at 157–59.

92. St. Amant v. Thompson, 390 U.S. 727, 731 (1968).

93. Herbert v. Lando, 441 U.S. 153 (1979).

94. Harte-Hanks Communications, Inc. v. Connaughton, 491 U.S. 657 (1989).

95. Cabello-Rondon v. Dow Jones & Co., 2017 U.S. Dist. LEXIS 131114 (S.D.N.Y. Aug. 16, 2017), aff'd, 720 Fed. Appx. 87 (2d Cir. 2018).

96. Warner Brothers Entm't, Inc. v. Jones, 538 S.W.3d 781 (Tex. App. 2017).

97. Zimmerman v. Al Jazeera Am., LLC, 246 F. Supp. 3d 257 (D.D.C. 2017).

98. Rosenblatt v. Baer, 383 U.S. 75, 85 (1966).

99. *Id.* at 86.

100. *Id.* at 87.

101. 388 U.S. 130, 163 (1967) (Warren, C.J., concurring).

102. *Id.* at 163–64.

103. 418 U.S. 323, 345 (1974).

104. *Id.*

105. *Id.* at 344.

106. *Id.* at 345.

107. Renner v. Donsbach, 749 F. Supp. 987 (W.D. Mo. 1990).

108. Curtis Publ'g Co. v. Butts and Associated Press v. Walker, 388 U.S. 130, 163 (1967).

109. Wolston v. Reader's Digest Ass'n, 443 U.S. 157 (1979).

110. Time, Inc. v. Firestone, 424 U.S. 448 (1976).

111. Hutchinson v. Proxmire, 443 U.S. 111 (1979).

112. *Id.* at 135.

113. Chuy v. Philadelphia Eagles Football Club, 431 F. Supp. 254, 276 (E.D. Pa. 1977).

114. McKee v. Cosby, 874 F.3d 54, 61 (1st Cir. 2017).

115. McKee v. Cosby, 236 F. Supp. 3d 427 (D. Mass 2017).

116. *McKee*, 874 F.3d 54, 61.

117. Gertz v. Robert Welch, Inc., 418 U.S. 323, 351 (1974).

118. *Id.* at 345.

119. Tillman v. Freedom of Information Comm'n, 2008 Conn. Super. LEXIS 2120, *25 (Aug. 15, 2008).

120. Dun & Bradstreet, Inc. v. Greenmoss Builders, Inc., 472 U.S. 749 (1985).

121. *Id.* at 783.

122. *Id.* at 772.

123. Michael K. Cantwell, *Exploring the Issue of "Strict Liability" for Defamation*, MLRC Bulletin, Dec. 2012, at 3.

124. *Id.*

125. Obsidian Finance Group, LLC v. Cox, 812 F. Supp. 2d 1220 (D. Ore. 2011).

126. Obsidian Finance Group, LLC v. Cox, 740 F.3d 1284 (9th Cir. 2014).

127. *Id.* at 1290–91.

128. Restatement (Second) of Torts § 46 (1965) cmt. j.

129. *See, e.g.,* Gouin v. Gouin, 249 F. Supp. 2d 62 (D. Mass. 2003).

130. *See* Charles E. Cantu, *An Essay on the Tort of Negligent Infliction of Emotional Distress in Texas: Stop Saying It Does Not Exist*, 33 St. Mary's L.J. 455, 458 (2002).

131. Restatement (Second) of Torts § 46 (1965).

132. *Id.* cmt. d.

133. *Id.*

134. Showler v. Harper's Magazine Found., 222 Fed. Appx. 755 (10th Cir.), *cert. denied*, 552 U.S. 825 (2007).

135. Alvarado v. KOB-TV, LLC, 493 F.3d 1210, 1222 (10th Cir. 2007).

136. Hatfill v. New York Times, 532 F.3d 312 (4th Cir.), *cert. denied*, 555 U.S. 1085 (2008).

137. *See* Scott Shane & Eric Lichtblau, *New Details on F.B.I.'s False Start in Anthrax Case*, N.Y. Times, Nov. 26, 2008, at A23.

138. Marshall Cty. Coal Co. v. Oliver, No. 17-C-124, 2018 WL 1082525 (W.Va. Cir. Ct. Feb. 22, 2018).

139. Best v. Malec, 2010 U.S. Dist. LEXIS 58996 (N.D. Ill., June 11, 2010).

140. KOVR-TV, Inc. v. Superior Court, 37 Cal. Rptr. 2d 431 (Cal. App. 1995).

141. Estate of Duckett v. Cable News Network, 2008 U.S. Dist. LEXIS 88667 (M.D. Fla., July 31, 2008), *quoting* Williams v. City of Minneola, 575 So. 2d 683, 691 (Fla. Ct. App. 1991).

142. Restatement (Second) of Torts § 46(1) (1965).

143. New York Times Co. v. Sullivan, 376 U.S. 254 (1964).

144. Hustler Magazine, Inc. v. Falwell, 485 U.S. 46 (1988).

145. *See* Rodney Smolla, Smolla and Nimmer on Freedom of Speech § 24.10 (2012). *See also* Rodney A. Smolla, Jerry Falwell v. Larry Flynt: The First Amendment on Trial (1988).

146. Falwell v. Flynt, 797 F.2d 1270 (4th Cir.), *rehearing en banc denied*, 805 F.2d 484 (4th Cir. 1986).

147. Hustler Magazine, Inc. v. Falwell, 485 U.S. 46 (1988).

148. Snyder v. Phelps, 562 U.S. 443, 444 (2011).

149. *Id.* at 448.

150. Snyder v. Phelps, 580 F.3d 206 (4th Cir. Md. 2009).

151. *Snyder*, 562 U.S. at 452.

152. Honoring America's Veterans and Caring for Camp Lejeune Families Act, 38 U.S.C. § 101.

153. *See, e.g.,* Neilson v. Union Bank of Cal., N.A., 290 F. Supp. 2d 1101, 1142 (C.D. Calif. 2003).

154. *See, e.g.,* Dowty v. Riggs, 385 S.W.3d 117 (Ark. 2010).

155. *See, e.g.,* Nelson v. Harrah's Entm't, Inc., 2008 U.S. Dist. LEXIS 46524 (N.D. Ill., June 13, 2008).

156. *See* Camper v. Minor, 915 S.W.2d 437, 440 (Tenn. 1996).

157. *Id.*

158. Hyde v. City of Columbia, 637 S.W.2d 251 (Mo. Ct. App. 1982).

159. Ann C. Motto, *First Amendment: "Equity Will Not Enjoin a Libel": Well, Actually, Yes, It Will*, 11 Seventh Cir. Rev. 271 (Spring 2016).

160. Kinney v. Barnes, 443 S.W.3d 87 (Tex. 2014), *cert. denied*, 135 S. Ct. 1164 (2015).

161. *In re* Janzen, 2015 Wash. App. LEXIS 2550 (Wash. Ct. App. Oct. 22, 2015).

162. Hassell v. Bird, 203 Cal. Rptr. 3d 203 (Cal. Ct. App. 2016).

163. McCarthy v. Fuller, 810 F.3d 456, 462 (7th Cir. 2015), *cert. denied*, 136 S. Ct. 1726 (2016).

164. *Id.* at 464 (Sykes, J., concurring).

165. Sindi v. El-Moslimany, 896 F.3d 1, 3 (1st Cir. 2018).

166. *Id.*

167. *Id.*

168. *See, e.g.,* Bassett v. Jensen, 319 F. Supp. 3d 568 (D. Mass 2018).

169. Lee Levine & Jonathan R. Donnellan, *Defamation*, Comm. L. Digital Age 2018 (Nov. 8, 2018).

170. *Sindi*, 896 F.3d at 33.

CHAPTER 5 BOXED FEATURES

i. Fowler V. Harper & Fleming James Jr., Law of Torts § 5.28, at 456 (1956).

ii. *See* Restatement of Torts § 606 (1938).

iii. Restatement (Second) of Torts § 566 (1977) cmt. a.

iv. Milkovich v. Lorain Journal Co., 497 U.S. 1, 14 (1990).

v. Gertz v. Robert Welch, Inc., 418 U.S. 323, 351 (1974).

vi. *Milkovich*, 497 U.S. 1.

vii. *See, e.g.,* Mark S. Sableman, *Fair Comment, the "Brightest Jewel in The Crown of Law," as Protection for Free Speech and Against Abusive SLAPP Suits,* 61 J. Mo. B. 132 (May–June 2005).

viii. Milkovich v. Lorain Journal Co., 497 U.S. 1, 4 (1990).

ix. 47 U.S.C. §§ 230 (c)(1), (e)(3).

x. 28 U.S.C. §§ 4101–4105 (2012).

xi. TV Azteca v. Ruiz, 490 S.W. 3d 29 (Tex. 2016), *cert. denied,* 137 S.Ct. 2290 (2017).

CHAPTER 5

1. Gertz v. Robert Welch, Inc., 418 U.S. 323, 339–40 (1974).

2. The expression "SLAPP" was initially coined by two University of Denver professors. *See* Penelope Canan & George W. Pring, *Studying Strategic Lawsuits Against Public Participation: Mixing Quantitative and Qualitative Approaches,* 22 Law & Soc'y Rev. 385 (1988).

3. *See, e.g.,* Cal. Code Civ. Proc. § 425.16 (stating, in part, "The Legislature finds and declares that there has been a disturbing increase in lawsuits brought primarily to chill the valid exercise of the constitutional rights of freedom of speech and petition for the redress of grievances. The Legislature finds and declares that it is in the public interest to encourage continued participation in matters of public significance, and that this participation should not be chilled through abuse of the judicial process. . . . A cause of action against a person arising from any act of that person in furtherance of the person's right of petition or free speech under the United States or California Constitution in connection with a public issue shall be subject to a special motion to strike, unless the court determines that the plaintiff has established that there is a probability that the plaintiff will prevail on the claim").

4. Davis v. Cox, 351 P.3d 862 (2015); Leiendecker v. Asian Women United of Minn., 895 N.W.2d 623 (2017).

5. Steve Miller, *Heavyweight Lobby Group Tries Again to Reduce Power of State's Anti-SLAPP Law,* Texas Monitor, Mar. 15, 2019, texasmonitor.org/heavyweight-lobby-group-tries-again-to-reduce-power-of-states-anti-slapp-law/.

6. Typically, these cases end up in federal court because of diversity jurisdiction, which has two requirements—jurisdictional amount exceeds $75,000, and no plaintiff shares a state of citizenship with any defendant. *See* 28 U.S.C. § 1332 (a).

7. William James Seidleck, Comment: *Anti-SLAPP Statutes and the Federal Rules: Why Preemption Analysis Shows They Should Apply in Federal Diversity Suits,* 166 U. Pa. L. Rev. 547 (Jan. 2018).

8. *See, e.g.,* Sarver v. Chartier, 813 F.3d 891 (9th Cir. 2016); Travelers Cas. Ins. Co. v. Hirsh, 831 F.3d 1179 (9th Cir. 2016) (Kozinski, J., concurring).

9. Howard Wasserman, *Deepening Split on SLAPP Laws in Federal Court,* PrawfsBlawg, Dec. 15, 2018, prawfsblawg.blogs.com/prawfsblawg/2018/12/deepening-split-on-slapp-laws-in-federal-court.html. *See also* Kelley Drye, *Trump Awarded Nearly $300,000 in Attorney's Fees and Costs Following His Successful Anti-SLAPP Motion Against Stormy Daniels,* Drye Wit, Dec. 12, 2018, www.dryewit.com/2018/12/trump-awarded-nearly-300000-in-attorneys-fees-and-costs-following-his-successful-anti-slapp-motion-against-stormy-daniels/.

10. Kevin T. Baine *et al., Defamation Law Case Summaries for PLI,* 2 Comm. L. in the Digital Age 32–39 (2014); Royalty Network, Inc. v. Harris, 756 F.3d 1351 (11th Cir., 2014). *See also* Carbone v. Cable News Network, 910 F.3d 1345 (11th Cir. 2018).

11. Abbas v. Foreign Policy Group, LLC, 783 F.3d 1328, 1332 (2015).

12. *Id.* at 1338.

13. Competitive Enter. Inst. v. Mann, 150 A.3d 1213 (D.C. App. 2016).

14. *Id.*

15. *Id.* at 1240–41.

16. *See, e.g.,* Deripaska v. Associated Press, 282 F.Supp. 3d 133 (D.D.C. 2017).

17. *Defamation and Related Claims,* Comm. L. in the Digital Age 2016 (Nov. 10, 2016).

18. Los Lobos Renewable Power, LLC v. AmeriCulture, Inc., 885 F.3d 659 (10th Cir.), *cert. denied*, 1139 S. Ct. 591 (2018).

19. *But see, e.g.,* Lee v. Dong-A Ilbo, 849 F.2d 876 (4th Cir. 1988) (ruling that the privilege does not extend to official reports issued by governments other than those in the United States).

20. Allen v. Ray, 87 A.3d 890 (Pa. Super. Ct. 2013) (table).

21. Tacopina v. O'Keeffe, 2015 U.S. Dist. LEXIS 118546 (S.D.N.Y. Sept. 4, 2015), *aff'd*, 645 Fed. Appx. 7 (2d Cir. 2016).

22. Hurst v. Capital Cities Media, Inc., 754 N.E.2d 429 (Ill. App. 2001).

23. Wiemer v. Rankin, 790 P.2d 347 (Idaho 1990).

24. DMC Plumbing and Remodeling v. Fox News Network, 2012 U.S. Dist. LEXIS 167318 (E.D. Mich. Nov. 26, 2012); *New Developments 2012*, MLRC Bulletin, Dec. 2012, at 60–61.

25. Milligan v. United States, 670 F. 3d 686, 698 (6th Cir. 2012).

26. Marshall Cty. Coal Co. v. Oliver, 2018 WL 1082525 (W.Va. Cir. Ct. Feb. 22, 2018).

27. Kevin T. Baine *et al., Defamation Law Case Summaries for PLI*, 2 Comm. L. in the Digital Age 15 (2014); Barhoum v. NYP Holdings, Inc., 2014 Mass. Super. LEXIS 52 (Mass. Super. Ct. 2014).

28. *Barhoum*, 2014 Mass. Super. LEXIS 52.

29. Lee v. TMZ Prods., Inc., 2015 U.S. Dist. LEXIS 104387 (D.N.J. 2015).

30. Lee v. TMZ Prods., Inc., 710 Fed. Appx. 551 (3d Cir. 2017).

31. Olsen v. Providence Journal Co., 261 F.Supp. 3d 362, 368 (D.R.I. 2017).

32. *Id.*

33. *Defamation and Related Claims*, Comm. L. in the Digital Age 2018 (Nov. 9, 2018).

34. Adelson v. Harris, 876 F.3d 413, 414 (2d Cir. 2017).

35. *Id.*

36. Fridman v. BuzzFeed, Inc., 97 N.Y.S.3d 476 (N.Y. App. Div. 2018).

37. *Defamation and Related Claims, supra* note 33.

38. *New Developments 2012*, MLRC Bulletin, Dec. 2012, at 61.

39. To see if the fair report privilege applies in your state, you can read your state's defamation law or search for state cases that have ruled on the fair

report privilege. See Chapter 1 for more information on finding cases and statutes.

40. Whitney v. California, 274 U.S. 357, 375 (1927) (Brandeis, J., concurring).

41. Fowler V. Harper & Fleming James Jr., Law of Torts § 5.28, at 456 (1956).

42. *See* Gertz v. Robert Welch, Inc., 418 U.S. 323, 339–40 (1974).

43. Ollman v. Evans, 750 F.2d 970 (D.C. Cir. 1984).

44. *Id.*

45. Janklow v. Newsweek, 788 F.2d 1300, 1305 (8th Cir. 1986).

46. Spelson v. CBS, Inc., 581 F.Supp. 1195 (N.D. Ill. 1984); Liberty Lobby, Inc. v. Anderson, 746 F.2d 1563 (D.C. Cir. 1984), *vacated on other grounds*, 477 U.S. 242 (1986); Henderson v. Times Mirror Co., 669 F.Supp. 356 (D. Colo. 1987); Dow v. New Haven Indep., Inc., 549 A.2d 683 (Conn. 1987).

47. Milkovich v. Lorain Journal Co., 497 U.S. 1, 4 (1990).

48. *Id.* at 1.

49. *Id.* at 18.

50. *Id.*

51. *Id.* at 21.

52. *Id.* at 17.

53. Dallas Morning News v. Tatum, 554 S.W.3d 614 (Tex. 2018), *cert. denied*, 139 S. Ct. 1216 (Feb. 19, 2019).

54. *Id.*

55. Madsen v. Buie, 454 So. 2d 727, 729 (Fla. Dist. Ct. App. 1984).

56. Couloute v. Ryncarz, 2012 U.S. Dist. LEXIS 20534 (S.D.N.Y. Feb. 15, 2012).

57. *New Developments 2012*, MLRC Bulletin, Dec. 2012, at 52.

58. Redmond v. Gawker Media, LLC, 2012 Cal. App. Unpub. LEXIS 5879 (Cal. App. Aug. 10, 2012) (unpublished).

59. Hustler Magazine, Inc. v. Falwell, 485 U.S. 46 (1988).

60. Greenbelt Cooperative Publ'g Ass'n, Inc. v. Bressler, 398 U.S. 6, 7–8 (1970).

61. Seaton d/b/a Grand Resort Hotel & Convention Ctr. v. TripAdvisor, 2012 U.S. Dist. LEXIS 118584 (E.D. Tenn., Aug. 22, 2012)

62. Grand Resort Hotel & Convention Ctr. v. TripAdvisor, 728 F.3d 592, 594 (6th Cir. 2013).

63. *Id.* at 596.

64. *Id.*

65. Mark Mooney, *Trump Defamation by Twitter Case Tossed Out*, CNNMoney, Feb. 4, 2017, money.cnn .com/2017/01/10/media/trump-cheryl-jacobus-twitter-defame/.

66. *Id.*

67. Silberman v. Georges, 456 N.Y.S.2d 395 (1982).

68. New Times, Inc. v. Isaacks, 91 S.W.3d 844, 850 (Tex. 2002).

69. New Times, Inc. v. Isaacks, 146 S.W.3d 144 (Tex. 2004), *cert. denied*, 545 U.S. 1105 (2005).

70. 47 U.S.C. §§ 230 (c)(1), (e)(3).

71. RonNell Andersen Jones, *Developments in the Law of Social Media*, Comm. L. in the Digital Age (2016).

72. *Legal Guide for Bloggers, Section 230 Protections*, Electronic Frontier Found., www.eff.org/issues/ bloggers/legal/liability/230.

73. *Id.*

74. Although this was not a libel case (the underlying right of publicity is discussed in Chapter 6), the court's ruling broadly applied to how Section 230 is used by services like Facebook to defend libel and privacy claims.

75. Fraley v. Facebook, Inc., 830 F.Supp. 2d 801–02 (N.D. Cal. 2011).

76. Jones v. Dirty World Entm't Recordings, 755 F.3d 398, 401 (6th Cir. 2014).

77. *Id.* at 417.

78. *Id.*

79. Doe No. 14 v. Internet Brands, Inc., 824 F. 3d 846, 850 (9th Cir. 2016).

80. *Id.* at 851.

81. Edwards v. National Audubon Society, 556 F.2d 113 (2d Cir. 1977) (ruling that "when a responsible, prominent organization . . . makes serious charges against a public figure, the First Amendment protects the accurate and disinterested reporting of those charges, regardless of the reporter's private views of their validity. . . . We do not believe that the press may be required under the First Amendment to suppress newsworthy statements merely because it has serious doubts regarding their truth"). *Id.* at 120.

82. Dan Laidman, *When the Slander Is the Story: The Neutral Report Privilege in Theory and Practice*, 17 UCLA Ent. L. Rev. 74, 76 (2010).

83. Eli Segal & Michael E. Baughman, *#MeToo and the Media*, Pepper Hamilton, LLC, May 2018, www .pepperlaw.com/publications/metoo-and-the-media-2018-06-05/.

84. McKinney v. Avery Journal, Inc., 393 S.E.2d 295 (N.C. 1990).

85. Auvil v. CBS, 140 F.R.D. 450 (E.D. Wash. 1991).

86. See Firth v. State of New York, 775 N.E.2d 463 (N.Y. 2002), which outlines the principles of applying the single-publication rule to the internet and is often used as a precedent to support similar cases in other states and in the federal court system.

87. Masson v. New Yorker Magazine, Inc., 501 U.S. 496, 523 (1991).

88. Cardillo v. Doubleday & Co., Inc., 518 F.2d 638 (2d Cir. 1975) (ruling that the passages of a book whose authors wrote that a habitual criminal was involved in various other criminal activities did not constitute actual malice).

89. Eriq Gardner, *Joe Arpaio Called "Libel-Proof" as CNN, HuffPo and Rolling Stone Push for Lawsuit Dismissal*, Hollywood Rep., Mar. 15, 2019, www .hollywoodreporter.com/thr-esq/joe-arpaio-called-libel-proof-as-cnn-huffpo-rolling-stone-push-lawsuit-dismissal-1195142.

90. Liberty Lobby, Inc. v. Anderson, 746 F.2d 1563, 1568 (D.C. Cir. 1984), *vacated on other grounds*, 477 U.S. 242 (1986).

91. *Id.*

92. Logan v. District of Columbia, 447 F.Supp. 1328 (D.D.C. 1978).

93. Mourning v. Family Publ'ns. Serv., 411 U.S. 356, 382 (1973). *See also* Adickes v. Kress & Co., 398 U.S. 144, 157 (1970); United States v. Diebold, Inc., 369 U.S. 654, 655 (1962).

94. *See* Anderson v. Liberty Lobby, Inc., 477 U.S. 242 (1986).

95. Washington Post Co. v. Keogh, 365 F.2d 965, 968 (D.C. Cir. 1966).

96. Hutchinson v. Proxmire, 443 U.S. 111, 120 n.9 (1979).

97. Anderson v. Liberty Lobby, Inc., 477 U.S. at 244, 256.

98. Bell Atlantic Corp. v. Twombly, 550 U.S. 544 (2007).

99. Ashcroft v. Iqbal, 556 U.S. 662 (2009).

100. Suja A. Thomas, *The New Summary Judgment*

Motion: The Motion to Dismiss Under Iqbal and Twombly, Ill. Pub. L. and Legal Theory Res. Papers Series (Oct. 27, 2009), papers.ssrn.com/sol3/papers .cfm?abstract_id=1494683.

101. Schatz v. Republican State Leadership Committee, 669 F.3d 50, 57 (1st Cir. 2012).

102. Mayfield v. NASCAR, 674 F. 3d 369 (4th Cir. 2012).

103. Michel v. NYP Holdings, Inc., 816 F. 3d 686 (11th Cir. 2016).

104. William H.J. Hubbard, *The Empirical Effects of Twombly and Iqbal*, 14 J. Empirical Legal Stud. 474 (2017).

105. *See, e.g.,* Keeton v. Hustler Magazine, Inc., 465 U.S. 770 (1984) (overturning a lower court ruling dismissing a libel suit filed by a resident of New York against an Ohio corporation in a New Hampshire court). *See also* New York Times Co. v. Sullivan, 376 U.S. 254 (1964) (where the trial and first appeal were heard in Alabama courts).

106. Young v. New Haven Advocate, 315 F.3d 256, 261 (4th Cir. 2002), *cert. denied*, 538 U.S. 1035 (2003).

107. *Id.* at 263.

108. *Id.*

109. *See, e.g.,* Baines v. Daily News 2018 WL 1546555 (table) (N.Y. Sup. Ct. Mar. 28, 2018); Hearst Newspapers, LLC v. Status Lounge, Inc., 541 S.W.3d 881 (Tex. App. 2017).

110. John C. Martin, *The Role of Retraction in Defamation Suits*, 1993 U. Chi. Legal F. 293, 294 (1993).

111. Two states' retraction statutes apply only to newspapers. *See* Minn. Stat. Ann. 548.06 (1987); S.D. Codified Laws 20–11–7 (1995). Two others include media other than newspapers but exclude radio and television. *See* Wis. Stat. 895.05 (1998); Okla. Stat. tit. 12, § 1446a.

112. Dennis Hale, *The Impact of State Prohibitions of Punitive Damages on Libel Litigation: An Empirical Analysis*, 5 Vand. J. Ent. L. & Prac. 96, 100 (2003).

113. Boswell v. Phoenix Newspapers, Inc., 730 P.2d 186 (Ariz. 1986).

114. Ariz. Rev. Stat. §§ 12–653.02 and 12.653.03.

115. Ariz. Const., art. 18, § 6.

116. RonNell Andersen Jones, *Developments in the Law of Social Media*, Comm. L. in the Digital Age (2016).

117. Hassell v. Bird, 203 Cal. Rptr. 3d 203 (Ct. App. 2016).

118. Hassell v. Bird, 420 P.3d 776, 882 (Cal. 2018), *cert. denied*, 139 S. Ct. 940 (2019).

119. Eric Goldman, *The California Supreme Court Didn't Ruin Section 230 (Today)—Hassell v. Bird*, Technology & Marketing Law Blog, July 2, 2018, blog.ericgoldman.org/archives/2018/07/the-california-supreme-court-didnt-ruin-section-230-today-hassell-v-bird.htm.

120. Eriq Gardner, *The N.Y. Times Struggles to Defend Dismissal of Sarah Palin Defamation Lawsuit*, Hollywood Rep., Sept. 21, 2018, www.hollywood reporter.com/thr-esq/ny-times-struggles-defend-dismissal-sarah-palin-defamation-lawsuit-1146008.

121. Palin v. New York Times Co., 264 F.Supp. 3d 527, 536 (S.D.N.Y. 2017).

122. *Defamation and Related Claims*, Comm. L. in the Digital Age 2018 (Nov. 9, 2018).

123. *Id.*

124. *Id.*

125. In its entirety, the column reads as follows:

> Yesterday in the Franklin County Common Pleas Court, judge Paul Martin overturned an Ohio High School Athletic Assn. decision to suspend the Maple Heights wrestling team from this year's state tournament.
>
> It's not final yet—the judge granted Maple only a temporary injunction against the ruling—but unless the judge acts much more quickly than he did in this decision (he has been deliberating since a Nov. 8 hearing) the temporary injunction will allow Maple to compete in the tournament and make any further discussion meaningless.
>
> But there is something much more important involved here than whether Maple was denied due process by the OHSAA, the basis of the temporary injunction. When a person takes on a job in a school, whether it be as a teacher, coach, administrator or even maintenance worker, it is well to remember that his primary job is that of educator.
>
> There is scarcely a person concerned with school who doesn't leave his mark in some way on the young people who pass his way—many are the lessons taken away from school by students which weren't learned from a lesson plan or out of a book. They come from personal experiences with and observations of their superiors and peers, from watching actions and reactions. Such

a lesson was learned (or relearned) yesterday by the student body of Maple Heights High School, and by anyone who attended the Maple-Mentor wrestling meet of last Feb. 8. A lesson which, sadly, in view of the events of the past year, is well they learned early.

It is simply this: If you get in a jam, lie your way out.

If you're successful enough, and powerful enough, and can sound sincere enough, you stand an excellent chance of making the lie stand up, regardless of what really happened.

The teachers responsible were mainly head Maple wrestling coach, Mike Milkovich, and former superintendent of schools H. Donald Scott.

Last winter they were faced with a difficult situation. Milkovich's ranting from the side of the mat and egging the crowd on against the meet official and the opposing team backfired during a meet with Greater Cleveland Conference rival Metor [sic], and resulted in first the Maple Heights team, then many of the partisan crowd attacking the Mentor squad in a brawl which sent four Mentor wrestlers to the hospital.

Naturally, when Mentor protested to the governing body of high school sports, the OHSAA, the two men were called on the carpet to account for the incident.

But they declined to walk into the hearing and face up to their responsibilities, as one would hope a coach of Milkovich's accomplishments and reputation would do, and one would certainly expect from a man with the responsible poisition [sic] of superintendent of schools.

Instead they chose to come to the hearing and misrepresent the things that happened to the OHSAA Board of Control, attempting not only to convince the board of their own innocence, but, incredibly, shift the blame of the affair to Mentor.

I was among the 2,000-plus witnesses of the meet at which the trouble broke out, and I also attended the hearing before the OHSAA, so I was in a unique position of being the only non-involved party to observe both the meet itself and the Milkovich-Scott version presented to the board. Any resemblance between the two occurrances [sic] is purely coincidental.

To anyone who was at the meet, it need only be said that the Maple coach's wild gestures during the events leading up to the brawl were passed off by the two as "shrugs," and that Milkovich claimed he was "Powerless to control the crowd" before the melee.

Fortunately, it seemed at the time, the Milkovich-Scott version of the incident presented to the board of control had enough contradictions and obvious untruths so that the six board members were able to see through it.

Probably as much in distasteful reaction to the chicanery of the two officials as in displeasure over the actual incident, the board then voted to suspend Maple from this year's tournament and to put Maple Heights, and both Milkovich and his son, Mike Jr. (the Maple Jaycee coach), on two-year probation.

But unfortunately, by the time the hearing before Judge Martin rolled around, Milkovich and Scott apparently had their version of the incident polished and reconstructed, and the judge apparently believed them.

"I can say that some of the stories told to the judge sounded pretty darned unfamiliar," said Dr. Harold Meyer, commissioner of the OHSAA, who attended the hearing. "It certainly sounded different from what they told us."

Nevertheless, the judge bought their story, and ruled in their favor.

Anyone who attended the meet, whether he be from Maple Heights, Mentor, or impartial observer, knows in his heart that Milkovich and Scott lied at the hearing after each having given his solemn oath to tell the truth.

But they got away with it. Is that the kind of lesson we want our young people learning from their high school administrators and coaches? I think not.

126. In its entirety, the column reads as follows:

So I guess we're down to just one form of death still considered worthy of deception.

I'm told there was a time when the word "cancer" was never mentioned. Oddly, it was considered an embarrassing way to die.

It took a while for honesty to come to the AIDS epidemic. Ironically, the first person I knew to die of AIDS was said to have cancer.

We're open these days with just about every form of death except one—suicide.

When art expert Ted Pillsbury died in March, his company said he suffered an apparent heart attack on a country road in Kaufman County.

But what was apparent to every witness on the scene that day was that Pillsbury had walked a few paces from his car and shot himself.

Naturally, with such a well-known figure, the truth quickly came out.

More recently, a paid obituary in this newspaper reported that a popular local high school student died "as a result of injuries sustained in an automobile accident."

When one of my colleagues began to inquire, thinking the death deserved news coverage, it turned out to have been a suicide.

There was a car crash, all right, but death came from a self-inflicted gunshot wound [page break] in a time of remorse afterward.

And for us, there the matter ended. Newspapers don't write about suicides unless they involve a public figure or happen in a very public way.

But is that always best?

I'm troubled that we, as a society, allow suicide to remain cloaked in such secrecy, if not outright deception.

Some obituary readers tell me they feel guilty for having such curiosity about how people died. They're frustrated when obits don't say. "Morbid curiosity," they call it apologetically.

But I don't think we should feel embarrassment at all. I think the need to know is wired deeply in us. I think it's part of our survival mechanism.

Like a cat putting its nose to the wind, that curiosity is part of how we gauge the danger out there for ourselves and our loved ones.

And the secrecy surrounding suicide leaves us greatly underestimating the danger there.

Did you know that almost twice as many people die each year from suicide as from homicide?

Think of how much more attention we pay to the latter. We're nearly obsessed with crime. Yet we're nearly blind to the greater threat of self-inflicted violence.

Suicide is the third-leading cause of death among young people (ages 15 to 24) in this country.

Do you think that might be important for parents to understand?

In part, we don't talk about suicide because we don't talk about the illness that often underlies it—mental illness.

I'm a big admirer of Julie Hersh. The Dallas woman first went public with her story of depression and suicide attempts in my column three years ago.

She has since written a book, Struck by Living. Through honesty, she's trying to erase some of the shame and stigma that compounds and prolongs mental illness.

Julie recently wrote a blog item titled "Don't omit from the obit," urging more openness about suicide as a cause of death.

"I understand why people don't include it," she told me. "But it's such a missed opportunity to educate."

And she's so right.

Listen, the last thing I want to do is put guilt on the family of suicide victims. They already face a grief more intense than most of us will ever know.

But averting our eyes from the reality of suicide only puts more lives at risk.

Awareness, frank discussion, timely intervention, treatment—those are the things that save lives.

Honesty is the first step.

CHAPTER 6 BOXED FEATURES

i. Griswold v. Connecticut, 381 U.S. 479, 481 (1965).

ii. Katz v. United States, 389 U.S. 347 (1967) (Harlan, J., concurring).

iii. State courts or federal courts applying state law to follow *Gertz* rather than *Hill* and *Cantrell*, thus not requiring private false light plaintiffs to prove actual malice, include Alabama, Delaware, Kansas, Utah, West Virginia and the District of Columbia. MEDIA L. RESOURCE CTR., MEDIA PRIVACY AND RELATED LAW 50-STATE SURVEY 2018–2019 (2019).

iv. Daniels v. FanDuel, Inc., 884 F.3d 672, *aff'd*, 909 F.3d 876 (7th Cir. 2018).

v. Daniels v. FanDuel, Inc., 109 N.E.3d 390, *aff'd*, 909 F.3d 876 (7th Cir. 2018).

vi. Jennifer Rothman, *Seventh Circuit Dismisses Athletes' Case in Fantasy Sports Suit*, ROTHMAN'S ROADMAP TO THE RIGHT OF PUBLICITY, Nov. 30, 2018, www .rightofpublicityroadmap.com/news-commentary/ seventh-circuit-dismisses-athletes-case-fantasy- sports-suit.

vii. Jane Kirtley, *Privacy and Data Protection 2018*, Comm. L. in the Digital Age 2018 (2018).

viii. Case C-131/12, Google Spain SL v. Agencia Española de Protección de Datos (Court of Justice of European Union, 2014), curia.europa.eu/juris/document/document.jsf?docid=152065&doclang=en.; *see also* Jeffrey Toobin, *The Solace of Oblivion*, New Yorker, Sept. 29, 2014, www.newyorker.com/magazine/2014/09/29/solace-oblivion.

ix. *Search Removals Under European Privacy Law*, Google, Mar. 31, 2019, www.google.com/transparencyreport/removals/europeprivacy/.

CHAPTER 6

1. Riley v. California, 573 U.S. 373, 385 (2014).

2. *Id.*

3. Carpenter v. United States, 138 S. Ct. 2206 (2018).

4. Jeffery A. Smith, *Moral Guardians and the Origins of the Right to Privacy*, 10 Journalism & Comm. Monographs 65 (2008).

5. Samuel D. Warren & Louis D. Brandeis, *The Right to Privacy*, 4 Harv. L. Rev. 193 (1890).

6. Warren and Brandeis rested their contention on an English case, Prince Albert v. Strange, 64 Eng. Rep. 293 (V.C. 1848), on appeal, 64 Eng. Rep. 293 (1849). But not until 2001 did English courts explicitly recognize a right to privacy. *See* Douglas v. Hello! Ltd., [2001] W.L.R. 992, 1033, ¶ 110 ("We have reached a point at which it can be said with confidence that the law recognizes and will appropriately protect a right of personal privacy") (per Sedley, L.J.).

7. Warren & Brandeis, *supra* note 5, at 197; *See also* Dorothy J. Glancy, *The Invention of the Right to Privacy*, 21 Ariz. L. Rev. 1 (1979).

8. *See* Don R. Pember, Privacy and the Press (1972).

9. U.S. Const. amend. IV.

10. Carpenter v. United States, 138 S. Ct. 2206, 2213 (2018).

11. U.S. Const. amend. III, V.

12. Griswold v. Connecticut, 381 U.S. 479, 481 (1965).

13. *Id.* at 483.

14. Roe v. Wade, 410 U.S. 113 (1973).

15. *Id.* at 153.

16. *Id.*

17. Olmstead v. United States, 277 U.S. 438 (1928).

18. *Id.* at 478 (Brandeis, J., dissenting).

19. Silverman v. United States, 365 U.S. 505 (1961).

20. Katz v. United States, 389 U.S. 347 (1967) (Harlan, J., concurring).

21. Daniel T. Pesciotta, *I'm Not Dead Yet: Katz, Jones, and the Fourth Amendment in the 21st Century*, 63 Case W. Res. 187, 198 (2012).

22. Carpenter v. United States, 138 S. Ct. 2206, 2237 (2018).

23. O'Connor v. Ortega, 480 U.S. 709 (1987).

24. Ray Lewis, Comment: *Employee E-mail Privacy Still Unemployed: What the United States Can Learn From the United Kingdom*, 67 La. L. Rev. 959 (2007); *see also* Smyth v. Pillsbury Co., 914 F. Supp. 97, 101 (E.D. Pa. 1996).

25. City of Ontario v. Quon, 560 U.S. 746 (2010).

26. *See* Comsys, Inc. v. Pacetti, 893 F. 3d 468 (7th Cir. 2018).

27. Kyllo v. United States, 533 U.S. 27 (2001).

28. United States v. Jones, 565 U.S. 400 (2012).

29. Riley v. California, 573 U.S. 373, 393 (2014).

30. Carpenter v. United States, 138 S. Ct. 2206 (2018).

31. *Id.* at 2219.

32. *Id.* at 2206.

33. United States v. Miller, 425 U.S. 435 (1976); Smith v. Maryland, 442 U.S. 735 (1979).

34. *Id.*

35. *Carpenter*, 138 S. Ct. at 2217–18.

36. *Id.* at 2223 (Kennedy, J., dissenting), 2246 (Alito, J., dissenting).

37. *Id.* at 2235 (Thomas, J., dissenting).

38. *Id.* at 2261 (Gorsuch, J., dissenting).

39. *Privacy*, Merriam-Webster, Mar. 31, 2019, www.merriam-webster.com/dictionary/privacy.

40. William L. Prosser, *Privacy*, 48 Cal. L. Rev. 383 (1960).

41. Media L. Resource Ctr., Media Privacy and Related Law 50-State Survey 2018–2019 (2019).

42. Restatement (Second) of Torts § 652I.

43. *See, e.g.*, Restatement (Third) of Unfair Competition § 46 cmt. d (right of publicity limited to "natural persons").

44. Restatement (Second) of Torts § 652B.

45. Media L. Resource Ctr., Media Privacy and Related Law 50-State Survey 2016–2017 (2017).

46. *Current Unmanned Aircraft State Law Landscape*, Nat'l Conference of State Legislatures, Sept.. 10, 2018, www.ncsl.org/research/transportation/ current-unmanned-aircraft-state-law-landscape .aspx.

47. Webb v. CBS Broad., Inc., 2009 U.S. Dist. LEXIS 38597, at *9 (N.D. Ill., May 7, 2009).

48. *See, e.g.,* Broughton v. McClatchy Newspapers, Inc., 588 S.E.2d 20 (N.C. App. 2003).

49. Boring v. Google, Inc., 362 F. App'x 273 (3d Cir.), *cert. denied*, 562 U.S. 836 (2010).

50. Hill v. Colorado, 530 U.S. 703 (2000).

51. Cal. Civ. Code § 1708.8.

52. Tracy Bloom, *New Laws Set to Take Effect in California for 2014*, KTLA, Dec. 31, 2013, ktla. com/2013/12/31/new-laws-set-to-go-into-effect- in-california-for-2014/.

53. Shulman v. Group W Prods., Inc., 74 Cal. Rptr. 2d 843, *opinion modified*, 1998 Cal. LEXIS 4846 (Cal. 1998).

54. United States v. Maldonado-Norat, 122 F. Supp. 2d 264 (D.P.R. 2000).

55. Medical Laboratory Mgmt. Consultants v. Am. Broad. Cos., Inc., 306 F.3d 806, 819 (9th Cir. 2002).

56. Belluomo v. KAKE TV & Radio, Inc., 596 P.2d 832 (Kan. App. 1979).

57. Machleder v. Diaz, 538 F. Supp. 1364 (S.D.N.Y. 1982).

58. Desnick v. Am. Broad. Cos., Inc., 44 F.3d 1345 (7th Cir. 1995).

59. Carter v. Superior Court of San Diego Cty., 2002 Cal. App. Unpub. LEXIS 5017 (Ct. App. 2002).

60. Dietemann v. Time, Inc., 449 F.2d 245, 249 (9th Cir. 1971).

61. *Id.*

62. Restatement (Second) of Torts § 652E cmt. b, illus. 1.

63. Solano v. Playgirl, Inc., 292 F.3d 1078, 1082 (9th Cir.), *cert. denied*, 537 U.S. 1029 (2002).

64. See Restatement (Second) of Torts § 652E.

65. *Id.* at § 652I cmt. c.

66. *Id.* at § 652D cmt. a.

67. *Solano*, 292 F.3d 1078.

68. *See, e.g., id.*

69. *See, e.g.,* Austin Eberhardt Donaldson Corp. v. Morgan Stanley Dean Witter Trust FSB, 2001 U.S. Dist. LEXIS 1090 (N.D. Ill. 2001).

70. Howard v. Antilla, 294 F.3d 244 (1st Cir. 2002).

71. Michael Sewell, Note and Comment: *Invasion of Privacy in Texas: Public Disclosure of Embarrassing Private Facts*, 2 Tex. Wesleyan L. Rev. 411 (1995).

72. Moriarty v. Greene, 732 N.E.2d 730 (Ill. App. Ct. 2000).

73. Kelson v. Spin Publ'ns, Inc., 1988 U.S. Dist. LEXIS 4675 (D. Md. 1988).

74. Peoples Bank & Trust Co. v. Globe Int'l, 978 F.2d 1065 (8th Cir. 1992), *on remand*, Mitchell v. Globe Int'l Publ'g, Inc., 817 F. Supp. 72 (W.D. Ark.), *cert. denied*, 510 U.S. 931 (1993).

75. Time, Inc. v. Hill, 385 U.S. 374 (1967).

76. *Id.*

77. Cantrell v. Forest City Pub. Co., 419 U.S. 245 (1974).

78. State courts or federal courts applying state law to follow *Hill* and *Cantrell* rather than *Gertz*, thus requiring private false light plaintiffs to prove actual malice, include Arkansas, California, Connecticut, Florida, Georgia, Illinois, Indiana, Iowa, Kentucky, Maine, Michigan, Mississippi, Montana, Nebraska, Nevada, New Jersey, Oklahoma, Oregon, Pennsylvania, Tennessee and Washington. *See, e.g.,* Lohrenz v. Donnelly, 223 F. Supp. 2d, 25 (2002).

79. Clark v. E! Entm't TV, 2018 U.S. Dist. LEXIS 49588 (M.D. Tenn. 2018), *appeal dismissed*, 2018 U.S. App. LEXIS 19250 (6th Cir. 2018).

80. State courts or federal courts applying state law to follow *Gertz* rather than *Hill* and *Cantrell*, thus not requiring private false light plaintiffs to prove actual malice, include Alabama, Delaware, Kansas, Utah, West Virginia and the District of Columbia. Media L. Resource Ctr., Media Privacy and Related Law 50-State Survey 2016–2017 (2017).

81. *See* Harvey L. Zuckman et al., Modern Commc'ns L. 357–61 (1999).

82. *See id.* at 360–61 (1999).

83. *E.g.,* Veilleux v. NBC, 206 F.3d 92, 134 (1st Cir. 2000), said opinion could be a false light defense, while Boese v. Paramount Pictures Corp., 952 F. Supp. 550, 558–59 (N.D. Ill. 1996), said opinion is not a false light defense.

84. Sarver v. Chartier, 813 F.3d 891, 901–02 (9th Cir. 2016).

85. *Id.*

86. Kelli L. Sager, *Address at the 2014 Practising Law Institute's Communication in the Digital Age* (Nov. 13, 2014).

87. *Id. See also* Kelli L. Sager & Karen A. Henry, *Developments in Misappropriation and Right of Publicity Law—2014*, 2 Comm. L. in the Digital Age 3–18 (2014).

88. Media L. Resource Ctr., Media Privacy and Related Law 50-State Survey 2018–2019 (2019).

89. Restatement (Third) of Unfair Competition § 46.

90. N.Y. Civil Rights Law §§ 50–51.

91. Haelan Labs., Inc. v. Topps Chewing Gum, Inc., 202 F.2d 866 (2d Cir. 1953).

92. *See* J. Thomas McCarthy, The Rights of Publicity and Privacy , 2d §§ 1:27, 4:7 (2018).

93. Some states, such as Georgia, New Jersey and Utah, and the U.S. Court of Appeals for the Second Circuit have decided by common law that the right of publicity survives after death. Statutes in 10 states say the same. Some states, such as Illinois and Ohio, and the U.S. Courts of Appeals for the Sixth and Seventh Circuits say by common law that the right of publicity ends when a person dies. Five states agree by statute: Arizona, Massachusetts, New York, Rhode Island and Wisconsin. *Id.*

94. By statute: California, Florida, Illinois, Indiana, Kentucky, Nebraska, Nevada, Ohio, Oklahoma, Pennsylvania, Tennessee, Texas, Virginia and Washington. By common law: Connecticut, Georgia, Michigan, New Jersey and Utah. *Id.*

95. For example, Virginia limits the right of publicity to 20 years after a person's death, Indiana and Oklahoma allow the right to last 100 years after a person's death and Nebraska has no stated duration. *Id.* § 9:18.

96. *New Developments 2012*, MLRC Bulletin, Dec. 2012, 68–71.

97. Milton H. Greene Archives v. Marilyn Monroe, LLC, 692 F. 3d 983 (9th Cir. 2012).

98. Hebrew Univ. of Jerusalem v. General Motors, LLC, 903 F. Supp. 2d 932 (C.D. Cal 2012).

99. *See, e.g.,* Jennifer Rothman, *Whitney Houston Estate Settles With IRS Over Right of Publicity Valuation*, Rothman's Roadmap to the Right of Publicity, Jan. 5, 2018, www.rightofpublicityroadmap.com/news-commentary/whitney-houston-estate-settles-irs-over-publicity-valuation; Paisley

Park Entm't. v. George Ian Boxill, 253 F. Supp. 3d 1037 (2017).

100. Peter J. Reilly, *We May Have to Wait a Year for Decision in Michael Jackson Estate Tax Case*, Forbes, July 27, 2018, www.forbes.com/sites/peterjreilly/2018/07/27/we-may-have-to-wait-a-year-for-decision-in-michael-jackson-estate-tax-case/#307a459a7f94.

101. Eriq Gardner, *Robin Williams Restricted Exploitation of His Image for 25 Years After Death*, Hollywood Rep., Mar. 30, 2015, www.hollywoodreporter.com/thr-esq/robin-williams-restricted-exploitation-his-785292.

102. *In re* Estate of Reynolds, 327 P. 3d 213 (Ariz. Ct. App. 2014).

103. Eriq Gardner, *Minnesota Lawmaker Proposes "Prince Act" So Others Can't Exploit Prince*, Hollywood Rep., May 9, 2016, www.hollywoodreporter.com/thr-esq/minnesota-lawmaker-proposes-prince-act-892154.

104. *See, e.g.,* Dalbec v. Gentleman's Companion, Inc., 828 F.2d 921 (2d Cir. 1987).

105. Jennifer Rothman, *Harris Faulkner Hamster Case Settles*, Rothman's Roadmap to the Right of Publicity, Oct. 7, 2016, www.rightofpublicityroadmap.com/news-commentary/harris-faulkner-hamster-case-settles.

106. *See* J. Thomas McCarthy, The Rights of Publicity and Privacy, 2d § 3:7 (2018).

107. Jackson v. Odenat, 9 F. Supp. 3d 342 (S.D.N.Y. Mar. 24, 2014).

108. Martin v. Wendy's Int'l, Inc., 2017 WL 1545684 (N.D. Ill. Apr. 28, 2017), *aff'd*, 714 F. App'x 590 (7th Cir.), *cert. denied*, 139 S. Ct. 104 (2018).

109. Martin v. Wendy's Int'l, Inc., 714 F. App'x 590 (7th Cir. 2018).

110. C.B.C. Distribution and Mktg., Inc. v. Major League Baseball Advanced Media, LP, 505 F.3d 818 (8th Cir. 2007), *cert. denied*, 553 U.S. 1090 (2008).

111. Dobrowolski v. Intelius, Inc., 2017 WL 3720170 (N.D. Ill. Aug. 29, 2017).

112. Midler v. Ford Motor Co., 849 F.2d 460 (9th Cir. 1988). A federal district court denied Midler punitive damages, but the jury awarded $400,000 in compensatory damages. The Ninth Circuit affirmed. Midler v. Young & Rubicam, Inc., 944 F.2d 909 (9th Cir. 1991), *cert. denied*, 503 U.S. 951 (1992).

113. White v. Samsung Elec. Am., Inc., 971 F.2d 1395 (9th Cir. 1992), *cert. denied*, 508 U.S. 951 (1993).

114. Wendt v. Host Int'l, Inc., 125 F.3d 806 (9th Cir. 1997), *cert. denied*, 531 U.S. 811 (2000).

115. *Norm and Cliff Cheered by Lawsuit*, CHI. TRIB., June 22, 2001, at C2.

116. *See, e.g.,* Cardtoons, L.C. v. Major League Baseball Players Ass'n, 95 F.3d 959 (10th Cir. 1996).

117. *See* Lohan v. Take-Two Interactive Software, Inc., 97 N.E.3d 389 (N.Y. 2018); Gravano v. Take-Two Interactive Software, Inc., 97 N.E.3d 396 (N.Y. 2018).

118. *Id.*

119. *Lohan*, 97 N.E.3d at 395.

120. ETW Corp. v. Jireh Publ'g, Inc., 332 F.3d 915, 924 (6th Cir. 2003).

121. Leviston v. Jackson III, a/k/a 50 Cent, 980 N.Y.S.2d 716 (2013).

122. Zacchini v. Scripps-Howard Broad. Co., 433 U.S. 562, 578 (1977).

123. *Id.*

124. *Id.*

125. *See* Mark S. Lee, *Agents of Chaos: Judicial Confusion in Defining the Right of Publicity-Free Speech Interface*, 23 LOYOLA L.A. ENT. L. REV. 471, 488 (2003).

126. Paulsen v. Personality Posters, Inc., 299 N.Y.S.2d 501 (Sup. Ct. 1968); Montana v. San Jose Mercury News, Inc., 40 Cal. Rptr. 2d 639 (Ct. App. 1995).

127. Factors Etc., Inc. v. Pro Arts, Inc., 579 F.2d 215 (2d Cir. 1978); Brinkley v. Casablancas, 438 N.Y.S.2d 1004 (App. Div. 1981); Titan Sports, Inc. v. Comics World Corp., 870 F.2d 85 (2d Cir. 1989).

128. Eriq Gardner, *Lindsay Lohan Loses Lawsuit Against Pitbull Over Hit Song*, HOLLYWOOD REP., Feb. 21, 2013, www.hollywoodreporter.com/thr-esq/lindsay-lohan-loses-lawsuit-pitbull-423228.

129. Rogers v. Grimaldi, 875 F.2d 994, 999 (2d Cir. 1989).

130. Parks v. LaFace Records, 329 F.3d 437, 442 (6th Cir. 2003), *cert. denied*, 540 U.S. 1074 (2003).

131. *See* Campbell v. Acuff-Rose Music, Inc., 510 U.S. 569 (1994); Pierre N. Leval, *Toward a Fair Use Standard*, 103 HARV. L. REV. 1105, 1111 (1990).

132. For a thorough and critical discussion of the Three Stooges decision, see F. Jay Daugherty, *All the World's Not a Stooge: The "Transformativeness" Test for Analyzing a First Amendment Defense to a Right of Publicity Claim Against Distribution of a Work of Art*, 27 COL. J. L. & ARTS 1 (2003).

133. Comedy III Prods., Inc. v. Gary Saderup, 106 Cal. Rptr. 2d 126, 140 (2001), *cert. denied*, 534 U.S. 1078 (2002).

134. Steve Berkowitz, *Payouts for College Athletes From EA Sports Distributed Soon*, USA Today, Nov. 7, 2015, www.usatoday.com/story/sports/college/2015/11/07/ncaa-college-ea-sports-lawsuit-payouts/75367410/.

135. Keller v. Elec. Arts, Inc., 2010 U.S. Dist. LEXIS 10719 (N.D. Calif. Feb. 8, 2010), *aff'd*, 724 F.3d 1268 (9th Cir. 2013), *cert. dismissed*, 573 U.S. 589 (2014).

136. Hart v. Elec. Arts, Inc., 808 F. Supp. 2d 757 (D.N.J. 2011).

137. *Id.* at 787.

138. Hart v. Elec. Arts, Inc., 717 F.3d 141 (3d Cir. 2013), *cert. dismissed*, 573 U.S. 989 (2014).

139. Anne Bucher, *EA, NCAA Video Game Likeness Class Action Settlement*, TOP CLASS ACTIONS, Oct. 24, 2014, topclassactions.com/lawsuit-settlements/open-lawsuit-settlements/42811-ea-ncaa-video-game-likeness-class-action-settlement/.

140. Derek Svendsen, *Former Student-Athletes File Lawsuit to Protect Their Rights of Publicity: Recap of Marshall v. ESPN* (filed 10/3/14), SPORT IN LAW, Oct. 15, 2014, heitnerlegal.com/2014/10/15/former-student-athletes-file-lawsuit-to-protect-their-rights-of-publicity-recap-of-marshall-v-espn-filed-10314/.

141. Marshall v. ESPN, 668 F. App'x 155 (Mem.) (6th Cir. 2016).

142. Steve Berkowitz, *Judges Who Ruled Against EA Sports Set to Hear NCAA Appeal in O'Bannon*, USA TODAY, Jan. 23, 2015, www.usatoday.com/story/sports/college/2015/01/23/obannon-class-action-lawsuit-ncaa-appeal-keller-case/22242583/.

143. Davis v. Elec. Arts, Inc., 2018 WL 3956212 (N.D. Cal. Aug. 17, 2018).

144. *Id.*

145. De Havilland v. FX Networks, 230 Cal. Rptr. 3d 625 (Ct. App. 2018), *cert. denied*, 139 S. Ct. 800 (2019).

146. *Id.* at 638.

147. Moore v. Weinstein Co., LLC, 545 F. App'x 405 (6th Cir. 2013).

148. Winter v. DC Comics, 69 P.3d 473 (Cal. 2003).

149. *Id.* at 478 (*quoting* Comedy III Prods., Inc. v. Gary Saderup, Inc., 106 Cal. Rptr. 2d 126, 140 (2001)).

150. Doe v. TCI Cablevision, 110 S.W.3d 363 (Mo. 2003), *on remand*, Doe v. McFarlane, 207 S.W.3d 52 (Mo. Ct. App. 2006).

151. Seale v. Gramercy Pictures, 949 F. Supp. 331 (E.D. Pa. 1996), *aff'd without opinion*, 156 F.3d 1225 (3d Cir. 1998).

152. Rosemont Enter., Inc. v. Random House, Inc., 294 N.Y.S.2d 122 (Sup. Ct. 1968), *judgment aff'd*, 301 N.Y.S.2d 948 (App. Div. 1969).

153. *See, e.g.,* Tyne v. Time Warner Entm't Co., 336 F.3d 1286 (11th Cir. 2003).

154. Booth v. Curtis Publ'g Co., 223 N.Y.S.2d 737 (Sup. Ct.), *aff'd*, 228 N.Y.S.2d 468 (1962).

155. Cher v. Forum Int'l, 692 F.2d 634 (9th Cir. 1982), *cert. denied*, 462 U.S. 1120 (1983).

156. Jordan v. Jewel Food Stores, Inc., 743 F.3d 509 (7th Cir. 2014).

157. Pratt v. Everalbum, Inc., 283 F. Supp. 3d 664 (N.D. Ill 2017).

158. Netzer v. Continuity Graphic Assoc., Inc., 963 F. Supp. 1308 (S.D.N.Y. 1997).

159. Roe v. Amazon.com, 170 F. Supp. 3d 1028 (S.D. Ohio 2016).

160. *Id.* at 1035.

161. Roe v. Amazon.com, 714 F. App'x 565 (6th Cir. 2017).

162. Brents v. Morgan, 299 S.W. 967 (Ky. Ct. App. 1927).

163. Restatement (Second) of Torts § 652D.

164. Michaels v. Internet Entm't Grp., 5 F. Supp. 2d 823, 842 (C.D. Cal. 1998).

165. Media L. Resource Ctr., Media Privacy and Related Law 50-State Survey 2016–2017 (2017). Four states have rejected the tort—Nebraska, New York, North Carolina and Virginia.

166. Restatement (Second) of Torts § 652D, requires the private facts to be disseminated "to the public at large, or to so many persons that the matter must be regarded as substantially certain to become one of public knowledge."

167. *See* Patrick J. McNulty, *The Public Disclosure of Private Facts: There Is Life After* Florida Star, 50 Drake L. Rev. 93, 100 (2001).

168. See Beaumont v. Brown, 257 N.W.2d 522, 531 (Mich. 1977), *overruled in part on other grounds*, Bradley v. Saranac Board of Education, 565 N.W.2d 650 (1997).

169. *See, e.g.,* Jones v. U.S. Child Support Recovery, 961 F. Supp. 1518 (D. Utah 1997). A debt collection agency sent a "wanted" poster to the employer of a divorced parent who was behind on child support payments.

170. *See, e.g.,* Y.G. v. Jewish Hosp. of St. Louis, 795 S.W.2d 488 (Mo. Ct. App. 1990). A couple, pregnant with triplets after an in vitro fertilization process, were invited to and attended a social gathering for couples who were part of a hospital's in vitro program. The hospital promised there would be no publicity. However, a television station reporting team was at the gathering, photographing and trying to interview the couple. The couple's pictures were part of the station's television report. The couple had not told anyone they were part of the in vitro program.

171. *See, e.g.,* Baugh v. CBS, Inc., 828 F. Supp. 745 (N.D. Cal. 1993). Without permission, a television program taped and showed the aftermath of a domestic violence incident.

172. *See, e.g.,* Michaels v. Internet Entm't Grp., 5 F. Supp. 2d 823, 842 (C.D. Cal. 1998). Musician Bret Michaels brought a private facts suit against an internet adult entertainment company for distributing a videotape showing Michaels and actress Pamela Anderson Lee having sex. Michaels and Lee made the tape, which an unknown person apparently stole and sold to the internet company.

173. Restatement (Second) of Torts § 652D cmt. c.

174. *See* M.G. v. Time Warner, Inc., 107 Cal. Rptr. 2d 504, 511 (Cal. App. 2001).

175. Sandler v. Calcagni, 565 F. Supp. 184 (D. Me. 2008).

176. *Id.* at 198.

177. Joe Mullin, *Revenge Porn Is "Just Entertainment," Says Owner of IsAnybodyDown,* Ars Technica, Feb. 4, 2013, arstechnica.com/tech-policy/2013/02/revenge-porn-is-just-entertainment-says-owner-of-isanybodydown.

178. Woodrow Hartzog, *How to Fight Revenge Porn*, Atlantic, May 10, 2013, www.theatlantic.com/technology/archive/2013/05/how-to-fight-revenge-porn/275759/.

179. *43 States + DC + One Territory Have Revenge Porn Laws*, Cyber Civil Rights Initiative, Mar. 29, 2019, www.cybercivilrights.org/revenge-porn-laws/. The seven states without revenge porn laws are Indiana, Massachusetts, Mississippi, Montana, Nebraska, South Carolina and Wyoming. *Id.*

180. Restatement (Second) of Torts § 652D cmts. g, h.

181. The Restatement also adopted the test. *Id.* cmt. h.

182. Virgil v. Time, Inc., 527 F.2d 1122 (9th Cir. 1975), *cert. denied*, 425 U.S. 998 (1976).

183. Virgil v. Sports Illustrated, Inc., 424 F. Supp. 1286 (S.D. Cal. 1976).

184. Michaels v. Internet Entm't Grp., Inc., 5 F. Supp. 2d 823 (C.D. Cal. 1998).

185. Tina Gehres, *Gehres Law Group Reviews the Constitutional Issues in Hulk Hogan v. Gawker*, GEHRES L. GRP., Mar. 22, 2016, gehreslaw.com/tag/hulk-hogan-civil-case/.

186. Gawker Media, LLC v. Bollea, 129 So. 3d 1196 (Fla. Dist. Ct. App. 2014).

187. Thomas Leatherbury, *2015–16 Developments in Newsgathering and Privacy Liability*, COMM. L. IN THE DIGITAL AGE, Nov. 10, 2016.

188. Sydney Ember, *Gawker and Hulk Hogan Reach $31 Million Settlement*, N.Y. TIMES, Nov. 2, 2016, www.nytimes.com/2016/11/03/business/media/gawker-hulk-hogan-settlement.html?_r=1.

189. Max Kennerly, *Hulk Hogan v. Gawker Legal FAQ—In Their Lawyers' Words*, LITIGATION & TRIAL, May 26, 2016, www.litigationandtrial.com/2016/05/articles/attorney/hogan-v-gawker-legal-faq/.

190. Cindy Boren, *The Erin Andrews Verdict: It's Not About the $55 Million in Peephole Lawsuit*, WASH. POST, Mar. 8, 2016, www.washingtonpost.com/news/early-lead/wp/2016/03/08/the-erin-andrews-verdict-its-not-about-the-55-million-in-peephole-lawsuit/?utm_term=.46a6f3f942d7.

191. Kevin Draper, *Jason Pierre-Paul and ESPN Settle Invasion of Privacy Suit*, DEADSPIN, Feb. 3, 2017, deadspin.com/jason-pierre-paul-and-espn-settle-invasion-of-privacy-s-1791981170.

192. Diaz v. Oakland Tribune, 188 Cal. Rptr. 762 (1983).

193. David Kravets, *Shamed by Mugshot Sites, Arrestees Try Novel Lawsuit*, Wired, Dec. 12, 2012, www.wired.com/2012/12/mugshot-industry-legal-attack/.

194. *See* Taha v. Bucks Cty., 9 F. Supp. 3d 490 (E.D. Pa. 2014).

195. Gabiola v. Sarid, 2017 U.S. Dist. LEXIS 157699 (N.D. Ill. Sept. 26, 2017).

196. Sidis v. F-R Publ'g Corp., 113 F.2d 806 (2d Cir.), *cert. denied*, 311 U.S. 711 (1940).

197. Florida Star v. B.J.F., 491 U.S. 524, 541 (1989).

198. *Id.* at 524.

199. *Id.*

200. *Id.*

201. *See* Green v. Chicago Tribune Co., 675 N.E.2d 249 (Ill. App. Ct. 1996), *appeal denied*, 679 N.E.2d 379 (Ill. 1997).

202. Cox Broad. Corp. v. Cohn, 420 U.S. 469 (1975).

203. Oklahoma Publ'g Co. v. Dist. Court, 430 U.S. 308 (1977).

204. Smith v. Daily Mail, 443 U.S. 97 (1979).

205. Bartnicki v. Vopper, 532 U.S. 514 (2001).

206. *See, e.g., In re* DoubleClick, Inc. Privacy Litigation, 154 F. Supp. 2d 497 (S.D.N.Y. 2001).

207. Geoffrey A. Fowler, *It's the Middle of the Night. Do You Know Who Your iPhone Is Talking To?*, WASH. POST, May 28, 2019, www.washingtonpost.com/technology/2019/05/28/its-middle-night-do-you-know-who-your-iphone-is-talking/?utm_term=.b8e8ea31da8d.

208. Fed. Trade Comm'n, *FTC Issues Final Commission Report on Protecting Consumer Privacy* (Mar. 26, 2012), ftc.gov/opa/2012/03/privacyframework.shtm.

209. Declan McCullagh, *FTC Says Current Privacy Laws Aren't Working*, CNET NEWS, June 22, 2010, www.cnet.com/news/ftc-says-current-privacy-laws-arent-working/.

210. Fed. Trade Comm'n, *Data Brokers: A Call for Transparency and Accountability* (May 2014), www.ftc.gov/system/files/documents/reports/data-brokers-call-transparency-accountability-report-federal-trade-commission-may-2014/140527databrokerreport.pdf.

211. *Id.*

212. Spokeo, Inc. v. Robins, 136 S. Ct. 1540 (2016).

213. *Id.*

214. Jane Kirtley, *Private Data Collection: Global Privacy and Data Protection*, COMM. L. IN THE DIGITAL AGE 2016 (2016).

215. Video Privacy Protection Act, 18 U.S.C.A. § 2710(b).

216. *In re* Hulu Privacy Litigation, 2012 U.S. Dist. LEXIS 112916 (N.D. Cal. 2012).

217. Jane Kirtley, *Private Data Collection: Global Privacy and Data Protection*, COMM. L. IN THE DIGITAL AGE 2016, 13 (2016); *see also* Dale Bish & Lauren Gallo White, *Ninth Circuit Narrowly Defines "Personally Identifiable Information" Under the VPPA*, WSGR DATA ADVISOR, Jan. 24, 2018, www.wsgrdataadvisor.com/2018/01/ninth-circuit-vppa/.

218. Daisuke Wakabayashi, *California Passes Sweeping Law to Protect Online Privacy*, N.Y. TIMES, June 28, 2018, www.nytimes.com/2018/06/28/technology/california-online-privacy-law.html.

219. Justices Kennedy, Thomas, Alito and Gorsuch all wrote dissenting opinions in this case. Justice Kennedy's dissent, joined by Justices Thomas and Alito, is the only one excerpted for this chapter in the interest of space. While not entirely inclusive, it captures most of the arguments and positions made in the other individual dissents.

CHAPTER 7 BOXED FEATURES

i. *Sample FOIA Request Letters*, Nat'l Freedom of Info. Coalition, www.nfoic.org/sample-foia-request-letters.

ii. New York Open Meetings Law, N.Y. Pub. Off. Law § 103 (1976).

iii. 532 U.S. 514, 518–19 (2001).

iv. *The First Amendment Handbook*, Reporters Comm. for Freedom of the Press, www.rcfp.org/resources/first-amendment-handbook/.

v. Wilson v. Layne, 526 U.S. 603, 607 (1999).

vi. Charles Ornstein, *NY Hospital to Pay $2.2 Million Over Unauthorized Filming of 2 Patients*, N.Y. Times, Apr.21,2016,www.nytimes.com/2016/04/22/nyregion/new-york-hospital-to-pay-fine-over-unauthorized-filming-of-2-patients.html.

vii. *Id.*

CHAPTER 7

1. Pell v. Procunier, 417 U.S. 817, 833 (1974).

2. Branzburg v. Hayes, 408 U.S. 665, 728 (1972).

3. Fed. Housekeeping Statute, 5 U.S.C. § 301.

4. Harold C. Relyea, *Access to Government Information in the United States*, Report for Congress, Jan. 7, 2005, fas.org/sgp/crs/97-71.pdf.

5. 5 U.S.C. ch. 5, subch. I § 500 *et seq.*

6. Zemel v. Rusk, 381 U.S. 1 (1965).

7. 5 U.S.C. § 552.

8. Federal Advisory Committee Act, 5 U.S.C. app. §§ 1–15, Pub. L. 92–463, 86 Stat. 770 (1972).

9. Government in the Sunshine Act, 5 U.S.C. § 552b (1976).

10. Privacy Act, 5 U.S.C. § 552a (1974).

11. Branzburg v. Hayes, 408 U.S. 665 (1972).

12. Houchins v. KQED, 438 U.S. 1, 14 (1978).

13. The earliest adopters likely were Utah (1898) and Florida (1905).

14. Electronic Freedom of Information Act, Pub. L. No. 104–231, 110 Stat. 3048, §§ 1–12 (1996) (codified as amended in various sections of 5 U.S.C. § 552).

15. OPEN FOIA Act, Pub. L. 111–83 § 564, 123 Stat. 2184 (2009) (establishing criteria for new exemptions to FOIA).

16. Issue Brief: *State Freedom of Information Laws*, Soc. of Amer. Archivists, Sept. 2015, www2.archivists.org/statements/issue-brief-state-freedom-of-information-laws.

17. Michael Roffe, *Post-9/11 Info Access*, Freedom F. Inst., July 2010, www.freedomforuminstitute.org/first-amendment-center/topics/freedom-of-the-press/freedom-of-information-overview/post-911-info-access.

18. Nicholas Kusnetz, *State Integrity Investigation Spurs Proposals for Reform*, St. Integrity 2015, Jan. 20, 2016, publicintegrity.org/state-politics/state-integrity-investigation-spurs-proposals-for-reform.

19. H.R. 2048, Pub. L. 114–23 (2015).

20. *See, e.g.,* Erwin Chemerinsky, *Protect the Press: A First Amendment Standard for Safeguarding Aggressive Newsgathering*, 33 Univ. Richmond L. Rev. 1143 (2000).

21. Branzburg v. Hayes, 408 U.S. 665 (1972).

22. *See* N.Y. Civil Liberties Union v. N.Y. City Transit Auth., 684 F.3d 286 (2d Cir. 2011) (access right applies to administrative hearing on violation of transit rules); Detroit Free Press v. Ashcroft, 303 F.3d 681 (6th Cir. 2002) (access right applies to executive branch deportation proceeding); N.J. Media Grp., Inc. v. Ashcroft, 308 F.3d 198 (3d Cir. 2003) (access right applies to deportation hearings).

23. *N.Y. Civil Liberties Union*, 684 F.3d 286.

24. Richmond Newspapers, Inc. v. Virginia, 448 U.S. 555 (1980); Globe Newspaper Co. v. Superior Court for Norfolk Cty., 457 U.S. 596 (1982); Press-Enterprise Co. v. Superior Court of California for Riverside Cty., 478 U.S. 1 (1986).

25. Guardian News & Media, LLC v. Ryan, 2017 WL 4180324 (D. Ariz. Sept. 21, 2017). *See also* Cal. First Amend. Coal. v. Woodford, 299 F.3d 868 (9th Cir. 2002).

26. Ala. Dep't of Corrections v. Advance Local Media, 918 F.3d 1161 (11th Cir. 2019).

27. *See, e.g.,* Nation Magazine v. U.S. Dep't of Defense, 762 F. Supp. 1558 (S.D.N.Y. 1991); Flynt v. Rumsfeld, 180 F. Supp. 2d 174 (2002).

28. Cindy Gierhart, *New York City Settles for $18 Million Over RNC Arrests of Journalists, Protesters*, Meta-News, Jan. 16, 2014, www.rcfp.org/new-york-city-settles-18-million-over-rnc-arrests-journalists-protes/.

29. Bell v. Keating, 697 F.3d 445 (7th Cir. 2012).

30. *See* Askins v. U.S. Dep't of Homeland Sec., 899 F.3d 1035 (9th Cir. 2018).

31. *Id.* at 1045.

32. Beacon Journal Publ'g Co., Inc. v. Blackwell, 389 F.3d 683 (6th Cir. 2004), *cert. dismissed*, 544 U.S. 915 (2005).

33. PG Publ'g Co. v. Aichele, 705 F.3d 91 (3d Cir.), *cert. denied*, 569 U.S. 1018 (2013).

34. City of Oak Creek v. Ah King, 436 N.W.2d 285 (Wis. 1989).

35. Leigh v. Salazar, 677 F.3d 892 (9th Cir. 2012).

36. Leigh v. Salazar, 954 F. Supp. 2d 1090 (D. Nev. 2013).

37. Ketcham v. U.S. Nat'l Park Serv., 2016 U.S. Dist. LEXIS 178823 (D. Wyo., May 5, 2016).

38. Sigma Delta Chi v. Speaker, Md. House of Delegates, 310 A.2d 156 (Md. 1973).

39. *Id.*

40. *See also* Ronald L. Goldfarb, TV or Not TV: Television, Justice, and the Courts 56–95 (1998).

41. *See* Turner v. Lieutenant Driver, 848 F.3d 678 (5th Cir. 2017); Gericke v. Begin, 753 F.3d 1 (1st Cir. 2014); Am. Civil Liberties Union of Ill. v. Alvarez, 679 F.3d 583 (7th Cir. 2012); Glik v. Cunniffe, 655 F.3d 78 (1st Cir. 2011); Smith v. City of Cumming, 212 F.3d 1332 (11th Cir. 2000); Fordyce v. City of Seattle, 55 F.3d 436 (9th Cir. 1995).

42. *Gericke*, 753 F.3d 1.

43. *Glik*, 655 F.3d 78.

44. Buehler v. City of Austin, 824 F.3d 548 (5th Cir. 2016), *cert. denied*, 137 S. Ct. 1579 (2017); Spoor v. Hamoui, 2017 U.S. Dist. LEXIS 2546 (M.D. Fla., Jan. 9, 2017).

45. Am. Civil Liberties Union of Ill. v. Alvarez, 679 F.3d 583 (7th Cir.), *cert. denied*, 568 U.S. 651 (2012).

46. Fields v. City of Philadelphia, 862 F.3d 353, 355 (3d Cir. 2017).

47. *Id.* at 359.

48. *Id.* at 360.

49. *Id.* at 365.

50. State v. Russo, 407 P.3d 137 (Haw. Dec. 14, 2017).

51. *Ex parte* Thompson, 414 S.W.3d 872 (Tex. App 2013), *aff'd*, 442 S.W.3d 325 (2014).

52. Letter from James Madison to W. T. Barry (Aug. 4, 1822), in The Writings of James Madison, 1819–1836, at 103 (Galliard Hunt ed. 1910).

53. *See, e.g.*, Shannon E. Martin, Freedom of Information: The News the Media Use (2008).

54. 5 U.S.C. § 522 (1966).

55. Dep't of the Air Force v. Rose, 425 U.S. 352, 361 (1976).

56. Amended in 1976.

57. Electronic Freedom of Information Act of 1996, Pub. L. No. 104–231, 110 Stat. 3048, §§ 1–12 (1996) (codified as amended in various sections of 5 U.S.C. § 552).

58. Honest Leadership and Open Government Act of 2007, Pub. L. No. 110–81, 121 Stat. 735 (2007).

59. FOIA Improvement Act, Pub. L. No. 114–85 (2016).

60. Am. Oversight v. Gen. Serv. Admin., 311 F. Supp. 3d 327 (D.D.C. 2018).

61. 5 U.S.C. § 552(f)(1).

62. *See, e.g.*, Kissinger v. Reporters Comm. for Freedom of the Press, 445 U.S. 136, 156 (1980). *But cf.* United States v. Clarridge, 811 F. Supp. 697 (D.D.C. 1992) (holding that the Tower Commission was an "agency" for purposes of 18 U.S.C. § 1001); Nat'l Sec. Archive v. Archivist of the U.S., 909 F.2d 541 (D.C. Cir. 1990) (holding that FOIA does not reach Office of Counsel to the President). The Sunshine Act incorporates FOIA's definition of "agency."

63. Goland v. CIA, 607 F.2d 339, 345 (D.C. Cir. 1978). In Forsham v. Harris, 445 U.S. 169, 178 (1980), the Supreme Court declared that Congress "did not provide any definition of 'agency records.'"

64. Note: *A Control Test for Determining "Agency Record" Status Under the Freedom of Information Act*, 85 Colum. L. Rev. 611, 616 (1985).

65. *See, e.g.*, Note: *The Definition of "Agency Records" Under the Freedom of Information Act*, 31 Stan. L. Rev. 1093, 1093 (1979); Note: *What Is a Record? Two Approaches to the Freedom of Information Act's Threshold Requirement*, 1978 B.Y.U. L. Rev. 408, 408; Nichols v. United States, 325 F. Supp. 130, 134 (D. Kan. 1971), *aff'd on other grounds*, 460 F.2d 671 (10th Cir.), *cert. denied*, 409 U.S. 966 (1972).

66. *Forsham*, 445 U.S. at 178.

67. *Id.* at 184.

68. *Goland*, 607 F.2d 339.

69. *Id.* at 347.

70. *See e.g.*, Mark Carreau, *Another Shuttle, Another Breach*, Houston Chron., July 9, 2003, at A1; Lee Hockstader, *Release of Challenger Tape Ordered*, Wash. Post, July 30, 1988, at A8; John Schwartz & Matthew L. Wald, *Earlier Shuttle Flight Had Gas Enter Wing on Return*, N.Y. Times, July 9, 2003, at A14; Ralph

Vartabedian, *E-Mail to Columbia Discounted Danger*, L.A. Times, July 1, 2003, at A12.

71. *See, e.g.,* Jake Lucas, *How Times Reporters Use the Freedom of Information Act*, N.Y. Times, July 21, 2018, www.nytimes.com/2018/07/21/insider/information-freedom-reporters-pruitt.html.

72. David Cuillier & Charles N. Davis, The Art of Access: Strategies for Acquiring Public Records (2010). *See also* www.theartofaccess.com.

73. *How to Use the Federal FOIA Act*, Reporters Comm. for Freedom of the Press, www.rcfp.org/open-government-guide/.

74. *FOI Letter Generator*, Reporters Comm. for Freedom of the Press, www.rcfp.org/foia-letter-generator/.

75. Citizens for Responsibility and Ethics in Washington v. Fed. Election Comm., 711 F.3d 180 (D.C. Cir. 2013).

76. Amer. Fed. of Teachers v. U.S. Dep't of Educ., SPLC, Oct. 17, 2018, www.splcenter.org/seeking-justice/case-docket/american-federation-teachers-et-al-v-us-department-education. *See also* Erica L. Green, *Education Secretary Considers Using Federal Funds to Arm Schools*, N.Y. Times, Aug. 22, 2018, www.nytimes.com/2018/08/22/us/politics/betsy-de vos-guns.html; ED Press Secretary (@EDPressSec), Twitter, Aug. 31, 2018, twitter.com/EDPressSec/status/1035632557126287360.

77. Reporters Comm. for Freedom of the Press v. FBI, 877 F.3d 399 (D.C. Cir. 2017).

78. Amy Harder, *Citizens Group Wins FOIA Battle With Nuclear Agency*, Reporters Comm. for Freedom of the Press, Apr. 4, 2008, www.rcfp.org/browse-media-law-resources/news/citizens-group-wins-foia-battle-nuclear-agency.

79. Amer. Civil Liberties Union v. CIA, 710 F.3d 422 (D.C. Cir. 2013), *aff'd*, 640 Fed. App'x 9 (D.C. Cir. 2016).

80. Electronic Freedom of Information Act Amendments of 1996, Pub. L. No. 104–231, 110 Stat. 3048, §§ 1–12 (1996) (codified as amended in various sections of 5 U.S.C. § 552).

81. TPS, Inc. v. Dep't of Def., 330 F.3d 1191 (9th Cir. 2003).

82. *See, e.g.,* Richard Matthews et al., *State-by-State Report on Permanent Public Access to Electronic Government Information*, Univ. of Ga. L. (2003), digitalcommons.law.uga.edu/cgi/viewcontent.cgi?article=1009&context=law_lib_artchop.

83. Freedom of Info. Found. of Texas, *Withholding Information*, Texas Pub. Info. Act, foift.org/resources/texas-public-information-act.

84. 5 Ill. Comp. Stat. 140/1–1.

85. Tennessee Public Records Act, T.C.A. § 10–7–301 (6).

86. Lake v. City of Phoenix, 218 P.3d 1004, 1007 (Ariz. 2009).

87. *Id.*

88. O'Neill v. City of Shoreline, 240 P.3d 1149 (Wash. 2010).

89. Nissen v. Pierce Cty., 357 P.3d 45 (Wash. 2015).

90. *Id.* at 56 (emphasis in original).

91. *Id.* at 57.

92. Associated Press v. Canterbury, 688 S.E.2d 317 (W. Va. 2009); Howell Educ. Assoc. v. Howell Bd. of Educ., 789 N.W.2d 495 (Mich. App. 2010); Convertino v. U.S. Dep't of Justice, 674 F. Supp. 2d 97 (D.D.C. 2009).

93. City of San Jose v. Superior Court, 389 P.3d 848 (Cal. 2017); *Private Electronic Devices May Be Subject to Public Records Requests*, Cal. Sch. Bd. Ass'n, May 2017, www.csba.org/-/media/CSBA/Files/GovernanceResources/PolicyNews_Briefs/PolicyNews/201705MayPolicyNews.ashx?la=en.

94. Daxton R. "Chip" Stewart, *Let the Sunshine In, or Else: An Examination of the "Teeth" of State and Federal Open Meetings and Open Records Laws*, 15 Comm. L. & Pol'y 265, 307–08 (2010).

95. *State Agencies Oppose New State Records Law Proposal*, Apr. 4, 2019, KDWN, kdwn.com/2019/04/04/state-agencies-oppose-new-state-records-law-proposal/.

96. Klye Whitmire, *This Open Records Bill Would Make Alabama . . . Better*, AL.com, Apr. 1, 2019, www.al.com/news/2019/04/this-open-records-bill-would-make-alabama-better.html.

97. Government in the Sunshine Act, 5 U.S.C. § 552b (1976).

98. Federal Advisory Committee Act, 5 U.S.C. App. §§ 1–15 (1972).

99. Seven states provide access to government meetings and records in one law. They are Arkansas, Connecticut, Maine, Missouri, North Dakota, South Carolina and Virginia.

100. Susan Dente Ross, *Break Down or Breakthrough in Participatory Government? How State Open Meetings Laws Apply to Virtual Meetings*, 19 Newspaper Res. J. 31 (1998).

101. Swindle v. Remington, 2019 Ala. LEXIS 17 (Ala. Mar. 8, 2019).

102. Utah Code § 52-4-203(5); 25 O.S. § 312.C.

103. *See, e.g., Sound Recordings Allowed,* Reporters Comm. for Freedom of the Press, www.rcfp.org/open-government-sections/1-sound-recordings-allowed/.

104. The Michigan Open Meetings Act and Freedom of Information Act, 1976 PA 267, MCL 15.261 *et seq.* (1976), www.legislature.mi.gov/documents/Publications/OpenMtgsFreedom.pdf.

105. Acosta v. City of Costa Mesa, 718 F.3d 800 (9th Cir. 2013).

106. *See* Use of Recording Devices in Connection With Telephone Service, 2 F.C.C.R. 502 (1986).

107. *See id.*

108. 18 U.S.C. § 2511(2)(d).

109. Steve Cain, *A Practical Guide to Taping Conversations in the 50 States and D.C.*, Expert Pages, expertpages.com/news/taping_conversations.htm.

110. *Id.*

111. The 12 states are California, Connecticut, Florida, Illinois, Maryland, Massachusetts, Michigan, Montana, Nevada, New Hampshire, Pennsylvania and Washington. See *Laws on Recording Conversations in All 50 States*, MWL, June 18, 2019, www.mwl-law.com/wp-content/uploads/2013/03/LAWS-ON-RECORDING-CONVERSATIONS-CHART.pdf.

112. *See Reporter's Recording Guide*, Reporters Comm. for Freedom of the Press, Summer 2012, www.rcfp.org/wp-content/uploads/imported/RECORDING.pdf.

113. Vermont v. Geraw, 795 A.2d 1219 (Vt. 2002).

114. Vermont v. Brooks, 601 A.2d 963 (Vt. 1991).

115. Kearney v. Salomon Smith Barney, 137 P.3d 914 (Cal. 2006).

116. 47 C.F.R. § 73.1206.

117. Bartnicki v. Vopper, 532 U.S. 514, 518–19 (2001).

118. 18 U.S.C. § 2511(1)(c).

119. *Bartnicki*, 532 U.S. at 525.

120. *Id.* at 534, 535.

121. Wiretap Act, 18 U.S.C. §§ 2510(2), 2511(1)(a), (c), (d).

122. Bowens v. Aftermath Entm't, 254 F. Supp. 2d 629 (E.D. Mich. 2003), *summary judgment granted*, 364 F. Supp. 2d 641 (E.D. Mich. 2005).

123. Vera v. O'Keefe, 2012 U.S. Dist. LEXIS 112406 (S.D. Cal. Aug. 9, 2012).

124. Rick Ungar, *James O'Keefe Pays $100,000 to ACORN Employee He Smeared*, Forbes, Mar. 8, 2013, www.forbes.com/sites/rickungar/2013/03/08/james-okeefe-pays-100000-to-acorn-employee-he-smeared-conservative-media-yawns.

125. For a useful summary of state wiretapping laws, see *Laws on Recording Conversations in All 50 States*, MWL, June 18, 2019, www.mwl-law.com/wp-content/uploads/2013/03/LAWS-ON-RECORDING-CONVERSATIONS-CHART.pdf.

126. United States v. Vespe, 389 F. Supp. 1359 (D. Del. 1975).

127. People v. Melongo, 6 N.E. 3d 120 (Ill. 2014).

128. *See, e.g.,* Miller v. NBC, 232 Cal. Rptr. 668, 677 (Cal. Ct. App. 1986): "The essence of the cause of action for trespass is an 'unauthorized entry' onto the land of another."

129. Fla. Publ'g Co. v. Fletcher, 340 So.2d 914 (Fla. 1976) (finding owner's silence during unauthorized intrusion is implied consent); *but see* Ayeni v. Mottola, 35 F.3d 680 (2d Cir. 1994) (finding a "clearly established" right to be free from intrusion of unauthorized persons).

130. Milligan v. United States, 670 F.3d 686 (6th Cir. 2012).

131. *Miller*, 232 Cal. Rptr. 668, 682.

132. *Id.* at 684 (*quoting* Dietemann v. Time, Inc., 449 F.2d 245, 249 (1971)).

133. Hanlon v. Berger, 526 U.S. 808 (1999).

134. Nancy L. Trueblood, Comment: *Curbing the Media: Should Reporters Pay When Police Ride-Alongs Violate Privacy?*, 84 Marq. L. Rev. 541, 560 n.131 (2000). ("At trial, Paul Berger was acquitted of federal charges of violating laws protecting eagles and found guilty of misdemeanor use of a pesticide.")

135. *Obituaries*, St. Petersburg (Fla.) Times, Apr. 20, 2003, at 21A.

136. Wilson v. Layne, 526 U.S. 603, 607 (1999).

137. *Id.* at 611 (1999).

138. *Id.*

139. *Id.* at 613.

140. *Id.* at 614.

141. *See, e.g.,* Shulman v. Grp. W Prods., Inc., 955 P.2d 469 (Cal. 1998) (ruling that outfitting a nurse with a wireless microphone, then videotaping her rescue of two people in an overturned automobile at the bottom of an embankment, then broadcasting the tape, constituted intrusion).

142. Shane Anderson, *Federal Judge Rules Against Wyoming's "Date Trespass" Laws on First Amendment*

Grounds, Star Tribune, Oct. 30, 2018, trib.com/news/local/crime-and-courts/federal-judge-rules-against-wyoming-s-data-trespass-laws-on/article_6c736e53-4e12-5cca-bfbc-2bdd71e3ac92.html. *See* W. Watersheds Project v. Michael, 869 F.3d 1189 (10th Cir. 2017).

143. *W. Watersheds Project*, 869 F.3d at 1195–96.

144. Animal Enterprise Terrorism Act, 18 U.S.C.A. § 43 (West 2014).

145. United States v. Johnson, 875 F.3d 360, 368 (7th Cir. 2017).

146. Animal Legal Def. Fund v. Otter, 118 F. Supp. 3d 1195 (D. Idaho 2015). *See also* Animal Legal Def. Fund v. Herbert, No. 13-00679 (D. Utah Aug. 8, 2014) (denying the state's motion to dismiss a First Amendment and equal protection challenge to Utah's ag-gag law).

147. *Otter*, 118 F. Supp. 3d at 1199.

148. Idaho Code § 18-7042 (2016).

149. Iowa Code § 717A.3A (2016); Kan. Stat. Ann. § 47-1825 (2016); Mont. Code Ann. § 80-30-101 (2015); Mo. Rev. Stat. § 578.405.1 (2015); N.C. Gen. Stat. § 99A-2 (2016); N.D. Cent. Code § 12.1-21.1-03 (2016); Utah Code Ann. § 76-6-112 (Lexis Nexis 2016). *See also* Marshall Tuttle, *Finally a Solution? How Animal Legal Defense Fund v. Otter Could Affect the Constitutionality of Iowa's Ag-Gag Law*, 21 Drake J. Agric. L. 237 (2016); Matthew Shea, *Punishing Animal Rights Activists for Animal Abuse*, 48 Colum. J.L. & Soc. Probs. 337 (2015).

150. *Otter*, 118 F. Supp. 3d at 1201.

151. *Id.*

152. Animal Legal Def. Fund v. Wasden, 878 F.3d 1184 (9th Cir. 2018).

153. Animal Legal Def. Fund v. Otter, Case No. 14-cv-00104-BLW (May 18, 2016).

154. *Wasden*, 878 F.3d at 1207.

155. Heff Zalesin, *Paragliding Journalist Arrested After Photographing Kansas Feedlot*, Reporters Comm. for Freedom of the Press, July 15, 2013, www.rcfp.org/paragliding-journalist-arrested-after-photographing-kansas-feedlot/.

156. *George Steinmetz Wonders: Was It Worth Getting Arrested for National Geographic Cover Story Photos?*, Photo District News, May 1, 2014, pdnpulse.pdnonline.com/2014/05/george-steinmetz-wonders-worth-getting-arrested-national-geographic-cover-story-photos.html.

157. *Fact Sheet—Small Unmanned Aircraft Regulations (Part 107)*, Fed. Aviation Admin., June 21, 2016, www.faa.gov/news/fact_sheets/news_story.cfm?newsId=20516.

158. Bart Jansen, *FAA Seeks $1.9 Million Fine From Drone Company SkyPan*, USA Today, Oct. 6, 2015, www.usatoday.com/story/news/2015/10/06/faa-drone-fine-skypan-19-million/73441850.

159. Bart Jansen, *Drone-Photography Company Fined $200,000 by FAA*, USA Today, Jan. 17, 2017, www.usatoday.com/story/news/2017/01/17/faa-drone-skypan/96671342.

160. Paul Aitken, *FAA Enacts New Enforcement Action Protocols Against Drone Pilots*, DroneDJ, Mar. 29, 2019, dronedj.com/2019/03/29/new-enforcement-actions-against-drone-pilots/.

161. *Aerial Photographers: Drone Laws You Need to Know Before Flying*, SLR Lounge, Mar. 12, 2016, www.slrlounge.com/aerial-photographers-drone-laws-need-know-flying-infographic (citing laws in Arkansas, California, Florida, Mississippi, Tennessee, Texas, Chicago, New York City and Pittsburgh). See also Alissa M. Dolan & Richard M. Thompson II, *Integration of Drones Into Airspace: Selected Legal Issues*, Cong. Research Serv., R42940 (2013). See Fla. Stat. § 934.50 (2013); 2013 Idaho Sess. Laws 850–60; 725 Ill. Comp. Stat. 167/0 (2014); Tex. Gov't Code Ann. § 423.001.008; Utah Code Ann. §§ 63G-18-101-05; 2013 Va. Acts 755; Wis. Stat. § 942.10 (2013).

162. *Current Unmanned Aircraft State Law Landscape*, Nat'l Conf. of State Legislatures, Jan. 5, 2017, www.ncsl.org/research/transportation/current-unmanned-aircraft-state-law-landscape.aspx.

163. *California Governor Outlaws Paparazzi Drones, Days After Approving Police UAVs*, RT, Oct. 1, 2014, rt.com/usa/192120-california-bans-paparazzi-drones/.

164. Tex. Gov't Code Ann. § 423.001.008.

165. Isabella Lee, *Uniform Law Commission Offers Revised Approach to Trespass and Privacy Laws Relating to Drones*, UAV Coach, Feb. 28, 2019, uavcoach.com/ulc-drone-tort-law/.

166. Wis. Stat. § 942.10 (2015).

167. John Reitmeyer, *Move to Cover Drones in Trespassing, Invasion of Privacy Laws*, NJ Spotlight, Feb. 21, 2019, www.njspotlight.com/stories/19/02/20/bill-would-extend-trespassing-invasion-of-property-laws-to-cover-drones/.

168. *See* Memorandum for Heads of All Federal Departments and Agencies (Oct. 12, 2001) from Atty. Gen. John Ashcroft, U.S. Dep't of

JUSTICE, www.justice.gov/archive/oip/011012.htm: "I encourage your agency to carefully consider the protection of all such values and interests when making disclosure determinations under FOIA. Any discretionary decision by your agency to disclose information protected under FOIA should be made only after full and deliberate consideration of the institutional, commercial, and personal privacy interests that could be implicated by disclosure of the information. . . . When you carefully consider FOIA requests and decide to withhold records, in whole or in part, you can be assured that the Department of Justice will defend your decisions unless they lack a sound legal basis or present an unwarranted risk of adverse impact on the ability of other agencies to protect other important records."

169. *See, e.g.,* Brett Strohs, *Protecting the Homeland by Exemption: Why the Critical Infrastructure Information Act of 2002 Will Degrade the Freedom of Information Act,* 2002 DUKE L. & TECH. REV. 18 (2002).

170. *Memorandum for the Heads of Executive Departments and Agencies,* FED. REG., Jan. 26, 2009, www.federalregister.gov/documents/2009/01/26/E9-1639/memorandum-for-the-heads-of-executive-departments-and-agencies.

171. *U.S. Agencies Are Still Slow to Open Files,* BOSTON GLOBE, Mar. 15, 2010, at 2.

172. Ted Bridis, *Obama Administration Sets New Record for Withholding FOIA Requests,* PBS NEWSHOUR, Mar. 18, 2015, www.pbs.org/newshour/rundown/obama-administration-sets-new-record-withholding-foia-requests/.

173. Steven D. Schwinn, Auer *Deference, Limited, Hangs On (But* Chevron *May Soon Go),* CON. L. PROF BLOG, June 26, 2019, lawprofessors.typepad.com/conlaw/2019/06/auer-deference-limited-hangs-on-but-chevron-may-go.html.

174. *Id.*

175. *See* Exec. Order No. 12958, § 4.2 (b), www.fas.org/sgp/bush/drafteo.html.

176. CIA v. Sims, 471 U.S. 159, 183 (1985).

177. Am. Civil Liberties Union v. U.S. Dep't of Defense, 681 F.3d 61 (2d Cir. 2012).

178. Twitter v. Whitaker, 219 U.S. Dist. LEXIS 555 (N.D. Calif. Jan. 2, 2019), *pending sub nom.* Twitter v. Barr (N.D. Cal. 2019).

179. Steven D. Schwinn, *AG Barr Invokes States Secrets Privileges in Twitter Suit,* CON L. PROF BLOG, Mar. 18, 2019, lawprofessors.typepad.com/conlaw/2019/03/ag-barr-invokes-states-secrets-privileges-in-twitter-suit.html.

180. Am. Civil Liberties Union v. U.S. Dep't of Defense, 901 F.3d 125 (2d Cir. 2018).

181. Electronic Frontier Found. v. U.S. Dep't of Justice, No. 16-cv-02041-HSG (N.D. Calif. Mar. 26, 2019).

182. *See, e.g.,* Am. Civil Liberties Union v. Nat'l Security Admin., 493 F.3d 644 (6th Cir. 2007), *cert. denied* (2008); Am. Civil Liberties Union v. Nat'l Security Admin., 2017 U.S. Dist. LEXIS 44597 (S.D. N.Y. Mar. 27, 2017).

183. Dep't of the Air Force v. Rose, 425 U.S. 352, 369–70 (1976).

184. Milner v. Dep't of the Navy, 562 U.S. 562 (2011).

185. Ctr. for Investigative Reporting v. U.S. Dep't of Justice, No. 17-CV-06557-JSC, 2018 WL 3368884 (N.D. Cal. July 10, 2018).

186. Argus Leader Media v. Food Mktg. Inst., 889 F.3d 914 (8th Cir. 2018), *cert. granted* 139 S. Ct. 915 (2019).

187. Steven D. Schwinn, *Industry Group Has Standing to Appeal FOIA Ruling,* CON. L. PROF BLOG, June 24, 2019, lawprofessors.typepad.com/conlaw/2019/06/industry-group-has-standing-to-appeal-foia-ruling.html.

188. Chrysler v. Brown, 441 U.S. 281, 316 (1979).

189. *Id.* at 292.

190. Russell v. Dep't of the Air Force, 682 F.2d 1045, 1048 (D.C. Cir. 1982).

191. FOIA Improvement Act of 2016, Pub. L. No. 114–85 (2016).

192. Electronic Privacy Info. Ctr. v. U.S. Dep't of Justice, 584 F. Supp. 2d 65 (D.D.C. 2008).

193. Dep't of Interior and Bureau of Indian Affairs v. Klamath Water Users Protective Ass'n, 532 U.S. 1, 7 (2001) (*quoting* Dep't of Air Force v. Rose, 425 U.S. 352, 361 (1976)).

194. Cochran v. United States, 770 F.2d 949, 956 (11th Cir. 1985).

195. *See* Dep't of Justice v. Reporters Comm. for Freedom of the Press, 489 U.S. 749 (1989).

196. *Id.*

197. *Id.* at 765.

198. Nat'l Archives and Records Admin. v. Favish, 541 U.S. 157 (2004).

199. *Id.* at 173.

200. *Reporters Comm. for Freedom of the Press*, 489 U.S. at 773.

201. FCC v. AT&T, 562 U.S. 397 (2011).

202. Dodd-Frank Wall St. Reform and Consumer Protection Act, Pub. L. No. 111–201, July 21, 2010, www.govinfo.gov/content/pkg/PLAW-111publ203/pdf/PLAW-111publ203.pdf.

203. Freedom of Information Act, 5 U.S.C. § 552 (1966).

204. Privacy Act, 5 U.S.C. § 552a (1974).

205. Fed. Aviation Admin. v. Cooper, 566 U.S. 284 (2012).

206. Family Educational Rights and Privacy Act, 20 U.S.C. § 1232g. (The nickname "Buckley Amendment" refers to the U.S. senator who introduced the bill, James Buckley of New York.)

207. *See* 34 C.F.R. § 99.3.

208. United States v. Miami Univ., 294 F.3d 797 (6th Cir. 2002).

209. Downs v. Holder, 758 F.3d 994 (8th Cir. 2014).

210. Clery Act, 20 U.S.C. § 1092(f) (1990).

211. Red & Black Publ'g Co. v. Bd. of Regents, Univ. of Ga., 427 S.E.2d 257 (Ga. 1993); Doe v. Red & Black Publ'g Co., 437 S.E.2d 474 (Ga. 1993).

212. *Red & Black Publ'g Co.*, 427 S.E.2d 257.

213. Paula Lavigne & Dan Murphy, *Federal Report Cites Michigan State With Systemic "Serious Violations" of Campus-Safety Law*, ESPN, Jan. 30, 2019, www.espn.com/espn/story/_/id/25885611/us-department-education-cites-michigan-state-university-clery-act-violations-espn-lines.

214. *Id.*

215. Health Insurance Portability & Accountability Act, P. L. 104–191, 110 Stat. 1936 (1996).

216. Driver's Privacy Protection Act, 18 U.S.C. §§ 2721–2725 (1994).

217. Reno v. Condon, 528 U.S. 141 (2000).

218. Dahlstrom v. Sun-Times Media, LLC, 777 F.3d 937 (7th Cir. 2015), *cert. denied*, 136 S. Ct. 689 (2015).

219. This practice is so common that courts call it "upskirting." *See, e.g.,* New Jersey v. Nicholson, 169 A.3d 990 (N.J. App. 2017); Gary v. Georgia, 790 S.E.2d 150 (Ga. App. 2016).

220. Video Voyeurism Prevention Act, 18 U.S.C. § 1801 (2004).

221. *Video Voyeurism Laws*, Nat'l Ctr. for Victims of Crime, victimsofcrime.org/docs/Policy/Vid%20Voy%20Aug%202009.pdf?sfvrsn=0.

222. Connecticut v. Panek, 145 A.3d 924 (Conn. App. 2016).

223. *Ex parte* Thompson, 442 S.W.3d 325 (Tex. Crim. App. 2014).

224. Greg Tsioros, *Photography Laws in Texas: When Taking Pictures Becomes a Crime*, June 1, 2016, www.txcrimdefense.com/photography-laws-in-texas-when-taking-pictures-becomes-a-crime/.

225. The 13 states are Alabama, Arkansas, California, Delaware, Georgia, Hawaii, Kansas, Maine, Michigan, Minnesota, New Hampshire, South Dakota and Utah. *See Reporter's Recording Guide*, Reporters Comm. for Freedom of the Press, Summer 2012, www.rcfp.org/wp-content/uploads/imported/RECORDING.pdf.

226. *Id.*

227. 18 U.S.C. § 2510(1).

228. *See, e.g.,* Robert Valdes & Dave Roos, *How VoIP Works*, HowStuffWorks, May 9, 2001, computer.howstuffworks.com/ip-telephony.htm; Ruby Carlino, *Internet Phones: The Cheaper Alternative to Calling Home*, Database Systems Corp., www.databasesystemscorp.com/tech-cti-softphone_55.htm.

229. Wiretap Act, 18 U.S.C. § 2510 (2002) (defining the "aural transfer" that occurs in wire communication as "a transfer containing the human voice at any point between and including the point of origin and the point of reception").

230. Stored Communications Act, 18 U.S.C. §§ 2701–2711 (2000).

231. Eric Koester, *VoIP Goes the Bad Guy: Understanding the Legal Impact of the Use of Voice Over IP Communications in Cases of NSA Warrantless Eavesdropping*, 24 J. Marshall J. Computer & Info. L. 227, 234 (2006).

232. Electronic Communications Privacy Act, 18 U.S.C. § 2511.

233. Computer Fraud and Abuse Act, Pub. L. No. 99–508, 100 Stat. 1848 (1986) and 18 U.S.C. § 1030.

234. Pam Greenberg, *Computer Crime Statutes*, Nat'l Conf. of State Legislatures, June 14, 2018, www.ncsl.org/research/telecommunications-and-information-technology/computer-hacking-and-unauthorized-access-laws.aspx.

235. Jessup-Morgan v. America Online, Inc., 20 F. Supp. 2d 1105 (E.D. Mich. 1998).

236. *See, e.g.,* Pennsylvania v. Cline, 177 A.3d 922 (Pa. Super. Ct. 2017); Pennsylvania v. Byrd, 185 A.3d 1015 (Pa. Super. Ct. 2018).

237. Pennsylvania v. Patterson, 180 A.3d 1217, 1234 (Pa. Super. Ct. 2018).

238. Foreign Intelligence Surveillance Act, 50 U.S.C. § 1802.

239. Gabe Rottman & Linda Moon, *How Foreign Intelligence Surveillance Law Applies to the News Media*, Nov. 9, 2018, Reporters Comm. for Freedom of the Press, www.rcfp.org/how-foreign-intelligence-surveillance-law-applies-news-media.

240. Erin Coyle & Eric Robinson, *Chilling Journalism: Can Newsgathering Be Harassment or Stalking?* 22 Comm. L. & Pol'y 65 (2017).

241. K.S.A. 2016 Supp. 60-31a01 *et seq.*

242. *Id.*

243. Coyle & Robinson, *supra* note 242, nn.422–423. The states are Colorado, Delaware, Idaho, Illinois, Louisiana, Maine, New Jersey, Ohio and Vermont.

244. Galella v. Onassis, 353 F. Supp. 196 (S.D.N.Y. 1972).

245. Galella v. Onassis, 487 F.2d 986 (2d Cir. 1973).

246. Raef v. App. Div. of Sup. Ct. of Los Angeles, 240 Cal. App. 4th 1112 (Cal. App. Dep't Super. Ct. 2015).

247. *Id.* at 1120.

248. Wolfson v. Lewis, 924 F. Supp. 1413 (E.D. Pa. 1996).

249. Food Lion, Inc. v. Capital Cities, Inc./ABC, 964 F. Supp. 956, 959 (M.D. N.C. 1997).

250. *See generally* Jane Kirtley, *It's the Process, Stupid: Newsgathering Is the New Target*, Colum. Jour. Rev. (Sept./Oct. 2000).

251. *Id.* "The duty of loyalty recognized in this case requires an employee to use her efforts, while working, for the service of her employer. The jury found that each of the producers violated this duty by failing to make a good faith effort toward performing the job requirements of her employer Food Lion as a result of the time and attention she was devoting to her investigation for ABC and by performing specific acts on behalf of ABC which proximately resulted in damage to Food Lion."

252. *Id.*

253. *Food Lion, Inc.*, 964 F. Supp. at 959.

254. Food Lion, Inc. v. Capital Cities, Inc./ABC, 194 F.3d 505, 526 (4th Cir. 1999) (Niemeyer, J., dissenting).

255. According to one of the attorneys involved, ABC's bill from one of the law firms handling the appeal only was in the "six figures" (personal communication on file with authors).

256. *Hidden Cameras, Hard Choices*, "Primetime Live" (Feb. 12, 1997). After the trial portion of the case, ABC's "Primetime Live" broadcast interviews with members of the jury. One juror said that on a scale of 1 to 10, with 10 being the worst, ABC's wrongdoing was a 10. "Because the—the girls were telling stories to get into a man's personal business, and they even made up stories to get in." This same juror said she wanted the punitive damages levied against ABC to be $1 billion. *Id.*

257. Special Force Ministries v. WCCO Television, 584 N.W. 2d 789 (Minn. 1998).

258. Veilleux v. NBC, 8 F. Supp. 2d 23, 30 (D. Me. 1998).

259. Veilleux v. NBC, 206 F.3d 92, 105 (1st Cir. 2000).

260. Nancy Garland, *Settlement Reached in "Dateline" Suit*, Bangor Daily News, Sept. 1, 2000.

261. *What Twitter and Facebook Have in Common: The Users Spreading Fake News Are Over 65 and Conservative*, Associated Press, Jan. 24, 2019, www.marketwatch.com/story/heres-how-few-people-spread-almost-all-of-the-fake-news-on-twitter-2019-01-24.

262. RonNell Anderson Jones & Lyrissa Barnett Lidsky, *Recent Developments in the Law of Social Media Communications, in* 3 Comm. L. in the Digital Age 2012, at 75, 85 (2012).

263. *How Social Media Is [sic] Trying to Contain Misinformation Over Vaccines*, PBS NewsHour, Apr. 5, 2019, www.pbs.org/newshour/health/how-social-media-is-trying-to-contain-the-spread-of-misinformation-over-vaccines.

264. Record at 1279, Cohen v. Cowles Media Co. (No. 90–634) (testimony of Bernard Casserly, characterizing the use of confidential sources as "a way of life in the profession of journalism").

265. Record at 694, Cohen v. Cowles Media Co., 501 U.S. 663 (testimony of Arnold Ismach).

266. *See, e.g.,* Brief of Petitioner, Cohen v. Cowles Media Co., 501 U.S. 663 (1990). One of the best known examples of investigative journalism, The Washington Post's uncovering of the Watergate scandal, was driven by a confidential source the reporters dubbed "Deep Throat." *See* Bob Woodward, The Secret Man: The Story of Watergate's Deep Throat (2005).

267. Cohen v. Cowles Media Co., 501 U.S. 663 (1991).

268. *Id.*

269. *Id.* at 669.

270. John Zangas, *Medics, Journalist Acquitted in First Jury Trial of Inauguration Protesters*, DC Media Group, Dec. 21, 2017, www.dcmediagroup.us/2017/12/21/

medics-journalist-acquitted-first-jury-trial-inauguration-protesters/.

271. Christopher Mele, *Reporter Arrested in West Virginia After Persistently Asking Questions of Tom Price*, N.Y. Times, May 10, 2017, www.nytimes.com/2017/05/10/business/media/reporter-arrested-tom-price.html.

272. Julia Carrie Wong & Sam Levin, *Republican Candidate Charged With Assault After "Body-Slamming" Guardian Reporter*, Guardian, May 25, 2017, www.theguardian.com/us-news/2017/may/24/greg-gianforte-bodyslams-reporter-ben-jacobs-montana.

273. Nieves v. Bartlett, 139 S. Ct. 1715 (2019).

274. *Id.*

275. *Id.* at 1721.

276. *Id.* at 1724.

277. *Id.* at 1726.

278. *Id.* at 1736 (Sotomayor, J., *dissenting*).

279. *Id.*

280. Frank LoMonte, *Supreme Court Puts Journalists at Greater Risk When Covering Crime Scenes, Protests*, Brechner Report, June 4, 2019, medium.com/@frankbrechner/supreme-court-puts-journalists-at-greater-risk-when-covering-crime-scenes-protests-feb70110c553.

281. Joe Concha, *Dem Lawmakers Unveil Journalist Protection Act Amid Trump Attacks on Media*, Hill, Mar. 12, 2019, thehill.com/homenews/media/433709-dem-lawmakers-unveil-journalist-protection-act-amid-trump-attacks-on-media.

282. *Worldwide Roundup of Journalists Killed, Detained, Held Hostage or Missing in 2018*, Reporters Without Borders, Dec. 2018, rsf.org/en/news/rsfs-2018-round-dead ly-attacks-and-abuses-against-journalists-figures-all-categories; Reuters, *United States Added to List of Most Dangerous Countries for Journalists for First Time*, NBC News, Dec. 18, 2018, www.nbcnews.com/news/amp/ncna949676?__twitter_impression=true&fbclid=IwAR0U1tfqUyAlf6ZFNwjOjCZw-J5OY_Ni2QteOnsgjUKeWTpSlR7mxCzlYfu8.

283. Lynh Bui et al., *Five Dead in Capital Gazette Shooting; Jarrod Ramos Is in Custody, Police Say*, Wash. Post., June 29, 2018, www.washingtonpost.com/local/public-safety/heavy-police-activity-reported-around-capital-gazette-newsroom-in-annapolis/2018/06/28/32e0123e-7b05-11e8-93cc-6d3beccdd7a3_story.html?utm_term=.1d439129999c.

284. Julia Ainsley, *U.S. Officials Made List of Reporters, Lawyers, Activists to Question at Border*, NBC News, Mar. 6, 2019, www.nbcnews.com/politics/immigration/u-s-officials-made-list-reporters-lawyers-activists-question-border-n980301.

285. *Id.*

286. Khushbu Shah, *Georgia Lawmakers Consider Bill That Takes Aim at the State's Journalists*, Guardian, Apr. 11, 2019, www.theguardian.com/us-news/2019/apr/11/georgia-lawmakers-consider-bill-that-takes-aim-at-the-states-journalists?fbclid=IwAR1YaYO7fFpRNJri9pV3s4tNPujCgwQmvo5FvwkBgpPHQeDNoc1yZrKoUCl.

287. Donald Barbati, *N.J. Supreme Court Will Decide Whether OPRA Covers Police Dash Cam*, N.J. Public Safety Officers L. Blog, Jan. 30, 2018, www.njpublicsafetyofficers.com/2018/01/articles/nj-supreme-court-will-decide-whether-opra-covers-police-dash-cam-videos. (The case is Ganzweig v. Twp. of Lakewood filed with the N.J. Supreme Court on Jan. 29, 2018.)

288. Pa. State Police v. Grove, 161 A.3d 877 (Penn. 2017).

289. Knight First Amendment Inst. v. Trump, 302 F. Supp. 3d 541 (S.D.N.Y. 2018); *see also Federal Judge Rules Trump's Twitter Account Is a Public Forum*, Conversation, May 24, 2018, theconversation.com/federal-judge-rules-trumps-twitter-account-is-a-public-forum-97159.

290. Knight Inst. v. Trump: *Lawsuit Challenging President Trump's Blocking of Critics on Twitter*, Knight First Amendment Inst., Mar. 26, 2019, knightcolumbia.org/content/knight-institute-v-trump-lawsuit-challenging-president-trumps-blocking-critics-twitter.

291. *See, e.g.*, Trump v. Cummings, Case 1:19-cv-01136-APM, Memorandum Opinion (D.D.C. May 20, 2019), assets.documentcloud.org/documents/6019022/20-19-Opinion-House-v-Trump.pdf.

292. Zachary Basu, *Judge Rejects Trump Effort to Block Deutsche Bank Subpoena*, Axios, May 22, 2019, www.axios.com/deutsche-bank-subpoena-trump-financial-records-a6e8e4e6-f8a8-4464-8c8b-cb373e1ce5d7.html.

293. Bart Jansen, *Trump Executive Privilege Keeps Census Documents Secret*, USA Today, June 12, 2019, www.usatoday.com/story/news/politics/2019/06/12/president-trump-census-executive-privilege-contempt-barr-ross/1426645001.

294. Adam Liptak, *Supreme Court Leaves Census Question on Citizenship in Doubt*, N.Y. Times, June 27, 2019,

www.nytimes.com/2019/06/27/us/politics/census-citizenship-question-supreme-court.html; *see also* Dep't of Commerce v. New York, 239 S. Ct. 2551 (2019). (The remand to the Second Circuit is pending.)

295.   Toensing v. Attorney Gen., 178 A.3d 1000 (Vt. 2017).

296.   *Id.*

297.   West v. Puyallup, 410 P.3d 1197 (Wash. Ct. App. 2018).

CHAPTER 8 BOXED FEATURES

i.   Press-Enterprise (I) v. Super. Ct. of Calif., 464 U.S. 501 (1984); Press-Enterprise (II) v. Super. Ct. of Calif., 478 U.S. 1 (1986).

ii.   Satya Prakash, *CCTV in Courtrooms Only to Ensure Security: Apex Court*, Trib. News Serv., Feb. 14, 2018, www.tribuneindia.com/news/nation/cctv-in-courtrooms-only-to-ensure-security-apex-court/543609.html.

iii. Utkarsh Anand, *Shedding Reluctance, Supreme Court Agrees to Open Courtrooms to Cameras*, Indian Express, Mar. 29, 2017, indianexpress.com/article/india/no-audio-initially-no-rti-either-shedding-reluctance-sc-agrees-to-open-courtrooms-to-cameras-supreme-court-4590136.

iv.   Model Policy on Access and Use of Electronic Portable Devices in Courthouses and Courtrooms, Media L. Res. Ctr., 2010, www.utcourts.gov/committees/Tech_in_Courtrooms/MLRC%20Model%20Policy%20on%20Electronic%20Portable%20Devices%20in%20Courthouses%20.pdf.

v.   Jon Bruschke et al., *The Influence of Heterogeneous Exposure and Pre-deliberation Queries on Pretrial Publicity Effects*, 83 Commc'n Monographs 521 (2016); Jon Bruschke & William E. Loges, Free Press vs. Fair Trials: Examining Publicity's Role in Trial Outcomes 134–37 (2004).

vi.   Venkat Balasubramani, *Social Media Evidence Roundup*, Tech. & Marketing L. Blog, Jan. 18, 2013, blog.ericgoldman.org/archives/2013/01/social_media_ev_2.htm.

vii. Domville v. State, 103 So. 3d 184 (Fla. Ct. App. 2012).

viii. Quigley Corp. v. Karkus, 2009 U.S. Dist. LEXIS 41296 at *16 (E.D. Pa., May 19, 2009).

ix.   Ellen Nakashima, *FBI Paid Professional Hackers One-Time Fee to Crack San Bernardino iPhone*, Wash. Post., Apr. 12, 2016, www.washingtonpost.com/world/national-security/fbi-paid-professional-hackers-one-time-fee-to-crack-san-bernardino-iphone/2016/04/12/5397814a-00de-11e6-9d36-33d198ea26c5_story.html?utm_term=.33d992d3b0c7.

x.   Nicole Perlroth & Katie Benner, *Subpoenas and Gag Orders Show Government Overreach, Tech Companies Argue*, N.Y. Times, Oct. 4, 2016, www.nytimes.com/2016/10/05/technology/subpoenas-and-gag-orders-show-government-overreach-tech-companies-argue.html?_r=0.

xi.   Nick Wingfield, *Microsoft's Challenge to Government Secrecy Wins Dozens of Supporters*, N.Y. Times, Sept. 2, 2016, www.nytimes.com/2016/09/03/technology/microsofts-challenge-to-government-secrecy-wins-dozens-of-supporters.html.

xii. Pennekamp v. Florida, 328 U.S. 331 (1946).

xiii. *See, e.g.*, Bloom v. Illinois, 391 U.S. 194, 203 n.6 (1968).

xiv. *Press-Enterprise (II) v. Super. Ct. of California*, 478 U.S. 1 (1986).

xv.   Nebraska Press Ass'n v. Stuart, 427 U.S. 539 (1976).

xvi. Julia Zebley, *Canada Supreme Court Broadens Journalists' Rights to Protect Sources*, Paper Chase, Oct. 22, 2010, jurist.org/paperchase/2010/10/canada-supreme-court-broadens-journalists-rights-to-protect-sources.php.

xvii. *Id.*

xviii. Branzburg v. Hayes, 408 U.S. 665, 710 (1972).

xix. Becca Gmerek, *Society's Obsession With True Crime*, Red Summit Productions, July 30, 2018, medium.com/@RedSummitProductions/societys-obsession-with-true-crime-4f5e51cfd05c.

xx.   Adam Banner, *What Happens When Hollywood Gets "True Crime" Wrong?*, A.B.A. J., Sept. 27, 2017, www.abajournal.com/news/article/what_happens_when_hollywood_gets_true_crime_wrong.

xxi. *"Making a Murderer" Filmmakers Address Criticisms of Docuseries Ahead of New Season*, CBS News, Oct. 18, 2018, www.cbsnews.com/news/making-a-murderer-part-two-filmmakers-address-criticisms-of-netflix-docuseries/.

xxii. *Id.*

xxiii. W. Va. Code § 57-3-10.

CHAPTER 8

1.   Sheppard v. Maxwell, 384 U.S. 333, 362 (1966).

2.   *Court Finds Prosecutorial Misconduct but Allows Death Sentence to Stand*, Death Penalty Info. Ctr., Sept. 21, 2017, deathpenaltyinfo.org/node/6875.

3. People v. Owens, 420 P.3d 257 (Colo. 2018), *cert. denied sub nom.*, Colo. Indep. v. Dist. Ct. of Colo., 2019 U.S. LEXIS 950 (2019).

4. *Sheppard*, 384 U.S. 333.

5. *See, e.g.,* CNN Special Report: *Married to a Murderer: The Drew Peterson Story*, CNN, June 25, 2015.

6. Mark Wilson, *Adnan Syed, Subject of "Serial," Asks for Another Appeal*, FINDLAW, Jan. 14, 2015, blogs.findlaw .com/celebrity_justice/2015/01/adnan-syed-subject-of-serial-asks-for-another-appeal.html.

7. Zsoit Boda & Gabriella Szabó, *The Media and Attitudes Towards Crime and the Justice System*, EUR. J. CRIM., July 20, 2011, doi.org/10.1177/147737 0811411455.

8. Jim Redden, *Criminal Justice Series Wins Award*, PORTLAND TRIB., June 26, 2018, pamplinmedia.com/ pt/9-news/399236-293995-criminal-justice-series-wins-award.

9. *See, e.g.,* Terry Gross, *"Charged" Explains How Prosecutors and Plea Bargains Drive Mass Incarceration*, NPR FRESH AIR, Apr. 10, 2019, www .npr.org/2019/04/10/711654831/charged-explains-how-prosecutors-and-plea-bargains-drive-mass-incarceration.

10. Michael McLaughlin, *Overcrowding in Federal Prisons Harms Inmates, Guards: GAO Report*, HUFFPOST, Sept. 14, 2012, www.huffpost.com/entry/ prison-overcrowding-report_n_1883919.

11. *See, e.g.,* Daniel Romer et al., *Television News and the Cultivation of Fear of Crime*, 53 J. COMM. 88 (2003).

12. Romeo Vitelli, *New Research Explores How Media Bias Impacts the Right to a Fair Trial*, PSYCHOLOGY TODAY, Aug. 22, 2018, www.psychology today.com/us/blog/media-spotlight/201808/ how-trial-media-can-undermine-the-courtroom.

13. Elizabeth Sun, *The Dangerous Racialization of Crime in U.S. News Media*, CTR. FOR AM. PROGRESS, Aug. 29, 2018, www.americanprogress.org/issues/ criminal-justice/news/2018/08/29/455313/ dangerous-racialization-crime-u-s-news-media/.

14. *Id.*

15. The Fifth Amendment provides rules for indictment and due process and prohibits double jeopardy and self-incrimination. The Sixth protects the rights to counsel, to confront evidence and witnesses, and to a speedy, local, public trial. The Seventh ensures trial by jury.

16. Gannett v. DePasquale, 433 U.S. 368 (1979).

17. *Id.* at 378.

18. *Id.* at 383.

19. *Id.* at 415, 423.

20. *Id.* at 429.

21. Richmond Newspapers, Inc. v. Virginia, 448 U.S. 555 (1980).

22. *Id.* at 569.

23. *Id.* at 581.

24. *Id.* at 575.

25. *See, e.g., Tsarnaev Convicted on All Counts*, HERE & NOW, Apr. 8, 2015, hereandnow.wbur.org/2015/04/08/ tsarnaev-trial-verdict.

26. Rapid City Journal v. Delaney, 804 N.W.2d 388 (S.D. 2011).

27. Globe Newspaper Co. v. Super. Ct. for Norfolk Cty., 457 U.S. 596 (1982).

28. *Id.* at 606.

29. *Id.*

30. Press-Enterprise (I) v. Super. Ct. of Calif., 464 U.S. 501 (1984); Press-Enterprise (II) v. Super. Ct. of Calif., 478 U.S. 1 (1986).

31. *Press-Enterprise II*, 478 U.S. at 11.

32. *Id.*

33. Eugene Volokh, *Does the First Amendment Protect a Presumptive Right to Access Criminal Court Records*, VOLOKH CONSPIRACY, Oct. 25, 2018, reason.com/ volokh/2018/10/25/does-the-first-amendment-protect-a-presu.

34. Globe Newspaper Co. v. Super. Ct. for Norfolk Cty., 457 U.S. 596, 607 (1982); *Press-Enterprise I*, 463 U.S. at 510.

35. Presley v. Georgia, 558 U.S. 209, 214 (2010).

36. *Id.*

37. *Id.* at 215.

38. *See, e.g.,* People v. Ray, 2006 WL 6924824 (Colo. Dist. Ct. 2006); People v. Ray, 252 P.3d 1042 (Colo. 2011); People v. Owens, 2012 WL 2488070 (Colo. Dist. Ct. 2012); People v. Ray, 417 P.3d 939 (Colo. App. 2018); People v. Ray, 420 P.3d 257 (Colo. 2018), *cert. denied sub nom.*, Colo. Indep. v. Dist. Ct. for 18th Judicial Dist. of Colo., 139 S. Ct. 1165 (2019).

39. *Id.*

40. *Ray*, 2006 WL 6924824.

41. *Owens*, 2012 WL 2488070.

42. *In re:* People v. Owens, Case. No. 06CR705, Petition for Original Proceeding and Issuance of Rule to Show Cause Under C.A.R. 21, June 21, 2013, www.scribd .com/document/150184019/Sir-Mario-Owens-Ruling;

see Colo. Supreme Court Denies Motion to Open Files of Death-Row Inmates, Colo. Freedom of Info. Coalition, Sept. 19, 2013, coloradofoic.org/cfoic-joins-call-open-files-death-row-inmates/.

43. *Ray*, 420 P.3d 257.

44. *Ray*, 252 P.3d 1042.

45. *Owens*, 420 P.3d 257.

46. *Id.* at 258.

47. People v. Bryant, 94 P.3d 624, 625–26 (Colo. 2004).

48. Times-Call Publ'g Co. v. Wingfield, 410 P.2d 511 (Colo. 1966).

49. *Id.* at 513.

50. *Id.*

51. People v. Owens, 420 P.3d 257, 258 (Colo. 2018).

52. Colo. Indep. v. Dist. Ct. for the Eighteenth Judicial Dist., 139 S. Ct. 1165 (2019).

53. Gubarev v. BuzzFeed, 365 F. Supp. 3d 1250 (S.D. Fla. 2019).

54. *Id.* at 1260. See also Gubarev v. BuzzFeed, 340 F. Supp. 3d 1304 (S.D. Fla. 2018).

55. Chandler v. Florida, 449 U.S. 560 (1981).

56. *Courtroom Camera Pilot Program Grounded*, Reporters Comm. for Freedom of the Press., 2015, www.rcfp .org/journals/news-media-and-law-spring-2016/ courtroom-camera-pilot-prog/.

57. *Judicial Conference Says "No" to Expanding Cameras Pilot Program*, Fix the Ct., Mar. 15, 2016, fixthecourt. com/2016/03/judicial-conference-says-no-to-expanding-cameras-pilot-program/.

58. Michael Lambert, *Courtroom Camera Pilot Program Grounded*, Reporters Comm. for Freedom of the Press, Spring 2016, www.rcfp.org/ browse-media-law-resources/news-media-law/ news-media-and-law-spring-2016/courtroom-camera-pilot-prog.

59. *Id.*

60. Hollingsworth v. Perry, 558 U.S. 183 (2010).

61. Lisa Leff, *Court Won't Order California Officials to Appeal Ruling That Struck Down Gay Marriage Ban*, L.A. Times, Sept. 8, 2010.

62. Kathy Kirby, *Cameras in the Court: A State-by-State Guide*, RTDNA, Summer 2012, rtdna.org/article/ cameras_in_the_court_a_state_by_state_guide_ updated.

63. *See* Rule 2.450, Rules of Judicial Administration, Florida Rules of Court (2008); Florida v. Palm Beach Newspapers, 395 So. 2d 544 (1981).

64. *See* Electronic Access to the Courts, Sup. Ct. Rule 1:19 (Mass. 2012), www.mass.gov/courts/case-legal-res/ rules-of-court/sjc/sjc119.html.

65. Sup. Ct. Rule 10–8 & 10–9 (S.D. 2011).

66. Ill. Code of Judicial Conduct, Rule 63 (A) (7).

67. 735 Ill. Code Civil Procedure 5/Art. VII, Part 7, § 8–701, Broadcast or Televised Testimony.

68. C. Danielle Vinson & John S. Ertter, *Entertainment or Education: How Do Media Cover the Courts?* 7 Harv. Int'l J. Press/Politics 80 (2002).

69. Leslie Y. Garfield Tenzer, *Social Media, Venue and the Right to a Fair Trial*, SSRN, Feb. 4, 2019, papers.ssrn .com/sol3/papers.cfm?abstract_id=3328959.

70. James Podgers, *Social Media Is New Norm, but Courts Still Grappling With Whether to Let Cameras In*, A.B.A. J., Aug. 8, 2010, www.abajournal.com/news/article/ social_media_is_norm_but_courts_still_grappling_ with_whether_to_let_cameras/.

71. State v. Smith, No. M2010–01384–SC–R11–CD (2013).

72. *See, e.g., Juror Use of Social Media: A State-by-State Guide*, Blog L. Online, Sept. 13, 2010, bloglawonline .blogspot.com/2010/02/juror-use-of-social-media-state-by.html.

73. *See, e.g., Kan. Reporter Gets OK to Use Twitter to Cover Federal Gang Trial*, Associated Press, Mar. 6, 2009.

74. Nate Anderson, *Appeals Court: No Webcast for Joel Tenenbaum*, Ars Technica, Arp. 16, 2009, arstech nica.com/tech-policy/2009/04/appeals-court-no-webcast-for-joel-tenenbaum/.

75. Jaikumar Vijayan, *Appeals Court Blocks Internet Streaming Order in RIAA Music Piracy Case*, Computerworld, Apr. 16, 2009, www.computerworld.com/ article/2523464/appeals-court-blocks-internet-streaming-order-in-riaa-music-piracy-case.html.

76. *Ninth Circuit Begins Live Video Streaming En Banc Proceedings*, Reporters Comm. for Freedom of the Press, 2014, www.rcfp.org/journals/news-media-and-law-winter-2014/ninth-circuit-begins-live-v/.

77. Hilary Hylton, *Tweeting in the Jury Box: A Danger to Fair Trials?*, Time, Dec. 29, 2009, content.time.com/ time/nation/article/0,8599,1948971,00.html.

78. Meghan Dunn, *Jurors' Use of Social Media During Trials and Deliberations*, Fed. Judicial Ctr., Nov. 22, 2011, www.fjc.gov/sites/default/files/2012/DunnJuror .pdf.

79. Nixon v. Warner Commc'ns, 435 U.S. 589 (1978).

80. *Id.* at 608–11.

81. *Ala. Dep't of Corrections v. Advance Local Media*, 918 F.3d 1161 (11th Cir. 2019); Steven D. Schwinn, *Eleventh Circuit Orders Release of Alabama's Execution Protocol Under Common Law Right to Access*, CON. L. PROF BLOG, Mar. 20, 2019.

82. *Ala. Dep't of Corrections*, 918 F.3d at 1167.

83. United States v. Doe, 870 F.3d 991 (9th Cir. 2017).

84. Florida Star v. B.J.F., 491 U.S. 524 (1989).

85. Undisclosed, LLC v. State, 807 S.E. 2d 393 (Ga. 2017); Colin Miller, *The Supreme Court of Georgia's Ruling in Undisclosed, LLC v. The State*, EvidenceProf Blog, Nov. 2, 2017, lawprofessors.typepad.com/evidence prof/2017/11/on-monday-the-supreme-court-of-georgia-ruled-against-undisclosed-in-our-attempt-to-get-the-court-reporters-recording-of-the.html.

86. Robert Timothy Reagan et al., *Sealed Settlement Agreements in Federal District Court*, FED. JUDICIAL CTR. (2009).

87. Grube v. Trader, 420 P.3d 343 (Haw. 2018).

88. United States v. Silver, 184 F. Supp. 3d 33 (S.D.N.Y. Feb. 23, 2016).

89. Pennsylvania v. Curley, 2018 WL 2473504 (Pa. Super. Ct. 2018).

90. Ind. Code § 5–15–3–3, § 5–14–3–4.

91. State *ex rel.* Cincinnati Enquirer v. Winkler, 805 N.E.2d 1094 (Ohio 2004).

92. *See* Nast v. Michels, 730 P.2d 54 (Wash. 1986).

93. *Privacy Policy for Electronic Case Files*, U.S. COURTS, Mar. 2008, www.privacy.uscourts.gov/b4amend.htm; Alan Carlson & Martha Wade Steketee, *Public Access to Court Records: Implementing the CCJ/COSCA Guidelines Final Project Report* Oct. 15, 2005, STATE JUSTICE INST., it.ojp.gov/documents/d/2005-10-15%20Final%20 Report.pdf; Martha Wade Steketee & Alan Carlson, *Developing CCJ/COSCA Guidelines for Public Access to Court Records: A National Project to Assist State Courts*, STATE JUSTICE INST., Oct. 18, 2002, ncsc.contentdm.oclc .org/digital/collection/accessfair/id/210/.

94. *A Quiet Revolution in the Courts: Electronic Access to State Court Records*, Aug. 2002, www.cdt.org/ publications/020821courtrecords.shtml.

95. Anna M. Phillips, *Court Papers Going Online*, TAMPA BAY TIMES, Mar. 14, 2015.

96. *Access Case Records*, MINN. JUDICIAL BRANCH, www .mncourts.gov/Access-Case-Records.aspx.

97. Oonagh Doherty & Sara Tonneson, *How to Look Up Court Records on the Internet*, MASS. JUSTICE PROJECT, Mar. 30, 2010, www.masslegalservices.org/content/ how-look-court-records-internet-links-online-access-records-other-states.

98. *A Boon for Transparency in Maine's Court System*, BANGOR DAILY NEWS, June 21, 2018, bangordaily-news.com/2018/06/21/opinion/editorials/a-boon-for-transparency-in-maines-court-system/; L. Dieringer, *Okla. Supreme Court Issues Rule Allowing Greater Public Access to Online Court Records*, REPUBLIC, Dec. 14, 2011; Carmen Forman, *Virginia Supreme Court Announces Plans for Public Records, Statewide Case Search*, ROANOKE TIMES, Jan. 25, 2018, www.roanoke.com/news/politics/ general_assembly/virginia-supreme-court-announces-plans-for-public-records-statewide-case/article_67e30a88-60a1-5512-9c9a-6af586d 189eb.html.

99. Final Report Minn. Sup. Ct. Advisory Committee and Order on Rules of Public Access to Records of the Judicial Branch. Minn. Court Rules: Record Access Rules Order No. C4–85–1848, Minn. Statutes; Martha Wade Steketee & Alan Carlson, *Developing CCJ/COSCA Guidelines for Public Access to Court Records: A National Project to Assist State Courts*, STATE JUSTICE INST., Oct. 18, 2002, ncsc .contentdm.oclc.org/digital/collection/accessfair/ id/210/.

100. *Privacy/Public Access to Court Records*, NAT'L CTR. FOR STATE COURTS, www.ncsc.org/topics/access-and-fairness/privacy-public-access-to-court-records/ state-links.aspx.

101. U.S. DOJ v. Reporters Comm. for Freedom of the Press, 489 U.S. 749 (1989).

102. Daily Press v. Office of Exec. Sec'y, 800 S.E.2d 822 (Va. 2017).

103. *Court Fees*, MINN. JUDICIAL BRANCH, July 1, 2017, www.mncourts.gov/Help-Topics/Court-Fees.aspx.

104. General Rule 31, adopted Oct. 7, 2004, by the Washington Supreme Court. *See* www.courts .wa.gov/newsinfo/?fa=newsinfo.pressdetail &newsid=484.

105. Estes v. Texas, 381 U.S. 532 (1965).

106. *1963 Pulitzer Prizes: Journalism*, THE PULITZER PRIZES, www.pulitzer.org/awards/1963.

107. *Estes*, 381 U.S. at 539.

108. *Id.* at 585 (Harlan, J., concurring).

109. *Id.* at 595.

110. Patton v. Yount, 467 U.S. 1025 (1984).

111. Sheppard v. Maxwell, 384 U.S. 333 (1966).

112. *Id.* at 340.

113. *Id.* at 349 *et seq.*

114. *Id.* at 384.

115. *Id.* at 358.

116. *Id.* at 358–62.

117. *Media Barred From Hearing in Sean Taylor Murder Case*, CBS Miami, Apr. 6, 2011, miami.cbslocal.com/2011/04/06/media-barred-from-hearing-in-sean-taylor-murder-case/.

118. Batson v. Kentucky, 476 U.S. 79 (1986); J.E.B. v. Alabama, 511 U.S. 127 (1994).

119. Mu'Min v. Virginia, 500 U.S. 415 (1991).

120. Sluss v. Commonwealth, 381 S.W.3d 215 (Ky. 2012).

121. *Id.* at 222, 223 (emphasis added).

122. Sluss v. Commonwealth, 450 S.W.3d 279 (Ky. 2014).

123. *Id.* at 285.

124. Jess Sullivan, *Judge: Juror's Twitter Messages During Trial Not Prejudicial*, Daily Republic, Apr. 4, 2015, www.dailyrepublic.com/news/all-dr-news/solano-news/crime-solano-county-courts/judge-jurors-twitter-messages-during-trial-not-prejudicial/.

125. *Id.*

126. People v. Tanubagijo, 2017 WL 526485 (1st D. Cal. App., Feb. 9, 2017). *See* www.leagle.com/decision/incaco20170209030.

127. Katharine Q. Seelye, *Surveys Show Bias of Potential Jurors in Boston Bombing Trial*, Int'l N.Y. Times, Jan. 23, 2015, www.nytimes.com/2015/01/23/us/boston-marathon-case-surveys-tell-of-troubles-in-selection-of-a-jury.html.

128. *Id.*

129. Betterman v. Montana, 136 S. Ct. 1609 (2016).

130. *Id.* at 1614.

131. United States v. Velarde, 606 F. App'x 434 (10th Cir. 2015) (finding failure to file necessary pretrial motion for dismissal under Speedy Trial Act or to show delay caused prejudice).

132. State v. Schoenbeck, Case No. 1202020644 (Del. Ct. Com. Pl. 2014).

133. *Id.*

134. *See* Abraham Abramovsky & Jonathan I. Edelstein, *Anonymous Juries: In Exigent Circumstances Only*, 13 St. John's J. Legal Comment. 457 (1999).

135. United States v. Ross, 33 F.3d 1507, 1519 (11th Cir. 1994).

136. *See* Christopher Keleher, *The Repercussions of Anonymous Juries*, 44 U.S.F. L. Rev. 531 (2010).

137. United States v. Wecht, 537 F.3d 222 (3d Cir. 2008); United States v. Blagojevich, 612 F.3d 558 (7th Cir. 2010).

138. *The Right of Access to Juror Names and Addresses*, Reporters Comm. for Freedom of the Press, 2016, www.rcfp.org/journals/news-media-and-law-summer-2016/right-access-juror-names-an/#_ftn6.

139. *See, e.g.,* United States v. Shryock, 342 F.3d 948 (9th Cir. 2003), *cert. denied*, 541 U.S. 965 (2004).

140. Matt Zapotosky et al., *Manafort Jury Ends Second Day of Deliberations After Trump Defends His Ex-Campaign Chair*, Wash. Post., Aug. 17, 2018, www.washingtonpost.com/local/jury-begins-deliberations-in-paul-manaforts-tax--and-bank-fraud-trial/2018/08/16/d2b0f486-a170-11e8-8e87-c869fe70a721_story.html?utm_term=.25609ba6f442.

141. Commonwealth v. Cosby, No. 3932-16 (Pa. C.C.P. May 18, 2018).

142. Tex. Crim. Proc. Code Ann. § 35.29 (1994).

143. Mu'Min v. Virginia, 500 U.S. 415 (1991).

144. *Id.*

145. Butterworth v. Smith, 494 U.S. 624 (1990).

146. Chuck Murphy, *Good Intentions, Bad Results in Judge's Gag Order*, Denver Post, Aug. 5, 2012, at 18-A.

147. Jeremy P. Meyer & Kurtis Lee, *Judge Expands Gag Order in Shooting Case to Include University*, Denver Post, July 27, 2012, at 6-A; *Colo. Shooting Suspect Objects to Ending Gag Order*, Bismarck Trib., Feb. 6, 2013.

148. People v. Holmes, Order Regarding Defendant's Motion for Relief Designed to Enforce and Protect Mr. Holmes's Constitutional Rights Arising from Law Enforcement's Violation of This Court's Pre-Trial Publicity Order (D-224), Aug. 28, 2014, www.courts.state.co.us/Courts/District/Case_Details.cfm?Case_ID=.

149. *Court's Gag Order in Michigan Jail Corruption Case Reversed*, Prison Legal News, Apr. 1, 2016, at 58, www.prisonlegalnews.org/news/2016/apr/1/courts-gag-order-michigan-jail-corruption-case-reversed.

150. People v. Sledge, 2015 Mich. App. LEXIS 1831 (Mich. Ct. App. 2015).

151. Richmond Newspapers, Inc. v. Virginia, 448 U.S. 555 (1991).

152. *In re* Wall St. Journal, 601 F. App'x 215 (4th Cir. 2015).

153. Ruthann Robson, *West Virginia District Judge's Extensive "Gag" and Sealing Order in Blankenship Trial*, Con. L. Prof Blog, Jan. 8, 2015, lawprofessors .typepad.com/conlaw/2015/01/west-virginia-district-judges-extensive-gag-order-in-blankenship-trial .html.

154. United States v. Blankenship, 79 F. Supp. 3d 613, 618 (S.D. W. Va. 2015).

155. *Wall St. Journal*, 601 F. App'x at 218.

156. Sheppard v. Maxwell, 384 U.S. 333, 342 (1966).

157. Caperton v. Massey, 556 U.S. 868, 870 (2009).

158. Republican Party of Minn. v. White, 536 U.S. 765 (2002).

159. *Id.* at 787.

160. United States v. Bryan, 339 U.S. 323, 331 (1950).

161. Branzburg v. Hayes, 408 U.S. 665, 710 (1972) (Powell, J., concurring).

162. *See, e.g., National Security Letters*, Electronic Privacy Info. Ctr., epic.org/privacy/nsl/. See also Daniel J. Malooly, *Searches Under FISA: A Constitutional Analysis*, 35 Am. Crim. L. Rev. 411 (1997–1998).

163. Zurcher v. Stanford Daily, 436 U.S. 547 (1978).

164. *Id.* at 563–64.

165. Report of the Committee of the Judiciary: Free Flow of Info. Act, S. Rep. No. 113–118, at § B (2013).

166. *See Paying the Price: A Recent Census of Reporters Jailed or Fined for Refusing to Testify*, Reporters Comm. for Freedom of the Press, www.rcfp.org/ jailed-journalists/. *See also* Edmond J. Bartnett, *Columnist Loses in Contempt Case*, N.Y. Times, Oct. 1, 1958, at 30 (explaining the jailing of reporter Marie Torre for refusing to disclose a source of information); Ross E. Milloy, *Writer Who Was Jailed in Notes Dispute Is Freed*, N.Y. Times, Jan. 5, 2002, at A8 (detailing Vanessa Leggett's incarceration and release).

167. *In re* Grand Jury Subpoena (Miller), 397 F.3d 964 (D.C. Cir. 2005).

168. *New York Times Reporter Jailed*, CNN, Oct. 28, 2005, www.cnn.com/2005/LAW/07/06/reporters .contempt.

169. Miller v. United States, 545 U.S. 1150 (2005).

170. Carol D. Leonnig, *N.Y. Times Reporter Jailed*, Wash. Post, July 7, 2005, at A1.

171. Kevin Gosztola, *Chelsea Manning Believes Subpoena from WikiLeaks Grand Jury May Be "Perjury Trap,"* *According to Unsealed Documents*, Common Dreams, Mar. 22, 2019, www.commondreams.org/ views/2019/03/22/chelsea-manning-believes-subpoena-wikileaks-grand-jury-may-be-perjury-trap; Matthew Barakat, *Chelsea Manning Continues to Fight Grand Jury Subpoena*, Associated Press, Mar. 5, 2019, www.apnews.com/966c33f560564678 a8d0df58f900334f.

172. Sarah N. Lynch, *U.S. Appeals Court Denies Manning's Bail Request, Upholds Contempt Finding*, Reuters, Apr. 22, 2019, www.reuters.com/article/usa-manning/update-1-u-s-appeals-court-denies-mannings-bail-request-upholds-contempt-finding-idUSL1N2240Z5.

173. *In re* Grand Jury Subpoena, 875 F.3d 1179 (9th Cir. 2017).

174. Branzburg v. Hayes, 408 U.S. 665, 708 (1972).

175. *In re* Grand Jury Subpoena Issued to Twitter, Inc., 2017 WL 9485553 (N.D. Tex. Nov. 7, 2017), *report and recommendation adopted*, 2018 WL 2421867 (N.D. Tex. Dec. 11, 2017).

176. Smith v. Daily Mail, 443 U.S. 97, 107 (1979).

177. Kent v. United States, 383 U.S. 541, 556 (1966).

178. *In re* Gault, 387 U.S. 1, 33, 36–37 (1967).

179. Kristin N. Henning, *Eroding Confidentiality in Delinquency Proceedings: Should Schools and Public Housing Authorities Be Notified?* 79 N.Y.U. L. Rev. 520 (2004). States that presumptively close juvenile proceedings are Alabama, Alaska, Illinois, Kentucky, Massachusetts, Mississippi, New Jersey, New York, Oklahoma, Rhode Island, South Carolina, Tennessee, Vermont, West Virginia, Wisconsin and Wyoming, as well as the District of Columbia. States with presumptively open proceedings are Arizona, Arkansas, Colorado, Florida, Georgia, Iowa, Kansas, Maryland, Michigan, Montana, Nevada, New Mexico, North Carolina, Ohio and Washington. States with open proceedings for children over a certain age or charged with certain offenses are California, Delaware, Hawaii, Idaho, Indiana, Louisiana, Maine, Minnesota, Missouri, North Dakota, Pennsylvania, South Dakota, Texas, Utah and Virginia.

180. *Child Advocates Win Fight to Open Juvenile Courts*, 11Alive, Nov. 14, 2013, www.11alive.com/article/ news/local/investigations/dfcs/child-advocates-win-fight-to-open-juvenile-courts/316810114; Garrett Therolf, *L.A. Judge Orders Juvenile Courts Opened to Press*, L.A. Times, Feb. 1, 2012, articles.latimes.com/2012/feb/01/local/la-me-open-courts-20120131; Jack Brammer, *Ky.*

Senate Approves a Bill to Open Some Juvenile Court Proceedings to the Public, Lexington Herald Leader, Mar. 10, 2014, www.kentucky.com/news/politics-government/article44475858.html; W.M. Horne, *The Movement to Open Juvenile Courts: Realizing the Significance of Public Discourse in First Amendment Analysis*, 39 Ind. L. J. 659 (2012); Barbara White Stack, *The Trend Toward Opening Juvenile Court Is Now Gaining Momentum*, Post-Gazette, Sept. 23, 2001, old.post-gazette.com/nation/20010923opencourt0923p8.asp.

181. Commonwealth v. Barnes, 963 N.E.2d 1156 (Mass. 2012).

182. Kristen Rasmussen, *Access to Juvenile Justice*, Reporters Comm. for Freedom of the Press, Spring 2012, www.rcfp.org/rcfp/orders/docs/SJAJJ.pdf.

183. Commonwealth v. Chism, 2015 Mass. Super. LEXIS 14 (Mass. Super. Ct., Mar. 3, 2015); 23 Mass. L. Rep. 423 (Mass. Super. Ct., Jan. 23, 2015).

184. Ralph Ellis & Jason Hanna, *Teen Sentenced to at Least 40 Years in Massachusetts Teacher Killing*, CNN, Feb. 26, 2016, www.cnn.com/2016/02/26/us/massachusetts-teacher-killing-sentence/.

185. *Id.*; *see* Howard Snyder & Melissa Sickmund, *Juvenile Offenders and Victims: 2006 National Report*, NCJJ & U.S. DOJ, Office of Juv. Just. & Delinquency Prevention, Mar. 2006, www.ojjdp.ncjrs.gov/ojstatbb/nr2006/downloads/NR2006.pdf.

186. Shira Schoenberg, *Massachusetts Lawmakers to Consider Raising Juvenile Court Age*, MassLive, Feb. 6, 2017, www.masslive.com/politics/index.ssf/2017/02/massachusetts_lawmakers_to_con.html.

187. For a summary of these statutes, see *Rape Shield Statutes*, Am. Prosecutors Research Inst., May 1, 2003, www.arte-sana.com/articles/rape_shield_laws_us.pdf.

188. *Rape Shield Statutes*, Nat'l District Attorneys Ass'n, Mar. 2011, ndaa.org/wp-content/uploads/NCPCA-Rape-Shield-2011.pdf.

189. *See, e.g.*, Colo. Rape Shield Law § 18–3–407 (2)(a).

190. Batey v. Haas, 573 F. App'x 590 (6th Cir. 2014), *cert. denied*, 135 S. Ct. 2320 (2015).

191. United States v. Reynolds, 345 U.S. 1 (1953).

192. *State Secrets Privilege*, Electronic Frontier Found., Dec. 4, 2012, www.eff.org/nsa-spying/state-secrets-privilege; *see* Rory Eastburg, *Behind Closed Courtroom Doors: From Criminal Cases to Civil, the Bush Administration Sought Unprecedented Levels of Secrecy in the Courts*, News Media & The Law (Oct. 1, 2008).

193. Patrice McDermott & Amy Fuller, Secrecy Report Card 2008, Open the Government, 2008, www.openthegovernment.org/wp-content/uploads/other-files/otg/SecrecyReportCard08.pdf.

194. Pub. L. 95–511, 92 Stat. 1783, 50 U.S.C. ch. 36.

195. Ginnie Graham, *Courts Keeping Cases Secret*, Tulsa World, Aug. 10, 2008, www.tulsaworld.com/news/local/courts-keeping-cases-secret/article_e6f0b2ad-a19c-5f75-89ab-0551a6bd2951.html.

196. United States v. Daoud, 755 F.3d 479 (7th Cir. 2014), *cert. denied*, 135 S. Ct. 1456 (2015).

197. Mohamed v. Jeppesen Dataplan, 614 F.3d 1070 (9th Cir. 2010) (en banc).

198. *Id.* at 1086.

199. *Id.* at 1087.

200. Dhiab v. Trump, 852 F.3d 1087 (D.C. Cir. 2017).

201. Glenn Greenwald, *Obama Wins the Right to Invoke "State Secrets" to Protect Bush Crimes*, Salon, Sept. 8, 2010, www.salon.com/2010/09/08/obama_138/; Charlie Savage, *Court Dismisses a Case Asserting Torture by CIA*, N.Y. Times, Sept. 8, 2010, www.nytimes.com/2010/09/09/us/09secrets.html?_r=1&hp.

202. Press-Enterprise (I) v. Super. Ct., 464 U.S. 501, 510 (1984).

203. *See, e.g., In re* Globe Newspaper Co., 920 F.2d 88 (1st Cir. 1990).

204. *See, e.g.*, Don J. DeBenedictis, *The National Verdict*, A.B.A. J., Oct. 1994, at 52, 54 (citing poll finding 86 percent of those people questioned thought media had some effect on trial fairness); Edith Greene, *Media Effects on Jurors*, 14 L. & Human Behavior 439, 448 (1990).

205. *In re* Charlotte Observer, 882 F.2d 850 (4th Cir. 1989).

206. Claire S.H. Lim, *Media Influence on Courts: Evidence From Civil Case Adjudication*, 17 Am. L. and Econ. Rev. 87 (2015), pdfs.semanticscholar.org/8b06/55851fb15f178af482bd53513f64935bd2ad.pdf; Jon Bruschke & William Loges, Free Press vs. Fair Trials: Examining Publicity's Role in Trial Outcomes (2004); Vincent Carroll, *Overreacting to Pretrial Publicity*, Denv. Post, Aug. 19, 2012, www.denverpost.com/ci_21331048/overreacting-pretrial-publicity?IADID=.

207. ABC, Inc. v. Stewart, 360 F.3d 90 (2d Cir. 2004).

208. *AMD v. Intel Antitrust Case*, are.berkeley.edu/~sberto/AMDIntel.pdf.

209. AMD v. Intel Corp., 2006 U.S. Dist. LEXIS 72722 (D. Del. Sept. 26, 2006).

210. *In re* Intel Corp. Microprocessor Antitrust Litigation, Consolidated Action: Motion to Intervene for Purpose of Unsealing Judicial Records and for Partial Reassignment, C.A. No. 05–441-JJF (D. Del. Aug. 21, 2008).

211. Intel Corp. v. AMD, 524 U.S. 241 (2004).

212. Associated Press, *Oops! Law Firm Leaks Facebook Settlement Amount*, Fox News, Feb. 12, 2009, www.foxnews.com/story/oops-law-firm-leaks-facebook-settlement-amount.

213. Greg Sandoval & Declan McCullagh, *Judge Seals Courtroom in MPAA DVD-Copying Case*, CNET News, Apr. 24, 2009, www.cnet.com/news/judge-seals-courtroom-in-mpaa-dvd-copying-case/. *See also* Bill Rosenblatt, *MPAA Wins Settlement in RealDVD Case*, Mar. 4, 2010, copyrightandtechnology.com/2010/03/04/mpaa-wins-settlement-in-realdvd-case/.

214. Peña Rodriguez v. Colorado, Oyez, www.oyez.org/cases/2016/15-606 (finding that juror reliance on racial animus jeopardizes a fair trial and overcomes the Rules of Evidence that preclude admission of testimony into the deliberative process of the jury).

215. Nebraska Press Ass'n v. Stuart, 427 U.S. 539 (1976).

216. Federated Publ'ns, Inc. v. Kurtz, 615 P.2d 440 (Wash. 1980).

217. Federated Publ'ns, Inc. v. Swedberg, 633 P.2d 74 (Wash. 1981), *cert. denied*, 456 U.S. 984 (1982).

218. *Nebraska Press Ass'n*, 427 U.S. 539.

219. Butterworth v. Smith, 494 U.S. 624 (1990).

220. Multimedia Holdings Corp. v. Circuit Court of Fla., 544 U.S. 1301 (2005). *See Justice Kennedy Denies Application for Stay in Prior Restraint Case, First Coast News v. Circuit Court of Florida, St. Johns County*, Media L. Prof Blog, Apr. 25, 2005, lawprofessors.typepad.com/media_law_prof_blog/2005/04/justice_kennedy.html.

221. Multimedia Holdings Corp., 544 U.S. at 1304.

222. Seattle Times v. Rhinehart, 467 U.S. 20 (1984).

223. Alabama Gas Corp. v. Advertiser Co., CV-2014-000488.00 (Ala. Cir. Ct., Sept. 23, 2014), s3.documentcloud.org/documents/1303999/filing.pdf.

224. *See, e.g.,* Greg Hurley, *Managing High Profile Cases*, Nat'l Ctr. for St. Cts., 2017, www.ncsc.org/sitecore/content/microsites/trends/home/Monthly-Trends-Articles/2017/Managing-High-Profile-Cases.aspx.

225. *Media Relations Resource Guide*, Nat'l Ctr. for St. Cts., www.ncsc.org/Topics/Media/Media-Relations/Resource-Guide.aspx.

226. *The Supreme Court of Florida: Florida State Courts Annual Report, July 1, 2016–June 30, 2017*, Office of the St. Cts. Admin., 2018, www.flcourts.org/content/download/218125/1974696/florida-courts-annual-report-2016-17.pdf.

227. Maane Khatchatoutian, *Mark Boal Settles Bowe Bergdahl Lawsuit, Won't Turn Over Tapes*, Variety, Dec. 13, 2016, variety.com/2016/film/news/mark-boal-bowe-bergdahl-lawsuit-settled-1201941202.

228. *See, e.g.,* Nathan Swinton, *Privileging a Privilege: Should the Reporter's Privilege Enjoy the Same Respect as the Attorney-Client Privilege?*, 19 Geo. J. Legal Ethics 979 (2006).

229. *See generally* David Rudenstine, *A Reporter Keeping Confidences: More Important Than Ever*, 29 Cardozo L. Rev. 1431 (2008).

230. Branzburg v. Hayes, 408 U.S. 665, 710 (1972).

231. *Id.*

232. *Id.* at 709.

233. *Id.* at 710.

234. *Id.* at 712.

235. *Id.* at 725.

236. *Id.*

237. *Id.*, quoting Time, Inc. v. Hill, 385 U.S. 374, 389 (1967).

238. *Id.* at 739.

239. *Id.* at 743.

240. *See, e.g.,* United States v. Lloyd, 71 F.3d 1256 (7th Cir. 1995) (finding that a district court did not abuse discretion in quashing a subpoena in a criminal case); LaRouche v. NBC, 780 F.2d 1134 (4th Cir. 1986) (finding that a lower court correctly applied privilege when it quashed subpoenas for journalists in a libel case); United States v. Caporale, 806 F.2d 1487 (11th Cir. 1986) (recognizing qualified privilege in a criminal case); Zerilli v. Smith, 656 F.2d 705 (D.C. Cir. 1981) (recognizing existence of federal privilege in a civil case in which journalists were not parties); Miller v. Transamerican Press, Inc., 621 F.2d 721 (5th Cir. 1980) (finding that journalists have a First Amendment privilege, although it is not absolute); United States v. Cuthbertson, 630 F.2d 139 (3d Cir. 1980) (stating that federal

privilege exists in both civil and criminal cases); Silkwood v. Kerr-McGee, 563 F.2d 433 (10th Cir. 1977) (recognizing privilege and finding that a documentary filmmaker could assert it); Cervantes v. Time, Inc., 464 F.2d 986 (8th Cir. 1972) (determining that a magazine could assert privilege in a libel case); Bursey v. United States, 466 F.2d 1059 (9th Cir. 1972) (finding that newspaper employees could assert privilege to quash grand jury subpoenas); Baker v. F & F Investment Co., 470 F.2d 778 (2d Cir. 1972) (recognizing privilege in a civil case).

241. Castellani v. Scranton Times, 956 A.2d 937 (Pa. 2008).

242. Alharbi v. TheBlaze, Civil Action No. 14-11550-PBS (D. Mass. Aug. 9, 2016).

243. *Eric Holder Says Putting Reporter James Risen Through Hell Is a Good "Example" of DOJ Process for Leak Investigations*, Techdirt, Feb. 19, 2015, www .techdirt.com/articles/20150218/17531730067/.

244. United States v. Sterling, 724 F.3d 482 (4th Cir. 2013), *cert. denied*, 572 U.S. 1149 (2014).

245. *Id.*; *see also* Charlie Savage, *Court Tells Reporter to Testify in Case of Leaked C.I.A. Data*, N.Y. Times, July 19, 2013, at A1.

246. Alan Feuer, *Times Reporter Can't Be Compelled to Testify in Baby Hope Case, Court Rules*, N.Y. Times, Oct. 20, 2016, www.nytimes.com/2016/10/21/ nyregion/times-reporter-baby-hope-case.html.

247. Phoenix Newspapers, Inc. v. Arizona, No. 1 CA–SA 16–0096 (Ariz. Ct. App., Aug. 11, 2016).

248. State v. Benson, 44 Media L. Rep. 2094 (Del. Super. Ct. 2016).

249. Peck v. City of Boston (*In re* Slack), 768 F. Supp. 2d 189 (D.D.C. 2011).

250. Keefe v. City of Minneapolis v. Star Tribune Media Co., 2012 U.S. Dist. LEXIS 187017, at *12–*13 (D. Minn. May 25, 2012).

251. Amended Memo. Op. and Order Re: Cowles Publishing Motion to Quash Subpoena Duces Tecum, Jacobson v. John Doe, Case No. CV-12-2098 (Idaho Dist. Ct., July 10, 2012).

252. Chevron Corp. v. Berlinger, 629 F.3d 297 (2d Cir. 2011).

253. *In re* McCray, 928 F. Supp. 2d 748 (S.D.N.Y. 2013), *aff'd*, 991 F. Supp. 2d 464 (S.D.N.Y. 2013).

254. *In re* McCray, 928 F. Supp. 2d 748 (S.D.N.Y. 2013).

255. Branzburg v. Hayes, 408 U.S. 665, 706 (1972).

256. Bill Kensworthy, *State Shield Laws and Leading Cases*, Freedom Forum Inst., Apr. 2011, www.freedom foruminstitute.org/first-amendment-center/topics /freedom-of-the-press/state-shield-statutes-leading-cases/.

257. Marina Riker, *Media Shield Law 2015: Who's Really a Journalist?*, (Honolulu) Civil Beat, Feb. 20, 2015, www.civilbeat.org/2015/02/media-shield-law-2015-whos-really-a-journalist/.

258. Anthony L. Fargo, *A Federal Shield Law That Works*, 8 J. Int'l Media and Ent. L. 35 (2018–19).

259. *Id.*

260. *Id.* at 36. *See* New York Times Co. v. Gonzales, 459 F. 3d 160 (2d Cir. 2006); Reporters Comm. for Freedom of the Press v. AT&T, 593 F. 2d 1030 (D.C. Cir. 1978). *See also* Julie Posetti, *Protecting Journalism Sources in the Digital Age*, UNESCO Series on Internet Freedom, 2017, unesdoc.unesco. org/images/0024/002480/248054E.pdf.

261. James Warren, *Guess Which State Passed a Landmark Shield Law to Protect Reporters?*, Poynter, Oct. 1, 2015, danielzolnikov.com/press-release-governor-signs-bill-protecting-freedom-of-the-press/.

262. Cindy Gierhart, *Colorado Considers Bill to Bolster Reporter Shield Law*, Reporters Comm. for Freedom of the Press, Jan. 16, 2014, rcfp.org/colorado-considers-bill-bolster-reporter-shield-law/; Nate Rabner, *Journalists Urge Expansion of Media Shield Law in Maryland to Protect Against Out-of-State Subpoenas*, Fox News, Feb. 3, 2015, www.foxnews .com/politics/journalists-urge-expansion-of-media-shield-law-in-maryland-to-protect-against-out-of-state-subpoenas; Marina Riker, *Media Shield Law 2015: Who's Really a Journalist?*, (Honolulu) Civil Beat, Feb. 20, 2015, www.civilbeat.org/2015/02/ media-shield-law-2015-whos-really-a-journalist/.

263. Abby Hamblin, *Dozens of San Diego Inmates Dead, A Journalist Subpoenaed After Reporting On It*, San Diego Union-Trib., May 28, 2018, www .sandiegouniontribune.com/opinion/the-conversa tion/sd-kelly-davis-san-diego-county-jail-deaths-20180209-htmlstory.html.

264. Randy Dotinga, *County Loses Another Bid to Haul a Journalist Into Court*, Voice of San Diego, May 28, 2018, www.voiceofsandiego.org/topics/news/ county-loses-another-bid-to-haul-a-journalist-into-court/.

265. Gubarev v. BuzzFeed, Inc., 2017 U.S. Dist. LEXIS 209697 (S.D. Fla. Dec. 21, 2017).

266. *Id.*, 2017 U.S. Dist. LEXIS 209697, at *10.

267. *Id.*, 2017 U.S. Dist. LEXIS 209697, at *11–12.

268. Andy Mannix, *Battle Over "First 48" TV Footage Now Embroils Up to 12 Court Cases*, Star Trib., Mar. 18, 2016, www.startribune.com/battle-over-first-48-footage-turning-into-drama-for-prosecutors/372623831.

269. *Television Program's Refusal to Disclose Footage Raises Questions Over Minnesota Shield Law*, Silha Ctr. Bull., Jun. 20, 2016, silha.umn.edu/news/SILHACENTERTVprogramandMinnShieldLawUniversityofMinnesota.html.

270. People v. Juarez, 80 N.Y.S.3d 913 (App. Div. 2018).

271. Lisa Provence, *Kessler Subpoenaed C-VILLE Reporter*, C-Ville Wkly., May 22, 2018, www.c-ville.com/kessler-subpoenaed-c-ville-reporter/#.WwyBiakh1E5.

272. Minn. Stat. Ann. § 595.023.

273. Matera v. Superior Court, 825 P.2d 971 (Ariz. Ct. App. 1992).

274. Mike Masnick, *Pennsylvania Court Says Bloggers Protected by Journalist Shield Law*, Techdirt, Mar. 30, 2017, www.techdirt.com/articles/20170328/00200337021/pennsylvania-court-says-bloggers-protected-journalist-shield-law-dont-have-to-reveal-commenter-ip-addresses.shtml.

275. Javens v. Does, 2017 WL 3314269 (Pa. Com. Pl. Mar. 9, 2017).

276. Too Much Media v. Hale, 993 A.2d 845 (N.J. App. Div. 2010).

277. Too Much Media v. Hale, 20 A.3d 364, 382 (N.J. 2011).

278. *New Jersey Shield Law Does Not Extend to Blogger*, 16:3 Silha Ctr. Bull. (Sum. 2011), silha.umn.edu/news/Summer2011/StateShieldLaws.html.

279. Johns-Byrne Co. v. TechnoBuffalo, No. 2011-L-009161 (Ill. Cir. Ct. Jan. 13, 2012); *see* James C. Goodale et al., *Reporter's Privilege—Recent Developments 2011–2012*, in 2 Comm. L. in the Digital Age 2012, at 25–26 (2012).

280. Ashley I. Kissinger, Katharine Larsen & Matthew E. Kelley, *Protections for Anonymous Online Speech*, in 2 Comm. L. in the Digital Age 2012, at 534 (2012).

281. Kevin Ellis, *Judge Gives Online Commenters First Amendment Protection*, First Amend. Coalition, July 28, 2010, firstamendmentcoalition.org/2010/07/judge-gives-online-commenters-first-amendment-protection/. *See also* Samantha Fredrickson, *Anonymous Bloggers Protected by Shield Law, Judge Finds*, Reporters Comm. for Freedom of the Press, Sept. 4, 2008, www.rcfp.org/browse-media-law-resources/news/anonymous-bloggers-protected-shield-law-judge-finds.

282. Obsidian Finance Grp. v. Cox, 2011 U.S. Dist. LEXIS 137548 (D. Ore. Nov. 30, 2011).

283. *Id.*, 2011 U.S. Dist. LEXIS 137548, at *13.

284. Obsidian Finance Grp. v. Cox, 2012 U.S. Dist. LEXIS 43125, at *20 (D. Ore. Mar. 27, 2012).

285. Lipsky v. Durant, 2012 WL 11953251 (Tex. Dist. Ct. Feb. 16, 2012).

286. Republic of Kazakhstan v. Does 1–100, 368 P.3d 524 (Wash. Ct. App. 2016).

287. People v. McKee, 24 N.E. 3d 75 (Ill. 2014); Ken Schmetterer & Joe Roselius, *Reporter's Privilege*, Editor & Publisher, Mar. 16, 2015, www.editorandpublisher.com/Features/Article/Reporter-s-Privilege.

288. Brokers' Choice of America v. NBCUniversal, 757 F.3d 1125 (10th Cir. 2014).

289. The states are Delaware, Minnesota and New York.

290. United States v. Nixon, 418 U.S. 683 (1974).

291. 42 U.S.C. § 2000aa.

292. Charlie Savage, *Holder Tightens Rules on Getting Reporters' Data*, N.Y. Times, July 12, 2013, www.nytimes.com/2013/07/13/us/holder-to-tighten-rules-for-obtaining-reporters-data.html?_r=1&.

293. *Id.*

294. *N.J. Newspaper Cries Foul After Police Seize Stolen Water Meter*, NBC New York, Dec. 21, 2016, www.nbcnewyork.com/news/local/Newspaper-Water-Meter-Seized-NJ-New-Jersey-New-Brunswick-407766655.html.

295. United States v. Cotterman, 709 F.3d 952 (9th Cir. 2013), *cert. denied*, 571 U.S. 1156 (2014).

296. *Audrey Hudson Wins Settlement in Reporter Privacy Rights Case*, Harris, Wiltshire & Grannis, LLP, Sept. 30, 2014, www.hwglaw.com/audrey-hudson-wins-settlement-in-reporter-privacy-rights-case.

297. *Government Obtains Wide AP Phone Records in Probe*, Associated Press, May 13, 2013, www.ap.org/ap-in-the-news/2013/govt-obtains-wide-ap-phone-records-in-probe; Charlie Savage & Leslie Kaufman, *Phone Records of Journalists Seized by U.S.*, N.Y. Times, May 13, 2013, www.nytimes.com/2013/05/14/us/phone-records-of-journalists-of-the-associated-press-seized-by-us.html.

298. La Monica Everett-Haynes, *Experts Evaluate the "New Media" and Courts*, Univ. of Ariz. News, Sept. 9, 2008, uanews.org/node/21471.

299. Bridget Flynn, *The Latest on Cameras in the Supreme Court*, SCOTUS Now, Sept. 21, 2018, blogs.kentlaw .iit.edu/iscotus/latest-cameras-supreme-court/.

300. Ashley Killough, *Neil Gorsuch Says He Has an "Open Mind" on Cameras in the Supreme Court*, CNN Politics, Mar. 21, 2017, www.cnn.com/2017/03/21/ politics/gorsuch-cameras-supreme-court; Sam Baker, *Justice Sotomayor No Longer Backs Television Cameras in Supreme Court*, Hill, Feb. 7, 2013, thehill.com/homenews/news/281765-soto-mayor-no-longer-backs-cameras-in-supreme-court; *Battles to Gain Camera/Audio Access to State and Federal Courtrooms Continue*, Silha Ctr. Bull., Fall 2011, silha.umn.edu/news/Fall2011/battles-togain.html.

301. Mike Cavender, *SCOTUS Camera Bill Resurfaces*, Jan. 16, 2017, RTDNA, https://rtdna.org/article/ scotus_camera_bill_resurfaces; *see, e.g.*, Anthony E. Mauro, *Let the Cameras Roll: Cameras in the Court and the Myth of Supreme Court Exceptionalism*, 1 Reynolds Cts. & Media L.J. 259 (2011).

302. *See* Gustavo A. Gelpi Jr. & Valeria M. Pelet del Toro, *Trial by Google: Juror Misconduct in the Age of Social Media*, Fed. Lawyer (Jan./Feb. 2018), www.fedbar.org/Resources_1/Federal-Lawyer-Magazine/2018/JanuaryFebruary/Trial-by-Google-Juror-Misconduct-in-the-Age-of-Social-Media. aspx?FT=.pdf.

303. *See* Amy J. St. Eve & Michael A. Zuckerman, *Ensuring an Impartial Jury in the Age of Social Media*, 11 Duke L. & Tech. Rev. 1, 2 (2012); Katie L. Dysart & Camalla M. Kimbrough, *#Justice? Social Media's Impact on the U.S. Jury System*, A.B.A., Aug. 22, 2013, apps.americanbar.org/litigation/commit-tees/trialevidence/articles/summer2013-0813-justice-social-media-impact-us-jury-system.html.

304. Timothy J. Fallon, *Mistrial in 140 Characters or Less? How the Internet and Social Networking Are Undermining the American Jury System and What Can Be Done to Fix It*, 38 Hofstra L. Rev. 935, 948 (2010).

305. John Schwartz, *As Jurors Turn to Web, Mistrials Are Popping Up*, N.Y. Times, Mar. 17, 2009, www.nytimes. com/2009/03/18/us/18juries.html.

306. Dimas-Martinez v. State, 385 S.W.3d 238, 246 (Ark. 2011).

307. United States v. Tsarnaev, 157 F. Supp. 3d 57, 66 (D. Mass. 2016).

308. *See* Joshua Dubin, *Juror Misconduct in the Age of Social Technology*, Champion, Mar. 2017; Robin H. Jones & Eli Lightner II, *Combating Jurors' Improper Internet Usage and Winning*, A.B.A., Nov. 3, 2011, apps.americanbar.org/litigation/committees/ commercial/articles/fall2011-jurors-improper-internet-usage.html; Thaddeus Hoffmeister, *Google, Gadgets, and Guilt: Juror Misconduct in the Digital Age*, 83 U. Colo. L. Rev. 410 (2012).

309. Amy J. St. Eve et al., *More From the #Jury Box: The Latest on Juries and Social Media*, 12 Duke L. & Tech. Rev. 64, 90 (2014).

310. Cohen v. California, 403 U.S. 15 (1971).

311. Jack Denton, *The State v. Hip-Hop*, Pacific Standard, Apr. 26, 2019, psmag.com/social-justice/the-state-v-hip-hop.

312. Charles E. Kubrin & Erik Nielson, *Rap on Trial*, 4 Race and Just. 185, Mar. 7, 2014.

313. *Id. See also* Shankar Vedantam et al., *Rap on Trial: How an Aspiring Musician's Words Led to Prison Time*, NPR, May 7, 2018, www.npr .org/2018/05/07/608161616/rap-on-trial-how-an-aspiring-musicians-words-led-to-prison-time.

314. State v. Skinner, 95 A.3d 236 (N.J. Sup. Ct. 2014).

315. Peter Hart, *Treating Rhymes as Crimes: The War on Hip-Hop*, Nat'l Coalition Against Censorship, Apr. 23, 2015, ncac.org/news/blog/ treating-rhymes-as-crimes-the-war-on-hip-hop.

CHAPTER 9 BOXED FEATURES

i. FCC, Ajit Pai Bio, May 2, 2019, www.fcc.gov/about/ leadership/ajit-pai#bio.

ii. FCC, *Michael O'Rielly Bio*, May 2, 2019, www.fcc .gov/about/leadership/mike-orielly#bio.

iii. FCC, *Brendan Carr Bio*, May 2, 2019, www.fcc.gov/ about/leadership/brendan-carr.

iv. FCC, *Jessica Rosenworcel Bio*, May 2, 2019, www.fcc .gov/about/leadership/jessica-rosenworcel#bio.

v. FCC, *Geoffrey Starks Bio*, May 2, 2019, www.fcc.gov/ about/leadership/geoffrey-starks#bio.

vi. FCC, *What We Do*, May 1, 2019, www.fcc.gov/ about-fcc/what-we-do.

vii. Geoffrey Starks, *Q&A With FCC Commissioners at the National Association of Broadcasters Show, Las Vegas, NV*, FCC, Apr. 11, 2019.

viii. John Eggerton, *MBG Sues Nexstar Over Station Sales: Minority Broadcaster Alleges Mistreatment Following FCC-Friendly Spin-off*, Broadcasting &

CABLE, Apr. 10, 2019, www.broadcastingcable.com/news/mgb-sues-nexstar-over-station-sales.

ix. Gene Maddaus, *Nexstar Accused of Sabotaging Black-Owned TV Station Group*, VARIETY, Apr. 2, 2019, variety.com/2019/biz/news/nexstar-sued-black-owned-tv-company-1203179793/.

x. *Id.*

xi. Michael O'Rielly, *Affirmatively Expand Permissible Foreign Ownership*, FCC BLOG, Mar. 3, 2015, www.fcc.gov/blog/affirmatively-expand-permissible-foreign-ownership.

xii. *Id.*

xiii. FCC, SPORTS BLACKOUTS (May 9, 2019), www.fcc.gov/guides/sports-blackouts.

xiv. Kathleen Kirby, *Communication Law 2016*, COMM. L. IN THE DIGITAL AGE 2016 (2016).

xv. FCC, FCC PROPOSES TO MODERNIZE MVPD DEFINITION (Dec. 19, 2014), www.fcc.gov/document/fcc-proposes-modernize-mvpd-definition.

xvi. FCC, ANNUAL ASSESSMENT OF THE STATUS OF COMPETITION IN THE MARKET FOR THE DELIVERY OF VIDEO PROGRAMMING (May 6, 2016), transition.fcc.gov/Daily_Releases/Daily_Business/2016/db0506/DA-16-510A1.pdf. *See also* Applications of Comcast Corp., General Electric Co., and NBC Universal, Inc. for Consent to Assign Licenses and Transfer Control of Licenses, MB Docket No. 10–56, Memorandum Opinion and Order, 26 FCC RCD. 4238, 4357, App. A (2011).

xvii. *Id.*

xviii. FCC, *Independent Programming NOI* (Feb. 18, 2016), www.fcc.gov/document/independent-programming-noi.

CHAPTER 9

1. FCC, *Remarks of FCC Chairman Ajit Pai at the National Association of Broadcasters Show, Las Vegas, NV* (April 9, 2019), www.fcc.gov/document/chairman-pai-remarks-national-association-broadcasters-show.

2. Joseph Burstyn, Inc. v. Wilson, 343 U.S. 495, 503 (1952).

3. *Remarks of FCC Chairman Ajit Pai, supra* note 1.

4. JOSEPH TUROW, MEDIA TODAY: MASS COMMUNICATION IN A CONVERGING WORLD 334 (6th ed. 2017).

5. *Id.*

6. Wireless Ship Act of 1910, Pub. L. 262, 36 Stat. 629.

7. *See* THOMAS G. KRATTENMAKER, TELECOMMUNICATIONS LAW AND POLICY 3–4 (1994).

8. Radio Act of 1912, Pub. L. 264, 37 Stat. 302.

9. *Id.*

10. United States v. Zenith Radio Corp., 12 F.2d 614 (N.D. Ill. 1926).

11. Radio Act of 1927, Pub. L. 69–632, ch. 169, 44 Stat. 1162.

12. FRC v. Nelson Bros., 289 U.S. 266 (1933).

13. *Id.*

14. Communications Act of 1934, Ch. 652, 48 Stat. 1064.

15. 47 U.S.C. § 153(6).

16. 47 U.S.C. § 605.

17. Nat'l Broad. Co. v. United States, 319 U.S. 190 (1943).

18. *Id.*

19. *Id.*

20. *Id.* at 213.

21. *Id.*

22. Great Lakes Broad., 3 F.R.C. Ann. Rep. 34 (1929).

23. Editorializing by Broad. Licensees, 13 F.C.C. 1246 (1949).

24. *Id.* at 1257–58.

25. Red Lion Broad. Co., Inc. v. FCC, 395 U.S. 367, 391 (1969).

26. *Red Lion Broad. Co.* at 367.

27. Miami Herald Publ'g Co. v. Tornillo, 418 U.S. 241 (1974).

28. Syracuse Peace Council, 2 F.C.C.R. 5043 (1987).

29. Syracuse Peace Council v. FCC, 867 F.2d 654 (D.C. Cir. 1989), *cert. denied*, 493 U.S. 1019 (1990).

30. Radio-Television News Dirs. Ass'n v. FCC, 229 F.3d 269 (D.C. Cir. 2000).

31. 47 U.S.C. § 399; FCC v. League of Women Voters of California, 468 U.S. 364 (1984).

32. Dylan Matthews, *Everything You Need to Know About the Fairness Doctrine in One Post*, WASH. POST, Aug. 23, 2011, www.washingtonpost.com/blogs/ezra-klein/post/everything-you-need-to-know-about-the-fairness-doctrine-in-one-post/2011/08/23/gIQAN8CXZJ_blog.html.

33. FCC v. League of Women Voters of Calif., 468 U.S. 364, 376 n.11 (1984).

34. *Id.*

35. FCC v. Pacifica Found., 438 U.S. 726 (1978).

36. *See* Robinson v. Am. Broad. Co., 441 F.2d 1396, 1399 (6th Cir. 1971).

37. *See, e.g.,* 47 U.S.C. §§ 302(a), 307(d), 309(a) and 316(a).

38. Peter J. Boyer, *Under Fowler, F.C.C. Treated TV as Commerce*, N.Y. Times, Jan. 19, 1987, www.nytimes .com/1987/01/19/arts/under-fowler-fcc-treated-tv-as-commerce.html.

39. *Guiding Principles*, FirstNet, 2014–2018.firstnet.gov/ principles.

40. *Id.*

41. David E. Hubler, *Improving First Responders' Interagency Communications*, EDM Digest, June 21, 2019, edmdigest.com/original/improving-interagency-communications/.

42. Jeff Bratcher, *FirstNet Core Delivers on the Promise of a Dedicated Network for Public Safety*, FirstNet, Mar. 27, 2018, www.firstnet.gov/newsroom/blog/firstnet-core-delivers-promise-dedicated-network-public-safety.

43. FCC, *What We Do* (May 1, 2019), www.fcc.gov/ about-fcc/what-we-do.

44. FCC, *Rulemaking Process* (May 4, 2019), www.fcc.gov/ about-fcc/rulemaking-process.

45. 47 U.S.C. § 309(j); 47 C.F.R. §§ 73.5000–73.5009; Competitive Bidding Order, 13 F.C.C.R. 15920 (1998).

46. 47 U.S.C. §§ 308(b), 319(a).

47. 47 U.S.C. § 310(b).

48. Telecommunications Act of 1996, Pub. L. No. 104–104, § 202(h), 110 Stat. 56, 111–12 (1996); Consolidated Appropriations Act of 2004, Pub. L. No. 108–99, § 629, 118 Stat. 3, 99–100 (2004) (Appropriations Act) (amending Sections 202(c) and 202(h) of the 1996 act). In 2004, Congress revised the then-biennial review requirement to require such reviews quadrennially. *See* Appropriations Act § 629, 118 Stat. at 100.

49. *See* Jonathan Obar, *Beyond Cynicism: A Review of the FCC's Reasoning for Modifying the Newspaper/ Broadcast Cross-ownership Rule*, 14 Comm. L. Pol'y 479, 485 (2009).

50. FCC, *Remarks of FCC Chairman Ajit Pai at the National Association of Broadcasters Show, Las Vegas, NV* (Apr. 9, 2019), www.fcc.gov/document/chairman-pai-remarks-national-association-broadcasters-show.

51. *2014 Quadrennial Regulatory Review—Review of the Commission's Broadcast Ownership Rules and Other Rules Adopted Pursuant to Section 202 of the Telecommunications Act of 1996*, Second Report and Order, 31 FCC Rcd. 9864 (2016); *2014 Quadrennial Regulatory Review—Review of the Commission's Broadcast Ownership Rules and Other Rules Adopted Pursuant to Section 202 of the Telecommunications Act of 1996*, Order on Reconsideration, 32 FCC Rcd. 9802 (2017).

52. *Id.*

53. *Commission Launches Modernization of Media Regulation Initiative*, Public Notice, 32 FCC Rcd. 4406 (2017).

54. *Id.*

55. *Amendment of Section 73.3555(e) of the Commission's Rules, National Television Multiple Ownership Rule*, Order on Reconsideration, 32 FCC Rcd. 3390 (2017).

56. Dan Kirkpatrick, *D.C. Circuit Upholds FCC Reinstatement of UHF Discount*, CommLawBlog, July 25, 2018, www.commlawblog.com/2018/07/articles/ broadcast/d-c-circuit-upholds-fcc-reinstatement-of-uhf-discount/.

57. Timothy Karr, *D.C. Circuit Dismisses Challenge to FCC's Obsolete UHF Discount*, Free Press, July 25, 2018, www.freepress.net/news/press-releases/dc-circuit-dismisses-challenge-fccs-obsolete-uhf-discount.

58. Free Press v. FCC, 735 F. App'x 731 (2018).

59. Kirkpatrick, *supra* note 56.

60. Public Notice: *Media Bureau Establishes Pleading Cycle for Applications to Transfer Control of Tribune Media Company to Sinclair Broadcast Group, Inc. and Permit-But-Disclose Ex Parte Status for the Proceeding*, 32 FCC Rcd. 5481 (7) (2017).

61. Jacey Fortin & Jonah Engel Bromwich, *Sinclair Made Dozens of Local News Anchors Recite the Same Script*, N.Y. Times, Apr. 2, 2018, www.nytimes .com/2018/04/02/business/media/sinclair-news-anchors-script.html.

62. Cecilia Kang, *F.C.C. Watchdog Looks Into Changes That Benefited Sinclair*, N.Y. Times, Feb. 15, 2018, www.nytimes.com/2018/02/15/technology/fcc-sinclair-ajit-pai.html?module=inline.

63. Kathleen A. Kirby, Developments in Electronic Media, Address to the Practicing Law Institute: Communication Law in the Digital Age 2018 (Nov. 8, 2018).

64. Sheelah Kolhatkar, *The Growth of Sinclair's Conservative Media Empire*, New Yorker, Oct. 15, 2018, www.newyorker.com/magazine/2018/10/22/ the-growth-of-sinclairs-conservative-media-empire.

65. *Id.*

66. *Applications of Tribune Media Company and Sinclair Broadcast Group*, Hearing Designation Order, 33 FCC Rcd. 6830 (11) (2018).

67. *2014 Quadrennial Regulatory Review—Review of the Commission's Broadcast Ownership Rules and Other Rules Adopted Pursuant to Section 202 of the Telecommunications Act of 1996*, Order on Reconsideration, 32 FCC Rcd. 9802 (2017).

68. *Id.*

69. *Id.*

70. *Id.*

71. *Id.*

72. Gautham Nagesh, *FCC Bans Ad Sales Pacts Between Same-Market TV Stations*, Wall Street J., Mar. 31, 2014, www.wsj.com/articles/SB100014240527023041572045794734925659893 78.

73. Prometheus Radio Project v. FCC, 824 F.3d 33 (3d Cir. 2016).

74. *2014 Quadrennial Regulatory Review—Review of the Commission's Broadcast Ownership Rules and Other Rules Adopted Pursuant to Section 202 of the Telecommunications Act of 1996*, Order on Reconsideration, 32 FCC Rcd. 9802 (2017).

75. *Id.*

76. John Eggerton, *Divided FCC Eliminates Main Studio Rule*, Broadcasting & Cable, Mar. 16, 2018, www.broadcastingcable.com/news/divided-fcc-eliminates-main-studio-rule-169598.

77. Geoffrey Starks, *Q&A With FCC Commissioners at the National Association of Broadcasters Show, Las Vegas, NV*, FCC, Apr. 11, 2019.

78. *2018 Quadrennial Regulatory Review of the Commission's Broadcast Ownership Rules and Other Rules Adopted Pursuant to Section 202 of the Telecommunications Act of 1996*, Report and Order, MB Docket No. 18–349, Nov. 21, 2018.

79. Consolidated Appropriations Act of 2004, Pub. L. 108–99, § 629, 118 Stat. 3, 86ff.

80. 47 U.S.C. § 396(g)(1)(D).

81. Corp. for Public Broad., *About CPB* (May 4, 2019), www.cpb.org/aboutcpb.

82. 47 U.S.C. § 396(g)(1)(A).

83. FCC v. League of Women Voters of California, 468 U.S. 364 (1984).

84. *Id.* at 402.

85. 47 U.S.C. § 399B.

86. 47 U.S.C. § 399b(A).

87. Minority TV Project, Inc. v. FCC, 649 F. Supp. 2d 1025 (N.D. Cal. 2009), *aff'd*, 736 F.3d 1192 (9th Cir. 2013), *cert. denied*, 573 U.S. 946 (2014).

88. 47 U.S.C. § 326.

89. *See* Justin Levine, *A History and Analysis of the Federal Communications Commission's Response to Radio Broadcast Hoaxes*, 52 Fed. Comm. L.J. 273, 277–79 (2000); Hadley Cantril, The Invasion From Mars (1940).

90. 47 C.F.R. § 73.1217.

91. *See, e.g.,* 47 C.F.R. § 73.1940.

92. Paramount Pictures Corp., 3 F.C.C.R. 245, 246 (Mass Media Bureau 1988).

93. *Id.*

94. Time-Telepictures Television, 17 F.C.C.R. 16273 (2002).

95. Multimedia Entm't, Inc., 9 F.C.C.R. 2811 (Political Programming Branch 1994).

96. Infinity Broad., 18 F.C.C.R. 18603 (Media Bureau 2003).

97. Arkansas Educ. Television Comm'n v. Forbes, 523 U.S. 666 (1998).

98. 47 U.S.C. § 315(b).

99. 47 U.S.C. §§ 317, 507.

100. Farmers Educ. and Coop. Union v. WDAY, Inc., 360 U.S. 525 (1959).

101. 47 U.S.C. § 312(a)(7).

102. CBS v. FCC, 453 U.S. 367 (1981).

103. *Id.*

104. *Id.* at 387.

105. *Id.* at 387–88.

106. Children's Television Act of 1990, Pub. L. 101–437, 104 Stat. 996.

107. 47 C.F.R. §§ 73.520, 73.671.

108. Children's Television Programming, 6 F.C.C.R. 7199 (1990).

109. Children's Television Report and Policy Statement, 50 F.C.C.2d 1, 13–14 (1974). The commission's current rules also prevent displaying a website address during a children's show if the website uses the show's characters to sell products or the site offers products featuring the show's characters.

110. Children's Television Programming, 6 F.C.C.R. 2111 (1991); Children's Television Programming, 6 F.C.C.R. 5093 (1991).

111. *Revision of Programming Policies*, 11 F.C.C.R. at 10660.

112. *Revision of Programming Policies*, 11 F.C.C.R. at 10730.

113. FCC, Michael O'Rielly, *It's Time to Reexamine the FCC's Kid Vid Requirements* (Jan. 26, 2018), www.fcc.gov/news-events/blog/2018/01/26/its-time-reexamine-fccs-kid-vid-requirements.

114. *Children's Television Programming Rules*, Notice of Proposed Rulemaking, FCC 18–93 (rel. July 13, 2018).

115. *Id.*

116. Wiley Rein, LLP, *FCC Releases Draft Order Modifying Children's Programming Rules*, WileyRein.com, June 20, 2019, www.wileyrein.com/newsroom-articles-FCC-Releases-Draft-Order-Modifying-Childrens-Programming-Rules.html.

117. Dade Hayes, *FCC's Vote to Ease "Kid Vid" Rules Draws Pushback And Democrats' Dissent*, Deadline, July 10, 2019, deadline.com/2019/07/fcc-vote-to-ease-kid-vid-rules-draws-pushback-and-democrats-dissent-1202644411/.

118. FCC, Annual Assessment of the Status of Competition in the Market for the Delivery of Video Programming, (May 6, 2016), transition.fcc.gov/Daily_Releases/Daily_Business/2016/db0506/DA-16-510A1.pdf.

119. *See* James C. Goodale & Rob Frieden, All About Cable and Broadband § 1.02 (2019).

120. Frontier Broad. Co., 24 F.C.C. 251 (1959).

121. Carter Mountain Transmission Corp., 32 F.C.C. 459 (1962), *aff'd*, 321 F.2d 359 (D.C. Cir. 1963), *cert. denied*, 375 U.S. 951 (1963).

122. United States v. Sw. Cable Co., 392 U.S. 157 (1968).

123. Cable Communications Policy Act of 1984, Pub. L. No. 98–549, 98 Stat. 2779.

124. Cable Television Consumer Protection and Competition Act of 1992, Pub. L. No. 102–385, 106 Stat. 1460.

125. Telecommunications Act of 1996, Pub. L. No. 104–104, 110 Stat. 56.

126. Turner Broad. Sys., Inc. v. FCC, 512 U.S. 622 (1994).

127. Denver Area Educ. Telecomm. Consortium, Inc. v. FCC, 518 U.S. 727 (1996) (plurality opinion).

128. *See* United States v. Playboy Entm't Grp., Inc., 529 U.S. 803 (2000).

129. *Major Pay-TV Providers Lost About 1,325,000 Subscribers in 1Q 2019*, Leichtman Res. Group, May 14, 2019, www.leichtmanresearch.com/major-pay-tv-providers-lost-about-1325000-subscribers-in-1q-2019/.

130. Nat'l Ass'n of Broads. v. FCC, 740 F.2d 1190 (D.C. Cir. 1984).

131. Satellite Home Viewer Improvement Act of 1999, Pub. L. No. 106–13, § 1001–12, 113 Stat. 1501. The act was upheld in Satellite Broad. and Comm'n Ass'n v. FCC, 275 F.3d 337 (4th Cir. 2001), *cert. denied*, 536 U.S. 922 (2002).

132. Direct Broadcast Satellite Public Interest Obligations, 13 F.C.C.R. 23254 (1998); 47 C.F.R. § 100.5.

133. Direct Broadcast Satellite Public Interest Obligations, 19 F.C.C.R. 5647 (2004).

134. 47 U.S.C. §§ 534 (commercial stations), 535 (non-commercial stations).

135. 512 U.S. 622 (1994).

136. Turner Broad. Sys., Inc. v. FCC, 520 U.S. 180 (1997).

137. United States v. O'Brien, 391 U.S. 367 (1968).

138. *Turner Broad. Sys., Inc.*, 520 U.S. at 180.

139. Cablevision Sys. Corp. v. FCC, 570 F.3d 83 (2d Cir. 2009), *cert. denied*, 560 U.S. 918 (2010).

140. *In the Matter of Implementation of Section 103 of the STELA Reauthorization Act of 2014, Totality of the Circumstances Test*, Notice of Proposed Rulemaking, MB Docket No. 15–216 (rel. Sep. 2, 2015).

141. *Id.*

142. *Id.*

143. Tennis Channel, Inc. v. FCC, 827 F.3d 137 (2016).

144. Game Show Network, LLC v. Cablevision Sys. Corp., DA 12–739 (rel. May 9, 2012).

145. *In the Matter of Game Show Network, LLC v. Cablevision Systems Corp., Initial Decision of Chief Administrative Law Judge Richard L. Sippel*, MB Docket No. 12–122, File No. CSR-8529-P (rel. Nov. 23, 2016).

146. *In the Matter of Game Show Network, LLC v. Cablevision Systems Corp.*, Memorandum Opinion and Order, MB Docket No. 12–122, File No. CSR-8529-P (rel. July 14, 2017).

147. *In the Matter of Word Network Operating Company d/b/a The Word Network v. Comcast Corp. and Comcast Cable Comm's, LLC*, Memorandum Opinion and Orders, MB Docket No. 12–122, File No. CSR-8938-P (rel. Oct. 27, 2017 and May 23, 2018).

148. 47 U.S.C. § 531.

149. *See, e.g.,* Denver Area Educ. Telecomm. Consortium, Inc. v. FCC, 518 U.S. 727, 761–62 (1996).

150. 47 U.S.C. §§ 531(e) (public access), 532(c)(2) (leased access).

151. Cable Television Consumer Protection and Competition Act of 1992, Pub. L. No. 102–385, § 25, 106 Stat. 1460.

152. Daniels Cablevision, Inc. v. United States, 835 F. Supp. 1 (D.D.C. 1993).

153. Halleck v. Manhattan Cmty. Access Corp., 882 F.3d 300, 304 (2d Cir. 2018).

154. Manhattan Cmty. Access Corp. v. Halleck, 204 L. Ed. 2d 405, 411 (2019).

155. *Id.* at 418.

156. Reno v. ACLU, 521 U.S. 844 (1997).

157. Telecommunications Act of 1996, Pub. L. No. 104–104, Title V, §§ 501–61, 110 Stat. 56, 133–43 (codified at 18 U.S.C. §§ 1462, 1465, 2422 and at scattered sections of 47 U.S.C.).

158. *Reno*, 521 U.S. at 869.

159. *Id.* at 853.

160. Miller v. California, 413 U.S. 15 (1973).

161. Appropriate Framework for Broadband Access to the Internet Over Wireline Facilities, 20 F.C.C.R. 148653 (2005).

162. United States v. Sw. Cable Co., 392 U.S. 157 (1968); United States v. Midwest Video Corp., 406 U.S. 649 (1972) (*Midwest I*); United States v. Midwest Video Corp., 440 U.S. 689 (1979) (*Midwest II*).

163. NCTA v. Brand X Internet Servs., 545 U.S. 967 (2005).

164. Telecommunications Act of 1996, 47 U.S.C. §§ 201–09, 251(a)(1).

165. High-Speed Access to the Internet Over Cable and Other Facilities, 17 F.C.C.R. 4798 (2002).

166. *In the Matter of Protecting and Promoting the Open Internet,* Report and Order on Remand, Declaratory Ruling, and Order, 30 FCC Rcd. 5601 (2015).

167. *In the Matter of Restoring Internet Freedom*, Declaratory Ruling, Report and Order, 33 FCC Rcd. 311 (2018).

168. *Id.*

169. *Id.*

170. Lee Drutman & Zander Furnas, *Who's Putting the Most Money Against Net Neutrality?* Daily Dot, Sept. 5, 2014, www.dailydot.com/politics/lobbyists-net-neutrality-fcc/.

171. Broadband Industry Practices, 223 F.C.C.R. 13028 (2008).

172. Comcast Corp. v. FCC, 600 F.3d 642, 644 (D.C. Cir. 2010).

173. *In re* Preserving the Open Internet, 25 F.C.C.R 17905 (2010).

174. Verizon v. FCC, 740 F.3d 623, 628 (D.C. Cir., 2014).

175. Recent Case: *Telecommunications Law, Internet Regulation: D.C. Circuit Holds That Federal Communication Commission Violated Communications Act in Adopting Open Internet Rules*, 127 Harv. L. Rev. 2565, 2574 (2014).

176. 47 C.F.R. Title II, § 20.15.

177. Protecting and Promoting the Open Internet, 80 Fed. Reg. 19737 (Apr. 13, 2015).

178. Protecting and Promoting the Open Internet, 2015 FCC LEXIS 1008 (Mar. 12, 2015) (Wheeler, Chair, concurring).

179. *Id.* (Pai, dissenting).

180. *List of Pending Appellate Cases*, FCC, Feb. 24, 2016, transition.fcc.gov/Daily_Releases/Daily_Business/2016/db0224/DOC-337898A1.pdf.

181. U.S. Telecomm. Ass'n v. FCC, No. 15–1063, 2016 WL 3251234 (rel. June 14, 2016).

182. Alina Selyukh & David Greene, *Tackling Net Neutrality Violations "After the Fact,"* NPR, May 5, 2017, www.npr.org/sections/alltech considered/2017/05/05/526916610/fcc-chief-net-neutrality-rules-treating-internet-as-utility-stifle-growth.

183. *In the Matter of Restoring Internet Freedom*, Declaratory Ruling, Report and Order, 33 FCC Rcd. 311 (2018).

184. Brian Heater, *Lawsuit Filed by 22 State Attorneys General Seeks to Block Net Neutrality Repeal*, TechCrunch, Jan. 16, 2018, techcrunch.com/2018/01/16/lawsuit-filed-by-22-state-attorneys-general-seeks-to-block-net-neutrality-repeal/; *see also* Jordan Crook, *Internet Association Wants in on the Lawsuit Challenging Net Neutrality Repeal*, TechCrunch, Mar. 22, 2018, techcrunch.com/2018/03/22/internet-association-wants-in-on-the-lawsuit-challenging-net-neutrality-repeal/.

185. Heather Morton, *Net Neutrality Legislation in States*, Nat'l Conf. of St. Legislatures, Jan. 23, 2019, www.ncsl.org/research/telecommunications-and-information-technology/net-neutrality-legislation-in-states.aspx.

186. *Id.*

187. H.R. 1644, Save the Internet Act of 2019, 116th Congress (2019–20), May 10, 2019, www.congress.gov/bill/116th-congress/house-bill/1644.

188. David Shepardson, *U.S. House Approves Net Neutrality Bill but Legislation Faces Long Odds*, REUTERS, Apr. 10, 2019,www.reuters.com/article/us-usa-internet/u-s-house-approves-net-neutrality-bill-but-legislation-faces-long-odds-idUSKCN1RM24X.

189. *See Revitalization of the AM Radio Service*, Notice of Proposed Rulemaking, 28 FCC Rcd. 15221 (2013); *Revitalization of the AM Radio Service*, First Report and Order, Further Notice of Proposed Rulemaking, and Notice of Inquiry, 30 FCC Rcd. 12145 (2015); *Revitalization of the AM Radio Service*, Third Report and Order, 32 FCC Rcd. 7736 (2017).

190. Alli Romano, *Nielsen's Brad Kelly on the Importance of AM/FM Radio During Natural Disasters*, MEDIAVILLAGE, June 26, 2018, www.mediavillage.com/article/natural-disasters-reaffirm-importance-of-amfm-radio/.

191. *Amendment of Part 74 of the Commission's Rules Regarding FM Translator Interference*, Notice of Proposed Rulemaking, FCC 18–60 (rel. May 10, 2018).

192. Gary Krakow, *Radio Is Going Digital, but Dueling Standards Complicate Transition*, NBC NEWS, Mar. 12, 2019, www.nbcnews.com/id/3078252/ns/technology_and_science-tech_and_gadgets/t/radio-going-digital/#.XM8NrS-ZPys.

193. *In Re Authorizing Permissive Use of the "Next Generation" Broadcast Television Standard*, Report and Order and Further Notice of Proposed Rulemaking, 32 FCC Rcd. 9930 (2017).

194. John Eggerton, *FCC's Pai Proposes ATSC 3.0 Rollout*, BROADCASTING & CABLE, Feb. 2, 2017, www.broadcastingcable.com/news/washington/fccs-pai-proposes-atsc-30-rollout/163020.

195. Kathleen A. Kirby, *Electronic Media Regulation*, COMM. L. IN THE DIGITAL AGE (2018).

196. *Phoenix Rises: Broadcasters Launching ATSC 3.0 "Model Market,"* ADVANCED TELEVISION SYS. COMMITTEE, May 11, 2019, www.atsc.org/newsletter/phoenix-rises-broadcasters-launching-atsc-3-0-model-market/.

197. Luke Bouma, *Next Gen ATSC 3.0 TV Is Starting to Roll Out This Year in 40 Markets*, CORDCUTTERSNEWS, Apr. 8, 2019, www.cordcuttersnews.com/next-gen-atsc-3-0-tv-is-launching-in-this-year-40-markets/.

198. *See Incentive Auction Closing and Channel Reassignment Public Notice: The Broadcast Television Incentive Auction Closes; Reverse Auction and Forward Auction Results Announced; Final Television Band Assignments Announced; Post-Auction Deadlines Announced*, Public Notice, 32 FCC Rcd. 2786 (2017).

199. *Id.*

200. Bipartisan Budget Act of 2015, Pub. L. No. 114–74 §§ 1001–08 (2015).

CHAPTER 10 BOXED FEATURES

i. John Herrman, *How the U.K. Won't Keep Porn Away From Teens*, N.Y. TIMES, May 3, 2019, www.nytimes.com/2019/05/03/style/britain-age-porn-law.html.

ii. *Id.*

iii. Jim Waterson, *UK Online Pornography Age Block Triggers Privacy Fears*, GUARDIAN, Mar. 16, 2019, www.theguardian.com/culture/2019/mar/16/uk-online-porn-age-verification-launch.

iv. Miller v. California, 413 U.S. 15, 22 (1973).

v. Eli Rosenberg, *One in Four Teens Are Sexting, A New Study Shows. Relax, Researchers Say, It's Mostly Normal*, WASH. POST, Feb. 27, 2018, www.washingtonpost.com/news/the-switch/wp/2018/02/27/a-new-study-shows-one-in-four-teens-are-sexting-relax-experts-say-its-mostly-normal/?utm_term=.80ff7b048309.

vi. *See, e.g.*, A.H. v. State, 949 So. 2d 234 (Fla. Dist. Ct. App. 2007).

vii. Sameer Hinduja and Justin W. Patchin, *State Sexting Laws*, CYBERBULLYING, May 16, 2019, cyberbullying.org/state-sexting-laws.pdf.

viii. Ronak Patel, *Taking It Easy on Teen Pornographers: States Respond to Minors' Sexting*, 13 J. HIGH TECH L. 574 (2013).

ix. David Grossman, *Whatever Happened to the V-Chip? Long Irrelevant, the Small Piece of Hardware Was Once Seen as a Generational Savior*, POPULAR MECHANICS, Mar. 12, 2018, www.popularmechanics.com/culture/tv/a19408909/20-years-ago-v-chip/.

x. Implementation of Section 551 of the Telecommunications Act of 1996; Video Programming Ratings, 13 F.C.C.R. 8232, 8237 (1998).

xi. Grossman, *supra* note ix.

xii. YouTube, *More Updates on Our Actions Related to the Safety of Minors on YouTube*, CREATOR BLOG, Feb. 28, 2019, youtube-creators.googleblog.com/2019/02/more-updates-on-our-actions-related-to.html.

xiii. Chavie Lieber, *YouTube Has a Pedophilia Problem, and Its Advertisers Are Jumping Ship*, VOX, Mar. 1,

2019, www.vox.com/the-goods/2019/2/27/18241961/youtube-pedophile-ring-child-safety-advertisers-pulling-ads.

CHAPTER 10

1. Jacobellis v. Ohio, 378 U.S. 184, 197 (1964) (Stewart, J., concurring).

2. Geoffrey R. Stone, Sex and the Constitution: Sex, Religion, and Law from America's Origins to the Twenty-First Century loc 6080 (2017) (ebook).

3. *Jacobellis*, 378 U.S. at 191.

4. *46 States + DC + One Territory Have Revenge Porn Laws*, Cyber Civil Rights Initiative, May 14, 2019, www.cybercivilrights.org/revenge-porn-laws/. The four states without revenge porn laws are Massachusetts, Mississippi, Montana, and Nebraska.

5. *Obscene*, Merriam-Webster, May 14, 2019, www.merriam-webster.com/dictionary/obscene.

6. Martin Cogan, *In the Beginning, There Was a Nipple*, ESPN, Jan. 28, 2014, espn.go.com/espn/feature/story/_/id/10333439/wardrobe-malfunction-beginning-there-was-nipple.

7. *See* Margaret A. Blanchard, Revolutionary Sparks: Freedom of Expression in Modern America (1992).

8. Heywood Broun & Margaret Leech, Anthony Comstock 265 (1927).

9. Robert Corn-Revere, *New Age Comstockery*, 4 CommLaw Conspectus 173, 173 (1996).

10. An Act for the Suppression of Trade in, and Circulation of, Obscene Literature and Articles of Immoral Use, ch. 258, § 2, 17 Stat. 598, 599 (1873).

11. Amendment to the Comstock Act, ch. 186, § 1, 19 Stat. 90.

12. Margaret A. Blanchard, *The American Urge to Censor*, 33 Wm. & Mary L. Rev. 741, 749 (1992).

13. L.R. 3 Q.B. 360, 371 (1868).

14. United States v. Kennerley, 209 F. 119, 120–21 (1913).

15. *Id.* at 121.

16. United States v. One Book Called "Ulysses," 5 F. Supp. 182, 184, 185 (S.D.N.Y. 1933), *aff'd sub nom.* United States v. One Book Entitled Ulysses, 72 F.2d 705 (2d Cir. 1934).

17. United States v. One Book Entitled Ulysses, 72 F.2d 705, 706–07 (2d Cir. 1934).

18. *Id.* at 705–06.

19. Stone, *supra* note 2, at loc 3272.

20. *Id.*

21. Roth v. United States, 354 U.S. 476, 484, 485, 497 (1957); *see also* Chaplinsky v. New Hampshire, 315 U.S. 568, 571–72 (1942).

22. *Roth*, 354 U.S. at 489.

23. Stone, *supra* note 2, at loc 5300–5341.

24. Jacobellis v. Ohio, 378 U.S. 184, 197 (1964) (Stewart, J., concurring).

25. *See e.g.*, Memoirs v. Massachusetts, 383 U.S. 413 (1966); Ginzburg v. United States, 383 U.S. 463 (1966); Mishkin v. New York, 383 U.S. 502 (1966).

26. Miller v. California, 413 U.S. 15 (1973).

27. *Id.* at 18.

28. *Id.* at 22.

29. Roth v. United States, 354 U.S. 476, 487 n.20 (1957).

30. Smith v. United States, 431 U.S. 291, 305 (1977); Hamling v. United States, 418 U.S. 87, 104–05 (1974); United States v. Salcedo, 2019 U.S. App. LEXIS 14069 (5th Cir. May 10, 2019).

31. Ward v. Illinois, 431 U.S. 767 (1977).

32. Mishkin v. New York, 383 U.S. 502, 508–09 (1966).

33. United States v. Thomas, 74 F.3d 701 (6th Cir.), *cert. denied*, 519 U.S. 820 (1996).

34. United States v. Kirkpatrick, 663 F. App'x 237 (2016).

35. *Id.*

36. United States v. Kilbride, 584 F.3d 1240 (9th Cir. 2009).

37. *Id.*

38. Ashcroft v. ACLU, 535 U.S. 564, 597 (2002) (Kennedy, J., concurring in the judgment).

39. *Id.* at 590 (Breyer, J., concurring in part and concurring in the judgment).

40. *Id.* at 586–89 (O'Connor, J., concurring in part and concurring in the judgment).

41. Miller v. California, 413 U.S. 15, 25 (1973).

42. Jenkins v. Georgia, 418 U.S. 153 (1974).

43. Ward v. Illinois, 431 U.S. 767 (1977).

44. *Jenkins*, 418 U.S. at 160.

45. United States v. Guthrie, 720 F. App'x. 199 (2018).

46. United States v. Salcedo, 2019 U.S. App. LEXIS 14069 (5th Cir. May 10, 2019).

47. Pope v. Illinois, 481 U.S. 497 (1987).

48. Luke Records, Inc. v. Navarro, 960 F.2d 134 (11th Cir.), *cert. denied*, 506 U.S. 1022 (1992).

49. Butler v. Michigan, 352 U.S. 380, 383 (1957).

50. *Id.*

51. Ginsberg v. New York, 390 U.S. 629 (1968).

52. 18 U.S.C. § 2256(8).

53. John Herrman, *How the U.K. Won't Keep Porn Away From Teens*, N.Y. Times, May 3, 2019, www.nytimes.com/2019/05/03/style/britain-age-porn-law.html.

54. New York v. Ferber, 458 U.S. 747 (1982).

55. *Id.* at 758.

56. 18 U.S.C. §§ 2251(a), 2252(b)(4), 2256(8).

57. 18 U.S.C. § 2256(2)(A).

58. John A. Humbach, *"Sexting" and the First Amendment*, 37 Hastings Const. L.Q. 433, 446 (2010).

59. United States v. Knox, 32 F.3d 733, 737 (3d Cir. 1994), *cert. denied*, 513 U.S. 1109 (1995).

60. *Id.*

61. Ashcroft v. Free Speech Coal., 535 U.S. 234 (2002).

62. United States v. Williams, 553 U.S. 285 (2008).

63. United States v. Anderson, 759 F. 3d 891 (8th Cir. 2014).

64. *Id.* at 896.

65. 18 U.S.C. § 2259.

66. *See* Emily Bazelon, *Money Is No Cure*, N.Y. Times, Jan. 27, 2013, § 8 (Magazine), at 22.

67. United States v. Monzel, 641 F.3d 528 (D.C. Cir.), *cert. denied*, 565 U.S. 1072 (2011); United States v. Kearney, 672 F.3d 81 (1st Cir. 2012), *cert. dismissed*, 568 U.S. 1223 (2013); United States v. Aumais, 656 F.3d 147 (2d Cir. 2011); United States v. Crandon, 173 F.3d 122 (3d Cir.), *cert. denied*, 528 U.S. 855 (1999); United States v. Burgess, 684 F.3d 445 (4th Cir.), *cert. denied*, 568 U.S. 968 (2012); United States v. Evers, 669 F.3d 645 (6th Cir. 2012); United States v. Laraneta, 700 F.3d 983 (7th Cir. 2012), *cert. denied*, 571 U.S. 898 (2013); United States v. Fast, 709 F.3d 712 (8th Cir. 2013); United States v. Kennedy, 643 F.3d 1251 (9th Cir. 2011); United States v. McGarity, 669 F.3d 1218 (11th Cir.), *cert. denied*, 568 U.S. 921 (2012).

68. *In re* Amy Unknown, 701 F.3d 749 (5th Cir. 2012) (en banc), *vacated and remanded sub nom.* Paroline v. United States, 572 U.S. 434 (2014).

69. 18 U.S.C. § 3663A (2012).

70. Paroline v. United States, 572 U.S. 434 (2014).

71. *Id.*

72. *Id.* at 454 (Roberts, C.J., dissenting).

73. *Id.* at 461 (Sotomayor, J., dissenting).

74. Mary Margaret Giannini, *Continuous Contamination: How Traditional Criminal Restitution Principles and §2259 Undermine Cleaning Up the Toxic Waste of Child Pornography Possession*, 40 New. Eng. J. on Crim. & Civ. Confinement 21, 25–26 (2014).

75. Stanley v. Georgia, 394 U.S. 557 (1969).

76. *Id.* at 568.

77. Joseph Burstyn, Inc. v. Wilson, 343 U.S. 495 (1952).

78. Times Film Corp. v. City of Chicago, 365 U.S. 43 (1961).

79. Freedman v. Maryland, 380 U.S. 51 (1965).

80. Pub. L. No. 91–452, 84 Stat. 922 (1970), codified at 18 U.S.C. §§ 1961–1968 (as amended by USA PATRIOT Act of 2001, Pub. L. No. 107–56, § 813, 115 Stat. 272, 382).

81. *See* Teresa Bryan *et al.*, *Racketeer Influenced and Corrupt Organizations*, 40 Am. Crim. L. Rev. 987 (2003).

82. Alexander v. United States, 509 U.S. 544 (1993).

83. 18 U.S.C. § 1464.

84. FCC v. Pacifica Found., 438 U.S. 726, 739 (1978).

85. *Id.* at 740.

86. *Id.* at 727.

87. Enforcement of Prohibitions Against Broad. Indecency, 8 F.C.C.R. 704, 705 n.10 (1993).

88. Pub. L. 69–632, ch. 169, § 29, 44 Stat. 1162 (1927); ch. 652, § 326, 48 Stat. 1064 (1934).

89. 18 U.S.C. § 1464.

90. 47 U.S.C. § 503(b)(1)(D).

91. *See, e.g.*, *Application of The Jack Straw Memorial Foundation for Renewal of the License of Station KRAB-FM, Seattle, Wash.*, 21 Rad. Reg. 2d (P&F) 505 (1971).

92. Sonderling Broad. Corp., 41 F.C.C.2d 777, 782 (1973), *aff'd*, Illinois Citizens Comm. for Broad. v. FCC, 515 F.2d 397 (D.C. Cir. 1974).

93. George Carlin, FCC Transcript: *Filthy Words*, law2.umkc.edu/faculty/projects/ftrials/conlaw/filthy-words.html (last visited May 18, 2019).

94. Pacifica Found., 56 F.C.C.2d 94 (1975) (the words, as listed in the FCC's decision, are "shit, piss, fuck, cunt, cocksucker, motherfucker, and tits").

95. Citizen's Complaint Against Pacifica Found. Station WBAI (FM), N.Y, N.Y., 56 F.C.C.2d 94 (1975).

96. FCC v. Pacifica Found., 438 U.S. 726, 750 (1978).

97. *Id.*

98. *Id.*

99. Pacifica Found., 2 F.C.C.R. 2698, 2699 (1987).

100. *In re* Infinity Broad. Corp. of Pa., 2 F.C.C.R. 2705 (1987); *In re* Pacifica Found., 2 F.C.C.R. 2698 (1987); *In re* Regents of the Univ. of Calif., 2 F.C.C.R. 2703 (1987); New Indecency Enforcement Standards to Be Applied to All Broad. & Amateur Radio Licensees, 2 F.C.C.R. 2726 (1987).

101. 2 F.C.C.R. 2726 (1987). The D.C. Circuit upheld the FCC's more expansive indecency definition. Action for Children's Television v. FCC, 852 F.2d 1332 (D.C. Cir. 1988) (*ACT I*).

102. FCC v. Pacifica Found., 438 U.S. 726, 772 (1978).

103. *In re* Indus. Guidance on the Comm'n's Case Law Interpreting 18 U.S.C. § 1464 & Enforcement Policies Regarding Broad. Indecency, 16 F.C.C.R. 7999, 8002–03 (2001).

104. *In re* Complaints Against Various Broad. Licensees Regarding Their Airing of the "Golden Globe Awards" Program, 19 F.C.C.R. 4975, 4976 (2004).

105. *Id.*

106. *In re* Complaints Regarding Various Television Broad. Between Feb. 2, 2002 & Mar. 8, 2005, 21 F.C.C.R. 2664 (2006).

107. *See* Fox Television Stations, Inc. v. FCC, 613 F.3d 317, 324 (2d Cir. 2010), *vacated by, remanded by* FCC v. Fox Television Stations, Inc., 567 U.S. 239 (2012).

108. FCC v. Fox Television Stations, Inc., 556 U.S. 502 (2009).

109. Fox Television Stations, Inc., 613 F.3d at 324.

110. *Id.*

111. *Fox Television Stations, Inc.*, 556 U.S. 502.

112. *Id.*

113. *Fox Television Stations, Inc.*, 613 F.3d at 323.

114. Complaints Against Various Television Licensees Concerning Their Feb. 1, 2004, Broad. of the Super Bowl XXXVIII, 19 F.C.C.R. 19230 (2004).

115. CBS Corp. v. FCC, 535 F.3d 167, 174 (3d Cir. 2008), *vacated and remanded*, 556 U.S. 1218 (2009).

116. *CBS Corp.*, 556 U.S. 1218.

117. CBS Corp. v. FCC, 663 F.3d 122 (3d Cir. 2011), *cert. denied*, 567 U.S. 953 (2012).

118. FCC v. Fox Television Stations, Inc., 567 U.S. 239, 258 (2012).

119. FCC Reduces Backlog of Broadcast Indecency Complaints by 70% (More Than One Million Complaints); Seeks Comment on Adopting Egregious Cases Policy, FCC, Apr. 1, 2013, www.fcc.gov/document/fcc-cuts-indecency-complaints-1-million-seeks-comment-policy.

120. *Issued a Notice of Apparent Liability for Forfeiture Proposing a $325,000 Penalty Against WDBJ Television, Inc. for Its Willful Violation of Federal Indecency Restrictions*, Notice of Apparent Liability for Forfeiture, 30 FCC Rcd. 3024 (4) (2015).

121. Eugene Volokh, *FCC Proposes $325,000 Fine for Accidental Inclusion of Porn on Video Capture in News Story*, Wash. Post, March 24, 2015, www.washingtonpost.com/news/volokh-conspiracy/wp/2015/03/24/fcc-proposes-325000-fine-for-accidental-inclusion-of-porn-on-video-capture-in-news-story/.

122. *Id.*

123. 47 C.F.R. § 73.3999.

124. Action for Children's Television v. FCC, 58 F.3d 654 (D.C. Cir. 1995) (*en banc*), *cert. denied*, 516 U.S. 1043 (1996) (*ACT III*).

125. Cruz v. Ferre, 755 F.2d 1415 (11th Cir. 1985), citing FCC v. Pacifica Found., 438 U.S. 726 (1978).

126. *See, e.g.*, Cmty. Television of Utah, Inc. v. Roy City, 555 F. Supp. 1164 (D. Utah 1982); HBO, Inc. v. Wilkinson, 531 F. Supp. 987 (D. Utah 1982).

127. 47 U.S.C. § 532(h) (franchising authorities may prohibit leased access programming that is "obscene or is in conflict with community standards in that it is lewd, lascivious, filthy or indecent, or is otherwise unprotected by the Constitution of the United States"); 47 U.S.C. § 544(d)(i) (franchising authorities may require a franchise to prohibit obscene or "otherwise unprotected" programming); 47 U.S.C. § 558 (franchising authorities may enforce state or local laws forbidding obscenity and "other similar laws").

128. 47 U.S.C. § 544(d)(2).

129. Various Complaints Against the Cable/Satellite Television Program "Nip/Tuck," 20 F.C.C.R. 4255, 4255 (2005), quoting Violent Television Programming and Its Impact on Children, Notice of Inquiry, 19 F.C.C.R. 14394, 14403 (2004).

130. Denver Area Educ. Telecomm. Consortium, Inc. v. FCC, 518 U.S. 727 (1996) (ruling on Pub. L. No. 102-385, § 10, 106 Stat. 1486).

131. *Id.*

132. 47 U.S.C. § 531(e).

133. Telecommunications Act of 1996, Pub. L. 104-104, §§ 504, 505, 110 Stat. 136.

134. Implementation of Section 505 of the Telecommunications Act of 1996, 12 F.C.C.R. 5212 (1997).

135. United States v. Playboy Entm't Grp., Inc., 529 U.S. 803 (2000).

136. *2018 Year in Review*, Pornhub Insights, Dec. 11, 2018, www.pornhub.com/insights/2018-year-in-review.

137. Geoffrey R. Stone, *Sexual Expression and Free Speech: How Our Values Have (D)evolved*, A.B.A., May 14, 2019, www.americanbar.org/groups/crsj/publications/human_rights_magazine_home/the-ongoing-challenge-to-define-free-speech/sexual-expression-and-free-speech/.

138. Pub. L. No. 104–104, § 502, 110 Stat. 56 (1996) (codified at 47 U.S.C. §§ 223(a)(1)(B)(ii), 223(d)).

139. Reno v. ACLU, 521 U.S. 844 (1997).

140. *Id.* at 877.

141. Pub. L. No. 105–277, §§ 1401–1406, 112 Stat. 1681 (codified at 47 U.S.C. § 231).

142. ACLU v. Reno, 31 F. Supp. 2d 473 (E.D. Pa. 1999).

143. ACLU v. Reno, 217 F.3d 162 (3d Cir. 2000).

144. Ashcroft v. ACLU, 535 U.S. 564 (2002).

145. ACLU v. Ashcroft, 322 F.3d 240 (3d Cir. 2003).

146. Ashcroft v. ACLU, 542 U.S. 656 (2004).

147. ACLU v. Gonzales, 478 F. Supp. 2d 775 (E.D. Pa. 2007).

148. ACLU v. Mukasey, 534 F.3d 181 (3d Cir. 2008), *cert. denied*, 555 U.S. 1137 (2009).

149. ACLU v. Ashcroft, 322 F.3d at 268.

150. Mukasey v. ACLU, 555 U.S. 1137 (2009).

151. Pub. L. 104–208, 110 Stat. 3009.

152. 18 U.S.C. § 2256(8)(B), (D).

153. Ashcroft v. Free Speech Coalition, 535 U.S. 234 (2002).

154. Pub. L. 108–21, §§ 102–601, 117 Stat. 650.

155. United States v. Williams, 553 U.S. 285 (2008).

156. Pub. L. No. 106–554, 114 Stat. 2763A-335 (2000).

157. United States v. Am. Library Ass'n, 539 U.S. 194 (2003).

158. Derek Hawkins, *Backpage.com Shuts Down Adult Services Ads After Relentless Pressure From Authorities*, Wash. Post, Jan. 10, 2017, www.washingtonpost.com/news/morning-mix/wp/2017/01/10/backpage-com-shuts-down-adult-services-ads-after-relentless-pressure-from-authorities/?utm_term=.227390c60d61.

159. Steven Koff, *Backpage.com Still Appears to Be Running Ads for Prostitutes, Sexual Services*, Cleveland.com, Jan. 12, 2017, www.cleveland.com/metro/index.ssf/2017/01/backpagecom_might_not_have_act.html.

160. Doe v. Backpage.com, LLC, 817 F.3d 12 (1st Cir. 2016), *cert. denied*, 137 S. Ct. 622 (2017); Backpage.com, LLC v. McKenna, 881 F. Supp. 2d 1262 (W.D. Wash. 2012).

161. Pub. L. No. 115–164, 132 Stat. 1253 (2018) (codified as amended at 18 U.S.C. §§ 1591, 2421A and 47 U.S.C. §230).

162. Cecilia Kang, *In Reversal, Tech Companies Back Sex Trafficking Bill*, N.Y. Times, Nov. 3, 2017, www.nytimes.com/2017/11/03/technology/sex-trafficking-bill.html.

163. Aja Romano, *A New Law Intended to Curb Sex Trafficking Threatens the Future of the Internet as We Know It*, July 2, 2018, Vox, www.vox.com/culture/2018/4/13/17172762/fosta-sesta-backpage-230-internet-freedom.

164. Woodhull Freedom Found. v. United States, 334 F. Supp. 3d 185 (D.D.C. 2018); *see also* Alex F. Levy, *Constitutional Challenge to FOSTA Dismissed for Lack of Standing (Guest Blog Post)*, Tech. & Marketing Blog, Oct. 8, 2018, blog.ericgoldman.org/archives/2018/10/constitutional-challenge-to-fosta-dismissed-for-lack-of-standing-guest-blog-post.htm. (The appeal was filed Oct. 12, 2018.)

165. *BREAKING: Woodhull Freedom Foundation Appeals FOSTA Ruling*, Woodhull Freedom Found., May 18, 2019, www.woodhullfoundation.org/2018/10/09/breaking-woodhull-freedom-foundation-appeals-fosta-ruling/.

166. Ryan Tarinelli, *Online Sex Ads Rebound, Months After Shutdown of Backpage*, AP News, Nov. 29, 2018, www.apnews.com/159434f052eb40dd87b9dd9b65da53f5.

167. *See e.g.*, Lura Chamberlain, Note: *FOSTA: A Hostile Law With a Human Cost*, 87 Fordham L. Rev. 2171 (2019).

CHAPTER 11 BOXED FEATURES

i. Chris Stokel-Walker, *Forget Apple vs. Samsung, An Even Bigger Patent War Has Just Begun*, Wired, July 2, 2018, www.wired.co.uk/article/apple-samsung-iphone-patents.

ii. Geoff Duncan, *Why Are Apple and Samsung Throwing Down? A Timeline of the Biggest Fight in Tech*, Digital Trends, Apr. 4, 2014, www.digitaltrends.com/mobile/apple-vs-samsung-patent-war-timeline.

iii. Samsung Electronics Co., Ltd. v. Apple Inc., 137 S. Ct. 429 (2016).

iv. *Id.*

v. Reuters, *Jury Awards Apple $539 Million in Samsung Patent Case*, N.Y. Times, May 24, 2018, www.nytimes .com/2018/05/24/business/apple-samsung-patent-trial.html.

vi. Roger Fingas, *Apple Versus Samsung Patent Trial Finally Completely Over*, Apple Insider, June 27, 2018, appleinsider.com/articles/18/06/27/apple-versus-samsung-iphone-design-patent-trial-finally-completely-over.

vii. 18 U.S.C. § 102(a).

viii. U.S. Copyright Office, *Copyright Basics* (May 23, 2019), www.copyright.gov/circs/circ01.pdf.

ix. Star Athletica, LLC v. Varsity Brands, Inc., 137 S. Ct. 1002 (2017).

x. 17 U.S.C. § 106.

xi. *Fair Use: What Is Transformative?*, Nolo, May 24, 2019, www.nolo.com/legal-encyclopedia/fair-use-what-transformative.html.

CHAPTER 11

1. President Barack Obama, Remarks at the Export-Import Bank's Annual Conference (Mar. 11, 2010), obamawhitehouse.archives.gov/the-press-office/remarks-president-export-import-banks-annual-conference.

2. 17 U.S.C. § 102(a).

3. U.S. Const. art. I, § 8, cl. 8.

4. Obama, *supra* note 1.

5. 15 U.S.C. § 1127.

6. *Id.*

7. 8 Anne, C. 19 (1710).

8. U.S. Const. art. I, § 8, cl. 8.

9. Act of May 31, 1790, ch. 15, 1 Stat. 124.

10. Wheaton v. Peters, 33 U.S. 591 (1834).

11. Act of Feb. 3, 1831, 4 Stat. 436 (musical compositions); Copyright Act of 1865, 13 Stat. 540 (photographs); Act of July 8, 1870, 16 Stat. 212 (paintings).

12. Pub. L. No. 60–349, 35 Stat. 1075.

13. Berne Convention Implementation Act of 1988, Pub. L. 100–568, 102 Stat. 2853.

14. Digital Millennium Copyright Act of 1998, Pub. L. 105–304, 112 Stat. 2860.

15. 17 U.S.C. § 1201.

16. *See, e.g.,* 321 Studios v. MGM Studios, Inc., 307 F. Supp. 2d 1085 (N.D. Cal. 2004).

17. 17 U.S.C. § 1202.

18. 18 U.S.C. § 102(a).

19. *See* Burrow-Giles Lithographic Co. v. Sarony, 111 U.S. 53 (1884).

20. Boisson v. Banian, Ltd., 273 F.3d 262, 268 (2d Cir. 2001).

21. ABS Entm't, Inc. v. CBS Corp., 908 F.3d 405, 414 (5th Cir. 2018).

22. 17 U.S.C. § 102(a).

23. *Id.*

24. Star Athletica, L.L.C. v. Varsity Brands, Inc., 137 S. Ct. 1002 (2017).

25. U.S. Copyright Off., *Useful Articles*, www.copyright .gov/register/va-useful.html.

26. Gene Quinn & Steve Brachmann, *Copyrights at the Supreme Court: Star Athletica v. Varsity Brands*, IPWatchdog, Mar. 22, 2017, www.ipwatchdog .com/2017/03/22/copyrights-supreme-court-star-athletica-v-varsity-brands/id=79767/.

27. *Star Athletica*, 137 S. Ct. at 1007.

28. Bruce Keller, *Communications Law in the Digital Age: Intellectual Property*, Comm. L. in the Digital Age (2016).

29. ABS Entm't, Inc. v. CBS Corp., 908 F.3d 405 (5th Cir. 2018).

30. *Id.* at 423.

31. 17 U.S.C. § 301.

32. *See* Wheaton v. Peters, 33 U.S. 591 (1834).

33. Feist Publ'ns, Inc. v. Rural Tel. Serv. Co., Inc., 499 U.S. 340 (1991).

34. *See, e.g.,* Am. Dental Ass'n v. Delta Dental Plans Ass'n, 126 F.3d 977 (7th Cir. 1997).

35. 17 U.S.C. § 103.

36. *See* 17 U.S.C. § 102(b).

37. *Feist Publ'ns*, 499 U.S. 340.

38. PhantomALERT, Inc. v. Google, Inc., No. 15-cv-03986-JCS (N.D. Cal., Mar. 8, 2016).

39. Media.net Advert., FZ-LLC v. NetSeer, Inc., 156 F. Supp. 3d 1052 (N.D. Cal. 2016).

40. 17 U.S.C. § 105.

41. 17 U.S.C. § 201(a).

42. 17 U.S.C. § 201(b).

43. 17 U.S.C. §§ 101, 201.

44. 17 U.S.C. § 101.

45. Cmty. for Creative Non-Violence v. Reid, 490 U.S. 730 (1989).

46. *Who Owns the Intellectual Property Developed by an Independent Contractor?*, HG, May 23, 2019, www .hg.org/legal-articles/who-owns-the-intellectual-property-developed-by-an-independent-contractor-7502.

47. 17 U.S.C. § 201(c).

48. N.Y. Times Co., Inc. v. Tasini, 533 U.S. 483 (2001).

49. 17 U.S.C. § 106.

50. Sony Corp. of Am. v. Universal City Studios, Inc., 464 U.S. 417 (1984).

51. Audio Home Recording Act of 1992, Pub. L. No. 102–563, 106 Stat. 4244 (codified at 17 U.S.C. §§ 1001–1010).

52. Tom Huddleston, Jr., *"Game of Thrones" Creator George R.R. Martin Almost Quit Writing for Real Estate*, CNBC, Apr. 14, 2019, www.cnbc.com/2019/04/12/ how-game-of-thrones-creator-george-rr-martin-overcame-failure.html.

53. Peter Mayer Publishers, Inc. v. Shilovskaya, 11 F. Supp. 3d 421 (S.D.N.Y. 2014).

54. ABS Entm't, Inc. v. CBS Corp., 908 F.3d 405 (2018).

55. *Id.* at 418.

56. Rearden, LLC v. Walt Disney Co., 293 F. Supp. 3d 963 (N.D. Cal. 2018).

57. *Id.*

58. Agence France Presse v. Morel, 934 F. Supp. 2d 547 (S.D.N.Y. 2013).

59. *Id.*

60. Joseph Ax, *Photographer Wins $1.2 Million From Companies That Took Pictures Off Twitter*, REUTERS, Nov. 22, 2013, www.reuters.com/article/ 2013/11/22/us-media-copyright-twitter-idUSBRE 9AL16F20131122.

61. 17 U.S.C. § 106(4).

62. WNET, Thirteen v. Aereo, Inc., 712 F. 3d 676, 685 (2d Cir. 2013), *rev'd and remanded sub nom.* ABC, Inc. v. Aereo, Inc., 573 U.S. 431 (2014).

63. Teleprompter Corp. v. CBS, 415 U.S. 394 (1974); Fortnightly Corp. v. United Artists Television, Inc., 392 U.S. 390 (1968).

64. 17 U.S.C. § 111.

65. 17 U.S.C. § 119; Satellite Home Viewer Improvement Act of 1999, Pub. L. No. 106–113, §§ 1001–1012, 113 Stat. 1501.

66. *ABC, Inc.*, 573 U.S. 431.

67. *Id.*

68. Corinee Lestch, *Aereo Suspends Video Streaming After Supreme Court Decision*, N.Y. DAILY NEWS, June 29, 2014, www.nydailynews.com/news/ national/aereo-suspends-streaming-service-supreme-court-decision-article-1.1847702.

69. Matthew Syrkin, *U.S. Television on the Internet and the New "MVPDs,"* HUGHES, HUBBARD & REED, Mar. 18, 2015, www.hugheshubbard.com/news/u-s-television-on-the-internet-and-the-new-mvpds-updated.

70. John Eggerton, *Ninth Circuit Reverses FilmOn X Decision*, BROADCASTING & CABLE, Mar. 16, 2018, www.broadcastingcable.com/news/ninth-circuit-reverses-filmon-x-decision-164275.

71. Fox TV Stations, Inc. v. Aereokiller, LLC, 851 F.3d 1002, 1006 (2017).

72. 17 U.S.C. § 106.

73. Perfect 10, Inc. v. Amazon.com, Inc., 508 F.3d 1146 (9th Cir. 2007).

74. Goldman v. Breitbart News Network, LLC, 302 F. Supp. 3d 585 (S.D.N.Y. 2018).

75. Jeffrey Neuburger, *New York Court Rebuffs Ninth Circuits' Copyright "Server Test," Finds Embedded Tweet Displaying Copyrighted Image to be Infringement*, NEW MEDIA AND TECH. L. BLOG, Mar. 2, 2018, newmedialaw.proskauer.com/2018/03/02/ new-york-court-rebuffs-ninth-circuits-copyright-server-test-finds-embedded-tweet-displaying-copyrighted-image-to-be-infringement/.

76. *Goldman*, 508 F.3d at 593.

77. *Id.*

78. Jeffrey P. Cunard et al., *Intellectual Property 2018: Select Developments*, COMM. L. IN THE DIGITAL AGE (2018).

79. Digital Performance Right in Sound Recordings Act, Pub. L. No. 104–39, 109 Stat. 336, *as amended by* DMCA, Pub. L. 105–304, 112 Stat. 2860.

80. 17 U.S.C. § 108.

81. U.S. Copyright Off., *Reproduction of Copyright Works by Educators and Librarians* (June 2, 2019), www .copyright.gov/circs/circ21.pdf.

82. 17 U.S.C. § 109(a).

83. The Supreme Court provides a brief history and interpretation of the first-sale doctrine in Quality King Distribs., Inc. v. L'Anza Research Int'l, Inc., 523 U.S. 135 (1998).

84. Kirtsaeng v. John Wiley & Sons, Inc., 568 U.S. 519 (2013).

85. 17 U.S.C. § 109(b)(1)(A); Computer Software Rental Amendments, Pub. L. No. 101–650, tit. viii, 104 Stat. 5089, 5134–35; Record Rental Amendment of 1984, Pub. L. No. 98–450, 98 Stat. 1727.

86. Capitol Records, LLC v. ReDigi, Inc., 934 F. Supp. 2d 640 (S.D.N.Y. 2013), *aff'd*, 910 F.3d 649 (2d Cir. 2018), *cert. denied*, 2019 WL 2124143 (June 24, 2019).

87. 17 U.S.C. §§ 203(a), 304(c).

88. Daisy Buchanan, *Adele's Spotify Boycott Isn't Selfish—It's Savvy and Her Fans Need to Pipe Down*, Telegraph, Nov. 20, 2015, www.telegraph.co.uk/women/life/adeles-spotify-boycott-isnt-selfish---its-savvy-and-her-fans-nee/.

89. Amy X. Wang, *Trump Signs Landmark Music Bill Into Law*, Rolling Stone, Oct. 11, 2018, www.rollingstone.com/music/music-news/trump-signs-music-modernization-act-736185/.

90. The Orrin G. Hatch-Bob Goodlatte Music Modernization Act (MMA), Pub. L. 115–264, 132 Stat. 3676 (Oct. 11, 2018).

91. *Summary of H.R. 1551, the Music Modernization Act*, Copyright Alliance, May 24, 2019, copyrightalliance.org/wp-content/uploads/2018/10/CA-MMA-2018-senate-summary_CLEAN.pdf.

92. *Id.*

93. Mitch Glazier, *Creators and Tech Companies: Let's Fix the DMCA Together* (Guest Column), Variety, May 6, 2019, variety.com/2019/music/news/digital-copyright-act-creators-tech-lets-fix-dmca-together-riaa-1203205595/.

94. U.S. Const. art I, § 8, cl. 8.

95. *See* 3 Melville B. Nimmer & David Nimmer, Nimmer on Copyright § 9.01 (2012).

96. Laurie Richter, *Reproductive Freedom: Striking a Fair Balance Between Copyright and Other Intellectual Property Protections in Cartoon Characters*, 21 St. Thomas L. Rev. 441, 451–52 (2009).

97. 17 U.S.C. § 302(a).

98. 17 U.S.C. § 302(c).

99. Eldred v. Ashcroft, 537 U.S. 186 (2003).

100. *Id.*

101. This was "due to (i) failure to comply with copyright formalities, (ii) lack of subject matter protection, or (iii) lack of national eligibility due to the absence of copyright relations with the" United States. Dan Laidman, *Golan v. Holder and the Controversial New Efforts to Update IP Law*

102. 17 U.S.C. § 104A.

103. Laidman, *supra* note 101.

104. Golan v. Holder, 565 U.S. 302 (2012).

105. *Id.* at 311.

106. 17 U.S.C. § 401(c).

107. Rimini Street, Inc. v. Oracle USA, Inc., 139 S. Ct. 873 (2019).

108. *Id.*

109. Fourth Estate Pub. Benefit Corp. v. Wall-Street.com, LLC, 139 S. Ct. 881 (2019).

110. Arnstein v. Porter, 154 F.2d 464 (2d Cir. 1946).

111. Shyamkrishna Balganesh, *The Questionable Origins of the Copyright Infringement Analysis*, 68 Stan. L. Rev. 791 (April 2016).

112. *See, e.g.,* Sid & Marty Krofft Television Prods., Inc. v. McDonald's Corp., 562 F.2d 1157 (9th Cir. 1977); Comput. Assocs. Int'l v. Altai, Inc., 982 F. 2d 693, 713 (2d Cir. 1992).

113. Kory Grow, *Robin Thicke, Pharrell Lose Multi-Million Dollar "Blurred Lines" Lawsuit*, Rolling Stone, Mar. 10, 2015, www.rollingstone.com/music/news/robin-thicke-and-pharrell-lose-blurred-lines-lawsuit-20150310.

114. Josh H. Escovedo, *The Blurred Lines of an Infringement Action*, IP L. Blog, Mar. 6, 2015, www.theiplawblog.com/2015/03/articles/copyright-law/the-blurred-lines-of-an-infringement-action/.

115. *Id.*

116. 17 U.S.C. § 504(c).

117. *See, e.g.,* Kalem Co. v. Harper Bros., 222 F. 55 (1911) (producer of infringing film violated copyright law although movie theaters, not producer, showed film to public); 17 U.S.C. §§ 106, 501(a).

118. Sony Corp. of Am. v. Universal City Studios, Inc., 464 U.S. 417 (1984).

119. *Id.*

120. Cartoon Network, LP v. CSC Holdings, Inc., 536 F.3d 121 (2d Cir. 2008), *cert. denied*, 557 U.S. 946 (2009).

121. Flava Works, Inc. v. Gunter, 689 F.3d 754 (7th Cir. 2012).

122. A&M Records, Inc. v. Napster, Inc., 239 F.3d 1004 (9th Cir. 2001).

123. MGM Studios, Inc. v. Grokster, Ltd., 545 U.S. 913 (2005).

for the Internet Age, Davis Wright Tremaine, Mar. 12, 2012, www.lexology.com/library/detail.aspx?g=2d5e85f7-9b48-4c6a-beff-c63c25335859.

124. *See* 35 U.S.C. § 271(b).

125. Columbia Pictures Indus., Inc. v. Fung, 710 F.3d 1020 (9th Cir.), *cert. dismissed*, 571 U.S. 1007 (2013).

126. Universal City Studios Prods., LLLP v. TickBox TV, LLC, No. CV 17-7496-MFW, 2018 U.S. Dist. LEXIS 40756 (C.D. Cal. Jan. 30, 2018).

127. Gene Maddaus, *TickBox Agrees to $25 Million Judgment in Copyright Infringement Case*, Variety, Sept. 11, 2018, variety.com/2018/digital/news/tickbox-copyright-suit-25-million-1202936712/.

128. 17 U.S.C. § 507.

129. *See, e.g.,* Dam Things From Denmark v. Russ Barrie & Co., 290 F.3d 548, 560 (3d Cir. 2002).

130. *See* Pierre N. Leval, *Toward a Fair Use Standard*, 103 Harv. L. Rev. 1105, 1105 (1990).

131. 17 U.S.C. § 107.

132. Leval, *supra* note 130, at 1110.

133. Campbell v. Acuff-Rose Music, Inc., 510 U.S. 569, 578 (1994).

134. Harper & Row Publishers, Inc. v. Nation Enters., 471 U.S. 539 (1985).

135. *See* 4 Melville Nimmer & David Nimmer, Nimmer on Copyright § 13.05[A][1] (2012).

136. *Campbell*, 510 U.S. at 579.

137. *Id.* at 569.

138. See Nimmer & Nimmer, *supra* note 135, at § 13.05[C][1].

139. Brownmark Films, LLC v. Comedy Partners, 682 F.3d 687 (7th Cir. 2012).

140. Keeling v. Hars, 809 F. 3d 43 (2d Cir. 2015), *cert. denied*, 136 S. Ct. 2519 (2016).

141. Barcroft Media, Ltd. V. Coed Media Grp., LLC, 297 F. Supp. 3d 339 (S.D.N.Y. 2017).

142. White v. West Publ'g Corp., 29 F. Supp. 3d 396 (S.D.N.Y. 2014).

143. Fox News Network, LLC v. TVEyes, Inc., 43 F. Supp. 3d 379 (S.D.N.Y. 2014).

144. Fox News Network, LLC v. TVEyes, Inc., 883 F.3d 169 (2d Cir.), *cert. denied*, 139 S. Ct. 595 (2018).

145. *Id.*

146. Authors Guild v. Google, Inc., 804 F.3d 202 (2d Cir. 2015), *cert. denied*, 136 S. Ct. 1658 (2016).

147. Authors Guild v. HathiTrust, 902 F. Supp. 445 (S.D.N.Y. 2012).

148. *Authors Guild*, 804 F.3d 202.

149. *See* 4 Melville Nimmer & David Nimmer, Nimmer on Copyright § 13.05[A][2] (2012).

150. Salinger v. Random House, Inc., 811 F.2d 90 (2d Cir. 1987), *cert. denied*, 484 U.S. 890 (1988).

151. 17 U.S.C. § 107; Pub. L. No. 102–492, 106 Stat. 3145.

152. A.V. v. iParadigms, LLC, 562 F.3d 630 (4th Cir. 2009).

153. *Id.* at 642.

154. *See* Fox News Network, LLC v. TVEyes, Inc., 43 F. Supp. 3d 379 (S.D.N.Y. 2014); White v. West Publ'g Corp., 29 F. Supp. 3d 396 (S.D.N.Y. 2014).

155. Bill Graham Archives v. Dorling Kindersley, Ltd., 448 F.3d 605 (2d Cir. 2006).

156. Benny Evangelista, *Consumers Can Now Pass Go, Collect Any App*, S.F. Chron., July 27, 2010, at D1.

157. Basic Books, Inc. v. Kinko's Graphics Corp., 758 F. Supp. 1522, 1534 (S.D.N.Y. 1991).

158. Campbell v. Acuff-Rose Music, Inc., 510 U.S. 569, 587 (1994).

159. *See, e.g.,* Authors Guild, Inc. v. Google, Inc., 954 F. Supp. 2d 282 (S.D.N.Y. 2013), *aff'd*, 804 F.3d 202 (2d Cir. 2015), *cert. denied*, 136 S. Ct. 1658 (2016); Authors Guild, Inc. v. HathiTrust, 755 F.3d 87 (2d Cir. 2014).

160. Pub. L. 105–304, 112 Stat. 2860.

161. 17 U.S.C. § 512(c).

162. Perfect 10, Inc. v. Google, Inc., 2010 U.S. Dist. LEXIS 75071 (C.D. Cal., July 26, 2010), *aff'd*, 653 F.3d 976 (9th Cir. 2011), *cert. denied*, 565 U.S. 1245 (2012).

163. UMG Recordings, Inc. v. Veoh Networks, Inc., 718 F.3d 1006 (9th Cir. 2013); *see also* Io Group, Inc. v. Veoh Networks, Inc., 586 F. Supp. 2d 1132 (N.D. Cal. 2008).

164. Viacom Int'l, Inc. v. YouTube, Inc., 940 F. Supp. 2d 110 (S.D.N.Y. 2013), *on remand from* Viacom Int'l, Inc. v. YouTube, Inc., 676 F.3d 19 (2d Cir. 2012); *see* Meg James, *YouTube Prevails in Viacom Copyright Suit*, L.A. Times, Apr. 19, 2013, at B3.

165. Capitol Records, LLC v. Vimeo, LLC, 972 F. Supp. 2d 537 (S.D.N.Y. 2014), *aff'd in part, vacated in part*, 826 F.3d 2d Cir. 2016), *cert. denied*, 137 S. Ct. 1374 (2017).

166. Evan Sheres, *Disabling the "Red Flag" Doctrine: Missed Opportunity to Establish Reasonable Precedent in* Capitol Records v. Vimeo, Copyright All., Sept. 25, 2013.

167. *Capitol Records*, 972 F. Supp. 2d 537.

168. Capitol Records, LLC v. Vimeo, No. 09-CV-101015, 2018 U.S. Dist. LEXIS 153998 (S.D.N.Y. Sept. 10, 2018).

169. BMG Rights Mgmt. (US), LLC v. Cox Commc'ns, Inc., 881 F.3d 293 (4th Cir. 2018).

170. BWP Media USA, Inc. v. Clarity Digital Grp., LLC, 820 F. 3d 1175 (10th Cir. 2016).

171. 15 U.S.C. § 1127.

172. Qualitex Co. v. Jacobson Prods. Co., Inc., 514 U.S. 159 (1995).

173. Ride the Ducks, LLC v. Duck Boat Tours, Inc., 2005 U.S. Dist. LEXIS 4422 (E.D. Pa. Mar. 21, 2005), *aff'd*, 138 F. App'x. 431 (3d Cir. Pa. 2005).

174. *See* Anne Gilson LaLonde, Gilson on Trademarks § 10A.09[5] (2019).

175. 15 U.S.C. § 1051 *et seq.*

176. 15 U.S.C. § 1125(a).

177. 15 U.S.C. § 1052.

178. PACCAR, Inc. v. TeleScanTechnologies, LLC, 319 F.3d 243 (6th Cir. 2003).

179. Bebe Stores, Inc. v. May Dep't Stores Int'l, 313 F.3d 1056 (8th Cir. 2002) (per curiam).

180. Standard Brands, Inc. v. Smidler, 151 F.2d 34 (2d Cir. 1945).

181. *See* Anne Gilson LaLonde & Jerome Gilson, Gilson on Trademarks § 2.04[1] (2019).

182. Sara Lee Corp. v. Kayser-Roth Corp., 81 F.3d 455, 464 (4th Cir. 1996).

183. Circuit City Stores, Inc. v. CarMax, Inc., 165 F.3d 1047 (6th Cir. 1999).

184. Japan Telecom, Inc. v. Japan Telecom Am., Inc., 287 F.3d 866, 873 (9th Cir. 2002).

185. Viacom Int'l, Inc. v. IJR Capital Invs., LLC, 891 F.3d 178 (5th Cir. 2018).

186. *Id.*

187. Boston Beer Co., LP v. Slesar Bros. Brewing Co., Inc., 9 F.3d 175 (1st Cir. 1993).

188. M. Fabrikant & Sons, Ltd. v. Fabrikant Fine Diamonds, Inc., 17 F. Supp. 2d 249 (S.D.N.Y. 1998).

189. Anne Gilson LaLonde & Jerome Gilson, Gilson on Trademarks § 2.08[1] (2019).

190. Harley-Davidson, Inc. v. Grottanelli, 164 F.3d 806 (2d Cir. 1999).

191. Small Bus. Assistance Corp. v. Clear Channel Broad., Inc., 210 F.3d 278 (5th Cir. 2000).

192. *See* Sung In, Note: *Death of a Trademark: Genericide in the Digital Age*, 21 Rev. Litig. 159 (2002).

193. *See, e.g.,* George K. Chamberlin, Annotation: *When Does Product Mark Become Generic Term or "Common Descriptive Name" So as to Warrant Cancellation of Registration of Mark*, 55 A.L.R. Fed. 241 (2004).

194. *See* Anne Gilson LaLonde & Jerome Gilson, Gilson on Trademarks § 2.02[6] (2019).

195. 15 U.S.C. § 1051.

196. 15 U.S.C. § 1052 (b), (c), (d), (e).

197. 15 U.S.C. § 1091.

198. 15 U.S.C. § 1052(a).

199. *In re* Tam, 808 F.3d 1321 (D.C. Cir. 2015), *aff'd sub nom.*, Matal v. Tam, 137 S. Ct. 1744 (2017).

200. *Id.*

201. *Id.* at 1327–28.

202. *Matal*, 137 S. Ct. at 1748.

203. *In re* Brunetti, 877 F.3d 1330 (D.C. Cir., 2017), *cert. granted*, 139 S. Ct. 782 (2019).

204. *Id.*

205. David G. Savage, *Supreme Court Debates Whether FUCT Clothing Line Can Trademark Its Name*, L.A. Times, Apr. 15, 2019, www.latimes.com/politics/la-na-pol-supreme-court-trademark-free-speech-dispute-fuct-20190415-story.html.

206. Iancu v. Brunetti, 2019 U.S. LEXIS 4201, 13 (2019).

207. *Id.* at 32 (Sotomayor, J., dissenting).

208. *Id.* at 54 (Sotomayor, J., dissenting).

209. 15 U.S.C. §§ 1052, 1072, 1115.

210. 15 U.S.C. § 1115(a), (b).

211. 15 U.S.C. § 1058.

212. 15 U.S.C. § 1059.

213. Pub. L. 106–113, 113 Stat. 1536.

214. E. & J. Gallo Winery v. Spider Webs, Ltd., 286 F.3d 270 (5th Cir. 2002).

215. Brookfield Commc'ns, Inc. v. West Coast Entm't Corp., 174 F.3d 1036 (9th Cir. 1999).

216. Ty, Inc. v. Perryman, 306 F.3d 509, 513 (7th Cir. 2002), *cert. denied*, 538 U.S. 971 (2003).

217. Infostream Grp., Inc. v. Avid Life Media, Inc., 2013 U.S. Dist. LEXIS 161940 (C.D. Cal., 2013).

218. Alzheimer's Disease and Related Disorders Ass'n v. Alzheimer's Found. of Am., Inc., 307 F. Supp. 3d 260 (S.D.N.Y. 2018).

219. 15 U.S.C. § 1125(a)(1) (Lanham Act—U.S. trademark law).

220. *See, e.g.,* Triangle Publ'ns v. Knight-Ridder Newspapers, Inc., 626 F.2d 1171 (5th Cir. 1978).

221. Deere & Co. v. MTD Prods., Inc., 41 F.3d 39 (2d Cir. 1994).

222. Facebook, Inc. v. Teachbook.com, LLC, 819 F. Supp. 2d 764, 781 (N.D. Ill. 2011).

223. *Tacking*, MarkLaw, www.marklaw.com/index.php/ trademark-terms-t/308-tacking.

224. *Pepsi Logo Timeline: The Evolution of the Company's Brand*, Huff. Post, Dec. 18, 2014, www.huffing tonpost.com/2012/12/28/pepsi-logo-timeline_ n_2279676.html.

225. *Id.*

226. Hana Fin., Inc. v. Hana Bank, 135 S. Ct. 907 (2015).

227. Mark Wilson, *What Is Trademark Tacking*, FindLaw, Jan. 21, 2015, blogs.findlaw.com/free_enterprise/ 2015/01/what-is-trademark-tacking.html.

228. *See* Application of E.I. DuPont de Nemours & Co., 476 F.2d 1357, 1361 (C.C.P.A. 1973).

229. 15 U.S.C. §§ 1125(c), 1127.

230. Anne Gilson LaLonde & Jerome Gilson, Gilson on Trademarks § 5A.01[5], [6] (2019).

231. Moseley v. V Secret Catalogue, Inc., 537 U.S. 418 (2003).

232. *Id.* at 434.

233. 15 U.S.C. § 1115(b).

234. 15 U.S.C. § 115(b)(4).

235. Overstock.com v. NoMoreRack.com, 2014 U.S. Dist. LEXIS 89620 (2014).

236. Webceleb, Inc. v. Procter & Gamble Co., 554 F. App'x 606 (9th Cir. 2014).

237. New Kids on the Block v. News Am. Publ'g, Inc., 971 F.2d 302 (9th Cir. 1992).

238. 15 U.S.C. § 1125(c)(3).

239. Colin Lecher, *The Oracle v. Google Case May Go to the Supreme Court*, Verge, Oct. 9, 2014, www.theverge.com/2014/10/9/6953215/oracle-v-google-case-supreme-court-hearing.

240. Oracle Am., Inc. v. Google, Inc., 872 F. Supp. 2d 974 (N.D. Cal. 2012).

241. Oracle Am., Inc. v. Google Inc., 750 F.3d 1339 (Fed. Cir. 2014), *cert. denied*, 135 S. Ct. 2887 (2015).

242. *Id.*

243. Bruce Keller, *Communications Law in the Digital Age: Intellectual Property*, Comm. L. in the Digital Age (2016).

244. Oracle Am., Inc. v. Google LLC, 886 F.3d 1179 (Fed. Cir. 2018), *petition for cert. docketed*, ___ U.S. ___ (Jan. 25, 2019).

245. *Id.* at 1210.

246. Michael Barclay, *EFF Asks the Supreme Court to Clean Up the Oracle v. Google Mess*, Electronic Frontier Found., Feb. 25, 2019, www.eff.org/deep links/2019/02/eff-asks-supreme-court-clean-oracle-v-google-mess.

CHAPTER 12 BOXED FEATURES

i. Va. State Bd. of Pharmacy v. Va. Citizens Consumer Council, 425 U.S. 748, 771–72 (1976).

ii. Cent. Hudson Gas & Elec. Corp. v. Pub. Serv. Comm'n of N.Y., 447 U.S. 557, 569–70 (1980).

iii. Sorrell v. IMS Health, Inc., 564 U.S. 552 (2011).

iv. Cent. Hudson Gas & Elec. Corp. v. Pub. Serv. Comm'n of New York, 447 U.S. 557, 561 (1980).

v. Jacob Bunge, *Roundup Sellers Boost Advertising as Lawsuits Mount for Weedkiller*, Wall St. J., May 1, 2019, www.wsj.com/articles/roundup-sellers-boost-advertising-as-lawsuits-mount-for-weedkiller-11556738038.

vi. *Monsanto Sued for False Advertising*, Matthews & Assocs., n.d., www.dmlawfirm.com/monsanto-sued-for-false-advertising/.

vii. *Jury Awards Groundskeeper $289.2 Million in Landmark Monsanto Roundup Verdict*, Baum, Hedlund, Aristei, Goldman, July 7, 2017, www.baumhedlund law.com/toxic-tort-law/monsanto-roundup-lawsuit/ california-glyphosate-warning/.

viii. Malcolm C. Weiss & Shannon Oldenburg, *Judge Halts Monsanto Warning Label on First Amendment Grounds*, Nickel Rep., Mar. 7, 2018, www.huntonnick elreportblog.com/2018/03/judge-halts-monsanto-warning-label-on-first-amendment-grounds/.

ix. Carey Gillam, *Monsanto Ordered to Pay $2 Billion to Cancer Victims,* U.S. Right to Know, May 13, 2019, usrtk.org/monsanto-roundup-trial-tacker/ monsanto-ordered-to-pay-2-billion-to-cancer-victims/. *But see In re*: Monsanto Co. v. Office of Envtl. Health Hazard Assessment, Case No. 16 CE CG 00183, Tentative Ruling for Dept. 403, Fresno Super. Ct. Cal., Jan. 26, 2017 (dismissing suit against Monsanto).

x. *See, e.g.,* Bob Egelko, *Monsanto Wants Roundup Cancer Lawsuits Moved Out of California*, San Francisco Chron., May 30, 2019, www.sfchronicle.com/bayarea/ article/Monsanto-wants-Roundup-cancer-lawsuits-moved-out-13907970.php.

xi. Barry J. Seldon & Khosrow Doroodian, *A Simultaneous Model of Cigarette Advertising: Effects on Demand and Industry Response to Public Policy*, 71 Rev. Econ. & Stat. 673 (1989); Jon P. Nelson & John R. Moran, *Advertising and U.S. Alcoholic Beverage Demand: System-Wide Estimates*, 27 Applied Econ. 1225 (1995).

xii. *See, e.g.,* Rosalind M. Kendellen, *The Food and Drug Administration Retreats From Patient Package Inserts for Prescription Drugs*, 40 Food Drug Cosm. L.J. 172 (1985) (showing the FDA's motivation for establishing a package insert plan for consumers). *But see* 1 Antitrust & Trade Reg. Rep. (BNA) No. 1277, at 199 (Aug. 7, 1986).

xiii. Cent. Hudson Gas & Elec. Corp. v. Pub. Serv. Comm'n, 447 U.S. 557, 569 (1980).

xiv. Posadas de Puerto Rico Assocs. v. Tourism Co. of Puerto Rico, 478 U.S. 328, 342 (1986).

xv. Lorillard Tobacco Co. v. Reilly, 533 U.S. 525, 557 (2001).

xvi. *Unfair Commercial Practices*, Your Europe, n.d., europa.eu/youreurope/citizens/consumers/unfair-treatment/unfair-commercial-practices/index_en.htm.

xvii. *Id.*

xviii. *Consumer Rights and Law: The Directive on Consumer Rights*, Eur. Comm'n, ec.europa.eu/justice/consumer-marketing/rights-contracts/directive/index_en.htm.

xix. Council Directive 2005/29.

xx. James C. Miller III, FTC Policy Statement on Deception, FTC, Oct. 14, 1983, www.ftc.gov/public-statements/1983/10/ftc-policy-statement-deception.

xxi. Reuters, *Philip Morris Suspends Media Campaign After Using Young "Influencers" to Sell New Tobacco Device*, CNBC, May 11, 2019, www.cnbc.com/2019/05/11/philip-morris-suspends-social-media-campaign.html.

xxii. Jakejames Lugo, *Philip Morris Suspends Influencer Marketing Efforts Following Shady Practices*, Influencer Update, May 16, 2019, www.influencerupdate.biz/news/68120/philip-morris-suspends-influencer-marketing-efforts-following-shady-practices/.

xxiii. Chris Kirkham, *Tobacco Giant Halts Marketing Blitz After Product Was Pitched by 21-year-old Model*, Global News, May 10, 2019, globalnews.ca/news/5266134/philip-morris-marketing-younger-model/.

xxiv. *Id.*

xxv. *Id.*

xxvi. Reuters, *supra* note xxi.

xxvii. *Id.*

xxviii. Reuters, *The Philip Morris Files*, Reuters Investigates, 2019, www.reuters.com/investigates/section/pmi/.

CHAPTER 12

1. Va. State Bd. of Pharmacy v. Va. Citizens Consumer Council, 425 U.S. 748, 762, 763, 764 (1976).

2. *Id.*

3. Sorrell v. IMS Health, Inc., 564 U.S. 552 (2011).

4. U.S. Const. art. 1, § 8.

5. Citizens United v. FEC, 558 U.S. 310 (2010).

6. Valentine v. Chrestensen, 316 U.S. 52, 53 (1942).

7. *Id.* at 53.

8. *Id.* at 53, 55.

9. *Id.* (emphasis added).

10. *Id.* at 55.

11. Breard v. Alexandria, 341 U.S. 622 (1951).

12. *Id.* at 645.

13. N.Y. Times Co. v. Sullivan, 376 U.S. 254 (1964).

14. *Id.* at 266.

15. *Id.*

16. Bigelow v. Virginia, 421 U.S. 809, 819 (1975) (emphasis added).

17. *Id.*

18. *Id.* at 817.

19. *Id.* at 820.

20. Va. State Bd. of Pharmacy v. Va. Citizens Consumer Council, 425 U.S. 748 (1976).

21. *Id.* at 755.

22. *Id.* at 761.

23. *Id.* at 772 n. 24.

24. *Id.* at 762.

25. *Id.* at 772 n. 24, 776.

26. Linmark Assocs. v. Twp. of Willingboro, 431 U.S. 85 (1977); Carey v. Population Servs. Int'l, 431 U.S. 678 (1977); Bates v. State Bar, 433 U.S. 350 (1977).

27. *Bates*, 433 U.S. at 380–81.

28. Ohralik v. Ohio State Bar Ass'n, 436 U.S. 447, 456 (1978).

29. Cent. Hudson Gas & Elec. Corp. v. Pub. Serv. Comm'n, 447 U.S. 557, 561 (1980) (emphasis added).

30. *Id.* at 561 (emphasis added).

31. C. Campbell et al., *Ads Aren't Ads Anymore: A Proposed Typology of Evolving and Varied New Forms of Online "Advertising*," 54 J. Advert. Res. 7 (2014); A. Mitra et al., *Can Consumers Recognize Misleading Advertising Content in a Media Rich Online Environment?*, 25 Psychol. & Marketing 655 (2008).

32. Nicole Perrin, *U.S. Native Advertising 2019*, eMarketer, Mar. 20, 2019, www.emarketer.com/content/us-native-advertising-2019; Jayson DeMers, *Is Native Advertising Sustainable for the Long Haul?*, Forbes, Mar. 1, 2018, www.forbes.com/sites/jaysondemers/2018/03/01/is-native-advertising-sustainable-for-the-long-haul/.

33. B.W. Wojdynski, *Native Advertising: Engagement, Deception, and Implications for Theory*, in The New Advertising: Branding, Content and Consumer Relationships in a Data-Driven Social Media Era 203–236 (R. Brown, V. K. Jones & B. M. Wang eds., 2016).

34. L. Moses, *The Wall Street Journal Launches Native Ad Studio*, AdWeek, Mar. 10, 2014, www.adweek.com/news/press/wall-street-journal-launches-native-ad-studio-156212.

35. Sam Sabin, *DeGeneres, Minaj Among Celebrities Whose Social Posts Drew FTC Interest in Past Year*, Morning Consult, Oct. 5, 2018, morningconsult.com/2018/10/05/degeneres-minaj-among-celebrities-whose-social-posts-drew-ftc-interest-in-past-year/.

36. Peter Horst, *Gillette's Controversial "Toxic Masculinity" Ad and the Opportunity It Missed*, Forbes, Jan. 18, 2019, www.forbes.com/sites/peterhorst/2019/01/18/gillettes-controversial-toxic-masculinity-ad-and-the-opportunity-it-missed/#57aef3ff5506.

37. Carl Jones, *Getting Ads Banned Is a Planned PR and Advertising Strategy*, Drum, Nov. 21, 2018, www.thedrum.com/opinion/2018/11/21/getting-ads-banned-planned-pr-and-advertising-strategy; Sam Pudwell, *Gillette Ad: What's Wrong With Controversy in PR?*, Red Lorry Yellow Lorry, Jan. 16, 2019, www.rlyl.com/us/gillette-ad-pr-controversy-2/. *See also* Anne M. Cronin, Public Relations Capitalism 105–16 (2018).

38. Test Masters Educ. Servs., Inc. v. Robin Singh Educ. Servs., Inc., 799 F.3d 437, 453 (5th Cir. 2015), *cert. denied*, 137 S. Ct. 499 (2016).

39. 16 C.F.R. § 255.5.

40. Jordan v. Jewel Food Stores, Inc., 743 F.3d 509 (7th Cir. 2014).

41. Va. State Bd. of Pharmacy v. Va. Citizens Consumer Council, Inc., 425 U. S. 748, 762 (1976).

42. Jordan v. Jewel Food Stores, Inc., 83 F. Supp. 3d 761 (N.D. Ill. 2015).

43. Sarver v. Chartier, 813 F.3d 891 (9th Cir. 2016) (citing *Va. State Bd. of Pharmacy*, 425 U.S. at 762).

44. Enigma Software Grp., LLC v. Bleeping Comput., LLC, 194 F. Supp. 3d 263 (S.D.N.Y. 2016).

45. *Id.* at 294.

46. *Id.*

47. Pittsburgh Press Co. v. Pittsburgh Comm'n on Human Relations, 413 U.S. 376, 389 (1973).

48. Cent. Hudson Gas & Elec. Corp. v. Pub. Serv. Comm'n of N.Y., 447 U. S. 557, 569–70 (1980) (emphasis added).

49. *See* United States v. O'Brien, 391 U.S. 367 (1968).

50. Posadas de Puerto Rico Assocs. v. Tourism Co. of Puerto Rico, 478 U.S. 328, 340 (1986).

51. *Cent. Hudson*, 447 U.S. at 566.

52. *Posadas*, 478 U.S. at 341.

53. *Id.* at 341–43.

54. *Id.* at 345–46.

55. Bd. of Trs. of the State Univ. of N.Y. v. Fox, 492 U.S. 469 (1989).

56. *Id.* at 477.

57. *Id.* at 480.

58. Rubin v. Coors Brewing Co., 514 U.S. 476, 491 (1995).

59. 44 Liquormart, Inc. v. Rhode Island, 517 U.S. 484, 529 (1996) (Thomas, J., concurring in Parts I, II, VI and VII, and in judgment).

60. Lorillard Tobacco Co. v. Reilly, 533 U.S. 525, 536, 561 (2001).

61. Thompson v. Western States Medical Center, 535 U.S. 357 (2002) (Breyer, J., dissenting).

62. Sorrell v. IMS Health, Inc., 564 U.S. 552, 572 (2011).

63. *44 Liquormart*, 517 U.S. at 503.

64. *Id.* at 500.

65. *Id.* at 518.

66. *Sorrell*, 564 U.S. at 552.

67. Vt. Stat. Ann., Tit. 18, § 4631(d).

68. *Sorrell*, 564 U.S. at 583.

69. *Id.* at 565.

70. *Id.* at 566.

71. *Id.* at 565–57.

72. *Id.* at 579.

73. *Id.* at 585–86.

74. Robert L. Kerr, *Desperately Seeking Coherence: The Lower Courts Struggle to Determine the Meaning of Sorrell for the Commercial Speech Doctrine*, 7 U. Balt. J. Media L. & Ethics 1 (2019).

75. Hunter B. Thomson, *Whither* Central Hudson? *Commercial Speech in the Wake of* Sorrell v. IMS Health, 47 Columbia J.L. & Soc. Probs. 171 (2013–14).

76. *One Year Later: The Consequences of Sorrell v. IMS Health Inc.*, Justice Watch, July 2, 2012, afjjustice watch.blogspot.com//2012/07/one-year-later-consequences-of-sorrell.html.

77. *Id.*

78. Retail Dig. Network, LLC v. Appelsmith, 810 F.3d 638 (9th Cir. 2016), *aff'd* 861 F.3d 839 (9th Cir. 2017).

79. Crazy Ely W. Vill., LLC v. City of Las Vegas, 618 F. App'x 904 (9th Cir. 2015).

80. Am. Meat Inst. v. USDA, 760 F.3d 18, 26 (D.C. Cir. 2014).

81. *Id.*

82. Riley v. Nat'l Fed'n of the Blind of N.C., Inc., 487 U.S. 781, 796–97 (1988).

83. Eugene Volokh, *The Law of Compelled Speech*, 97 Tex. L. Rev. 355 (2018).

84. *Id.*

85. Wieman v. Updegraff, 344 U.S. 183 (1952). *See also* Shelton v. Tucker, 364 U.S. 479 (1960) (disclosure of memberships and contributions); Keyishian v. Bd. of Regents of Univ. of State of N.Y., 385 U.S. 589 (1967) (subversive speech).

86. Zauderer v. Office of Disciplinary Counsel of Sup. Ct. of Ohio, 471 U.S. 626, 651 (1985).

87. *Id.*

88. *Id.*

89. Sarah C. Haan, *Facebook's Alternative Facts*, 105 Va. L. Rev. Online 18 (2019).

90. *See* Sarah C. Haan, *The Post-Truth First Amendment*, 94 Indiana L.J. (forthcoming 2019), available at papers.ssrn.com/sol3/papers.cfm?abstract_id=3209366 (arguing that the application of a common ideology approach embroils courts in the current "post-truth" controversy in which "facts are a matter of perspective").

91. *See, e.g.*, Dwyer v. Cappell, 762 F.3d 275, 282–85 (3d Cir. 2014); *see also* Entm't Software Ass'n v. Blagojevich, 469 F.3d 641, 652 (7th Cir. 2006) (quoting *Zauderer* as authorizing disclaimers aimed at preventing deception without further analysis); United States v. Wenger, 427 F.3d 840, 849 (10th Cir. 2005).

92. *See, e.g.*, Am. Meat Inst. v. USDA, 760 F.3d 18, 20 (D.C. Cir. 2014); Disc. Tobacco City & Lottery, Inc. v. United States, 674 F.3d 509, 559 n.8 (6th Cir. 2012); Pharm. Care Mgmt. Ass'n v. Rowe, 429 F.3d 294, 310 n.8 (1st Cir. 2005); Nat'l Elec. Mfrs. Ass'n v. Sorrell, 272 F.3d 104, 115 (2d Cir. 2001).

93. Nat'l Inst. of Family and Life Advocates v. Becerra, 138 S. Ct. 2361 (2018).

94. *Id.* at 2377.

95. *Id.* (emphasis added).

96. CTIA—The Wireless Ass'n v. City of Berkeley, 138 S. Ct. 2708 (2018).

97. CTIA—The Wireless Ass'n v. City of Berkeley, 854 F.3d 1105 (9th Cir. 2017).

98. *Id.* at 1119.

99. *Id.* at 1117.

100. CTIA—The Wireless Assoc. v. City of Berkeley, Cal., 2019 WL 2750838 (9th Cir. July 2, 2019).

101. Am. Beverage Ass'n v. City & Cty. of San Francisco, 871 F.3d 884, 887 (9th Cir. 2017).

102. *Id.* at 895.

103. Rich Samp, *Soda Warning Case Tests How High Court's* NIFLA *Decision Affects Commercial Speech Mandates*, Forbes, Sept. 27, 2018, www.forbes.com/sites/wlf/2018/09/27/soda-warning-case-tests-how-high-courts-nifla-decision-affects-commercial-speech-mandates/#1d3530df15ae.

104. Capital Broad. Co. v. Mitchell, 333 F. Supp. 582 (D.D.C. 1971).

105. Lorillard Tobacco Co. v. Reilly, 533 U.S. 525, 569 (2001).

106. Nicopure Labs v. FDA, 266 F. Supp. 3d 360 (D.D.C. 2017). *See also Effective and Compliance Dates Applicable to Retailers, Manufacturers, Importers and Distributors of Deemed Tobacco Products*, FDA, Aug. 9, 2018, www.fda.gov/tobacco-products/compliance-enforcement-training/effective-and-compliance-dates-applicable-retailers-manufacturers-importers-and-distributors-deemed.

107. Juliet Eilperin, *FDA Delays Enforcement of Stricter Standards for E-cigarette, Cigar Industry*, Wash. Post., May 2, 2017, www.washingtonpost.com/politics/fda-suspends-enforcement-of-stricter-standards-for-e-cigarette-cigar-industry/2017/05/02/be7e557a-2ed6-11e7-9534-00e4656c22aa_story.html?utm_term=.86eaa43eec2a.

108. Faircloth v. FDA, 2017 U.S. Dist. LEXIS 159641 (S.D.W.Va. 2017).

109. Posadas de Puerto Rico Assocs. v. Tourism Co. of Puerto Rico, 478 U.S. 328, 340 (1986).

110. United States v. Edge Broad., 509 U.S. 418 (1993).

111. *Id.* at 428.

112. *Id.* at 435.

113. Rubin v. Coors Brewing Co., 514 U.S. 476 (1995).

114. *Id.* at 490.

115. 44 Liquormart, Inc. v. Rhode Island, 517 U.S. 484, 507 (1996).

116. *Id.* at 496.

117. *Id.* at 509.

118. *Id.* at 497.

119. *Id.* at 505.

120. Educ. Media Co. at Va. Tech., Inc. v. Insley, 731 F.3d 291 (4th Cir. 2013).

121. Educ. Media Co. at Va. Tech. v. Swecker, 2008 U.S. Dist. LEXIS 124685 (E.D. Va., June 19, 2008), *vacated*, 602 F.3d 583 (4th Cir. 2010).

122. Sorrell v. IMS Health, Inc., 564 U.S. 552 (2011).

123. Vt. Stat. Ann., Tit. 18, § 4631 (Supp. 2010).

124. *Sorrell*, 564 U.S. at 580.

125. Calif. Penal Code § 26820.

126. Tracy Rifle & Pistol, LLC v. Harris, 339 F. Supp. 3d 1007, 1012–13 (E.D. Cal. 2018).

127. *Id.* at 1014.

128. Tracy Rifle & Pistol, LLC v. Harris, 118 F. Supp. 3d 1182 (E.D. Cal. 2015).

129. Seattle Mideast Awareness Campaign v. King Cty., 781 F.3d 489 (9th Cir. 2015).

130. *Id.* at 503.

131. Am. Freedom Def. Initiative v. Mass. Bay Transp. Auth., 781 F.3d 571 (1st Cir. 2015), *cert. denied*, 136 S. Ct. 793 (2016).

132. Am. Freedom Def. Initiative v. Se. Penn. Transp. Auth., 92 F. Supp. 3d 314 (E.D. Pa. 2015).

133. *Id.* at 321.

134. *Id.*

135. First Nat'l Bank of Boston v. Bellotti, 435 U.S. 765 (1978).

136. *See, e.g.*, FEC v. Nat'l Right to Work Comm., 459 U.S. 197 (1982); FEC v. Nat'l Conservative Political Action Comm., 470 U.S. 480 (1985); FEC v. Mass. Citizens for Life, Inc., 479 U.S. 238 (1986); Austin v. Mich. State Chamber of Commerce, 494 U.S. 652 (1990).

137. Citizens United v. FEC, 558 U.S. 310 (2010).

138. Nike, Inc. v. Kasky, 539 U.S. 654 (2003).

139. Kasky v. Nike, Inc., 45 P.3d 243, 258 (Cal. 2002).

140. *See, e.g.*, Bates v. State Bar of Ariz., 433 U.S. 350 (1977).

141. *Id.*

142. Kiser v. Kamdar, 831 F.3d 784 (6th Cir. 2016).

143. Peter Horst, *Gillette's Controversial "Toxic Masculinity" Ad and the Opportunity It Missed*, Forbes, Jan. 18, 2019, www.forbes.com/sites/peterhorst/2019/01/18/gillettes-controversial-toxic-masculinity-ad-and-the-opportunity-it-missed/#57aef3ff5506.

144. Carl Jones, *Getting Ads Banned Is a Planned PR and Advertising Strategy*, Drum, Nov. 21, 2018, www.thedrum.com/opinion/2018/11/21/getting-ads-banned-planned-pr-and-advertising-strategy; Sam Pudwell, *Gillette Ad: What's Wrong With Controversy in PR?*, Red Lorry Yellow Lorry, Jan. 16, 2019, www.rlyl.com/us/gillette-ad-pr-controversy-2/. *See also*, Anne M. Cronin, Public Relations Capitalism 105–16 (2018).

145. Olivia Petter, *Gillette Sales Unchanged After Controversial Advert About Toxic Masculinity*, Indep., Jan. 25, 2019, www.independent.co.uk/life-style/gillette-advert-toxic-masculinity-sales-impact-a8745966.html.

146. Pizza Hut, Inc. v. Papa John's Int'l, Inc., 227 F.3d 489, 492 (5th Cir. 2000).

147. *Id.* at 498.

148. *Id.* at 501–02.

149. Va. State Bd. of Pharmacy v. Va. Citizens Consumer Council, 425 U.S. 748, 771–72 (1976); Cent. Hudson Gas & Elec. Corp., v. Pub. Serv. Comm'n, 447 U.S. 557, 564, 566 (1980); Zauderer v. Office of Disciplinary Counsel, 471 U.S. 626, 652–53 (1985); Cincinnati v. Discovery Network, 507 U.S. 410, 434 (1993); Lorillard Tobacco Co. v. Reilly, 533 U.S. 535, 576 (2001).

150. *Va. State Bd. of Pharmacy*, 425 U.S. at 777–78 (Stewart, J. concurring).

151. Lorillard Tobacco Co. v. Reilly, 533 U.S. 535, 576 (2001).

152. Va. State Bd. of Pharmacy v. Va. Citizens Consumer Council, 425 U.S. 748, 771–72 (1976).

153. Zauderer v. Office of Disciplinary Counsel, 471 U.S. 626, 652–53 (1985).

154. Cincinnati v. Discovery Network, 507 U.S. 410, 434 (1993) (emphasis added).

155. Pub. Citizen v. La. Attorney Disciplinary, 632 F. 3d 212, 218 (5th Cir. 2011). *See also* Am. Beverage Ass'n v. San Francisco, 871 F.3d 884, 893 (9th Cir. 2017); Ocheesee Creamery v. Putnam, 851 F.3d 1228, 1235–36 (11th Cir. 2017); Dwyer v. Cappell, 762 F.3d 275, 281–83 (3d Cir. 2014); Greater Baltimore Ctr. for Pregnancy Concerns v. Mayor of Baltimore, 721 F.3d 264, 283 (4th Cir. 2013).

156. Karlene Lukovitz, *Canada Dry Maker Faces False Advertising Lawsuits*, MARKETINGDAILY, July 5, 2018, www.mediapost.com/publications/article/321742/canada-dry-maker-faces-false-advertising-lawsuits.html.

157. *See* Cent. Hudson Gas & Elec. Corp. v. Pub. Serv. Comm'n, 447 U.S. 557 (1980); FTC Act of 1914; Everette MacIntyre (FTC member), *Statement on Fair Advertising Landmarks*, BEFORE N.Y. BAR ASS'N, Jan. 22, 1963 (marking the 25th anniversary of the Wheeler-Lea amendment to the FTC Act that "so greatly strengthened the authority of the FTC to protect businessmen and the public from false advertising and other deceptive and unfair acts"), www.ftc.gov/system/files/documents/public_statements/683461/19620122_macintyre_fair_advertising_landmarks.pdf.

158. *See, e.g.,* Lorillard Tobacco Co. v. Reilly, 533 U.S. 525, 540–41 (2001) (reading the U.S. Constitution's Article VI Supremacy Clause and express language of federal statutes to preempt contravening state or local actions).

159. 15 U.S.C. 1125, § 43 (a)(1)(A)(B).

160. Lexmark v. Static Control, 572 U.S. 118 (2014).

161. *Id.* at 131–32.

162. 21 U.S.C.S. § 301 et seq.

163. Aaron Taube, *Coca-Cola Loses Huge False-Advertising Case in Supreme Court*, BUS. INSIDER, Jun. 12, 2014, www.businessinsider.com/scotus-revives-false-ad-claims-against-coke-2014-6.

164. POM Wonderful, LLC v. Coca-Cola Co., 573 U.S. 102, 119 (2014).

165. *Lexmark*, 572 U.S. at 188.

166. Eric Goldman, *Supreme Court Changes False Advertising Law Across the Country*, FORBES, Mar. 26, 2014, www.forbes.com/sites/ericgoldman/2014/03/26/supreme-court-changes-false-advertising-law-across-the-country/#782612674671.

167. Grubbs v. Sheakley Grp., Inc., 807 F.3d 785 (6th Cir. 2015).

168. *Id.* at 801.

169. Radiance Found., Inc. v. NAACP, 786 F.3d 316, 320 (4th Cir. 2015).

170. L.A. Taxi Coop., Inc. v. Uber Techs., Inc., 114 F. Supp. 3d 852, 858 (N.D. Cal. 2015).

171. 15 U.S.C. § 1125.

172. Roscoe B. Starek III, *Myths and Half-Truths About Deceptive Advertising*, ADDRESS TO THE NAT'L INFOMERCIAL MARKETING ASS'N, Oct. 15, 1996, www.ftc.gov/speeches/starek/nima96d4.htm.

173. Margaret E. Krawiec et al., *FTC Enforcement Trends in Consumer Protection*, SKADDEN, LLP, Feb. 11, 2019, www.skadden.com/insights/publications/2019/02/ftc-enforcement-trends-in-consumer-protection.

174. *Id.*

175. *Id.*

176. *Id.* (emphasis added).

177. *Three Home Loan Advertisers Settle FTC Charges; Failed to Disclose Key Loan Terms in Ads*, FTC, Jan. 8, 2009, www.ftc.gov/opa/2009/01/anm.shtm.

178. *Id.*

179. *Decision and Order: Am. Nationwide Mortgage Co.*, Docket No. C-2429, FTC, Feb. 17, 2009, www.ftc.gov/sites/default/files/documents/cases/2009/01/090108americancmpt.pdf.

180. FTC v. Corzine, No. Civ.-S-94-1446 (E.D. Cal. 1994).

181. *Uber Settles FTC Allegations That It Made Deceptive Privacy and Data Security Claims*, FTC, Aug. 15, 2017, www.ftc.gov/news-events/press-releases/2017/08/uber-settles-ftc-allegations-it-made-deceptive-privacy-data.

182. *Uber Agrees to Expanded Settlement With FTC Related to Privacy, Security Claims*, FTC, Apr. 12, 2018, www.ftc.gov/news-events/press-releases/2018/04/uber-agrees-expanded-settlement-ftc-related-privacy-security.

183. *Decision and Order in the Matter of Uber Techs.*, Docket No. C-4662, FTC, Oct. 25, 2018, www.ftc.gov/system/files/documents/cases/152_3054_c-4662_uber_technologies_revised_decision_and_order.pdf.

184. *Complaint in the Matter of Uber Techs.*, Docket No. C-4662, FTC, Oct. 26, 2018, www.ftc.gov/system/files/documents/cases/152_3054_c-4662_uber_technologies_revised_complaint.pdf. *See also In re* Uber Techs., 304 F. Supp. 3d 1351 (Apr. 4, 2018).

185. *Uber to Pay $20 Million Over Claims It Misled Drivers Over How Much They Would Earn*, Guardian, Jan. 19, 2017, www.theguardian.com/technology/2017/jan/19/uber-settlement-ftc-driver-earnings-car-leases.

186. *In re* Volkswagen "Clean Diesel" Mktg., 328 F. Supp. 3d 963 (N.D. Cal. 2018).

187. *FTC Charges Volkswagen Deceived Consumers With Its "Clean Diesel" Campaign*, FTC, Mar. 29, 2016, www.ftc.gov/news-events/press-releases/2016/03/ftc-charges-volkswagen-deceived-consumers-its-clean-diesel.

188. *Rite Aid Settles FTC Charges That It Failed to Protect Medical and Financial Privacy of Customers and Employees*, FTC, July 27, 2010, www.ftc.gov/opa/2010/07/riteaid.shtm.

189. *Three CortiSlim Defendants to Give Up $4.5 Million in Cash and Other Assets*, FTC, Sept. 21, 2005, www.ftc.gov/news-events/press-releases/2005/09/three-cortislim-defendants-give-45-million-cash-and-other-assets.

190. Lesley Fair, *Substantiation: The Science of Compliance*, FTC, Dec. 15, 2011, www.ftc.gov/news-events/blogs/business-blog/2011/12/science-reliance-compliance.

191. *Complaint in the Matter of Tropicana Products, Inc.*, Docket No. C-4145, FTC, 2005, www.ftc.gov/os/caselist/0423154/050825comp0423154.pdf.

192. Warner-Lambert Co. v. FTC, 562 F.2d 749 (1977), *cert. denied*, 435 U.S. 950 (1978).

193. *Id.* at 762, 764.

194. Michael B. Mazis, FTC v. Novartis: *The Return of Corrective Advertising?*, 20 J. Pub. Pol'y & Mktg. 114 (2001).

195. *Id.*

196. *FTC Charges Marketers With Making Unsubstantiated Claims That They Could Eliminate Consumers' Debt*, FTC, Dec. 2, 2010, www.ftc.gov/opa/2010/12/ffdc.shtm.

197. Sam Fulwood III & Henry Weinstein, *"Joe Camel" Ads Illegally Target Youths, FTC Says*, L.A. Times, May 29, 1997, www.latimes.com/archives/la-xpm-1997-05-29-mn-63716-story.html.

198. *Id.*

199. Stuart Elliott, *Joe Camel, A Giant in Tobacco Marketing, Is Dead at 23*, N.Y. Times, July 11, 1997, www.nytimes.com/1997/07/11/business/joe-camel-a-giant-in-tobacco-marketing-is-dead-at-23.html.

200. *Privacy & Data Security Update (2016)*, FTC, Jan. 2017, www.ftc.gov/reports/privacy-data-security-update-2016#general.

201. *Id.*

202. 15 U.S.C. § 6501 *et seq.*

203. *Two App Developers Settle FTC Charges They Violated Children's Online Privacy Protection Act*, FTC, Dec. 17, 2016, www.ftc.gov/news-events/press-releases/2015/12/two-app-developers-settle-ftc-charges-they-violated-childrens.

204. 16 C.F.R. § 312 *et seq.*; *see also* Seena Gressin, *COPPA: When Persistence Doesn't Pay*, Bus. Blog, Dec. 17, 2015, www.ftc.gov/news-events/blogs/business-blog/2015/12/coppa-when-persistence-doesnt-pay.

205. Jessica Guynn, *FTC Calls on Online Ad Industry to Agree on Do-Not-Track Standard*, L.A. Times, Apr. 17, 2013, www.latimes.com/business/la-xpm-2013-apr-17-la-fi-tn-ftc-online-ad-industry-do-not-track-20130417-story.html.

206. *FTC Testifies on Do Not Track Legislation*, FTC, Dec. 2, 2010, www.ftc.gov/opa/2010/12/dnttestimony.shtm.

207. Dawn Chmielewski, *How "Do Not Track" Ended Up Going Nowhere*, Vox, Jan. 4, 2016, www.vox.com/2016/1/4/11588418/how-do-not-track-ended-up-going-nowhere.

208. Elizabeth Schulze, *$5 Billion Fine Is a "Bargain" for Facebook, Top US Senators Say*, CNBC, May 7, 2019, www.cnbc.com/2019/05/07/facebook-ftc-fine-of-up-to-5-billion-is-a-bargain-top-senators-say.html.

209. *See, e.g.*, *Facebook Settles FTC Charges That It Deceived Consumers by Failing to Keep Privacy Promises*, FTC, Nov. 29, 2011, www.ftc.gov/news-events/press-releases/2011/11/facebook-settles-ftc-charges-it-deceived-consumers-failing-keep.

210. *FTC Completes Review of CAN-SPAM Rule*, FTC, Feb. 12, 2019, www.ftc.gov/news-events/press-releases/2019/02/ftc-completes-review-can-spam-rule.

211. 15 U.S.C. §§ 7701–7713 (2004).

212. *Id.*

213. 15 U.S.C. § 7704(a)(1).

214. *FTC Approves New Rule Provision Under the CAN-SPAM Act*, FTC, May 12, 2008, www.ftc.govopa/2008/05/canspam.shtm.

215. 16 C.F.R. § 255.5.

216. These states are Alaska, Arizona, Arkansas, California, Colorado, Connecticut, Delaware, Florida, Georgia, Idaho, Illinois, Indiana, Iowa, Kansas, Louisiana, Maine, Maryland, Michigan, Minnesota, Missouri, Nevada, New Mexico, North Carolina, North Dakota, Ohio, Oklahoma, Pennsylvania, Rhode Island, South Dakota, Tennessee, Texas, Utah, Virginia, Washington, West Virginia, Wisconsin and Wyoming.

217. Va. Code Ann. § 18.2–152.3:1.

218. *See Virginia: Spam Law Struck Down on Grounds of Free Speech*, N.Y. Times, Sept. 13, 2008, at A17.

219. Jaynes v. Virginia, 666 S.E.2d 303, 314 (Va. 2008), *cert. denied*, 556 U.S. 1152 (2009).

220. 47 U.S.C. § 227(b)(1)(A) (1991).

221. Nack v. Walburg, 715 F.3d 680 (8th Cir. 2013), law.justia.com/cases/federal/appellate-courts/ca8/11-1460/11-1460-2013-05-21.html.

222. Zauderer v. Office of Disciplinary Counsel of Sup. Ct. of Ohio, 471 U.S. 626, 651 (1985).

223. *.Com Disclosures: Information About Online Advertising*, FTC, May 2000, www.ftc.gov/os/2000/05/0005dotcomstaffreport.pdf; *.Com Disclosures: How to Make Effective Disclosures in Digital Advertising*, FTC, Mar. 2013, ftc.gov/os/2013/03/130312dotcomdisclosures.pdf.

224. Sam Sabin, *DeGeneres, Minaj Among Celebrities Whose Social Posts Drew FTC Interest in Past Year*, Morning Consult, Oct. 5, 2018, morningconsult.com/2018/10/05/degeneres-minaj-among-celebrities-whose-social-posts-drew-ftc-interest-in-past-year/.

225. Sam Sabin, *A Year After Major Actions, FTS's Influencer Marketing Guidelines Still Overlooked*, Morning Consult, Oct. 4, 2018, morningconsult.com/2018/10/04/a-year-later-ftcs-influencer-marketing-guidelines-still-largely-ignored/.

226. *Enforcement Policy Statement on Deceptively Formatted Advertisements*, FTC, 2015, www.ftc.gov/system/files/documents/public_statements/896923/151222deceptiveenforcement.pdf; *Native Advertising: A Guide for Businesses*, FTC, Dec. 2015, www.ftc.gov/tips-advice/business-center/guidance/native-advertising-guide-businesses.

227. *Lord & Taylor Settles FTC Charges It Deceived Consumers Through Paid Article in an Online Fashion Magazine and Paid Instagram Posts by 50 "Fashion Influencers,"* FTC, Mar. 15, 2016, www.ftc.gov/news-events/press-releases/2016/03/lord-taylor-settles-ftc-charges-it-deceived-consumers-through.

228. *Complaint in the Matter of Lord & Taylor, LLC*, Docket No. C-4576, FTC, Mar. 15, 2016, www.ftc.gov/system/files/documents/cases/160523lordtaylorcmpt.pdf.

229. *FTC Approves Final Lord & Taylor Order Prohibiting Deceptive Advertising Techniques*, FTC, May 23, 2016, www.ftc.gov/news-events/press-releases/2016/05/ftc-approves-final-lord-taylor-order-prohibiting-deceptive.

230. Patrick Coffee, *FTC Slams Lord & Taylor for Not Disclosing Paid Social Posts and Native Ads*, AdWeek, Mar. 15, 2016, www.adweek.com/news/advertising-branding/ftc-slamslord-taylor-deceiving-customers-not-disclosing-its-native-ads-170229.

231. *Agreement Containing Consent Order, In re Machinima, Inc.*, File No. 1423090, FTC, Mar. 17, 2016.

232. *See Closing Letter, Microsoft/Starcom*, File No. 142-3090, FTC, Aug. 26, 2015, www.ftc.gov/system/files/documents/closing_letters/nid/150902machinima_letter.pdf.

233. Paul Fletcher, *Report: Nearly 40% of Publishers Ignore FTC's Native Advertising Rule*, Forbes, Mar. 19, 2017, www.forbes.com/sites/paulfletcher/2017/03/19/nearly-40-percent-of-publishers-ignore-ftcs-native-advertising-rules/#67d0ed2967db.

234. Aaron Burstein, *FTC Puts "Influencers" on Notice: Disclose Marketing Relationships in Social Media Post*, Broad. L. Blog, Apr. 26, 2017, www.broadcastlawblog.com/2017/04/articles/ftc-puts-influencers-on-notice-disclose-marketing-relationships-in-social-media-posts/?utm_source=David+Oxenford%2C+Esq+-+Broadcast+Law+Blog&utm_campaign=84656aaedb-RSS_EMAIL_CAMPAIGN.

235. Tracy P. Marshall & Sheila A. Millar, *FTC Issues Staff Report on Native Advertising*, Nat'l L. Rev., Jan. 3, 2018, www.natlawreview.com/article/ftc-issues-staff-report-native-advertising.

236. *See, e.g., Closing Letter, AnnTaylor Stores Corp.*, File No. 102–3147, FTC, Apr. 20, 2010, www.ftc.gov/os/closings/100420anntaylor-closingletter.pdf; *Closing Letter, Cole Haan*, File No. 142-3041, FTC, Mar. 20, 2014, www.ftc.gov/system/files/documents/closing_letters/cole-haan-inc./140320colehaanclosingletter.pdf.

237. *Guides Concerning the Use of Endorsements and Testimonials in Advertising*, 16 C.F.R. pt. 255 (2014), ftc.gov/os/2009/10/091005revisedendorsement-guides.pdf; *The FTC's Endorsement Guides: What*

People Are Asking, FTC, Sept. 2017, www.ftc.gov/tips-advice/business-center/guidance/ftcs-endorsement-guides-what-people-are-asking.

238. Minority TV Project v. FCC, 573 U.S. 946 (2014).

239. Minority TV Project v. FCC, 736 F.3d 1192, 1204 (9th Cir. 2013).

240. *The Public and Broadcasting: Offensive Advertising*, FCC, Dec. 2018, www.fcc.gov/media/radio/public-and-broadcasting#OFFENSIVE.

241. Greater New Orleans Broad. Ass'n, Inc. v. United States, 527 U.S. 173 (1999).

242. *Id.*

243. Van Hollen v. FEC, 811 F.3d 486 (D.C. Cir. 2016).

244. *Id.* at 500.

245. *Id.* at 488.

246. Coyne Beahm, Inc. v. FDA, 966 F. Supp. 1374 (M.D.N.C. 1997).

247. *Id.* at 1399.

248. Family Smoking Prevention and Tobacco Control Act (FSPTCA), Pub. L. No. 111–31, 123 Stat. 1776 (2009).

249. Steven Reinberg, *U.S. Abandons Effort to Place Graphic Labeling on Cigarettes*, HEALTHDAY, Mar. 20, 2013, consumer.healthday.com/cancer-information-5/lung-cancer-news-100/u-s-abandons-effort-to-place-graphic-labeling-on-cigarettes-674641.html.

250. Discount Tobacco City & Lottery Co. v. United States, 674 F.3d 509 (6th Cir. 2012), *cert. denied*, 569 U.S. 946 (2013); R.J. Reynolds Tobacco Co. v. FDA, 696 F.3d 1205 (D.C. Cir. 2012).

251. *R.J. Reynolds Tobacco Co.*, 696 F.3d 1205.

252. *See, e.g., Discount Tobacco City*, 674 F.3d 524–25.

253. *Discount Tobacco City*, 674 F.3d 509; *R.J. Reynolds Tobacco Co.*, 696 F.3d 1205.

254. *The Facts on the FDA's New Tobacco Rule*, FDA, Apr. 8, 2017, www.fda.gov/ForConsumers/ConsumerUpdates/ucm506676.htm

255. Nicopure Labs v. FDA, 266 F. Supp. 3d 360 (D.D.C. 2017); Cigar Ass'n of Am. v. FDA, 315 F. Supp. 3d 143 (D.D.C. 2018).

256. *Cigar Ass'n of Am.*, 315 F. Supp. 3d at 164–67.

257. Hoban v. FDA, 2018 WL 3122341 (D.Minn. 2018).

258. Stephanie Strom, *U.S. Judge Rejects Gruesome Cigarette Labels*, N.Y. TIMES, Feb. 29, 2012, www.nytimes.com/2012/03/01/business/us-judge-rejects-gruesome-cigarette-labels.html.

259. Mark Bittman, *The Right to Sell Kids Junk*, OPINIONATOR, Mar. 27, 2012, opinionator.blogs.nytimes.com/2012/03/27/the-right-to-sell-kids-junk/.

260. David Oxenford, *What Do New Drug Ad Price Disclosures Mean for TV?*, BROAD. L. BLOG, May 15, 2019, www.broadcastlawblog.com/2019/05/articles/what-do-new-drug-ad-price-disclosures-mean-for-tv/?utm_source=David+Oxenford%2C+Esq+-+Broadcast+Law+Blog&utm_campaign=df3be43517-RSS_EMAIL_CAMPAIGN&utm_medium=email&utm_term=0_550fd6c4c6-df3be43517-70342789.

261. *Id.*

262. *ANA Strongly Opposes New HHS Ad Disclosure Rule*, ANA, May 9, 2019, www.ana.net/blogs/show/id/rr-blog-2019-05-ANA-Strongly-Opposes-New-HHS-Ad-Disclosure-Rule+.

263. *Id.*

264. *See, e.g.,* William D. Araiza, *Invasion of the Content Neutrality Rule*, BROOKLYN L. SCH., Feb. 15, 2019, papers.ssrn.com/sol3/papers.cfm?abstract_id=3335261.

265. *See, e.g.,* Mark Robertson, *Proposed Federal Alcohol Labeling Revisions Retain Constitutionally Suspect Review Standards*, FORBES, Apr. 8, 2019, www.forbes.com/sites/wlf/2019/04/08/proposed-federal-alcohol-labeling-revisions-retain-constitutionally-suspect-review-standards/#4e40048323c2; Sarah C. Haan, *The Post-Truth First Amendment*, 94 INDIANA L.J. (forthcoming 2019), available at papers.ssrn.com/sol3/papers.cfm?abstract_id=3209366; Valerie C. Brannon, *Assessing Commercial Disclosure Requirements Under the First Amendment*, CONG. RES. SERV., Apr. 23, 2019, fas.org/sgp/crs/misc/R45700.pdf.

266. Mark Robertson, *Proposed Federal Alcohol Labeling Revisions Retain Constitutionally Suspect Review Standards*, FORBES, Apr. 8, 2019, www.forbes.com/sites/wlf/2019/04/08/proposed-federal-alcohol-labeling-revisions-retain-constitutionally-suspect-review-standards/#4e40048323c2.

267. *Id.*

268. Eugene Volokh, *The Law of Compelled Speech*, 97 TEX. L. REV. 355, 395 (2018–19). *See also* R. Randall Kelso, *Clarifying Viewpoint Discrimination in Free Speech Doctrine*, S. TEX. COLLEGE OF L., Jan. 23, 2019, papers.ssrn.com/sol3/papers.cfm?abstract_id=3360691 (arguing that the Court's review of compelled speech cases has caused "unnecessary confusion" among lower courts).

269. Nick Sibilla, *FDA Crackdown on Calling Almond Milk "Milk" Could Violate the First Amendment*, Forbes, Jan. 31, 2019, www.forbes.com/sites/nicksibilla/2019/01/31/fda-crackdown-on-calling-almond-milk-milk-could-violate-the-first-amendment/#743f3ccc7b70.

270. *U.S. Non-Dairy Milk Sales Grow 61% Over the Last Five Years*, Mintel, Jan. 4, 2018, www.mintel.com/press-centre/food-and-drink/us-non-dairy-milk-sales-grow-61-over-the-last-five-years.

271. Allison Shoemaker, *Some Dairy Farmers Would Rather You Call It "Nut Juice" Than Almond Milk*, Takeout, Feb. 19, 2019, thetakeout.com/dairy-farmers-rather-you-call-it-nut-juice-almond-milk-1832732529.

272. Kevin Pang, *Meat Association Would Like Fake Meat Companies to Not Use the Word Meat*, Takeout, Feb. 26, 2018, thetakeout.com/meat-association-would-like-fake-meat-companies-to-not-1823344442.

273. Dan Flynn, *The Ban Against Lab-Grown Food Using "Meat" on the Label Grows to 7 States*, Food Safety News, Apr. 5, 2019, www.foodsafetynews.com/2019/04/the-ban-against-lab-grown-food-using-meat-on-the-label-grows-to-7-states/. *See also* Greg Henderson, *Montana's Real Meat Act*, Drovers, Apr. 1, 2019, www.drovers.com/article/montanas-real-meat-act. The states are Arkansas, Mississippi, North Dakota, South Dakota, Wyoming and Missouri, which was the first. Similar bills are pending in Indiana, Montana, Nebraska, Tennessee and Virginia.

274. *Id.*

275. Dan Flynn, *More "Fake Meat" Skirmishes Breaking Out as Missouri Settlement Takes Time*, Food Safety News, Mar. 4, 2019, www.foodsafetynews.com/2019/03/more-fake-meat-skirmishes-breaking-out-as-missouri-settlement-takes-time/. The case is Turtle Island Foods v. Missouri.

276. 7 U.S.C.S. § 1639i (2019). Dan Charles, *Congress Just Passed a GMO Labeling Bill. Nobody's Super Happy About It*, NPR: All Things Considered, July 14, 2016, www.npr.org/sections/thesalt/2016/07/14/486060866/congress-just-passed-a-gmo-labeling-bill-nobodys-super-happy-about-it.

277. Michael Halagarda & Stanislaw Popek, *Consumer Response to Genetically Modified Foods*, Sci. Direct, June 22, 2018, www.sciencedirect.com/science/article/pii/B9780081005965218842.

278. Clifford Fisher & Claire Lee, *A Constitutional Food Fight: Commercial Speech & Organic/Non-GMO Labeling*, 4 Int'l J. of Bus. and Applied Soc. Sci. (2018).

279. *See, e.g., In re* Kind, LLC "Healthy & All Natural" Litig., 287 F. Supp. 3d 457 (2018).

280. 83 Fed. Reg. 60562 (Nov. 26, 2018).

281. *Rubin v. Coors Brewing Co.*, 514 U.S. 476 (1995).

282. Marc Robertson, *Revisions Retain Constitutionally Suspect Review Standards*, Forbes, Apr. 8, 2019, www.forbes.com/sites/wlf/2019/04/08/proposed-federal-alcohol-labeling-revisions-retain-constitutionally-suspect-review-standards/#60eb3d8d23c2.

283. *Id.*

284. *Modernization of the Labeling and Advertising Regulations for Wine, Distilled Spirits, and Malt Beverages; Comment Period Extension*, Doc. 2019-05148, Fed. Reg., Mar. 19, 2019, www.federalregister.gov/documents/2019/03/19/2019-05148/modernization-of-the-labeling-and-advertising-regulations-for-wine-distilled-spirits-and-malt; *TTB Extends Comment Deadline for Modernization of the Labeling & Advertising Regulations for Wine, Distilled Spirits & Malt Beverages 90 Days*, Distillery Trail, Mar. 19, 2019, www.distillerytrail.com/blog/ttb-extends-comment-deadline-for-modernization-of-the-labeling-advertising-regulations-for-wine-distilled-spirits-malt-beverages-90-days/.

CASE INDEX

SUBJECT INDEX